MARKETING

REAL PEOPLE, REAL CHOICES

4TH CANADIAN EDITION

MICHAEL R.
SOLOMON
Saint Joseph's University

GREG W.
MARSHALL
Rollins College

ELNORA W.
STUART
The University of
South Carolina
Upstate

J. BROCK
SMITH
University of
Victoria

SYLVAIN
CHARLEBOIS
University of Guelph

BHUPESH
SHAH
Seneca College

PEARSON

Toronto

Vice-President, Editorial Director: Gary Bennett
Editor-in-Chief: Nicole Lukach
Senior Acquisitions Editor: Nick Durie
Senior Marketing Manager: Leigh-Anne Graham
Developmental Editor: Catherine Belshaw
Project Manager: Lesley Deugo
Production Editor: Lila Campbell
Copy Editor: Julie van Tol
Proofreaders: Susan Bindernagel, Kelli Howey
Compositor: Element, LLC
Photo Researcher/Permissions Editor: Terri Rothman, M.L.S.
Permissions Editor: Freedman & Sister Communications
Manufacturing Coordinator: Susan Johnson
Art Director: Julia Hall
Cover and Interior Designer: Miriam Blier
Cover illustration: Miriam Blier

Credits and acknowledgments for material borrowed from other sources and reproduced, with permission, in this textbook appear on the appropriate page within text.

If you purchased this book outside the United States or Canada, you should be aware that it has been imported without the approval of the publisher or the author.

10 9 8 7 6 5 4 [V0TX]

Library and Archives Canada Cataloguing in Publication

Marketing: Real people, real choices / Michael R. Solomon ... [et al.].— 4th Canadian ed.

Previous edition issued under title: Marketing: real people, real decisions.

Includes bibliographical references and index.

ISBN 978-0-13-262631-6

1. Marketing—Textbooks.   2. Marketing—Canada—Textbooks.   I. Solomon, Michael R

HF5415.M3696 2013   658.8   C2011-905711-5

ISBN 13: 978-0-13-262631-6

▶Brief Contents

▶Contents

CHAPTER 11 Advertising, Public Relations, Promotions, Direct Marketing, and Personal Selling 386

Real People Profiles: Hesham Shafie, A Decision Maker at Brand Momentum Inc. 386

CHAPTER 12 Deliver Value through Supply Chain Management, Channels of Distribution, and Logistics 440

Real People Profiles: Heather Mayo, A Decision Maker at Sam's Club 440

About the Authors

MICHAEL R. SOLOMON, Ph.D., joined the Haub School of Business at Saint Joseph's University in Philadelphia as Professor of Marketing in 2006, where he also serves as Director of the Center for Consumer Research. From 1995 to 2006, he was the Human Sciences Professor of Consumer Behavior at Auburn University. Prior to joining Auburn in 1995, he was Chairman of the Department of Marketing in the School of Business at Rutgers University, New Brunswick, New Jersey. Professor Solomon's primary research interests include consumer behavior and lifestyle issues; branding strategy; the symbolic aspects of products; the psychology of fashion, decoration, and image; services marketing; and the development of visually oriented online research methodologies. He currently sits on the editorial boards of the *Journal of Consumer Behaviour*, the *European Business Review*, and the *Journal of Retailing*, and he recently completed a six-year term on the Board of Governors of the Academy of Marketing Science. In addition to other books, he is also the author of Prentice Hall's text *Consumer Behavior: Buying, Having, and Being*, which is widely used in universities throughout the world. Professor Solomon frequently appears on television and radio shows such as *The Today Show, Good Morning America*, Channel One, the *Wall Street Journal* Radio Network, and National Public Radio to comment on consumer behavior and marketing issues.

GREG W. MARSHALL, Ph.D., is the Charles Harwood Professor of Marketing and Strategy in the Crummer Graduate School of Business at Rollins College, Winter Park, Florida. For three years he also served as Vice President for Strategic Marketing for Rollins. Prior to joining Rollins, he served on the faculties of Oklahoma State University, the University of South Florida, and Texas Christian University. He earned a BSBA in Marketing and an MBA from the University of Tulsa, and a Ph.D. in Marketing from Oklahoma State University. Professor Marshall's research interests include sales force selection, performance, and evaluation; decision making by marketing managers; and intraorganizational relationships. He is editor of the *Journal of Marketing Theory and Practice* and former editor of the *Journal of Personal Selling & Sales Management*, and currently serves on the editorial boards of the *Journal of the Academy of Marketing Science, Journal of Business Research*, and *Industrial Marketing Management*. Professor Marshall is a Distinguished Fellow and President of the Academy of Marketing Science, Past-President of the American Marketing Association Academic Division, and a Fellow and Past-President of the Society for Marketing Advances. His industry experience prior to entering academe includes product management, field sales management, and retail management positions with firms such as Warner-Lambert, the Mennen Company, and Target Corporation.

ELNORA W. STUART, Ph.D., is Professor of Marketing at the University of South Carolina Upstate. Prior to joining USC Upstate in 2008, she was Professor of Marketing and the BP Egypt Oil Professor of Management Studies at the American University in Cairo, Professor of Marketing at Winthrop University in Rock Hill, South Carolina, and on the faculty of the University of South Carolina. She is also a regular visiting professor at Instituto de Empresa in Madrid, Spain. She earned a BA in Theatre/Speech from the University of North Carolina at Greensboro and both a Master of Arts in Journalism and Mass Communication, and a Ph.D. in Marketing from the University of South Carolina. Professor Stuart's research has been published in major academic journals including the *Journal of Consumer Research, Journal of Advertising, Journal of Business Research*, and *Journal of Public Policy and Marketing*. For over 25 years she has served as a consultant for numerous businesses and not-for-profit organizations in the United States and in Egypt.

BROCK SMITH is a Professor of Marketing and Entrepreneurship, Winspear Scholar, and Entrepreneurship Area Champion at the Peter B. Gustavson School of Business at the University of Victoria where he has taught marketing, marketing research, and new venture marketing courses for more than 20 years. Winner of the 1992 Academy of Marketing Science Doctoral Dissertation Award, he has published articles relating to marketing strategy and entrepreneurial cognition in leading journals such as the *Journal of Marketing, Industrial Marketing Management, Psychology and Marketing*, the *Academy of Management Journal*, and *Entrepreneurship Theory & Practice*.

SYLVAIN CHARLEBOIS is Associate Dean and Professor in the College of Management and Economics at the University of Guelph. Dr. Charlebois is an award-winning researcher and teacher. He also served as the Director of the Johnson-Shoyama Graduate School of Public Policy (Regina Campus). His current research interest lies in the broad area of food distribution, security, and safety. He has published many peer-reviewed journal articles and his research has been featured in a number of newspapers and on television. Dr. Charlebois is a member of the National Advisory Board of the Canadian Food Inspection Agency. He has been asked to act as an advisor on food safety policies in North America and Europe.

BHUPESH SHAH earned his B.Sc. (Anthropology/Microbio-Biochem) from the University of Toronto and his MBA (Marketing/Finance) from York University. After 15 years of marketing management positions in the retail, packaged goods and equipment industries, he has returned to the classroom to teach marketing and other business-related courses at Seneca College. Bhupesh also puts theory to practice via his strategy consulting business.

▶Preface

What's new in the fourth Canadian edition is what's new in marketing: more on metrics, more on new marketing tools and techniques, a rethinking of advertising and promotions, and even stronger links to the real world of marketing by showing how concepts are linked with marketing planning.

Here's just a sample of what we changed.

Focus on marketing metrics:
- Marketing Metrics boxed features illustrate how marketers specify and measure desired outcomes.
- Specific exercises in every chapter and revised pedagogical material includes focused in-class and homework activities and research that encourage improved critical thinking and decision-making skills.

Heightened attention to social networking as a marketing communication option of increasing importance:
- New Tech and Trends boxed feature highlights cutting-edge trends in technology in every chapter.
- Covers emerging topics such as geospatial platforms, user-generated content (UCG), augmented reality, owned/earned/paid media, and multichannel strategies.

Rethinking how companies are approaching advertising and promotion:
- Major revision and recasting of the entire promotion/marketing communication series of Chapters 10, 11, and 12.

Linking marketing planning with concepts:
- The addition of Part Openers that add value in two ways: (1) providing a brief overview of the key learning to come within the part chapters, and (2) linking those learning elements to application in a threaded example marketing plan.
- Marketing Plan Template, available both in the text and on MyMarketingLab, walks students through the steps to creating strategic and compelling marketing plans.

Features of the Fourth Canadian Edition of *Marketing: Real People, Real Choices*

Focus on Decision Making

The Real People, Real Choices approach and unique decision-making focus features real marketers at real companies in the chapter openers, and it walks students through the critical thinking questions and ethics issues faced by real marketers on a daily basis in the form of new Applying boxes.

Meet Real Marketers

Many of the Real People, Real Choices vignettes are new to this edition, featuring a variety of decision makers from CEOs to brand managers, including many Canadians. Here is just a sample of the marketers we feature:

- Richard Hill, Yellow Point Lodge

- Jay Minkoff, First Flavor

- Ryan Garton, Discover Financial Services

- Julie Cordua, (RED)

- Catharine Downes, North Shore Credit Union

- Jeff Quipp, Search Engine People Inc.

- Michael Pepperdine, Sitka

- Michael Monello, Campfire

- Hesham Shafie, Brand Momentum Inc.

Ethics and Sustainability in Marketing

Because the roles of ethics and sustainability in business and marketing are so important, we focus on these topics in every chapter of the book. These Ethical and Sustainable Decisions in the Real World boxes feature real-life examples of ethical and sustainable decisions marketers are faced with on a day-to-day basis.

Cutting-Edge Technology

With technology evolving at a rapid-fire pace, it's now more important than ever for today's marketers to stay on the cutting edge of the latest technological developments. Viral marketing campaigns are just the tip of the iceberg! Tech and Trends boxes feature the most current technological advances and explain how companies are using them to creatively get their messages out to consumers.

An Easy-to-Follow Marketing Plan Template

Marketing: Real People, Real Choices, Fourth Canadian edition includes a template of a marketing plan you can use as you make your way through the book. The template provides a framework that will enable you to organize marketing concepts by chapter and create a solid marketing plan of your own.

End-of-Chapter Study Map

Each chapter now has an integrated study map for students that includes an Objective Summary, Key Terms, and student assessment opportunities of several types—Concepts: Test Your Knowledge; Activities: Apply What You've Learned; Marketing Metrics Exercise (more on this one below); Choices: What Do You Think?; and Miniproject: Learn By Doing. By completing these assessments, students and instructors achieve maximum assurance of learning.

Measuring the Value of Marketing through Marketing Metrics

Just how do marketers add value to a company, and can that value be quantified? More and more, businesses demand accountability, and marketers respond as they develop a variety of "scorecards" that show how specific marketing activities directly affect their company's ROI—return on investment. On the job, the decisions that marketers make increasingly come from data and calculations and less from instinct. Each end-of-chapter section includes exercises that provide real-world examples of the measures marketers use to help them make good decisions.

New and Updated End-of-Chapter Cases in This Edition

Each chapter concludes with an exciting Marketing in Action minicase about a real firm facing real marketing challenges. Questions at the end let you make the call to get the company on the right track.

All New CBC Video Cases

Each part concludes with all new CBC Video Cases drawn from the CBC's *The National* and *Marketplace* programs. The case summaries demonstrate for students how the concepts they have learned in the book apply to the real world, while the questions at the end of each case provide students with the opportunity to apply what they have learned and develop their critical thinking skills.

Instructor Resources

The following instructor supplements are available for downloading from a password-protected section of Pearson Canada's online catalogue (www.pearsoned.ca/highered). Navigate to your book's catalogue page to view a list of those supplements that are available. See your local sales representative for details and access.

Instructor's Manual

The *Instructor's Manual* includes a chapter overview, objectives, a detailed lecture outline, support for end-of-chapter material, along with additional student projects and assignments. It also includes teaching notes for the end-of-chapter cases and end-of-part CBC video cases.

Test Item File

Available in Microsoft Word format, this test bank includes more than 1200 questions—100+ questions per chapter. Questions range from multiple choice and true/false to essay and application. All questions offer level of difficulty and page references and are linked to the book's learning objectives. These questions are also available in MyTest format.

MyTest

MyTest from Pearson Canada is a powerful assessment-generation program that helps instructors easily create and print quizzes, tests, exams, as well as assignment or practice handouts. Questions and tests can all be authored online, allowing instructors ultimate flexibility and the ability to efficiently manage assessments anytime, from anywhere. MyTest for the Fourth Canadian edition of *Marketing: Real People, Real Choices* includes over 1200 multiple choice, true/false, and short answer questions. These questions are also available in Microsoft Word format on the Instructor's Resource Centre.

PowerPoint Presentation

This presentation includes outlines and key points from each chapter. The slides provide instructors with visual talking points designed to engage students and stimulate classroom discussion. These slides were designed for instructors who like to customize their Power-Points using their own materials or the image library featured on the Instructor's Resource Centre. A student version of these PowerPoint slides is also available on MyMarketingLab.

PowerPoints for Personal Response Systems (PRS)

These Q&A style slides are designed for classrooms using "clickers" or classroom response systems.

CBC Video Library

The CBC Video Library is a compilation of video segments drawn from the CBC's *The National* and *Marketplace* programs upon which the video cases in the book are based.

Image Library

The Image Library consists of many of the figures and exhibits featured in the text. These are ideal for PowerPoint customization.

Study on the Go

At the end of each chapter, you will find a unique QR code providing access to Study on the Go, an unprecedented mobile integration between text and online content. Students link to Pearson's unique Study on the Go content directly from their smartphones, allowing them to study whenever and wherever they wish! Go to one of the sites below to see how you can download an app to your smartphone for free. Once the app is installed, your phone will scan the code and link to a website containing Pearson's Study on the Go content, including the popular study tools Glossary Flashcards, Audio Summaries, and Quizzes, which can be accessed anytime.

ScanLife
http://get.scanlife.com
NeoReader
http://get.neoreader.com
QuickMark
http://www.quickmark.com.tw/

The Moment You Know

Educators know it. Students know it. It's that inspired moment when something that was difficult to understand suddenly makes perfect sense. Our MyLab products have been designed and refined with a single purpose in mind—to help educators create that moment of understanding with their students.

MyMarketingLab

MyMarketingLab delivers **proven results** in helping individual students succeed. It provides **engaging experiences** that personalize, stimulate, and measure learning for each student. And it comes from a **trusted partner** with educational expertise and an eye on the future.

MyMarketingLab can be used by itself or linked to any learning management system. To learn more about how MyMarketingLab combines proven learning applications with powerful assessment, visit www.mymarketinglab.com.

MyMarketingLab—the moment you know.

CourseSmart

CourseSmart is a new way for instructors and students to access textbooks online, anytime, from anywhere. With thousands of titles across hundreds of courses, CourseSmart helps instructors choose the best textbook for their class and give their students a new option for buying the assigned textbook as a lower cost eTextbook. For more information visit www.coursesmart.com.

Technology Specialists

Pearson's Technology Specialists work with faculty and campus course designers to ensure that Pearson technology products, assessment tools, and online course materials are tailored to meet your specific needs. This highly qualified team is dedicated to helping schools take full advantage of a wide range of educational resources by assisting in the integration of a variety of instructional materials and media formats. Your local Pearson Canada sales representative can provide you with more details on this service program.

Pearson Custom Library

For enrollments of at least 25 students, you can create your own textbook by choosing the chapters that best suit your own course needs. To begin building your custom text, visit www.pearsoncustomlibrary.com. You may also work with a dedicated Pearson Custom editor to create your ideal text—publishing your own original content or mixing and matching Pearson content. Contact your local Pearson representative to get started.

Acknowledgments

We would first like to express our thanks to the US authors of this text, Michael R. Solomon, Greg W. Marshall, and Elnora W. Stuart, for their vision of a marketing text that reflects the activities and priorities of real marketers. We hope we have maintained their vision in the fourth Canadian edition.

We would also like to thank the many other people who have made significant contributions to this book. We greatly appreciate the time that each of the "real people" generously spent to help us write the Real People, Real Choices profiles. Without their willingness to be involved, we could not have provided students with the decision-maker focus that is so central to this book.

We are grateful to the following reviewers, instructors, and real marketers who provided valuable feedback during the development of this edition:

Deepa Acharya, Mount Royal University
H. Onur Bodur, Concordia University
Marc Boivin, University of Calgary
Jack Brown, Georgian College
Brahm Canzer, CEGEP John Abbott College
Kerry Dale Couet, Grant MacEwan University
Dean Cowell, Centennial College
Ian Fisher, Sheridan College
Ray Friedman, Lethbridge College
Darryl Hammond, Red River College
Rosalie Hilde, College of New Caledonia
Don Hill, Langara College
Athena Hurezeanu, Seneca College
Tom Jopling, British Columbia Institute of Technology
Deborah Lawton, Thompson Rivers University
David MacLeod, NBCC Moncton
David Moscovitz, Vanier College
David Moulton, Douglas College
Margaret Osborne, Seneca College
Charles Royce, McGill University
Reginald Sheppard, University of New Brunswick
Les Smith, Fleming College
Rae Verity, Southern Alberta Institute of Technology
Keith Wallace, Kwantlen Polytechnic University

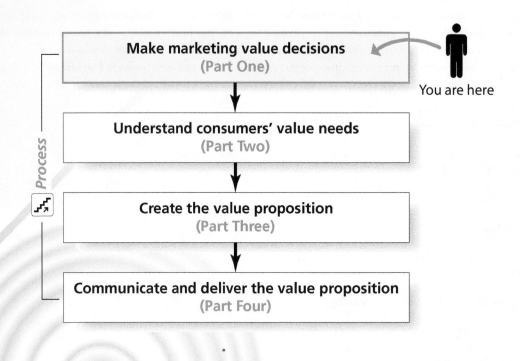

Make marketing value decisions
(Part One)

You are here

Understand consumers' value needs
(Part Two)

Process

Create the value proposition
(Part Three)

Communicate and deliver the value proposition
(Part Four)

Make Marketing Value Decisions

Part One Overview

Welcome to the first set of chapters in *Marketing: Real People, Real Decisions*! The book is divided into four major "Parts." Each Part focuses on key elements of marketing as a value-adding factor in any organization's success. Each Part Opener (like this one) provides you with a brief overview of the focus of the content within that Part. It also relates and applies this content to the development of a marketing plan for a fictitious company called S&S Smoothie.[1] The full marketing plan for S&S Smoothie can be found in the Appendix. The S&S Smoothie marketing plan gives you an example of how marketing analysis, decisions, and rationale come together to achieve organizational objectives. The Part Openers also link each Part's content to the bigger picture of marketing planning and help you understand the who, what, when, where, why, and how related to the way that particular material fits into the big picture of marketing. Don't be concerned right now if the notion of a marketing plan is brand new to you; very soon, we'll bring you up to speed on what marketing planning is all about.

You will notice right away that this book is about *people making marketing decisions*, as opposed to merely about the marketing

of products, firms, ideas, or other items of value. The Real People, Real Choices vignettes that begin each chapter help you connect marketing to actual people making marketing decisions. The vignettes are chosen to fit the chapters so the material that you will cover in a particular chapter will help you better understand the issues and concepts involved in making effective decisions; and along the way we will show you how some of the concepts you are learning apply to the Real People decision. At the end of each chapter is a short summary of what the actual decision maker decided, and why, so you can compare your thinking to those getting paid to make the decision. The actual decision made is not necessarily the best decision, and, ultimately, customers are the judges. However, if you read the vignettes, give some thought to the advantages and disadvantages of the alternatives presented, and try to apply what you are learning in the chapter, your own decision-making skills will significantly improve.

Part One offers two chapters that kick off your study of marketing. The term marketing conjures up two common misconceptions. Some people will tell you that marketing is all about advertising. Others tend to equate marketing with selling something to someone. As you will learn in this Part, marketing is first and foremost a decision-making process—one that is focused on identifying, creating, and delivering value for customers and other stakeholders. At the end of Part One you will also recognize that leading businesses achieve their success not only by creating economic value, but also by creating social and environmental value.

Marketing Plan Connection:
S&S Smoothie

The S&S Smoothie Company Canada Ltd. was founded in September 2008 in Toronto with the goal of creating and marketing healthy "smoothie" beverages for sale to health-conscious consumers. S&S Smoothie expects to take advantage of an increasing desire for healthy foods both in Canada and internationally—and to ride the wave of consumer interest in low-carb alternatives.

The abbreviated marketing plan example found in the Appendix for the fictitious S&S Smoothie Company is flagged to indicate which plan elements correspond to each of the Parts within this text. The "Build a Marketing Plan" guide on the inside covers of this book is also cross-referenced to chapters by section of the marketing plan.

In the chapters within Part One, there are major learning elements that guide you in developing four initial parts of a marketing plan: internal environmental analysis, external environmental analysis, SWOT analysis, and setting marketing objectives. Let's take a look at each of these elements.

Internal Environmental Analysis

Chapter 2 provides an overview of marketing planning from the perspective of a marketing firm. Surprisingly, accomplishing a useful internal environmental analysis is often more challenging than is the analysis of the external environment. It's like the old saying, "We have found the enemy and it is us!" Some firms do not have a culture that supports honest self-reflection, and instead they tend to sweep problems under the rug. This is, of course, very dangerous, since future marketing planning depends on a realistic assessment of the firm and its internal capabilities.

When you review the case of S&S Smoothie, take special note of their mission, how the firm is set up and who the key players are, the nature of their organizational culture, and how they are currently deploying the four Ps (product, promotion, price, and place) of the marketing mix. What is evidently working well for them already? What likely could be improved through marketing planning?

External Environmental Analysis

In Chapter 2 you will also gain solid knowledge of the global environment in which marketers today do business. In contrast to the internal environment, the external environment consists of elements that are largely outside the direct control of a firm and its managers. The company operates within its external environment, but in most instances it can do little to directly shape and form that environment. Because of this, it becomes incredibly important that firms accurately identify the external factors that are likely to have the greatest impact on success and then to proactively take these factors into account when developing plans and forecasts.

Key elements in the external environment include:
- *Competitive environment*—Who do you compete with and how?
- *Economic environment*—In what ways do economic forces impact the marketing success of the firm?
- *Technological environment*—What is the role of advancing technology on the business?
- *Political and legal environment*—How do these elements impact decisions the firm makes about products and markets?
- *Sociocultural environment*—What is the impact of changing societal tastes and values on the marketplace?

One of the most challenging aspects of doing external environmental analysis is that the information gathered is not static. It is constantly changing! This means that marketers need to continually scan the elements of the external environment for trends and (hopefully) make changes to their marketing plans before the trends get away from them.

As you review S&S Smoothie's marketing plan, try to imagine which of the external environmental elements identified are most likely to change in the near future, and how the changes would impact their plan.

SWOT Analysis

A SWOT analysis (**S**trengths, **W**eaknesses, **O**pportunities, and **T**hreats) is a convenient way of summarizing your situation analysis. You will note that the S&S Smoothie example has a very succinct set of 3–4 bulleted items under each of the SWOT subheadings. This is what you should strive for in a SWOT—a succinct prioritization of the main internal and external situational factors that you believe, based on your analysis, are most important to future planning for the firm. Be sure to specify the implications of these factors by explaining why they are important to your firm and what you need to think about or do as a result.

Marketing Objectives

An objective is something that you set out to accomplish. You will learn in Chapter 2 that for objectives to be useful they must meet several important criteria. A well-stated objective is specific, measurable, and realistically attainable. Objectives are not very useful to marketers for planning purposes if they are vague, if you don't know what metrics tell you that you've succeeded, or if they are impossible to accomplish. S&S Smoothie has identified four important marketing objectives. See if you think they meet these criteria.

MyMarketingLab

Now, if you are working on a marketing plan as part of your course, you can go to MyMarketingLab to apply what you learn in Part One to your own marketing plan project.

Welcome to the World of Marketing:
Create and Deliver Value

Real People **Profiles**

Richard Hill

▼ A Decision Maker
at Yellow Point Lodge

Richard Hill learned the hospitality business at the knee of a master, his father Gerry Hill, the original "custodian" of Yellow Point Lodge. In the mid-1930s, Gerry Hill started the Yellow Point Lodge near Ladysmith, British Columbia, with seven tiny cabins, a small cookhouse, and a dining room. The lodge was built on the north end of 185 acres overlooking a pristine, rocky promontory of land, with a 270-degree view of the Pacific Ocean and some of the Gulf Islands. Richard grew up at Yellow Point but left after high school to pursue a career in rock and roll.

Richard returned to Yellow Point in 1984 to help his father run the lodge and learn the family business. Richard Hill is now the owner and manager of Yellow Point Lodge and has assumed the mantle of "custodian" of this unique property. In 1990 he married Sandi Bastian, a friend from his teens, and together they are raising their children with the same values with which Richard was raised.

The cost of running Yellow Point Lodge has increased significantly in the past few years but revenues have not increased, in part because Richard wondered whether increasing prices or otherwise changing the hospitality concept would wreck what he and his customers love about the lodge.

Yellow Point Lodge is a rustic, all-inclusive camp for adults seeking to get away from the city for rest and relaxation. The menu has not changed in 50 years and the customers like it that way. Roast beef on Friday nights, seafood on Saturday, roast turkey on Sundays—and if you don't eat your veggies, you don't get dessert. This isn't a luxury resort; accommodations range from a basic lodge room to cabins that sleep two, four, six, or eight people, to beach-front shacks with bathroom facilities up the hill and outdoor showers designed for reasonable modesty. For the more adventuresome, there is a salt water swimming pool, a hot tub, tennis courts, mountain bikes, and kayaks. For those who just want to curl up with a good book, there is a large open room with a huge fireplace, lots of overstuffed chairs and couches, and shelves of good books and board games. The concept isn't for everyone, but those who like it, like it a lot.

Situated just 40 minutes south of the BC Ferry terminal at Nanaimo, Yellow Point Lodge is fully booked from May through September, and has good occupancy the rest of the year. At about $100 a night per person, all in, Yellow Point Lodge guests are intensely loyal. Most guests have been

Here's my ~~problem~~.

coming to Yellow Point for the same week, or part of a week, every year for 20 or more years, with some not having missed a year in over 50. For these guests, Yellow Point is their summer cabin, which Richard just happens to look after the other weeks of the year. Guests are so devoted to what Richard offers that they formed a society, "The Friends of Yellow Point," who organize work parties to help Richard maintain the property to keep his costs down. When the old lodge burned down in October 1985, the Friends of Yellow Point helped Richard, his father, and a professional crew rebuild it.

With soaring property values, Richard's 185 acres are now worth more than $20 million, and Richard's tax bill for holding this land has increased substantially. Other cost pressures are also making it difficult to maintain the value proposition so dearly loved by his guests. However, almost all of the guests are long-time guests, and a lot of the value they receive from Richard's offering is in the memories they have of summers past and the long-standing relationships they have with the other guests, who once a year get together at Yellow Point. In light of this situation, Richard considered three options to better align revenues with costs:

Things to remember

Richard's guests don't like change and are quick to let Richard know if something isn't quite right—by which they mean it isn't like it used to be five, ten, or twenty years ago. His customers are generally not wealthy people and seek a "few frills" experience that is rich in relational value. The waiting list to secure one of the very basic beach shacks is years, if not decades, long during the peak summer season.

Richard considered his **Options** 1·2·3

1 Option
Raise the price. One option is to simply raise the prices. With such strong demand for the Yellow Point experience, and fierce loyalty by the long-time guests, Richard thought that he might be able to raise prices by 10 or 15 percent to match the cost increases. This would be a relatively unobtrusive option, as the experience would not change for the guests. The challenge, however, lies in that most of Richard's guests are middle-class professionals, such as teachers or government employees, and many are retired and on a fixed income. Richard wondered at what price point the Yellow Point experience would be considered too expensive. As soon as some of the regular guests stop coming, the value of those long-standing relationships erodes, and there is less incentive to return. It could become just another place where you don't know anyone. With higher prices, the Lodge might attract

a different clientele, but those people might have higher expectations for luxury accommodation that Richard could not easily provide.

2 Option
Increase capacity. Richard could develop the property by adding more cabins or extending the "main lodge" to accommodate more visitors. Yellow Point Lodge has easy access for visitors. It isn't too far for anyone, whether they fly into Victoria or Nanaimo, or drive. Richard thought that there was sufficient demand for expansion, given that he was almost fully booked for six months of the year, and guests joked that they had put "their" weeks in their wills. However, expansion would erode the value proposition for the current guests who like knowing each other and like the feeling that the facility is all theirs. With 200 guests spread around the current facility, there is a feeling of spaciousness and it is quite easy to find a quiet spot to be by yourself.

3 Option
Protect the land and decrease its value. The third option Richard looked at was to find a way to decrease his tax obligation while still maintaining the integrity of the resort. Relatively new tax law made the option of protecting some or all of the land with an ecological covenant a viable alternative. A covenant would prevent Richard, or anyone else in the future, from cutting trees (other than for safety) on the land. The land would be much less valuable with such a covenant placed on it, thereby reducing Richard's tax liability. Richard would still own the land and his guests would have use of the trails, and the old growth forest, part of a rapidly diminishing coastal Douglas fir zone, would be preserved in perpetuity. Richard still wanted to be able to maintain the lodge and his cabins and expand those facilities if appropriate, so he could not put a covenant on all the land. This was a viable option, but it would mean reducing the value of his very valuable land forever. By doing this, Richard would be taking the decision out of the hands of his kids. This would make their lives easier, because they wouldn't be forced to decide, and it might keep family relationships intact in case his kids didn't agree on the best course of action. On the other hand, it would be decreasing their financial inheritance.

You Choose

Which **Option** would you choose, and **why?**
1. ☐YES ☐NO   2. ☐YES ☐NO   3. ☐YES ☐NO

See what **option** Richard chose on **page 39** ➡

1

Welcome to Brand You

At the beginning of each chapter, we will introduce you to a marketing professional like Richard Hill, in a feature called Real People, Real Decisions. We will tell you about a decision the marketer had to make and give you the options she or he considered. Think about these options as you read through the chapter so you can build an argument for selecting one of the options. These vignettes and others introduced in class by your instructor will allow you to practise making and defending marketing decisions based on appropriate analysis; application of marketing theory, concepts, and principles; and your own judgment. Do not worry if you think that you might not have good judgment yet. That comes with experience and practice in making marketing decisions. These vignettes give you a chance to practise and develop your own decision making and decision defending ability. There are no "right answers" in business, so while we will tell you at the end of each chapter what decision was actually made, and why, those decisions are not necessarily the best decisions that could have been made. Ultimately, consumers are the only judges who matter.

What Marketing Is and How Value Creation Is Central to the Marketing Concept

> I have a TV screen of some 32 inches
> TV dinner and an easy chair
> From where I view a disaster
> And switch the channel fast
> And thank my lucky star I wasn't there
> The world's in a hurry but I don't have to worry
> There's a movie on with a happy end
> I've seen it before but I can see it some more
> So I don't have to go out and pretend

Alex wakes up with a groan as the Hellacopters blare out a song from the next bedroom. Why does her roommate have to download these loud ringtones onto her cellphone and then leave it on so early in the morning? She throws back the Laura Ashley sheets and rolls out of her new Sleep Number bed that she bought at Sleep Country Canada. As Alex stumbles across the room in her Dalia Cami pyjamas by La Vie en Rose, her senses are further assaulted as she catches a waft of Amanda's trademark Magic by Celine perfume. She pours herself a steaming cup of Starbucks' Caffé Verona, and stirs in a heaping mound of Splenda. As she starts to grab a Yoplait from the SubZero, she checks her BlackBerry and gets reminded of her job interview with lululemon athletica—yeah for Monster.ca! Good thing she texted her friends last night to get advice on what to wear. Alex does a quick scan of *The Globe and Mail* Online, then Googles the manager who will be interviewing her. Hopefully he won't look her up on Facebook—some of those photos aren't exactly professional. Alex slips into her Ann Taylor suit, slides on her Prada shoes, grabs her Coach briefcase, and climbs into her Scion. Traffic is a bear, but she doesn't care—she has her iTunes.

Marketing is all around us. Indeed, some might say that we live in a branded world. Like Alex, you have encounters with many marketers even before you leave for the day via products, ads, the Web, charitable causes, podcasts, and other ways you receive information or interact with brands.

What's more, like Alex, *you* are a product. That may sound a bit weird, but companies like Monster and Facebook couldn't exist if you were not a product with value. We are going to use that word a LOT in this book, so let's define it now. **Customer value** refers to the benefits a customer receives from buying and using a good or service in relation to the costs and sacrifices of buying and using it. For example, consider a new chair from Ikea. The benefits include that it looks good and it is comfortable. The cost and sacrifices include the price you paid, the hassle of getting it home, the time it takes to assemble, the inconvenience of taking the box to the recycling depot, and the angst of figuring out what you are supposed to do with the Styrofoam. Customers look at value over the life of the product—from when they start looking for it, to when they have finished using it and have had it disposed of.

You have "market value" as a person—qualities that set you apart from others and abilities other people want and need. After you finish this course, you'll have even more value, because you'll know about the field of marketing and how this field relates to you as a future business person and consumer. Although our main focus is understanding how to make effective marketing decisions for organizations, what you learn here equally applies to "brand you," and we hope you will get some ideas about what you can do to increase your value to employers, partners, and maybe even to society. You probably already knew that celebrities like Justin Bieber, Sidney Crosby, Mike Meyers, and Avril Lavigne (Exhibit 1.1) are "brands"—but so is everyone else (albeit not quite as effectively). We "position" ourselves for job interviews, we are "on the market" when we break up with a boyfriend or girlfriend; some people hire image consultants to devise a "marketing strategy" for them, while others undergo plastic surgery or makeovers to improve their "product image." So, the principles of marketing apply to you, just as they apply to coffee, cars, computers, and produce. While there are some differences in how we go about marketing each of these, the basic ideas are the same. Marketing is a fundamental part of our lives both as consumers and as business people. We are going to take you behind the scenes so that you can learn what goes on before consumers can make their goods and services choices. In this chapter and the next, we are going to introduce you to a lot of concepts. If you feel overwhelmed, don't worry, these concepts will be explained in detail in the rest of the text. These introductory chapters are just intended to give you an overview of the big picture before getting into the details. Let's start with the "what and how" before we talk about the "who and where."

Exhibit 1.1

Marketing concepts apply to the branding of people, like Justin Bieber and you.

customer value

The benefits a customer receives from buying and using a good or service in relation to the costs and sacrifices of buying and using it.

What Is Marketing?

Marketing. Lots of people talk about it, but what is it? When you ask people to define marketing, you get many answers, and there are many misconceptions about what marketing is. Some say, "That's what happens when a pushy salesperson tries to sell me something I don't want." Others say, "Oh, that's simple—TV commercials." Others might say "merchandising," "pricing," "packaging," or "telephone soliciting."

As you can see, the term *marketing* means different things to different people (in England, it is even used as a synonym for shopping). Each of these responses has a

Courtesy of the Pepsi-Cola Company

Exhibit 1.2

PepsiCo hopes that the product, price, distribution, and communication decisions it makes for Aquafina result in a value proposition preferred by customers.

marketing

Marketing is the activity, set of institutions, and processes for creating, communicating, delivering, and exchanging offerings that have value for customers, clients, partners, and society at large.

Richard Hill

APPLYING ▽ Customer Value

Richard Hill needs to understand what his customers value most about the Yellow Point Lodge experience before he can decide how to adapt his offering. His customers appear to highly value the simplicity of the experience, the consistency of the experience, and their relationships with other customers. ➡

grain of truth to it, but they are very incomplete. There is an official definition of **marketing** adopted in 2007 by the American Marketing Association (AMA, which has many Canadian chapters):

"Marketing is the activity, set of institutions, and processes for creating, communicating, delivering and exchanging offerings that have value for customers, clients, partners, and society at large."[2]

Focus on Value Creation

The basic idea of this somewhat complicated definition of marketing is that marketing is all about creating and delivering value, and doing this for all parties involved in an exchange (at the very least both the customer and the organization). It involves a decision-making process, and these decisions are typically (but not always) made by people who have official marketing roles in areas of an organization, such as a marketing department, a sales department, a marketing communications department, or a new product development department. Decision makers in organizations like PepsiCo (Exhibit 1.2) make product, price, distribution, and communication decisions that result in a product (good or service) offering that is intended to be better than competitive offers, at least in the minds of some customers (otherwise no product would be sold).

Another way of defining *marketing* that is more consistent with this focus on value creation is, *Marketing is the process of achieving individual and organizational objectives by creating superior customer value for one or more target markets with a sustainable strategy.*

This definition suggests that the "prime directive" of marketing is to achieve objectives. We do that by creating superior customer value—offers that are perceived as being more valuable to customers than any other solutions (competing brands), or even more valuable than the money in their wallet. To create a transaction or an economic exchange of value, both parties need to believe that the exchange is fair—that what they get is worth more to them than what they give up. Of course, each of us has our own perceptions of how to best satisfy our needs, what is valuable, and what exchanges are "worth it." As we will explore more fully in Chapter 2, that calculation involves many considerations beyond the functional or utilitarian use of the product. Many consumers have bought some version of Apple's iPod or iPod Touch, believing that the value received in terms of "coolness," prestige, design, and interface is well worth the price premium over competitive offerings. One enterprising entrepreneur in England recently offered deluxe 61-step car washes for $10 000. Not everyone can afford a $10 000 car wash, but lots of customers thought that the two-week process was worth it; the entrepreneur had nine months worth of business lined up shortly after opening.[3] Marketers need to regularly conduct research to keep up with changing consumer perspectives and preferences. Another challenge is to figure out how much value to offer to the customer (how good a deal) and how much value to keep in his or her company (as profit or contribution from the sale of the product). Value from the seller's perspective goes beyond profit. Some organizations seek prestige among rivals, take pride in doing what they do well, or make important societal or environmental contributions. Because value is such a complicated but important concept, now more than ever marketers search for new and better ways to accurately measure just what kind of value they deliver. They also try to learn how this stacks up to the competition, and in some cases even whether the relationship they have with a customer possesses enough value for them to continue it.

The alternative definition of marketing presented above also focuses on the idea of creating value for specific **target markets**, groups of people that have different needs, wants, or preferences from other groups of people and would seek a different value proposition (solution). Not everyone would want a $10 000 car wash, but apparently some people (some billionaires) do. This definition also suggests that we want to develop a sustainable strategy, not in the environmental sense (although, as we will see later in this chapter, it often makes good business sense to make decisions that are good for the environment), but in the sense of making a set of decisions that will allow us to compete effectively until our objectives have been achieved, which for most organizations is a long-term perspective.

Marketing Is About Creating Customer Value

One important part of our definition of marketing is that it is about creating value for diverse **stakeholders**. The term *stakeholders* here refers to buyers, sellers, investors in a company, community residents, and even citizens of the nations where goods and services are made or sold; in other words, any person or organization that has a "stake" in the outcome of an economic **exchange**.

One important stakeholder is the **consumer**. A consumer is the ultimate user of a good or service. Consumers can be individuals or organizations (although we usually use the term "customer" when referring to an organization), whether a company, government, charity, or association. So while some like to say "the customer is king" (or queen), it's important to recognize that marketing is not just about satisfying customer needs, it is about satisfying the needs of all the parties involved in an exchange. The seller needs to make a profit to stay in business to be able to continue offering the goods and services valued by the customer. That is why the customers of European airline Ryanair usually don't complain too much about being charged £15 for checked luggage or £10 to pay with a credit card. When a flight from London to Munich is as little as £6, return, customers recognize that money must be made somewhere for the airline to stay in business.

Similarly, a not-for-profit organization needs to match its supply of resources with customer demand. This is the philosophy behind the **marketing concept**. The marketing concept suggests that organizational objectives such as long-term profitability are best met by first understanding what customers need (value sought) and then determining the associated costs of satisfying those needs (creating and delivering that value)—thus, creating exchanges of mutual satisfaction. Central to the philosophy reflected in the marketing concept is an understanding that organizations exist to create value for consumers where it is neither efficient nor effective for consumers to attempt to satisfy their needs themselves.[4]

A **need** is the difference between a consumer's actual state and some ideal or desired state. When the difference is big enough, the consumer is motivated to take action to satisfy the need. When you are hungry, you buy a snack. If you're not happy with your hair, you get a new look. As we will see in Chapter 4, needs are related to physical conditions, such as being cold, hungry, or scared, and psychological conditions, such as being liked, communicating with others, or being fulfilled. The specific way a need is satisfied depends on an individual's history, learning experiences, and cultural environment. A **want** is a desire for a particular product used to satisfy a need in specific ways that are culturally and socially influenced. For example, two classmates' stomachs rumble during a noon-hour class, and both need food. How each of them satisfies this need may be quite different. One

target market
The group(s) of consumers or customers on which an organization focuses its marketing plan and toward which it directs its marketing efforts.

stakeholder
People or organizations who influence or are influenced by marketing decisions.

exchange
The process by which some transfer of value occurs between a buyer and a seller.

consumer
The ultimate user of a good or service.

marketing concept
A business orientation that focuses on achieving organizational objectives by understanding customer needs, and creating and delivering value in exchanges that satisfy the needs of all parties.

need
The recognition of any difference between a consumer's actual state and some ideal or desired state.

want
The desire to satisfy needs in specific ways that are culturally and socially influenced.

Exhibit 1.3

Consumers with the same needs may have very different wants.

benefit
The outcome sought by a customer that motivates buying behaviour (that satisfies a need or want).

demand
Customers' desire for products coupled with the resources to obtain them.

market
All the customers and potential customers who share a common need that can be satisfied by a specific product, who have the resources to exchange for it, who are willing to make the exchange, and who have the authority to make the exchange.

marketplace
Any location or medium used to conduct an exchange.

might crave a salad or a bag of trail mix to go. The other might buy a cheeseburger and fries. Or the want may be even more specific: I want Mountain Country Cranberry Trail Mix (Exhibit 1.3) or a McDonald's cheeseburger. Consumers are motivated by needs but make purchase decisions based on wants.

A product delivers a **benefit** when it satisfies a need or want. For marketers to be successful, they must develop products that provide one or more benefits. The challenge is to identify what benefits people look for, develop a product that delivers those benefits, and then convince buyers that it does so better than a competitor's product. As the management expert Peter Drucker wrote, "The aim of marketing is to make selling superfluous."[5] What Drucker means is, if we succeed in creating a product that meets the needs of the customer, he or she will happily buy it without any "persuasion" from a salesperson. The salesperson may still be required to make the customer aware of the product and its relative merits in meeting the customer's needs. Ultimately, the marketer's value proposition (the benefits offered in relation to the costs and sacrifices) needs to be seen, by at least some customers, as being more valuable than the money those customers have in their pocket (or their bank account).

Everyone can want your product, but that doesn't ensure sales unless they have the means to obtain it. When you couple desire with the buying power or resources to satisfy a want, the result is **demand**. So the potential customers for a snappy, red BMW convertible are the people who want the car, minus those who can't afford to buy or lease one. A **market** consists of all the consumers who share a common need that can be satisfied by a product purchase and who have the resources, willingness, and authority to make the purchase.

A **marketplace** used to be a location where face-to-face buying and selling occurred. The marketplace may still be a street corner or an open air market, but in today's "wired" world, buyers and sellers might not ever see each other. Increasingly, the modern marketplace takes the form of a glitzy shopping mall, a mail-order catalogue, a television shopping network, an eBay auction site, or an e-commerce Web site. Indeed, a marketplace may not even exist in the physical world. Residents of cyberworlds like *Second Life* and *Habbo Hotel* buy and sell virtual real estate, home furnishings, and bling for their digital avatars; in 2010 alone they bought about $1.6 billion worth of virtual goods that exist only on a computer server (see Exhibit 1.4).

Marketing and Exchange Relationships

At the heart of every marketing act, big or small, is something we refer to as an "exchange relationship." An exchange occurs when something is obtained for something else in return. The buyer receives an object, service, or idea that satisfies a need, and the seller receives something he or she believes is of equivalent economic value. Usually this is money, but it could be other goods or services. Almost anything of value can be exchanged, including, if you remember the beginning of the chapter, you! (your time, your ideas, and the things you can do; see Exhibit 1.4). Politicians exchange promises for votes, athletes and performers exchange performances for ticket sales and exchange their images via endorsements for product sales. Places like Canada's Wonderland or Prince Edward Island exchange experiences for customers' time and money. Not-for-profit organizations like Covenant House (Exhibit 1.5) exchange services for the time of their clients and exchange the concept of making a difference to the problem of homelessness for the money of their donators.

For an exchange to occur, at least two people or organizations must be willing to make a trade, and each must have something the other wants. Both parties must agree on the value of the exchange and how it will be carried out. Each party also must be free to accept or reject the other's terms for the exchange. Under these conditions, a gun-wielding robber's offer to "exchange" your money for your life does not constitute a valid economic exchange.

To complicate things a bit more, everyone does not always agree on the terms of the exchange. Consider, for example, music piracy, which is a huge headache for music producers. On the one hand, they claim that they lose billions of dollars a year when consumers download songs without paying for them. On the other hand, a lot of people think the producers charge way too much for new songs and consider downloading a fair, socially valid (albeit illegal) act.

In recent years, many firms have transformed the way they do business. They now regard consumers as *partners* in the transaction rather than as passive "victims" and recognize that *it is more expensive to attract new customers than it is to retain current ones.* Although this notion has transformed the way many companies do business, it doesn't always hold true. In recent years, companies have been working harder to calculate the true value of their relationships with customers by asking, how much is this customer *really* worth to us? Firms recognize that it can be very costly in terms of both money and human effort to get new customers, and they do whatever it takes to keep their best customers loyal to the company.

Companies like the North Shore Credit Union, featured in the Real People profile of Chapter 6, calculate the **lifetime value of a customer** and look at how much profit they expect to make from a particular customer, including each and every purchase he or she will make from them now and in the future. To calculate lifetime value, companies estimate the amount the person will spend and then subtract what it will cost to maintain this relationship. In the long run, firms may decide to "fire" customers whose life-time value is negative. This concept will be explored further in Chapter 6.

Exhibit 1.4

Some transactions today, like those of the online game *Second Life,* are virtual exchanges.

lifetime value of a customer
How much profit companies expect to make from a particular customer, adding the contribution of each and every purchase s/he will make from them now and in the future and subtracting the cost to the company of maintaining this relationship.

The Who and Where of Marketing

This book is about marketing, and, more specifically, about making effective marketing decisions that create value for others. But who makes these decisions? Marketers come from many different places. Although many have earned marketing degrees, others have all sorts of backgrounds, sometimes with formal training and sometimes without. You will see this in the Real People profiles that are featured in each chapter. Fashion retailers may have training in design. Advertising creative executives often have a fine arts background, while copywriters often have degrees in English. E-marketers who design interactive Web pages for products and companies may have studied computer science. Even accountants often end up in marketing roles, as someone needs to make marketing decisions for accounting firms.

Marketers work in a variety of locations. They work in consumer goods companies like Taco Bell or Black & Decker, or at service companies like Tourism Saskatoon, Intrawest (Exhibit 1.6), or the Bank of Montreal. You will see them in retail organizations like lululemon athletica or Frontrunners and at companies that manufacture products for other companies, like Bombardier or Nortel. You will see them in government organizations like the Canadian Tourism Commission, not-for-profit organizations like the Canadian Cancer Society, large organizations like IBM Canada, and small startups like Sitka Surfboards, who make custom surfboards and boarding apparel. Marketing principles are also used to get people to endorse ideas or to change their behaviours in positive ways. Many organizations work hard to convince consumers to use seat belts, engage in safe

THIS CHRISTMAS, HELP GIVE STREET KIDS A HOME.

COVENANT HOUSE covenanthouse.ca

Exhibit 1.5

Not-for-profit organizations like Covenant House exchange services for time, and the concept of making a difference for the money of donors.

Exhibit 1.6

Marketing is important to service companies like Intrawest, as well as in most contexts you can think of.

sex, not litter, not smoke, and not drink and drive. Finally, sports and the arts are hotbeds of activity for marketing. A big part of these efforts involves promoting athletes like Sidney Crosby and artists like Avril Lavigne—who themselves create customer experiences.

Marketing's Role in the Firm: Cross-Functional Relationships

What role do marketers play in a firm? The importance organizations assign to marketing activities varies a lot. Top management in some firms is very marketing oriented (especially when the chief executive officer comes from the marketing ranks), whereas in other companies marketing is an afterthought. However, analysts estimate that at least one-third of CEOs come from a marketing background—so stick with us!

Sometimes a company uses the term *marketing* when what it really means is sales or advertising. In some organizations, particularly small, not-for-profit ones, there may be no one in the company specifically designated as "the marketing person." In contrast, some firms realize that marketing applies to all aspects of the firm's activities. As a result, there has been a trend toward integrating marketing with other business functions (such as management and accounting) instead of making it a separate function.

No matter what size the firm, a marketer's decisions affect, and are affected by, the firm's other operations. Marketing managers must work with financial and accounting officers to figure out whether products are profitable, to set marketing budgets, and to determine prices. They must work with people in manufacturing to be sure that products are produced on time and in the right quantities. Marketers also must work with research-and-development specialists to create products that meet consumers' needs.

Where Do You Fit In? Careers in Marketing

Marketing is an incredibly exciting, diverse discipline that brims with opportunities. There are many paths to a marketing career; we've tried to summarize the most typical ones here. Check out Table 1.1 to start thinking about which path might be best for you. Okay, now that you've gotten a glimpse of who marketers are and where they work, it's time to dig into what marketing really is.

Table 1.1 | Careers in Marketing

Marketing Field	Where Can I Work?	What Entry-Level Position Can I Get?	What Course Work Do I Need?
Advertising	**Advertising agency:** Media, research, and creative departments; account work **Large corporation:** Advertising department: brand/product management **Media:** Magazine, newspaper, radio, and television selling; management consulting; marketing research	Account coordinator (traffic department); assistant account executive; assistant media buyer; research assistant; assistant brand manager	Undergraduate business degree
Brand Management	**Any size corporation:** Coordinate the activities of specialists in production, sales, advertising, promotion, R&D, marketing research, purchasing, distribution, package development, and finance	Associate brand manager	M.B.A. preferred, but a few companies recruit undergraduates. Expect a sales training program in the field from one to four months and in-house classes and seminars.
Business-to-Business Marketing	**Any size corporation:** Only a few companies recruit on campus, so be prepared to search out job opportunities on your own, as well as interview on campus.	Sales representative; market research administrator; product manager; pricing administrator; product administrator; assistant marketing manager; sales administrator; assistant sales manager; sales service administrator	Undergraduate business degree. A broad background of subjects is generally better than concentrating on just one area. A technical degree may be important or even required in high-technology areas. Courses in industrial marketing and marketing strategy are very helpful.
Direct–Response Marketing	**Any size corporation:** Marketing-oriented firms, including those offering consumer goods, industrial products, financial institutions, and other types of service establishments. Entrepreneurs seeking to enter business for themselves.	Direct-response marketing is expanding rapidly and includes direct mail, print and broadcast media, telephone marketing, catalogues, in-home presentations, and door-to-door marketing. Seek counsel from officers and directors of the Direct Marketing Association and the Direct Selling Association.	Undergraduate business degree. Supplemental work in communications, psychology, and/or computer systems recommended.
Supply-Channel Management	**Any size corporation, including transportation corporations:** The analysis, planning, and control of activities concerned with the procurement and distribution of goods. The activities include transportation, warehousing, forecasting, order processing, inventory control, production planning, site selection, and customer service.	Physical distribution manager; supply chain manager; inventory-control manager; traffic manager; distribution-centre manager; distribution-planning analyst; customer service manager; transportation marketing; and operations manager	Undergraduate business degree and M.B.A. Broad background in the core functional areas of business, with particular emphasis in distribution-related topics such as logistics, transportation, purchasing, and negotiation.
International Marketing	**Large corporations:** Marketing department at corporate headquarters	Domestic sales position with an international firm may be the best first step toward international opportunities.	M.B.A. A broad background in marketing is recommended, with some emphasis on sales management and market research.
Marketing Models and Systems Analysis	**Large corporations:** Consult with managers who are having difficulty with marketing problems.	Undergraduate: Few positions available unless you have prior work experience. Graduate: market analyst, market research specialist, and management scientist.	M.B.A. Preparation in statistics, mathematics, and the behavioural sciences.

(continued)

Table 1.1	Careers in Marketing *(continued)*		
Marketing Field	**Where Can I Work?**	**What Entry-Level Position Can I Get?**	**What Course Work Do I Need?**
Marketing Research	**Any size corporation:** Provide management with information about consumers, the marketing environment, and the competition	Assistant market analyst or assistant product analyst level.	M.B.A. or an M.S. in Marketing Research although prior experience and training may improve an undergraduate's chances.
New Product Planning	**Any size corporation:** Marketing of consumer products, consumer industries, advertising agencies, consulting firms, public agencies, medical agencies, retailing management	Assistant manager or director of product planning or new product development.	M.B.A.
Retail Management	**Retail corporations**	Assistant buyer positions; department manager positions	Undergraduate business degree
Sales and Sales Management	**Profit and nonprofit organizations:** Financial, insurance, consulting, and government	Trade sales representative who sells to a wholesaler or retailer; missionary sales representative in manufacturing who sells to retailers or decision makers (e.g., pharmaceutical representative); technical sales representative who sells to specified accounts within a designated geographic area.	Undergraduate business degree; M.B.A.; *Helpful courses*: consumer behaviour, psychology, sociology, economics, anthropology, cost accounting, computer science, statistical analysis, communications, drama, creative writing. Language courses if you're interested in international marketing; engineering or physical science courses if you're interested in technical selling.
Services Marketing	**Any size corporation:** Banking and financial service institutions, health care organizations, leisure-oriented businesses, and in various other service settings.	Assistant brand manager; assistant sales manager	Undergraduate business degree; M.B.A.; Additional course work in management policy, research, advertising and promotion, quantitative analysis, consumer behaviour, and the behavioural sciences should prove useful.

Source: This information was based on an excellent compilation prepared by the marketing faculty of the Marshall School of Business, University of Southern California at **http://www.marshall.usc.edu/marketing/resources/resources-overview.htm** (accessed June 11, 2010). For average salaries broken down by job type and state consult the *Aquent/AMA Survey of Marketing Professionals* at **http://www.marketingsalaries.com/aquent/Home.form** or commercial Web sites such as **payscale.com** and **riley-guide.com**.

What Can We Market?

Marketers' creations surround us. It seems that everywhere we turn we get bombarded by advertisements, stores, and products that compete fiercely and loudly for our attention and our dollars. Marketers filter much of what we learn about the world. Advertising influences our perceptions of beauty, how we should act, and what we should own. Marketing's influence extends from "serious" goods and services such as health care to "fun" things such as extreme skateboarding equipment and hip-hop music (though many people take these products as seriously as their health). In this book, we'll refer to any good, service, or idea that can be marketed as a **product** even though what you're buying may not take a physical form.

Consumer Goods and Services

Consumer goods are the tangible products that individual consumers purchase for personal or family use. **Services** are intangible products that we pay for and use but never

product
Any good, service, or idea that can be marketed.

consumer goods
The tangible products that individual consumers purchase for personal or family use.

services
Intangible products that are exchanged directly between the producer and the customer.

own. Service transactions contribute on average more than 60 percent to the gross national product of all industrialized nations. As will be discussed in Chapter 7, marketers need to understand the special challenges that arise when marketing an intangible service rather than a tangible good.

Popular culture consists of the music, movies, sports, books, celebrities, and other forms of entertainment that the mass market consumes. The relationship between marketing and popular culture is a two-way street. Marketers influence what is popular, but products and the communication of those products also reflect the key social beliefs and values of the times. Introduction of the TV dinner signalled changes in family structure, such as a movement away from the traditional family dinner hour filled with conversation about the day's events. Cosmetics made of natural materials and not tested on animals reflected social concerns about pollution and animal rights. Condoms marketed in pastel carrying cases intended for female buyers signalled changing attitudes toward sexual responsibility.

Marketing applies to more than just canned peas or cola drinks. Some of the best marketers come from the ranks of services companies such as American Express or not-for-profit organizations such as Greenpeace. Politicians, athletes, and performers use marketing to their advantage (just think about that $30 T-shirt you may have bought at a hockey game or rock concert). Ideas such as political systems (democracy, totalitarianism), religion (Christianity, Islam), and art (realism, abstract) also compete for acceptance in a "marketplace."

Business-to-Business Goods and Services

Business-to-business marketing is the marketing of goods and services from one organization to another. Although we usually relate marketing to the thousands of consumer goods begging for our dollars every day, the reality is that businesses and other organizations buy a lot more goods than consumers do. They purchase these **industrial goods** for further processing or to use in their own business operations. For example, automakers buy tons of steel to use in the manufacturing process, and they buy computer systems to track manufacturing costs and other information essential to operations.

Similarly, there is a lot of buzz about **e-commerce** and the buying and selling of products—books, CDs, cars, and so forth—on the Internet. However, just like in the off-line world, much of the real online action is in the area of business-to-business marketing.

Not-for-Profit Marketing

As we noted earlier, you don't have to be a businessperson to use marketing principles. Many **not-for-profit organizations** including museums, zoos, and even churches practise the marketing concept. The United Church of Canada, for example, recently spent $10.5 million on a campaign asking viewers to contemplate controversial topics such as gay marriage, kinky sex, and whether it is blasphemous or devout to have a bobblehead Jesus Christ on your car dashboard.[6] Although controversial itself, the campaign was aimed at supporting The United Church's positioning as a 'safe haven' for open-ended dialogue (Exhibit 1.7).

Idea, Place, and People Marketing

Marketing principles also encourage people to endorse ideas or change their behaviours in positive ways. Many organizations work hard to convince consumers to use seat belts, not to litter our highways, to engage in safe sex, or to believe that one political system is preferable to another. The Resource Recovery Fund Board of Nova Scotia (RRFB), for example, is a not-for-profit that works closely with the provincial government department Nova Scotia Environment. RRFB recently introduced an upbeat TV and online campaign aimed at improving household waste disposal practices to reduce landfill waste by 25 percent by

popular culture
The music, movies, sports, books, celebrities, and other forms of entertainment consumed by the mass market.

business-to-business marketing
The marketing of those goods and services that business and organization customers need to produce other goods and services, for resale or to support their operation.

industrial goods
Goods individuals or organizations buy for further processing or for their own use when they do business.

e-commerce
The buying or selling of goods and services electronically, usually over the Internet.

not-for-profit organizations
Organizations with charitable, educational, community, and other public service goals that buy goods and services to support their functions and to attract and serve their members.

Used with permission of The United Church of Canada.

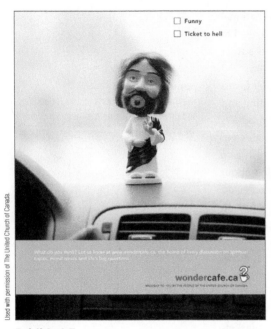

Exhibit 1.7

Not-for-profit organizations like The United Church of Canada use marketing concepts to communicate ideas and increase membership or clients.

2015.[7] The ads, like the one in Exhibit 1.8, encourage residents to recycle and even offer incentives.

In addition to ideas, places and people also are marketable. We are all familiar with tourism marketing that promotes exotic resorts like Club Med ("the antidote for civilization"). For many developing countries like Thailand, tourism provides an important opportunity for economic growth.

You may have heard the expression, "Stars are made, not born." There's a lot of truth to that. Lady Gaga may have a killer voice and Daniel Sedin may have a red-hot hockey stick, but talent alone doesn't make thousands or even millions of people buy CDs or arena seats. Entertainment events do not just happen—people plan them. Whether for a concert or a hockey game, the application of sound marketing principles helps ensure that patrons will continue to support the activity and buy tickets. Today, sports and the arts are hotbeds of marketing activity.

Some of the same principles that go into "creating" a celebrity apply to you, too. Everyday people "package" themselves when they sum up their accomplishments on Facebook or LinkedIn and join professional groups to link with as many "stakeholders" as they can. You may not do it purposefully, but just like marketers of other products, the decisions that you make in how you present yourself to others reflect a value proposition—what you have to offer in exchange for other people's time, thoughts, and, in the case of potential employers, money.

Courtesy of the Resource Recovery Fund Board of Nova Scotia

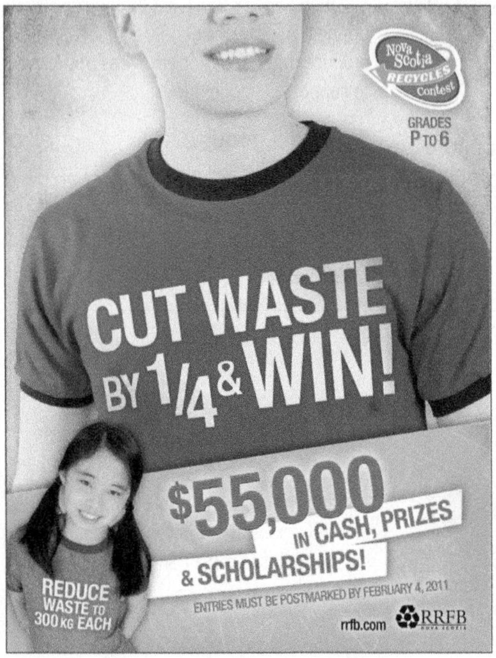

Exhibit 1.8

Ideas such as recycling can also be marketed.

2 Marketing as a Decision-Making Process

OBJECTIVE

Explain how marketing is a decision-making process and describe the planning and the marketing mix tools that managers use in the marketing process.

(pp. 16-27)

Marketing is fundamentally a *decision-making process* that allows individuals and organizations to achieve objectives by creating value that satisfies stakeholder needs and wants. As such, marketing decision making involves a series of steps that entail both careful thought (planning) and action (executing). When it's done right, marketing is a strategic decision-making process in which marketing managers determine the most appropriate set of decisions for a particular organization, at a particular time, that will help the organization meet its long-term objectives. This decision-making process is summarized in Figure 1.1 with more detail provided in Figure 1.2. Collectively, these decisions are usually summarized and justified in a marketing plan. This is a document that describes the marketing environment, outlines the marketing objectives and strategy, and identifies who will be responsible for carrying out each part of the marketing strategy. In Chapter 2, we will expand on Figure 1.2 to give you a template that you can use to construct your own marketing plan, helping to bring this important process to life. If you want, you can even use it to develop a plan to market "Brand You"!

Understand the Opportunity

Marketing decisions start with understanding the situation, or context, in which the decisions need to be made. As depicted in Figure 1.2, and explored more fully in Chapter 2, situational analysis involves identifying opportunities to create value for the organization by creating value for customers. This first involves understanding factors relating to the

Figure 1.1 The Marketing Decision Process

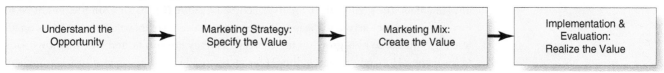

markets in which an organization competes, such as understanding general trends in that market (political or regulatory, economic, sociocultural, technological, and other trends), consumer or organizational buying behaviour, industry dynamics, and the strategies and likely reactions of competitors. Then, marketing decision makers need to assess factors relating to their own organization and their ability to create value and compete effectively in those markets. These internal factors include understanding the relative effectiveness of their current marketing strategy, their resources, competencies, and expertise, and the values or mission of the organization. The decision context is better understood by the application of marketing theory, concepts, and principles—which you will learn about in this text.

Marketing Strategy: Specify the Value

As will be discussed in more detail in Chapter 2, marketers make marketing strategy decisions to achieve the objectives of their organization. Strategy is the set of decisions that explain *what* an organization is going to do in order to achieve its objectives (and better

Figure 1.2 A Marketing Decision Framework

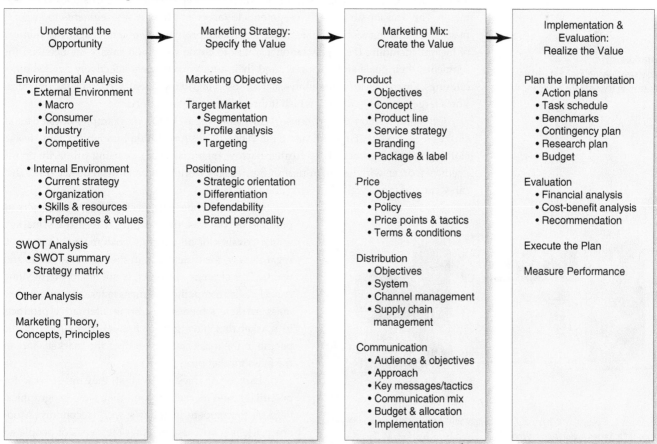

strategy also explains why). Tactics are the decisions that explain *how* the strategies will be implemented. The goal of the Canadian Football League (CFL), for example, might be to increase attendance across the league. One strategy to achieve this might be to focus on attracting families, so kids grow up to be fans when they are adults, and take their own kids to the games. How might this be done? One tactic could be a "kids go free" program where one free ticket for kids is offered for every paying adult.

Segmentation

The most critical decision marketers make in developing marketing strategy is the selection of the specific group of customers on which they will focus their customer value creation efforts. A **market segment** is a distinct group of customers within a larger market who have similar needs, wants, preferences, and behaviours, who seek similar product solutions, and whose needs differ from other customers in the larger market. Parents with young children, for example, typically seek different entertainment products than teenagers and young adults.

As will be discussed in more detail in Chapter 6, **market segmentation** is a process of dividing the overall market into groups of consumers who are sufficiently similar, within the groups, to want a similar solution to their particular needs and wants, and sufficiently different, between the groups, so that each group seeks a different solution to its needs and wants. The challenge for marketers is to identify groups with real differences in underlying needs, wants, preferences, value sought, and behaviour so products can be designed to uniquely appeal to a particular group.

Targeting

Marketers need to decide how many market segments to focus on when creating their products (offers of value). Some companies, like Buckley's (Exhibit 1.9) decide to focus on a single segment, or very few segments; others, like PepsiCo or IBM, focus on several segments. The decision about which segments to target and how many segments to target is made by evaluating each of the segments in terms of profitability potential against a number of factors, including the organization's ability to create value and satisfy the needs of the segments, their goals and resources, and their ability to compete effectively against other offerings. On the basis of this analysis, the chosen market segment(s) become the organization's target market(s) toward which it directs its marketing efforts.

Canadian fashion design house 11th Floor Apparel Ltd, for example, doesn't make clothes for everyone. First, following the vision of designer Linda Lundström, they design clothing only for women. They further narrow their market by focusing primarily on the needs of women with less-than-perfect figures and working women who need clothes that can wear and travel well.

Some firms choose to reach as many customers as possible by offering their products to a **mass market**, which consists of all possible customers in a market, regardless of the differences in their specific needs and wants. This strategy, however, is not tenable in the long run. Usually, competitors of mass marketers, or even the mass marketers themselves, bring alternative products to market that have greater appeal to a subset of the people in the mass market, eroding the market share of the mass market product.

Many companies know that they must look for potential target markets beyond their own geographical borders to compete in today's world economy. Modern marketers are busy meeting the needs of people all

market segment

A distinct group of customers within a larger market who have similar needs, wants, preferences, and behaviours, who seek similar product solutions, and whose needs differ from other customers in the larger market.

market segmentation

A process of dividing the overall market into groups of consumers who seek very different solutions for their needs and wants than other groups of consumers.

mass market

All possible customers in a market, regardless of the differences in their specific needs and wants.

Courtesy of Novartis Consumer Health Canada, Inc.

Exhibit 1.9

Buckley's focuses on people who have cold or flu symptoms. Their positioning is reflected in the statement "It Tastes Awful. And It Works."

around the world, especially when the demand for products at home flattens. Expanding internationally is desirable, for example, to Tim Hortons, the iconic Canadian coffee and donut chain. Tim Hortons announced plans to take the Tim Hortons brand global in the next four years, building on relationships forged with the British and US military in Afghanistan.[8]

One trend for multinational companies is to focus on selling products to developing countries, a trend some refer to as B2–4B ("business to four billion"), which refers to the approximate number of potential customers in these markets. Hewlett-Packard (HP), for example, believes that much of the firm's future growth could come from developing countries. The company has begun to implement a plan to sell, lease, or donate $1 billion in goods and services to governments, development agencies, and not-for-profit groups in these areas. In fact, to satisfy the needs of this market, HP is developing low-power or solar-powered devices that will connect to the Internet wirelessly or via satellites. But HP's developing world efforts are not just philanthropic (see Exhibit 1.10). It believes that this kind of investment will allow HP to tap into the huge potential markets that will develop in these countries.[9]

Throughout the text we will emphasize marketers' need to think globally—even if they only act locally. Smart marketers know that, whether in developing world countries or developed countries, long-term success means finding customers wherever they are, from Montreal to Manila.

Positioning the Offering

After choosing the target market(s), marketers need to develop an offering that appeals to the needs, wants, and preferences of that target market better than alternatives provided by competitors. This process starts with positioning the product. **Positioning** is how the marketing organization wants its brand to be known in the minds of the target customers—what value it offers relative to competitors and why that offer is superior to others for a particular target market. It involves specifying a competitive advantage that enables an offering to be differentiated from others in the marketplace.

The first step is for the organization to identify what it does really well. A **distinctive competency** is a firm's capability that is superior to that of its competition. For example, Coca-Cola's success in global markets—Coke commands 50 percent of the world's soft-drink business—is related to its distinctive competencies in distribution and marketing communications. Coke's distribution system got a jump on the competition during World War II. To enable US soldiers fighting overseas to enjoy a five-cent Coke, the US government assisted Coca-Cola in building 64 overseas bottling plants. Coke's skilful marketing communications program, a second distinctive competency, has contributed to its global success. In addition to its television commercials, Coke blankets less-developed countries such as Tanzania with signs posted on roads and on storefronts so that even people without televisions will think of Coke when they get thirsty.

The second step is to turn a distinctive competency into a **differential benefit**—value that competitors don't offer. Differential benefits set products apart from competitors' products by providing something unique that customers want. Differential benefits provide reasons for customers to pay a premium for a firm's products and exhibit a strong brand preference. For many years, loyal Apple computer users benefited from superior graphics capability compared to their PC-using counterparts. Later, when PC manufacturers caught

Richard Hill

APPLYING ▽ Target Market Selection

Selecting among alternative target markets is one of Richard Hill's dilemmas at Yellow Point Lodge. He needs to figure out how to attract new consumers without turning off long-loyal consumers at the same time. These different market segments may have conflicting needs, wants, and preferences.

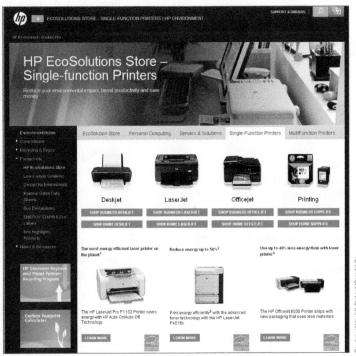

Exhibit 1.10

HP is designing products with smaller footprints to help expand into new markets.

Courtesy of Hewlett-Packard (Canada) Co.

positioning
How an organization wants its brand to be known to its customers as being different and better than competing brands.

distinctive competency
A capability of a firm that is superior to that of its competition.

differential benefit
Providing an outcome or result valued by customers that competitors are not able to offer as well.

up with this competitive advantage, Apple relied on its inventive product designers to create another differential benefit—futuristic-looking computers in a multitude of colours. This competitive advantage even tempted many loyal PC users to take a bite of the Apple.

Note that a differential benefit does not necessarily mean simply offering something different. For example, Mennen marketed a deodorant with a distinctive feature: it contained vitamin D. Unfortunately, consumers did not see any reason to pay for the privilege of spraying a vitamin under their arms. Despite advertising claims, consumers saw no benefit, and the product failed. The moral is, *effective product benefits must be both different from the competition and things that customers want*. A firm that delivers these desired benefits provides value to its customers and other stakeholders.

Positioning also involves developing strategy to defend the competitive advantage that has been, or will be, created and specifying the unique competencies, resources, or know-how that allow a firm to sustain its superiority and differential benefit.

Finally, the positioning of a brand often involves developing a **brand personality**. Mike's Hard Lemonade, for example, takes it name from Mike, a sociable, fun-loving young man who likes to party. In Norway, VOSS Water (www.vosswater.com) has developed a personality of sophistication (Exhibit 1.11). Its water comes from a "virgin aquifer that has been shielded for centuries under ice and rock in the untouched wilderness of Central Norway." At prices ranging up to $22.00 for a 0.5 L bottle, customers are putting a significant premium on that personality![10]

brand personality
A distinctive image that captures a good or service's character and benefits.

Marketing Mix: Create the Value

Once the desired positioning is established, marketers need to create the value proposition reflected in the offer. To do this, marketers make a set of decisions about the product itself, its price, the place it is available for purchase, and the activities that introduce it to consumers. These decisions, collectively called the **marketing mix** decisions, create the value promised by the product positioning and are intended to be sufficiently motivating (valuable) to create a desired exchange response among members of the target market. Just as every college student seems to have an iPod, every government official seems to have a BlackBerry. The marketing mix decisions made by Apple and RIM created an interesting value proposition for the marketplace.

The marketing mix decisions are commonly known as the **four Ps**: product, price, promotion (communication), and place (distribution). Together, the bundle of marketing mix elements represents an offer of value to the consumer—what the customer will receive in an exchange. Some marketers consider a fifth P, "people" or relationships, as a distinct consideration. Others, including the authors of this book, view managing exchange relationships as being so central to what marketers do that it should be integrated into all the other marketing decisions and not treated as a separate decision.

Just as a radio DJ puts together a collection of separate songs (a musical mix) to create a certain mood, the idea of a mix in this context reminds us that no *single* marketing activity is sufficient to accomplish the organization's objectives, and consistency among the decisions is critical to the overall marketing (or music) program. We will examine these components of the marketing mix in detail later in this book. For now, let's briefly look at each element of the marketing mix to gain some insight into its meaning and role in creating value.

marketing mix
A combination of the product itself, the price of the product, the place where it is made available, and the activities that introduce it to consumers, which creates a desired response among a set of predefined consumers.

four Ps
Product, price, promotion, and place.

Product

The product is a good, service, idea, place, person—whatever is offered for exchange. Notice, therefore, that the concept of product, as defined in marketing, is broader than its usage in everyday language, where it primarily signifies a tangible good.

Product strategy decisions begin with objectives: What do you want to achieve with your product decision? For most companies, this usually involves supporting the overall positioning of the brand, developing new solutions for existing customers, developing new

Exhibit 1.11
Brand personality is what allows VOSS to sell a half-litre bottle of water for as much as $22.

solutions for new customers, and/or increasing sales of a particular product or product line (a set of related products).

While developing life-long customers is a goal for many marketing organizations, some take this too far. A recent study by the Harvard School of Public Health concluded that tobacco companies "deliberately changed the menthol levels in cigarettes depending upon whom they were marketing them to—lower levels for young smokers who preferred the milder brands and higher levels to 'lock in lifelong adult smokers.'"[11] Consequently, many marketers also have product policies—rules or guiding principles for the kinds of products they are willing to develop or offer their customers. Product policies increasingly centre on ethics and sustainability practices, which we will learn more about later in this chapter.

Next, marketers make decisions about the products they are going to offer their customer, such as key features, functions, design, and other attributes of the product that, together, create the benefits and experiences sought by the target customers. These decisions include how many variants or versions (models, types, sizes, colours, shapes, flavours) of a product they will offer. Honda, for example, chooses to compete with just a few models of cars, while General Motors has more than one hundred. Product decisions include what level of service will be provided. For nearly pure service companies like Disney or Flight Centre and online companies like Expedia.ca, the strategy to create the desired customer experience is central to what they do, but even packaged goods like cereal or consumer goods like a notebook computer can have important service aspects. Dell, for example, offers free delivery, online and phone-based technical support, and a range of options for getting your computer fixed if there is a problem, including in-home repair. Product decisions also include *branding strategy*—will a product be part of a family of products like Campbell's soups, an individual brand like BlackBerry (Exhibit 1.12), a store brand like President's Choice, or just be named for the product category, like "spaghetti"? Finally, product decisions include packaging and labelling decisions; be honest, how many times have you bought something because the package looked good?

Exhibit 1.12

The name of a brand, like BlackBerry® from Research In Motion® (RIM®), is one of the product decisions marketers must make.

Price

The **price** is an agreement between a buyer and seller on a product's economic value. It is based on the seller's assessment of the value of a product, what they would like to receive from the buyer in exchange for the product, and the buyer's assessment of its worth. Pricing strategy decisions start with *pricing objectives*—what do you want to accomplish with your pricing decisions? Are you trying to support a premium position like Gucci, be similar to your competitors, like Petro-Canada, or increase market share like Dell? Different pricing objectives suggest different *pricing policies*. Procter & Gamble (P&G) used to determine its prices based on what a product actually cost to develop plus a profit, but now it prices products by what consumers in different countries can afford. Walmart uses "Every Day Low Prices" as a retail policy. Marketers also have to come up with the actual price. *Price point* decisions need to take into consideration the cost of creating and delivering the product, competitors' prices, and what the customer is willing to pay, among other factors. There are also psychological considerations. Should the price of Croc shoes be $9.99, $17.54, or $30.00? Finally, marketers need to decide on pricing terms and conditions—when does the price need to be paid, how can it be paid, and are there any special deals or discounts?

price
The seller's assignment of value to a product.

Distribution

Distribution (place) concerns the availability of the product to the customer at the desired time and location. *Channels of distribution* involve firms that work together to get a product from a producer to a consumer. For consumer goods like Roots clothing products, a

distribution
The availability of the product to the customer at the desired time and location. Also known as *channels of distribution*.

distribution channel includes retailers such as Sears as well as their own Roots retail out-lets and the Roots Web site. Distribution decisions begin with specifying the distribution objectives, such as are you trying to make the product as widely available as possible, minimize the cost of getting the product to the customer, or make it easy for customers to compare your product with others—such as with an auto mall? To achieve one or another of these distribution objectives, marketers decide on a distribution system: what type of distribution system will be created, how many and what types of channel partners will be involved, and will it be a traditional approach or a nontraditional one? Channel relation-ship management decisions also need to be made: how will you identify, attract, motivate, and keep your channel partners working toward your common goals, and how will you deal with the conflict that is inherent between the roles of channel members? Finally, *sup-ply chain management* involves systems and processes to ensure efficient and effective value creation, from the sourcing of raw materials to the customer receiving the value. This in-cludes *logistics*, the physical distribution of goods to the customer, or a *service blueprint* for delivering a service experience.

Communication

communication
The coordination of communication efforts by a marketer to influence consumers or organizations about goods, services, or ideas.

Communication (promotion) refers to the marketing communication activities undertaken to inform consumers or organizations about goods, services, or ideas, and to encourage potential customers to buy these goods, services, or ideas. Unlike the other marketing mix decisions, communication strategy decisions start with deciding the *audience*, or target of the communication, not the *communication objective*. The audience is a specific subset of a target market whose members are the receivers of the communication. A communication campaign usually has many different elements targeted at different audiences, but we design the strategy for each audience. For each audience, we need to decide the commu-nication objectives. What do you want to achieve with your communication decisions? Is the objective to create awareness about your product, develop purchase intentions, encourage trial of the product, or develop trust with your customers? To achieve these or other communications objectives, marketers need to decide on an overall *approach* to the communication strategy. Will it be a push strategy, where retailers are encouraged to stock products that customers can find, or a pull strategy, where customers are encouraged to seek products from retailers or other channel members? Will it be one-way communication or will you seek feedback from customers and try to develop a relationship with them? Once the overall approach is decided, we need to decide the *key messages*, what we want to communicate to our audience, and the *tactics* we will use to get their attention. Then, we decide on the appropriate communications mix to get our message(s) to our audi-ence. Should we develop advertising for television, radio, or print publications; create promotions like Tim Hortons' "Roll Up the Rim to Win" contest; use public relations as Raincoast Books used to gain free publicity around Harry Potter book launches; commu-nicate using a sales force; create a Web site; or use viral marketing techniques such as de-veloping entertaining video clips that customers can send to their friends? Social media is fast becoming an integral element of the communications mix with sites such as Facebook and Twitter (and hundreds of others) offering low-cost, two-way access to thousands, if not millions, of customers. Online spending is approaching 20 percent of total communication expenditures (now second to television in terms of advertising expenditure), and some marketers now spend more on online communications than they do on traditional media, because that is where their customers are.

We also need to decide on a *creative strategy* that will get the attention of our audience, *schedule* the timing and placement of any advertising that is used, determine a *budget* to do all this, and develop a way to *evaluate* whether our communication strategy has been effective.

For example, Mike's Hard Lemonade Company's communication strategy supports the brand image by developing and supporting the "personalities" of Mike and the lemonade. Cute stories about Mike and lemons were included on the packaging, and the product was brought to consumers' attention with print advertising, in-store displays, and on-shelf signage. After Mike's initial success, television advertising was created that showed "lemons being hurt real bad in the making of this product" and investigators trying to determine "who has been hurting the lemons." These quirky, light-hearted ads helped make Mike's the leading brand in the Canadian cooler market. There is also a hip Internet site (www.mikeshardlemonade.com) that further supports the brand's personality.

So, this discussion and Figure 1.2 suggest that there are lots of decisions that marketers make for creating, communicating, and delivering value to customers and for managing customer relationships in ways that benefit the organization and its stakeholders. Once made, these decision need to be acted upon.

Implementation and Evaluation: Realize the Value

Before we can evaluate the relative merits of our proposed marketing decisions, we need to plan for their implementation, such as identifying the key *actions* that need to be done, assigning *tasks* to people to do them, and developing a schedule of when they need to be completed. Implementation decisions also involve developing performance *benchmarks* (targets) to help us assess if our strategy is working, and a *contingency* plan that outlines what we will do if things do not go as planned. Finally, we need to identify the key assumptions that we have made in developing our plan and outline how we will use *market research* to test those assumptions and ensure we are making informed decisions. We also need to specify and allocate a *budget* to make all this happen.

After planning the implementation, we then need to decide whether or not to proceed. This overall recommendation is based on an assessment of whether implementing the strategy is worth it from the organization's perspective (value to the organization). To make this decision, we need to do *financial analysis* and *cost-benefit analysis*, which you will learn more about in Chapter 2. This decision is usually made in contrast to other viable alternatives, to ensure that the best strategy is being considered. The alternatives typically come from different choices of target markets, different positioning, or different ways of creating value via the marketing mix. It may seem like a lot of wasted work to end up recommending not to implement, but you can't make an informed decision without first specifying the best strategy you can think of.

If you decide to implement the strategy, the next step is *execution*, getting it done, and then *measuring* performance against the plan. Throughout this text, we will show you examples of measures, or "metrics," that marketers use to assess their performance.

Add Value through the Value Chain

Many different players, both within and outside a firm, need to work together to create and deliver value to customers. The **value chain** is a useful way to appreciate all the players that work together to create value. This term refers to a series of activities involved in designing, producing, marketing, delivering, and supporting any product. In addition to marketing activities, the value chain includes business functions such as human resource management and technology development.[12]

value chain
A series of activities involved in designing, producing, marketing, delivering, and supporting any product. Each link in the chain has the potential to either add or remove value from the product the customer eventually buys.

The value chain concept reminds us that every product starts with raw materials that are of relatively limited value to the end customer. Each link in the chain has the potential to either add or remove value from the product the customer eventually buys. The successful firm is the one that can perform one or more of these activities better than other firms—this is its competitive advantage. For example, when you buy a new iPad at your local Apple store, do you think about all the people and steps involved in designing, manufacturing, and delivering that product to the store? Not to mention other people who create brand advertising, conduct consumer research to figure out what people like or dislike about their mobile music players, or even make the box it comes in or those little plastic peanuts that keep the unit from being damaged in shipment?

As Figure 1.3 shows, all these companies (and more) belong to Apple's value chain. This means that Apple must make a lot of decisions. What electronic components will go into its music players? What accessories will it include in the package? What trucking companies, wholesalers, and retailers will deliver the iPads to stores? What service will it provide to customers after the sale? And what marketing strategies will it use? In some cases, members of a value chain will work together to coordinate their activities to be more efficient and thus create a competitive advantage.

Consumer-Generated Value: From Audience to Community

One of the most exciting developments in the marketing world is the evolution of how consumers interact with marketers. In particular, we're seeing everyday people actually *generating* value instead of just buying it—consumers are turning into advertising directors, retailers, and new-product-development consultants. They create their own ads (some flattering, some not) for products, and post them on sites like YouTube. They buy and sell merchandise ranging from Beatles memorabilia to washing machines on eBay. They share ideas for new styles with fashion designers, and customize their own unique versions of products on Web sites. These changes mean that marketers need to adjust their thinking about customers. They need to stop thinking of buyers as a passive audience and start thinking of them as a community that is motivated to participate in both the production and the consumption of what companies sell. Some of these consumers are amafessionals (amateur professionals). They contribute ideas for the fun and challenge rather than to receive a paycheque, so their motivation is to gain *psychic income* rather than financial income. We'll talk more about this phenomenon later, but for now think about these recent examples of **consumer-generated content**:

consumer-generated content
Everyday people functioning in marketing roles, such as participating in creating advertisements, providing input to new product development, or serving as wholesalers or retailers.

- Frito-Lay Canada had its customers name a new product and create a video to introduce it to the market. A new flavour of Doritos appeared on store shelves packaged in white single-serving bags featuring the Doritos logo, a black dollar sign, and the words "Unidentified Flavour." On the back, the package read, "Doritos brand needs a new guru and the job is worth big bucks! Want it? Just name this flavour and send us a

Marketing Metrics

An Example of a Customer Service Scorecard

Item Text	1st Qtr.	Quarterly Scores 2nd Qtr.	3rd Qtr.
Satisfaction With			
C1 Employee responsiveness	60%	65%	68%
C2 Product selection	60%	62%	63%
C3 Service quality	60%	62%	55%
C4 Cleanliness of facility	75%	80%	85%
C5 Knowledge of employees	62%	62%	58%
C6 Appearance of employees	60%	62%	63%
C7 Convenience of location	60%	65%	68%

Source: Adapted from C.F. Lundby and C. Rasinowich, "The missing link," *Marketing Research*, Winter 2003, 14–19: 18.

Figure 1.3 Apple's Value Chain

Apple's value chain includes inbound logistics, operations, outbound logistics, marketing and sales, and service.

Inbound Logistics	Operations	Outbound Logistics	Marketing and Sales	Service
• Planar lithium battery (Sony) • Hard drive (Toshiba) • MP3 decoder and controller chip (PortalPlayer) • Flash memory chip (Sharp Electronics Corp.) • Stereo digital-to-analog converter (Wolfson Microelectronics Ltd.) • Firewire interface controller (Texas Instruments)	• Consumer research • New-product-development team • Engineering and production	• Trucking companies • Wholesalers • Retailers	• Advertising • Sales force	• Computer technicians

Source: Based on information from Erik Sherman, "Inside the Apple iPod Design Triumph," *Electronics Design Chain* (May 27, 2006), accessed at http://www.designchain.com/coverstory.asp?issue=summer02.

guru worthy advertising idea. For the whole story visit DoritosGuru.ca." Contestants submitted their flavour name and marketing ideas to the DoritosGuru.ca site (which simultaneously updated contest pages on Facebook.com and YouTube.com), and visitors voted for the five best concepts, and then for the winner. The response included 2100 video entries, which were seen by 30 000 Facebook fans and 1.5 million unique YouTube visitors. Eight Montreal university students won the $25 000 top prize for their "Scream Cheese" flavour name and video.[13]

• When the creators of the TV show *Lost* were trying to fit in a reference to Canada, they couldn't remember exactly how they had done it on the show before. So the show's writers asked the fans behind Lostpedia, a Wiki site about the show, who observed that every time one of the show's characters mentioned Canada, they were lying. Thus fans helped in the show's creative process.[14]

• Threadless.com invites customers and other designers to submit T-shirt designs to their Web site. Other members vote on which designs they like best, and each week Threadless produces T-shirts in the top six winning designs that the designers, members, and their friends can buy online. The appeal is unique T's—and the winning designers get $2500, tee credits, and the rights to their work. Threadless develops dozens of new items each month, with no advertising, no professional designers, no sales force, and no retail distribution.[15] Last year, Threadless shipped more than 100 000 T-shirts per month and made a profit of more than $30 million. They have 1.5 million followers on Twitter and 100 000 fans on Facebook, and they get 300 T-shirt design submissions per day. Some of their fans have voted on more than 100 000 T-shirt designs, showing extremely high commitment to the concept (Exhibit 1.13).[16]

online social networking
Using Internet technology to keep in contact with friends, relatives, and business associates.

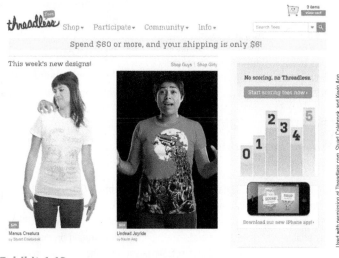

Exhibit 1.13

Threadless uses consumer-generated content to create highly valued T-shirts.

Social Networking & Web 2.0

The tremendous acceleration of **online social networking** fuels this community fire. In a social network, a user represents him- or herself via a profile on a Web site and provides and receives links to other members of the network to share input about common interests. The odds are you—and most of your classmates—checked your Facebook page before (or during?) class today. Facebook and other online social networking sites are recording strong profits as advertisers figure out that these sites are a great way to reach an audience that tunes in regularly and enthusiastically to catch up with friends, check out photos of what they did at that outrageous party Saturday night, proclaim opinions about political or social issues, or share discoveries of new musical artists. Specialized sites like LinkedIn, which helps people keep connected with business peers, attract more focused advertising from marketers looking to reach the particular profile of the people on a particular site. This communication becomes even more focused, and cost effective, when linked to the profiles of the people on the site; so Mountain Equipment Co-op, for example, can advertise to LinkedIn customers who are young professional males, living in British Columbia, who include the term "outdoor" in their profile.

Social networking is an integral part of the Web 2.0 experience, which is characterized by the following features: significantly increased interactivity among producers and users, enhanced experiences as the number of users increases (e.g., Facebook is more useful the more of your friends use it regularly), eyeballs as its currency (e.g., Google makes its money by charging advertisers according to the number of people who see their ads after they type in a search term), and being version-free and in perpetual beta. Unlike static Web sites or books, content is always a work in progress. Wikipedia, the online encyclopedia, gets updated constantly by users who "correct" others' errors, and it categorizes entries according to "folksonomy" rather than "taxonomy." In other words, sites rely on users rather than pre-established systems to sort contents. DailySplice is a Canadian company that allows users to create, publish, and aggregate podcasts in a personal multimedia "station," helping users stream the content that they want to watch or hear, when they want to watch or hear it.

Crowdsourcing—outsourcing tasks to an undefined, large group of people or community by posting an open call for assistance on the Internet (like Threadless does)—is increasingly being used by marketers to ensure that the "voice of the customer" is reflected in new product development and marketing mix decisions. This "wisdom of crowds" perspective (from a book by that name) argues that under the right circumstances, groups are smarter than the smartest people in them.[17] Detractors argue that people in the crowd are not necessarily very knowledgeable about your company, its positioning, or your strategy, so the thinking and results that are generated may not be particularly useful, and may be potentially litigious if the buyer does not check whether the ideas are original. When Gap unveiled a new logo in 2010, passionate customers let them know their disapproval via blogs, Facebook, and Twitter. The retailer invited people to submit their own design ideas for a new logo, then eventually dropped the idea entirely and went back to their original blue box logo.[18]

open source model
A practice used in the software industry in which companies share their software codes with anyone to assist in the development of a better product.

Open Source Business Models

Another, related, change is the rise of the **open source model** that turns some of our conventional assumptions about the value of products and services on its head. This model

Tech and Trends

Social Media

What isn't an app these days? Stickybits software turns a Coke can, iPhone, or box of detergent into an app that lets users link video, photos, text, or audio to any object that has a barcode. Some call these apps physical URLs; they enable user-generated clouds of content to form around products you encounter in the store or on the street. When you scan the barcode, you can upload your own content or see what others have already uploaded. Brands such as Ben & Jerry's, Campbell Soup, and Doritos already have content forming around their products. A similar app lets users link for good causes; when they participate in CauseWorld, they earn money for charity as they scan products from P&G and Kraft.[19] Before long, will we all be remembering to scan our cans?

started in the software industry where the Linux system grows by leaps and bounds—even IBM uses it now. Unlike the closely guarded code that companies like Microsoft use, open source developers post their programs on a public site, and a community of volunteers is free to tinker with it, develop other applications using the code, and then give their changes away for free. For example, the company that gives out (for free) the Mozilla Firefox Internet browser that competes with Microsoft, commands over 20 percent market share among users.[20] We'll talk more about this in Chapter 9 (pricing), and answer the question of how in the world you can make money from something when you give it away.

3 Making Decisions in a Sustainable World

OBJECTIVE
Understand key issues relating to making ethical marketing decisions in a sustainable world and be able to discuss different perspectives of marketing.
(pp. 27–32)

Marketing decisions (and all business decisions) are made in a global context. Even if you have a small, local business, your products are made with materials sourced in a global context, your competitors are increasingly global (particularly with the rise of Internet shopping), and customers evaluate your offering in light of what they know about these alternatives. They also evaluate your offering in light of what they know about your business practices—preferring to do business with sellers who act ethically and in the long-term interest of both the customer and society.

The Global Environment of Business

In his bestselling book *The World Is Flat: A Brief History of the 21st Century*, Thomas Friedman argues that in today's fiercely competitive and global marketplace, the world is indeed flat. Marketers must recognize that national borders are not as important as they once were, or risk disappearing off the face of the earth. Today, businesses like Bombardier and Research In Motion must seek new and improved ways to attract customers down the street and around the globe, and they need to meet the challenge of doing good while doing well.

It is no longer enough to just make money; today, we expect companies to benefit their communities at the same time. Just as we consider value from the customer's and seller's perspective, we need to consider value from society's perspective: are we making marketing (and business) decisions that benefit our society, and the world, in the long term? In many ways, we are at the mercy of marketers, because we trust them to sell us products that are safe and perform as promised. We also trust them to price and distribute these products fairly. Conflicts often arise in business when the pressure to succeed in the marketplace provokes dishonest business practices—such as when Canadian media mogul Conrad Black was charged in US courts of defrauding Hollinger International investors out of millions of dollars, or when shoddy lending practices by US and other banks led to the recent global economic crisis.

Marketing is *still* concerned with the firm's "bottom line," but now many managers consider the **triple bottom line**, a new way of looking at business that emphasizes the need to maximize three components:

triple bottom line
A business perspective that measures economic, social, and environmental value creation.

- *The financial bottom line*: Financial profits to stakeholders.

- *The social bottom line*: Contributing to the communities in which the company operates.

- *The environmental bottom line*: Creating sustainable business practices that minimize damage to the environment or that even improve it.

Richard Hill

Richard Hill understands the need to balance economic, social, and environmental objectives when deciding how to protect the business, history, and land of Yellow Point Lodge. He needs the business to prosper in order to protect the land from threat of development, and for the business to prosper he needs to balance the social and historical values of his current customers with the increased costs of running the Lodge. ➥

customer relationship management (CRM)

A systematic tracking of consumers' preferences and behaviours over time in order to tailor the value proposition as closely as possible to each individual's unique wants and needs. CRM allows firms to talk to individual customers and to adjust elements of their marketing programs in light of how each customer reacts.

attention economy

A perspective that consumer spending, and hence the economy, is driven by psychological attachment to brands, the relevance of information, and solutions. Consumers choose where to spend their attention and their money.

Is it possible to contribute in a positive way to society and the earth and still contribute to your paycheque? Walmart, North America's largest retailer, seems to think so. The huge company announced in 2010 its goal to cut 20 million metric tons of greenhouse gas emissions from its supply chain by the end of 2015—the equivalent of removing more than 3.8 million cars from the road for a year. It's asking suppliers to take a hard look at the carbon their products emit. Walmart will work with its vendors to make their manufacturing processes more efficient—and, hopefully, pass cost savings on to customers. The chain has introduced more modest initiatives already; for example, it's working to change the labels on clothing it sells to indicate the products can be washed in cold water (therefore lowering customers' electricity bills) and, in partnership with 20th Century Fox Home Entertainment, it eliminated the plastic knob in the centre of CD cases to cut greenhouse gas emissions.[21]

Many companies believe that having a triple-bottom-line orientation can be a source of competitive advantage. Mountain Equipment Co-op states on its Web site (in its Account-ability Report), "We have a long-standing focus on social, environmental, and economic sustainability. It's part of our mandate as a retail co-op. It's also what we believe."[22]

The MEC Accountability Report develops a sustainability agenda and then explains how this agenda is embedded in their five-year strategic plan, which contains the additional priorities:[23]

- Offer the best product quality, functionality, and form, at the most competitive price in each of the outdoor recreation activities we support. (Equipping Members)

- Have highly effective, knowledgeable, and engaged employees who make MEC an outstanding place to work. (Engaging Staff)

- Be a financially viable business in the short- and long-term. (Economic Performance)

- Represent the values of our membership and oversee a healthy and ethical co-operative that is living its Charter.

In this way MEC is a leading Canadian example of the triple-bottom-line perspective.

Customer Relationship Management

One outgrowth of this triple bottom line, value creation thinking is the concept of **customer relationship management (CRM)**. CRM involves establishing an ongoing relationship with customers, systematically tracking their preferences and behaviours over time, and being responsive in tailoring the value proposition as closely as possible to each individual's unique wants and needs. To do this, marketers need to establish a dialogue, or two-way communication, with customers. The advent of the Internet has facilitated this dialogue, making it much easier for organizations to find and communicate with customers, and for customers to engage with organizations. As will be further discussed in Chapter 10 (communications), there are still significant challenges in implementing CRM, not the least of which is motivating customers to want to engage in a relationship with your brand.

Although dot-com companies took a beating in the marketplace when the "bubble" burst in the early 2000s, many analysts believe that this was just a preliminary shakeout—the heyday of the Internet is yet to come. More recent success stories like Google, Skype, Twitter, Facebook, and Flickr seem to be proving analysts right. Indeed, some marketing analysts suggest that the Internet creates a *paradigm shift* for business. This means that companies must adhere to a new model to profit in a wired world. They argue that we live in an **attention economy**, one in which a company's success will be measured by its share of mind rather than share of market, where companies make money when they attract eyeballs rather than just dollars. For example, Google sells advertising to many other companies, so the more consumers it can persuade to "google" rather than "bing" or "yahoo," the more it can charge to place ads on search pages. Skype was valued by Microsoft at $8.5 billion, even though most of its customers use free services.[24]

This means that companies must find new and innovative ways to stand out from the crowd and become an integral part of consumers' lives rather than just being a dry company that makes and sells products. For example, major consumer packaged foods companies are drawing many more customers to their Web sites than in the past. More important, the sites are "sticky," meaning that they tend to keep visitors long enough to make a lasting impression on them and motivate them to come back for more (Exhibit 1.14). They do this by offering games, contests, and other promotions that transform their Web site into less of a store and more of a carnival. For example, the Wrigley company's Candystand.com site invites visitors to play games like Nut Vendor, where the player assumes the role of a ballpark peanut hawker. Candystand.com, like other sites, gathers customers' e-mail addresses (by permission) as they register for sweepstakes, and then lures them back with offers of new recipes, games, and products (Exhibit 1.15).[25] This is also true of service organizations. For example, Maximum Vegas (www.mgmgrand.com), an interactive Web site for the MGM Grand Hotel and Casino in Las Vegas, was designed by Canadian agency Diesel, in Montreal. This Web site, a Best of Show winner at the Digital Marketing Awards, offers a stunningly rich media experience that lets visitors tour the hotel and experience the sights and sounds as if they were really there.

Exhibit 1.14

Companies like Moosehead use "sticky" Web content to keep customers on their sites longer and motivate returns to the site.

Social Marketing Concept

Another result of this new way of long-term thinking is the **social marketing concept**, which maintains that marketers must satisfy customers' needs in ways that also benefit society while still delivering a profit to the firm. Many big and small firms alike practise this philosophy. Their efforts include satisfying society's environmental and social needs for a cleaner, safer environment by developing recyclable packaging, adding extra safety features such as car air bags, voluntarily modifying a manufacturing process to reduce pollution, and sponsoring campaigns to address social problems. For example, McCain Foods, one of the world's largest makers of frozen French fries, refuses to process genetically altered potatoes.[26] Mountain Equipment Co-op (MEC) will source products only from countries that aspire to fair labour practices (Exhibit 1.16), and they strive to sell as many Canadian-made products as possible, even reducing margins to a certain point. Alberta-based Servus Credit Union even handed out $200 000 in $10 increments to finance small good deeds.[27]

A very important trend now is for companies to think of ways to design and manufacture products with a focus on **sustainable development**, which we define as "meeting present needs without compromising the ability of future generations to meet their needs."[28] Some refer to this philosophy as *cradle to cradle.* This term describes the ideal condition where a product is made from natural materials and is fully reusable, recyclable, or biodegradable, so the net depletion of resources a company needs to make it is zero. When players in the 2010 World Cup ran onto the field, many wore Nike jerseys made from plastic bottles the company retrieved from landfills in Japan and Taiwan. Walmart is a leader in sustainability practices. The giant retail chain makes and sells photo frames from plastic waste products it generates, and it recycles materials left over from manufacturing its private label diapers into building materials when it constructs new stores. Sustainability is good business,

social marketing concept
A management philosophy that marketers must satisfy customers' needs in ways that benefit society and also deliver profit to the firm.

sustainable development
Meeting present needs without compromising the ability of future generations to meet their needs.

Exhibit 1.15

Game sites like Candystand are "sticky" (this one is built around candy, after all) so many advertisers find these media outlets an attractive place to advertise.

Courtesy of Mountain Equipment Co-Op, www.mec.ca

Exhibit 1.16

Mountain Equipment Co-op has adopted the social marketing concept by their commitment to reducing their ecological footprint and improving the human conditions of factory workers.

green marketing
The development of marketing strategies that support environmental stewardship.

ROI (return on investment)
The revenue or profit margin generated by an investment, divided by the cost of the investment.

because it reduces costs while conserving resources. Walmart estimates savings of $100 million in one year by switching to a recyclable variety of cardboard to ship goods to its stores.

Sustainability applies to many aspects of doing business, including social and economic practices (e.g., humane working conditions and diplomacy to prevent wars that deplete food supplies, atmospheric quality, and, of course, lives). One other crucial pillar of sustainability is the environmental impact of the product. **Green marketing**, the development of marketing strategies that support environmental stewardship by creating an environmentally founded differential benefit in the minds of consumers, is being practised by most forward-thinking firms today. Green marketing is one aspect of a firm's overall commitment to sustainability. A recent study on the impact of green marketing uncovered some interesting results:

- About half the companies reported that they are consciously taking steps to become more green.

- More than 80 percent of respondents indicated they expect to spend more on green marketing in the future.

- Companies with smaller marketing budgets tend to spend more on green marketing and also think green marketing is more effective than larger companies do.

- By far the most popular medium for green marketing was the Internet, with 74.2 percent of respondents having spent money online.

- Marketers that track marketing spending and its relation to sales believe people will pay more for green products.

- Marketers tend to lead green initiatives, with 50 percent of firm managers surveyed agreeing that control of the green (sustainability) program is in the hands of marketers.[29]

In addition to building long-term relationships and focusing on social responsibility, triple-bottom-line firms place a much greater focus on *accountability*, measuring just how much value marketing activities create. This means that marketers at these organizations ask hard questions about the true value of their efforts and their impact on the bottom line. These questions all boil down to the simple acronym of **ROI (return on investment)**. Marketers now realize that if they want to assess just how much value they are creating for the firm, they need to know exactly what they are spending and what the concrete results of their actions are.

However, it's not always so easy to assess the value of marketing activities. Many times managers state their marketing objectives using vague phrases like "increase awareness of our product" or "encourage people to eat healthier snacks." These goals are important, but their lack of specificity makes it pretty much impossible for senior management to determine marketing's true impact. Because management may view these efforts as costs rather than investments, marketing activities often are among the first to be cut out of a firm's budget. To win continued support for what they do (and sometimes to keep their jobs), marketers in triple-bottom-line firms do their best to prove to management that they are generating measurable value by aligning marketing activities with the firm's overall business objectives.[30]

Throughout the text we will discuss how marketers try to measure the value they are creating. One way they do this is through scorecards, which report in quantified terms how the company or a brand is doing in achieving its various goals. Scorecards like the one shown in the Marketing Metrics box on page 24 tend to be short and to the point, and they often use charts and graphs to summarize the information in an easy-to-read format. They might report "grades" on factors such as actual cost per sale, a comparison of Web site hits (the number of people who view a Web site), customers' satisfaction with a company's repair facilities, or even the percentage of customers who respond to direct mail pieces. Enlightened marketers typically adopt a *balanced scorecard* approach that, consistent with triple-bottom-line thinking, includes a variety of measures that capture economic, social, and environmental value creation.

Other Perspectives of Marketing

Not all organizations have adopted a triple-bottom-line orientation. Organizations that focus on the most efficient production and distribution of products, and not on whether these products best satisfy consumers' needs, have a **product orientation**. Sales of Procter & Gamble's Ivory Soap declined because P&G viewed the brand as plain old soap, not as a cleansing product that could provide other benefits as well. Ivory Soap lost business to newer deodorant and "beauty" soaps containing cold cream that appealed to different customer needs in this market.[31] The Ivory Soap example demonstrates how firms that focus narrowly on the product learn an important lesson the hard way—customers do not buy products, they buy benefits. We will explore this concept in more detail in Chapter 7 on product strategy.

product orientation
A management philosophy that emphasizes the most efficient ways to produce and distribute products.

Other firms adopt a **selling orientation**, which means that management views marketing as a selling function, or a way to move products out of warehouses so that inventories don't pile up. You have probably experienced aggressive salespeople who try to "hard sell" and get you to buy something without a lot of concern for your needs and wants. This is the type of salesperson depicted in movies like *Glengarry Glen Ross* or plays like *Death of a Salesman*. Companies that still follow a selling orientation tend to be successful at making one-time sales rather than building repeat business. In the end, such companies inevitably fail because their buyers do not come back. This is particularly true in Canada where there are not as many customers as in larger countries like the United States.

selling orientation
A managerial view of marketing as a selling function, or a way to move products out of warehouses to reduce inventory.

Other organizations have adopted a **consumer orientation**—being proactive and responsive in identifying and satisfying customers' needs and wants. Grocery retailer Thrifty Foods (now owned by Sobeys) enjoys a 25 percent market share on Vancouver Island by focusing on quality meats and produce, selection, value, and service. Over the past 23 years, founder Alex Campbell introduced unique services and programs for his customers, including home delivery, composting and recycling, and "kiddie-friendly" tills that offer Sesame Snaps and colouring books instead of candy. Montreal-based MEGA Brands Inc. with its brand Mega Bloks is proactive in identifying consumer needs and wants with respect to building block sets that will appeal to preschoolers, kids, and collectors. In addition to perennial favourites like farm- or space-themed sets (Exhibit 1.17), MEGA Brands also develops themed sets that are associated with popular TV shows like Power Rangers and Thomas the Tank Engine, comics like Spiderman, video games like Halo and Need for Speed, and other themes such as Hello Kitty and Smurfs.

consumer orientation
A management philosophy that focuses on ways to satisfy customers' needs and wants.

A consumer orientation is more progressive than a production or selling orientation, but it does not take into consideration the broader stakeholder relationship management, social marketing, and accountability considerations of the triple-bottom-line orientation.

Exhibit 1.17
By finding out what customers want and then making an exchange valued by both parties, Mega Bloks follows a consumer orientation.

business ethics
Rules of conduct for an organization.

4

OBJECTIVE
Be able to discuss
ethical issues
related to marketing
decisions.
(pp. 32–38)

Doing It Right: Ethical Behaviour in the Marketplace

Business ethics is the first step toward creating social profit. But what does ethical business behaviour mean to marketers and to their marketing strategies? Ethics are rules of conduct—how most people in a culture judge what is right and what is wrong. Business ethics are basic values that guide a firm's behaviour. These values govern all sorts of marketing planning decisions that managers make, including what goes into their products, where they source raw materials, how they advertise, and what type of pricing they establish.

Today in Canada, and in many other parts of the world, we are witnessing greater concern about business decisions based solely on short-term profits. It has been suggested that business operates in an "ethics era"—a period in which both executives and consumers are becoming concerned about the downside of "business as usual."[32] A report from the Canadian Democracy and Corporate Accountability Commission has revealed that 74 percent of Canadian shareholders believe that business executives should "embrace a broader social ethic" in their corporate responsibilities.[33] And this was before the recent economic collapse caused by questionable banking and accounting practices around the world. Developing sound business ethics is a major step toward creating a strong relationship with customers and others in the marketplace. Actions speak louder than words for most customers, so companies need to act ethically and not just profess to ethical values.

The emphasis on ethical business practices means that sometimes firms must make decisions that hurt them in the short term. Despite robust sales of a video game called Night Trap made by Sega, executives at Toys "R" Us pulled the product from store shelves. This costly action was taken after the store chain received complaints from parents who objected to their children playing a game in which scantily dressed sorority sisters fight off zombies who try to suck out their blood with a giant syringe.

Notions of right and wrong differ between organizations and cultures. Some businesses, for example, believe it is acceptable for salespeople to use any means to persuade customers to buy, even if it includes giving partly true or even false information, while other firms feel that anything less than total honesty with customers is wrong. Because each culture has its own set of values, beliefs, and customs, ethical business behaviour varies in different parts of the world. Transparency International (www.transparency.org), an organization dedicated to fighting corruption in business around the world, created an International Corruption Perceptions Index, which highlights the differences in the perceptions of corrupt business practices around the world. Out of the 91 countries ranked in their recent Index, Finland was identified as number one, the country perceived to have the least-corrupt business practices, and Canada ranked as number seven, ahead of both the United Kingdom (number 13) and the United States (number 16).

With many rules about doing business, both written and unwritten, floating around, how do marketers know what upper management, investors, and customers expect of them? In order to answer this question definitively, many firms develop their own **code of ethics**, or written standards of behaviour to which everyone in the organization must subscribe, as part of the planning process. These documents eliminate confusion about what the firm considers to be ethically acceptable behaviour by its people, and also set standards for how the organization interacts with its stakeholders. For example, the Dow Chemical Company's Code of Business Conduct, available in 20 different languages through its Web site (www.dow.com) is based on Dow's stated corporate values of integrity and respect for people. The code deals with the following issues: diversity; the environment; financial integrity; accurate company records; conflicts of interest; obligations to customers, competitors, and regulators; computer systems and telecommunications

code of ethics
Written standards of behaviour to which everyone in the organization must subscribe.

Figure 1.4 Code of Ethics of the American Marketing Association

The American Marketing Association helps its members adhere to ethical standards of business through its Code of Ethics.

Ethical Norms and Values for Marketers

PREAMBLE

The American Marketing Association commits itself to promoting the highest standard of professional ethical norms and values for its members (practitioners, academics, and students). Norms are established standards of conduct that are expected and maintained by society and/or professional organizations. Values represent the collective conception of what communities find desirable, important and morally proper. Values also serve as the criteria for evaluating our own personal actions and the actions of others. As marketers, we recognize that we not only serve our organizations but also act as stewards of society in creating, facilitating, and executing the transactions that are part of the greater economy. In this role, marketers are expected to embrace the highest professional ethical norms and the ethical values implied by our responsibility toward multiple stakeholders (e.g., customers, employees, investors, peers, channel members, regulators, and the host community).

ETHICAL NORMS

As Marketers, we must:

1. **Do no harm.** This means consciously avoiding harmful actions or omissions by embodying high ethical standards and adhering to all applicable laws and regulations in the choices we make.
2. **Foster trust in the marketing system.** This means striving for good faith and fair dealing so as to contribute toward the efficacy of the exchange process as well as avoiding deception in product design, pricing, communication, and delivery of distribution.
3. **Embrace ethical values.** This means building relationships and enhancing consumer confidence in the integrity of marketing by affirming these core values: honesty, responsibility, fairness, respect, transparency, and citizenship.

ETHICAL VALUES

Honesty—to be forthright in dealings with customers and stakeholders. To this end, we will:

- Strive to be truthful in all situations and at all times.
- Offer products of value that do what we claim in our communications.
- Stand behind our products if they fail to deliver their claimed benefits.
- Honor our explicit and implicit commitments and promises.

Responsibility—to accept the consequences of our marketing decisions and strategies. To this end, we will:

- Strive to serve the needs of customers.
- Avoid using coercion with all stakeholders.
- Acknowledge the social obligations to stakeholders that come with increased marketing and economic power.
- Recognize our special commitments to vulnerable market segments such as children, seniors, the economically impoverished, market illiterates, and others who may be substantially disadvantaged.
- Consider environmental stewardship in our decision making.

Fairness—to balance justly the needs of the buyer with the interests of the seller. To this end, we will:

- Represent products in a clear way in selling, advertising, and other forms of communication; this includes the avoidance of false, misleading, and deceptive promotion.
- Reject manipulations and sales tactics that harm customer trust.
- Refuse to engage in price fixing, predatory pricing, price gouging, or "bait-and-switch" tactics.
- Avoid knowing participation in conflicts of interest.
- Seek to protect the private information of customers, employees, and partners.

Ethical Norms and Values for Marketers *(continued)*

Respect—to acknowledge the basic human dignity of all stakeholders. To this end, we will:

- Value individual differences and avoid stereotyping customers or depicting demographic groups (e.g., gender, race, sexual orientation) in a negative or dehumanizing way.
- Listen to the needs of customers and make all reasonable efforts to monitor and improve their satisfaction on an ongoing basis.
- Make every effort to understand and respectfully treat buyers, suppliers, intermediaries, and distributors from all cultures.
- Acknowledge the contributions of others, such as consultants, employees, and coworkers, to marketing endeavors.
- Treat everyone, including our competitors, as we would wish to be treated.

Transparency—to create a spirit of openness in marketing operations. To this end, we will:

- Strive to communicate clearly with all constituencies.
- Accept constructive criticism from customers and other stakeholders.
- Explain and take appropriate action regarding significant product or service risks, component substitutions or other foreseeable eventualities that could affect customers or their perception of the purchase decision.
- Disclose list prices and terms of financing as well as available price deals and adjustments.

Citizenship—to fulfill the economic, legal, philanthropic, and societal responsibilities that serve stakeholders. To this end, we will:

- Strive to protect the ecological environment in the execution of marketing campaigns.
- Give back to the community through volunteerism and charitable donations.
- Contribute to the overall betterment of marketing and its reputation.
- Urge supply chain members to ensure that trade is fair for all participants, including producers in developing countries.

IMPLEMENTATION

We expect AMA members to be courageous and proactive in leading and/or aiding their organizations in the fulfillment of the explicit and implicit promises made to those stakeholders. We recognize that every industry sector and marketing sub-discipline (e.g., marketing research, e-commerce, Internet selling, direct marketing, and advertising) has its own specific ethical issues that require policies and commentary. An array of such codes can be accessed through links on the AMA Web site. Consistent with the principle of subsidiarity (solving issues at the level where the expertise resides), we encourage all such groups to develop and/or refine their industry and discipline-specific codes of ethics to supplement these guiding ethical norms and values.

Source: Copyright © American Marketing Association, http://www.marketingpower.com.

security; safeguarding important information; interactions with the public; and corporate social responsibility.

Professional associations also often establish codes of ethics to guide the behaviour of members. For instance, to help members of the marketing profession in North America and elsewhere adhere to ethical behaviour in their marketing efforts, the American Marketing Association (AMA), the largest professional marketing association in the world, has developed its own Code of Ethics, which is shown in Figure 1.4. In Canada, the Professional Marketing Research Society (www.pmrs-aprm.com), the professional organization for the marketing research community, has its own set of ethical standards that all members must adhere to, as does the Canadian Marketing Association (CMA) (see Figure 1.5). The code of ethics of the CMA is more specific than the AMA code of ethics, and includes statements relating to privacy, advertising to children, and considerations when marketing to teenagers. It also has stronger language, indicating what marketing *must* do as compared to should do.

The Dark Side of Marketing

Whether intentionally or not, some marketers do violate their bond of trust with consumers, and, unfortunately, the "dark side" of marketing often is the subject of harsh criticism.[34] In some cases, these violations are illegal, such as when a retailer adopts a "bait and switch" selling strategy, luring consumers into the store with promises of inexpensive products, with the sole intent of getting them to switch to higher-priced goods.

In other cases, marketing practices have detrimental effects on society even though they are not actually illegal. Some alcohol and tobacco companies advertise in low-income neighbourhoods where abuse of these products is a big problem. Others sponsor commercials depicting groups of people in an unfavourable light or sell products that encourage antisocial behaviour. An online game based on the Columbine High School massacre drew criticism from some who say it trivializes the actions of the two teen killers.[35]

Ethical and Sustainable Decisions in the Real World

Tap Zoo is a zoo simulation game developed by Streetview Labs where you can create a virtual zoo with all types of animals and attractions that you can place anywhere you choose, to make it amazing. It is a "free" App on the Apple iTunes store and popular with children. Parents all over the world, however, are receiving bills from Apple for hundreds of dollars in "in-app" purchases when their children answer yes to questions asking them if they would like "more stars" or another animal in their zoo. No password needed—just a charge of $1.19 to $189.99, each time the child answers yes, and with no warnings. Regular purchases on iTunes require a password to be entered and a confirmation that the account holder wants to make a purchase.

One review of the Tap Zoo game says, "While it's not bad on its own, too much of Tap Zoo feels designed to get you interested in playing so you'll spend $9.99 or more on stars to keep playing Tap Zoo. It's a little underhanded and greatly diminishes the game."[1] Parents hit with these charges think it is more than a little underhanded. The Web site of Tap Zoo's developer, Streetview Labs, has been flooded with complaints from users saying their children unwittingly racked up bills as large as US$1300.[2] One parent indicated in an Apple discussion forum that he "checked the developer's Web site and it appears they have acknowledged they have done the wrong thing and have supported people to seek refunds,"[3] but at least six months from the first of these complaints, this author observes (from his own kids racking up a large bill), that the software has not been modified.

Apple, by offering this application in their iTunes store, by having in-app purchases enabled as the default on their iTunes software, and by taking a 30 percent commission on these purchases, appears to condone the Streetview Labs marketing strategy. Is it enough that Apple's iTunes Web site provides the warning "PLEASE NOTE: this game lets you purchase items within the game for real money. Please disable in-app-purchases on your device if you do not want this feature to be accessible."[4] One Australian parent, Mr. Ravlen, did not think so. He thought it misleading of the computer giant to list the application as "free," and while Apple did credit $962 back into his account, their email said that this would be "a one-time exception."[5]

Is Streetview Labs' use of in-app purchases unethical behaviour or savvy marketing? Would your conclusions change if the app was not specifically targeting children? What role do regulatory bodies have in protecting children from marketing strategies that they may not fully understand?

Written by J. Brock Smith, from the following sources:

[1] http://www.appolicious.com/games/articles/3166-tap-zoo-iphone-game-tries-too-hard-for-the-pocketbook.

[2] http://www.theherald.com.au/news/local/news/general/how-a-free-iphone-game-cost-charlestown-dad-967/1941584.aspx.

[3] http://discussions.apple.com/message.jspa?messageID=12455663.

[4] http://itunes.apple.com/ar/app/tap-zoo/id360893304?mt=8#.

[5] http://www.theherald.com.au/news/local/news/general/how-a-free-iphone-game-cost-charlestown-dad-967/1941584.aspx.

ETHICS CHECK:
Find out what other students taking this course would do and why on **www.mypearsonmarketinglab.com**

Does Apple risk tarnishing its brand by not only allowing, but tacitly encouraging, in-app purchases?

☐ YES ☐ NO

Figure 1.5 Canadian Marketing Association Code of Ethics: Privacy

Below is part of the privacy principles advocated by the CMA to align with Canada's Federal privacy laws.

J1 Ten Privacy Principles:
1. **Accountability:** An organization is responsible for personal information under its control and shall designate an individual or individuals who are accountable for the organization's compliance with the following principles.
2. **Identifying Purposes:** The purposes for which personal information is collected shall be identified by the organization at or before the time the information is collected.
3. **Consent:** The knowledge and consent of the individual are required for the collection, use or disclosure of personal information, except where inappropriate.
4. **Limiting Collection:** The collection of personal information shall be limited to that which is necessary for the purposes identified by the organization. Information shall be collected by fair and lawful means.
5. **Limiting Use, Disclosure and Retention:** Personal information shall not be used or disclosed for purposes other than those for which it was collected, except with the consent of the individual or as required by law. Personal information shall be retained only as long as necessary for the fulfillment of those purposes.
6. **Accuracy:** Personal information shall be as accurate, complete and up-to-date as is necessary for the purposes for which it is being used.
7. **Safeguards:** Personal information shall be protected by security safeguards appropriate to the sensitivity of the information.
8. **Openness:** An organization shall make readily available to individuals specific information about its policies and practices relating to the management of personal information.
9. **Individual Access:** Upon request, an individual shall be informed of the existence, use and disclosure of his or her personal information and shall be given access to that information. An individual shall be able to challenge the accuracy and completeness of the information and have it amended as appropriate.
10. **Challenging Compliance:** An individual shall be able to address a challenge concerning compliance with the above principles to the designated individual or individuals accountable for the organization's compliance.

For guidance in the implementation of these principles and the key tenets of PIPEDA, marketers are encouraged to consult CMA's Canadian Privacy Compliance Guide and CMA Opt-Out Consent Guidelines.

Source: Canadian Marketing Association Code of Ethics and Standards of Practice, http://www.the-cma.org/?WCE=C=47|K=225849#10.

For some—hopefully, not many and, hopefully, not *you* after you read this book—marketing is a four-letter word. Let's briefly review some dimensions of the "dark side" of consumer behaviour also for which marketers come under attack.

Criticism: Marketing corrupts society. The marketing system comes under fire from both sides. On the one hand, some believe that marketers contribute to the moral breakdown of society by presenting images of selfish pleasure and encouraging materialism at the expense of things like spirituality and concern for the environment. On the other hand, some on the "left" side of the spectrum might argue that many who would otherwise be engaged in more significant action for social change have been distracted by these same promises of material pleasure.

A Response: A need is a basic biological motive, while a want represents one way that society has taught us to satisfy the need. For example, thirst is biologically based, but we are taught to want Coca-Cola to satisfy that thirst rather than wanting, say, goat's milk. Thus, the need is already there, with marketers simply recommending ways to satisfy it. Marketing's basic objective is to create awareness that needs exist, not to create needs. In a democratic society, anyone or any organization can suggest ways to satisfy any basic needs, even those needs related to spirituality or government.

Criticism: Advertising and marketing are unnecessary. It has been said that marketers arbitrarily link products to desirable social attributes, thereby fostering a materialistic society in which people measure us by what we own.

A Response: Products are designed to meet existing needs, and advertising only helps to communicate the availability of the goods.[36] Advertising is a service for which consumers are willing to pay, because the information it provides about a product and the alternatives might save the consumer both time and money.

Criticism: Marketers manipulate consumers through the promise of miracles. Through advertising, consumers are led to believe that products have properties enabling them to do special and mysterious things for consumers in a way that will transform their lives: beauty, control, success, good health, etc.

A Response: Advertisers simply do not know enough about people to be able to manipulate them in this way—the failure rate for new products ranges from 40 to 80 percent. Although people might think that advertisers have foolproof techniques to manipulate them, in reality, the industry is successful only when it tries to sell good products, and it is unsuccessful when selling poor ones.

Criticism: Marketers support addictive consumption. **Consumer addiction** is a physiological or psychological dependency on goods or services. These problems, of course, include alcoholism, drug addiction, and cigarette smoking. Many companies profit from addictive products or by selling solutions.

A Response: Clearly, there are marketers who produce products (goods and services) that are not good for people's health and well-being, or especially not when consumed in extreme quantities. There are consumers, however, who want to consume or use these products, even when fully aware of the risks. Although most people equate addiction with drugs, consumers can use virtually anything to relieve (at least temporarily) some problem or satisfy some need to the point that reliance on it becomes extreme. "Shopaholics" turn to shopping much the way addicted people turn to drugs or alcohol.[37] Numerous treatment centres in China, South Korea, and Taiwan (and now a few in the United States also) deal with cases of Internet addiction; some hard-core gamers have become so hooked they literally forget to eat or drink and die of dehydration. There is even a Chapstick addiction support group with approximately 250 active members![38] Many people still smoke, eat more fat than is good for them, and consume alcohol immoderately. As a society, we have to decide how to balance freedom of choice against regulation that prevents consumers making unwise decisions. In preserving freedom of choice, society is exposed to the potential of harm generated by the decisions of some marketers.

Criticism: Marketers exploit people. Sometimes people are used or exploited, willingly or not, for commercial gain in the marketplace. These situations range from travelling road shows that feature dwarfs and little people to the selling of body parts and babies on eBay. "Consumed consumers" are people who themselves become commodities.

A Response: This can happen. There are marketers who do not take a triple-bottom-line perspective and balance economic, social, and environmental objectives in the interest of their companies, their customers, and society as a whole. However, consumers have a strong voice and can stop buying brands whose values do not align with their own. When marketers make decisions that their consumers do not like, the consumers should let them know by making alternative consumption choices.

Exhibit 1.18

Some people feel that marketers manipulate consumers, while others argue that people should be held responsible for their own choices. This ad is critical of the current trend of lawsuits brought against fast-food companies by people who blame their health problems on the fast-food industry. What do you think?

consumer addiction
A physiological or psychological dependency on goods or services.

Despite the best efforts of researchers, government regulators, and concerned industry leaders, sometimes consumers are their own worst enemies (Exhibit 1.18). We tend to think of individuals as rational decision makers, calmly doing their best to obtain products and services that will maximize the health and well-being of themselves, their families, and society. In reality, however, consumers' desires, choices, and actions often result in negative consequences to individuals and society. Some of these actions are relatively harmless, but others have more onerous consequences.

Consumerism: People Fighting Back

Organized activities that bring about social and political change are not new to the Canadian scene. Women's right to vote, child labour laws, universal health care, minimum wage, and equal employment opportunities have all resulted from social movements in which citizens, public and private organizations, and business worked to change society. **Consumerism** is the social movement directed at protecting consumers from harmful business practices.

consumerism
A social movement that attempts to protect consumers from harmful business practices.

The modern consumerism movement in Canada began in the late 1940s, when the Consumers' Association of Canada (CAC) was established (www.consumer.ca). The mission of the CAC is to inform and educate consumers, and also to advocate on their behalf.[39] Since its inception, the CAC has been active in helping to establish protective legislation for consumers related to labelling and packaging, bans on the use of certain pesticides, and improved quality standards for agricultural and manufactured goods. Recent activities of the CAC have focused on fighting the practice of negative-option marketing by the cable industry, in which consumers were automatically charged for services that they did not sign up for unless they contacted the cable company to cancel. They have also conducted a national consumer survey regarding Canadians' perceptions of the quality of goods and services.

Conclusions

In this first chapter, you learned that marketing is primarily about creating value—both for customers and for the marketing organization—where marketers make strategic and tactical decisions related to the choice of target market focus and their positioning relative to competitors for the attention and consideration of those target customers, and marketing mix decisions related to products, pricing, communication, and distribution. These decisions are reflected and justified in a marketing plan which typically adheres to the outline of Figure 1.2 and answers the questions implicit in that figure. Be sure to read the Part Opener sections of the text as they walk you through the development of an example marketing plan found in the Appendix at the back of the book. This text is also organized around the decisions implicit in Figure 1.2 and the factors that are considered in making those decisions. Chapter 2 focuses on the environment of marketing decisions and introduces you to *SWOT analysis*, a useful tool for understanding the strategic implications of factors in the internal and external environment. Chapter 3 gives you an introduction to the research marketers do to make informed decisions. Chapters 4 and 5 examine key consumer and organizational buying behaviour concepts that help us develop better market segment profiles. Chapter 6 focuses on how to make target market and positioning decisions. Chapters 7 through 12 focus on the marketing mix decisions summarized in Figure 1.2. All the marketing decisions must support each other in the writing of a marketing plan, and the tools, concepts, and principles discussed throughout the text can be used to provide rationale for a particular course of action. We will show you how to do this in the Part Openers in relation to the S&S Smoothie company.

Here's my choice. . .

Real **People**, Real **Choices**

1 Option   2 Option   3 Option

Why do you think Richard chose option 3?

How It Worked Out at Yellow Point Lodge

Richard decided to implement Option 3: protect the land and decrease its value. Richard valued the land and his father's vision more than the money—which the government would take half of anyway. This option was most consistent with Richard's values and those of his father. It was also consistent with his guests' values and the value proposition they found so appealing.

Richard negotiated with The Land Conservancy and the Nanaimo Area Land Trust and signed the timber rights of the main lodge property (about 80 acres) into a conservation covenant. While Richard maintained ownership, this protected the property as part of the coastal Douglas fir zone. In making this land untouchable, Richard has ensured that neither he nor any future owner will be able to log or develop it.

There will be some tax advantage to doing this, but that was not Richard's primary motivation. He wanted the land protected. His decision also means that his children won't be faced with the increasing pressure to develop the land. By following in his father's footsteps as a "custodian" of the land instead of the "owner," Richard has been true to his and his family's values. He has also protected, to some extent, a pretty nice way of life for his children should they choose to be custodians of Yellow Point.

Objective Summary ➡ Key Terms ➡ Apply

CHAPTER 1
Study Map

---

1. Objective Summary   (pp. 6-16)

Explain what marketing is and how value creation is central to the marketing concept.

Marketing is the activity, set of institutions, and processes for creating, communicating, delivering, and exchanging offerings that have value for customers, clients, partners, and society at large. Therefore, marketing is all about delivering value to stakeholders; that is, to everyone who is affected by a transaction. Organizations that seek to ensure their long-term profitability by identifying and satisfying customers' needs and wants have adopted the marketing concept. Marketing is also about exchanges, or the transfer of value between a buyer and a seller.

Value is the benefits a customer receives from buying a good or service relative to the costs of buying, using, and disposing of it. Marketing communicates these benefits as the value proposition to the customer. For customers, the value proposition includes the whole bundle of benefits the product promises to deliver, not just the benefits of the product itself. Sellers determine value by assessing whether their transactions are profitable, whether they are providing value to stakeholders by creating a competitive advantage, and whether they are providing value through the value chain. Customers generate value when they turn into advertising directors, retailers, and new product development consultants, often through social networking. Society receives value from marketing activities when producers and consumers engage in ethical, profitable, and environmentally friendly exchange relationships.

Key Terms

customer value, p. 7

marketing, p. 8

target market, p. 9

stakeholder, p. 9

exchange, p. 9

consumer, p. 9

marketing concept, p. 9

need, p. 9

want, p. 9

benefit, p. 10

demand, p. 10

market, p.10

marketplace, p. 10

lifetime value of a customer, p. 11

product, p. 14

consumer goods, p. 14

services, p. 14

popular culture, p. 15

business-to-business marketing, p. 15

industrial goods, p. 15

e-commerce, p. 15

not-for-profit organizations, p. 15

2. Objective Summary (pp. 16–27)

Explain how marketing is a decision-making process and describe the planning and the marketing mix tools that managers use in the marketing process.

The strategic process of marketing planning begins with an assessment of factors within the organization and in the external environment that could help or hinder the development and marketing of products. On the basis of this analysis, marketers set objectives and develop strategies. Many firms use a target marketing strategy in which they divide the overall market into segments and then target the most attractive one. Then they design the marketing mix to gain a competitive position in the target market. The marketing mix includes product, price, place, and promotion. The product is what satisfies customer needs. The price is the assigned value or amount to be exchanged for the product. The place or channel of distribution gets the product to the customer. Promotion is the organization's efforts to persuade customers to buy the product.

Key Terms

market segment, p. 18

market segmentation, p. 18

mass market, p. 18

positioning, p. 19

distinctive competency, p. 19

differential benefit, p. 19

brand personality, p. 20

marketing mix, p. 20

four Ps, p. 20

price, p. 21

distribution, p. 22

communication, p. 22

value chain, p. 24

consumer-generated content, p. 25

online social networking, p. 26

open source model, p. 27

3. Objective Summary (pp. 27–32)

Understand key issues relating to making ethical marketing decisions in a sustainable world and be able to discuss different perspectives of marketing.

Many consumers today are concerned with the ethical practices of companies. As a result, astute marketers recognize that long-term profitability depends on making quality products while acting in an ethical and socially responsible manner. Marketing is *still* concerned with the firm's "bottom line," but now many managers also consider social profit, which is the net benefit both the firm and society receive from a firm's ethical practices and socially responsible behaviour.

The second part of social profit is social responsibility, a management process in which organizations engage in activities that have a positive effect on society and promote the public good. These activities include environmental stewardship, cause marketing, and encouraging cultural diversity. Firms like Mountain Equipment Co-op (MEC) that believe in social responsibility represent a business value system that goes beyond the short-term bottom line. Instead, they consider the short- and long-term effects of decisions on the company, its employees, consumers, the community, and the world at large.

Key Terms

triple bottom line, p. 28

customer relationship management (CRM), p. 28

attention economy, p. 29

social marketing concept, p. 29

sustainable development, p. 30

green marketing, p. 30

ROI (return on investment), p. 30

product orientation, p. 31

selling orientation, p. 31

consumer orientation, p. 31

4. Objective Summary (pp. 32–38)

Be able to discuss ethical issues related to marketing decisions.

Early in the twentieth century, firms followed a production orientation in which they focused on the most efficient ways to produce and distribute products. Beginning in the 1930s, some firms adopted a selling orientation that encouraged salespeople to aggressively sell products to customers. In the 1950s, organizations adopted a consumer orientation that focused on customer satisfaction. This led to the development of the marketing concept. Today, many firms are moving toward a triple-bottom-line orientation that includes not only a commitment to quality and value, but also a concern for both economic and social profit. There are, however, some firms that still have a production orientation or selling orientation or consumer orientation that have not always acted in the long-term interests of their customers and society. This has led some people to have concerns about the practice of marketing, such as concerns that marketing corrupts society, or leads to waste and conspicuous consumption.

Key Terms

business ethics, p. 32

code of ethics, p. 34

consumer addiction, p. 37

consumerism, p. 38

Chapter **Questions** and **Activities**

Concepts: Test Your Knowledge

1. Where do marketers work, and what role does marketing play in the firm?
2. Briefly explain what marketing is.
3. Explain needs, wants, and demands. What is the role of marketing in each of these?
4. What is value? How does marketing create different types of value?
5. Trace the evolution of the marketing concept.
6. Define the terms consumer goods, services, and industrial goods.
7. To what does the lifetime value of the customer refer, and how is it calculated?
8. What does it mean for a firm to have a competitive advantage? What gives a firm a competitive advantage?
9. What is involved in marketing planning?
10. List and describe the elements of the marketing mix.

Activities: Apply What You've Learned

1. **Creative Homework/Short Project** An old friend of yours has been making and selling vitamin-fortified smoothies to acquaintances and friends of friends for some time. He is now thinking about opening a shop in a small northern town, but he is worried about whether he'll have enough customers who want these smoothies to keep a business going. Knowing that you are a marketing student, he's asked you for some advice. What can you tell him about product, price, promotion, and place (distribution) strategies that will help him get his business off the ground?
2. **In class 10–25 Min.** for Teams Assume that you are employed by your city's Chamber of Commerce. One major focus of the chamber is to get industries to move to your city. As a former marketing student, you know that there are issues involving product, price, promotion, and place (distribution) that can attract business. Next week you and your consulting firm have an opportunity to speak to the members of the chamber, and your topic will be "Marketing a City." Develop an outline for that presentation.
3. **In Class 10–25 Min.** for Teams Successful firms have a competitive advantage because they are able to identify distinctive competencies and use these to create differential benefits for their customers. Consider your business school or your university. What distinctive competencies does it have? What differential benefits does it provide for students? What is its competitive advantage? What are your ideas as to how your university could improve its competitive position? Write an outline of your ideas.

4. **Creative Homework/Short Project** As a marketing professional, you have been asked to write a short piece for a local business newsletter about the state of marketing today. You think the best way to address this topic is to review how the marketing concept has evolved and to discuss the triple-bottom-line orientation. Write the short article you will submit to the editor of the newsletter.
5. **In Class 10–25 Min.** for Teams As university or college students, you and your friends sometimes discuss the various courses you are taking. One of your friends says to you, "Marketing's not important. It's just dumb advertising." Another friend says, "Marketing doesn't really affect people's lives in any way." As a role-playing exercise, present your arguments against these statements to your class.

Marketing Metrics: Exercise

The chapter discusses the growing importance of sustainability, and it notes that companies and consumers increasingly consider other costs in addition to the financial kind when they decide what to sell or buy. One of these cost categories is damage to the environment. How can marketers make it easier for shoppers to compute these costs? The answer is more apparent in some product categories than in others. For example, North American consumers often are able to compare the power consumption and annual costs of appliances by looking at their EnergyStar™ rating. In other situations, we can assess the *carbon footprint* implications of a product or service; this tells us how much CO_2 our purchase will emit into the atmosphere (e.g., if a person flies from Vancouver to Toronto). The average North American is responsible for 9.44 tons of CO_2 per year![40] A carbon footprint comes from the sum of two parts, the direct, or primary, footprint and the indirect, or secondary, footprint:

1. The *primary footprint* is a measure of our direct emissions of CO_2 from the burning of fossil fuels, including domestic energy consumption and transportation (e.g., cars and planes).
2. The *secondary footprint* is a measure of the indirect CO_2 emissions from the whole lifecycle of products we use, from their manufacture to their eventual breakdown.[41] Although many of us are more aware today that our consumption choices carry unseen costs, there is still a lot of confusion about the best way to communicate the environmental costs of our actions—and in many cases, consumers aren't motivated to take these issues into account unless the costs impact them directly and in the short term. What other metrics would you suggest that might address this important measurement problem?

Choices: What Do You Think?

1. ***Ethics*** Have you ever pirated software? How about music? Is it ethical to give or receive software instead of paying for it? Does the answer depend on the person's motivation and/or if the person could otherwise afford to buy the product?

2. ***Critical thinking*** The marketing concept focuses on the ability of marketing to satisfy customer needs. As a typical college student, how does marketing satisfy your needs? What areas of your life are affected by marketing? What areas of your life (if any) are not affected by marketing?

3. ***Critical thinking*** In both developed and developing countries, not all firms have implemented programs that follow the marketing concept. Can you think of firms that still operate with a production orientation? a selling orientation? What changes would you recommend for these firms?

4. ***Critical thinking*** Ideally, each member of a value chain adds value to a product before someone buys it. Thinking about a music CD you might buy in a store, what kind of value does the music retailer add? How about the label that signs the artist? The public relations firm that arranges a tour by the artist to promote the new CD? The production company that shoots a music video to go along with the cut?

5. ***Critical thinking*** User-generated commercials seem to be part of a broader trend toward user-generated content of all sorts. Examples include MySpace, Flickr (where users post photos and comment on others' pictures), blogging, and video-sharing sites like YouTube. Do you think this is a passing fad or an important trend? How (if at all) should marketers be dealing with these activities?

6. ***Ethics*** Some marketing or consumption activities involve the (literal) consumption of people—voluntarily or not. In one recent controversial incident, a man in Germany advertised on the Internet to find someone who wanted to be killed and eaten (we are not making this up). He actually found a willing volunteer and did just what he promised—he's now on trial for murder. If a person consents to be "consumed" in some way, is this still an ethical problem?

Miniproject: Learn by Doing

The purpose of this miniproject is to develop an understanding of the importance of marketing to different organizations.

1. Working as a team with two or three other students, select an organization in your community that practises marketing. It may be a manufacturer, a service provider, a retailer, a not-for-profit organization—almost any organization will do. Then schedule a visit with someone within the organization who is involved in the marketing activities. Arrange for a short visit during which the person can give your group a tour of the facilities and explain the organization's marketing activities.

2. Divide the following list of topics among your team and ask each person to be responsible for developing a set of questions to ask during the interview to learn about the company's program:

   - What customer segments the company targets
   - How it determines needs and wants
   - What its pricing strategies are, including any discounting policies it has
   - What promotional strategies it uses and what these emphasize to position the product(s)
   - How it distributes products and whether it has encountered any problems
   - What products it offers, including features, benefits, and goals for customer satisfaction
   - How marketing planning is done and who does it
   - Whether social responsibility is part of the marketing program and, if so, in what ways

3. Develop a team report of your findings. In each section of the report, share what you learned that is new or surprising to you compared to what you expected.

4. Develop a team presentation for your class that summarizes your findings. Conclude your presentation with comments on what your team believes the company was doing that was particularly good and what was not quite so good.

Marketing in **Action** Case Online Gambling

Online gambling is one of the fastest growing online businesses. Some argue that it is the single most important factor in the growth of e-commerce.[1] Canadians currently spend close to a billion dollars a year pursuing this activity. In Canada, the provinces of British Columbia and Quebec launched online-gambling sites in 2010. Ontario, Nova Scotia, and New Brunswick were poised to launch sites in 2011. However, the growth of this online business is not without controversy.

Online gambling in Canada is controlled by the provinces and territories. Any province that does offer Internet gambling cannot take bets from out of province residents unless that other province allowed it. However, the general public does not generally understand these controls and the rules related to this activity. Almost 30 percent of Canadians surveyed by Ipsos Reid in 2010 perceived the control to be with the federal govern-

ment, with approximately 25 percent believing it was uncontrolled. Over 70 percent of those surveyed believed it was illegal in their province. Clarification of the control and regulations is needed. Most survey respondents believed that this regulation should come from the federal government.[2]

The Ontario Lottery and Gaming Corporation estimates Ontarians spend about $400 million a year on unregulated online gambling. According to Emir Aly Crowne-Mohammed and Sanjay Roy, "it appears that 60% of the world's online gambling traffic is received by the Kahnawake Gaming Commission (a gambling commission created by the Kahnawake First Nation's people, an indigenous group in Quebec, Canada), despite the fact that the operation of an online gambling site is clearly illegal under Canadian criminal law, unless licensed and authorized by a provincial government."[3] Why is this regulation not enforced? One reason may be that regulation of any product offered on the Internet is difficult.

There is considerable controversy and uncertainty with respect to the legality of online gaming in both the US and Canada. The US justice department position is that Internet gambling, and the advertising of Internet gambling, in the United States, is illegal. Yet little appears to be done to enforce this law, and the world's largest poker site, PartyPoker.com, now runs radio and television advertisements in Las Vegas, and local billboards advertise Internet poker sites. Part of the confusion lies in the definition of gambling, which traditionally has meant real money being bet. PartyPoker.com offers free electronic currency for betting and makes their money on advertising to the hundreds of thousands of users.

In Canada, it is a crime for anyone except a provincial government to offer lotteries or games of chance that are accessed on or through a computer, but many provincial governments have chosen to operate Internet casinos and online slot machines to supplement their revenues.[4] The national Criminal Code, once uniform in its application, can now be seen to have regional interpretations, at least in regard to gambling. As a whole, Canadians appear to be ambivalent toward gambling, with many viewing gambling as an acceptable community activity, due perhaps to its perceived inevitability and its being a source of revenue for governments and charities. On the other hand, many Canadians feel there should be more restrictions on gambling, with the strength of such feelings varying with the type of gambling (e.g., VLTs), the location of venues ("not in my backyard"), and the perceived social costs of gambling.

Legislation exists in the US and in Canada to prohibit the advertising of Internet gambling sites. However, this is also surrounded with controversy and uncertainty. The US Justice Department's position is that online gambling, and the advertising of it, is illegal. In Canada, the Province of Ontario has a blanket prohibition on the advertising of Internet gambling sites. Enforcement of this position is achievable regarding "traditional" advertising; however, Internet advertising is problematic. Ontario has dealt with this by narrowing the definition of advertising to "instances where the advertising originates in Ontario or is primarily intended for Ontario residents."[5] In most jurisdictions, online gambling firms have been advertising on more mainstream Web sites and competing for advertising space with more popular industries and on well-known portals.

Internet gambling, and the advertising of it, is hard to control. Is government-sponsored gambling contrary to the interests of the public good and contrary to the purpose of good government? Can socially responsible gambling coexist with an industry whose economic sustainability appears to be more and more dependent on those who develop gambling-related problems and harms?

Voluntary codes of practice and industry managed programs such as self-exclusion could be encouraged or reconsidered. Policing practices vary greatly from having engaged policing to not having policing at all.[6] Some jurisdictions prefer to assist people with problems by setting up self-help booths in gambling facilities. The efficiency of some of these strategies is questionable, at best. Self-regulation can take the form of cards with predefined limits or self-exclusion from the ability to gamble online. Can these exclusions also include advertising? Is responsible gambling a shared obligation of all stakeholders in legalized gambling, including regulators and gambling operators? Should gambling operators be required to implement a comprehensive responsible gambling program? Leading experts have argued that the structure of the Internet allows for operators to deliver responsible gaming programs that meet or exceed current standards in the bricks-and-mortar casinos.

Online gambling is big business. Regulation or self-regulation regarding use, advertising, and the use of the proceeds can be examined, but whether or not online gambling should be a business seems to have already been decided.

You Make the Call

1. When is government regulation appropriate or not appropriate when it comes to the marketing of products on the Internet?
2. Should provincial governments be in the online gaming market? Why or why not? Should they have a monopoly? Why or why not?
3. Develop a code of ethics for the Canadian online gaming industry.
4. Compare the key elements of your code of ethics to those of other students. Discuss the differences and update your own code where appropriate.

[1] Berzon, Alexandra. "Corporate News: Venture Bets on Chance Online Gambling Comes to U.S.," *Wall Street Journal,* June 20, 2011, B.4.

[2] Ipsos Reid. "Internet Gaming in Canada: Public Perception and Behaviour," April 2010, http://www.canadiangaming.ca/media_uploads/pdf/103.pdf

[3] Crowne-Mohammed, Emir Aly and Sanjay Roy. "Maintaining Provincial Monopolies: The Legality of Online Gambling Sites in Canada." *Canadian Gaming Lawyer Magazine,* May 2010.

[4] The Legalization of Gambling in Canada 06 July, 2005, at http://www.responsiblegambling.org/articles/legalization_of_gambling_in_canada_july_2005.pdf.

[5] Heydary, Javad. "Advertising for Online Gambling—Is it Legal?" *E-Commerce Times.* 04/28/05. http://www.ecommercetimes.com/story/42696.html.

[6] McMullan, John L. The Gambling Problem and Problem Gambling: Research, Public Policy And Citizenry. St. Mary's University. 2005, https://dspace.ucalgary.ca/bitstream/1880/47421/13/mcmullan.pdf.

Strategic Market Planning:
Take the Big Picture

Real People **Profiles**

Jay Minkoff

 **Profile**

▼ A Decision Maker
at First Flavor

Jay Minkoff is a serial entrepreneur who specializes in creating innovative marketing solutions. Currently, Jay is the co-founder and president of First Flavor, which provides the patent-pending Peel'n Taste flavour-sampling platform for marketing food, beverage, and flavoured products using edible film technology. Prior to this, he co-founded HomeBuilder.com, an online marketing and listing site for the home-building industry that was sold to Homestore Inc. (now Move.com) in 1999, and which he continued to manage until 2003. His previous business, Tri-State Publishing & Communications, publisher of the *Apartment Shoppers Guide* and *New Homes Guide* consumer real estate magazines, was sold to Primedia in 1996. That company was recognized in 1990 as 91st on *Inc. Magazine*'s list of the 500 fastest-growing companies in the country. Prior to this, Jay was a successful commercial real estate broker, having sold or financed over a quarter billion dollars of institutional properties.

A graduate of Tufts University, majoring in civil engineering, he holds an MBA in entrepreneurial management and real estate finance from The Wharton School at the University of Pennsylvania. Jay lives in Wynnewood, PA, with his wife and two daughters.

First Flavor had just completed product development of its marketing services product, the Peel 'n Taste Marketing System. This product provides marketers, for the first time, with the ability to use the sense of taste to market a consumer product. The company's technology allows it to infuse virtually any taste onto an edible flavour strip (à la popular breath strips). The consumer can "sample" the product—whether it's fruit juice, toothpaste, frozen desserts, or any beverage—simply by plucking a strip from a dispenser in a grocery aisle or peeling one off a magazine ad. The strip completely dissolves on the tongue and provides a realistic approximation of what the item will taste like. This new taste-sampling vehicle has the potential to be for the food and beverage industry what Scratch 'n Sniff was for the fragrance industry; it's a way to sample a sensory attribute without actually purchasing the product! Better yet, it can be included in any printed marketing medium.

As First Flavor started to see its first sales of Peel 'n Taste from consumer product manufacturers (Arm & Hammer toothpaste, Old Orchard fruit juice, Welch's grape juice, Sunny Delight Elations, etc.), the startup became aware of other uses for its capability of producing great-tasting edible film strips. Several different applications presented themselves. Here are a few examples:

• When people saw samples of edible films that tasted like Krispy Kreme glazed donuts, buttered popcorn, and butter pecan ice cream, some of them asked, how many calories do they have? and, can I use these when I'm on a diet? Jay realized that providing dieters with no-calorie edible film strips in indulgent flavours could be a new market for First Flavor given the size of the $30 billion diet industry.

Here's my problem...

- Several people during those early years also contacted the company about the use of the flavour strips by people with medical conditions that prevented them from swallowing (dysphagia) and thus from tasting food as well. Quite literally, one of their five senses was not being activated. First Flavor's strips could thus improve the quality of life for many people with an application that might generate a new revenue stream.

- One of First Flavor's clients had a line of herbal-flavoured water it wanted to sell on QVC (quality, value, and convenience). Because the water weighed so much, the expense of shipping the flavoured water was as great as its purchase price. The owner of the water company asked Jay if First Flavor could create "flavour strips" containing the flavouring used in the herbal-flavoured water. The consumer could simply drop a flavouring strip into a bottle of water to create the herbal flavour at home.

As entrepreneurs, Jay and his partners wanted to jump on all of these new opportunities. But they were concerned with losing focus while in the middle of launching First Flavor's first product, Peel 'n Taste. Also, they didn't think they would be able to secure intellectual property protection (such as patents) for any of these three new product ideas. In addition, as an undercapitalized company that Jay was primarily funding, First Flavor was also concerned with the cost of launching these other products. The decision regarding whether to diversify into new product categories was a major strategic crossroads for the young company.

Things to remember

First Flavor's new technology allows it to duplicate virtually any taste in an edible strip that dissolves on a person's tongue. This provided several potential benefits, including novelty/entertainment, risk reduction (people could taste a product before they bought it), and a new way to promote a product in-store or even in print media (by attaching a flavour strip to a mailing or a magazine ad). Jay has to understand which application(s) hold the most promise and also to decide on a strategic focus so that First Flavor can identify marketing objectives based on what the company hopes to accomplish in the short term and then farther into the future.

Jay considered his Options 1·2·3

1 Option **Investigate all three new business ideas and start product development even as Peel 'n Taste was still a fledgling product trying to gain market acceptance.** This strategy could create new revenue opportunities and give the company other options to fall back upon if Peel 'n Taste took off slower than First Flavor hoped. And since the new applications couldn't be patented, the extra lead time would give First Flavor a first-to-market advantage. On the other hand, these other initiatives would drain the company's limited financial resources. Also, management needed to stay focused on maximizing the market's acceptance of Peel 'n Taste at this crucial point in its young life cycle.

2 Option **Continue to focus on introducing Peel 'n Taste into the market until it gained market acceptance. This product would provide the company with the cash flow to invest in new product launches at a later point.** A single approach would keep management and staff focused on the company's initial mission. It would reduce costs and thus the initial investment required to bring the company to profitability. Still, it's not clear how long this process would take. There may be missed market opportunities if another company picked up on one or more of these ideas and brought them to market first.

3 Option **Pick just one or two of these new products and investigate the opportunity of launching it with limited resources and management attention while Peel 'n Taste remained the company's primary focus.** This more selective approach would minimize the cost of launching a new product. Management's time and attention would be diverted, but not on such a significant basis. And this strategy would force First Flavor to look at each of the opportunities more critically because it would have to pick only one to push forward. Still, there was the problem of the "road not taken." Two of the ideas would not get implemented in the near future, and First Flavor faced a possible loss of first-mover advantage in the marketplace for these new products.

Put yourself in Jay's shoes. Which option would you choose, and why?

You Choose

Which **Option** would you choose, and **why?**

1. ☐YES ☐NO   2. ☐YES ☐NO   3. ☐YES ☐NO

See what **option** Jay chose on **page 79**

45

1

OBJECTIVE

Explain how businesses develop plans at different levels within the organization.
(pp. 46–57)

The great success Jay Minkoff and First Flavor have had with its innovative product line didn't just happen by luck. A great deal of planning went into creating value with the innovative First Flavor Peel 'n Taste Marketing System. The company's ongoing business planning at all levels of the firm—strategic, marketing, and operational—drives the market success of its patent-pending technology; this process replicates the flavour of a product in quick-dissolving edible film strips that prospective customers can sample by tasting individually packaged pouches. Implementation of these plans led to First Flavor's ability to pitch easy integration of Peel 'n Taste into a variety of clients' promotional marketing programs in order to drive consumer trial—a powerful service. In this chapter, you will experience the power of effective business planning and lay the groundwork for your own capability to do the kind of planning that has led to Jay's success at First Flavor.

This chapter sets the stage for your ability to do great market planning. It's about the *process* of planning, and we even include a marketing plan template that shows you, step by step, how to build a plan and where to find the information throughout the book to be able to do it. For Jay Minkoff at First Flavor, or for any marketer engaged in planning for the future of the business, the knowledge you gain from going through this planning process is worth its weight in gold! You see, without ongoing market planning in a business, there's no real way to know where you want the firm to go, how it will get there, or even if it is on the right or wrong track right now. There's nothing like a clear map when you're lost in the wilderness.

As part of the planning process, firms like First Flavor must come to grips with their own resources and capabilities—or *internal environment*—in the *situational analysis* section of their marketing plan. Jay has to have a clear understanding of First Flavor's mission and marketing objectives before he can develop plans to invest in future products and markets for company growth.

Business Planning: Plan Well and Prosper

Jay Minkoff at First Flavor understands that planning is everything—well, almost. Part of Jay's role as a planner is to define his offering's distinctive identity and purpose. Careful planning enables a firm to speak in a clear voice in the marketplace so that customers understand what the firm is and what it has to offer that competitors don't have, especially as it decides how to create value for customers, clients, partners, and society at large.

We think this process is so important that we're launching into our exploration of marketing by starting with a discussion about what planners do and the questions they (both First Flavor and marketers in general) need to ask to be sure they keep their companies and products on course. In many ways, developing great business planning is like taking a great digital photo. The metaphor works because success in photography is built around capturing the right information in the lens of your camera, positioning the image correctly, and snapping the picture. A business plan is a lot like that.

This chapter extends our discussion of marketing by expanding on the marketing planning topics introduced in Chapter 1. While those of you who are marketing majors will likely take a whole course on marketing planning or marketing strategy, this chapter serves as a comprehensive introduction to marketing planning concepts. It is geared toward readers who like to see the big picture before getting into the details. However, because you have not seen the details yet, the big picture may still seem a bit fuzzy. You may find it useful to re-read this chapter near the end of your course, as you will get more out of it with more experienced eyes.

Whether a firm is a well-established company like Bombardier or a relatively new firm like First Flavor, planning for the future is key to prosperity. Sure, it's true that a firm can succeed even if it makes some mistakes in planning, and there are times when even the best planning cannot anticipate the future accurately. It's also true that some seat-of-the-pants businesses are successful. But without good planning for the future, firms will be less successful than they could be. In the worst-case scenario, a lack of planning can be fatal for both large and small businesses. So, like a Scout, it's always better to be prepared.

Business planning is an ongoing process of decision making that guides the firm both in the short term and the long term. Planning identifies and builds on a firm's strengths, and it helps managers at all levels make informed decisions in a changing business environment. *Planning* means that an organization develops objectives before it takes action. In large firms like Microsoft and Bombardier, which operate in many markets, planning is a complex process involving many people from different areas of the company's operations. At a very small business, like a cafe in your home town, however, planning is quite different. The owner of the cafe is often the chief cook, occasional dishwasher, and sole company planner. With more entrepreneurial firms, depending on the size of the firm and the complexity of its operations, the planning process falls somewhere in between those of the corporation and the cafe.

In this chapter, we'll look at the different steps in an organization's planning. First, we'll see how managers develop a **business plan** that includes the decisions that guide the entire organization or its business units. Then we'll examine the entire strategic planning process and the stages in that process that lead to the development and implementation of a **marketing plan**—a document that describes the marketing environment, outlines the marketing objectives and strategies, and identifies how the company will implement and control the strategies embedded in the plan. But first, let's reconsider one of the most important overarching issues in planning—ethics.

business planning
An ongoing process of making decisions that guide the firm both in the short term and for the long term.

business plan
A plan that includes the decisions that guide the entire organization.

marketing plan
A document that describes the marketing environment, outlines the marketing objectives and strategy, and identifies who will be responsible for carrying out each part of the marketing strategy.

Ethics Is Up Front in Marketing Planning

It's hard to overemphasize the importance of ethical marketing decisions. As we saw in Chapter 1, businesses touch many stakeholders, and they need to do what's best for all of them where possible. On a more selfish level, unethical decisions usually come back to bite you later. The consequences of low ethical standards become very visible when you consider a slew of highly publicized corporate scandals that have made news headlines since the turn of the century. These include the fall of Enron and WorldCom due to unsavory financial and management practices, Martha Stewart's stint as a jailbird for obstructing justice and lying about a well-timed stock sale, food safety concerns with products coming out of China, the subprime mortgage meltdown that contributed to the woes of AIG and other financial giants, and Earl Jones's infamous $50 million Ponzi scheme that robbed thousands of Canadians of their retirement nest eggs. And these are only a few especially high-profile examples!

The fallout from these and other cases raises the issue of how damaging unethical practices can be to society at large. The business press is filled with articles about accountability, corporate accounting practices, and government regulation as the public and corporate worlds rethink what we define as ethical behaviour. When major companies defraud the public, everyone suffers. Thousands of people lose their jobs, and in many cases the pensions they counted on to support them in retirement vanish overnight. Other stakeholders are punished as well, including stockholders who lose their investments and consumers who end up paying for worthless merchandise or services. Even confidence in our political system suffers when governments choose to bail out corporations that made poor decisions.

Levels of Planning

We all know, in general, what planning is; we plan a vacation or a great Saturday night party or how we are going to get work completed. When planning for a businesses, however, the process is more complex. Business planning usually occurs on an annual basis at three levels—strategic planning, marketing planning, and operational planning. Figure 2.1 outlines this process. The top level is "big picture" stuff, while the bottom level specifies the "nuts and bolts" actions the firm will need to take to achieve these lofty goals.

strategic planning
A managerial decision process that matches an organization's resources and capabilities to its market opportunities for long-term growth and survival.

Strategic planning is the managerial decision process that matches the organization's resources (i.e., manufacturing facilities, financial assets, and skilled workforce) and capabilities to its market opportunities for long-term growth. These decisions focus on the firm's ability to respond to changes and opportunities in its environment. In a strategic plan, the top management team (e.g., the chief executive officer or CEO, president, and other top executives) defines the firm's purpose (mission) and specifies what the firm hopes to achieve over the next few years (organizational objectives). Increasingly, this planning takes place in consultation with a cross-section of employees who bring varied perspectives and knowledge to the process. For example, a firm's strategic plan may set a goal of increasing the firm's total revenues by 20 percent in the next five years. Strategies are then developed for achieving those objectives. As we introduced in Chapter 1, **strategy** reflects *what* a firm is going to do to achieve an objective. For example, Michel Bendayan is vice president, Americas, for the Canadian toy company Mega Bloks, the second largest construction toy company in the world (after Lego). As described in the Marketing in Action case at the end of this chapter, in his earlier position as an international sales and marketing VP, Michel needed to decide how to develop a long-term brand in the Japanese market. Mega Bloks might have a goal, for example, of increasing total revenues by 20 percent in the next five years. Their strategy to achieve this growth may be to enter new markets with either new or existing products. **Tactics** reflect *how* a strategy is going to be enacted or realized. For example, Mega Bloks may decide to enter the Japanese market with a product line customized for the Japanese consumer.

strategy
What a firm is going to do to achieve an objective.

tactics
How a strategy is going to be enacted.

Figure 2.1 Levels of Planning

During planning, an organization determines its objectives and then develops courses of action to accomplish them. In larger firms, planning takes place at the strategic, functional, and operational levels.

Strategic Planning	**Functional** Planning (In Marketing Department, called Marketing Planning)	**Operational** Planning
Planning done by top-level corporate management	Planning done by top functional-level management such as the firm's chief marketing officer (CMO)	Planning done by supervisory managers
1. Define the mission 2. Evaluate the internal and external environment 3. Set organizational or SBU objectives 4. Establish the business portfolio (if applicable) 5. Develop growth strategies	1. Perform a situational analysis 2. Set marketing objectives 3. Develop marketing strategies 4. Implement marketing strategies 5. Monitor and control marketing strategies	1. Develop action plans to implement the marketing plan 2. Use marketing metrics to monitor how the plan is working

Source: Copyright American Marketing Association.

Strategic plans are usually developed for a period of three to five years and take a long-term view of the strategic health of the business. In large firms, strategic planning can actually occur at two different levels. First, there is overall corporate strategic planning, which determines the organization's different business and product pursuits. Second, the individual business units do strategic planning for their products. Strategic planning at the Walt Disney Company, for example, involves an assessment of resources and capabilities for starting new businesses. In addition to making movies and running theme parks, Disney is now in the cruise ship business and operates a number of Disney vacation resorts. Disney's corporate planning expanded its theme park business to Europe and Japan—separate business units. At Disney, there are separate strategic plans for each of the different Disney businesses. Similarly, Canada's Bombardier produces transportation vehicles ranging from commercial aircraft to high-speed trains, with each product class organized as a **strategic business unit (SBU)**, a semi-autonomous entity which operates as an independent business with its own mission and objectives, and with its own marketing strategy (Exhibit 2.1). Large multifaceted organizations like Bombardier find it more effective to organize their operations into SBUs, where focus can be given to specific business opportunities, technologies, product lines, and customers, rather than having to consider multiple opportunities, multiple technologies, multiple product lines, and varied customers all at once.

The next level of planning is **functional planning**. This level gets its name because the various functional areas of the firm—such as marketing, finance, and human resources—are involved. Vice presidents or functional directors usually do this planning. We refer to the functional planning that marketers do as *marketing planning*. The person in charge of such planning may have the title of Director of Marketing, Vice President of Marketing, or Chief Marketing Officer. Marketers like Jay Minkoff at First Flavor might set an objective to gain 40 percent of a particular market by successfully introducing three new products during the coming year. This objective would be part of a marketing plan. Marketing planning typically includes both a broad three- to five-year plan to support the firm's strategic plan and a detailed annual plan for the coming year. The marketing plan takes its direction from the strategic plan and develops lower-level strategies and tactics for achieving the objectives specified in the strategic plan. The marketing plan contains details regarding the marketing mix elements (product strategy, pricing strategy, channel of distribution strategy, marketing communication strategy), while the strategic plan does not contain this level of detail. What is sometimes confusing about strategies and tactics is that a tactic at the organizational

SBU
A semi-autonomous entity that operates as an independent business with its own mission and objectives—and its own marketing strategy.

functional planning
A decision process that concentrates on developing detailed plans for strategies and tactics for the short term, supporting an organization's long-term strategic plan.

Exhibit 2.1
Bombardier Learjet is an SBU of Bombardier.

Courtesy of Bombardier Inc.

(strategic plan) level becomes, or is reflected in, the strategy at the functional level, and functional-level tactics become, or are reflected in, operational strategies.

For example, at the strategic planning level, Mega Bloks' strategy may be to expand internationally. Their tactic to do this may be to enter the Japanese market with a product line customized for the Japanese consumer. At the marketing planning level, this becomes the strategy to achieve more specific marketing objectives such as "have 20 percent of sales come from new markets this year," and "earn a profit of $5 million from those new market sales." At the marketing planning level, the marketing mix decisions to achieve this market entry strategy are the tactics that specify how the strategy will be implemented and the objectives achieved. In the operational plan (see below), a marketing mix decision such as establishing a uniquely Japanese brand personality for Mega Bloks in Japan becomes the strategy (what you are going to do), while decisions reflecting how this will be done, such as hiring an advertising agency to create a Japanese anime cartoon character, are the tactics. So while strategies reflect what to do and tactics reflect how to do it, they are related across levels of analysis and differ in increasing levels of specificity.

In marketing, **operational planning** is conducted by people such as sales managers, marketing communications managers, brand managers, and marketing research managers. This level of planning focuses on the day-to-day execution of the functional plans and includes detailed annual, semiannual, or quarterly plans. Operational plans might show exactly how many units of a product a salesperson needs to sell per month, or how many television commercials the firm will place on certain networks during a season. At the operational planning level, for example, First Flavor may develop plans for a marketing campaign to promote the product by creating buzz via social networking outlets.

Of course, marketing managers don't just sit in their offices dreaming up plans without any concern for the rest of the organization. Even though we've described each layer separately, *all business planning is an integrated activity*. This means that the organization's strategic, functional, and operational plans must work together for the benefit of the whole, and always work within the context of the organization's mission and objectives. So planners at all levels must consider good principles of accounting, the value of the company to its stockholders, and the requirements for staffing and human resource management; that is, they must keep the "big picture" in mind even as they plan for their corner of the organization's world.

So far, we have a general understanding of the three levels of planning. Now we'll discuss in more detail strategic planning and the important role that marketing plays in it.

operational planning
Planning that focuses on the day-to-day execution of the functional plans and includes detailed annual, semiannual, or quarterly plans.

Strategic Planning: Guiding the Business

In firms with multiple SBUs, the first step in strategic planning is for top management to establish a mission for the entire corporation. Top managers then evaluate the internal and external environments of the business and set corporate-level objectives that guide decision making within each individual SBU. In small firms that are not large enough to have separate SBUs, strategic planning simply takes place at the overall firm level. Whether or not a firm has SBUs, the process of strategic planning is basically the same. Let's look at the planning steps in a bit more detail, guided by Figure 2.2.

Step 1: Define the Mission

Theoretically, top management's first step in the strategic planning stage is to answer questions such as these:

- What business are we in?
- What customers should we serve?
- How should we develop the firm's capabilities and focus its efforts?

In many firms, the answers to questions such as these become the lead items in the organization's strategic plan. The answers become part of a **mission statement**—a formal document that describes the organization's overall purpose and what it hopes to achieve in terms of its customers, products, and resources. For example, the mission of Mothers Against Drunk Driving (MADD) is "to stop drunk driving, support the victims of this violent crime, and prevent underage drinking."[1] The ideal mission statement is not too broad, too narrow, or too shortsighted. A mission that is too broad will not provide adequate focus for the organization. It doesn't do much good to claim, "We are in the business of making high-quality products" or "Our business is keeping customers happy"

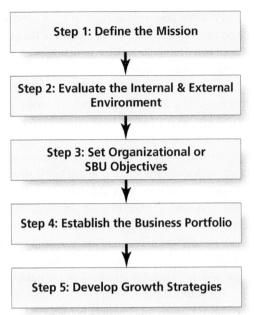

Step 1: Define the Mission

Step 2: Evaluate the Internal & External Environment

Step 3: Set Organizational or SBU Objectives

Step 4: Establish the Business Portfolio

Step 5: Develop Growth Strategies

Figure 2.2 Process Steps in Strategic Planning

The strategic planning process includes a series of steps that result in the development of growth strategies.

Jay Minkoff

APPLYING ▽ The Mission Statement

First Flavor's mission statement is "to facilitate the success of its clients through the innovative technology of its Peel 'n Taste Marketing System, creating opportunities for firms to build brands by effectively sampling and promoting their products to consumers." ➡

as it is hard to find a firm that doesn't make these claims. A mission statement that is too narrow may inhibit managers' ability to visualize possible growth opportunities. Imagine the disastrous consequences for McDonald's if its mission statement read, "We are in the hamburger business." They would not be able to adapt to new customer preferences for healthier choices. Similarly, eBay wants to be more than an online auction company. While revenues are up and may hit $10 billion this year, the company languishes as an obscure, faded Internet afterthought, according to Forrester Research, the technology industry gurus.[2] President and CEO John Donahoe is turning to 25-year-old entrepreneur Jack Abraham to help eBay redefine itself as a "cross-channel retail" business, not just an online auction site. eBay recently bought Abraham's retail aggregator company, Milo, for $75 million and wants to use Abraham's technology to put all off-line inventory online so a customer, standing in a store, can use their Web-enabled phone to compare prices, check if nearby stores have their size, make the purchase online, and then go to that store to pick it up. Last year, browsing and buying online represented just 9 percent of all retail sales in North America. On the other hand, cross-channel retail made up 33 percent, over $1 trillion and growing—a big opportunity that needs a big

mission statement

A formal statement in an organization's strategic plan that describes the overall purpose of the organization and what it intends to achieve in terms of its customers, products, and resources.

external environment

The uncontrollable elements outside of an organization that may affect its performance either positively or negatively. These include macro environment factors like regulatory or technology factors, consumer behaviour trends, industry factors such as industry concentration, and competitive factors such as the number and sophistication of competitors.

mission (Exhibit 2.2). Mission statements should also inspire customers and other stakeholders to want to do business with an organization. The mission of Campbell's Soup Company, for example, is "Together we will build the world's most extraordinary food company by nourishing people's lives everywhere, every day."[3]

Step 2: Evaluate the Internal & External Environment

The second step in strategic planning is an assessment of an organization's environment, both external and internal. This process is referred to as a *situational analysis*, *environmental analysis*, or sometimes a *business review*.

External Environment

The **external environment** consists of those uncontrollable elements outside of the organization that may

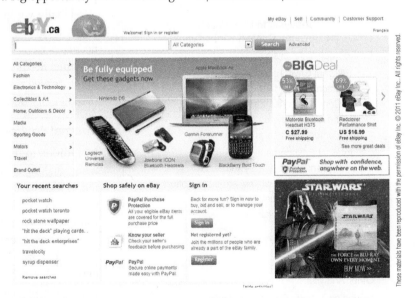

Exhibit 2.2

eBay wants to redefine its mission to take advantage of cross-channel retail opportunities.

affect it either positively or negatively. While this can include everything from consumers to government regulations to competitors to the economy, there are four main categories of considerations. The first is looking for trends or issues in the *macro or general environment* that might have a positive or negative effect on your organization. These may be **p**olitical (including legal or regulatory), **e**conomic, **s**ocial or cultural, **t**echnological, or **o**ther (**PESTO**) trends or issues that might impact a particular industry and business. Mega Bloks, for example, might need to understand political or legal issues relating to foreign ownership of joint ventures before deciding how to enter the Japanese market.

Similarly, Mega Bloks has to consider the implications of children, all around the world, being increasingly interested in electronic games. McDonald's has to consider the implications of governments imposing "fat" taxes or regulating the use of trans fats in the preparation and consumption of food, and consider the social trend toward healthier lifestyles. Canadian lumber companies have to consider the relative strength of the Canadian dollar when developing export strategies. Media producers need to understand the implications of RSS (Really Simple Syndication) feed technology, as teenagers and young adults increasingly seek to customize information and entertainment products accessed via the Internet.

The external environment also includes detailed *consumer analysis*. We will be examining these issues in much more detail in Chapters 4 and 5, but this is where you would look for trends, issues, or considerations with respect to changing consumer segments, segment profiles, and segment sizes. While sociocultural trends are more general across society, consumer analysis is focused on understanding specific market segments. For example, Mega Bloks would need to understand the extent to which "North American" products are perceived positively among consumers in key Japanese market segments.

The external environment also includes *industry analysis*. Industry considerations might include factors like industry size and competitiveness, industry structure, industry dynamics (trends, norms, etc.), stage of the product life cycle (see Chapter 8), and industry key success factors. Again, we are just looking for factors that might positively or negatively impact our strategic decisions. For example, a new entrant into the computer printer industry should understand that manufacturers make little, if any, money on selling the printers, but they make significant margins selling ink. By pricing new printers below the cost of the replacement ink, some manufacturers are encouraging customers to throw away perfectly good printers. This industry practice needs to be understood in the context of the sociocultural environment: at what point do consumers punish companies that don't follow sustainable business practices?

Finally we give consideration to *competitive analysis*—identifying the key competitors, understanding their strategies and strengths and weaknesses, as well as anticipating likely future strategic changes. Mega Bloks, for example, needs to understand and anticipate Lego's marketing strategy in Japan, as well as the strategies of domestic competitors, to make an informed market-entry decision.

Internal Environment

In addition to the need to understand factors in the external environment when making marketing decisions, marketers need a solid understanding of their own organization and its abilities to create value and compete effectively. As illustrated in Figure 2.3, the **internal environment** is all the controllable elements inside an organization that influence how well the organization operates. Marketers need to understand the current strategy of the organization and assess how well that strategy is working: How superior is the current value created by the firm's products? How effective is the current marketing mix? What is the relative market share of these products? What has been their financial performance? Marketers also need to understand the *resources and competencies of the organization*: its technology,

PESTO
Political (including legal or regulatory), economic, social or cultural, technological, or other trends or issues that might impact a particular industry and business.

internal environment
The controllable elements inside an organization—including its people, its facilities, and how it does things—that influence the operations of the organization.

Figure 2.3 Analysis to Understand the Decision Context

> **Analysis to Understand the Decision Context (Opportunity)**
>
> Environmental Analysis
> - External Environment
>   - Macro
>   - Consumer analysis
>   - Industry analysis
>   - Competitive analysis
> - Internal Environment
>   - Current strategy & performance
>   - Organization systems, structure, culture
>   - Skills & resources
>   - Preferences & values
>
> SWOT Analysis
> - SWOT summary
> - Strategy matrix
>
> Other Analysis
> Marketing Theory, Concepts, Principles

intellectual capital, and other assets. For example, firms need to have appropriate technical skills to compete in their industry. Their employees need to have appropriate skills, abilities, and training to produce the firm's products. A firm's physical facilities can be an important asset for creating customer value, as can its level of financial stability, its relationships with suppliers and channel members, its corporate reputation, and its ownership of strong brands in the marketplace. Marketers also need to understand the *organization* of the firm—its structure, culture, and systems (how they get work done). Some firms, for example, have a positive work climate that encourages creativity, innovation, and teamwork. Other firms find they have a "chilly" climate, characterized by negativity, work-to-rule, and in-fighting among employees, which can seriously affect product quality and relationships with customers, suppliers, distributors, and other stakeholders. Finally the *beliefs, values, and preferences of senior management* in an organization need to be understood for marketers to consider organization-appropriate alternatives in making key marketing decisions.

Step 3: Set Organizational or SBU Objectives

After they construct a mission statement and understand the decision environment, top management sets organizational or strategic business unit (SBU) objectives. Organization and SBU objectives are a direct outgrowth of the mission statement and broadly identify what the firm hopes to accomplish within the general time frame of the firm's long-range business plan.

To be effective, objectives need to be *specific, measurable* (so firms can tell whether they've met them or not), and *attainable*. Attainability is especially important. Firms that establish "pie in the sky" objectives they can't realistically obtain can create frustration for their employees (who work hard but get no satisfaction for accomplishment) and other stakeholders in the firm, such as vendors and shareholders who are affected when the firm doesn't meet its objectives. That a firm's objectives are sustainable is also critical—what's the point of investing in attaining an objective for only a very short term? This often happens when a firm underestimates the likelihood a competitor will come to market with a better offering. Without some assurance that an objective is sustainable, the financial return on an investment likely will not be positive.

Objectives may relate to revenue and sales, profitability, the firm's standing in the market, return on investment, productivity, product development, customer relations and satisfaction, and social responsibility. To ensure measurability, objectives are often stated in numerical terms. For example, a firm might have as an objective a 10-percent increase in profitability. It could reach this objective by increasing productivity, by reducing costs, or by selling off an unprofitable division. Or it might meet this 10-percent objective by developing new products, investing in new technologies, or entering a new market. If you are a business major, you will learn a lot more about setting and specifying objectives in your organizational behaviour and business strategy courses.

For many years, one of Procter & Gamble (P&G)'s objectives was to have a number-one brand in every product category in which it competed. This objective was specific and, clearly, it was attainable, since P&G could boast of market leaders such as Crest in the toothpaste category, Folgers in coffee, Pampers in diapers, and Head & Shoulders in shampoo. It also was measurable in terms of the share of market of P&G's products versus those competitors sold. However, in the long run, this objective is very difficult to sustain because of competitive activity and ever-changing consumer tastes. Sure enough, over time, some P&G brands continued to hold a respectable market share, but they dropped from the number-one position. Should P&G withdraw from a product category simply because its brand is not number one? Management realized the answer to this question was clearly "no," and the objective morphed from category leadership into one focused on profitability for each brand. [4]

Step 4: Establish the Business Portfolio

For companies with several different SBUs, strategic planning includes making decisions about how to best allocate resources across these businesses to ensure growth for the total

Jay Minkoff

APPLYING ▽ Portfolio Analysis

First Flavor needs to evaluate the potential of new markets in addition to its initial focus on selling flavour strips to manufacturers for use in in-store product sampling to determine whether it should expand its portfolio to other applications. ➡

business portfolio
The group of different products or brands owned by an organization and characterized by different income-generating and growth capabilities.

portfolio analysis
A tool management uses to assess the potential of a firm's business portfolio.

BCG growth–market share matrix
A portfolio analysis model developed by the Boston Consulting Group that assesses the potential of successful products to generate cash that a firm can then use to invest in new products.

Figure 2.4 BCG Matrix
The Boston Consulting Group's (BCG) growth–market share matrix is one way a firm can examine its portfolio of different products or SBUs. By categorizing SBUs as stars, cash cows, question marks, or dogs, the matrix helps managers make good decisions about how the firm should grow.

Source: Product Portfolio Matrix, © 1970, The Boston Consulting Group.

organization. As Figure 2.4 illustrates, each SBU has its own focus within the firm's overall strategic plan, and each has its own target market and strategies for reaching its objectives. Just like an independent business, each SBU is a separate *profit centre* within the larger corporation; that is, each SBU within the firm is responsible for its own costs, revenues, and profits.

Just as the collection of different stocks an investor owns is called a portfolio, the range of different businesses that a large firm operates is called its **business portfolio**. As we saw with Bombardier, these different businesses usually represent very different product lines, each of which operates with its own budget and management. Having a diversified business portfolio reduces the firm's dependence on one product line or one group of customers. For example, if travel suffers and Disney has a bad year in theme-park attendance and cruises, its managers hope that the lost sales will be made up by stay-at-homers who watch Disney's television networks and DVDs.

Portfolio analysis is a tool management uses to assess the potential of a firm's business portfolio. It helps management decide which of its current SBUs should receive more, or less, of the firm's resources, and which of its SBUs are most consistent with the firm's overall mission. There are a host of portfolio models available for use. To exemplify how one works, let's examine the especially popular model the Boston Consulting Group (BCG) developed: the **BCG growth–market share matrix.**

The BCG model focuses on determining the potential of a firm's existing successful SBUs to generate cash that the firm can then use to invest in other businesses. The BCG matrix in Figure 2.4 shows that the vertical axis represents the attractiveness of the market: the *market growth rate.* Even though the figure shows "high" and "low" as measurements, marketers might ask whether the total market for the SBU's products is growing at a rate of 10, 50, 100, or 200 percent annually.

The horizontal axis in Figure 2.4 shows the SBU's current strength in the market through its relative market share. Here, marketers might ask whether the SBU's share is 5, 25, or perhaps 75 percent of the current market. Combining the two axes creates four quadrants, representing four different types of SBUs. Each quadrant of the BCG grid uses a symbol to designate business units that fall within a certain range for market growth rate and market share. Let's take a closer look at each cell in the grid:

- **Stars** are SBUs with products that have a dominant market share in high-growth markets. Because the SBU has a dominant share of the market, stars generate large revenues, but

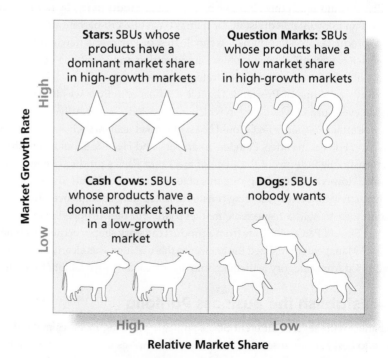

they also require large amounts of funding to keep up with production and promotion demands. Because the market has a large growth potential, managers design strategies to maximize market share in the face of increasing competition. The firm aims at getting the largest share of loyal customers so that the SBU will generate profits that it can reallocate to other parts of the company. For example, in recent years, Disney has viewed its television operations as a star, so it invested heavily in such franchise players as *Hannah Montana* and *Narnia*. Likewise, at Disney/Pixar, *Toy Story 3* and the re-release of *Toy Story 1* and *2* in 3D continued the sensational success of that business unit as a contributor to overall Disney profits (Exhibit 2.3).

- **Cash cows** have a dominant market share in a low-growth-potential market. Because there's not much opportunity for new companies, competitors don't often enter the market. At the same time, the SBU is well established and enjoys a high market share that the firm can sustain with minimal funding. Firms usually milk cash cows of their profits to fund the growth of other SBUs. Of course, if the firm's objective is to increase revenues, having too many cash cows with little or no growth potential can become a liability. For Disney, its theme parks unit fits into the cash cow category in that sales have been basically steady or only slightly increasing/decreasing for an extended period of time.

- **Question marks,** sometimes called "problem children," are SBUs with low market shares in fast-growth markets. When a business unit is a question mark, it suggests that the firm has failed to compete successfully. Perhaps the SBU's products offer fewer benefits than competing products. Or maybe its prices are too high, its distributors are ineffective, or its advertising is too weak. The firm could pump more money into marketing the product and hope that market share will improve. But the firm may find itself "throwing good money after bad" if it gains nothing but a negative cash flow and disappointment. For Disney, its brick and mortar Disney Stores are in the question-mark category, as their performance compared to the overall specialty retail market has lagged in recent years. The online version of the Disney Store, in contrast, performs much better.

- **Dogs** have a small share of a slow-growth market. They are businesses that offer specialized products in limited markets that are not likely to grow quickly. When possible, large firms may sell off their dogs to smaller firms that may be able to nurture them, or they may take the SBU's products off the market. Disney, being a savvy strategic planner, apparently identified its Miramax film studio as a long-term dog (to Pluto and Goofy: no pun intended), as they announced in 2009 that they planned to shut it down.

Like Disney, Jay Minkoff at First Flavor could use the BCG matrix to evaluate his product lines in order to make important decisions about where to invest for future growth. He would look across First Flavor's various offerings to assess the market growth rate and relative market share, determine the degree to which each is a cash generator or a cash user, and decide whether to invest further in these or other business opportunities.

Step 5: Develop Growth Strategies

Although the BCG matrix can help managers decide which SBUs they should invest in for growth, it doesn't tell them much about *how* to make that growth happen. Should the growth of an SBU come from finding new customers, from developing new variations of the product, or from some other growth strategy? Part of the strategic planning at the SBU level entails evaluating growth strategies.

Exhibit 2.3

The recent acquisition of Marvel Comics by Disney most likely will add to the entertainment company's stable of stars.

Figure 2.5 Product-Market Growth Matrix

Marketers use the product-market growth matrix to analyze different growth strategies.

Product Emphasis

	Existing **Products**	New **Products**
Existing Markets	**Market penetration strategy** • Seek to increase sales of existing products to existing markets	**Product development strategy** • Create growth by selling new products in existing markets
New Markets	**Market development strategy** • Introduce existing products to new markets	**Diversification strategy** • Emphasize both new products and new markets to achieve growth

(Market Emphasis, left axis)

market penetration strategies
Growth strategies designed to increase sales of existing products to current customers, nonusers, and users of competitive brands in served markets.

market development strategies
Growth strategies that introduce existing products to new markets.

product development strategies
Growth strategies that focus on selling new products in served markets.

diversification strategies
Growth strategies that emphasize both new products and new markets.

Exhibit 2.4

By appealing to older consumers, Red Bull is attempting a market development strategy.

Courtesy of © Red Bull Media House

Marketers use the product-market growth matrix shown in Figure 2.5 to analyze different growth strategies. The vertical axis in Figure 2.5 represents opportunities for growth, either in existing markets or in new markets. The horizontal axis considers whether the firm would be better off putting its resources into existing products or if it should acquire new products. The matrix provides four fundamental marketing strategies: market penetration, market development, product development, and diversification.

- **Market penetration strategies** seek to increase sales of existing products to existing markets such as current users, nonusers, and users of competing brands within a market. For example, Campbell's can advertise new uses for soup in lunches and dinners, encourage current customers to eat more soup, and prod nonusers to find reasons to buy soup. The firm might try to increase sales by cutting prices, improving distribution, or conducting promotions aimed at attracting users of competing soup brands.

- **Market development strategies** introduce existing products to new markets. This strategy can mean expanding into a new geographic area, or it may mean reaching new customer segments within an existing geographic market. For example, the wildly popular Wii home gaming system by Nintendo has also become popular with older consumers because its active functionality during the game provides an opportunity for a light and fun physical workout. Wii exercise sessions have become especially popular in retirement homes where the activity takes on a strong social and community-building flavour. And because the technology part of Wii is so straightforward and user-friendly, even the most technophobic of seniors are not reluctant to join in the Wii events.[5] (For another example, see Exhibit 2.4.)

- **Product development strategies** create growth by selling new products in existing markets. *Product development* may mean extending the firm's product line by developing new variations of the item, or it may mean altering or improving the product to provide enhanced performance. Many business-class hotels, for example, have upgraded their rooms with more comfortable beds promising a great night's sleep. These new-age beds carry their own brand names—Heavenly Bed at Westin, the Revive Collection at Marriott, and Sweet Sleeper at Sheraton. Radisson's Sleep Number beds even allow each occupant to adjust the firmness of his or her side with a remote control device.[6] This product development strategy is geared to creating growth by taking market share from competitors.

- **Diversification strategies** emphasize both new products and new markets to achieve growth. After a long period of sluggish performance in the fast-food market, McDonald's has re-energized itself over the past several years through successful strategic planning. For example, feeling that it was maxing out in the hamburger business in the late 1990s, McDonald's sought to attract different customers with lines of business that diversified its portfolio of food offerings. Among those are Donatos Pizza, Boston Market, and a controlling interest in Chipotle Mexican Grills. Interestingly, now that its core hamburger and fries business is back on track, McDonald's has begun to divest some of these other brands and is shifting from diversification back to more of a product development strategy around the core McDonald's brand.[7] The Rocky Mountaineer (Exhibit 2.5) has also implemented a diversification strategy by developing a single level glass dome service called SilverLeaf. This service has been introduced as a mid-level price point between GoldLeaf Service (two level glass-domed coach) and Redleaf Service (single level classic rail coach). SilverLeaf Service offers enhancements and a larger viewing area in comparison to RedLeaf Service.

For Jay Minkoff at First Flavor, the product-market growth matrix can be a very important way to analyze where his future opportunities lie. Consider these options for future growth. Is he primarily focused on growing totally new customers for the First Flavor Peel 'n Taste Marketing System (market development)? Or will he eventually also be moving current users into new product lines as the company creates them (product development)? And to what degree does the First Flavor Peel 'n Taste Marketing System afford him the chance to grow current customers in usage of existing product lines (market penetration)? Jay has to weigh these options for future product-market investment against the potential returns of each over both the short and long term.

To review what we've learned so far, strategic planning includes developing the mission statement, assessing the internal and external environment, setting objectives, establishing the business portfolio, and developing growth strategies. In the next section, we'll look at marketers' functional plans—marketing planning—and learn about a situational analysis tool, SWOT analysis.

Exhibit 2.5

Rocky Mountaineer has developed a diversification strategy by targeting new customers with new short-haul experiences.

2 The Marketing Planning Process

OBJECTIVE

Describe the steps in the marketing planning process and explain how to conduct SWOT analysis to understand a decision context.

(pp. 57–69)

Until now, we have focused on fairly broad strategic plans. This big-picture perspective, however, does not provide details about how to reach the objectives we set. Strategic plans "talk the talk" but put pressure on lower-level functional-area managers, such as the marketing manager, production manager, and finance manager, to "walk the walk" by developing the functional plans—the nuts and bolts—to achieve organizational and SBU objectives. Since this is a marketing course and marketing book, our focus at the functional planning level is naturally on developing marketing plans, which is the next step in planning, as we showed back in Figure 2.1.

Marketing planning uses the output of the strategic planning process as an input; that is, the strategic planning process provides the context in which marketing planning is conducted. While the process (the steps) are similar, an important distinction between strategic planning and marketing planning is that marketing professionals focus much of their planning efforts on issues related to the *marketing mix*—the firm's product, price, promotional approach, and distribution (place) methods.

Solid planning means that a firm has a viable product at a price consumers are willing to pay, the means to get that product to the place consumers want it, and a way to communicate (promote) the product to the right consumers; that is, offer them a product that is perceived by the intended customers as being more valuable than the money (or other compensation) being asked for it.

The marketing planning process culminates in the development of a formal document called the marketing plan. Let us briefly examine the marketing plan template shown in Figure 2.6. You will see that it matches the marketing decision framework of Figure 1.2.

Figure 2.6 Marketing Plan Template

Executive Summary
Table of Contents

Situational Analysis
- **Environmental Analysis**
  - External Environment
  - Internal Environment
- **SWOT Analysis**
  - SWOT Summary
  - Strategy Matrix

Marketing Objectives
Marketing Strategies
- Identify Market Segments
- Select Target Markets and Positioning
- Develop Detailed Target Market Profiles

Marketing Mix Strategies for Each Target Market
- Product Strategies
- Pricing Strategies
- Communication Strategies
- Distribution & Supply Chain Strategies

Implementation & Control Plan
- Action Plan
- Task Schedule & Responsibilities
- Control Metrics & Benchmarks
- Contingency Plans
- Research Plan

Step 1: Perform a Situational Analysis to Understand the Decision Context

The marketing planning process begins with a thorough analysis of the marketing environment or decision context facing the firm. To do this, the situational analysis conducted for the strategic plan is reviewed and updated and any constraints, assumptions, or other decision parameters that need to be taken into consideration are identified. A strategic assessment of the situation is then conducted to identify the key facts, factors, or observations in the external and internal environments that have the most important implications or bearing on the marketing planning. Some environmental considerations are more important to understand than others. For example, Jay Minkoff at First Flavor might choose to focus on different products, depending on whether he was able to get patent protection on the base technologies. Richard Hill, at Yellow Point Lodge, needs to find a strategy consistent with the strong sense of history and tradition of his long-loyal customers. The challenge is in identifying the most important considerations on which to base your marketing strategy.

SWOT analysis
An analysis of an organization's strengths and weaknesses and the opportunities and threats in its external environment.

SWOT analysis is one tool often used by marketers (and other planners) in this task. SWOT analysis seeks to identify meaningful strengths (S) and weaknesses (W) in the organization's internal environment, and opportunities (O) and threats (T) from the external environment. In conducting a SWOT analysis, marketers start with an examination of the facts or observations made in a situational analysis and try to identify the implications of each of these considerations. For each fact or observation, several questions must be considered. Why is it important to understand this information? How does it impact a decision that I need to make? Is it a strength of my organization that will help me create superior customer value or defend my desired positioning, or is it a weakness that undermines that ability and would need to be addressed or mitigated (reduced in effect)? Is it an opportunity in the external environment that my organization could exploit or take advantage of in creating or defending value creation, or is it a threat that impedes or otherwise limits my organization's ability to compete effectively?

If the implication does not have a direct bearing on a decision that you have to make, it probably isn't very important and does not need to be included in the SWOT analysis. Determining the strategic implications and what is important and not important can take many years of experience—and you have to practise doing SWOT analysis to gain that experience.

Fatal Business Flaws

There are, however, factors you can look for in your SWOT analysis that are likely to be strategic issues, because marketing and business strategy research has found that there are six basic reasons why organizations fail.[8] Identifying a "fatal flaw" can help you focus on an issue that either needs to be addressed or mitigated (reduce its impact) when developing your marketing strategy:

1. **Failure to innovate:** no differentiation. Organizations that do not create offers that are superior in some way to those already available usually do not survive very long. Lack of differentiation and the inability to create and defend sustainable competitive advantage is a strategic issue that can be observed in an organization's current strategy relative to its competitive environment.

2. **Failure to create value:** not a large enough market segment that wants a particular offer. Sometimes the current strategy of an organization does not create sufficient customer value to attract customers. Insufficient value creation is a strategic issue that is sometimes observed in an analysis of an organization's current strategy relative to segment profile analysis.

3. **Failure to persist over time:** insufficient margins, volume, or resources. Often related to the failure to create value, but also sometimes related to the inability to communicate that value. Some organizations are not able to make sufficient margins or generate sufficient sales volume. Many startup organizations fail because they do not have the financial, technical, human, or management resources to compete effectively over time. This is particularly true of businesses with high fixed costs (those that require significant investment in buildings, equipment, people, technology, or overhead—such as software creation or car manufacturing), because it can take many months or years to recover those initial investments. More established organizations can fail because their markets change over time: competition increases, demand decreases, or they can't or don't keep up with changing technology. The inability to compete effectively is an important strategic issue that can be observed in both the internal and external environment.

4. **Failure to maintain uniqueness:** offers are imitable or substitutable. Some organizations fail to protect the value they have created and competitors are able to better satisfy customer demand with similar offers or substitutes. Organizations that are unable to limit direct competition by means of intellectual property protection; strong supplier, distributor, or customer relationships; cost structure advantages (such as economies of scale); switching costs; unique knowledge; greater customization or niche (small market) focus; strong brand name; or some other market entry barrier may not be able to defend their positioning.

5. **Failure to prevent "appropriation" of value:** holdup or slack. Some organizations get held hostage by powerful stakeholders, such as strong unions, single source suppliers, or key distributors. These stakeholders are able to negotiate terms that erode the profitability of the organization. Holdup issues might be evident in an industry or competitive analysis. Other organizations are wasteful or inefficient with their resources (slack), often because the management team does not have sufficient experience in that industry to be effective. This might be evident in an analysis of the organization structure, systems, and culture or in the current strategy and performance.

6. **Failure to be flexible and adapt:** inability to deal with uncertainty and ambiguity. Uncertainty is being able to anticipate events, but not their timing. For example, a chicken satay vendor could anticipate that, at some point in time, despite their best food-safety efforts, a customer will get food poisoning from eating the chicken. Effective organizations create risk management plans, crisis management plans, and have insurance and other "due diligence" interventions to limit the impact of potential risks. In highly volatile, fast-changing industries (like fashion or biotechnology) this can be difficult to do, and some events cannot even be anticipated (such as terrorist attacks, currency devaluations, or stock crashes), so managers need to be capable of adapting to changing circumstances. The degree of uncertainty is often assessed in an industry analysis, and the inability of management to plan or adapt could be an issue in an assessment of an organization's management and systems.

Using SWOT Analysis

Marketers use SWOT analysis to help them make strategic and tactical decisions. Internal strengths and external opportunities provide rationale to support a particular course of action. Internal weaknesses and external threats provide reasons why a particular course

Ethical and Sustainable Decisions in the Real World

Successful marketing strategies depend on understanding a firm's environment, and that means learning as much as you can about the competition. But sometimes companies cross the ethical boundary in doing this. For example, Mark Hill, a former vice president of strategic planning and co-founder of WestJet, used an access code from a former Air Canada employee to get information on Air Canada operations. On learning about this, Air Canada hired a private investigator to look through Hill's home garbage, seeking all documents relating to Air Canada, including reconstructing private, shredded documents. This incident was reported to Hill by an observant neighbour, and the next time the private investigator came, Hill had planted false information in his garbage.

Both companies sued. Air Canada launched a $5-million lawsuit against WestJet alleging that WestJet had used information from a confidential Air Canada Web site. WestJet countersued for $5 million, alleging that Air Canada had obtained sensitive data from Hill's garbage. Air Canada raised the stakes by increasing its claim to $220 million, and WestJet launched a $30-million countersuit, claiming Air Canada was abusing the court process in WestJet's legal action of corporate espionage. After two years of legal battle, the Ontario Superior Court ruled against WestJet's claim regarding court abuse. In May of 2006, WestJet apologized to Air Canada for spying and agreed to pay $5.5 million in legal fees and contribute $10 million to children's charities (Exhibit 2.6).[9]

Exhibit 2.6

WestJet was accused of improperly logging on to an Air Canada internal employee Web site many times in one year and downloading and analyzing the carrier's operational data. Of course, it is illegal to do so in Canada.

> **ETHICS CHECK:** ↖
> Find out what other students taking this course **would do** and **why** on **www.mypearsonmarketinglab.com**

↓

While this case was extreme, do you think a company should be allowed to get insider information to learn about its competition?

☐ **YES** ☐ **NO**

of action might not be appropriate. Weaknesses and threats, however, are not absolute; both can be addressed or mitigated through marketing strategy. Meal Exchange, for example, is a not-for-profit organization dedicated to motivating post-secondary students to increase their involvement in fighting social problems like hunger (www.meal exchange.com). The organization works with colleges and universities so that students can donate the unused money on their meal cards to local food banks, which could then purchase food for those in need. Differences in college and university policies regarding the redemption of meal cards might be a threat in the external environment of Meal Exchange that could limit expansion plans for the organization. However, this threat might be mitigated or overcome by supporters of the Meal Exchange concept lobbying college and university administrators to change their policies so that participation in the Meal Exchange program is possible.

The key to SWOT analysis is not to get bogged down in analysis paralysis. Firms face hundreds, if not thousands, of internal and external environmental considerations that shape and impact their business. You will want to identify the top six to ten issues that might have the greatest implications for the marketing decisions that you have to make. Ask yourself, does this fact or piece of information have a major implication for a decision I have to make? If not, it's probably not worth documenting in a SWOT analysis.

A SWOT summary is a list of the most important issues and their implications. To help him make his market-entry decision, Michel Bendayan at Mega Bloks needs to conduct a situational analysis, and SWOT analysis is a useful tool for identifying the environmental factors critical to the decision. An illustrative example of a SWOT analysis summary for this decision is shown in Table 2.1.

Table 2.1	Illustrative SWOT Summary for Mega Bloks

Internal Environment:

Current Strategy & Performance
— World market-share leader in preschool segment (**S**)
  • Ability to leverage international brand name in new markets
— Weak sales and lack of distribution network (**W**)
  • Status quo not really an option, market may require unique strategy

Organization (structure, systems, culture)
— Asia, Australia, and Africa are all under one international marketing director (**W**)
  • May limit ability to focus on Japan and customize Japanese lines
— Product innovation culture (**S**)
  • Ability to compete on innovative new product development
— Rapid growth in past five years (**S, W**)
  • Has gained significant international experience that supports its ability to enter the Japanese market
  • *But hard to maintain focus and organizational culture with such growth; high degree of Japanese customization may be difficult to implement*

Resources & Competencies
— Second largest construction block company in the world (after Lego) (**S**)
  • Has the experience and resources needed for international expansion
— 3000 employees, 75 to 100 product lines, in 100 countries (**S**)
  • Has the people, expertise, and resources to develop custom product lines
— Basic product not patentable—Lego had a patent (now expired) (**W**)
  • Hard to protect markets from competitors.

Management Preferences & Values
— Standardized products are preferable (inferred) (**?**)
  • *Mega Bloks has not previously customized products for a single country; doing so may create a precedent for a wholesale change in strategy that has significant cost implications. It might be possible to do it for one country but maybe not for all countries.*

External Environment:

Macro (General) Environment: PESTO
— American products are often considered prestige products in Japan (**O**)
  • May be value in offering North American–style product lines
— High quality consciousness in Japanese society (**T**)
  • *May need greater control over the supply chain*
— Greater awareness and importance of pop culture (**T**)
  • *May need Japanese brand personality*

Consumer Analysis
— Japanese consumers strongly nationalistic (**T**)
  • Prefer Japanese look and feel
— Japanese houses are much smaller than those in North America or even Europe (**T**)
  • Will likely require different packaging, but also maybe different product lines that enable blocks to be used for many designs

Industry Analysis
— Very large market (**O**)
  • Attractive market for achieving organizational goals.

(continued)

Table 2.1	Illustrative SWOT Summary for Mega Bloks *(continued)*

— Japanese retailers are more varied, fragmented, and relationship oriented (**T**)
  - This may require a partnership model with a strong Japanese distributor or significant investment in selling direct.
— Many Japanese toy manufacturers, among the largest in world (**T/O**)
  - May be able to license the Mega Blok brand and utilize the distribution network of an established toy company.
  - *Threat of a domestic competitor with greater local resources.*
— There is no patent or trademark protection on the shape & function of the blocks (**O/T**)
  - Mega Bloks can compete against Lego, anyone can compete with Mega Bloks
  - *Branding and distribution are the key sources of competitive advantage.*
Competitive Analysis
— Lego is a strong competitor in all markets (**T**)
  - They have the resources to copy any strategy if proven effective
— No current local competitor (**O**)
  - *By customizing the product line we reduce the threat of local competition*

Note: S: Strength; W: Weakness; O: Opportunity; T: Threat; ?: impact not clear; Italics: most significant implications for the decision faced by Michael Bendayan.

Step 2: Set Marketing Objectives

Based on the situational analysis, the business then develops a set of marketing objectives. Generally, marketing objectives are more specific to the firm's brands, sizes, product features, and other marketing mix–related elements than to the organization or SBU objectives. Think of the connection between business objectives and marketing objectives this way: Business objectives guide the entire firm's operations, while marketing objectives state what the marketing function must accomplish if the firm is ultimately to achieve these overall business objectives. So for Jay Minkoff at First Flavor, setting marketing objectives means deciding what he wants to accomplish in terms of First Flavor's marketing mix–related elements: product development, pricing strategies, or specific marketing communication approaches.

Marketing objectives normally include one or more sales objectives. After all, without sales, there are no profits, and without profits, there is no business. Some examples of sales objectives are: increase sales of our deluxe model toy by 15 percent during the next 12 months, increase our toy market share by 5 percent each year for the next three years, or sell one million toys during the holiday season.

If a firm has decided that its growth strategy is to focus on product development—new or improved products for existing customers—it will develop product objectives. Because it is more profitable to retain customers than it is to replace them, firms often set objectives for improvements in quality or service to develop customer loyalty. In the breakfast cereal market, where consumers are more fickle than loyal, firms like Kellogg and General Mills may set objectives for developing new brands to suit the tastes of specific market segments, or they may set goals for a new product to retain customers who are being lured away by a competitor's new honey-coated, fruit-and-fibre cereal. In other cases, a firm may decide to modify a product by taking advantage of trends, as when Frito-Lay Canada developed its line of "lite" snacks.

In some instances, firms find that their best opportunities for growth are stated in the form of market objectives. Michel Bendayan at Mega Bloks, for example, might set a target of gaining 30-percent share of the Japanese construction toy market within 18 months.

When marketers set specific, measurable objectives, they establish criteria against which performance can be measured. **Metrics** are the measures marketers use to assess their performance. Key measures of performance that are used by leading marketing firms around the world are identified in the Marketing Metrics box highlighted in this section.

metrics
Measurements or "scorecards" marketers use to identify the effectiveness of different strategies or tactics.

Marketing Metrics

Measuring Performance

A survey of leading marketing firms in five countries (United States, the United Kingdom, France, Germany, and Japan) found that *market share* is the metric that managers are most likely to report to the company's board of directors. Other commonly used metrics include the following:

- Perceived product/service quality
- Customer loyalty/retention
- Customer/segment profitability
- Relative price

Across the five countries, German companies are the heaviest users of metrics and Japanese firms the lightest. Of the companies surveyed, 97 percent of German firms said they report their market share to their boards, compared with 79 percent of American firms and only 57 percent of Japanese firms. Overall, firms that do business in multiple countries and those that have above-average marketing budgets are more likely to rely on metrics.[10]

Step 3: Develop Marketing Strategies

Once the marketing and other objectives are developed, the organization develops a marketing strategy aimed at achieving those objectives. As was discussed briefly in Chapter 1, marketing strategy begins with identifying, profiling, and selecting market segments that will be targeted by the strategy. As will be discussed in more detail in Chapter 6, choosing the right market to compete in and the right customer to attract is a critical task for a marketer; it is a task that combines art and science. Once the target market customers have been chosen, marketing strategy focuses on the positioning issues of strategic orientation, differentiation, defendability, and brand personality.

Strategic orientation is a discussion of how the organization will compete in its chosen market(s). This would include a discussion of growth strategies (as per above), customer value creation strategy (Chapter 1), or other strategy concepts that you will learn if you take another marketing course. Your SWOT analysis is another source of strategy alternatives. The SWOT strategy matrix in Figure 2.7 illustrates how you can develop strategy alternatives by

Figure 2.7 SWOT Strategy Matrix for Mega Bloks

	Strengths	**Weaknesses**
Opportunity	Utilize strengths to take advantage of opportunity: Utilize strong international experience, international brand name, and economies of scale to take advantage of the opportunity that North American brands are valued in Japan.	Address weaknesses to take advantage of opportunity: Address the weakness that the product is not patentable, and take advantage of the large Japanese market opportunity by developing a fully customized Japanese product line and brand personality. This will discourage local competition.
Threats	Utilize strengths to address or mitigate threats: Utilize product innovation culture to develop a line of flexible use, small-package products that address the space limitations of the Japanese market, then utilize international experience and channels to sell this line in Europe.	Address weaknesses to address or mitigate threats: Hire Japanese sales representatives to develop their own distribution network in Japan, and utilize this network to address the threat of Japanese retailers being more relationship oriented. Consider partnering in this endeavour with a large retailer to limit strategic exposure with Japanese toy manufacturers.

considering how to utilize your strengths or address your weaknesses to take advantage of opportunities, and how to address or mitigate threats in the external environment.

Differentiation is how a brand will be known to its customers as being better than competitive brands. A discussion of differentiation should be specific. It is not meaningful to say that an organization will differentiate itself on quality. What does that mean in your specific context? For a car it could mean greater reliability, durability, longevity, rust protection, or more comfortable seats, among many other considerations. For a restaurant it could mean better taste, greater variety, better ingredients, faster service, or better ambiance, among other considerations. You need to be specific in identifying what your organization will do better than others.

Defendability discusses sources of sustainable **competitive advantage** and the systems, competencies, technology, or other resources that enable an organization to defend its chosen positioning. It is important to understand that the underlying goal of *all* marketing strategies and plans is to create a competitive advantage for the firm—to take what the company does really well and outperform the competition, thus providing customers with a benefit the competition cannot provide. A competitive advantage gives consumers a reason to choose one product over another, again and again.

Finally, *brand personality* is a discussion of how the intended differentiation will be captured in the creation of brand meaning. Some brands, like the Apple Macintosh, have clear personalities. Imagine that Apple Macintosh was a person and he or she just walked into the room. Describe him or her in as much detail as possible. You can probably do that quite easily because Apple has spent considerable money developing the Mac Guy versus PC Guy series of advertisements (which can be found on its Web site: www.apple.com). In defining a brand personality, we specify what personality we are seeking to support the overall positioning of the brand. This personality gets developed in the marketing mix decisions that we subsequently make.

Develop Marketing Mix Strategies

As outlined in Chapter 1, a marketing plan then describes the marketing mix decisions relating to product, price, channel of distribution, and marketing communications (see Figure 1.2, on page 17). Rationale for these decisions comes from your SWOT and other analyses, your understanding of your target market profile, and the marketing theory, principles, and concepts that you will learn from reading this text and attending class. Marketing mix decisions were described in Chapter 1, but we will review them here by comparing the approaches of several different airlines.

- Because the product is the most fundamental part of the marketing mix—firms simply can't make a profit without something to sell—carefully developed *product strategies* are essential to achieving marketing objectives. Product strategies include decisions such as product design, packaging, branding, support services (e.g., maintenance), if there will be variations of the product, and what product features will provide the unique benefits targeted customers want. For example, product planners for JetBlue Airways decided to include in-seat video games and television as a key product feature during the flight. Their planes get you from point A to point B just as fast (or slow) as the other airlines—that is, the basic product is the same—but the flight seems shorter because there is more to do while you're in the air.

- The *pricing strategy* determines how much a firm will charge for a product. Of course, that price has to be one that customers are willing to pay. If not, all the other marketing efforts are futile. In addition to setting prices for the final consumer, pricing strategies usually establish prices the company will charge to wholesalers and retailers. A firm may base its pricing strategies on costs, demand, or the prices of competing products. WestJet uses a pricing strategy to successfully target customers who could not previously afford

competitive advantage
The ability of a firm to outperform the competition, providing customers with a benefit the competition cannot.

air travel. WestJet does not compete solely on price; however, consumers do perceive WestJet as a low-priced airline compared with Air Canada, and the airline reinforces this theme regularly in its ads targeting travellers on a tight budget.

- A *communication strategy* is how marketers communicate a product's value proposition to the target market. Marketers use communication strategies to develop the product's message and the mix of advertising, sales promotion, public relations and publicity, direct marketing, and personal selling that will deliver the message. Many firms use all these elements to communicate their message to consumers. Air Canada strives to portray an image of quality and convenience. In one recent campaign, customers paint images of Air Canada using their fingertips, reinforcing the concept that everything Air Canada offers its customers, and in particular its industry-leading video-on-demand in-flight entertainment system, global network, and state-of-the-art Executive First Suite, is easily accessible.[11]

- *Distribution strategies* outline how, when, and where the firm will make the product available to targeted customers (the *place* component). When they develop a distribution strategy, marketers must decide whether to sell the product directly to the final customer or to sell through retailers and wholesalers. And the choice of which retailers should be involved depends on the product, pricing, and promotion decisions. For example, if the firm produces a luxury good, it may wish to avoid being seen on the shelves of discount stores for fear that it will cheapen the brand image. Recently, the airline industry has made major changes in its distribution strategy. For many years, most customers bought their airline tickets through travel agencies or at the ticket counters of the major airlines. Today, most airlines actually penalize customers who don't opt for online purchase of "ticketless" flight reservations by charging them a "ticketing fee" of $5 or $10. This strategy has moulded the behaviour of many consumers to go online 24/7 to save money as well as experience the convenience of personally scheduling the flight they want.

Step 4: Develop an Implementation Plan

The preceding section of the marketing plan describes what to do. The implementation plan describes the tactics of how to do it. An action plan provides the details of what needs to be done, by whom (including who has final responsibility to ensure that it is done correctly), and when it needs to be done by. It is usually organized by marketing objective and the strategies outlined above to meet each objective. The implementation plan also involves control plans, including the metrics for how you will measure performance and benchmarks or targets that indicate success or lack of success. A contingency plan outlines how the strategy will be modified if benchmarks (targets) are not met. Unless already specified as part of the marketing mix, this section of the plan would also specify how exchange relationships will be initiated and managed. It might also describe the research plan—what research is

Tech and Trends

Social Networks and Marketing Planning

Many companies have begun to incorporate social networks into their larger marketing plans and strategies—typically, either to promote brands or to be on the lookout for complaints about services and products. But there are other ways marketers can mine the wealth of data that are available on social media platforms like Facebook or Yelp! Let's say, for example, that a marketing manager of a hotel wants to send a targeted e-mail to people looking for "hotels in Dublin." A search pulls up all the people on Twitter talking about and looking for hotels in Dublin. Twitter very nicely gives you an RSS feed of these results in the top right-hand corner. Copy the URL of this link.

Then you can add a subscription button in Google Reader (you can easily sign up if you don't have an account). Paste in the URL of the Twitter RSS feed, then click "Show Details" in the top right corner, where you will see a blank graph. After a few days this will show some fantastic data on what day of the week, month, and time people were talking about "hotels in Dublin." From this information you can determine when will be the very best time to send the e-mail. Faith and Begorrah! That's how you lure visitors to your little piece of Ireland. Timing can be everything, and the information found in social network sites can help marketers be more effective in implementing their strategies.[12]

needed to test key assumptions on which the plan is based, and what research is needed to make a better plan in the next planning cycle. Finally, it specifies the budget and how the budget will be allocated by activity.

Control is a big part of the implementation plan. Today's CEOs are keen to quantify just how an investment in marketing has an impact on the firm's success, financially and otherwise, over the long haul. You've heard of the term *return on investment (ROI)*—think of this overall notion as **return on marketing investment (ROMI)**. *In fact, it's critical to consider marketing as an investment rather than an expense*—this distinction drives firms to use marketing more strategically to enhance the business. For many firms nowadays, ROMI is the metric *du jour* to analyze how the marketing function contributes to the bottom line.

So, what exactly is ROMI? It is the revenue or profit margin (both are widely used) generated by investment in a specific marketing campaign or program, divided by the cost of that program (expenditure) at a given risk level (the risk level is determined by management's analysis of the particular program). Again, the key word is *investment*; that is, in the planning process, thinking of marketing as an investment rather than an expense keeps managers focused on using marketing dollars to achieve specific goals.[13]

But is ROMI always appropriate or sufficient to judge marketing's effectiveness and efficiency? Here are six common objections to relying exclusively on ROMI for measuring marketing success.

return on marketing investment (ROMI)
The revenue or profit margin generated by investment in a specific marketing campaign or program, divided by the cost of that program at a given risk level.

1. In a company's accounting statements, marketing expenditures tend to appear as a cost, not as an investment. This perpetuates the "marketing is an expense" mentality in the firm.

2. ROMI requires the profit to be divided by expenditure, yet all other bottom-line performance measures consider profit or cash flow *after* deducting expenditures.

3. Calculating ROMI requires knowing what would have happened if the marketing expenditure in question had never taken place. Few marketers have those figures.

4. ROMI has become a fashionable term for marketing productivity in general, yet much evidence exists that firms interpret the calculation of ROMI quite differently. When executives discuss ROMI with different calculations of it in mind, only confusion can result.

5. ROMI, by nature, ignores the effect of marketing assets of the firm (e.g., its brands) and tends to lead managers toward a more short-term decision perspective. That is, it typically considers only short-term incremental profits and expenditures without looking at longer-term effects or any change in brand equity.

6. And speaking of short-term versus long-term decisions, ROMI (like a number of other metrics focused on snapshot information; in this case, a particular marketing campaign) often can lead to actions by management that shore up short-term performance to the detriment of a firm's sustainability commitment. Ethics in marketing should not be an oxymoron—but often unethical behaviour is driven by the demand for quick, short-term marketing results.

For an organization to use ROMI properly it must (a) identify the most appropriate and consistent measure to apply, (b) combine review of ROMI with other critical marketing metrics (one example is marketing payback—how quickly marketing costs are recovered), and (c) fully consider the potential long-term impact of the actions ROMI drives (that is, their sustainability).[14]

Fortunately for the marketer, there are many other potential marketing metrics beyond ROMI that measure specific aspects of marketing performance. Just to give you a sense of a few of them, Table 2.2 provides some examples of metrics that managers apply across an array of marketing planning situations, including all the marketing mix variables.

TABLE 2.2	Examples of Marketing Metrics

- Cost of a prospect
- Value of a prospect
- ROI of a campaign
- Value of telesales
- Conversion rates of users of competitor products
- Long-term value of a customer
- Customer commitment to relationship/partnership
- Referral rate
- Response rates to direct marketing
- Perceived product quality
- Perceived service quality
- Customer loyalty/retention
- Customer turnover
- Customer/segment profitability
- Customer mindset/customer orientation
- Customer satisfaction
- Company/product reputation
- Customer word-of-mouth (buzz) activity
- Salesperson's self-ratings of effectiveness
- Timeliness and accuracy of competitive intelligence
- Usage rates of technology in customer initiatives
- Reach and frequency of advertising
- Recognition and recall of message
- Sales calls per day/week/month
- Order fulfillment efficiency/stock-outs
- Timeliness of sales promotion support

Step 5: Evaluate the Plan

Often it is not possible to determine if a plan makes sense until it is completely thought out and the implementation details are considered. In addition, in a large organization there may be competing plans for the allocation of the firm's resources. Consequently, the collective decisions represented in a marketing plan need to be evaluated, both to determine if the strategy should be implemented, and to be confident that the best strategy has been devised, given the circumstances.

Throughout the writing of a marketing plan, rationale is provided for each decision made using situational analysis; SWOT analysis; consumer analysis; and marketing theory, concepts, and principles. To make the overall recommendation to implement the marketing plan, financial analysis and cost-benefit analysis are required. Financial analysis involves developing projected (pro forma) financial statements, such as a pro forma income statement and balance sheet, and sometimes a cash flow statement or a statement of sources and uses of funds. Financial analysis might also include ratio analysis—a comparison of key figures in the financial statements. These topics are reviewed in the Appendix to Chapter 9, but are the primary focus of a managerial accounting course.

Cost-benefit analysis, as the name implies, is an analysis of all the advantages and disadvantages of implementing a particular course of action. Simple cost-benefit analysis involves a judgment-based (qualitative) assessment of the net benefit (advantages relative to disadvantages) of one course of action relative to alternatives. More sophisticated cost-benefit analysis involves assigning numerical values to (quantifying) the costs and benefits, and then using a decision rule or formula to calculate the net benefit of each alternative. This more sophisticated approach allows the analyst to assign different levels of importance (weights) to different costs and benefits, but it can sometimes be very difficult to assign a numerical value to some costs and benefits. For example, how might a reasonable numeric value be assigned to the potential loss of life from a poorly designed child's toy, or to the potential damage to an ecosystem from batteries that are not recycled?

Finally, a marketing plan typically includes a set of exhibits that provide details that support the recommendations made in the body of the plan. These exhibits include the SWOT analysis, detailed market segment profiles, and a pro forma income statement that shows the forecast sales volume and revenue and identifies the key expenses, as per the proposed marketing budget. Positioning maps (described in Chapter 6) are also often included to illustrate the relative positioning of an organization's brand(s).

Use the Marketing Planning Template

Ultimately, the planning process we've described in this section is documented in a formal, written marketing plan. You'll find a template for a marketing plan on the inside front and back covers of the book. The template will come in handy as you make your way through the book, as each chapter will give you information you can use to "fill in the blanks" of a marketing plan. You will note that the template is cross-referenced with the questions you must answer in each section of the plan, and it also provides you with a general road map of the topics covered in each chapter that need to flow into building the marketing plan. By the time you're done, we hope that all these pieces will come together and you'll understand how real marketers make real decisions.

As we noted earlier, a marketing plan should provide the best possible guide for the firm to successfully market its products. In large firms, top management often requires such a written plan, because putting the ideas on paper encourages marketing managers to formulate concrete objectives and strategies. In small entrepreneurial firms, a well-thought-out marketing plan is often the key to attracting investors who will help turn the firm's dreams into reality.

Operational Planning: Day-to-Day Execution of Marketing Plans

operational plans
Plans focusing on the day-to-day execution of the marketing plan.

Recall that planning happens at three levels: strategic, functional (such as marketing planning), and operational. In the previous section, we discussed marketing planning—the process by which marketers perform a situational analysis; set marketing objectives; and develop, implement, and control marketing strategies. But talk is cheap. The best plan ever written is useless if it's not properly carried out. That's what **operational plans** are for. They put the pedal to the metal by focusing on the day-to-day execution of the marketing plan.

The task of operational planning falls to the first-line managers we discussed earlier, such as sales managers, marketing communications managers, brand managers, and marketing research managers. Operational plans generally cover a shorter period of time than either strategic plans or marketing plans, perhaps only one or two months, and they include detailed directions for the specific activities to be carried out, who will be responsible for them, and time lines for accomplishing the tasks.

Significantly, many of the important marketing metrics managers use to gauge the success of plans actually get used at the operational planning level. For example, sales managers in many firms are charged with the responsibility of tracking a wide range of metrics related to the firm–customer relationship, such as number of new customers, sales calls per month, customer turnover, and customer loyalty. The data are collected at the operational level and then sent to upper management for use in planning at the functional level and above.

To summarize what we've discussed in this chapter, business planning, a key element of a firm's success, occurs in several different stages. Strategic planning takes place at both the corporate and the SBU level in large firms and in a single stage in smaller businesses. Marketing planning, one of the functional planning areas, comes next. Operational planning ensures proper implementation and control of the marketing plan. It is critical that firms approach the marketing planning process in a highly ethical manner, mindful of the importance of establishing an organizational code of ethics to eliminate ambiguity about which behaviours by organization members are acceptable and which are not. And it is also important that the application of metrics to provide effective control of marketing performance take into account not just short-term results but also impact on long-term sustainability issues. Most businesses do strategic planning and marketing planning in a global context. Consequently, we end this chapter with a dialogue on global and international marketing issues and considerations.

3 Strategic Marketing Mix Decisions in International Markets

OBJECTIVE

Understand the big picture of international marketing and the decisions firms must make when they consider globalization.

(pp. 69–79)

Whether you think of yourself as a member of a global community or only a resident of a small town, you are a citizen of the world and a participant in a global marketplace. You likely eat fruit from Peru, may sip wine from Australia, wear shoes made in Thailand, put your feet up on the cocktail table imported from Indonesia, and watch the World Cup football (soccer) match on an HDTV made in China. You may even have been one of the millions of people around the world who donated money to help the people of Haiti hit by an earthquake in 2010. And you may be looking for an exciting career with a firm that does business around the globe. With Internet shopping, consumers are increasingly choosing from global product offerings.

Like you, businesses make decisions in a global context. Even if they are a small, local business they may have global suppliers, be affected by global prices, and have customers who are more globally savvy than ever before.

In his bestselling book *The World Is Flat: A Brief History of the Twenty-first Century*, Thomas Friedman argues that technology creates a level playing field for all countries and that marketers must recognize that national borders are not as important as they once were. Today, businesses like eBay, Tim Hortons, and even small retailers like Rogers' Chocolates must seek new and improved ways to attract customers down the street and around the globe in order to stay relevant.

The global marketing game is exciting—the stakes are high and it's easy to lose your shirt. Competition comes from both local and foreign firms, and differences in national laws, customs, and consumer preferences can make your head spin. Like many companies that feel they are running out of growth opportunities in the North American marketplace, the retail giant Walmart aggressively expands its international presence. But you can be sure that when its planners plot future growth, they're keenly aware of competitors in their external environment who have other ideas. While the giant US retailer ranks number three in *Fortune* magazine's list of the top 500 global firms, other retailers hope to steal some of the chain's thunder. French company Auchan, now the world's 14th biggest retailer with 1,200 stores in 12 countries, is rapidly expanding into China, Russia, and Eastern Europe.[15] In China, Auchan outperforms Walmart as the firm opens an average of two new stores per month. The success attests to Auchan's understanding of the Chinese market, where middle-class consumers often assume that cheaper products are unsafe or counterfeit. Auchan has created an image of being a retailer with higher-quality products; the store aisles are wider and the lighting is better than that of its competitors.

Figure 2.8 Steps in the Decision Process for Entering Global Markets

Entering global markets involves a sequence of decisions.

Step 1: Whether to Go Global

↓

Step 2: Which Market(s) to Enter

↓

Step 3: Level of Commitment

↓

Step 4: How to Adapt Marketing Mix Strategies
• Localize
• Standardize

If a firm decides to expand beyond its home country, it must make important decisions about how to structure its business and whether to adapt its product marketing strategy to accommodate local needs. First, the company must decide on the level of its commitment, which dictates the type of entry strategy it will use. Is the firm better off to simply export to another country, to partner with another firm, or to go it alone in the foreign market? It also has to make specific decisions about the marketing mix for a particular product.

Figure 2.8 shows that when firms consider going global they must think about this in four steps:

- **Step 1.** "Go" or "no go"—is it in our best interest to focus exclusively on our home market or should we cast our net elsewhere as well?

- **Step 2.** If the decision is "go," which global markets are most attractive? Which country or countries offer the greatest opportunity for us?

- **Step 3.** What market-entry strategy and thus what level of commitment is best? As we'll see, it's pretty low risk to simply export products to overseas markets, while the commitment and the risk is substantial if the firm decides to build and run manufacturing facilities in other countries (though the payoff may be worth it).

- **Step 4.** How do we develop marketing mix strategies in the foreign markets—should we standardize what we do in other countries, or develop a unique, localized marketing strategy for each country?

Should We Go Global?

Many times, a firm decides to go global because domestic demand is declining while demand in foreign markets grows. For example, the market for personal computers has levelled off in Canada; more Canadians replace old or obsolete machines than buy a personal computer for the first time. In contrast, the demand is much greater in some parts of the world where consumers and businesses are only now beginning to tune in to the power of the Web. So it's no coincidence that a few years ago IBM sold its entire personal computing business to Lenovo, a Chinese company.

Of course, it isn't only Western countries that are going global. For years, China was a huge export market for Western firms as consumers there began to prosper and crave foreign goods (see Exhibit 2.7). Now the Chinese are turning the tables as they carve out a larger role in the global marketplace. Dozens of Chinese companies have global ambitions, including government-owned Chery Automobile. Chery, founded in 1997, is now the largest exporter of Chinese automobiles, reaching 500,000 in international sales, mainly in Europe, South-East Asia, South America, and the Middle East.[16] Chery has overseas plants in thirteen countries and has plans for further overseas market development. Other Chinese carmakers such as Great Wall and Geely are also hungrily looking to North America.[17] Watch for a flood of new, low-priced cars from Asia—including one that features a karaoke player in the dashboard!

Going global is not a simple task. Even a popular television show may have to make "adjustments" as it travels across borders. Consider, for example, the incredibly popular *Idol* TV shows (*Canadian Idol*, *American Idol*, Britain's *Pop Idol*, etc). More than 100 million people

Courtesy of Great Wall Motors

Exhibit 2.7

Great Wall Motors is a Chinese company that operates in the international and domestic market.

around the globe tune in to over 20 local versions of the *Idol* show, but sometimes the format has to be fine-tuned.[18] When a South African contestant was bluntly told to work on her clothes and her appearance, she broke down and told the judges she was too poor to afford nicer things. The station was swamped with calls from angry viewers who offered to donate clothing. Because the word "idol" has Hitler-like connotations for Germans, producers there had to change the show's title to *Germany Seeks the Superstar*. Similarly, use of the term "idol" is sacrilegious in Arabic countries and so it can't be used in those markets.

Expanding into foreign markets is not the right decision for all firms. For some, globalization may mean simply being a customer of large and small companies around the world as they import products they need to run their business. Still, even very small firms may want to consider global opportunities—as Internet platforms like eBay allow producers of locally made products to find buyers in many other markets. In this section we will look at the decisions firms must make as they consider their global opportunities.

Which Global Markets Are Most Attractive?

In Chapter 1, we saw how firms hope to create competitive advantage over rivals. When firms compete in a global marketplace, this challenge is even greater. There are more players involved, and typically local firms have a "home-court advantage." It's like soccer—increasing numbers of North Americans play the game, but they are up against an ingrained tradition of soccer fanaticism in Europe and South America where kids start dribbling a soccer ball when they start to walk.

If it wants to go global, a firm needs to examine the competitive advantage that makes it successful in its home country. Will this leg up "travel" well to other countries? For example, the many competitive advantages enjoyed by Silicon Valley companies such as Microsoft and HP have allowed the companies to be successful first in exporting their products to international markets. That success has led to direct investment in research facilities and service centres around the globe. In contrast, developing countries typically do not have engineering expertise, highly trained workers, or high-tech facilities, but they do have a large labour force and low wages. Thus, firms in these countries can compete better in the global marketplace with products that rely on low-cost manufacturing or even handmade crafts.

Many other factors influence the decision of whether or not to compete internationally, and where. The same situational analysis needed to make strategic planning decisions and strategic marketing decisions is needed to make internationalization decisions. For example, in the political-legal environment, national laws, international regulations, regional agreements, political stability, regulatory issues, and human rights issues need to be understood. Analysis of the economic environment would consider indicators of economic health, the level of economic development in different countries, and the **business cycle** in those countries. Analysis of the technological environment would consider how technology influences current and potential marketing strategies in the industry in different countries. For example, not all countries have the same level of Internet use as in North America, while cell phone use is often greater in some countries outside North America. This could have implications for a marketer's distribution and communication decisions. Analysis of the sociocultural environment would focus on differences in consumer and customer values, social norms, and buying behaviour that need to be understood. In the competitive environment, we need to know who our competitors are, and could be, and we need to evaluate their strengths and weaknesses, understand and monitor their marketing strategies, and try to predict their strategic decisions. This would include understanding the positioning of all of their brands. Industry analysis would focus on understanding the big picture—the

business cycle
The overall patterns of change in the economy—including periods of prosperity, recession, depression, and recovery— that affect consumer and business purchasing power.

Used with permission of Heinz Canada.

Exhibit 2.8

Large packaged-goods companies like Heinz continually scan the global environment to identify opportunities to sell their products in new markets. This ad is from Egypt.

overall structure of the industry in different countries, and the business models used to compete effectively (see Exhibit 2.8).

What Market-Entry Strategy and Thus What Level of Commitment Should We Adopt?

Just like a romantic relationship, a firm must determine the level of commitment it is willing to make to operate in another country. This commitment ranges from casual involvement to a full-scale "marriage." At one extreme, the firm simply exports its products, while at the other extreme it directly invests in another country by buying a foreign subsidiary or opening its own stores or manufacturing facility. This decision about the extent of commitment entails a trade-off between *control* and *risk*. Direct involvement gives the firm more control over what happens in the country, but its risk also increases if the operation is not successful.

Let's review four globalization strategies representing increased levels of involvement: exporting, contractual arrangements, strategic alliances, and direct investment. Table 2.3 summarizes these options.

Exporting

If a firm chooses to export, it must decide whether it will attempt to sell its products on its own or rely on intermediaries to represent it in the target country. These specialists, or **export merchants,** understand the local market and can find buyers and negotiate terms. An exporting strategy allows a firm to sell its products in global markets and cushions it against downturns in its domestic market. Because the firm actually makes the products at home, it is able to maintain control over design and production decisions.

Contractual Agreements

The next level of commitment a firm can make to a foreign market is a contractual agreement with a company in that country to conduct some or all of its business there. These agreements take several forms. Two of the most common are licensing and franchising.

In a **licensing agreement**, a firm gives another firm (the *licensee*) the right to produce and market its product in a specific country or region in return for royalties on goods sold. Because the licensee produces the product in its home market, it can avoid many of the barriers to entry that the licensor would have encountered. However, the licensor also loses control over how the product is produced and marketed, so if the licensee does a poor job this may tarnish the company's reputation. Licensors also have to accept the possibility that local licensees will alter its product to suit local tastes, as has been done with *Sesame Street* in India, France, Japan, and South Africa, where new characters have been introduced with names like Nac, Khokha, and Kami.

Franchising is a form of licensing that gives the franchisee the right to adopt an entire way of doing business in the host country. Again, there is a risk to the parent company if the *franchisee* does not use the same-quality ingredients or procedures, so firms monitor these operations carefully. McDonald's, perhaps the best known of all franchises, has over 30 000 restaurants that serve 52 million people in 119 countries. In India, where Hindus do not eat beef, all McDonald's have vegetarian and nonvegetarian burger-cooking lines and offer customers vegetarian specialties such as Pizza McPuff and McAloo Tikki

export merchants
Intermediaries a firm uses to represent it in other countries.

licensing agreement
An agreement in which one firm gives another firm the right to produce and market its product in a specific country or region in return for royalties.

franchising
A form of licensing involving the right to adapt an entire system of doing business.

| Table 2.3 | Market-Entry Strategies |

Strategy	Exporting Strategy	Contractual Agreements		Strategic Alliances	Direct Investment
Level of Risk	Low	Medium		Medium	High
Level of Control	Low	Medium		Medium	High
Options	Sell on its own — Rely on export merchants	Licensing — License a local firm to produce the product	Franchising — A local firm adopts your entire business model	Joint venture where firm and local partner pool their resources	Complete ownership often through buying a local company
Advantages	Low investment so lowest risk of financial loss — Can control quality of product — Avoid difficulties of producing some products in other countries	Avoid barriers to entry — Limit financial investment and thus risk	Local franchisee avoids barriers to entry — Limit financial investment and risk	Easy access to new markets — Preferential treatment by governments and other entities	Maximum freedom and control — Avoid import restrictions
Disadvantages	May limit growth opportunities — Perceived as a "foreign" product	Lose control over how product is produced and marketed, which could tarnish company and brand image — Potential unauthorized use of formulas, designs, or other intellectual property	Franchisee may not use the same quality ingredients or procedures, thus damaging brand image	High level of financial risk	Highest level of commitment and financial risk — Potential for nationalization or expropriation if government is unstable

Choosing a market-entry strategy is a critical decision for companies that want to go global. Decisions vary in terms of risk and control.

(a spiced-potato burger).[19] However, don't make the mistake of thinking that the only kind of franchise is a fast-food restaurant! There are thousands of franchise systems that offer business opportunities from pet care to tutoring services.

Strategic Alliances

Firms that choose to develop an even deeper commitment to a foreign market enter a **strategic alliance** with one or more domestic firms in the target country. These relationships often take the form of a **joint venture**, in which two or more firms create a new entity to allow the partners to pool their resources for common goals. Strategic alliances also allow companies easy access to new markets, especially because these partnerships often bring with them preferential treatment in the partner's home country. For example, General Motors has an alliance with the Chinese firm SAIC. In 2009, GM sold 1.83 million cars in China and it projects sales of over 2 million vehicles annually.[20]

Of course, joint ventures are not always successful. In India, where import taxes can be as high as 40 percent and retail shop rental rates are high, international marketers find their activities simply cannot be profitable. Thus, over a dozen global brands, including GAS, Replay, and the Etam women's apparel chain, have ended their joint venture or franchisee relationships in that country.

strategic alliance
Relationship developed between a firm seeking a deeper commitment to a foreign market and a domestic firm in the target country.

joint venture
A strategic alliance in which a new entity owned by two or more firms allows the partners to pool their resources for common good.

Direct Investment

An even deeper level of commitment occurs when a firm expands internationally through ownership, usually buying a business in the host country outright. Instead of starting from scratch in its quest to become multinational, buying part or all of a domestic firm allows a foreign firm to take advantage of a domestic company's political savvy and market position in the host country.

Sometimes firms have no option other than to invest directly in a local business. In most countries, McDonald's purchases its lettuce and pickles from local farms. When the company entered Russia in 1990, there were no private businesses to supply the raw ingredients for its burgers. McDonald's had to build its own facility, the McComplex, outside Moscow. As the country's economy booms, however, domestic businesses develop to take up the slack. Today, McDonald's purchases 80 percent of its ingredients from local farmers, some of whom have become millionaires as a result.[21]

How to Adapt Marketing Mix Strategies

Marketers like Mega Bloks that operate in two or more countries have a crucial decision to make: How necessary is it to develop a customized marketing mix for each country? The choice between standardization and localization (customization) can be difficult and complex. For example, as seen in Exhibit 2.9, Walmart chose standardized signs and store layout in its Japanese stores. While Japanese shoppers are confused about the term "rollback," they do understand that the sign reflects price discounts offered by the retailer. Procter & Gamble adopted a localized strategy for Asia, packing most of the shampoos it sells in single-use sizes to adapt to consumer preferences for trying new brands.[22]

Advocates of standardization argue that the world has become so small and tastes so homogeneous that basic needs and wants are the same everywhere.[23] A focus on the similarities among cultures certainly is appealing. After all, if no changes in a firm's marketing strategy had to be made to compete in foreign countries, it would realize large economies of scale, because it could spread the costs of product development and promotional materials over many markets. For example, Reebok created a new centralized product development centre to develop shoe designs that can easily cross borders.[24]

Widespread, consistent exposure also helps create a global brand by forging a strong, unified image all over the world: Coca-Cola signs are visible on billboards in London and on metal roofs deep in the forests of Thailand.

In contrast, those in favour of localization (customization) feel that the world is not *that* small, and that products and promotional messages should be tailored to local environments. These marketers feel that each culture is unique and that each country has a *national character*—a distinctive set of behavioural and personality characteristics.[25] Snapple failed in Japan because consumers there didn't like the drink's cloudy appearance. Similarly, Frito-Lay Inc. stopped selling Ruffles potato chips (too salty) and Cheetos (the Japanese didn't appreciate having their fingers turn orange after eating a handful).[26] A new product, Haggis Dogs with Chutneep (a turnip chutney) is gaining popularity in Scotland, but it might not be popular with

Exhibit 2.9

Walmart's experience in Japan highlights the role of standardization versus localization.

consumers outside the UK who do not have a tradition of eating a mixture of sheep organs, spices, and quality pork (see Exhibit 2.10).

International Marketing Mix Strategies

Once a firm decides whether it will adopt standardization or a localization strategy, it is time to plan the marketing mix to support that strategy.

Product Decisions

A firm seeking to sell a product in a foreign market has three choices: sell the same product in the new market, modify it for the market, or develop a brand-new product for the market. Let's take a closer look at each option.

- A *straight extension strategy* retains the same product for domestic and foreign markets. Coca-Cola sells the same formula in every country, and Gillette offers the same razor blades everywhere.

- A *product adaptation strategy* recognizes that in many cases people in different cultures do have strong and different product preferences. Sometimes these differences can be subtle, yet important. In India, Pizza Hut offers pizzas with traditional toppings such as paneer and tikka. Kellogg's, which markets the identical version of its Corn Flakes and Rice Krispies brands in both North America and Europe, had to remove the green "loops" from Froot Loops after research showed that Europeans felt they were too artificial looking.[27]

- A *product invention strategy* means that a company develops a new product as it expands to foreign markets. For example, in India, Coca-Cola and Pepsi now offer their versions of a traditional lemonade, Nimbu Panni.[28] In some cases, a product invention strategy takes the form of **backward invention**. For example, there are still nearly one and a half billion people on the earth without electricity, primarily in Africa, Asia, and the Middle East. This provides a challenge for firms to develop products such as refrigerators and air conditioning systems that can operate without electric power.[29]

Exhibit 2.10

Scottish entrepreneur Mark Shaw started Haggis Dog with the hopes of selling them throughout the United Kingdom.

backward invention
Product strategy in which a firm develops a product to serve the needs of people living in countries without electricity or other elements of a developed infrastructure.

Marketing Communications (Promotion) Decisions

Marketers must also decide whether it's necessary to modify how they speak to consumers in a foreign market. Some firms endorse the idea that the same message will appeal to everyone around the world, while others feel the need to customize it. The 2006 World Cup was broadcast in 189 countries to one of the biggest global television audiences ever. This mega-event illustrates how different marketers make different decisions—even when they create ads that run during the same game. MasterCard ran ads that appeared in

Exhibit 2.11

The Plant Billboard of Coca-Cola Philippines prominently features the contour bottle, already a globally recognized icon, and as such, can be used in both domestic and foreign markets.

39 countries, so its ad agency came up with a spot called "Fever," in which 100-odd cheering fans from 30 countries appear. There's no dialogue, so it works in any language. At the end, the words, "Football fever. Priceless" appeared under the MasterCard logo.[30] In 2009, Coke launched its first global ad campaign with the tagline "Open Happiness." More recently, Sprite followed with its global "The Spark" ad campaign (along with a new global package) in Europe, North America, Africa, and Asia.[31] The strength of these brands and recognition of their logos around the world is also a big advantage, because the logos remind customers of what the brand stands for without the need for translation. (See Exhibit 2.11.)

Fans of a localization strategy, on the other hand, feel that cultural differences translate into market differences, which may in turn call for different advertising strategies. When Tim Hortons moved into the US market, for example, it faced a completely undeveloped "morning market" for coffee and baked goods in that country. Many US customers were grabbing a cup of coffee at a local gas station on their way to work. Tim Hortons' strategy for this target market became one of creating a morning market by using an advertising tag line, "Morning people. Where do they come from?" This strategy contrasted with their focus on the target market for lunch menu items (such as sandwiches and chili) in the Canadian market, where Tim's already has a strong coffee and muffin/donut breakfast following.[32]

Price Decisions

Costs associated with transportation, tariffs, and differences in currency exchange rates often make the product more expensive for a company to make or sell in foreign markets compared to its home country. Aside from cost factors, sometimes a higher price is charged in international markets, because consumers there value the uniqueness of the product. Kokanee beer, for example, is sold for $1 more per six-pack than its American competitors, because American consumers place a higher value on a product that is Canadian.

One danger of pricing too high is that competitors will find ways to offer the product at a lower price, even if this is done illegally. **Grey market goods** are items that are imported without the consent of the trademark holder. While grey market goods are not counterfeit, they may be different from authorized products in warranty coverage and compliance with local regulatory requirements. The Internet offers exceptional opportunities for marketers of grey market goods from toothpaste to textbooks. But, as the saying goes, "If it seems too good to be true, it probably is."Consumers may be disappointed when they find grey

grey market goods
Items manufactured outside a country and then imported without the consent of the trademark holder.

market goods may not be of the same quality, so the deal they think they got may not look as good after they take delivery. On the other hand, the products may be identical, but priced differently in different markets to try to maximize revenues. Pharmaceuticals manufactured in the United States are often sold at a lower price in Canada, causing a significant grey market problem. Similarly, Canadian products, like some models of gas barbeques, are sold at a lower price at Home Depot in the United States than at Home Depot in Canada, because the US company buys in higher quantity. The Internet has also made pricing more transparent, making it difficult for marketers to support very different prices in different markets, thereby reducing the potential for grey marketing.

A company can also run into trouble if it tries to price a product too low to establish it in a new market. Some countries outlaw a practice called **dumping**, in which a company tries to get a toehold in a foreign market by pricing its products lower than they are priced at home—often removing excess supply from home markets and keeping prices higher there. In one case, Eastman Kodak accused Japanese rival Fuji Photo Film of selling colour photographic paper in the United States for as little as a quarter of what it charges in Japan.[33]

dumping
Pricing products lower in a foreign market than that offered in the home market.

Distribution Decisions

Manufacturers like Mega Bloks realize that establishing a reliable distribution system is essential if the marketer is to succeed in an international market. Establishing a reliable system might be especially difficult in developing countries where thousands of individual distributors (some who transport goods to remote rural areas on ox carts or bicycles) must be persuaded to take on the product. There are often problems finding a way to transport, package, refrigerate, or store goods for long periods of time in less developed countries. A reliable distribution system is also essential in developed countries, where competition for shelf space may be fierce. With more than 60 percent of all grocery retail controlled by two large firms in Canada (the Sobeys group and the Loblaw group), it can be very difficult for new entrants to get their products listed.

Ethics in the Marketing Mix

Marketing mix strategies are crucial to a firm's success in achieving its objectives, but marketing managers are also responsible for determining the most ethical way to price, package, communicate, and distribute their offerings to reach profit and market share objectives. Let's examine how ethical considerations can influence marketing mix decisions.

In product strategies, a key ethical decision concerns product safety. It may be tempting to cut costs on design, safety testing, and production in order to rush a new product to market or to beat competitors on price. However, responsible companies realize that product safety needs to be a priority. They do everything to ensure that their product meets safety standards when it goes to market, and they react swiftly if a product is found to be unsafe after it is on the market. In any month in Canada, there are several product recalls. Manufacturers recognize safety problems with their products and ask consumers to return them. You can log on to the CBC Web site to check out the latest product recalls (www.cbc.ca/consumer/recalls).

The term "green" describes efforts by firms to choose packages, product designs, and other aspects of the marketing mix that are earth friendly but still profitable (see Exhibit 2.12). The Canadian government, through Environment Canada, encourages Canadian companies to practise green marketing through such programs as the EcoLogo. This program promotes stringent, environmentally friendly guidelines for industries, ranging from automotive products to office supplies. If a business meets the guidelines, it may use the EcoLogo on its product to signal its environmental soundness to consumers. Companies that have been granted the right to use the EcoLogo include Frigidaire Canada, which manufactures energy-efficient dishwashers and washing machines, and Fuji Graphics Systems, which has developed photo processing systems that are gentle to the environment.[34]

Green marketing practices can indeed be successful for a firm's bottom line. For example, Electrolux found that profits from its solar-powered lawn mowers, chain saws

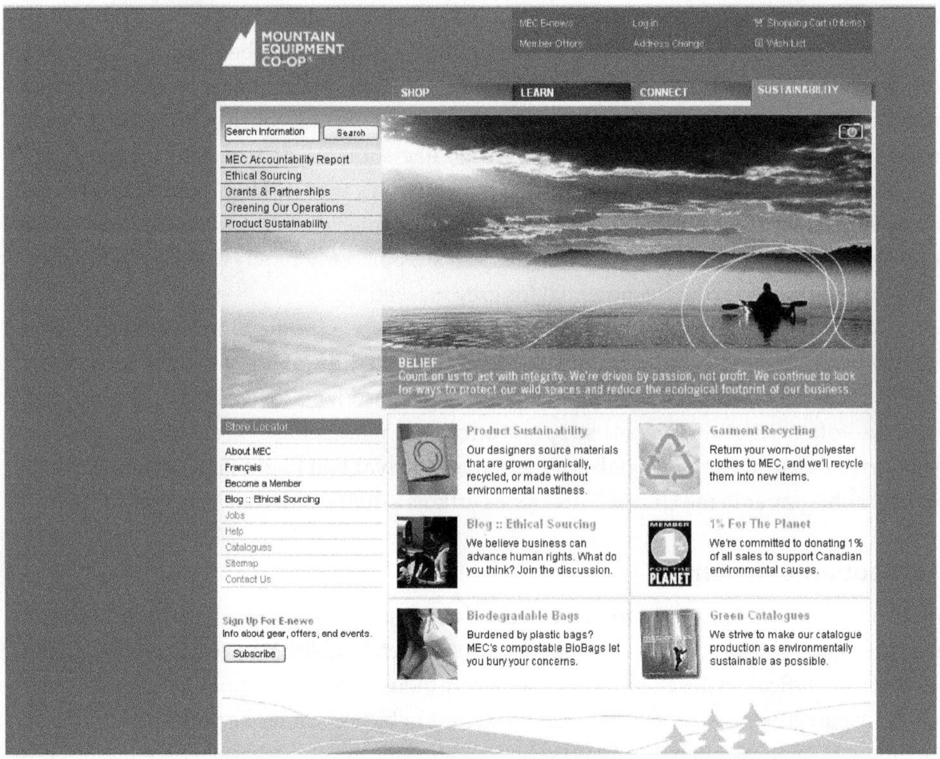

Exhibit 2.12

Mountain Equipment Co-op is one of many Canadian firms that does well by "doing good."

price fixing

An illegal business practice in which competing firms decide in advance on a common price for their product.

lubricated with vegetable oil, and water-conserving washing machines were actually 3.8 percent higher than profits from the company's conventional products.[35]

As we will see in Chapter 9, the potential for unethical pricing strategies is so great that many shady pricing practices are illegal. For example, firms that compete in a market in which there are only a few other firms are not allowed to decide in advance on a common price for their product. This practice, called **price fixing**, eliminates price competition that otherwise would keep prices down.

Price gouging—raising the price of a product to take advantage of its popularity or scarcity (such as after a natural disaster) is not illegal, but many consider it to be unethical. When Chrysler introduced its PT Cruiser, some consumers paid up to $10 000 over the sticker price to get the car. Some Canadian consumers think oil companies are price gouging with unreasonably high gasoline prices—particularly when the price goes up just before a long weekend.

Marketing management's decisions on how to communicate the firm's products are likely to draw the most criticism from consumers. To promote ethical behaviour on the part of advertisers, and to provide consumers with a forum for expressing complaints about advertising, the Canadian advertising industry follows a process of self-regulation through Advertising Standards Canada (ASC, www.adstandards.com). The Canadian Code of Advertising Standards, which ASC administers, has specific guidelines regarding unfair or deceptive advertising to ensure the accuracy and appropriateness of claims. In doing so, it complements Canadian laws relating to deceptive advertising and other anti-competitive practices administered by the Canadian Competition Bureau. In 2010, the Canadian Competition Bureau participated with members of the International Consumer Protection and Enforcement Network to do an in-depth assessment of advertising on social media sites, questioning whether all advertisers targeting these platforms are above board.[36]

ASC also enforces guidelines with respect to appropriate gender portrayal in ads. These Gender Portrayal Guidelines state that advertising should not include sexual exploitation and should always portray women and men as equals. KIA, for example, stirred controversy with an ad that implied that a young female police officer was making out with a KIA driver she had pulled over. KIA eventually pulled the ad after significant public backlash. Although these guidelines were originally intended to fight negative portrayals of women in advertising, complaints by consumers have increasingly related to the portrayal of men.

Channels of distribution decisions can also create ethical dilemmas. For example, because their size gives them bargaining power in the channel of distribution, many large retail chains are forcing manufacturers to pay a **slotting allowance**, a fee paid in exchange for agreeing to place the manufacturer's products on the retailer's valuable shelf space. While the retailers claim that such fees pay the cost of adding products to their inventory, many manufacturers feel slotting fees are unethical. Certainly, the practice prevents smaller manufacturers that cannot afford the slotting allowances from reaching consumers.

Firms also make ethical decisions when implementing their marketing strategy, and there are vast differences in what people consider ethical business behaviour around the world. Business leaders who have experienced a sheltered life in North American companies are often shocked to find that they cannot expect the same ethical standards of others in the global community. Westerners, for example, are often painfully honest and will say that they cannot meet a deadline or attend a meeting or provide the needed services. In other cultures the answer, even if untrue, will always be "yes." Westerners see such dishonest answers as unethical, but in some areas of the world, people just believe that saying "no" to any request is extremely rude—even if there's no way they intend to honour the request.

In many least developed and developing countries, salaries for mid-level people are sadly very low and the economy runs on a system we would call blatant bribery. Some of these "payments" are only petty corruption and the "favours" are inconsequential, while others may involve high-level government or business officials and can have devastating consequences. The 2014 and 2018 FIFA World Cup decision, for example, was marred by a scandal where three of the decision makers were found to have accepted bribes in exchange for their votes.

Some businesspeople give bribes to speed up required work, secure a contract, or avoid having a contract cancelled. Such payments are a way of life in many countries because many people consider them as natural as giving a waiter a tip for good service. This practice is illegal for American companies, and the *Canadian Foreign Public Officials Act* makes it illegal for a Canadian company to bribe foreign officials, either directly or indirectly.

slotting allowance
A fee paid by a manufacturer to a retailer in exchange for agreeing to place products on the retailer's shelves.

Summary

In this chapter, we have examined the process by which marketers make marketing planning decisions in the context of business strategy. Central to this process is situational analysis, which gives us an understanding of the strategic issues and considerations in an organization's internal and external environment. SWOT analysis was introduced as a useful analytic tool for conducting situational analysis, and you learned that the strengths, weaknesses, opportunities, and threats identified in SWOT analysis, as well as their strategic implications, provide the rationale in support of (or against) alternative courses of action and marketing mix approaches. The Real People profiles that begin each chapter of this text, and the Marketing in Action Cases at the end of each chapter of this text, provide you with opportunities to practise doing situational analyses and using SWOT analyses to make strategic marketing decisions. Even if your instructor does not discuss these situations in class, take the time to think about them, develop rationale for a particular course of action, and discuss and defend your recommendations with others in your class. It is this practice in making marketing decisions that will make you an effective marketer.

This chapter concluded with a discussion of marketing strategy decisions in an international context, and those are the decisions faced by Michel Bendayan and other senior Mega Bloks managers in the Marketing in Action Case at the end of this chapter.

Here's my choice. . .

Real **People**, Real **Choices**

Why do you think Jay chose option 2?

1 Option   2 Option   3 Option

How It Worked Out at First Flavor

Jay and his partners decided to defer the flavouring strip concept, as they felt that it required a more capital-intensive consumer product launch rather than working through a corporate partner with an existing supply chain. Focusing on their core marketing services product, Peel 'n Taste First Flavor was able to achieve profitability for the first time in Q1 2010 as a result of new orders.

To learn the whole story, visit www.mypearsonmarketinglab.com.

Objective Summary ➡ **Key Terms** ➡ **Apply**

CHAPTER 2
Study Map

---

1. Objective Summary (pp. 46–57)

Explain how businesses develop plans at different levels within the organization.

Strategic planning is the managerial decision process in which top management defines the firm's purpose and specifies what the firm hopes to achieve over the next five or so years. For large firms that have a number of self-contained business units, the first step in strategic planning is for top management to establish a mission for the entire corporation. Top managers then evaluate the internal and external environment of the business and set corporate-level objectives that guide decision making within each individual SBU. In small firms that are not large enough to have separate SBUs, strategic planning simply takes place at the overall firm level. For companies with several different SBUs, strategic planning also includes (1) making decisions about how to best allocate resources across these businesses to ensure growth for the total organization, and (2) developing growth strategies.

Planning takes place at three key levels. Strategic planning is the managerial decision process that matches the firm's resources and capabilities to its market opportunities for long-term growth. Functional planning gets its name because the various functional areas of the firm such as marketing, finance, and human resources get involved. And operational planning focuses on the day-to-day execution of the functional plans and includes detailed annual, semiannual, or quarterly plans.

Key Terms

business planning, p. 47

business plan, p. 47

marketing plan, p. 47

strategic planning, p. 48

strategy, p. 48

tactics, p. 48

SBU, p. 49

functional planning, p. 49

operational planning, p. 50

mission statement, p. 51

external environment, p. 51

PESTO, p. 52

internal environment, p. 52

business portfolio, p. 54

portfolio analysis, p. 54

BCG growth–market share matrix, p. 54

market penetration strategies, p. 56

market development strategies, p. 56

product development strategies, p. 56

diversification strategies p. 56

2. Objective Summary (pp. 57–69)

Describe the steps in the marketing planning process and explain how to conduct SWOT analysis to understand a decision context.

Marketing planning is one type of functional planning. Marketing planning begins with an evaluation of the internal and external environments. Marketing managers then set marketing objectives, usually related to the firm's brands, sizes, product features, and other marketing mix–related elements. Next, marketing managers select the target market(s) for the organization and decide what marketing mix strategies they will use. Product strategies include decisions about products and product characteristics that will appeal to the target market. Pricing strategies state the specific prices to be charged to channel members and final consumers. Promotion strategies include plans for advertising, sales promotion, public relations, publicity, personal selling, and direct marketing used to reach the target market. Distribution (place) strategies outline how the product will be made available to targeted customers when and where they want it. Once the marketing strategies are developed, they must be implemented. Control is the measurement of actual performance and comparison with planned performance. Maintaining control implies the need for concrete measures of marketing performance called "marketing metrics."

SWOT analysis is an analytic tool used to help identify strategic issues and considerations in the internal and external environment. Strengths and weaknesses relating to internal environment considerations such as current strategy; organization structure and culture; skills and resources; management preferences and values; and particularly, the implications of these strengths and weaknesses, all provide rationale for or against particular courses of marketing action. Opportunities and threats in the external environment relating to the macro environment, the industry, customers, and competitors, as well as their implications, also provide rationale for or against particular courses of marketing action.

Key Terms

SWOT analysis, p. 58

metrics, p. 62

competitive advantage, p. 64

return on marketing investment (ROMI), p. 66

operational plans, p. 68

3. Objective Summary (pp. 69–79)

Understand the big picture of international marketing and the decisions firms must make when they consider globalization.

Marketing decisions are made in a global context, and marketers need to understand political, legal, economic, sociocultural, technological, and other macro environment conditions in different markets. As well, they must understand consumer preferences, industry dynamics, competitive offerings and strategy, and their own ability to create value in these markets before deciding whether or not to pursue international or global markets. If internationalization is chosen, marketers then need to decide how to enter these markets and what level of commitment and risk they are prepared to accept. Another issue is the degree of standardization of products and the extent to which marketing mix variables need to be adapted for local situations.

Key Terms

business cycle, p. 71

export merchants, p. 72

licensing agreement, p. 72

franchising, p. 72

strategic alliance, p. 73

joint venture, p. 73

backward invention, p. 75

grey market goods, p. 76

dumping, p. 77

price fixing, p. 78

slotting allowance, p. 79

Chapter Questions and Activities

Concepts: Test Your Knowledge

1. What are strategic, functional, and operational planning? How does strategic planning differ at the corporate and SBU levels?
2. What is a mission statement? What is a SWOT analysis? What role do these play in the planning process?
3. What is a strategic business unit (SBU)? How do firms use the Boston Consulting Group model for portfolio analysis in planning for their SBUs?
4. Describe the four business growth strategies: market penetration, product development, market development, and diversification.
5. Explain the steps in the marketing planning process.
6. How does operational planning support the marketing plan?
7. What are the elements of a formal marketing plan?
8. What is an action plan? Why are action plans such an important part of marketing planning? Why is it so important for marketers to break the implementation of a marketing plan down into individual elements through action plans?
9. What is return on marketing investment (ROMI)? How does considering marketing as an investment instead of an expense affect a firm?
10. Give several examples of marketing metrics. How might a marketer use each metric to track progress of some important element of a marketing plan?

11. How does internationalization impact marketing planning decisions?
12. How is a firm's level of commitment related to its level of control in a foreign market? Describe the four levels of involvement that are options for a firm: exporting, contractual agreements, strategic alliances, and direct investment.
13. What are the arguments for standardization of marketing strategies in the global marketplace? What are the arguments for localization? What are some ways a firm can standardize or localize its marketing mix?

Activities: Apply What You've Learned

1. Assume that you are the marketing director for a small firm that manufactures educational toys for children. Your boss, the company president, has decided to develop a mission statement. He's admitted that he doesn't know much about developing a mission statement and has asked you to help guide him in this process. Write a memo outlining exactly what a mission statement is, why firms develop such statements, how firms use mission statements, and your thoughts on what the firm's mission statement might be.
2. As a marketing student, you know that large firms often organize their operations into a number of strategic business units (SBUs). A university might develop a similar structure in which different academic schools or departments are seen as separate businesses. Consider how your university might divide its total academic units into separate SBUs. What would be the problems with implementing such a plan? What would be the advantages and disadvantages for students and for faculty? Be prepared to share your analysis of university SBUs to your class.
3. An important part of planning is a SWOT analysis, understanding an organization's strengths, weaknesses, opportunities, and threats. Choose a business in your community with which you are familiar. Develop a brief SWOT analysis for that business.
4. Select one of the following product categories. Think about how a firm's offering in the product category would need to differ for least developed countries, developing countries, and developed countries. Develop recommendations for the product, pricing, promotion, and distribution in these different markets.

   a. Shampoo
   b. Automobiles
   c. Diapers
   d. Washing machines
   e. Athletic shoes

5. Consider the pros and cons of localization and standardization of marketing strategies. Are the advantages and disadvantages different for different products? In different countries? Organize a debate in your class to argue the merits of the standardization perspective versus the localization perspective.

Marketing Metrics: Exercises

Most marketers today feel pressure to measure (quantify) their level of success in marketing planning. In your opinion, is it easy to measure marketing's success (compared to, say, measuring the success of a firm's financial management or production quality)? Explain your viewpoint.

1. The Boston Consulting Group matrix identifies products as stars, cash cows, question marks, and dogs. Do you think this is a useful way for organizations to examine their businesses? What are some examples of product lines that fit in each category?
2. In this chapter, we talked about how firms do strategic, functional, and operational planning. Yet some firms are successful without formal planning. Do you think planning is essential to a firm's success? Can planning ever hurt an organization?
3. Most planning involves strategies for growth. But is growth always the right direction to pursue? Can you think of some organizations that should have contraction rather than expansion as their objective? Do you know of any organizations that have planned to get smaller rather than larger in order to be successful?

Many Western firms see their futures in the growing populations of developing countries, where eight out of 10 consumers now live. Consumers from countries such as Brazil, India, China, and Russia offer new opportunities for firms because growing numbers of them are accumulating small but significant amounts of disposable income. Firms like world-wide cosmetics giant Beirsdorf, producer of Nivea products, are adapting their products and their marketing activities to meet the needs of these populations. Often this means selling miniature or even single-use packages of shampoo, dishwashing detergent, or fabric softener for only a few cents. The huge Swiss company Nestlé sells shrimp-flavoured instant soup cubes for two cents each in Ghana, while the financial company Allianz, in a joint program with CARE, sells micro-insurance for five cents a month to the very poor in India.

But how do these firms measure their success in these new markets? Firms normally use such marketing metrics as customer awareness or satisfaction, increases in market share or profits, or return on marketing investment (ROMI). These metrics may not be right for the new markets in the developing world where many millions of people buy streamlined versions of a firm's products at a fraction of their usual price.

What do you think? Develop a list of possible metrics that firms might use to measure their success in these new, developing markets.

Miniproject: Learn by Doing

The purpose of this miniproject is to gain an understanding of marketing planning through actual experience.

1. Select one of the following for your marketing planning project:

   • Yourself (in your search for a career)
   • Your university
   • A specific department in your university

2. Next, develop the following elements of the marketing planning process:

   • A mission statement
   • A SWOT analysis

- Objectives
- A description of the target market(s)
- A positioning strategy
- A brief outline of the marketing mix strategies—the product, pricing, distribution, and promotion

strategies—that satisfy the objectives and address the target market

3. Prepare a brief outline of a marketing plan using the basic template provided in this chapter as a guide.

Marketing in **Action** Case   Real Choices at Mega Bloks

Michel Bendayan is now vice president, Americas, for Mega Bloks (www.megabloks.com), the publicly traded, Montreal-based company that is the second-largest construction-toy manufacturer in the world after Lego. Mega Bloks is a world-wide organization employing over 3000 people, and selling a line of 75 to 100 Mega Bloks items in four sizes in 100 countries. Sales of Mega Bloks have grown exponentially in the past five years and Mega Bloks is now the world market-share leader in the preschool construction toy segment.

Michel had been a director of international sales and marketing since 2003, and then took over responsibility for Asia, Australia, and Africa in addition to his previous focus on Eastern Europe and the Middle East. Before joining Mega Bloks in 1998, he worked for Hasbro Canada as assistant product manager for the Parker Brothers and Milton Bradley brands. Prior to that, he completed a B.Com. degree from McGill University in 1994.

As international sales and marketing director, Michel determines international marketing strategy and product launch tactics. His role includes identifying new distributors, working on getting product listings, understanding retail and consumer preferences and trends, and working with retailers to grow the sales of Mega Bloks products.

Soon after taking over the Asia portfolio, Michel learned that Mega Bloks' sales in Japan were weak. The Japanese toy market is the second largest in the world after the United States, and construction toys represent a much smaller proportion of that market than in either the United States or Europe, suggesting to Michel that there was an opportunity to increase Mega Bloks' sales in Japan. For the previous five years, Mega Bloks had worked with three different Japanese distributors, but had only marginal sales success. Michel didn't know if the problem was with the distributors, the product line, or both.

One thing he had learned in the European market was that European consumers and distributors were quite different from those in North America. Focus group research had found that European consumers liked simple, compact box packaging (similar to that of Lego or Playmobil) that showed a picture of the product or the product in use, and had little writing. In North America, most consumers were influenced either by the flashiness of the packaging—bolder colours, graphic callouts, and bold text that highlighted product benefits—or the size of the packaging, bigger or more interesting being better. Consequently, Mega Bloks packaged their North American products in either bulk bags or shaped theme packaging such as a set of Bloks that came in a dump truck or in a container shaped like a bear. North American consumers tend to like detailed information on the packaging that explains who the product is for and how it is used, but such detailed text makes European packaging very cluttered as it has to be presented in multiple languages. European distributors considered Mega Bloks to be a premium foreign brand while in North America it is positioned as a high quality but value brand.

Conducting similar research, Michel found that Japanese consumers were even more quality oriented than Europeans and would reject toys with the slightest scratches or dented boxes. Japanese consumers demand the use of Japanese script on the packaging, and while North American products are often considered prestigious, Japanese consumers want a Japanese look and feel to the packaging. Because Japanese households have even less space than European households, and rooms often have multiple uses, consumers demand efficient and utilitarian packaging—wanting to be able to easily put toys back in their boxes or containers and put them out of sight. Japanese consumers are also much more conscious of and involved with pop-culture characters (for example, Power Rangers). Differences were also found with Japanese retailers, who were much more varied (for example, hypermarkets, supermarkets, convenience stores), fragmented (lots of different channels), and much more relationship oriented. Although there are fewer specialty toy stores, many Japanese toy manufacturers are among the largest toy companies in the world.

With a desire to develop a strong long-term brand in the Japanese market, Michel and his colleagues considered three distribution alternatives and three product line alternatives:

1) Distribution alternative one (D1) *was to continue to work through small distributors.*

  Even though the previous distributors did not understand the product line well and lacked focus and commitment to the product lines, Michel thought there might be some better small distributors and it might be easier to get the interest and attention of smaller distributors than the larger ones who already had strategic relationships with the large Japanese toy manufacturers. On the other hand, these small distributors were often small because they did not have access to as many channels and were not embedded in a large corporate network.

2) Distribution alternative two (D2) *was to sell direct.*

  Michel thought that the Japanese market was potentially big enough for Mega Bloks to consider developing its own sales and distribution company in Japan. He thought that such an investment could pay off in the long run as it would be closer to the customer and would not be reliant

(continued)

Marketing in **Action** Case   Real Choices at Mega Bloks

on others. The risk, however, was that no one in the Mega Bloks organization knew a lot about Japanese business practices or Japanese consumers, and it would take months, or even years, to establish the key retail relationships needed for the sales reps to be effective.

3) Distribution alternative three (D3) *was to partner with a large Japanese manufacturer or distributor.*

This alternative was attractive, as a strategic partner could offer local expertise, knowledge of the Japanese consumer, and access to a large distribution network. The downside was that Mega Bloks would be a much smaller organization, it might not get the attention needed, and all the "help" would come at the expense of significantly higher margins demanded by the partner organization.

With respect to the product line, Bendayan considered three alternatives:

1) Product line alternative one (P1) *was to sell the existing US or European product lines.*

It would be easiest and fastest to sell the current lines without any customization, and the European lines had already been customized to reflect space issues. While international brands were popular in Japan, Bendayan did not know if this would be true for children's toys. He didn't know if Japanese consumer preferences would accept the brand without modification; it might be perceived as too "Western."

2) Product line alternative two (P2) *was to sell existing product lines but customize the packaging for the Japanese market.*

The easiest customization option was to change the packaging to portray a Japanese image, but retain the current product lines that were the most popular sellers in Europe and North America. This approach had worked well in Europe where European consumers responded well to new, cleaner package designs and packing that facilitated storage such as bags or plastic boxes.

3) Product line alternative three (P3) *was to develop an entirely new product line for the Japanese market.*

This option would be the most expensive and would take a year or more to implement. The key advantage would be that a new product line could be designed to specifically appeal to Japanese consumers. Such a new line would also have stronger appeal to Japanese distributors. The downside was that minimum order quantities and sales would need to be achieved to justify the production costs. If standard products were sold, it would not matter as much if sales targets were missed.

You Make the Call

1. What are the strategic issues and considerations that Michel Bendayan should take into consideration when deciding how to enter the Japanese market? Conduct situational and SWOT analyses to identify these issues and considerations.

2. What market entry strategy would you recommend for Mega Bloks? Of the distribution alternatives presented, which makes most sense to you and why?

3. What product strategy would you recommend for Mega Bloks? Of the product line alternatives presented, which makes most sense to you and why?

4. What other elements of the marketing mix might need to be customized, and how?

CBC Video Case

Junk Food

For many years food manufacturers have been packing extra vitamins and minerals in their products. Health Canada, who traditionally kept stricter and more prohibitive laws as compared to the US and Europe, is now considering changing its rules. Health Canada is updating its food and drug regulations dealing with fortified food; among the proposals is one that would allow food manufacturers to add vitamins and minerals to a wider range of packaged and processed foods.

With Health Canada potentially allowing products for sale in this country that are fortified with vitamins and minerals, the case raises a few issues. One of the concerns is whether fortified food is a marketing gimmick by the food industry.

The CBC video asks teenagers why they relish junk food and some of their responses include: "Because it is good," "it is tasty," and "yummy."

The concern is whether teenagers would consume more junk food because it now comes with added vitamins. The case interviews a few consumers on their opinions regarding fortified junk food and their responses include: "Dressing it up with vitamins does not do anything for me," and "Even though it has vitamins, it still has a high fat content." These responses indicate that consumers may recognize that fortified junk food is still junk food.

This new proposal is not met well by some health professionals. One obesity expert says "The new rules might lead to fortified junk food and that would mislead consumers." He is concerned with the potential consumer perception that getting the vitamins from junk food eliminates the need for consuming foods that provide other health benefits. He quotes a possible consumer perception as: "If a

chocolate bar gives me my Vitamin C, I don't need an orange."

However, focus groups results indicate that "Canadians would not consume more junk food just because it came packaged with vitamins."

As well, Canada's food industry says that "Canadian baby boomers are demanding a wider range of healthier products." For example, cranberry juice fortified with vitamins and tea extracts would most likely be an acceptable product for this market.

The case also provides examples of common foods such as yogurts with fortified vitamins that have been marketed in the US and Europe and are not yet available in the Canadian market.

The presenter concludes the case by stating that dieticians and health professionals remind consumers that it is an apple a day, and not a Twinkie packed with potassium, that keeps the doctor away.

Questions

1. Does the addition of vitamins and minerals to existing food present a viable marketing opportunity? Is there a market for fortified food? Does fortified food add value to an existing product? Which target market(s) would you direct your product to?

2. What are the pros and cons of introducing a fortified product into the marketplace? Is there a need for more nutrients in the average Canadian diet? Are fortified foods responding to a real need or is it just a marketing gimmick?

3. What is the difference between a need and a want? Does fortified food represent a need or a want?

Source: This case was prepared by Kas Roussy and is based on "Junk Food," *National*, CBC video, Toronto, 13 May 2009 (time:2:07 min).

MyMarketingLab

To view the CBC videos go to
pearsoned.ca/mymarketinglab.com

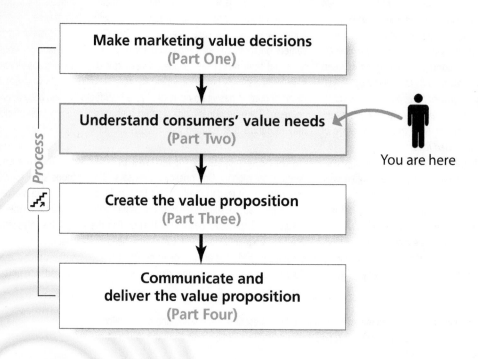

Make marketing value decisions
(Part One)

Process

Understand consumers' value needs
(Part Two)

You are here

Create the value proposition
(Part Three)

Communicate and
deliver the value proposition
(Part Four)

Understand Consumers' Value Needs

Part Two
Overview

Part Two continues the focus on making marketing decisions by providing insights in Chapter 3 on how marketers conduct research to gather the information they need to make excellent decisions. Information is the fuel that drives the engine of marketing decision making, and bad input information generally leads to bad output in the form of poor decisions by marketers. In Chapter 3, you learn about the steps in the marketing research process and gain insights on effective approaches to collecting data. In marketing, a useful and convenient way to consider markets and customers is by splitting them up as end-user consumer markets, which are composed of folks that purchase products for their own personal consumption or use, and business markets, which are composed of a variety of organizational customers who are purchasing products and services for use within their enterprise.

Chapter 4 provides insights on consumer behaviour, including the interesting topics of how and why individuals make their purchase decisions. Chapter 5 outlines the process of business-to-business (B2B) purchasing, which has numerous important differences from end-user consumer buying. Although you're probably more familiar with marketing from a consumer's perspective, the truth is that B2B accounts for a huge volume of transactions around the world—most students work for a B2B firm at some point during their professional careers. Finally, in Chapter 6 you have the opportunity to explore target marketing, a fascinating process that includes market segmentation, selection of target markets, and positioning. Because consumer markets are more diverse than ever on many dimensions, doing market segmentation has become increasingly complex. Fortunately, today's more sophisticated research methodologies allow marketers to derive very precise profiles of their markets so that they can laser target the ones that offer the best return on investment. Marketers use positioning strategies to influence how a particular market segment perceives a good or service in comparison to the competition.

Marketing Plan Connection:
Tricks of the Trade

Recall that the Appendix at the end of the book provides you with an abbreviated marketing plan example for the fictitious S&S Smoothie Company. That plan is flagged to indicate what elements from the plan correspond to each of the Parts within the book. In addition, in Chapter 2 you found a guide called "Build a Marketing Plan," which can be used as a template for marketing planning. It is also cross-referenced to chapters by section of the marketing plan.

In the chapters within Part Two, there are major learning elements that guide you in developing three critical elements of your marketing plan: marketing objectives, target market strategies, and positioning the offering. But before you deal with those elements, a good bit of information is required. This information is attained via marketing research designed to find out all it can about the consumer marketplace and the business marketplace so you can make better decisions as a marketer.

Marketing Research

As you will read in Chapter 3, "Information is the fuel that runs the marketing engine." Nowhere is the value of working with good information for decision making more apparent than in marketing planning. In the S&S Smoothie marketing plan, you will notice that research has been used to gather information about such things as customer awareness and loyalty, the sociocultural environment, and customer demographics. The results of marketing research—assuming the research is conducted properly—are invaluable in allowing you to decide on the best marketing objectives, the right target markets, and the most attractive positioning of your offering for those markets.

Marketing Objectives

The information from the situation analysis and from research on consumer and B2B markets leads an organization to formulate appropriate marketing objectives. You learned in Chapter 1 that good objectives must be specific, measurable, attainable, and sustainable over time. The following are the marketing objectives set by S&S Smoothie:

- To increase the awareness of S&S Smoothie products by at least 10 percent among the target market.
- To increase gross sales by 50 percent over the next two years.
- To introduce two new product lines over the next three years: a line of low-carb smoothies and a line of gourmet flavoured smoothies.
- To increase distribution of S&S Smoothie products to include new retail outlets both in Canada and globally.

Consumer and Business-to-Business
Target Markets

Consumer markets consist of end-users of products and services—people like you who buy things for your own use at the nearby Shoppers Drug Mart or online. Chapter 4 gives you the lowdown on consumer behaviour. In S&S Smoothie's case, most (but not all) of their marketing planning is for the consumer market. To develop successful target marketing strategies, they (and you) need to be able to actually describe the market segments in each category that have the most potential. Perusal of the S&S Smoothie marketing plan in the Appendix will reveal that they do a great job of specifying which consumer segments they want to target. In Chapter 5 you will learn that B2B markets differ from consumer markets in that the purchaser of the product or service is buying it for resale or for use in their own business. In the past, S&S Smoothie has targeted two categories of reseller markets: (1) health clubs and gyms, and (2) small, upscale specialty food markets. To increase distribution and sales of its products, they aim to target several different B2B customers in the future: hotels and resorts in Canada and selected international markets, golf and tennis clubs, and college and university campuses. The final element in targeting in Chapter 6 is positioning, influencing how a particular market segment perceives a good or service in comparison to the competition. To develop a positioning strategy, marketers must clearly understand the criteria target customers use to evaluate the different brands in a product category, and then convince those customers that their brand will better meet their needs. One way to think of positioning is that it is the application of the marketing mix (four Ps) elements in a unique way to appeal to a particular target market. S&S Smoothie seeks to position its products as the first-choice smoothie beverage for the serious health-conscious consumer, including those who are seeking to lower their carbohydrate intake. The justification for this positioning is as follows: Many smoothie beverages are available. The S&S Smoothie formula provides superior flavour and nutrition in a shelf-stable form. S&S Smoothie has developed its product, packaging, pricing, and promotion to communicate a superior, prestige image. This positioning is thus supported by all its marketing strategies.

MyMarketingLab

Now, if you are working on a marketing plan as part of your course, you can go to MyMarketingLab to apply what you learn in Part Two to your own marketing plan project.

Marketing Research:
Gather, Analyze, and Use Information

Real People **Profiles**

Ryan Garton

| Profile |

▼ A **Decision Maker** at Discover Financial Services

Ryan Garton is Director, Consumer Insights, at Discover Financial Services. Promoted to his current position in January 2008, Ryan and the Consumer Insights team are responsible for all market research activities for the firm, including brand and advertising tracking and effectiveness, new product development, innovation screeners, financial attitudes and usage studies, overall voice of the customer, and other ad hoc quantitative and qualitative studies as requested by business lines. Prior to this assignment, Ryan joined Discover Financial Services as Director, Corporate Brand Strategy, where he and his team of brand specialists were responsible for overall corporate brand strategy for all Discover Card products and programs, including Discover More Card, Miles by Discover, Discover Open Road Card, Discover Motiva Card, and Stored Value card products. Additionally, the team was responsible for brand and marketing strategy for Discover Banking products, such as student loans, deposits, and personal loans. The Brand team

is also responsible for integrating product development, innovation cycles, marketing strategy, and ensuring communication efforts are fully leveraged across all business activities.

Prior to joining Discover Financial Services, Ryan had an 11-year career at United Airlines that spanned several marketing leadership roles in international marketing—STAR Alliance, market research, product development, and brand marketing strategy—where he and his team were responsible for all United branding, the new United aircraft livery, development of Airport Lounge products, EasyCheck-in, sub-brand development (TED), and overall partnership strategy (e.g., Starbucks, PepsiCo, and AOL). His assignment prior to joining the Marketing Division was the Marketing and Sales Manager for the Midwest Region–Chicago, where he was responsible for revenue and profitability within United's largest North American Region.

Before his airline career, Ryan worked for The Gallup Organization in survey research and political tracking. He worked with several key accounts, including Volkswagen, NationsBank, CNN News, and numerous political polls. He has an MBA from the University of Nebraska with an emphasis on International Marketing & Strategy, and an undergraduate degree from St. Olaf College in economics and political science.

Here's my problem.

Ryan's problem at Discover Card was simple: too much of a good thing. The company had a lot of very good new product and services ideas: new card products, new technologies to help people manage their finances and bills, enhancements to its Web site, new insurance products, and new banking products. However, Ryan lacked an integrated approach to determining which of the ideas would be most likely to fit cardholders' desires, fit with the Discover brand image as the card that is all about cashback and other rewards to cardholders, and suit company resources (financial and technical).

In fact, Ryan had such a good thing that he didn't have the internal resources to evaluate each product idea. In particular, he was missing a crucial piece of the puzzle: customer input. Typically, Discover would prioritize new product ideas using metrics such as revenue projections, resource consumption estimates, and internal assessments of strategic fit. But these estimates largely occur in a vacuum, because they don't include the "reality check" that actual users could provide.

Ryan knew he had to seriously consider whether it was worthwhile to invest crucial resources to develop a system that could screen a large number of new product ideas with input from current or potential users of these products. He convened a cross-functional team of colleagues from Consumer Insights, Brand Strategy, and New Product Strategy to outline what this new screening process might look like. The "old" process was one where Ryan would gather these business partners together to look at the available financial information and technology resources. They would then determine the best course of action, typically without necessarily considering consumers' needs.

Things to remember

Like many companies, Discover Financial collected a lot of data from different sources to stay on top of changes in the financial services industry and to monitor the types of credit card options competitors offered to customers. But (also like many companies) the recognition that consumers' preferences should play a role when decisions are made regarding which products to take to market is a fairly new one for Discover. The marketing research process also gets more complicated when more input is included, so Ryan has to decide if his internal organization has the resources to make the best use of all the information. He also recognizes that internal decision-making often has a "political" side to it, as executives often have a vested interest in which paths the company will choose to follow.

Ryan considered his Options 1·2·3

1 Option **Don't muddy the waters.** Continue to use the same project prioritization process that Discover had been using for many years. A passive approach would not put additional roadblocks in front of project timelines; new card features and other offerings could get to market faster because they wouldn't have to undergo another evaluation. Decision makers wouldn't have to learn a new process. But decisions made about new features would continue to rely on internal projections and the intuition of managers without benefiting from input by actual consumers.

2 Option **Modify the current process to include existing consumer input Discover can easily access.** The team could look more carefully at feedback the company received in blogs, letters, and telephone calls to help it gauge the likelihood of success. Again, this extra layer of information wouldn't significantly hold up the progress of product ideas in the pipeline. And, if the information contradicted management's priorities, at least this would be a red flag to force decision makers to take a second look. However, some of the new ideas broke new ground, so there was no primary or syndicated research to indicate if they would fly. Consumers can't spontaneously provide feedback about products that don't yet exist.

3 Option **Engage an outside firm to assist Discover in developing a new process.** Ideally, Ryan wanted to test consumers' reactions to several key measures: market potential, consumer likeability, brand fit, and comparisons with launches by other financial services companies. This new process would involve hiring an outside firm to apply a standardized set of measures to assess all potential offerings so Discover could use an "apples to apples" comparison. Decision makers could access one score for each concept that encompassed all relevant research results. They could more easily identify how a concept might be improved so that cardholders would think more highly of it. And the score would include an assessment of how well each concept fits with the Discover brand.

But this radical new approach would be politically challenging within the organization, because it would challenge some internal stakeholders' existing beliefs and priorities regarding which offerings they would like to develop. And a new approach would involve a big financial investment, most likely in the neighbourhood of $100 000. There would also be a potential cost in that it would add weeks to the decision-making process, so a competitor might get to market with the idea first.

Now, put yourself in Ryan Garton's shoes.

You Choose

Which **Option** would you choose, and **why?**
1. ☐YES ☐NO   2. ☐YES ☐NO   3. ☐YES ☐NO

See what **option** Ryan chose on **page 111**

marketing research ethics
Taking an ethical and above-board approach to conducting marketing research that does no harm to the participant in the process of conducting the research.

marketing information system (MIS)
A process that first determines what information marketing managers need and then gathers, sorts, analyzes, stores, and distributes relevant and timely marketing information to system users.

Knowledge Is Power

By now we know that successful planning means that managers make informed decisions to guide the organization. But how do marketers actually make these choices? Specifically, how do they find out what they need to know to develop marketing objectives, select a target market, position (or reposition) their product, and develop product, price, promotion, and place strategies?

Here's an answer—information. Information is the fuel that runs the marketing engine. To make good decisions, marketers must have information that is accurate, up to date, and relevant. We are now in Part 2 of the book, called "Understand Consumers' Value Needs." To understand these needs, marketers first need to conduct *marketing research* to identify them. In this chapter, we will discuss some of the tools that marketers use to get that information. In the chapters that follow, we will look at consumer behaviour, how and why organizations buy, and then how marketers sharpen their focus via target marketing strategies.

A marketer who conducts research to learn more about her customers shouldn't encounter any ethical challenges, right? Well, maybe. In reality, several aspects of marketing research are fraught with the *potential* for ethics breaches. **Marketing research ethics** refers to taking an ethical and above-board approach to conducting marketing research that does no harm to the participant in the process of conducting the research.

When the organization collects data, important issues of privacy and confidentiality come into play. Marketers must be very clear when they work with research respondents about how they will use the data and give respondents full disclosure on their options for confidentiality and anonymity. For example, it is unethical to collect data under the guise of marketing research when your real intent is to develop a database of potential customers for direct marketing. Firms who abuse the trust of respondents run a serious risk of damaging their reputation when word gets out that they are engaged in unethical research practices. This makes it difficult to attract participants in future research projects—and it "poisons the well" for other companies when consumers believe that they can't trust them.

The Marketing Information System

Many firms use **marketing information systems (MIS)** to collect information. The MIS is a process that first determines what information marketing managers need, and then it gathers, sorts, analyzes, stores, and distributes relevant and timely marketing information to users. As you can see in Figure 3.1, the MIS includes three important components:

- Four types of data (internal company data, marketing intelligence, marketing research, and acquired databases)
- Computer hardware and software to analyze the data and to create reports
- Output for marketing decision makers

Various sources "feed" the MIS with data, and then the system's software "digests" it. The MIS analysts use the output to generate a series of

Ethical and Sustainable Decisions in the Real World

Consumers are increasingly looking for "green" products. To have a positive impact on the environment is on the minds of many, and marketers have capitalized on this opportunity for some time now. As a result, many companies are convinced they need labels to show how environmentally focused they are. Packaging is altered and labels and promotional materials clearly indicate whether or not products help preserve the environment—but do they really? How can a consumer tell whether or not a product is environmentally friendly? If competitive products claim to be environmentally friendly, how can we tell if one product is more environmentally friendly than the other?

As regulators, investors and, most importantly, consumers demand ever-more assurance about how companies advertise, many companies are wondering whether the self-penned note on their environmental and sustainability stance is enough. As a result, marketers in Canada and around the world are considering new methods to validate how environmentally friendly their products really are. In essence, many companies feel the need to provide accurate and comprehensive information directly to consumers so they, in turn, can make informed choices. Companies are enticed to do so in order to offer added value to the consumer, and eventually they charge a premium for it. Regrettably, some companies falsely advertise their products as being environmentally friendly without providing any evidence to its customers. Some companies have been susceptible to misleading advertising terms that have done a great job generalizing a message that cannot be generalized. In other words, consumers tend to have very simplistic ideas about what is green.

As an example, Frito-Lay announced in 2010 they would sell their Sun Chips brand in the first completely compostable bag in Canada and in the United States. Clearly, the launch was consistent with Frito-Lay's ongoing efforts to make their products environmentally friendly. Many consumers found the bags to be too noisy, thus creating noise pollution. Also, the label on bags mentioned "World's First 100% compostable chip package," without explaining the details of why the packaging is eco-friendly. They eventually went back to the old bags for five of the six Sun Chips flavours (Vranica, *The Wall Street Journal*, December 23 2010, page B10). With proper research, Frito-Lay could have dealt with these issues before the launch.

Many, if not all, companies support the environment, but far fewer are willing to go to the trouble of providing concrete evidence to consumers that their products can have a positive impact on the environment. Given the rising sales of environmentally friendly products, even in the worst recession most consumers have ever seen, consumer demand may play a stronger role in how these products are marketed. With market research, marketers may gather the data required to build their cases and assure consumers how the offered product may have a positive impact on the environment. It is no longer a matter of whether the product is "green" or not, but rather how significant its impact is to the environment. It is a really a matter of sustainability.

ETHICS CHECK: Find out what other students taking this course **would do** and **why** on www.mypearsonmarketinglab.com.

regular reports for various decision makers. For example, Frito-Lay's MIS generates daily sales data by product line and by region. Its managers then use this information to evaluate the market share of different Frito-Lay products compared to one another and to competing snack foods in each region where the company does business.[1]

Let's take a closer look at each of the four different data sources for the MIS.

1. Internal Company Data

The *internal company data system* uses information from within the organization to produce reports on the results of sales and marketing activities. Internal company data include a firm's sales records—information such as which customers buy which products in what

If you were in Frito-Lay's marketing department, what would you do in order to make sure the next-generation compostable bag is successful?

☐YES ☐NO

Figure 3.1 The Marketing Information System

A firm's marketing information system (MIS) stores and analyzes data from a variety of sources and turns the data into information for useful marketing decision making.

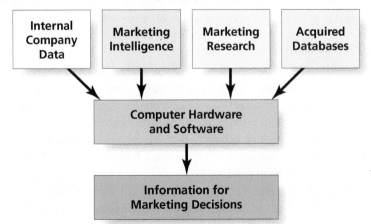

quantities and at what intervals, which items are in stock and which are back-ordered because they are out of stock, when items were shipped to the customer, and which items have been returned because they are defective.

Often, an MIS allows salespeople and sales managers in the field to access internal records through a company **intranet**. This is an internal corporate communications network that uses Internet technology to link company departments, employees, and databases. Intranets are secured so that only authorized employees have access. When salespeople and sales managers in the field can use an intranet to access their company's MIS, they can better serve their customers, because they have immediate access to information on pricing, inventory levels, production schedules, shipping dates, and the customer's sales history. But equally important, because salespeople and sales managers are the ones in daily direct contact with customers, the company intranet enters their reports directly into the system. This means the reports can provide an important source of information to upper management on changes in sales patterns or on new sales opportunities.

Marketing managers at the head office also can see daily or weekly sales data by brand or product line from the internal company data system. They can view monthly sales reports to measure progress toward sales goals and market share objectives. For example, managers and buyers at Loblaw headquarters in Mississauga use up-to-the-minute sales information they obtain from store cash registers around the country so they can quickly detect problems with products, promotions, and even in the firm's distribution system.

intranet
An internal corporate communication network that uses Internet technology to link company departments, employees, and databases.

2. Marketing Intelligence

As we saw in Chapter 1, to make good decisions, marketers need to have information about the marketing environment. Thus, a second important element of the MIS is the **marketing intelligence system**, a method by which marketers get information about what's going on in the world that is relevant to their business. Although the name *intelligence* may suggest cloak-and-dagger spy activities, in reality nearly all the information companies need about their environment, including the competitive environment, is available by monitoring everyday sources: Web sites, industry trade publications, or simple observations of the marketplace. And because salespeople are the ones "in the trenches" every day—talking with customers, distributors, and prospective customers—they too can provide valuable information. Retailers often hire "mystery shoppers" to visit their stores and those of their competitors, posing as customers to see how people are treated. Other information may come from speaking with organizational buyers about competing products, attending trade shows, or simply purchasing competitors' products.

marketing intelligence system
A method by which marketers get information about everyday happenings in the marketing environment.

Marketing managers may use marketing intelligence data to predict fluctuations in sales due to economic conditions, political issues, and events that heighten consumer awareness, or to forecast the future so that they will be on top of developing trends. For example, the global economic recession has had an impact on how consumers spend their vacation, even in Canada. The stay-at-home consumer and the so-called "staycation" phenomenon has been one of the strongest trends of the recession. As a result, supermarkets across Canada have managed to offer more finger foods and ready-to-eat products for consumers wanting to feel away from home, at home. The furniture industry capitalized on home entertainment units as well.[2]

3. Marketing Research

Marketing research refers to the process of collecting, analyzing, and interpreting data about customers, competitors, and the business environment to improve marketing effectiveness. (See Exhibit 3.1.) Although companies collect marketing intelligence data continually to keep managers abreast of happenings in the marketplace, marketing research also is called for when managers need unique information to help them make specific decisions. Whether their business is selling cool stuff to teens or coolant to factories, firms succeed when they know what customers want, when they want it, where they want it—and what competing firms are doing about it. In other words, the better a firm is at obtaining valid marketing information, the more successful it will be. Therefore, virtually all companies rely on some form of marketing research,

marketing research
The process of collecting, analyzing, and interpreting data about customers, competitors, and the business environment in order to improve marketing effectiveness.

though the amount and type of research conducted varies dramatically. In general, marketing research data available in an MIS include syndicated research reports and custom research reports.

Syndicated research is general information that specialized firms collect on a regular basis and then sell to other firms. The Q Scores Company, for instance, reports on consumers' perceptions of over 1700 celebrity performers for companies that want to feature a well-known person in their advertising. The company also rates consumer appeal of cartoon characters, sports stars, and even deceased celebrities.[3] Other examples of syndicated research reports include Nielsen's television ratings and Arbitron's radio ratings. Environics Research Group and Ipsos Reid are two syndicated research firms in Canada that combine information about consumers' buying behaviour and their media usage with geographic and demographic characteristics.

As valuable as it may be, syndicated research doesn't provide all the answers to marketing questions, because the information it collects typically is broad but shallow; it gives good insights about general trends, such as who is watching what television shows or what brand of perfume is hot this year. In contrast, **custom research** is research a single firm conducts to provide answers to specific questions. This kind of research is especially helpful for firms when they need to know more about why certain trends have surfaced.

Some firms maintain an in-house research department that conducts studies on its behalf. Many firms, however, hire outside research companies that specialize in designing and conducting projects based on the needs of the client. These custom research reports are another kind of information an MIS includes. Marketers may use marketing research to identify opportunities for new products, to promote existing ones, or to provide data about the quality of their products, who uses them, and how.

Exhibit 3.1
For many years, automakers such as Ford Canada have conducted extensive market research on consumers' car preferences.

4. Acquired Databases

A large amount of information that can be useful in marketing decision making is available in the form of external databases. Firms may acquire these databases from any number of sources. For example, some companies are willing to sell their customer database to noncompeting firms. Government databases, including the massive amounts of economic and demographic information Statistics Canada compiles, are available at little or no cost. Provincial, regional, and local agencies may make information available for a fee.

In recent years, the use of such databases for marketing purposes has come under increased government scrutiny as some consumer advocates protest against the potential invasion of privacy these may cause. Using the data to analyze consumer trends is one thing—using it for outbound mailings and unsolicited phone calls and e-mails has evoked a backlash resulting in a plethora of "do not call" lists and anti-spam laws. As a matter of fact, in 2011, the Canadian Radio-television and Telecommunications Commission forced Bell Canada to pay a record $1.3 million fine when it found the company broke the law by contacting Canadians on the do-not-call list to sell them television, telephone, and internet services.[4] Maybe you have noticed that when you sign up for most anything on the Web that requires your contact information, you receive an invitation to "opt out" of receiving promotional mailings from the company or from others who may acquire your contact information from the organization later. By law, if you decide to opt out, companies cannot use your information for marketing purposes.

The Marketing Decision Support System

As we have seen, a firm's marketing information system generates regular reports for decision makers on what is going on in the internal and external environment. But

syndicated research
Research by firms that collect data on a regular basis and sell the reports to multiple firms.

custom research
Research conducted for a single firm to provide specific information its managers need.

Ryan Garton

APPLYING ▾ MDSS

Ryan has to decide on the best system to integrate data from different sources so that Discover can make intelligent choices as it competes in the credit card marketplace. ➡

Figure 3.2 The MDSS

Although an MIS provides many reports managers need for decision making, it doesn't answer all their information needs. The marketing decision support system (MDSS) is an enhancement to the MIS that makes it easy for marketing managers to access the MIS and find answers to their questions.

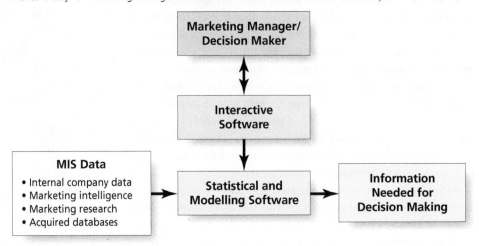

marketing decision support system (MDSS)

The data, analysis software, and interactive software that allow managers to conduct analyses and find the information they need.

sometimes these reports are inadequate. Different managers may want different information, and in some cases, the problem they must address is too vague or unusual for the MIS process to easily answer. As a result, many firms beef up their MIS with a **marketing decision support system (MDSS)**. An MDSS includes analysis and interactive software that allows marketing managers, even those who are not computer experts, to access MIS data and conduct their own analyses, often over the company intranet. Figure 3.2 shows the elements of an MDSS.

Typically an MDSS includes sophisticated statistical and modelling software tools. Statistical software allows managers to examine complex relationships among factors in the marketplace. For example, a marketing manager who wants to know how consumers perceive her company's brand in relation to the competition's brand might create a "perceptual map," or a graphic presentation of the various brands in relationship to each other. You'll see an example of a perceptual map in Chapter 6.

Modelling software allows decision makers to examine possible or preconceived ideas about relationships in the data—to ask "what-if" questions. For example, media modelling software allows marketers to see what would happen if they made certain decisions about where to place their advertising. A manager may be able to use sales data and a model to find out how many consumers stay with her brand and how many switch, thus developing projections of market share over time. Table 3.1 gives some examples of the different marketing questions an MIS and an MDSS might answer.

Table 3.1	Examples of Questions an MIS and an MDSS Might Answer

Questions an MIS Answers	Questions an MDSS Answers
What were our company sales of each product during the past month and the past year?	Has our decline in sales simply reflected changes in overall industry sales, or is there some portion of the decline that industry changes cannot explain?
What changes are happening in sales in our industry, and what are the demographic characteristics of consumers whose purchase patterns are changing the most?	Do we see the same trends in our different product categories? Are the changes in consumer trends very similar among all our products? What are the demographic characteristics of consumers who seem to be the most and the least loyal?
What are the best media for reaching a large proportion of heavy, medium, or light users of our product?	If we change our media schedule by adding or deleting certain media buys, will we reach fewer users of our product?

2 Searching for Gold: Data Mining

OBJECTIVE
Understand data mining and how marketers can put it to good use.
(pp. 95–96)

As we have explained, most MIS include internal customer transaction databases and many include acquired databases. Often, these databases are extremely large. To take advantage of the massive amount of data available, a sophisticated analysis technique called **data mining** is now a priority for many firms. This refers to a process in which analysts sift through data (often measured in terabytes—much larger than kilobytes or even gigabytes) to identify unique patterns of behaviour among different customer groups (Figure 3.3).

data mining
Sophisticated analysis techniques to take advantage of the massive amount of transaction information now available.

Data mining uses computers that run sophisticated programs so that analysts can combine different databases to understand relationships among buying decisions, exposure to marketing messages, and in-store promotions. These operations are so complex that often companies need to build a *data warehouse* (which can cost more than $10 million) simply to store and process the data.[5] Powerful consumer data generators Google, Yahoo!, Facebook, and Twitter are evaluating how best to use their substantial databases for data mining. For example, Yahoo! collects between 12 and 15 terabytes of data each day, and Facebook has access to valuable information that its over 50 million users post. Both firms want to use the data to facilitate targeted advertising by clients who are willing to pay big money to get their online ads in front of people who are likely to buy.[6]

Tracking consumers' behaviour via cookies happens all the time. A "cookie" is a small piece of information sent by a Web server to store on a Web browser so it can later be read back from that browser. With this technology, companies can track what consumers are doing. They can actually track click behaviours and online flow patterns.

You will notice that privacy and confidentiality in marketing research are very important concepts. Often, a research project needs to be approved by an ethics board of some sort. All universities have ethics board. Students and professors are asked to submit marketing research projects to the board prior to data collection.

Even cellular providers are getting into the data mining act. Signals among phones and base stations can be detected by commercial sensing devices. But the detailed records of who is calling whom belong entirely to the phone companies. Right now, they make little use of that data, in part because they fear alienating subscribers who worry about

Figure 3.3 Uses of Data Mining

Data mining has four important applications for marketers:[7]

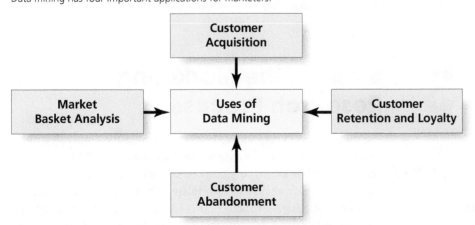

Tan et al., *Introduction to Data Mining*; Nate Nead, "Customer Acquisition vs. Retention," November 9, 2009, http://www.digitalsignage.com/blog/2009/11/09/signage-customer-acquisition-vs-retention/; Martin, Brat, "The new nutritionist: your grocer," *The Wall Street Journal*, July 27, 2010, p. D10.

privacy infringement. But cellular operators have begun signing deals with business partners who are eager to market products based on specific phone users' location and calling habits. If *reality mining* catches on, phone companies' calling records will become precious assets. And these will only grow in value as customers use their phones to browse the Web, purchase products, and update their Facebook pages—and as marketers apply reality mining's toolkit to these activities.[8]

1. **Customer acquisition:** Many firms include demographic and other information about customers in their database. For example, a number of supermarkets offer weekly special price discounts for store "members." These stores' membership application forms require that customers indicate their age, family size, address, and so on. With this information, the supermarket determines which of its current customers respond best to specific offers and then sends the same offers to noncustomers who share the same demographic characteristics.

2. **Customer retention and loyalty:** The firm identifies big-spending customers and then targets them for special offers and inducements other customers won't receive. Keeping the most profitable customers coming back is a great way to build business success, because keeping good customers is less expensive than constantly finding new ones.[9]

3. **Customer abandonment:** Strange as it may sound, sometimes a firm wants customers to take their business elsewhere, because servicing them actually costs the firm too much. Today, this is popularly called "firing a customer." For example, a department store may use data mining to identify unprofitable customers—those who are not spending enough or who return most of what they buy. In recent years, data mining has allowed food distributor Safeway to monitor customer purchasing habits to recommend healthier alternatives to the food products they buy. Loyalty cards allowed the company to gather data and achieve this objective.[10]

4. **Market basket analysis:** Focused promotional strategies are developed based on the records of which customers have bought certain products. Hewlett-Packard, for example, carefully analyzes which of its customers recently bought new printers and targets them to receive e-mails about specials on ink cartridges and tips to get the most out of their machines.

So far, we have looked at the MIS and the MDSS, the overall systems that provide the information marketers need to make good decisions. We've seen how MIS and MDSS data include internal company data, marketing intelligence data gathered by monitoring everyday sources, acquired databases, and information gathered to address specific marketing decisions through the marketing research process. In the rest of the chapter, we'll look at the steps that marketers take when they conduct marketing research.

3 Steps in the Marketing Research Process

OBJECTIVE

List and explain the steps and key elements of the marketing research process.

(pp. 96–110)

The collection and interpretation of strategic information is hardly a one-shot deal that managers engage in "just out of curiosity." Ideally, marketing research is an ongoing process, a series of steps marketers take, repeatedly, to learn about the marketplace. Whether a company conducts the research itself or hires another firm to do it, the goal is the same: to help managers make informed marketing decisions. Figure 3.4 shows the steps in the research process, and we'll go over each of these now.

Step 1: Define the Research Problem

The first step in the marketing research process is to clearly understand what information managers need. We refer to this step as defining the research problem. You should note that the word *problem* here does not necessarily refer to "something that is wrong," but instead it refers to the overall questions for which the firm needs answers. Defining the problem points to three components:

1. **Specify the research objectives:** What questions will the research attempt to answer?

2. **Identify the consumer population of interest:** What are the characteristics of the consumer group(s) of interest?

3. **Place the problem in an environmental context:** What factors in the firm's internal and external business environment might influence the situation?

It's not as simple as it may seem to provide the right kind of information for each of these pieces of the problem. Suppose a luxury car manufacturer wants to find out why its sales have fallen off dramatically over the past year. The research objective could revolve around any number of possible questions: Is the firm's advertising failing to reach the right consumers? Is the right message being sent? Do the firm's cars have a particular feature (or lack of one) that's turning customers away? Is there a problem with the firm's reputation for providing quality service? Do consumers believe the price is right for the value they get? The particular objective researchers choose depends on a variety of factors, such as the feedback the firm gets from its customers, the information it receives from the marketplace, and sometimes even the intuition of the people who design the research.

Often the focus of a research question comes from marketplace feedback that identifies a possible problem. Mercedes-Benz is a great example of a firm that for years has continually monitored drivers' perceptions of its cars. When the company started to get reports from its dealers in the 1990s that more and more people viewed Mercedes products as "arrogant" and "unapproachable," even to the point at which they were reluctant to sit in showroom models, the company undertook a research project to better understand the reasons for this perception.

The *research objective* determines the consumer population the company will study. In the case of Mercedes, the research could have focused on current owners to find out what they especially like about the car. Or it could have been directed at nonowners to understand their lifestyles, what they look for in a luxury automobile, or their beliefs about the company itself that keep them from choosing its cars. So what did Mercedes find out? Research showed that although people rated its cars very highly on engineering quality and status, many were too intimidated by the elitist Mercedes image to consider actually buying one. Mercedes dealers reported that a common question from visitors to showrooms was, "May I actually sit in the car?" Based on these findings, Mercedes in recent years has worked hard to adjust perceptions by projecting a slightly more down-to-earth image in its advertising, and it ultimately created new downsized classes of vehicles to appeal to consumers who want something a little less ostentatious.[11]

Step 2: Determine the Research Design

Once we isolate specific problems, the second step of the research process is to decide on a "plan of attack." This plan is the **research design**, which specifies exactly what information

Figure 3.4 Steps in the Marketing Research Process

The marketing research process includes a series of steps that begins with defining the problem or the information needed and ends with the finished research report for managers.

Define the Research Problem
- Specify the research objectives
- Identify the consumer population of interest
- Place the problem in an environmental context

Determine the Research Design
- Determine whether secondary data are available
- Determine whether primary data are required
  —Exploratory research
  —Descriptive research
  —Causal research

Choose the Method to Collect Primary Data
- Determine which survey methods are most appropriate
  —Mail questionnaires
  —Telephone interviews
  —Face-to-face interviews
  —Online questionnaires
- Determine which observational methods are most appropriate
  —Personal observation
  —Unobtrusive measures
  —Mechanical observation

Design the Sample
- Choose between probability sampling and nonprobability sampling

Collect the Data
- Translate questionnaires and responses if necessary
- Combine data from multiple sources (if available)

Analyze and Interpret the Data
- Tabulate and cross-tabulate the data
- Interpret or draw conclusions from the results

Prepare the Research Report
- In general, the research report includes the following:
  —An executive summary
  —A description of the research methods
  —A discussion of the results of the study
  —Limitations of the study
  —Conclusions and recommendations

research design
A plan that specifies what information marketers will collect and what type of study they will do.

Figure 3.5 Marketing Research Designs

For some research problems, the secondary research may provide the information needed. At other times, one of the primary research methods may be needed.

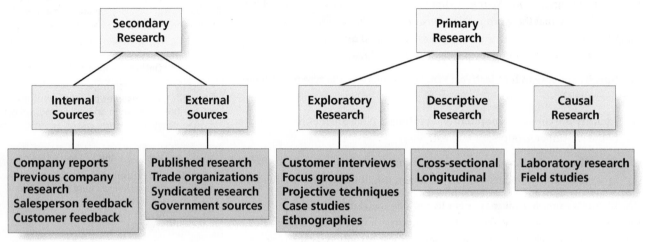

marketers will collect and what type of study they will do. Figure 3.5 summarizes many of the types of research designs in the researcher's arsenal. As you can see, research designs fall into two broad categories: *secondary research* and *primary research*. All marketing problems do not call for the same research techniques, and marketers solve many problems most effectively with a combination of techniques.

Secondary Research

The first question marketers must ask when they determine their research design is whether the information they require to make a decision already exists. For example, a coffee producer who needs to know the differences in coffee consumption among different demographic and geographic segments of the market may find that the information it needs is already available from one or more studies already conducted by the National Coffee Association, the leading trade association of US coffee companies and a major generator of industry research. We call data that have been collected for some purpose other than the problem at hand **secondary data**.

Many marketers thrive on going out and collecting new, "fresh" data from consumers. However, if secondary data are available, it saves the firm time and money because the expense to design and implement a study has already been incurred. Sometimes, the data that marketers need may be "hiding" right under the organization's nose in the form of company reports; previous company research studies; feedback received from customers, salespeople, or stores; or even in the memories of longtime employees. More typically, though, researchers need to look elsewhere for secondary data. They may obtain reports published in the popular and business press, studies that private research organizations or government agencies conduct, and published research on the state of the industry from trade organizations.

For example, many companies subscribe to reports such as the *National Consumer Study*, a national survey conducted by syndicated research firm Experian Simmons. Simmons publishes results that it then sells to marketers, advertising agencies, and publishers. Access to their data is even available in some college libraries. This database contains over 60 000 data variables with usage behaviour on all major media, over 450 product categories, and over 8000 brands. Data from Experian Simmons can give a brand manager a profile of who uses a product, identify heavy users, or even provide data on what magazines a target market reads.[12] Of course, marketers can readily turn to the Internet for numerous external information sources. Table 3.2 lists several Web sites helpful to marketers when they look for secondary research topics.

secondary data

Data that have been collected for some purpose other than the problem at hand.

Table 3.2	Helpful Internet Sites for Marketing Research

URL	Description
www.opinionresearch.com	Opinion Research Corporation offers numerous industry and trend reports that are useful as secondary data sources.
http://www.google.com/intl/en/analytics/	Google Analytics provides rich insights into Web site traffic and marketing effectiveness.
http://www.statcan.gc.ca/start-debut-eng.html	Statistics Canada publishes data on a regular basis on a variety of topics, industries, and trends.
http://bbm.ca	Offers ratings on listenership for TV and radio.
www.marketingpower.com	The American Marketing Association provides many resources to its members on a variety of industry topics.
www.dialog.com	Dialog sorts companies by location, size, and industry. The user can request telemarketing reports, preaddressed mailing labels, and company profiles.
www.lexisnexis.com	LexisNexis is a large database featuring information from sources such as Dun & Bradstreet, *The New York Times,* CNN, National Public Radio transcripts, Market Research Intelligence Association, Ipsos, and TNS.

Primary Research

Of course, secondary research is not always the answer. When a company needs to make a specific decision, it often needs to collect **primary data**—information it gathers directly from respondents to address a specific question at hand. Primary data include demographic and psychological information about customers and prospective customers, customers' attitudes and opinions about products and competing products, and their awareness or knowledge about a product and their beliefs about the people who use those products. In the next few sections, we'll talk briefly about the various design options for conducting primary research.

primary data
Data from research conducted to help make a specific decision.

Primary Data	Secondary Data
Cost method	More affordable
Generating new information	Reprocess and reuse collected information
Latest information	Past information
Completely tailor-made	Obtained effortlessly
Time consuming	Readily available

Exploratory (Qualitative) Research

Marketers use **exploratory research** to come up with ideas for new strategies and opportunities or perhaps just to get a better handle on a problem they are currently experiencing with a product. Because the studies are usually small scale and less costly than other techniques, marketers may use exploratory research to test their hunches about what's going on without too much risk.

exploratory research
A technique that marketers use to generate insights for future, more rigorous studies.

Exploratory studies often involve in-depth probing of a few consumers who fit the profile of the "typical" customer. Researchers may interview consumers, salespeople, or other employees about products, services, ads, or stores. They may simply "hang out" and watch what people do when they choose among competing brands in a store aisle. Or they may locate places where the consumers of interest tend to be and ask questions in these settings. For example, some researchers find that younger people often are too suspicious or skeptical in traditional research settings, so they may interview them while they wait in line to buy concert tickets or in clubs.[13]

We refer to most exploratory research as *qualitative*: that is, the results of the research project tend to be nonnumeric and instead might be detailed verbal or visual information about consumers' attitudes, feelings, and buying behaviours in the form of words rather than in numbers. For example, when DuPont wanted to know how women felt about panty hose, marketers asked research participants to collect magazine clippings that expressed their emotions about the product.

Intuit, the software company that produces the personal finance software packages Turbo-Tax and Quicken, used personal interviews to better understand consumers' frustrations when they try to install and use its products. When customers told researchers that the software itself should "tell me how to do it," they took this advice literally and developed software that used computer audio to give verbal instructions. Intuit's probing went one step beyond interviews. Its researchers left respondents microcassette recorders so that whenever they were having problems, they could simply push a button and tell the company of their frustration.

focus group

A product-oriented discussion among a small group of consumers led by a trained moderator.

The **focus group** is the technique that marketing researchers use most often for collecting exploratory data. Focus groups typically consist of five to nine consumers who have been recruited because they share certain characteristics (they all play golf at least twice a month, are women in their twenties, and so on). These people sit together to discuss a product, ad, or some other marketing topic a discussion leader introduces. Typically, the leader records (by videotape or audiotape) these group discussions, which may be held at special interviewing facilities that allow for observation by the client who watches from behind one-way glass.

Today it's common to find focus groups in cyberspace as well. Firms such as Del Monte, Coca-Cola, and Disney use online focus group sites that often bear some resemblance to other social-networking sites, where members create profile pages and post to discussion boards. Companies use them to administer polls, chat in real time with consumers, and even ask members to go to the store to try out specific products. Del Monte handpicked 400 members for its private network, which the company uses to help create products, test marketing campaigns, and stir up buzz. The rapid back and forth between the company and the online community allows for real-time data collection that can help substantially shorten the product development cycle.[14]

case study

A comprehensive examination of a particular firm or organization.

The **case study** is a comprehensive examination of a particular firm or organization. In business-to-business (B2B) marketing research in which the customers are other firms, for example, researchers may try to learn how one particular company makes its purchases. The goal is to identify the key decision makers, to learn what criteria they emphasize when choosing among suppliers, and perhaps to learn something about any conflicts and rivalries among these decision makers that may influence their choices. That in itself is often challenging. Other methods mentioned could also be applied to business-to-business research, but the sample size and the number of respondents tend to be much lower than research involving consumers.

ethnography

An approach to research based on observations of people in their own homes or communities.

An **ethnography** is a different kind of in-depth report. It uses a technique marketers borrow from anthropologists. Ethnography involves fieldwork in which the researcher lives among the population being studied. Some marketing researchers visit people's homes or participate in real-life consumer activities to get a handle on how they really use products. Imagine having a researcher follow you around while you shop and then while you use the products you bought to see what kind of consumer you are. This is basically marketers' version of a reality show—though, hopefully, the people they study are a bit more "realistic"! Ethnographies can be conducted in businesses as well, if your unit of analysis is organizations. But most professional marketers would agree that trying to benchmark one organizational culture against another is too overwhelming a task.

Descriptive (Quantitative) Research

descriptive (quantitative) research

A tool that probes more systematically into the problem and bases its conclusions on large numbers of observations.

In **quantitative research**, researchers use tools such as questionnaires or equipment to collect numerical data. We've seen that marketers have many tools in their arsenal, including focus groups and observational techniques, to help them better define a problem or opportunity.

These are usually modest studies of a small number of people, enough to get some indication of what is going on but not enough for the marketer to feel confident about generalizing what she observes to the rest of the population.

The next step in marketing research, then, often is to conduct **descriptive research**. This kind of research probes systematically into the marketing problem and bases its conclusions on a large sample of participants. Results typically are expressed in quantitative terms—averages, percentages, or other statistics that result from a large set of measurements. In such quantitative approaches to research, the project can be as simple as counting the number of Listerine bottles sold in a month in different regions of the country, or as complex as statistical analyses of responses to a survey mailed to thousands of consumers. In each case, marketers conduct the descriptive research to answer a specific question, in contrast to the "fishing expedition" that may occur in exploratory research.

Marketing researchers who employ descriptive techniques most often use a **cross-sectional design**. This approach usually involves the systematic collection of responses to a consumer survey instrument, such as a *questionnaire*, from one or more samples of respondents at one point in time. The data may be collected on more than one occasion but generally not from the same pool of respondents.

In contrast to these one-shot studies, a **longitudinal design** tracks the responses of the same sample of respondents over time. Market researchers sometimes create consumer panels to get information; in this case, a sample of respondents that are representative of a larger market agrees to provide information about purchases on a weekly or monthly basis. Major consumer packaged goods firms like Procter & Gamble, Unilever, Colgate-Palmolive, and Johnson & Johnson, for instance, recruit consumer advisory panels on a market-by-market basis to keep their fingers on the pulse of local shoppers. Although longitudinal studies can be quite beneficial for marketers, such an approach can be cost prohibitive.

Causal Research

It's a fact that purchases of both diapers and beer peak between 5:00 PM and 7:00 PM. Can we say that purchasing one of these products caused shoppers to purchase the other as well—and, if so, which caused which? Does taking care of a baby drive a parent to drink? Or is the answer simply that this happens to be the time when young fathers stop at the store on their way home from work to pick up some brew and Pampers?[15]

The descriptive techniques we've examined do a good job of providing valuable information about what is happening in the marketplace, but by its very nature, descriptive research can only *describe* a marketplace phenomenon—it cannot tell us *why* it occurs. Sometimes marketers need to know if something they've done has brought about some change in behaviour. For example, does placing one product next to another in a store mean that people will buy more of each? We can't answer this question through simple observation or description.

Causal research attempts to identify cause-and-effect relationships. Marketers use causal research techniques when they want to know if a change in something (e.g., placing cases of beer next to a diaper display) is responsible for a change in something else (e.g., a big increase in diaper sales). They call the factors that might cause such a change *independent variables* and the outcomes *dependent variables*. The independent variable(s) cause some change in the dependent variable(s). In our example, then, the beer display is an independent variable, and sales data for the diapers are a dependent variable—that is, the study would investigate whether an increase in diaper sales "depends" on the proximity of beer. Researchers can gather data and test the causal relationship statistically.

To rule out alternative explanations, researchers carefully design **experiments** that test predicted relationships among variables in a controlled environment. Because this approach tries to eliminate competing explanations for the outcome, researchers may bring respondents to a laboratory so they can control precisely what the participants

cross-sectional design
A type of descriptive technique that involves the systematic collection of quantitative information.

longitudinal design
A technique that tracks the responses of the same sample of respondents over time.

causal research
A technique that attempts to understand cause-and-effect relationships.

experiment
A technique that tests prespecified relationships among variables in a controlled environment.

experience. For example, a study to test whether the placement of diapers in a grocery store influences the likelihood that male shoppers will buy them might bring a group of men into a testing facility and show them a "virtual store" on a computer screen. Researchers would ask the men to fill a grocery cart as they click through the "aisles." The experiment might vary the placement of the diapers—next to shelves of beer in one scenario or near paper goods in a different scenario. The objective is to see which placement gets the guys to put diapers into their carts.

Step 3: Choose the Method to Collect Primary Data

When the researcher decides to work with primary data, the next step in the marketing research process is to figure out just how to collect it. We broadly describe primary data collection methods as either *survey* or *observation*. There are many ways to collect data, and marketers try new ones all the time. A few marketing researchers now even turn to sophisticated brain scans to directly measure our brains' reactions to various advertisements or products. These "neuromarketers" hope to be able to tell companies how people will react to their brands by scanning consumers' brains rather than collecting data the old-fashioned way—by asking them.[16] These techniques are still in their infancy, so for now we still rely on other methods to collect primary data.

Survey Methods

Survey methods involve some kind of interview or other direct contact with respondents who answer questions. Questionnaires can be administered on the phone, in person, through the mail, or over the Internet. Table 3.3 summarizes the advantages and disadvantages of different methods for collecting data.

Questionnaires

Questionnaires differ in their degree of structure. With a totally *unstructured questionnaire*, the researcher loosely determines the items in advance. Questions may evolve from the respondent's answers to previous questions. At the other extreme, the researcher uses a *completely structured questionnaire*. She asks every respondent the exact same questions and each participant responds to the same set of fixed choices. You have probably experienced this kind of questionnaire, where you might have had to respond to a statement by saying if you "strongly agree," "somewhat agree," and so on. *Moderately structured questionnaires* ask each respondent the same questions, but the respondent is allowed to answer the questions in her own words.

Mail questionnaires are easy to administer and offer a high degree of anonymity to respondents. On the downside, because the questionnaire is printed and mailed, researchers have little flexibility in the types of questions they can ask and little control over the circumstances under which the respondent answers them. Mail questionnaires also take a long time to get back to the company and are likely to have a much lower response rate than other types of data collection methods, because people tend to ignore them.

Telephone interviews usually consist of a brief phone conversation in which an interviewer reads a short list of questions to the respondent. There are several problems with using telephone interviews as a data collection method. The respondent also may not feel comfortable speaking directly to an interviewer, especially if the survey is about a sensitive subject.

Another problem with this method is that the growth of **telemarketing**, in which businesses sell directly to consumers over the phone, has eroded consumers' willingness to participate in phone surveys (Exhibit 3.2). In addition to aggravating people by barraging

Exhibit 3.2
Telemarketing can involve both inbound and outbound calling. Outbound calling is used to make direct contact with the customer.

telemarketing
The use of the telephone to sell directly to consumers and business customers.

Table 3.3	Advantages and Disadvantages of Data Collection Methods		
Data Collection Method	**Advantages**	**Disadvantages**
Mail questionnaires	• Respondents feel anonymous • Low cost • Good for ongoing research	• May take a long time for questionnaires to be returned • Low rate of response; many may not return questionnaires • Inflexible questionnaire • Length of questionnaire limited by respondent interest in the topic • Unclear whether respondents understand the questions • Unclear who is responding • No assurance that respondents are being honest
Telephone interviews	• Fast • High flexibility in questioning • Low cost • Limited interviewer follow-up	• Decreasing levels of respondent cooperation • Limited questionnaire length • High likelihood of respondent misunderstanding • Respondents cannot view materials • Cannot survey households without phones • Consumers screen calls with answering machines and caller ID • Do-not-call lists allow many research subjects to opt out of participation
Face-to-face interviews	• Flexibility of questioning • Can use long questionnaires • Can determine whether respondents have trouble understanding questions • Can use visuals or other materials	• High cost • Interviewer bias a problem • Take a lot of time
Online questionnaires	• Instantaneous data collection and analysis • Questioning very flexible • Low cost • No interviewer bias • No geographic restrictions • Can use visuals or other materials	• Unclear who is responding • No assurance that respondents are being honest • Limited questionnaire length • Unable to determine whether respondent is understanding the question • Self-selected samples

them with telephone sales messages, some unscrupulous telemarketers disguise their pitches as research. They contact consumers under the pretense of doing a study when, in fact, their real intent is to sell the respondent something or to solicit funds for some cause. This is called **outbound calling**, a strategy in which an organization calls prospects directly. This in turn prompts increasing numbers of people to use voice mail and caller ID to screen calls, which further reduces the response rate. And, as we noted earlier, the CRTC's *do-not-call list* allows many potential research subjects to opt out of participation both in legitimate marketing research and unscrupulous telemarketing.[17] Telemarketing also encompasses **inbound calling**. Very different from outbound calling, inbound calls are generated by advertising, publicity, or the efforts of outside salespeople. Customers would call in to gather more information, or simply to order a product and get a service of some sort. This is recognized as being a reactive strategy whereas outbound calling is considered to be more proactive.

outbound calling
Encompasses telemarketing, lead generating, and other steps necessary in the sales process.

inbound calling
A customer-initiated call to place an order or get some information about a product or a service.

In *face-to-face interviews*, a live interviewer asks questions of one respondent at a time. Although in "the old days" researchers often went door-to-door to ask questions, that's much less common today because of fears about security and because the large numbers of two-income families make it less likely to find people at home during the day. Typically, today's face-to-face interviews occur in a **mall intercept**—a study in which researchers recruit shoppers in malls or other public areas. You've probably seen this going on in your local mall, where a smiling person holding a clipboard stops shoppers to see if they are willing to answer a few questions.

mall intercept

A study in which researchers recruit shoppers in malls or other public areas.

Mall intercepts offer good opportunities to get feedback about new package designs, styles, or even reactions to new foods or fragrances. However, because only certain groups of the population frequently shop at malls, a mall-intercept study does not provide the researcher with a representative sample of the population (unless the population of interest is mall shoppers). In addition to being more expensive than mail or phone surveys, respondents may be reluctant to answer questions of a personal nature in a face-to-face context.

Online questionnaires are growing in popularity, but the use of such questionnaires is not without concerns. Many researchers question the quality of responses they will receive—particularly because (as with mail and phone interviews) no one can be really sure who is typing in the responses on the computer. In addition, it's uncertain whether savvy online consumers are truly representative of the general population.[18] However, these concerns are rapidly evaporating as research firms devise new ways to verify identities; present surveys in novel formats, including the use of images, sound, and animation; and recruit more diverse respondents.[19]

Observational Methods

As we said earlier, the second major primary data collection method is *observation*. This term refers to situations where the researcher simply records the consumer's behaviours.

When researchers use *personal observation*, they simply watch consumers in action to understand how they react to marketing activities. When they suspect that subjects will probably alter their behaviour if they know someone is watching them, researchers may use **unobtrusive measures** to record traces of physical evidence that remain after people have consumed something. For example, instead of asking a person to report on the alcohol products currently in her home, the researcher might go to the house and perform a "pantry check" by actually counting the bottles in her liquor cabinet. Another option is to sift through garbage to search for clues about each family's consumption habits. The "garbologists" can tell, for example, which soft drink accompanied what kind of food (Exhibit 3.3). Since people in these studies don't know that researchers are looking through products they've discarded, the information is totally objective—although a bit smelly!

unobtrusive measure

Measuring traces of physical evidence that remain after some action has been taken.

Mechanical observation is a primary data-collection method that relies on nonhuman devices to record behaviour. For example, one of the classic applications of mechanical observation is the Nielsen Company's famous use of "people meters"—boxes the company attaches to the television sets of selected viewers to record patterns of television watching. The data Nielsen obtains from these devices indicate who is watching which shows. These "television ratings" help network clients determine how much to charge advertisers for commercials and which shows to cancel or renew. The service is so popular that Nielsen tripled the size of its reporting panel between 2007 and 2011—currently about 12 000 homes are involved in the data collection in Canada.[20]

Online Research

The Internet rewrote some of the rules of the marketing research process. Many companies find that the Web is a superior way to collect data—it's fast, it's relatively cheap, and it lends itself well to forms of

© Louie Psihoyos/Science Faction/Corbis

Exhibit 3.3

Garbologists search for clues about consumption activities unobtrusively.

Tech and Trends

Measuring Multimedia Activity

Who watches old-fashioned TV anymore? As more and more people tune into Hulu or YouTube instead of catching their favourite shows on network television, TV ratings alone grossly underestimate actual viewership of program content. CTVglobemedia and Rogers Media were the Canadian broadcasters of the most recent Winter Olympics in Vancouver. But NBCUniversal, the American broadcaster for the games, used the occasion to do some groundbreaking market research. The company measured how viewers actually watched the games across the full array of diverse media platforms today, including mobile devices and the Web. "To some extent, these Olympics are starting to influence how people use new technology," said Alan Wurtzel, president of research and media development, NBCUniversal. "About half of people who used mobile [to watch NBC Olympics content] are using it for the first time."

As more people start to get information and entertainment from venues other than the living room TV, measuring the overall activity will play a large role in whether big networks such as NBC can get advertisers to pay significant dollars for it. To capture the full scope, the network unveiled a metric dubbed "TAMi," or *total audience measurement index*. The data capture in basic fashion the numbers of people watching Olympics content on TV, online, via mobile, and through video-on-demand. Results are far from perfect, and some of the numbers may represent duplication of viewership. Even so, NBC is rolling out TAMi across all its program offerings as a means of helping advertisers track cross-media promotions. "It gives you an insight that you normally wouldn't have about TV viewership across platforms," Wurtzel said.[21]

---

research from simple questionnaires to online focus groups. In fact, some large companies like Procter & Gamble now collect a large portion of their consumer intelligence online. Developments in online research are happening quickly, so let's take some time now to see where things are headed.

There are two major types of online research. One type is information we gather by tracking consumers while they surf the Web. The second type is information we gather through questionnaires on Web sites, through e-mail, or from focus groups that virtual moderators conduct in chat rooms.

The Internet offers an unprecedented ability to track consumers as they search for information. Marketers can better understand where people look when they want to learn about products—and which advertisements they stop to browse along the way. How can marketers do this? **Cookies** are text files a Web site sponsor inserts into a user's hard drive when the user connects with the site. Cookies remember details of a visit to a Web site and they track which pages the user visits. Some sites request or require that visitors "register" on the site by answering questions about themselves and their likes and dislikes. In such cases, cookies also allow the site to access these details about the customer.

cookie
Text file inserted by a Web site sponsor into a Web surfer's hard drive that allows the site to track the surfer's moves.

This technology allows Web sites to customize services, such as when Amazon.com recommends new books to users on the basis of what books they have ordered in the past. Consider this one. A shopper at the retail site figleaves.com takes a close look at a frilly pair of women's slippers. Next, a recommendation pops up for a man's bathrobe. Is this a mistake—or is the site showing the shopper just what she wanted to see? These surprising connections will happen more often as e-marketers adopt a newer generation of **predictive technology** that uses shopping patterns of large numbers of people to determine which products are likely to be purchased if others are. So, why the bathrobe? ATG, a Cambridge, Massachusetts, e-commerce software company that crunches data for figleaves.com, has found that certain types of female shoppers at certain times of the week are likely to be shopping for men. Like all Web recommendations, this one will be wrong a good portion of the time. But as marketers scrutinize online shoppers in greater detail, they're edging closer to their ultimate goal: teaching computers to blend data smarts with something close to the savvy of a flesh-and-blood sales clerk.[22] Most consumers have no idea that technologies such as cookies allow Web sites to gather and store all this information. You can block cookies or curb them, although this can make life difficult if you are trying to log on to many sites, such as online newspapers or travel agencies that require this information to admit you. The information generated from tracking consumers' online journeys has become a product as well—companies sell records to other companies that want to target prospects.

predictive technology
Analysis techniques that use shopping patterns of large numbers of people to determine which products are likely to be purchased if others are.

But consumers increasingly are concerned about the sharing of these data. In a study of 10 000 Web users, 84 percent objected to the reselling of their information to other companies. Although Internet users can delete cookie files manually or install anticookie software on their computers, many people feel there is a need for privacy regulation and for cookies to limit potential abuses.

The Canadian Marketing Association has worked on the Canadian privacy landscape for many years now and has been actively involved in various national and international forums discussing privacy issues and the protection of personal information.[23] Privacy rights proponents in Canada advocate the following guiding principles:

- Information about a consumer belongs to the consumer.

- Consumers should be made aware of information collection.

- Consumers should know how information about them will be used.

- Consumers should be able to refuse to allow information collection.

- Information about a consumer should never be sold or given to another party without the permission of the consumer.

No data collection method is perfect, and online research is no exception—though many of the criticisms of online techniques also apply to off-line techniques. One potential problem is the representativeness of the respondents. Although the number of Internet users continues to grow, many segments of the consumer population, mainly the poor and elderly, do not have equal access to the Internet. In addition, in many studies (just as with mail surveys or mall intercepts) there is a self-selection bias in the sample. That is, because respondents have agreed to receive invitations to take part in online studies, by definition they tend to be the kind of people who like to participate in surveys. As with other kinds of research, such as live focus groups, it's not unusual to encounter "professional respondents"—people who just enjoy taking part in studies (and getting paid for it). Online research specialists such as Harris Interactive, Survey Sampling International, and Greenfield Online address this problem by monitoring their participants and regulating how often they are allowed to participate in different studies over a period of time.

There are other disadvantages of online research. Hackers can actually try to influence research results. Competitors can learn about a firm's marketing plans, products, advertising, and so forth when they intercept information from these studies (though this can occur in off-line studies just as easily). Because cheating has become so rampant, some companies today use fraud-busting software that creates a digital fingerprint of each computer involved in a survey to identify respondents who fake responses or professionals who game the industry by doing as many surveys as possible.[24]

Data Quality: Garbage In, Garbage Out

We've seen that a firm can collect data in many ways, including focus groups, ethnographic approaches, observational studies, and controlled experiments. But how much faith should marketing managers place in what they find out from the research?

All too often, marketers who commission a study assume that because the researchers give them a massive report full of impressive-looking numbers and tables, they must be looking at the "truth." Unfortunately, there are times when this truth is really just one person's interpretation of the facts. At other times, the data researchers use to generate recommendations are flawed. As the expression goes, "Garbage in, garbage out!"[25] That is, your conclusions can only be as good as the information you use to make them. Typically, three factors influence the quality of research results—validity, reliability, and representativeness.

Validity is the extent to which the research actually measures what it was intended to measure. This was part of the problem underlying the famous New Coke fiasco in the 1980s, in which Coca-Cola underestimated people's loyalty to its flagship soft drink after it replaced

validity
The extent to which research actually measures what it was intended to measure.

"Old Coke" with a new, sweeter formula. In a blind taste test, the company assumed testers' preferences for one anonymous cola over another was a valid measure of consumers' preferences for a cola brand. Coca-Cola found out the hard way that measuring taste only is not the same as measuring people's deep allegiances to their favourite soft drinks. After all, Coke is a brand that elicits strong consumer loyalty and is nothing short of a cultural icon. Tampering with the flavours was like assaulting Mom and apple pie. Sales eventually recovered after the company brought back the old version as "Coca-Cola Classic."[26]

Reliability is the extent to which the research measurement techniques are free of errors. Sometimes, for example, the way a researcher asks a question creates error by biasing people's responses. Imagine that an attractive female interviewer working for Trojan condoms stopped male college students on campus and asked them if they used contraceptive products. Do you think their answers might change if they were asked the same questions on an anonymous survey they received in the mail? Most likely, their answers would be different because people are reluctant to disclose what they actually do when their responses are not anonymous. Researchers try to maximize reliability by thinking of several different ways to ask the same questions, by asking these questions on several occasions, or by using several analysts to interpret the responses. Thus, they can compare responses and look for consistency and stability.

Reliability is a problem when the researchers can't be sure the consumer population they're studying even understands the questions. For example, kids are difficult subjects for market researchers because they tend to be undependable reporters of their own behaviour, they have poor recall, and they often do not understand abstract questions. In many cases, the children cannot explain why they prefer one item over another (or they're not willing to share these secrets with grown-ups).[27] For these reasons, researchers have to be especially creative when they design studies involving younger consumers. Figure 3.6 shows part of a completion test a set of researchers used to measure children's preferences for television programming in Japan.

Representativeness is the extent to which consumers in the study are similar to a larger group in which the organization has an interest. This criterion underscores the importance of **sampling**—the process of selecting respondents for a study. The issue then becomes how large the sample should be and how to choose these people. We'll talk more about sampling in the next section.

reliability
The extent to which research measurement techniques are free of errors.

representativeness
The extent to which consumers in a study are similar to a larger group in which the organization has an interest.

sampling
The process of selecting respondents for a study.

probability sample
A sample in which each member of the population has some known chance of being included.

Step 4: Design the Sample

Once the researcher defines the problem, decides on a research design, and determines how to collect the data, the next step is to decide from whom to obtain the needed information. Of course, he or she *could* collect data from every single customer or prospective customer, but this would be extremely expensive and time consuming, if possible at all (this is what Statistics Canada spends millions of dollars to do every 5 years). Not everyone has the resources of the Canadian government to poll everyone in their market. So they typically collect most of their data from a small proportion or sample of the population of interest. Based on the answers from this sample, researchers generalize to the larger population. Whether such inferences are accurate or inaccurate depends on the type and quality of the study sample. There are two main types of samples: probability and nonprobability samples.

Probability Sampling

In a **probability sample**, each member of the population has some known chance of being included. Using a probability sample ensures that the sample represents the population and that inferences we make about the population from what members of the sample say or do are justified. For example, if a

Figure 3.6 Completion Test
It can be especially difficult to get accurate information from children. Researchers often use visuals such as this Japanese completion test to encourage children to express their feelings. The test asked boys to write in the empty balloon what they think the boy in the drawing will answer when the girl asks, "What program do you want to watch next?"

larger percentage of males than females in a probability sample say they prefer action movies to "chick flicks," one can infer with confidence that a larger percentage of males than females in the general population also would rather see a character get sliced and diced (okay, we wouldn't really use these descriptions in a study, but you get the idea).

The most basic type of probability sample is a *simple random sample* in which every member of a population has a known and equal chance of being included in the study. For example, if we simply take the names of all 40 students in your class and put them in a hat and draw one out, each member of your class has a one in 40 chance of being included in the sample. In most studies, the population from which the sample will be drawn is too large for a hat, so marketers use a computer program to generate a random sample from a list of members.

Sometimes researchers use a *systematic sampling procedure* to select members of a population; they select the nth member of a population after a random start. For example, if we want a sample of 10 members of your class, we might begin with the second person on the roll and select every fourth name after that—the 2nd, the 6th, the 10th, the 14th, and so on. Researchers know that studies that use systematic samples are just as accurate as those that use simple random samples. But unless a list of members of the population of interest is already in a computer data file, it's a lot simpler just to create a simple random sample.

Yet another type of probability sample is a *stratified sample*, in which a researcher divides the population into segments that relate to the study's topic. For example, imagine you want to study what movies most theatregoers like. You have learned from previous studies that men and women in the population differ in their attitudes toward different types of movies—men like action flicks and women like romances. To create a stratified sample, you would first divide the population into male and female segments. Then you would randomly select respondents from each of the two segments in proportion to their percentage of the population. In this way, you have created a sample that is proportionate to the population on a characteristic that you know will make a difference in the study results.

Nonprobability Sampling

nonprobability sample
A sample in which personal judgment is used to select respondents.

Sometimes researchers do not believe the time and effort required to develop a probability sample is justified, perhaps because they need an answer quickly or they just want to get a general sense of how people feel about a topic. They may choose a **nonprobability sample**, which entails the use of personal judgment to select respondents—in some cases they just ask whomever they can find. With a nonprobability sample, some members of the population have no chance at all of being included. Thus, there is no way to ensure that the sample is representative of the population. Results from nonprobability studies can be generally suggestive of what is going on in the real world but are not necessarily definitive.

convenience sample
A nonprobability sample composed of individuals who just happen to be available when and where the data are being collected.

A **convenience sample** is a nonprobability sample composed of individuals who just happen to be available when and where the data are being collected. For example, if you simply stand in front of the student association's office and ask students who walk by to complete your questionnaire, the "guinea pigs" you get to agree to do it would be a convenience sample.

Finally, researchers may also use a *quota sample* that includes the same proportion of individuals with certain characteristics as in the population. For example, if you are studying attitudes of students in your university, you might just go on campus and find first-, second-, third-, and fourth-year students in proportion to the number of members of each class in the university. The quota sample is much like the stratified sample except that with a quota sample, the researcher uses his or her individual judgment to select respondents.

Step 5: Collect the Data

At this point, the researcher has determined the nature of the problem she needs to address. She has decided on a research design that will specify how to investigate the problem and what kinds of information (data) she will need. The researcher has also selected the data collection and sampling methods. Once she has made these decisions, the next task is to actually collect the data.

Garbage (Collector) In, Garbage Out

We noted earlier that the quality of your conclusions is only as good as the data you use. The same logic applies to the people who collect the data: the quality of research results is only as good as the poorest interviewer in the study. Careless interviewers may not read questions exactly as written, or they may not record respondent answers correctly. So marketers must train and supervise interviewers to make sure they follow the research procedures exactly as outlined. In the next section, we'll talk about some of the problems in gathering data, and some solutions. (See Exhibit 3.4.)

Challenges to Gathering Data in Foreign Countries

Conducting market research around the world is big business for Canadian firms. In 2010, among the top Canadian research firms, a significant amount of revenue came from projects outside Canada.[28] Because international research is very costly, federal and provincial agencies also assist companies in market research abroad. However, market conditions and consumer preferences vary world-wide, and there are major differences in the sophistication of market research operations and the amount of data available to global marketers. In Mexico, for instance, because there are still large areas where native tribes speak languages other than Spanish, researchers may end up bypassing these groups in surveys. In Egypt, where the government must sign off on any survey, the approval process can take months or years. And in many developing countries, infrastructure is an impediment to executing phone or mail surveys and lack of online connectivity blocks Web-based research.

For these and other reasons, choosing an appropriate data collection method is difficult. In some countries, many people may not have phones, or low literacy rates may interfere with mail surveys. Understanding *local customs* can be a challenge, and *cultural differences* also affect responses to survey items. Both Danish and British consumers, for example, agree that it is important to eat breakfast. However, the Danish sample may be thinking of fruit and yogurt while the British sample has toast and tea in mind. Sometimes marketers can overcome these problems by involving local researchers in decisions about the research design.

Another problem with conducting marketing research in global markets is *language*. Sometimes translations just don't come out right. In some cases, entire subcultures within a country might be excluded from the research sample. In fact, this issue is becoming more and more prevalent inside Canada due to multiculturalism, as citizens for whom English is not their primary language increase as a percentage of the population.

To overcome language difficulties, researchers use a process of **back-translation**, which requires two steps. First, a native speaker translates the questionnaire into the language of the targeted respondents. Then they translate this new version back into the original language to ensure that the correct meanings survive the process. Even with precautions such as these, researchers must interpret data they obtain from other cultures with care.

Step 6: Analyze and Interpret the Data

Once marketing researchers collect the data, what's next? It's like a spin on the old "if a tree falls in the woods" question: "If results exist but there's no one to interpret them, do they

Exhibit 3.4
The Canadian Marketing Association has worked closely with its members and legislators to ensure marketing practices remain ethical and are deemed appropriate to Canadian consumers.

back-translation
The process of translating material to a foreign language and then back to the original language.

Ryan Garton

APPLYING ▽ Data Analysis

Ryan's decision relates to the process by which Discover will incorporate consumer data with other sources and how much weight each data component will carry when researchers process information from both internal and external sources.

have a meaning?" Well, let's leave the philosophers out of it and just say that marketers would answer "no." Data need interpretation if the results are going to be useful.

To understand the important role of data analysis, let's take a look at a hypothetical research example. Say a company that markets frozen foods wishes to better understand consumers' preferences for varying levels of fat content in their diets. They conducted a descriptive research study where they collected primary data via telephone interviews. Because they know that dietary preferences relate to gender, they used a stratified sample that included 175 males and 175 females.

Typically, marketers first tabulate the data as Table 3.4 shows—that is, they arrange the data in a table or other summary form so they can get a broad picture of the overall responses. The data in Table 3.4 show that 43 percent of the sample prefers a low-fat meal. In addition, there may be a desire to cross-classify or cross-tabulate the answers to questions by other variables. Cross-tabulation means that we examine the data we have broken down into subgroups, in this case males and females separately, to see how results vary between categories. The cross-tabulation in Table 3.4 shows that 59 percent of females versus only 27 percent of males prefer a meal with a low fat content. In addition, researchers may wish to apply additional statistical tests, which you'll probably learn about in subsequent courses (something to look forward to).

Based on the tabulation and cross-tabulations, the researcher interprets the results and makes recommendations. For example, the study results in Table 3.4 may lead to the conclusion that females are more likely than males to be concerned about a low-fat diet. Based on these data, the researcher might then recommend that the firm target females when it introduces a new line of low-fat foods.

Step 7: Prepare the Research Report

The final step in the marketing research process is to prepare a report of the research results. In general, a research report must clearly and concisely tell the readers—top management, clients, creative departments, and many others—what they need to know in a way that they can easily understand and that won't put them to sleep (kind of like a good textbook). A typical research report includes the following sections:

Table 3.4 | Examples of Data Tabulation and Cross-Tabulation Tables

Fat Content Preference (number and percentages of responses)		
Questionnaire Response	Number of Responses	Percentage of Responses
Do you prefer a meal with high fat content, medium fat content, or low fat content?		
High fat	21	6
Medium fat	179	51
Low fat	150	43
Total	350	100

Fat Content Preference by Gender (number and percentages of responses)						
Questionnaire Response	Number of Females	Percentage of Females	Number of Males	Percentage of Males	Total Number	Total Percentage
Do you prefer a meal with high fat content, medium fat content, or low fat content?						
High fat	4	2	17	10	21	6
Medium fat	68	39	111	64	179	51
Low fat	103	59	47	27	150	43
Total	175	100	175	100	350	100

- An executive summary of the report that covers the high points of the total report
- An understandable description of the research methods
- A complete discussion of the results of the study, including the tabulations, cross-tabulations, and additional statistical analyses
- Limitations of the study (no study is perfect)
- Conclusions drawn from the results and the recommendations for managerial action based on the results

Why do you think Ryan chose option 3?

Here's my choice. . .

Real **People**, Real **Choices**

1 Option **2** Option **3** Option

How It Worked Out at Discover Card

Discover went with Option 3. The firm's leadership decided it was worth taking on additional costs and delays to maximize the chances that consumers would adopt new card offerings. After all, a new product that bombs can cost a company millions of dollars, so investing up front to prevent this can be well worth the money and time.

Ryan's team undertook the first Innovation Screening in Discover's history. The company interviewed numerous marketing research companies and eventually selected Ipsos, which had impressive prior experience in working with clients from the financial services industry. This company also maintained an online panel that would allow them to create a statistically representative panel of over 1600 respondents who were current customers of Discover as well as those who used competing card products. The consumer panelists evaluated a total of 16 concepts: three benchmark cards (card products that Chase, Citibank, and American Express already had in the market), seven new product ideas, and six new feature ideas. Each respondent evaluated three concepts, for a total of about 300 evaluations per concept. In order to get at the true potential of the ideas, participants assessed them without being told which card company was thinking about introducing them. At a later point in the study, they rated the attractiveness of these ideas when they were paired with actual card companies.

The consumer research showed that, in fact, some of management's initial estimates about the likely appeal of new products were significantly off the mark. Some were less appealing than sponsors assumed, while some showed evidence of greater demand than Discover's internal finance teams predicted; one potential product moved from the back of the list to be Discover's highest priority based on this work. In addition, when the team tested some new offerings that competing card companies had recently launched, it found that they weren't all that appealing, and indeed, about a year later the other companies closed these down. Ryan was gratified that Discover lived up to its name and invested in discovering what its customers actually liked and disliked.

How Discover Card Measures Success

Discover Card developed a number of key metrics for its evaluation process. Consumers rated each new concept on these dimensions:

- Intent to sign up for the new product
- Intensity of liking for the product
- Price versus perceived value

- Uniqueness of the product versus competitive offers

- Believability

- Ability of the concept to fulfill a need compared to the card product already in use

The team went on to develop an IPP (intent for product purchase) index score that combined a consumer's responses to several of the key variables. It created a second index it called "Brand Right," which combined measures of brand fit and customer need. Brand fit is crucial; the team knew from past research that the best new offerings still require more marketing funds (advertising, direct mail, incentives, etc.) to gain acceptance if customers don't believe that they are consistent with an existing brand's image. It measured customer need through some questions in the study that related to whether or not respondents felt the product Discover was considering would fill a need that one of the cards they already used wasn't filling. For example, the respondent would be asked to indicate if "... this is a new idea that solves a problem for me today."

Then Ryan and the team plotted the IPP index against the "Brand Right" index to highlight to leadership which proposed products and services were likely to be a hit with consumers and to be best fits with Discover.

To learn the whole story, visit www.mypearsonmarketinglab.com.

Objective Summary ➥ Key Terms ➥ Apply

CHAPTER 3
Study Map

1. Objective Summary (pp. 90-94)

Explain the role of a marketing information system and a marketing decision support system in marketing decision making.

A marketing information system (MIS) is composed of internal data, marketing intelligence, marketing research data, acquired databases, and computer hardware and software. Firms use an MIS to gather, sort, analyze, store, and distribute information needed by managers for marketing decision making. The marketing decision support system (MDSS) allows managers to use analysis software and interactive software to access MIS data and to conduct analyses and find the information they need.

Key Terms

marketing research ethics, p. 90

marketing information system (MIS), p. 91

intranet, p. 92

marketing intelligence system, p. 92

marketing research, p. 92

syndicated research, p. 93

custom research, p. 93

marketing decision support system (MDSS), p. 94

2. Objective Summary (pp. 95-96)

Understand data mining and how marketers can put it to good use.

When marketers mine data, they methodically sift through large datasets, using computers that run sophisticated programs, to understand relationships among things like consumer buying decisions, exposure to marketing messages, and in-store promotions. Data mining leads to the ability to make important decisions about which customers to invest in further and which to abandon.

Key Terms

data mining, p. 95

3. Objective Summary (pp. 96-110)

List and explain the steps and key elements of the marketing research process.

The research process begins by defining the problem and determining the research design or type of study. Next, researchers choose the data-collection method; that is, whether there are secondary data available or if primary research with a communication study or through observation is necessary. Then researchers determine what type of sample is to be used for the study and collect the data. The final steps in the research are to analyze and interpret the data and prepare a research report.

Exploratory research typically uses qualitative data collected by individual interviews, focus groups, or observational methods such as ethnography. Descriptive research includes cross-sectional and longitudinal studies. Causal research goes a step further by designing controlled experiments to understand cause-and-effect relationships between independent marketing variables, such as price changes, and dependent variables, such as sales.

Researchers may choose to collect data via survey methods and observation approaches. Survey approaches include mail questionnaires, telephone interviews, face-to-face interviews, and online questionnaires. A study may use a probability sample such as a simple random or stratified sample, in which inferences can be made to a population on the basis of sample results. Nonprobability sampling methods include a convenience sample and a quota sample. The researcher tries to ensure that the data are valid, reliable, and representative.

Online research accounts for a rapidly growing proportion of all marketing research. Online tracking uses cookies to record where consumers go on a Web site. Consumers have become increasingly concerned about privacy and how this information is used and made available to other Internet companies. The Internet also provides an attractive alternative to traditional communication data-collection methods because of its speed and low cost. Many firms use the Internet to conduct online focus groups.

Key Terms

research design, p. 98

secondary data, p. 99

Chapter **Questions** and **Activities**

Concepts: Test Your Knowledge

1. What is a marketing information system (MIS)? What types of information are included in a marketing information system? How does a marketing decision support system (MDSS) allow marketers to easily get the information they need?

2. What is data mining? How is it used by marketers?

3. What are the steps in the marketing research process? Why is defining the problem to be researched so important to ultimate success with the research project?

4. What techniques are used to gather data in exploratory research? How can exploratory research be useful to marketers?

5. What are some advantages and disadvantages of telephone interviews, mail questionnaires, face-to-face interviews, and online interviews?

6. When considering data quality, what are the differences among validity, reliability, and representativeness? How do you know the data have high levels of these characteristics?

7. How do probability and nonprobability samples differ? What are some types of probability samples? What are some types of nonprobability samples?

8. What is a cross-tabulation? How are cross-tabulations useful in analyzing and interpreting data?

9. What is a cookie? What ethical and privacy issues are related to cookies?

10. What important issues must researchers consider when planning to collect their data online?

Activities: Apply What You've Learned

1. Your firm is planning to begin marketing a consumer product in several global markets. You have been given the responsibility of developing plans for marketing research to be conducted in South Africa, Spain, and China. In a role-playing situation, present the difficulties you expect to encounter, if any, in conducting research in each of these areas.

2. As an account executive with a marketing research firm, you are responsible for deciding on the type of research to be used in various studies conducted for your clients. For each of the following client questions, list your choices of research approaches.

   a. Will television or magazine advertising be more effective for a local bank to use in its marketing communication plan?
   b. Could a new package design for dry cereal do a better job of satisfying the needs of customers and, thus, increase sales?
   c. Are consumers more likely to buy brands that are labelled as environmentally friendly?
   d. How do female consumers determine if a particular perfume is right for them?
   e. What types of people read the local newspaper?
   f. How frequently do consumers switch brands of soft drinks?
   g. How will an increase in the price of a brand of laundry detergent affect sales?
   h. What are the effects of advertising and sales promotion in combination on sales of a brand of shampoo?

3. Your marketing research firm is planning to conduct surveys to gather information for a number of clients. Your boss has asked you and a few other new employees to do some preliminary work. She has asked each of you to choose three of the topics (from among those listed next) that will be included in the project and to prepare an analysis of the advantages and disadvantages of these communication methods of collecting data: mail questionnaires, telephone interviews, face-to-face interviews, and online questionnaires.

   a. The amount of sports nutrition drinks consumed in a city.
   b. Why a local bank has been losing customers.
   c. How heavily the company should invest in manufacturing and marketing home fax machines.
   d. The amount of money being spent "across the border" for lottery tickets.
   e. What local doctors would like to see changed in the city's hospitals.
   f. Consumers' attitudes toward several sports celebrities.

4. For each of the topics you selected in question 3, how might a more passive (observation) approach be used to support the communication methods employed?

Marketing Metrics: Exercise

It's a fact that many marketers tend to overly on click-through rates—basically, the mere number of pages a visitor to a Web site lands on—to provide a metric of the success of a firm's online/interactive marketing initiatives. According to Forrester senior analyst Emily Riley, "Brand marketers gravitate toward metrics that measure quantity, not quality. Clicks and impressions, metrics that are easy to track, measure little more than campaign volume."

Consider what you learned in this chapter about approaches to marketing research. What other two or three data collection approaches to measuring the success of a Web site might be fruitful in providing more meaningful data than just clicks? Hint: Even though the metric relates to the Web, non-Web-based research approaches may still be appropriate.

Choices: What Do You Think?

1. Some marketers attempt to disguise themselves as marketing researchers when their real intent is to sell something to the consumer. What is the impact of this practice on legitimate researchers? What do you think might be done about this practice?
2. Do you think marketers should be allowed to conduct market research with young children? Why or why not?
3. Are you willing to divulge personal information to marketing researchers? How much are you willing to tell, or where would you draw the line?
4. What is your overall attitude toward marketing research? Do you think it is a beneficial activity from a consumer's perspective? Or do you think it merely gives marketers new insights on how to convince consumers to buy something they really don't want or need?
5. Sometimes firms use data mining to identify and abandon customers who are not profitable because they don't spend enough to justify the service needed or because they return a large proportion of the items they buy. What do you think of such practices? Is it ethical for firms to prune out these customers?
6. Many consumers are concerned about online tracking studies and their privacy. Do consumers have the right to "own" data about themselves? Should governments limit the use of the Internet for data collection?
7. One unobtrusive measure mentioned in this chapter involved going through consumers' or competitors' garbage. Do you think marketers should have the right to do this? Is it ethical?
8. Consider the approach to tracking consumers' exposure to promotions via portable people meters, or PPMs. How would you feel about participating in a study that required you to use a PPM? What would be the advantage of a PPM approach versus keeping a written diary of television shows you watched and ads you saw?

Miniprojects: Learn by Doing

Miniproject 1

The purpose of this miniproject is to familiarize you with marketing research techniques and to help you apply these techniques to managerial decision making.

1. With a group of three other students in your class, select a small retail business or fast-food restaurant to use as a

"client" for your project. (Be sure to get the manager's permission before conducting your research.) Then choose a topic from among the following possibilities to develop a study problem:

- Employee–customer interactions
- The busiest periods of customer activity
- Customer perceptions of service
- Customer likes and dislikes about offerings
- Customer likes and dislikes about the environment in the place of business
- Benefits customers perceive to be important
- Age groups that frequent the place of business
- Buying habits of a particular age group
- How customer complaints are handled

2. Develop a plan for the research.

   a. Define the problem as you will study it.
   b. Choose the type of research you will use.
   c. Select the techniques you will use to gather data.
   d. Develop the mode and format for data collection.

3. Conduct the research.
4. Write a report (or develop a class presentation) that includes four parts:

   a. Introduction—a brief overview of the business and the problem studied
   b. Methods—the type of research used, the techniques used to gather data (and why they were chosen), the instruments and procedures used, the number of respondents, duration of the study, and other details that would allow someone to replicate your study
   c. Results—a compilation of the results (perhaps in table form) and the conclusions drawn

d. Recommendations—a list of recommendations for actions management might take based on the conclusions drawn from the study

Miniproject 2

As we discussed in this chapter, monitoring changes in demographics and other consumer trends is an important part of the marketing intelligence included in an MIS. Today, much of this information is gathered by government research and is available on the Internet.

Statistics Canada provides tabled data for cities and counties across the nation at its site, www.statcan.gc.ca. On the home page, choose Statistical Abstract. In addition, most provinces produce their own statistical abstract publications that are available on the Web. You should be able to locate the statistical abstract for your province by using a search engine such as Google and entering something like "Saskatchewan Statistical Abstract." Using both provincial data and Canadian census data, develop a report on a city or county of your choice that answers these questions:

1. What is the total population of the city or county?
2. Describe the population of the area in terms of age, income, education, ethnic background, marital status, occupation, and housing.
3. How does the city or county compare to the demographic characteristics of the entire Canadian population?
4. What is your opinion of the different Web sites you used? How useful are they to marketers? How easy were they to navigate? Was there information that you wanted that was not available? Was there more or less information from the sites than you anticipated? Explain.

Marketing in **Action** Case   Real Choices at IMMI

Marketing executives claim, "Half the money I spend on advertising is wasted; I just don't know which half." With more than half of all ad dollars spent on broadcast media like television and radio, advertisers need to have a way to determine the exposure and effectiveness of these media. The people meters and diaries that firms have used to track television and radio audiences for decades provide some estimates, but they do not track the other media (like the Internet) that are also key today.

Integrated Media Measurement Inc., also known as IMMI, uses existing technologies to measure broadcast audiences in a new way. IMMI recruits adults and teens, aged 13 to 54, to carry a special cell phone at all times for two years. The phone captures 10 seconds of audio from its surroundings every 30 seconds, 24 hours a day, seven days a week. The samples are then compressed into small digital files and uploaded to the company's servers where they are compared to samples of the media being measured using a technology called **acoustic matching**. This allows IMMI to measure the number of people

who have been exposed to an advertisement not only on television or radio but also on digital video recorders, game players, cell phones, DVDs, and CDs. Based on the data, IMMI produces real-time reports that get to individual behaviour, not just group averages, thus connecting advertising to consumer behaviour more accurately than possible with older methodologies. IMMI can answer questions such as the following: How many people are actually watching my network including outside the home and with time-shifting devices? How many people actually see my commercial? What songs cause radio listeners to change stations? What programs cause TV viewers to change channels?

Of course, IMMI's research methodology is not without potential problems. For example, IMMI only tracks audible media—not print or Internet advertising. Furthermore, many people are unwilling to participate in the study because they feel the technology is an invasion of their privacy. IMMI has been able to recruit an initial 3000 panelists, but it will have to

(continued)

Marketing in **Action** Case   Real Choices at IMMI

work hard to replenish that group when its two-year participation ends. While the cell phones only track broadcast media, many people are concerned that the company will also record their personal phone conversations.

For IMMI and for advertisers, the future is unclear. IMMI founders agree that this is not the last step in the attempt to more accurately understand media usage and advertising effectiveness. Surely better methodologies will follow. IMMI must consider its future and plan now in order to remain on top.

You Make the Call

1. What is the decision facing IMMI?
2. What factors are important in understanding this decision situation?
3. What are the alternatives?
4. What decision(s) do you recommend?
5. What are some ways to implement your recommendation?

Based on: "How It Works," http://immi.com/howItWorks.html; Jason Pontin, "Are Those Commercials Working? Just Listen," *New York Times,* September 9, 2007; http://immi.com;09stream.html.

Chapter 4

Consumer Behaviour:
How and Why We Buy

Real People **Profiles**

Julie Cordua

Profile

▼ A Decision Maker at (RED)

Julie Cordua was the vice president of marketing at (RED), a new brand created by U2 lead singer Bono and Bobby Shriver to engage business in the fight against AIDS in Africa. (RED) partners with the world's best brands to make uniquely branded products from which up to 50 percent of profits are directed to the Global Fund to finance African HIV/AIDS programs focusing on women and children. In her role at (RED), Julie was responsible for building the (RED) brand through innovative marketing programs, including public relations, advertising, events, and co-branding.

Prior to joining (RED), Julie spent the bulk of her career in marketing in the wireless industry. She was the senior director of buzz marketing and part of the startup team at HELIO, a new mobile brand for young, connected consumers. Before HELIO, Julie spent five years at Motorola in the Mobile Devices division in Chicago. At Motorola, she led the global category marketing group and was part of the team that orchestrated the RAZR launch in 2002.

Julie started her career in public relations at Hill & Knowlton in Los Angeles. She holds a BA in communications with an emphasis in business administration from UCLA and an MBA from the Kellogg School at Northwestern University. She currently is the Executive Director, DNA Foundation and lives in Manhattan Beach, California, with her husband.

Here's my problem...

(RED) is not a charity or "campaign." It is an economic initiative that aims to deliver a sustainable flow of private sector money to the Global Fund.

Launch product partners included Converse, Gap, Motorola, Emporio Armani, Apple, and American Express (UK only). In its first year, (RED) added Hallmark, Dell, and Microsoft as partners. These companies were chosen because they were strong international consumer brands that could drive significant awareness and sell large volumes of products. And, more importantly, they were the few brave companies that were willing to take a risk on the idea of (RED) before it was a proven concept.

By fall 2007, with a successful first year behind it, (RED) was evaluating how to ensure sustained success for the brand. Some of the main inputs Julie needed were more insights about how shoppers related to the (RED) concept and awareness of how to do social marketing/charity in general. The company had not done this research before launch, so Julie decided it was time to do an extensive consumer research study in the United States.

Specifically, Julie wanted to know what consumers thought about the following (and how their beliefs affected their purchasing/participation actions):

- A corporation's role in solving social issues
- Churches/community organizations' roles in solving social issues
- An individual's role in solving social issues (via donation or volunteering)
- Government's role in solving social issues
- Celebrity involvement in solving social issues
- The idea of combining charity with capitalism (buying and contributing at the same time)

The research project included three components: (1) interviews with a variety of consumers to qualitatively understand their thoughts on the relationship between shopping and charity and what they knew about (RED); (2) a nation-wide quantitative survey to identify major attitudinal and behavioural trends across the population; and (3) ethnographies where researchers spent time with people going about their daily lives, which helped bring some of the key learning from the survey to life.

The research showed that teens are the most open to the idea of cause marketing. This finding made sense to Julie; this is a group that has grown up with the idea of "creative capitalism" and has no concept of a separation between doing good and having what you want. Also, this group looks up to celebrities more than any other age segment; they cited famous people across music, film, TV, and sports as major influences on their opinions and behaviours. However, when describing how they relate to (RED), they often commented that the current partner brands were not relevant to them.

A surprisingly large portion of the population rejected the idea of combining charity and capitalism. These "traditionalists" believed that social issues were best taken care of by the government or churches and community organizations. They were highly skeptical of corporations that promoted an ability to do good by buying a product. These consumers wanted a more traditional way to get involved—donations, volunteering, or simply through paying taxes and allowing their government to address the issues.

With these insights in hand, Julie and her colleagues, including the head of business development, several outside advisors, and the CEO, had

Things to remember
A sizeable portion of consumers have strong negative attitudes toward big corporations. They don't necessarily want to deal with companies that are now aligned with (RED) as part of their charitable activities.

to decide if the (RED) model—partnering with mass market international brands for long-term deals—was the optimal way to generate the most money for the Global Fund.

Julie considered her **Options** 1·2·3

1 Option
Expand the (RED) model based on what the research revealed about the teen market. Complement the bigger deals involving mainstream brands with the introduction of smaller "special edition" deals with younger, more relevant brands. Engage celebrities that specifically appeal to the younger demographic. If young people bought into the concept now, this would build loyalty, and they would remain long-term fans of the brand. On the down side, this investment in smaller brands would require additional resources and divert (RED)'s small staff from its primary task of working with larger companies.

2 Option
Stick with the existing (RED) model. Continue to partner only with large, international brands that make significant marketing and contribution commitments. Use celebrity engagement to draw attention to (RED). This option would let (RED) tap into the growing sentiment toward combining charity and social enterprise. It would provide opportunities for significant exposure for (RED) through large-scale marketing programs.

On the other hand, this approach might alienate those who prefer more traditional avenues of giving to charity and might not give to the Global Fund. And, with such a mass-market approach, (RED) might not maximize engagement with the high-potential teen segment with its long-term value.

3 Option
Expand the (RED) model to include more traditional non-profit aspects, such as donation and volunteering, in order to appeal to all consumer groups and increase engagement. This would allow (RED) to expand its reach to a much broader audience and potentially drive more revenue for the Global Fund through donations. But such an expansion might create brand confusion since (RED) is all about shopping and doing good at the same time. Julie feared that the company might not be able to be "all things to all people" by appealing to both those who endorse the idea of "creative capitalism" and those who want to contribute via more traditional avenues.

Now, put yourself in Julie's shoes. Which option would you choose, and why?

You Choose

Which **Option** would you choose, and **why**?

1. ☐YES ☐NO **2.** ☐YES ☐NO **3.** ☐YES ☐NO

See what **option** Julie chose on **page 141** ➡

consumer behaviour
The process involved when individuals or groups select, purchase, use, and dispose of goods, services, ideas, or experiences to satisfy their needs and desires.

1

Decisions, Decisions

Nothing is more important than understanding consumers and how they make decisions when you need to plan marketing strategy. In this chapter, we'll look at the consumer decision-making process and the multitude of factors that influence those choices. And we'll show how understanding consumers boosts ROI, as these insights help marketers to figure out the best way to win customers by meeting their needs.

We include consumer insights in many parts of the marketing plan—from what type of product to offer to where to advertise. This knowledge is key when we select a target market. For example, Julie Cordua's understanding of (RED)'s consumer base showed her that teens were the most receptive to social marketing and thus an ideal target for the organization's message.

The Consumer Decision-Making Process

Compelling new products, clever packaging, and creative advertising surround us, clamouring for our attention—and our money. But consumers don't all respond in the same way. Each of us is unique, with our own reasons for choosing one product over another. Remember, the focus of the marketing concept is to satisfy consumers' wants and needs. To accomplish that crucial goal, first we need to appreciate what those wants and needs are. What causes one consumer to step into Boston Pizza for a huge cholesterol-laden meal, while another opts for a quick Starbucks latte and Danish pastry, and a third eats a healthy serving of "natural" Kashi cereal and fruit at Cora's? And what, other than income, will cause one consumer to buy that box of Kashi cereal only when it's "a deal" while her neighbour never even looks at the price?

Consumer behaviour is the process individuals or groups go through to select, purchase, use, and dispose of goods, services, ideas, or experiences to satisfy their needs and desires. Marketers recognize that consumer decision making is an ongoing process—it's much more than what happens at the moment a consumer forks over the cash and in turn receives a good or service.

Let's go back to the shoppers who want to buy a box of dry cereal. Although this may seem like a simple purchase, in reality the process includes quite a few steps that cereal marketers need to understand. The first decision is that of where to buy the cereal. If you eat a lot of it, you may choose to make a special trip to a warehouse-type retailer that sells supersized boxes rather than just pick up a box at the local supermarket. Of course, if you get a craving for cereal in the middle of the night, you may dash to the local convenience store. Then, there is deciding on the type of cereal. Do you eat only low-fat, high-fibre bran cereals, or do you go for the sugar-coated varieties with marshmallows? Of course, you may also like to have a variety of cereals available so you can "mix and match."

Marketers also need to know how and when you consume their products. Do you eat cereal only for breakfast, or do you snack on it while sitting in front of the TV at night? Do you eat certain kinds of cereal only at certain times (like sugary "kids' cereals" as comfort food when you're pulling an all-nighter)? What about storing the product (if it lasts long enough for that)? Do you have a kitchen pantry where you can store supersized boxes, or is space an issue?

And there's more. Marketers also need to understand the many factors that influence each of these steps in the consumer behaviour process—internal factors unique to each of us, situational factors at the time of purchase, and the social influences of people around us. In this chapter, we'll talk about how all these factors influence how and why consumers do what they do. But first we'll look at the types of decisions consumers make and the steps in the decision-making process.

Not All Decisions Are the Same

Traditionally, researchers assumed that we carefully collect information about competing products, determine which products possess the characteristics or attributes important to our needs, weigh the pluses and minuses of each alternative, and arrive at a satisfactory decision (Exhibit 4.1). But how accurate is this picture of the decision-making process? Is this the way you buy cereal?

Although it does seem that people take these steps when they make an important purchase such as a new car, is it realistic to assume that they do this for everything they buy, like that box of cereal? Today we realize that decision makers actually employ a set of approaches that range from painstaking analysis to pure whim, depending on the importance of what they are buying and how much effort they choose to put into the decision.[1] Researchers find it convenient to think in terms of an "effort" continuum that is anchored on one end by *habitual decision making*, such as the decision to purchase a box of cereal, and at the other end by *extended problem solving*, such as the decision to purchase a new car.

When consumers engage in extended problem solving, we do, indeed, carefully go through the steps outlined in Figure 4.1: problem recognition, information search, evaluation of alternatives, product choice, and postpurchase evaluation. When making habitual decisions, however, we make little or no conscious effort. We may not search much if at all for more information, and we may not bother to compare alternatives. Rather, we make the purchase automatically. You may, for example, simply throw the same brand of cereal in your shopping cart week after week without thinking about it. Figure 4.2 provides a summary of the differences between extended problem solving and habitual decision making.

Many decisions fall somewhere in the middle and are characterized by *limited problem solving*, which means that we do *some* work to make the decision but not a great deal. This probably describes how you decide on a new pair of running shoes or a new calculator for math class. We often rely on simple "rules of thumb" instead of painstakingly learning all the ins and outs of every product alternative. Rather than devoting a week of your life to learning all there is to know about calculators, you may use a simple rule like, buy a well-known electronics brand.

Just how much effort do we put into our buying decisions? The answer depends on our level of **involvement**—how important we perceive the consequences of the purchase to be. As a rule, we are more involved in the decision-making process for products that we think are risky in some way. **Perceived risk** may be present if the product is expensive or complex and hard to understand, such as a new computer or a sports car. Perceived risk also can play a role when we think that making a bad choice will result in embarrassment or social rejection. For example, a person who wears a pair of Crocs shoes on a job interview may jeopardize the job if the interviewer doesn't approve of his footwear.

When perceived risk is low, as when buying a box of cereal, we experience a small amount of involvement in the decision-making process. In these cases, we're not overly concerned about which option we choose because it is not especially important or risky. The worst-case scenario is that you don't like the taste and pawn off the box on your

Exhibit 4.1
Aldo shoes, made by a Canadian-founded company that operates world-wide, are very popular. What do consumers consider when buying shoes from Aldo? What kind of decision-making process do they go through?

involvement
The relative importance of perceived consequences of the purchase to a consumer.

perceived risk
The belief that choice of a product has potentially negative consequences, whether financial, physical, and/or social.

Figure 4.1 The Consumer Decision-Making Process
The consumer decision-making process involves a series of steps.

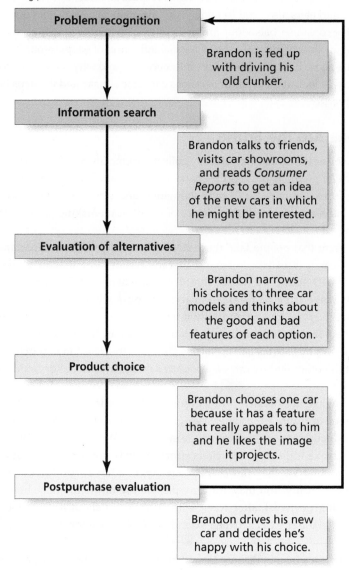

Figure 4.2 Extended Problem Solving versus Habitual Decision Making
Decisions characterized as extended problem solving versus habitual decision making differ in a number of ways.

	Extended Problem Solving	*Habitual Decision Making*
Product	New car	Box of cereal
Level of involvement	High (important decision)	Low (unimportant decision)
Perceived risk	High (expensive, complex product)	Low (simple, low-cost product)
Information processing	Careful processing of information (search advertising, magazines, car dealers, Web sites)	Respond to environmental cues (store signage or displays)
Learning model	Cognitive learning (use insight and creativity to use information found in environment)	Behavioural learning (ad shows product in beautiful setting, creating positive attitude)
Needed marketing actions	Provide information via advertising, salespeople, brochures, Web sites Educate consumers to product benefits, risks of wrong decisions, etc.	Provide environmental cues at point-of-purchase, such as product display

unsuspecting roommate! In *low-involvement* situations, the consumer's decision is often a response to environmental cues, such as when you decide to try a new type of cereal because the grocery store prominently displays it at the end of the aisle. Under these circumstances, managers must concentrate on how a product is displayed to influence the decision maker at the time of purchase. For example, a cereal marketer may decide to spend extra money to be sure its brand stands out in a store display or to feature a cool athlete like Olympic speed skater Clara Hughes on the box so consumers notice it (Exhibit 4.2).

For *high-involvement* purchases, such as when we buy a house or a car, we are more likely to carefully process all the available information and to have thought about the decision well before we buy the item. The consequences of the purchase are important and risky, especially because a bad decision may result in significant financial losses, aggravation, or embarrassment. Most of us would not just saunter into a real estate agent's office at lunchtime and casually plunk down a deposit on a new house. For high-involvement products, managers must start to reduce perceived risk by educating the consumer about why their product is the best choice well in advance of the time that the person is ready to make a decision.

To understand each of the steps in the decision-making process, we'll follow the fortunes of a consumer named Brandon, who, as Figure 4.1 shows, is in the market for a new ride—a highly involving purchase decision, to say the least.

Exhibit 4.2
Clara Hughes, a highly successful Canadian athlete, can be displayed on many different products.

Step 1: Problem Recognition

Problem recognition occurs whenever a consumer sees a significant difference between his or her current state of affairs and some desired or ideal state. A woman whose 10-year-old Hyundai lives at the mechanic's shop has a problem, as does the man who thinks he'd have better luck getting dates if he traded his Hyundai in for a new sports car. Brandon falls into the latter category—his old clunker runs okay, but he wants to sport some wheels that will get him admiring stares instead of laughs.

Do marketing decisions have a role in consumers' problem recognition? Although most problem recognition occurs spontaneously or when a true need arises, marketers often develop creative advertising messages that stimulate consumers to recognize that their current state (that old car) just doesn't equal their desired state (a shiny, new convertible). Figure 4.3 provides examples of marketers' responses to consumers' problem recognition and the other steps in the consumer decision-making process.

problem recognition
The process that occurs whenever the consumer sees a significant difference between his current state of affairs and some desired or ideal state; this recognition initiates the decision-making process.

Step 2: Information Search

Once Brandon recognizes his problem—he wants a newer car!—he needs adequate information to resolve it. **Information search** is the step of the decision-making process in which the consumer checks his memory and surveys the environment to identify what options are out there that might solve his problem. Advertisements in newspapers, on TV, or on the radio, information we "Google" on the Internet, or a video we find on YouTube often provide valuable guidance during this step. Brandon might rely on recommendations from his friends, Facebook drivers' clubs, information he finds at www.caranddriver.com, in brochures from car dealerships, or on the manufacturers' Web sites.

information search
The process whereby a consumer searches for appropriate information to make a reasonable decision.

The Internet as a Search Tool

Increasingly, consumers use the Internet to search for information about products. Search engines, sites such as Google (www.google.com) and Bing (www.yahoo.ca), help us locate useful information as they search millions of Web pages for key words and return a list of sites that contain those key words.

Figure 4.3 Responses to Decision-Process Stages

Understanding the consumer decision process means marketers can develop strategies to help move the consumer from recognizing a need to being a satisfied customer.

Stage in the Decision Process	Marketing Strategy	Example
Problem recognition	Encourage consumers to see that existing state does not equal desired state	• Create TV commercials showing the excitement of owning a new car
Information search	Provide information when and where consumers are likely to search	• Target advertising on TV programs with high target-market viewership • Provide sales training that ensures knowledgeable salespeople • Make new-car brochures available in dealer showrooms • Design exciting, easy-to-navigate, and informative Web sites • Provide information on blogs and social networks to encourage word-of-mouth strategies • Use search marketing to ensure that your Web site has preferential search engine positioning • Participate in consumer review/advisory Web sites such as caranddriver.com
Evaluation of alternatives	Understand the criteria consumers use in comparing brands and communicate own brand superiority	• Conduct research to identify most important evaluative criteria • Create advertising that includes reliable data on superiority of a brand (e.g., fuel efficiency, safety, comfort)
Product choice	Understand choice heuristics used by consumers and provide communication that encourages brand decision	• Advertise "Made in Canada" (country of origin) • Stress long history of the brand (brand loyalty)
Postpurchase evaluation	Encourage accurate consumer expectations	• Provide honest advertising and sales presentations

search marketing
Marketing strategies that involve the use of Internet search engines.

search engine optimization (SEO)
A systematic process of ensuring that your firm comes up at or near the top of lists of typical search phrases related to your business.

search engine marketing (SEM)
Search marketing strategy in which marketers pay for ads or better positioning.

Of course, the problem for marketers is that consumers seldom follow up on more than a page or two of results they get from these searches—we're all bombarded by too much information these days to ever look at all of it. This has led marketers to develop sophisticated **search marketing** techniques. With **search engine optimization (SEO),** marketers first find what key words consumers use most in their searches. Then they edit their site's content or HTML to increase its relevance to those key words so they can try to place their site high up in the millions of sites the search might generate. With **search engine marketing (SEM),**

Ethical and Sustainable Decisions in the Real World

Considering a new TV? What brand is best? Will you be happy with the new state-of-the-art, 50-inch Samsung 3D or should you go with the lower-priced Sylvania? Many consumers turn to Internet review sites such as Epinions, Google, FourSquare, and Yelp to help them make important purchase decisions. Sites that provide customer reviews of products and retailers are sprouting up all over, as research has shown that these sites do influence consumers' purchases. Retailers such as Best Buy and Walmart even advertise the availability of customer reviews on their own Web sites. But buyer beware—review sites are not without their critics.

Consumers who use review Web sites assume the reviews are written by ordinary consumers who are "just like me." In reality, some reviews may be written by the companies that produce the products. And there are other issues as well. At least one review site has been accused of allowing businesses that advertise on their site to give better placement to positive reviews of their products, while placing negative reviews at the bottom where consumers are less likely to see them. Other companies say they have been pressured to buy advertising on the review site, and some have claimed that their ratings actually fell when they refused to be a paid advertiser. As a marketer, what would you do?

ETHICS CHECK: 🖎
Find out what other students taking this course **would do** and **why** on **www.mypearsonmarketinglab.com**

What policies should review sites have toward companies that do and that do not advertise on their sites? If your business were reviewed on a Web site, would you buy advertising in order to get preferential treatment?

☐ **YES** ☐ **NO**

---

the search engine company charges marketers to display **sponsored search ads** that appear at the top or beside the search results.

Comparison shopping agents (or shopbots) such as Shopzilla.com and NexTag.com are Web applications that can help online shoppers to find what they are looking for at the lowest price. In addition to listing where a product is available and the price, these sites often provide customer reviews and ratings of the product and the sellers. They enable consumers to view both positive and negative feedback about the product and the online retailer from other consumers. Increasingly, consumers also search out other consumers' opinions and experience through networking Web sites, such as YouTube and Facebook. We'll talk more about these sites and others similar to them later in the chapter.

Behavioural Targeting

During information search, the marketer's goal is to make the information consumers want and need about their product easily accessible. The challenge today is in getting the right message to the right consumer. One answer to this challenge is **behavioural targeting**, a strategy that presents individuals with advertisements based on their Internet use. In other words, with today's technology it has become fairly easy for marketers to tailor the ads you see to Web sites you've visited.

Cable TV stations offer the newest behavioural targeting strategy.[2] Using existing systems in digital set-top boxes, cable companies can deliver ads to specific households based on such demographic data as income, ethnicity, gender, and household size. For example, an ad for diapers would only go to households with infants, while one for the Lexus SC convertible (starting price of over $68 000) would target high-income households. In addition, a viewer will be able to press a button on her remote to get more information about a product, see a movie trailer, view a demonstration video of a new product, or order a sample or a coupon.

Some critics regard this as a mixed blessing because of privacy issues. While most agree that using demographic information is acceptable, many fear that viewing habits will be tracked and also used in behavioural targeting. What do you think?

Step 3: Evaluation of Alternatives

Once Brandon has identified his options, it's time to decide on a few true contenders. There are two components to this stage of the decision-making process. First, a consumer armed with information identifies a small number of products in which he is interested. Then, he narrows down his choices by first deciding which of the possibilities are feasible and then comparing the pros and cons of each remaining option.

sponsored search ads
Paid ads that appear at the top or beside the Internet search engine results.

comparison shopping agents (shopbots)
Web applications that help online shoppers find what they are looking for at the lowest price and provide customer reviews and ratings of products and sellers.

behavioural targeting
The marketing practice by which marketers deliver advertisements for products a consumer is looking for by watching what the consumer does online.

Brandon has always wanted a red Ferrari. But, after he allows himself to daydream for a few minutes, he returns to reality and reluctantly admits that an Italian sports car is probably not in the cards for him right now. He decides that the cars he likes, and can actually afford, are the Scion, the Ford Focus, and the Honda Element. He has narrowed down his options by considering only affordable cars that come to mind or that his buddies suggest.

Now it's decision time! Brandon has to look more systematically at each of the three possibilities and identify the important characteristics, or **evaluative criteria**, that he will use to decide among them. The criteria may be power, comfort, price, the style of the car, and even safety. Keep in mind that marketers often play a role in educating consumers about which product characteristics they should use as evaluative criteria—usually they will "conveniently" emphasize the dimensions in which their product excels. To make sure customers like Brandon come to the "right" conclusions in their evaluation of the alternatives, marketers must understand which criteria consumers use, and which are more or less important. With this information, sales and advertising professionals can point out a brand's superiority on the most important criteria as *they* have defined them.

Step 4: Product Choice

When Brandon examines his alternatives and takes a few test drives, it's time to "put the pedal to the metal." Deciding on one product and acting on this choice is the next step in the decision-making process. After agonizing over his choice for a few weeks, Brandon decides that even though the Element and the Scion have attractive qualities, the Focus has the affordability he needs, and its carefree image is the way he wants others to think of him. All this thinking about cars is "driving" him crazy, and he's relieved to make a decision to buy the Focus and get on with his life.

So, just how do consumers like Brandon choose among the alternatives they consider? These decisions often are complicated because it's hard to juggle all the product characteristics in your head; one car offers better gas mileage, another is $2000 cheaper, while another boasts a better safety record. How do we make sense of all these qualities and arrive at a decision?

We saw earlier that consumers often rely on decision guidelines when they weigh the merits of competing brand claims that companies make. These **heuristics,** or mental rules-of-thumb, provide consumers with shortcuts that simplify the decision-making process. One such heuristic is "price = quality"; many people willingly buy the more expensive brand because they assume that if it costs more, it must be better (even though this isn't always true).

Perhaps the most common heuristic is **brand loyalty**; this occurs when we buy the same brand over and over, and as you can guess, it's the Holy Grail for marketers. Consumers who have strong brand loyalty feel that it's not worth the effort to consider competing options. People form a preference for a favourite brand and then may never change their mind in the course of a lifetime. Needless to say, this makes it extremely difficult for rivals to persuade them to switch.

Still another heuristic is based on *country-of-origin*. We assume that a product has certain characteristics if it comes from a certain country (Exhibit 4.3). In the car category, many people associate German cars with fine engineering and Swedish cars with safety. Brandon assumed that the Japanese-made Honda would be a bit more reliable than the Ford, so he factored that into his decision.

Sometimes a marketer wants to encourage a country association even when none exists. For example, Canadian-based firm lululemon athletica offers consumers an attractive, trendy, almost European-sounding line of athletic clothing. Häagen-Dazs ice cream comes from that exotic Scandinavian area that is . . . New Jersey.

evaluative criteria
The dimensions consumers use to compare competing product alternatives.

heuristics
A mental rule of thumb that leads to a speedy decision by simplifying the process.

brand loyalty
A pattern of repeat product purchases, accompanied by an underlying positive attitude toward the brand, based on the belief that the brand makes products superior to those of its competition.

Step 5: Postpurchase Evaluation

In the last step of the decision-making process, the consumer evaluates just how good a choice he made. Everyone has experienced regret after making a purchase ("What was I *thinking*?"), and (hopefully) we have all been pleased with something we've bought. The evaluation of the product results in a level of **consumer satisfaction/dissatisfaction**. This refers to the overall feelings, or attitude, a person has about a product after she purchases it.

Just how do we decide if we're satisfied with what we bought? The obvious answer would be, that's easy—the product is either wonderful or it isn't. However, it's a little more complicated than that. When we buy a product, we have some *expectations* of product quality. How well a product or service meets or exceeds these expectations determines customer satisfaction. In other words, we tend to assess product quality by comparing what we have bought to a pre-existing performance standard. We form this standard via a mixture of information from marketing communications, informal information sources such as friends and family, and our own prior experience with the product category. That's why it's very important that marketers create accurate expectations of their product in advertising and other communications.

Even when a product performs to expectations, consumers may suffer anxiety or regret, or **cognitive dissonance,** after making a purchase. When we have rejected product alternatives with attractive features, we may second-guess our decision. Brandon, for example, might begin to think, "maybe I should have chosen the Honda Element—everyone says Hondas are great cars." To generate satisfied customers and remove dissonance, marketers often seek to reinforce purchases through direct mail or other personalized contacts after the sale.

So, even though Brandon's new Focus is not exactly as powerful as a Ferrari, he's still happy with the car, because he never really expected a fun little car to eat up the highway like a high-performance sports car that costs ten times as much. Brandon has "survived" the consumer decision-making process: he recognized a problem, conducted an informational search to resolve it, identified the (feasible) alternatives available, made a product choice, and then evaluated the quality of the decision.

Apart from understanding the mechanics of the consumer decision-making process, marketers also try to ascertain what influences in consumers' lives affect this process. There are three main categories: internal, situational, and social influences. In Brandon's case, for example, the evaluative criteria he used to compare cars and his feelings about each were influenced by

1. Internal factors such as the connection he learned to make between a name like Ford Focus and an image of "slightly hip, yet safe and solid"

2. Situational factors such as the way the Ford salesperson treated him

3. Social influences such as his prediction that his friends would be impressed when they saw him cruising down the road in his new wheels.

Figure 4.4 shows the influences in the decision-making process and emphasizes that all these factors work together to affect the ultimate choice each person makes. Now, let's consider how each of these three types of influences work, starting with internal factors.

Courtesy of Roots Canada Ltd.

Exhibit 4.3

Roots, established in 1973, is a recognizably Canadian brand. There are Roots stores throughout Canada, in the United States, and in Asia.

consumer satisfaction/dissatisfaction
The overall feelings, or attitude, a person has about a product after she purchases it.

cognitive dissonance
The anxiety or regret a consumer may feel after choosing from among several similar attractive choices.

Figure 4.4 Influences on Consumer Decision Making

A number of different factors in consumers' lives influence the consumer decision-making process. Marketers need to understand these influences and which ones are important in the purchase process.

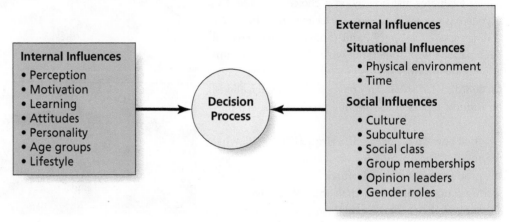

2 Internal Influences on Consumers' Decisions

OBJECTIVE

Explain how internal factors influence consumers' decision-making processes.
(pp. 128–134)

Like Brandon, your dream car may be a sporty Ferrari. However, your roommate dreams of a pimped-out Escalade and your dad is set on owning a big Mercedes. As the saying goes, "That's why they make chocolate and vanilla." We can attribute much of these differences in opinion to internal influences on consumer behaviour—those things that cause each of us to interpret information about the outside world, including which car is the best, differently from one another. Let's see how internal factors relating to the way people absorb and interpret information influence the decision-making process.

Perception

perception
The process by which people select, organize, and interpret information from the outside world.

Perception is the process by which people select, organize, and interpret information from the outside world. We receive information in the form of sensations, the immediate response of our sensory receptors—eyes, ears, nose, mouth, and skin—to basic stimuli such as light, colour, odour, touch, and sound. We try to make sense of the sensations we receive as we interpret them in light of our past experiences. For example, when we encounter a new product, we look at and perhaps touch the product or its package. Then we interpret that product based on our past experiences—or lack of experiences—with similar products.

Take the computer keyboard, for example. When typewriters were introduced in the 1870s, the keys got stuck if you typed too fast. Then in 1874, an inventor named Christopher Latham Sholes developed the QWERTY keyboard (named for the first six letters on the top row); this layout arranged the letters of the alphabet so that it decreased how fast a person could type. We don't have physical keys in computers and cell phones, so why do we still use QWERTY keyboards? Because we're used to them and it would be a hassle to learn a different configuration.

We are bombarded with information about products—thousands of ads, in-store displays, special offers, our friends' opinions, and on and on. The perception process has important implications for marketers: As we absorb and make sense of the vast quantities of information that compete for our attention, the odds are that any single message will get lost in the clutter. And, if we do notice the message, there's no guarantee that the meaning we give it will be the same one the marketer intended. The issues that marketers need to understand during this process include *exposure*, *attention*, and *interpretation*.

Exposure

The stimulus must be within range of people's sensory receptors to be noticed; in other words, people must be physically able to see, hear, taste, smell, or feel the stimulus. For example, the lettering on a highway billboard must be big enough for a passing motorist to read easily, or the message will be lost. **Exposure** is the extent to which a person's sensory receptors are capable of registering a stimulus.

Many people believe that even messages they can't see will persuade them to buy advertised products. Claims about **subliminal advertising**, messages hidden in ice cubes (among other places), have been surfacing since the 1950s. Canadian food retailers like Loblaw, Sobeys, Metro, and Safeway are known to use scent, music, and even lighting to lure consumers to buy products they may not really need. There is very little evidence to support the argument that this technique actually has any effect at all on our perceptions of products. But still, concerns persist. Most recently, Ferrari was accused of having a logo that sported a barcode design, which in turn looked like the logo of Marlboro, a well-known tobacco company. For a few years now, many countries around the world have prevented tobacco companies from sponsoring major sporting and social events. Ferrari actually decided to remove the barcode in 2010,[3] but no evidence is available to suggest that Ferrari's logo did in fact generate more sales for Marlboro. The short story is, hidden messages are intriguing and fun to think about (if a little scary), but they don't work. Sorry for the letdown.

Information search is often an ongoing process, and this stage may be more extensive and intensive for some consumers than others. It ends with the identification of alternatives for consideration, called the **consideration set**.

Evaluation of Alternatives

Once consumers have identified the set of products they are interested in, they narrow down their choices by deciding which of all the possibilities are feasible and evaluating the remaining alternatives. Emma might want a top-of-the-line notebook, like a Dell XPS, but she realizes that her student budget doesn't allow for such a purchase. As she looks around, she decides that the notebooks she likes in her price range are the Apple MacBook, the Compaq Presario, and the Gateway Solo. She has narrowed down her options by considering only affordable notebooks.

Now, Emma has to choose. It's time for her to look more systematically at each of the three possibilities and identify the important characteristics, or evaluative criteria, she will

exposure
The extent to which a stimulus is capable of being registered by a person's sensory receptors.

subliminal advertising
Supposedly hidden messages in marketers' communications.

consideration set
The set of alternative brands the consumer is considering for the decision process.

Marketing Metrics

Clickstream Analysis

Conventional Internet metrics have relied on counting the number of eyeballs viewing a Web site. Research shows, however, that conversion rates and average order value are better measures for a Web site's success. A new method allows companies to conduct funnel-based analysis of where revenue is lost when consumers drop off. One such method is **clickstream analysis**, which helps companies analyze where customers enter their Web sites and where they exit. The managers at Playboy.com are using clickstream data to increase site subscription and convert free visitors into paying members. Play boy.com can now examine exactly where it converts customers on the Web site and where it loses them by specifically tracking each user's movements around the site. The company receives reports from the clickstream provider about how traffic comes in from other Web sites, how the site compares with those of competitors, and where conversions are specifically failing.[4]

clickstream analysis
A means of measuring a Web site's success by tracking customers' movement around the site.

use to decide among them. These may be the power of the computer, its weight, the size of the monitor, the battery life, the warranty offered, or even the computer's design or colour options. During her evaluation, Emma learns that the Apple product, the MacBook, seems to her to have a lot of the features she is looking for. It appears that it has all the great features of other notebooks, but with much greater speed.

Marketers often play a role in educating consumers about which product characteristics should be used as evaluative criteria—usually, they emphasize the dimensions in which their product excels. Where Compaq Presario might focus on price because it is one of the least expensive notebook computers available, Apple is educating consumers about the value of their new operating system.

Attention

attention
The extent to which a person devotes mental processing to a particular stimulus.

As you drive down the highway, you pass hundreds of other cars. But to how many do you pay attention? Probably only one or two—the bright pink and purple VW Bug and the Honda with the broken taillight that cut you off at the exit ramp. **Attention** is the extent to which we devote mental-processing activity to a particular stimulus. Consumers are more likely to pay attention to messages that speak to their current needs. For example, you're far more likely to notice an ad for a fast-food restaurant when you're hungry, while smokers are more likely than non-smokers to block out messages about the health hazards of smoking.

Grabbing consumers' attention is becoming harder than ever, because people's attention spans are shorter than ever. Now that we are accustomed to *multitasking*, flitting back and forth between our e-mails, TV, IMs, and so on, advertisers have to be more creative by mixing up the types of messages they send. That's why we see, on the one hand, long (60-second) commercials that almost feel like miniature movies and short (some as brief as five seconds) messages that are meant to have surprise value—they are usually over before commercial-haters can zap or zip past them. Indeed, brief blurbs that are long enough to tantalize viewers but short enough not to bore them are becoming commonplace. In contrast to the old days when most commercials on television networks were 30-second spots, today more than one-third run for only 15 seconds.[5]

Interpretation

interpretation
The process of assigning meaning to a stimulus based on prior associations a person has with it and assumptions he or she makes about it.

Interpretation is the process of assigning meaning to a stimulus based on prior associations we have with it and assumptions we make about it. Extra Strength Maalox Whip Antacid flopped, even though a spray can is a pretty effective way to deliver this kind of tummy ache relief. But to consumers, aerosol whips mean dessert toppings, not medication.[6] If we don't interpret the product the way it was intended because of our prior experiences, the best marketing ideas will be "wasted."

Motivation

motivation
An internal state that drives us to satisfy needs by activating goal-oriented behaviour stimulus.

Motivation is an internal state that drives us to satisfy needs. Once we activate a need, a state of tension exists that drives the consumer toward some goal that will reduce this tension by eliminating the need.

Think again about Brandon and his old car. He began to experience a gap between his present state (he owns an old car) and a desired state (he craves a car that gets him noticed and is fun to drive). This activated the need for a new car, which in turn motivated Brandon to test different models, to talk with friends about different makes, and finally to buy a new car.

hierarchy of needs
An approach that categorizes motives according to five levels of importance, the more basic needs being on the bottom of the hierarchy and the higher needs at the top.

Psychologist Abraham Maslow developed an influential approach to motivation.[7] He formulated a **hierarchy of needs** that categorizes motives according to five levels of importance, the more basic needs being on the bottom of the hierarchy and the higher needs at the top. The hierarchy suggests that before a person can meet needs at a given level, he

Figure 4.5 Maslow's Hierarchy of Needs and Related Products

Abraham Maslow proposed a hierarchy of needs that categorizes motives. Savvy marketers know they need to understand the level of needs that motivates a consumer to buy a particular product or brand.

Hobbies, travel, education (U.S. Army—"Be all you can be.")

Cars, furniture, credit cards, stores, country clubs, liquors (Royal Salute Scotch—"What the rich give the wealthy.")

Clothing, grooming products, clubs, drinks (Pepsi—"You're in the Pepsi generation.")

Insurance, alarm systems, retirement investments (Allstate Insurance—"You're in good hands with Allstate.")

Medicines, staple items, generics (Quaker Oat Bran—"It's the right thing to do.")

Higher-Level Needs

Self-Actualization
Self-fulfillment, enriching experiences

Ego Needs
Prestige, status, accomplishment

Belongingness
Love, friendship, acceptance by others

Safety
Security, shelter, protection

Physiological
Water, sleep, food

Lower-Level Needs

Source: Maslow's Hierarchy of Needs and Related Products—Maslow's *Hierarchy of Needs: Motivation and Personality,* 3rd ed., by A.H. Maslow, 1987. Reprinted by permission of Prentice Hall, Inc., Upper Saddle River, NJ.

must first meet the lower level needs—somehow those hot new Seven jeans don't seem as enticing when you don't have enough money to buy food.

As you can see from Figure 4.5, people start at the lowest level with basic physiological needs for food and sleep. Then they progress to higher levels to satisfy more complex needs, such as the need to be accepted by others or to feel a sense of accomplishment. Ultimately, they can reach the highest-level needs, where they will be motivated to attain such goals as self-fulfillment. As the figure shows, if marketers understand the level of needs relevant to consumers in their target market, they can tailor their products and messages to them.

Learning

Learning is a change in behaviour caused by information or experience. Learning about products can occur deliberately, as when we set out to gather information about different MP3 players before we buy one brand. We also learn even when we don't try. Consumers recognize many brand names and can hum many product jingles, for example, even for products they themselves do not use. Psychologists who study learning have advanced several theories to explain the learning process, and these perspectives are important because a major goal for marketers is to "teach" consumers to prefer their products. Let's briefly review the most important perspectives on how people learn.

Behavioural Learning

Behavioural learning theories assume that learning takes place as the result of connections we form between events. In one type of behavioural learning, **classical conditioning**, a person perceives two stimuli at about the same time. After a while, the person transfers his response from one stimulus to the other. For example, an ad shows a product and a breathtakingly beautiful scene so that (the marketer hopes) you will transfer the positive feelings you get when you look at the scene to the advertised product. Hint: Did you ever notice that

learning
A relatively permanent change in behaviour caused by acquired information or experience.

behavioural learning theories
Theories of learning that focus on how consumer behaviour is changed by external events or stimuli.

classical conditioning
The learning that occurs when a stimulus eliciting a response is paired with another stimulus that initially does not elicit a response on its own but will cause a similar response over time because of its association with the first stimulus.

operant conditioning
Learning that occurs as the result of rewards or punishments.

cognitive learning theory
Theory of learning that stresses the importance of internal mental processes and that views people as problem solvers who actively use information from the world around them to master their environment.

observational learning
Learning that occurs when people watch the actions of others and note what happens to them as a result.

attitude
A learned predisposition to respond favourably or unfavourably to stimuli on the basis of relatively enduring evaluations of people, objects, and issues.

affect
The feeling component of attitudes; refers to the overall emotional response a person has to a product.

cognition
The knowing component of attitudes; refers to the beliefs or knowledge a person has about a product and its important characteristics.

behaviour
The doing component of attitudes; involves a consumer's intention to do something, such as the intention to purchase or use a certain product.

car ads often show a new auto on a beautiful beach at sunset or speeding down a mountain road with brightly coloured leaves blowing across the pavement?

Another common form of behavioural learning is **operant conditioning**, which occurs when people learn that their actions result in rewards or punishments. This feedback influences how they will respond in similar situations in the future. Just as a rat in a maze learns the route to a piece of cheese, consumers who receive a reward, such as a prize in the bottom of a box of cereal, will be more likely to buy that brand again. We don't like to think that marketers can train us like lab rats, but that kind of feedback does reward us for the behaviour. Will that be Havarti or Swiss for you?

Cognitive Learning

In contrast to behavioural theories of learning, **cognitive learning theory** views people as problem solvers who do more than passively react to associations between stimuli. Supporters of this viewpoint stress the role of creativity and insight during the learning process. *Cognitive learning* occurs when consumers make a connection between ideas, or by observing things in their environment.

Observational learning occurs when people watch the actions of others and note what happens to them as a result. They store these observations in memory and at some later point use the information to guide their own behaviour. Marketers often use this process to create advertising and other messages that allow consumers to observe the benefits of using their products. Health clubs and manufacturers of exercise equipment feature well-muscled men and women pounding away on treadmills, while mouthwash makers show that fresh breath is the key to romance.

Now we've discussed how the three internal processes of perception, motivation, and learning influence how consumers absorb and interpret information. But the results of these processes—the interpretation the consumer gives to a marketing message—differ depending on unique consumer characteristics. Let's talk next about some of these characteristics: existing consumer attitudes, the personality of the consumer, and consumer age groups.

Attitudes

An **attitude** is a lasting evaluation of a person, object, or issue.[8] Consumers have attitudes toward brands, such as whether McDonald's or Wendy's has the best hamburgers. They also evaluate more general consumption-related behaviours such as whether high-fat foods, including hamburgers, are a no-no in a healthy diet. A person's attitude has three components: affect, cognition, and behaviour.

Affect is the *feeling* component of attitudes. This term refers to the overall emotional response a person has to a product. Affect is usually dominant for expressive products, such as perfume, where we choose a fragrance if it makes us feel happy.

Cognition, the *knowing* component, refers to the beliefs or knowledge a person has about a product and its important characteristics. You may believe that a Mercedes is built better than most cars, or (like Brandon) that a Ford Focus is slightly hip, yet solid. Cognition is important for complex products, such as computers, for which we may develop beliefs on the basis of technical information. (See Exhibit 4.4.)

Behaviour, the *doing* component, involves a consumer's intention to do something, such as the intention to purchase or use a certain product. For products such as cereal, consumers act (purchase and try the product) on the basis of limited information and then form an evaluation of the product simply on the basis of how the product tastes or performs.

Exhibit 4.4
Cognitive learning theory views people as problem-solvers. Marketing messages facilitate this process when they provide factual information to help consumers make decisions.

Personality and the Self: Are You What You Buy?

Personality is the set of unique psychological characteristics that consistently influences the way a person responds to situations in the environment. One adventure-seeking consumer may always be on the lookout for new experiences and cutting-edge products, while another is happiest in familiar surroundings using the same brands over and over. Today, popular online matchmaking services like eHarmony, lavalife, and flirtbox.ca offer to create your "personality profile" and then hook you up with other members whose profiles are similar.

It makes sense to assume that consumers buy products that are extensions of their personalities. That's why marketers try to create brand personalities that will appeal to different types of people. For example, consider the different "personalities" fragrance marketers invent. A brand with a "wholesome, girl-next-door" image such as Clinique's Happy would be hard to confuse with the sophisticated image of Christian Dior's Dolce Vita. We'll talk more about this in a later chapter.

A person's **self-concept** is his attitude toward himself. The self-concept is composed of a mixture of beliefs about one's abilities, and observations of one's own behaviour and feelings (both positive and negative) about one's personal attributes, such as body type or facial features. The extent to which a person's self-concept is positive or negative can influence the products he buys and even the extent to which he fantasizes about changing his life.

Self-esteem refers to how positive a person's self-concept is. Alberto Culver uses a self-esteem pitch to promote its Soft & Beautiful, Just for Me hair relaxer for children. The company's Web site "Mom's Blog" encourages mothers to provide affirmation of their daughters' beauty to encourage their self-esteem. The site also provides "conversation starters" to help parents talk to their daughters about self-image.[9]

Age

A person's age is another internal influence on purchasing behaviour. For instance, many of us feel we have more in common with those our own age because we share a common set of experiences and memories about sporting events, whether these involve the 1972 Canada–USSR summit series, Canada Cup in 1987, or the Vancouver Olympics Gold Medal hockey game between Canada and the United States in 2010.

Goods and services often appeal to a specific age group. Although there are exceptions, it is safe to assume that most buyers of Lil' Kim's CDs are younger than those who buy Celine Dion's albums. Thus, many marketing strategies appeal to the needs of different age groups such as children, teenagers, the middle-aged, and the elderly. These various needs result in different types of consumer behaviour, both offline and now online as many people incorporate the Web into their shopping patterns.

Age is important, but actually, regardless of how old we are, what we buy often depends more on our current position in the **family life cycle**—the stages through which family members pass as they grow older. Singles (of any age) are more likely to spend money on expensive cars, entertainment, and recreation. Couples with small children purchase baby furniture, insurance, and a larger house, while older couples whose children have "left the nest" are more likely to buy a retirement home on Vancouver Island.

Lifestyle

A **lifestyle** is a pattern of living that determines how people choose to spend their time, money, and energy, and that reflects their values, tastes, and preferences. We express our lifestyles in our preferences for activities such as sports, interests

personality
The set of unique psychological characteristics that consistently influences the way a person responds to situations in the environment.

self-concept
An individual's self-image that is composed of a mixture of beliefs, observations, and feelings about personal attributes.

family life cycle
A means of characterizing consumers within a family structure on the basis of different stages through which people pass as they grow older.

lifestyle
The pattern of living that determines how people choose to spend their time, money, and energy and that reflects their values, tastes, and preferences.

Exhibit 4.5

Marketers recognize that it's often helpful to group is people into market segments based on similarities in lifestyle preferences. For example, skateboarding has morphed from an activity we associate with the lawbreaking daredevils from the movie *Dogtown and Z-Boys* depicted to become a full-fledged lifestyle, complete with a full complement of merchandise that boarders need to live the life.

Tech and Trends

Social Networks

Has social media gone to the dogs? Mattel hopes so. The toy company is targeting pet owners, especially those who think their pets are totally—or at least pretty close to—human, with its first foray into the pet products market. Puppy Tweets is a high-tech toy that attaches to a dog's collar and sends Tweets to the pet's Twitter page. No, Puppy Tweets doesn't know what a pet is thinking. Instead, the toy responds to the dog's movement or barking to randomly send one of 500 Tweets. With Tweets such as "I bark because I miss you. There, I said it. Now hurry home" and "I finally caught that tail I've been chasing, and . . . OOUUUCHH!" Mattel's toy may be only the beginning of new products that use social media to allow people to interact with their pets.[10]

such as music, and opinions on politics and religion. Consumers often choose goods, services, and activities that they associate with a certain lifestyle. (See Exhibit 4.5.) Brandon may drive a Ford Focus, hang out in Internet cafes, and go extreme skiing during spring break, because he views these choices as part of a cool student lifestyle.

If lifestyles are so important, how do marketers identify them so that they can reach consumers who share preferences for products that they associate with a lifestyle that appeals to them? *Demographic* characteristics, such as age and income, tell marketers *what* products people buy, but they don't reveal *why*. Two consumers can share the same demographic characteristics, yet be totally different people—all 20-year-old male university students are hardly identical to one another. That's why it is often important to further profile consumers in terms of their passions and how they spend their leisure time. Socio-economic differences between market segments ought to be considered as well. Consumers with less means will of course behave differently and have different priorities.

To breathe life into demographic analyses, marketers turn to **psychographics**, which groups consumers according to psychological and behavioural similarities. One way to do this is to describe people in terms of their activities, interests, and opinions (**AIOs**). (See Exhibit 4.6.) These dimensions are based on preferences for vacation destinations, club memberships, hobbies, political and social attitudes, tastes in food and fashion, and so on. Using data from large samples, marketers create profiles of customers who resemble one another in terms of their activities and patterns of product use.[11]

psychographics
The use of psychological, sociological, and anthropological factors to construct market segments.

AIOs
Measures of consumer activities, interests, and opinions used to place consumers into dimensions.

3 Situational and Social Influences on Consumers' Decisions

OBJECTIVE
Show how situational factors and consumers' relationships with other people influence consumer behaviour
(pp. 134–141)

We've seen that internal factors such as how people perceive marketing messages, their motivation to acquire products, and their unique personalities, age groups, family life cycle, and lifestyle influence the decisions they make. In addition, situational and social influences—factors external to the consumer—have a big impact on the choices consumers make and how they make them.

Situational Influences

When, where, and how consumers shop—what we call situational influences—shape their purchase choices. Some important situational cues are our physical surroundings and time pressures.

Marketers know that dimensions of the physical environment, including factors such as decor, smells, lighting, music, and even temperature, can influence consumption to a certain degree. One study found that pumping certain odours into casinos actually increased the amount of money patrons fed into slot machines.[12] **Sensory marketing** is becoming big busi-

sensory marketing
Marketing techniques that link distinct sensory experiences such as a unique fragrance with a product or service.

Exhibit 4.6

Social groups are a good source of marketing information.

ness. Westin Hotels spray a blend of green tea, geranium, and black cedar into hotel lobbies while Sheraton uses a combination of jasmine, clove, and fig. Sony scents its stores with orange, vanilla, and cedar, and Cadillac puts that "new car" smell into its autos artificially, all to influence the consumer's decision process.[13] These strategies tend to be more observable than subliminal messages we discussed earlier.

Let's see how some other situational factors influence the consumer decision-making process.

The Physical Environment

It's no secret that physical surroundings strongly influence people's moods and behaviours. Despite all their efforts to pre-sell consumers through advertising, marketers know that the store environment influences many purchases. For example, one classic study showed that consumers decide on about two out of every three of their supermarket product purchases in the aisles (so always eat before you go to the supermarket).[14] A more recent study in Germany showed that almost 70 percent of shoppers decide what to buy at the point of sale.[15] The messages consumers receive at the time and their feelings about being in the store strongly influence these decisions.

Two dimensions, *arousal* and *pleasure*, determine whether a shopper will react positively or negatively to a store environment. In other words, the person's surroundings can be either dull or exciting (arousing) and either pleasant or unpleasant. Just because the environment is arousing doesn't necessarily mean it will be pleasant—we've all been in crowded, loud, hot stores that are anything but. Maintaining an upbeat feeling in a pleasant context is one factor behind the success of theme parks such as Disney World or Canada's Wonderland near Toronto, which try to provide consistent doses of carefully calculated stimulation to visitors.[16]

The importance of surroundings explains why many retailers focus on packing as much entertainment as possible to support their stores. For example, Mountain Equipment Co-Op (MEC), a consumers' cooperative founded in 1971 and based out of Vancouver, promotes a lifestyle outside their stores to generate more revenues. MEC developed and launched a series of biking and paddling events across the country to promote sports and,

Exhibit 4.7

As consumers are exposed to more and more advertising, advertisers must work harder to get their attention. Messages put on bathroom walls, a medium created by Zoom Media, offer a way to reach consumers when they are a captive audience.

time poverty
Consumers' belief that they are more pressed for time than ever before.

culture
The values, beliefs, customs, and tastes a group of people practise.

of course, their products. In these events, participants compete for prizes. A company called Zoom Media even sells ad space on restroom walls in stadiums (Exhibit 4.7). According to the company's president, "It's a decided opportunity for an advertiser to reach a captive audience."[17]

Time

Time is one of consumers' most limited resources. We talk about "making time" or "spending time," and we remind one another that "time is money." Marketers know that the time of day, the season of the year, and how much time a person has to make a purchase affects decision making.

Indeed, many consumers believe that they are more pressed for time than ever before. This sense of **time poverty** makes consumers responsive to marketing innovations that allow them to save time, including services such as one-hour photo processing, drive-through lanes at fast-food restaurants, and ordering products on the Web. A number of Web sites, including Apple's iTunes and even Walmart, now offer consumers the speed and convenience of downloading music or movies. These sites allow consumers to browse thousands of titles, preview selections, and order and pay for them—all without setting foot inside a store. This saves the customer time, plus the "store" is always open.

Social Influences on Consumers' Decisions

Although we are all individuals, we are also members of many groups that influence our buying decisions. Families, friends, and classmates often sway us, as do larger groups with which we identify, such as ethnic groups and political parties. Now let's consider how social influences such as culture, social class, influential friends and acquaintances, and trends within the larger society affect the consumer decision-making process.

Culture

As we saw in Chapter 2, we think of **culture** as a society's personality. It is the values, beliefs, customs, and tastes a group of people produce or practise. Although we often assume that what people in one culture (especially our own) think is desirable or appropriate will be appreciated in other cultures as well, that's far from the truth. Middle Eastern youth may not agree with US politics, but they love Western music and find Arab TV music channels boring. Enter MTV Arabia, a 24-hour free satellite channel. To be sure, many Canadian, US, and European videos have to be cleaned up for the Arab audience and many are simply too edgy to air. To meet the values of the Middle Eastern audience, bad language and shots of kissing, revealing outfits, or people in bed are blurred or removed and sometimes replaced by more acceptable copy.[18] Culture matters.

Rituals

Every culture associates specific activities and products with its *rituals*, such as weddings and funerals. Some companies are more than happy to help us link products to cultural events. Consider the popularity of the elaborate weddings Disney stages for couples who want to re-enact their own version of a popular fairy tale. At Disney World, the princess bride wears a tiara and rides to the park's lakeside wedding pavilion in a horse-drawn coach, complete with two footmen in grey wigs and gold lamé pants. At the exchange of vows, trumpets blare as Major Domo (he helped the Duke in his quest for Cinderella) walks up the aisle with two wedding bands in a glass slipper on a velvet pillow. Disney stages about 2000 of these extravaganzas each year.[19]

In most countries, rituals are involved in the celebration of holidays. Canadians purchase and cook turkeys, cranberry sauce, and pumpkin pies to have the perfect Thanksgiving dinner. In Christian cultures, the Christmas ritual is so strongly tied to gifts, Christmas trees, lights, and decorations that it becomes the make-or-break sales season of the year for retailers. In many Muslim countries, the Ramadan season means fasting during the day but consuming gigantic amounts of food after sunset each day. And New Year's Eve parties all around the globe must include fancy party dresses and champagne. Is it any wonder that marketers of so many companies study consumer rituals?

Values (Again)

As we also saw earlier, cultural values are deeply held beliefs about right and wrong ways to live.[20] Marketers who understand a culture's values can tailor their product offerings accordingly. Consider, for example, that the values for collectivist countries differ greatly from those of individualistic cultures where immediate gratification of one's own needs comes before all other loyalties. In collectivist cultures, loyalty to a family or a tribe overrides personal goals. Collectivist cultures put value on self-discipline, accepting one's position in life, and honouring parents and elders. Individualist cultures, on the other hand, stress equality, freedom, and personal pleasure. Canada would fit in this latter category. Today, we see the economic growth of some collectivist countries such as India, Japan, and China making many consumers more affluent—and individualistic. For marketers, this means growth opportunities for products such as travel, luxury goods, sports activities like tennis and golf, and entertainment.

Exhibit 4.8

Asics appeals to social pressure to create desire for its running shoes.

Subcultures

A **subculture** is a group that coexists with other groups in a larger culture but whose members share a distinctive set of beliefs or characteristics, such as members of a religious organization or an ethnic group. **Microcultures** are groups of consumers who identify with a specific activity or art form (Exhibit 4.8). These build around music groups such as Nickelback, media creations such as *World of Warcraft*, or leisure activities such as extreme sports. Social media has been a real boon to subcultures and microcultures; it provides an opportunity for like-minded consumers to share their thoughts, photographs, videos, and so on. More on these important new sharing platforms later in the book.

For marketers, some of the most important subcultures are racial and ethnic groups, because many consumers identify strongly with their heritage, and products that appeal to this aspect of their identities appeal to them. To grow its business, cereal maker General Mills targets Hispanic consumers. The company hopes to reach mothers who want better ways to nurture their children through its *Que Vida Rica* marketing program that tells mothers about the benefits of its products and offers nutrition tips and recipe suggestions. Advertising for General Mills' Nature Valley brand shows Hispanic couples "savouring nature instead of conquering it."[21]

Social networks such as Facebook, Twitter, and others do influence subcultures and will likely continue to influence how reference groups are created and evolve. Today's marketers cannot afford to underestimate the power of these networks and how quickly they can change the market landscape.

Emerging Lifestyle Trends: Consumerism and Environmentalism

Powerful new social movements within a society also contribute to how we decide what we want and don't want. One such influence is consumerism, the social movement directed toward protecting consumers from harmful business practices. Many consumers are

subculture

A group within a society whose members share a distinctive set of beliefs, characteristics, or common experiences.

microcultures

Groups of consumers who identify with a specific activity or art form.

becoming very aware of the social and environmental consequences of their purchases—and making their decisions accordingly.

Organized activities that bring about social and political change are not new to the Canadian scene. Women's right to vote, child labour laws, minimum wage, equal employment opportunity, and the ban on nuclear weapons testing all have resulted from social movements in which citizens, public and private organizations, and businesses worked to change society. In today's connected world, criticisms from consumerists can be especially damaging. A company's best way to combat such attacks and maintain a good image is to be proactive by practising good business.

Related to the consumerism movement is **environmentalism**; this is a social movement that grows out of the world-wide growing concern for the many ways in which our consumption behaviours impact the physical world in which we live. Environmentalists seek solutions that enable companies to manage resources responsibly.

Climate change is on everyone's minds these days. The United Nations Climate Change Conference series, the most recent held in Cancun in 2010, has made the environment a high priority for many governments around the world. Consumers, of course, are becoming more environmentally conscious of how they consume. Other than the Kyoto protocol in 1997, no other major agreement on climate change has been reached. In recent years, the United Nations has made some progress, but political swings and economic downturns have made it increasingly challenging for nations to ratify a new agreement. In the meantime, consumers are looking for environmentally friendly products and some are even proactively asking for them. That is why corporate and social responsibilities along with sustainability have become strategic priorities for many Canadian companies. Global concerns are mounting, and a lot of businesses are acting even in the absence of government regulations, because they understand that consumers will reward companies that do. Many firms now assume a position of **environmental stewardship** when they make socially responsible business decisions that also protect the environment. A green marketing strategy describes efforts to choose packages, product designs, and other aspects of the marketing mix that are earth-friendly but still profitable. One potential red flag in all of this rush to do good is concerns about **greenwashing**. This refers to instances where a company claims its products are better for the environment than they really are in order to appeal to consumers' new focus on eco-friendly brands. Although many companies make sincere efforts to clean up their acts, many consumers are skeptical about green claims for this reason.

Green marketing practices can indeed result in black ink for a firm's bottom line. As mainstream marketers recognize this change, they are starting to alter their practices to satisfy consumers' desires for healthy and earth-friendly products. Coca-Cola, for example, demonstrated its commitment to the environment during the 2010 Vancouver Olympics. As a matter of fact, the Vancouver Games were the most environmentally focused games in history. Many facilities and sports venues were built with recycled materials exclusively. Coca-Cola sponsored a 100-percent environmentally sustainable, carbon-neutral cafe. It featured bottles, furniture, and other products made from recycled material. Going even further, Coke made every aspect of its involvement with the Olympics green—from staff uniforms to delivery trucks to compostable coffee cups.[22]

Social Class

Social class is the overall rank of people in a society. People who are within the same class tend to exhibit similarities in occupation, education, and income level, and they often have similar tastes in clothing, decorating styles, and leisure activities. Class members also share many political and religious beliefs.

Many marketers design their products and stores to appeal to people in a specific social class. Working-class consumers tend to evaluate products in more utilitarian terms like sturdiness or comfort instead of trendiness or aesthetics. They are less likely to experiment with new products or styles, such as modern furniture or coloured appliances, because they

environmentalism
A broad philosophy and social movement that seeks conservation and improvement of the natural environment.

environmental stewardship
A position taken by an organization to protect or enhance the natural environment as it conducts its business activities.

greenwashing
A practice in which companies promote their products as environmentally friendly when in truth the brand provides little ecological benefit.

social class
The overall rank or social standing of groups of people within a society according to the value assigned to factors such as family background, education, occupation, and income.

tend to prefer predictability to novelty.[23] Marketers need to understand these differences and develop product and communication strategies that appeal to different social classes.

Luxury goods often serve as **status symbols**; visible markers that provide a way for people to flaunt their membership in higher social classes (or at least to make others believe they are members). The bumper sticker, "He who dies with the most toys wins," illustrates the desire to accumulate these badges of achievement. However, it's important to note that, over time, the importance of different status symbols rises and falls. For example, when James Dean starred in the movie *Giant*, the Cadillac convertible was the ultimate status symbol car in North America. Today, wealthy consumers who want to let the world know of their success are far more likely to choose a Mercedes Benz, a BMW, or an Escalade. The "in" car five years from now is anyone's guess—perhaps with today's emphasis on the environment the Prius and other hybrids will emerge as the new status symbols.

In addition, today, traditional status symbols are available to a much wider range of consumers around the world with rising incomes. This change fuels demand for mass-consumed products that still offer some degree of panache or style (Exhibit 4.9). Think about the success of companies like Nokia, H&M, Zara, ING, Dell Computers, Gap, Nike, EasyJet, or L'Oréal. They cater to a consumer segment that analysts have labelled **mass-class**. This term refers to the hundreds of millions of global consumers who now enjoy a level of purchasing power that's sufficient to let them afford high-quality products offered by well-known multinational companies.

Client: Grupo Damm Product: A.K.Damm Alsatian beer Agency: Caldas Naya (Barcelona) Creative Director: Gustavo Caldas Account Director: Fabiana Casañas Copywriter: Gustavo Caldas Art Director: Juanjo CasaÁvas/Gustavo Caldas Client supervisor: Anabel Lope/Victor Caballí Photographer: Mike Diver/Pedro Aguilar (London) Make Up/Costumes: Natasha Lawes Assistant: Zaheer Anwari

Exhibit 4.9

This Spanish beer ad makes a statement about social class.

Group Membership

Anyone who's ever "gone along with the crowd" knows that people act differently in groups than they do on their own. When there are more people in a group, it becomes less likely that any one member will be singled out for attention, and normal restraints on behaviour may evaporate (think about the last wild party you attended). In many cases, group members show a greater willingness to consider riskier alternatives than they would if each member made the decision alone.[24]

A **reference group** is a set of people a consumer wants to please or imitate. Consumers "refer to" these groups when they decide what to wear, where they hang out, and what brands they buy. This influence can take the form of family and friends, respected Canadian heroes like Maurice Richard, Terry Fox, Pierre E. Trudeau, global celebrities like Angelina Jolie and Brad Pitt, or even (dare we say it!) your professors.

Opinion Leaders

If, like Brandon, you are in the market for a new car, is there a certain person to whom you'd turn for advice? An **opinion leader** is a person who influences others' attitudes or behaviours because they believe that he possesses expertise about the product.[25] Opinion leaders usually exhibit high levels of interest in the product category. They continually update their knowledge as they read blogs, talk to salespeople, or subscribe to podcasts about the topic. Because of this involvement, opinion leaders are valuable information sources.

Unlike commercial endorsers, who are paid to represent the interests of just one company, opinion leaders have no "axe to grind" and can impart both positive and negative information about the product (unless they're being compensated to blog on behalf of a brand, which is not unheard of these days!). In addition, these knowledgeable consumers

status symbols
Visible markers that provide a way for people to flaunt their membership in higher social classes (or at least to make others believe they are members).

mass-class
The hundreds of millions of global consumers who now enjoy a level of purchasing power that's sufficient to let them afford high-quality products—except for big-ticket items like university educations, housing, or luxury cars.

reference group
An actual or imaginary individual or group that has a significant effect on an individual's evaluations, aspirations, or behaviour.

opinion leader
A person who is frequently able to influence others' attitudes or behaviours by virtue of his or her active interest and expertise in one or more product categories.

often are among the first to buy new products, so they absorb much of the risk and reduce uncertainty for others who are not as courageous.

Gender Roles

gender roles
Society's expectations regarding the appropriate attitudes, behaviours, and appearance for men and women.

Some of the strongest pressures to conform come from our **gender roles**—society's expectations regarding the appropriate attitudes, behaviours, and appearance for men and women.[26] Of course, marketers play a part in teaching us how society expects us to act as men and women. Marketing communications and products often portray women and men differently. These influences teach us what the "proper" gender roles of women or men should be and which products are appropriate for each gender. Some of these "sex-typed" products have come under fire from social groups. For example, feminists claim the Barbie doll reinforces unrealistic ideas about what women's bodies should look like—even though a newer version of the doll isn't quite as skinny and buxom as the original doll.

Sex roles constantly evolve—in a complex society like ours we often encounter contradictory messages about "appropriate" behaviour. We can clearly see this in the messages girls have been getting from the media for the last several years: it's cool to be overly provocative. Role models like Justin Bieber, Lady Gaga, Paris Hilton, Lindsay Lohan, and Britney Spears convey standards about how far pre-teens and teens should go to broadcast their sexuality (Exhibit 4.10). Now we see signs of a backlash. At the Pure Fashion Web site, girls get style tips including skirts and dresses that fall no more than four fingers above the knee and no tank tops without a sweater or jacket over them. Several other sites, such as ModestApparelUSA.com, advocate a return to styles that leave almost everything to the imagination.[27] Is our culture moving from a celebration of "girls gone wild" to "girls gone mild"?

metrosexual
A straight, urban male who is keenly interested in fashion, home design, gourmet cooking, and personal care.

Men's sex roles are changing too. For one, men are concerned as never before with their appearance. Guys spend $7.7 billion on grooming products globally each year. In Europe, 24 percent of men younger than age 30 use skincare products—and 80 percent of young Korean men do.[28] In fact, no doubt one of the biggest marketing buzzwords over the past few years is the **metrosexual**—a straight, urban male who is keenly interested in fashion, home design, gourmet cooking, and personal care. But just how widespread is the metrosexual phenomenon? Clearly, our cultural definition of masculinity is evolving as men try to redefine sex roles while they stay in a "safety zone" of acceptable behaviours bounded by danger zones of sloppiness at one extreme and effeminate behaviour at the other. For example, a man may decide that it's okay to use a moisturizer but draw the line at an eye cream that he considers too feminine.[29] And, much like the "girls gone mild" trend we just discussed, some cultural observers report the emergence of "retrosexuals"—men who want to emphasize their old-school masculinity as they get plastic surgery to create a more rugged look that includes hairier chests and beards, squarer chins, and more angular jaw lines.[30]

Rick Madonik/Getstock.com

Exhibit 4.10
Lady Gaga is arguably one of the most intriguing figures in the music industry in recent years. She has influenced many on how to behave and, ultimately, how and what to buy.

Trends will always affect consumer behaviour. The Canadian population is becoming older and more diverse. In fact, the number of Canadians with Asian roots is growing at an impressive rate. Demographics and the aging population is a systemic force marketers cannot ignore. It means many consumers will have a fixed income and won't be able to afford premium products. That is why Target has bought Zellers and will enter the Canadian market in the near future. Growth opportunities are more challenging to find.

Consumers are becoming less loyal. The changing role of women is also altering the Canadian retail landscape. More women are earning more than their employed spouses, which in turn changes how households make decisions on major items such as dishwashers, TVs, cars, even houses. Internet and social networking sites like Facebook and Twitter are also changing the way consumers buy, and set values. We are in the era of immediacy and quick purchasing. To cope with these changes, marketers will need to adapt quickly as well.

Now that you've learned about consumer behaviour, read "Real People, Real Choices: How It Worked Out" to see which strategy Julie selected to promote the (RED) brand.

Here's my choice. . .

Real **People**, Real **Choices**

Why do you think Julie chose option 1?

1 Option   2 Option   3 Option

How It Worked Out at (RED)

Julie chose Option 1. (RED) continued to seek out major international brands to partner with, but it is now complementing those partnerships with smaller special editions that appeal to a younger age group. The company decided that this expansion of its business model is necessary to keep (RED) fresh and relevant in the consumer marketplace. Teens are clearly the emerging consumer group that will drive (RED)'s success in the future. One of the first examples of this strategy is the release of a (PRODUCT) RED skateboard in the spring of 2008. (RED) is also looking at adding other action sports products and teen-focused fashion brands to the collection.

How (RED) Measures Success

(RED) implemented a brand-tracking study that will allow the organization to measure awareness, consideration, preference, and brand momentum with its key consumer targets over time. Through this study Julie can determine whether or not (RED)'s investment in key consumer groups via new partnerships and marketing programs is paying off. Are they more aware of (RED)? Do they prefer (RED) products over non-(RED) products? Are they more likely to choose brands that join (RED)? If (RED) is able to move the needle on these measures, this feedback will give Julie powerful ammunition when she pitches the idea to brands that haven't yet signed up for the program.

To learn the whole story, visit www.mypearsonmarketinglab.com.

Objective Summary ➡ Key Terms ➡ Apply

1. Objective Summary (pp. 120–128)

Define consumer behaviour and explain the purchase decision-making process.

Consumer behaviour is the process individuals or groups go through to select, purchase, use, and dispose of goods, services, ideas, or experiences to satisfy their needs and desires. Consumer decisions differ greatly, ranging from habitual, repeat (low-involvement) purchases to complex, extended problem-solving activities for important, risky (high-involvement) purchases. When consumers make important purchases, they go through a series of five steps. First, they recognize there is a problem to be solved. Then, they search for information to make the best decision. Next, they evaluate a set of alternatives and judge them on the basis of various evaluative criteria. At this point, they are ready to make their purchasing decision. Following the purchase, consumers decide whether the product matched their expectations.

Key Terms

consumer behaviour, p. 120

involvement, p. 121

perceived risk, p. 121

problem recognition, p. 123

information search, p. 123

search marketing, p. 124

search engine optimization (SEO), p. 124

search engine marketing (SEM), p. 124

sponsored search ads, p. 125

comparison shopping agents or shopbots, p. 125

behavioural targeting, p. 125

evaluative criteria, p. 126

heuristics, p. 126

brand loyalty, p. 126

consumer satisfaction/dissatisfaction, p. 127

cognitive dissonance, p. 127

2. Objective Summary (pp. 128–134)

Explain how internal factors influence consumers' decision-making processes.

Several internal factors influence consumer decisions. Perception is how consumers select, organize, and interpret stimuli.

Motivation is an internal state that drives consumers to satisfy needs. Learning is a change in behaviour that results from information or experience. Behavioural learning results from external events, while cognitive learning refers to internal mental activity. An attitude is a lasting evaluation of a person, object, or issue and includes three components: affect, cognition, and behaviour. Personality traits such as innovativeness, materialism, self-confidence, sociability, and the need for cognition may be used to develop market segments. Marketers seek to understand a consumer's self-concept in order to develop product attributes that match some aspect of the consumer's self-concept. The age of consumers, family life cycle, and their lifestyle also are strongly related to consumption preferences. Marketers may use psychographics to group people according to activities, interests, and opinions that may explain reasons for purchasing products.

Key Terms

perception, p. 128

exposure, p. 129

subliminal advertising, p. 129

consideration set, p. 129

clickstream analysis, p. 129

attention, p. 130

interpretation, p. 130

motivation, p. 130

hierarchy of needs, p. 130

learning, p. 131

behavioural learning theories, p. 131

classical conditioning, p. 131

operant conditioning, p. 132

cognitive learning theory, p. 132

observational learning, p. 132

attitude, p. 132

affect, p. 132

cognition, p. 132

behaviour, p. 132

personality, p. 133

self-concept, p. 133

family life cycle, p. 133

lifestyle, p. 133

psychographcs, p. 134

AIOs, p. 134

3. Objective Summary (pp. 134–141)

Show how situational factors and consumers' relationships with other people influence consumer behaviour.

Situational influences include our physical surroundings and time pressures. Dimensions of the physical environment, including decor, smells, lighting, music, and even temperature, can influence consumption. The time of day, the season of the year, and how much time one has to make a purchase also affect decision making. Consumers' overall preferences for products are determined by the culture in which they live and their membership in different subcultures. Consumerism is a social movement directed toward protecting consumers from harmful business practices. Environmentalism, another social movement, seeks ways to protect the natural environment. Firms practise environmental stewardship when they make decisions that protect the environment. Green marketing strategies include earth–friendly packaging and product designs. Social class, group memberships, and opinion leaders are other types of social influences that affect consumer choices. A reference group is a set of people a consumer wants to please or imitate, and this affects the consumer's purchasing decisions. Purchases also often result from conformity to real or imagined group pressures. Another way social influence is felt is in the expectations of society regarding the proper roles for men and women. Such expectations have led to many gender-typed products.

Key Terms

sensory marketing, p. 134

time poverty, p. 136

culture, p. 136

subculture, p. 137

microcultures, p. 137

environmentalism, p. 138

environmental stewardship, p. 138

greenwashing, p. 138

social class, p. 138

status symbols, p. 139

mass-class, p. 139

reference group, p. 139

opinion leader, p. 139

gender roles, p. 140

metrosexual, p. 140

Chapter Questions and Activities

Concepts: Test Your Knowledge

1. What is consumer behaviour? Why is it important for marketers to understand consumer behaviour?
2. Explain habitual decision making, limited problem solving, and extended problem solving. What is the role of perceived risk in the decision process?
3. What are the steps in the consumer decision-making process?
4. What is search engine marketing and how is it related to the consumer decision process?
5. What is perception? Explain the three parts of the perception process: exposure, attention, and interpretation. For marketers, what are the implications of each of these components?
6. What is motivation? What is the role of motivation in consumer behaviour?
7. What is behavioural learning? What is cognitive learning? How is an understanding of behavioural and cognitive learning useful to marketers?
8. What are the three components of attitudes? What is personality?
9. Explain what lifestyle means. What is the significance of family life cycle and lifestyle in understanding consumer behaviour and purchasing decisions?
10. What are cultures, subcultures, and microcultures? How do cultures, subcultures, and microcultures influence consumer behaviour? What is the significance of social class to marketers?

11. What are reference groups, and how do they influence consumers? What are opinion leaders?
12. What are gender roles? How do metrosexuals differ from other male consumers?
13. What is consumerism? What is environmentalism? How do firms respond to these social movements?

Activities: Apply What You've Learned

1. Assume that you are in the marketing department of a manufacturer of one of the products listed below. You know that internal factors including (1) perception, (2) motivation, (3) learning, (4) attitudes, and (5) personality influence consumers' decision making. With your classmates, develop your ideas about why each of these internal factors is important in the purchase of the product and how you might use these factors in developing marketing strategies for your firm. Report your ideas to your class.

   a. Automobiles
   b. Designer jeans
   c. An iPad or other tablet book
   d. Fragrances (for men or for women)
   e. Furniture

2. Sometimes advertising or other marketing activities cause problem recognition by showing consumers how much better off they would be with a new product or by pointing

out problems with products they already own. Discuss problem recognition for the following product categories. Make a list of some ways marketers might try to stimulate problem recognition for each product. Present your ideas to your class.

a. Life insurance
b. Mouthwash
c. A new automobile
d. A health club membership

3. Assume that you are a marketing manager for a major hotel chain with outlets in major tourism sites around the world. You are concerned about the effects of current consumer trends, including changing ethnic populations, changing roles of men and women, increased concern for time and for the environment, and decreased emphasis on status goods. Others in your firm do not understand or care about these changes. They believe that the firm should continue to do business just as it always has. Develop a role-playing exercise to discuss these two different points of view for your class. Be sure to include the importance of each of these trends to your firm and offer suggestions for marketing strategies to address these trends.

4. This chapter indicated that consumers go through a series of steps (from problem recognition to postpurchase evaluation) as they make purchases. Write a detailed report describing what you would do in each of these steps when deciding to purchase one of the following products:

a. An iPhone or similar device
b. A university education
c. A fast-food lunch

Then make suggestions for what marketers might do to make sure that consumers like you who are going through each step in the consumer decision process move toward the purchase of their brand. (Hint: Think about product, place, price, and promotion strategies.)

5. In 1991, a survey of American consumers found that almost two-thirds believe in the existence of subliminal advertising, and over one-half are convinced that this technique can get them to buy things they don't really want. Conduct your own survey on perceptions of subliminal advertising with students in your school. You may wish to ask them what they know about subliminal advertising, how much subliminal advertising they believe exists today, and whether they feel subliminal advertising works; that is, whether it causes people to buy things they don't really want. Report the results of your research to your class.

6. In this chapter we learned that some products are status symbols and serve as visible markers that provide a way for people to flaunt their membership in higher social classes. Using the Internet and magazines (your library probably has a collection of magazines), find ads and Web sites for status symbol products. Examine how the Web sites and the ads communicate that the product is a status symbol. How do they relate to a higher social class? Make a list of the products and the visuals and words that are used to promote the status symbol products.

7. In different cultures, perceptions about the proper roles for men and women; that is, gender roles, can vary greatly. Select one of the countries listed below or some other country of your choice. Conduct research to learn about the beliefs about gender roles held by people in that country. You should be able to find some information about the country on the Internet. If possible, find someone who is a native of the country or has visited the country. Prepare a report on the results of your research and the implications for global marketers.

a. France
b. China
c. Japan
d. Mexico
e. Egypt

Marketing Metrics: Exercise

Marketers use some or all of a variety of metrics to better understand how consumers make decisions involving a marketer's brand. Below is a list of some of these metrics. Which of these metrics would be useful to better understand each item listed after the metrics? Explain how the metrics suggested could be used.

a. A firm's existing customers
b. Potential new customers for a firm
c. The market potential market for a new product

- Awareness is the percentage of all customers who recognize or know the name of a brand. Unaided brand recognition for toothpaste may be measured by asking consumers to name all the brands of toothpaste that come to mind. Aided recognition is measured by asking consumers questions such as, "Have you heard of Tom's of Maine toothpaste?"
- Top of Mind Awareness (TOMA) is the first brand that comes to mind when a consumer thinks of a product category. Marketers measure TOMA with questions such as, "What brand comes to mind when you think of toothpaste?"
- Brand Knowledge is measured by asking consumers if they have specific knowledge about a brand. To measure brand knowledge, marketers may ask consumers if they believe the brand possesses certain attributes or characteristics.
- Measures of Attitudes toward a brand may include survey questions about (1) beliefs that the brand possesses certain characteristics, (2) the relative importance of those characteristics to the product category, and (3) the overall measure of how much the consumer likes the brand.
- Intentions are consumers' stated willingness to buy or their likelihood of certain behaviour. A consumer survey may ask, "If you are in the market for a new pair of shoes, what is the likelihood that you would purchase a pair of Nike shoes?"
- Purchase habits measure consumers' self-reported behaviour. Marketers ask consumers questions such as, "On average, how many times a month do you eat out? Which restaurant did you go to the last time you ate out? How much do you normally spend on a dinner out with your family?"
- Loyalty is a measure of consumers' commitment to a specific brand. Marketers measure loyalty by asking such questions as, "If on your next trip to the store you

plan to purchase hand soap and your favourite brand of hand soap is not available, would you buy another brand or wait until you find your favourite brand to make the purchase?"

- Customer satisfaction is generally based on a survey in which consumers are asked if they are (1) very satisfied, (2) somewhat satisfied, (3) neither satisfied nor dissatisfied, (4) somewhat dissatisfied, or (5) very dissatisfied with a brand.

Choices: What Do You Think?

1. Demographic or cultural trends are important to marketers. What are some current trends that may affect the marketing of the following products?

   a. Housing
   b. Food
   c. Education
   d. Clothing
   e. Travel and tourism
   f. Automobiles

2. What are the core values of your culture? How do these core values affect your behaviour as a consumer? Are they collectivist or individualistic? What are the implications for marketers?

3. Consumers often buy products because they feel pressure from reference groups to conform. Does conformity exert a positive or a negative influence on consumers? With what types of products is conformity more likely to occur?

4. Retailers often place impulse purchase items such as magazines and candy bars near the entrance to the store or near the checkout area. How would you describe the decision process for these products? Why are these locations effective? What are the problems with these decisions?

5. Behavioural targeting on the Internet involves tracking where people go online and then feeding them advertising information that's related to what they're looking for. Now, cable TV providers are also considering their own version of behavioural targeting. While proponents of this approach argue that it's a very efficient and convenient way for people to conduct information-search, others who are concerned about a potential invasion of privacy aren't so enthusiastic. What are some other arguments for and against behavioural targeting? What's your opinion? Do you mind having marketers know what sites you visit or what TV shows and movies you watch in return for receiving more relevant information on products?

6. Today, consumers are increasingly demanding "green" products. And marketers are responding with more and more products to meet that demand. Some companies, however, are "greenwashing" their products; that is, they are claiming they are more environmentally friendly than they really are. What are some examples of products that you suspect are being greenwashed? What should be done about this problem? Should there be laws about greenwashing or should marketers do more to patrol their own actions?

Miniproject: Learn by Doing

The purpose of this miniproject is to increase your understanding of the roles of personal, social, and situational factors in consumer behaviour.

1. Select one of the following product categories (or some other product of your choice):
   - Hairstyling
   - Large appliances, such as refrigerators or washing machines
   - A restaurant
   - Banking
   - Fine jewellery

2. Visit three stores or locations where the product may be purchased. (Try to select three that are very different from each other.) Observe and make notes on all the elements of each retail environment.

3. At each of the three locations, observe people purchasing the product. Make notes about their characteristics (e.g., age, race, gender, and so on), their social class, and their actions in the store in relation to the product.

4. Prepare a report for your class describing the situational variables and individual consumer differences among the three stores and how they relate to the purchase of the product. Present your findings to your class.

Marketing in **Action** Case   Real Choices at Lexus

In 1983, at a top-secret meeting, Toyota chairman Eiji Toyoda suggested that the time was right for Toyota to introduce a true luxury automobile that would challenge the best luxury vehicles in the world. A six-year development process followed that involved 60 designers and 450 prototypes at a cost of over $1 billion. In 1989, the Lexus was launched. In 1999, Lexus sold its millionth car in the United States, and within a little over a decade, Lexus became America's best-selling line of luxury vehicles.

Following its success in the United States, Toyota introduced the Lexus in markets outside America, and today the luxury cars are available in over 40 different countries. Since its introduction, the Lexus has repeatedly won top awards and accolades for customer satisfaction, dependability, appeal, design, and engineering from the Motoring Press Association, J.D. Power and Associates studies, *The Robb Report, Popular Science, Car and Driver, Popular Mechanics, Automobile Magazine,* and *Motor Trend.*

Why has Lexus been such a success? According to President and CEO, North America, Atsushi Niimi, "Lexus is a success story because there is no compromise in its manufacture, as it always reflects the voice of the customer." Toyota President Ray Tanguay noted, "Manufacturing Lexus demands a deep understanding of what customers want, expect, and deserve in a luxury vehicle. We call it the relentless pursuit of perfection."

How did Toyota listen to the voices of its consumers? As early as 1985 while the Lexus was only a concept, Toyota sent a study team to the United States to conduct focus groups with potential customers. More recently, Lexus Great Britain introduced a unique program that helps Lexus consultants better understand customers by giving them a taste of luxury. Staff from Lexus centres are pampered at top-class hotels in order to experience for themselves the kind of quality and service their customers expect. In another program, Lexus GB gets feedback from actual customers. Thousands of UK Lexus owners are invited to spend the day at luxury spa hotels to share their opinions on where Lexus is succeeding and where it could be better—all while enjoying the spa facilities.

Such attention to providing the best for luxury car owners has led to Lexus's latest innovation: the Advanced Parking Guidance System. Most consumers find parallel parking a real pain; or worse, they simply avoid parallel parking spaces altogether.

Enter the 2007 Lexus LS 460 sedan. The car actually parks itself—or almost. In theory, a driver only need pull up ahead of the empty parking space, make a few minor adjustments on a computer screen, and lift his or her foot off the brake. As the car backs up, the steering wheel turns as needed, and, "voila," the car is in the space, just where you want it to be. Of course, the LS isn't perfect. It must have a parking space considerably (about six feet) longer than the car, so it isn't useful in those tight city spots. And the system won't work on downward inclines—only on level ground where it can move at a "creeping" speed. As you might expect, the price of the Lexus with the Advanced Parking Guidance System is over $70,000—not a price tag to be taken lightly.

The question many observers ask is whether the parking capability of the Lexus is truly a benefit luxury car owners want and will use—or is it just a gimmick? And were customers really asking for this feature? Some argue that the Lexus automatic parking capability isn't really useful and that Lexus should have waited to introduce the feature until the company had worked out all the kinks in the system. Has Lexus stepped away from its focus on customer needs, and if so, what should the company do now?

You Make the Call

1. What is the decision facing Lexus?
2. What factors are important in understanding this decision situation?
3. What are the alternatives?
4. What decision(s) do you recommend?
5. What are some ways to implement your recommendation?

Sources: Based on: "Lexus History," Conceptcarz.com, http://www.conceptcarz.com/view/makehistory/94,0/Lexus_History.aspx; "Lexus Luxury Lifestyle Training," Carpages, http://www.carpages.co.uk/lexus/lexus-lifestyle-12-11-05.asp; Trevor Hoffman, "First Luxury Lexus Built outside Japan Rolls Off the Line in Cambridge, Ontario," Automobile.com, http://car-reviews.automobile.com/news/worlds-first-lexus-built-outside-of-japan-rolls-off-canadian-line/456/; "Lexus," Wikipedia, http://wikipedia.org/wiki/Lexus.

Chapter 5

Business-to-Business Markets:
How and Why Organizations Buy

Brad Tracy

Profile

▼ A Decision Maker
at NCR Corporation

Brad Tracy is VP of Americas Marketing Deployment for NCR Corporation, headquartered in Dayton, Ohio. In this role, Brad has the responsibility for developing and deploying NCR marketing programs for NCR's full portfolio of products throughout the Americas region (that is, North and South America). This includes solutions and best practices for the retail, financial, hospitality, health care, and travel industries. He joined NCR in 1988 as a retail sales representative in Portland, Oregon. His experience includes positions in sales, product management, product marketing, and industry marketing. Prior to his current assignment, he led the Global Marketing team for NCR's retail solutions division, responsible for all aspects of marketing for NCR retail products. Brad holds a Bachelor of Science degree in business administration from the University of Oregon.

Here's my problem...

NCR had just released a new generation point-of-sale (POS) workstation that was ahead of the competition by almost a year. The POS workstation is the computer that drives the retail checkout process. It is responsible for accepting input from the scanners and other peripherals, pricing the merchandise, offering discounts, calculating tax, and finalizing the transaction via cash, credit, debit, or other financial instrument. The official launch occurred in January at a major trade show. This launch was to be followed up by other industry shows and events, webinars, and advertising. As Brad and his colleagues planned these events, they questioned NCR's participation in a particular trade show because this would entail a significant amount of resources. The company had sent representatives to the event for many years, and many of its customers regularly participated in the show. While it had traditionally been a great venue for meeting with key clients and marketing NCR's newest solutions, in recent years attendance had been waning and other competing shows had grown in popularity. Suffering from this downturn in attendance and increased competition, the event had decided to combine with another event to boost the number of attendees. This combination involved moving the venue from its traditional location and renaming the combined show.

With a superior solution to promote and a legacy of attending the show, the retail division's sales managers made an impassioned case for NCR's continued participation. They felt that this venue would be their last chance to demonstrate the new workstation before the competition responded with its own next-generation product. NCR would miss a golden opportunity to capitalize on its market leadership. In the end, the discussions became quite political as these managers argued their case. The discussion was extremely difficult as a number of key sales leaders were pushing to attend while Brad felt it would be best to skip the show.

Complicating this situation, NCR's retail division (the organization responsible for developing and selling solutions to retailers) had "shared" a booth with another division in prior years. Despite being told of the retail division's concerns, the other division proceeded on the assumption that retail would again participate and fund a significant portion of the event. As the event drew closer, this group pushed hard to force the retail division to continue to fund the event.

Things to remember

Especially in B2B contexts, trade shows are a major element in a firm's marketing mix. Show attendees gather a lot of information about competing products as they contemplate purchases, but they also use these venues as an opportunity to connect personally with company representatives.

Brad considered his Options 1·2·3

1 Option **Attend the show as in past years.** This would allow Brad's division to reinforce the product launch and further solidify its market leadership while the competition again showed an outdated product. But attending the show would consume limited sales and marketing resources. The *cost per touch* (that is, the number of potential clients the team could talk to at the show divided by the total cost of exhibiting at the show) would increase as the number of people attending the show declined.

2 Option **Skip the show this year and reallocate sales and marketing resources to one or more of the other alternatives for marketing the new workstation.** The freed-up budget would allow NCR to attend two smaller but more targeted events in which the company had not previously participated. Because these events are highly targeted and have more of a conference format, they tend to be more intimate, and NCR's representatives could spend more quality time with retail clients. However, while costs for these smaller shows would be lower, since NCR hadn't been to these shows before Brad didn't know what kinds of opportunities to interact with customers would actually occur, so it was hard to predict the cost per touch.

3 Option **Forgo the show this year and find out whether the changes in venue and sponsorship would really diminish the value of the event.** If it turned out that the newly combined show continued to draw enough attendees, NCR could participate the following year. Sitting it out would let the retail division conserve its limited marketing resources. On the other hand, NCR would miss the window to further exploit its market leadership by showcasing its new POS product. And, if Brad decided not to attend, the division would lose its position in the booth selection process. This loss of "seniority" could mean a poor position on the show floor in subsequent years, which would result in decreased foot traffic if NCR's booth was in an out-of-the-way location.

Now, put yourself in Brad's shoes: which option would you choose, and why?

You Choose

Which **Option** would you choose, and **why**?

1. ☐YES ☐NO   2. ☐YES ☐NO   3. ☐YES ☐NO

See what **option** Brad chose on **page 169** ➡

business-to-business (B2B) markets
The group of customers that include manufacturers, wholesalers, retailers, and other organizations.

organizational markets
Another name for business-to-business markets.

1

Business Markets: Buying and Selling When the Customer Is Another Firm

You might think most marketers spend their days dreaming up the best way to promote cutting-edge products for consumers, like new apps for your iPhone, a new power drink to keep you fit, or some funky shoes to add to your closet collection. But this is not the whole picture. Many marketers know that the "real action" also lies in products that companies sell to businesses and organizations rather than to end-user consumers like you: software applications to make a business more efficient, group medical insurance, safety shoes for industrial plants, or the First Flavor Peel 'n Taste Marketing System used by brands from Bacardi to Campbell's Soup. In fact, some of the most interesting and lucrative jobs for young marketers are in businesses you've never heard of because these companies don't deal directly with consumers.

Like an end consumer, a business buyer makes decisions, but with an important difference—the purchase may be worth millions of dollars, and both the buyer and the seller have a lot at stake (maybe even their jobs). A consumer may decide to buy two or three T-shirts at one time, each emblazoned with a different design. *Fortune* 500 companies such as Petro-Canada, Canadian Tire, and Tim Hortons buy hundreds, even thousands, of employee uniforms embroidered with their corporate logos in a single order.

Consider these transactions. Dell makes computer network servers to sell to its business customers. Procter & Gamble contracts with several advertising agencies to promote its brands at home and around the globe. The Toronto Symphony Orchestra buys costumes, sets, and programs. Swiss Chalet restaurants buy chickens from food processors across the country. The Government of Canada places an order for 3000 new HP laser printers. Perhaps at the extreme, Lufthansa CityLine purchases Bombardier's CRJ200 regional jets to add to their fleet—at a price that can exceed $40 million each.[1]

All the above exchanges have one thing in common: they're part of business-to-business (B2B) marketing. This is the marketing of goods and services that businesses and other organizations buy for purposes other than personal consumption. Some firms resell these goods and services, so they are part of a *channel of distribution*, a concept we'll revisit in Chapter 12. Other firms use the goods and services they buy in order to produce still other goods and services that meet the needs of their customers, or to support their own operations. These **business-to-business (B2B) markets**, also called **organizational markets**, include manufacturers, wholesalers, retailers, and a variety of other organizations, such as hospitals, universities, and governmental agencies.

To put the size and complexity of business markets into perspective, let's consider a single product—a pair of jeans. A consumer may browse through several racks of jeans and ultimately purchase a single pair, but the buyer who works for the store at which the consumer shops had to purchase many pairs of jeans in different sizes, styles, and brands from different manufacturers. Each of these manufacturers purchases fabrics, zippers, buttons, and thread from other manufacturers, who, in turn, purchase the raw materials to make these components. In addition, all the firms in this chain need to purchase equipment, electricity, labour, computer systems, legal and accounting services, insurance, office supplies, packing materials, and countless other goods and services. So, even a single purchase of a pair of 7 For All Mankind jeans is the culmination of a series of buying and selling activities among many organizations—many people have been keeping busy while you're out shopping!

In this chapter, we'll look at the big picture of the business marketplace—a world in which the fortunes of business buyers and sellers can hang in the balance of a single transaction—along with characteristics of B2B demand. Then, we'll learn about different types of B2B customers. And finally, we'll examine different business buying situations and the elements of the business buying decision process.

Factors That Make a Difference in Business Markets

In theory, the same basic marketing principles should hold true in both consumer and business markets—firms identify customer needs and develop a marketing mix to satisfy those needs. For example, take the company that made the desks and chairs in your classroom. Just like a firm that markets consumer goods, the classroom furniture company first must create an important competitive advantage for its target market of colleges and universities. Next, the firm develops a marketing mix strategy, beginning with a product: classroom furniture that will withstand years of use by thousands of students while it provides a level of comfort that a good learning environment requires (and you thought those hardback chairs were intended just to keep you awake during class). The firm must offer the furniture at prices that colleges and universities will pay and that will allow the firm to make a reasonable profit. Then the firm must develop a sales force or other marketing communication strategy to make sure your university (and hundreds of others) considers—and hopefully chooses—its products when it furnishes classrooms.

Although marketing to business customers does have a lot in common with consumer marketing, there are differences that make this basic process more complex.[2] Figure 5.1 summarizes the key areas of difference and Table 5.1 provides a more extensive set of comparisons between the two types of markets.

Figure 5.1 Key Differences in Business versus Consumer Markets

There are a number of differences between business and consumer markets. To be successful, marketers must understand these differences and develop strategies specific to organizational customers.

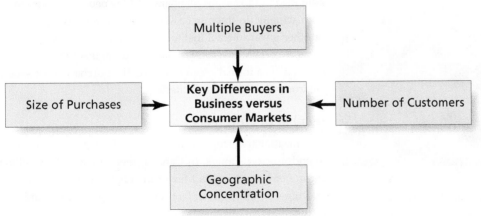

Table 5.1	Differences between Organizational and Consumer Markets

Organizational Markets	Consumer Markets
• Purchases made for some purpose other than personal consumption	• Purchases for individual or household consumption
• Purchases made by someone other than the user of the product	• Purchases usually made by ultimate user of the product
• Decisions frequently made by several people	• Decisions usually made by individuals
• Purchases made according to precise technical specifications based on product expertise	• Purchases often based on brand reputation or personal recommendations with little or no product expertise
• Purchases made after careful weighing of alternatives	• Purchases frequently made on impulse
• Purchases based on rational criteria	• Purchases based on emotional responses to products or promotions
• Purchasers often engage in lengthy decision processes	• Individual purchasers often make quick decisions
• Interdependencies between buyers and sellers; long-term relationships	• Buyers engage in limited-term or one-time-only relationships with many different sellers
• Purchases may involve competitive bidding, price negotiations, and complex financial arrangements	• Most purchases made at "list price" with cash or credit cards
• Products frequently purchased directly from producer	• Products usually purchased from someone other than producer of the product
• Purchases frequently involve high risk and high cost	• Most purchases are relatively low risk and low cost
• Limited number of large buyers	• Many individual or household customers
• Buyers often geographically concentrated in certain areas	• Buyers generally dispersed throughout total population
• Products often complex; classified based on how organizational customers use them	• Products: consumer goods and services for individual use
• Demand derived from demand for other goods and services, generally inelastic in the short run, subject to fluctuations, and may be joined to their demand for other goods and services	• Demand based on consumer needs and preferences, is generally price-elastic, steady over time and independent of demand for other products
• Promotion emphasizes personal selling	• Promotion emphasizes advertising

Courtesy of Canadian Tire Corporation

Exhibit 5.1

Canadian Tire sells to consumers, but they buy many products from businesses, including their delivery trucks.

Multiple Buyers

In business markets, products often have to do more than satisfy an individual's needs. They must meet the requirements of everyone involved in the company's purchase decision. If you decide to buy a new chair for your room or apartment, you're the only one who has to be satisfied. For your classroom, the furniture must satisfy not only students but also faculty, administrators, campus planners, and the people at your school who actually do the purchasing. If your school is a provincial or other governmental institution, the furniture may also have to meet certain government-mandated engineering standards. If you have a formal green initiative, the purchase must satisfy environmentally friendly criteria.

Number of Customers

Organizational customers are few and far between compared to end-user consumers. In Canada, there are about 15 million consumer households but fewer than half a million businesses and other organizations. Not-for-profit organizations are also included in this category.

Size of Purchases

B2B products dwarf consumer purchases both in the quantity of items ordered and how much they cost (Exhibit 5.1). A company that rents uniforms to other businesses, for example, buys hundreds of large drums of laundry detergent each year to launder its uniforms. In contrast, even a hard-core soccer mom who deals with piles of dirty socks and shorts only goes through one container of detergent every few weeks.

Organizations purchase many products, such as a highly sophisticated piece of manufacturing equipment or computer-based marketing information systems, which can cost a million dollars or more. Recognizing such differences in the size of purchases allows marketers to develop effective marketing strategies. Although it makes perfect sense to use mass-media advertising to promote laundry detergent to consumers who buy it at their nearby Zellers, selling thousands of dollars' worth of laundry detergent to Marriott Hotels or a million-dollar machine tool to Northrop Grumman is best handled by a strong personal sales force. There is more on the differences in promotion approaches to businesses versus consumers later in the book.

Geographic Concentration

Another difference between business markets and consumer markets is *geographic concentration*, meaning that many business customers are located in a small geographic area rather than being spread out across the country. Whether they live in the heart of Vancouver or in a small fishing village in Manitoba, consumers buy and use toothpaste and televisions. This is not necessarily so for B2B customers, who may be almost exclusively located in a single region of the country. The Canadian commercial jet aircraft industry is centred in the Montreal area (Bombardier and dozens of subcontractors). For B2B marketers who wish to sell to these markets, this means that they can concentrate their sales efforts and perhaps even locate distribution centres in a single geographic area.

B2B Demand

Demand in business markets differs from consumer demand. Most demand for B2B products is derived, inelastic, fluctuating, and joint. Understanding how these factors influence B2B demand is important for marketers when they forecast sales and plan effective marketing strategies. Let's look at each of these concepts in a bit more detail.

Derived Demand

Consumer demand is based on a direct connection between a need and the satisfaction of that need. But business customers don't purchase goods and services to satisfy their own needs. Businesses instead operate on **derived demand**, because a business's demand for goods and services comes either directly or indirectly from consumers' demand for what it produces.

To better understand derived demand, take a look at Figure 5.2. Demand for forestry products comes from the demand for paper that publishers buy to make the textbooks you use in your classes. The demand for textbooks comes from the demand for education (yes, education is the "product" you're buying—with the occasional party or campus event thrown in as a bonus). As a result of derived demand, the success of one company may depend on another company in a different industry. The derived nature of business demand means that marketers must constantly be alert to changes in consumer trends that ultimately will have an effect on B2B sales. So if fewer students attend college or university and fewer books are sold, the forestry industry has to find other sources of demand for its products.

Inelastic Demand

Inelastic demand means that it usually doesn't matter if the price of a B2B product goes up or down—business customers still buy the same quantity. Demand in B2B

derived demand
Demand for business or organizational products caused by demand for consumer goods or services.

inelastic demand
Demand in which changes in price have little or no effect on the amount demanded.

Figure 5.2 Derived Demand

B2B demand is derived demand; that is, the demand is derived directly or indirectly from consumer demand for another good or service. Some of the demand for forestry products is derived indirectly from the demand for education. At least until the day when all textbooks are only available online, publishers will need to buy paper.

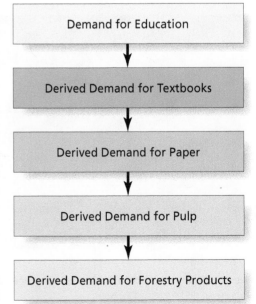

Used with permission of Metro Ontario Inc.

Exhibit 5.2

Grocers like Metro manage an inelastic demand, as consumers need food to survive.

markets is mostly inelastic because what a firm sells often is just one of the many parts or materials that go into producing the consumer product. It is not unusual for a large increase in a business product's price to have little effect on the final consumer product's price.

For example, you can buy a limited edition Porsche Boxster S "loaded" with options for about $60 000.[3] To produce the car, Porsche purchases thousands of different parts. If the price of tires, batteries, or stereos goes up or down, Porsche will still buy enough to meet consumer demand for its cars. As you might imagine, increasing the price by $30 or $40 or even $100 won't change consumer demand for Boxsters—so demand for parts remains the same. (If you have to ask how much it costs, you can't afford it!)

But B2B demand isn't always inelastic. Sometimes a consumer good or service requires only one or a few materials or component parts to produce. If the price of the part increases, demand may become elastic if the manufacturer of the consumer good passes the increase on to the consumer. Currently, for example, the price of corn is skyrocketing, largely due to the demand for ethanol-based fuel and high-fructose corn syrup sweetener (which is a cheaper substitute for sugar in many products). As a result, other food products, overall, that use corn or corn by-products are much more expensive. (See Exhibit 5.2.)

Fluctuating Demand

Business demand also is subject to greater fluctuations than is consumer demand. There are two reasons for this. First, even modest changes in consumer demand can create large increases or decreases in business demand. Take, for example, air travel. A rise in jet fuel prices, causing higher ticket prices and a shift by some consumers from flying to driving vacations, can cause airlines to postpone or cancel orders for new equipment. This change, in turn, creates a dramatic decrease in demand for planes from manufacturers such as Boeing and Airbus (Exhibit 5.3).

joint demand
Demand for two or more goods that are used together to create a product.

A product's life expectancy is another reason for fluctuating demand. Business customers tend to purchase certain products infrequently. They may only need to replace some types of large machinery every 10 or 20 years. Thus, demand for such products fluctuates—it may be very high one year when a lot of customers' machinery wears out but low the following year because everyone's old machinery works fine. One solution to keeping production more constant is to use price reductions that encourage companies to order products before they actually need them.

Joint Demand

Joint demand occurs when two or more goods are necessary to create a product. For example, Porsche needs tires, batteries, and spark plugs to make that limited edition Boxster S that piqued your interest earlier. If the supply of one of these parts decreases, Porsche will be unable to manufacture as many automobiles, and so it will not buy as many of the other items either.

Types of Business-to-Business Customers

As we noted before, many firms buy products in business markets so they can produce other goods. Other B2B customers resell, rent, or lease goods and services. Still other customers,

Photo courtesy of Bombardier Inc. and used under license

Exhibit 5.3

The CRJ1000, which costs over $30 million, is sold by Canadian-based Bombardier to many airlines from around the world.

Figure 5.3 The Business Marketplace

The business marketplace consists of three major categories of customers: producers, resellers, and organizations. B2B marketers must understand the different needs of these customers if they want to build successful relationships with them.

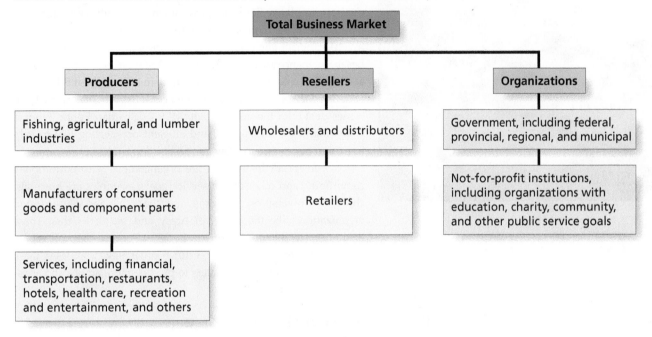

including governments and not-for-profit institutions such as the Red Cross or a local church, serve the public in some way. In this section, we'll look at the three major classes of B2B customers that Figure 5.3 shows (producers, resellers, and organizations). Then we'll look at how marketers classify specific industries.

Producers

Producers purchase products for the production of other goods and services that they, in turn, sell to make a profit. For this reason, they are customers for a vast number of products, from raw materials to goods that still other producers manufacture. For example, Dell buys microprocessor chips from Intel and AMD that go into its line of computers, and Marriott buys linens, furniture, and food to produce the accommodations and meals its hotel guests expect.

producers
The individuals or organizations that purchase products for use in the production of other goods and services.

Resellers

Resellers buy finished goods for the purpose of reselling, renting, or leasing to consumers and other businesses. Although resellers do not actually produce goods, they do provide their customers with the time, place, and possession utility we talked about in an earlier chapter, because they make the goods available to consumers when and where they want them. For example, Walmart buys toothpaste, peanuts, kids' shoes, and about a gazillion other products to sell in its over 4000 stores world-wide.

resellers
The individuals or organizations that buy finished goods for the purpose of reselling, renting, or leasing to others to make a profit and to maintain their business operations.

Government and Not-for-Profit Organizations

Governments and not-for-profit institutions are two other types of organizations in the business marketplace. **Government markets** make up the largest single business and organizational market in Canada. The Canadian government market includes 10 provinces, 3 territories, more than 5000 municipalities and townships, plus the federal government. In Canada, the government is everywhere. We also have many Crown corporations, like Farm Credit Canada, the Business Development Bank of Canada, and Canada Post. Provinces also have Crown corporations, which employ thousands of people as well. Just in the Province of Saskatchewan alone, more than 11 000 people work for Crown corporations.

government markets
The federal, provincial, regional, and municipal governments that buy goods and services to carry out public objectives and to support their operations.

Exhibit 5.4

The Canadian government buys products for its employees and for major events like for the Canada Day celebrations on Parliament Hill.

And, of course, there are thousands more government customers around the globe, and many of those governments are just about the only customers for certain products; for example, jet bombers and nuclear power plants. But many government expenditures are for more familiar items. Pens, pencils, and paper for offices; cots, bedding, and toiletries for jails and prisons; and cleaning supplies for routine facilities maintenance are just a few examples of items consumers buy one at a time but that governments purchase in bulk (Exhibit 5.4).

The MERX system (www.merx.com) in Canada helps businesses deal with the government. MERX Canadian Public Tenders is a straightforward, speedy, and efficient prospecting tool to help Canadian businesses to grow and respond to tenders.

Not-for-profit institutions are organizations with educational, community, and other public service goals; examples are hospitals, churches, universities, museums, and charitable and cause-related organizations like the Salvation Army and the Red Cross. These institutions tend to operate on low budgets. Because nonprofessional part-time buyers who have other duties often make purchases, these customers may rely on marketers to provide more advice and assistance before and after the sale.

The North American Industry Classification System

North American Industry Classification System (NAICS)

The numerical coding system that the United States, Canada, and Mexico use to classify firms into detailed categories according to their business activities.

In addition to looking at B2B markets within these three general categories, marketers rely upon the **North American Industry Classification System (NAICS)** to identify their customers. This is a numerical coding of industries that the United States, Canada, and Mexico developed. Table 5.2 shows the NAICS coding system. NAICS replaced the US Standard Industrial Classification (SIC) system in 1997 so that the North American Free Trade Agreement (NAFTA) countries could compare economic and financial statistics.[4] The NAICS reports the number of firms, the total dollar amount of sales, the number of employees, and the growth rate for industries, all broken down by geographic region; an example is the Golden Horseshoe region in Ontario. Many firms use the NAICS to assess potential markets and determine how well they are doing compared to others in their industry group.

Firms may also use the NAICS to find new customers. A marketer might first determine the NAICS industry classifications of his current customers and then evaluate the sales potential of other firms occupying these categories. For example, Brad Tracy may find that several of NCR's large customers are in the grocery industry. To find new customers, he could contact other firms in the same industrial group.

Table 5.2 | North American Industry Classification System

		Frozen Fruit Example		Cellular Telecommunications Example
• Sector (two digits)	31–33	Manufacturing	51	Information
• Subsector (three digits)	311	Food manufacturing	513	Broadcasting and Telecommunications
• Industry group (four digits)	3114	Fruit and vegetable preserving and speciality food manufacturing	5133	Telecommunications
• Industry (five digits)	31141	Frozen food manufacturing	51332	Wireless Telecommunications Carriers (except satellite)
• U.S. Industry (six digits)	311311	Frozen fruit, juice, and vegetable manufacturing	513322	Cellular and Other Wireless Telecommunications

2

OBJECTIVE

Appreciate
opportunities for
using e-commerce
and social media in
business-to-business
settings.
(pp. 157–160)

Business-to-Business E-Commerce and Social Media

We know that the Internet transformed marketing—from the creation of new products to providing more effective and efficient marketing communications to the actual distribution of some products. This is certainly true in business markets as well. **Business-to-business (B2B) e-commerce** refers to Internet exchanges between two or more businesses or organizations. This includes exchanges of information, goods, services, and payments. It's not as glitzy as consumer e-commerce, but it sure has changed the way businesses operate. Using the Internet for e-commerce allows business marketers to link directly to suppliers, factories, distributors, and their customers, radically reducing the time necessary for ordering and delivery of goods, tracking sales, and getting feedback from customers.

In the simplest form of B2B e-commerce, the Internet provides an online catalogue of goods and services that businesses need. Companies find that their Internet site is important to deliver online technical support, product information, order status information, and customer service to corporate customers. Many companies, for example, save millions of dollars a year when they replace hard-copy manuals with electronic downloads. And, of course, B2B e-commerce creates some exciting opportunities for a variety of B2B service industries.

business-to-business (B2B) e-commerce
Internet exchanges between two or more businesses or organizations.

Intranets, Extranets, and Private Exchanges

Although the Internet is the primary means of B2B e-commerce, many companies maintain intranets, which provide more secure means of conducting business. As we said in an earlier chapter, this term refers to an internal corporate computer network that uses Internet technology to link a company's departments, employees, and databases. Intranets give access only to authorized employees. They allow companies to process internal transactions with greater control and consistency because of stricter security measures than those they can use on the entire Web. Businesses also use intranets for video conferences, distributing internal documents, communicating with geographically dispersed branches, and training employees.

In contrast to an intranet, an **extranet** allows certain suppliers, customers, and others outside the organization to access a company's internal system. A business customer that a company authorizes to use its extranet can place orders online. Extranets can be especially useful for companies that need to have secure communications between the company and its dealers, distributors, and/or franchisees.

As you can imagine, intranets and extranets are very cost efficient. Sun Life's extranet allows its corporate customers to enroll new employees and check eligibility and claim status themselves. This saves Sun Life money because it can hire fewer customer service personnel, there are no packages of insurance forms to mail back and forth, and Sun Life doesn't even have to input policyholder data into the company database.

In addition to saving companies money, extranets allow business partners to collaborate on projects (such as product design) and build relationships. Companies like HP and Procter & Gamble swap marketing plans and review ad campaigns with their advertising agencies through extranets (Exhibit 5.5). They can exchange ideas quickly without having to spend money on travel and meetings. GE's extranet, the Trading Process Network,

extranet
A private, corporate computer network that links company departments, employees, and databases to suppliers, customers, and others outside the organization.

Exhibit 5.5

HP exchanges information and ideas efficiently through its extranet system.

Courtesy of Hewlett-Packard (Canada) Co.

began as a set of online purchasing procedures and has morphed into an extensive online extranet community that connects GE with large buyers such as Pratt & Whitney in Montreal.

Some of the most interesting online activity in the B2B world takes place on **private exchanges**. These are systems that link a specially invited group of suppliers and partners over the Web. A private exchange allows companies to collaborate with suppliers they trust—without sharing sensitive information with others.

Walmart, IBM, and HP are among the giant firms that operate private exchanges. Many other companies are getting on board as well. For example, the director of inventory control for Rona can click a mouse and instantly receive an up-to-the-minute listing of the screwdrivers, hammers, and other products its suppliers have in stock. In addition, the suppliers Rona invites to participate in its private exchange (and only those suppliers) can submit bids when Rona stores start to run low on hammers. In the "old days" before Rona implemented this process it would take 7 to 10 days to purchase more hammers, and Rona's suppliers could only guess how many they should have on hand to supply the store chain at any given time. The system benefits everyone, because Rona keeps tighter controls on its inventories, and its suppliers have a more accurate picture of the store's needs so they can get rid of unneeded inventory and streamline their costs.

The Dark Side of B2B E-Commerce

Doing business the Web-enabled way sounds great—perhaps too great. There are also security risks because so much information gets passed around in cyberspace. You've no doubt heard all the recent stories about hackers obtaining vast lists of consumers' credit card numbers from retailers and other sources. But companies have even greater worries. When hackers break into company sites, they can destroy company records and steal trade secrets. Both business-to-consumer (B2C) and B2B e-commerce companies worry about *authentication* and ensuring that transactions are secure. This means making sure that only authorized individuals are allowed to access a site and place an order. Maintaining security also requires firms to keep the information transferred as part of a transaction, such as a credit card number, from criminals' hard drives.

Well-meaning employees also can create security problems. They can give out unauthorized access to company computer systems by being careless about keeping their passwords into the system a secret. For example, hackers can guess at obvious passwords—nicknames, birthdates, hobbies, or a spouse's name. To increase security of their Internet sites and transactions, most companies now have safeguards in place—firewalls and encryption devices, to name the two most common methods.

A *firewall* is a combination of hardware and software that ensures that only authorized individuals gain entry into a computer system. The firewall monitors and controls all traffic between the Internet and the intranet to restrict access. Companies may even place additional firewalls within their intranet when they wish only designated employees to have access to certain parts of the system. Although firewalls can be fairly effective (even though none is totally foolproof), they require costly, constant monitoring.

Encryption means scrambling a message so that only another individual (or computer) with the right "key" can unscramble it; otherwise, it looks like gobbledygook. The message is inaccessible without the appropriate encryption software—kind of like a decoder ring you might find in a cereal box. Without encryption, it would be easy for unethical people to get a credit card number by creating a "sniffer" program that intercepts and reads messages. A sniffer finds messages with four blocks of four numbers, copies the data, and voila!—someone else has your credit card number.

Despite firewalls, encryption, and other security measures, Web security for B2B marketers remains a serious problem. The threat to intranet and extranet usage goes beyond competitive espionage. The increasing sophistication of hackers and Internet criminals who create viruses and worms and other approaches to disrupting individual computers and

private exchanges
Systems that link an invited group of suppliers and partners over the Web.

entire company systems means that all organizations—and consumers—are vulnerable to attacks and must remain vigilant.

B2B and Social Media

Trade shows will always be great vehicles to promote products and services to other businesses. But another way B2B marketers drive brand awareness and generate buzz is by playing games—yes, *games*. Check out Office Depot's "Strange Little Office Beings" as an example of a viral game that appeals to business customers' playful sides. As we'll see in Chapter 11, a viral technique refers to, for instance, a message that people spread to others (just like catching a cold, but more fun).[5] And speaking of viral, there's hardly a B2B firm of any size today that doesn't promote itself through social networking sites such as LinkedIn, Twitter, and Facebook.

When it comes to developing an effective B2B social media marketing strategy, one size definitely does not fit all. A recent study of more than 2300 people and the social media resources used for business-relevant information found that the following five resources were the most turned to by people at work looking for information:

1. Webinars and podcasts
2. Online ratings and reviews of business products or services
3. Company pages on social networking sites such as Facebook or LinkedIn
4. Company blogs
5. Searches of business-related information on social media sites

However, use of these formats varied considerably across company size, job role, and industry. Social media channels were most effective to reach and engage prospects at mid-to-large-size companies. Respondents who work at small companies with fewer than 100 employees were less likely to use almost all social media resources for business, with one exception—online ratings and reviews. Also, while the use of Twitter for business was 60 percent lower than for webinars or podcasts overall, Twitter is indeed a viable channel to reach senior managers at mid-to-large-size companies. Among those using any type of social media for business, 41 percent use Twitter. Certain industries (advertising and marketing, computers and software, and the Internet) and job roles (marketing and consulting) are also heavier users of social media for business than other industries (health care, legal, and retail) and job responsibilities (accounting, finance, customer support, and sales).[6]

Among the social media sites, the one that has become most associated with B2B networking is LinkedIn. Here are key reasons why it is the site *du jour* for so many businesspeople.

LinkedIn reduces the separation gap. Like other social networking sites, LinkedIn allows you to connect with people you know. However, it has one distinct benefit—it also allows you to see the degree of separation between you and others with whom you are not yet connected. This allows you to discover who your connections are connected with, and many times they're just the people you need to know.

LinkedIn is primarily for corporate professionals. Sites like Facebook mainly cater to people looking to have fun, post pictures, take quizzes, and so on. After all, the site was created by college kids to reach out to other kids. Most people do not use Facebook as a business tool, and most members aren't on it to network or build their brand. However, LinkedIn was created for business professionals. Almost everyone on LinkedIn is a member of the white-collar business world, which not only helps you to reach a large audience; it helps you to reach your target audience.

LinkedIn can lead to quality introductions. When you are trying to land a big account or grow your business, sometimes all it takes is an introduction to the right person. LinkedIn addresses this very need. It has a unique tool that allows you to ask people you are connected with to connect you with people they know in a professional way. A quality introduction like this is a great way to get your foot in the door and gives you more credibility than a cold call would.

Trade Shows Gone Virtual

Trade shows are a staple in the B2B world. Traditionally, firms ship samples of their latest and greatest wares to a convention centre and company reps man a booth for several days of prospecting and networking. But tight travel budgets and busier-than-ever clients have caused many firms to shift to virtual trade shows, where exhibitors and attendees participate through their Web browsers. The events resemble virtual worlds such as Second Life and may last only a few hours or span several days. There are presentations from speakers, exhibit halls, and even lounges—sans virtual cocktails—where attendees can "mingle" with other participants.

Setting up a virtual booth is quick and easy. Exhibitors choose from predesigned displays, add their company logos, and upload promotional materials. When a visitor clicks on a company's booth, employees (who are logged into their own computers but may be multitasking) receive an alert. They can talk to the visitor through a chat window or, if both parties have Web cameras, by video.

Procuring a booth at a virtual trade show isn't always cheap, but it tends to be less than its brick-and-mortar counterpart, which can exceed $15 000 before travel costs. A virtual booth costs $3000 to $8000, on average. Importantly, virtual shows often provide more detailed data about attendees than a physical event can—a rich source of information for follow-up by sales and marketing.

Still, the virtual expos don't get nearly as many visitors as in-person events—maybe a couple thousand versus 8000 or so. And because of the lower costs—admission is usually free—attendees at virtual expos tend to be smaller companies rather than large corporations. But the intimacy of virtual trade shows sometimes allows smaller firms to get more attention than they would receive at a big expo, a benefit for both parties. Although the absence of real face-to-face interaction is a downside, given that companies are tightening their budgets for many B2B buyers and sellers virtual shows have become the primary channel for initial contact, and the medium is projected to continue growing for the foreseeable future.[7]

LinkedIn can help you reconnect with alumni and colleagues. LinkedIn has an extensive and comprehensive search engine that will allow you to locate and reconnect with past colleagues and peers. Who knows what company your old roommate from college works for, or what quality connections your long-lost coworker can offer you? LinkedIn can help you to revive these old relationships to network and build your brand.

LinkedIn is a professional site. Because it was designed specifically for business professionals, LinkedIn users follow good business manners. Unlike on the other social networking sites, you won't have to weed your way through party pictures and drunken status updates in order to reach your target audience.[8]

3 Business Buying Situations and the Business Buying Decision Process

OBJECTIVE
Identify and describe the different business buying situations and the business buying decision process. (pp. 160–168)

So far we've talked about how B2B markets are different from consumer markets and about the different types of customers that make up business markets. In this section, we'll discuss some of the important characteristics of business buying situations. This is important because just like companies that sell to end consumers, a successful B2B marketer needs to understand how her customers make decisions. Armed with this knowledge, the company is able to participate in the buyer's decision process from the start.

The Buyclass Framework

Like end-user consumers, business buyers spend more time and effort on some purchases than on others. This usually depends on the complexity of the product and how often they need to make the decision. A **buyclass** framework identifies the degree of effort required of the firm's personnel to collect information and make a purchase decision. These classes, which apply to three different buying situations, are straight rebuys, modified rebuys, and new-task buys (Figure 5.4).

buyclass
One of three classifications of business buying situations that characterize the degree of time and effort required to make a decision.

Figure 5.4 Elements of the Buyclass Framework

The classes of the buyclass framework relate to three different organizational buying situations: straight rebuy, modified rebuy, and new-task buy.

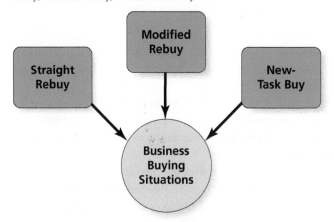

Straight Rebuy

A **straight rebuy** refers to the routine purchase of items that a B2B customer regularly needs. The buyer has purchased the same items many times before and routinely reorders them when supplies are low, often from the same suppliers. Reordering the items takes little time. Buyers typically maintain a list of approved vendors that have demonstrated their ability to meet the firm's criteria for pricing, quality, service, and delivery. GE Healthcare's customers routinely purchase its line of basic surgical scrubs (the clothing and caps doctors and nurses wear in the operating room) without much evaluation on each occasion.

Because straight rebuys often contribute the "bread and butter" revenue a firm needs to maintain a steady stream of income, many business marketers go to great lengths to cultivate and maintain relationships with customers who submit reorders on a regular basis (Exhibit 5.6). Salespeople may regularly call on these customers to personally handle orders and to see if there are additional products the customer needs. The goal is to be sure that the customer doesn't even think twice about just buying the same product every time she is running low. Rebuys keep a supplier's sales volume up and help cover selling costs.

Modified Rebuy

Life is sweet for companies whose customers automatically do straight rebuys. Unfortunately, these situations do not last forever. A **modified rebuy** occurs when a firm decides to shop around for suppliers with better prices, quality, or delivery times. This situation also can occur when the organization confronts new needs for products it already buys. A buyer who purchased many BlackBerry smartphones from Research In Motion (RIM), based in Waterloo, Ontario, for example, may have to reevaluate several other options if the firm upgrades its cellular telecommunications system.

Modified rebuys require more time and effort than straight rebuys. The buyer generally knows the purchase requirements and she has a few potential suppliers in mind. Marketers know that modified rebuys can mean that some vendors get added to a buyer's approved supplier list while others may be dropped. So even if in the past a company purchased its smartphones from RIM, this doesn't necessarily mean it will

straight rebuy
A buying situation in which business buyers make routine purchases that require minimal decision making.

modified rebuy
A buying situation classification used by business buyers to categorize a previously made purchase that involves some change and that requires limited decision making.

Freight from a network unlike any other. Check.

Give your business a competitive advantage with Purolator Freight®, offering premium services, including individual skid-level tracking for your less-than-truckload (LTL) shipments. Our suite of specialized online tools gives you maximum control over your orders, helping you effectively manage your inventory in transit and the needs of your customers with greater precision. With the resources, support and coast-to-coast coverage of Canada's largest courier company, we will help take your business wherever it needs to go. To learn more about our network unlike any other, visit purolator.com/freight

Purolator Freight

purolator.com/freight

Courtesy of Purolator, Inc.

Exhibit 5.6

By offering its customers the capability to send heavier shipments, Purolator hopes that its business customers will routinely use the company for all its straight-rebuy purchases.

do so in the future. Other firms like Apple, Palm, and Google's Android may gain approved supplier status going forward, and the race is on. Astute marketers routinely call on buyers to detect and define problems that can lead to winning or losing in such situations.

New-Task Buy

A first-time purchase is a **new-task buy**. Uncertainty and risk characterize buying decisions in this classification, and they require the most effort because the buyer has no previous experience on which to base a decision.

Your university, for example, may decide (if it hasn't done so already) to go into the "distance learning" business—delivering courses to off-site students. Buying the equipment to set up classrooms with two-way video transmission is an expensive and complex new-task buy for a school. The buyer has to start from scratch to gather information on purchase specifications that may be highly technical and complex and require detailed input from others. In new-task buying situations, not only do buyers lack experience with the product, but they also are often unfamiliar with firms that supply the product. Supplier choice is critical, and buyers gather much information about quality, pricing, delivery, and service from several potential suppliers.

A prospective customer's new-task buying situation represents both a challenge and an opportunity. Although a new-task buy can be significant in and of itself, many times the chosen supplier gains the added advantage of becoming an "in" supplier for more routine purchases that will follow. A growing business that needs an advertising agency for the first time, for example, may seek exhaustive information from several firms before it selects one, but then it may continue to use the chosen agency's services for future projects without bothering to explore other alternatives.

Marketers know that to get the order in a new-buy situation, they must develop a close working relationship with the business buyer. There are many situations in which marketers focus on selling their product by wooing people who recommend their products—over and above the end consumers who actually buy them. To use an example close to home, think about all of the goods and services that make up the higher-education industry. For instance, even though you are the one who shelled out the money for this extremely awesome textbook, your professor was the one who made the exceptionally wise decision to assign it. She made this choice (did we mention it was a really wise choice?) only after carefully considering numerous textbooks and talking to several publishers' sales representatives.

Professional Buyers and Buying Centres

Just as it is important for marketers of consumer goods and services to understand their customers, it's essential that B2B marketers understand who handles the buying for business customers. Trained professional buyers typically carry out buying in B2B markets. These people have titles such as *purchasing agents, procurement officers,* or *directors of materials management.*

While some consumers like to shop 'til they drop almost every day, most of us spend far less time roaming the aisles. However, professional purchasers do it all day, every day—it's their job and their business to buy! These individuals focus on economic factors beyond the initial price of the product, including transportation and delivery charges, accessory products or supplies, maintenance, and other ongoing costs. They are responsible for selecting quality products and ensuring their timely delivery. They shop as if their jobs depend on it—because they do.

Many times in business buying situations, several people work together to reach a decision. Depending on what they need to purchase, these participants may be production workers, supervisors, engineers, administrative assistants, shipping clerks, or financial officers. In a small organization, everyone may have a voice in the decision. The **buying centre** is the group of people in the organization who participate in the decision-making process.

new-task buy
A new business-to-business purchase that is complex or risky and that requires extensive decision making.

Brad Tracy

APPLYING   The Buyclass Framework

How would you categorize the purchase of a new POS workstation for most companies? What does your answer imply about the factors that will influence its purchase?

buying centre
The group of people in an organization who participate in a purchasing decision.

Although this term may conjure up an image of "command central" buzzing with purchasing activity, a buying centre is not a place at all. Instead, it is a cross-functional team of decision makers. Generally, the members of a buying centre have some expertise or interest in the particular decision, and as a group they are able to make the best decision.

Hospitals, for example, frequently make purchase decisions through a large buying centre. When they need to purchase disposable protective masks, one or more physicians, the director of nursing, and purchasing agents may work together to determine quantities and select the best products and suppliers. A separate decision regarding the types of pharmaceutical supplies to stock might call for a different cast of characters to advise the purchasing agent, likely including pharmacists and pharmacy technicians. Marketers must continually identify which employees in a firm take part in every purchase decision and develop relationships with them all. (See Exhibit 5.7.)

Depending on the complexity of the purchase and the size of the buying centre, a participant may assume one, several, or all of the six roles that Table 5.3 shows. Let's review them now.

Exhibit 5.7

Canada Post, a federal Crown corporation, buys many products from other businesses so it can render a service to the general public.

- The *initiator* begins the buying process by first recognizing that the firm needs to make a purchase. A production employee, for example, may notice that a piece of equipment is not working properly and notify a supervisor that it is slowing up the production line. At other times, the initiator may suggest purchasing a new product because it will improve the firm's operations. Depending on the initiator's position in the organization and the type of purchase, the initiator may or may not influence the actual purchase decision. For marketers, it's important to make sure that individuals who might initiate a purchase are aware of improved products they offer.

- The *user* is the member of the buying centre who actually needs the product. The user's role in the buying centre varies. For example, an administrative assistant may give her input on the features a new copier should have because she will be chained to it for several hours a day. Marketers need to inform users of their products' benefits, especially if the benefits outweigh those that competitors offer.

- The *gatekeeper* is the person who controls the flow of information to other members. Typically the gatekeeper is the purchasing agent who gathers information and materials

Table 5.3	Roles in the Buying Centre	
Role	**Potential Player**	**Responsibility**
• Initiator	• Production employees, sales manager, almost anyone	• Recognizes that a purchase needs to be made
• User	• Production employees, secretaries, almost anyone	• Individual(s) who will ultimately use the product
• Gatekeeper	• Buyer/purchasing agent	• Controls flow of information to others in the organization
• Influencer	• Engineers, quality control experts, technical specialists, outside consultants	• Affects decision by giving advice and sharing expertise
• Decider	• Purchasing agent, managers, CEO	• Makes the final purchase decision
• Buyer	• Purchasing agent	• Executes the purchase decision

from salespeople, schedules sales presentations, and controls suppliers' access to other participants in the buying process. For salespeople, developing and maintaining strong personal relationships with gatekeepers is critical to being able to offer their products to the buying centre.

- An *influencer* affects the buying decision when she dispenses advice or shares expertise. Highly trained employees like engineers, quality-control specialists, and other technical experts in the firm generally have a great deal of influence in purchasing equipment, materials, and component parts the company uses in production. The influencers may or may not wind up using the product. Marketers need to identify key influencers in the buying centre and persuade them of their product's superiority.

- The *decider* is the member of the buying centre who makes the final decision. This person usually has the greatest power within the buying centre; she often has power within the organization to authorize spending the company's money. For a routine purchase, the decider may be the purchasing agent. If the purchase is complex, a manager or even the chief executive officer (CEO) may be the decider. Quite obviously, the decider is critical to a marketer's success and deserves a lot of attention in the selling process.

- The *buyer* is the person who has responsibility to execute the purchase. Although the buyer often has a role in identifying and evaluating alternative suppliers, this person's primary function is to handle the details of the transaction. The buyer obtains competing bids, negotiates contracts, and arranges delivery dates and payment plans. Once a firm makes the purchase decision, marketers turn their attention to negotiating the details of the purchase with the buyer. Successful marketers are well aware that providing exemplary service in this stage of the purchase can be a critical factor in achieving future sales from this client.

The Business Buying Decision Process

We've seen that there are a number of players in the business buying process, beginning with an initiator and ending with a buyer. To make matters even more challenging to marketers, members of the buying team go through several stages in the decision-making process before the marketer gets an order. The *business buying decision process*, as Figure 5.5 shows, is a series of steps similar to those in the consumer decision process we discussed in Chapter 4. To help understand these steps, let's say you've just started working at the Way Radical Skateboard Company and your boss just assigned you to the buying centre for the purchase of new software for Web-page design—a new-task buy for your firm.

Step 1: Recognize the Problem

As in consumer buying, the first step in the business buying decision process occurs when someone sees that a purchase can solve a problem. For straight rebuy purchases, this may occur because the firm has run out of paper, pens, or garbage bags. In these cases, the buyer places the order, and the decision-making process ends. Recognition of the need for modified rebuy purchases often comes when the organization wants to replace outdated existing equipment, from changes in technology or from an ad, brochure, or some other marketing communication that offers the customer a better product or one at a lower price. Two events may occur in the problem-recognition step. First, a firm makes a request or requisition, usually in writing. Then, depending on the complexity of the purchase, the firm may form a buying centre.

The need for new-task purchases often occurs because the firm wants to enhance its operations in some way or because a smart salesperson tells the business customer about a new product that will increase the efficiency of the firm's operations or improve the firm's end products. In the case of Way Radical's new software purchase,

Figure 5.5 Steps in the Business Buying Decision Process

The steps in the business buying decision process are the same as those in the consumer decision process. But for business purchases, each step may be far more complex and require more attention from marketers.

Step 1: Recognize the problem
- Make purchase requisition or request
- Form buying centre, if needed

↓

Step 2: Search for Information
- Develop product specifications
- Identify potential suppliers
- Obtain proposals and quotations

↓

Step 3: Evaluate the Alternatives
- Evaluate proposals
- Obtain and evaluate samples

↓

Step 4: Select the Product and Supplier
- Issue purchase order

↓

Step 5: Evaluate Postpurchase
- Survey users
- Document performance

Ethical and Sustainable Decisions in the Real World

The fair trade movement in Canada has grown significantly over the past few decades. Fair trade is an organized social movement and market-based approach that fosters better trading conditions for farmers in developing countries. As a result, it promotes sustainability and connects the northern hemisphere with poorer countries. Fair trade has focused its activities around commodities like coffee, cacao, tea, and handcrafted products.

The response from consumers and from marketers to fair trade has been mixed and fair trade's increasing popularity has drawn criticism from both ends of the political spectrum. The fair trade movement has had problems getting its labelling policies structured around the world and this has influenced how consumers perceive these products. Since the fair trade movement doesn't really monitor how systems are supporting farmers, there is no evidence that participating farmers get higher prices on average. But these products in Canada do cost more to buy. So, is it okay to charge more for these products? How could you guarantee that farmers get more revenues from these products? How can marketers market these products differently between organizations and make sure the proper information gets to the consumer?

ETHICS CHECK: 🖎
Find out what other students taking this course **would do** and **why** on **www .mypearsonmarketinglab .com**

---

the marketing department had previously hired an outside agency to design and maintain its Web page. The company became dissatisfied with the outside supplier and decided to move the design function in-house. Now the company needs to select new software to create a truly Way Radical Web site.

Step 2: Search for Information

In the second step of the decision process (for purchases other than straight rebuys), the buying centre searches for information about products and suppliers. Members of the buying centre may individually or collectively refer to reports in trade magazines and journals, seek advice from outside consultants, and pay close attention to marketing communications from different manufacturers and suppliers. As in consumer marketing, it's the job of marketers to make sure that information is available when and where business customers want it—placing ads in trade magazines, mailing brochures and other printed material to prospects, and having a well-trained sales force regularly calling on customers to build long-term relationships. For Way Radical's purchase, you may try to find out what software your outside supplier uses (if the supplier will tell you), talk to the information technology experts in your firm, or review ads and articles in trade magazines.

There are thousands of specialized publications out there that cater to just about any industry you can think of. Usually sponsored by leading industry trade associations, each is bursting with information from competing companies that cater to a specific niche. Who needs that fluffy romance novel at the beach? Try leafing through the latest issue of *Chemical Processing* or *Meat and Poultry Magazine* instead.

Of course, sometimes B2B marketers try to get the information about their product into the hands of buyers via less-specialized media. For example, Sleeman Breweries, known for its interesting commercials and focus on the Sleeman family, sells most of its products to businesses—retail stores. The company launched an aggressive advertising campaign drawing attention to its bootlegging past, featuring John Sleeman, even though the company does not sell to consumers directly (Exhibit 5.8).

Business buyers often develop **product specifications**; that is, a written description of the quality, size, weight, colour, features, quantity, training, warranty, service terms, and delivery requirements for the purchase. When the product needs are complex or technical, engineers and other experts are the key players who identify specific product characteristics required and determine whether the organizations can get by with standardized/off-the-shelf items or if they need to acquire customized/made-to-order goods and services. Although excellent Web-design software is available off the shelf, for some computer applications, like the one Way Radical needs, custom-designed software may be necessary.

Once the product specifications are in hand, the next step is to identify potential suppliers and obtain written or verbal proposals, or *bids*, from one or more of them. For standardized

Brad Tracy

APPLYING ▽ The Search for Information

Brad knows that prospective customers need a lot of information about a complex purchase like a POS workstation. He needs to decide upon the best places to make this information available, including which trade shows NCR should attend. ➥

product specifications
A written description of the quality, size, weight, and other details required of a product purchase.

At Moosehead we believe our independence is our greatest strength, allowing us to brew quality beer without compromise, the way we always have, since 1867.

www.moosehead.ca

Exhibit 5.8
Even though Moosehead Breweries does not sell its products to consumers directly, it does advertise to the greater public.

customer reference program
A formalized process by which customers formally share success stories and actively recommend products to other potential clients, usually facilitated through an online community.

or branded products in which there are few, if any, differences in the products of different suppliers, this may be as simple as an informal request for pricing information, including discounts, shipping charges, and confirmation of delivery dates. At other times, the potential suppliers receive a formal written *request for proposal* or *request for quotation* that requires detailed information from vendors. For the Way Radical software, which is likely to be a custom-designed software package, you will probably need specific, detailed pricing information.

Step 3: Evaluate the Alternatives

In this stage of the business buying decision process, the buying centre assesses the proposals it receives. Total spending for goods and services can have a major impact on the firm's profitability, so, all other things being equal, price can be a primary consideration. Pricing evaluations must take into account discount policies for certain quantities, returned-goods policies, the cost of repair and maintenance services, terms of payment, and the cost of financing large purchases. For capital equipment, cost criteria also include the life expectancy of the purchase, the expected resale value, and disposal costs for the old equipment. In some cases, the buying centre may negotiate with the preferred supplier to match the lowest bidder.

Although a firm often selects a bidder because it offers the lowest price, there are times when it bases the buying decision on other factors. For example, in its lucrative B2B market, American Express wins bids for its travel agency business because it offers extra services other agencies don't or can't offer, such as a corporate credit card, monthly reports that detail the company's total travel expenses, and perks tied to AMEX's customer loyalty program.

The more complex and costly the purchase, the more time buyers spend searching for the best supplier—and the more marketers must do to win the order. In some cases, a company may even ask one or more of its current customers to participate in a **customer reference program**. In these situations, customers formally share success stories and actively recommend products to other potential clients, often as part of an online community composed of people with similar needs.

Marketers often make formal presentations and product demonstrations to the buying centre group. In the case of installations and large equipment, they may arrange for buyers to speak with or even visit other customers to examine how the product performs. For less complex products, the buying firm may ask potential suppliers for samples of the products so its people can evaluate them personally. The buying centre may ask salespeople from various companies to demonstrate their software for your Way Radical group so that you can all compare the capabilities of different products.

Step 4: Select the Product and Supplier

Once buyers have assessed all proposals, it's time for the rubber to hit the road. The next step in the buying process is the purchase decision, when the group selects the best product and supplier to meet the firm's needs. Reliability and durability rank especially high for equipment and systems that keep the firm's operations running smoothly without interruption. For some purchases, warranties, repair service, and regular maintenance after the sale are important. For Way Radical, the final decision may be based not only on the capabilities of the software itself but also on the technical support the software company provides. What kind of support is available and at what cost to the customer?

One of the most important decisions a buyer makes is how many suppliers can best serve the firm's needs. Sometimes having one supplier is more beneficial to the organization than having multiple suppliers. **Single sourcing**, in which a buyer and seller work quite closely, is particularly important when a firm needs frequent deliveries or specialized products. Single sourcing also helps assure consistency of quality of materials input into the production process. But reliance on a single source means that the firm is at the mercy of the chosen supplier to deliver the needed goods or services without interruption. If the single source doesn't come through, the firm's relationship with its own end users will very likely be affected.

However, using one or a few suppliers rather than many has its advantages. A firm that buys from a single supplier becomes a large customer with a lot of clout when it comes to negotiating prices and contract terms. Having one or a few suppliers also lowers the firm's administrative costs because it has fewer invoices to pay, fewer contracts to negotiate, and fewer salespeople to see than if it uses many sources.

In contrast, **multiple sourcing** means buying a product from several different suppliers. Under this system, suppliers are more likely to remain price competitive. And if one supplier has problems with delivery, the firm has others to fall back upon. The automotive industry practises this philosophy: A vehicle manufacturer often won't buy a new product from a supplier unless the vendor's rivals also are capable of making the same item! This policy tends to stifle innovation, but it does ensure a steady supply of parts to feed to the assembly line.

Sometimes supplier selection is based on **reciprocity**, which means that a buyer and seller agree to be each other's customers by saying, essentially, I'll buy from you, and you buy from me. For example, a firm that supplies parts to a company that manufactures trucks would agree to buy trucks from only that firm.

The Canadian government frowns on reciprocal agreements and often determines that such agreements between large firms are illegal because they limit free competition—new suppliers simply don't have a chance against the preferred suppliers. Reciprocity between smaller firms—that is, firms that are not so large as to control a significant proportion of the business in their industry—is legal in Canada if both parties voluntarily agree to it. In other countries, reciprocity is a practice that is common and even expected in B2B marketing.

Outsourcing occurs when firms obtain outside vendors to provide goods or services that might otherwise be supplied in-house. For example, Cara Operations, based in Vaughan, Ontario, is the largest company that provides catering services to airlines. It delivers food to accommodate thousands of flights every day across the country. You may have seen their trucks when going to the airport. Airlines are a major category of clientele for Cara Operations.

Outsourcing is an increasingly popular strategy, but in some cases it can be controversial. Many critics object when Canadian companies contract with companies or individuals in remote places like China or India to perform work they used to do at home. These tasks range from complicated jobs like writing computer code to fairly simple ones like manning reservations desks, staffing call centres for telephone sales, and even taking drive-through orders at fast-food restaurants. (Yes, in some cases it's actually more efficient for an operator in India to relay an order from a customer for a #3 Burger Combo to the restaurant's cooks than for an on-site person to take the order!)

Controversy aside, many companies find that it's both cost-efficient and productive to call on outsiders from around the world to solve problems their own scientists can't handle. We call this process **crowdsourcing**: put simply, a way to harness "crowds" to "source" solutions to business problems. Among the more interesting areas for crowdsourcing by marketers are brainstorming and feedback (www.kluster.com), brand names (www.namethis.com), product redesign (www.redesignme.com), and logo design (www.99designs.com), which hawks itself as follows: "Need a logo? No problem. Simply turn your logo/design project needs into

---

single sourcing
The business practice of buying a particular product from only one supplier.

multiple sourcing
The business practice of buying a particular product from several different suppliers.

reciprocity
A trading partnership in which two firms agree to buy from one another.

outsourcing
The business buying process of obtaining outside vendors to provide goods or services that otherwise might be supplied in-house.

crowdsourcing
A practice in which firms outsource marketing activities (such as selecting an ad) to a community of users.

reverse marketing
A business practice in which a buyer firm attempts to identify suppliers who will produce products according to the buyer firm's specifications.

a contest on 99designs. Submit a brief and determine a fee for the contest winner (minimum is around $150), then sit back and watch the crowd go to work. More than 40,000 designers use 99designs. After all the submissions are in you can choose a design. What could be simpler?"[9]

Yet another type of buyer-seller partnership is **reverse marketing**. Instead of sellers trying to identify potential customers and then "pitching" their products, buyers try to find suppliers that can produce specifically needed products and then attempt to "sell" the idea to the suppliers. The seller aims to satisfy the buying firm's needs. Often large poultry producers practise reverse marketing. Lilydale supplies baby chickens in many provinces, as well as chicken food, financing for chicken houses, medications, and everything else necessary for farmers to lay "golden eggs" for the company. This assures the farmer that she will have a buyer, while at the same time guaranteeing Lilydale's chicken supply.

Step 5: Evaluate Postpurchase

Just as consumers evaluate purchases, an organizational buyer assesses whether the performance of the product and the supplier lives up to expectations. The buyer surveys the users to determine their satisfaction with the product as well as with the installation, delivery, and service the supplier provides. For producers of goods, this may relate to the level of satisfaction of the final consumer of the buying firm's product. Has demand for the producer's product increased, decreased, or stayed the same? By documenting and reviewing supplier performance, a firm decides whether to keep or drop the supplier. Many suppliers recognize the importance of conducting their own performance reviews on a regular basis. Measuring up to a customer's expectations can mean winning or losing a big account. Many a supplier has lost business because of a history of late deliveries or poor equipment repairs and maintenance.

An important element in postpurchase evaluation is measurement. When you think about measuring elements of a customer's experience with a company and its products and brands, we'll bet you automatically think about end-user consumers—like travellers' views of their Marriott Hotel stay or the taste of that new Starbucks coffee flavour. Similarly, in the B2B world, managers pay a lot of attention to the feedback they get about the purchases they've made. Here are some metrics organizational buyers use to measure how well a product or service performs:

- *Satisfaction* Yes, customer satisfaction is still very relevant in B2B and in the buying centre; ultimately, it is the user of the product that should provide this feedback. You can bet that if users are dissatisfied, they will quickly relay this information to the rest of the buying centre.

- *Quality* Is the product meeting, exceeding, or falling short of expectations, and (for the latter) what can be done to correct the deficiency?

- *Customer Engagement* It is important to find ways to get and keep customers involved in your business after the sales have been made through customer reference programs or other means.

- *Purchase Intentions* A common metric is to determine the general budgetary plan a client has for the year ahead, leading to the ability to determine what appropriate sales goals might be going forward.

- *Promptness and Effectiveness of Problem Resolution* The complexities of the B2B market ensure that problems will occur between vendor and client. The true test is how well and how quickly problems are resolved when they do come up.

A final tip: Remember that B2B customers are busy professionals. They have even less time to fill out lengthy questionnaires than do end-user consumers. Make sure you collect feedback efficiently in a manner most comfortable to the client.[10]

Here's my choice. . .

Real **People**, Real **Choices**

Why do you think Brad chose option 2?

Option 1 Option 2 Option 3

How It Worked Out at NCR

Brad selected Option 2. NCR's retail division passed on the show and reallocated its sales and marketing resources to the two smaller events. As it turned out, NCR was only one of a number of large vendors that made this decision. Like a snowball effect, this drop-off, in turn, decreased the number of retail customers who chose to attend. Additionally, the change in venue and combination with another trade event failed to generate incremental attendance necessary for continued operation. A few days after the show, the organizers announced they were discontinuing it.

The new events NCR did attend delivered mixed results. One show was sponsored by a national trade association and it drew a solid number of customers and prospects. The number of vendors was limited as only show sponsors (including NCR) participated. Because there was less competition for customers' attention, Brad's staff were able to dramatically increase the quality and length of their interactions with visitors to the booth. However, the second event, sponsored by a trade publication, did not draw the expected number of attendees. Vendor attendees slightly outnumbered retail attendees so the quantity, quality, and duration of NCR's interactions were disappointing. Moving forward, the division will continue to focus its resources in two areas: 1) large industry leading shows that have sustainable momentum with its targeted customers; and 2) small focused conference events that offer the opportunity to have high-quality interactions with attendees.

How NCR Measures Success

NCR evaluates its promotional efforts in terms of their value to the company's organizational objectives. This process involves looking closely at expected costs and benefits and comparing these forecasts to what a trade show or other marketing effort actually achieved. But this equation is a bit more complicated, because each event is only one of many touchpoints with a customer that ultimately determines whether the company will win the business. Therefore, NCR must use several measures that taken together help its analysts to approximate the impact of a trade show or other initiative. These measures include the following:

- Number of attendees

- Number of interactions (meetings, discussions, or booth tours) with existing customers

- Number of interactions (meetings, discussions, or booth tours) with potential new customers

- Overall cost

- Cost per attendee

- Cost per interaction

- Number of leads captured

- Number of discrete new opportunities (customer projects where NCR has a solution offering that can be proposed)

Objective Summary ➡ Key Terms ➡ Apply

1. Objective Summary (pp. 150–156)

Understand the characteristics of business-to-business markets, business-to-business market demand, and how marketers classify business-to-business customers.

B2B markets include business or organizational customers that buy goods and services for purposes other than personal consumption. There are a number of major and minor differences between organizational and consumer markets. To be successful, marketers must understand these differences and develop strategies that can be effective with organizational customers. For example, business customers are usually few in number, may be geographically concentrated, and often purchase higher-priced products in larger quantities. Business demand derives from the demand for another good or service, is generally not affected by price increases or decreases, is subject to great fluctuations, and may be tied to the demand and availability of some other good. Business customers include producers, resellers, governments, and not-for-profit organizations. Producers purchase materials, parts, and various goods and services needed to produce other goods and services to be sold at a profit. Resellers purchase finished goods to resell at a profit as well as other goods and services to maintain their operations. Governments and other not-for-profit organizations purchase the goods and services necessary to fulfill their objectives. The North American Industry Classification System (NAICS), a numerical coding system developed by NAFTA countries, is a widely used classification system for business and organizational markets.

Key Terms

business-to-business (B2B) markets, p. 150

organizational markets, p. 150

derived demand, p. 153

inelastic demand, p. 153

joint demand, p. 154

producers, p. 155

resellers, p. 155

government markets, p. 155

North American Industry Classification System (NAICS), p. 156

2. Objective Summary (pp. 157–160)

Appreciate opportunities for using e-commerce and social media in business-to-business settings.

Business-to-business (B2B) e-commerce refers to Internet exchanges between two or more businesses or organizations. This includes exchanges of information, goods, services, and payments. Using the Internet for e-commerce allows business marketers to link directly to suppliers, factories, distributors, and their customers, radically reducing the time necessary for order and delivery of goods, tracking sales, and getting feedback from customers. Besides the Internet itself, intranets, extranets, and private exchanges also provide useful means for firms and their employees, customers, and suppliers to conduct business. As with the consumer side, B2B e-commerce has a potential "dark side" fraught with problems such as security breaches, fraud, password theft, sophisticated hackers, and nasty viruses. Despite firewalls, encryption, and other security measures, overall Web security for B2B marketers remains a serious issue with high potential for financial loss. Social media usage has made its way into B2B, especially through the use of LinkedIn. LinkedIn was developed specifically for professional business users. However, don't ignore opportunities to connect your business via Facebook, Twitter, and other more consumer-focused social network sites.

Key Terms

business-to-business (B2B) e-commerce, p. 157

extranet, p. 157

private exchanges, p. 158

3. Objective Summary (pp. 160–168)

Identify and describe the different business buying situations and the business buying decision process.

The buyclass framework identifies the degree and effort required to make a business buying decision. Purchase situations can be straight rebuy, modified rebuy, and new-task buying. A buying centre is a group of people who work together to make a buying decision. The roles in the buying centre are (1) the initiator, who recognizes the need for a purchase; (2) the user, who will ultimately use the product; (3) the gatekeeper, who controls the flow of information to others; (4) the influencer, who shares advice and expertise; (5) the decider, who makes the final decision; and (6) the buyer, who executes the purchase.

Key Terms

buyclass, p. 160

straight rebuy, p. 161

modified rebuy, p. 161

new-task buy, p. 162

buying centre, p. 162

product specifications, p. 165

Chapter **Questions** and **Activities**

Concepts: Test Your Knowledge

1. How do B2B markets differ from consumer markets? How do these differences affect marketing strategies?
2. Explain what we mean by derived demand, inelastic demand, fluctuating demand, and joint demand.
3. How do we generally classify B2B markets? What is the NAICS?
4. Describe new-task buys, modified rebuys, and straight rebuys. What are some different marketing strategies each calls for?
5. What are the characteristics of business buyers?
6. What is a buying centre? What are the roles of the various people in a buying centre?
7. What are the steps in the business buying decision process? What happens in each step?
8. How are the steps in the business buying decision process similar to the steps in the consumer buying process? How are they different?
9. What is single sourcing? multiple sourcing? outsourcing?
10. Explain how reciprocity and reverse marketing operate in B2B markets.
11. Explain the role of intranets, extranets, and private exchanges in B2B e-commerce.
12. Describe the security issues firms face in B2B e-commerce. What are some safeguards firms use to reduce their security risks?

Activities: Apply What You've Learned

1. As a director of purchasing for a firm that manufactures motorcycles, you have been notified that the price of an important part used in the manufacture of the bikes has nearly doubled. You see your company having three choices: (1) buying the part and passing the cost on to the customer by increasing your price; (2) buying the part and absorbing the increase in cost, thereby keeping the price of your bikes the same; and (3) buying a lower-priced part that will be of lower quality. Prepare a list of pros and cons for each alternative. Then, explain your recommendation and justification for it.
2. Assume that you are the marketing manager for a small securities firm (a firm that sells stocks and bonds) whose customers are primarily businesses and other organizations. Your company has so far not made use of the Internet to provide information and service to its customers. You are considering whether this move is in the best interests of your firm. Write a memo outlining the pros and cons of e-commerce for your firm, the risks your firm would face, and your recommendations.
3. Assume you are a sales manager for a firm that is a distributor of hospital equipment and supplies. Your company offers its customers a wide range of products—everything from disposable rubber gloves to high-tech patient monitors. Thus, purchases made by your customers include straight rebuys, modified rebuys, and new-task purchases. Your job is to explain to your new salesperson the differences among these types of purchases and how to be effective in "getting the business" for all three types of purchases. In a role-playing exercise with another classmate, provide the needed information and advice.
4. As chief marketing officer (CMO) for a four-year-old software firm specializing in applications for use in billing and scheduling systems in medical offices, you are interested in providing a forum for your clients to share their success stories and best practices. You believe that building a community of this type can lead to numerous leads and referrals for new business. What characteristics might a customer reference program have that would best serve you, your firm, and its customers? Be as specific as you can about what this program would be like and how it would work to gain the desired references.

Marketing Metrics: Exercise

B2B customers are very busy professionals and notoriously reluctant to take time to provide data to marketers. In order to measure important issues described in the chapter such as client satisfaction, quality, customer engagement, repurchase intentions, and problem resolution turnaround and effectiveness, marketers must employ the most user-friendly and efficient data collection methods available—or the customer will be highly unlikely to provide the needed data.

Review what you learned in Chapter 3 about approaches to collecting data, and propose an approach to collecting the above information from a busy B2B customer in a way that is most likely to result in his or her cooperation. Be as specific as you can in describing your chosen approach and explain why you selected it.

Choices: What Do You Think?

1. E-commerce is dramatically changing the way B2B transactions take place. What are the advantages of B2B e-commerce to companies? to society? Are there any disadvantages of B2B e-commerce?
2. The practice of buying business products based on sealed competitive bids is popular among all types of business buyers. What are the advantages and disadvantages of this practice to buyers? What are the advantages and disadvantages to sellers? Should companies always give the business to the lowest bidder? Why or why not?
3. When firms implement a single sourcing policy in their buying, other possible suppliers do not have an opportunity. Is this ethical? What are the advantages to the company? What are the disadvantages?
4. Many critics say that strict engineering and other manufacturing requirements for products purchased by governments increase prices unreasonably and that taxpayers end up paying too much because of such policies. What are the advantages and disadvantages of such purchase restrictions? Should governments loosen restrictions on their purchases?
5. In the buying centre, the gatekeeper controls information flow to others in the centre. Thus, the gatekeeper determines which possible sellers are heard and which are not. Does the gatekeeper have too much power? What policies might be implemented to make sure that all possible sellers are treated fairly?
6. Some critics complain that outsourcing sends much-needed jobs to competitors overseas while depriving Canadian workers of these opportunities. Should a company consider this factor when deciding where to obtain raw materials or brainpower in order to compete efficiently?

Miniproject: Learn by Doing

The purpose of this miniproject is to gain knowledge about one B2B market using the NAICS codes and other government information.

1. Select an industry of interest to you and use the NAICS information you find on the Internet or in your library.
   a. What are the codes for each of the following classifications?
   NAICS Sector (two digits)
   NAICS Subsector (three digits)
   NAICS Industry Group (four digits)
   NAICS Industry (five digits)
   b. What types of products are or are not included in this industry?
2. Locate the *Industrial Outlook* or *Standard & Poor's Industry Surveys* in your library to find the answers to the following:
   a. What was the value of industry shipments (sales) for Canada in the latest year reported?
   b. What were world-wide sales for the industry in the most recent year reported?
3. Statistics Canada publishes a number of economic censuses. These include the following publications: *Census of Retail Trade, Census of Wholesale Trade, Census of Service Industries, Census of Transportation, Census of Manufacturers, Census of Mineral Industries*, and *Census of Construction Industries*. Use the appropriate publication to determine the value of shipments in your industry for the most recent year reported.
4. *Ward's Business Directory* provides useful industry-specific information. Use it to find the names and addresses of the top four public companies in the industry and their sales revenues.
5. *Compact Disclosure* provides information from company annual reports on CD-ROM (usually available in your school library). Use it or some other similar source to provide the following for the four companies you listed in question 4:
   a. Income statements
   b. Net sales, gross profits, and income before tax

Marketing in **Action** Case   Real Choices at The Filter

How often do Web site recommendations work for the average customer? Yahoo.com offers advice as customers browse the music and video catalogue and suggests the shopping habits of other buyers. In many cases, the connections proposed do not seem to be helpful. How are these recommendations decided? "Recommendations—from friends, from newspapers, from colleagues—are the most common way to find new content," says Doug Merrill, former Google engineering VP. One of the independent purveyors of digital decision making is The Filter. Merrill further states, "However, there is more information available than there are people to recommend. The Filter analyzes data to provide measurably better, more relevant recommendations, automatically." Based in Bath, England, The Filter is a six-year-old privately held company that provides recommendation technology for various companies on the Web.

Martin Hopkins is a physicist who is a passionate fan of music. In 2004, he owned an online media-recommendation endeavour born out of his frustration administering his own digital music collection of over 10 000 tracks. One of the roots of his frustration is the boredom that resulted from not being able to efficiently find the music he wanted to hear. Hopkins developed an algorithm using artificial intelligence that learned his likes and dislikes and then suggested playlists. This software would later become the foundation for the decision-making procedure that controls The Filter's recommendation engine.

The Filter markets what they consider to be a better way of recommending music and videos on the Internet. Its client list includes firms such as Sony Music, Nokia, and Comcast. In 2010, The Filter entered into a deal with Dailymotion, a Web site of over 66 million monthly users, to make video-to-video recommendations. During the trial and optimization period, over 5 billion video views were captured and over 1 billion recommendations were delivered. There are many other firms promoting their own recommendation engines. Netflix uses its extensive database of customer-posted opinions not only to help people find what they're looking for, but also to offer selections that users might have not considered. The Filter uses a similar philosophy to be superior to search engines and, ultimately, to get customers to purchase more recommended items.

The Filter attempts to compete with other companies by guiding customers toward the choices that are not obvious. The reasoning behind this is that anybody can recommend the popular, so The Filter is using this method to form a competitive advantage. One of the program's advantages is that it only deals with digital media that can be tracked after purchase by a customer. This advantage allows The Filter to monitor postpur-chase consumption behaviour. For instance, some customers only listen to or watch parts of the media acquired. This type of knowledge could make a significant difference in what the software recommends.

Initially, The Filter aimed its services at individual users; however, it did not collect sufficient business to be profitable. At that point, the direction shifted to promote its recommendation engine to media firms. The pressure is on to prove that its recommendation algorithms do provide the kind of improvements claimed. The ultimate goal for The Filter is to market its service to companies in other industries. The firm has to define its long-term strategy and find ways to ensure profitability well into the future.

You Make the Call

1. What is the decision facing The Filter?
2. What factors are important in understanding this decision situation?
3. What are the alternatives?
4. What decision(s) do you recommend?
5. What are some ways to implement your recommendation?

Sources: Based on Devin Leonard, "Tech Entrepreneur Peter Gabriel Knows What You Want," *Bloomberg Businessweek*, April 8, 2010, http://www.businessweek.com/magazine/content/10_16/b4174046688330.htm; The Filter, *Wikipedia*, http://en.wikipedia.org/wiki/The_Filter; Rachel Carr and Arielle Himy, "The Filter Recommendation Engine Launched on Dailymotion to Further Boost User Engagement," *Marketwire*, March 2, 2010, http://www.marketwire.com/press-release/Filter-Recommendation-Engine-Launched-on-Dailymotion-Further-Boost-User-Engagement-1124739.htm; Erick Schonfeld, "The Filter Reboots as Recommendation Engine for Hire, Ex-Googler Doug Merrill Joins Board," *TechCrunch*, February 8, 2010, http://techcrunch.com/2010/02/08/the-filter-reboots-doug-merrill/.

Sharpen the Focus:
Target Marketing Strategies and Customer Relationship Management

Real People **Profiles**

Catharine Downes

▼ A Decision Maker at North Shore Credit Union

Catharine Downes is the Assistant Vice President, Marketing, for North Shore Credit Union (NSCU) in British Columbia (www.nscu.com) and is responsible for brand, promotions, marketing communications, research, products, segmentation, and online services. She joined the credit union to head up the Marketing team in 2006, following extensive experience in marketing leadership roles at technology firms focused on banking systems, customer relationship management, and analytic software solutions for the financial services and credit union sectors. Catharine holds an MA in English from McMaster University, moved to BC while completing her postgraduate studies, and has been enjoying the West Coast lifestyle ever since (even the rain!). In addition to time with her husband and two children, when she's not in her self-confessed workaholic mode, Catharine putters in her garden, keeps up with the latest fiction and films, and dreams of her next travel destination.

The NSCU is a full-service financial institution offering banking, investment, loan, and insurance solutions through a branch network spanning North and West Vancouver, Squamish, Whistler, Pemberton, Vancouver, and Burnaby in British Columbia. Founded in 1941, NSCU has 40 000 members, 300 employees, and nearly $2.4 billion in assets under adminis-

tration. The organization's vision is to become a premium financial services boutique, catering to the unique needs of its West Coast marketplace. Reflecting the interests of its current and prospective clients, NSCU operates in a financially responsible and environmentally sustainable manner, while actively contributing to the physical, mental, environmental, and financial wellness of the communities it serves.

Traditionally, most of the big banks and almost all of the credit unions in Canada utilized an undifferentiated (mass) targeting strategy, appealing to a wide spectrum of people. The majority of retail financial institutions (banks and credit unions) grew their business by attracting customers from all economic and social walks of life. Particular attention was paid to retaining the 20 percent of customers who generated 80 percent of the profit, but all customers were typically sought, valued, and serviced. In the 1990s; however, some financial institutions realized that they were actually losing money by managing relationships with customers with frequent low-value transactions, and not paying sufficient attention and resources to attracting and keeping their most profitable customers.

Industry research highlighted a key underserved demographic—the "mass affluent"—individuals with between $100 000 and $500 000 in liquid, investable assets. This was insufficient wealth to attract the attention of private banking providers, but it clearly warranted an enhanced level of services to respond to their more complex financial needs—particularly in the area of wealth management. Some of the large Canadian retail banks introduced "private banking lite"–type offerings, but none made this target market the core of their business strategy.

Here's my problem. . .

Real **People**, Real **Choices**

In 2005, president and CEO Chris Catliff articulated a bold new vision for the credit union, premised on delivering a well-constructed offering for mass affluent and emerging wealthy individuals who embraced an active West Coast lifestyle. This focus demanded a disciplined approach and a willingness to differentiate the banking experience based on client needs—a seismic shift in traditional credit union system practices. It required that NSCU look to elevate its brand and operational capabilities to provide holistic, comprehensive financial solutions that went well beyond traditional day-to-day banking and friendly customer service. The goals were to grow NSCU's assets under administration to $3 billion by 2015; continue strong profitability while reinvesting in expanding the business and raising the brand profile; maintain high levels of employee engagement; and deliver a relevant, integrated, and exceptional banking experience for increasingly discerning clients.

Changes on the credit union landscape also opened new opportunities. In 2008, British Columbia implemented unlimited deposit insurance protection for BC credit unions through the Credit Union Deposit Insurance Corporation—a game-changing decision that attracted the attention of wealthier clients. Further changes will be in the offing if proposed new federal legislation enables credit unions to expand beyond their provincial boundaries to operate as federal cooperative banks in future.

Initial efforts focused on building NSCU's internal capabilities and infrastructure. Branches were remodelled to provide a more welcoming experience emphasizing advisory relationships and financial planning; facilities featured natural West Coast materials; a boutique-level of attention was paid to design; and business processes were streamlined. The standards for staff professionalism, knowledge, and experience were raised, with a focus on employee training, education, and professional development, including a requirement for advisors to earn CFP (Certified Financial Planner) or PFP (Personal Financial Planner) designations. Roughly 20 percent of members were "assigned" to dedicated financial advisors, who served as primary relationship managers in an integrated team approach to advisory services, with access to investment, insurance, and small business specialists when needed by their clients.

Within this context of renewal and repositioning, the NSCU marketing team was faced with the strategic decision of what targeting strategy to employ. Should they continue to utilize an undifferentiated (mass) targeting strategy, appealing to a broad spectrum of people in their current market? Or should they develop a more targeted strategy focused on the new West Coast affluent? Growth might also be achieved by expanding into new markets, either with the current mass targeting strategy or with a more focused approach.

Things to remember

Many customers perceive banking services to be quite similar and undifferentiated. The large banks and most of the credit unions offer a wide range of products and service to a wide range of similar customers. This makes it difficult to get noticed in the marketplace.

Credit unions are member based. They exist to serve their membership, which for NSCU includes both "West Coast affluent" and "making ends meet" customers.

By increasing focus and attention on the more profitable West Coast affluent members, in either current or new markets, NSCU might alienate or put off other members. It is not clear how those other members would react to a change in focus, or how NSCU's competitors would react.

Catharine and the NSCU marketing team considered their **Options** 1·2·3

Option 1

Continue to utilize an undifferentiated (mass) targeting strategy in their current market. This strategy had served NSCU very well for almost 70 years. This approach would not prevent NSCU from developing and promoting specific financial, wealth management, and insurance products to different segments within an appeal to a broad customer base, but it does suggest that the credit union should be catering to all segments equally within their community. NSCU has developed strong connections with its local communities and is known for its corporate social responsibility and community giving, but Downes wondered if that was enough on which to grow the business. NSCU had made strides in modernizing the branches and in developing a stronger service culture and more personalized banking experiences, but so had others. Defending this basis of differentiation would be difficult with a diffuse, undifferentiated mass marketing strategy.

Option 2

Develop a more targeted strategy focused on the West Coast affluent. A more targeted strategy would recognize that some customers are more profitable to serve than others. By focusing on the West Coast affluent, NSCU could reasonably expect to grow their business with these customers by providing them with an enhanced banking experience that would be more "local" and responsive than could be provided by the larger banks. The whole banking experience could be enhanced to meet the expectations of the affluent in ways that it would be difficult for traditional banks to match and this could be the basis for differentiating the NSCU product in the marketplace.

This strategy, however, might alienate the traditional "making ends meet" NSCU members. Downes doesn't know how these traditional credit union members would react. Would they be happy with an improved level of service for everyone or would they move their business to another credit union or bank that was more traditional in their offering and less up-market?

Option 3

Develop a more focused strategy and expand into new markets. Rather than continue to be all things to all people, NSCU could focus on profitable market niches in new markets and offer more focused and tailored product (banking experience) on which to compete in the new markets against established competitors. There were increasingly affluent customers in other parts of BC's Lower Mainland, and NSCU could focus on expansion in these markets. Downes also observed that a number of West Coast affluent customers were moving to the interior of British Columbia. NSCU could follow them and target other affluent customers in those markets. In future, expansion into other provinces might be possible, if pending federal legislation is enacted. The disadvantage of a more tailored expansion strategy is that the farther afield from the credit union's current trade area, the greater the challenges of building brand awareness, establishing a credible presence, and winning the business of enough affluent consumers quickly enough to justify the cost of expansion.

You Choose

Which **Option** would you choose, and **why**?

1. ☐YES ☐NO   2. ☐YES ☐NO   3. ☐YES ☐NO

See what **option** Catharine chose on page 211.

175

market fragmentation
The creation of many consumer groups due to a diversity of distinct needs and wants in modern society.

target marketing strategy
Dividing the total market into different segments on the basis of customer characteristics, selecting one or more segments, and developing products to meet the needs of those specific segments.

1

Target Marketing Strategy: Process Overview

By now, you've read over and over that the goal of the marketer is to create value, build customer relationships, and satisfy needs. But in our modern, complex society, it's naive to assume that everyone's needs are the same. Understanding people's needs is an even more complex task today because technological and cultural advances in modern society create a condition of **market fragmentation**. This means that people's diverse interests and backgrounds divide them into numerous groups with distinct needs and wants. Because of this diversity, the same good or service will not appeal to everyone.

Consider, for example, the effects of fragmentation in the health and fitness industry—one that has gained increasing attention due to recent data about skyrocketing rates of obesity among adults and children. Back in the 1960s, dieting was simple. Pritikin was a best-selling weight loss system that emphasized very low fat and high fibre, and health-conscious consumers thought that this combination would surely yield a lean body and good health. Today's consumers, however, have a cornucopia of diets from which to choose including such brands as NutriSystem, Weight Watchers, Jenny Craig, the Atkins diet, and many more. Calories, fat, carbs, or all of the above—which to cut?

Marketers must balance the efficiency of mass marketing, where they serve the same items to everyone, with the effectiveness that comes when they offer each individual exactly what he or she wants. Mass marketing certainly costs much less; when we offer one product to everyone we eliminate the need for separate advertising campaigns and distinctive packages for each item. However, consumers see things differently; from their perspective, the best strategy would be to offer the perfect product just for them. Unfortunately, that's often not realistic. To this day, Burger King touts its longtime motto "Have It Your Way," but BK can only deliver this promise to a point. "Your way" is fine as long as you stay within the confines of familiar condiments such as mustard or ketchup. Don't dream of topping your burger with blue cheese, mango sauce, or some other "exotic" ingredient.

Instead of trying to sell something to everyone, marketers select a **target marketing strategy** in which they divide the total market into different segments based on customer characteristics, select one or more segments, and develop products to meet the needs of those specific segments. Figure 6.1 illustrates the three-step process of segmentation, targeting, and positioning, and it's what we're going to check out in this chapter.

Identify and Select Market(s)

One of the challenges in developing a target marketing strategy is determining what market you are in and what market you should be segmenting. For example, should beer marketers be segmenting the beer market, the alcoholic beverage market, or the social beverage market? Kodak redefined itself from being in the film business to being in the imaging business—leading Kodak to venture into new markets. Deciding what "market" you are competing in has significant implications for the segments you might identify. You must also consider the geographic scope of the market—are you segmenting the

Figure 6.1 Steps in the Target Marketing Process

Pre) Select Markets	1. Market Segmentation	2. Market Targeting	3. Market Positioning	Post) Create and Execute Marketing Mix Programs
a. Define your market b. Understand customers: needs and wants; benefits, features, and attributes sought; and purchase and consumption behaviour	a. Identify groups: geographic, behavioural, pyschographic, and demographic segmentation b. Describe (profile) the groups: who, what, when, where, why	a. Evaluate segment attractiveness: size, growth, strategic fit, competitive or comparative advantage, level of competition, and defendability b. Decide which one(s) to target	Decide how you want to compete, be differentiated, and be known for value creation in the minds of consumers	

beverage market in North America, Canada, or in one or more provinces? The decision about how to define the markets you are competing in is typically done at the executive (strategic planning) level of an organization. As an entrepreneur or consultant, you may need to make this decision yourself—based on your experience; your understanding of the consumer, competitive, and technological environments; and your understanding of the mission, strategic directions, and competencies of your organization.

Criteria for Identifying Market Segments

Before discussing how to segment a market, let's review the criteria for a successful segmentation scheme. There is no right or wrong way to segment a market, but some segmentation schemes are more useful than others for identifying market opportunities and being able to position products that uniquely appeal to a well-defined group of consumers or customers—the term used to describe organizational or business-to-business buyers.

A viable segmentation approach should satisfy the requirements outlined in Figure 6.2.

1. Members of the segment must be similar to each other in their product needs and wants, such that the same marketing programs (product offers) would be appealing to most members of the group.

2. At the same time, consumers in each segment should be sufficiently different from consumers in other segments so that different marketing programs or product offers would be appealing to the different segments. Segment differences need to be actionable—that is, they require different product, pricing, distribution, and/or communication strategies to create a product offer that appeals to each segment. Without real differences in consumer needs and wants, firms might as well use a mass-marketing strategy. For example, it's a waste of time to develop two separate lines of skin care products for working and non-working women, if both segments have the same needs and wants with respect to skin care.

3. The segment must be large enough now and in the future to warrant targeting. What is large enough is a judgment call, and usually depends on the size of the company doing the segmentation scheme. Large organizations like Procter & Gamble may be interested only in market segments with sales potential in the millions of dollars. A smaller company may be interested in segments with sales potential in the tens or hundreds of thousands of dollars. In considering the BC market, for example, the Beef Information Centre evaluated the Chinese Canadian community as a possible

- Similar Enough Within the Group
- Different Enough Between the Groups
- Large Enough
- Measurable Market
- Reachable

Figure 6.2 Criteria for Effective Segmentation Approaches

Beef Information Centre.

Exhibit 6.1

Chinese Canadian consumers were identified as a large segment for the Beef Information Centre of British Columbia.

segment. Chinese Canadians spend more money on food than any other ethnic group, and if just 25 percent of the close to 300 000 Chinese Canadians in British Columbia ate one more beef meal a month, sales of beef in British Columbia would increase by 77 000 kilograms per year. This analysis led the organization to target the Chinese Canadian segment in Vancouver through magazine ads like the one in Exhibit 6.1, recipes distributed at grocery stores, and the sponsorship of a Chinese cooking show on TV.

4. The segment must represent a measurable market—that is, people in the segment have purchasing power: the authority, willingness, and ability to make a purchase decision. Children, for example, may not have the authority to make a purchase. Religious or cultural beliefs may impact willingness to buy (such as beef-based hamburgers in India). Low-income consumers may not have the ability to buy.

5. Finally, the segment must be reachable. Marketers must be able to identify consumers or organizational customers in the segment and communicate the product offer to them in a cost-effective manner. It is easy to select television programs or magazines that will efficiently reach older consumers, consumers with specific levels of education, certain ethnic groups, or residents of major cities, because the media they prefer are easy to identify. It would be more difficult, however, for marketing communications to effectively and efficiently reach left-handed blond people with tattoos who listen to hip-hop. Therefore, our segments need to be defined in such a way that we can actually find those customers to present them with our offer.[1]

segmentation

The process of dividing a larger market into smaller pieces based on one or more meaningfully shared characteristics.

2

OBJECTIVE

Understand the need for market segmentation and the approaches available to do it.

(pp. 178–193)

Step 1: Segmentation

Segmentation is the central tenet or cornerstone of marketing strategy. Because consumers have different needs and wants and the same marketing program is unlikely to appeal to all consumers, marketers identify the key groups in a market, choose which group(s) to focus on (target), decide how they want their brand to compete and be known by these consumers (positioning), and design marketing programs (make marketing mix decisions) to create product offers that uniquely appeal to the chosen target groups. There are very few, if any, products with universal appeal. Even for products as popular as cola soft drinks, some consumers choose Coca-Cola over Pepsi or Pepsi over Coke, some prefer diet colas and others flavoured colas (e.g., Dr. Pepper, Vanilla Coke; Exhibit 6.2), some prefer caffeine-enhanced colas like Jolt, and others prefer non–soft drink beverages. Theresa Bergeron, president of Thermohair Inc. (Exhibit 6.3), has developed a product line of specialty socks made of kid (baby goat) mohair. Not everyone would be interested in a $25 pair of durable, warm, comfortable socks, but people involved in outdoor recreational sports like hiking and camping might be.

Doing a good job at segmentation is the first step in the target marketing process, and taking a different approach to segmentation than your competitors can often provide competitive advantage. During the late 1990s, for example, Converse began falling well behind its competitors such as Reebok and Nike, which successfully targeted the younger demographic

demographic as they tied their shoes (pun intended!) to popular athletes who acted as marketing machines for the brands. Converse needed to find a way to appeal to the younger generation as they sought markets beyond traditional sports. The marketers at Converse (which Nike acquired in 2003) identified the segment of socially aware and involved Generation Y consumers—people born between 1979 and 1994 who were "optimistic rebels" looking for a "blank canvas for self-expression."[2] Converse gained considerable market share when they reminded these consumers that the cultural icons that they admired, such as Kurt Cobain, once wore Converse shoes, and that Converse was a hip brand with deep roots with the avant-garde.

So, just how do marketers segment a market? We'll show you how to do this for consumer markets and then for organizational (business-to-business) markets for which the process is quite similar. But we will discuss some of the differences shortly.

Segment Consumer Markets

Several **segmentation variables**, or bases for segmentation, can be used to group consumers into actionable segments. For example, consider the sports shoe industry. At one time, it was sufficient to divide the sports shoe market into athletes and nonathletes. But take a walk through any sporting goods store today, and you'll quickly see that the athlete market has fragmented in many directions. Shoes designed for jogging, basketball, tennis, cycling, cross training, and even skateboarding beckon us from the aisles. Some sports, such as running, are more popular in some provinces than others, so marketers consider geography. Not everyone is willing or able to pay $150 for the latest running shoe, so marketers consider disposable and discretionary income. Men may be more likely to participate in some sports, such as basketball, whereas women may be more likely than men to want the latest aerobics styles, so marketers also consider gender. Not all age groups are going to be equally interested in buying specialized athletic shoes, and some kids may be more inclined to "extreme" sports than others. As this example shows, the larger consumer "pie" can be sliced into smaller pieces in a number of ways, including geographic, demographic, psychological, and behavioural differences (see Figure 6.3). These segmentation variables are used to identify the groups. Then we create detailed descriptions or profiles of the groups.

In the sections that follow, we'll consider each of these segmentation approaches in turn, but first a note of caution. When it comes to marketing to some groups—in particular, lower income individuals, the poorly educated, non-native language speakers, and children—it is incumbent on marketers to exercise the utmost care not to take undue advantage of their circumstances. Ethical marketers are sensitive to the different conditions in which people find themselves and proactively work to uphold a high level of honesty and trust with all segments of the public. Doing so is nothing short of marketing's social responsibility.

Segment by Behaviour

People may use the same product for different reasons, on different occasions, and in different amounts. Savvy marketers realize that if the objective is to create groups that want very different product offers, it makes sense to try to group them by the similarity of their needs, wants and preferences, the benefits they seek, the features and attributes they desire, or their purchasing or consumption behaviour. This approach to segmentation is called **behavioural segmentation**, and marketers as diverse as Research In Motion and McDonald's have found it a useful place to start because it identifies groups that require distinct

Exhibit 6.2

Coca-Cola developed Vanilla Coke to appeal to a flavoured-cola-seeking market segment.

segmentation variables
Dimensions that divide the total market into fairly homogeneous groups, each with different needs and preferences.

Exhibit 6.3

Thermohair Inc. focuses on a narrow segment interested in warm, comfortable, durable socks that are made for cold weather (they even have a rib-free line for people with circulation problems).

Figure 6.3 Segmenting Consumer Markets

Consumer markets can be segmented by demographic, psychographic, or behavioural criteria.

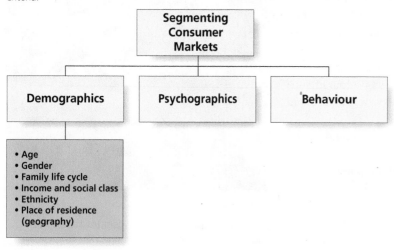

behavioural segmentation
A technique that divides consumers into segments on the basis of how they act toward, feel about, or use a good or service.

benefit segmentation
A segmentation approach that groups consumers or customers based on the benefits or value they seek in buying and using products.

usage segmentation
A segmentation approach that groups consumers or business customers based on the amount of a product purchased or consumed or how the product is used.

80/20 rule
A marketing rule of thumb that 20 percent of purchasers typically account for 80 percent of a product's sales.

marketing programs. Research by Digital Consumer Projects in New York reflects this understanding that behavioural segmentation usually produces more actionable segments; they found that an individual's online behaviour matters more than demographics when it comes to online shopping, finding that there are seven behavioural segments, including "surfers," "loiterers," and "quickies."[3] (See Exhibit 6.4.)

Behavioural segmentation divides consumers on the basis of how they act toward, feel about, or use a product or service. **Benefit segmentation**, or value segmentation, is a powerful behavioural segmentation approach where consumers are grouped by the benefits they seek in a product category. For example, Peachtree Network, a company that operated online grocery stores across Canada, originally segmented its market into three benefit segments: busy people, people with mobility difficulties, and people who liked and were motivated to use the technology behind the service.[4] In many industries, consumers seek different types of benefits from products and can be grouped accordingly. For example, the following benefit-based groups (among others) might be identified as restaurant industry segments: convenience seekers, fun seekers, health oriented, fine-dining experience seekers, novelty seekers, cost oriented, family oriented, image or status oriented, or culture seekers. Each of us may fall into more than one of these benefit-seeking categories at different times or in different contexts, but restaurant owners know that different consumers seek different benefits from a restaurant and select restaurants based on the benefits they wish to receive at a particular time. That is why restaurants are usually clearly positioned to appeal to one or more of these benefit segment groups. Think of all the restaurants you know—what benefit(s) do they primarily focus on delivering? The advantage of segmenting by benefits is that the resulting groups are usually seeking very different product solutions, which makes the segmentation scheme very actionable in terms of designing appropriate marketing programs.

Another common approach to behavioural segmentation is product **usage segmentation**. In this approach, groups are identified based on how they use a product or how much they use a product. Baking soda, for example, is marketed to a variety of end-use segments, including deodorizing fridges, sinks, or rugs; cooking; and teeth brushing. Airlines often identify consumer and business traveller segments, which is a proxy for describing the frequency of product use (light users versus heavy users) and how consumers use the service. Many marketers (particularly those in business-to-business markets) abide by a rule of thumb called the **80/20 rule**: 20 percent of purchasers account for 80 percent of the product's sales (this ratio is just an approximation). Therefore, it often makes more sense to focus on the smaller number of people who are heavy users of a product rather than on the larger number who are just casual users. This is what NSCU is thinking of doing by targeting the West Coast affluent.

While the 80/20 rule still generally holds in the majority of situations, the Internet's ability to offer an unlimited choice of goods to billions of people

Exhibit 6.4

Palm and other PDA manufacturers often use behavioural segmentation to target segments that use communication devices differently.

is starting to change how marketers think about segmentation. A new approach called the **long tail** is turning traditional thinking about the virtues of selling in high volume on its head. The basic idea is that we no longer need to rely solely on the big hits (like blockbuster movies or bestselling books) to find profits. Companies can also make money by selling small amounts of items that only a few people want—if they sell enough different items. For example, Amazon.com maintains an inventory of 3.7 million books compared to the 100 000 or so you'll find at a Chapters retail store. Most of these will sell only a few thousand copies (if that), but the 3.6 million books that Chapters *doesn't* carry make up a quarter of Amazon's revenues! Similarly, about a fifth of the videos Netflix delivers to its customers are older or obscure titles that Blockbuster does not stock. Other examples of long tail include successful microbreweries and TV channels that make money on reruns of old shows.

Some marketers find it useful to divide the market into users and nonusers of a good or service so that they can reward current users (as Air Canada does with frequent flyer miles) or try to win over new ones. However, nonusers are often not clearly identifiable and reachable, thus failing to satisfy the fifth criterion for identifying market segments outlined above. And current users may not be a very homogeneous group, which is the first criterion (see Figure 6.2), and they may not reflect the users desired by the marketing organization.

Another way to segment a market based on behaviour is to look at **usage occasions**, or the context in which consumers use the product most. Many products are associated with specific occasions, including time of day and holidays, whether for a business function or casual situation. Greeting cards, for example, are a product associated with specific occasions. Carlton Cards, Canada's leading greeting card marketer, experiences peak demand related to four special occasions: Christmas, Valentine's Day, Mother's Day, and Easter. In addition to meeting the demand for these occasions with specialized cards, advertising, and in-store promotions, Carlton engages in marketing efforts designed to encourage the giving of cards on other occasions, such as Earth Day. Similarly, ski resorts like Mont Tremblant, which experiences heavy demand during vacation periods, might offer great bargains during the off-season to tempt vacationers who would otherwise just visit the resort during Christmas vacation.

Being strongly associated with a particular occasion can be a mixed blessing for a product. On the one hand, sales can be almost guaranteed at that time (think about how many people cook a whole turkey on Thanksgiving); on the other hand, a product can become locked into an occasion (few people cook whole turkeys as a standard menu item). For the past 10 years, Ocean Spray has worked hard to expand cranberry consumption beyond the holiday season, introducing new cranberry foods like Craisins Dried Cranberries, spritzers, and cranberry-based beverages. Now it's trying to increase consumption frequency by communicating the health benefits of its products and encouraging consumers to take the Ocean Spray Cranberry Cocktail "One Glass A Day Challenge" (Exhibit 6.5).

In a similar vein, Google enables its advertising clients to target certain ads to certain segments of search engine users, based on data such as Google domain, query entered, IP address, and language preference. This way, companies can have Google automatically sort and send the intended ad to certain market segments. Thus, it is possible for advertisers on Google to tailor their automatically targeted ads based on seasonality—you will see more TurboTax ads on Google pages during tax season, even if people aren't querying tax software.[5]

Segment by Psychographics

Consumers and customers often make purchase decisions that reflect or support their attitudes, values, interests, opinions, emotions, personality, and lifestyles. Discussed in Chapter 4, these concepts are collectively referred to as *psychographics*. **Psychographic segmentation** groups consumers by these and other variables that are related to an individual's psychology, mental state, or self and is concerned with consumers' motivation to buy products.

---

long tail
A new approach to segmentation based on the idea that companies can make money by selling small amounts of items that only a few people want, provided they sell enough different items.

usage occasions
Indicator used in one type of market segmentation based on when consumers use a product most.

psychographic segmentation
A segmentation approach that groups people based on their attitudes, beliefs, values, lifestyles, or other psychological orientations.

Exhibit 6.5

Ocean Spray wants to expand cranberry consumption beyond traditional holiday usage occasions.

Grouping consumers by their psychological orientation to a purchase often results in a useful segmentation scheme that meets the criteria of Figure 6.2, since differences in these psychological considerations usually reflect differences in needs and wants and are precursors to purchase and consumption behaviour. For example, Covenant House, a charitable organization that helps homeless people, recognized that donors care more about the homeless than nondonors do, and believe their donations will make a difference. With this understanding, Taxi Advertising and Design of Toronto developed a series of highly effective (and award-winning) campaign elements to increase the number of people who care about the homeless, thus increasing the pool of potential donors. One showed black and white images of homeless people sitting alone on the ground in a transit shelter replaced by images of young children in the same position, with the tag line, "How old do they have to be before you give a damn?" The Covenant House print ad in Exhibit 6.6 is another execution of the concept, enabling readers to physically take people off the street.

Over the years, Harley-Davidson has done a great job of understanding buyers on the basis of psychographics. A Harley user's profile includes both thrill-seeking and affinity for a countercultural image (at least on weekends). In fact, your doctor, banker, lawyer, or even marketing professor may be a member of HOG (the Harley Owners Group). Over the past decade, the age of the typical Harley buyer has risen to about 46, older than the motorcycle industry average of 38. But because the company knows the psychographics of its target buyers, it isn't lulled into age stereotypes of safety and conservatism. Harley-Davidson knows that in spite of their older age, their buyers (Exhibit 6.7) are still a thrill-seeking bunch (they may just need a little more time and some Aspirin to recover after a long ride).

Lifestyles are a powerful segmentation variable because they capture a number of behavioural, psychographic, and demographic characteristics that reflect how different groups of people live, what they care about, and how they behave. Think about your high-school experience. Were there cliques or groups of students like Jocks, Nerds, Preppies, Stoners, and others who hung out together, dressed similarly, had similar attitudes and values, and behaved similarly? You could probably describe each of those groups in some detail. That's what marketers do. Some advertising agencies and manufacturers develop their own psychographic classifications of consumers, identifying lifestyle segments like Yuppies

An actual peel-off sticker was placed on this magazine ad.

When readers peeled the sticker off, a message was revealed.

Exhibit 6.6

Removable stickers of homeless children in this Covenant House public service announcement demonstrate that donations make a difference: "Your donation gets kids off the street."

(young urban professionals), Dinks (dual income, no kids), Shredders (boarders), Granolas (earthy, environmentally concerned peaceniks), Metrosexuals (urban heterosexual males who are sensitive, well educated, and in touch with their feminine side), and others. Products are communicated to people in these segments by showing how the brand supports or is consistent with a particular lifestyle. Beer marketers like Molson, for example, often use lifestyle advertising to demonstrate what your life (or at least your social life) would be like if you adopted their particular brand. Similarly, car marketers like Toyota, Mazda, Volvo, Saturn, and Mercedes try to show you a lifestyle that they suggest could be yours if you drive their cars. The Toyota hybrid ad in Exhibit 6.8 relates Toyota hybrid cars to a natural, environmentally-responsible lifestyle. Web-based services like GeoCities (geocities.yahoo.com) allow people to sort themselves into lifestyle communities based on specific shared interests. Online marketers can then target these specific lifestyle groups. Apple's use of lifestyle segmentation has been particularly effective. Apple positions Macs and iPods as being for people with a young, hip, unconventional outlook on life.

Exhibit 6.7

Harley-Davidson uses psychographic segmentation to understand that their buyers, while older, are still thrill-seekers with an affinity for countercultural image.

Other marketers choose to subscribe to larger services that divide the population into segments and sell pieces of this information to clients for specific strategic applications. The best known of these systems is **VALS (Values and Lifestyles)**. The original VALS system was based on social values and lifestyles. Today VALS is based on psychological traits that correlate with consumer behaviour. If you go to www.strategicbusinessinsights.com and click on "VALS Survey" you can complete a brief, free questionnaire to find out your own VALS type (you might be surprised).

VALS divides the US population into eight groups according to what drives them psychologically as well as by their economic resources. As Figure 6.4 shows, three primary consumer motivations are key to the system: ideals, achievement, and self-expression. Consumers who are motivated primarily by ideals are guided by knowledge and principles. Consumers who are motivated primarily by achievement look for goods and services that demonstrate success to their peers. Consumers who are motivated primarily by self-expression desire social or physical activity, variety, and risk.

VALS helps match products to particular types of people. For example, VALS survey data show that 12 percent of North American adults (many of whom are on the younger side) are Experiencers who tend to be thrill seekers. VALS helped Isuzu market its Rodeo sport-utility vehicle by repositioning it to Experiencers, many of whom believe it is fun to break rules. The company and its advertising agency repositioned the car as a vehicle that lets a driver break the rules by going off road. To do this, it used images like kids jumping into mud puddles or purposefully colouring outside the lines, illustrating "rule breaking." Isuzu sales increased significantly after this campaign.

VALS is one of the most comprehensive psychographic systems available, but because its conclusions are based on residents of the United States (there are also Japanese and UK versions), many Canadian firms prefer to use Canadian psychographic systems, such as the one developed by the Environics Research Group (www.environics.ca). Like VALS, Environics segments people on the basis of attitudes, values, and lifestyles.

Exhibit 6.8

Car manufacturers like Toyota often use lifestyle segmentation to identify groups of people interested in different types of cars.

VALS (Values and Lifestyles)
A psychographic system that divides people into eight segments.

The 12 "tribes" identified by Environics range from the Rational Traditionalists (who are motivated by financial independence, security, and stability, and whose key values include respect for authority, duty, and delayed gratification) to the Social Hedonists (who are motivated by experience seeking, and who value hedonism, immediate gratification, and sexual permissiveness).[6] While the Rational Traditionalists may be a good target market for certain financial and insurance services, the Social Hedonists would probably be a prime target for *Tribe Magazine* and such leisure activities as snowboarding. Another Canadian-based segmentation system is the Goldfarb segments (Figure 6.5) that identify six groups of Canadian adults: structured, discontented, fearful, resentful, assured, and caring.

Segment by Demographics

demographics
Variables that describe objective characteristics of a population or group.

Demographics are vital for identifying the best potential customers for a product or service because objective characteristics like a person's sex or age are (usually) easy to identify, and demographic information about a consumer market can be easily obtained from government sources like Statistics Canada (www.statcan.ca). Demographics are extremely useful in the development of profiles or descriptions of market segments (you will learn how to develop these profiles soon) because demographic variables help identify people in segments so that they can be reached with a marketer's communication strategy. Communications media publish demographic information about their viewers, listeners, or readers to help marketers decide which media are best for reaching which audiences.

However, with a few notable exceptions, demographic variables like age, sex, income, family structure, social class, ethnicity, geography, and education do not usually provide a good starting point or main basis for segmentation, because demographic-based segmentation schemes usually do not meet the criterion that the people within each group be similar enough that the same marketing programs (product offers) would appeal to most members of that group (first criterion, Figure 6.2). For example, one might be tempted to segment the music market by age, suggesting that teenagers may listen to different music than people in their twenties, forties, or sixties. However, while teenagers may be more likely than other age groups to listen to grunge or hip-hop music, not all teens like and listen to this style of music, and there are people in their twenties, thirties, forties, and perhaps even older, who do. By creating age segments we are suggesting that most people in a particular age category have similar needs, wants, preferences, and buying behaviour with respect to music and that they would likely purchase the same or similarly positioned artists or brands, which are different from the artists or brands that consumers in other segments would likely purchase. If you thought this were true, then age would be an appropriate basis for segmenting the music market. However, it might make more sense to segment the music market by psychographic variables such as values, attitudes, interests, opinions, or lifestyles, and then use age and other demographic variables to describe each of the psychographic groups created. This is a subtle but

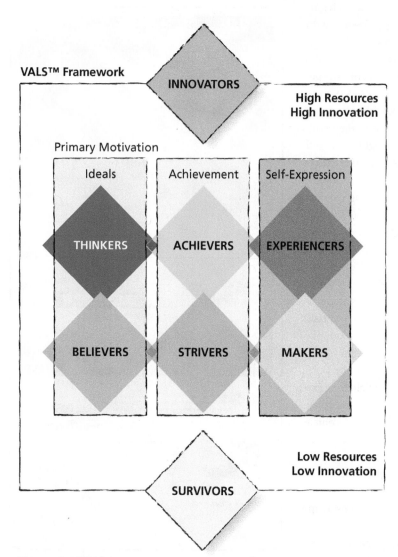

Figure 6.4 VALS
VALS uses psychological characteristics to segment the US market into eight unique consumer groups.

Figure 6.5 Goldfarb Segments

Goldfarb is a Canadian segmentation framework.

Segment	Percentage	Characteristics
Traditionalists		
Day-to-Day Watchers	24	Represent the status quo; don't like the fast pace; motivated by familiarity, loyalty, and security; influenced by quality, brand name, and authority figures.
Old-Fashioned Puritans	18	Prefer simpler times, express conservative values, motivated by price and quality, influenced by value-oriented messages, motivated by sales and other forms of discounts.
Responsible Survivors	12	Frugal shoppers who look for best price; have money but do not like to spend it; motivated by price; shop at low-end stores; heavy television viewers, so it is a good medium to reach them with.
Non-traditionalists		
Joiner Activists	16	Idealists; liberal-minded; careful decision makers; willing to spend; motivated by information, and therefore receptive to advertising messages; rational appeals have influence (quality, service, dependability, etc.).
Bold Achievers	15	Aggressive and confident individuals; success- and responsibility-oriented; innovators who lead in attitude and purchase decision; motivated by status, prestige, and success; products purchased reflect success; want higher-priced goods and exclusivity.
Self-indulgents	14	Resent authority; motivated by self-gratification, and therefore often buy impulsively (even on major purchases); price not a factor; want easy road to success; messages should stress gratification as source of motivation.

important point for creating useful segmentation schemes—demographics are extremely useful for describing market segments and for directing communication messages but are generally limited as the primary basis for segmentation. As Peter van Stolk, the Vancouver-based founder of Jones Soda (Exhibit 6.9, www.jonessoda.com), told the Beverage Forum in Manhattan, "It's not about demographics. It's psychographics. You didn't grow up with the computer and crack and AIDS. Our consumers did."[7]

There are some notable exceptions where demographic variables are related to differences in needs, wants, preferences, and purchase behaviour, and it would make sense to use these variables as the main basis for segmentation.

Segment by Demographics: Sex

It makes sense to segment the clothing, fashion, footwear, or fragrance industries by sex, for example, because physiological and socialization differences between men and women can result in different needs, wants, and preferences. However, men and women may also seek different benefits, features, or attributes, so, in many cases, starting with benefit segmentation would result in a similar segmentation scheme as if starting with sex. Socialization by sex starts at a very early age and markets need to be responsive to consumer preferences; even diapers come in pink for girls and blue for boys. As proof that consumers take these differences seriously, market researchers report that most parents refuse to put male infants in pink diapers.[8] Ford Canada recognizes that women and men may have different needs when it comes to purchasing and servicing cars and trucks, which is why the company is now focusing efforts on trying to better understand and serve the needs of Canadian women. Volvo has created a concept car designed by

Exhibit 6.9

Jones Soda targets psychographic segments.

Exhibit 6.10

Fuel magazine targets a segment of young males.

tweens

Boys and girls age 9–12 who are "in-between" stages in their development, when they are considered "too old for toys" but "too young for dating."

Exhibit 6.11

Boomers are willing to invest a lot of money, time, and energy to maintain their youthful image.

women for women.[9] Similarly, companies such as Home Depot Canada, Marriott Hotels, and Mr. Lube, which have traditionally focused on marketing to men, have started developing products and messages specifically targeting Canadian women. Youth Culture's *Fuel* magazine is focused on male teens (Youth Culture also publishes *Verve* for girls), its research finding that boys and girls liked and wanted to learn and read about different things (Exhibit 6.10). Its biggest hurdle has been convincing advertisers that boys do shop and develop brand loyalty, but for different products than girls.[10]

Segment by Demographics: Age

Consumers in different age groups have very different needs and wants with respect to *product categories*. Members of a generation tend to share the same outlook and spending priorities, and these outlooks and priorities change as people age (what you spend your discretionary money on is likely different from what your parents spend their discretionary money on). However, unless brands specifically reflect differences in product category needs and wants (such as the content of *Fuel* magazine being directed to the interests of teenage boys, and Disney's TV show *Hannah Montana* being directed to **tweens** (girls and boys age 9 to 12), age is less useful for identifying differences in *brand* preferences than for identifying differences in product category preferences.

Canadian demographer David Foot has identified several segments of Canadian consumers based on age. These include members of the baby boom (those people born in 1947–1966), the baby bust (generation X; those born in 1967–1979), the baby boom echo (generation Y; those born in 1980–1995), and the millennium busters (those born in 1996–2010).[11]

While each of these groups of consumers presents needs that some marketers are interested in, the largest demographic segment in Canada, the baby boomers, accounts for about one-third of the Canadian population and is, therefore, a segment of prime importance to many marketers. Several companies have achieved success by monitoring the changing needs of this group of consumers. Coca-Cola, for example, can attribute part of its success in North America to the fact that boomers drank a lot of pop when they were young. Coke has now modified its marketing efforts to keep up with the changing tastes of the boomers. It changed its product line to include juice and bottled water to cater to the concerns that aging boomers have for their health.[12]

Marketers need to remember one key characteristic of boomers; they invest a lot of money, time, and energy to maintain a youthful image (Exhibit 6.11). Boomer women in their fifties, for example, are becoming a hot new market for "reward cars": sexy, extravagant vehicles that are a reward for all those years of driving kids around in a minivan. Since many people are now retiring younger than age 65, these consumers are enjoying increased leisure time, making them an ideal target for travel and other leisure products. Health is also a major concern for these consumers; some of them may be experiencing failing health, and others are simply interested in maintaining good health as they age. The Healthwatch service provided by Shoppers Drug Mart, which provides advice from pharmacists, a database of individualized health information, and a health magazine, is a good example of a service targeted to the needs of these consumers. Boomers will arguably become the most important demographic segment in years to come. Companies seeking growth will want to consider boomers because of their wealth, time available, and the fact that most boomers had fewer children than their own parents. Exhibit 6.12 shows that many marketers are starting to tailor products to meet the needs of older consumers.

The group of consumers born between 1967 and 1979 are **Generation Xers,** sometimes labelled busters or the lost generation. Many of these people, now over 35 years old, have a cynical attitude toward marketing, and most don't have the spending power of boomers or even Gen Y. However, because **baby boomers** have taken and held on to the top jobs in the country, Gen Xers have had to be much more entrepreneurial. They have been responsible for upwards of 70 percent of the new start-up businesses in North America. According to 2010 Investors Group's research, 62 percent of Gen Xers believe they will have to fund their own retirement and half (51 percent) expect they will have to fund their own medical and personal care.[13]

Gen Y (the echo boom) comprises the children of the baby boomers, typically born between 1980 and 1995. The largest proportion of the estimated 9.2 million Gen Y's in Canada are now late teens and young adults, and represent a lucrative group of consumers, the second-fastest growing segment in Canada.[14]

Gen Y is the first generation to grow up online, and is ethnically diverse and more socially and environmentally aware than earlier generations. These consumers tend to spend their money on items such as clothing, personal grooming, entertainment, sports, and eating out. (See Exhibit 6.13.) Montreal-based La Senza successfully targeted Gen Y girls when they were tweens with La Senza Girl stores and now tries to attract them to their regular stores. Banks such as TD Canada Trust, the Royal Bank, and CIBC have savings programs and debit cards specifically aimed at kids.[15] VanCity Credit Union recently targeted youth with a banking service "Not for the majority," offering free banking service to anyone under the age of 25. The campaign is backed with a combination of street marketing, Web promotions, contests, special events, and a text messaging campaign targeting 5000 youth in Vancouver who had been given cellphones by research company Digital Youth in exchange for volunteering to receive promotional messages and advertising.

Gen Y are hard to reach because they resist reading, increasingly turn off the TV, and, on average, spend four or more hours online a day. When they do watch TV, they tend toward alternative fare such as the late-night lineup. As a result, marketers are increasingly using online marketing techniques and guerrilla marketing techniques to reach these consumers. The older part of Gen Y, those born in the early to mid-1980s, are now either in graduate school or have joined the workforce and are starting to make major purchases on their own. The younger college- and university-age group is an important target group for companies like DirectProtect, which sells insurance to students, and brewers such as Moosehead, Molson, and Labatt, who realize that many of the heavy users of their products can be found on campuses across Canada.

Teens are also an attractive segment. The 12 to 17 age group now represents more than 26 million consumers in North America, who spend almost $200 billion.[16]

Exhibit 6.12

A phone with a feature adapted specifically to the needs of older callers.

Generation X
The group of consumers born between 1965 and 1978.

baby boomers
The segment of people born between 1946 and 1964.

Gen Y
The children of baby boomer parents is the second largest demographic segment in Canada.

Courtesy of Siblings

Exhibit 6.13

Siblings stores target tweens and young teens.

Tech and Trends

Ford Fiesta Looks for Gen Y "Where They Live"

Ford's Fiesta launched in Canada in 2010, but a year earlier the company gave away 100 of the cars to influential Gen Y's in the hope of building some buzz from the ground up. The "recruitment call" went out for 100 "agents" to receive the car in April 2009, complete Ford-assigned "missions," and chronicle their experiences through their social networks such as Facebook, Flickr, and YouTube. The company has dubbed this effort its "Fiesta Movement," and it's the anchor of a plan to build excitement and spread the word about the arrival of the new Ford Fiesta to the next generation of customers—clearly strong targets for this economy-priced vehicle. Sam De La Garza, small car marketing manager for Ford, says, "Socially vibrant campaigns are so important because of their power in delivering authentic and genuine messages across a broad spectrum of media, which will only help us deliver a more positive consumer experience when the car launches in North America next year."

The company set up a Web site where people could upload a two- to five-minute video to explain why they want to become one of the agents. By 2010, Gen Y will account for 28 percent of North America's driving population (a total of about 77 million new drivers). The movement gives Ford an opportunity to connect with the group before they have established brand loyalty, while the company also appeals to their affinity for social networking and technology. Using social networking as a way to reach Gen Y is a sound strategy, provided that the company is upfront about its relationship with the agents and is willing to let them craft the message as they see fit.[17]

Much of this money goes to consumer electronics like iPhones or "feel good" products like cosmetics, posters, and fast food—with the occasional nose ring or tattoo thrown in as well. Many marketers are attracted to this group, hoping to groom them into lifelong customers. Avon, for example, has developed a new product line called mark (www.meetmark.com), so named in celebration of young women making their mark in the world today. Apple is a masterful marketer to teens, yet its product line appeals to other age groups as well. The iPod in its various forms (Exhibit 6.14) enables teens to be content creators and empowers them to be masters of their own music world. This satisfies a strong need among this age group for individuality.

Segment by Demographics: Family Life Cycle

Because family needs and expenditures change over time, one way to segment consumers is to consider the stage of the family life cycle they occupy (you learned about the family life cycle in Chapter 4). Not surprisingly, consumers in different life cycle segments (such as young adults, married with children, empty nesters) are unlikely to need the same products, or at least in the same quantities. For example, many food companies cater to the needs of people who live alone by providing single-portion frozen and prepared foods but also offer "jumbo" packs for those people who live in larger households.

As we age and move into new life situations, different product categories ascend and descend in importance to us. Young singles and newlyweds are the most likely to exercise, to go to bars, concerts, and movies, and to consume alcohol. Young families are heavy users of disposable diapers and toys and games for children. They are also interested in household appliances, furniture, and such vehicles as minivans or SUVs. Older couples and singles are more likely to use maintenance services, and older people are a prime market for retirement communities and golf products. Condominiums that are built in Canadian cities, for example, are often designed with different family structures in mind. Some target single divorced men and women, others go after young families and include amenities such as on-site day care, and still others target vacation home buyers. Canadian department stores also consider family life cycle by specifically targeting brides- and grooms-to-be with wedding registry services.

Exhibit 6.14

The iPod and iPhone are iconic symbols of modern youth—stylish, nonconforming, and an expression of a clear difference from the past.

Segment by Demographics: Income and Social Class

The distribution of wealth is of great interest to marketers, because it determines which groups have the greatest buying

Ethical and Sustainable Decisions in the Real World

Most major brands are gearing up to more deeply target consumers in emerging markets. China has 1.3 billion people. India has 1.1 billion. Other nations such as Brazil and Russia offer the dazzling prospect of massive revenue for savvy brands. Coca-Cola is particularly known for successful targeting, for many reasons, including the firm's ability to identify untapped target markets and win over consumers not only by aggressively pursuing them, but also by wanting to know them.

Currently 30 million people, one in three of India's population, constitute the BOP "bottom-of-pyramid" marketplace. The BOP refers to the masses in developing countries that account for over 65 percent of the world's population. Buyers at the BOP behave differently not only from their counterparts in developed countries but also from the upper- and middle-income consumers in their own societies.

Now, Coke is reaching out to this group in India with Vitingo, a new drink aimed at lower-income consumers. Coke isn't alone as it pursues this target market, and for good reason. Statistics show that 40 million Indian families are moving from outright poverty to the BOP demographic every year. Remember, that's not 40 million people, it's 40 million families. Like Coke, Glaxo Smith Kline, the pharmaceutical firm, knows there is no greater brand advocate than a family member. In fact, GSK is launching its own milk-based drink in India, Asha, designed to appeal to the BOP demographic. Also like Coke, GSK is doing more than offering a product. It is selling the product to a specific group of consumers that the brand values and actively targets. Says Zubair Ahmed, managing director at GSK India: "We are building a robust go-to-market model to ensure the products reach the right consumers because it's not enough just to have the right products."

Other familiar brands investing in India's BOP market are Nestlé, Pepsi, and Hindustan Unilever, all with the idea that the successful brands of tomorrow are already courting these up-and-coming BOP consumers that will provide important revenue streams in the years to come.

ETHICS CHECK:
Find out what other students taking this course **would do** and **why** on **www.mypearsonmarketinglab.com**

Is it appropriate for firms such as Coke and GSK to target the BOP market in countries like India?

☐**YES** ☐**NO**

---

power. It should come as no surprise that many marketers yearn to capture the hearts and wallets of high-income consumers. In Canada, the average family income is about $77,300, but the top quartile of the population has a household income above $178 300.[18] These high-income consumers are a good target market for such luxury products as expensive jewellery, as well as financial services of brokers and investment products. At the same time, other marketers target lower-income consumers—the majority of Canadian consumers. The Hudson's Bay Company successfully targets these income groups with its Bay and Zellers department stores, as will Target when it takes over Zellers in 2013.

In the past, it was popular for marketers to consider social class segments, such as upper class, middle class, and lower class. However, many consumers do not buy according to where they actually fall in that framework, but rather according to the image they wish to portray. For example, over the years, readily available credit has facilitated the sale of many BMWs to consumers whose income doesn't easily support the steep price tag. The recent global financial crisis nipped a good portion of this free-flowing credit, and it remains to be seen over the long run how much the new era of credit austerity changes consumer buying behaviour.

Segment by Demographics: Ethnicity

As was discussed in Chapter 4, many Canadian marketers are adopting a multicultural approach to their marketing activities in recognition of the ethnic diversity of the Canadian population. Ethnicity can have a strong impact on a consumer's preferences for products and services, such as magazines or television shows, foods, apparel, and choice of leisure activities.

French Canadian consumers, who account for about 22 percent of Canadians, are the second-largest ethnic market in Canada (after those people of British origin) and are, therefore, an important segment for marketers.[19] Most French Canadian consumers live in Quebec, but there are also large segments of French Canadian consumers in New Brunswick and Ontario. As will be discussed further in Chapter 8, national marketers often decide to specifically target the French-Canadian market through the development of different products to suit the needs of this group and the use of French-language advertising. For example, MusiquePlus and MusiMax are the French-language music video TV stations owned by CHUM, the same company that operates MuchMusic and MuchMoreMusic in the English-Canadian market. While MusiquePlus and MusiMax show many of the same videos as do the English stations, French music and programming is featured to appeal to the music tastes of French-Canadian consumers. As the vice president of sales for CHUM Specialty Television observes, "They are not MuchMusic and MuchMoreMusic in French. They have an identity of their own with a more regional than national focus."[20] So when Procter & Gamble was looking for a French-Canadian spokesperson for Cover Girl cosmetics, it chose Geneviève Borne, a MusiquePlus VJ, because of her appeal to female French-Canadian teens.

Over 1.2 million people in Canada are of Aboriginal origin; they are located in various regions throughout the country, and 42 percent live off-reserve.[21] The Aboriginal population is growing at four times the rate of any other segment, with half of the Aboriginal people in Canada currently under the age of 25. The income of Aboriginal consumers is rising faster than that of other Canadians, and there are more than 20 000 Aboriginal-owned businesses.[22] The combined income of Aboriginal households, business, and government sectors is expected to rise sharply in the next five years to $32 billion (more than the combined GDP of Newfoundland and Labrador and Prince Edward Island).[23]

The banking sector in Canada has also been proactive in targeting both Aboriginal consumers and business owners. All the major Canadian banks operate branches in Aboriginal communities, with services targeted to meet their needs, as illustrated by the ad for the Royal Bank in Exhibit 6.15. The Aboriginal Peoples Television Network (APTN) and *Spirit* magazine are examples of media targeting Aboriginal peoples. A key challenge in marketing to Aboriginal peoples is to recognize the ethnic diversity within this group: Inuit, Métis, and First Nations (such as Cree, Maliseet, Dene, Anishinabe, Mohawk, Haida) have significantly different languages, histories, traditions, and environments that influence current thinking, attitudes, and behaviours. As this segment has traditionally been misunderstood and under-researched, it is particularly important to conduct research (see Chapter 3) to understand these consumers.

Other than people of British, French, and Aboriginal origins, the three largest ethnic groups in Canada are German, Italian, and Chinese. Of these three, the fastest growing is the Chinese Canadian community.[24] Tropicana Products Ltd. considers the Chinese Canadian community to be one of the most important target markets for its orange juice product. It communicates with this target with Chinese-language print ads placed in Chinese-Canadian newspapers and promotions such as coupons for 68 cents (both six and eight are considered to signify prosperity in the Chinese culture). The company is careful to avoid the use of the number four (which signifies death) in any of its pricing and advertising.[25]

Other large ethnic groups in Canada include the South Asian community, which accounts for 2.8 percent of the population, and the black community, which makes up 2.1 percent of the Canadian population.[26] Bell Canada provides customer service representatives who speak Hindi, Punjabi, Urdu, and Tamil to better serve its South Asian customers. To reach the over 351 000 people in Canada of Jewish origin, companies such as Baskin-Robbins offer kosher food products, Hallmark offers cards and festive products targeted to Jewish holidays, and the Liquor Control Board of Ontario offers 80 different types of kosher wines.[27]

Partners in Your Future

Original art by Natalie Rostad

*R*oyal Bank Financial Group has long been a leading provider of services to Aboriginal communities through our specialized products, educational programs, career opportunities and initiatives to assist Aboriginal economic development. We have specialized teams all across Canada that understand the financial requirements of Aboriginal peoples.

Our Aboriginal Banking initiatives reflect the bank's commitment to all of its customers - understanding their financial services requirements, offering flexible solutions, and treating clients as they want to be treated. We are committed to ensuring your financial and banking requirements are being met. Royal Bank will continue to be "Partners in Your Future".

ROYAL BANK

Exhibit 6.15

Aboriginal consumers are an important segment for the Royal Bank.

Segment by Demographics: Geography

People's preferences for products and services often depend on which region of the country they live in. For example, a recent study of how upper-income people across Canada spend their money showed significant regional differences. Compared to the average Canadian, upper-income people living in Edmonton were more likely to spend their money on skiwear and snowmobile suits; in Saskatoon it would be home exercise equipment; in Montreal, leather and fur coats and jackets; in Halifax, art goods and decorative ware; in St. John's, snow blowers; while those in the north were more likely to purchase outboard motor boats. Similarly, a study of snacking behaviour found that Maritimers consume more potato chips than consumers in other regions (almost double the national average), and Quebec consumers eat less than half of the average amount of corn chips of consumers in other regions.[28]

Recognition of these kinds of regional differences can lead marketers to focus efforts on one or more regions, or to have different marketing strategies in different regions. When marketers want to segment regional markets even more precisely, they sometimes combine geography with demographics by using a technique called **geodemography**. A basic assumption of geodemography is that "birds of a feather flock together"; people who live near one another share similar characteristics. Sophisticated statistical techniques identify geographic areas that share the same preferences for household items, magazines, and other products. This allows marketers to construct segments consisting of households with a common pattern of preferences, so that a company can home in on those customers who are most likely to be interested in its specific offerings—in some cases, so precisely that families living on one block will be included in a segment whereas those on the next block will not.

One Canadian geodemographic system, PSYTE, is a large database developed by Compusearch Micromarketing Data and Systems. This system classifies Canadian consumers into 60 clusters, based on postal code and demographic information. The resulting clusters include boomers and teens, conservative homebodies, young city singles, brie and chablis, and suburban nesters.[29] PSYTE system is used by Canada Post in its GeoPost Plus program, which allows marketers to target direct mail to clusters of consumers that match their target segment. For example, the boomers-and-teens segment is described as "late middle-aged consumers who are university and college educated with children over the age of six. Mostly double income families who live in their own homes." The cluster named young city singles are "young singles and some couples who rent predominantly newer, downtown apartments and other dwellings." Using a geodemographic system like GeoPost Plus, a marketer of home improvement products like outdoor paint and fencing can identify precisely which postal codes will be the best prospects for direct mail advertising for their product, while avoiding other postal codes where residents aren't likely to be interested.

geodemography
Segmentation technique that combines geography with demographics.

Segment Business-to-Business Markets

We've reviewed the segmentation variables marketers use to divide up the consumer pie, but how about all those business-to-business markets out there? Adding to what we learned about business markets in Chapter 5, it's important to know that segmentation also helps **B2B marketers** better understand their customers. Though the specific variables may differ, the underlying logic of classifying the larger market into manageable pieces that share relevant characteristics is the same whether the product you sell is pesto or pesticides.

B2B marketers
Marketers who work in business-to-business markets.

Segment by Organizational Behaviour

Just as in consumer segmentation, it is often fruitful to consider the behaviour of the people making business and organization decisions. Organizational buying behaviour was the focus of Chapter 5, and it is important to recognize that organizations act and behave in ways that are both similar to and different from consumers, and that the way they behave and operate is influenced by the types of products and services they both sell and need. Consequently, one way to segment business-to-business markets is by the unique way each operates.

Exhibit 6.16

Grand & Toy targets behaviour-based business segments.

Organization buying and consumption behaviour is influenced by the production technology used; the type of purchases made; the business customer's degree of technical, financial, or operations expertise; how they make purchase decisions and who is involved in those decisions; whether the prospect is a current user or nonuser of the product; and the frequency or size of the transactions. These operating variables are all useful bases of segmentation. For example, Grand & Toy (Exhibit 6.16) recognized the differences in the buying behaviour of large and small businesses when it launched The Stockroom (www.thestockroom.ca), an Internet-based office supplies store that targets small businesses. While the Grand & Toy Web site is geared to the needs of large businesses (offering benefits like large volume discounts), The Stockroom site caters to small businesses with its products and pricing policies. The general manager of The Stockroom describes the company's approach this way: " . . . we felt it was important to take a very aggressive, focused stance, purely aimed at the small business segment."[30]

Business marketers also must consider how different customers will use their products or services. They must focus on identifying different end-use applications for these offerings. The personal computer industry is a good example of how firms can segment a market based on end use. Some major PC manufacturers, such as Dell, have divided the market into four segments—corporate, small business, government, and home or home office—each with its own computer-use profile. IBM segments its mainframe market into user "verticals"—different applications (such as health care or manufacturing) for which the mainframe computers might be used.

Segment by Industrial Psychographics

industrial psychographics
The application of psychographics to the business-to-business context.

Being concerned with psychology, thinking, feeling, and other mental states, the concept of psychographics relates only indirectly to organizations, but it does relate to the people who run and work in those organizations. **Industrial psychographics**, the application of psychographics to the business-to-business context, has mainly been applied to understanding buyers (purchasing agents or multiple people in a buying centre) to help salespeople better understand their one-on-one relationships with clients. It may also be fruitful to segment business markets by the mission, goals, and values of an organization and its management team, since purchase and consumption decisions and behaviours are likely to be consistent with those missions, goals, and values. This is the thinking of Steve Munden, director of research at the Toronto-based marketing firm Warrillow and Co. Munden is developing a psychographic profile of Generation Xers who own small- and medium-sized businesses. These entrepreneurs are people in their mid-twenties to thirties who are increasingly leaving the workforce to take control of their lives and find financial independence. Munden thinks a psychographic profile of these entrepreneurs will help his clients better target these business organizations—as the beliefs, values, and orientation of these entrepreneurs are expected to play a large role in their company's purchase decisions.[31]

Segment by Organizational Demographics

Demographic data help business marketers understand the needs and characteristics of their potential customers. For example, a manufacturer of work uniforms needs to know which industries currently provide uniforms for employees. For each industry that uses uniforms, from chemical processing to pest control, a marketer needs to know how many companies are potential customers, the number of employees in each company, what types of uniforms are needed, and so on. That information enables the manufacturer to offer its services to the prospects that are most likely to be interested in outfitting employees in its protective clothing.

Many industries use the North American Industry Classification System (NAICS) to obtain information about the size and number of companies operating in a particular industry. Other government information sources, such as Statistics Canada and Strategis (www.strategis.gc.ca), provide valuable business demographic information.

3

Step 2: Targeting

We've seen that the first step in a target marketing strategy is segmentation, in which the firm divides the market into smaller groups that share certain characteristics. The next step is targeting, in which marketers evaluate the attractiveness of each potential segment and decide in which of these groups they will invest resources to try to turn them into customers. The customer group or groups they select are the firm's target market.

In this section, we'll review the three phases of targeting: evaluate market segments, develop segment profiles, and choose one or more target segments (see Figure 6.6).

Evaluate Market Segments

Just because a marketer identifies a segment does not necessarily mean that it's a useful target. A viable market segment should satisfy the criteria identified in Figure 6.2 (page 177) but also meet two other key requirements before being added to the consideration set:

- Is the segment actionable? Marketers must know something about the characteristics of the customers in each segment—their number (segment size), purchasing power, buying behaviour, and consumption behaviour—before they decide if it's worth their efforts to target them, and these characteristics need to be actionable in the sense that they allow the marketer to create an offer that uniquely appeals to a particular segment and that the differences between the groups are meaningful enough to warrant a separate marketing strategy.

- Can the marketer adequately serve the needs of the segment? Does the firm have the expertise and resources to satisfy the segment better than the competition? Some years ago, consumer-products manufacturer Warner-Lambert (now a part of Pfizer) made the mistake of trying to enter the pastry business by purchasing Entenmann's Bakery. Entenmann's sells high-end boxed cakes, cookies, pastries, and pies in supermarkets. Unfortunately, Warner-Lambert's expertise at selling Listerine mouthwash and Trident gum did not transfer to baked goods and it soon lost a lot of dough on the deal.

Develop Segment Profiles

Once a marketer identifies a set of usable segments, the next task is to develop a brief **segment profile**, or description of each segment, with sufficient depth to be able to understand the segment so that it can be evaluated and either be targeted or rejected. Years ago, when the R.J. Reynolds Company made plans to introduce a new brand of cigarettes called Dakota that it would target to women, it created a segment profile of a possible customer group, the "Virile Female." The profile included these characteristics: her favourite pastimes are

Catharine Downes

APPLYING ▽ Market Segments

Catharine Downes of NSCU is confident that the West Coast affluent market segment is actionable. NSCU knows a lot about their attitudes, interests, and opinions, knows where they live, and knows their media habits and their consumption behaviours. NSCU could tailor their financial services offering to this target market and communication that offer to this segment. ➡

segment profile
A description of the "typical" customer in a segment.

Figure 6.6 Phases of Targeting
Targeting involves three distinct phases of activities.

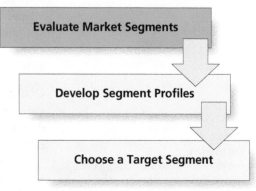

cruising, partying, going to hot-rod shows and tractor pulls with her boyfriend, and watching evening soap operas, and her chief aspiration is to get married in her early 20s.[32] Just as consumer behaviour changes over time, so do segment profiles. Does the "Virile Female" still exist in your community?

To make this "typical" customer more tangible or real, marketers often put a name to the customer and then describe him or her in as much detail as possible. In 2010, Buick's marketers named their target consumers Greg and Laurie Robbins. They say they're in their early 40s with two kids, and, together, they make $130 000 a year and live in a $363 000 house. They are Facebook fans of Target, Starbucks, Apple, J. Crew, Whole Foods, and the Westin. This (fictional) couple is younger than Buick's current user and their interests extend beyond the golf course, which is where many older Buick drivers spend their time. To woo this target customer, the company is cutting back on ads in golf magazines and instead promoting Buick in culinary- and travel-related venues and on *The Wall Street Journal*'s iPad application. The goal of this psychographic exercise is to "Put a Buick in the Robbins's garage where a Lexus is probably parked now."[33]

One useful template for developing these profiles is illustrated in Figure 6.7. A detailed profile would normally include a description of (1) who is in the segment (using demographics, psychographics, and geographic variables); (2) what people or organizations in this segment want (benefits, features, and attributes) and why (needs, motivations); (3) when and where they expect to buy and use the product; (4) how they typically buy the product (such as purchase decision process, influences, sources of information, media preferences); and (5) how they typically use the product (consumption behaviour). In addition, marketers try to estimate the size of each segment and its expected growth rate. (An example of the application of this framework can be found in the S&S Smoothie marketing plan in the Appendix to this text.) For the purposes of selecting market segments to target, these profiles are usually created based on experience and judgment. Sophisticated marketers, however, use market research and analytic tools such as **cluster analysis** to verify profile assumptions or to more scientifically identify the segments and their characteristics. The profiles of the segment(s) chosen for targeting (see below) are developed in much more detail and provide, in part, the basis for making marketing mix decisions.

To estimate the size and growth of a segment, marketers try to forecast each segment's **market potential.** This is the maximum demand expected among consumers or customers in that segment for a particular product. To determine market potential, the firm must identify the number of consumers or customers in the segment and how much they spend in the product category. Then it must determine the sales potential for its product if it targets this segment—how many consumers or customers would buy this product during the forecast period and with what frequency or quantity. This number is the total dollar potential. The firm then projects its market share—what percentage share of the market is likely to buy its particular brand(s). Multiplying total dollar potential by market share gives the likely actual dollar amount the firm might make. Forecasting is an advanced topic that you will likely learn more about in senior-level courses. For the initial, brief profiles, an estimate of the relative size of each segment is expected. This would be based on experience, observation, analysis, and/or market research.

Choose One or More Target Segments

Once marketers have divided a market into actionable segments and developed a brief profile of each segment, they need to evaluate the attractiveness of each potential segment and decide which one or more of these segments they will target with marketing programs. The consumer or customer group(s) selected are the firm's **target market(s).**

Earth's Own Food Company, previously SoyaWorld, a Canadian soy beverage marketer, has attained 60 percent of the dairy alternative market by carefully considering

cluster analysis
Computer software that groups survey respondents based on the commonality of their answers to questions, putting respondents with similar answers in the same group, while maximizing the differences between the groups or segments.

market potential
The maximum demand expected among consumers in a segment for a product or service.

target market
A group that a marketing organization focuses on when developing marketing programs.

Figure 6.7 Framework for Creating Rich Segment Profiles.

Who are they?
- What are their demographic characteristics?
- What are their psychographic characteristics?
- What are their geodemographic characteristics?
- How price sensitive are they?

What do they want and why?
- What are the benefits, features, attributes, or characteristics sought by consumers in this segment?
- What do they need and want?
- What motivates the purchase and consumption decision?

When do they buy and use it?
- What triggers the purchase decision?
- What is the context in which they buy the product?
- How often do they buy the product?
- What time of day, part of the week, or month, or year is it purchased?
- What time of day, part of the week, or month, or year is it used or consumed?

Where do they buy and use it?
- What stores or other distribution channels do they use?
- Where are they when they use the product?

How do they buy and use it?
- How do they decide what to buy? (decision-making process used)
- What or who influences the purchase decision?
- What media do they use/access in making the decision?
- Is it a thinking (cognitive) or feeling (emotional) decision?
- Is it a high-involvement (important or risky) decision or a low involvement (not important or risky) decision?
- How do they use or consume the product?
- How much of it do they use?

Segment Size
- What is the market potential?
- What is the expected growth rate of the segment?

specific target markets. Soy beverages make up the fastest-growing beverage category in Canada, and Earth's Own has identified three main targets in the total market: the mainstream dairy market, the Asian market, and the organic market. For the mainstream dairy segment, Earth's Own introduced So Good, a soy beverage with an improved taste that comes in several flavours. Since the product was being promoted as an alternative to milk, So Good was packaged to look like milk and was placed in the dairy cases of major supermarkets. Billboards, TV, and magazine ads, such as the one shown in Exhibit 6.17, were all used to reach the mainstream market. Earth's Own targets Asian consumers with its Sunrise brand, a product that has a more traditional soy taste. For the organic target segment, it offers So Nice, a soy beverage, and Rice Choice, a fortified rice beverage. To reach the organic and Asian segments, the Earth's Own products are distributed through specialty retailers, such as Chinese grocery stores and health food stores, in addition to selected larger grocery stores.[34] In this section, we'll review how marketers like Earth's Own assess the customer groups in the market and the selection strategies they use for effective targeting.

Target Market Selection

There are three basic criteria for deciding which market segments are attractive to an organization: segment size and growth, the external decision environment, and the internal

Exhibit 6.17

Earth's Own Food Company targets the mainstream dairy market with the So Good soy beverage.

undifferentiated targeting strategy

Appealing to a broad spectrum of people.

differentiated targeting strategy

Developing one or more products for each of several distinct customer groups and making sure these offerings are kept separate in the marketplace.

concentrated targeting strategy

Focusing a firm's efforts on offering one or more products to a single segment.

decision environment (see SWOT analysis in Chapter 2). Figure 6.8 summarizes these criteria.

Choose a Targeting Strategy

A basic targeting decision revolves around how finely tuned the target should be: Should the company go after one large segment or focus on meeting the needs of one or more smaller segments? Let's look at four targeting strategies, which Figure 6.9 summarizes.

A company like Walmart that selects an **undifferentiated targeting strategy** appeals to a broad spectrum of people. If successful, this type of operation can be very efficient because production, research, and promotion costs benefit from economies of scale—it's cheaper to develop one product or one advertising campaign than to choose several targets and create separate products or messages for each. But the company must be willing to bet that people have similar needs so the same product and message will appeal to many customers. This is the approach Henry Ford used in offering the Model-T Ford—"in any colour, so long as it was black." Today it is difficult to create a single product or offering that has very broad appeal. Consumers expect choices, there are many distribution channels from which to purchase products, and there are many focused-communication outlets that let marketers cost-effectively communicate to increasingly narrow target markets. Companies with new-to-the-world innovations are the ones that most commonly practise undifferentiated marketing, but segments in these markets quickly develop as competitors enter these markets with differentiated products and consumers become more knowledgeable and demanding about the product category. When competitors are using a differentiated strategy, it makes it difficult for the original innovator to continue using an undifferentiated strategy.

A company that chooses a **differentiated targeting strategy** develops one or more products for each of several customer groups with different product needs. A differentiated strategy is called for when consumers choose among well-known brands that have distinctive images, and the company can identify one or more segments that have distinct needs for different types of products.

Despite its highly publicized product safety issues in 2010, Toyota historically has been a leader in differentiated strategy with distinct product lines that cater to multiple customer groups. Its Lexus product line caters to consumers who want luxury, performance, and the newest technology. The Prius hybrid provides value to drivers who want to save gas money and the environment. And finally, the Scion product line caters to younger drivers who look for a relatively inexpensive car that is highly customizable and stylish.[35]

Differentiated marketing can also involve connecting one product with different segments by communicating differently to appeal to those segments. Using the "Got Milk?" campaign as an example, one of their most classic ads featured Aerosmith's Steven Tyler in order to appeal to both aging boomers who got into the band in the 1970s and Gen Yers who discovered the band in the 1990s with Run-DMC's remake of "Walk This Way."

When a firm offers one or more products to a single segment, it uses a **concentrated targeting strategy**. Smaller firms that do not have the resources or the desire to be all things to all people often do this. Blacksocks.com is a mail-order sock company that only makes black dress socks; it targets businessmen who are too busy to go to the store and buy new socks when their old ones wear out. Blacksocks ships 3-packs of black socks once a month to its "sockscribers." The company argues that every guy who wears a business suit wears socks, and most wear black socks. For these busy men, going to the store just to buy socks is boring, time consuming, and simply unnecessary.[36] Periodically, the company wrestles with the dilemma of whether or not to also sell white socks, because this expansion will dilute the brand (and force the company to change its name!). (See Exhibit 6.18 on page 199.) This

Figure 6.8 Criteria for Choosing Target Market Segments

1. *Segment Size and Growth.* When choosing market segments to target, one consideration is the size and growth of the segment. The segment must be "the right size"—large enough to be profitable now and in the future, but small enough that an organization can compete effectively in it. It is a lot easier to compete in a high-growth segment than in a low- or declining-growth segment because in a high-growth segment, new customers do not have to be taken away from existing competitors.

2. *External Environment.* While segment size and growth is part of the external environment, marketers tend to give that issue special attention because of its strategic importance. There are, however, other external environment considerations when choosing market segments. One is the level of competition. Large and high-growth segments are highly attractive to other competitors, and a smaller organization may not have the resources to compete effectively against them. It may make sense for smaller companies, with more limited resources, to focus on smaller segments (market niches) and not compete directly with larger competitors. This was the strategy of Sun Microsystems when it focused on the computer segment of engineering and scientific workstations in the early 1990s. As a small company, it was able to dominate a very small, but high growth, niche and grow with that niche to become a dominant player in the overall computer market. Similarly, when Toyota introduced the Echo subcompact car into the Canadian market, the target segment was described demographically as "60/40 male/female, 40% married, median age 32, 48% university educated with an average household income $42 000." In addition, the segment displayed the following psychographic traits: idealistic, experimental, independent, educated, urban, and not brand loyal. This is likely a fairly small segment, even on a national level, and it suggests that even large companies may decide to focus on small segments if they can create unique value there better than competitors can. It may be more profitable to be a "big fish in a small pond," and being that "big fish" may discourage other competitors from entering the market segment.

   Related to the extent and level of competition is the industry structure. A local monopoly (or near monopoly) like Rogers Cable may choose to focus on large, less well-defined segments because there are no direct competitors (other than satellite TV services) focusing their strategies on more narrow segments. Where there is extensive competition, different competitors will focus on increasingly narrow market segments, making it difficult for others to compete effectively in multiple segments.

   A segment with many substitute products may limit the price and, hence, profits in that segment. Segments where there are few buyers or buyers with otherwise strong bargaining positions might also be unattractive as these buyers can keep prices down and play one supplier off another. Segments with strong suppliers (large, concentrated, or with few competitors or substitutes) may similarly be unattractive. Finally, segment attractiveness is also related to the stage of the product life cycle—where mature and declining markets are less attractive than new and growing ones.

3. *Internal Environment.* The marketer must also be able to adequately serve the needs of the segment and have the expertise and resources to do so better than the competition. Some years ago, Exxon made the mistake of trying to enter the office products business, a growing segment. The company's expertise at selling petroleum products did not transfer to copying machines, and the effort was unsuccessful. Four Seasons Hotels, on the other hand, was able to transfer its expertise in exceptional accommodation services aimed at a tightly defined, luxury lifestyle audience to an entirely new market sector, residential properties. The attractiveness of a segment depends on a company's ability to create value in that segment and defend their strategy in it. This requires an assessment of the strengths and weaknesses of the organization relative to the needs of the consumers and competition in that segment (see SWOT analysis in Chapter 2).

US company is even more focused than the Canadian company JustWhiteShirts.com, which has been selling white shirts (and black socks) online since 1990 and has since expanded its selection to include dress shirts, sports shirts, jackets and blazers, ties, casual accessories, and much more.

Niche marketing is a type of concentrated targeting strategy where the market segment chosen is relatively small. Jones Soda, for example, focuses on the alternative soft drink niche by offering a series of soft drink products for people who want a premium beverage that stands out, is individualized, expresses personality, and makes a fashion statement. Niche marketing is becoming the norm in many markets as it allows many competitors to each make unique appeals and be the product of choice for some group of consumers.

niche marketing
A type of concentrated targeting strategy where the market segment chosen is relatively small.

Figure 6.9 Choose a Targeting Strategy

Marketers must decide on a targeting strategy. Should the company go after one total market, one or several market segments, or even target customers individually?

Undifferentiated Marketing

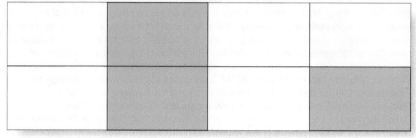

Differentiated Marketing

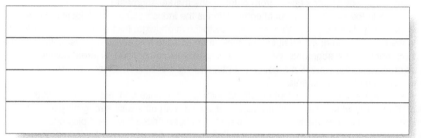

Concentrated Marketing

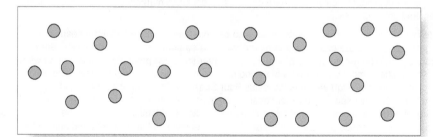

Customized Marketing

custom marketing strategy
An approach that tailors specific products and the messages about them to individual customers.

Ideally, marketers should be able to define segments so precisely that they can offer products and services that exactly meet the needs of every individual or firm. **Custom marketing strategy**, also called micro-marketing strategy, is tailoring specific products and the messages about them to individual customers or locations. A custom marketing strategy is often used in business markets by companies, such as aircraft manufacturer Bombardier, that often work with one or a few large clients and develop products that only these customers will use. In consumer markets, this level of concentration shows up (we hope!) in personal or professional services by doctors, lawyers, and hair stylists, for example. In most consumer markets, individualized marketing strategies are neither practical nor possible when products are mass produced. However, advances in technology coupled with the new emphasis on building solid relationships with customers have enabled mass customization. Clothing manufacturers like Levi Strauss and the high-end German clothier Engelhorn, for example, use digital imaging technology to do body scans of customers that enable the creation of perfectly fitting jeans, swimwear, or other clothing products. Calgary-based Critical Mass has worked with Nike to develop NIKEiD, an interactive part of the Nike Web site where consumers can design and purchase their own running shoes.[37] Dell uses the Internet to provide custom-built computers; customers choose among various options and Dell makes the computer to order. Individualized communication has also been enabled by Internet and e-mail technologies. Online retailers, such as HMV.com, for example, are able to send customized messages to users regarding the status of their orders, upcoming promotions that may be of interest based on the products they have bought in the past, and announcements of new releases.

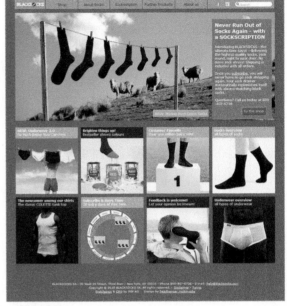

4

Step 3: Positioning

OBJECTIVE

Understand how marketers develop and implement a positioning strategy (pp. 199–207)

The final, crucial stage of the target marketing process is providing consumers in a targeted market segment with a product (good or service) that meets their unique needs and expectations. Positioning means developing a marketing strategy that clearly differentiates a firm's **brand** from its competitors along key dimensions of value that are important to target consumers or customers. To position a brand, marketers have to clearly understand the criteria target consumers use to evaluate competing brands and then convince them that their brand or organization will better meet those needs. In addition, the organization has to come up with a way to communicate this "position" to its target market. The high-performance sportswear company Under Armour, for example, was able to effectively communicate its positioning when Al Pacino and Jamie Foxx were shown to be wearing the brand in the film *Any Given Sunday*. The president of Under Armour just a happened to know someone who was auditioning for a part in the movie, and he sent along some samples for the casting director as a gift.

Exhibit 6.18

Blacksocks practises a highly concentrated targeting strategy.

brand
One particular company's version of a product (good or service).

Steps in Positioning

When developing a positioning strategy, marketers often focus on four elements: strategic orientation, differentiation, defendability, and brand personality.

Strategic Orientation

Strategic orientation (or strategic thrust) is the overall approach to how you plan to compete and create value for your customers. There are numerous frameworks or typologies that summarize key marketing and positioning strategies, and they all have different perspectives on how organizations can develop competitive advantage. One of these suggests that firms can focus on one or more of the following strategies: product leadership, customer intimacy, or operational excellence.[38]

strategic orientation
The overall approach to how you plan to compete and create value for your customers.

Product leadership is a strategy of competing by continually bringing innovative and useful new products or technologies to market. Adopted by companies such as 3M, Apple, and Nike, it is concerned with product innovation, quality, performance superiority, and other forms of functional value (see Chapter 1). Positioning consistent with a product leadership strategy focuses on dimensions such as the following:

product leadership
A strategy of competing by continually bringing innovative and useful new products or technologies to market.

- Quality (e.g., Ford: "Quality is Job 1"; Gillette: "The best a man can get")

- Reliability or durability (e.g., Timex: "It takes a lickin' and keeps on tickin'")

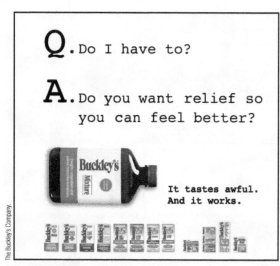

Exhibit 6.19

Buckley's cough syrup is positioned on the outcome "it works," consistent with a product leadership strategy.

customer intimacy
A strategy concerned with creating tailored solutions for narrowly defined market segments.

operational excellence
A strategy focused on cost effectiveness, efficiency, and customer convenience.

symbolic-expressive value
Differentiating your brand by the psychological meaning associated with it.

- Key features or attributes (e.g., Honda Civic: "Better gas mileage. A Civic responsibility")
- Innovation (e.g., Lexus: "The relentless pursuit of excellence"; GE: "Progress is our most important product")
- Performance (e.g., BMW: "The ultimate driving machine"; Apple: "The power to do your best")
- Outcomes (e.g., Buckley's: "It tastes awful. And it works"; Exhibit 6.19)

Customer intimacy, or customer responsiveness, is a strategy concerned with creating tailored solutions for narrowly defined market segments. Companies such as Kraft, Nordstrom, Marriott, and Levi Strauss aim to excel at providing superior customer experiences and/or personalized or customized interactions through outstanding service quality, customer support, flexibility, and customization. Concerned with the creation of experiential or emotional value, customer intimacy positioning strategies focus on dimensions such as the following:

- Sensory experience (e.g., KFC: "Finger lickin' good"; A&W: "That frosty mug sensation")
- Excitement, adventure (e.g., Nike: "Just do it"; Pontiac: "We drive excitement"; Club Med: "Do it now, do it fast, and do everything at the same time")
- Fun or pleasure (e.g., McDonald's: "I'm lovin' it"; Lay's: "Betcha can't eat just one")
- Emotion (e.g., Harlequin: "Live the emotion"; Hallmark: "When you care enough to send the very best")
- Social value (e.g., De Beers: "Diamonds are forever"; AT&T: "Reach out and touch someone")
- Responsiveness, customized, personalized (e.g., Burger King: "Have it your way"; Speedy Muffler: "At Speedy you're a somebody")
- Safety or security (e.g., Allstate: "You're in good hands with Allstate"; Michelin: "Because so much is riding on your tires")
- Novelty, knowledge, or fantasy (e.g., Disney Online: "Where the magic comes to you"; Microsoft: "Where do you want to go today?")

Operational excellence is a strategy focused on cost effectiveness, efficiency, and customer convenience. Companies such as Zellers, WestJet Airlines, Dell, and Ikea are tenacious at lowering costs and customer prices while making it more convenient to do business with them. Concerned with the creation of cost-sacrifice value, operational excellence positioning strategies focus on dimensions such as the following:

- Price (e.g., Zellers: "The lowest price is the law"; Buy.com: "Canada's low price Internet superstore")
- Value (e.g., Ikea: "Swedish for common sense")
- Convenience (e.g., 7-Eleven: "Oh thank heaven"; American Express: "Don't leave home without it")
- Personal investment of time, effort, or energy (e.g., Yellow Pages: "Let your fingers do the walking")
- Risk (e.g., Levi's Jeans: "Have you ever had a bad time in Levi's?"; Listerine mouthwash: "Even your best friends won't tell you")

Another common positioning strategy is concerned with **symbolic-expressive value**—differentiating your brand by the psychological

Exhibit 6.20

The Body Shop's image is closely tied to natural and ethical products and practices. Their customers identify with this approach, consistent with a symbolic-expressive value strategy.

meaning associated with it. Some products (luxury goods, for example) appeal to consumers' self-concepts and self-worth; that is, they make us feel good about ourselves. Other products (such as music or comfort foods, among many others) have personal meaning— associations with people or events that only have meaning to a particular consumer (such as an association with Tide because your Mom used it). Products can also provide a means of self-expression; products such as Calvin Klein fragrances, Roots clothing, a Volkswagen Beetle, or The Body Shop lotions allow consumers to reflect or express their personalities, tastes, and values (Exhibit 6.20). Still other products focus on social meaning—how others see us. Products such as BMW cars, Birks jewellery, and Lee Valley Tools are purchased because of their prestige, status, or image. Brands can also be positioned on one or more of these four symbolic meaning dimensions. For example:

- Self identity/concept/worth (e.g., L'Oréal: "Because I'm worth it")

- Personal meaning: (e.g., Kodak: "Share moments. Share life")

- Self-expression (e.g., Canon: "Express yourself")

- Social meaning (e.g., Grey Poupon: "Pardon me. Do you have any Grey Poupon?"; Rolls-Royce: "Trusted to deliver excellence")

There are many other marketing strategy frameworks or typologies that you will learn about in a marketing strategy course. However, there are some other ways to differentiate products and establish a brand's position in the marketplace. These include strategies that emphasize:

- Product class leadership: e.g., BMW "The Ultimate Driving Machine."

- Relative positioning: The Pepsi Challenge claims "More people prefer the taste of Pepsi over Coke." (This is an example of head-to-head competitive positioning, where other organizations try to associate their brand with the market leader.)

- Use occasions: Wrigley's gum is an alternative at times when smoking is not permitted.

- Users: Sunny Delight is the "Goodness kids go for."

Differentiation

While strategic orientation explains how you will compete, differentiation explains how, specifically, your offer will be different from and better than competitive offerings, at least in the minds of your target customers. A **brand concept** is how a firm wants to be differentiated. WestJet, for example, wants to be known as the airline brand that provides the best value—low prices and good service from friendly, personable staff (Exhibit 6.21). BC Ethic, the apparel manufacturer known for re-popularizing the retro, button-down bowling shirt style worn by Seinfeld's Kramer,[39] positions its shirts as being "cool" and supports that differentiation by offering customized embroidered shirts free to music artists like the Barenaked Ladies and Cypress Hill. Most successful organizations are able to differentiate themselves on more than one dimension of value to customers. Starbucks, for example, competes on quality (an affordable luxury), selection and customization (you can have it your way), convenience (many locations), and atmosphere (replacing bars as a place to socialize with friends).

It isn't good enough to simply say that you are going to offer high quality or better service. Those descriptions are too superficial. Marketers need to explain exactly what is different and better about their quality or their service. For a doctor's office, for example, service quality

Catharine Downes

APPLYING ▽ Strategic Orientation

Catharine Downes and the NSCU are considering targeting the West Coast affluent consumers with a customer intimacy / customer responsiveness strategy where they would be more "local" and more responsive and adaptive to the financial needs of this particular segment than the larger banks. ➡

brand concept
How the marketer wants the brand to be positioned.

Smiles from coast to coast.

Fast, fun and friendly—as Canada's national low-fare leader we'll get you to your destination for less.

westjet.com
CALL YOUR TRAVEL AGENT, BOOK ONLINE
OR CALL 1.800.538.5696

WESTJET
Value in Canada's skies

Courtesy of WestJet

Exhibit 6.21

WestJet competes with a value positioning.

brand image
How consumers perceive the positioning of the brand.

perceptual map
A picture of where products or brands are "located" in consumers' minds.

Catharine Downes

APPLYING ▽ Differentiation

NSCU's customer intimacy/customer responsiveness strategy alternative would see them be more "local" and more responsive to the West Coast affluent than the larger banks. Specifically, they could differentiate the NSCU by redesigning the physical space of NSCU branches to reflect affluent West Coast architecture, furniture, and fixtures. They could provide amenities like lattes and cappuccino, and tailor their financial services to include niche commercial and residential mortgage products, integrated wealth management and insurance solutions, and owner-operated business solutions. There may be other ways of specifically differentiating their service, but the key is to be specific in explaining what makes you different and better than your competitors. ➥

might specifically mean that patients don't wait more than 5 minutes for a scheduled appointment, phones are answered by the third ring, and an hour a day is unscheduled to accommodate emergency cases.

Much of marketing communication strategy (Chapter 10) involves establishing a brand's differentiation in the minds of its customers, but sometimes the intended result is not achieved. **Brand image** is the perceived positioning of a product by consumers. Canadian consumers, for example, perceived Knorr soups, sauces, and marinades as being "refined, polished, and sophisticated"—but Unilever wanted its Knorr brand to be more accessible and work as an everyday solution. The company developed its "A Little Bit More" campaign to reinforce the idea that Knorr products have more interesting ingredients than competitors' brands and offer numerous opportunities for everyday culinary creativity. The phrase "a little bit more" in Knorr's communication strategy is its slogan or tag line—which usually communicates the unique selling proposition or key point of differentiation underlying a brand's positioning. We will see other examples of this shortly.

To decide your differentiation, you need to understand your competitor's positioning: what competitors are out there, and how does the target market perceive them? Aside from direct competitors in the product category, are there other goods or services that provide similar benefits? Sometimes, the indirect competition can be more important than the direct, especially if it represents an emerging consumer trend. For years, McDonald's developed positioning strategies based only on its direct competition, which it defined as other large fast-food hamburger chains (translation: Burger King and Wendy's). McDonald's failed to realize that, in fact, many indirect competitors fulfilled consumers' needs for a quick, tasty, convenient meal—from supermarket delis to frozen microwavable single-serving meals to call-ahead takeout from full-service restaurants like T.G.I. Friday's, Outback, and Chili's. Only recently, McDonald's has begun to understand that it must react to this indirect competition by serving up a wider variety of adult-friendly food and shoring up lagging service. Their latest home run is the McCafe concept, with coffee products aimed squarely at taking business away from morning mainstays Starbucks and Tim Hortons.

How do marketers determine where competitors' products (and their own) actually stand in the minds of consumers? One solution is to ask consumers what characteristics are important and how competing offers would rate on these attributes. Marketers use this information to construct a **perceptual map**, a picture of where products or brands are "located" in consumers' minds.

For example, suppose you want to construct a perceptual map of women's magazines as perceived by Canadian women, to give you some guidance while developing an idea for a new magazine. After interviewing a sample of female readers, you determine questions women ask when selecting a magazine. Is it "service oriented," emphasizing family, home, and personal issues, or is it "fashion forward," oriented toward personal appearance and fashion? Is it for "upscale" women, who are older and established in their careers, or for relatively "downscale" women, who are younger and just starting out in their careers?

The perceptual map in Figure 6.10 illustrates how these ratings might look for certain major women's magazines. It depicts the aggregate or average perception of how brands are perceived by multiple consumers on the dimensions of upscale/downscale and service/fashion, and it should be recognized that no individual consumer may hold these average perceptions. The shaded areas in Figure 6.10 represent two segments of consumers who seek the benefits and attributes offered by the set of magazines encircled. These are only two of many dimensions on which consumers compare magazines; marketers typically produce a series of positioning maps to understand how their and other brands are perceived by consumers. Other dimensions on which to position magazines might include cost (high/low), age appropriateness (young/old), sex appropriateness (mainly for men/mainly for women), and content (serious/frivolous), among other possible dimensions.

The map also provides some guidance as to where your new women's magazine might be positioned. You might decide to compete directly with either the cluster of service magazines

Figure 6.10 Perceptual Maps

Perceptual maps are used to Illustrate the perceived positioning of competing brands in a market.

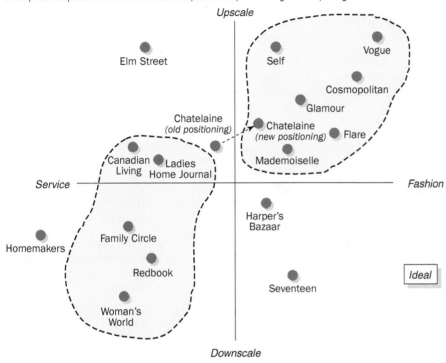

in the middle left or the fashion magazines in the upper right. In this case, you would have to determine what benefits your new magazine might offer that these existing magazines do not. *Chatelaine*, for example, repositioned itself in 1999 from a service-type magazine to a more urban, contemporary, youth- and fashion-oriented publication. This repositioning moved *Chatelaine* further away from its nearest Canadian competitor, *Canadian Living*.

To introduce a new magazine, you might try to locate an unserved area in this perceptual map. A **blue ocean strategy** is where you create a new market and get to define the playing field before competitors enter. *Elm Street*, a relatively new entrant to the Canadian women's magazine scene, has tried to position itself for the upscale woman who is interested in articles on a broad range of topics, a part of the market that it felt was unserved. An unserved area of the map represents either an unserved segment and, hence, a potential opportunity for marketers, or a positioning that is not in demand by a segment of consumers. According to Figure 6.10 (see "ideal"), there may be room for a magazine targeted to downscale "cutting-edge" fashion, perhaps for younger women.

Positioning maps are similar to perceptual maps, except that they may include factual as well as perceptual information. By including factual information in the map, marketers can illustrate how brands actually compete in a marketplace.

Defendability

The choice of strategic orientation and the basis of differentiation is dependent on an organization's ability to defend that positioning. Analysis of your ability to defend a particular positioning requires an assessment of the strengths and weaknesses of your own organization and your ability to create sustainable competitive advantage, and the opportunities and threats in the external environment—in particular, consumer behaviour and your assessment of the strategies, capabilities, and likely reactions of your competitors (recall SWOT analysis from Chapter 2). Based on this analysis, you need to explain how you are going to be able to compete the way you said you will compete, how you will be able to create the value you said you will create, and how you will be able to maintain or enhance the basis of differentiation that sets you apart from others in the minds of your target

blue ocean strategy
A positioning strategy where you create a new market and get to define the playing field before competitors enter.

positioning maps
Illustration of the positioning of competing brands that draws on facts about each brand, such as characteristics or key attributes.

Table 6.1	Positioning Strategy Implementation			
	Product Leadership	**Customer Intimacy**	**Operational Excellence**	**Symbolism/Meaning**
Strategy	Innovate, bring new products to market quickly that have superior features, functions, performance, or outcomes	Develop exceptional customer experiences and tailored, customized solutions	Provide the best value by reducing costs, lowering prices, and making it easy to do business with you	Develop superior symbolism or meaning for your product that creates psychological attachment to your brand
Structure	Flat, organic, flexible	Decentralized, empowerment close to customer contact	Strong centralized decisions focused on process or system improvements	Centralized decision making to control corporate and brand image, strong brand management structure
Culture	Entrepreneurial, creative, rewards innovation	Customer oriented, flexible, rewards customer satisfaction and loyalty	Bureaucratic, run by accountants, cost savings are rewarded.	Culture reflects and supports brand positioning. Brand management is rewarded.
Resource	Research & development	Customer research	Procurement	Marketing communications
Focus	New product development, production, distribution	Service quality, customer support, flexible manufacturing	Distribution, scale efficiencies, manufacturing efficiencies	Product quality, brand management, customer research

customers. This explanation typically centres on having the requisite resources, people, core competencies (know how), and/or the situation.

Different strategic orientations require different organizational strengths (capabilities), focus, and resource allocation, and they are often associated with different organizational cultures (Table 6.1). This makes it difficult to be the industry leader in more than one of these areas. At issue is whether an organization has the skills, abilities, resources, organizational structure, and culture to create the intended offer such that it will be perceived as superior by members of the target market on the differentiation dimensions reflected in the positioning strategy; whether the organization can communicate this effectively to the target market; and whether it can continue to do this until its goals are met as an organization. Marketers need to explain how they are going to be able to sustain the basis for value creating differentiation in the minds of its target customers.

For example, what allows NSCU to defend their customer-intimacy strategy positioning for "West Coast affluent" consumers, because other banks or credit unions could do this too? First, NSCU is geographically focused. Other banks and credit unions may need to support a consistent image across regions. Second, NSCU is membership based. If their members want to focus on a particular segment that reflects a large proportion, but not all, of the membership base, NSCU can do so. The larger banks have a broader mandate and may not have the ability (from licensing regulations) or the desire (from a public relations perspective) to focus on any one segment among the many who utilize their services. Third, NSCU has the resources to effect this change; by being geographically focused they have a more intimate knowledge of local real estate and business markets, they could train existing staff to be more responsive and adaptive to the needs of the West Coast affluent, and can enhance their core competencies in financial planning know-how through recruitment or staff training. Finally, there is some advantage in being the first to focus. The other banks and credit unions would look to be copying NSCU if they also chose to specifically focus on the West Coast affluent.

Bring a Product to Life: The Brand Personality

The final element of a positioning strategy for many marketers, particularly those implementing a customer-intimacy or symbolic-expressive value creation strategy, is creating a brand personality. Brands, like people, can be described in terms of personality traits. These descriptions might include words like cheap, elegant, sexy, bold, or wimpy. A positioning strategy often tries to create a brand personality for a product or service— a distinctive image that captures its character, soul, and benefits. An advertisement for *Elle* magazine, which bills itself as the number-one fashion magazine for women, once said, "She is not a reply card. She is not a category. She is not shrink-wrapped. *Elle* is not a magazine. She is a woman." When the Mark Anthony Group was developing a name for its lemonade-based alcohol product, it did research with consumers to determine what name would communicate the right brand personality. The "person" it chose for its hard lemonade, "Mike," is described as a "fun, party, happy-go-lucky guy who is infatuated with lemons."[40] Other organizations use mascots or characters to help create brand personality. Energizer has the Energizer Bunny. Cell phone companies have focused on various animals to promote brand personality, from lizards to fish to beavers. In 2011, Telus developed a Facebook campaign where Canadians were given a chance to vote for which of 27 "critters" would be the next Telus campaign star. Brand personalities are often reflected in logos. The clothing ad from Chile in Exhibit 6.22 pits a shark against the more familiar crocodile—with bloody results.

One of the most effective marketing campaigns to establish brand personality has been Apple's Mac–PC campaign that depicts PC as an overweight, middle-aged accountant-type person and Mac as a personable, creative, and sophisticated young adult. In a series of interactions between Mac and PC, the audience learns the key basis of differentiation between Macs and all the PC brands. You can see the ads on Apple's Web site (www.apple.com), and on YouTube you will find many parodies of these ads—evidence of their resonance with their target audience.

brand personality
A distinctive image that captures a product or service's character and benefits.

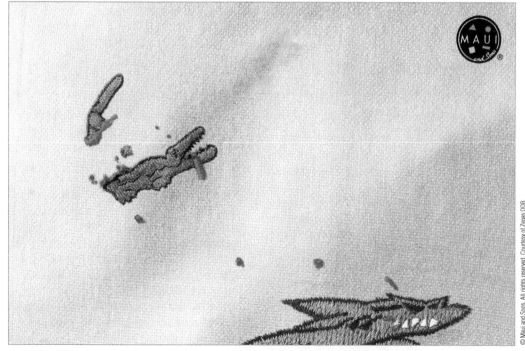

Exhibit 6.22
Brand personalities are often reflected in logos.

Photography by Daniel Couto. Used with permission of Johnson & Johnson

Exhibit 6.23

Listerine was able to change its brand personality using its action-hero campaign and significantly regained market share.

repositioning

Modifying a brand image to keep up with changing times.

Marketing researchers find that most consumers have no trouble describing what a product would be like "if it came to life."[41] People tend to anthropomorphize (ascribe human attributes) to many things around us: pets, cars, and brands. Try it. If Air Canada walked into the room would Air Canada be male or female? How old would she or he be? Thin or overweight? Is Air Canada married or unmarried? Is s/he friendly or cold and aloof? service oriented or self-serving? What does s/he do with her spare time? What does s/he care about? What kind of house does s/he live in and what kind of car does s/he drive? What colour is Air Canada's hair? Now try it again for WestJet. How do the brand personalities differ?

A change strategy is **repositioning**, and it's fairly common to see a company try to modify its brand image to keep up with changing times. For example, after 124 years of positioning itself as the brand that "kills the germs that cause bad breath," Listerine lost market leadership in the 1980s to Scope and private label brands, in part because the brand was perceived as being cold, old-fashioned, authoritarian, serious, and stuffy—much like Margaret Thatcher, the British prime minister at the time.[42] In the 1990s, Listerine tried many times to reposition its brand, but it could not shake its authoritarian brand personality, and consumers closed their ears to bad-breath lectures. Earlier this decade, Listerine research identified that consumers were now much more aware of plaque, tartar, and gingivitis and that a shift to healthier gums positioning could be compelling and ownable. Research also found that the use of Listerine reduces gingivitis better than brushing and flossing alone. The challenge was then to develop a new brand personality that was both lighthearted and powerful. By developing a parody of a comic book action hero that fights the evil gingivitis, Listerine was able to transform its image and is now perceived by consumers as powerful, larger than life, immortal, and unfailing (Exhibit 6.23).

Marketing Metrics

Brand Personality

How do you measure the personality of a brand? Professor David Aaker offers the Aaker Brand Personality Scale, where 42 questions relate to five dimensions of brand personality: sincerity, excitement, competence, sophistication, and ruggedness. This scale was used in a "Measuring the Value of Product Placement" study conducted by CTV Market Research and Group M (a unit of marketing giant WPP Group, comprising its media networks Mediaedge:cia and MindShare). The objective of the study was to determine what impact placement/integration has on a brand's personality. The study used CTV's nightly entertainment show *e-Talk Daily* as a test vehicle. A total of 300 people aged 18 to 54 who are viewers of *e-Talk Daily* or similar programs, participated in the study.

They were divided into groups and shown one of four test tapes in which the marketers' involvement ranged from no ad exposure, to a 30-second commercial, to a 30-second commercial augmented by either product placement or product integration. Product placement and integration was found to have a discernible impact on brand personality, product recall, and purchase intent. One of the brand participants, LG, found that their ranking in the excitement category of Aaker's Brand Personality Scale grew 32 percent following the integration. Mark Husak, managing partner of MindShare Canada in Toronto, calls this "one of the most important findings" of the study. "It allows us to relate back to some specific marketing strategies to understand how that dimension works."[43]

Implementing the Positioning Strategy

The success of a target marketing strategy hinges on a marketer's ability to identify and select appropriate target markets and then devise a positioning that will set apart their offer from those of their competitors that will be highly appealing to the target market, and that can be defended. Because everything else depends on segmentation and positioning decisions, segmentation and positioning, together, are the two most important concepts in marketing.

The marketing mix decisions relating to product, pricing, distribution, and communication are then made in a way that supports the desired positioning. For example, Montreal-based G.I. Energy Drinks developed the following strategy when it introduced the Guru energy drink. The company segmented the market in terms of age and psychographics, and

Exhibit 6.24

Many Canadian energy drinks, such as Generator and Guru, reach target segments by being sold at raves.

then targeted a segment of 16- to 24-year-olds, whose profiles indicated they were into "new-age" beverages that would give them a feeling of energy without unhealthy additives. The company reached these consumers by selling its drinks at raves in Montreal and Toronto (see Exhibit 6.24), advertising in club culture magazines, and sponsoring events like snowboarding demonstrations. A company spokesperson describes the Guru positioning strategy this way: "We really feel the best way to reach people is through trial and onsite promotions. . . . We want to provide the consumer with a drink that will enhance the activity they are already participating in."[44] Marketing decisions are the focus of the remainder of this text.

The target marketing process is ongoing. Over time, an organization may find that it needs to change the segments it targets or adapt to changing needs or wants of people in their chosen segments. Marketers need to monitor these changes and adjust their positioning strategies when necessary. Sometimes marketers redo a product's position to respond to marketplace changes. For example, in response to the trend for dual-income families not being home to eat lunch, the Campbell's Soup Company is trying to reposition itself from being a soup company to being a food company. Its Power2Cook campaign (www.power2cook.ca) uses traditional advertising, direct marketing, and a re-tooled Web site to teach young and busy cooks, male and female, how to prepare tasty meals using Campbell products.

Positioning is not easy. The main challenges are (1) vague positioning, where companies do not clearly articulate their main point(s) of differentiation; (2) confused positioning, where the positioning strategy keeps changing (like McDonald's), making it difficult for consumers or customers to understand what the brand is supposed to mean to them; (3) off-target positioning, where companies do not differentiate themselves on dimensions important to consumers or customers; and (4) over positioning, where companies position themselves too narrowly, either appealing to too small a market segment or being unable to change or adapt their positioning with changing market conditions.

5

OBJECTIVE

Explain how marketers increase long-term success and profits by practising customer relationship management.

(pp. 208–211)

Customer Relationship Management (CRM): Toward a Segment of One

We've talked about how marketers identify a unique group of consumers and then develop products specifically to meet their needs. And we talked about how marketers today build products to meet the needs of individual consumers by using mass customization techniques. As we discussed in Chapter 1, currently many highly successful marketing firms embrace **customer relationship management** (CRM) programs that involve systematically tracking consumers' preferences and behaviours over time in order to tailor the value proposition as closely as possible to each individual's unique wants and needs. CRM allows firms to talk to individual customers and to adjust elements of their marketing programs in light of how each customer reacts.[45] The CRM trend facilitates one-to-one marketing, which includes several steps.[46]

customer relationship management
A systematic tracking of consumers' preferences and behaviours over time in order to tailor the value proposition as closely as possible to each individual's unique wants and needs. CRM allows firms to talk to individual customers and to adjust elements of their marketing programs in light of how each customer reacts.

1. Identify customers and get to know them in as much detail as possible.

2. Differentiate among these customers in terms of both their needs and their value to the company.

3. Interact with customers and find ways to improve cost efficiency and the effectiveness of the interaction.

4. Customize some aspect of the goods or services that you offer to each customer. This means treating each customer differently based on what has been learned through customer interactions.[47]

Table 6.2 suggests some specific activities to implement these four steps of one-to-one marketing. Remember, successful one-to-one marketing depends on CRM, which allows a company to identify its best customers, stay on top of their needs, and increase their satisfaction.[48]

CRM: A New Perspective on an Old Problem

CRM is about communicating with customers, and about customers being able to communicate with a company, "up close and personal." CRM systems are applications that use computers, specialized computer software, databases, and often the Internet to capture information at each **touchpoint**, which is any point of direct interface between customers and a company (online, by phone, or in person).

touchpoint
Point of direct interface between customers and a company (online, by phone, or in person).

These systems include everything from Web sites that let you check on the status of a bill or package to call centres that solicit your business. When you log on to the FedEx Web site to track a lost package, that's part of a CRM system. When you get a phone message from the dentist reminding you about your appointment tomorrow to get a filling fixed, that's CRM. And when you get a call from the car dealer asking how you like your new vehicle, that's also CRM. Remember how in Chapter 3 we said information is the fuel that runs the marketing engine? It is through CRM that companies act upon and manage the information they gather from their customers.

- Amazon.com is the world champion master of the happy customer approach to CRM. For loyal users, Amazon tracks visits so it can customize advertisements, product promotions, and discounts for each shopper. And, if you happen to have a passion for, say, grunge bands of the 1990s, the Web site is quick to recommend that new retrospective on Pearl Jam the next time you visit.[49]

Table 6.2	The Four Steps of One-to-One Marketing

Step	Suggested Activities
Identify	Collect and enter names and additional information about your customers.
	Verify and update, deleting outdated information.
Differentiate	Identify top customers.
	Determine which customers cost the company money.
	Find higher-value customers who have complained about your product more than once.
	Find customers who buy only one or two products from your company but a lot from other companies.
	Rank customers into A, B, and C categories based on their value to your company.
Interact	Call the top three people in the top 5 percent of dealers, distributors, and retailers that carry your product and make sure they're happy.
	Call your own company and ask questions; see how hard it is to get through and get answers.
	Call your competitors and compare their customer service with yours.
	Use incoming calls as selling opportunities.
	Initiate more dialogue with valuable customers.
	Improve complaint handling.
Customize	Find out what your customers want.
	Personalize your direct mail.
	Ask customers how and how often they want to hear from you.
	Ask your top 10 customers what you can do differently to improve your product.
	Involve top management in customer relations.

Source: Adapted by permission of *Harvard Business Review* from Don Peppers, Martha Rogers, and Bob Dorf, "Is Your Company Ready for One-to-One Marketing?" *Harvard Business Review* (January–February 1999), 151–60. Copyright © 1999 by the Harvard Business School Publishing Corporation. All rights reserved.

- Coca-Cola launched its My Coke Rewards online program, the multiyear customer-loyalty marketing blitz into which it poured millions of dollars.

- At Holt Renfrew CRM is central to the "company culture" of putting the customer at the core of everything they do, but one thing they do very well is events designed to connect with consumers and create an emotional attachment to the brand. The retailer, for example, recently invited 100 of its best customers to a private dinner with designer Michael Kors.[50]

Characteristics of CRM

In addition to having a different mind-set, companies that successfully practise CRM have different goals, use different measures of success, and look at customers in some different ways. Followers of CRM look at four critical elements, as portrayed in Figure 6.11: share of customer, lifetime value of a customer, customer equity, and customer prioritization. Let's have a look at each of these ideas now.

Share of Customer

Historically, marketers measured success in a product category by their market share. For example, if people buy 100 million pairs of athletic shoes each year, a firm that sells 10 million of them claims a 10 percent market share. If the shoemaker's marketing objective is to increase market share, it may lower the price of its shoes, increase its advertising, or offer customers a free basketball with every pair of shoes they purchase. These tactics may increase sales in the short run. Unfortunately, they may not do much for the long-term success

Figure 6.11 Characteristics of CRM

Followers of CRM look at share of customer, lifetime value of a customer, customer equity, and customer prioritization.

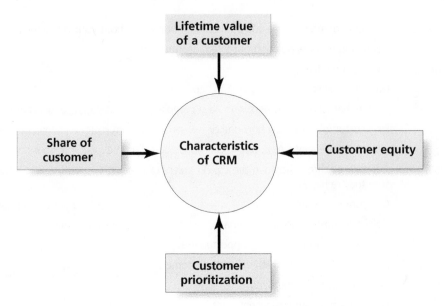

of the shoemaker. In fact, they may actually decrease the value of the brand because they cheapen its image with giveaways.

Because it is always easier and less expensive to keep an existing customer than to get a new customer (yes, we've said that already), CRM firms try to increase their **share of customer**, not share of market. Let's say that a consumer buys six pairs of shoes a year—two pairs from each of three different manufacturers. Assume one shoemaker has a CRM system that allows it to send letters to its current customers inviting them to receive a special price discount or a gift if they buy more of the firm's shoes during the year. If the firm can get the consumer to buy three or four or perhaps all six pairs from it, it has increased its share of customer. And that may not be too difficult, because the customer already likes the firm's shoes. Without the CRM system, the shoe company would probably use traditional advertising to increase sales, which would be far more costly than the customer-only direct-mail campaign. So the company can increase sales and profits at a much lower cost than it would spend to get one, two, or three new customers.

Lifetime Value of a Customer

As you'll recall from Chapter 1, the **lifetime value of a customer** is the potential profit a single customer's purchase of a firm's products generates over the customer's lifetime. It just makes sense that a firm's profitability and long-term success are going to be far greater if it develops long-term relationships with its customers so that those customers buy from it again and again. Costs will be far higher and profits lower if each customer's purchase is a first-time sale.

How do marketers calculate the lifetime value of a customer? They first estimate a customer's future purchases across all products from the firm over the next 20 or 30 years. The goal is to try to figure out what profit the company could make from the customer in the future (obviously, this will just be an estimate). For example, an auto dealer might calculate the lifetime value of a single customer by first calculating the total revenue the customer will generate for the company during his or her life. This figure includes the number of automobiles he will probably buy times their average price, plus the service the dealership would provide over the years, and even possibly the income from auto loan financing. The lifetime value of the customer would be the total profit the revenue stream generates.

share of customer
The percentage of an individual customer's purchase of a product that is a single brand.

lifetime value of a customer
The potential profit a single customer's purchase of a firm's products generates over the customer's lifetime.

Catharine Downes

APPLYING ▽ CRM

Catharine Downes and NSCU understand CRM and the concepts of lifetime value of a customer and customer equity, which is why they are examining the strategic repositioning of targeting West Coast affluent members. These are the high-value customers from which the credit union derives most of its earnings. ➡

Customer Equity

Today an increasing number of companies, just like NSCU, consider their relationships with customers as financial assets. These firms measure success by calculating the value of their **customer equity**—the financial value of a customer throughout the lifetime of the relationship.[51] To do this, they compare the investments they make to acquire customers and then to retain them to the financial return they'll get on those investments.

customer equity
The financial value of a customer relationship throughout the lifetime of the relationship.

Focus on High-Value Customers

Using a CRM approach, the organization prioritizes its customers and customizes its communications to them accordingly. For example, any banker will tell you that not all customers are equal when it comes to profitability. Some generate a lot of revenue because they bank interest on loans or credit cards, while others basically just use the bank as a convenient place to store a small amount of money and take out a little bit each week to buy beer. Banks use CRM systems to generate a profile of each customer based on factors such as value, risk, attrition, and interest in buying new financial products. This automated system helps the bank decide which current or potential customers it will target with certain communications or how much effort it will expend to retain an account—all the while cutting its costs by as much as a third. It just makes sense to use different types of communication contacts based on the value of each individual customer. For example, personal selling (the most expensive form of marketing communication per contact) may constitute 75 percent of all contacts with high-volume customers, while direct mail or telemarketing is more often the best way to talk to low-volume customers.

Here's my choice. . .

Real **People**, Real **Choices**

1 ②2 3
Option   Option   Option

Why do you think Catharine chose option 2?

How It Worked Out at NSCU

The NSCU Marketing team has moved forward with implementing Option 2: developing a more targeted strategy focused on the West Coast affluent with the marketing team shifting its efforts to support delivery of a differentiated experience to the target affluent customer, in concert with the organizational efforts to overhaul the look and feel of NSCU branches and raise the bar on staff professionalism and knowledge (particularly for advisory personnel).

Marketing segment analytics were the engine used to assign "mass affluent" and "emerging wealthy" members to a dedicated financial advisor. This has helped NSCU ensure that it has the right people assigned to the right sales channel; with its most experienced, highest-cost financial/investment advisors devoting their time and efforts to increasing the credit union's share-of-wallet among existing affluent members and creating a group of brand advocates that generate word-of-mouth referrals to NSCU.

Differentiated marketing communication tactics were employed to reinforce the one-to-one "trusted advisor" relationships. All correspondence, promotional offers, and a unique "for assigned members only" monthly e-newsletter are personalized, provide more sophisticated content appropriate to larger wealth portfolios, and appear as if they've been sent from the financial advisor's desk, all building a greater personal connection and providing a persistent reminder of the value the advisor can provide in proactive value-added advice.

Marketing promotion has persistently focused on NSCU's wealth management services, financial planning, and advisory capabilities in all its integrated communication tactics and across all media channels, with very little promotion of everyday banking services. These efforts are geared at broadening awareness of the wide range of products and services NSCU can offer, as well as the calibre of experience and expertise its financial, investment, insurance, and small business advisors provide. Advertising buys, sponsorships, and events are all directly linked to ensuring exposure is tightly focused on affluent audiences, with a corresponding reduction (though not elimination) of "mass market" spend and participation in broad-based community events with communication messages focused on our ability to improve members' financial well-being and being better at providing expert financial advice.

Five years after the creation of NSCU's bold new vision, the credit union has nearly doubled in size, growing from $1.3 billion to $2.36 billion in assets under administration. Deposit growth of customers with over $100 000 at NSCU (a key driver of credit unions' ability to expand lending and realize profit targets) had increased from 59% to 80%.

With this marketing strategy continuing, the Marketing team is poised to also support the adoption of elements of Option 3, carrying the same focus on affluent markets while expanding into new geographic markets. In 2011, the credit union will open its first *de novo* (new) branch in more than six years in the affluent Vancouver west side, with plans for further expansion of the branch network into similar affluent Lower Mainland neighbourhoods in future.

To learn the whole story, visit www.mypearsonmarketinglab.com.

Objective Summary ➡ Key Terms ➡ Apply

CHAPTER 6
Study Map

1. Objective Summary (pp. 176–178)

Identify the steps in the target marketing process.

Marketers must balance the efficiency of mass marketing, serving the same items to everyone, with the effectiveness of offering each individual exactly what she wants. To accomplish this, instead of trying to sell something to everyone, marketers follow these steps:

1. select a target marketing strategy, in which they divide the total market into different segments based on customer characteristics;
2. select one or more segments; and
3. develop products to meet the needs of those specific segments.

Key Terms

market fragmentation, p. 176
target marketing strategy, p. 176

2. Objective Summary (pp. 178–193)

Understand the need for market segmentation and the approaches available to do it.

Market segmentation is often necessary in today's marketplace because of market fragmentation—that is, the splintering of a mass society into diverse groups due to technological and cultural differences. Most marketers can't realistically do a good job of meeting the needs of everyone, so it is more efficient to divide the larger pie into slices in which members of a segment share some important characteristics and tend to exhibit the same needs and preferences. Marketers frequently find it useful to segment consumer markets on the basis of demographic characteristics, including age, gender, family life cycle, social class, race or ethnic identity, and place of residence. A second dimension, psychographics, uses measures of psychological and social characteristics to identify people with shared preferences or traits. Consumer markets may also be segmented on the basis of how consumers behave toward the product, for example, their brand loyalty, usage rates (heavy, moderate, or light), and usage occasions. Business-to-business markets are often segmented on the basis of industrial demographics, type of business based on the North American Industry Classification (NAICS) codes, and geographic location.

Key Terms

segmentation, p. 178
segmentation variables, p. 179
behavioural segmentation, p. 180
benefit segmentation, p. 180
usage segmentation, p. 180
80/20 rule, p. 180
long tail, p. 181
usage occasions, p. 181

psychographic segmentation, p. 181

VALS (Values and Lifestyles), p. 184

demographics, p. 184

tweens, p. 186

Generation X, p. 187

baby boomers, p. 187

Gen Y, p. 187

geodemography, p. 191

B2B marketers, p. 191

industrial psychographics, p. 192

3. Objective Summary (pp. 193–199)

Explain how marketers evaluate segments and choose a targeting strategy.

To choose one or more segments to target, marketers examine each segment and evaluate its potential for success as a target market. Meaningful segments have wants that are different from those in other segments, can be identified, can be reached with a unique marketing mix, will respond to unique marketing communications, are large enough to be profitable, have future growth potential, and possess needs that the organization can satisfy better than the competition.

After marketers identify the different segments, they estimate the market potential of each. The relative attractiveness of segments also influences the firm's selection of an overall marketing strategy. The firm may choose an undifferentiated, differentiated, concentrated, or custom strategy based on the company's characteristics and the nature of the market.

Key Terms

segment profile, p. 193

cluster analysis, p. 194

market potential, p. 194

target market, p. 194

undifferentiated targeting strategy, p. 196

differentiated targeting strategy, p. 196

concentrated targeting strategy, p. 196

niche marketing, p. 197

custom marketing strategy, p. 198

4. Objective Summary (pp. 199–207)

Understand how marketers develop and implement a positioning strategy.

After marketers select the target market(s), they must determine how they wish to compete relative to the competition—that is, decide their value creation strategy (strategic orientation) and how they will be specifically different from, and better than, their competitors (differentiation). Marketers must also decide and explain how they will defend that positioning and maintain the competitive advantage on which their positioning strategy is based. Finally, marketers give thought to how they want their brand to be perceived by their customers (brand image) and that often includes consideration of brand personality. Marketers can compare brand positions by using such research techniques as perceptual mapping. In developing and implementing the positioning strategy, firms analyze the competitors' positions, determine the competitive advantage offered by their product, tailor the marketing mix in accordance with the positioning strategy, and evaluate responses to the marketing mix selected. Marketers must continually monitor changes in the market that might indicate a need to reposition the product.

Key Terms

brand, 199

strategic orientation, p. 199

product leadership, p. 199

customer intimacy, p. 200

operational excellence, p. 200

symbolic-expressive value, p. 200

brand concept, p. 201

brand image, p. 202

perceptual map, p. 202

blue ocean strategy, p. 203

positioning maps, p. 203

brand personality, p. 205

repositioning, p. 206

5. Objective Summary (pp. 208–211)

Explain how marketers increase long-term success and profits by practising customer relationship management.

Companies using customer relationship management (CRM) programs establish relationships and differentiate their behaviour toward individual customers on a one-to-one basis through dialogue and feedback. Success is often measured one customer at a time using the concepts of share of customer, lifetime value of the customer, and customer equity. In CRM strategies, customers are prioritized according to their value to the firm, and communication is customized accordingly.

Key Terms

customer relationship management (CRM), p. 208

touchpoint, p. 208

share of customer, p. 210

lifetime value of a customer, p. 210

customer equity, p. 211

Chapter **Questions** and **Activities**

Concepts: Test Your Knowledge

1. What is market segmentation, and why is it an important strategy in today's marketplace?
2. List and explain the major ways to segment consumer markets.
3. What are some of the ways marketers segment industrial markets?
4. List the criteria marketers use to determine whether a segment may be a good candidate for targeting.
5. Explain undifferentiated, differentiated, concentrated, and customized marketing strategies. What is mass customization?
6. What is product positioning? What do marketers mean by creating a brand personality? How do marketers use perceptual maps to help them develop effective positioning strategies?
7. Explain the concept of strategic orientation and the value creation strategy of customer intimacy.
8. How can marketers defend their positioning strategies?
9. What is CRM? How do firms practise CRM?
10. Explain the concepts of share of customer, lifetime value of a customer, customer equity, and customer prioritization.

Activities: Apply What You've Learned

1. Assume that a small regional beer brewery has hired you to help them with their target marketing. They are pretty unsophisticated about marketing—you will need to explain some things to them and provide ideas for their future. In the past, the brewery has simply produced and sold a single beer brand to the entire market—a mass-marketing strategy. As you begin work, you come to believe that the firm could be more successful if it developed a target marketing strategy. Write a memo to the owner outlining the following:

   - The basic reasons for doing target marketing in the first place
   - The specific advantages of a target marketing strategy for the brewery
   - An initial "short list" of possible target segment profiles

2. As the marketing director for a company that is planning to enter the business-to-business market for photocopy machines, you are attempting to develop an overall marketing strategy. You have considered the possibility of using mass marketing, concentrated marketing, differentiated marketing, and custom marketing strategies.

   - Prepare a summary explaining what each type of strategy would mean for your marketing plan in terms of product, price, promotion, and distribution channel.
   - Evaluate the desirability of each type of strategy.
   - What are your final recommendations for the best type of strategy?

3. As an account executive for a marketing consulting firm, your newest client is a university—your university. You have been asked to develop a positioning strategy for the university. Develop an outline of your ideas, including the following:

   - Who are your competitors?
   - What are the competitors' positions?
   - What target markets are most attractive to the university?
   - How will you position the university for those segments, relative to the competition?

4. Assume that a firm hires you as marketing manager for a chain of retail bookstores. You believe that the firm should develop a CRM strategy. Outline the steps you would take in developing that strategy.

Marketing Metrics: Exercise

In the chapter discussion about CRM, you read about four key characteristics of CRM: share of customer, lifetime value of a customer, customer equity, and customer prioritization. Each of these elements is discussed in the context of monitoring and assessing the effectiveness of a CRM initiative.

Consider Scene, a relatively new loyalty partnership between Cineplex and Scotiabank. Go to their Web site (www.scene.ca) and explore how it works. In what ways could Cineplex measure the four elements of CRM above within the context of a reward program such as this? How would data be collected for each element, and how might management at Cineplex utilize that data to provide loyal customers with a very strong relationship with the organization?

Choices: What Do You Think?

1. Some critics of marketing have suggested that market segmentation and target marketing lead to an unnecessary proliferation of product choices that wastes valuable resources. These critics suggest that if marketers didn't create so many different product choices, there would be more resources to feed the hungry and house the homeless and provide for the needs of people around the globe. Are the results of segmentation and target marketing harmful or beneficial to society as a whole? Should firms be concerned about these criticisms? Why or why not?
2. One of the criteria for a usable market segment is its size. This chapter suggested that to be usable, a segment must be large enough to be profitable now and in the future and that some very small segments get ignored because they can never be profitable. So how large should a segment be? How do you think a firm should go about determining if a segment is profitable? Have technological advances made it possible for smaller segments to be profitable? Do firms ever have a moral or ethical obligation to develop products for small, unprofitable segments? When?
3. A few years ago, Anheuser-Busch Inc. created a new division dedicated to marketing to Hispanics and announced it would boost its ad spending in Hispanic media by two-thirds

to more than $60 million, while Miller Brewing Co. signed a $100 million, three-year ad package with Spanish-language broadcaster Univision Communications Inc. But Hispanic activists immediately raised public-health concerns about the beer ad blitz on the grounds that it targets a population that is disproportionately likely to abuse alcohol. Surveys of Hispanic youth show that they are much more likely to drink alcohol, get drunk, and to engage in binge drinking than their white or black peers. A senior executive at Anheuser-Busch responded, "We would disagree with anyone who suggests beer billboards increase abuse among Latino or other minority communities. It would be poor business for us in today's world to ignore what is the fastest-growing segment of our population."

Manufacturers of alcohol and tobacco products have been criticized for targeting unwholesome products to certain segments of the market—the aged, ethnic minorities, the disabled, and others. Do you view this as a problem in Canada? Should a firm use different criteria in targeting such groups? Should the government oversee and control such marketing activities?

2. Customer relationship management (CRM) relies on data collected from customers to create customized or one-to-one experiences for those customers. Data are collected at various touchpoints—places in which the customer interfaces with the firm to provide information, such as at a checkout lane, on the phone, on the Web site, and so on. Do firms have an obligation to explain to customers that they are collecting information from them to populate and drive their CRM initiative, or is it inherently obvious in today's world that such practices are routine? In general, what is your personal viewpoint of database-driven positioning strategies? What are the potential pros and cons to the company and to the customer?

Miniproject: Learn by Doing

This miniproject will help you to develop a better understanding of how firms make target marketing decisions. The project focuses on the market for women's beauty-care products.

1. Gather ideas about different dimensions useful for segmenting the women's beauty products market. You may use your own ideas, but you probably will also want to examine advertising and other marketing communications developed by different beauty care brands.
2. Based on the dimensions for market segmentation that you have identified, develop a questionnaire and conduct a survey of consumers. You will have to decide which questions should be asked and which consumers should be surveyed.
3. Analyze the data from your research and identify the different potential segments.
4. Develop segment profiles that describe each potential segment.
5. Generate several ideas for how the marketing strategy might be different for each segment based on the profiles. Develop a presentation (or write a report) outlining your ideas, your research, your findings, and your marketing strategy recommendations.

Marketing in **Action** Case — Real Choices at Spitz International

Spitz International Inc. is the new name for Alberta Sunflower Seeds Limited, but we all know them as Canada's number one sunflower seed company—"Spitz." The company was started in 1982 by Tom and Emmy Droog as a sunflower seed supplier for the bird seed market. The Droogs arrived in Canada from Holland in 1972, speaking no English and with only $125 in their pocket. Today sales have grown to more than $30 million a year.

In 1990, the Droogs introduced Spitz, a line of roasted confection sunflower seed snacks for humans. Sales success was immediate. Yearly sales increases of 300 and 400 percent between 1990 and 1995 still did not meet the demand for this new snack. The company increased its market share by eliminating its competition—buying out Sid's Sunflower Seeds in Regina in 1993 and Tasty Seeds in Winkler, Manitoba, in 2005.

Today, this privately held company commands a 75 percent market share in the Canadian confectionary sunflower and pumpkin seed category and is the third-largest-selling sunflower seed brand in the United States.

Myles Hamilton was appointed vice president in 2006, and has now taken over the day-to-day operations from Tom and Emmy. Hamilton has been tasked with doubling the total company sales over the next three years with a goal of making Spitz North America's leading sunflower and pumpkin seed brand. He brings expertise to the position with a background that includes 6 years at P&G in sales and marketing roles and 15 years with Frito-Lay, a large US snack food company, during which time he served most of his tenure as vice president of Frito-Lay Western Canada. To expand Spitz's sales and bring them to the top of the sunflower seed snack food market, Hamilton is considering either targeting current markets with new products, finding new markets for existing products, or both.

Innovation has always been the name of the game for Spitz. The company was first in the North American sunflower industry to come up with flavours and resealable bags. North American competitors have matched these innovations and have now developed some of their own, enhancing the product to increase sales. One option would be to follow the US trend toward coated kernels—chocolate, honey roasted, or candy. Another option would be to follow the lead of Sunseeds in South Dakota, which infuses their seeds with popular energy boosters such as caffeine, ginseng, taurine, and lysine—similar to those found in energy drinks. Sunflower seeds could be made even healthier by infusing the product with vitamins and minerals. Another option would be to more actively pursue the

(continued)

Marketing in **Action** Case | Real Choices at Spitz International

baking or salad markets. Health-oriented consumers are finding new ways to use seed kernels in baking or as salad, and coated and/or infused seeds might expand the possibilities—maybe even replacing chocolate chips!

There may also be opportunities to enter new markets. The company recently entered the Quebec market, changing their packaging and working the French translation into their new logo and new look. They are also planning on expanding current distribution from 41 states in the United States to full distribution across all states. There is potential to expand beyond North America and into China, where they already process pumpkin seeds.

Hamilton knew that the place to start was to segment the seed consumption market and then choose which segments to focus on, and with what positioning.

You Make the Call

1. If you were Myles Hamilton and the Spitz company, what would you do and why?
2. How might the seed consumption market be segmented?
3. Which segment(s) should the Spitz company be targeting?

Source: This case was written by Bev Duthie and Brock Smith, drawing on the following sources: Gina Teel, "Sunflower power," *Times Colonist,* 22 May 2007: B1; and www.spitz.

CBC Video Case

Electric Future

The North American auto industry is at a cross-roads with consumers and governments seeking cars with fewer emissions and better mileage. Two main questions are raised:

"How will the demand for cleaner, greener cars revolutionize the auto industry?"

"How soon can you be plugging in your car instead of pumping gas?"

The five-year prediction is that by 2014, as the economy improves, the car industry will be over-hauled with new concept cars, new car manufacturers, and new dealer distribution systems.

Susan Ormiston, the video case presenter, suggests that a look into the present will help predict the future. GM dealers with a 40-year history have closed offices because of consumer loyalties that began shifting in the 1990s due to imports. Changes in consumer preferences have affected the auto business, with GM and Chrysler closing franchises and foreseeing dramatic changes in the auto industry.

The next generation of car buyers is predicted to consider different vehicles, like electric cars. A consumer driving short distances every day may consider the electric car as a viable option, whereas a consumer driving longer distances may not find it suitable.

The change for electric cars is happening faster in certain markets like California, where emission controls and fuel efficiency standards have already begun. In San Francisco, an entrepreneur by the name of Scott Painter predicts a retail revolution. Painter is not your traditional car dealer, but rather builds auto buying companies online. His company "Zag.com" links consumers on the internet to car dealers and partners with the Automobile Association to guarantee a fixed price.

For example, if a customer is shopping for a base model of a Malibu, the system will look for a dealer in the area with an upfront price, and will also research a dealer with higher membership satisfaction in that area. The price obtained via the Internet is guaranteed, implying that the consumer is certified to obtain that specific model at the online price.

Research indicates that 95% of buyers research their purchases online. Painter believes the old practice of haggling over price with dealers will have less appeal, as the consumer will be able to compare fixed prices online. Good competitive upfront pricing will likely be the key to a car dealer's success, rather than its location (as was the case in the past).

Painter also sees another distinctive trend. More consumers will dump their affection for SUVs as they move to fuel efficiencies. These shifting consumer preferences imply that cars over the next five years will look very different.

Some of the expected car manufacturers include Tesla, which is changing the image of the slow moving electric vehicle. Tesla Motors is making and selling an electric sports car that is a pure, electric plug-in that can be fully charged in just 3.5 hours.

It is quiet, fast, boasts that it can go 400 km on a single battery charge, and sells for US$100,000. The sedan version of this roadster is expected to be released in Canada in late 2011.

Elon Musk of Tesla Motors states that, like many new high-technology products, introductory prices are very high and thus only the wealthy can afford it. He adds that Tesla is changing an industry and recognizes its challenge to stay viable and produce affordable cars.

Other companies entering the electric car industry with promises of plug-in include: GM (Chevy Volt in late 2010) and Ford (Magna by 2012).

But, the real competition comes from offshore. Nissan and Toyota are each planning new electric vehicles by 2012. China is also expected to have an impact as it is expected to produce 0.5 billion electric cars with its BYD in less than two years.

A new electrical infrastructure is evolving with charge points that resemble a parking meter, where you can plug in rather than gas up. Dave O'Brien, CEO of Toronto Hydro, predicts quick changes. Electric car owners will plug in their cars overnight to get fuelled, and will have the possibility to plug in during the day at various stations that will be located in parking lots of shopping malls, large offices, and major highway stations.

The auto industry crisis is giving rise to new opportunities with change occurring faster than predicted.

Questions

1. What environmental forces are changing the auto industry? What are the key factors changing the nature of the auto industry? When are these changes likely to occur?

2. What are the main distinctive consumer trends that are expected to alter the auto industry within the next five years? Identify and describe the changes in consumer behaviour. How will consumers purchase cars? What will likely motivate customers to change their purchasing habits?

3. Which consumer groups are likely to be the first to adopt the newer electric cars? Describe the typical innovator?

4. What target market strategies are likely to be adopted with this new product introduction?

Source: This case was prepared by Susan Ormiston and is based on "Electric Future," *National,* CBC video, Toronto, 19 May 2009 (time: 13:40 min).

MyMarketingLab

To view the CBC videos go to
pearsoned.ca/mymarketinglab.com

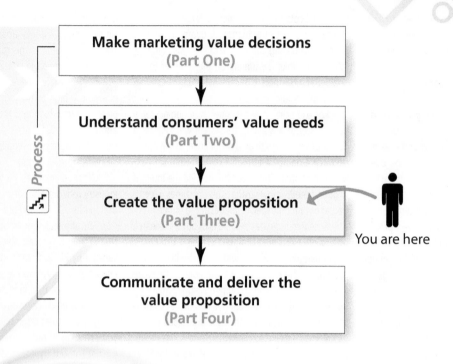

Make marketing value decisions
(Part One)

↓

Understand consumers' value needs
(Part Two)

↓

Process

Create the value proposition
(Part Three)

You are here

↓

**Communicate and deliver the
value proposition**
(Part Four)

Create the Value Proposition

Part Three
Overview

Part Three focuses on the value offering a firm brings to the market. This offering—which often is generically referred to as simply the "product"—can be in the form of an actual physical good, service, or other intangible. Services and other intangible offerings comprise a very large percentage of the purchase transactions nowadays throughout the world and, as a result, the phrase "service economy" is commonly used to describe today's marketplace. It has often been said that among the four elements of the marketing mix—product, price, promotion, and distribution—if the product itself isn't right, the other three elements of the mix probably won't overcome that deficiency in the mind of the consumer.

Making decisions about developing new products and the adoption and diffusion of those products is critical to any marketer, and this is the topic of Chapter 7. Chapter 8 then addresses important issues of the product life cycle, branding, packaging, and long-term product management.

Finally, a big part of creating the value proposition is making decisions about how to price the offering. Remember that value is like a give/get ratio—the customer gives something up (money, for instance) in the belief that your good or service will have benefits that equal or exceed the value of the price paid. Chapter 9 provides you with great ideas on how to go about pricing your offering.

Marketing Plan Connection: S&S Smoothie
Tricks of the Trade

Recall that the Appendix at the end of the book provides you with an abbreviated marketing plan example for the fictitious S&S Smoothie Company. That plan is flagged to indicate what elements from the plan correspond to each of the Parts within the book. In addition, inside the front and back covers, you will find a guide called "Build a Marketing Plan," which can be used as a template for marketing planning. It is also cross-referenced to chapters by section of the marketing plan.

In the chapters within Part Three, there are major learning elements that guide you in developing two critical elements of your marketing plan: your product strategies in which you outline how you will develop and manage the offering (both physical product and service components) and your pricing strategies.

Recall that S&S Smoothie seeks to position its products as the first-choice smoothie beverage for the serious health-conscious consumer, including those who are seeking to lower their carbohydrate intake. The justification for this positioning is as follows. Many smoothie beverages are available. The S&S Smoothie formula provides superior flavour and nutrition in a shelf-stable form. S&S Smoothie has developed its product (including packaging) and pricing in support of this positioning strategy. Let's review what they're doing with these two marketing mix elements to support that positioning.

Product Strategies

To increase its leverage in the market and to meet its sales objectives, S&S Smoothie needs additional products. Two new product lines are planned:

1. **S&S Smoothie Gold:** This product will be similar to the original S&S Smoothie beverage, but it will come in six unique flavours:

   a. Piña Colada
   b. Chocolate Banana
   c. Apricot Nectarine Madness
   d. Pineapple Berry Crush
   e. Tropical Tofu Cherry
   f. Peaches and Dreams

To set the product apart from the original-flavour Smoothie beverages in store refrigerator cases, labels will include the name of the beverage and the logo in gold lettering. The bottle cap will be black. The nutritional content, critical to the success of new products in this category, will be similar to that of the original S&S Smoothie beverages. The packaging for S&S

Smoothie Gold will also be similar to that used for the original product, utilizing the unique easy-to-hold, hourglass-shaped, frosted glass bottle and providing the new beverage with the same upscale image.

2. Low-Carb S&S Smoothie: The Low-Carb S&S Smoothie beverage will have approximately 50 percent fewer grams of carbohydrates than the original Smoothie beverage or the S&S Smoothie Gold. Low-Carb S&S Smoothie will come in the following four flavours:

   a. Strawberry
   b. Blueberry
   c. Banana
   d. Peach

Packaging for the Low-Carb S&S Smoothie will be similar to other S&S Smoothie beverages but will include the term "Low-Carb" in large type. The label will state that the beverage has 50 percent fewer carbs than regular smoothies.

Pricing Strategies

The current pricing strategy will be maintained for existing and new products. This pricing is appropriate for communicating a high-quality product image for all S&S Smoothie products. The company feels that creating different pricing for the new beverages would be confusing and create negative attitudes among consumers. Thus, there is no justification for increasing the price of the new products.

MyMarketingLab

Now, if you are working on a marketing plan as part of your course, you can go to MyMarketingLab to apply what you learn in Part Three to your own marketing plan project.

Create the Product

Palo Hawken

Profile

▼ A Decision Maker at Bossa Nova Superfruit Company

Palo Hawken is co-founder and vice president of research and innovation at Bossa Nova. His dream from an early age was to become an inventor, which led him to pursue both a degree in physics from UC Santa Cruz and a degree in industrial design from the Rhode Island School of Design. When he completed his degree at RISD in 1996, he was invited to join his mentor and former professor Stephan Copeland to help develop his consulting business. After three years of working at the Copeland studio, primarily in the contract furniture industry for companies like Steelcase, Knoll, and Innovant, Palo moved to New York to start a furniture company. It was not a very successful venture, but it eventually led him to Los Angeles, where he met Alton Johnson and joined forces to launch Bossa Nova. Palo's specialty is harnessing the underappreciated power of design from formulation, to functionality, to packaging, to maximize any given market opportunity.

Bossa Nova Beverage Group was born out of the founder Alton Johnson's fascination with the fruits of Brazil. While visiting there on business, he was constantly served platters of local fruits with unrecognizable flavours and names that invariably were accompanied by intriguing stories of health and healing. Because many of these legends seemed too good to be true, he initiated one of the first university studies to analyze them in greater depth. The results were compelling enough to launch a multiyear R&D effort to find the best way to commercialize the two most promising items: the açai and guarana fruits.

In the summer of 2004, Bossa Nova was completing a regional, southern California test market of its launch product: a line of premium, guarana-flavoured carbonated energy drinks. This line had four SKUs: a rainforest refresher and an energy drink in both regular and diet versions. At the same time, Bossa Nova was also putting the finishing touches on the crowning achievement of its R&D department—the world's first juice from an unknown Brazilian palm berry called açai. Açai had been overlooked by those outside Brazil for decades as it was notoriously hard to work with—spoiling within hours of picking and containing naturally occurring fats that looked and smelled awful. But it was also rumoured to be the world's highest-antioxidant fruit (the company's university research partners confirmed this finding). In the fall of 2004, after years of work, Bossa Nova had finally commercialized a method for extracting the bright purple, antioxidant-rich juice from the brownish pulp.

Here's my problem.

Palo and his partner had succeeded in creating a compelling (and expensive) new ingredient, but he wasn't sure how it fit into the product line Bossa Nova was currently selling. If indeed the company had just created the highest antioxidant juice ingredient in the world, what was the product that best took advantage of this opportunity? Palo's role as head of product development was to make sure the new company could capitalize on this opportunity with the right new product strategy.

Palo considered his **Options** 1·2·3

1

Option

Add the new açai juice ingredient to one of the four products Bossa Nova was already making to create a carbonated "antioxidant superfruit refresher." This would create a unique health proposition in the carbonated beverage category, not known for substantive health or functional claims. This option lent itself to an easy and rapid product development cycle because Bossa Nova would be leveraging its current product platform rather than having to create a new manufacturing process. It would be fairly easy to stimulate sales because the company would be working with the same buyers, making it unnecessary to forge relationships with new retail customers. On the other hand, the powerful health story of açai could get lost in an essentially unhealthy product platform (basically, sugar water). And the new ingredient would only be included in one of the company's four SKUs, so it wouldn't create the splash Palo hoped for. In addition, the dark açai juice looked murky and intimidating in the cobalt blue bottle that gave Bossa Nova's energy drinks so much life. The company's technical people weren't sure how to change that property of the juice.

2

Option

Go all out: Create a new line of pure açai juices in a new package that would showcase its world-class nutritional features and benefits. Açai would not be an ingredient in an energy drink (as in Option 1); it would be the core ingredient of a whole new product line. At that time the market leader in premium antioxidant juices, POM Wonderful, was pulling in about $20–$30 million annually in sales by promoting its antioxidant

message, and Palo saw Bossa Nova as a fast follower that could grab a piece of that market. Adding a new product line could diversify the firm's product portfolio, which would also build brand awareness in two places in the store instead of one (on the carbonated, 4-pack dry shelf, and in the fresh juice case in the produce department). Bossa Nova could help define the emerging beverage category of premium, functional antioxidant juices.

3

Option

On the other hand, another product line could overextend Bossa Nova; it would force the company to spread already scarce capital and human resources across two product lines rather than focusing on one. This option would also be risky because the current product line wasn't yet firmly established in the market. Finally, the brand wasn't originally designed to embody the health message of the new açai juice line; it was too playful and needed more science/credibility, which Palo was unclear on how to achieve.

Rewrite, reraise, and rebuild. Rewrite the business plan to focus on developing a single product line that could stake the claim to the title of highest-antioxidant juice in the world. This option was the riskiest, because it entailed raising a significant amount of capital, selling off the existing carbonated inventory, rebranding the company, and generally moving back to square one. If this option were successful, it would result in a strong seductive product concept with a radical value proposition (both a "world's first . . ." and a "world's highest. . ."). The company would also be able to ride the coattails of $5 million of advertising by POM Wonderful designed to educate consumers about the benefits of antioxidants. Of course, this choice would entail huge risk; it would mean a decision to jettison a small but successful product line and remake/rebrand a new company that had already burned through $500 000 in seed capital. And, although the new açai juice ingredient was the world's highest-antioxidant juice, it was very expensive to produce and the margins were dangerously low.

Now, put yourself in Palo's shoes: Which option would you pick, and why?

You Choose

Which **Option** would you choose, and **why**?

1. ☐YES ☐NO   2. ☐YES ☐NO   3. ☐YES ☐NO

See what **option** Palo chose on **page 258**

221

good
A tangible product that we can see, touch, smell, hear, or taste.

intangibles
Experience-based products.

attributes
Include features, functions, benefits, and uses of a product. Marketers view products as a bundle of attributes that includes the packaging, brand name, benefits, and supporting features in addition to a physical good.

1 OBJECTIVE
Articulate the value proposition
(pp. 222–223)

Build a Better Mousetrap—And Add Value

"Build a better mousetrap and the world will beat a path to your door," is an old adage about the power of innovation. The truth is that just because a product is better there is no guarantee it will succeed. For decades, the Woodstream Company built Victor brand wooden mousetraps. Then the company decided to build a better one. Woodstream's product-development people researched the eating, crawling, and nesting habits of mice (hey, it's a living). They built prototypes of different mousetraps to come up with the best-possible design and tested them in homes. Then the company unveiled the sleek-looking "Little Champ," a black plastic, miniature inverted bathtub with a hole. When the mouse went in and ate the bait a spring snapped upward—and the mouse was history.

Sounds like a great new product (unless you're a mouse), but the Little Champ failed. Woodstream studied mouse habits, *not* consumer preferences. The company later discovered that husbands set the trap at night, but in the morning it was the wives who disposed of the trap holding the dead mouse. Unfortunately, many of them thought the Little Champ looked too expensive to throw away, so they felt they should empty the trap for reuse. This was a task most women weren't willing to do—they wanted a trap they could happily toss into the garbage.[1]

Woodstream's failure in the "rat race" underscores the importance of creating products that provide the benefits people want rather than just new gizmos that sound like a good idea. It also tells us that any number of products, from low-tech cheese to high-tech traps, potentially deliver these benefits. Despite Victor's claim to be the "World's Leader in Rodent Control Solutions," in this case, cheese and a shoe box could snuff out a mouse as well as any high-tech trap.

We need to take a close look at how products successfully trap consumers' dollars by providing value. Chapter 1 showed us that the *value proposition* is the consumer's perception of the benefits she will receive if she buys a good or service. So, the marketer's task is twofold: first, to create a better value than what's out there already, and second, to convince customers that this is true.

As we defined it in Chapter 1, a *product* is a tangible good, service, idea, or some combination of these that satisfies consumer or business customer needs through the exchange process; it is a bundle of attributes including features, functions, benefits, and uses. Products can be physical goods, services, ideas, people, or places. A **good** is a *tangible* product, something that we can see, touch, smell, hear, taste, or possess. It may take the form of a pack of cookies, a digital camera, a house, a fancy new smartphone, or a chic but pricey Coach handbag. In contrast, **intangible** products—services, ideas, people, places—are products that we can't always see, touch, taste, smell, or possess.

Marketers think of the product as more than just a thing that comes in a package. They view it as a bundle of **attributes** that includes the packaging, brand name, benefits, and supporting features in addition to a physical good. We are now in Part Three of this book, called "Create the Value Proposition." The key word here is *create*, and a large part of the marketer's role in creating the value proposition is to develop and market products appropriately.

In this chapter, we'll first examine what a product is and see how marketers classify consumer and business-to-business products. Then we'll go on to look at services as products, and from there, at new products, how marketers develop new products, and how markets accept them (or not). In the chapters that follow, we'll look at how marketers manage and assign a price to goods and services.

2 Layers of the Product

OBJECTIVE

Explain the layers of a product.

(pp. 223–224)

No doubt you've heard someone say, "It's the thought, not the gift, that counts." This means that the gift is a sign or symbol that the gift giver has remembered you (or possibly it means that you hate the gift but are being polite!). When we evaluate a gift, we may consider the following: Was it presented with a flourish? Was it wrapped in special paper? Was it obviously a "re-gift"—something the gift giver had received as a gift for herself but wanted to pass on to you? These dimensions are a part of the total gift you receive, in addition to the actual goodie in the box.

Like a gift, a product is everything that a customer receives in an exchange. As Figure 7.1 shows, we distinguish among three distinct layers of the product—the core product, the actual product, and the augmented product. When they develop product strategies, marketers need to consider how to satisfy customers' wants and needs at each of these three layers; that is, how they can create value. Let's consider each layer in turn.

Figure 7.1 Layers of the Product

A product is everything a customer receives—the basic benefits, the physical product and the packaging, and the "extras" that come with the product.

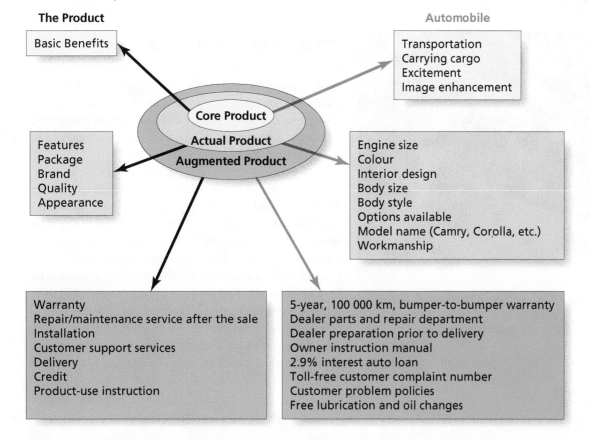

The Product

Basic Benefits

Features
Package
Brand
Quality
Appearance

Warranty
Repair/maintenance service after the sale
Installation
Customer support services
Delivery
Credit
Product-use instruction

Core Product
Actual Product
Augmented Product

Automobile

Transportation
Carrying cargo
Excitement
Image enhancement

Engine size
Colour
Interior design
Body size
Body style
Options available
Model name (Camry, Corolla, etc.)
Workmanship

5-year, 100 000 km, bumper-to-bumper warranty
Dealer parts and repair department
Dealer preparation prior to delivery
Owner instruction manual
2.9% interest auto loan
Toll-free customer complaint number
Customer problem policies
Free lubrication and oil changes

The Core Product

core product
All the benefits the product will provide for consumers or business customers.

The **core product** consists of all the benefits the product will provide for consumers or business customers. As we noted in Chapter 1, a *benefit* is an outcome that the customer receives from owning or using a product. Wise old marketers (and some young ones, too) will tell you, "A marketer may make and sell a 12.0 mm drill bit, but a customer buys a 12.0 mm hole." This tried-and-true saying tells us that people buy the core product, in this case, the ability to make a hole. If a new product, such as a laser, comes along that provides that outcome in a better way or more cheaply, the drill-bit maker has a problem. The moral of this story? *Marketing is about supplying benefits,* not *attributes.*

Many products actually provide multiple benefits. For example, the primary benefit of a car is transportation—all cars (in good repair) provide the ability to travel from point A to point B. But products also provide customized benefits—benefits customers receive because manufacturers add "bells and whistles" to win customers. Different drivers seek different customized benefits in a car. Some simply want economical transportation, others appreciate an environmentally friendly hybrid car, and still others want a top-of-the-line SUV or hot sports car that will be the envy of their friends.

The Actual Product

actual product
The physical good or the delivered service that supplies the desired benefit.

The second layer—the **actual product**—is the physical good or the delivered service that supplies the desired benefit. For example, when you buy a washing machine, the core product is the ability to get clothes clean, but the actual product is a large, square, metal apparatus. When you get a medical exam, the core service is maintaining your health, but the actual one is a lot of annoying poking and prodding. The actual product also includes the unique features of the product, such as its appearance or styling, the package, and the brand name. Sony makes a wide range of televisions from tiny, battery-powered TVs for camping trips, to massive plasma televisions that can display a resolution rivalling reality—but all offer the same core benefit of enabling you to catch Phil Dunphy's antics on the latest episode of *Modern Family.*

augmented product
The actual product plus other supporting features such as a warranty, credit, delivery, installation, and repair service after the sale.

The Augmented Product

Finally, marketers offer customers an **augmented product**—the actual product plus other supporting features such as a warranty, credit, delivery, installation, and repair service after the sale. Marketers know that adding these supporting features to a product is an effective way for a company to stand out from the crowd (see Exhibit 7.1).

For example, Apple revolutionized the music business when it created its iTunes Music Store that enables consumers to download titles directly to their digital music and video libraries. It also conveniently saves you the trouble of correctly inserting, labelling, and sorting new music on your iPod because it does that automatically. Plus, because so many of us tote around an MP3 player, you don't even have to worry about where to store all those stacks of CDs. Apple's augmented product (convenience, extensive selection, and ease of use) pays off handsomely for the company in sales and profits, and customers adore the fact that you can do it all on your laptop if you want. You crave a track or video clip and two minutes later you've got it.

Exhibit 7.1
Are record albums doomed to the fate of the dinosaur? Maybe, but old-style phonograph records from the '80s and earlier are something of a cult product on sites like eBay, and connoisseurs of real "albums" swear that the analogue sound is "richer" (static and all) than the crisp digital recordings of today.

3 How Marketers Classify Products

OBJECTIVE
Describe how
marketers classify
products.
(pp. 225–228)

So far we've learned that a product may be a tangible good or an intangible service or idea, and that there are different layers to the product through which a consumer can derive value. Now we'll build on these ideas as we look at how products differ from one another. Marketers classify products into categories, because they represent differences in how consumers and business customers feel about products and how they purchase different products. Such an understanding helps marketers develop new products and a marketing mix that satisfies customer needs.

Generally, products are either consumer products or business-to-business products, although sometimes consumers and businesses buy the same products, such as toilet paper, vacuum cleaners, and light bulbs. In these cases, though, businesses tend to buy a lot more of them at once. Of course, as we saw, customers differ in how they decide on a purchase, depending on whether the decision maker is a consumer or a business purchaser. Let's first consider differences in consumer products based on how long the product will last and on how the consumer shops for the product. Then we will discuss the general types of business-to-business products.

How Long Do Products Last?

Marketers classify consumer goods as durable or nondurable depending on how long the product lasts. You expect a refrigerator to last many years, but a litre of milk will last only a week or so until it turns into a science project. **Durable goods** are consumer products that provide benefits over a period of months, years, or even decades, such as cars, furniture, and appliances. In contrast, we consume **nondurable goods**, such as gasoline, newspapers and food, in the short term.

We are more likely to purchase durable goods under conditions of *high involvement* (as we saw in Chapter 4), while nondurable goods are more likely to be *low-involvement* decisions. When consumers buy a computer or a house, they will spend a lot of time and energy on the decision process. When they offer these products, marketers need to understand consumers' desires for different product benefits and the importance of warranties, service, and customer support. So they must be sure that consumers can find the information they need. One way is to provide a "Frequently Asked Questions" (FAQs) section on a company Web site. Another is to host a Facebook page, Twitter feed, message board, or blog to build a community around the product. When a company itself sponsors such forums, odds are that the content will be much more favourable and the firm can keep track of what people say about its products. For example, the section of the Microsoft Web site called "Microsoft Technical Communities" allows users to interact with Microsoft employees, experts, and peers in order to share knowledge and news about Microsoft products and related technologies.[2]

In contrast, consumers usually don't "sweat the details" so much when they choose among nondurable goods. There is little, if any, search for information or deliberation. Sometimes, this means that consumers buy whatever brand is available and reasonably priced. In other instances, they base their decisions largely on past experience. Because a certain brand has performed satisfactorily before, customers see no reason to consider other brands, and they choose the same one out of habit. For example, even though there are other brands available, most consumers buy that familiar yellow bottle of French's Mustard again and again. In such cases, marketers can probably be less concerned with developing new product features to attract customers; they should focus more on creating new uses for the existing product, as well as pricing and distribution strategies. In fact, mustard has had

durable goods
Consumer products that provide benefits over a long period of time, such as cars, furniture, and appliances.

nondurable goods
Consumer products that provide benefits for a short time because they are consumed (such as food) or are no longer useful (such as newspapers).

something of a "condiment field day" in recent years as it is extremely low in calories and fat compared to its mayonnaise and ketchup competitors!

How Do Consumers Buy Products?

Marketers also classify products based on where and how consumers buy the product. Figure 7.2 portrays product classifications in the consumer and business marketplaces. We'll consider the consumer market first. In these contexts we think of both goods and services as convenience products, shopping products, specialty products, or unsought products. Recall that in Chapter 4 we talked about how consumer decisions differ in terms of effort they put into habitual decision making to limited problem solving to extended problem solving. We can use this idea when we want to understand why it's important to classify products. For example, it's a good guess that shoppers don't put a lot of thought into buying convenience products, so a company that sells products like white bread might focus its strategy on promoting awareness of a brand name as opposed to providing the detailed "spec sheet" we might expect to find for a smartphone.

A **convenience product** typically is a nondurable good or service that consumers purchase frequently with a minimum of comparison and effort. As the name implies, consumers expect these products to be handy, and they will buy whatever brands are easy to obtain. In general, convenience products are low priced and widely available. You can buy a litre of milk or a loaf of bread at almost any grocery store, drug store, or convenience store. Consumers generally already know all they need or want to know about a convenience product, devote little effort to purchases, and willingly accept alternative brands if their preferred brand is not available in a convenient location. Most convenience product purchases are the results of habitual consumer decision making. What's the most important thing for marketers of convenience products? You guessed it—make sure the product is easily obtainable in all the places where consumers are likely to look for it.

There are several types of convenience products:

convenience product
A consumer good or service that is usually low priced, widely available, and purchased frequently with a minimum of comparison and effort.

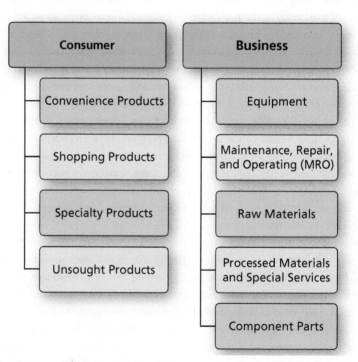

Figure 7.2 Classification of Products
Products are classified differently depending on whether they are in the consumer or business market.

- **Staples** such as milk, bread, and gasoline are basic or necessary items that are available almost everywhere. Most consumers don't perceive big differences among brands. When selling staples, marketers must offer customers a product that consistently meets their expectations for quality and make sure it is available at a price comparable to the competition's prices. While a staple is something we usually decide to buy in advance (or at least before the fuel needle sits on "E" for too long), we buy **impulse products** on the spur of the moment. When you throw a copy of *People* magazine into your shopping cart because it has a cool photo of Lady Gaga on the cover, you're acting on impulse. When they want to promote impulse products, marketers have two challenges: to create a product or package design that is enticing and that "reaches out and grabs the customer," and to make sure their product is highly visible, for example, by securing prime end-aisle or checkout-lane space.

- As the name suggests, we purchase **emergency products** when we're in dire need; examples include bandages, umbrellas, and something to unclog the bathroom sink. Because we need the product badly and immediately, price and sometimes product quality may be irrelevant to our decision to purchase. If you ever go to Disney World in Florida during the summer months, chances are at some point you will get caught in a sudden downpour. When that happens, Disney knows that any umbrella at any price may do and the company stocks its concessions with the product. The company also rolls out the Mickey Mouse ponchos, because once the sky opens up everybody's gotta have one.

- In contrast to convenience products, **shopping products** are goods or services for which consumers will spend time and effort to gather information on price, product attributes, and product quality. They are likely to compare alternatives before they buy. The purchase of shopping products is typically a limited problem-solving decision. Often consumers have little prior knowledge about these products. Because they gather new information for each purchase occasion, consumers are only moderately brand loyal; they will typically switch whenever a different brand offers new or better benefits. They may visit several stores and devote considerable effort to comparing products.

In business-to-consumer e-commerce, consumers sometimes can shop more efficiently when they use **intelligent agents** or *shopbots*—computer programs that find sites selling a particular product. Some of these programs also provide information on competitors' prices, and they may even ask customers to rate the various e-businesses that they have listed on their site so consumers can learn from other shoppers which sellers are good and which are less than desirable. We should note, however, that some sites do not wish to compete on price and don't give shopbots access to their listings.

Specialty products have unique characteristics that are important to buyers at almost any price. You can buy a mop at Canadian Tire for well under $10, right? Yet the iRobot Corporation has models of its Scooba Floor Washing Robot that sell for upwards of $500! They also make equally pricey robot vacuums, pool cleaners, and gutter cleaners.[3] Other examples of specialty products include Rolex watches and Alienware laptops.

Consumers usually know a good deal about specialty products, and they tend to be loyal to specific brands. Generally, a specialty product is an extended problem-solving purchase that requires a lot of effort to choose. That means firms that sell these kinds of products need to create marketing strategies that make their product stand apart from the rest.

Unsought products are goods or services (other than convenience products) for which a consumer has little awareness or interest until a need arises. For college graduates with their first "real" jobs, retirement plans and disability insurance are unsought products. It requires a good deal of advertising or personal selling and is a real challenge to find convincing ways to interest people in these kinds of products—just ask any life insurance salesperson. One solution may be to make pricing more attractive; for example, reluctant consumers may be

staples
Basic or necessary items that are available almost everywhere.

impulse products
A product people often buy on the spur of the moment.

emergency products
Products we purchase when we're in dire need.

shopping products
Goods or services for which consumers spend considerable time and effort gathering information and comparing alternatives before making a purchase.

intelligent agents
Computer programs that find sites selling a particular product.

specialty products
Goods or services that have unique characteristics and are important to the buyer and for which she will devote significant effort to acquire.

unsought products
Goods or services for which a consumer has little awareness or interest until the product or a need for the product is brought to her attention.

more willing to buy an unsought product for "only pennies a day" than if they have to think about their yearly or lifetime cash outlay.

How Do Businesses Buy Products?

Although consumers purchase products for their own use, as we saw in Chapter 5, organizational customers purchase items to use in the production of other goods and services or to facilitate the organization's operation. Marketers classify business-to-business products based on how organizational customers use them. As with consumer products, when marketers know how their business customers use a product, they are better able to design products and craft the entire marketing mix. Let's briefly review the five different types of business-to-business products Figure 7.2 depicts.

equipment
Expensive goods, which last for a long time, that an organization uses in its daily operations.

Equipment refers to the products an organization uses in its daily operations. *Heavy equipment*, sometimes called *installations* or *capital equipment*, includes items such as buildings and robotics Ford uses to assemble automobiles. Installations are big-ticket items and last for a number of years. Computers, photocopy machines, and water fountains are examples of *light* or *accessory equipment*; they are portable, cost less, and have a shorter life span than capital equipment. Marketing strategies for equipment usually emphasize personal selling and may mean custom-designing products to meet an industrial customer's specific needs.

maintenance, repair, and operating (MRO) products
Goods that a business customer consumes in a relatively short time.

Maintenance, repair, and operating (MRO) products are goods that a business customer consumes in a relatively short time. *Maintenance products* include light bulbs, mops, cleaning supplies, and the like. *Repair products* are items such as nuts, bolts, washers, and small tools. *Operating supplies* include computer paper and oil to keep machinery running smoothly. Although some firms use a sales force to promote MRO products, others rely on catalogue sales, the Internet, and telemarketing in order to keep prices as low as possible.

raw materials
Products of the fishing, lumber, agricultural, and mining industries that organizational customers purchase to use in their finished products.

Raw materials are products of the fishing, lumber, agricultural, and mining industries that organizational customers purchase to use in their finished products. For example, a food company may transform soybeans into tofu, and a steel manufacturer changes iron ore into large sheets of steel used by other firms to build automobiles, washing machines, and lawn mowers. And turning one industry's waste materials into another's raw material is a great business model. Did you know that producers use cotton seeds left over from making textiles to make mayonnaise (check the ingredients on the back for cottonseed oil)?[4]

processed materials
Products created when firms transform raw materials from their original state.

Firms produce **processed materials** when they transform raw materials from their original state. Organizations purchase processed materials that become a part of the products they make. A builder uses treated lumber to add a deck onto a house, and a company that creates aluminum cans for Red Bull buys aluminum ingots for this purpose.

In addition to tangible materials, some business customers purchase *specialized services* from outside suppliers. Specialized services may be equipment-based, such as repairing a copy machine or fixing an assembly line malfunction, or non-equipment based, such as market research and legal services. These services are essential to the operation of an organization but are not part of the production of a product.

component parts
Manufactured goods or subassemblies of finished items that organizations need to complete their own products.

Component parts are manufactured goods or subassemblies of finished items that organizations need to complete their own products. For example, a computer manufacturer needs silicon chips to make a computer, and an automobile manufacturer needs batteries, tires, and fuel injectors. As with processed materials, marketing strategies for component parts usually involve nurturing relationships with customer firms and on-time delivery of a product that meets the buyer's specifications.

To review, we now understand what a product is. We also know how marketers classify consumer products based on how long they last and how they are purchased, and we've seen how they classify business-to-business products according to how they use them. In the next section we'll learn about the marketing of services.

4

OBJECTIVE

Understand the importance of services as products.

(pp. 229-243)

Marketing What Isn't There

What do a Lady Gaga concert, a postsecondary education, a Jays baseball game, and a visit to Disney World have in common? Easy answer—each is a product that combines experiences with physical goods to create an event that the buyer consumes. You can't have a concert without musical instruments (or bizarre masks, in Lady Gaga's case), a postsecondary education without textbooks (Thursday night parties don't count), a Jays game without a hot dog, or a Disney experience without the mouse ears. But these tangibles are secondary to the primary product, which is some act that, in these cases, produces enjoyment, knowledge, or excitement.

Exhibit 7.2

The call-centre industry employs more than 18 000 people in New Brunswick, representing nearly one in 20 employed people in the province.[5]

In this section, we'll consider some of the challenges and opportunities that face marketers whose primary offerings are intangibles: services and other experience-based products that we can't touch. The marketer whose job is to build and sell a better football, automobile, or smartphone—all tangibles—deals with issues that are somewhat different from the job of the marketer who wants to sell tickets to a basketball game, limousine service to the airport, or allegiance to a hot new rock band. In the first part of this section, we'll discuss services, a type of intangible that also happens to be the fastest-growing sector in our economy. As we'll see, all services are intangible, but not all intangibles are services. Then we'll look at a few other types of intangibles as well.

What Is a Service?

Services are acts, efforts, or performances exchanged from producer to user without ownership rights. Like other intangibles, a service satisfies needs when it provides pleasure, information, or convenience. In 2009, service industry jobs accounted for over 75 percent of all employment in Canada and over two-thirds of the gross domestic product (GDP).[6] If you pursue a marketing career, it's highly likely that you will work somewhere in the services sector of the economy. Got your interest? (Exhibit 7.2)

Of course, the service industry includes many consumer-oriented services, ranging from dry cleaning to body piercing. But it also encompasses a vast number of services directed toward organizations. Some of the more common business services include vehicle leasing, information technology services, insurance, security, Internet transaction services (Amazon.ca, Google, online banking, etc.), legal advice, food services, consulting, cleaning, and maintenance. In addition, businesses also purchase some of the same services as consumers, such as electricity, telephone service, and gas (although as we saw in Chapter 5, these purchases tend to be in much higher quantities).

The market for business services has grown rapidly, because it is often more cost effective for organizations to hire outside firms that specialize in these services than to hire a workforce and handle the tasks themselves.

Characteristics of Services

Services come in many forms, from those done to you, such as a massage or a teeth cleaning, to those done to something you own, such as a computer upgrade by the Geek Squad

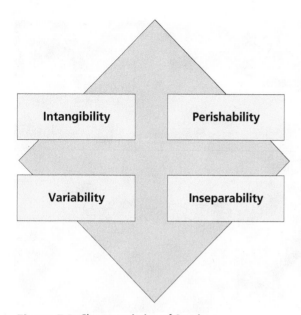

Figure 7.3 Characteristics of Services
Services have four unique characteristics versus products.

intangibility
The characteristic of a service that means customers can't see, touch, or smell good service.

perishability
The characteristic of a service that makes it impossible to store for later sale or consumption.

capacity management
The process by which organizations adjust their offerings in an attempt to match demand.

variability
The characteristic of a service that means that even the same service performed by the same individual for the same customer can vary.

or getting your Subaru WRX Sti modded. Regardless of whether they affect our bodies or our possessions, all services share four characteristics summarized in Figure 7.3: intangibility, perishability, inseparability, and variability. The discussion that follows shows how marketers address the unique issues related to these characteristics of services that are not encountered when marketing tangible goods.

Intangibility

The title of this section is "Marketing What Isn't There." The essence is that unlike a can of pop or a flat screen TV—both of which have physical, tangible properties—services do NOT assume a tangible form. **Intangibility** means customers can't see, touch, or smell good service. Unlike the purchase of a tangible good, we can't inspect or handle services before we buy them. This makes it much more difficult for consumers to evaluate many services. Although it may be easy to evaluate your new haircut, it is far less easy to determine whether the dental hygienist did a great job when she cleaned your teeth.

Because they're buying something that isn't there, customers look for reassuring signs before they purchase—so marketers must ensure that these signs are readily available. That's why they try to overcome the problem of intangibility by providing *physical cues* to reassure the buyer. These cues might be the "look" of the facility, its furnishings, logo, stationery, business cards, appearance of its employees, or well-designed advertising and Web sites.

Perishability

Perishability refers to the characteristic of a service that makes it impossible to store for later sale or consumption—it's a case of use it or lose it. When rooms go unoccupied at a ski resort, there is no way to make up for the lost opportunity to rent them for the weekend. Marketers try to avoid these problems when they use the marketing mix to encourage demand for the service during slack times. One popular option is to reduce prices to increase demand for otherwise unsold services. Airlines do this when they offer more lower-priced seats in the final days before a flight by direct e-mail to customers who sign up for last-minute deals or online through outlets like Redtag.ca. In a last-ditch effort to fill their ships to the highest possible capacity, Disney Cruise Lines offers Walt Disney World Resort employees discounts in excess of 50 percent off about a week before the ship sets sail. We'll talk more about these and other pricing tactics in Chapter 9.

Because perishability is a given when it comes to offering a service, organizations may attempt to match supply and demand via **capacity management**. This strategy may mean adjusting the product, or it may mean adjusting the price. In the summer, for example, Whistler Mountain Bike Park in BC combats its perishability problem when it opens its lifts to mountain bikers who tear down the sunny slopes. Rental car companies offer discounts on days of the week when business travel is light, and many hotels offer special weekend packages to increase weekend occupancy rates. Las Vegas might add free meals, room discounts, show passes, or other incentives to lure travellers during slow weeks, yet during a big convention or major boxing match prices go sky high and amenities disappear.

Variability

An NHL goalkeeper may be hot one Saturday and ice cold the next, and the same is true for most services. **Variability** means that over time even the same service the same individual performs for the same customer changes—even only in minor ways (Exhibit 7.3). It's rare when you get exactly the same cut from a hairstylist each time you visit him. Even your physician might let a rough day get in the way of her usual charming bedside manner with patients.

It's difficult to standardize services because service providers and customers vary. Think about your experiences in your college classes. A school can standardize its offerings to some degree—course catalogues, course content, and classrooms are fairly controllable. Professors, however, vary in their training, life experiences, and personalities, so there is little hope of being able to make teaching uniform (not that we'd want to do this anyway). And because students with different backgrounds and interests vary in their needs, the lecture that you find fascinating might put your friend to sleep (trust us on this). The same is true for customers of organizational services. Differences in the quality of individual security guards or cleaning personnel mean variability in how organizations deliver these services.

The truth is, if you really stop and think about it, we don't necessarily *want* standardization when we purchase a service. Most of us desire a hairstyle that fits our face and personality or a personal trainer who will address our unique physical training needs. Businesses like McDonald's, Wendy's, and Burger King want unique advertising campaigns to set them apart from each other, not cookie-cutter messages. Because of the nature of the tasks service providers perform, customers often appreciate the one that customizes its service for each individual.

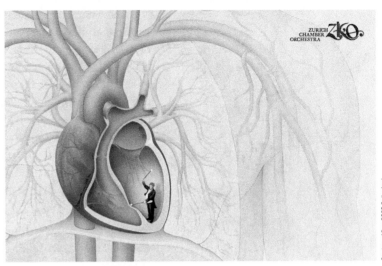

Exhibit 7.3

A symphony orchestra provides an intangible service that is also variable from one performance to another.

Inseparability

In services, **inseparability** means that it is impossible to divide the production of a service from the consumption of that service. Think of the concept of inseparability this way: A firm can manufacture goods at one point in time, distribute them, and then sell them later (likely at a different location than the original manufacturing facility). In contrast, by its nature, a service can take place only at the time the actual service provider performs an act on either the customer or the customer's possession. Nobody wants to eat a meal at a restaurant that was prepared yesterday at another location—that's inseparability. And you can't bulk up haircuts or empty seats on airplanes as inventory for future use!

Still, it's difficult if not impossible to detach the expertise, skill, and personality of a provider or the quality of a firm's employees, facilities, and equipment from the offering itself. The central role that employees play in making or breaking a service underscores the importance of the **service encounter**, or the interaction between the customer and the service provider.[7] The most expertly cooked meal is just plain mush if a surly or incompetent waiter brings it to the table.

To minimize the potentially negative effects of bad service encounters and to save on labour costs, some service businesses turn to **disintermediation**, which means removing the "middleman" and thus eliminating the need for customers to interact with people at all. Examples include self-checkouts at the supermarket or home improvement store, self-service gas pumps, and bank ATMs. Even salad and dessert bars reduce reliance on a restaurant server. Although some consumers resist dealing with machines, pumping their own gas, or fixing their own salad, most prefer or at least don't mind the speed and efficiency disintermediation provides. The remaining consumers who want a Caesar salad prepared table-side by a server with old fashioned flair, or a fill-up that includes an oil check and a clean windshield, provide marketing opportunities for full-service restaurants and the few gas stations that still provide these higher levels of service—usually at a higher price.

inseparability
The characteristic of a service that means that it is impossible to separate the production of a service from the consumption of that service.

service encounter
The actual interaction between the customer and the service provider.

disintermediation
A service that requires the customer to obtain an outcome without the intervention of a human provider.

The Internet provides many opportunities for disintermediation, especially in the financial services area. Banking customers can access their accounts, transfer funds from one account to another, and pay their bills with the click of a mouse. Many busy consumers can check out mortgage interest rates and even apply for a loan at their convenience—a much better option than taking an afternoon off from work to sit in a mortgage company or bank office. Online brokerage services are popular, as many consumers seek to handle their investments themselves so they can avoid the commission a full-service brokerage firm charges. Insurance companies like Allstate and Sun Life aggressively lead consumers to the Web site instead of to an agent's office to get rate quotes.

The Service Encounter

Earlier we said that a service encounter occurs when the customer comes into contact with the organization—which usually means she interacts with one or more employees who represent that organization. The *service encounter* has several dimensions that are important to marketers.[8]

First, there is the social contact dimension—one person interacting with another person. The physical dimension is also important; customers often pay close attention to the environment where they receive the service. But, despite all the attention (and money) firms pay to create an attractive facility and deliver a quality product, this social contact is "the moment of truth"—it is the employee who often determines whether the customer will come away with a positive or a negative impression of the service. Our interactions with service providers can range from the most superficial, such as when we buy a movie ticket, to telling a psychiatrist (or bartender) our most intimate secrets. In each case, though, the quality of the service encounter exerts a big impact on how we feel about the service we receive. Because services are intimately tied to company employees who deliver the service, *the quality of a service is only as good as its worst employee*. The employee represents the organization; her actions, words, physical appearance, courtesy, and professionalism reflect its values. Customers entrust themselves and/or their possessions to the care of the employee, so it is important that employees look at the encounter from the customer's perspective.

However, the customer also plays a part in the type of experience that results from a service encounter. When you visit a doctor, the quality of the health care you receive depends not only on the physician's competence, it's also influenced by your ability to accurately and clearly communicate the symptoms you experience and how well you follow the regimen she prescribes to treat you. The business customer must provide accurate information to her accounting firm. And even the best personal trainer is not going to make the desired improvements in a client's physique if the client refuses to do the workout designed for her.

How We Classify Services

When they understand the characteristics of different types of services, marketers can develop strategies to ramp up customer satisfaction. As Table 7.1 shows, we classify services in terms of whether the service is performed directly on the customer or on something the customer owns, and whether the service consists of tangible or intangible actions. Customers themselves receive tangible services to their bodies—a haircut or a heart transplant. The education (we hope!) you are receiving in this course is an intangible service directed at the consumer. A customer's possessions are the recipient of tangible services such as the repair of a favourite carpet. Other intangible services directed at a consumer's possessions include insurance and home security.

In reality, most products are a combination of goods and services. The purchase of a "pure good" like a Cadillac Escalade still has service components, such as bringing it to the dealer for maintenance work or using its OnStar service to figure out how to find the dealer

Table 7.1	Classification of Services by Inputs and Tangibility

	Tangible Services	Intangible Services
Customer	Haircuts	Postsecondary education
	Plastic surgery	Religious services
	Manicure	TV program
	Personal training	Flower-arranging course
		Marriage counselling
Possessions	Dry cleaning	Banking
	Auto repair	Accounting Services
	Housecleaning	Insurance
	Package delivery	Home security service

Marketers classify services according to whether the customer or his possessions are the recipients of the service and whether the service itself consists of tangible or intangible elements.

in the first place. The purchase of a "pure service" like a makeover at a department store has product components; for example, the lotions, powders, and lipsticks the cosmetologist uses to create the "new you."

The service continuum in Figure 7.4 shows that either tangible or intangible elements dominate some products, such as salt versus teaching, whereas others such as a commercial airline flight tend to include a mixture of goods and services. A product's placement on this continuum gives some guidance as to which marketing issues are most likely to be relevant. As the product approaches the tangible pole of this continuum, there is fairly little emphasis on service. The physical product itself is the focal point, and we choose one option over others because of the product's function or image. But as the product gets near the intangible pole, the issues we've discussed, such as intangibility and inseparability, shape the service experience. In the middle of the continuum, both goods and services contribute substantially to the quality of the product, because these products rely on people to satisfactorily operate equipment that will in turn deliver quality service. As you move across the service continuum from tangibles to intangibles, it's useful to consider the various products within the context of three categories: goods-dominated products, equipment- or facility-based services, and people-based services.

Goods-Dominated Products

Even if this means only that the company maintains a toll-free telephone line for questions or provides a 30-day warranty against defects, companies that sell tangible products still must provide support services. Automobile, major appliance, and electronics manufacturers can realize a competitive advantage when they provide customers with better support than the competition. Services may be even more important for marketers of business-to-business tangibles. Business customers often will not even consider buying from manufacturers who don't provide services like employee training and equipment maintenance. For example, hospitals that buy lifesaving patient care and monitoring equipment costing hundreds of thousands of dollars demand not only in-service training for their nursing and technician personnel but also quick response to breakdowns and regular maintenance of the equipment.

Equipment- or Facility-Based Services

As we see in Figure 7.4, some products include a mixture of tangible and intangible elements. While a restaurant is a balanced product because it includes the preparation and

Figure 7.4 The Service Continuum

Products vary in their level of tangibility. Salt is a tangible product, teaching is an intangible product, and the products fast-food restaurants offer include both tangible and intangible elements.

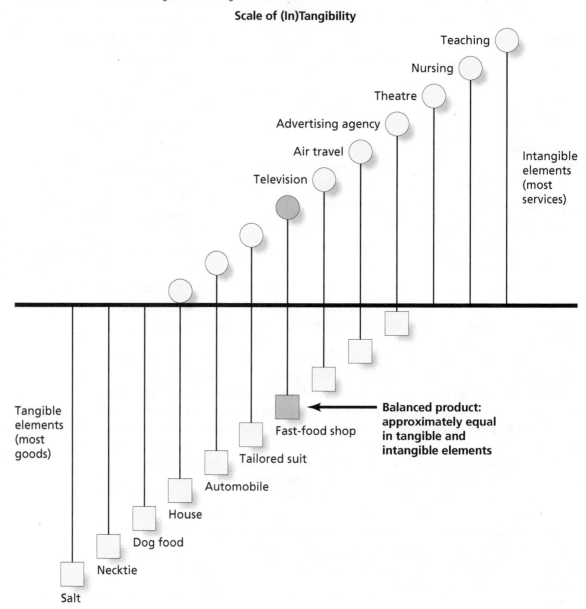

Adapted from G. Lynn Shostack, "How to Design a Service," *European Journal of Marketing*, 16, no. 1 (1982): 52. Emerald Publishing.

delivery of the food to your table plus the food itself, the tangible elements of the service are less evident for other products. Many hospitals and hotels fall in the middle of the continuum not because customers take a tangible good away from the service encounter, but because these organizations rely on expensive equipment or facilities to deliver a product. Other services such as automatic car washes, amusement parks, museums, movie theatres, health clubs, tanning salons, and zoos also must be concerned with operational, locational, or environmental factors (Exhibit 7.4).

- **Operational factors:** Clear signs and other guidelines must show customers how to use the service. In particular, firms need to minimize waiting times. Marketers employ a number of tricks to give impatient customers the illusion that they aren't waiting too long. One hotel chain, responding to complaints about the long wait for elevators, installed mirrors in the lobby: People tended to check themselves out until the elevators arrived, and lo and behold, protests decreased.[9]

- **Locational factors:** These are especially important for frequently purchased services, such as dry cleaning or retail banking, that we obtain at a fixed spot. When you select a bank, a restaurant, or a health club, its location often factors into your decision. Marketers of these services make sure their service sites are convenient and in neighbourhoods that are attractive to prospective customers.

- **Environmental factors:** Service managers who operate a storefront service that requires people to come to their location realize they must create an attractive environment to lure customers. One trend is for such services to adopt a more retail-like philosophy, borrowing techniques from clothing stores or restaurants to create a pleasant environment as part of their marketing strategy. Banks, for example, increasingly create signature looks for their branches through the careful use of lighting, colour, and art.[10]

Exhibit 7.4

An amusement park is an equipment-based service that includes both tangible and intangible elements.

People-Based Services

At the intangible end of the continuum are people-based services. Take, for example, the ultimate father-son bonding experience through good grooming—a trip to First Choice Haircutters (Exhibit 7.5).

Because people have less and less time to get things done, the importance of people-based services is increasing. Self-improvement services such as those wardrobe consultants and personal trainers offer are increasingly popular, and in some locales even professional dog walkers and mobile pet washing trucks do a brisk business. Many of us hire someone to do our legal work, repair our cars and appliances, or do our tax returns.

Exhibit 7.5

While services strive for consistency, the providers are inherently unique and different.

Core and Augmented Services

When we buy a service, we may actually purchase a *set* of services. The **core service** is a benefit that a customer gets from the service. For example, when your car breaks down, repairing the problem is a core service you seek from an auto dealer or a garage. In most cases though, the core service alone just isn't enough. To attract customers, a service firm often tries to offer **augmented services**—additional service offerings that differentiate the firm from the competition. When the auto dealership provides pickup and delivery of your car, a free car wash, or a customer lounge with donuts and coffee, it gains your loyalty as a customer.

And what about your own postsecondary education? Over the last decade, increased competition for students prompted many colleges and universities to emphasize a whole variety of augmented products such as full-service gyms and fitness centres, comprehensive on-site health services, upgraded dining options, writing and editing centres for term paper development, expanded hours for campus support departments, more variety of housing options including boutique and upscale residences, user-friendly grant and scholarship counselling, and convenient bill payment plans. With so many augmented services, hopefully in their spare moments students even squeeze in a few classes along the way!

core services
The basic benefit of having a service performed.

augmented services
The core service plus additional services provided to enhance value.

Physical Elements of the Service Encounter: Servicescapes and Other Tangibles

servicescape
The actual physical facility where the service is performed, delivered, and consumed.

As we noted earlier in the chapter, because services are intangible, marketers have to be mindful of the *physical evidence* that goes along with them. An important part of this physical evidence is the **servicescape**: the environment in which the service is delivered and where the firm and the customer interact. Servicescapes include facility exteriors—elements such as a building's architecture, the signage, parking, and even the landscaping. They also include interior elements, such as the design of the office or store, equipment, colours, air quality, temperature, and smells. For hotels, restaurants, banks, airlines, and even schools, the servicescape is quite elaborate. For other services, such as an express mail drop-off, a dry cleaner, or an Interac machine, the servicescape can be very simple.

Marketers know that carefully designed servicescapes can have a positive influence on customers' purchase decisions, their evaluations of service quality, and their ultimate satisfaction with the service. Thus, for a service such as a pro basketball game, much planning goes into designing not only the actual court but also the exterior design and entrances of the stadium, landscaping, seating, restrooms, concession stands, and ticketing area. Similarly, marketers pay close attention to the design of other tangibles that facilitate the performance of the service or provide communications. For the basketball fan, these include the signs that direct people to the stadium, the game tickets, the programs, the team's uniforms, and the hundreds of employees who help to deliver the service.

Nowadays, for many consumers, the first tangible evidence of a business (service or otherwise) is its Web site. Web sites send a strong cue to customers about you, and sites that are unattractive or frustratingly dysfunctional provide a horrible first impression of the company and its service. Searchability is important, as is paying attention to **search engine optimization (SEO)**: a systematic process of ensuring that your firm comes up at or near the top of lists of typical search phrases related to your business. SEO is critical, because if your organization's name doesn't come up when someone Googles, she'll just click on one of the competitors that does appear on the list (try Googling our book's title *Real People, Real Choices*, and see what happens).

search engine optimization (SEO)
A systematic process of ensuring that your firm comes up at or near the top of lists of typical search phrases related to your business.

How We Provide Quality Service

If a service experience isn't positive, it can turn into a *disservice* with nasty consequences. Quality service ensures that customers are satisfied with what they have paid for. However, satisfaction is relative because the service recipient compares the current experience to some prior set of expectations. That's what makes delivering quality service tricky. What may seem like excellent service to one customer may be mediocre to another person who has been "spoiled" by earlier encounters with an exceptional service provider. So, marketers must identify customer expectations and then work hard to exceed them.

In air travel, lots of "little things" that used to be considered a normal part of service are now treated by most airlines as extras. Many fliers believe the airlines are "nickel and diming" them for extra bag weight, blankets and pillows, small snacks and drinks, and prime seat locations. WestJet, though, has continued to offer all these perks as part of the basic service. Thus, by essentially doing nothing different from what they've always done, WestJet now stands out from the crowd and exceeds customer expectations. No surprise that WestJet has been named J.D. Power 2011 Customer Service Champion—one of only 40 companies to be recognized.[11]

Of course, it's not always so easy to meet or exceed customer expectations. The stories we hear from friends and acquaintances may influence our standards, and these may not always be realistic in the first place.[12] In some cases, there is little that marketers can do to soothe ruffled feathers. Exaggerated customer expectations, such as providing a level of personal service impossible for a large company to accomplish, account for about 75 percent of the complaints service businesses report. However, providing customers with logical explanations for service failures and compensating them in some way can substantially reduce dissatisfaction.

Service Quality Attributes

Because services are inseparable, in that an organization doesn't produce one until the time a customer consumes it, it is difficult to estimate how good a service will be until you buy it. Most service businesses cannot offer a free trial. Because services are variable, it is hard to predict consistency of quality and there is little or no opportunity for comparison shopping. The selection process for services is somewhat different than for goods, especially for services that are highly intangible—such as those on the right end of the continuum in Figure 7.4. Service marketers have to come up with creative ways to illustrate the benefits their service will provide. A useful way to begin to develop approaches to marketing services effectively is to consider three types of service quality attributes: search qualities, experience qualities, and credence qualities.

- **Search qualities** are product attributes that the consumer can examine prior to purchase. These include colour, style, price, fit, smell, and texture. Tangible goods, of course, are more likely to have these characteristics, so services need to build them in by paying attention to details such as the style of flight attendants' uniforms or the decor of a hotel room.

- **Experience qualities** are product attributes that customers identify during or after consumption. For example, we can't really predict how good a vacation will be until we have it, so marketers need to reassure customers *before* the fact that they are in for a positive experience. A travel agency may invest in a slick presentation complete with alluring images of a tropical resort and perhaps even supply enthusiastic recommendations from other clients who had a positive experience at the same location. On the other hand, the last thing a marketer wants to do is overpromise and then fall short in the actual delivery—so conveniently cropping out that construction site that's located right next to the resort may not be a great idea.

- **Credence qualities** are product attributes we find difficult to evaluate even *after* we've experienced them. For example, most of us don't have the expertise to know if our doctor's diagnosis is correct.[13] To a great extent, the client must trust the service provider. That is why tangible clues of professionalism, such as diplomas, an organized office, or even the professional's attire (for example, a physician in a lab coat instead of blue jeans) count toward purchase satisfaction.

search qualities
Product characteristics that the consumer can examine prior to purchase.

experience qualities
Product characteristics that customers can determine during or after consumption.

credence qualities
Product characteristics that are difficult to evaluate even after they have been experienced.

How We Measure Service Quality

Because the customer's experience of a service determines if she will return to the provider in the future, service marketers feel that measuring positive and negative service experiences is the "Holy Grail" for the services industry. Marketers gather consumer responses in a variety of ways. For example, some companies hire "mystery shoppers" to check on hotels and airlines and report back. These shoppers usually work for a research firm, although some airlines reportedly recruit "spies" from the ranks of their most frequent flyers. Some firms also locate "lost customers" (former patrons) so they can find out what turned them off and correct the problem.

SERVQUAL

The **SERVQUAL** scale is one popular instrument to measure consumers' perceptions of service quality. SERVQUAL identifies five dimensions, or components, of service quality:

- *Tangibles:* the physical facilities and equipment and the professional appearance of personnel

SERVQUAL
A multiple-item scale used to measure service quality across dimensions of tangibles, reliability, responsiveness, assurance, and empathy.

- *Reliability*: the ability to provide dependably and accurately what was promised

- *Responsiveness:* the willingness to help customers and provide prompt service

- *Assurance:* the knowledge and courtesy of employees, and the ability to convey trust and confidence

- *Empathy:* the degree of caring and individual attention customers receive[14]

Thousands of service businesses apply the SERVQUAL scale. They usually administer it in a survey format through a written, online, or phone questionnaire. Firms often track SERVQUAL scores over time to understand how their service quality is (hopefully) improving. They also can use this measure to apply the gap analysis approach we describe next.

Gap Analysis

gap analysis
A marketing research method that measures the difference between a customer's expectation of a service quality and what actually occurred.

Gap analysis (no, nothing to do with a Gap clothing store) is a measurement approach that gauges the difference between a customer's expectation of service quality and what actually occurs. By identifying specific places in the service system where there is a wide gap between what customers expect and what they receive, services marketers can get a handle on what needs improvement. Figure 7.5 illustrates where the gaps can occur in service, both on the consumer's side (often referred to as "in front of the curtain") and on the marketer's side ("behind the curtain"). Some major gaps include the following:[15]

- **Gap between consumers' expectations and management's perceptions:** A major quality gap occurs when the firm's managers don't understand what its customers' expectations are in the first place. Many service organizations have an *operations orientation* rather than a *customer orientation*. For example, banks often used to close branches at midday to balance transactions because that's more efficient for them, even though it's not convenient for customers who want to do their banking during their lunch hour. Today more and more banks are open late and on weekends.

Marketing Metrics

From Social Media to Social CRM

Based on extensive survey results from both consumers and business executives, the IBM Institute for Business Value (IBV) uncovered significant gaps between what customers want and what businesses think customers want in their social media engagement. According to their 2011 CRM study, consumers desire tangible value such as coupons and discounts, while businesses feel that they want to learn about new products. They used gap analysis to learn more about customers. Figure 7.5 highlights the significant perception gap.[16]

Most customers want to use social media for personal reasons—to connect with friends and family, not with companies. Consumers are willing to interact with businesses if they believe it is to their benefit. Have you noticed that many successful social media campaigns often include some type of prize or incentive? Even recent TV commercials feature stories where customers who tweet about their brand are surprised with prizes in coffee shops or airports. While

that is an interesting business tactic to introduce customers to social media, it can get expensive and have questionable long-term returns.

Survey results show that businesses are three times more likely to think consumers are interested in interacting with them to feel part of a community. It's clear that businesses are overestimating consumers' desire to engage with them to feel connected to their brand. In reality, these two activities are among the least interesting from a consumer's perspective.

So . . . what does this data tell marketers? First, they should ensure they are getting continuous direct consumer feedback about their social media initiatives. Are they working? What needs to change? What is the perceived value to the customer (as compared to the expected value from the company's perspective)? As the report suggests, businesses need to stay laser focused on customer value to avoid falling into the perception gaps they've uncovered.

Figure 7.5 The Gap Model of Service Delivery

A gap analysis identifies specific places in the service system where there is a wide gap between what customers expect and what they receive, allowing marketers to get a handle on what needs improvement.

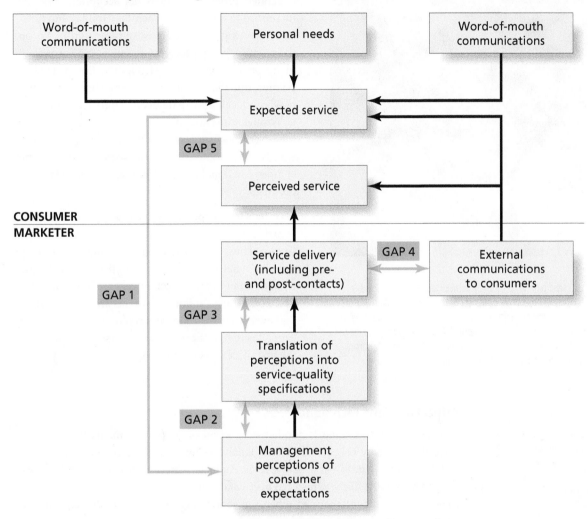

A. Parasuraman, Valarie A. Zeithaml, and Leonard L. Berry, "A Conceptual Model of Service Quality and its Implications for Future Research," *Journal of Marketing* (Fall 1985), pp. 41–50.

- **Gap between management's perception and quality standards the firm sets:** Quality suffers when a firm fails to establish a quality-control program. Successful service firms, such as American Express, Four Seasons, and WestJet, develop written quality goals. American Express found that customers complained most about its responsiveness, accuracy, and timeliness. The company established 180 specific goals to correct these problems, and it now monitors how fast employees answer phones in an effort to be more responsive.

- **Gap between established quality standards and service delivery:** One of the biggest threats to service quality is poor employee performance. When employees do not deliver the service at the level the company specifies, quality suffers. Teamwork is crucial to service success. Unfortunately, many companies don't clearly specify what they expect of employees. Merrill Lynch addressed this problem when the brokerage firm assembled its operations personnel into quality groups of 8 to 15 employees each to clarify its expectations for how its personnel should interact with clients.

Exhibit 7.6

Disney Parks and Resorts is a real champion of consistency between standards and delivery. Disney makes all employees, or "Cast Members" (whether they sell ice cream on Main Street USA or they come in from another company to fill an executive role), go through "Traditions" training, as well as many other training programs, to help ensure that all Disney cast members know how they should interact with guests. They follow up frequently with refresher seminars and meetings to remind everyone of the company's history and traditions.

- **Gap between service quality standards and consumers' expectations:** Sometimes a firm makes exaggerated promises or does not accurately describe its service to customers. When the Holiday Inn hotel chain developed an advertising campaign based on the promise that guests would receive "No Surprises," many operations personnel opposed the idea. They pointed out that no service organization, no matter how good, can anticipate every single thing that can go wrong. Sure enough, the campaign was unsuccessful. A services firm is better off when it communicates exactly what the customer can expect and how the company will make it right if it doesn't deliver on its promises.

- **Gap between expected service and actual service:** Sometimes consumers misperceive the quality of the service. Thus, even when communications accurately describe what service quality the firm provides and what customers can expect, buyers are less than satisfied. Some diners at fine restaurants are so demanding that even their own mothers couldn't anticipate their every desire (that's probably why they're eating out in the first place). See Exhibit 7.6.

The Critical Incident Technique

critical incident technique
A method for measuring service quality in which marketers use customer complaints to identify critical incidents—specific face-to-face contacts between consumer and service providers that cause problems and lead to dissatisfaction.

The **critical incident technique** is another way to measure service quality.[17] Using this approach, the company collects and closely analyzes very specific customer complaints. It can then identify *critical incidents*—specific contacts between consumers and service providers that are most likely to result in dissatisfaction.

Some critical incidents happen when the service organization simply can't meet a customer's expectations. For example, it is impossible to satisfy a passenger who says to a flight attendant, "Come sit with me. I don't like to fly alone." In other cases, though, the firm is capable of meeting these expectations but fails to do so. For example, the customer might complain to a flight attendant, "My seat won't recline."[18] A service provider can turn a potentially dissatisfied customer into a happy one if it addresses the problem or perhaps even tells the customer why the problem can't be solved at this time. Customers tend to be fairly forgiving if the organization gives them a reasonable explanation for the problem.

Strategic Issues When We Deliver Service Quality

We've seen that delivering quality is the goal of every successful service organization. What can the firm do to maximize the likelihood that a customer will choose its service and become a loyal customer? Because services differ from goods in so many ways, decision makers struggle to market something that isn't there. But, just as in goods marketing, the first step is to develop effective marketing strategies. Table 7.2 illustrates how three different types of service organizations might devise effective marketing strategies.

Of course, no one (not even your marketing professor) is perfect, and mistakes happen. Some failures, such as when your dry cleaner places glaring red spots on your new white sweater, are easy to see at the time the firm performs the service. Others, such as

Table 7.2	Marketing Strategies for Service Organizations		
	Dry Cleaner	City Opera Company	A University
Marketing objective	Increase total revenues by 20 percent within one year by increasing business of existing customers and obtaining new customers	Increase to 1000 the number of season memberships to opera productions within two years	Increase applications to undergraduate and graduate programs by 10 percent for the coming academic year
Target markets	Young and middle-aged professionals living within a five-kilometre radius of the business	Clients who attend single performances but do not purchase season memberships Other local residents who enjoy opera but do not normally attend local opera performances	Primary market: prospective undergraduate and graduate students who are Canadian residents Secondary market: prospective undergraduate and graduate students living in foreign countries
Benefits offered	Excellent and safe cleaning of clothes in 24 or fewer hours	Experiencing professional-quality opera performances while helping ensure the future of the local opera company	High-quality education in a student-centred campus environment
Strategy	Provide an incentive offer to existing customers, such as one suit cleaned for free after 10 suits cleaned at regular prices Use newspaper, direct mail advertising, and Groupon or LivingSocial to communicate a limited-time discount offer to all customers	Correspond with former membership holders and patrons of single performances, encouraging them to purchase new season memberships Arrange for opera company personnel and performers to be guests for local television and radio talk shows	Increase number of recruiting visits to local high schools; arrange a special day of events for high-school counsellors to visit campus Communicate with alumni, encouraging them to recommend the university to prospective students they know

when the dry cleaner shrinks your sweater, are less obvious and you recognize them only at a later time when you're running late and get a "surprise." But no matter when or how you discover the failure, the important thing is that the firm takes fast action to resolve the problem. A timely and appropriate response means that the problem won't occur again (hopefully) and that the customer's complaint will be satisfactorily resolved. The key is speed; research shows that customers whose complaints are resolved quickly are far more likely to buy from the same company again than they are from those that take longer to resolve complaints.[19]

To make sure that they keep service failures to a minimum and to ensure that when they do blow it they can recover quickly, managers should first understand the service and the potential points at which failures are most likely to occur so they can plan how to recover ahead of time. That's why it's so important to identify critical incidents. In addition, employees should be trained to listen for complaints and be empowered to take appropriate actions immediately. Many hoteliers allow front desk employees the discretion to spend up to a certain amount per service failure to compensate guests for certain inconveniences.

The Future of Services

As we look into the future, we recognize that service industries will continue to play a key role in the growth of both Canada and the global economy. In fact, in recent years, the

new dominant logic for marketing
A reconceptualization of traditional marketing to redefine service as the central (core) deliverable and the actual physical products purveyed as comparatively incidental to the value proposition.

accelerating impact of service as an integral part of any firm's value proposition has led some analysts to argue that there is now a **new dominant logic for marketing**. This means that we need to rethink our traditional distinction between services and goods. Instead, we need to recognize that a service is the central (core) deliverable in *every* exchange; any physical products involved are relatively minor in terms of their contribution to the value proposition.[20] (See Exhibit 7.7.) Figure 7.6 indicates several trends for us to consider that will provide both opportunities and challenges for the marketers of services down the road (that means you). In the future, we can expect services that we can't even imagine yet. Of course, they will also provide many new and exciting job opportunities for future marketers.

- **Changing demographics:** As the population ages, service industries that meet the needs of older consumers will see dramatic growth. Companies that offer recreational opportunities, health care, and living assistance for seniors will be in demand.

- **Globalization:** The globalization of business will increase the need for logistics and distribution services to move goods around the world (we'll talk more about these in Chapter 12) and for accounting and legal services that facilitate these global exchanges (see Exhibit 7.8). In addition, global deregulation will affect the delivery of services by banks, brokerages, insurance, and other financial service industries because globalization means greater competition. For example, many "medical tourists" now journey to countries like Thailand and India to obtain common surgical procedures that may cost less than half what they would in the United States. Meanwhile, hospitals in the United States often look more like luxury spas as they offer amenities such as adjoining quarters for family members, choice of different ethnic cuisines, and in-room Internet access. In the hotel industry, demand for luxury properties is growing around the world. Hyatt International is expanding aggressively in China with 14 luxury properties either open or scheduled to open. Hyatt expects to have as many as 24 properties there within a decade.[21]

- **Technological advances:** Changing technology provides opportunities for growth and innovation in global service industries such as telecommunications, health care, banking, and Internet services. And we can also expect technological advances to provide opportunities for services that we haven't even thought of yet but that will dramatically change and improve the lives of consumers. Best Buy's Geek Squad makes the company a ton of money by showing people how to set up and use their home computers—with

Figure 7.6 Factors That Shape the Future of Services
Changing demographics, globalization, technological advances, and proliferation of information all impact services.

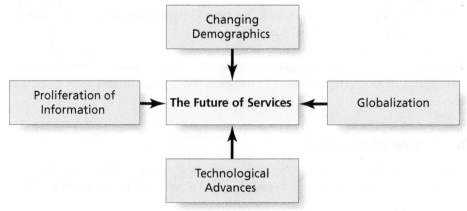

new advances there will always be "clueless" customers who need help to keep up with progress! Meanwhile, social media Web sites, smartphones, blogs, and the Internet in general all are central to successfully marketing all kinds of intangibles. In the political realm, the 2011 federal election was a breakthrough in the use of digital platforms as handlers for all parties' candidates invested heavily to support these real-time methods of communicating with tech-savvy voters about their candidate's ideas and position on the issues *du jour*.

Exhibit 7.7

This Australian ad promotes the idea of safe driving.

- **Proliferation of information:** In many ways, we have become an information society. The availability of, flow of, and access to information are critical to the success of organizations. These changes will provide greater opportunities for database services, artificial intelligence systems, communications systems, and other services that facilitate the storage and transfer of knowledge.

Exhibit 7.8

Non-profit organizations often use vivid imagery to communicate the importance of their causes.

OBJECTIVE

Understand the
importance and types
of product innovations.
(pp. 244–246)

5 "New and Improved!" The Process of Innovation

OBJECTIVE

Understand the
importance and types
of product innovations.
(pp. 244–246)

"New and improved!" What exactly do we mean when we use the term *new product*? The US Federal Trade Commission says that (1) a product must be entirely new or changed significantly to be called new, and (2) a product may be called new for only six months. In Canada, the Competition Bureau is responsible for determining if a product can be termed "new" or not. This is handled on a case-by-case basis.

innovation
A product that consumers perceive to be new and different from existing products.

That definition is fine from a legal perspective. From a marketing standpoint, though, a new product or an **innovation** is *anything* that customers perceive as new and different. An innovation may be a game-changing product with cutting-edge style like the Apple iPhone that is an iPhone *and* an iPod, or the Gillette Fusion MVP razor that looks like a device from Star Trek. It can also be an innovative communications approach such as Skype VoIP telephony over the Internet, or a new way to power a vehicle such as hydrogen fuel cell cars like the BMW Hydrogen 7, the Ford Focus FCV, or the Honda FCX Clarity. An innovation may be a completely new product that provides benefits never available before, such as personal computers when they were first introduced, or it may simply be an existing product with a new style, in a different colour, or with some new feature, like blue Smarties.

Types of Innovations

Innovations differ in their degree of newness, and this helps to determine how quickly the target market will adopt them. Because innovations that are more novel require us to exert greater effort to figure out how to use them, they are slower to spread throughout a population than new products that are similar to what is already available.

As Figure 7.7 shows, marketers classify innovations into three categories based on their degree of newness: continuous innovations, dynamically continuous innovations, and discontinuous innovations. However, it is better to think of these three types as ranges along a continuum that goes from a very small change in an existing product to a totally new product. We can then describe the three types of innovations in terms of the amount of change they bring to people's lives. For example, the first automobiles caused tremendous changes in the lives of people who were used to getting places by "horse power." While a more recent innovation like GPS systems that feed us driving directions by satellite is undoubtedly cool, in a relative sense, we have to make fewer changes in our lives to adapt to them (other than not having to ask a stranger for directions when we're lost). And how about the Lexus LS 460 that can actually parallel park itself?[22]

Tech and Trends

Airlines Introduce Handheld Devices to Improve Service

The beleaguered airline industry is looking for any ways it can use handheld technology to improve performance with customers (and save time and money in the process!). Airline agents are increasingly going mobile at airports, with tools in hand to help passengers check in and print boarding passes, and eventually help sell augmented services (which is where much of their profit comes from).

American Airlines recently equipped its agents at several airports with mobile devices. The plan is to eventually assign them at every gate. Delta introduced agents with mobile devices last year, too, and the airline has since increased the number of devices to 900 units used at all domestic airports.

Services in place or planned via the devices include printing boarding passes, providing flight and gate information, displaying maps of other airports, printing bag tags, making upgrade purchases and other bundled offerings, adding passengers to standby lists, rebooking cancelled flights, issuing meal vouchers, and paying for oversized bags that shouldn't have cleared security.

Despite the industry's generally bad service reputation, one thing they have done well over time is integrating technology into the service encounter. As travellers, we've all been trained to use the Internet to buy tickets and self-serve kiosks to check in and print boarding passes. Our expectations are very low for having an actual human encounter throughout the process. With the handhelds, the airlines can reintroduce a human touchpoint and maximize opportunities for up-sale to travellers while at the same time speeding along the airport process.[23]

Continuous Innovations

A **continuous innovation** is a modification to an existing product, such as when Crocs reinvigorated the market for clogs by offering a version of the comfy shoe with big holes punched in it. This type of modification can set one brand apart from its competitors. For example, people associate Volvo cars with safety, and Volvo comes out with a steady stream of safety-related innovations. Volvo was the first car to offer full front and side air bags, and beginning with some of its 2009 models you can get "Low Speed Collision Avoidance" and "Volvo City Safety." The cars have a radar system that monitors the distance of the car to the car in front of you, and if you get too close, the car's computer automatically applies the brakes.[24]

The consumer doesn't have to learn anything new to use a continuous innovation (see Exhibit 7.9). From a marketing perspective, this means that it's usually pretty easy to convince consumers to adopt this kind of new product. For example, the current generation of high-definition plasma flat-screen monitors didn't require computer users to change their behaviours. We all know what a computer monitor is and how it works. The system's continuous innovation simply gives users the added benefits of taking up less space and being easier on the eyes than old-style monitors.

A **knockoff** is a new product that copies, with slight modification, the design of an original product. Firms deliberately create knockoffs of clothing and jewellery, often with the intent to sell to a larger or different market. For example, companies may copy the *haute couture* clothing styles of top designers and sell them at lower prices to the mass market. It's likely that a cheaper version of the gown Jennifer Aniston wears to the Academy Awards ceremony will be available at numerous Web sites within a few days after the event. It is difficult to legally protect a design (as opposed to a technological invention), because an imitator can argue that even a very slight change—different buttons or a slightly wider collar on a dress or shirt—means the knockoff is not an exact copy.

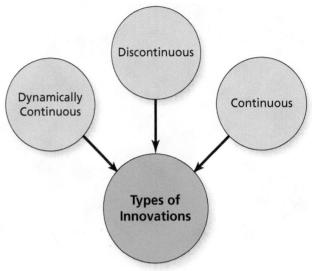

Figure 7.7 Types of Innovations

Three types of innovations are continuous, dynamically continuous, and discontinuous, based on their degree of newness.

continuous innovation
A modification of an existing product that sets one brand apart from its competitors.

knockoff
A new product that copies, with slight modification, the design of an original product.

dynamically continuous innovation
A change in an existing product that requires a moderate amount of learning or behaviour change.

Dynamically Continuous Innovations

A **dynamically continuous innovation** is a pronounced modification to an existing product that requires a modest amount of learning or change in behaviour to use it. The history of audio equipment is a series of dynamically continuous innovations. For many years, consumers enjoyed listening to their favourite Frank Sinatra songs on record players. In the 1960s, they swooned as they listened to the Beatles on a continuous-play eight-track tape (requiring the purchase of an eight-track tape player, of course). Then came cassette tapes to listen to the Eagles (oops, now a cassette player is needed). In the 1980s, consumers could hear Metallica songs digitally mastered on compact discs (that, of course, required the purchase of a new CD player).

In the 1990s, recording technology moved one more step forward with MP3 technology; it allowed Madonna fans to download music from the Internet or to exchange electronic copies of the music with others, and when mobile MP3 players hit the scene in 1998, fans could download the tunes directly into a portable player. Then, in November 2001, Apple Computer introduced its first iPod. With the original iPod, music fans could take 1000 songs with them wherever they went. By 2006, iPods could hold 15 000 songs, 25 000 photos, or 150 hours of video, and in 2010, iPods could hold 40 000 songs, 25 000 photos, or 200 hours of video.[25] Music fans go to the Apple iTunes music store or elsewhere to download songs and get suggestions for new music they might enjoy. Of course, today you can do all this on your smartphone—you don't even need an iPod to have a portable music player. From radio to smartphone—an amazing journey in dynamically continuous innovation! (See Exhibit 7.10.)

Trevor Schoenfeld writer/co-creator. Courtesy of Lisa Greenberg, co-creator.

Exhibit 7.9

A continuous innovation makes the product easier to use.

Exhibit 7.10

Convergence is one of the most talked-about forms of dynamically continuous innovations in the digital world. This term means the coming together of two or more technologies to create new systems that provide greater benefit than the original technologies alone. Originally, the phone, organizer, and camera all came together in the Palm Treo and then the BlackBerry. Cable companies now provide cellular service, home phone lines, and high-speed Internet. Today, devices like Apple's iPad integrate numerous functions on one platform.

discontinuous innovation
A totally new product that creates major changes in the way we live.

Discontinuous Innovations

To qualify as a **discontinuous innovation**, the product must create *major changes* in the way we live. Consumers must learn a great deal to use a discontinuous innovation because no similar product has ever been on the market. Major inventions such as the airplane, the car, and the television radically changed modern lifestyles. Another discontinuous innovation, the personal computer—facilitated by the advent of the Internet—changed the way we shop and allowed more people to work from home or anywhere else. What's the next discontinuous innovation? Is there a product out there already that will gain that distinction? Usually, marketers only know for sure through 20–20 hindsight; in other words, it's tough to plan for the next big one (what the computer industry calls "the killer app").

How Do We Measure Innovation?

Innovation is a complicated item to try to measure. This is because it involves not only marketing, but the firm's overall culture, leadership, and processes in place that foster innovation. Here's a short list of measures that, when taken as a whole, can provide a firm's "innovation report card":

Firm Strategy

* How aware are organization members of a firm's goals for innovation?
* How committed is the firm and its leadership to those goals?
* How actively does the firm support innovation among its organization members? Are there rewards and other incentives in place to innovate? Is innovation part of the performance evaluation process?
* To what degree do organization members perceive that resources are available for innovation (money and otherwise)?

Firm Culture

* Does the organization have an appetite for learning and trying new things?
* Do organization members have the freedom and security to try things, fail, and then go forward to try different things?

Outcomes of Innovation

* What is the number of innovations launched in the past three years?
* What percentage of revenue is attributable to launches of innovations during the past three years?[26]

new product development (NPD)
The phases by which firms develop new products including idea generation, product concept development and screening, marketing strategy development, business analysis, technical development, test marketing, and commercialization.

OBJECTIVE

Show how firms develop new products.
(pp. 246–252)

New Product Development

Building on our knowledge of different types of innovations, we'll now turn our attention to how firms actually develop new products. There are seven phases in the process of **new product development** (or **NPD**), as shown in Figure 7.8: idea generation, product concept development and screening, marketing strategy development, business analysis, technical development, test marketing, and commercialization. Let's take a look at what goes on during each of these phases.

Phase 1: Idea Generation

In the initial **idea generation** phase of product development, marketers use a variety of sources to come up with great new product ideas that provide customer benefits and that are compatible with the company mission. Sometimes ideas come from customers. Ideas also come from salespeople, service providers, and others who have direct customer contact.

Often firms use marketing research activities such as the *focus groups* we discussed in Chapter 3 in their search for new product ideas. For example, a company such as TSN that is interested in developing new channels or changing the focus of its existing channels might hold focus-group discussions across different groups of sports-minded viewers to get ideas for new types of programs.

idea generation
The first step of product development in which marketers brainstorm for products that provide customer benefits and are compatible with the company mission.

Phase 2: Product Concept Development and Screening

The second phase in developing new products is **product concept development and screening**. Although ideas for products initially come from a variety of sources, it is up to marketers to expand these ideas into more complete product concepts. Product concepts describe what features the product should have and the benefits those features will provide for consumers.

Everyone knows that McDonald's makes the world's best French fries—a fact that has annoyed archrival Burger King (BK) for decades. Unfortunately for BK, the chain achieved technical success but not commercial success when the chain invested heavily to out-fry McDonald's. BK's food engineers came up with a potato stick coated with a layer of starch that makes the fry crunchier and keeps the heat in to stay fresh longer. Burger King created 19

product concept development and screening
The second step of product development in which marketers test product ideas for technical and commercial success.

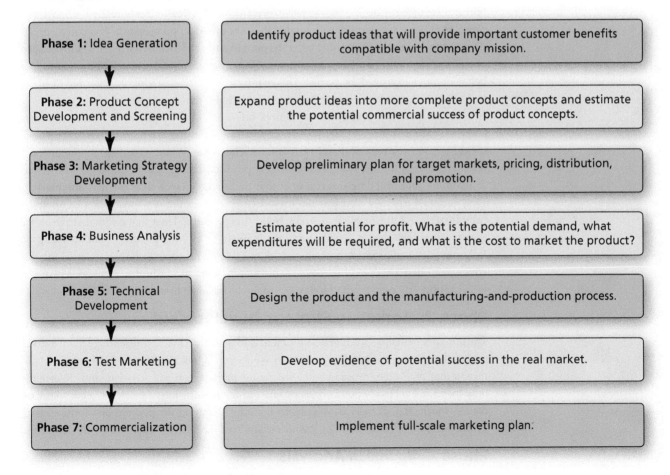

Figure 7.8 Phases in New Product Development
New product development generally occurs in seven phases.

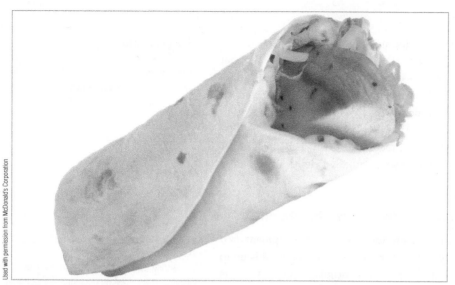

Exhibit 7.11

Some companies encourage their designers to "think outside the box" by exposing them to new ideas, people, and places. The director of culinary innovation at McDonald's is a trained chef. He runs the chain's test kitchen and is challenged with the tricky assignment of finding new menu concepts that work within the context of a McDonald's restaurant. Recently, he came up with a simple idea: He took the breaded chicken the chain uses in its Chicken Selects strips, topped it with shredded cheese and lettuce, added a few squirts of creamy ranch dressing, and wrapped it in a flour tortilla. McDonald's dubbed it the "Snack Wrap" and put it on the menu at a starter price of $1.29. A hit was born—the Snack Wrap is one of the most successful new product launches in company history with sales exceeding projections by 20 percent!

pages of specifications for its new contender, including a requirement that there must be an audible crunch present for seven or more chews. The $70 million rollout of the new product included a "Free Fryday" when BK gave away 15 million orders of fries to customers, placed lavish advertising during the Super Bowl, and engineered official proclamations by the governors of three states. Unfortunately, the new fry was a "whopper" of a product failure. Burger King blamed the product failure on inconsistent cooking by franchisees and a poor potato crop, but a more likely explanation is that consumers simply did not like the fry as well as those they might find at certain (golden) archrivals. Just because it's new doesn't always make it better.

On the other hand, did you know that Sony was originally working *with* archrival Nintendo to create a new video game system? Executives from both sides were happy because Nintendo had the market, the intellectual property, and the know-how to do it and Sony had the financial means. However, Nintendo eventually decided not to move forward with the deal and essentially ditched Sony. The man at Sony who would have headed the joint project approached the company's president and told him that Sony could enter the market anyway without the big N's help because of the headway it had already made. Sony's CEO reportedly felt dishonoured by Nintendo's behaviour and approved the project. This rebuff resulted in Sony's highly regarded PlayStation, which went on to seriously challenge Nintendo for gaming supremacy.[27]

In new product development, failures often come as frequently (or more so) than successes (see Exhibit 7.11). BK's French fry failure illustrates the importance of screening ideas for *both* their technical and their commercial value. When screening, marketers and researchers examine the chances that a new product concept might be successful, while at the same time weeding out concepts that have little chance to make it in the market. They estimate *technical success* when they decide whether the new product is technologically feasible—is it possible to actually build this product? Then they estimate *commercial success* when they decide whether anyone is likely to buy the product. And speaking of technology-driven product innovation, look at Table 7.3 for some examples of "pushing the envelope"—new products that have their roots in some old-fashioned ones. But proceed with caution; any new product today can easily be obsolete tomorrow!

Phase 3: Marketing Strategy Development

The third phase in new product development is to develop a marketing strategy to introduce the product to the marketplace, a process we began to talk about back in Chapter 1. This means that marketers must identify the target market, estimate its size, and determine how they can effectively position the product to address the target market's needs. And, of course, marketing strategy development includes planning for pricing, distribution, and promotion expenditures both for the introduction of the new product and for the long run.

Phase 4: Business Analysis

business analysis
The step in the product development process in which marketers assess a product's commercial viability.

Once a product concept passes the screening stage, the next phase is a **business analysis**. Even though marketers have evidence that there is a market for the product, they still must

| Table 7.3 | Products Yesterday, Today, and Tomorrow |

YESTERDAY	TODAY	TOMORROW
Typewriter	Personal Computer	**Dragon Naturally Speaking 10** This software for computers, MP3 players, and cell phones allows you to send e-mails and instant messages, and surf the Web with voice commands. *$100,* **www.shop.nuance.com**.
Drinking Fountain	Bottled Water	**AquaSafeStraw** This portable, reusable straw removes 99.9 percent of waterborne bacteria from any water. $45, **www.aquasafestraw.com**.
Wine Cork	Synthetic Cork and Screwcap	**Skybar Wine Preservation and Optimization System** A wine bar that stores, refrigerates, pours, and preserves three bottles of wine for up to 10 days after opening. *$1,000,* **www.skybarhome.com**.
Blackboard	Dry-Erase Board	**Interactive Smart Board** This whiteboard lets you write in multiple colors, erase, zoom, and move objects around with your fingers or with one of its ink-free pens. *From $700 to $4,450,* **www.smarttech.com**.
Payphone	Cell Phone	**Google's Nexus One** This smartphone with a 3.7-inch touchscreen, a 5-megapixel camera, and Wi-Fi connectivity will help you forget the scary parts of the movie *Phone Booth. $529,* **www.google.com/phone**.
Mechanical Bell	Electronic Bell (Alarm Clock)	**Soleil Sun Alarm Ultima SA-2008** The 10-watt bulb grows brighter as wake-up time approaches, just like the sunrise. *$90,* **www.soleilsunalarm.com**.
Boombox	Sony Walkman	**Sony Ericsson Portable Bluetooth Speaker MBS-100** Set the speakers around the room, keep your MP3 player or smartphone in your pocket, and DJ from the dance floor. *$64,* **www.amazon.com**.
Hotel Key	Electronic Keycard	**Openways** This system sends a series of tones to a cell phone that will unlock doors. The manufacturer planned to install it in three major U.S. hotel chains and two Las Vegas casinos in 2010. **www.openways.com**.
Road Map	GPS Navigation Device	**Garmin nüvi 1690** This GPS provides real-time fuel prices, movie times, and Google Local search, along with hands-free calling. *$500,* **www.target.com**.
Cheque book	Debit Card	**RedLaser App** This iPhone application lets you scan a barcode for an item, comparison-shop online, and purchase with your phone. *$2,* **www.iTunes.com**.
Lick-and-Stick Stamp	Peel-and-Press Stamp	**Stamps.com** Pay a monthly service charge on this site, and you can print official USPS postage directly onto your envelopes. No licking, no peeling, no nothing. *$16 per month,* **www.stamps.com**.
Photo Film	Digital Camera	**Sony Cyber-shot DSC-HX5V/B** This still camera was the first of its kind to include GPS, a compass, and full advanced video codec high-definition video capability. *$350,* **www.sonystyle.com**.

Source: Lauren Parajon, "Last Tech," *Southwest Airlines Spirit Magazine,* March 2010, pp. 82–92. Prices are as of this writing.

Tech and Trends

Facebook for NPD

During Phase Two of the new product development process—product concept development and screening—marketers frequently engage in qualitative research approaches, such as focus groups, to enhance the development process. In the past, these have largely been in person rather than via social networking. Today, however, Facebook looms as an effective way to get feedback. Some firms offer free product samples on their Facebook pages, but Splenda (the artificial sweetener folks) took a different approach. The company planned to introduce a pocket-size spray form of the product it called Splenda Mist. It turned to Facebook to gather valuable input from its target, women 25 years and older, as well as from those outside its target. Splenda used the data to plan the next stages of the product rollout.

"It's another tool in which to expose a product idea, concept, or actual product to a particular target in a very efficient way," said Ivy Brown, group product director at Splenda. Tom Arrix, VP-US sales at Facebook, said that other consumer-products companies were taking note of the ever-expanding possibilities the social network has to offer. "There are conversations on an ongoing basis about brands out there," Arrix said. "Innovative brand teams can come into a platform like Facebook, glean insights, and make real-time decisions." Facebook offers marketers the following guidelines for conducting market research on their site:

- The Facebook experience won't replace a formal focus group, but it can provide plenty of information that you wouldn't necessarily gather in street sampling.
- As people interact with you in such an engagement, reach of your product can be extended. Just as in the off-line world, if you are giving participants samples, you want to make sure you don't run out.
- Once you've invited people in, don't abandon them. Give them regular product updates to encourage a sense of ownership.[28]

find out if the product can make a profitable contribution to the organization's product mix. How much potential demand is there for the product? Does the firm have the resources it will need to successfully develop and introduce the product?

The business analysis for a new product begins with assessing how the new product will fit into the firm's total product mix. Will the new product increase sales, or will it simply cannibalize sales of existing products? Are there possible synergies between the new product and the company's existing offerings that may improve visibility and the image of both? And what are the marketing costs likely to be?

Phase 5: Technical Development

technical development
The step in the product development process in which company engineers refine and perfect a new product.

prototypes
Test versions of a proposed product.

patent
A legal mechanism to prevent competitors from producing or selling an invention, aimed at reducing or eliminating competition in a market for a period of time.

test marketing
Testing the complete marketing plan in a small geographic area that is similar to the larger market the firm hopes to enter.

If it survives the scrutiny of a business analysis, a new product concept then undergoes **technical development** in which a firm's engineers work with marketers to refine the design and production process (Exhibit 7.12). For example, when Sharp Electronics began to look into the next big product innovation in home television, it soon settled on the potential of adding a fourth colour pixel (yellow) to the standard palette of red, green, and blue. The company labelled the innovation "Quattron technology" and introduced it in 2010 via an innovative promotional campaign that featured actor George Takei (Sulu in the original *Star Trek* series) dressed in an engineer's lab coat talking in very scientific terms about the distinct advantages of Quattron over competitors' mere three-pixel sets. The translation of technical developments into terms that consumers can easily understand and respond to is a critical marketing function, and Sharp did this brilliantly without ever attempting to show the new screen in its ads (after all, how could you view the fourth colour if you don't already have a Quattron set?). The reaction on Takei's face when he sees the picture and says "Oh man, you have to see it" was enough to drive consumers into Best Buy and other electronics retailers in droves to see if they could tell the difference between Quattron and all the other sets lined up on the wall.[29]

The better a firm understands how customers will react to a new product, the better its chances of commercial success. For this reason, typically, a company's research and development (R&D) department usually develops one or more physical versions or **prototypes** of the product. Prospective customers may evaluate these mockups in focus groups or in field trials at home.

Prototypes also are useful for people within the firm. Those involved in the technical development process must determine which parts of a finished good the company will make and which ones it will buy from other suppliers. If it will be manufacturing goods, the company may have to buy new production equipment or modify existing machinery. Someone has to develop work instructions for employees and train them to make the product. When it's a matter of a new service process, technical development includes decisions such as which activities will occur within sight of customers versus in the "backroom," and whether the company can automate parts of the service to make delivery more efficient.

Technical development sometimes requires the company to apply for a **patent**. Because patents legally prevent competitors from producing or selling the invention, this legal mechanism may reduce or eliminate competition in a market for many years so that a firm gains some "breathing room" to recoup its investments in technical development.

Phase 6: Test Marketing

The next phase of new product development is **test marketing**. This means the firm tries out the complete marketing plan—the distribution, advertising, and sales promotion—in a small geographic area that is similar to the larger market it hopes to enter.

Exhibit 7.12

New flavours need to undergo rigorous technical development so companies can be sure they will satisfy consumers' expectations.

There are both pluses and minuses to test marketing. On the negative side, test marketing is extremely expensive. It can cost over a million dollars to conduct a test market even in a single city. A test market also gives the competition a free look at the new product, its introductory price, and the intended promotional strategy—and an opportunity to get to the market first with a competing product. On the positive side, when they offer a new product in a limited area, marketers can evaluate and improve the marketing program. Sometimes, test marketing uncovers a need to improve the product itself. At other times, test marketing indicates product failure; this advanced warning allows the firm to save millions of dollars by "pulling the plug."

For years, Listerine manufacturer Warner-Lambert (now owned by McNeil-PPC) wanted to introduce a mint-flavoured version of the product to compete with Procter & Gamble's Scope (it originally introduced this alternative under the brand Listermint). Unfortunately, every time Warner-Lambert tried to run a test market, P&G found out and poured substantial extra advertising and coupons for Scope into the test market cities. This counter-attack reduced the usefulness of the test market results for Warner-Lambert when its market planners tried to decide whether to introduce Listermint nation-wide. Because P&G's aggressive response to Listermint's test marketing actually *increased* Scope's market share in the test cities, there was no way to determine how well Listermint would actually do under normal competitive conditions. Warner-Lambert eventually introduced Listermint nationally but achieved only marginal success, so the company pulled it from the market. Today, Listerine itself is available in mint flavour as well as several other choices.[30]

As we saw in Chapter 3, because of the potential problems and expense of test marketing, marketers instead may use special computer software to conduct simulated tests that imitate the introduction of a product into the marketplace. These simulations allow the company to see the likely impact of price cuts and new packaging—or even to determine where in the store it should try to place the product. The process entails gathering basic research data on consumers' perceptions of the product concept, the physical product, the advertising, and other promotional activity. The test market simulation model uses that information to predict the product's success much less expensively (and more discreetly) than a traditional test market. As this simulated test market technology improves, traditional test markets may become a thing of the past.

Phase 7: Commercialization

The last phase in new product development is **commercialization**. This means the launching of a new product, and it requires full-scale production, distribution, advertising, sales promotion—the works. For this reason, commercialization of a new product cannot happen overnight. A launch requires planning and careful preparation. Marketers must implement trade promotion plans that offer special incentives to encourage dealers, retailers, or other members of the channel to stock the new product so that customers will find it on store shelves the very first time they look. They must also develop consumer sales promotions such as coupons. Marketers may arrange to have point-of-purchase displays designed, built, and delivered to retail outlets. If the new product is especially complex, customer service employees must receive extensive training and preparation.

As launch time nears, preparations gain a sense of urgency—like countdown to blastoff at NASA. Sales managers explain special incentive programs to salespeople. Soon the media announce to prospective customers why they should buy and where they can find the new product. All elements of the marketing program, ideally, come into play like a carefully planned lift-off of a Delta rocket.

Innovation genius and Apple CEO Steve Jobs was never one to squelch pre-commercialization hype about his new product introductions. It has been estimated that Apple achieved pre-launch publicity worth over $500 million on the iPhone before it spent a penny on any advertising. The introduction of the iPad in 2010 was no exception to the Apple hype-creation machine. Jobs claimed that the iPad would offer an experience superior to that

commercialization
The final step in the product development process in which a new product is launched into the market.

Ethical and Sustainable Decisions in the Real World

When P&G's new Pampers Dry Max diaper was introduced in 2009, it was hailed by company executives as "the iPod of baby care." It was supposed to be a breakthrough innovation: a diaper that could legitimately claim to be 20 percent thinner and way more absorbent than its Pampers predecessors or the competition, based on credible consumer tests. Dry Max uses revamped, more permeable material, which allowed P&G to eliminate the traditional mesh liner and a considerable amount of wood-based fibre that was in the old Pampers, resulting in considerably less environmental impact.

But since the introduction, a group of mostly Internet-centred critics have been increasingly vocal. Review boards like www.diapers.com quickly lit up with highly negative comments by users (one source says the online reviews are 5 to 1 negative). Anti–Dry Max Facebook pages cropped up; the main page for critics boasts more than 7000 members. The noise undercut what P&G had expected to be positive buzz about the most significant inno-

ETHICS CHECK:
Find out what other students taking this course **would do** and **why** on www .mypearsonmarketinglab .com

vation in 24 years for Pampers, P&G's largest global brand that has sales approaching $9 billion.

So what is the "big deal," so to speak? Basically, according to information released from a $5 million class-action lawsuit on the matter filed against P&G in mid-2010, the key issue is increased cases of diaper rash, sometimes severe, among babies who wear Dry Max. P&G is "shifting blame to parents" for the rashes, according to the complaint, "implying that [the parents] fail to change their children's diapers with sufficient frequency." In general, P&G has taken a tough stance; it denies that Dry Max contributes to increased cases of diaper rash and cites data that the malady affects more than 2.5 million babies, or one in four, at any given moment, and of those, 250 000 cases typically are severe. The company claims that a small number of vocal critics dominate the online activity and cites evidence that one person has posted complaints on at least 75 sites, with more than 50 posts on P&G's own Pampers Village.

The marketers at P&G for Dry Max need to get on top of this situation quickly in order to avoid broad and long-term damage to the Pampers brand new product introduction.

If you were in charge of marketing for Dry Max at P&G, would you recall all the new Pampers Dry Max diapers?

☐YES ☐NO

product adoption
The process by which a consumer or business customer begins to buy and use a new good, service, or idea.

diffusion
The process by which the use of a product spreads throughout a population.

tipping point
In the context of product diffusion, the point when a product's sales spike from a slow climb to an unprecedented new level, often accompanied by a steep price decline.

of netbooks, and that the 75+ million people who already owned iPhones and iPod touches already knew how to use the iPad, which uses the same operating system and touch-screen interface. Some analysts think the iPad is a tougher sell than its prior product brethren in part because it is a more complex innovation than those. The questions about the iPad's introduction provide a perfect segue to the next section on adoption and diffusion of innovation.

7 Adoption and Diffusion of New Products

OBJECTIVE
Explain the process of product adoption and the diffusion of innovations.
(pp. 252–258)

In the previous section, we talked about the steps marketers take to develop new products from generating ideas to launch. Now we'll look at what happens *after* that new product hits the market—how an innovation spreads throughout a population.

A painting is not a work of art until someone views it. A song is not music until someone sings it. In the same way, new products do not satisfy customer wants and needs until the customer uses them. **Product adoption** is the process by which a consumer or business customer begins to buy and use a new good, service, or idea.

The term **diffusion** describes how the use of a product spreads throughout a population. One way to understand how this process works is to think about a new product as if it were a computer virus that spreads from a few computers to infect many machines. A brand like UGG, for example, might just slog around—sometimes for years and years. At first only a small number of people buy it, but change happens in a hurry when the process reaches the moment of critical mass. This moment of truth is called the **tipping point**.[31] For example, Sharp created the low-price, home/small-office fax in 1984 and sold about 80 000 in that year. There was a slow climb in the number of users for the next three years. Then, suddenly, in 1987 enough people had faxes that it made sense for everyone to have one—Sharp sold a million units that year as it reached its tipping point. Along with such diffusion almost always comes steep price declines—today you can buy a fax machine at Amazon for about $80.[32] The question, of course, is how long a market for traditional fax machines can be sustained, given all the other document transmission possibilities today, including scan and send via e-mail attachment. That's a question we'll take up in the next chapter.

After they spend months or even years to develop a new product, the real challenge to firms is to get consumers to buy and use the product, and to do so quickly so they can recover the costs of product development and launch. To accomplish this, marketers must understand the product adoption process. In the next section, we'll discuss the stages in this process. We'll also see how consumers and businesses differ in their eagerness to adopt new products and how the characteristics of a product affect its adoption (or "infection") rate.

Stages in Consumers' Adoption of a New Product

Whether the innovation is better film technology or a better mousetrap, individuals and organizations pass through six stages in the adoption process. Figure 7.9 shows how a person goes from being unaware of an innovation through the stages of awareness, interest, evaluation, trial, adoption, and confirmation. At every stage, people drop out of the process, so the proportion of consumers who wind up using the innovation on a consistent basis is a fraction of those who are exposed to it.

Awareness

Awareness that the innovation exists at all is the first step in the adoption process. To educate consumers about a new product, marketers may conduct a massive advertising campaign: a **media blitz**. For example, let's revisit our discussion of Sharp's new Quattron technology. To raise awareness that it was going to incorporate this new attribute in its AQUOS TV line, the company fed bits and pieces about the product into a variety of outlets, including previews of George Takei's "Oh, my!" commercial on Twitter, Facebook, and YouTube. Within three days the ad had been viewed more than 100 000 times via Sharp's dedicated YouTube channel—remember, that's FREE promotion for Sharp![33]

media blitz
A massive advertising campaign that occurs over a relatively short time frame.

At this point, some consumers will say, so there's a new television set out there, or so what? Many of these consumers, of course, will fall by the wayside and thus drop out of the adoption process. But this strategy works for new products when at least some consumers see a new product as something they want and need and just can't live without.

Interest

For some of the people who become aware of a new product, a second stage in the adoption process is *interest*. In this stage, a prospective adopter begins to see how a new product might satisfy an existing or newly realized need (see Exhibit 7.13). Interest also means

Figure 7.9 Six Stages in Consumers' Adoption of a New Product
Consumers pass through six *stages* in the adoption of a new product—from being unaware of an innovation to becoming loyal adopters. The right marketing strategies at each stage help ensure a successful adoption.

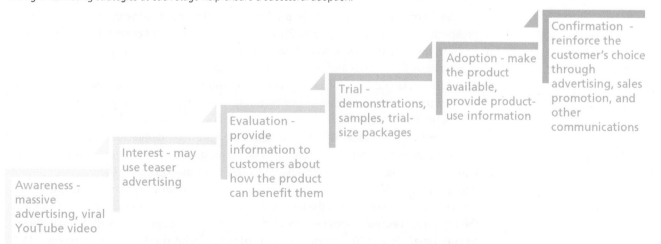

Exhibit 7.13

In the interest stage, a prospective adopter begins to see how a new product might satisfy an existing or newly realized need. This juice drink bills itself as "a new way to eat fruit."

impulse purchase

A purchase made without any planning or search effort.

that consumers look for and are open to information about the innovation. Volkswagen's Jetta, for instance, developed a certain panache with the young 20s crowd a number of years ago, in 2000 or so. But, as those 20- and 30-something car buyers of today started having families and needed bigger cars with more carrying space, they began to lose interest in the Jetta. To get the lucrative young-parent group interested in the product again, Volkswagen reverted to a stronger emphasis on safety and also touted the quality and reliability virtues of German engineering. Today the brand has become successful in its positioning, which takes advantage of German mechanical prowess but at a lower price point than the other cars from Deutschland.[34] Marketers often design teaser advertisements that give prospective customers just enough information about the new product to make them curious and to stimulate their interest. Despite marketers' best efforts, however, some more consumers drop out of the process at this point.

Evaluation

In the *evaluation* stage, we weigh the costs and benefits of the new product. On the one hand, for complex, risky, or expensive products, people think about the innovation a great deal before they will try it. For example, a firm will carefully evaluate spending hundreds of thousands of dollars on manufacturing robotics prior to purchase. Marketers for such products help prospective customers see how such products can benefit them.

But as we've seen in the case of impulse products, sometimes little evaluation may occur before someone decides to buy a good or service. A person may do very little thinking before she makes an **impulse purchase** like the virtual Tamagotchi (Japanese for "cute little egg") pets. For these goods, marketers design the product to be eye-catching and appealing to get consumers to notice the product quickly. Tamagotchis certainly did grab the attention of consumers—40 million of them bought the first generation of Tamagotchis. Toymaker Bandai Co. has since come out with a new generation of Tamagotchis—the current version allows the pet owner to control aspects of the Tamagotchi's life such as career choices and who they eventually become. Bandai's newest tagline for the product is "Start livin' the Tamagotchi life!"—a not-too-veiled reference to virtual worlds such as Second Life.[35] Some potential adopters will evaluate an innovation positively enough to move on to the next stage. Those who do not think the new product will provide adequate benefits drop out at this point.

Trial

Trial is the stage in the adoption process when potential buyers will actually experience or use the product for the first time. Often marketers stimulate trial when they provide opportunities for consumers to sample the product. Even if the trial is satisfactory, however, some prospective buyers still won't actually adopt the new product because it costs too much. Initially, this was the case with GPS systems in cars. Consumers could try out the system in rental cars from Hertz and Avis, but the price to have this option in new vehicles (over $2000) understandably put off most prospective customers. Today, as prices dip below $100 at Walmart and elsewhere, many more consumers buy the units for their own cars and order them with new vehicles.[36]

Travel through some US airports and you'll see Dell demonstration kiosks—a big departure from the company's usual focus on online direct marketing. That's because there is a drawback to online directing marketing: some consumers just can't stand to buy without first touching, holding, and using a product—in short, conducting a "trial." Interestingly, people also buy Dells right at the kiosks. In retrospect, this is not too surprising, given that the passenger demographics tend toward 24 to 49 years of age, most with annual household incomes above $70 000—just the type of people who want the latest computer. Dell also showcases the PC gaming power of its higher-end computers at Gamestop locations around the country, in part because of its acquisition of Alienware, a long-time champion of high-powered PC gaming. For gamers, it's really important to touch, feel, and experience the product first-hand before they buy.[37]

Adoption

In the *adoption* stage, a prospect actually buys the product (Hallelujah!). If the product is a consumer or business-to-business good, this means buying the product and learning how to use and maintain it. If the product is an idea, this means that the individual agrees with the concept.

Does this mean that all individuals or organizations that first choose an innovation are permanent customers? That's a mistake many firms make. Marketers need to provide follow-up contacts and communications with adopters to ensure they are satisfied and remain loyal to the new product over time.

Confirmation

After she adopts an innovation, a customer weighs expected versus actual benefits and costs. Favourable experiences make it more likely that she will become a loyal adopter as her initially positive opinions result in *confirmation*. Of course, nothing lasts forever—even a loyal customer may decide that a new product no longer meets her expectations and reject it (sort of like dropping a boyfriend). Some marketers feel that reselling the customer in the confirmation stage is important. They provide advertisements, sales presentations, and other communications to reinforce a customer's choice.

Innovator Categories

As we saw earlier, *diffusion* describes how the use of a product spreads throughout a population. Of course, marketers prefer their entire target market to immediately adopt a new product, but this is not the case. Consumers and business customers differ in how eager or willing they are to try something new, lengthening the diffusion process by months or even years. Some people like to try new products. Others are so reluctant you'd think they're afraid of anything new (do you know anyone like that?). As Figure 7.10 shows, there are five categories of adopters: innovators, early adopters, early majority, late majority, and laggards.[38] To understand how the adopter categories differ, we'll focus on an example of the adoption of one specific technology from the past that has had a big impact on all of us today—Wi-Fi (wireless fidelity).

Innovators

Innovators make up roughly the first 2.5 percent of adopters. This segment is extremely adventurous and willing to take risks with new products. Innovators are typically well educated, younger, better off financially than others in the population, and worldly. Innovators who were into new technology knew all about Wi-Fi before other people had heard of it. Because innovators pride themselves on trying new products, they purchased laptops with Wi-Fi cards way back in 1999 when Apple Computer first introduced them in its laptops.

innovators
The first segment (roughly 2.5 percent) of a population to adopt a new product.

early adopters
Those who adopt an innovation early in the diffusion process, but after the innovators.

Early Adopters

Early adopters, approximately 13.5 percent of adopters, buy product innovations early in the diffusion process but not as early as innovators. Unlike innovators, early adopters

Figure 7.10 Categories of Adopters
Because consumers differ in how willing they are to buy and try a new product, it often takes months or years for most of the population to adopt an innovation.

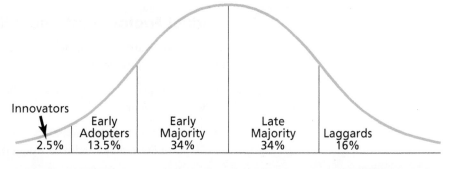

are very concerned about social acceptance, so they tend to gravitate toward products they believe will make others think they are cutting-edge or fashionable. Typically, they are heavy media users and often are heavy users of the product category. Others in the population often look to early adopters for their opinions on various topics, making early adopters key to a new product's success. For this reason, marketers often target them in their advertising and other communications efforts.

Columnists who write about personal technology for popular magazines like *Business-Week* were testing Wi-Fi in mid2000. They experienced some problems (like PCs crashing when they set up a wireless network at home), but still they touted the benefits of wireless connectivity. Road warriors adopted the technology as Wi-Fi access spread into airports, hotels, city parks, and other public spaces. Intel, maker of the Centrino mobile platform, launched a major campaign with Condé Nast's *Traveler* magazine and offered a location guide to T-Mobile hotspots nation-wide.

Early Majority

early majority
Those whose adoption of a new product signals a general acceptance of the innovation.

The **early majority**, roughly 34 percent of adopters, avoid being either first or last to try an innovation. They are typically middle-class consumers and are deliberate and cautious. Early majority consumers have slightly above-average education and income levels. When the early majority adopts a product, we no longer consider it new or different—it is, in essence, already established. By 2002, Wi-Fi access was available in over 500 Starbucks cafes, and monthly subscription prices were dropping rapidly (from $30 to $9.95 per month).

Late Majority

late majority
The adopters who are willing to try new products when there is little or no risk associated with the purchase, when the purchase becomes an economic necessity, or when there is social pressure to purchase.

Late majority adopters, about 34 percent of the population, are older, even more conservative, and typically have lower-than-average levels of education and income. The late majority adopters avoid trying a new product until it is no longer risky. By that time, the product has become an economic necessity or there is pressure from peer groups to adopt. By 2004, Wi-Fi capability was being bundled into almost all laptops and you could connect in mainstream venues like McDonald's restaurants and sports stadiums. Cities across the country began considering blanket Wi-Fi coverage throughout the entire town through WiMax technology.

Laggards

laggards
The last consumers to adopt an innovation.

Laggards, about 16 percent of adopters, are the last in a population to adopt a new product. Laggards are typically lower in social class than other adopter categories and are bound by tradition. By the time laggards adopt a product, it may already be superseded by other innovations. By 2006, it would have seemed strange if Wi-Fi or a similar capability was not part of the standard package in even the lowest-priced laptop computer, and people began to become annoyed if Wi-Fi access wasn't available just about everywhere they might go.[39]

Understanding these adopter categories allows marketers to develop strategies that will speed the diffusion or widespread use of their products. For example, early in the diffusion process, marketers may put greater emphasis on advertising in special-interest magazines to attract innovators and early adopters. Later they may lower the product's price or come out with lower-priced models with fewer "bells and whistles" to attract the late majority. We will talk more about strategies for new and existing products in the next chapter.

Product Factors That Affect the Rate of Adoption

Not all products are successful, to say the least. Let's see if you've ever heard of these classic boo-boos in new product introduction:

- Crystal Pepsi—Same Pepsi taste but clear in colour. Consumers didn't equate the look with the flavour.
- Clairol Look of Buttermilk shampoo—Consumers pondered what exactly was the "Look of Buttermilk" and why would they want it?

- Betamax video player—Sony refused to allow anyone to make the players and the entire rest of the industry went to VHS format.

- Snif-T-Panties—Yes, women's underwear that smelled like bananas, popcorn, whiskey, or pizza. What were they thinking![40]

The reason for most product failures is really pretty simple—consumers did not perceive that the products satisfied a need better than competitive products already on the market. If you could predict which new products will succeed and which will fail, you'd quickly be in high demand as a marketing consultant by companies worldwide. That's because companies make large investments in new products, but failures are all too frequent. Experts suggest that as much as 95 percent of all new products fail.[41] As you might expect, a lot of people try to develop research techniques that enable them to predict whether a new product will be hot or not.

Researchers identify five characteristics of innovations that affect the rate of adoption: relative advantage, compatibility, complexity, trialability, and observability.[42] The degree to which a new product has each of these characteristics affects the speed of diffusion. It may take years for a market to widely adopt a new product. Let's take a closer look at the humble microwave oven—a product that was highly innovative in its early days but now is generally a low-priced staple of every kitchen (and every college apartment and residence)—as an example to better understand why each of these five factors is important.

- **Relative advantage** describes the degree to which a consumer perceives that a new product provides superior benefits. In the case of the microwave oven, consumers in the 1960s did not feel that the product provided important benefits that would improve their lives. But by the late 1970s, that perception had changed because more women had entered the workforce. The 1960s woman had all day to prepare the evening meal, so she didn't need the microwave. In the 1970s, however, when many women left home for work at 8:00 AM and returned home at 6:00 PM, an appliance that would "magically" defrost a frozen chicken and cook it in 30 minutes provided a genuine advantage.

- **Compatibility** is the extent to which a new product is consistent with existing cultural values, customs, and practices. Did consumers see the microwave oven as being compatible with existing ways of doing things? Hardly. Cooking on paper plates? If you put a paper plate in a conventional oven, you'll likely get a visit from the fire department. By anticipating compatibility issues early in the new-product development stage, marketing strategies can address such problems in planning communications programs, or there may be opportunities to alter product designs to overcome some consumer objections.

- **Complexity** is the degree to which consumers find a new product or its use difficult to understand. Many microwave users today haven't a clue about how a microwave oven cooks food. When appliance manufacturers introduced the first microwaves, they explained that this new technology causes molecules to move and rub together, which creates friction that produces heat. Voilà! Cooked pot roast. But that explanation was too confusing for many people to understand in the 1950s and 60s.

- **Trialability** is the ease of sampling a new product and its benefits. Marketers took a very important step in the 1970s to speed up adoption of the microwave oven—product trial. Just about every store that sold microwaves invited shoppers to visit the store and sample an entire meal cooked in a microwave.

- **Observability** refers to how visible a new product and its benefits are to others who might adopt it. The ideal innovation is easy to see. For example, for a generation of kids, scooters like the Razor became the hippest way to get around as soon as one preteen saw her friends flying by. That same generation observed its friends trading Pokémon

Palo Hawken

APPLYING ▽ Complexity

Palo and his colleagues realized they were better off with a simple, focused message to make it more likely that consumers would adopt their new Bossa Nova beverage product. ➡

relative advantage
The degree to which a consumer perceives that a new product provides superior benefits.

compatibility
The extent to which a new product is consistent with existing cultural values, customs, and practices.

complexity
The degree to which consumers find a new product or its use difficult to understand.

trialability
The ease of sampling a new product and its benefits.

observability
How visible a new product and its benefits are to others who might adopt it.

cards and wanted to join in. In the case of the microwave, it wasn't quite so readily observable for its potential adopters—only close friends and acquaintances who visited someone's home would likely see an early adopter using it. But the fruits of the microwave's labours—tasty food dishes—created lots of buzz at office water coolers and social events and its use spread quickly.

Now that you've learned the basics of creating a product, read "Real People, Real Choices: How It Worked Out" to see which strategy Palo Hawken selected for Bossa Nova.

Here's my choice. . .

Real **People**, Real **Choices**

Why do you think Palo chose Option 3?

1 Option   2 Option   3 Option

How It Worked Out at Bossa Nova

Bossa Nova clung to Options 1 and 2 for many months. Then Palo and his colleagues took the leap and chose Option 3. They created Bossa Açai juice in three flavours. Bossa Nova took its first order from Whole Foods Market and went on to be picked up by most other grocery retailers in the United States.

To learn the whole story, visit www.mypearsonmarketinglab.com.

Objective Summary ➡ Key Terms ➡ Apply

CHAPTER 7
Study Map

1. Objective Summary (pp. 222-223)

Articulate the value proposition.

Products can be physical goods, services, ideas, people, or places. A good is a *tangible* product, something that we can see, touch, smell, hear, taste, or possess. In contrast, *intangible* products—services, ideas, people, places—are products that we can't always see, touch, taste, smell, or possess. Marketers think of the product as more than just a thing that comes in a package. They view it as a bundle of attributes that includes the packaging, brand name, benefits, and supporting features in addition to a physical good. The key issue is the marketer's role in creating the value proposition in order to develop and market products appropriately.

Key Terms

good, p. 222

intangibles, p. 222

attributes, p. 222

2. Objective Summary (pp. 223-224)

Explain the layers of a product.

A product may be anything tangible or intangible that satisfies consumer or business-to-business customer needs. Products include goods, services, ideas, people, and places. The core product is the basic product category benefits and customized benefit(s) the product provides. The actual product is the physical good or delivered service, including the packaging and brand name. The augmented product includes both the actual product and any supplementary services, such as warranty, credit, delivery, installation, and so on.

Key Terms

core product, p. 224

actual product, p. 224

augmented product, p. 224

3. Objective Summary (pp. 225–228)

Describe how marketers classify products.

Marketers generally classify goods and services as either consumer or business-to-business products. They further classify consumer products according to how long they last and by how they are purchased. Durable goods provide benefits for months or years, whereas nondurable goods are used up quickly or are useful for only a short time. Consumers purchase convenience products frequently with little effort. Customers carefully gather information and compare different brands on their attributes and prices before buying shopping products. Specialty products have unique characteristics that are important to the buyer. Customers have little interest in unsought products until a need arises. Business products are for commercial uses by organizations. Marketers classify business products according to how they are used, for example, equipment; maintenance, repair, and operating (MRO) products; raw and processed materials; component parts; and business services.

Key Terms

durable goods, p. 225

nondurable goods, p. 225

convenience product, p. 226

staples, p. 227

impulse products, p. 227

emergency products, p. 227

shopping products, p. 227

intelligent agents, p. 227

specialty products, p. 227

unsought products, p. 227

equipment, p. 228

maintenance, repair, and operating (MRO) products, p. 228

raw materials, p. 228

processed materials, p. 228

component parts, p. 228

4. Objective Summary (pp. 229–243)

Understand the importance of services as products.

Services are products that are intangible and that are exchanged directly from producer to customer without ownership rights.

Generally, services are acts that accomplish some goal and may be directed either toward people or toward an object. Both consumer services and business-to-business services are important parts of the economy. Important service characteristics include the following: (1) intangibility (they cannot be seen, touched, or smelled), (2) perishability (they cannot be stored), (3) variability (they are never exactly the same from one time to the next), and (4) inseparability from the producer (most services are produced, sold, and consumed at the same time).

In reality, most products are a combination of goods and services. Some services are goods-dominant (i.e., tangible products are marketed with supporting services). Some are equipment- or facility-based (i.e., the creation of the service requires elaborate equipment or facilities). Other services are people-based (i.e., people are actually a part of the service marketed).

Like goods, services include both a core service, or the basic benefit received, and augmented services, including innovative features and convenience of service delivery. Banking and brokerages, computer software, music, travel, dating services, career services, distance learning, and medical care are among some of the services available on the Internet. Marketers know that both the social elements of the service encounter (i.e., the employee and the customer) and the physical evidence including the servicescape are important to a positive service experience.

The customer's perception of service quality is related to prior expectations. Because services are intangible, evaluation of service quality is more difficult, and customers often look for cues to help them decide whether they have received satisfactory service. Marketers improve customers' perceptions of services by designing important search qualities, experience qualities, and credence qualities.

SERVQUAL is a multiple-item scale used to measure consumer perceptions of service quality across dimensions of tangibles, reliability, responsiveness, assurance, and empathy. Gap analysis measures the difference between customer expectations of service quality and what actually occurred. Using the critical incident technique, service firms can identify the specific contacts between customers and service providers that create dissatisfaction. When service quality does fail, marketers must understand the points at which failures occur and take fast action.

Services industries will continue to play a key role in the growth of both Canada and the global economy. There is now a new dominant logic for marketing that redefines service as the central (core) deliverable and the actual physical products sold as comparatively incidental to the value proposition. Services will provide many new and exciting job opportunities for future marketers as changing demographics, globalization, technological advance, and the proliferation of information all shape the future of services.

Key Terms

intangibility, p. 230

perishability, p. 230

capacity management, p. 230

variability, p. 230

inseparability, p. 231

service encounter, p. 231

disintermediation, p. 231

5. Objective Summary (pp. 244–246)

Understand the importance and types of product innovations.

Innovations are anything consumers perceive to be new. Understanding new products is important to companies because of the fast pace of technological advancement, the high cost to companies for developing new products, and the contributions to society that new products can make. Marketers classify innovations by their degree of newness. A continuous innovation is a modification of an existing product, a dynamically continuous innovation provides a greater change in a product, and a discontinuous innovation is a new product that creates major changes in people's lives.

Key Terms

6. Objective Summary (pp. 246–252)

Show how firms develop new products.

In new product development, marketers generate product ideas from which product concepts are first developed and then screened. Next they develop a marketing strategy and conduct a business analysis to estimate the profitability of the new product. Technical development includes planning how the product will be manufactured and may mean obtaining a patent. Next, the effectiveness of the new product may be assessed in an actual or a simulated test market. Finally, the product is launched, and the entire marketing plan is implemented.

Key Terms

7. Objective Summary (pp. 252–258)

Explain the process of product adoption and the diffusion of innovations.

Product adoption is the process by which an individual begins to buy and use a new product, whereas the diffusion of innovations is how a new product spreads throughout a population. The stages in the adoption process are awareness, interest, trial, adoption, and confirmation. To better understand the diffusion process, marketers classify consumers—according to their readiness to adopt new products—as innovators, early adopters, early majority, late majority, and laggards.

Five product characteristics that have an important effect on how quickly (or if) a new product will be adopted by consumers are relative advantage, compatibility, product complexity, trialability, and observability. Similar to individual consumers, organizations differ in their readiness to adopt new products based on characteristics of the organization, its management, and characteristics of the innovation.

Key Terms

Chapter **Questions** and **Activities**

Concepts: Test Your Knowledge

1. What is the difference between the core product, the actual product, and the augmented product?
2. What is the difference between a durable good and a nondurable good? What are the main differences among convenience, shopping, and specialty products?
3. What is an unsought product? How do marketers make such products attractive to consumers?
4. What types of products are bought and sold in business-to-business markets?
5. What are intangibles? How do basic marketing concepts apply to marketing of intangibles?
6. What is the service continuum? What are goods-dominated services, equipment- or facility-based services, and people-based services?
7. What are core and augmented services? How do marketers increase market share with augmented services?
8. What dimensions do consumers and business customers use to evaluate service quality? How do marketers measure service quality?
9. What is the so-called "new dominant logic for marketing"? Why is it especially relevant to someone just starting a career in business (either in marketing or otherwise)?
10. What is a new product? Why is understanding new products so important to marketers? What are the types of innovations?
11. List and explain the steps marketers undergo to develop new products.
12. What is a test market? What are some pros and cons of test markets?
13. Explain the stages a consumer goes through in the adoption of a new product.
14. List and explain the categories of adopters.
15. What product factors affect the rate of adoption of innovations?
16. Explain how organizations may differ in their willingness to buy and use new industrial products.

Activities: Apply What You've Learned

1. Assume that you are the director of marketing for the company that has developed a tablet to outdo the iPad. How would you go about convincing the late majority to go ahead and adopt it—especially since they still haven't quite caught onto the iPad yet?
2. Assume that you are employed in the marketing department of a firm that is producing a hybrid automobile. In developing this product, you realize that it is important to provide a core product, an actual product, and an augmented product that meets the needs of customers. Develop an outline of how your firm might provide these three product layers in the hybrid car.
3. You are currently a customer for a postsecondary education, a very expensive service product. You know that a service organization can create a competitive advantage by focusing on how the service is delivered after it has been purchased—making sure the service is efficiently and comfortably delivered to the customer. Develop a list of recommendations for your school for improving the delivery of its service. Consider both classroom and non-classroom aspects of the educational product.
4. Firms go to great lengths to develop new product ideas. Sometimes new ideas come from brainstorming, in which groups of individuals get together and try to think of as many different, novel, creative—and hopefully profitable—ideas for a new product as possible. With a group of other students, participate in brainstorming for new product ideas for one of the following (or some other product of your choice):

   • A backpack with some desirable new features
   • A combination shampoo and body wash
   • A new type of university

   Then, with your class, screen one or more of the ideas for possible further product development.

Marketing Metrics: Exercise

The chapter provides a discussion on measuring innovation and outlines some important metrics related to firm strategy, firm culture, and outcomes of innovation—an "Innovation Report Card." Apple is often cited as an example of a highly innovative firm—one that is highly engaged in new product development and continuous product innovation. Their success, both with consumers and in the financial markets, has been incredible in recent years. Between the unveiling of the iPad in late January 2010 and its first sale in early April, Apple's stock rose more than 10 percent by riding on the hype around the new product. Most firms would like to come even close to the success Apple achieves through innovation.

Review the questions in the chapter section "Measuring Innovation." Your job is to go to the Apple Web site and also to review some articles and news stories online about Apple's new product introductions. Look for evidence to be able to answer the metrics questions related to innovation as applied to Apple. How does Apple score on the "Innovation Report Card"?

Choices: What Do You Think?

1. Technology is moving at an ever-increasing speed, and this means that new products enter and leave the market faster than ever. What are some products you think technology might be able to develop in the future that you would like? Do you think these products could add to a company's profits?
2. In this chapter, we talked about the core product, the actual product, and the augmented product. Does this mean that marketers are simply trying to make products that are really the same seem different? When marketers understand these three layers of the product and develop products with this concept in mind, what are the benefits to consumers? What are the hazards of this type of thinking?

3. Discontinuous innovations are totally new products—something seldom seen in the marketplace. What are some examples of discontinuous innovations introduced in the past 50 years? Why are there so few discontinuous innovations? What products have companies recently introduced that you believe will end up being regarded as discontinuous innovations?
4. Consider the differences in marketing to consumer markets versus business markets. Which aspects of the processes of product adoption and diffusion apply to both markets? Which aspects are unique to one or the other? Provide evidence of your findings.
5. In this chapter, we explained that knockoffs are slightly modified copies of original product designs. Should knockoffs be illegal? Who is hurt by knockoffs? Is the marketing of knockoffs good or bad for consumers in the short run? in the long run?
6. Many not-for-profit and religious organizations have found that they can be more successful by marketing their ideas. What are some ways that these organizations market themselves that are similar to and différent from the marketing by for-profit businesses? Is it ethical for houses of worship and religious organizations to spend money on marketing? Why or why not?

Miniproject: Learn by Doing

What product characteristics do consumers think are important in a new product? What types of service components do they demand? Most important, how do marketers know how to develop successful new products? This miniproject is designed to let you make some of these decisions.

1. Create (in your mind) a new product item that might be of interest to students such as yourself. Develop a written description and possibly a drawing of this new product.
2. Show this new product description to a number of your fellow students who might be users of the product. Ask them to tell you what they think of the product. Some of the questions you might ask them are the following:

- What is your overall opinion of the new product?
- What basic benefits would you expect to receive from the product?
- What about the physical characteristics of the product? What do you like? dislike? What would you add? delete? change?
- What do you like (or would you like) in the way of product packaging?
- What sort of services would you expect to receive with the product?
- Do you think you would try the product? How could marketers influence you to buy the product?

Develop a summary based on what you found. Include your recommendations for changes in the product and your beliefs about the potential success of the new product.

Marketing in **Action** Case   Real Choices at KFC

If there is no bread, is it really a sandwich? That's the question that many customers are asking the Kentucky Fried Chicken (KFC) fast-food retail chain. In 2010, KFC released its latest addition to its menu, the "Double Down." KFC promotes the new item in its advertisements, stating that it is "so much 100-percent premium chicken, we didn't have room for a bun." The sandwich is an attempt to grow revenue in a very competitive business. The United States has the largest fast-food market in the world. Many competitors offer products that are considered the same, and the rivallry compels prices that constrain profit margins.

KFC began in a gas station in North Corbin, Kentucky, during the Great Depression. The success of the eating establishment called Sanders Court & Café led to expansion. The first Kentucky Fried Chicken retail store opened in 1952 in South Salt Lake, Utah. Eventually expanding to Canada, by the early 1960s Kentucky Fried Chicken was sold in over 600 franchised outlets. Since that time, the fast-food restaurant has changed ownership multiple times. Today the brand is owned by Yum! Brands and is based in Louisville, Kentucky. There are more than 14 000 KFC outlets in more than 80 countries and territories around the world, serving some 12 million customers each day.

According to KFC.com, the Double Down "features two thick and juicy boneless white meat chicken filets (Original Recipe® or Grilled), two pieces of bacon, two melted slices of Monterey Jack and pepper jack cheese and Colonel's Sauce." Although it was initially offered on a limited-time basis, KFC decided to add the item to its menu permanently. The company's change of course was related to strong sales driven in part by people eating the sandwich on YouTube and popular television personality Stephen Colbert consuming one on *The Colbert Report* television show. KFC reports that the launch is one of their most successful ever.

From a nutritional standpoint, the Double Down is 540 calories, 32 grams of fat, and 1380 milligrams of sodium. The grilled version is 460 calories, 23 grams of fat and 1430 milligrams of sodium. The level of sodium in the sandwich is drawing a great deal of concern from customers and health advocacy organizations. Many critics are questioning why KFC introduced this option in the midst of building its brand image as a fast-food restaurant offering healthier menu choices. Lona Sandon, a registered dietitian and spokesperson for the American Dietetic Association, says, "You are getting large amounts of total fat and saturated fat by eating a sandwich like this, and this is very detrimental to your overall heart health."

The fast-food retail market is in a constant state of competitive fervour. Are sandwiches like the Double Down the future of fast-food chains? The dilemma for companies like KFC is, how do you appeal to both the healthy market and the indulgent market? Many customers prefer healthy choices when considering fast food. However, there are also numerous diners to whom the appeal of fat, salt, and processed carbs is irresistible. The choice of menu items must lead to long-term profitability. KFC will have to deal with any public relations concerns and the bottom line.

You Make the Call

1. What is the decision facing KFC?
2. What factors are important in understanding this decision situation?
3. What are the alternatives?
4. What decision(s) do you recommend?
5. What are some ways to implement your recommendation?

Sources: Based on Sam Sifton, "On Ingesting KFC's New Product, the 'Double Down,'" *The New York Times*, April 12, 2010, http://dinersjournal.blog s.nytimes.com/2010/04/12/on-ingesting-kfcs-new-product-the-double-down/ ?scp=1&sq=new%20product&st=cse; KFC, Wikipedia, http://en.wikipedia .org/wiki/Kfc; Double Down (sandwich), Wikipedia, http://en.wikipedia.org/ wiki/Double_Down_(sandwich); Rosemary Black, "KFC's New 'Double Down' Sandwich Swaps Bun for Two Deep-Fried Chicken Breasts, Extra Calories," *New York Daily News*, August 26, 2009; Gerrick D. Kennedy, "KFC's Double Down: A Cheesy, Sodium-Filled Sandwich—Will You Be Buying?" *Los Angeles Times*, April 12, 2010, http://dinersjournal.blogs.nytimes.com/2010/04/12/ on-ingesting-kfcs-new-product-the-double-down/?scp=1&sq=new%20 product&st=cse.

Manage the Product

Jeff Quipp

Profile

▼ A Decision-Maker

at Search Engine People Inc.

Jeff Quipp is the founder and CEO of Search Engine People Inc. (SEP), Canada's largest search marketing firm. From its inception in 2001 in the basement of Jeff's home, SEP has grown to become a force in the Canadian marketing agency scene. In each of 2009, 2010, and 2011, SEP was acknowledged as one of the 100 fastest growing companies in Canada by *Profit* magazine, a feat he claims is a result of practising what they preach.

SEP's service offerings include SEO (search engine optimization), SEM (search engine marketing or paid search marketing), SMM (social media marketing), analytics and call tracking, conversion optimization, and site mobile optimization.

Prior to launching SEP, Jeff spent time in the Bell Group of companies in various roles, including manager Traffic and Distribution for Sympatico-Lycos Inc. These experiences combined to ready Jeff for the opportunity that would become Search Engine People Inc.

Jeff holds a BA in Economics, and an MBA from Wilfrid Laurier University. He currently resides in Ajax, Ontario, with his wife and three children.

SEP was launched in September 2001 as a sole proprietorship. At that time, search was still in its infancy, and few companies had any idea what the acronym "SEO" meant. The sales process was, therefore, more about education, and the search engine optimization category could be defined as a cottage industry in the introductory phase of the product life cycle. Competition was minimal.

At the time, most of the people working in this industry were technically inclined and had little business savvy. Since this category was new and continuously evolving, colleges and universities could not adapt curriculums fast enough to train potential employees. SEP chose to differentiate itself by bringing a great deal of business savvy and acumen to the table, and by training new hires from scratch. New hires, however, would often take 6–12 months to get to a level of competency where they could "pay for themselves." To make ends meet, SEP worked with clients of all sizes, from small, one-person operations to multinationals. The strategy worked, however, and SEP became one of the best-known brands in the industry, growing by 100 percent and more in most years.

Here's my problem...

During the growth stage, the industry became "mainstream," and many more firms, both large and small, began entering the category. Competition increased sharply, for both clients and trained employees. Some of the firms entering the market were exceptionally well financed and well known (e.g., large advertising agencies, Yellow Pages Group, etc.) and could offer very lucrative salaries (given that they could avoid substantial training costs and time for employees lured from other firms). At the same time, by 2008, SEPs leadership position in the market made its 24 "SEP-trained" employees prime candidates to be "headhunted." This threatened to erode or even arrest its revenues.

The big question then became, how, with so much competition entering the market at all levels, could SEP evolve to protect and continue to grow its client and employee base as it matured through its life cycle?

Things to remember

Jeff needed to define a strategy that would allow SEP to continue to grow as it matured through its product life cycle.

While SEP's competitive advantage is threatened due to the well known and well financed companies entering the market, price is only one aspect of a product.

2 Option **Focus on better understanding client/employee needs.** In Jeff's experience, price is not the primary motive for clients and employees to remain with SEP; there are always other motives stronger than price. Some of the motives for employees would be location, flexibility, and opportunity for growth. Some of the motives for clients would be results (ROI), professionalism, ability and willingness to customize reporting, and business savvy. If SEP could identify the main motives driving each client and employee, and devise solutions specifically for each, then perhaps employee and client retention would remain very high despite the increased competition that is so common in the growth stage of the life cycle. But what if price was the primary motivation?

3 Option **Create a school.** If schools could not teach the necessary subjects adequately, then perhaps SEP, with its familiarity with the subject matter, could forge a school to teach the topics. SEP could then identify the best students for possible future employment with the company. Running a school would further define SEP as an authority in the online marketing space and consequently allow the company to retain its lead as the market grows. On the other hand, SEP's exceptional growth already had them in a resource crunch, so they might not have the time to properly set up a school.

Now, put yourself in Jeff's shoes. Which option would you choose, and why?

Jeff considered his Options 1·2·3

1 Option **Recruit from those same competitors.** If competitors could target and recruit from SEP, then surely SEP could employ a similar strategy and, likewise, target and recruit from competitors. If performed successfully, new employees would presumably be mostly trained already and paying for themselves much more quickly. SEP could then largely forgo the time and money associated with training, and move forward much faster. Competitors would have a higher cost of entry into this market and possible lag behind as SEP captured more market share. However, if SEP could easily recruit someone away from competitors, then perhaps those employees might not be the "best" candidates.

You Choose

Which **Option** would you choose, and **why**?

1. ☐YES ☐NO 2. ☐YES ☐NO 3. ☐YES ☐NO

See what **option** Jeff chose on **page 289** ➡

product management
The systematic and usually team-based approach to coordinating all aspects of a product's marketing initiative including all elements of the marketing mix.

1

OBJECTIVE

Explain the different product objectives and strategies a firm may choose.
(pp. 266–272)

Product Planning: Use Product Objectives to Decide on a Product Strategy

What makes one product fail and another succeed? It's worth repeating what we said in Chapter 2: *Firms that plan well succeed.* Product planning plays a big role in the firm's *marketing planning.* Strategies that the product plan outlines spell out how the firm expects to develop a value proposition that will meet marketing objectives. Product planning is guided by the continual process of **product management**, which is the systematic and usually team-based approach to coordinating all aspects of a product's marketing initiative, including all elements of the marketing mix. In some companies, product management is sometimes also called *brand management*, and the terms refer to essentially the same thing. The organization members that coordinate these processes are called *product managers* or *brand managers.* We'll discuss the role of these individuals in more detail later in the chapter.

As more and more competitors enter the global marketplace and as technology moves forward at an ever-increasing pace, firms create products that grow, mature, and then decline at faster and faster speeds. This means that smart product management strategies are more critical than ever. Marketers just don't have the luxury of trying one thing, finding out it doesn't work, and then trying something else.

In Chapter 7, we talked about how marketers think about products—both core and augmented—and about how companies develop and introduce new products. In this chapter, we'll finish the product part of the story as we see how companies manage products, and then we'll examine the steps in product planning that Figure 8.1 outlines. These steps include developing product objectives and the strategies required to successfully market products as they evolve from "new kids on the block" to tried-and-true favourites—and, in some cases, finding new markets for these favourites. Next, we'll discuss branding and packaging, two of the more important tactical decisions product planners make. Finally, we'll examine how firms organize for effective product management. Let's start with how firms develop product-related objectives.

When marketers develop product strategies, they make decisions about product benefits, features, styling, branding, labelling, and packaging. But what do they want to accomplish? Clearly stated product objectives provide focus and direction. They should support the broader marketing objectives of the business unit in addition to being consistent with the firm's overall mission. For example, the objectives of the firm may focus on return on investment (ROI). Marketing objectives then may concentrate on building market share and/or the unit or dollar sales volume necessary to attain that return on investment. Product objectives need to specify how product decisions will contribute to reaching a desired market share or level of sales.

To be effective, product-related objectives must be measurable, clear, and unambiguous—and feasible. Also, they must indicate a specific time frame.

Consider, for example, how fgf Brands, the manufacturer of International Fabulous Flats flatbreads, might state its product objectives:

- In the upcoming fiscal year, reduce the fat and calorie content of our products to satisfy consumers' health concerns.

- Introduce three new items this quarter to the product line to take advantage of increased consumer interest in South Asian foods.

- During the coming fiscal year, improve the Stone Baked Pizza Crust line to the extent that consumers will rate them better-tasting than the competition.

Planners must keep in touch with their customers so that their objectives accurately respond to their needs. An up-to-date knowledge of competitive product innovations also is important to develop product objectives. Above all, these objectives should consider the *long-term implications* of product decisions. Planners who sacrifice the long-term health of the firm to reach short-term sales or financial goals choose a risky course. Product planners may focus on one or more individual products at a time, or they may look at a group of product offerings as a whole. In this section, we'll briefly examine both of these approaches. We'll also look at one important product objective: product quality.

Develop Product Objectives
- For individual products
- For product lines and mixes

Design Product Strategies

Make Tactical Product Decisions
- Product branding
- Packaging and labelling design

Figure 8.1 Steps to Manage Products
Effective product strategies come from a series of orderly steps.

Objectives and Strategies for Individual Products

Everybody loves the MINI Cooper. But it wasn't just luck or happenstance that turned this product into a global sensation. Just how do you launch a new car that's only 361 cm long and makes people laugh when they see it? BMW deliberately called attention to the small size and poked fun at the car. The original launch of the MINI Cooper a few years back included bolting the MINI onto the top of a Ford Excursion with a sign, "What are you doing for fun this weekend?" BMW also mocked up full-size MINIs to look like coin-operated kiddie rides you find outside grocery stores with a sign proclaiming: "Rides $16 850. Quarters only." The advertising generated buzz in the 20- to 34-year-old target market and today the MINI is no joke.

As a smaller brand, the MINI didn't have a huge advertising budget—in fact it was the first launch of a new car in modern times that didn't include TV advertising. Instead, the MINI launched with print, outdoor billboards, and Web ads. The aim wasn't a heavy car launch but more of a "discovery process." Ads promoted "motoring" instead of driving, and magazine inserts included MINI-shaped air fresheners and pullout games. *Wired* magazine ran a cardboard foldout of the MINI, suggesting readers assemble and drive it around their desks making "putt-putt" noises. *Playboy* came up with the idea of a six-page MINI "centrefold" complete with the car's vital statistics and hobbies. By the end of its first year on the market, the MINI was the second most memorable new product of the year!

Some product strategies focus on a single new product. (As an interesting sidebar, enough customers have complained about the cramped quarters in the MINI's back seat—it is, after all, a "mini"—that BMW has since introduced a larger MINI. Now that's an oxymoron—something like a "jumbo shrimp"!)[1] Strategies for individual products may be quite different for new products, for regional products, or for mature products. For new products, not surprisingly, the objectives relate to successful introduction (see Exhibit 8.1). After a firm experiences success with a product in a local or regional market, it may decide to introduce it

Exhibit 8.1

In 2010, the five most memorable new products were Microsoft's Windows 7, Mars's Pretzel M&M's, Motorola Droid, McDonald's McCafé Real Fruit Smoothie, and Apple's iPad. Each of these products owes its success largely to exceptionally well-executed product planning and management.

nationally. Alexander Keith's, for example, started out in 1820 as a regional beer you could buy only in Nova Scotia. It took over 175 years before it was introduced to the rest of Canada and another 14 before they decided to ship to the US.

For mature products like cheddar Goldfish snack crackers that Campbell's Soup Company manufactures under its Pepperidge Farm label, product objectives may focus on bringing new life to a product while holding on to the traditional brand personality. For Goldfish, "The snack that smiles back," this means introducing a host of spin-offs—peanut butter flavoured, giant sized, multicoloured, and colour changing, to name a few. The Goldfish brand has been around since 1962, but it continues to stay fresh with 25 varieties it sells in more than 40 countries. In fact, people eat over 75 billion Goldfish per year—if strung together, enough to wrap around the earth 30 times![2]

Objectives and Strategies for Multiple Products

Although a small firm might get away with a focus on one product, a larger firm often sells a set of related products. This means that strategic decisions affect two or more products simultaneously. The firm must think in terms of its entire portfolio of products. As Figure 8.2 shows, product planning means developing *product line* and *product mix* strategies to encompass multiple offerings.

A **product line** (or product family) is a firm's total product offering to satisfy a group of target customers. For example, Procter & Gamble's (P&G's) line of cleaning products includes three different liquid dish detergent brands: Dawn stresses grease-cutting power, Ivory emphasizes mildness, and Joy is for people who want shiny dishes. To do an even better job of meeting varying consumer needs, each of the three brands comes in more than one formulation. In addition to regular Dawn, you can also buy Dawn with Bleach Alternative, Dawn Simple Pleasures (smells nice, with botanicals), Dawn Direct Foam (detergent comes out already foaming so "One pump and my dishes are done"), and Dawn Plus with Power Scrubbers ("Finally, an answer to tough, stuck-on food").[3]

product line
A firm's total product offering designed to satisfy a single need or desire of target customers.

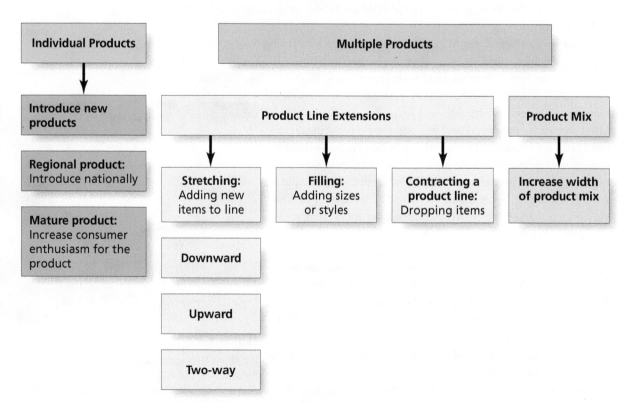

Figure 8.2 Objectives for Single and Multiple Products
Product objectives provide focus and direction for product strategies. Objectives can focus on a single product or group of products.

The **product line length** is determined by the number of separate items within the same category. We describe a large number of variations in a product line as a *full line* that targets many customer segments to boost sales potential. A *limited-line strategy*, with fewer product variations, can improve the firm's image if consumers perceive it as a specialist with a clear, specific position in the market. A great example is Rolls-Royce Motor Cars, which BMW now owns. Rolls-Royce makes expensive, handcrafted cars built to each customer's exact specifications, and for decades it has maintained a unique position in the automobile industry. Every Rolls Phantom that rolls out the factory door is truly a unique work of art.[4]

product line length
Determined by the number of separate items within the same category.

Organizations may decide to extend their product line by adding more brands or models when they develop product strategies. For example, Patagonia, Gap, and Roots extended their reach when they added children's clothing. When a firm stretches its product line, it must decide on the best direction to go. If a firm's current product line includes middle and lower-end items, an *upward line stretch* adds new items—higher-priced entrants that claim better quality or offer more bells and whistles. Hyundai decided it could tap the market for bigger, more luxurious cars and SUVs, and stretched its line upward in the form of models such as the Azera sedan, Tucson and Santa Fe SUVs, and the Entourage minivan. It positions each of these against top-end products by Toyota and Honda but prices its cars thousands of dollars less. Hyundai does the same thing in the sedan category; it offers its popular Sonata as an alternative to the pricier Accord and Camry. These product-line changes positioned Hyundai for considerable success with value-conscious consumers during the recent recession, and Hyundai (and its sister firm, Kia) took away considerable market share from Toyota and other brands—even before Toyota ran into problems with its allegedly faulty accelerators.[5]

Conversely, a *downward line stretch* augments a line when it adds items at the lower end. Here the firm must take care not to blur the images of its higher-priced, upper-end offerings. Rolex, for example, may not want to run the risk of cheapening its image with a new watch line to compete with Timex or Swatch.

In some cases, a firm may decide that its target is too small a market. In this case, the product strategy may call for a *two-way stretch* that adds products at both the upper and lower ends. Marriott Hotels, for example, added Fairfield Inns and Courtyard at the lower end and J.W. Marriott and Ritz Carlton at the upper end to round out its product line.

A *filling-out strategy* adds sizes or styles not previously available in a product category. Kraft Canada did this when it introduced 100-calorie "Thinsations" versions of its popular Oreo and Chips Ahoy! cookies. In other cases, the best strategy may be to *contract* a product line, particularly when some of the items are not profitable. For example, Heinz scrapped its "Bite Me" brand of frozen pizza snacks because of poor sales. The product, targeted to teens, failed to meet company expectations.[6]

We've seen that there are many ways a firm can modify its product line to meet the competition or take advantage of new opportunities. To further explore these strategic decisions, let's return to the "glamorous" world of dish detergents. What does P&G do if the objective is to increase market share? One possibility would be to expand its line of liquid dish detergents—as the company did with its Dawn brand when it introduced Dawn Direct Foam and other extensions. If the line extension meets a perceived consumer need the company doesn't currently address, this would be a good strategic objective.

But whenever a manufacturer extends a product line or a product family, there is risk of **cannibalization**. This occurs when the new item eats up sales of an existing brand as the firm's current customers simply switch to the new product. That may explain why P&G met consumer demands for an antibacterial dish liquid by creating new versions of the existing brands Joy and Dawn.

cannibalization
The loss of sales of an existing brand when a new item in a product line or product family is introduced.

Product Mix Strategies

A firm's **product mix** describes its entire range of products. For example, in addition to a deep line of shaving products, P&G's acquisition of Gillette a few years back gave P&G Oral-B toothbrushes, Braun oral care products, and Duracell batteries.

product mix
The total set of all products a firm offers for sale.

product mix width
The number of different product lines the firm produces.

When they develop a product mix strategy, planners usually consider the **product mix width**: the number of different product lines the firm produces. If it develops several different product lines, a firm reduces the risk of putting all its eggs in one basket. Normally, firms develop a mix of product lines that have some things in common, as can be seen in Figure 8.3.

◄──────────── **Width of Product Mix** ────────────►

Fabric and Home Care	Beauty Care	Health Care/Baby and Family Care	Snacks and Beverages
Ace Laundry and Bleach	Ausonia	Actonel	Folgers
Alomatik	Aussie	Asacol	Millstone
Ariel	Camay	Bounty	Pringles
Bold	Clairol's Herbal Essences	Charmin	Punica
Bonux	Cover Girl	Codi	Sunny Delight
Bounce	Evax	Crest	Torengos
Cascade	Giorgio	Didronel	
Cheer	Head & Shoulders	Dodot	
Dash	Hugo Boss	Eukanuba	
Dawn	Infasil	Fixodent	
Daz	Infusion 23	Iams	
Downy	Ivory Personal Care	Kandoo	
Dryel	Lacoste	Luvs	
Era	Laura Biagiotti	Macrobid	
Fairy	Lines Feminine Care	Metamucil	
Febreze	Max Factor	Pampers	
Flash	Mum Always Whisper	Pepto-Bismol	
Gain	Muse	Puffs	
Hi Wash	Natural Instincts and Hydrience	PUR	
Ivory Dish	Naturella	Scope	
Joy	Nice 'n Easy	Tempo	
Lang	Noxzema	ThermaCare	
Lenor	Olay	Vicks	
Maestro Limpio	Old Spice		
Mr. Clean/Proper	Orkid		
Myth	Pantene		
Rindex	Pert		
Salvo	Physique		
Swiffer	Rejoice		
Tide	Safeguard		
Viakal	Secret		
Vizir	SK-II		
	Sure		
	Tampax		
	Vidal Sassoon		
	Wash&Go		
	Zest		

(Left vertical axis label: Length of Product Line)

Figure 8.3 Product Line Length and Product Mix Width
A product line is a firm's total offerings that satisfy one need, whereas the product mix includes all products that a firm offers. Here we see an example of both for a selection of Procter & Gamble's extensive family of products.

Wine and spirits distributor Constellation Brands' entry into the US mainstream supermarket wine space through its acquisition of Robert Mondavi is an example of a successful product mix expansion strategy. Americans and Canadians drink more wine (and hard liquor) of late (perhaps to help them forget the recession), and the Mondavi brand gives Constellation the crown jewel in the $4+ billion *supermarket wine channel* (i.e., mass market wines that people buy in large volume where they shop for groceries rather than at specialty wine shops).[7]

Quality as a Product Objective: The Science of TQM

Product objectives often focus on **product quality**; the overall ability of the product to satisfy customers' expectations. Quality is tied to how customers *think* a product will perform, and not necessarily to some technological level of perfection. Product quality objectives coincide with marketing objectives for higher sales and market share and to the firm's objectives for increased profits.

In 1980, just when the economies of Germany and Japan were finally rebuilt from World War II and were threatening American markets, an NBC documentary on quality titled *If Japan Can Do It, Why Can't We?* demonstrated to the American public, and to American CEOs, the poor quality of American products.[8] So began the **total quality management (TQM)** revolution in American industry.

TQM is a business philosophy that calls for company-wide dedication to the development, maintenance, and continuous improvement of all aspects of the company's operations. Indeed, some of the world's most admired, successful companies—top-of-industry firms such as AMD, 3M, Bombardier, and Coca-Cola—endorse a total quality focus.

Product quality is one way that marketing adds value to customers. However, TQM as an approach to doing business is far more sophisticated and effective than simply paying attention to product quality. TQM firms promote the attitude among employees that *everybody* working there serves its customers—even employees who never interact with people outside the firm. In such cases, employees' customers are *internal customers*—other employees with whom they interact. In this way, TQM maximizes customer satisfaction by involving all employees, regardless of their function, in efforts to continually improve quality. For example, TQM firms encourage all employees, even the lowest-paid factory workers, to suggest ways to improve products—and then reward them when they come up with good ideas.

Quality Guidelines

Around the world, many companies look to the uniform standards of the International Organization for Standardization (ISO) for quality guidelines. This Geneva-based organization developed a set of criteria in 1987 to improve and standardize product quality in Europe. The **ISO 9000** is a broad set of guidelines that establishes voluntary standards for quality management. These guidelines ensure that an organization's products conform to the customer's requirements. In 1996, the ISO developed **ISO 14000** standards, which concentrate on "environmental management." This means the organization works to minimize any harmful effects it may have on the environment. Because members of the European Union and other European countries prefer suppliers with ISO 9000 and ISO 14000 certification, Canadian companies must comply with these standards to be competitive there.[9]

One way that companies can improve quality is to use the **Six Sigma** method. The term *Six Sigma* comes from the statistical term *sigma*, which is a standard deviation from the mean. Six Sigma refers to six standard deviations from a normal distribution curve. In practical terms, that translates to no more than 3.4 defects

product quality
The overall ability of the product to satisfy customers' expectations.

total quality management (TQM)
A management philosophy that focuses on satisfying customers through empowering employees to be an active part of continuous quality improvement.

ISO 9000
Criteria developed by the International Organization for Standardization to regulate product quality in Europe.

ISO 14000
Standards of the International Organization for Standardization concerned with "environmental management" aimed at minimizing harmful effects on the environment.

Six Sigma
A process whereby firms work to limit product defects to 3.4 per million or fewer.

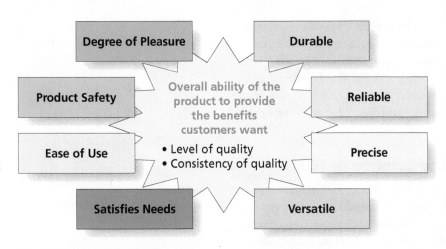

Figure 8.4 Product Quality
Some product objectives focus on quality, which is the ability of a product to satisfy customer expectations—no matter what those expectations are.

per million—getting it right 99.9997 percent of the time. As you can imagine, achieving that level of quality requires a very rigorous approach (try it on your term papers—even when you use spell check!), and that's what Six Sigma offers. The method involves a five-step process called "DMAIC" (*define, measure, analyze, improve,* and *control*). The company trains its employees in the method, and, as in karate, they progress toward "black belt" status when they successfully complete all the levels of training. Employees can use Six Sigma processes to remove defects from services, not just products. In these cases a "defect" means failing to meet customer expectations. For example, hospitals use Six Sigma processes to reduce medical errors, and airlines use the system to improve flight scheduling.

It's fine to talk about product quality, but exactly what is it? Figure 8.4 summarizes the many meanings of quality. In some cases, product quality means durability. For example, athletic shoes shouldn't develop holes after their owner shoots hoops for a few weeks. Reliability also is an important aspect of product quality—just ask Maytag and the "lonely repairman" it featured in its commercials for years. For many customers, a product's versatility and ability to satisfy their needs are central to product quality.

For other products, quality means a high degree of precision. For example, purists compare HDTVs in terms of the number of pixels and their refresh rate. Quality, especially in business-to-business products, also relates to ease of use, maintenance, and repair. Yet another crucial dimension of quality is product safety. Finally, the quality of products such as a painting, a movie, or even a wedding gown relates to the degree of aesthetic pleasure they provide. Of course, evaluations of aesthetic quality differ dramatically among people. To one person, the quality of a mobile device may mean simplicity, ease of use, and a focus on reliability in voice signal (think a basic Samsung or LG flip phone), while to another it's the cornucopia of applications and multiple communication modes available (think Apple iPhone).

2 Marketing Throughout the Product Life Cycle

OBJECTIVE
Understand how firms manage products throughout the product life cycle.
(pp. 272–276)

product life cycle (PLC)
A concept that explains how products go through four distinct stages from birth to death: introduction, growth, maturity, and decline.

Many products have very long lives, while others are "here today, gone tomorrow." The **product life cycle (PLC)** is a useful way to explain how the market's response to a product and marketing activities change, over the life of a product. In Chapter 7, we talked about how marketers go about introducing new products, but the launch is only the beginning. Product marketing strategies must evolve and change as they continue through the product life cycle.

Alas, some brands don't have long to live. Who remembers the Nash car or Evening in Paris perfume? In contrast, other brands seem almost immortal. For example, Coca-Cola has been the number-one cola brand for more than 120 years, General Electric has been the number-one light bulb brand for over a century, and Kleenex has been the number-one tissue brand for over 80 years.[10] Let's take a look at the stages of the PLC.

The Introduction Stage

Like people, products are born, they "grow up" (well, most people grow up, anyway), and eventually they die. We divide the life of a product into four separate stages. The first stage we see in Figure 8.5 is the **introduction stage**. Here customers get the first chance to purchase the good or service. During this early stage, a single company usually produces the product. If it clicks and is profitable, competitors usually follow with their own versions.

During the introduction stage, the goal is to get first-time buyers to try the product. Sales (hopefully) increase at a steady but slow pace. As is also evident in Figure 8.5, the company usually does not make a profit during this stage. Why? Research and development (R&D) costs and heavy spending for advertising and promotional efforts cut into revenue. There may also be higher distribution costs due to the lower quantities initially being shipped.

As Figure 8.6 illustrates, during the introduction stage, pricing may be high to recover the R&D costs (demand permitting) or low to attract large numbers of consumers. For example, the introductory base price of the Lexus GS 450h was $54,900, nearly the same as the BMW 550i's base price of $57,400 at the time. Lexus intended the price to appeal to consumers who are willing to pay for the GS 450h's unique combination of comfort, great gas mileage, and superb performance. The high price is also necessary so that Lexus can recover its R&D costs for this revolutionary new engineering design, and ultimately develop more hybrid products like the LS 600h L, which hit the market at $104 000.

How long does the introduction stage last? As we saw in Chapter 7's microwave oven example, it can be quite long. A number of factors come into play, including marketplace acceptance and the producer's willingness to support its product during start-up. Sales for hybrid cars started out pretty slowly except for the Prius, but now with gas prices at astronomical levels and sales reaching new heights, hybrids are well past the introduction stage. Now, electric cars like the Chevy Volt and the Nissan Leaf have replaced them.

It is important to note that many products never make it past the introduction stage. For a new product to succeed, consumers must first know about it. Then they must believe that it is something they want or need. Marketing during this stage often focuses on informing consumers about the product, how to use it, and its promised benefits. However, this isn't nearly as easy as it sounds. Would you believe that the most recent data indicate that as many as 95 percent of new products introduced each year fail? Shocking as that number is, it's true. Ever heard of Parfum Bic or Pierre Cardin frying pans? These product blunders, which must have seemed good to some product manager at the time but sound crazy now, certainly didn't last on shelves very long. Ever heard of the Microsoft "Kin" mobile phone, positioned as a product for teens and tweens? It was both introduced and subsequently withdrawn from the market in 2010—sales were abysmal (if you have one, keep it—it could be worth a fortune as a collector's item). It's noteworthy that these (as are many) product failures were backed by big companies and attached to already well-known brands. Just think of the product introduction risks for startups and unknown brands![11]

introduction stage
The first stage of the product life cycle in which slow growth follows the introduction of a new product in the marketplace.

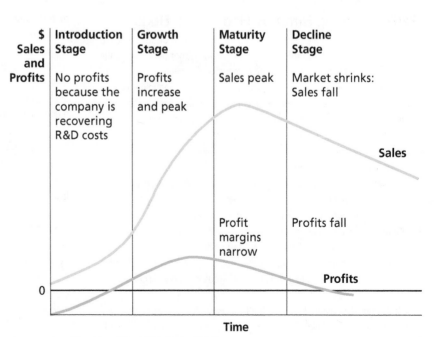

Figure 8.5 The Product Life Cycle (PLC)
The PLC helps marketers understand how a product changes over its lifetime and suggests how to modify their strategies accordingly.

Figure 8.6 Marketing Mix Strategies through the Product Life Cycle

Marketing mix strategies—the Four Ps—change as a product moves through the life cycle.

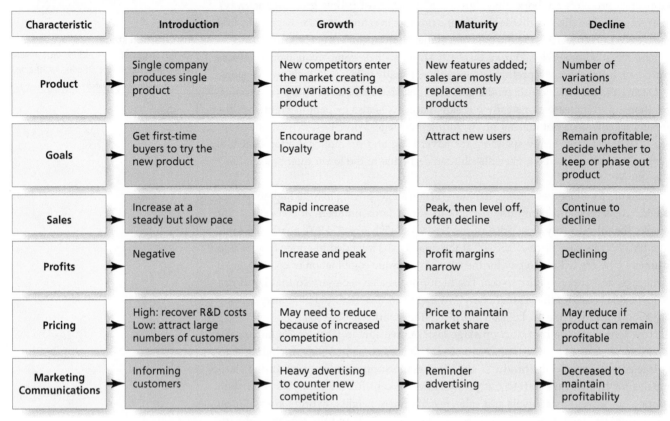

Characteristic	Introduction	Growth	Maturity	Decline
Product	Single company produces single product	New competitors enter the market creating new variations of the product	New features added; sales are mostly replacement products	Number of variations reduced
Goals	Get first-time buyers to try the new product	Encourage brand loyalty	Attract new users	Remain profitable; decide whether to keep or phase out product
Sales	Increase at a steady but slow pace	Rapid increase	Peak, then level off, often decline	Continue to decline
Profits	Negative	Increase and peak	Profit margins narrow	Declining
Pricing	High: recover R&D costs Low: attract large numbers of customers	May need to reduce because of increased competition	Price to maintain market share	May reduce if product can remain profitable
Marketing Communications	Informing customers	Heavy advertising to counter new competition	Reminder advertising	Decreased to maintain profitability

Tech and Trends

iPad's Branding Strategy Had Some "Bugs"

In its inimitable way, Apple generated an amazing amount of buzz in 2010 with its new iPad tablet. But this time, some of it might not have been quite the conversation it wanted. Many women immediately tweeted, posted, and blogged that the name evokes awkward associations with feminine hygiene products. In the hours after the iPad launch announcement, "iTampon" became one of the most popular trending topics on Twitter. Apple's communication team fielded a wave of queries on the subject but characteristically declined to comment.

Various marketing experts and pundits quickly weighed in that a lot of women, when they hear the word "pad," are automatically going to associate it with feminine hygiene products. Michael Cronan, a naming consultant in Berkeley, Calif., whose company has helped come up with brands like TiVo and Kindle, said many naming experiments show that women tend to reflexively relate words like "pad" and "flow" to bodily concerns. He's not sure Apple could have found an alternative that ties in as perfectly to its famous brands. "I think we're going to get over this fairly quickly and we'll get on with enjoying the experience."

If this wasn't enough drama for Apple, in iPad's first few days out of the chute, it turns out that folks of both sexes from Boston to Ireland complained that the verbalization of "iPad," in their regional brogue, sounds almost indistinguishable from "iPod," Apple's music player. In addition, there were more serious conflicts. It turns out two other high-tech companies already market products—albeit relatively obscure ones—called iPad and laid claim to the trademark. Fujitsu, the Japanese technology firm, applied for the iPad trademark in the United States and already was selling a $2000 hand-held device that shop clerks use to check inventory. Swiss semiconductor company STMicroelectronics owned the iPad trademark in Europe, where it uses the name as an acronym for integrated passive and active devices—which sounds less fun than playing games on a tablet.

Naming conflicts have not stopped Apple before. In 2007, on the eve of the introduction of the iPhone, technology giant Cisco Systems pointed out that it already sold an Internet handset called the iPhone. Legend has it that Apple CEO Steve Jobs personally strong-armed Cisco into submission by peppering Cisco executives with calls at all hours and telling them he was prepared to claim that Cisco was underutilizing the trademark. Cisco surrendered the trademark with a vague promise to market their products jointly—a partnership that never materialized.

"Jobs is a very tough businessman and tough negotiator," said Charles Giancarlo, a former Cisco executive who dealt directly with him on the issue. "I feel sorry for the poor guy at Fujitsu who is going to be negotiating with Steve directly."

As for the "iTampon" crowd—likely by now the technological wonders of the tablet have long since erased any confusion about what product category the brand represents.[12]

The Growth Stage

In the **growth stage**, sales increase rapidly while profits increase and peak. Marketing's goal here is to encourage brand loyalty by convincing the market that this brand is superior to others. In this stage, marketing strategies may include the introduction of product variations to attract market segments and increase market share (see Exhibit 8.2). The smartphone is an example of a product that is still in its growth stage, as world-wide sales continue to increase. Continual new product introductions (Android phones, iPhones, and others) fuel what seems, for now, to be an endless growth opportunity due to relentless product innovation as manufacturers continue to build in more and more communication features and developers create more useful apps.

When competitors appear on the scene, marketers must advertise heavily and also rely on other forms of promotion. Price competition may develop, which drives profits down. Some firms may seek to capture a particular segment of the market by positioning their product to appeal to a certain group. And, if it initially set the price high, the firm may now reduce it to meet increasing competition. This was seen with e-readers, where Amazon's Kindle2 was the big seller. After Barnes & Noble' introduced the Nook e-reader at $259, Amazon quickly followed suit. When the iPad launched, both the Kindle2 and the Nook dropped their prices to $199.

The Maturity Stage

The **maturity stage** of the product life cycle is usually the longest. Sales peak and then begin to level off and even decline while profit margins narrow. Competition gets intense when remaining competitors fight for market share (see Exhibit 8.3). Firms may resort to price reductions and reminder advertising ("Did you brush your teeth today?") to maintain market share. Because most customers have already accepted the product, they tend to buy to replace a "worn-out" item or to take advantage of product improvements. For example, almost everyone in Canada owns a TV (there are still more homes without indoor toilets than without a TV set), which means most people who buy a new set replace an older one—especially when television stations nationwide stopped using analogue signals and began to broadcast exclusively in a digital format in August 2011. TV manufacturers hope that a lot of the replacements will be sets with the latest and greatest new technology—Samsung would love to sell you a 3D television to replace that worn-out basic model. During the maturity stage, firms try to sell their product through as many outlets as possible because availability is crucial in a competitive market. Consumers will not go far to find one particular brand if satisfactory alternatives are close at hand.

To remain competitive and maintain market share during the maturity stage, firms may tinker with the marketing mix in order to extend this profitable phase for their product. Food manufacturers constantly monitor consumer trends, which of late have been heavily skewed toward healthier eating. This has resulted in all sorts of products that trumpet their low-carb, organic, or no trans-fat credentials.

The Decline Stage

We characterize the **decline stage** of the product life cycle by a decrease in product category sales. The reason may be obsolescence forced by new technology—where (other than in a museum) do you see a typewriter today? Although a single firm may still be profitable, the market as a whole begins to shrink, profits decline, there are fewer variations of the product, and suppliers pull out. In this stage, there are usually many competitors but none has a distinct advantage.

---

growth stage
The second stage in the product life cycle, during which consumers accept the product and sales rapidly increase.

maturity stage
The third and longest stage in the product life cycle, during which sales peak and profit margins narrow.

decline stage
The final stage in the product life cycle, during which sales decrease as customer needs change.

Jeff Quipp

APPLYING ▽ The Growth Stage of the Product Life Cycle

As SEP starts to enter the growth stage, Jeff needs to consider how to use the marketing mix to tweak its position in the market for the long term. ➡

Scary smart.

The big, fluffy chocolate you've always loved and ... ... than the average of the leading chocolate brands. Simply brilliant. www.3musketeers.com

3 Musketeers

A Lighter Way to Enjoy Chocolate

ALSO AVAILABLE IN *Mint*

Exhibit 8.2

New products often have an advantage at the starting gate if they are offshoots of a well-known brand.

Used with permission of The Procter & Gamble Company

FRESH BLADE. MORE COMFORTABLE SHAVE

Gillette
Fusion
POWER

Gillette
The Best a Man Can Get

Exhibit 8.3

Disposable razor blades are a mature product, so companies like Gillette need to keep introducing new variations to maintain consumers' interest.

A firm's major product decision in the decline stage is whether to keep the product at all. An unprofitable product drains resources that it could use to develop newer products. If the firm decides to keep the product, it may decrease advertising and other marketing communications to cut costs, and reduce prices if the product can still remain profitable. If the firm decides to drop the product, it can eliminate it in two ways: (1) phase it out by cutting production in stages and letting existing stocks run out, or (2) simply dump the product immediately. If the established market leader anticipates that there will be some residual demand for the product for a long time, it may make sense to keep the product on the market. The idea is to sell a limited quantity of the product with little or no support from sales, merchandising, advertising, and distribution and just let it "wither on the vine."

Now that e-commerce is a significant factor for marketing, some products that would have died a natural death in brick-and-mortar stores continue to sell online to a cadre of fans, backed by zero marketing support (translation: high profits for the manufacturer). Online purveyors such as candydirect.com sell Beeman's gum direct to consumers. In the "old days" (that is, B.I.—before the Internet), a brand like Beeman's would have been doomed by aggressive marketing budgets for all the crazy and continuous new product introductions in the category by behemoth gum competitors Wrigley and American Chicle. The life cycle of many products has certainly been lengthened by eBay—yes, you can buy Beeman's there too (as well as occasionally its sister products Clove and Blackjack gum), hopefully with current expiration dates for freshness!

Create Product Identity: Branding Decisions

OBJECTIVE

Discuss how branding strategies create product identity.
(pp. 276–283)

Successful marketers keep close tabs on their products' life cycle status, and they plan accordingly. Equally important, though, is to give that product an *identity* and a *personality*. For example, the word "Disney" evokes positive emotions around fun, playfulness, family, and casting day-to-day cares out the window. Folks pay a whole lot of money at Disney's theme parks in Florida and California to act on those emotions. Disney achieved its strong identity through decades of great branding. Branding is an extremely important (and expensive) element of product strategies. In this section, we'll examine what a brand is and how certain laws protect brands. Then we'll discuss the importance of branding and how firms make branding decisions.

What's in a Name (or a Symbol)?

brand

A name, a term, a symbol, or any other unique element of a product that identifies one firm's product(s) and sets it apart from competition.

How do you identify your favourite **brand**? By its name? By the logo (how the name appears)? By the package? By some graphic image or symbol, such as Nike's swoosh? A brand is a name, a term, a symbol, or any other unique element of a product that identifies one firm's product(s) and sets it apart from the competition. Consumers easily recognize the Coca-Cola logo, the Jolly Green Giant (a *trade character*), and the triangular, red Nabisco logo (a *brand mark*) in the corner of the box. Branding provides the recognition factor products need to succeed in regional, national, and international markets.

A brand name is probably the most used and most recognized form of branding—the name that uniquely identifies the brand owner as the source of the good or service. Smart marketers use brand names to maintain relationships with consumers "from the cradle to the grave." McDonald's would like nothing better than to bring in kids for their Happy Meal and then convert them over time to the more adult Southwest Salad (hopefully followed by a Mocha Frappe). A good brand name may position a product because it conveys a certain image or personality (Ford Mustang) or describes how it works (Drano). Brand names such as Caress and Shield help position these different brands of bath soap by saying different things about the benefits they promise. Irish Spring soap provides an unerring image of freshness (can't you just smell it now?). The Nissan Xterra combines the word *terrain* with the letter *X*, which many young people associate with extreme sports, to give the brand name a cutting-edge, off-road feel. Apple's use of "i-everything" is a brilliant branding strategy, as it conveys individuality and personalization—characteristics that Gen Y buyers prize.

How does a firm select a good brand name? Good brand designers say there are four "easy" tests: *easy to say, easy to spell, easy to read, and easy to remember*—like P&G's Tide, Cheer, Dash, Bold, Gain, Downy, and Ivory Snow (P&G is probably the undisputed branding king of all time). And the name should also "fit" four ways:

1. *Fit the target market*
2. *Fit the product's benefits*
3. *Fit the customer's culture,* and
4. *Fit legal requirements.*

A firm can claim protection for a brand even if it has not legally registered it. In Canada, *common-law protection* exists if the firm has used the name and established it over a period of time (sort of like a common-law marriage). Although a registered trademark prevents others from using it on a similar product, it may not bar its use for a product in a completely different type of business. Consider the range of "Quaker" brands: Quaker Oats (cereals), Quaker Funds (mutual funds), Quaker State (motor oil), Quaker Bonnet (gift food baskets), and Quaker Safety Products Corporation (firemen's clothing). A court applied this principle when Apple Corp., the Beatles' music company, sued Apple Computers in 2006 over its use of the Apple logo. The plaintiff wanted to win an injunction to prevent Apple Computer from using the Apple logo in connection with its iPod and iTunes products; it argued that the application to music-related products came too close to the Beatles' musical products. The judge didn't agree; he ruled that Apple Computer clearly used the logo to refer to the download service, not to the music itself.[13]

trademark
The legal term for a brand name, brand mark, or trade character; trademarks legally registered by a government obtain protection for exclusive use in that country.

Why Brands Matter

A brand is *a lot* more than just the product it represents—the best brands build an emotional connection with their customers. Think about the most popular energy drinks; they're branded Red Bull and Cheetah Power Surge, not some functionally descriptive name like Neurotransmitter Inhibitor or Keep You Awake. The point is that these brands evoke the feeling of power, not the utility of the drink.

Marketers spend huge amounts of money on new-product development, advertising, and promotion to develop strong brands. When they succeed, this investment creates **brand equity**. This term describes a brand's value over and above the value of the generic version of the product. For example, how much extra will you pay for a golf shirt with a Ralph Lauren or Lacoste logo on it than for the same shirt with no logo? The difference reflects the polo player or gator's brand equity in your mind.

brand equity
The value of a brand to an organization.

Brand equity means that a brand enjoys customer loyalty because people believe it is superior to the competition. For a firm, brand equity provides a competitive advantage because it gives the brand the power to capture and hold on to a larger share of the market and to sell at prices with higher profit margins. For example, among pianos, the Steinway name has such powerful brand equity that its market share among concert pianists is 95 percent.[14]

Marketers identify different levels of loyalty, or lack thereof, by observing how customers feel about the product. At the lowest level, customers really have no loyalty to a brand and they will change brands for any reason—often they will jump ship if they find

Figure 8.7 The Brand Equity Pyramid
The brand equity pyramid shows one way to think about escalating levels of attachment to a brand.

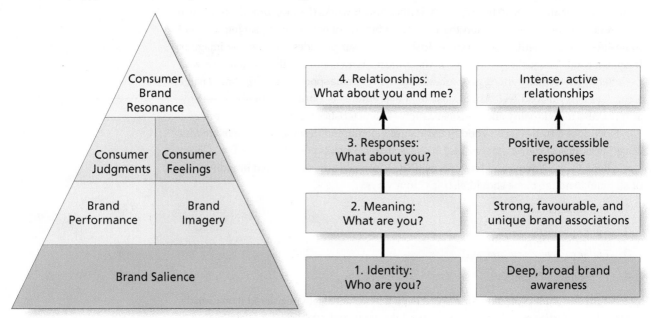

Kevin Lane Keller, *Building Customer-Based Brand Equity: A Blueprint for Creating Strong Brands,* Working Paper Series, Report 01-107, p.7. Copyright © 2001 Marketing Science Institute. Reprinted by permission.

something else at a lower price. At the other extreme, some brands command fierce devotion, and loyal users will go without rather than buy a competing brand.

Figure 8.7 shows one way to think about these escalating levels of attachment to a brand. At the lowest levels of the "brand equity pyramid," consumers become aware of a brand's existence. Moving up the pyramid, they might look at the brand in terms of what it literally does for them or how it performs relative to competitors. Going up still farther, they may think more deeply about the product and form beliefs and emotional reactions to it. The truly successful brands, however, are those that make the long climb to the top of the pyramid—they "bond" with their customers so that people feel they have a real relationship with the product. Here are some of the types of relationships a person might have with a product.

- *Self-concept attachment:* The product helps establish the user's identity. (For example, do you feel better in Ralph Lauren or Sean John clothing?)

- *Nostalgic attachment:* The product serves as a link with a past self. (Does eating the inside of an Oreo cookie remind you of childhood? How about a vintage T-shirt with a picture of Strawberry Shortcake or Mayor McCheese—both recent fashion hits?)[15]

- *Interdependence:* The product is a part of the user's daily routine. (Could you get through the day without a Tim Hortons coffee?)

- *Love:* The product elicits emotional bonds of warmth, passion, or other strong emotion. (Hershey's Kiss, anyone?)[16]

Ultimately, the way to build strong brands is to forge strong bonds with customers—bonds based on **brand meaning**. This concept encompasses the beliefs and associations that a consumer has about the brand. In many ways, the practice of brand management revolves around the management of meanings. Brand managers, advertising agencies, package designers, name consultants, logo developers, and public relations firms are just some of the collaborators in a global industry devoted to the task of *meaning management.* Table 8.1 summarizes some important dimensions of brand meaning.

brand meaning
The beliefs and associations that a consumer has about the brand.

Table 8.1	Dimensions of Brand Meaning
Dimension	**Example**
Brand identification markers	Coca-Cola's red and white colours, the Nike swoosh logo, Harley-Davidson's characteristic sound
Product attribute and benefit	Starbucks as good coffee; Canada Goose parkas and warmth
Gender	TNA, Harley-Davidson, Old Spice and masculinity; lululemon and femininity
Social class	Mercedes and the old-guard elite; Jell-O and the lower-middle class
Age	Facebook, LinkedIn, iCarly, iPod, Adult Swim
Reference group	Dockers and the casual workforce; Williams-Sonoma and the serious cook
Life stage	Dewar's and the coming of age; Parent's Soup and new mothers
Lifestyles and taste subcultures	BMW and the yuppie; Red Bull and the club culture
Place	Tim Hortons and Canada; Poutine and rural Quebec
Time and decade	Betty Crocker and the 1950s; VW and the 1960s countercultural revolution
Trends	Pottery Barn and cocooning; Starbucks and small indulgences
Traditions and rituals	May 24 weekend and outdoor activities

Nowadays, for many consumers, brand meaning builds virally as people spread its story online. "Tell to sell," once a mantra of top Madison Avenue ad agencies, is making a comeback as marketers seek to engage consumers with compelling stories rather than peddle products in hit-and-run fashion with interruptive advertising like 30-second commercials—which Gen Y and younger largely block out anyway. The method of **brand storytelling** captures the notion that powerful ideas do self-propagate when the audience is connected by digital technology. It conveys the constant reinvention inherent in interactivity, in that whether it's blogging, content creation through YouTube or other means, or social media, there will always be new and evolving perceptions and dialogues about a brand real-time. A cadre of startup firms have emerged over the last few years to aid companies in storytelling about their brand (we'll meet one of them, Campfire, in a later chapter).[17]

brand storytelling
Marketers seek to engage consumers with compelling stories about brands.

If we could name the key elements that make a brand successful, what would they be? Here is a list of 10 characteristics of the world's top brands:[18]

1. Excels at delivering the benefits customers truly desire

2. Stays relevant

3. Pricing strategy is based on consumers' perceptions of value

4. Properly positioned

5. Consistent

6. Portfolio and hierarchy make sense

7. Makes use of and coordinates a full repertoire of marketing activities to build equity

8. Managers understand what the brand means to consumers

9. Is given proper support, and that support is sustained over the long run

10. Sources of brand equity are monitored

Products with strong brand equity provide exciting opportunities for marketers. A firm may leverage a brand's equity via **brand extensions**—new products it sells with the same brand name. Because of the existing brand equity, a firm is able to sell its brand extension at a higher price than if it had given it a new brand, and the brand extension will attract new customers immediately. Of course, if the brand extension does not live up to the quality or attractiveness of its namesake, brand equity will suffer as will brand loyalty and sales.

brand extensions
A new product sold with the same brand name as a strong existing brand.

sub-branding
Creating a secondary brand within a main brand that can help differentiate a product line to a desired target group.

One other related approach is **sub-branding**, or creating a secondary brand within a main brand that can help differentiate a product line to a desired target group. Dodge, like many domestic automobile brands, has had its problems recently. Although the brand features a line of sedans, Dodge is by far best known for the Ram truck. To help clarify things for consumers, in 2009 Dodge made Ram a sub-brand (minus the Dodge name) that is marketed separately from all other Dodge products. Now the Dodge name is all about cars, which sport a new Dodge logo to clearly differentiate them, while Ram trucks have the same Ram symbol as before but now displayed more prominently than ever. In terms of future positioning, the trucks will focus on hard-core commercial and recreational users and the cars on young attitudes and lifestyles rather than age groups or price classes.[19]

Sometimes a brand's meaning simply becomes so entrenched with a particular consumer group that it can be tough to find ways to branch out and achieve new users through extensions. Take, for example, Quiksilver, whose original line of wetsuits and swimwear was aimed squarely at teenage boys who identified with the surf and skate cultures. But now, Quiksilver hopes to appeal to women who may have never hit the waves with items from sweaters to jeans. The new line is in Quiksilver's 650+ stores as well as Nordstrom and other high-end retail outlets. The competition will be fierce, though—Urban Outfitters, Anthropologie, and Liz Claiborne Lucky Brand Jeans are formidable in the 20-something female market and are aimed at the same genre of retailer as Quiksilver uses for its new line.[20]

Branding Strategies

Because brands contribute to a marketing program's success, a major part of product planning is to develop and execute branding strategies. Marketers have to determine which branding strategy approach(es) to use. Figure 8.8 illustrates the options: individual or family brands, national or store brands, generic brands, licensing, and cobranding. This decision is critical but it is not always an easy or obvious choice.

family brand
A brand that a group of individual products or individual brands share.

Individual Brands versus Family Brands

Part of developing a branding strategy is to decide whether to use a separate, unique brand for each product item—an *individual brand strategy*—or to market multiple items under the same brand name—a **family brand** or *umbrella brand* strategy. Individual brands may do a better job of communicating clearly and concisely what the consumer can expect from the product, while a well-known company like Apple may find that its high brand equity in other categories (like computers) can sometimes "rub off" on a new brand (like the iPod and iPhone). The decision often depends on characteristics of the product and whether the company's overall product strategy calls for the introduction of a single, unique product or for the development of a group of similar products (see Exhibit 8.4). For example, Microsoft serves as a strong umbrella brand for a host of diverse, individually branded products like Windows 8, Office, Xbox 360, and Bing, while P&G prefers to brand each of its household products separately.

But there's a potential dark side to having too many brands, particularly when they become undifferentiated in the eyes of the consumer due to poor positioning. Over the last decade, venerable General Motors continually suffered from muddy differentiation among the eight brands in its portfolio—namely, Chevrolet, GMC, Pontiac, Saturn, Cadillac, Buick, Hummer, and Saab. The brands often competed

Figure 8.8 Branding Strategies
Marketing managers have several options for which branding strategy or strategies to employ.

with each other—both for customers and a slice of GM's marketing budget. For example, at one time GM had four mainstream, midsize sedans. It backed its top-selling Chevy Malibu with an aggressive ad campaign, while the Buick LaCrosse, Pontiac G6, and Saturn Aura struggled to build the awareness and recognition these lines needed to compete. Fast forward to today. When GM got into financial difficulty and was "bailed out" by the government, one of the first moves for the leaner, meaner GM was to cut out all the fat in its product lines. Of the models listed above, only the Malibu is still around.[21]

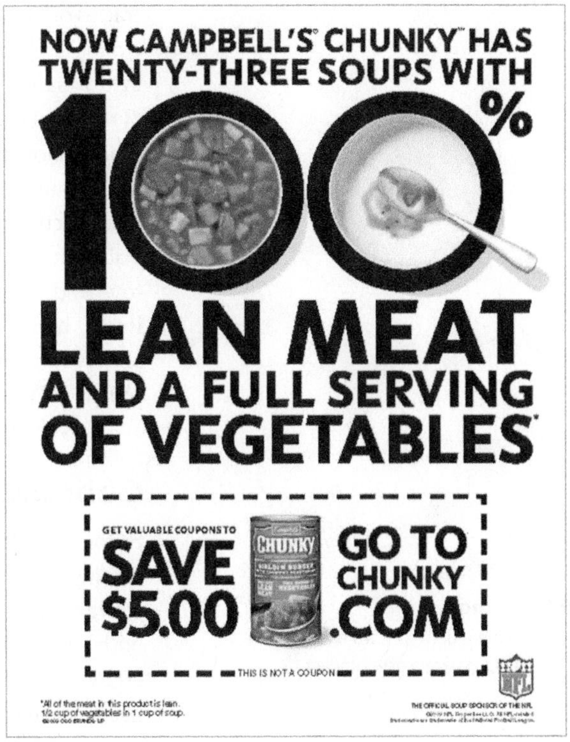

Courtesy of Campbell Soup Company; The NFL shield design is a registered trademark of the National Football League, and is used with permission.

Exhibit 8.4

Campbell's uses a family branding strategy to identify its Chunky line of soups.

National and Store Brands

Retailers today often are in the driver's seat when it comes to deciding what brands to stock and push. In addition to choosing from producers' brands, called **national or manufacturer brands**, retailers decide whether to offer their own versions. **Private-label brands**, also called *store brands*, are the retail store or chain's exclusive trade name. Canadian Tire, for example, sells store brand Motomaster Long-life antifreeze/coolant and Yardworks lawn mowers along with national brands such as Prestone and MTD. During the recent recession, store brands gained substantially in popularity for many value-conscious shoppers, and the projection is that many consumers will not switch back to the parallel national brands as the economy rebounds, because they are satisfied with the private labels.

In addition, if you stock a unique brand that consumers can't find in other stores, it's much harder for shoppers to compare "apples to apples" across stores and simply buy the brand where they find it sold for the lowest price. Loblaws, Canada's largest supermarket chain, sells over 4000 food items under the "premium quality" President's Choice label, from cookies to beef, olive oil, curtains, and kitchen utensils. Sales of President Choice items run from 30 to 40 percent of total store volumes. Under the private label, Loblaws can introduce new products at high quality but for lower prices than brand names. It can also keep entire categories profitable by its mix of pricing options. Competitors that sell only national brands can cut prices on those brands, but that hurts their overall profitability. Loblaws can bring prices down on national brands but still make money on its private-label products.[22]

national or manufacturer brands
Brands that the product manufacturer owns.

private-label brands
Brands that a certain retailer or distributor owns and sells.

Generic Brands

An alternative to either national or store branding is **generic branding**, which is basically no branding at all. Generic branded products are typically packaged in white with black lettering that names only the product itself (for example, "Green Beans"). Generic branding is one strategy to meet customers' demand for the lowest prices on standard products such as dog food or paper towels. Generic brands first became popular during the inflationary period of the 1980s when consumers became especially price conscious because of rising prices. Lately, they have experienced resurgence with the soft economy. Walmart has set the pharmacy business on end by offering some types of generic prescriptions, such as basic antibiotics, for $4.00.[23]

generic branding
A strategy in which products are not branded and are sold at the lowest price possible.

Licensing

As we saw in Chapter 2, some firms choose to use a **licensing** strategy to brand their products. This means that one firm sells another firm the right to use a legally protected brand name for a specific purpose and for a specific period of time. Why should an organization sell its name? Licensing can provide instant recognition and consumer interest in a new product, and this strategy can quickly position a product for a certain target market as it

licensing
An agreement in which one firm sells another firm the right to use a brand name for a specific purpose and for a specific period of time.

trades on the high recognition of the licensed brand among consumers in that segment. For example, distiller Brown-Forman licensed its famous Jack Daniel's bourbon name to T.G.I. Friday's to use on all sorts of menu items from shrimp to steak to chicken. In addition to this "Jack Daniel's Grill," Friday's features menu items inspired by the popular Food Network reality show *Ultimate Recipe Showdown*.[24]

A familiar form of licensing occurs when movie producers license their properties to manufacturers of a seemingly infinite number of products. Each time a blockbuster Harry Potter movie hits the screens, a plethora of Potter products packs the stores. In addition to toys and games, you can buy Harry Potter candy, clothing, all manner of back-to-school items, home items, and even wands and cauldrons. And in 2010, Harry and the gang showed up in the form of an attraction at Universal Orlando called "The Wizarding World of Harry Potter."[25]

Cobranding

cobranding
An agreement between two brands to work together to market a new product.

Frito-Lay sells K.C. Masterpiece–flavoured potato chips, and Post sells Oreo O's cereal. Strange marriages? Not at all! Actually, these are examples of a great strategy called **cobranding**, as are the Tim Hortons and Cold Stone Creamery stores. Cobranding benefits both partners when combining the two brands provides more recognition power than either enjoys alone (see Exhibit 8.5). For example, Panasonic markets a line of digital cameras that use Leica lenses, which are legendary for their superb image quality. Panasonic is known for its consumer electronics. Combining the best in traditional camera optics with a household name in consumer electronics helps both brands.

ingredient branding
A form of cobranding that uses branded materials as ingredients or component parts in other branded products.

A new and fast-growing variation on cobranding is **ingredient branding**, in which branded materials become "component parts" of other branded products.[26] This was the strategy behind the classic "Intel inside" campaign that convinced millions of consumers to ask by name for a highly technical computer part (a processor) that they wouldn't otherwise recognize if they fell over it.[27] Today, consumers can buy Breyer's ice cream with Reese's peanut butter cups, M&M's candies, Twix cookies, or Snickers bars in it. The practice of ingredient branding has two main benefits. First, it attracts customers to the host brand because the ingredient brand is familiar and has a strong brand reputation for quality. Second, the ingredient brand's firm can sell more of its product, not to mention the additional revenues it gets from the licensing arrangement.[28]

Brand Metrics

Recall from our earlier discussion that brand equity represents the value of a product with a particular brand name compared to what the value of the product would be without that brand name (think Coca-Cola versus generic supermarket soda). Companies, marketing research firms, and creative agencies create metrics of brand equity because this is an important way to assess whether a branding strategy has been successful. For example, Harris Interactive conducts its EquiTrend study twice a year to measure the brand equity of over 1000 brands. The company interviews over 25 000 consumers to determine how they feel about competing brands.[29] Each year, *BusinessWeek* applies its brand equity formulas to come up with a list of its top 100 global brands. In 2009, the top 10 in order of brand value were Coca-Cola, Microsoft, IBM, GE, Nokia, McDonald's, Google, Toyota, Intel, and Disney. Of these, McDonald's and Google moved up in the

Exhibit 8.5

Jelly Belly cobrands with other companies to offer new flavour options.

How Healthy Is Your Brand? Why Old Metrics Don't Apply and What Marketers Need to Do About It

If you ask marketers how healthy their brand is, they can usually rattle off numbers like last quarter's sales numbers or their current market share. But today that isn't enough. A brand's health can no longer be measured in years, quarters, or months. It must be managed in real time. Because the health of any brand is more vulnerable in the digital age as consumer opinion travels faster and farther, spreading like a video of a kitten playing on a piano.

Today, a brand's health is strengthened or weakened by every interaction and exposure with a consumer, which requires a more vigilant approach to managing brand perception. Indeed, 77% of marketers report that they feel their brand is at least somewhat at risk from not being engaged in social media. What's more shocking is that 73% of marketers do not even report social-media intelligence to management.

To keep track of their always-on, anytime, anywhere, unfettered-public-opinion-sharing customers, marketers must demand a new dashboard to augment classic brand metrics. There are four factors of digital influence that marketers must consider monitoring:

Volume: Brand perceptions are typically measured using representative samples of consumers. But why settle for a mere sample when more than 77% of Canadians use social media to create at least 30 billion influence impressions on products and services?

Velocity: Marketers usually perform brand-tracking studies once a year or quarterly. But that's too infrequent to monitor the impact of real-time consumer opinion, as Kenneth Cole's Twitter fiasco demonstrated — resulting in a 64% decline in brand equity scores in just three days.

Visibility: Consumers are now empowered to voice their unfiltered opinions about a brand to the general public. Already, 25% of search results for the world's 20 largest brands are linked to user-generated content.

Volatility: Brand sentiment can be increasingly unpredictable in this digital age. Gap learned this the hard way with its new logo unveiling, which received such negative consumer response online that it returned to the old logo one week later.

Source: Chris Stutzman, "How Healthy Is Your Brand," *Adage.com*, May 18, 2011, http://adage.com/article/cmo-strategy/cmos-healthy-brand/227628/.

---

rankings versus 2008, while Toyota, Intel, and Disney moved down. The estimated brand value for Coca-Cola was $68.7 billion (with a "b") in 2009.[30]

If consumers have strong, positive feelings about a brand and are willing to pay extra to choose it over others, you are in marketing heaven. Each of the following approaches to measuring brand equity has some good points and some bad points:

1. *Customer mind-set metrics* focus on consumer awareness, attitudes, and loyalty toward a brand. However, these metrics are based on consumer surveys and don't usually provide a single objective measure that a marketer can use to assign a financial value to the brand.

2. *Product-market outcomes metrics* focus on the ability of a brand to charge a higher price than the price an unbranded equivalent charges. This usually involves asking consumers how much more they would be willing to pay for a certain brand compared to others. These measures often rely on hypothetical judgments and can be complicated to use.

3. *Financial market metrics* consider the purchase price of a brand if it is sold or acquired. They may also include subjective judgments about the future stock price of the brand.

4. A team of marketing professors proposed a simpler measure that they claim reliably tracks the value of a brand over time. Their *revenue premium metric* compares the revenue a brand generates with the revenue generated by a similar private-label product (that doesn't have any brand identification). In this case, brand equity is just the difference in revenue (net price times volume) between a branded good and a corresponding private label.[31]

4 Create Product Identity: The Package and Label

OBJECTIVE

Explain how packaging and labelling contribute to product identity.

(pp. 284–287)

How do you know if the soda you are drinking is "regular" or "caffeine free"? How do you keep your low-fat grated cheese fresh after you have used some of it? Why do you always leave your bottle of new "fresh, sexy, enticing" blue Glow by JLO perfume out on your dresser so everyone can see it? The answer to all these questions is effective packaging and labelling. So far, we've talked about how marketers create product identity with branding. In this section, we'll learn that packaging and labelling decisions also help to create product identity. We'll also talk about the strategic functions of packaging and some of the legal issues that relate to package labelling.

What Packages Do

A **package** is the covering or container for a product, but it's also a way to create a competitive advantage. So, the important functional value of a package is that it protects the product. For example, packaging for computers, TV sets, and stereos protects the units from damage during shipping and warehousing. Cereal, potato chips, or packs of grated cheese wouldn't be edible for long if packaging didn't provide protection from moisture, dust, odours, and insects. The multilayered, soft box you see in Figure 8.9 prevents the chicken broth inside from spoiling. In addition to protecting the product, effective packaging makes it easy for consumers to handle and store the product. Figure 8.9 shows how packaging serves a number of different functions (see also Exhibit 8.6).

Over and above these utilitarian functions, however, the package communicates brand personality. Effective product packaging uses colours, words, shapes, designs, and pictures to provide brand and name identification for the product. In addition, packaging provides product facts including flavour, fragrance, directions for use, suggestions for alternative uses (for example, recipes), safety warnings, and ingredients. Packaging may also include warranty information, a **QR code,** and a toll-free telephone number for customer service. All of these can serve as a point of difference when everything else is very similar.

A final communication element is the barcode that is seen on most consumer packaging. The QR code is now used to share information with mobile phone and tablet users. Scanning a QR code could take a user to a Web site, play a video, show some contact or product usage information, and even provide an augmented reality experience. A **Universal Product Code (UPC)** is the set of black bars or lines printed on the side or bottom of most items sold in grocery stores and other mass-merchandising outlets. The UPC is a national system of product identification, assigning each product a unique 10-digit number. These numbers supply specific information about the type of item (grocery item, meat, produce, drugs, or a discount coupon), the manufacturer (a five-digit code), and the specific product (another five-digit code). At checkout counters, electronic scanners read the UPC bars and automatically transmit data to a computer in the cash register so that retailers can easily track sales and control inventory.

package
The covering or container for a product that provides product protection, facilitates product use and storage, and supplies important marketing communication.

QR code (quick response)
A two-dimensional code consisting of modules arranged in a square pattern that can be read by a QR barcode reader (and camera phones). The QR codes hold more data than a typical barcode and don't have to be scanned at one particular angle.

Universal Product Code (UPC)
The set of black bars or lines printed on the side or bottom of most items sold in grocery stores and other mass-merchandising outlets. The UPC, readable by scanners, creates a national system of product identification.

Courtesy of General Mills Canada Corporation

Exhibit 8.6

A range of package sizes allows a company to expand its product line.

Figure 8.9 Functions of Packaging

Great packaging provides a covering for a product, and it also creates a competitive advantage for the brand.

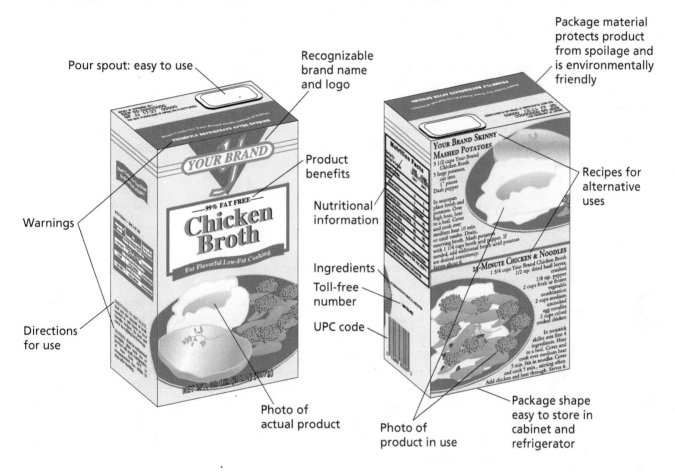

Pour spout: easy to use

Recognizable brand name and logo

Package material protects product from spoilage and is environmentally friendly

Product benefits

Warnings

Nutritional information

Recipes for alternative uses

Ingredients

Toll-free number

UPC code

Directions for use

Photo of actual product

Photo of product in use

Package shape easy to store in cabinet and refrigerator

Effective Package Design

Should the package have a zip-lock, feature an easy-to-pour spout, be compact for easy storage, be short and fat so it won't fall over, or be tall and skinny so it won't take up much shelf space? Effective package design involves a multitude of decisions (see Exhibit 8.7).

Planners must consider the packaging of other brands in the same product category. For example, when P&G introduced Pringles potato chips, it packaged them in a cylindrical can instead of in bags like Lay's and others. This was largely out of necessity, since P&G doesn't have all the local trucks to deliver to stores that Frito-Lay does, and the cans keep the chips fresher much longer. However, P&G discovered that not all customers will accept a radical change in packaging, and retailers may be reluctant to adjust their shelf space to accommodate such packages. To partly answer the concern, Pringles now comes in an amazing array of products and package types and sizes including Stix, Snack Stacks, Grab & Go, and 100 Calorie (apportioned for those who want a snack while they also watch their weight).[32]

Who says people don't judge a book by its cover? NXT, a new brand of shaving gel targeted at younger men, makes a glitzy statement on the shelf. It's sold in an arresting triangular container that lights up from the bottom to illuminate air bubbles suspended in the clear gel. The plastic is tinted blue, and when its base lights up (yes, this package requires batteries!), the whole thing looks like a miniature lava lamp or tiny fishless aquarium. How does NXT afford such a fancy container? It doesn't spend a dime on traditional advertising—the brand counts

Exhibit 8.7

A waterproof camera is a packaging innovation, and a differential advantage for Pentax.

Ethical and Sustainable Decisions in the Real World

Because of the power of branding, marketers constantly are on the lookout for new trends and ways they can connect to those trends through their packaging and labelling. One of the hottest consumer trends now is "organic" food, as in organically grown agricultural products. A lot of products use the word "organic" on their product labels. Unfortunately for consumers, there is no precise definition of "organic," so a lot of food products that carry this label may really be stretching it. Recently, the US Department of Agriculture (USDA) has addressed this controversial topic as it tries to categorize ingredients as organic or not organic.

Also, unfortunately for consumers, the big food companies are pressuring the USDA to add a whole bunch of ingredients to the organic list; these include numerous nonorganic ingredients they want to use in products that qualify to bear the "USDA Organic" seal. Remarkably, some of these are artificial food colourings that will ensure your organic food has pleasing eye appeal.

Assume you are a retailer like Whole Foods whose business (and reputation) is built around giving consumers true healthy choices. You have to decide whether to feature the "USDA Organic" designation as part of your product strategy. Under the circumstances, what would you do?

ETHICS CHECK: ↖

Find out what other students taking this course **would do** and **why** on www.mypearsonmarketinglab.com

Would you describe products labelled USDA Organic as organic to your customers even if they may contain nonorganic ingredients?

☐ **YES** ☐ **NO**

Courtesy of Pacific Natural Foods.

on its innovative package to sell the gel in the grocery aisle. What's NXT? NXT body wash and NXT deodorant, of course.[33]

Firms that wish to act in a socially responsible manner must also consider the environmental impact of packaging. Shiny gold or silver packaging transmits an image of quality and opulence, but certain metallic inks are not biodegradable. Some firms are developing innovative *green packaging* that is less harmful to the environment than other materials. Of course, there is no guarantee that consumers will accept such packaging. They didn't take to plastic pouch refills for certain spray bottle products even though the pouches may take up less space in landfills than the bottles do. They didn't like pouring the refill into their old spray bottles. Still, customers have accepted smaller packages of concentrated products such as laundry detergent, dishwashing liquid, and fabric softener.

What about the shape: square, round, triangular, or hourglass? How about an old-fashioned apothecary jar that consumers can reuse as an attractive storage container? What colour should it be? White to communicate purity? Yellow because it reminds people of lemon freshness? Brown because the flavour is chocolate? Sometimes we can trace these decisions back to personal preferences. The familiar Campbell's Soup label—immortalized as art by Andy Warhol—is red and white because a company executive many years ago liked the football uniforms at Cornell University!

Finally, there are many specific decisions brand managers must make to ensure a product's packaging reflects well on its brand and appeals to the intended target market. What graphic information should the package show? Should there be a picture of the product on the package? Should cans of green beans always show a picture of green beans? Should there be a picture that demonstrates the results of using the product, such as beautiful hair? Should there be a picture of the product in use, perhaps a box of crackers that shows them with delicious-looking toppings arranged on a silver tray? Should there be a QR code on the back that links to a Web site offering recipes or coupons? (See Exhibit 8.8.) Of course, all these decisions rest on a marketer's understanding of consumers, their ingenuity, and perhaps on a little creative luck.

Exhibit 8.8

Pacific Natural Foods, known for its award-winning natural and organic food and beverages, puts recipes, cooking demos, and easy-to-access shopping lists at consumers' finger tips with a QR code on their packaging.

Labelling Regulations

The *Consumer Packaging and Labelling Act* controls package communications and labelling in Canada. This law aims to make labels more helpful to consumers by providing useful information. An example would be the laws around bilingual labelling. Generally speaking, "all" mandatory label information must be shown in English and French, except the dealer's name and address which can appear in either language.

More recently, the requirements of the *Food and Drug Regulations* forced food marketers to make sweeping changes in how they label products. In 2002, the *Food and Drug Regulations* were amended to make nutrition labelling mandatory on most pre-packaged foods, update requirements for nutrient content claims, and permit the use of diet-related health claims on foods. These regulations force marketers to be more accurate when they describe the contents of their products. Juice makers, for example, must state how much of their product is real juice rather than sugar and water.

As of August 4, 2012, the *Food and Drug Regulations* also require that all food labels list the sources of common food allergens, gluten, and sulphites when they are present in a pre-packaged product. This applies to imported and domestically produced foods. In Canada, approximately five to six percent of young children and three to four percent of adults suffer from some kind of food allergy.

5
OBJECTIVE
Describe how marketers structure organizations for new and existing product management.
(pp. 287–288)

Organize for Effective Product Management

Of course, firms don't create great packaging, brands, or products—people do. Like all elements of the marketing mix, product strategies are only as effective as their managers make them and carry them out. In this section, we'll talk about how firms organize to manage existing products and to develop new products.

Manage Existing Products

In small firms, a single marketing manager usually handles the marketing function. She is responsible for new-product planning, advertising, working with the company's few sales representatives, marketing research, and just about everything else. But in larger firms, there are a number of managers who are responsible for different brands, product categories, or markets. Depending on the organization's needs and the market situation, product management may include brand managers, product category managers, and market managers. Let's take a look at how each operates.

Brand Managers

Sometimes a firm sells several or even many different brands within a single product category. In the detergent aisle in the supermarket, for example, P&G manufactures and markets the Bounce, Cheer, Downy, Dreft, Era, Febreze, Gain, Ivory, and Tide brands. In such cases, each brand may have its own **brand manager** who coordinates all marketing activities for a brand, including positioning, identifying target markets, research, distribution, sales promotion, packaging, and evaluating the success of these decisions. While this job title and assignment is still common throughout industry, some big firms are changing the way they allocate responsibilities. For example, today P&G's brand managers are called "business managers" and have responsibility for managing the complete business of key retail clients across all product lines. Brand managers still are responsible for positioning

brand manager
An individual who is responsible for developing and implementing the marketing plan for a single brand.

of brands and developing brand equity, but they also work heavily with folks from sales, finance, logistics, and others to serve the needs of the major retailers that comprise the majority of P&G's business.

By its very nature, the brand management system is not without potential problems. Acting independently and sometimes competitively against each other, brand managers may fight for increases in short-term sales for their own brand. They may push too hard with coupons, cents-off packages, or other price incentives to a point at which customers will refuse to buy the product when it's not "on deal." Such behaviour can hurt long-term profitability and damage brand equity.

Product Category Managers

Some larger firms have such diverse product offerings that they need more extensive coordination. Take IBM, for example. Originally known as a computer manufacturer, IBM now generates much of its revenue from a wide range of consulting and related client services across the spectrum of IT applications (and the company doesn't even sell personal computers anymore!). In cases such as IBM, organizing for product management may include **product category managers**, who coordinate the mix of product lines within the more general product category and who consider the addition of new-product lines based on client needs.

product category managers
Individuals who are responsible for developing and implementing the marketing plan for all the brands and products within a product category.

Market Managers

Some firms have developed a **market manager** structure in which different people focus on specific customer groups rather than on the products the company makes. This type of organization can be useful when firms offer a variety of products that serve the needs of a wide range of customers. For example, Saputo, a company that specializes in dairy products, specialty cheeses, and snack-cakes, sells some products directly to consumer markets, others to manufacturers, and still others to the food service industry. It serves its customers best when it focuses separately on each of these very different markets.

market manager
An individual who is responsible for developing and implementing the marketing plans for products sold to a particular customer group.

Organize for New-Product Development

You read in Chapter 7 about the steps in new-product development and learned earlier in this chapter about the importance of the introductory phase of the product life cycle. Because launching new products is so important, the management of this process is a serious matter. In some instances, one person handles new-product development, but within larger organizations new-product development almost always requires many people. Often, especially creative people with entrepreneurial skills get this assignment.

The challenge in large companies is to enlist specialists in different areas to work together in **venture teams**. These teams focus exclusively on the new-product development effort. Sometimes the venture team is located away from traditional company offices in a remote location called a "skunk works." This colourful term originated with the Skonk Works, an illicit distillery in the comic strip *Li'l Abner*. Because illicit distilleries were bootleg operations, typically located in an isolated area with minimal formal oversight, organizations adopted the colourful description "skunk works" to refer to a small and often isolated department or facility that functions with minimal supervision (not because of its odour).[34]

venture teams
Groups of people within an organization who work together to focus exclusively on the development of a new product.

Here's my choice. . .

Real **People**, Real **Choices**

1 Option   2 Option   3 Option

Why do you think Jeff chose option 2?

How It Worked Out at Search Engine People Inc.

Jeff chose Option 2, understanding client and employee needs better so that they could devise solutions that address those needs. SEP knew that clients didn't care as much about price as they did about results. Accordingly, the company focused much time and effort of being the absolute best in the market. They knew definitively before taking on a new client that they could exceed their objectives, because they did their research or due diligence in advance. If the client was price sensitive initially, SEP would let them sign on with their competitors, and realize on their own that price was only part of the equation. Many potential clients that opted for competitors initially, eventually found their way back to SEP. At the end of the day, results mattered—price did not!

SEP's office location became a key advantage to recruiting and retaining quality employees, because there weren't any other companies of their size and in their category in the Durham region, and people living in Durham really didn't want to spend 2–3 hours commuting to a big city each day. SEP also added a games room and gym at the office, brought in a massage therapist weekly, let people work flexible schedules, and held many company-sponsored events. They also spent a great deal more time trying to identify, in the interview process, individuals who were loyal and had high EQ (emotional intelligence).

SEP didn't want to recruit from competitors as, they reasoned, any employee that could be lured away from competitors could also be easily recruited away from SEP (loyalty—it's a trait). Also, those they could recruit wouldn't be exceptional, otherwise their current employer would have taken extraordinary steps to keep them and SEP would be left recruiting the most undesirable candidates.

SEP's exceptional growth already had them in a resource crunch, so creating a school was not a viable option. There were far too many opportunities for SEP to chase, so they limited themselves to those directly related to their core business. The school wasn't a core business and would have required much time and effort—time they just didn't have.

To learn the whole story, visit www.mypearsonmarketinglab.com.

Objective Summary ➡ Key Terms ➡ Apply

CHAPTER 8
Study Map

1. Objective Summary (pp. 266–272)

Explain the different product objectives and strategies a firm may choose.

Objectives for individual products may be related to introducing a new product, expanding the market of a regional product, or rejuvenating a mature product. For multiple products, firms may decide on a full- or a limited-line strategy.

Often companies decide to extend their product line with an upward, downward, two-way stretch, or with a filling-out strategy, or they may decide to contract a product line. Firms that have multiple product lines may choose a wide product mix with many different lines or a narrow mix with few. Product quality objectives refer to the durability, reliability, degree of precision, ease of use and repair, or degree of aesthetic pleasure.

Key Terms

product management, p. 266

product line, p. 268

product line length, p. 269

cannibalization, p. 269

product mix, p. 269

product mix width, p. 270

product quality, p. 271

total quality management (TQM), p. 271

ISO 9000, p. 271

ISO 14000, p. 271

Six Sigma, p. 271

2. Objective Summary (pp. 272–276)

Understand how firms manage products throughout the product life cycle.

The product life cycle explains how products go through four stages from birth to death. During the introduction stage, marketers seek to get buyers to try the product and may use high prices to recover research and development costs. During the growth stage, characterized by rapidly increasing sales, marketers may introduce new-product variations. In the maturity stage, sales peak and level off. Marketers respond by adding desirable new-product features or market-development strategies. During the decline stage, firms must decide whether to phase a product out slowly, to drop it immediately, or, if there is residual demand, to keep the product.

Key Terms

product life cycle (PLC), p. 272

introduction stage, p. 273

growth stage, p. 275

maturity stage, p. 275

decline stage, p. 275

3. Objective Summary (pp. 276–283)

Discuss how branding strategies create product identity.

A brand is a name, term, symbol, or other unique element of a product used to identify a firm's product. A brand should be selected that has a positive connotation and is recognizable and memorable. Brand names need to be easy to say, spell, read, and remember, and should fit the target market, the product's benefits, the customer's culture, and legal requirements. To protect a brand legally, marketers obtain trademark protection. Brands are important because they help maintain customer loyalty and because brand equity or value means a firm is able to attract new customers. Firms may develop individual brand strategies or market multiple items with a family or umbrella brand strategy. National or manufacturer brands are owned and sold by producers, whereas private-label or store brands carry the retail or chain store's trade name. Licensing means a firm sells another firm the right to use its brand name. In a cobranding strategy, two brands form a partnership in marketing a new product.

Key Terms

brand, p. 276

trademark, p. 277

brand equity, p. 277

brand meaning, p. 278

brand storytelling, p. 279

brand extensions, p. 279

sub-branding, p. 280

family brand, p. 280

national or manufacturer brands, p. 281

private-label brands, p. 281

generic branding, p. 281

licensing, p. 281

cobranding, p. 282

ingredient branding, p. 282

4. Objective Summary (pp. 284–287)

Explain how packaging and labelling contribute to product identity.

Packaging is the covering or container for a product and serves to protect a product and to allow for easy use and storage of the product. The colours, words, shapes, designs, pictures, and materials used in package design communicate a product's identity, benefits, and other important product information. Package designers must consider cost, product protection, and communication in creating a package that is functional, aesthetically pleasing, and not harmful to the environment. Product labelling in Canada is controlled by a number of federal laws aimed at making package labels more helpful to consumers.

Key Terms

package, p. 284

QR code, p. 284

Universal Product Code (UPC), p. 284

5. Objective Summary (pp. 287–288)

Describe how marketers structure organizations for new and existing product management.

To successfully manage existing products, the marketing organization may include brand managers, product category managers, and market managers. Large firms, however, often give new-product responsibilities to new-product managers or to venture teams, groups of specialists from different areas who work together for a single new product.

Key Terms

brand manager, p. 287

product category managers, p. 288

market manager, p. 288

venture teams, p. 288

Chapter **Questions** and **Activities**

Concepts: Test Your Knowledge

1. What are some reasons a firm might determine it should expand a product line? What are some reasons for contracting a product line? Why do many firms have a product mix strategy?
2. Why is quality such an important product strategy objective? What are the dimensions of product quality? How has e-commerce affected the need for quality product objectives?
3. Explain the product life cycle concept. What are the stages of the product life cycle?
4. How are products managed during the different stages of the product life cycle?
5. What is a brand? What are the characteristics of a good brand name? How do firms protect their brands?
6. What is a national brand? a store brand? individual and family brands?
7. What does it mean to license a brand? What is cobranding?
8. What are the functions of packaging? What are some important elements of effective package design?
9. What should marketers know about package labelling?
10. Describe some of the ways firms organize the marketing function to manage existing products. What are the ways firms organize for the development of new products?

Activities: Apply What You've Learned

1. The Internet allows consumers to interact directly through blogs and other means with other people so they can praise products they like and slam those they don't. With several of your classmates, conduct a brief survey of students and of older consumers. Find out if consumers complain to each other about poor product quality. Have they ever used a Web site to express their displeasure over product quality? Make a report to your class.
2. You may think of your college or university as an organization that offers a line of different educational products. Assume that you have been hired as a marketing consultant to examine and make recommendations for extending its product line. Develop alternatives that the college or university might consider:
   a. Upward line stretch
   b. Downward line stretch
   c. Two-way stretch
   d. Filling-out strategy

   Describe how each might be accomplished. Evaluate each alternative.
3. Assume that you are the vice president of marketing for a firm that markets a large number of specialty food items (gourmet sauces, marinades, relishes, and so on). Your firm is interested in improving its marketing management structure. You are considering several alternatives: using a brand manager structure, having product category managers, or focusing on market managers. Outline the advantages and disadvantages of each type of structure. What is your recommendation?
4. Assume that you are working in the marketing department of a major manufacturer of athletic shoes. Your firm is introducing a new product, a line of disposable sports clothing. That's right—wear it once and toss it! You wonder if it would be better to market the line of clothing with a new brand name or use the family brand name that has already gained popularity with your existing products. Make a list of the advantages and disadvantages of each strategy. Develop your recommendation.
5. Assume that you have been recently hired by Kellogg, the cereal manufacturer. You have been asked to work on a plan for redesigning the packaging for Kellogg's cereals. In a role-playing situation, present the following report to your marketing superior:
   a. Discussion of the problems or complaints customers have with current packaging
   b. Several different package alternatives
   c. Your recommendations for changing packaging or for keeping the packaging the same

Marketing Metrics: Exercise

The chapter introduces you to the concept of brand equity, an important measurement of the value vested in a product's brand in and of itself. Different formulas for calculating brand equity exist. One well-publicized approach is that of Interbrand, which annually publishes its "Best 100 Global Brands" list. Go to the location on the Interbrand Web site where they provide these rankings for the present and past years (http://www.interbrand.com/best-global-brands). Peruse the list of brands and select any five in which you have interest. For each, observe whether brand equity has been trending up or down over the past few years. How does Interbrand explain the changes (or stability) in each? Do you agree with Interbrand's assessment or do you have another opinion about why your brand's equity is what it is?

Choices: What Do You Think?

1. Brand equity means that a brand enjoys customer loyalty, perceived quality, and brand name awareness. To what brands are you personally loyal? What is it about the product that creates brand loyalty and, thus, brand equity?
2. Quality is an important product objective, but quality can mean different things for different products, such as durability, precision, aesthetic appeal, and so on. What does quality mean for the following products?

   a. Automobile
   b. Pizza
   c. Running shoes
   d. Hair dryer
   e. Deodorant
   f. Postsecondary education

3. Many times firms take advantage of their popular, well-known brands by developing brand extensions, because they know that the brand equity of the original or parent brand will be transferred to the new product. If a new product is of poor quality, it can damage the reputation of the parent brand, while a new product that is of superior quality can enhance the parent brand's reputation. What are some examples of brand extensions that have damaged and that have enhanced the parent brand equity?
4. Sometimes marketers seem to stick with the same packaging ideas year after year regardless of whether they are the best possible design. Following is a list of products. For each one, discuss what, if any, problems you have with the package of the brand you use. Then think of ways the package could be improved. Why do you think marketers don't change the old packaging? What would be the results if they adopted your package ideas?

   a. Dry cereal
   b. Laundry detergent
   c. Frozen orange juice
   d. Litre of milk
   e. Potato chips
   f. Loaf of bread

5. You learned in this chapter that it's hard to legally protect brand names across product categories; Quaker and Apple, for example, and also Delta, which is an airline and a faucet. But what about the ethics of borrowing a name and applying it to some unrelated products? Think of some new business you might like to start up. Now consider some possible names for the business that are already in use as brands in other unrelated categories. Do you think it would be ethical to borrow one of those names? Why or why not?

Miniproject: Learn by Doing

In any grocery store in any town, you will surely find examples of all the different types of brands discussed in this chapter: individual brands, family brands, national brands, store brands, and cobranded and licensed products. This miniproject is designed to give you a better understanding of branding as it exists in the marketplace.

1. Go to a typical grocery store in your community.
2. Select two product categories of interest to you: ice cream, cereal, laundry detergent, soup, paper products, and so on.
3. Make a list of the brands available in each product category. Identify what type of brand each is. Count the number of shelf facings (the number of product items at the front of each shelf) for each brand.
4. Arrange to talk with the store manager at a time that is convenient with him or her. Ask the manager to discuss the following:

   a. How the store decides which brands to carry
   b. Whether the store is more likely to carry a new brand that is an individual brand versus a family brand
   c. What causes a store to drop a brand
   d. The profitability of store brands versus national brands
   e. Other aspects of branding that the store manager sees as important from a retail perspective

5. Present a summary to your class on what you learned about the brands in your two product categories.

Marketing in **Action** Case   Real Choices at Starbucks

The Starbucks story began as a local coffee bean roaster and retailer of whole bean and ground coffee, tea, and spices. From 1971, a lone store in Seattle's Pike Place Market has grown into the largest coffeehouse company in the world. The Seattle-based Starbucks Corporation is an international coffee and coffeehouse chain with 16 635 stores in 49 countries, including 11 068 in the United States, nearly 1000 in Canada, and more than 800 in Japan. The Starbucks product selection includes drip brewed coffee, espresso-based hot drinks, other hot and cold drinks, coffee beans, salads, hot and cold sandwiches and paninis, pastry, snacks, and items such as mugs and tumblers.

One of the prominent Starbucks brands that suffered in the recession at the beginning of the 21st century is the Frappuccino. At its height, annual sales of this specialty drink exceeded $2 billion annually. However, sales have declined over the past few years. In 2010, the Frappuccino brand was estimated to represent between 15 percent and 20 percent of annual sales at Starbucks retail outlets. Dunkin' Donuts, McDonald's, along with many other smoothie chains are gearing up to snatch market share away from Starbucks with their own drinks. Since the Frappuccino plays such an important role in Starbucks' product mix, the company takes these challenges very seriously.

Frappuccino is a registered trademark of the Starbucks Corporation and it has been a brand for over 15 years. The blended ice beverage is a mixture of frappé and cappuccino, an Italian-style coffee with a topping of frothed milk. Starbucks sells it at the counter and also in bottles. Like the terms "Kleenex" and "Band-Aid," the word "Frappuccino" has become almost generic and many customers think the product is also available at other coffee purveyors.

Starbucks has tried various strategies to extend the brand name. Two new Frappuccino-flavoured ice creams are available on supermarket shelves. Vanilla Frappuccino Light, a bottled beverage, was created in a joint venture with PepsiCo. In addition, Starbucks globally introduced new blends, such as Black Sesame Frappuccino in China, and Red Bean Frappuccino in other Asian markets. Still other plans are in the works including new bottled versions, new "wacky" ingredients, and other products under the same brand banner.

The chain also is looking closely at a "however-you-want-it-Frappuccino" customization program at a premium price. Customization empowers the consumer to co-create value by beginning with an empty slate and personalizing the beverage with his or her own choice of milk, coffee intensity, syrup, and any optional toppings. Annie Young-Scrivner, global chief marketing officer for Starbucks, observes that one of the target markets for the Frappuccino is an 18- to 24-year-old woman. The customization option allows calorie-counting customers to create a nonfat milk, light syrup, and no whipped cream version with only 160 calories. According to Young-Scrivner, this market is ideal for the custom-made Frappuccino. She told *The Wall Street Journal*, "Millennials (otherwise known as Gen Y) are the iPod age group... accustomed to selecting exactly what they want. Now, they can choose an extra shot of espresso, no whipped cream, or a dab more caramel, for instance."

With any product extension strategy, there are inevitable challenges. The Frappuccino has an involved preparation process and takes longer to produce than other Starbucks beverages. This may present a problem if the new program is successful. The extra time needed for baristas to customize each drink may lead to long lines, customer irritation, more complicated employee training, and slower-than-expected sales growth. Starbucks has questions to answer concerning—among other things—pricing, training, and competition.

You Make the Call

1. What is the decision facing Starbucks?
2. What factors are important in understanding this decision situation?
3. What are the alternatives?
4. What decision(s) do you recommend?
5. What are some ways to implement your recommendation?

Sources: Based on Bruce Horovitz, "Starbucks' Strategy: Whip It Good," *USA Today*, April 27, 2010, p. 3B; Starbucks Corporation Official Web site, "Company Profile" (http://www.starbucks.com/about-us/company-information); Starbucks, *Wikipedia*, http://en.wikipedia.org/wiki/Starbucks (accessed April 28, 2010); Kevin Helliker, "At Long Last, Customized Frappuccino," *Wall Street Journal* (Eastern Edition), New York, March 17, 2010 p. D.3.

Price the Product

Real People **Profiles**

Mike Pepperdine

Profile

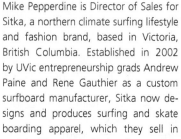

▼ A Decision Maker at Sitka

Mike Pepperdine is Director of Sales for Sitka, a northern climate surfing lifestyle and fashion brand, based in Victoria, British Columbia. Established in 2002 by UVic entrepreneurship grads Andrew Paine and Rene Gauthier as a custom surfboard manufacturer, Sitka now designs and produces surfing and skate boarding apparel, which they sell in three flagship stores (Victoria, Vancouver, and Auckland, New Zealand), as well as through commissioned sales representatives, manufacturer's agents, and distributors in 6 countries around the world. Sitka also offers a skateboard line and a surfboard line aimed at the discerning boarder who cares about quality. For the past 9 years Sitka has experienced double-digit growth and, as their Web site describes, has grown into a tight-knit family "thriving off each others' stoke."

Mike Pepperdine is an avid surfer who worked for years in a variety of marketing roles, first for Carmanah Technologies (a world leader in LED lighting applications), and then as an account executive for Suburbia Studios, a boutique advertising agency. Growing up in Summerland BC, he was a typical "ski bum" but gained valuable experience in marketing and retail sales working in his father's ski and snowboard shop. He joined his former UVic classmates Andrew and Rene at Sitka to be their Western Canada regional sales representative, and in 2010 he assumed responsibilities for Sitka's global brand sales.

Although Sitka has been experiencing double-digit growth in Canada, Australia, New Zealand, Japan, and other international locations, they have experienced significant challenges in breaking into the US market. The United States, and California in particular, is the self-proclaimed surfing capital of the world and the surfing industry adage is that you have to be successful there to be successful anywhere. While Sitka has had a US sales manager for the past five years, they have yet to make serious inroads into the US market and are currently losing money in the US market.

The current US sales manager lives in a small seaside town in Washington State. He represents Sitka and supports the Sitka line with three of his own sales representatives but he also represents a competing line of surfing apparel, plus some other complementary products. For the first five years he did this on a purely commission basis, helping Rene and Andrew break into the US market. For the past year he has been placed on a retainer, where Sitka pays him a fixed sum to represent the line, plus a commission on sales.

So far, the US sales do not cover the retainer fee and Mike is wondering whether a new approach to the US market is needed or whether they should abandon it completely. The challenge with the US market is multifaceted, but it boils down to price and positioning, especially in the T-shirt line where the challenge is the biggest. Sitka sells very high-quality T's made from bamboo and other sustainable sources of fibre. In other markets, Sitka sells their T's in high-end boutique retail stores (such as in Whistler or Banff) that focus on a boarding lifestyle segment that isn't very price sensitive and care a lot about style, image, and the "cool" factor. Sitka marks up their T's to a $12.50 distributor price. The distributors sell it to retailers for about $17.50, and the retailers sell it to customers for $27 to $34.

In the US market, the Sitka brand has been positioned with more mainstream brands like Rip Curl, Billabong, and O'Neill. These mainstream brands sell a lot more product and have much greater economies of scale, selling T's to the distributors for about $7.50, who in turn sell to the retailers for about $12.50, who then sell to the customers at $18 to $24. The high Canadian dollar has helped Sitka buy product more competitively in recent years, but it has hurt their US sales: the $17.50 wholesale price of T's was about US$12.50 four years ago. Now Sitka T's are 25 to 30 percent more expensive than the large volume US and Australian surfing brand T's. But Mike wondered if this was a pricing issue or a positioning and distribution issue. Sitka does not want to compete

Here's my problem.

with Rip Curl, Billabong, and O'Neill, who have gone more mainstream in their market appeal.

Sitka wants to be an elite, exclusive brand—that discerning customers wear to show that they are boarding apparel fashion leaders, not followers—that is sold in high-end surfing boutique stores. So far, their US sales manager has not had a lot of success getting the brand into the high-end US stores. Part of the reason may be that the Sitka product line reflects northern surfing climate (their signature hoodie, jackets, and other cold weather apparel) and northern symbolism (woodsman chic), and is loosely tied to its Canadian origin in brand meaning (such as through their Sitka Spruce tree logo, choice of sustainable materials, and "the story" of the Sitka brand). This works well in Canada and other international markets with similar climate or where Canadian brand meaning resonates with consumers (such as in Japan), but it does not appear to work well in the United States, where consumers seek American symbolism (even from Australian brands).

As Director of Sales for Sitka, Mike Pepperdine is responsible for developing Sitka's global sales strategy and helping the management team decide what to do about the US market.

Mike Pepperdine and the Sitka team considered their **Options** 1·2·3

1 Option — **Abandon the US market and focus on existing markets.** The US sales manager is not selling much Sitka product. His three reps are focused on Northern California, the Rockies, and the Pacific Northwest, but the economies in these regions have suffered considerably from the recent economic crisis, and customers appear to be much more price conscious than they were before. Sitka is not in the high-end boutiques and their positioning does not resonate as well with US customers. There is a lot more competition in the US market, from very large companies, and from other boutique brands like Sitka, that were more aligned with American culture.

Sitka was far from saturating the potential in existing markets. Sales in Western Canada were strong, but there were opportunities in Ontario, Quebec, and Eastern Canada that offered high growth potential. Sitka had recently opened a store in New Zealand, but there were opportunities in other cities and resort towns in that country. Sitka did not have their own store in Japan, but distributors were also doing well with the brand over there. Mike thought that these existing markets provided significant growth potential for Sitka, would leverage existing brand presence and relationships, and would provide some economies in marketing communications and brand support.

But could they be a credible brand without a presence in the US market, or should they strategically withdraw to enter later with a larger brand, and perhaps a more competitive cost structure? Mike also recognized that the Sitka founders, Andrew and Rene, felt some loyalty to the US sales manager who had been a mentor to them as they were just starting out, and part of the Sitka culture was to develop strong relationships and support their representatives, distributors, and retail accounts. Abandoning the US market would mean abandoning these relationships.

2 Option — **Abandon the US market and focus on new markets.** Related to the first option, Mike also recognized that there was significant potential for entering new markets. The resources currently spent in the US could be spent pursuing opportunities in Europe and Asia. Mike had recently had enquiries from European distributors. One distributor thought that he could generate $1 million in sales in Scandinavia. Another saw great opportunity in Portugal and another in Belgium.

The big advantage of entering new markets was the ability to utilize distributors. Distributors pay for the samples and marketing materials, they take the risk in developing the market, they typically place one or two large orders a year (simplifying Sitka's manufacturing), and they pay for half the order when it is placed and the other half when it is shipped. This helps Sitka's cash flow considerably. In markets served by Sitka's own sales representatives, Sitka carries the cost of the inventory until it is sold. Sitka makes a lower margin when using distributors (selling T's for example to distributors at $12.50 instead of $17.50 to retailers when they use their own sales force) but they potentially sell much greater volume, with lower risk, and using other people's money.

3 Option — **Change their strategy in the US market.** The US market may still be viable if a different strategy was used to penetrate that market. The current US sales manager is telling Mike that Sitka's US pricing is not competitive, at least in the current retail accounts where Sitka is competing head to head against much larger, more mainstream, surfing and boarding apparel brands. Sitka could follow the current strategy but try to operate with lower margins, hoping to cover their fixed costs with higher US volume. But this is risky. Even when the Canadian dollar was lower in value, Sitka struggled with US sales. In the current set-up Sitka takes the risk of product not selling and has to finance the US inventory. Lowering their price to drive volume may only result in having more unsold product at the end of the season and greater inventory carrying costs. On the other hand, it may not be possible to maintain the current margins if consumers don't value the uniqueness of the brand. Distributors have been an effective way to enter other international markets, but the Sitka team has not found a US distributor to approach. Sitka's competitors all use their own sales forces to sell direct to retail.

This leaves the option of replacing the US sales manager with someone who might focus more attention on the Sitka brand and try to get the brand into higher-end surfing and skateboard retailers. Although the economies of Washington State and Oregon are depressed right now, these states have climates similar to British Columbia, have some affinity to woodsman chic, and have cold climate surfers and boarders. It isn't clear, however, whether the current sales manager just isn't trying hard enough, whether Sitka hasn't invested enough resources to crack the US market, or whether Sitka is trying to do the impossible. A refocus on the US market might be kick started by participating in the "Agenda," the top surfing lifestyle and apparel trade show in the United States. The Agenda is held in Huntington Beach, California and would cost Sitka about $10 000 to attend, so Mike knew that he needed to figure out his overall strategy before deciding to attend.

You Choose

Which **Option** would you choose, and **why**?

1. ☐YES ☐NO   2. ☐YES ☐NO   3. ☐YES ☐NO

See what **option** Mike chose on **page 336**

1

OBJECTIVE

Explain the importance of pricing, the process of making pricing decisions, and how marketers set objectives for their pricing strategies. (pp. 296–302)

"Yes, But What Does It Cost?"

As Mike Pepperdine and the founders of Sitka understand, the question of what to charge for a product is a central part of marketing decision making. What to charge for a product, whether it is a good, service, or idea, is a key strategic decision and a central part of a marketing plan. In this chapter, we'll examine the set of decisions associated with the price element of the marketing mix, how those decisions are made, and the role of demand, costs, revenues, and the environment in the pricing decision process. We will start by discussing what price is, why pricing decisions are important, and the context in which pricing decisions are made. Then we will examine pricing objectives, pricing policy (or strategy), price points and tactics, and implementation terms and conditions—which, collectively, are the key pricing decisions. These key decisions are illustrated in Figure 9.1. Then we'll look at the dynamic world of pricing on the Internet and at some psychological, legal, and ethical aspects of pricing.

What Is Price?

"If you have to ask how much it is, you can't afford it!" We've all heard that, but how often do you buy something without asking the price? If price weren't an issue, we'd all drive dream cars, take trips to exotic places, and live like royalty. In the real world, though, most of us need to at least consider a product's price before we buy it. As we said in Chapter 1, price is the value that customers give up, or exchange, to obtain a desired product. Payment may be in the form of money, goods, services, favours, votes, or anything else that has *value* to the other party. Often, the monetary value of a product is called something other than price, sometimes to hide the idea that you are being charged a price or perhaps to assume an air of greater respectability. For example, colleges and universities charge *tuition* for an education, a lawyer or accountant charges a *professional fee*, and students who join a chapter of the American Marketing Association pay *dues*. No matter what it is called, it's still a price.

As we also explained in Chapter 1, marketing is the process that creates exchanges of things of value. We usually think of this exchange as people trading money for a good or a service. But in some marketplace practices, price can mean exchanges of nonmonetary value as well. Long before societies minted coins, people exchanged one good or service for another. This practice of bartering was the basis for the economic development of Canada, with the Hudson's Bay Company trading goods to Northwest trappers for furs. Bartering still occurs today, facilitated by the Internet. The Barter Network (based in Toronto) and the Community Exchange System (based in Quebec) are two of many online barter networks that service B2B customers. An estimated 450 000 North American businesses barter $10 billion worth of goods and services each year.[1] Consumer sites like UsedEverywhere (UsedCalgary, UsedSoon, etc.) and Kijiji also allow people to offer items for barter. No money changes hands, but there still is an exchange of value (just ask the Canada Revenue Agency). In 2006, a Vancouver-based blogger named Kyle MacDonald managed to use multiple barters to trade a paper clip for a rural house in Saskatchewan.[2]

Because price is what customers give up to buy and use a product, other nonmonetary costs are important to both marketers and consumers or customers. Psychological costs, for example, involve the stress, anxiety, or mental difficulty of buying and using a good or service. How difficult is it to assemble that Ikea couch that you bought? Did you take that into consideration when thinking about the value proposition? How stressful is it to use a chainsaw? How much of a hassle was it to buy that new stereo online or recycle all the Styrofoam that it was packed in? Was getting that new bag on sale worth the anxiety of finding a parking spot at a crowded mall? In Chapter 4, you learned about cognitive dissonance, the postpurchase regret or remorse that consumers often experience when making important, involving, risky, or close-alternative purchase decisions. That is also a **psychological cost**. Psychological costs are particularly relevant when marketing ideas, such as not smoking. Health Canada uses shocking or disturbing images such as the one in Exhibit 9.1 to increase the perceived psychological cost of smoking.

In addition to psychological costs, consumers invest time, effort, and energy into finding solutions that meet their needs and wants. Convenience-store operators, such as Mac's or 7-Eleven, and Internet companies, such as Chapters.ca, for example, focus on saving customers time. Apple recognizes that a nonmonetary cost is the time it takes to learn how to use something. They design products to work "right out of the box."

Organizations that follow an operational excellence strategy (Chapter 6), or another cost-based differentiation strategy, focus on making the cost to the customer as low as possible. This includes nonmonetary costs. When evaluating purchase alternatives, consumers take into account other economic costs such as operating costs, switching costs, and opportunity costs. **Operating costs** are those involved in using the product, such as toner in a printer. **Switching costs** are involved in moving from one brand to another, such as getting new cheques printed if you switch banks. **Opportunity costs** are the benefits and value you give up or miss out on by engaging in one activity or buying one product and not another, such as the income you forgo while in school.

Risk is another nonmonetary cost and physical, social, financial, and strategic risks (among others) are all part of the "cost" consideration for consumers and customers. As consumers, we read labels to assess whether products are safe to use (physical risk). We try to assess whether the hair cut we are about to get will make us look terrible (social risk). We try to assess whether that online vendor is really going to deliver what we paid for, or to use PayPal or a credit card to reduce our financial exposure to nonperformance (financial risk). Finally, and more common in B2B contexts, but still an issue in consumer buying, we try to assess whether our investment in a particular technology, system, or process will allow us to achieve our objectives—will it work as expected and deliver the desired outcomes for the expected length of time (strategic risk)?

The Importance of Pricing Decisions

How important are good pricing decisions? Pricing is probably the least understood and least appreciated element of the marketing mix. Marketers like to talk about advertising and other communication elements. It's fun to think about changing technology and how firms invest in new-product development. Even decisions about channels of distribution seem to be more exciting than setting the right price. Yet price has a major strategic impact on the firm—it determines the net value received by the customer in an exchange (benefits minus costs) versus the net value (profit) received by the firm.

Figure 9.1 Key Pricing Strategy Decisions

psychological costs
The stress, anxiety, or mental difficulty of buying and using a product.

operating costs
Costs involved in using a product.

switching costs
Costs involved in moving from one brand to another.

opportunity cost
The value of something that is given up to obtain something else.

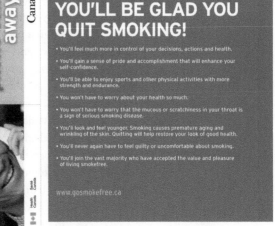

Exhibit 9.1

Health Canada tries to increase the perceived psychological cost of smoking.

Exhibit 9.2

Poor pricing decisions can hurt an entire industry.

Good pricing decisions are critical to a firm's success in the marketplace. For most organizations, the only source of profit is through the price charged for products. If customers are not willing to pay the price asked for a firm's product, the firm will not make a profit and will have failed its shareholders. But sometimes it is difficult to know what to do. Consider the plight of Angela Kim and her husband Sung Bae who independently own an Esso gas station in Courtney, British Columbia. A new Costco opened in the small town and started selling gasoline for $0.98 per litre while other gas stations were selling it at $1.29. The local Shell station matched that price, and others lowered their prices to within 3 cents of that figure. But Kim and Bae had bought their last tanker of gasoline from Esso at $1.23 per litre. They dropped their price to $1.19 a litre but lost thousands of dollars a day at that price and sold less gasoline (postponing the next automatic order for more gasoline at a potentially lower price), and faced having to consider closing if the price war went on too long.[3] If they had matched their competitors' pricing, Kim and Bae would have lost money even faster, and if they had held their price steady, they would have sold even less gasoline.

North American air travel pricing also shows how poor pricing decisions can hurt an entire industry (Exhibit 9.2). A fierce price war in the late 1980s and early 1990s combined with a doubling of labour and fuel costs resulted in billions of dollars in losses and the bankruptcy of many airlines,[4] or the takeover of many airlines, such as Canadian Airlines taking over Wardair in 1986 and then being taken over themselves by Air Canada in 1999. The survivors continued to discount in the face of new low-cost airlines like Southwest Airlines and WestJet only to be hit with significant reductions in demand following the terrorist attacks of 2001 as well as the more recent global economic challenges and volcanic disruptions, which led to more bankruptcies, including Toronto-based Skyservice and Halifax-based Go Travel South in 2010.[5] The industry is still feeling the impact of the pricing decisions of the early 1990s that caused consumers to wait for last-minute specials and for airlines to compete on price.

Marketers have long known that even during the best economic times, most consumers rank "reasonable price" as the most important consideration when making a purchase and deciding where to shop.[6] Price is even more important during recessions, when consumers have less to spend and count their pennies carefully. This is why Internet price comparison sites like Shopzilla, Shopbot, and PriceGrabber are becoming increasingly popular, and why many other Internet sites, even Canada Post, provide price comparison functionality. Buying professionals also know that, when all else is equal, getting a low price keeps costs down and helps make their firm's product competitive. This is why smaller businesses form buying groups, using online services like Mega.[7]

Brothers Anthony and Andrew Sukow recognized the consumer- and business-buying focus on price when they started Advanced Ecommerce Research Systems (AERS), a Canadian company that analyzes 10.5 billion consumer purchasing decisions on eBay (see Marketing Metrics box on page 300). AERS (http://www.researchadvanced.com/) sells information about current pricing and pricing trends on everything bought on eBay to help customers make more effective pricing and selling decisions. (Another example is Terapeak: see Exhibit 9.3.)

Ok, so we know, from Figure 9.1, a bit about what decisions need to be made with respect to pricing, and we know that these decisions are important and have strategic implications. But how do we make these decisions? Figure 9.2 shows a six-step process to price planning: developing pricing objectives, estimating demand, determining costs, evaluating the pricing environment, choosing a pricing strategy, and developing pricing tactics. These six steps provide the outline for the discussion of pricing in this chapter.

Step 1: Develop Pricing Objectives

The first crucial step in price planning is to develop pricing objectives. These are the broader objectives of the firm, such as maximizing shareholder value, as well as its overall marketing objectives, such as increasing market share. Figure 9.3 provides examples of different types of pricing objectives. Let's take a closer look at these.

Profit Objectives

As we discussed in Chapter 2, often a firm's overall objectives relate to a certain level of profit it hopes to realize. This is usually the case in B2B marketing. When pricing strategies are determined by **profit objectives**, the focus is on a target level of profit growth or a desired net profit margin. A profit objective is important to firms that believe profit is what motivates shareholders and bankers to invest in a company. Because firms usually produce an entire product line and/or a product mix, profit objectives may focus on pricing for the firm's entire portfolio of products. In such cases, marketers develop pricing strategies that try to maximize the profits of the entire portfolio rather than focusing on the costs or profitability of each individual product. For example, it may be better to price one product especially high and lose sales on it if that decision causes customers to instead purchase a product that has a higher profit margin. However, with profit maximization as your objective, it is difficult to determine if you have been successful. That is why marketers like to include **SMART objectives** in their planning. These are ones that are specific, measurable, attainable, relevant, and time-bounded, allowing marketers to more readily determine if they have been met. A target level of profit is also a common objective in not-for-profit organizations or social enterprises. Your college or university bookstore, for example, likely has a target return or target profitability in mind when they price textbooks. They need to make enough profit to stay in business but want to provide students with access to the books at the lowest possible price.

Cannibalization, a subject we discussed in Chapter 8, is also something to worry about. For example, what happens when a firm that markets several brands of hair care products offers a special price promotion of 15 percent off on one of its shampoos? If customers who normally buy another of the firm's offerings are attracted to the price-off promotion and buy the discounted brand, the promotion can mean a loss to the firm instead of the desired increase in sales and profits.[8]

Figure 9.2 Process of Price Planning

Successful price planning includes a series of orderly steps beginning with setting pricing objectives.

Step 1: Set Pricing Objectives
- Profit
- Sales
- Market share
- Competitive effect
- Customer satisfaction
- Image enhancement

Step 2: Estimate Demand
- Shifts in demand
- Price elasticity of demand

Step 3: Determine Costs
- Variable costs
- Fixed costs
- Break-even analysis
- Marginal analysis
- Markups and margins

Step 4: Examine the Pricing Environment
- The economy
- The competition
- Government regulation
- Consumer trends
- The international environment

Step 5: Choose a Pricing Strategy
- Based on cost
- Based on demand
- Based on the competition
- Based on customers' needs
- New-product pricing

Step 6: Develop Pricing Tactics
- For individual products
- For multiple products
- Distribution-based tactics
- Discounting for channel members

profit objectives
Pricing products with a focus on a target level of profit growth or a desired net profit margin.

SMART objectives
Objectives that are specific, measurable, attainable, relevant, and time-bounded.

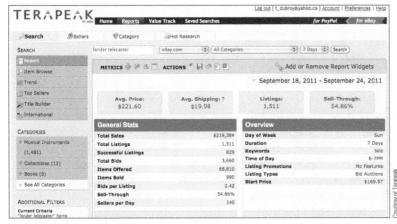

Exhibit 9.3

Terapeak offers software that displays metrics based on eBay sales, showing statistics like average price or top sellers for any product successfully sold on the platform.

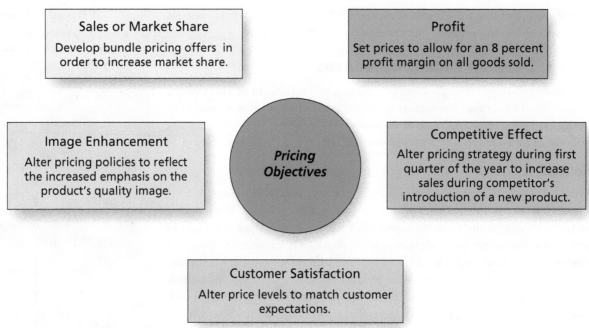

Figure 9.3 Pricing Objectives
The first step in price planning is to develop pricing objectives that support the broader objectives of the firm.

Although profits are an important consideration in the pricing of all goods and services, they are critical when the product is a fad. Fad products, from pet rocks to Beanie Babies, have a short market life, making a profit objective essential in order to allow the firm to recover its investment quickly. In such cases, the firm must harvest profits before customers lose interest and move on to the next app, electronic pet, doll, cartoon idol, or other fad product. Teen Buzz, for example, offers a free Mosquito ringtone that generally only kids can hear. Originally developed in the UK as a loitering deterrent, kids now use the Mosquito ringtone in class to alert them to incoming text messages without their teachers' knowledge.[9] A company that hawks a tone like this has to move quickly to unload its "inventory" before the next cool idea replaces it.

sales or market share objective
Pricing products to maximize sales or to attain a desired level of sales or market share.

Sales or Marketing Share Objectives

Often the objective of a pricing strategy is to maximize sales (either in dollars or in units) or to increase market share. Does setting a price intended to increase unit sales or market

---

eBay Sales

Advanced Ecommerce Research Systems (AERS) is in the business of providing marketing metrics for eBay sellers. For organizations that want to better understand both their competitors and consumer behaviour in product verticals (wide or narrowly focused markets), AERS offers SectorView, a trend analysis and decision support tool that provides live updates for monitoring and reacting to fast-changing eBay consumer behaviour.

For sellers seeking to improve their selling success and become more profitable, AERS offers Terapeak, software that monitors "sold" listings to identify the highest, lowest, and average sold prices for any item. It identifies the most effective selling techniques, the most effective key words, and most effective listing techniques, as well as the best time to list and sell. It is designed to answer the following three basic questions. What items should I sell on eBay? How should I price each item to maximize my profits? When listing each item, which tactics should I use to make more money?

As described on their Web site (http://www.terapeak.com/product/terapeak-ebay/features), Terapeak helps users make smarter pricing decisions.

share simply mean pricing the product lower than the competition? Sometimes, yes. Providers of cable, Internet, and satellite TV services such as Rogers, Bell, Shaw, Telus, and others relentlessly offer consumers better deals that include more of the services. Similarly, mobile phone providers compete with deals that include a set number of minutes for a standard fee, free night-time and weekend minutes, rollover minutes, and low- or no-cost phones to keep them ahead in the "mobile wars." But lowering prices is not always necessary to increase market share. If a company's product has a competitive advantage, keeping the price at the same level as other firms may satisfy sales objectives. And such "price wars" can have a negative effect when consumers switch from one producer to another simply because the price changes.

Exhibit 9.4

The Travelocity.ca Price & Service Guarantee is a promise to stand behind customers and support them always, even when they're on the road.

Competitive Effect Objectives

Sometimes strategists design the pricing plan to dilute the competition's marketing efforts. In these cases, a firm may deliberately try to pre-empt or reduce the impact of a rival's pricing changes. That's what happened when new low-fare airline JetBlue entered Delta's hub Atlanta market with flights from Atlanta to Los Angeles. Delta slashed its fares in response, forcing JetBlue to abandon the Atlanta market.[10] The earlier example of Costco entering the Courtney, BC, market with extremely low prices for gasoline may also have been for competitive effect—serving notice to other retailers that there is a new top dog in town to follow.

Customer Satisfaction Objectives

Many quality-focused firms believe that profits result from making customer satisfaction the primary objective. Travelocity.ca, for example, offers a "Travelocity.ca Price & Service Guarantee" (see Exhibit 9.4). It is a promise to stand behind customers and support them always.[11] Firms like Travelocity.ca believe that if they focus solely on short-term profits they will lose sight of their objective to retain customers for the long term. General Motors, for example, tried to put customer satisfaction first with its Saturn brand of car and a one price, "no haggling, no negotiation, and no deals," Saturn experience and developed a loyal core of Saturn owners. Unfortunately, when GM faced bankruptcy in 2009, the Saturn division was shut down.[12]

Image Enhancement Objectives

Consumers often use price to make inferences about the quality of a product. In fact, marketers know that price is often an important means of communicating not only quality but also image to prospective customers. The image enhancement function of pricing is particularly important with **prestige products** (or luxury products) that have a high price and appeal to status-conscious consumers. Most of us would agree that the high price tag on a Rolex watch, a Louis Vuitton handbag, or a Rolls-Royce car, although representing the higher costs of producing the product, is vital to shaping an image of an extraordinary product that only the wealthy can afford. The Burton Snowboard company, like many other boarding companies, sets high prices on its products to communicate an elite image and uniqueness in the boarding subculture (Exhibit 9.5).

    Image objectives don't have to be upscale. East-Side Mario's is going back to its "Badda Boom Badda Bing" roots after an unsuccessful attempt to reposition the brand to attract more sophisticated diners. They have refocused on families, offering low prices, value, and fun.[13]

prestige products
Products that have a high price and that appeal to status-conscious consumers.

Courtesy of Burton Snowboards

Exhibit 9.5

Pricing of Burton snowboards and clothing is consistent with a positioning objective.

Costs	Demand
Revenue	Pricing Environment

Figure 9.4 Factors in Price Setting

To set the right price, marketers must understand a variety of quantitative and qualitative factors.

demand curve

A plot of the quantity of a product that customers will buy in a market during a period of time at various prices if all other factors remain the same.

Flexibility of Price Objectives

It is important that pricing objectives be *flexible*. Often, it is necessary to develop pricing objectives (and strategies) tailored to different geographic areas and time periods. There may be varying levels of competition in different parts of the country, making it necessary to lower prices in the areas with the heaviest competition. Some geographic regions may have greater sales potential, making it wise for firms to develop pricing objectives aimed at obtaining a larger market share in those areas. Mortgage lenders may do this by offering lower rates in areas where new housing starts are booming.

Market conditions can change during the year, requiring price adjustments for seasonal and other reasons. Accommodation rental rates in Whistler, British Columbia, are much higher during the winter than during the summer; rates in Summerside, Prince Edward Island, or Grand Bend, Ontario, are higher during the summer vacation months.

These are only some of the factors that marketers must consider when making pricing decisions. In the next section, we will examine the impact of other factors in the decision environment, first focusing on the role of costs and consumer or customer demand.

2 Costs, Demand, Revenue, and the Pricing Environment

OBJECTIVE

Describe how marketers use costs, demands, revenue, and the pricing environment to make pricing decisions.
(pp. 302–316)

Once a marketer decides on its pricing objectives, it is time to begin the actual process of price setting. In order to set the right price, marketers must understand a variety of quantitative and qualitative factors that can mean success or failure for the pricing strategy. As shown in Figure 9.4, these include an estimate of demand, knowledge of costs and revenue, and an understanding of the pricing environment.

Step 2: Estimate Demand and Value

The second step in price planning is to estimate demand and perceived value. Marketers first need to know what range of prices consumers or customers consider reasonable given the nature of the offer, the benefits received, the nonmonetary costs associated with buying and using the product, and the nature and positioning of competitive offers. If you are a marketing manager at Electronic Arts, for example, it would be helpful to know what alternatives your customers think about when deciding whether or not to purchase the latest offering in the Need For Speed product line, what they would expect to pay, and what premium, if any, they would be willing to pay compared to those alternatives. Using research to answer these questions, across many customers and segments of customers, marketers learn what the market will bear in terms of price.

They also learn about demand for the product at different price levels. Demand refers to customers' desire for a product: how much of a product are they willing to buy as the price of the product goes up or down? Knowing what volume of sales might be expected at different price levels helps marketers decide what price is most appropriate; therefore, one of the earliest steps marketers take in price planning is to estimate demand for their products.

Economists use a graph of a **demand curve** to illustrate the effect of price on the quantity demanded of a product. The demand curve, which can be a curved or straight line, shows the quantity of a product that customers will buy in a market during a period of time at various prices if all other factors remain the same.

Figure 9.5 shows demand curves for normal and prestige products. The vertical axis for the demand curve represents the different prices that a firm might charge for a product (*P*).

Figure 9.5 Demand Curves for Normal and Prestige Products

For normal products, there is an inverse relationship between price and demand. For prestige products, demand will increase—to a point—as price increases, or will decrease as price decreases.

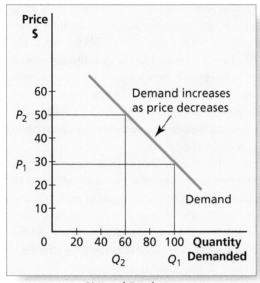

Normal Products

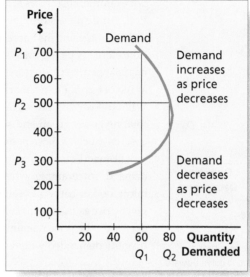

Prestige Products

The horizontal axis shows the number of units or quantity (Q) of the product demanded. The demand curve for most goods (shown on the left side of Figure 9.5) slopes downward and to the right. As the price of the product goes up (P_1 to P_2), the number of units that customers are willing to buy goes down (Q_1 to Q_2). If prices decrease, customers will buy more. This is the law of demand. For example, if the price of bananas goes up, customers will probably buy fewer of them. And if the price gets really high, customers will eat their cereal without bananas.

There are, however, exceptions to this typical price-quantity relationship. In fact, there are situations in which (otherwise rational) people desire a product more as it *increases* in price. For prestige products such as luxury cars or jewellery, a price hike may actually result in an *increase* in the quantity consumers demand, because they see the product as more valuable and, therefore, more exclusive. In such cases, the demand curve slopes upward. The right-hand side of Figure 9.5 shows the backward-bending demand curve we associate with prestige products. In that case, if the price decreases, from P_2 to P_3, consumers perceive the product to be less desirable and demand may decrease from Q_2 to Q_1. On the other hand, if the price increases from P_3 to P_1, consumers think the product is more desirable and quantity increases from Q_1 to Q_2. Still, the higher-price/higher-demand relationship has its limits. If the firm increases the price too much (say from P_2 to P_1), making the product unaffordable for all but a few buyers, demand will begin to decrease. The direction the backward-bending curve takes shows this.

Shifts in Demand

The demand curves we've shown assume that all factors other than price stay the same. But what if they don't? What if the company improves the product? What happens when there is a glitzy new advertising campaign that turns a product into a "must-have" for a lot of people? What if stealthy *paparazzi* catch Brad Pitt using the product at home? Any of these things could cause an *upward shift* of the demand curve. An upward shift in the demand curve means that at any given price, demand is greater than before the shift occurs. And the demand shift might even be more precipitous if Shiloh Nouvel Jolie-Pitt were also to make an appearance in the pic!

Mike Pepperdine

APPLYING   Price Objectives

To begin to think about the US market in relation to Sitka's global strategy, Mike Pepperdine needed to think about Sitka's overall marketing objectives and then their pricing objectives. Mike wanted to support a prestige positioning for the Sitka brand that would suggest an image enhancement pricing objective, but he didn't know if that would work in the highly competitive US market. Mike wondered if Sitka should consider a market share objective to increase their sales volume, at a lower profit per unit, in order to drive production volume and lower the cost per unit.

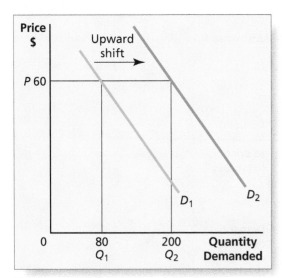

Figure 9.6 Shift in Demand Curve

Changes in the environment or in company efforts can cause a shift in the demand curve. A great advertising campaign, for example, can shift the demand curve upward.

Exhibit 9.6

Demand is influenced by many factors. In the real world, factors other than the price and marketing activities influence demand; for example, if it rains, the demand for umbrellas increases and the demand for golf tee times falls. The development of new products may influence demand for old ones. Even though a few firms may still produce phonographs, the introduction of digital music players has all but eliminated the demand for vinyl records and turntables on which to play them.

Figure 9.6 shows the upward shift of the demand curve as it moves from D_1 to D_2. At D_1, before the shift occurs, customers will be willing to purchase the quantity Q_1 (80 units, in Figure 9.6) at the given price, P ($60, in Figure 9.6). For example, customers at a particular store may buy 80 barbecue grills at $60 a grill. But then the store runs a huge advertising campaign featuring Jim Carrey on his patio using the barbecue grill and the demand curve shifts from D_1 to D_2. (The store keeps the price at $60.) Take a look at how the quantity demanded has changed, to Q_2. In our example, the store is now selling 200 barbecue grills at $60 per grill. From a marketing standpoint, this shift is the best of all worlds. Without lowering prices, the company can sell more of its product. As a result, total revenues go up and so do profits, unless, of course, the new promotion costs as much as those potential additional profits.

Demand curves may also shift downward. That's what happens to grill demand, for example, when there are media stories about harmful effects of burnt food or barbecues setting homes on fire. Sales of barbecues decline at any given price as risk-averse consumers seek alternative ways to prepare food. Then, even with the price remaining at $60, the curve would shift downward and the quantity demanded would drop so that the store could sell only 30 or 40 grills.

Estimate Demand

It's extremely important for marketers to understand and accurately estimate demand (see Exhibit 9.6). A firm's production scheduling is based on anticipated demand that must be estimated well in advance of when products are brought to market. In addition, all marketing planning and budgeting must be based on reasonably accurate estimates of potential sales. So how do marketers reasonably estimate potential sales? There are a number of sophisticated approaches to forecasting that are beyond the scope of this introductory text. One simple approach, however, is when marketers predict total demand first by identifying the number of buyers or potential buyers for their product and then multiply that estimate times the average amount each member of the target market is likely to purchase. Table 9.1 shows how a small business, such as a startup pizza restaurant, estimates demand in markets it expects to reach. For example, the pizza entrepreneur may estimate that there are 180 000 consumer households in his market who would be willing to buy his pizza and that each household would purchase an average of six pizzas a year. The total annual demand is 1 080 000 pizzas.

Once the marketer estimates total demand, the next step is to predict what the company's market share is likely to be. The company's estimated demand is then its share of the whole (estimated) pie. In our pizza example, the entrepreneur may feel that she can gain 3 percent of this market, or about 200 pizzas per month—not bad for a new startup business. Of course, such projections need to take into consideration other factors that might affect demand, such as new competitors entering the market, the state of the economy, and changing consumer tastes like a sudden demand for low-carb take-out food.

Price Elasticity of Demand

Marketers also need to know how their customers are likely to react to a price change. In particular, it is critical to understand whether a change in price will have a large or a small impact

© Photodisc/Thinkstock

on demand. How much can a firm increase or decrease its price if it sees a marked change in sales? If the price of a pizza goes up one dollar, will people switch to subs and burgers? What would happen if the pizza went up two dollars? or even five dollars? **Price elasticity of demand** is a measure of the sensitivity of customers to changes in price. If the price changes by 10 percent, what will be the percentage change in demand for the product? The word *elasticity* indicates that changes in price usually cause demand to stretch or retract like a rubber band. We calculate price elasticity of demand as follows:

Table 9.1	Estimating Demand for Pizza	
Number of families in market		180,000
Average number of pizzas per family per year		6
Total annual market demand		1,080,000
Company's predicted share of the total market		3%
Estimated annual company demand		32,400 pizzas
Estimated monthly company demand		2,700
Estimated weekly company demand		675

price elasticity of demand
The percentage change in unit sales that results from a percentage change in price.

$$\text{Price elasticity of demand} = \frac{\text{percentage change in quantity demanded}}{\text{percentage change in price}}$$

Sometimes customers are very sensitive to changes in price and a price change results in a substantial change in the quantity they demand. In such instances, we have a case of **elastic demand**. In other situations, a change in price has little or no effect on the quantity consumers are willing to buy. We describe this as inelastic demand. Let's use the formula in an example. Suppose the pizza maker finds (from experience or from marketing research) that lowering the price of his pizza 10 percent (from $10 per pizza to $9) will cause a 15 percent increase in demand. He would calculate the price elasticity of demand as 15 divided by 10, which is 1.5. If the price elasticity of demand is greater than one, demand is elastic; that is, consumers respond to the price decrease by demanding more. Or, if the price increases, consumers will demand less. Figure 9.7 shows these calculations.

elastic demand
Demand in which changes in price have large effects on the amount demanded.

As Figure 9.7 illustrates, when demand is elastic, changes in price and in total revenues (total sales) work in opposite directions. If the price is increased, revenues decrease. If the price is decreased, total revenues increase. With elastic demand, the demand curve shown in Figure 9.7 is more horizontal. With an elasticity of demand of 1.5, a decrease in price will increase the pizza maker's total sales. We saw earlier that in some instances demand is *inelastic* so that a change in price results in little or no change in demand. For example, if the 10 percent decrease in the price of pizza resulted in only a 5 percent increase in pizza sales, then the price elasticity of demand calculated would be 5 divided by 10, which is 0.5 (less than one), and our pizza maker faces inelastic demand. When demand is inelastic, price and revenue changes are in the same direction; that is, increases in price result in increases in total revenue, while decreases in price result in decreases in total revenue. With inelastic demand, the demand curve in Figure 9.7 becomes more vertical. Generally, the demand for necessities, such as food and electricity, is inelastic. Even large price increases do not cause us to buy less food or to give up our lights and hot water (though we may take fewer bubble baths).

If demand is price inelastic, can marketers keep raising prices so that revenues and profits will grow larger and larger? And what if demand is elastic—does it mean that marketers can never raise prices? The answer to these questions is no (surprise!). Elasticity of demand for a product often differs for different price levels and with different percentages of change. As a general rule, pizza makers and other companies can determine the *actual* price elasticity only after they have tested a pricing decision and calculated the resulting demand (as Taco Bell did with its value menu). Only then will they know whether a specific price change will increase or decrease revenues.

To estimate what demand is likely to be at different prices for new or existing products, marketers often do research. One approach is to conduct a study in which consumers tell marketers how much of a product they would be willing to buy at different prices. For example, researchers might ask participants if they would download fewer iTunes songs if the

---

Elastic demand

Price changes from $10 to $9.

$10 − 9 = $1

1/10 = 10% change in price

Demand changes from 2700 per month to 3100 per month

$$3100$$
$$-\ 2700$$

Increase   400 pizzas

Percentage increase   400/2700 = .148 ~ 15% change in demand

$$\text{Price elasticity of demand} = \frac{\text{percentage change in quantity demanded}}{\text{percentage change in price}}$$

$$\text{Price elasticity of demand} = \frac{15\%}{10\%} = 1.5$$

Inelastic demand

Price changes from $10 to $9.

$10 − 9 = $1

1/10 = 10% change in price

Demand changes from 2700 per month to 2835 per month

$$2835$$
$$-\ 2700$$

Increase   135 pizzas

Percentage increase   135/2700 = 0.05 ~ 5% change in demand

$$\text{Price elasticity of demand} = \frac{\text{percentage change in quantity demanded}}{\text{percentage change in price}}$$

$$\text{Price elasticity of demand} = \frac{5\%}{10\%} = 0.5$$

Figure 9.7 Price Elasticity of Demand

Marketers know that elasticity of demand is an important pricing metric.

price per track goes from $1.29 to $1.75, or how many bags of their favourite chocolate chip cookies they would buy at $3, $4, or $5. At other times, researchers conduct *field studies* in which they vary the price of a product in different stores and measure how much is actually purchased at the different price levels.

Other factors can affect price elasticity and sales. Consider the availability of *substitute* goods or services. If a product has a close substitute, its demand will be elastic; that is, a change in price will result in a change in demand, as consumers move to buy the substitute product. For example, all but the most die-hard cola fans might consider Coke and Pepsi close substitutes. If the price of Pepsi goes up, many people will buy Coke instead. Marketers of products with close substitutes are less likely to compete on price, because they recognize that doing so could result in less profit as consumers switch from one brand to another.

Changes in prices of other products also affect the demand for an item, a phenomenon we label **cross-elasticity of demand**. When products are substitutes for each other, an increase in the price of one will increase the demand for the other. For example, if the price of bananas goes up, consumers may instead buy more strawberries, blueberries, or apples. However, when products are *complements*—that is, when one product is essential to the use of a second—an increase in the price of one decreases the demand for the second. So if the price of gasoline goes up, consumers may drive less, carpool, or take public transportation. Thus demand for tires (as well as gasoline) will decrease.

As a final note on demand, consumer insights are critical to understanding demands. The current recessionary economic environment is driving changes in consumers' budgets and in their spending habits. How is this affecting demand and how will it affect demand

cross-elasticity of demand

When changes in the price of one product affect the demand for another item.

in the future? While we talk about demand in terms of the relationship of price to quantity demanded, such relationships cannot be fully understood or used in pricing without a full understanding of exactly how consumers respond not only to the offering and its price but also to the offerings of competitors, the marketing communications, and the influence of other consumers. We will revisit this idea later in the chapter.

Step 3: Determine Costs

Estimating demand helps marketers determine possible prices to charge for a product. It tells them how much of the product they think they'll be able to sell at different prices. Knowing this brings them to the third step in determining a product's price: making sure the price will cover costs. Before marketers can determine price, they must understand the relationship of cost, demand, and revenue for their product. In this next section, we'll talk about different types of costs that marketers must consider in pricing. Then we'll show two types of analyses that marketers use to make pricing decisions.

Variable and Fixed Costs

It's obvious that the cost of producing a product plays a big role when firms decide what to charge for it. If an item's selling price is lower than the cost to produce it, it doesn't take a rocket scientist to figure out that the firm will lose money. Before looking at how costs influence pricing decisions, we need to understand the different types of costs that firms incur. First, a firm incurs **variable costs**—the per-unit costs of production that will fluctuate, depending on how many units or individual products a firm produces. For example, if it takes 25-cents worth of nails, a variable cost, to build one bookcase, it will take 50-cents worth for two, 75-cents worth for three, and so on. For the production of bookcases, variable costs would include the cost of lumber and paint as well as the wages the firm would pay factory workers. Figure 9.8 shows some examples of the variable cost per unit, or average variable cost, and the total variable costs at different levels of production (for producing 100, 200, and 500 bookcases). If the firm produces 100 bookcases, the average variable cost per unit is $50, and the total variable cost is $5000 ($50 × 100). If it doubles production to 200 units, the total variable cost now is $10 000 ($50 × 200).

In reality, calculating variable costs is usually more complex than what we've shown here. As the number of bookcases the factory produces increases or decreases, average variable costs may change. For example, if the company buys just enough lumber for one bookcase, the lumberyard will charge top dollar. If it buys enough for 100 bookcases,

variable costs
The costs of production (raw and processed materials, parts, and labour) that are tied to and vary, depending on the number of units produced.

Figure 9.8 Variable Costs at Different Levels of Production

Variable Costs to Produce 100 Bookcases		Variable Costs to Produce 200 Bookcases		Variable Costs to Produce 500 Bookcases	
Wood	$13.25	Wood	$13.25	Wood	$9.40
Nails	0.25	Nails	0.25	Nails	0.20
Paint	0.50	Paint	0.50	Paint	0.40
Labour (3 hours × $12.00 per hr)	$36.00	Labour (3 hours × $12.00 per hr)	$36.00	Labour (2½ hours × $12.00 per hr)	$30.00
Cost per unit	$50.00	Cost per unit	$50.00	Cost per unit	$40.00
Multiply by number of units	100	Multiply by number of units	200	Multiply by number of units	500
Cost for 100 units	$5000	Cost for 200 units	$10 000	Cost for 500 units	$20 000

One bookcase = one unit.

the guys at the lumberyard will probably offer a better deal. And if it buys enough for thousands of bookcases, the company may cut variable costs even more. Even the cost of labour goes down with increased production as manufacturers are likely to invest in labour-saving equipment that allows workers to produce bookcases faster. Figure 9.8 shows this is the case. By purchasing wood, nails, and paint at a lower price (because of a volume discount) and by providing a means for workers to build bookcases more quickly, the company reduces the cost per unit of producing 500 bookcases to $40 each.

Variable costs don't always go down with higher levels of production. Using the bookcase example, at some point the demand for the labour, lumber, or nails required to produce the bookcases may exceed the supply; for example, the bookcase manufacturer may have to pay employees higher overtime wages to keep up with production or the manufacturer may have to buy additional lumber from a distant supplier that will charge more to cover the costs of shipping. In either case, the cost per bookcase rises.

fixed costs
Costs of production that do not change with the number of units produced.

Fixed costs are costs that *do not* vary with the number of units produced—costs that remain the same whether the firm produces 1000 bookcases this month or only 10. Fixed costs include rent or the cost of owning and maintaining the factory, utilities to heat or cool the factory, and the costs of equipment such as hammers, saws, and paint sprayers used in the production of the product. While the cost of factory workers to build the bookcases is part of a firm's variable costs, the salaries of a firm's executives, accountants, human resources specialists, marketing managers, and other personnel not involved in the production of the product are fixed costs. So, too, are other costs such as advertising and other marketing activities, at least in the short term. All these costs are constant no matter how many items the factory manufactures. **Average fixed cost** is the fixed cost per unit—the

average fixed cost
The fixed cost per unit produced.

total fixed costs divided by the number of units (bookcases) produced. Although total fixed costs remain the same no matter how many units are produced, the average fixed cost will decrease as the number of units produced increases. Say, for example, that a firm's total fixed costs of production are $300 000. If the firm produces one unit, it applies the total of $300 000 to the one unit. If it produces two units, it applies $150 000, or half of the fixed costs, to each unit. If it produces 10 000 units, the average fixed cost per unit is $30.00, and so on. As we produce more units, average fixed costs go down and so does the price we must charge to cover fixed costs.

Of course, like variable costs, in the long term, total fixed costs may change. The firm may find that it can sell more of a product than it has manufacturing capacity to produce, so it builds a new factory, its executives' salaries go up, and more money goes into purchasing manufacturing equipment.

total costs
The total of the fixed costs and the variable costs for a set number of units produced.

Combining variable costs and fixed costs yields **total costs** for a given level of production. As a company produces more and more of a product, both average fixed costs and average variable costs may decrease. Average total costs may decrease, too, up to a point. As we said, as output continues to increase, average variable costs may start to increase. These variable costs ultimately rise faster than average fixed costs decline, resulting in an increase to average total costs. As total costs fluctuate with differing levels of production, the price that producers have to charge to cover those costs changes accordingly. Therefore, marketers need to calculate the minimum price necessary to cover all costs—the *break-even price*.

Break-Even Analysis

break-even analysis
A method for determining the number of units that a firm must produce and sell at a given price to cover all its costs.

Break-even analysis is a technique marketers use to examine the relationship between costs and price. This method lets them determine what sales volume the company must reach at a given price before it will completely cover its total costs and past which it will begin to turn a profit. Simply put, the **break-even point** is the point at which the company doesn't lose any money and doesn't make any profit. All costs are covered, but there isn't a penny extra. A break-even analysis allows marketers to identify how many units of a product they will have to sell at a given price to exceed the break-even point and be profitable. Figure 9.9 uses our bookcase example to demonstrate break-even analysis assuming the manufacturer

break-even point
The point at which the total revenue and total costs are equal and beyond which the company makes a profit; below that point, the firm will suffer a loss.

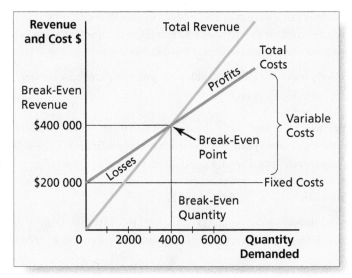

Figure 9.9 Break-Even Analysis Assuming a Price of $100

Using break-even analysis, marketers can determine what sales volume must be reached before the company makes a profit. This company needs to sell 4000 bookcases at $100 each to break even.

charges $100 per unit. The vertical axis represents the amount of costs and revenue in dollars and the horizontal axis shows the quantity of goods the manufacturer produces and sells. In this break-even model, we assume that there is a given total fixed cost and that variable costs do not change with the quantity produced.

In this example, let's say that the total fixed costs (the costs for the factory, the equipment, and electricity) are $200 000 and that the average variable costs (for materials and labour) are constant. The figure shows the total costs (variable costs plus fixed costs) and total revenues if varying quantities are produced and sold. The point at which the total revenue and total costs lines intersect is the break-even point. If sales are above the break-even point, the company makes a profit. Below that point, the firm will suffer losses.

To determine the break-even point, the firm first needs to calculate the **contribution per unit**, or the difference between the price the firm charges for a product (the revenue per unit) and the variable costs. This figure is the amount the firm has after it pays for the wood, nails, paint, and labour to contribute to meeting the fixed costs of production. For our example, we will assume that the firm sells its bookcases for $100 each. Using the variable costs of $50 per unit that we had before, contribution per unit is $100 − $50 = $50. Using the fixed cost for the bookcase manufacturing of $200 000, we can now calculate the firm's break-even point in units of the product:

$$\text{Break-even point (in units)} = \frac{\text{total fixed costs}}{\text{contribution per unit to fixed costs}}$$

$$\text{Break-even point (in units)} = \frac{\$200\,000}{\$50} = 4000 \text{ units}$$

We see that the firm must sell 4000 bookcases at $100 each to meet its fixed costs and to break even. We can also calculate the break-even point in dollars. This shows us that to break even the company must sell $400 000 worth of bookcases:

$$\text{Break-even point (in dollars)} = \frac{\text{total fixed costs}}{1 - \dfrac{\text{variable cost per unit}}{\text{price}}}$$

$$\text{Break-even point (in dollars)} = \frac{\$200\,000}{1 - \dfrac{\$50}{\$100}} = \frac{\$200\,000}{1 - 0.5} = \frac{\$200\,000}{0.5} = \$400\,000$$

contribution per unit
The difference between the price the firm charges for a product and the variable costs.

After the firm's sales have met and passed the break-even point, it begins to make a profit. How much profit? If the firm sells 4001 bookcases, it will make a profit of $50. If it sells 5000 bookcases, we calculate the profit as follows:

$$\text{Profit} = \text{quantity above break-even point} \times \text{contribution margin}$$
$$= \$1\,000 \times 50$$
$$= \$50\,000$$

Often a firm will set a *profit goal*—the dollar profit figure it wants to earn. Its managers may calculate the break-even point with a certain dollar profit goal in mind. In this case, it is not really a "break-even" point we are calculating, because we're seeking profits. It's more of a target amount. If our bookcase manufacturer thinks it is necessary to realize a profit of $50 000, his calculations look like this:

$$\frac{\text{Break-even point (in units)}}{\text{with target profit included}} = \frac{\text{total fixed costs} + \text{target profit}}{\text{contribution per unit to fixed costs}}$$

$$\text{Break-even point (in units)} = \frac{\$200\,000 + 50\,000}{\$50} = 5\,000 \text{ units}$$

Sometimes we express the target return or profit goal as a *percentage of sales*. For example, a firm may say that it wants to make a profit of at least 10 percent on sales. In such cases, it first calculates what the 10 percent profit is in dollars: 10 percent of $100 is $10. Then, the firm adds this profit amount to the variable cost when it calculates break-even point. In our example, the company wants to earn 10 percent of the selling price of the bookcase, or per unit. We would simply add this $10 to the variable costs of $50 and calculate the new target amount as we calculated the break-even point before. The contribution per unit becomes as follows:

$$\frac{\text{Contribution per unit with}}{\text{target profit included}} = \text{selling price} - (\text{variable costs} + \text{target profit})$$
$$= \$100 - (\$50 + \$10) = \$40$$

$$\text{Break-even point (in units)} = \frac{\text{total fixed costs}}{\text{contribution per unit to fixed costs}}$$

$$\text{Break-even point (in units)} = \frac{\$200\,000}{\$40} = 5\,000 \text{ units}$$

Break-even analysis does not provide an easy answer for pricing decisions. Yes, it provides answers about how many units the firm must sell to break even and to make a profit, but without knowing whether demand will equal that quantity at that price, companies can make big mistakes. It is, therefore, useful for marketers to estimate the demand for their product and then perform a marginal analysis. Now let's see how to do that.

Marginal Analysis

marginal analysis
A method that uses cost and demand to identify the price that will maximize profits.

Marginal analysis provides a way for marketers to look at cost and demand at the same time and to identify the output and the price that will generate the maximum profit. Figure 9.10 shows the various cost and revenue elements we consider in marginal analysis. Like Figure 9.9, the vertical axis in Figure 9.10 represents the cost and revenues in dollars, and the horizontal axis shows the quantity produced and sold. Figure 9.10 shows the average revenue, average cost, marginal revenue, and marginal cost curves.

marginal cost
The increase in total cost that results from producing one additional unit of a product.

When they do a marginal analysis, marketers examine the relationship of **marginal cost** (the increase in total costs from producing one additional unit of a product) to **marginal revenue** (the increase in total income or revenue that results from selling one additional unit of a product). Average revenue is also the demand curve and thus represents the amount customers will buy at different prices—people buy more only if price (and thus revenue) decrease. Thus, both average revenue and marginal revenue decrease with each additional unit sold.

marginal revenue
The increase in total income or revenue that results from selling one additional unit of a product.

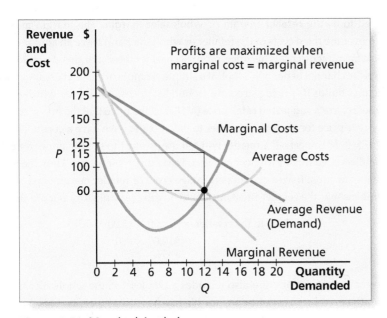

Figure 9.10 Marginal Analysis

Marginal analysis allows marketers to consider both costs and demand in calculating a price that maximizes profits.

If the manufacturer produces only one bookcase, the average total cost per unit is the same as the marginal cost per unit. After the first unit, the cost of *producing each additional unit* (marginal cost) and the average cost at first decrease. Eventually, however, both marginal costs and average costs begin to increase, since, as we discussed earlier, both average fixed costs and average variable costs may increase in the long term.

Profit is maximized at the point at which marginal cost is *exactly* equal to marginal revenue. At that point, the cost of producing one unit is exactly equal to the revenue to be realized from selling that one unit. If, however, the company produces one additional unit, the cost of producing that unit is *greater than* the revenue from the sale of the unit, and total profit actually begins to decrease. So it's a no-brainer that firms should maintain production and sales at the point of maximum profit.

One word of caution when you use marginal analysis: although in theory the procedure is straightforward, in the real world things seldom are. Production costs may vary unexpectedly because of shortages, inclement weather, unexpected equipment repairs, and so on. Revenues may also unexpectedly move up and down because of the economy, what the competition is doing, or a host of other reasons. Predicting demand, an important factor in marginal analysis, is never an exact science. This makes marginal analysis a less-than-perfect way to determine the best price for a product. Indeed, it is theoretically sounder than break-even analysis, but most firms find the break-even approach more useful on a day-to-day basis.

Markups and Margins: Pricing through the Channel

So far we have talked about costs simply from the perspective of a manufacturer selling directly to a consumer. But in reality, most products are not sold directly to the consumers or business buyers of the product. Instead, a manufacturer may sell a consumer good to a wholesaler, distributor, or jobber who in turn sells to a retailer who finally sells the product to the ultimate consumer. In organizational markets, the manufacturer may sell his product to a distributor who will then sell to the business customer. Each of these members of the channel of distribution buys a product for a certain amount and adds a **markup** amount to create the price at which they will sell a product. This markup amount is the **gross margin**,

markup
An amount added to the cost of a product to create the price at which a channel member will sell the product.

gross margin
The markup amount added to the cost of a product to cover the fixed costs of the retailer or wholesaler and leave an amount for a profit.

retailer margin
The margin added to the cost of a product by a retailer.

wholesaler margin
The amount added to the cost of a product by a wholesaler.

list price or manufacturer's suggested retail price (MSRP)
The price the end customer is expected to pay as determined by the manufacturer; also referred to as the suggested retail price.

Mike Pepperdine

APPLYING ▽ Markups and Margins

The crux of Sitka's challenge in the US market is one of markups and margins. They currently sell their product through distribution channels that are expecting 80–100 percent markups on their cost. With a higher cost structure than their larger competitors, Sitka is faced with three choices—reducing their markup (on cost); replacing the distributors who take a 30 percent markup; or finding retailers who are willing to reduce their markup—if they want to be competitive in the retail price of their T's. Distributors perform important functions for Sitka, and replacing the middlemen means that Sitka would have to perform those functions themselves. Of course Mike may choose not to compete on price and try to find higher-end distributors that only sell exclusive brands priced more similarly to Sitka's products.

Sitka marks up their T's to a $12.50 distributor price. The distributors sell it to retailers for about $17.50, and the retailers sell it to customers for $27 to $34. ➡

also referred to as the **retailer margin** or **wholesaler margin**. The margin must be great enough to cover the fixed costs of the retailer or wholesaler and leave an amount for a profit.

When a manufacturer sets his price, he must consider these margins. To understand pricing through the channel better, we'll look at a simple example of channel pricing. Many times, a manufacturer builds its pricing structure around list prices. A **list price**, which we also refer to as a **manufacturer's suggested retail price (MSRP)**, is the price that the manufacturer sets as the appropriate price for the end consumer to pay. Let's say we have a consumer good with an MSRP of $10. This means the retailer will sell the product to the consumer for $10. But, as we said, retailers need money to cover their fixed costs and their profits. Thus, the retailer may determine that he must have a certain percentage gross or retailer margin; say, 30 percent.

This means that the retailer must be able to buy the product for no more than

$$\text{Price to the retailer} = \$10.00 \times (1.00 - 0.30)$$
$$= \$10.00 \times 0.70$$
$$= \$7.00$$

If the channel of distribution also includes a wholesaler, the wholesaler must be able to mark up the product in order to pay for his fixed costs and profits. This means that the wholesaler must also have a certain percentage gross or wholesaler margin; say, 20 percent. This means that the wholesaler must be able to buy the product for no more than:

$$\text{Price to the wholesaler} = \$7.00 \times (\$1.00 - 0.20)$$
$$= \$7.00 \times 0.80$$
$$= \$5.40$$

Thus, the manufacturer will sell the product not for $10 but for $5.40. Of course, the manufacturer may sell the product to the wholesaler for less than that, but he cannot sell it for more and still meet the margin requirements of the retailer and the wholesaler. If the manufacturer's variable costs for producing the product are $3, then his contribution to fixed costs is $2.40. It is this amount that is used to calculate the break-even point.

Step 4: Examine the Pricing Environment

In addition to demand and costs, marketers look at factors in the firm's external environment when they set prices. Only then can marketers set a price that not only covers costs but also provides a *competitive advantage*—a price that meets the needs of customers better than the competition. This section will discuss some important external influences on pricing strategies—the economic environment, competition, and consumer trends. Before we begin this discussion, it is especially important to note that price decisions are interdependent and must take into account demand and costs and the pricing environment together, as a whole.

The Economy

Broad economic trends, like those we discussed in Chapter 2, tend to direct pricing strategies. The business cycle, inflation, economic growth, and consumer confidence all help to determine whether one pricing strategy or another will succeed. Should a firm keep prices stable, reduce them, or even raise them in today's recessionary economy? Of course, the upswings and downturns in a national economy do not affect all product categories or all regions equally. Marketers need to understand how economic trends will affect their particular business. In general, during recessions, consumers grow more price sensitive (see Exhibit 9.7). They switch brands to get a better price and patronize discount stores and warehouse outlets. They are less likely to take luxury vacations and instead are happy with a "staycation" where they entertain the family at home. Many consumers lose their jobs and others are fearful of losing theirs. Even wealthy households, relatively unaffected by the recession, tend to cut back on their consumption. As a result, to keep factories in operation during periods of recession, some firms find it necessary to cut prices to levels at which they cover their costs but don't make a profit.

During the global recession that started in 2008, many consumers were affected, either directly or indirectly, by the sub-prime mortgage crisis and discovered that they could no longer spend as freely as they had become accustomed to doing. On the other hand, some companies actually found ways to profit from the credit crunch. For example, in the United States, Sekurus Inc. created a product for used car dealers to install in vehicles they sell to poor credit risks. It's a box underneath the dashboard that flashes a light when a payment is due. If the buyer doesn't make the payment and punch in a code when the dealer receives it, the car won't start and the repo man pays a visit.[14] Walmart removed many national brands from its shelves to make more space for its own brands when it found that shoppers were increasingly opting for the lower-priced versions. But this proved to be a mistake as it aggravated customers, and Walmart quickly responded by returning hundreds of national brands to its stores.[15]

Procter & Gamble, the world's biggest consumer-product maker, produces many premium-priced brands, some at prices twice the category average. But during the 2008 recession, P&G found sales, market share, and profits declining as consumers switched to store brands and other cheaper options. P&G responded with a number of price-cutting and product enhancement strategies. For example, P&G began offering larger packs of Duracell batteries and more absorbent Pampers diapers without increasing prices (Exhibit 9.8). The company also repositioned Cheer detergent as a bargain brand. But will customers return to premium brands after the recession? In Canada, probably yes, as the recession was not as extensive as in the United States. Many experts believe, however, that the recession of 2008 will likely have a permanent effect on American consumers, who are now spending less and saving more.[16]

There are also some economic trends that allow firms to increase prices, altering what consumers see as an acceptable or unacceptable price range for a product. *Inflation* may give marketers causes to either increase or decrease prices. First, inflation gets customers accustomed to price increases. Customers may remain insensitive to price increases, even when inflation goes away, allowing marketers to make real price increases, not just those that adjust for the inflation. Of course, during periods of inflation, consumers may grow fearful of the future and worry about whether they will have enough money to meet basic needs. In such a case, they may cut back on purchases. Then, as in periods of recession, inflation may cause marketers to lower prices and temporarily sacrifice profits to maintain sales levels.

The Competition

Marketers try to anticipate how the competition will respond to their pricing actions. They know that consumers' expectations of what constitutes a fair price largely depend on what the competition charges. However, it's not always a good idea to

Exhibit 9.7

Consumers are very price sensitive when economic conditions are bleak.

Exhibit 9.8

P&G responded to the recent recession by maintaining prices but increasing value.

fight the competition with lower and lower prices. Pricing wars such as those in the fast-food industry can change consumers' perceptions of what is a "fair" price, leaving them unwilling to buy at previous price levels.

Most industries, such as the airline, restaurant, and wheat farming, consist of a number of firms. These industries can belong to one of three industry structures—oligopoly, monopolistic competition, or pure competition. The industry structure a firm belongs to will influence price decisions. In general, firms like Delta Airlines that do business in an oligopoly—in which the market has few sellers and many buyers—are more likely to adopt *status quo* pricing objectives in which the pricing of all competitors is similar. Such objectives are attractive to oligopolistic firms, because avoiding price competition allows all players in the industry to remain profitable.

In a business such as the restaurant industry that is characterized by monopolistic competition—in which there are a lot of sellers each offering a slightly different product—it is more possible for firms to differentiate products and to focus on nonprice competition. Then each firm prices its product on the basis of its cost without much concern for matching the exact price of competitors' products. People don't tend to "comparison shop" between the prices of a coffee at Starbucks or Second Cup before deciding which chain to patronize. Of course, this doesn't mean that firms in an oligopoly can just ignore pricing by the competition. When one fast-food chain offers a "value meal," others often respond with their own versions.

Organizations like wheat farmers that function in a purely competitive market have little opportunity to raise or lower prices. Rather, supply and demand directly influence the price of wheat, soybeans, corn, or fresh peaches. When bad weather decreases the supply of crops, prices go up. And prices for almost any kind of fish have increased dramatically since health-conscious consumers began to turn away from red meat.

Of course, the elements of the pricing environment are interdependent. When the economy turns down and firms are faced with declining sales from a recession, many will simply lower their prices and sacrifice profits to drive sales. Other firms in the industry have to decide whether to maintain their current prices or follow suit and lower prices. The trick is to balance the two—maintain customer loyalty and the corresponding sales while ensuring an adequate level of profits. Starbucks, for example, tried to keep its more price sensitive customers during the recent recession by raising the prices of some products like Frappuccinos and Caramel Macchiatos, while lowering the prices of more popular beverages such as lattes and brewed coffee.[17]

Government Regulation

Another important factor in the environment that influences how marketers develop pricing strategies is government regulations. Governments in Canada and other countries develop two different types of regulations that have an effect on pricing. First, a large number of regulations increase the costs of production. Regulations for health care, environmental protection, occupational safety, and highway safety, just to mention a few, cause the costs of producing many products to increase. Other regulations such as those imposed by Health Canada and the Canadian Food Inspection Agency also increase the costs of developing and producing food and pharmaceutical products.

In addition, some regulations directly address prices. Electricity and natural gas prices are regulated in Canada, and the leader of the Ontario NDP said she would regulate gasoline prices in Ontario if the NDP won the next provincial election.[18] The federal government recently introduced legislation to regulate the Canadian credit card and debit card industry. Positioned as a self-regulating code of conduct, unless there is non-conformance, the legislation promotes fair business practices and ensures that merchants and consumers understand the costs and benefits associated with credit and debit cards.[19]

Consumer Behaviour & Trends

As we discussed in Chapter 4, marketers need to understand consumer behaviour to make informed marketing decisions, and this includes pricing decisions. We saw earlier in this chapter how some consumer factors influence demand, but marketers also need to consider other consumer factors when making price decisions. For example, consumers often base purchase decisions on their **internal reference price**, or what they perceive to be the customary or fair price (see Exhibit 9.9). If the price is above their expectations, they will perceive it as a rip-off, while if it is below expectations, consumers may think the product quality is unsatisfactory. Consider soft drinks, which are on sale so often that many consumers feel cheated when faced with paying a nondiscounted price.

Many older shoppers have outdated internal reference prices. They remember paying 20 cents for a chocolate bar, 80 cents for a loaf of bread, and $3.50 for a movie. This is why it is important for marketers to set pricing expectations and show that the prices they charge are fair. Gasoline retailers do this by showing you why gasoline costs what it does and that their margin is only about 3 percent. Other marketers may show their price compared to competitors' prices in advertising. Similarly, a retailer will display a product next to a higher-priced version of the same or a different brand, expecting one of two different results. On the one hand, if the prices (and other characteristics) of the two products are fairly close, it is likely that the consumer will feel the product quality is similar—called an *assimilation effect*. The customer might think that since the price is about the same, they must be alike, and choose the item that is priced lower, because the low price made it attractive next to the high-priced alternative. This is why store brands of deodorant, vitamins, pain relievers, and shampoo sit beside national brands (see Exhibit 9.10), often accompanied by a shelf sign pointing out how much shoppers can save by purchasing the store brands.

On the other hand, if the prices of the two products are far apart, a *contrast effect* may result. In this case, the consumer feels that the large difference in price means that there is a large difference in quality, and splurge to get the one they perceive as better quality. Using this strategy, an appliance store may place an advertised $800 refrigerator next to an $1199 model to make the customer believe that the "bottom of the line" model just won't do.

Consumers also make *price-quality inferences* about a product when they use price as a cue or an indicator for quality. If consumers are unable to judge the quality of a product through examination or prior experience—direct evidence—they will usually assume that the higher-priced product is the higher-quality product. Does it make sense to believe that a product is better quality just because it has a higher price tag? The answer is, sometimes. In many cases, it is true that a higher-priced product is better. Many of us have bought a bargain-priced pair of sneakers, a private-label

Exhibit 9.9
Most consumers have an internal reference price when it comes to buying food staples like bread.

internal reference price
A set price or a price range in consumers' minds that they refer to in evaluating a product's price.

Exhibit 9.10
Reference pricing strategies: Pharmacists sometimes need to explain why a brand-name drug costs more than a generic drug.

brand of cereal, or a less expensive brand of cellophane tape only to be disappointed. These experiences lead rational decision makers to associate price with quality, when quality cannot be otherwise perceived, especially when they have little prior experience in evaluating the item.

Consumer trends also can strongly influence prices. Culture and demographics determine how consumers think and behave, and so these factors have a large impact on all marketing decisions. Take, for example, the buying habits of the women who opted for a career in their twenties but who are hearing the ticking of their biological clocks as they enter their late thirties and forties. Couples who have babies later in their lives are often better off financially than younger parents, and on average they will have fewer children to spoil, so they are more willing to spend whatever it costs to give their babies the best.

Another important trend is that even well-off people no longer consider it shameful to hunt for bargains—in fact, it's becoming fashionable to boast that you found one. As a marketing executive for a chain of shopping malls observed, "Everybody loves to save money. It's a badge of honour today." Luxury consumers are looking for prestigious brands at low prices, though they're still willing to splurge for some high-ticket items. Industry analysts have called this new interest in hunting for sales "strategic shopping."[20]

The International Environment

As we discussed in Chapter 2, the marketing environment often varies widely from country to country. This can have important consequences in developing pricing strategies. Can prices be standardized for global markets or must there be localization in pricing? For some products such as jet airplanes, companies such as Boeing and Airbus standardize their prices. This is possible, first, because about the only customers for the wide-bodies and other popular jets are major airlines and governments of countries who buy for their military or for use by government officials, two groups that are able to pay. Second, companies building planes have little or no leeway in cutting their costs without sacrificing safety.

For other products, including most consumer goods, unique environmental factors in different countries mean marketers must adapt their pricing strategies. As we noted in Chapter 2, the economic conditions in developing countries often mean that consumers simply cannot afford $3 or $4 or more for a bottle of shampoo or laundry detergent. As a result, marketers offer their brands at lower prices, often by providing them in one-use packages called sachets that sell for just a few cents. In other cases, companies must save on costs by using less expensive ingredients in their brands in order to provide toothpaste or soap that is affordable.

The competitive environment in different countries also contributes to different pricing strategies. In countries such as China, long-established manufacturers of packaged foods and toiletries have been successful for decades by providing products at affordable prices. New entrants into these markets must price their products more or less in line with the local firms.

price subsidies
Government payments made to protect domestic businesses or to reimburse them when they must price at or below cost to make a sale. The subsidy can be a cash payment or tax relief.

Another factor that can have an effect on a firm's pricing in the international environment is government regulation. In some countries, the government dictates what the prices of products such as pharmaceuticals will be. With this kind of government control, a firm's only options are to use cheaper ingredients to produce the product or not to make their products available. Governments may also offer **price subsidies** (through outright payment or a tax relief) to local industries to make them more competitive. Prairie farmers face this situation as low grain prices and US and European subsidies have combined to put Canadian farmers at a severe competitive disadvantage. For years, American forest companies have claimed that Canada's software lumber is unfairly subsidized and have successfully lobbied for import restrictions.[21]

Finally, channels of distribution often vary both in the types and sizes of available intermediaries and in the availability of an infrastructure to facilitate product distribution. Often these differences can mean that trade margins will be higher, as will the cost of getting the products to consumers.

3

OBJECTIVE
Understand key
pricing strategies.
(pp. 317–324)

Pricing the Product: Establishing Strategies

An old Russian proverb says, "There are two kinds of fools in any market. One doesn't charge enough. The other charges too much."[22] In modern business, there seldom is any one-and-only, now-and-forever, best pricing strategy. Like playing a chess game, making pricing moves and countermoves requires thinking two and three moves ahead. Figure 9.11 provides a summary of the different pricing strategies and tactics.

Step 5: Choose a Pricing Strategy

The next step in price planning is to choose a pricing strategy. As Figure 9.11 suggests, some strategies are more consistent with particular pricing objectives. In addition, some strategies work for certain products, with certain customer groups, in certain competitive markets. When is it best for the firm to undercut the competition and when to just meet the competition's prices? When is the best pricing strategy one that covers costs only and when is it best to use one based on demand?

Strategies for Profit or Return Objectives

Cost-based strategies are typically associated with a target profit or return objectives. By understanding a product's cost structure, marketers can set prices to achieve a desired profit. Marketers use *cost-based strategies* because they are simple to calculate and are relatively safe, in that they ensure that the price will cover the costs the company incurs in producing and marketing the product.

Cost-based pricing methods, however, have drawbacks. They do not consider such factors as the nature of the target market, demand, competition, the product life cycle, and the product's image. In addition, although the calculations for setting the price may be simple and straightforward, it may be difficult to estimate costs accurately. Think about such firms as Bombardier and McCain, which produce many products. How do they allocate the costs for the plant, equipment, design engineers, maintenance, and marketing personnel so that the pricing plan accurately reflects the cost of production for any particular product? For example, how do you allocate the salary of a marketing executive who deals with many different products? Should the cost be divided equally among all products? Should costs be based on the actual number of hours spent working on each product? Or should costs be assigned based on the revenues generated by each product? There is no one right answer. However, even with these limitations, cost-based pricing strategies are often a marketer's best choice.

The most common cost-based pricing approach to pricing a product is **cost-plus pricing**, in which a marketer totals the unit costs for the product and then adds an amount to cover desired profit. Many marketers, especially retailers and wholesalers, use cost-plus pricing because of its simplicity—users need only estimate the unit cost and add the markup. To calculate cost-plus pricing, marketers usually calculate either a markup on cost or a markup on selling price. With both methods, you calculate the price by adding a predetermined percentage to the cost, but, as the names of the methods imply, for the one the calculation uses a percentage of the costs and for the other a percentage of the selling price. Which of the two methods is used seems often to be little more than a matter of "the way our company has always done it." You'll find more information about cost-plus pricing and how to calculate markup on cost and markup on selling price in Appendix 9A, Marketing Math, at the end of this chapter.

cost-plus pricing
A method of setting prices in which the seller totals all the unit costs for the product and then adds the desired profit per unit.

Profit Objectives
 Cost Based
  Cost-Plus Pricing
  Price-Floor Pricing
 Demand Based
  Target Cost Pricing
  Yield Management
  Variable (Custom) Pricing
  Skimming (New products)
 Experience Based
  Experimental Pricing
  Judgment
Sales or Market Share Objectives
 Value Pricing (Everyday low pricing)
 Frequent Discounting
 Penetration Pricing (New products)
 Trial Pricing (New products)
Competitive Effect Objectives (Stability)
 Price Leadership or Follower
 Premium Pricing
 Umbrella Pricing (Pricing below the competition)
 Price Bundling
Customer Satisfaction Objectives
 Variable (Custom) Pricing
 Cost of Ownership Pricing
 Value Pricing (Everyday low pricing)
 Price Bundling
Image Enhancement / Positioning Objectives
 Premium Pricing
 Prestige/Image Pricing
Everyday Low Pricing

Figure 9.11 Pricing Strategies

Marketers develop successful pricing programs by choosing from a variety of pricing strategies and tactics.

Cost-based pricing methods do not take into account any factors except costs and profits. But there are times when firms need to consider other factors, such as the advantage of having a plant operating at its peak capacity, which keeps a skilled workforce fully employed. **Price-floor pricing** is a method for calculating price that considers both costs and what can be done to ensure that a plant can operate at its capacity. It is sometimes used when the state of the economy or other temporary market conditions make it impossible for a firm to sell enough units of its product at a price that covers fixed costs (those that do not change with the number of units produced), variable costs (the additional cost to make one more unit of a product), and profit goals to keep its plants operating at full capacity. In such circumstances, it may be possible to sell part of the units produced at a lower price, one that covers only the variable costs of production. If the price-floor price can be set above the marginal costs, then the firm can use the difference to increase profits or to help cover its fixed costs.

price-floor pricing
A method for calculating price in which, to maintain full plant operating capacity, a portion of a firm's output may be sold at a price that covers only marginal costs of production.

For example, assume that a jeans firm, operating at full capacity, can produce 400 000 pairs of jeans a year. The average variable costs per unit are $20; the price that covers fixed costs, variable costs, and a desired level of profits is $30 per pair. Due to a downturn in the economy, the firm finds that it can sell only 350 000 units at this price. Using price-floor pricing, the firm can sell the additional 50 000 pairs of jeans at a price as low as $20 and maintain full-capacity operations.

If it adopts this approach, the firm will not make anything on the additional units, but it will not lose anything either. If it sells the additional 50 000 pairs at $25, then it will not only cover the variable costs but will also increase its total profits—50 000 × $5, or $250 000—not a bad deal. But several risks accompany price-floor pricing. Selling the additional 50 000 pairs of jeans at a lower cost might cannibalize full-price sales and, if the lower price is offered to some retailers and not others, it might anger those not included and undermine customer loyalty.

Firms that produce their own national brands as well as manufacture private-label brands sold through various retailers and distributors may use price-floor pricing for the private-label end of the business. Thus, Frigidaire may sell 70 percent of its refrigerators under the Frigidaire name and the rest to Sears for sale under its own Kenmore brand name. The consumers in Exhibit 9.11 look at specifications to compare models of different prices.

demand-based pricing
A price-setting method based on estimates of demand at different prices.

Cost-based strategies are quite popular, because they ensure that prices take into account an organization's costs. However, when firms base price strategies on cost, they are operating under the old production orientation and not a marketing orientation, because cost-based strategies do not take into consideration customer demand.

Strategies Based on Demand

Demand-based pricing means that the firm bases the selling price on an estimate of volume or quantity that it can sell in different markets at different prices. To use any of the pricing strategies based on demand, firms must determine how much product they can sell in each market and at what price. As we noted earlier, marketers often use customer surveys, in which consumers indicate whether they would buy a certain product and how much of it they would buy at various prices. They may obtain more accurate estimates by conducting an experiment like the ones we described in Chapter 3. For example, a firm might actually offer the product at different price levels in different test markets and gauge the reaction.

Exhibit 9.11
Price-floor pricing is a method for calculating price that considers both costs and what can be done to ensure that a plant can operate at capacity.

A strength of demand-based pricing strategies is that their use assures a firm that it will be able to sell what it produces at the determined price, because the price is based on research findings about customer demand rather than on the seller's costs. A major disadvantage is the difficulty of estimating demand accurately. Although sales forecasting is a topic covered in advanced marketing courses, it is important to know that estimating demand can be difficult. This is because the size of markets is often not known and needs to be estimated, the market share a firm might expect to capture needs to be estimated, and these projections need to take into consideration other factors that can affect demand, such as new competitors entering the market, the state of the economy, and changing consumer tastes. Dell is one company that uses demand pricing.[23] Dell revises the price of its computers when necessary to offset decreasing sales. The computer company reviews its prices frequently (often a few times a month) in an attempt to keep tabs on customer thinking and give customers the value they want.

Four specific demand-based pricing strategies are target cost pricing, yield management pricing, variable (custom) pricing, and skimming pricing. We'll talk about those next.

Today firms are finding that they can be more successful if they match price with demand using a process called **target costing**. With target costing, a firm first determines the price at which customers would be willing to buy the product and then it works backward to design the product in such a way that it can produce and sell the product at a profit. With target costing, a product's cost, and thus its price, is strongly tied to its design—70 to 80 percent of a product's costs are determined by its final design.

Firms first use marketing research to identify the quality and functionality needed to satisfy attractive market segments and what price they are willing to pay *before the product is designed*. As Table 9.2 shows, the next step is to determine what margins retailers and dealers require, as well as the profit margin the company requires. Based on this information, managers can calculate the target cost—the maximum it can cost the firm to manufacture the product. In addition, the company may break down this total target cost into different product functions or components, allocating more of the cost to product features consumers consider critical. If the firm can meet customer quality and functionality requirements, and control costs to meet the required price, it will manufacture the product. If not, it abandons the product.

One reason that target costing is practised more today is the global economy—competitor firms can bring "me too" products to market so quickly, usually within months, that there is little time to recover development costs, much less create brand loyalty. Success is tied to designing costs out of a product.

Yield-management pricing is another type of demand-based pricing strategy most commonly used by airlines, hotels, and cruise lines (Exhibit 9.12). With yield-management pricing, firms charge different prices to different customers to manage capacity while maximizing revenues. Many service firms practise yield-management pricing be-

target costing
A process in which firms identify the quality and functionality needed to satisfy customers and what price they are willing to pay before the product is designed; the product is manufactured only if the firm can control costs to meet the required price.

yield-management pricing
A practice of charging different prices to different customers to manage capacity while maximizing revenues.

Table 9.2	Target Costing Using a Jeans Example

Step 1: Determine the price customers are willing to pay for the jeans. $39.99

Step 2: Determine the markup required by the retailer. 40% = 0.40

Step 3: Calculate the maximum price the retailer will pay, the markup amount.
Price to the Retailer = Selling price × (1.00 − markup percentage)
Price to the Retailer = $39.99 × 0.60 = $23.99

Step 4: Determine the profit required by the firm. 15% = 0.15

Step 5: Calculate the target cost, the maximum cost of producing the jeans.
Target Cost = Price to the Retailer × (1.00 − profit percentage)
Target Cost = $23.99 × 0.85 = $20.39

With target costing, a firm first determines the price at which customers would be willing to buy the product and then works backward to design the product in such a way that it can produce and sell the product at a profit.

Exhibit 9.12
Hotels like Quebec City's Fairmont Le Château Frontenac use a yield-management pricing strategy to maximize revenues.

cause they recognize that different customers have different sensitivities to price—some customers will pay top dollar for an airline ticket while others will travel only if there is a discount fare. The goal of yield-management pricing is to accurately predict the proportion of customers who fall into each category and allocate the percentages of the airline's or hotel's capacity accordingly so that no product goes unsold.

For example, an airline may have two prices for seats: the full fare ($899) and the discount fare ($299). The airline must predict how many seats it can fill at full fare and how many can be sold at only the discounted fare. The airline begins months ahead of the date of the flight with a basic allocation of seats—perhaps it will place 25 percent in the full-fare "bucket" and 75 percent in the discount-fare bucket. While the seats in the full-fare bucket cannot be sold at the discounted price, the seats allocated for the discounted price can be sold at the full fare.

As flight time gets closer, the airline might make a series of adjustments to the allocation of seats in the hope of selling every seat on the plane at the highest price possible. If the Toronto Maple Leafs need to book the flight, chances are some of the discount seats will be sold at full fare, decreasing the number available at the discounted price. If, as the flight date nears, the number of full-fare ticket sales falls below the forecast, some of those seats will be moved to the discount bucket. This process continues until the day of the flight as the airline attempts to have every seat filled when the plane takes off. This is why you may be able to get a fantastic price on an airline ticket through discount travel agencies like Priceline.com or Cheapticketscanada. com if you wait until the last minute to buy your ticket.

This strategy is similar to a price discrimination strategy where different segments are targeted for different pricing levels—such as the price difference between men's and women's haircuts and men's and women's dry cleaning.

variable pricing
A flexible pricing strategy that reflects what individual customers are willing to pay.

Variable pricing, or custom pricing, is a strategy of tailoring the price of a product to reflect variability in market demand and what different customers are willing to pay. The price of gasoline, for example, is often set higher during periods of peak demand—like long weekends. Variable pricing is common in B2B marketing contexts where prices are typically negotiated in new buy or modified rebuy situations or submitted as sealed bids (typical of government purchases). Coca-Cola has been experimenting with the concept of variable pricing in vending machines—the price determined by the ambient temperature outside the machine—with a rationale that consumers may be willing to pay more for a cold Coke when it is hot outside.[24] Variable pricing could be considered a profit-oriented strategy as it ensures that products are sold at the highest price each customer is willing to pay. However, it could also be considered a customer satisfaction–based strategy, as it also ensures that customers get the best "deal" they are able to negotiate.

While variable pricing can result in maximized profit and satisfied customers, the negotiation process can be time consuming, and consumers have different levels of negotiating skills. This leaves some customers with cognitive dissonance, wondering if they got the best price.

skimming price
Charging a very high, premium price for a new product.

Skimming pricing means taking the top or best part of something—like the cream that separates and rises to the top of non-homogenized milk, used for making ice cream and whipped cream. In pricing new products, one strategy is to set a skimming price, which means that the firm charges a high, premium price for its new product, expecting demand from the top-spending, least price-sensitive, target market. For example, when Top-Flite introduced its new Strata golf balls with a new dimple design and more solid core for better flight with metal clubs, the price was three times that of regular balls. Pro shops still couldn't keep them in stock.[25]

If a product is highly desirable and offers unique benefits, and early adopters are not price sensitive during the introductory stage of the product life cycle, a skimming pricing strategy allows a firm to quickly recover research, development, and promotion costs, resulting in earlier profitability than under other pricing strategies (Exhibit 9.13). For skimming pricing to be successful, however, there should be little chance that competitors can get into the market quickly. With highly complex, technical products, it may be quite a while before competitors can develop and test new products and get them into production. This is the case for patented pharmaceutical products that have a lock on the market for 25 years.

A skimming pricing strategy is most successful when the market consists of several customer segments with different levels of price sensitivity. There must be a substantial number of initial product customers who have very low price sensitivity. After a period of time, the price can go down, and a second segment of the market with a slightly higher level of price sensitivity will purchase, and so on. For example, hand calculators that once commanded $200 can now be bought for less than $2—accessible to almost everyone.

Because of the difficulty in forecasting demand for products at different prices, many marketers, and in particular retailers, use their own experience to set prices. Experience-based pricing strategies are when a marketer tries different levels of pricing to see what the demand is. **Experimental pricing** is often used in market pre-tests where different prices are used in different geographic markets to generate the data to create a demand curve at different price levels. It is also used, less formally, by retailers who try one price for a product, and then make adjustments to the price to see what price level seems to generate the greatest profitability. This is also called trial-and-error pricing. Marketers also use **judgment** in setting prices—drawing on past experience with similar products or their understanding of the market segment to set prices.

Exhibit 9.13

Manufacturers of new-to-the-world, high-technology products like 3D TVs often use a skimming pricing strategy to recover research and development costs quickly.

Courtesy of LG Electronics Canada

experimental pricing
A strategy of experimenting with prices until the price that generates the highest profitability is found.

judgment
A pricing strategy that draws on past experience of the marketer in setting appropriate prices.

Strategies for Market Share Objectives

Other pricing strategies are more appropriate for meeting market share objectives. **Value-based pricing**, for example, is practised by retailers such as Walmart and Zellers (soon Target) that offer everyday low pricing (EDLP), which promises ultimate value to consumers—without having to negotiate or bargain for it. As discussed in Chapter 1, customer *value* is the benefits received by a customer relative to the costs and sacrifices necessary to obtain those benefits. This means that, in the customers' eyes, the product's price is justified by what they receive.

Value-based pricing begins with customers, then considers the competition, and then determines the best pricing strategy. Smart marketers know that the firm that wins is not necessarily the one with the lowest prices but rather the one that delivers the most value.

This has been the strategy behind the success of WestJet Airlines. Modelled after Southwest Airlines, WestJet focuses on everyday low fares, short distances, and good customer service to attract budget-conscious leisure travellers throughout Canada. It started with understanding the target market—what it would take to get people out of their cars for short-haul trips—then made marketing mix decisions to deliver the value bundle sought by those customers: no-frills, direct flights at rock-bottom prices, to and from under-utilized airports, using standard aircraft, serviced by personable staff offering fun and lighthearted (perhaps even irreverent) customer interactions.

value-based pricing
A pricing strategy in which a firm sets prices that provide ultimate value to customers.

In practice, when marketers use EDLP strategies, consumers feel they get more for their money. Marketers hope that will make them see the price as reasonable and encourage them to remain loyal rather than snapping up whatever happens to be on sale. Deal-oriented consumers, however, have been conditioned to choose products because they are "on special" rather than because they are superior to others. The problem with deals or frequent price promotions is that consumers learn to wait for sales or stock up on products when they are on sale, thus making it difficult for companies to maintain "regular" margins and production volumes.

frequent discounting
A strategy of frequently using sale prices to increase sales volume.

The approach of using sales, coupons, and other discounts to stimulate sales is a **frequent discounting** strategy. Retailers like Future Shop that have weekly sale extravaganzas use this strategy to entice consumers into their stores where they may purchase both sale and non-sale items. The problem with frequent discounting is that it conditions consumers to wait for the sale price. If they can wait, consumers will not pay the "regular" price for a two-litre bottle of Coca-Cola, knowing that it goes on sale for 99 cents periodically and is in the $1.79 range regularly.

penetration pricing
A pricing strategy in which a firm introduces a new product at a very low price to encourage more customers to purchase it.

Another market share–based strategy is **penetration pricing**. Penetration pricing, the opposite of skimming pricing, is when a new product is introduced at a very low price, as Intel did with its first Pentium processor chip.[26] Because rivals were way behind in developing competitive chips, Intel had used a skimming strategy for the 486 processor. However, when the Pentium 1 was introduced, Intel knew that Motorola was working with IBM and Apple to develop comparable chips, and it set a low price for the Pentium 1 to sell more in a short period of time and derail Motorola's debut.[27] This strategy worked well for Intel. The low price encouraged demand and sales in the early stages of the product life cycle. If the marketing objective is to beef up market share, penetration pricing makes sense.

Another reason marketers use penetration pricing is to discourage competitors from entering the market. The firm that is first out with a new product has an important advantage. Experience has shown that a *pioneering brand* often is able to maintain dominant market share for the life of the product. Competitors looking at the market may feel that the potential for developing a profitable alternative is not good. Bayer aspirin and Hoover vacuum cleaners are examples of brands that were first to market, kept their leads for decades, and still dominate their fields. These pioneering brands don't need to do much talking to tell consumers who they are. Keeping prices low may even act as a *barrier to entry* to potential competitors, because the cost of developing and manufacturing a new similar product prevents a satisfactory return.

trial pricing
Pricing a new product low for a limited period of time to lower the risk for a customer.

Trial pricing is when a new product carries a low price for a limited period of time to lower the risk for a customer, and then the price is increased to "regular" levels.[28] In trial pricing, the idea is to win customer acceptance first and make profits later. A low enough introductory price may be a preferred alternative to giving out free samples, as the trial price will bring some positive contribution to the organization. A number of years ago, Via Rail launched a "Miss Mom's Cooking Campaign" targeting university students. The campaign was based on the assumption that many first-year students are missing Mom's home cooking and clean laundry. Ads featured empty fridges and piles of dirty laundry. Flyers were distributed to university residences encouraging students to visit a special Web site where they would receive a special reduced fare on a train ticket "home to Mom." According to Via Rail executives, the objective of this reduced fare was to encourage trial, so that later on when students started their careers they would be aware of Via Rail.[29]

Telecommunications companies like Telus and Bell use trial pricing on their Internet, phone, and TV packages, offering a discounted rate for an initial period of time (usually six months) before increasing the price for the duration of an annual or longer contract. Trial pricing also works for services. Health clubs and other service providers frequently offer trial memberships or special introductory prices. They hope that customers will try the service at a low price and be converted to a regular-price customer.

Strategies for Competitive Effect Objectives

Competitive effect pricing strategies are those that are competitor focused. To achieve competitive effect objectives, a firm can adopt a price leadership (follower) strategy, a parity pricing strategy, a premium pricing strategy, an umbrella pricing strategy, or a price bundling strategy.

Before Walmart came to Canada, Zellers was clearly the price leader in discount stores (their tag line was "The lowest price is the law"). Other discount stores would price their products similarly to Zellers.[30] A firm that chooses a **price leadership (follower)** strategy is either the industry leader or it follows the industry leader by setting the same or similar prices. Usually, firms practise a price leadership strategy when they're in an oligopoly with relatively few producers—such as the Canadian petroleum industry or cell phone industry. In such industries, it is in the best interest of all firms to minimize price competition for everyone to make a profit. Price leadership strategies are popular, because they provide an acceptable and legal way for firms to agree on prices without ever talking with each other.

> **price leadership (follower)**
> The firm that sets prices first in an industry; other major firms in the industry follow the leader by staying in line.

Even when there isn't a single industry price leader, firms may adopt a **parity pricing strategy**—they try to keep their price about equal to key competitors' prices. Gasoline retailers attempt to maintain a parity pricing structure by responding quickly to competitive price moves; consumers often view this rapid response as *price fixing*. Numerous national and provincial investigations of gasoline prices have found no evidence of price fixing, and the petroleum companies are spending millions of dollars educating consumers about the cost structure of gasoline.[31]

> **parity pricing strategy**
> A pricing strategy where organizations keep their prices about equal to key competitors' prices.

Premium pricing is when firms choose to price their products higher than competitive offerings. While this strategy helps to portray a premium or quality positioning, it also helps firms achieve the competitive effect of market leadership and price stability. IBM computers, for example, are priced 10 to 15 percent higher than competitive offerings, in part because IBM's industry leadership allows them to, and it protects the pricing in the industry and enables competitors to compete on price without entering a price war. For similar reasons, Microsoft computer peripherals, such as optical mice, are priced 10 to 20 percent higher than competitive products. Coca-Cola is counting on its market leadership position, brand equity, and customer loyalty to support a new premium pricing strategy, pricing Coke products above the competition in an attempt to increase margins and profits.[32]

> **premium pricing**
> Firms choose to price their products higher than competitive offerings.

The opposite of premium pricing is **umbrella pricing**, or pricing below the competition. By using rock-bottom prices on popular movies, music, and games, electronics stores such as Future Shop have been able to get shoppers into their stores, where many will buy the high-profit electronics equipment sold by the retailer. Umbrella pricing is a strategy of ducking under the competition's price by a standard percentage. Corel Corporation, for example, consistently prices its office software suite at least 20 percent below that of Microsoft.

> **umbrella pricing**
> A strategy of ducking under a competitor's price by a fixed percentage.

Price bundling is selling two or more goods or services as a single package for one price. As a strategy, it is an attempt to pre-empt competition and prevent consumers or customers from entering a discrete purchase decision for the product included with the one intended for purchase. Hewlett-Packard bundles computer systems, for example, to include a system unit, a monitor, and a printer. By including the monitor or printer "free" with the system unit purchase, HP ends up not competing with Lexmark, Canon, or other computer peripheral manufacturers. Price bundling could also be used to achieve customer satisfaction objectives by including another product of value to customers with their intended purchase. Porter Airlines, for example, bundles specific flights to promote their VIPorter

> **price bundling**
> Selling two or more goods or services as a single package for one price.

Free one-way flight.

When you book and take two return flights from Toronto to Montréal between September 1 and November 15, you'll earn enough VIPorter points for a free one-way flight anywhere Porter flies.

VIPorter offer!

* Book and travel between September 1 and November 15. Earn 2,000 VIPorter points for every eligible flight. 7500 VIPorter Points are required to redeem for a one-way flight. Originating airport and final destination airport are either YTZ-YUL or YUL-YTZ.

Exhibit 9.14

Price bundling often entices customers to spend more than if they bought only one product. This strategy is even used by airlines.

cost of ownership
A pricing strategy that considers the lifetime cost of using the product.

prestige pricing
A strategy where prices are set significantly higher than competing brands.

SHRINK **COSTS.**
WATCH BUSINESS
GROW.
HP LASERJET. IT PAYS YOU BACK.

The less your business spends, the more it can grow. After just one year, the HP LaserJet CM3530 Color Multifunction Printer pays for itself by saving energy, paper and toner. Learn more at **hp.ca/paysback**

HP LASERJET CM3530 COLOR MFP

hp HIT PRINT INTELLIGENTLY

Exhibit 9.15

Hewlett-Packard bases its pricing on customer needs using a cost-of-ownership strategy.

frequent flyer points program (Exhibit 9.14). We will discuss the tactical use of price bundling shortly.

Pricing Strategies to Achieve Customer Satisfaction Objectives

When firms develop pricing strategies that cater to the needs of customers, they are less concerned with short-term successes than with keeping customers for the long term. Firms truly dedicated to customer satisfaction look at the wants and needs of customers in developing pricing strategies. Three pricing strategies we have already discussed can be used to achieve customer satisfaction objectives: variable pricing, value pricing, and price bundling. Another strategy to achieve customer satisfaction objectives is to consider total **cost of ownership**. The cost of ownership is the price consumers pay for a product, plus the cost of maintaining and using the product, less its resale (or salvage) value. Sanyo, for example, bases the price of its rechargeable batteries on customer cost of ownership—comparing the cost of using regular batteries to the use of Sanyo's rechargeable ones and setting a price lower than the cost of multiple regular batteries. In 2010, HP launched its "HP LaserJet Pays You Back" global marketing campaign to illustrate the significant cost savings—up to $2,500 in less than one year—that are possible when using an HP Color LaserJet Multifunction Printer (MFP). Over time, the printer pays for itself through money saved and then continues to pay customers back through energy conservation, solutions that help reduce paper waste and high-capacity cartridges which require fewer replacements. HP's goal is to encourage customers around the world to view an HP LaserJet as a business investment that delivers both near- and long-term return-on-investment (ROI). (See Exhibit 9.15.)

Pricing Strategies to Achieve Image Enhancement/Positioning Objectives

There are three common pricing strategies for achieving image enhancement (positioning) objectives. We have already discussed value pricing (everyday low pricing), which is used to support a value positioning strategy, in addition to being a way of increasing market share. We have also already discussed premium pricing as a competitive effect-based strategy, but premium pricing could also be used to support a premium positioning strategy where higher-than-competition pricing is intended to support inferences of higher quality or another basis of superiority. Related to premium pricing is **prestige pricing**, which is pricing products significantly higher than competitive brands to make them status symbols. Rolex, for example, uses a prestige pricing strategy for its watches, which retail for $5000 to $10 000 (or more!). Prestige pricing is part of an exclusive positioning strategy, where only the very wealthy or privileged can purchase the brand.

4

OBJECTIVE

Understanding pricing tactics and how to set price points.

(pp. 325-330)

Pricing the Product: Pricing Tactics and Setting Price Points

Once marketers have developed pricing strategies, the next step in price planning is to actually set prices by applying pricing tactics and to set the terms and conditions associated with that price.

Step 6: Develop Pricing Tactics

In practice, prices are set in the range determined by the product's costs, what customers are willing to pay, and the price of competitive or substitute products. However, as seen in Figure 9.12, there are a number of considerations for setting prices within this range.

Pricing for Individual Products

How marketers present a product's price to the market can make a big difference in the attractiveness of the offering. Here are two tactics:

- With *two-part pricing*, two separate types of payments are required to purchase the product. For example, golf and tennis clubs charge yearly or monthly fees plus fees for each round of golf or tennis. Cellular phone and Internet service providers offer customers a set number of minutes of usage for a monthly fee plus a per-minute rate for extra usage.

- *Payment pricing* makes products appear more attainable by breaking up the total price into smaller amounts payable over time. For example, many customers now opt to lease rather than buy a car. The monthly lease amount is an example of payment pricing, which tends to make people less sensitive to the total price of the car (Exhibit 9.16).[33]

Pricing for Multiple Products

A firm may sell several products that consumers typically buy together. When people buy a burger, pizza, or taco for lunch, they often purchase a drink, fries, or salad as well. Similarly, when someone buys a personal computer, a USB drive is usually not far behind. We have previously discussed price bundling as a pricing strategy. As a price tactic, price bundling is enhancing the perceived value of a purchase by combining two or more goods or services into a single offer, at a lower price than the individual items. A music buff, for example, can buy tickets to an entire concert series for a lower price than buying tickets to each concert separately. A movie ticket may include a drink and popcorn. Even an all-you-can-eat special at the local diner is an example of price bundling. Price bundling is an increasingly popular pricing tactic for consumer electronics, small and large appliances, and even automobiles, where the tangible product is bundled with an extended warranty package. The tangible product is priced near cost while more significant margins are made on the extended warranty. The thinking behind price bundling as a tactic is that whatever revenue a seller loses from the reduced prices, it makes up in increased total purchases.

Captive pricing is a tactic a firm uses when it has two products that work only when used together. The firm sells one item at a very low price and then makes its profit on the second high-margin item. Gillette uses captive pricing to sell its shaving products. The Gillette Fusion ProGlide razor is sold for a

captive pricing
A pricing tactic for two items that must be used together; one item is priced very low and the firm makes its profit on another, high-margin item essential to the operation of the first item.

Pricing for Individual Products
- Two-part pricing
- Payment pricing

Pricing for Multiple Products
- Price bundling
- Captive pricing

Geographic Pricing
- F.O.B. pricing
- Zone pricing
- Uniform delivered pricing
- Freight absorption pricing

Psychological Pricing
- Odd (even) number pricing
- Price lining

Price Discounts
- Trade or functional discounts
- Quantity discounts
- Cash discounts
- Seasonal discounts

Figure 9.12 Pricing Tactics

Exhibit 9.16

Auto manufacturers know that a per-month price for a new car makes people less sensitive to the total price of the car.

relatively low price but the disposable blades sell for $4.50 or more per blade set—and the typical user buys 30 blades a year. Although the blade and razor business generates only a third of corporate revenues for Gillette, the company's use of captive pricing tactics in this category delivers two-thirds of its profits (Exhibit 9.17).

Geographic Pricing

Geographic pricing is a tactic that establishes how firms handle the cost of shipping products to customers near, far, and wide. Characteristics of the product, customers, and competition may make it advisable to charge all customers the same price, or it may make better sense to vary the prices charged to customers in different locations, regardless of the overall pricing strategy selected.

F.O.B. Pricing

Often, pricing is stated as f.o.b. factory or f.o.b. delivered—f.o.b. stands for *free on board*, which means the supplier will pay to have the product loaded onto a truck or some other carrier. Also—and this is important—title passes to the buyer at the f.o.b. location. Thus, *f.o.b. factory* or **f.o.b. origin** means that the cost of transporting the product from the factory to the customer's location is the responsibility of the customer; **f.o.b. delivered** means that the seller pays both the cost of loading and transporting to the customer, which is included in the selling price.

The f.o.b. origin pricing creates many different prices, because the purchase price for each customer changes with shipping costs. But with f.o.b. delivered pricing, every customer pays the same price. Another option combines f.o.b. origin and f.o.b. delivered—sometimes, a seller's terms indicate that title to the product is transferred at the seller's location, but the seller will pay the freight. This plan is called *f.o.b. factory, freight prepaid*.

Sellers often prefer *f.o.b. factory* pricing because of its simplicity. The marketer doesn't have to take into account the costs of shipping to different customers at varying distances from the factory. It also allows flexibility in how a product gets shipped, because pricing does not depend on a particular shipping method. In addition, the fact that the title is transferred before shipping shifts the risk of damage to the transit company and the customer.

---

f.o.b. origin pricing
A pricing tactic in which the cost of transporting the product from the factory to the customer's location is the responsibility of the customer.

f.o.b. delivered pricing
A pricing tactic in which the cost of loading and transporting the product to the customer is included in the selling price, paid by the manufacturer.

zone pricing
A pricing tactic in which customers in different geographic zones pay different transportation rates.

Zone Pricing

Another geographic pricing tactic is **zone pricing**. Like f.o.b. factory pricing, zone pricing means that distant customers pay more than customers who are close to the factory. However, in zone pricing, there are a limited number of different prices charged, based on geographic zones established by the seller. All customers located in each zone pay the same transportation charge.

Zone pricing simplifies geographic cost differences, which is important in certain markets. It would be nearly impossible for Canada Post's express courier service to charge one price if a package shipped from Winnipeg went to Toronto, a different price if it went to Mississauga, and another if it went to Don Mills, Ontario. Therefore, XPRESSPOST charges different rates for shipping packages from any single location to different zones across the country.

Uniform Delivered Pricing

With **uniform delivered pricing**, an average shipping cost is added to the price, no matter what the buyer's location or distance from the manufacturer's plant—within reason. Catalogue sales, home television shopping, e-commerce, and other types of nonstore retail sales usually use uniform delivered pricing.

Freight Absorption Pricing

Freight absorption pricing means the seller takes on part or all of the cost of shipping. This strategy is good for high-ticket items, when the cost of shipping is a negligible part of the sales price and the profit margin. Marketers are most likely to use freight absorption pricing in highly competitive markets or when such pricing allows them to enter new markets.

Psychological Tactics

Marketers need to take into consideration consumer behaviour when making pricing decisions, and this will be discussed further later in the chapter. As we saw in Chapter 4, part of understanding consumer behaviour is understanding consumer psychology. Two pricing tactics that draw on consumer psychology are odd (even) number pricing, and price lining.

Odd (Even) Number Pricing

We usually see prices reported in dollars and cents—$1.99, $5.98, $23.67, or even $599.99. Exhibit 9.18 shows this common practice. We see prices in even dollar amounts—$2, $10, or $600—far less often. The reason? Marketers have assumed that there is a psychological response to odd prices that differs from the responses to even prices. Research on the difference in perceptions of odd versus even prices has been inconclusive and has produced no substantive evidence that the use of odd prices is superior to even prices. But that doesn't mean that marketers should change this practice.

At the same time, there are some instances in which even prices are the norm or perhaps even necessary. Theatre and concert tickets, admission to sporting events, and lottery tickets tend to be priced in even amounts, so that ticket sellers don't have to make change. Professional fees are normally expressed as even dollars. If a lawyer charged $99.99 per hour, the client might wonder why he or she has a "bargain-priced" fee and may think less of the quality of the legal advice. Many luxury items such as jewellery, golf course fees, and resort accommodations use even dollar prices to set them apart from less costly substitutes.

Price Lining

Marketers often apply their understanding of the psychological aspects of pricing in a practice called **price lining**. This means that similar items in a product line sell at different prices, called price points. If you want to buy a laptop computer, you will find that most manufacturers have one "stripped-down" model for about $450. Other laptop systems are offered at prices around $650, $850, $1150, $1350, $1550, and $1750. While consumers can spend much more than $1750 on a laptop computer system, computer manufacturers have found that most consumers are prepared to pay $1150 to $1550 for a laptop.

Exhibit 9.17

Gillette practises captive pricing with its razors. Once customers buy the handles, they are "captive" to the company's blade prices. Many computer printer companies follow the same strategy with computer ink.

uniform delivered pricing
A pricing tactic in which a firm adds a standard shipping charge to the price for all customers regardless of location.

freight absorption pricing
A pricing tactic in which the seller absorbs the total cost of transportation.

Exhibit 9.18

Most companies offer prices in odd dollar amounts because they think customers will be more inclined to buy.

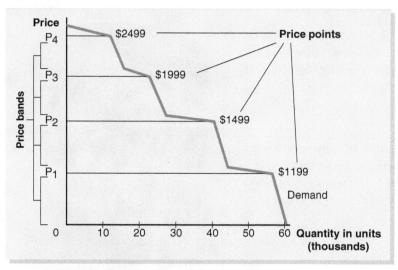

Figure 9.13 Price Lining

Sometimes firms will offer products at standard price levels to match customer.expectations.

price lining

The practice of setting a limited number of different specific prices, called price points, for items in a product line.

list price

The price the end customer is expected to pay as determined by the manufacturer.

trade or functional discounts

Discounts off the list price of products to members of the channel of distribution that perform various marketing functions.

Rather than competing on price, these manufacturers compete on the features offered at each price point.

Why is price lining a good practice? From the marketer's standpoint, price lining is a way to maximize profits. In theory, a firm would charge each individual customer the highest price that customer was willing to pay. If the most one specific person would be willing to pay is $1499 for a personal computer, then that would be their price. If another person would be willing to pay $1999, that would be their price. But charging each consumer a different price is usually not possible (it takes too long to negotiate the price). Having a limited number of prices that generally fall at the top of the range customers find acceptable is a more workable alternative. Firms that use price lining assume that demand is inelastic within certain ranges, but that if prices go above that range, demand will become elastic and customers will balk.

Figure 9.13 shows an assumed demand curve for a product for which price lining is a good strategy. This figure shows price points within price bands for different computers in a manufacturer's product line.

Price Discounts

Marketers also use price discounts as a tactic in setting prices—both with customers and channel intermediaries—and for customers or distributors to get these discounts, they have to meet certain terms and conditions.

Trade or Functional Discounts

Whether a firm sells to businesses or directly to consumers, most pricing structures are built around list prices. A **list price** is set by the manufacturer for the end customer to pay. In pricing for members of the channel, marketers recognize that pricing must ensure that retailers and wholesalers can cover their costs of doing business and make a profit (Exhibit 9.19).

When manufacturers develop pricing tactics for channel intermediaries, they often use **trade or functional discounts**, because the channel members perform selling, credit, storage, and transportation services that the manufacturer would otherwise have to provide. Often, setting functional discounts is simplified when a firm uses set percentage discounts off the list price for each channel level.

Let's look at an example of a channel of distribution that includes a manufacturer which sells to wholesalers, that in turn sell to smaller retailers. The manufacturer may state trade discounts as list price less 40/20. The first number means that 40 percent of the list price is to cover the overhead and profit requirements for the retailer—the manufacturer is suggesting that the wholesalers sell to their retail customers at list less 40 percent. If the list price of a product were $200, the price to the retailers would be

$$\$200 - (40\% \times 200) = \$200 - \$80 = \$120$$

Exhibit 9.19

In pricing to retailers, bicycle manufacturers have to consider the amount retailers must have to operate their business and make a profit.

The second number, the 20, is the discount percentage allowed for wholesalers to cover their costs of doing business and profit. Thus, the manufacturer's selling price to the wholesaler is discounted from the retailer's price and would be

$$\$120 - (20\% - 120) = \$120 - \$24 = \$96$$

Note that although we talk about trade discounts being determined by manufacturers, in reality the manufacturer has little if any control over the percentage discounts. In most industries, these are standard percentages based on the margins retailers and wholesalers require to cover their overhead and profits.

Quantity Discounts

Firms that sell to distribution channel members or end-user business customers often offer **quantity discounts**, or reduced prices, for purchases of larger quantities. Marketers commonly use quantity discounts as a way to encourage larger purchases from distribution channel partners.

Sometimes marketers offer buyers **cumulative quantity discounts**, which are based on a total quantity bought within a specified time period, such as a year. Cumulative quantity discounts encourage a buyer to stick with a single seller instead of moving from one supplier to another. Cumulative quantity discounts may be rebates, in which case the firm sends the buyer a rebate cheque at the end of the discount period. In other cases, the discount is a credit against future orders. In either case, the buyer must wait until the end of the discount period to receive the discount. This delay makes cumulative quantity discounts less attractive, because the buyer must pay the nondiscounted price for the goods all year long and not realize the discount until the end of the period. For businesses that operate with low gross margins, this can create some financial hardships.

Noncumulative quantity discounts are based only on the quantity purchased with each individual order. Noncumulative discounts encourage larger single orders, but do little to tie the buyer and the seller together. When a competitor makes a better discount offer, the buyer may switch. In most cases, noncumulative quantity discounts mean that the buyer pays a reduced price for the goods purchased—there is a simple cash discount. In other cases the discount offer is made in terms of free goods. For example, a grocer who buys 10 cases of peanut butter may get one case free.

Sometimes, offering quantity discounts can create problems for a manufacturer among their distribution channels. If a large customer like Costco can get larger discounts than smaller retailers by purchasing in larger volumes, the smaller distributors may not be able to compete. Managing pricing across distribution channels with different expectations of margins is a challenging task. This is why some manufacturers, particularly those producing electronic goods, like Sony or LG, offer many variations (stock keeping units, or SKUs) of their products. Different channels get different products so customers can't do direct price comparisons.

Cash Discounts

Using money costs money, as anyone who's ever taken out a mortgage or a college loan understands. When a firm borrows money, it must pay interest for every day it has the use of the money. Conversely, if a firm has excess cash, it is able to invest that cash and make money from its money. Thus, having cash is an advantage. For this reason many firms try to entice their customers to pay their bills quickly by offering *cash discounts*. For example, a firm selling to a retailer may state that the terms of the sale are "2 percent 10 days, net 30 days." This means that if the retailer pays the producer for the goods within 10 days, the amount due is cut by 2 percent. The total amount is due within 30 days, and after 30 days, the payment is late.

quantity discounts
A pricing tactic of charging reduced prices for larger quantities of a product.

cumulative quantity discounts
Discounts based on the total quantity bought within a specified time period.

noncumulative quantity discounts
Discounts based only on the quantity purchased in individual orders.

Tech and Trends

Virtual Wallets

History shows a series of innovations in how consumers buy shoes, toothpaste, and candy bars. Coins replaced bartering and were the first currency. Paper money followed coins, and in the 1950s the credit card was introduced. Today Canadians use plastic more than money, and some airlines and restaurants won't even take cash. So what's next? Most likely the transition to digital cash. In the future, money as we know it may cease to exist. Instead, consumers will carry virtual wallets, with their credit card and bank information stored on remote computers. And since everyone, it seems, has a cell phone, that's the obvious access vehicle. ShopSavvy is one new cell phone app that uses the phone camera to scan an item's bar code, checks to see if it's available for a lower price online, and then buys it with a credit card number and shipping information stored on a Web site. MasterCard, with its partner Obopay, now makes it possible for consumers to send money to anyone via cell phone text messages. In Malaysia, Visa has begun installing chips into cell phones so that consumers can swipe their cell phone instead of their credit card. And Starbucks has an iPhone app that allows its customers to upload money and then swipe their phone at the cash register to pay for their double macchiato.[34]

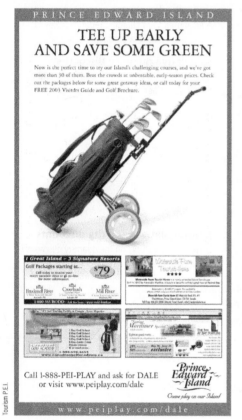

Exhibit 9.20

Tourism PEI, like other destination marketing organizations, promotes seasonal discounts to attract visitors.

Seasonal Discounts

Seasonal discounts are price reductions offered during certain times of the year. Products such as snow blowers, lawn mowers, and water skiing equipment are priced in this way. If such products are sold only during a few months of the year, then the manufacturer must either build a large plant that has to be shut down during the off-season or build a large warehouse to store inventory until the season comes around again. Both of these options are unattractive; so to entice retailers and wholesalers to buy off-season and store the product at their locations until the right time of the year, a firm may offer seasonal discounts. Seasonal discounting is also used extensively by tourist attractions and destinations—enticing visitors in slower seasons (Exhibit 9.20).

Other Terms and Conditions

In setting prices, marketers also have to set other terms and conditions. One of these is whether they are going to accept cash only or also accept credit card, debit card, or other forms of payment. Credit and debit card acceptance makes it more convenient for customers to pay for products, but the credit card companies and banks charge the seller a commission ranging from 1 to 4 percent for processing the transaction and guaranteeing payment. Marketers also have to decide what currencies they are willing to accept. Canadian retailers that target tourists, for example, are often willing to accept US dollars, but few are equipped or willing to provide change in US dollars, because of the hassle of keeping two sets of cash registers and currencies stocked and the exchange rate risk of dealing in multiple currencies. Businesses that have a larger international trade find it advantageous to make it as easy as possible for customers to buy and do business in their own currency.

5 Pricing and Electronic Commerce

As we have seen, price planning is a complex process in any firm. But if you are operating in the "wired world," get ready for even more pricing options! Because sellers are connected to buyers around the globe as never before through the Internet, corporate networks, and wireless setups, marketers can offer deals they tailor to a single person at a single moment. On the other hand, they're also a lot more vulnerable to smart consumers, who can easily check out competing prices with the click of a mouse.

Many experts suggest that technology is creating a consumer revolution that might change pricing forever—and perhaps create the most efficient market ever. The music industry provides the most obvious example. Music lovers from around the globe purchase and download billions of songs from numerous Internet sites including the iTunes Music Store.[35] And mobile music is just beginning—43 percent of mobile users across the globe access music through their phones. In the United States, consumers spent $1.1 billion on recorded music for their phones in 2007. This figure is about 12 percent of the $9 billion people spent globally on mobile music; analysts expect the total to jump to $17.5 billion by 2012.[36] And many of the sellers find that it is easy to compete on price.

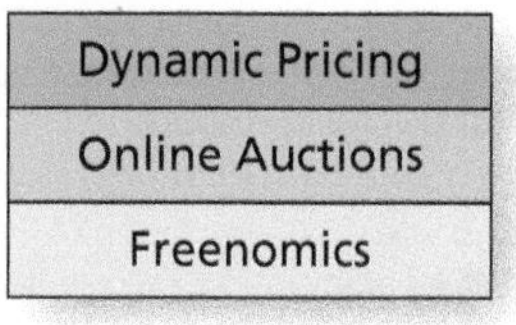

The Internet also enables firms that sell to other businesses (B2B firms) to change their prices rapidly as they adapt to changing costs. For consumers who have lots of stuff in the attic they need to put in someone else's attic, the Internet means an opportunity for consumers to find ready buyers. And for B2C firms, firms that sell to consumers, the Internet offers other opportunities. In this section, we will discuss some of the more popular Internet pricing strategies shown in Figure 9.14.

Dynamic Pricing Strategies

One of the most important opportunities the Internet offers is **dynamic pricing**, in which the seller can easily adjust the price to meet changes in the marketplace. If a bricks-and-mortar retail store like Sitka wants to change prices, employees/workers must place new price tags on items, create and display new store signage and media advertising, and input new prices into the store's computer system. For B2B marketers, employees/workers must print catalogues and price lists and distribute to salespeople and customers. These activities can be very costly to a firm, so they simply don't change their prices very often.

Online Auctions

Most consumers are familiar with eBay. But what about Ubid4it, Bazaario, and eBid? These too are some of the many online auctions that allow shoppers to bid on everything from bobbleheads to health-and-fitness equipment to a game-worn, Sidney Crosby jersey. Auctions provide a second Internet pricing strategy. Perhaps the most popular auctions are the consumer-to-consumer (C2C) auctions, such as those on eBay. The eBay auction is an *open auction*, meaning that all the buyers know the highest price bid at any point in time. On many Internet auction sites, the seller can set a *reserve price*, a price below which the item will not be sold.

A *reverse auction* is a tool used by firms to manage their costs in B2B buying. While in a typical auction buyers compete to purchase a product, in reverse auctions, sellers compete for the right to provide a product at, hopefully, a low price.

Freenomics: What If We Just Give It Away?

It turns out that one of the most exciting revolutions in e-commerce is happening in the area of pricing. Once again the Internet is changing the way we look at doing business.[37] In this case this is because the Net makes it possible to give products away FOR FREE.

It turns out that a business model based on pricing goods at zero or close to zero actually makes dollars and sense. For example, indie music groups like The New Pornographers, Arcade Fire, Hot Panda, and even mainstream bands like the Barenaked Ladies understand that when they make their music freely available online they build a fan base that flocks to their concerts and buys their merchandise. Many online video games are free to players because they are ad-supported, and almost everything Google "sells," such as unlimited search, Gmail, and Picasa, is actually free to consumers.

This new business model of **freenomics** is based on the idea that economists call *externalities*; this means that the more people you get to participate in a market, the more profitable it is. So, for example, the more people Google convinces to use its Gmail e-mail service, the more eyeballs it attracts, which in turn boosts the rates advertisers are willing

Dynamic Pricing
Online Auctions
Freenomics

Figure 9.14 Internet Pricing Strategies

The Internet provides an opportunity to use some unique pricing strategies.

dynamic pricing
A pricing strategy in which the price can easily be adjusted to meet changes in the marketplace.

online auctions
E-commerce that allows shoppers to purchase products through online bidding.

freenomics
The business model of offering a basic good or service for free in order to build a customer base to which added value offerings can be sold.

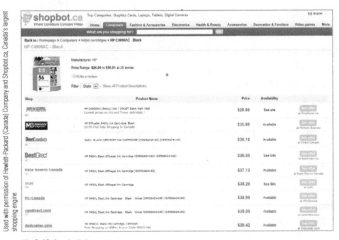

Exhibit 9.21

The Internet makes comparison shopping for products like an HP toner cartridge much easier for consumers.

to pay to talk to those people. Following are a few examples of how freenomics is changing the way at least some savvy marketers think about pricing.

The hugely successful European discount airline Ryanair, for example, currently flies passengers from London to Barcelona for about $20. The company's CEO says he hopes eventually to turn all of his flights into a free ride. Don't lose any sleep over the airline's profitability—it makes money when it sells ancillary services *a la carte* such as food, beverages, extra fees for preloading, checked baggage, and flying with an infant. Ryanair charges extra for credit card transactions, sells in-flight advertising, and the plan is to introduce gambling so that passengers who are riding for free will drop a bundle while en route to their destinations.

The singer Prince launched his new *Planet Earth* album by putting a free copy of the CD, normally worth about $19 retail (but significantly less in terms of actual cost), into 2.8 million copies of London's *Daily Mail* newspaper. This investment was more than recovered by an increase in expected ticket sales to the 21 shows held at London's O2 Arena.

In another example, US cable giant Comcast gave about nine million subscribers free set-top digital video recorders. How do you make money by giving away DVRs? Try adding installation fees to put the boxes in, and charge customers a monthly fee to use the box. Comcast also hopes to lure new customers with the offer, and then sell them other services like high-speed Internet. All told, Comcast earns back the cost of its free DVR in 18 months, and then the company goes into the black.

Pricing Advantages for Online Shoppers

The Internet also creates unique pricing challenges for marketers, because consumers and business customers are gaining more control over the buying process. Access to sophisticated "shopbots" and search engines means that consumers are no longer at the mercy of firms that dictate a price they must accept. The result is that customers have become more price sensitive. Many computer-savvy computer shoppers find that shopbots provide them with the best price on both hardware and software. As one illustration, a Shopbot.ca comparison study found that the price of a ViewSonic VT2430 LCD TV ranges from a high of $299.99 at Newegg.ca and to a low of $246.99 at PC Canada, before tax and shipping.[38] Similarly, the price of a Pink Canon SD1400 IS 4183B001 Powershot Digital Camera (Exhibit 9.21) was $201.96 at Tiger Direct Canada and $284.97 at TechDepot Canada.[39]

Detailed information about what products actually cost manufacturers, available from sites such as Consumerreports.org, can give consumers more negotiating power when shopping for new cars and other big-ticket items. Finally, e-commerce can, potentially, lower consumers' costs because of the gasoline, time, and aggravation they save when they avoid a trip to the mall.

OBJECTIVE

Describe the legal and ethical aspects of pricing.

(pp. 332-335)

Legal and Ethical Aspects of Pricing

The free enterprise system is founded on the idea that the marketplace will regulate itself. Supplies of goods and services will be made available if there is an adequate profit incentive and prices will rise or fall according to demand. Unfortunately, some business people are greedy and/or unscrupulous. The federal and provincial governments have found it necessary to enact legislation to protect consumers and to protect businesses from predatory rivals.

The Competition Bureau, a unit of Industry Canada, is responsible for ensuring that Canadian businesses (including foreign businesses that operate in Canada) adhere to federal laws that are designed to maintain and encourage fair competition. Most of these laws are found within statutes of the *Competition Act*, but others are found in the *Consumer Packaging and Labelling Act*, the *Textile Labelling Act*, and the *Precious Metals Marking Act*. The *Competition Act* was recently amended to enable civil (as well as criminal) action to more quickly and effectively stop unfair, deceptive, or otherwise anti-competitive behaviour. In the next section, we will discuss these behaviours and some of the more important regulations to combat them. A more detailed discussion is available on the Competition Bureau Web site (www. competitionbureau.gc.ca).

Deceptive Pricing Practices

Unscrupulous businesses may attempt to advertise or promote prices in a deceptive way. The Competition Act specifies that sellers cannot make a representation to the public that is false or misleading in a material respect. Thus, a retailer or other supplier must not claim that its prices are lower than a competitor's, unless it is true. Firms cannot promote a going-out-of-business sale unless they are going out of business. Similarly, sellers cannot make false or misleading representation as to the ordinary selling price of a product. For example, a retailer cannot promote a 50-percent-off sale unless it has sold a substantial volume of the product at the "regular" or higher price within a reasonable period of time. An "introductory low price" cannot be promoted unless the price goes up to its "regular" level within a reasonable period of time. What is "reasonable" and "substantial" is a matter for the civil courts to decide. In 2011, the Canadian Competition Bureau fined Bell Canada $10 million for misleading price advertising, finding that the advertised prices for Bell's phone, TV, and Internet bundles were not available because of additional mandatory fees hidden in 1600 words of small print. The Canadian Competition Bureau asserted that Bell had been using misleading advertising in its printed material, on its Web site, and in some television and radio spots since 2007.[40] Similarly, women's fashion retailer Suzy Shier Inc. paid a $1 million fine for misleading consumers about how much they were saving on items marked "on sale" (Exhibit 9.22).[41]

Another deceptive pricing practice is the **bait and switch**, a tactic in which a retailer advertises an item at a very low price—the *bait*—to lure customers into the store, does not have reasonable quantities available, and then tries to get customers to buy a different, more expensive, item—the *switch*. They might tell the customer, "The advertised item is really poor quality. It doesn't have important features. There have been a lot of problems with that one. I can tell you're a really smart shopper—you know poor quality when you see it." Simply encouraging consumers to purchase a higher-priced item is an acceptable sales technique—called "trading up"—but it is a civil offence to advertise a lower-priced item when there are not reasonable quantities available. It is not considered bait and switch when a product is not available because of circumstances beyond the retailer's control or when customers are offered a "rain cheque"—a promise to fulfill at a later date when supplies are replenished.

Other deceptive practices are selling a product at a price above the advertised price and double ticketing, or the selling of a product at a price that exceeds the lowest of two or more prices tagged on, or applied to, a product. Selling at a price above the advertised price is a civil court issue, while double ticketing is a criminal offence.

Predatory Pricing

Predatory pricing is a strategy of selling products at unreasonably low prices to drive a rival out of the market or substantially reduce competition, then raising prices to recoup

Exhibit 9.22
Suzy Shier Inc. was fined $1 million for misleading price advertising.

bait and switch
An illegal marketing practice in which an advertised price special is used as bait to get customers into the store with the intention of switching them to a higher-priced item.

predatory pricing
The strategy of selling products at unreasonably low prices to drive competitors out of business.

Courtesy of Costco Wholesale Canada Ltd.

Exhibit 9.23
Costco's low operating costs and tremendous buying power translate to low markups and exceptional values for its members.

loss-leader pricing
The pricing strategy of setting prices below cost to attract customers into a store.

price discrimination
The illegal practice of offering the same product of like quality and quantity to different business customers at different prices, thus lessening competition.

price maintenance
The collaboration of two or more firms in setting prices, usually to keep prices high.

the sacrificed returns and earn higher profits. Although predatory pricing is a criminal offence under section 50(1)(c) of the *Competition Act*, setting prices for the purpose of taking business away from competitors is normal competition. Although there are many comments about possible predatory pricing expressed on the Internet, it is very difficult to prove that low prices are "unreasonable" or that an intentional "strategy" is being followed, and few organizations have been charged under this section of the act. Recall the Costco gasoline pricing example discussed earlier in the chapter—even though Costco was selling gasoline at a price below some competitor's cost, Costco was not intentionally trying to drive the local Esso station owners out of business.

A low price is not necessarily a predatory price. **Loss-leader pricing**, for example, is a retailer's strategy of offering products at or below cost to draw consumers into its store. Once in the store, the consumers are expected to buy other items with higher margins. This is what Costco (Exhibit 9.23) was doing with its gasoline prices in Courtney BC—driving traffic to the store. Grocery stores often use loss-leader pricing for staples like milk, eggs, and rice, but have also turned to loss-leader pricing of DVD rentals, contributing to the demise of video stores like Blockbuster.[42]

Price Discrimination

The *Competition Act* also prohibits **price discrimination**, which is a supplier practice of granting price concessions or other advantages to one purchaser, but not making them available to competing purchasers that are buying articles of like quality and quantity.[43] It applies only to the sale of goods, not leases, licences, or the consignment of goods or the sale of services. Dry cleaners charge more to clean a woman's shirt than a man's shirt. Movie theatres charge students and seniors less than other adults. These practices are not illegal. Price discrimination only applies to competing business purchasers, not end users or consumers, and it does not apply to concessions (such as discounts, rebates, guarantees, or shipping costs) negotiated on a particular transaction. As with the predatory pricing statute, price discrimination, a criminal offence, is difficult to prove. The Consumers Group for Fair Gas Prices, for example, took the case of Porter's Automotive Parts and Service in Foxtrap, Newfoundland, to the Competition Bureau, alleging that the major Canadian gasoline suppliers were selling gas to their own corporate-owned gas stations at a lower price than to the independents. The Competition Bureau found no evidence to support the allegation that gas suppliers had charged Porter's a higher price than another dealer in the area buying a similar volume.[44]

Price Maintenance

Price maintenance, or price fixing, occurs when two or more companies conspire to keep prices at a certain level. Rough diamond seller De Beers, for example, currently faces a price-fixing class action law suit that alleges that they have led a world-wide diamond cartel that has had anti-competitive impact on Canadian consumers.[45] A criminal offence under section 61 of the *Competition Act*, price maintenance can take two forms: horizontal and vertical.

Horizontal Price Fixing

Horizontal price fixing occurs when competitors making the same product jointly determine what price they will charge. This kind of price fixing keeps prices high by eliminating competition. In industries such as the Canadian gasoline industry, in which there are few sellers, there may be no specific price-fixing agreement, but sellers will still charge the same price to "meet the competition." Such parallel pricing is not of itself considered price fixing. There must be an exchange of pricing information between sellers to indicate price-fixing actions. This was the situation in Quebec where the Canadian Competition Bureau recently charged 38 individuals and 14 companies over gasoline price fixing. Fines ranged from $10,000 to $50,000, and six people were put in jail.[46] Also recently, Air Canada was among 12 global airlines that were fined a total of $1.1 billion by European Union regulators for collusion in setting cargo prices on European flights.[47]

Vertical Price Fixing

Sometimes manufacturers or wholesalers attempt to force retailers to charge a certain price for their product. This is called *vertical price fixing*, a criminal offence under the *Competition Act*. Retail stores are free to set whatever price they choose without interference or coercion by the manufacturer or wholesaler. Manufacturers and wholesalers can provide a "suggested retail price," but they cannot retaliate against retailers who choose not to follow the suggestion. Manufacturers or wholesalers are free to set prices when they own the retail outlet. The same is true for consignment selling, in which retailers do not actually ever own the product but simply agree to offer it for sale and to accept a percentage of the selling price for their efforts.

Bid rigging is collusion between suppliers responding to a request for bids or tenders, where the suppliers reduce or eliminate competition in the bidding process and trade off opportunities to "win" the business with margins that are higher than would otherwise be attained. This might include any of the following: suppliers agreeing to submit token bids that are priced too high, suppliers abstaining from bidding or withdrawing bids, pre-selected suppliers submitting the lowest bid on a systematic or rotating basis, or suppliers not competing in designated geographic regions or for specific customers. These activities are all criminal offences. Les Entreprises Promecanic Ltd., a Montreal refrigeration company, recently pleaded guilty to three counts of bid rigging for high-rise building ventilation systems. They admitted to colluding with competitors to pre-determine the winners of about $8 million in contracts.[48]

bid rigging
Collusion between suppliers responding to bid requests to lessen competition and secure higher margins.

Ethical and Sustainable Decisions in the Real World

In the United States, some states frown on loss-leader practices and have passed legislation called unfair sales acts (also called *unfair trade practices acts*). These laws or regulations prohibit wholesalers and retailers from selling products below cost. The aim is to protect small wholesalers and retailers from larger competitors because the "big fish" like Costco have the financial resources that allow them to offer loss leaders or products at very low prices—knowing that the smaller firms can't match these bargain prices. Canada does not have similar legislation, enabling larger firms with greater buying power to offer loss leaders with impunity. Loss leaders provide bargains to many consumers but it makes it difficult for small retailers like Angela Kim and her husband Sung Bae who are losing thousands of dollars a day while Costco heavily discounts gasoline. What would you do? Should Canada restrict the use of loss-leader pricing in the *Competition Act*?

ETHICS **CHECK:**
Find out what other students taking this course **would do** and **why** on **www.mypearsonmarketinglab.com**

If you were advising the federal government with respect to loss-leader pricing, would you recommend that the practice be curtailed?

☐YES ☐NO

Here's my choice...

Real **People**, Real **Choices**

1 Option   2 Option   **3** Option

Why do you think Mike chose option 3?

How It Worked Out at Sitka

Mike Pepperdine and Sitka decided to implement Option 3, change their strategy in the US market. They retained their US sales manager, but more in a sales representative capacity for the US Pacific Northwest. Mike decided to personally pursue some "dream" accounts in the States—that is, the best and most sought-after stores. His thinking was that if Sitka can gain a following in those places and build the brand that way, growth will come more organically. Mike didn't change Sitka's USA pricing structure as the more upscale "dream accounts" carried other brands priced similarly to Sitka's offering. Initial forays have been positive, but it requires quite a bit of his time to establish and maintain these key relationships.

To learn the whole story, visit www.mypearsonmarketinglab.com.

Objective Summary ➡ Key Terms ➡ Apply

CHAPTER 9
Study Map

1. Objective Summary (pp. 296–302)

Explain the importance of pricing, the process of making pricing decisions, and how marketers set objectives for their pricing strategies.

Pricing is important to firms because it creates profits and influences customers to purchase or not. Prices may be monetary or nonmonetary, as when consumers or businesses exchange one product for another. Effective pricing objectives are designed to support corporate and marketing objectives and are flexible. Pricing objectives often focus on a desired level of profit growth or profit margin, on sales (to maximize sales or to increase market share), on competing effectively, on increasing customer satisfaction, or on communicating a certain image.

Key Terms

psychological costs, p. 297

operating costs, p. 297

switching costs, p. 297

opportunity cost, p. 297

profit objectives, p. 299

SMART objectives, p. 299

sales or market share objective, p. 300

prestige products, p. 300

2. Objective Summary (pp. 302–316)

Describe how marketers use costs, demands, revenue, and the pricing environment to make pricing decisions.

In developing prices, marketers must estimate demand and determine costs. Marketers often use break-even analysis and marginal analysis to help in deciding on the price for a product. Break-even analysis uses fixed and variable costs to identify how many units must be sold at a certain price in order to begin making a profit. Marginal analysis uses both costs and estimates of product demand to identify the price that will maximize profits. Marketers must also consider the requirements for adequate trade margins for retailers, wholesalers, and other members of the channel of distribution. Like other elements of the marketing mix, pricing is influenced by a variety of external environmental factors. This includes economic trends such as inflation and recession and the firm's competitive environment—that is, whether the firm does business in an oligopoly, a monopoly, or a more competitive environment. Government regulations can also affect prices by increasing the cost of production or through actual regulations of a firm's pricing strategies. Consumer trends that influence how consumers think and behave may also influence pricing. While marketers of some products may develop standardized pricing strategies for global markets, unique environmental factors in different countries mean marketers must localize pricing strategies.

Key Terms

demand curve, p. 302

price elasticity of demand, p. 305

elastic demand, p. 305

cross-elasticity of demand, p. 306

variable costs, p. 307

fixed costs, p. 308

average fixed cost, p. 308

total costs, p. 308

break-even analysis, p. 308

break-even point, p. 308

contribution per unit, p. 309

marginal analysis, p. 310

marginal cost, p. 310

marginal revenue, p. 310

markup, p. 311

gross margin, p. 311

retailer margin, p. 312

wholesaler margin, p. 312

list price or manufacturer's suggested retail price (MSRP), p. 312

internal reference price, p. 315

price subsidies, p. 316

3. Objective Summary (pp. 317–324)

Understand key pricing strategies.

Though easy to calculate and "safe," frequently used cost-based strategies do not consider demand, the competition, the stage in the product life cycle, plant capacity, or product image. The most common cost-based strategy is cost-plus pricing. Pricing strategies based on demand, such as target costing and yield-management pricing, can require that marketers estimate demand at different prices in order to be certain they can sell what they produce. Strategies based on the competition may represent industry wisdom but can be tricky to apply. A price leadership strategy is often used in an oligopoly. Firms that focus on customer needs may consider everyday low price or value pricing strategies. New products may be priced using a high skimming price to recover research, development, and promotional costs, or a penetration price to encourage more customers and discourage competitors from entering the market. Trial pricing means setting a low price for a limited time.

To implement pricing strategies with individual products, marketers may use two-part pricing or payment pricing tactics. For multiple products, marketers may use price bundling, wherein two or more products are sold and priced as a single package. Captive pricing is often chosen when two items must be used together; one item is sold at a very low price and the other at a high, profitable price. Distribution-based pricing tactics, including f.o.b., basing-point, and uniform delivered pricing,

address differences in how far products must be shipped. Similar pricing tactics are used for products sold internationally. Pricing for members of the channel may include trade or functional discounts, cumulative or noncumulative quantity discounts to encourage larger purchases, cash discounts to encourage fast payment, and seasonal discounts to spread purchases throughout the year or to increase off-season or in-season sales.

Key Terms

cost-plus pricing, p. 317

price-floor pricing, p. 318

demand-based pricing, p. 318

target costing, p. 319

yield-management pricing, p. 319

variable pricing, p. 320

skimming price, p. 320

experimental pricing, p. 321

judgment, p. 321

value-based pricing p. 321

frequent discounting, p. 322

penetration pricing, p. 322

trial pricing, p. 322

price leadership (follower), p. 323

parity pricing strategy, p. 323

premium pricing, p. 323

umbrella pricing, p. 323

price bundling, p. 323

cost of ownership, p. 324

prestige pricing, p. 324

4. Objective Summary (pp. 325–330)

Understand pricing tactics and how to set price points.

Pricing tactics for individual products include two-part pricing and payment pricing. For multiple products, pricing tactics include captive pricing, zone pricing, and freight absorption pricing. Consumers may express emotional or psychological responses to prices. Customers may use an idea of a customary or fair price as an internal reference price in evaluating products. Sometimes marketers use reference pricing strategies by displaying products with different prices next to each other. A price-quality inference means that consumers use price as a cue for quality. Customers respond to odd prices differently than to even-dollar prices. Marketers may practise price lining strategies in which they set a limited number of different price ranges for a product line. With luxury products, marketers may use a prestige pricing strategy, assuming that people will buy more if the price is higher. Marketers also discount from the list price to encourage larger orders or to reward distributors who focus more of their attention on a particular manufacturer's products, but managing pricing across distribution channels with different margin expectations can be challenging.

Key Terms

captive pricing, p. 325

f.o.b. origin pricing, p. 326

f.o.b. delivered pricing, p. 326

zone pricing, p. 326

uniform delivered pricing, p. 327

freight absorption pricing, p. 327

price lining, p. 327

list price, p. 328

trade or functional discounts, p. 328

quantity discounts, p. 329

cumulative quantity discounts, p. 329

noncumulative quantity discounts, p. 329

5. Objective Summary (pp. 330–332)

Understand the opportunities for Internet pricing strategies.

E-commerce may offer firms an opportunity to initiate dynamic pricing—meaning prices can be changed frequently with little or no cost. Auctions offer opportunities for customers to bid on items in C2C, B2C, and B2B e-commerce. The Internet allows buyers to compare products and prices, gives consumers more control over the price they pay for items, and has made customers more price-sensitive.

Key Terms

dynamic pricing, p. 331

online auctions, p. 331

freenomics, p. 331

6. Objective Summary (pp. 332–335)

Describe the legal and ethical aspects of pricing.

Most marketers try to avoid unethical or illegal pricing practices. One deceptive pricing practice is the illegal bait-and-switch tactic. Federal regulations also prohibit predatory pricing, price discrimination, bid rigging, and horizontal or vertical price fixing.

Key Terms

bait and switch, p. 323

predatory pricing, p. 323

loss-leader pricing, p. 324

price discrimination, p. 324

price maintenance, p. 324

bid rigging, p. 335

Chapter Questions and Activities

Concepts: Test Your Knowledge

1. What is price, and why is it important to a firm? What are some examples of monetary and nonmonetary prices?
2. Describe and give examples of some of the following types of pricing objectives: profit, market share, competitive effect, customer satisfaction, and image enhancement.
3. Explain how the demand curves for normal products and for prestige products differ. What are demand shifts and why are they important to marketers? How do firms go about estimating demand? How can marketers estimate the elasticity of demand?
4. Explain variable costs, fixed costs, average variable costs, average fixed costs, and average total costs.
5. What is break-even analysis? What is marginal analysis? What are the comparative advantages of break-even analysis and marginal analysis for marketers?
6. What are trade margins? How do they relate to the pricing for a producer of goods?
7. How does recession affect consumers' perceptions of prices? How does inflation influence perceptions of prices? What are some ways that the competitive environment, government regulations, consumer trends, and the global environment influence a firm's pricing strategies?
8. Explain cost-plus pricing, target costing, and yield-management pricing. Explain how a price leadership strategy works.
9. For new products, when is skimming pricing more appropriate, and when is penetration pricing the best strategy? When would trial pricing be an effective pricing strategy?
10. Explain two-part pricing, payment pricing, price bundling, captive pricing, and distribution-based pricing tactics. Give an example of when each would be a good pricing tactic for marketers to use.
11. Why do marketers use trade or functional discounts, quantity discounts, cash discounts, and seasonal discounts in pricing to members of the channel?
12. What is dynamic pricing? Why does the Internet encourage the use of dynamic pricing?
13. Explain these psychological aspects of pricing: price-quality inferences, odd-even pricing, internal reference price, price lining, and prestige pricing.
14. Explain how unethical marketers might use bait-and-switch tactics, price fixing, and predatory pricing. What is loss-leader pricing? Why is it not price discrimination when men and women get charged different amounts to have a shirt dry cleaned?

Activities: Apply What You've Learned

1. Assume that you are the director of marketing for a firm that manufactures candy bars. Your boss has suggested that the current economic conditions merit an increase

in the price of your candy bars. You are concerned that increasing the price might not be profitable because you are unsure of the price elasticity of demand for your product. Develop a plan for the measurement of price elasticity of demand for your candy bars. What findings would lead you to increase the price? What findings would cause you to rethink the decision to increase prices? Develop a presentation for your class outlining (1) the concept of elasticity of demand, (2) why raising prices without understanding the elasticity would be a bad move, (3) your recommendations for measurement, and (4) the potential impact on profits for elastic and inelastic demand.

2. As the vice president for marketing for a firm that markets computer software, you must regularly develop pricing strategies for new software products. Your latest product is a software package that automatically translates any foreign language e-mail messages to the user's preferred language. You are trying to decide on the pricing for this new product. Should you use a skimming price, a penetration price, or something in between? Argue in front of your class the pros and cons for each alternative.

3. Assume that you have been hired as the assistant manager of a local store that sells fresh fruits and vegetables. As you look over the store, you notice that there are two different displays of tomatoes. In one display the tomatoes are priced at $1.89 per kilogram, and in the other the tomatoes are priced at $1.39 per kilogram. The tomatoes look very much alike. You notice that many people are buying the $1.89 tomatoes. Write a report explaining what is happening and give your recommendations for the store's pricing strategy.

4. We know that marketers must consider not only the monetary costs of products but also the nonmonetary costs. Take, for example, the cost of your postsecondary education. While you pay tuition and other fees, there are also nonmonetary costs that students must bear. Talk with five to 10 of your fellow students. Ask them what nonmonetary costs they feel are important and would like reduced. Develop a report with your recommendations for how your university might change policies or practices that would reduce nonmonetary costs.

5. Select one of the product categories below. Identify two different firms that offer consumers a line of product offerings in the category. For example, Dell, HP, and Toshiba each market a line of laptop computers while Hoover, Eureka, and Bissell offer lines of vacuum cleaners. Using the Internet or by visiting a retailer who sells your selected product, research the product lines and pricing of the two firms. Based on your research, develop a report on the price lining strategies of the two firms. Your report should discuss (1) the specific price points of the product offerings of each firm and how the price lining strategy maximizes revenue, (2) your ideas for why the specific price points were selected, (3) how the price lining strategies of the two firms are alike and how they are different, and (4) possible reasons for differences in the strategies.

   a. Laptop computers
   b. Vacuum cleaners
   c. Refrigerators
   d. HD televisions

6. Assume that you are the VP of marketing for a firm that produces refrigerated prepared pasta dishes for sale to consumers through various retail channels. You are considering producing a new line of all-natural, one-serving pasta dishes. Your research suggests that consumers would only be willing to buy the pasta if the price is less than $6.00 per package. You will be selling the pasta through specialty food brokers who will distribute to natural food stores that will sell to consumers. The natural food stores require a 30 percent retailer margin and the brokers require a 20 percent wholesaler margin.

   a. Assuming the natural food stores will sell the product for $5.99 per package, what price will the specialty food brokers charge the food stores for the product?
   b. What price will the manufacturer charge the specialty food brokers?
   c. If the manufacturer costs are $0.95 per package, what will the manufacturer's contribution per unit be?

Marketing Metrics: Exercise

Contribution analysis and break-even analysis are surely the most important and most frequently used marketing metrics. These analyses are essential to determine if a firm's marketing opportunity will mean a financial loss or be profitable. As explained in the chapter, *contribution* is the difference between the selling price per unit and the variable cost per unit. Break-even analysis that includes contribution tells marketers how much must be sold to break even or to earn a desired amount of profit.

Happy Days Dairy is a producer of high-quality organic yogurt, sour cream, and crème fraiche. They are considering marketing a new line of drinkable yogurt for children. The new yogurt will be offered in packages of 125 ml individual containers and it will be available in four flavours.

The company plans to use TV and newspaper advertising to promote the new product. Distribution will be through major supermarket chains, which currently have over 90 percent of the Canadian yogurt market. The suggested retail price for each 125 ml individual container will be $0.60. Because the retailer requires a 30 percent markup, Happy Days' price to the supermarkets will be $0.42 per 125 ml container. The unit variable costs for the product including packaging will be $0.15.

The company estimates its advertising and promotion expenses for the first year will be $1 500 000.

1. What is the contribution per unit for the new children's yogurt product?
2. What is the break-even unit volume for the first year that will cover the planned advertising and promotion? the break-even in dollars?
3. How many units of the yogurt must Happy Days sell to earn a profit of $800 000?

Choices: What Do You Think?

1. Governments sometimes provide price subsidies to specific industries; that is, they reduce a domestic firm's costs so that it can sell products on the international market at a lower price. What reasons do governments (and politicians) use for these government subsidies? What are the

benefits and disadvantages to domestic industries in the long run? to international customers? Who would benefit and who would lose if all price subsidies were eliminated?

2. In many oligopolistic industries, firms follow a price leadership strategy in which an accepted industry leader sets, raises, or lowers prices and the other firms follow. Why is this good policy for the industry? In what ways is this good or bad for consumers? What is the difference between price leadership and price fixing? Should governments allow industries to use price leadership strategies?

3. Many very successful retailers use a loss-leader pricing strategy, in which they advertise an item at a price below their cost and sell the item at that price to get customers into their store. They feel that these customers will continue to shop with their company and that they will make a profit in the long run. Do you consider this an unethical practice? Who benefits and who is hurt by such practices? Do you think the practice should be made illegal, as some jurisdictions have done? How is this different from bait and switch pricing?

4. Consumers often make price-quality inferences about products. What does this mean? What are some products for which you are likely to make price-quality inferences? Do such inferences make sense?

5. In pricing new products, marketers may choose a skimming or a penetration pricing strategy. While it's easy to see the benefits of these practices for the firm, what are the advantages and/or disadvantages of the practice for consumers? for an industry as a whole?

Miniprojects: Learn by Doing

The purpose of this miniproject is to help you become familiar with how consumers respond to different prices by conducting a series of pricing experiments. For this project, you should first select a product category that students such as yourself normally purchase. It should be a moderately expensive purchase such as athletic shoes, a bookcase, or a piece of luggage. You should next obtain two photographs of items in this product category or, if possible, two actual items. The two items should not appear to be substantially different in quality or in price.

Note: You will need to recruit separate research participants for each of the activities listed in the next section.

• Experiment 1: Reference Pricing

a. Place the two products together. Place a sign on one with a low price. Place a sign on the other with a high price (about 50 percent higher will do). Ask your research participants to evaluate the quality of each of the items and to tell which one they would probably purchase.

b. Reverse the signs and ask other research participants to evaluate the quality of each of the items and to tell which one they would probably purchase.

c. Place the two products together again. This time place a sign on one with a moderate price. Place a sign on the other that is only a little higher (less than 10 percent higher). Again, ask research participants to evaluate the quality of each of the items and to tell which one they would probably purchase.

d. Reverse the signs and ask other research participants to evaluate the quality of each of the items and to tell which one they would probably purchase.

• Experiment 2: Odd-Even Pricing.

For this experiment, you will only need one of the items from experiment 1.

a. Place a sign on the item that ends in $.99 (for example, $62.99). Ask research participants to tell you if they think the price for the item is very low, slightly low, moderate, slightly high, or very high. Also ask them to evaluate the quality of the item and to tell you how likely they would be to purchase the item.

b. This time place a sign on the item that is slightly lower but that ends in $.00 (for example, $60.00). Ask different research participants to tell you if they think the price for the item is very low, slightly low, moderate, slightly high, or very high. Also ask them to evaluate the quality of the item and to tell you how likely they would be to purchase the item. Develop a presentation for your class in which you discuss the results of your experiments and what they tell you about how consumers view prices.

Marketing in **Action** Case   Fashion Cutlery Inc.

Heather Adams just had another sleepless night. Fashion Cutlery, a Canadian firm that she founded two years ago, faced a crisis that could spell the end of her company. About nine months ago, Fashion Cutlery received a large order from Walmart for boxed cutlery for four people in a specific pattern of service. Since this order was key to the growth of the small firm, Fashion Cutlery agreed to produce the order but only to ship a small part of it to the Walmart distribution centre and retain the balance of the order to be shipped as the stores sold the cutlery. This approach is used by large retail chains, where possible, to shift inventory costs and risks to their suppliers. Last week, Heather received an email from the Walmart buyer stating that after being on the shelves for three months, the Fashion Cutlery was not generating the gross profit dollars required by Walmart to continue carrying the item. Walmart knew that fewer units of Fashion Cutlery would be sold but had forecast that the higher dollar contribution per sale would allow the product to maintain its place on the shelves. The buyer indicated that Walmart would not need the balance of the stock held by Fashion Cutlery and went on to request permission to return the stock from the store shelves.

Two years earlier, Heather had identified an opportunity to create a new line of quality stainless-steel cutlery targeted at baby boomer and Gen X couples who entertained a lot and wanted modern, attractive cutlery without the maintenance required of silverware. Heather thought she understood the industry quite well as her father and brother own a major import business selling kitchenware to large North American retailers. Heather knew that the styling of less-expensive cutlery had not changed a great deal in the last 50 years while the more-expensive products reflect the modern, fresh look that fits in with the current life styles of North Americans, especially the foody baby boomers and Gen Xers—fashion-conscious consumers who love food, like to prepare it, and enjoy entertaining to show off their culinary prowess. While upscale cutlery is still a popular engagement or wedding gift, the popularity of silverware was waning as busy people didn't have time to keep it polished. Heather was aware also that stainless steel cutlery varies greatly in quality, depending on how much nickel and chrome is blended into the steel. But most producers of cutlery do not specify the quality of the steel used, and customers cannot really judge the quality, other than by inference, assuming that heavier cutlery is better, an assumption supported by the fact that heavier cutlery comes at higher prices.

After spending considerable time and money attending major trade shows, visiting upscale retailers in fashion capitals like New York, Paris, and Milan, and otherwise researching the products currently available on the market, Heather saw an opportunity to create boxed sets (four place settings) of premium stainless steel cutlery designed by a leading Canadian designer. It could be made in China of 18-8 stainless steel (top quality steel that has 18% nickel and 8% chrome), and priced at a suggested retail price of $29.95 per box.

Heather was optimistic about that product, despite being told by her father that boxed cutlery had not been a profitable item for his distribution company as the mass merchandisers bought cutlery on price, and many of them, such as Home Hardware and Canadian Tire, sell cutlery as loss leaders to attract customers to their stores. Heather thought that her product was a compelling value for the money and comparable in styling, weight, and quality of steel with cutlery that retails for $100 or more, and Oprah had liked it enough to feature it on her show! Heather decided that her main competitor was Oneida, a well-known, long-established producer of stainless and silver plate cutlery. Oneida has offerings at several price points, but she thought that the direct competition would come from a 24-piece box which retails for $25.95 at most mass merchandise stores and $21.00 at Walmart. This box contains service for four as well, but with an additional four pieces for serving.

Heather wanted Fashion Cutlery's product to be available at every major retailer of cutlery in Canada, and after receiving and approving the samples provided by her supplier, Heather used her family's contacts to obtain appointments with the buyers of the major mass merchandisers. In general, the buyers were impressed with Heather's knowledge of her product, the competition, and how the major chains operate, and with her strong belief in her product. She was able to obtain orders with a number of major chains, including Walmart, Target, and Costco in the United States—a major feat for a new, small Canadian company.

Sales volume at Target had been acceptable. Attracting a slightly more affluent customer than Walmart, Target sold the cutlery at the suggested retail price and was generally happy with the Fashion Cutlery product. Fashion Cutlery was also doing very well at Costco, the warehouse-style retailer that uses an aggressive discount price structure, selling Fashion Cutlery for less than the suggested retail price—about $2 less than Target, but $2 more than Walmart.

To find out more about what was going on after receiving the e-mail from Walmart, Heather decided to visit a Walmart store just across the Canadian border. She found a large display of her product at above eye level on the shelves (eye level is ideal for attracting customer attention). Her main competitor, Oneida, had an equally large display, but at eye level. Fashion Cutlery sold for at least $4.00 more than any other brand, and Walmart shoppers tend to be very price conscious, looking for the lowest priced product. Walmart advertising encourages this type of customer. She also realized that while the side panel of the Fashion Cutlery box noted the fact that the product used 18-8 stainless steel, that the technical process produced knives with additional strength, and that the product carried a 50-year guarantee, there was nothing on the box suggesting that the product was comparable in quality, styling, weight, and steel quality with other high-end products.

With some effort Heather found a sales associate and asked if she would recommend Oneida or Fashion Cutlery for purchase. The sales associate said that while she knew the Oneida name and that the company has been in business for a very long time, she knew nothing about Fashion Cutlery. She also pointed out that you get more pieces for less money when buying Oneida.

Armed with this information, Heather went home to consider what she had learned and how she might respond to Walmart. With a Master's degree in social work but no formal marketing education, Heather wondered why the sales results at Walmart were so different from those at Costco and Target. Was it that the price was too high for Walmart customers? Were there other explanations?

Note: This case was written by Maurice Borts and is used by permission.

You Make the Call

1. What are some reasons why the sales results at Walmart are so different from those at Costco and Target?
2. How might the concept of segmentation be useful to Heather?
3. How might Heather better manage prices in distribution channels with different margin expectations?
4. How should Heather respond to Walmart?

APPENDIX 9A

Marketing Math

To develop marketing strategies to meet the goals of an organization effectively and efficiently, it is essential that marketers understand and use a variety of financial analyses and costs. This Appendix provides an overview of how marketers view costs as well as an overview of basic financial analysis.

A MARKETER'S VIEW OF COSTS

It is very important for marketers to understand the profit model and how marketers view costs. If you have taken an accounting course, you are likely familiar with the calculation for net income shown in Figure 9A.1. Marketers look at the financial world a bit differently to make marketing decisions (Figure 9A.1). Marketers split the cost of goods sold (i.e., the total cost to make and sell the products that have been sold by an organization in a particular time period) into two components: fixed costs and variable costs.

Fixed costs are the costs incurred to make and sell the first unit of a product. They do not vary with the number of units produced and they have to be paid up front, even if the organization does not sell any of the units produced. Fixed costs include rent, plant and equipment, utilities and overhead, advertising and other marketing communication expenses, the salaries of a firm's executives, managers, and employees, and any other costs that have to be paid up front and do not change with the level of production.

Variable costs are the costs that change depending on the number of units produced. That is, they are the costs involved in making and selling one more unit of a product (other than the first). Variable costs for a manufacturer of bookcases like Palliser Furniture, for example, would include construction materials such as wood, nails, and glue; finishing materials like paint or varnish; packaging (boxes, shrinkwrap, etc); piecework labour (wages paid by the number of pieces finished or hourly wages allocated to the number of units produced); shipping; and sales commission (wages paid to sales staff based on the number of units sold).

In reality, calculating variable costs is often quite complex. For example, as the number of bookcases a factory produces increases or decreases, the variable costs may change. If the company buys just enough lumber for one bookcase, the lumberyard will charge top dollar. If it buys enough for 100 bookcases, it will get a better deal. And if it buys enough for thousands of bookcases, it may cut variable costs even more. Even the cost of labour goes down with increased production, as manufacturers are likely to invest in labour saving equipment that allows workers to produce bookcases faster. At some point diseconomies of scale will be reached, and using the bookcase example, the demand for the labour, lumber, or nails required to produce the bookcases may exceed the supply, causing the average cost per bookcase to rise. Because variable costs are related to the number of units produced, marketers often use the average variable cost across a production range, or they use sensitivity analysis to calculate financial impacts of different production level scenarios.

Marketers split these costs up to make pricing decisions. At a minimum, the price charged must cover the variable costs—otherwise the company loses money on each transaction. The difference between the price charged by a manufacturer and its variable costs is its **contribution margin (CM)**. It is called a contribution margin because these funds, in excess of the variable costs, contribute to paying off the fixed costs incurred up front. The contribution margin for each unit sold times the number of units sold is the **total contribution** received by the organization. The total contribution less fixed costs is net profit before tax. Marketers know that they have to cover all their fixed costs to stay in business. As we will see below, marketers sometimes use the concept of **total unit cost** (variable costs plus average fixed costs per unit) to ensure that prices cover all the costs incurred.

BREAK-EVEN ANALYSIS

Break-even analysis is a technique marketers use to examine the relationship between cost and price and to determine what sales volume must be reached at a given price before the company breaks even. The break-even point is the point at which the company doesn't lose any money and doesn't make any profit; all costs are covered, but there isn't a penny extra. A break-even analysis allows marketers to identify how many units of a product they will have to sell at a given price to begin to be profitable.

Accounting View	Marketing View
Sales Revenue – Costs of Goods = Gross Margin	Sales Revenue – Variable Costs = Contribution Margin per Unit
Gross Margin – Operating Expenses = Net Income Before Taxes (Operating Income)	Contribution Margin × Units Sold = Total Contribution Margin
	Total Contribution Margin – Fixed Costs = Net Income Before Taxes (Operating Income)

Figure 9A.1 Marketing Versus Accounting Views of Costs

contribution margin (CM)
The price an organization receives less its variable costs.

total contribution
Contribution margin multiplied by the number of units sold.

total unit cost
Variable costs plus average fixed costs per unit.

break-even analysis
A method for determining the number of units that a firm must produce and sell at a given price to cover all its costs.

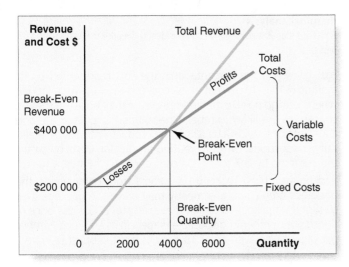

Figure 9A.2 Break-Even Analysis

Using break-even analysis, marketers can determine what sales volume to reach before the company makes a profit. This company needs to sell 4000 bookcases at $100 each to break even.

Figure 9A.2 demonstrates break-even analysis for a bookcase manufacturer like Palliser. The vertical axis represents the amount of costs and revenue in dollars, and the horizontal axis shows the quantity of goods produced and sold. In this break-even model, we assume that there is a given total fixed cost and that variable costs do not change with the quantity produced.

In this example, the total fixed costs (for the factory, the equipment, and electricity) are $200 000, and the average variable costs (for materials and labour) are constant. The figure shows the total costs (variable costs plus fixed costs) and total revenues if varying quantities are produced and sold. The point at which the total revenue and total costs lines intersect is the *break-even point*. If sales are above the break-even point, the company makes a profit. Below that point, the firm suffers a loss.

To determine the break-even point, the firm first needs to calculate the *contribution per unit,* or the difference between the price the firm charges for a product (the revenue per unit) and the variable costs. This *contribution margin* is the amount the firm has after paying for the wood, nails, paint, and labour to contribute to meeting the fixed costs of production. For our example, assuming that the firm sells its bookcases for $100 each and that variable costs are $50 per unit, contribution per unit is $100 − $50 = $50. Using the fixed cost for the bookcase manufacturing of $200 000, we can now calculate the firm's break-even point in units of the product.

$$\text{Break-even point (in units)} = \frac{\text{total fixed cost}}{\text{contribution per unit to fixed costs}}$$

$$\text{Break-even point (in units)} = \frac{\$200\ 000}{\$50} = 4000 \text{ units}$$

Thus, the firm must sell 4000 bookcases at $100 each to meet its fixed costs and to break even. In a similar way, we can calculate the break-even point in dollars. This shows us that to break even, the company must sell $400 000 worth of bookcases.

$$\text{Break-even point (in dollars)} = \frac{\text{total fixed cost}}{1 - \dfrac{\text{variable cost per unit}}{\text{price}}}$$

$$\text{Break-even point (in dollars)} = \frac{\$200\ 000}{1 - \dfrac{\$50}{\$100}} = \frac{\$20\ 000}{1 - 0.5}$$

$$= \frac{\$20\ 0000}{0.5} = \$400\ 000$$

Now that we understand the profit model and how marketers view costs, we can discuss how marketers determine or set pricing objectives, strategies, price points, and terms and conditions.

Using Break-Even Analysis to Set Price Objectives

Marketers who seek to achieve a target level of profit or target return on investment use the concept of break-even analysis in setting specific price objectives. Often a firm will set a *profit goal*, which is the dollar profit figure it desires to earn. The "break-even" point may be calculated with that dollar goal added to the fixed costs. This is not really a break-even point because it includes profits; but by adding the desired profit to fixed costs in the break-even equation, marketers can determine how many units would need to be sold at a particular contribution margin (price − variable costs) to achieve that level of profit. For example, if the bookcase manufacturer feels it is necessary to realize a profit of $50 000, the firm's calculations would be as follows:

$$\begin{array}{l}\text{Break-even point} \\ \text{(in units with target} \\ \text{amount included)}\end{array} = \frac{\text{total fixed cost} + \text{target profit}}{\text{contribution per unit to fixed costs}}$$

$$\text{Break-even point (in units)} = \frac{\$200\ 000 + \$50\ 000}{\$50}$$

$$= 5000 \text{ units}$$

Sometimes the target return or profit goal is expressed as a *percentage of sales*. For example, a firm may say that it wants to make a profit of at least 10 percent on sales. In such cases, this profit is added to the variable cost in calculating the break-even point. In our example, the company wants to earn 10 percent of the selling price of the bookcase, or 10% × $100 = $10 per unit. We add this $10 to the variable costs of $50 and calculate the new target amount as we calculated the break-even point before. The contribution per unit becomes:

$$\begin{array}{l}\text{Contribution per unit} = \text{selling price} \\ \qquad\qquad - (\text{variable costs} + \text{target profit})\end{array}$$

$$= \$100 - (\$50 + \$10) = \$40$$

$$\text{Break-even point (in units)} = \frac{\text{total fixed cost}}{\text{contribution per unit to fixed costs}}$$

$$\text{Break-even point (in units)} = \frac{\$200\ 000}{\$40} = 5000 \text{ units}$$

Marketers who want to maximize profits sometimes use a technique called **marginal analysis**, where demand is forecast at different price levels and the profit expected in each price–demand scenario is calculated. Although the procedure is straightforward, it is often difficult to develop sufficiently accurate forecasts, and variable costs can fluctuate with shortages, inclement weather, and other uncontrollable events.

COST-PLUS PRICING

As discussed earlier in this chapter, the most common cost-based approach to pricing a product is cost-plus pricing, in which a marketer totals the unit cost for the product and then adds an amount to cover desired profit. The first step requires that the unit cost be estimated reasonably well and that the level of output does not change much. For this and the other examples, we will consider how a small manufacturer and a retailer price a line of jeans. As Table 9A.1 shows, we will assume that the jeans manufacturer has a fixed cost of $2 000 000 to make 400 000 pairs of jeans, or $5 per pair. Variable costs for the jeans are $20 per pair, making the total cost $25 per pair.

The second step is to calculate the markup. There are two methods for calculating the markup percentage: markup on cost and the more popular markup on selling price. In *markup on cost pricing*, just as the name implies, a percentage of the cost is added to the cost to determine the selling price.

Markup on cost: For markup on cost, the calculation is:

Price = total cost + (total cost × markup percentage)

In our jeans example, if the manufacturer wants a profit of $2 000 000, what markup percentage would it use? The $2 000 000 is 20 percent of the $10 million total cost. To find the price, the calculation would be:

Price = $25 + ($25 × 0.20) = $25 + $5 = $30

(Note that in the calculations, the markup percentage is expressed as a decimal; that is, 20% = 0.20.)

Markup on selling price: As we noted, sometimes firms use a different calculation method—markup on selling price. Wholesalers and retailers more frequently use markup on selling price in pricing their products because the markup percentage becomes the seller's gross margin. For example, if a retailer knows it needs a 40 percent margin to cover overhead and profits, the retailer will calculate its price as a 40 percent markup on selling price.

Let's say a retailer buys the jeans from the manufacturer for $30 per pair. If the retailer requires a 40 percent markup on selling price, we would calculate the retailer's price as follows.

$$\text{price} = \frac{\text{cost}}{1 - \text{markup percentage}}$$

As we see in Table 9A.1, the price of jeans with the markup on selling price is $50.00.

Just to compare the difference in the final prices of the two markup methods, Table 9A.2 also shows what would happen if the retailer uses a markup on cost method. Using the same product cost and price with a 40 percent markup on cost would yield $42, a much lower price. The markup on selling price gives you the percentage of the selling price represented by the markup ($20 is 40 percent of the selling price of $50). The markup on

marginal analysis
A method that uses costs and demand to identify the price that will maximize profits.

cost gives you the percentage of the cost represented by the markup ($12 is 40 percent of the cost of $42). But what happens when costs go up? Do marketers increase their prices? If they do, consumers are likely to rebel. One solution is to keep the price constant but provide a bit less of the product. Frito-Lay, maker of salty snack foods, offset increasing production costs by cutting the contents by 6.7 to 7.5 percent per bag of Fritos, Cheetos, and potato chips. To keep consumers from complaining that packages aren't full, a company may make the package ever-so-slightly smaller. In a similar move, Procter & Gamble once reduced the number of disposable diapers in its Luvs and Pampers packages by an average of 13 percent. Let the buyer beware!

BASIC FINANCIAL ANALYSIS

To develop marketing strategies to meet the goals of an organization effectively and efficiently, it is essential that marketers understand and use a variety of financial analyses. This section of the Appendix provides some of these basic financial analyses, including a review of the income statement and balance sheet as well as some basic performance ratios. In addition, this section includes an explanation of some of the specific calculations that marketers use routinely in determining price.

Income Statement and Balance Sheet

The two most important documents used to explain the financial situation of a company are the income statement and the balance sheet. The *income statement* (which is sometimes referred to as the *profit and loss statement*) provides a summary of the revenues and expenses of a firm—that is, the amount of income a company received from sales or other sources, the amount of money it spent, and the resulting income or loss that the company experienced.

The major elements of the income statement are:

Gross sales: the total of all income the firm receives from the sales of goods and services.

Net sales revenue: the gross sales minus the amount for returns and promotional or other allowances given to customers.

Cost of goods sold (sometimes called the cost of sales): the cost of inventory or goods that the firm has sold.

Gross margin (also called *gross profit*): the amount of sales revenue that is in excess of the cost of goods sold.

Operating expenses: expenses other than the cost of goods sold that are necessary for conducting business. These may include salaries, rent, depreciation on buildings and equipment, insurance, utilities, supplies, and property taxes.

Operating income (sometimes called *income from operations*): the gross margin minus the operating expenses. Sometimes accountants prepare an *operating statement*, which is similar to the income statement except that the final calculation is the operating income—that is, other revenues or expenses and taxes are not included.

Table 9A.1	Markup on Cost: An Example for a Jeans Manufacturer

Fixed Costs	
Management and other non-production-related salaries	$750 000
Rent	600 000
Insurance	50 000
Depreciation on equipment	70 000
Supplies	30 000
Advertising	500 000
Total fixed costs	$2 000 000
Number of units (pairs of jeans) produced	400 000
Fixed costs per unit	$5.00
Variable Costs	
Cost of materials (fabric, zipper, thread, etc.)	$7.00
Cost of production labour	10.00
Cost of utilities and supplies used in production process	3.00
Variable cost per unit (pair of jeans)	$20.00
Total cost (fixed cost per unit plus variable cost per unit)	$25.00

Markup on Cost

Formula: Price = total cost + (total cost × markup percentage)

Price = $25.00 + ($25.00 × 0.20) = $25.00 + $5.00 = $30.00

Table 9A.2	Markup on Cost and Markup on Selling Price: An Example of a Retailer's Pricing

Markup on Selling Price		Markup on Cost	
Retailer's cost for a pair of jeans	$30.00	Retailer's cost for a pair of jeans	$30.00
Markup percentage	40%	Markup percentage	40%

Markup on Cost —
Formula: Price = total cost
+ (total cost × markup percentage)

Formula: $\text{Price} = \dfrac{\text{cost}}{(1.00 - \text{markup percentage})}$

$\text{Price} = \dfrac{\$30.00}{(1.00 - .40)} = \dfrac{\$30.00}{0.60} = \$50.00$

Price 5 $30.00 1 ($30.00 3 0.40)
= $30.00 + $12.00 = $42.00

Other revenue and expenses: income and/or expenses other than those required for conducting the business. These may include such items as interest income/expenses and any gain or loss experienced on the sale of property or plant assets.

Taxes: the amount of income tax the firm owes calculated as a percentage of income.

Net income (sometimes called *net earnings* or *net profit*): the excess of total revenue over total expenses.

Table 9A.3 shows the income statement for an imaginary company, DLL Incorporated. DLL is a typical merchandising firm. Note that the income statement is for a specific year and includes income and expenses from January 1 through December 31 inclusive. The following comments explain the meaning of some of the important entries included in this statement.

- DLL Inc. has total or gross sales during the year of $253 950. This figure was adjusted, however, by deducting the $3000 worth of goods returned and special allowances given to customers and by $2100 in special discounts. Thus the actual or net sales generated by sales is $248 850.

- The cost of goods sold is calculated by adding the inventory of goods on January 1 to the amount purchased during the year and then subtracting the inventory of goods on December 31. In this case, DLL had $60 750 worth of inventory on hand on January 1. During the year the firm made purchases in the amount of $135 550. This amount, however, was reduced by purchase returns and allowances of $1500 and by purchase discounts of $750, so the net purchase is only $133 300.

Table 9A.3	DLL Inc. Income Statement for the Year Ended December 31, 20XX		
Gross Sales			$253 950
Less: Sales Returns and Allowances	$ 3 000		
Sales Discounts	2 100	5 100	
Net Sales Revenue			$248 850
Cost of Goods Sold			
Inventory, January 1, 20XX		$ 60 750	
Purchases	$135 550		
Less: Purchase Returns and Allowances	1 500		
Purchase Discounts	750		
Net Purchases	$133 300		
Plus: Freight-In	2 450	135 750	
Goods Available for Sale		196 500	
Less: Inventory, December 31, 20XX		60 300	
Cost of Goods Sold			$136 200
Gross Margin			112 650
Operating Expenses			
Salaries and Commissions		15 300	
Rent		12 600	
Insurance		1 500	
Depreciation		900	
Supplies		825	
Total Operating Expenses			31 125
Operating Income			81 525
Other Revenue and (Expenses)			
Interest Revenue		1 500	
Interest Expense		(2 250)	(750)
Income before Tax			80 775
Taxes (40%)			32 310
Net Income			$ 48 465

There is also an amount on the statement labelled "Freight-In." This is the amount spent by the firm in shipping charges to get goods to its facility from suppliers. Any expenses for freight from DLL to its customers (Freight-Out) would be an operating expense. In this case, the Freight-In expense of $2450 is added to net purchase costs. Then these costs of current purchases are added to the beginning inventory to show that during the year the firm had a total of $196 500 in goods available for sale. Finally, the inventory of goods held on December 31 is subtracted from the goods available, for a total cost of goods sold of $136 200. For a manufacturer, calculation of the cost of goods sold would be a bit more complicated and would probably include separate figures for such items as inventory of finished goods, the "work-in-process" inventory, the raw materials inventory, and the cost of goods delivered to customers during the year.

- The cost of goods sold is subtracted from the net sales revenue to get a gross margin of $112 650.

- Operating expenses for DLL include the salaries and commissions paid to its employees, rent on facilities and/or equipment, insurance, depreciation of capital items, and the cost of operating supplies. DLL has a total of $31 125 in operating expenses, which is deducted from the gross margin. Thus DLL has an operating income of $81 525.

- DLL had both other income and expenses in the form of interest revenues of $1500 and interest expenses of $2250, making a total other expense of $750, which was subtracted from the operating income, leaving an income before tax of $80 775.

- Finally, the income before tax is reduced by 40 percent ($32 310) for taxes, leaving a net income of $48 465. The 40 percent is an average amount for federal and provincial corporate income taxes incurred by most firms.

The *balance sheet* lists the assets, liabilities, and stockholders' equity of the firm. Whereas the income statement represents what happened during an entire year, the balance sheet is like a snapshot; it shows the firm's financial situation at one point in time. For this reason, the balance sheet is sometimes called the *statement of financial position*.

Table 9A.4 shows DLL Inc.'s balance sheet for December 31. Assets are any economic resource that is expected to benefit the firm in the short or long term. Current assets are items that are normally expected to be turned into cash or used up during the next 12 months or during the firm's normal operating cycle. Current assets for DLL include cash, securities, accounts receivable (money owed to the firm and not yet paid) inventory on hand, prepaid insurance, and supplies: a total of $84 525. Long-term assets include all assets that are not current assets. For DLL, these are property, plant, equipment, furniture, and fixtures less an amount for depreciation, or $45 300. The total assets for DLL are $129 825.

A firm's liabilities are its economic obligations, or debts that are payable to individuals or organizations outside the firm. Current liabilities are debts due in the coming year or in the firm's normal operating cycle. For DLL, the current liabilities—the accounts payable, unearned sales revenue, wages payable, and interest payable—total $72 450. Long-term liabilities (in the case of DLL, a note in the amount of $18 900) are all liabilities that are not due during the coming cycle. Stockholders' equity is the value of the stock and the corporation's capital or retained earnings. DLL has $15 000 in common stock and $23 475 in retained earnings for a total stockholders' equity of $38 475. Total liabilities always equal total assets—in this case, $129 825.

IMPORTANT FINANCIAL PERFORMANCE RATIOS

How do managers and financial analysts compare the performance of a firm from one year to the next? How do investors compare the performance of one firm with that of another? Often, a number of different financial ratios provide important information for such comparisons. Such ratios are percentage figures comparing various income statement items to net sales. Ratios provide a better way to compare performance than simple dollar sales or cost figures for two

Table 9A.4	DLL Inc. Balance Sheet: December 31, 20XX			
Assets				
Current Assets				
Cash		$ 4275		
Marketable Securities		12 000		
Accounts Receivable		6 900		
Inventory		60 300		
Prepaid Insurance		300		
Supplies		150		
Total Current Assets			84 525	
Long-Term Assets—Property, Plant and Equipment				
Furniture and Fixtures	$42 300			
Less: Accumulated Depreciation	4 500	37 800		
Land		7 500		
Total Long-Term Assets			45 300	
Total Assets			$129 825	
Liabilities				
Current Liabilities				
Accounts Payable	$70 500			
Unearned Sales Revenue	1 050			
Wages Payable	600			
Interest Payable	300			
Total Current Liabilities		72 450		
Long-Term Liabilities				
Note Payable		18 900		
Total Liabilities			91 350	
Stockholders' Equity				
Common Stock		15 000		
Retained Earnings		23 475		
Total Stockholders' Equity			38 475	
Total Liabilities and Stockholders' Equity			$129 825	

reasons. They enable analysts to compare the performance of large and small firms, and they provide a fair way to compare performance over time, without having to take inflation and other changes into account. In this section we will explain the basic operating ratios. Other measures of performance that marketers frequently use and that are also explained here are the inventory turnover rate and return on investment (ROI).

Operating Ratios

Measures of performance calculated directly from the information in a firm's income statement (sometimes called an operating statement) are called the *operating ratios*. Each ratio compares some income statement item to net sales. The most useful of these are the *gross margin ratio, the net income ratio, the operating expense ratio, and the returns and allowances ratio*. These ratios vary widely by industry but tend to be important indicators of how a firm is doing within its industry. The ratios for DLL Inc. are shown in Table 9.A5.

- The *gross margin ratio* shows what percentage of sales revenues are available for operating and other expenses and for profit. With DLL, this means that 45 percent, or nearly half, of every sales dollar is available for operating costs and for profits. The *net income ratio* (sometimes called the *net profit ratio*) shows what percentage of sales revenues are income or profit. For DLL, the net income ratio is 19.5 percent. This means that the firm's profit before taxes is about 20 cents of every dollar.

- The *operating expense ratio* is the percentage of sales needed for operating expenses. DLL has an operating expense ratio of 12.5 percent. Tracking operating expense ratios from one year to the next or comparing them with an industry average gives a firm important information about how efficient its operations are.

- The *returns and allowances ratio* shows what percentage of all sales are being returned, probably by unhappy customers. DLL's returns and allowances ratio shows that only a little over 1 percent of sales are being returned.

Inventory Turnover Rate

The *inventory turnover rate*, also referred to as the stockturn rate, is the number of times inventory or stock is turned over

(sold and replaced) during a specified time period, usually a year. Inventory turnover rates are usually calculated on the basis of inventory costs, sometimes on the basis of inventory selling prices, and sometimes by number of units.

For our example, DLL Inc., we know that for the year, the cost of goods sold was $136 200. Information on the balance sheet enables us to find the average inventory. By adding the value of the beginning inventory to the ending inventory and dividing by 2, we can compute an average inventory. In the case of DLL, this would be

$$\frac{\$60\ 750 + \$60\ 300}{2} = \$60\ 525$$

Thus

$$\text{Inventory turnover rate} \atop \text{(in cost of goods sold)} = \frac{\text{costs of goods sold}}{\text{average inventory at cost}}$$

$$= \frac{\$136\ 200}{\$60\ 525} = 2.25 \text{ times}$$

Return on Investment (ROI)

Firms often develop business objectives in terms of return on investment, and ROI is often used to determine how effective (and efficient) the firm's management has been. First, however, we need to define exactly what a firm means by investment. In most cases, firms define investment as the total assets of the firm. To calculate the ROI we need the net income found in the income statement and the total assets (or investment), which is found on the firm's balance sheet.

Return on investment is calculated as follows:

$$\text{ROI} = \frac{\text{net income}}{\text{total investment}}$$

For DLL Inc., if the total assets are $129 825, then the ROI is

$$\frac{\$48\ 465}{\$129\ 825} = 37.3\%$$

Sometimes return on investment is calculated by using an expanded formula.

$$\text{ROI} = \frac{\text{net profit}}{\text{sales}} \times \frac{\text{sales}}{\text{investment}}$$

Table 9A.5	(Hypothetical) Operating Ratios for DLL Inc.					
Gross margin ratio	=	$\dfrac{\text{gross margin}}{\text{net sales}}$	=	$\dfrac{\$112\ 650}{248\ 850}$	=	45.3%
Net income ratio	=	$\dfrac{\text{net income}}{\text{net sales}}$	=	$\dfrac{\$48\ 465}{248\ 850}$	=	19.5%
Operating expense ratio	=	$\dfrac{\text{total operating expenses}}{\text{net sales}}$	=	$\dfrac{\$31\ 125}{248\ 850}$	=	12.5%
Returns and allowances ratio	=	$\dfrac{\text{returns and allowances}}{\text{net sales}}$	=	$\dfrac{\$3000}{248\ 850}$	=	1.2%

$$\text{ROI} = \frac{\$48\ 465}{\$248\ 850} \times \frac{\$248\ 850}{\$129\ 825} = 37.3\%$$

This formula makes it easy to show how ROI can be increased and what might reduce ROI. For example, there are different ways to increase ROI. First, if the management focuses on cutting costs and increasing efficiency, profits may be increased while sales remain the same.

$$\text{ROI} = \frac{\text{net profit}}{\text{sales}} \times \frac{\text{sales}}{\text{investment}}$$

$$\text{ROI} = \frac{\$53\ 277}{\$248\ 850} \times \frac{\$248\ 850}{\$129\ 825} = 41.0\%$$

But ROI can be increased just as much without improving performance simply by reducing the investment—by maintaining less inventory, for instance.

$$\text{ROI} = \frac{\text{net profit}}{\text{sales}} \times \frac{\text{sales}}{\text{investment}}$$

$$\text{ROI} = \frac{\$48\ 465}{\$248\ 850} \times \frac{\$248\ 850}{\$114\ 825} = 42.2\%$$

Sometimes, however, differences among the total assets of firms may be related to the age of the firm or the type of industry, which makes ROI a poor indicator of performance. For this reason, some firms have replaced the traditional ROI measures with *return on assets managed* (ROAM), *return on net assets* (RONA), or *return on stockholders' equity* (ROE).

PRICE ELASTICITY

Price elasticity, discussed in Chapter 9, is a measure of the sensitivity of customers to changes in price. Price elasticity is calculated by comparing the percentage change in quantity to the percentage change in price.

$$\text{Price elasticity of demand} = \frac{\text{percentage change in quantity}}{\text{percentage change in price}}$$

$$E = \frac{(Q_2 - Q_1)/Q_1}{(P_2 - P_1)/P_1}$$

where Q = quantity and P = price.

For example, suppose the manufacturer of jeans increased its price from $30 a pair to $35. But instead of 40 000 pairs being sold, sales declined to only 38 000 pairs. The price elasticity would be calculated as follows:

$$E = \frac{(38\ 000 - 40\ 000)/40\ 000}{(\$35 - 30)/\$30} = \frac{-0.05}{0.167} = 0.30$$

Note that elasticity is usually expressed as a positive number even though the calculations create a negative value.

In this case, a relative small change in demand (5 percent) resulted from a fairly large change in price (16.7 percent), indicating that demand is inelastic. At 0.30, the elasticity is less than 1.

On the other hand, what if the same change in price resulted in a reduction in demand to 30 000 pairs of jeans? Then the elasticity would be

$$E = \frac{(38\ 000 - 40\ 000)/40\ 000}{(\$35 - 30)/\$30} = \frac{-0.05}{0.167} = 1.50$$

In this case, because the 16.7 percent change in price resulted in an even larger change in demand (25 percent), demand is elastic. The elasticity of 1.50 is greater than 1. Note: Elasticity may also be calculated by dividing the change in quantity by the average of Q1 and Q2 and dividing the change in price by the average of the two prices. We, however, have chosen to include the formula that uses the initial quantity and price rather than the average.

Economic Order Quantity

The amount a firm should order at one time is called the *economic order quantity* (EOQ). Every time a firm places an order, there are additional costs. By ordering larger quantities less frequently, the firm saves on these costs. But it also costs money to maintain large inventories of needed materials. The EOQ is the order volume that provides both the lowest processing costs and the lowest inventory costs. The EOQ can be calculated as follows:

1. Determine the *order processing cost*. This is the total amount it costs a firm to place an order from beginning to end. Typically, this might include the operating expenses for the purchasing department, costs for follow-up, costs of record keeping of orders (data processing), costs for the receiving department, and costs for the processing and paying of invoices from suppliers. The simplest way to calculate this is to add up all these yearly costs and then divide by the number of orders placed during the year.

2. Next, calculate the *inventory carrying cost*. This is the total of all costs involved in carrying inventory. These costs include the costs of capital tied up in inventory, the cost of waste (merchandise that becomes obsolete or unusable), depreciation costs, storage costs, insurance premiums, property taxes, and opportunity costs.

The formula for calculating EOQ is

$$\text{EOQ} = \sqrt{\frac{2 \times \text{units sold (or annual usage)} \times \text{ordering cost}}{\text{unit cost} \times \text{inventory carrying cost (\%)}}}$$

For example, suppose an office supply store sells 6000 cases of pens a year at a cost of $12 a case. The cost to the store for each order placed is $60. The cost of carrying the pens in the warehouse is 24 percent per year (this is a typical inventory carrying cost in many businesses). Thus, the calculation is

$$\text{EOQ} = \sqrt{\frac{2 \times 6000 \times \$60}{\$12 \times 0.24}} = \sqrt{\frac{\$720\ 000}{\$2.88}} = 500$$

The firm should order pens about once a month (it sells 6000 cases a year or 500 cases a month).

CBC ⬤ Video Case

ELECTRIC CARS

Ontario is looking to give potential purchasers of electrical cars a jump start by offering an attractive incentive to buy.

The Ontario provincial government unveiled a new program that offers a rebate to anyone buying an electric car or plug-in hybrid. This program is predicted to begin next summer and will help early movers by offering a rebate between $4,000 and $10,000 off the purchase price of a new car. The rebate is based on the size of the vehicle's battery; the bigger the car battery, the bigger the discount. The hope is to make 5 percent of all vehicles electric by the year 2020.

The technology (i.e., new electric cars) is expected to come to market next year, and it will be quite expensive. The Chevy Volt is expected to start at a base price of $40,000. Ford, Chrysler, Nissan, and Toyota are all racing to roll out electrics in the next coming years. Tesla, which already has a sports model available, is looking to launch a sedan version at $50,000.

This video case raises some concerns:

"Will the incentive be sufficient to drive consumers to buy vehicles that cost more upfront and will be slower and have less range?"

Others also question Ontario's motives, since the government is part owner of GM—the maker of the Volt.

Lastly, there is also the concern as to where car owners will go to plug in when a car needs a charge. The details regarding the accessibility of charge stations for plug-in requirements are not fully clear.

The new technology is here. But, will this incentive be sufficient to entice potential consumers to purchase electric cars? How quickly will the market for new electric cars grow?

Questions

1. What types of consumers are likely to be the first to buy these new electric cars? Answer in relation to the adopter categorization on the basis of relative time of adoption of innovations.

2. What stage of the adoption process does this new program influence? Refer to the five stages that a consumer goes through in the process of adopting a new product.

3. What do you believe will be the strongest motivations to entice the purchase of an electric car? Do you think the Ontario incentive program is attractive? Do you think this rebate program will cause a jump start for the electric car market?

4. Comment on the introductory prices for the new electric cars? What type of pricing strategy is being adopted with these new products? Do you believe that the introductory prices are supported? Are the prices in line with the offerings? Do you think enough buyers will want the product at the introductory prices?

Source: This case was prepared by Cameron MacIntosh and is based on "Electric Cars," *National*, CBC video, Toronto, 15 July 2009 (time: 2:01 min).

MyMarketingLab

To view the CBC videos go to
pearsoned.ca/mymarketinglab.com

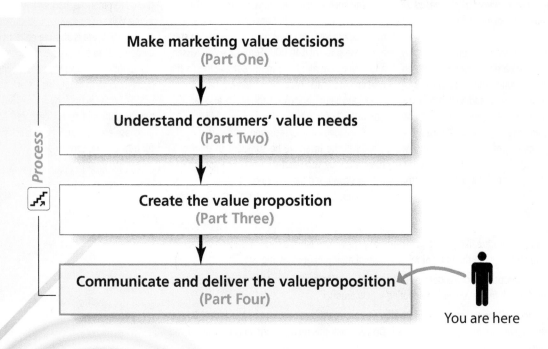

Make marketing value decisions
(Part One)

Understand consumers' value needs
(Part Two)

Create the value proposition
(Part Three)

Communicate and deliver the valueproposition
(Part Four)

Process

You are here

Communicate and Deliver the Value Proposition

Part Four Overview
Now that you have your offering developed and priced—all with a great value proposition that you think will be a home run with your target market—it's time to make important decisions about how you'll communicate that value proposition to your potential purchasers. The chapters in Part Four take you on a fascinating journey through the various marketing communication approaches you can employ to get your message out there. Should you advertise on TV, send free samples of your product in the mail, use Facebook to sponsor a consumer do-it-yourself advertising contest, or something else? Making the right choice of approach is critical, largely because most of the available promotion tools come at a very high cost to the marketer!

Chapter 10 introduces you to these options for communicating the marketing message—called the promotion mix.

You'll enjoy learning about building buzz in the marketplace and using various forms of new media to do the trick. Then, in Chapter 11, you'll get some great guidelines on doing "mass" communication through advertising, public relations, and consumer sales promotion—communicating "one to many," as well as "one to one" communication through trade sales promotion, direct marketing, and personal selling. Finally, Chapter 12 will help you understand the concept of the value chain and the key elements in a supply chain. The concepts of wholesaling and retailing will also be addressed in this chapter.

The overarching theme of the chapters in Part Four is how to go about making a decision on which elements of the promotion mix will be most effective for communicating the value proposition of your offering to your target markets and how to deliver the value proposition.

Marketing Plan Connection:
Tricks of the Trade

Recall that the Appendix at the end of the book provides you with an abbreviated marketing plan example for the fictitious S&S Smoothie Company. That plan is flagged to indicate what elements from the plan correspond to each of the Parts within the book. In addition, you will find a guide called "Build a Marketing Plan," which can be used as a template for marketing planning. It is also cross-referenced to chapters by section of the marketing plan.

In the chapters within Part Four, there are major learning elements that guide you in developing an integrated approach to marketing communication within your marketing plan. In doing so, not all possible promotion elements are appropriate for a given offering at a given time. Marketers must apply the different promotion elements based on the positioning strategy. That is, along with the other marketing mix elements, promotion helps communicate the positioning to the consumer. Recall that S&S Smoothie seeks to position its products as the first-choice smoothie beverage for the serious health-conscious consumer, including those who are seeking to lower their carbohydrate intake. The justification for this positioning is as follows. Many smoothie beverages are available. The S&S Smoothie formula provides superior flavour and nutrition in a shelf-stable form. S&S Smoothie has developed its product (including packaging) and pricing in support of this positioning strategy. Let's review how S&S Smoothie has chosen to support this positioning through promotional strategies.

Promotional Strategies

In the past, S&S Smoothie has used mainly personal selling to promote its products to the trade channel. To support this effort, signage has been provided for the resellers to promote the product at the point of purchase. Posters and stand-alone table cards show appealing photographs of the product in the different flavours and communicate the brand name and the healthy benefits of the product. Similar signage will be developed for use by resellers who choose to stock the S&S Smoothie Gold and the low-carb Smoothies.

Selling has previously been handled by a team of over 75 manufacturers' agents who sell to resellers. In addition, in some geographic areas, an independent distributor does the selling. To support this personal selling approach, S&S Smoothie plans for additional promotional activities to introduce its new products and meet its other marketing objectives. These include the following:

1. *Television advertising:* S&S Smoothie will purchase a limited amount of relatively inexpensive and targeted cable channel advertising. A small number of commercials will be shown during prime-time programs with high viewer ratings by the target market. Television advertising can be an important means of not only creating awareness of the product, but also enhancing the image of the product.

2. *Magazine advertising:* Because consumers in the target market are not avid magazine readers, magazine advertising will be limited and will supplement other promotion activities. During the next year, S&S Smoothie will experiment with limited magazine advertising in such titles as *Sports Illustrated.* The company will also investigate the potential of advertising in university newspapers.

3. *Sponsorships:* S&S Smoothie will attempt to sponsor several marathons in major cities. The advantage of sponsorships is that they provide visibility for the product while at the same time showing that the company supports activities of interest to the target market.

4. *Digital marketing:* S&S Smoothie will continue its use of social media to communicate with consumers and to monitor customers' postings about S&S products. In addition, S&S TV commercials will be available on the company Web site and on YouTube. In the latter part of the year, the company will sponsor a do-it-yourself ad competition through its Web site. The winning ads will be aired on cable TV.

5. *Sampling:* Sampling of S&S Smoothie beverages at select venues will provide an opportunity for prospective customers to become aware of the product and to taste the great flavours. Sampling will include only the two new products being introduced. Venues for sampling will include the following:

   a. Marathons

   b. Weight-lifting competitions

   c. Gymnastics meets

   d. Student unions located on selected college and university campuses

---

MyMarketingLab

Now, if you are working on a marketing plan as part of your course, you can go to MyMarketingLab to apply what you learn in Part Four to your own marketing plan project.

From One-to-Many to Many-to-Many:
Traditional and New Media

Real People **Profiles**

Michael Monello

Profile

▼ A Decision Maker at Campfire

Mike Monello is partner/executive creative director at Campfire, a communications agency based in New York. Mike started out as a DIY filmmaker, and in 1998 he created *The Blair Witch Project* with four other film school friends. This integrated, interactive experience forged a community around the film's mythology. With over $240 million in worldwide box-office receipts, it was a pop-culture phenomenon that changed the way marketers approach the Internet.

Excited by this marketing/entertainment hybrid, Mike co-founded Campfire, where he has been intimately involved in the creative development of every project that has come through the company's doors. From "Beta-7" for Sega, and "Art of the Heist" for Audi to "Frenzied Waters" for Discovery Channel's Shark Week, he's led work that has been awarded top honours at the One Show, Clio, Mixx, ad:Tech, and Addy awards. A vocal force in the world of transmedia storytelling, Mike has spoken at many prestigious events, including Futures of Entertainment at M.I.T. and SXSW Interactive.

Decision Time at Campfire

Campfire's growth has been completely organic. It started as a small group of associates and collaborators who would come together to work on a project and evolved to a "real" agency with offices in New York City. Campfire is a project-based agency that is not reliant on specific media platforms to generate revenue (30-second TV spots, or banner ads and Flash-based Web sites, for example). Most advertising agencies seek AOR (Agency of Record) relationships, where the client pays a monthly retainer fee to the agency for creative services. The AOR relationship, however, can create a structure that supports only the most common and "safe" work to be presented to the client, since entire teams of people depend on that retainer for their jobs.

Campfire's work centres around storytelling and experience, and the marketing programs it develops for clients aren't easily put into the usual traditional/digital silos. For example, Campfire's work for Verizon FiOS encompasses a 30-minute technology home makeover show, large block-party events, a robust online experience, local PR outreach, direct mail, casting events, and more. Most clients, including Verizon, usually build a roster of specialized agencies and put them in silos to develop their own particular pieces, so the traditional ad agency develops for TV and print while

Here's my problem..

the event agency does all the public events and sponsorships, the direct mail agency works on their pieces, branded content companies may be in the mix for product placement, digital agencies for online work, and so on. The results are almost never integrated beyond simple things like an overall look and feel and perhaps a tagline. Campfire's expertise is not in any one particular silo but in developing all these elements as part of the total integrated project. Campfire sits at the intersection of entertainment and marketing, and this is one reason why the company's position in the agency landscape is a bit of a mystery to some. Since its campaigns cross all media channels, Campfire has been called, at one time or another, a digital agency, a branded content agency, a transmedia agency, a social media agency, and, simply, a creative shop. That mystery has served Mike and his partners well, as it tends to attract clients who want to take bold chances; they often are willing to take risks with Campfire and approve projects that they would never accept from their traditional agencies.

In 2007, *Advertising Age* listed Campfire as one of "The Hottest Digital Agencies Around."[1] The company had only really been a full-time agency for about a year at that point, and it had never identified itself as a "digital agency." This was fantastic recognition that opened many new doors for the agency. As a result, Mike and his partners found themselves at a crossroads soon after when a potential client approached them to become their digital agency of record (AOR). Campfire had only seven employees at the time, and this was both a big opportunity as well as a significant change in the young agency's business model. While it had built Web sites, banner ads, and other more traditional media, these efforts were always in the service of a larger project. Campfire's leaders had to decide if they were to take the leap to become a full-service digital agency.

> **Things to remember**
> Campfire is largely a "new media" agency; this means that Mike and his colleagues employ a number of nontraditional channels to tell stories about their clients' brands. Mike has to choose between retaining that independence from "business as usual" and gaining access to resources (including employees and clients) that work in more established areas like television advertising.

its financial future. On the other hand, the culture and structure required to develop the kinds of projects Campfire is known for is quite different from that of a traditional digital shop. While most agencies have strong hierarchies with creative directors, account planning, account management, art directors and copywriter teams, studio creatives and more, Campfire develops projects with smaller teams of higher-level people whose skills and knowledge cross the boundaries of their titles. The agency would have to make adjustments to accommodate the new work as well as consider what building out that offering would mean for its own brand and differentiation in the marketplace.

2 Option
Partner with a smaller, more traditional agency and split the work according to capabilities in order to handle all the client's needs. Each agency could do what it does best with the added benefit of bridging strategy, research, and creative across both agencies, something that's often difficult for clients to manage on their own. While Campfire had worked successfully with partners in the past, the process would be complicated, and it would have to be managed very closely in order to keep it simple for the client. Dividing account services in particular could be tricky—who owns the overall creative strategy when there are disagreements between agencies?

3 Option
Walk away. Campfire could turn the client away gracefully, explain that the agency isn't structured to service the kind of work they require on an ongoing basis, and hope to keep the door open for a future project that more closely aligns with Campfire's services. Turning away any work is not easy for a growing agency, especially when you need the income. While Campfire would stay true to its brand, would it be tossing away a great opportunity to expand the scope of its business? After all, there are a lot more potential clients who want traditional digital work rather than the kind of fully integrated projects Campfire had done up to that time.

Now, put yourself in Mike's shoes. Which option would you choose, and why?

Mike considered his Options 1·2·3

1 Option
Become the client's digital AOR. To do this, Campfire would have to hire new creative, account, and production people and develop a more traditional digital offering. As a small agency built up organically, it would gain some breathing room in the race for new business, as well as a longer window into

You Choose

Which **Option** would you choose, and **why**?
1. ☐YES ☐NO   2. ☐YES ☐NO   3. ☐YES ☐NO

See what **option** Mike chose on **page 380.**

promotion
The coordination of a marketer's communication efforts to influence attitudes or behaviour.

1

OBJECTIVE

Understand the communication process and the traditional promotion mix.
(pp. 356–363)

One-to-Many: The Traditional Communication Model

Test your advertising memory:*

1. What energy drink "gives you wings"?
2. What store advertises "Home owners helping homeowners"
3. What character do Energizer battery ads feature?
4. At Burger King, you can have it "_____," whereas Harvey's makes your hamburger "_____."
5. Which paper towel brand is "The Quicker Picker-Upper"?

Did you get them all right? You owe your knowledge about these and a thousand other trivia questions to the efforts of people who specialize in marketing communications. Of course, today, these slogans are "old school" as marketers have followed consumers onto Facebook and Twitter and virtual worlds to talk with their customers.

As we said in Chapter 1, **promotion** is the coordination of marketing communication efforts to influence attitudes or behaviour. This function is one of the famous *four Ps* of the marketing mix and it plays a vital role—whether the goal is to sell hamburgers, insurance, ringtones, or healthy diets. Of course, virtually *everything* an organization says and does is a form of marketing communication. The ads it creates, the packages it designs, the uniforms its employees wear, and what other consumers say about their experiences with the firm contribute to the impression people have of the company and its products. In fact, savvy marketers should consider that *every element of the marketing mix is actually a form of communication*. After all, the price of a product, where it is sold, and, of course, the quality of the product itself contributes to our impression of it.

In previous chapters, we talked about creating, managing, and pricing tangible and intangible products. But it's not enough just to produce great products—successful marketing plans must also provide effective marketing communication strategies. Just what do we mean by communication? Today, messages take many forms: quirky television commercials, innovative Web sites, viral videos, sophisticated magazine ads, funky T-shirts, blimps blinking messages over football stadiums—even do-it-yourself, customer-made advertising. Some marketing communications push specific products (the Apple iPad) or actions (donating blood), whereas others try to create or reinforce an image that represents the entire organization (General Electric or the Catholic Church).

Marketing communication in general performs one or more of four roles:

1. It informs consumers about new goods and services.
2. It *reminds* consumers to continue using certain brands.
3. It *persuades* consumers to choose one brand over others.
4. It *builds* relationships with customers (Exhibit 10.1).

---

*Answers: (1) Red Bull energy drink, (2) Home Hardware, (3) the Energizer Bunny, (4) "your way," "a beautiful thing" (5) Bounty paper towels

Many marketing experts now believe a successful promotional strategy should blend several diverse forms of marketing communication. **Integrated marketing communication (IMC)** is the process that marketers use "to plan, develop, execute, and evaluate coordinated, measurable, persuasive brand communication programs over time"[2] to targeted audiences. The IMC approach argues that consumers come in contact with a company or a brand in many different ways before, after, and during a purchase. Consumers see these points of contact or *touchpoints*—described in Chapter 6 as a TV commercial, a company Web site, a coupon, an opportunity to win a sweepstakes, or a display in a store—as a whole, and as a single company that speaks to them in different places and different ways. IMC marketers understand that to achieve their marketing communication goals, they must selectively use some or all of these touchpoints to deliver a consistent message to their customers in a **multichannel promotional strategy** where they combine traditional advertising, sales promotion, and public relations activities with online buzz-building activities. A lot is different from most traditional marketing communication programs of the past that made little effort to coordinate the varying messages consumers received. When an advertising campaign runs independently of a sweepstakes, which in turn has no relation to a 10K marathon sponsorship, consumers often get conflicting messages that leave them confused and unsure of the brand's identity. With IMC, marketers seek to understand what information consumers want as well as how, when, and where they want it—and then to deliver information about the product using the best combination of communication methods available to them.

Exhibit 10.1

Promotion takes many forms, including humorous print ads like this one for a German company that makes pens.

It's great to talk about a multichannel strategy, but that still leaves a lot of questions about how we get our customers to understand what we're trying to say. And in today's high-tech world, these questions get even more complicated because the communications options available to marketers change literally almost every day—there will probably be new formats that appear on the scene between the time you start and finish this course!

It helps to understand these options when we look at how we as consumers get our information. Figure 10.1 shows three communication models. The first traditional communication model is a "one-to-many" view in which a single marketer develops and sends messages to many consumers, perhaps even millions of consumers, at once. The one-to-many approach involves traditional forms of mass media marketing communication such as *advertising*, including traditional mass media (TV, radio, magazines, and newspapers); *out-of-home* (like billboards); and Internet advertising. This model also benefits from *consumer sales promotions* such as coupons, samples, rebates, or contests and press releases and special events that *public relations* professionals organize.

Today, these traditional methods still work in some circumstances, but there are a lot of other options available that often mesh better with our "wired," 24/7 culture. When you take a break from posting on your friends' Facebook walls, you'll recognize that you also learn about products and services from your own social network, in addition to ads, billboards, or coupons. For this reason, we need to consider an *updated communications model* where marketing messages are what we think of as many-to-many. This newer perspective recognizes the huge impact of **word-of-mouth communication,** where consumers look to each other for information and recommendations. Many of us are more likely to choose a new restaurant based on users' reviews we read on Yelp than on a cool commercial we saw for the place on TV; ditto for nail salons, bike stores, and maybe even cars.

In the updated model, marketers add new tools to their communications toolbox, including *buzz-building* activities that use *viral* and *evangelical marketing techniques* as well as

integrated marketing communication (IMC)
A strategic business process that marketers use to plan, develop, execute, and evaluate coordinated, measurable, persuasive brand communication programs over time to targeted audiences.

multichannel promotional strategy
A marketing communication strategy where they combine traditional advertising, sales promotion, and public relations activities with online buzz-building activities.

word-of-mouth communication
Communication that takes place when consumers provide information about products to other consumers.

Figure 10.1 Three Models of Marketing Communications

Marketers today make use of the traditional one-to-many communication model and the updated many-to-many communication model as well as talking one-to-one with consumers and business customers.

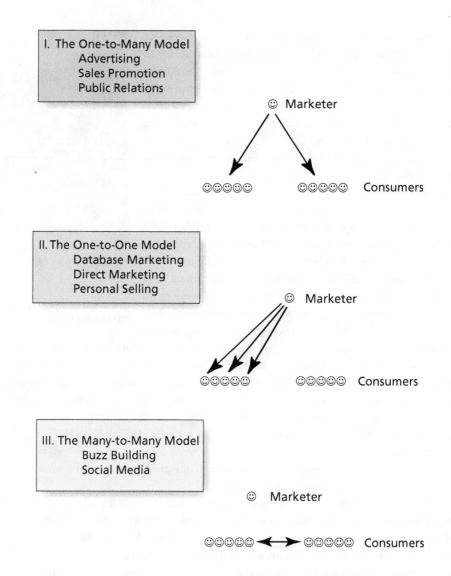

new social media platforms such as *brand communities*, *product review sites*, and *social networking sites*. The odds are that you're using many of these platforms already, though you may not call them by these names. By the end of this section, you will.

We also need to expand our traditional communication model to include *one-to-one marketing*, where marketers speak to consumers and business customers individually. The one-to-one forms of marketing communication include *personal selling*, *personal trade sales promotion* activities used to support personal selling, and a variety of *database marketing* activities that include direct marketing. In this chapter and the next, we'll examine each of these different ways to communicate with our customers.

The Communications Model

communications model
The process whereby meaning is transferred from a source to a receiver.

Wired or not, the **communications model** in Figure 10.2 is a good way to understand the basics of how any kind of message works. In this perspective, a *source* transmits a *message* through some *medium* to a *receiver* who (we hope) listens and understands the message. The basic idea is that *any* way a marketer reaches out to consumers—a hat with a Caterpillar tractor logo on it, a door-to-door sales pitch from a College Pro Painters representative, or a televised fashion show with supermodels strutting their stuff for Victoria's Secret—this is part of the basic communications process.

The communications model specifies the elements necessary for effective communication to occur: a source, a message, a medium, and a receiver. Regardless of how a marketer sends messages, her objective is to capture receivers' attention and relate to their needs.

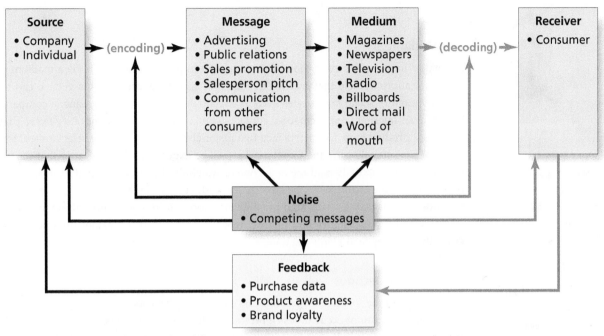

Figure 10.2 Communications Model

The communications model explains how organizations create and transmit messages from the marketer (the source) to the consumer (the receiver) who (we hope) understands what the marketer intends to say.

The Source Encodes

Let's start to explore this basic model from a good place: the beginning. **Encoding** is the process by which a source translates an idea into a form of communication that conveys the desired meaning. The **source** is the organization or individual that sends the message. It's one thing for marketers to form an idea about a product in their own minds, but it's not quite as simple to express the idea to their customers. To make their messages more believable or more attractive to consumers, marketers sometimes choose a real person (like the computer users that appeared in Microsoft's "Windows 7 Was My Idea" advertising), hire an actor or a model (William Shatner of *Star Trek* fame for Priceline.com or Queen Latifah for Cover Girl Cosmetics), or create a character (the Geico gecko with the Cockney accent) to represent the source.[3] (See Exhibit 10.2.)

In other cases, the message features actual customers. In advertising to counter negative consumers' responses to Toyota's massive recall, the company used ads in which Toyota customers told why they were going to continue to buy the cars.

The Message

The **message** is the actual content that goes from the source to a receiver. It includes information necessary to persuade, inform, remind, or build a relationship. Advertising messages may include both verbal and nonverbal elements, such as beautiful background scenery or funky music. The marketer must select the ad elements carefully so that the message connects with end consumers or business customers in its target market. Otherwise, effective communication simply does not occur and the organization just wastes its money.

encoding
The process of translating an idea into a form of communication that will convey meaning.

source
An organization or individual that sends a message.

message
The communication in physical form that goes from a sender to a receiver.

Exhibit 10.2

Many marketing messages rely on an expert or highly credible source to encourage recipients to take them seriously.

Mike Monello

medium
A communication vehicle through which a message is transmitted to a target audience.

receiver
The organization or individual that intercepts and interprets the message.

decoding
The process by which a receiver assigns meaning to the message.

noise
Anything that interferes with effective communication.

feedback
Receivers' reactions to the message.

The Medium

No matter how the source encodes the message, it must then transmit it via a **medium**, a communications vehicle that reaches members of a target audience. This vehicle can be television, radio, social media sites such as Facebook or Twitter, a magazine, a company Web site, an Internet blog, a personal contact, a billboard, or even a temporary tattoo that displays a product logo. Marketers face two major challenges when they select a medium. First, they must make sure the target market will be exposed to the medium—that the intended receivers actually read the magazine or watch the TV show where the message appears. Second, the attributes of the advertised product should match those of the medium. For example, magazines with high prestige are more effective to communicate messages about overall product image and quality, whereas specialized magazines do a better job when they convey factual information.[4]

The Receiver Decodes

If a tree falls in the forest and no one hears it, did it make a sound? Zen mysteries aside, communication cannot occur unless a **receiver** is there to get the message. The receiver is any individual or organization that intercepts and interprets the message. Assuming that the customer is even paying attention (a big assumption in our overloaded, media-saturated society), she interprets the message in light of her unique experiences. **Decoding** is the process whereby a receiver assigns meaning to a message; that is, she translates the message she sees or hears back into an idea that makes sense to her.

Marketers hope that the target consumer will decode the message the way they intended, but effective communication occurs only when the source and the receiver share a mutual frame of reference (Exhibit 10.4). Too often, sources and receivers aren't on the same page, and the results can range from mildly embarrassing to downright disastrous. As we saw in an earlier chapter, this mismatch is especially likely to happen when the source and the receiver don't share the same cultural background or language.

Noise

The communication model also acknowledges that **noise**—anything that interferes with effective communication—can block messages. As the many arrows between noise and the other elements of the communication model in Figure 10.2 indicate, noise can occur at any stage of communication. It can pop up at the encoding stage if the source uses words or symbols that the receiver will not understand. Or a nearby conversation may distract the receiver. There may be a problem with transmission of the message through the medium—especially if it's drowned out by the chorus of other marketers clamouring for us to look at *their* messages instead. Marketers try to minimize noise when they place their messages where there is less likely to be distractions or competition for consumers' attention. Calvin Klein, for example, will often buy a block of advertising pages in a magazine so that the reader sees only pictures of its clothing as she leafs through that section.

Feedback

To complete the communication loop, the source gets "**feedback**" from receivers. Feedback is a reaction to the message that helps marketers gauge the effectiveness of the message so they can fine-tune it. Sometimes consumers eagerly provide this feedback—especially if they are unhappy. They may call a toll-free number or post an e-mail to the manufacturer to resolve a problem. More often, though, marketers must actively seek their customers' feedback. The need for this "reality check" reminds us of the importance of conducting marketing research (as we discussed in Chapter 3) to verify that a firm's strategies are working. And keep in mind that even though nobody likes to be yelled at, we actually *want* customers to complain so that we have an opportunity to address their concerns before they say negative things to others.

The Traditional Promotion Mix

As we said earlier, promotion, or marketing communication, is one of the famous four Ps. Marketers use the term **promotion mix** to refer to the communication elements that the marketer controls. These elements of the traditional promotion mix include

- Advertising
- Sales promotion
- Public relations
- Personal selling
- Direct marketing

Exhibit 10.3

Mr. Clean employs a creative medium to get its message to customers.

Used with permission of Procter & Gamble Inc.

Just as a DJ combines different songs or phrases to create an entertainment experience, the term *mix* implies that a company's promotion strategy focuses on more than one element. And as we said, promotion works best when the marketer skilfully combines all of the elements of the promotion mix to deliver a single consistent message about a brand.

Another challenge is to be sure that the promotion mix works in harmony with the overall *marketing mix* to combine elements of promotion with place, price, and product to position the firm's offering in people's minds. For example, marketers must design ads for luxury products such as Prada bags or Lexus automobiles to communicate that same luxury character of the product, and the ads should appear in places that reinforce that upscale image. A chic commercial that appears before a showing of the latest *Hangover* movie just won't cut it.

Marketers have a lot more control over some kinds of marketing communication messages than they do others. As Figure 10.3 shows, *mass-media advertising* and *sales promotion* are at one end of the continuum, where the marketer has total control over the message she delivers. At the other end is *word-of-mouth (WOM) communication*, where everyday people rather than the company run the show. WOM is a vitally important component of the brand attitudes consumers form—and of their decisions about what and what not to buy. Sandwiched between the ends we find *personal selling* and *direct marketing*, where marketers have some but not total control over the message they deliver, and *public relations*, where marketers have even less control. Table 10.1 presents some of the pros and cons of each element of the promotion mix.

Mass Communications

Some elements of the promotion mix include messages intended to reach many prospective customers at the same time. Whether a company offers customers a coupon for 50-cents off or airs a television commercial to millions, it promotes itself to a mass audience. These are the elements of the promotion mix that use **mass communication**—that is, TV, radio, magazines, and newspapers.

promotion mix
The major elements of marketer-controlled communication, including advertising, sales promotion, public relations, personal selling, and direct marketing.

mass communication
Relates to television, radio, magazines, and newspapers.

Surrender, tough messes. Conquer them with our thick wipes.

Exhibit 10.4

For effective decoding to occur, the source and the receiver must share a mutual frame of reference. In this ad, the receiver needs to understand the meaning of a "white flag" in order for the message to make sense.

CLOROX® is a registered trademark of The Clorox Company. © 2012 The Clorox Company. Used with permission

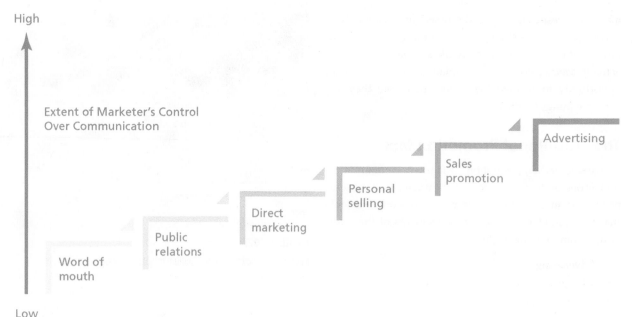

Figure 10.3 Control Continuum
The messages that consumers receive about companies and products differ in the amount of control the marketer has over the message she delivers to the consumer.

advertising
Nonpersonal communication from an identified sponsor using mass media.

- *Advertising:* **Advertising** is, for many, the most familiar and visible element of the promotion mix. It is nonpersonal communication from an identified sponsor using the mass media. The most important advantage of advertising is that it reaches large numbers of consumers at one time. In addition, advertising can convey rich and dynamic images that establish and reinforce a distinctive brand identity. This helps marketers bond with customers and boost sales. Advertising also is useful to communicate factual information about the product or to remind consumers to buy their favourite brand. However, it sometimes suffers from a credibility problem; cynical consumers tune out messages they think are biased or intended to sell them something they don't need. Advertising can also be very expensive, so firms must ensure that their messages deliver the best bang for the buck.

- *Sales promotion:* Consumer sales promotion includes programs such as contests, coupons, or other incentives that marketers design to build interest in, or encourage purchase of, a product during a specified period. Unlike other forms of promotion, sales promotion intends to stimulate immediate action (often in the form of a purchase) rather than build long-term loyalty.

- *Public relations:* Public relations describes a variety of communication activities that seek to create and maintain a positive image of an organization and its products among various *publics*, including customers, government officials, and shareholders. Public relations programs also include efforts to present negative company news in the most positive way so that this information will have less damaging consequences. In contrast to sales promotion, public relations components of the promotion mix usually do not seek a short-term increase in sales. Instead, they try to influence feelings, opinions, or beliefs for the long term.

Personal Communications

Sometimes marketers want to communicate with consumers on a personal, one-on-one level. The most immediate way for a marketer to make contact with customers is simply to tell them how wonderful the product is. This is part of the *personal selling* element of the promotion

Table 10.1	A Comparison of Elements of the Traditional Promotion Mix	

Promotional Element	Pros	Cons
Advertising	• The marketer has control over what the message will say, when it will appear, and who is likely to see it.	• Because of the high cost to produce and distribute, it may not be an efficient means of communicating with some target audiences. • Some ads may have low credibility and/or be ignored by audiences.
Sales promotion	• Provides incentives to retailers to support one's products. • Builds excitement for retailers and consumers. • Encourages immediate purchase and trial of new products. • Price-oriented promotions cater to price-sensitive consumers.	• Short-term emphasis on immediate sales rather than a focus on building brand loyalty. • The number of competing promotions may make it hard to break through the promotional clutter. • If consumers use too many price-related sales promotion activities, consumers' perception of a fair price for the brand may be lowered.
Public relations	• Relatively low cost • High credibility	• Lack of control over the message that is eventually transmitted, and no guarantee that the message will ever reach the target. • It is difficult to measure the effectiveness of PR efforts.
Personal selling	• Direct contact with the customer gives the salesperson the opportunity to be flexible and modify the sales message to coincide with the customer's needs. • The salesperson can get immediate feedback from the customer.	• High cost per contact with customer. • Difficult to ensure consistency of message when it is delivered by many different company representatives. • The credibility of salespeople often depends on the quality of their company's image, which has been created by other promotional strategies.
Direct marketing	• Targets specific groups of potential customers with different offers. • Marketers can easily measure the results. • Provides extensive product information and multiple offers within a single appeal. • Provides a way for a company to collect feedback about the effectiveness of its messages in an internal database.	• Consumers may have a negative opinion of some types of direct marketing. • Costs more per contact than mass appeals.

mix we mentioned previously. It is the direct interaction between a company representative and a customer that can occur in person, by phone, or even over an interactive computer link.

Salespeople are a valuable source of communication, because customers can ask questions and the salesperson can immediately address objections and describe product benefits. Personal selling can be tremendously effective, especially for big-ticket consumer items and for industrial products for which the "human touch" is essential.

Marketers also use direct mail, telemarketing, and other *direct marketing* activities to create personal appeals. Like personal selling, direct marketing provides direct communication with a consumer or business customer. Because direct marketing activities seek to gain a direct response from individual consumers, the source can target a communication to market segments of a few or, with today's technology, even segments of one.

2

OBJECTIVE

Understand
how marketers
communicate
using an updated
communication model
that incorporates buzz
marketing activities
and social media.

(pp. 364–373)

Many-to-Many: The New Media Communication Model

groundswell
A social trend in which people use technology to get the things they need from each other, rather than from traditional institutions like corporations.

It seems as if most of us are "on" 24/7 these days, whether we're checking our Facebook wall while on vacation or tweeting about the fabulous new restaurant we just discovered. Authors Charlene Li and Josh Bernoff refer to the changing communication landscape as the **groundswell**: "a social trend in which people use technology to get the things they need from each other, rather than from traditional institutions like corporations."[5] In other words, today's consumers are increasingly getting their information on running shoes, nightclubs, cars, new phones, or even last week's economics lecture from one another rather than from the original source.

The Web revolution is here! What has led to this new communication model and how is it changing marketing? Much of the answer lies in changing technology; everyone is online now. Millions of people around the globe surf the Web, talk with their friends, watch TV, and purchase products from traditional marketers, from Internet-only marketers, and from each other on their computers or their mobile phones with broadband Internet connections. For example, at last report, Facebook had over 750 million monthly active users, more than the population of any country except India and China. These users all have the potential to connect with each other and to share feedback—whether it's about how hard that statistics test was this morning or where they bought a great new swimsuit for summer and how much they paid for it. Marketers are no longer the only ones who talk about their products—millions of consumers have the ability and the desire to spread the good (or bad) news about the goods and services they buy. That's why we're moving from a one-to-many communication model to the new world of many-to-many.

At the same time, traditional advertising has diminished as a way to talk to customers. As consumers, especially younger ones, spend more and more time online, they don't lounge in front of the TV as much and they don't tend to read printed magazines. For those who do watch TV, there are literally hundreds of channels to choose from. This abundance of choice fragments the TV audience and makes the job of reaching a mass market both complex and costly.

As one telling example of this realignment, in 2010 Pepsi decided to forgo advertising on the Super Bowl for the first time in 23 years in order to put money into online formats, especially Facebook. The Pepsi Refresh Project combined online activities and a charitable campaign that Pepsi hoped would let young consumers know it was serious about doing good for the world—and increase its market share. Pepsi accepted one thousand ideas a month online from consumers on ways to improve their communities. The best ideas were chosen by online consumer voting. In all, Pepsi offered a total of $20 million in grants of between $5000 and $250 000 to implement the best ideas.[6] After the tremendous success of the Pepsi Refresh project (over 45 million votes were cast by more than 1 million Facebook users in the first nine months), Pepsi decided to expand the project in 2011 to Europe, Latin America, and Asia, as well as to continue to fund the project in the US and Canada.[7]

Like Pepsi, many other marketers are moving money away from traditional communication vehicles, such as TV advertising, and investing heavily in new media. In 2010, global advertisers spent over $60 billion on online advertising! Retailers also find that their online business is growing, but the Internet customer is harder to please and less loyal since she has easy access to competing prices and to the reviews of products and sellers from other online shoppers. The growth of Internet C2C shopping sites such as eBay and Craigslist means more and more consumers buy from each other than (gulp) pay retail prices. In order to better understand this new communication model and its consequences, we need to first look at how marketers encourage and enable consumers to talk about their products in "buzz" building activities. Then we'll look at some of the specific new media that pop up in the marketing communications landscape.

Buzz Building

Why do the heavy lifting when you can put your customers to work for you? The many-to-many communication model relies on consumers like you to talk to one another about goods, services, and organizations. Marketers think of **buzz** as everyday people helping the marketing efforts when they share opinions with their friends and neighbours.[8] The idea is nothing new. It's basically the so-called "office water-cooler effect" where coworkers dish about the latest TV sitcom on Monday morning.

buzz
Word-of-mouth communication that customers view as authentic.

The trick is to create buzz that works for you, not against you. How does this happen? Or, more specifically, how do marketers make sure it happens? Let's look at Volvo's recent online-only campaign called "The Naughty Volvo" to see buzz in action. The carmaker's goal was to get driving enthusiasts to talk about the new S60 model's innovative design and technology. The campaign was called "naughty" because instead of focusing on Volvo's traditional image of safety, it included online demonstrations of the S60's performance and handling. Online viewers could use a virtual dial to go from a "tame" test of the auto to one where the car swerved around a goldfish bowl or, in an even "naughtier" one, to drive the car in reverse (okay, maybe that's not so naughty). Fans could also submit their ideas for more "naughty" films.[9]

Companies today spend millions to create consumer positive buzz. Firms like Dell have named word-of-mouth (WOM) marketing managers, and the WOMMA (Word-of-Mouth Marketing Association) membership roster includes most of the top consumer brand companies.[10] According to advertising agency JWT Worldwide, over 85 percent of the top 1000 marketing firms now use word-of-mouth tactics.[11] Techniques to encourage consumers to spread information about companies and their products come under a variety of names such as *word-of-mouth marketing, viral marketing, buzz marketing*, and *evangelist marketing*.

As we've noted, buzz isn't *really* new. In fact, we can point to the fame of none other than the *Mona Lisa* portrait as one of the first examples of buzz marketing. In 1911, the painting was stolen from the Louvre museum in Paris. The theft created buzz around the globe while it catapulted da Vinci's masterpiece into the limelight (Note: we're not advocating that you arrange to get your product stolen to build buzz).

What *is* new is the magnifying effect that technology exerts on the spread of buzz. When you think of the effect of consumers talking one-on-one a century ago, imagine the exponential increase in influence of the individual consumer "connectors" or "e-fluentials" who use Facebook, blogs, and other social media to increase their reach.[12] How many online "friends" do you have? Compared to traditional advertising and public relations activities, these endorsements are far more credible and, thus, more valuable to the brand.

People like to share their experiences, good or bad, with others. Truly happy customers will share their excitement about a brand. Unfortunately, the unhappy ones will be even more eager to tell their friends about their unpleasant experiences. When Honda's PR staff set up a Facebook fan page for the new 2010 Honda Accord Crosstour, customers disliked the car's visual appearance and responded with such comments as "Oh god, it looks like the mutant redheaded offspring of a Chrysler Crossfire and a Pontiac Aztec."[13] By the way, that unpredictability is a good reason to think twice before you post those photos from last Saturday night on your Facebook page.

Of course, marketers don't necessarily create the buzz around their product anyway—sometimes they just catch a wave that's building and simply ride it home. WOMMA refers to buzz that comes from deliberate buzz marketing campaigns as "amplified WOM," while it calls buzz that occurs naturally "organic WOM." Organic buzz allowed Procter & Gamble to discover that its Home Café coffee maker had a tendency to start fires after 3000 people complained.[14] Naturally occurring buzz also can create negative publicity, as Southwest Airlines learned firsthand after director/actor Kevin Smith was removed from a Southwest plane because he was too fat to fit in his seat. He used Twitter to express his displeasure. Southwest responded to Smith's tweets, apologized, and offered him a seat.[15]

Ethical and Sustainable Decisions in the Real World

Social media sites like Facebook and Twitter are great places for users to get together with their friends, to talk about what they are doing right now ("dropping off my dry cleaning!"), and to share news. But sometimes the news isn't exactly true—and, unfortunately, the fun goes too far.

When Ed McMahon, Farrah Fawcett, and Michael Jackson died over the span of a few days, the Web was full of made-up death reports about various celebrities. Within a week, rumours that Harrison Ford had died at sea in his capsized yacht, George Clooney's private plane had nosedived, and Jeff Goldblum had fallen to his death on a movie set quickly spread on Twitter and Facebook. Most of the rumours started on a prank Web site called Fakeawish.com, where a user can enter a celebrity's name and then gets a list of fake stories to circulate about him or her.

But is this ethical? Does it damage the credibility of Web sites? Does it seriously harm any celebrities or their families? Should such prankster Web sites be allowed to exist? Should consumers participate in a prankster Web site such as Fakeawish?

What would you do?

ETHICS CHECK: ↖

Find out what other students taking this course **would do** and **why** on **www.mypearsonmarketinglab.com**

↓

Would you spread rumours about celebrities on the Web as an online prank?

☐ **YES** ☐ **NO**

viral marketing

Marketing activities that aim to increase brand awareness or sales by consumers passing a message along to other consumers.

Mike Monello

APPLYING ▽ Viral Marketing

A lot of Mike's work has involved viral marketing, where his team creates an engaging message and relies on viewers to disseminate it broadly. This was the key to the success of the groundbreaking *The Blair Witch Project*.

Ethical Problems in Buzz Marketing

Just as firms are discovering there are myriad opportunities for buzz marketing, there are equally large opportunities for unethical or at least questionable marketing behaviour. Some of these are the following:

- *Activities designed to deceive consumers.* Buzz works best when companies put unpaid consumers in charge of creating their own messages. As Table 10.2 shows, WOMMA considers hiring actors to create buzz deceptive and unethical. This is just what Sony Ericsson Mobile Communications did when the company hired 60 actors to go to tourist attractions. Their role was to act like tourists and get unsuspecting passersby to take their photos using the new Sony Ericsson camera phone, and then hype the phone. WOMMA now has rules that state that anyone talking up products should identify the client for whom they work.[16]

- *Directing buzz marketing at children or teens.* Some critics say buzz marketing should never do this, as these consumers are more impressionable and easier to deceive than adults.[17]

- *Buzz marketing activities that damage property.* Puma encouraged consumers to stencil its cat logo all over Paris. Such activities led to damage or vandalism, which the company will ultimately have to pay for. In addition, individual consumers could find themselves in trouble with the law, a problem that could ultimately backfire and damage the company image.

- *Stealth marketing activities that deliberately deceive or lie on behalf of clients.* WOMMA considers such activities—whether authoring a positive product review on a shopbot, pretending to read a new novel on the subway, or calling a supermarket to ask the manager why she is not stocking a certain product—to be unethical.

Viral Marketing

One form of buzz building is **viral marketing**. This term refers to marketing activities that aim to increase brand awareness or sales by consumers passing a message along to other consumers, hopefully in an exponential fashion—much like your roommate passes a cold on to you and you pass it along to all your other friends. Some of the earliest examples of viral marketing were messages at the bottom of e-mails by Yahoo! and Hotmail that advertised the free e-mail services, much like the tag today at the bottom of e-mails, "Sent from my BlackBerry device on the ___ network." Consumers could not choose whether

Table 10.2	Positive and Unethical Word-of-Mouth Marketing Strategies

Positive Word-of-Mouth Marketing Strategies

1. **Encouraging communications:**

   Developing tools to make telling a friend easier.

   Creating forums and feedback tools.

   Working with social networks.

2. **Giving people something to talk about:**

   Information that can be shared or forwarded.

   Advertising, stunts, and other publicity that encourages conversation.

   Working with product development to build WOM elements into products.

3. **Creating communities and connecting people:**

   Creating user groups and fan clubs.

   Supporting independent groups that form around your product.

   Hosting discussions and message boards about your products.

   Enabling grassroots organization such as local meetings and other real-world participation.

4. **Working with influential communities:**

   Finding people who are likely to respond to your message.

   Identifying people who are able to influence your target customers.

   Informing these individuals about what you do and encouraging them to spread the word.

   Good-faith efforts to support issues and causes that are important to these individuals.

5. **Creating evangelist or advocate programs:**

   Providing recognition and tools to active advocates.

   Recruiting new advocates, teaching them about the benefits of your products, and encouraging them to talk about those benefits.

6. **Researching and listening to customer feedback:**

   Tracking online and offline conversations by supporters, detractors, and neutrals.

   Listening and responding to both positive and negative conversations.

7. **Engaging in transparent conversation:**

   Encouraging two-way conversations with interested parties.

   Creating blogs and other tools to share information.

   Participating openly on online blogs and discussions.

8. **Co-creation and information sharing:**

   Involving consumers in marketing and creative (feedback on creative campaigns, allowing them to create commercials, etc.).

   Letting customers "behind the curtain" to have first access to information and content.

Unethical Word-of-Mouth Marketing Strategies

1. **Stealth Marketing**

   Any practice designed to deceive people about the involvement of marketers in a communication.

2. **Shilling**

   Paying people to talk about (or promote) a product without disclosing that they are working for the company; impersonating a customer.

3. **Infiltration**

   Using fake identities in an online discussion to promote a product.

   Taking over a Web site, conversation, or live event against the wishes or rules set by the proprietor.

4. **Comment Spam**

   Using automated software ("bots") to post unrelated or inappropriate comments to blogs or other online communities.

5. **Defacement**

   Vandalizing or damaging property to promote a product.

6. **Spam**

   Sending bulk or unsolicited e-mail or other messages without clear, voluntary permission.

7. **Falsification**

   Knowingly disseminating false or misleading information.

Source: Adapted from "Word-of-Mouth 101 in An Introduction to Word-of-Mouth Marketing," WOMMA, http://womma.org/wom101/. © WOMMA, 2011.

they wanted to participate in these viral marketing programs. Today, most viral marketing tactics are more subtle and consist of marketers' use of video clips, interactive games, or other activities that consumers will find so interesting or unique that they want to share them with their friends using digital technology. The recent phenomenon of "lipdubbing" at many colleges and universities is an example of viral marketing.

Brand Ambassadors and Evangelists

Many marketers realize that they can't create buzz by themselves; they recruit loyal customers as **brand ambassadors or brand evangelists** to help them. These zealous consumers can be the best salespeople a company can ever find—and they often work for free. They are

brand ambassadors or brand evangelists

Loyal customers of a brand recruited to communicate and be salespeople with other consumers for a brand they care a great deal about.

NO ONE GROWS KETCHUP LIKE HEINZ.

That's because every red, ripe tomato in every bottle is grown only from Heinz seeds. It's what helps us deliver the uniquely thick, rich flavor that America loves.

HEINZ. GROWN, NOT MADE.™

Exhibit 10.5

Advertising can convey rich and dynamic images that establish and reinforce a distinctive brand identity.

social media

Internet-based platforms that allow users to create their own content and share it with others who access these sites.

social networks

Sites used to connect people with other similar people.

heavy users, take a product seriously, care a great deal about it, and want it to succeed.[18] (See Exhibits 10.5 and 10.6.) In addition, they know the target audience better than anyone, because they are a part of it. A new twist in evangelist marketing is the brand party in the intimate settings provided by consumers' homes. For example, to introduce Windows 7, Microsoft enlisted nearly 60 000 hosts who held parties attended by an estimated 7 million consumers world-wide. Each Windows 7 host received an autographed edition of the operating system, a tote bag, a deck of cards, and other party favours.[19]

So how do marketers identify and motivate these loyal customers to be brand ambassadors? Sometimes they seek out customers who already blog about the product, sharing what they love about the brand. One way to motivate brand ambassadors is to give them special access or privileges to the company and its marketing strategies. Some might be recruited and featured through a brand contest, as done for the Ford Fiesta launch in the United States.[20]

New Social Media

In addition to buzz building, **social media** are an important part of the updated communications model. This term refers to Internet-based platforms that allow users to create their own content and share it with others who access these sites. It's hard to grasp just how much these new formats will transform the way we interact with marketers; they "democratize" messages, because they give individual consumers a seat at the table when organizations shape brand meanings and promote themselves in the marketplace. This makes it much easier for companies to tap into their brand evangelists to help spread the word. The flip side is that the bad stuff also gets out much quicker and reaches people a lot faster. In one survey, 72 percent of respondents said they would be compelled to share a negative online experience with friends and family, and 52 percent "who have had a bad experience are less likely to shop from that brand again in an offline channel."[21]

There's no doubt that social media is the place to be in marketing communications now, even if many organizations haven't quite figured out just what to do with these platforms. Traditional brands such as Energizer and Coke are scrambling to move hefty portions of their promotion budgets from traditional advertising into social media. Energizer Canada has kicked off the "Now that's positivenergy" campaign with the aid of Canadian ad agency TBWA, launching an online pledge campaign rallying consumers to "pay it forward" with acts of kindness, urging people to "Do Something Little. Help Something Big."[22]

Social media include blogs, forums, picture- and video-sharing sites, wikis, and podcasts, to name a few. While marketers can and do use all these types of sites, we are going to focus on just a few platforms: social networking sites, virtual worlds, product review sites, and geospatial mobile apps.

Social Networks

Social networks are sites used to connect people with other similar people. Successful networking sites ask users to develop profiles of themselves so that those with similar backgrounds, interests, hobbies, religious beliefs, racial identities, or political views can "meet" online. Social networks such as Facebook and LinkedIn are some of the most popular sites on the Internet, with millions of users from around the globe. Once a user has created a profile, it's easy to connect with old and new friends.

So what's in all this social networking for marketers? First, social networks make it easy for marketers to reach influential people such as journalists and consumers who are opinion leaders. But even more important is the opportunity social networks provide to create a brand community. We'll talk later about brand communities, but first, let's examine a couple of the most popular social media sites.

Facebook. Facebook is the most popular of all social networking sites with over 750 million monthly active users as we write this book—and no doubt tons more again as you're reading it. Users of Facebook first develop a profile that remains private unless they choose to connect with a "friend." While this social media site was originally created to allow US college students to keep in touch with their friends (in those days you had to have ".edu" in your e-mail address to join), it is no longer just for students. Among the 17 million Canadians on Facebook are many significant user segments including baby-boomer women and even grandparents who use the platform to locate long-lost friends (and keep tabs on their grandchildren).[23] Despite this "invasion," at least for now, Facebook is the social media site of choice for college and university students. In one recent survey of American students, an overwhelming 82 percent of males and 90 percent of females gave it the ultimate compliment, rating it "cool" and the go-to place over all other networking platforms, and even over Web sites in general, including Google.[24]

Exhibit 10.6

A brand community is a group of people who are organized around a lifestyle or idea that is representative of the brand. The brand community members are admirers of the brand and share in the rituals and traditions they associate with it. They feel connected to the brand and as a result they bond with each other. After near bankruptcy in 1983, Harley focused on building a brand community. The Harley Owners Group, fondly referred to as H.O.G., is credited with helping to turn the company around. Harley supports riders' passions for their bikes by sponsoring huge rallies around the country where members can meet up. In 2010, Harley enjoyed revenues of over $4 billion.

A major advantage for marketers is that you can establish Facebook groups around topics and you can recruit fans for your product. Many firms are rolling out promotions that tap into this fan base. A typical one is the campaign by TELUS to choose the next critter to appear in their ads. In the past TELUS, had hippos, dolphins, and frogs representing their brand but they were looking for a new star. A Facebook contest was created where fans got to vote for which critter would take centre stage in TELUS's ads. TELUS would also donate $1 for every vote to the Nature Conservancy of Canada (up to $100 000), and every time a vote was cast, the user would be entered into a draw to win an African Safari grand prize or one of 10 BlackBerry Playbooks. In addition, after voting, the fan got a promo code for $100 off any smartphone.[25]

Twitter: **Twitter** is a free microblogging service that lets users post short text messages with a maximum of 140 characters. People who subscribe to an individual's Twitter feed are called "followers." Users can follow anyone they like, unlike Facebook where you have to be recognized and accepted as a "friend." Attesting to its popularity, Twitter now has 175 million registered users who "tweet" 155 million posts a day.[26]

Twitter
A free social networking and microblogging service that lets users send and read text-based posts with a maximum of 140 characters.

The good news for marketers is that one in five (20 percent) tweets posted on Twitter is either a question or a comment about a brand-related product or service.[27] Thus, it is especially important that marketers monitor Twitter to understand what consumers say about their products. Unlike other social media, Twitter is a broadcast medium, which means that marketers can send messages to hundreds of thousands of people at a time. They can use this platform to alert customers to deals and to generate sales. Dell, for example, used Twitter to tell followers about exclusive deals; these tweets generated over $3 million in revenue in 24 months.[28]

Virtual Worlds

What if a sophisticated video game like *Madden Football* married a chatroom that enables multiple participants to talk to each other in real time? Suppose they had a baby. This would probably be a **virtual world**. This term refers to an online, highly engaging digital environment where **avatars**—graphic representations of users—live and interact with other avatars

virtual worlds
Online, highly engaging digital environments where avatars live and interact with other avatars in real time.

avatars
Graphic representations of users of virtual worlds.

Marketing Metrics

A Simple Way to Calculate Social Media Return on Investment

Social media return on investment (ROI) is simply a measurement of efficiency. It's a lot of things to a lot of people: "return on inactivity," "return on innovation" and "return on engagement." However, in a stricter sense, social media ROI is defined as a measure of the efficiency of a social media marketing campaign. This definition might sound complicated, but in reality, it's quite simple.

What Does ROI Really Mean?

In the financial world, ROI is used to measure the financial efficiency of an investment. ROI is based on the financial formula:

ROI = (return − investment) / investment

This means that if you increase your return while keeping your investment the same, then you increase your ROI. This is good. If you decrease your return while keeping your investment the same, then the ROI goes down. That's bad. A high ROI is better than a low ROI.

Because the ROI formula uses only two inputs—the return and the investment—the ROI formula is an easy way to measure and compare marketing campaigns. A marketing campaign with a high ROI is considered better and more efficient than a marketing campaign with a lower ROI.

It's important to understand that ROI measures the efficiency of an investment because then you also understand that ROI cannot be defined using alternative definitions. "Return on inactivity" does not help you measure the efficiency of your campaign.

Social Media ROI Uses the Return and the Investment

Now, all we need is to take our social media return (the amount of value that we got from our social media campaign) and our social media investment (the amount of money that we invested in our social media campaign) and run it through the financial ROI formula.

Social media ROI = (SM return − SM investment)/ SM investment

Simple, right? Not so fast. The social media investment is clearly defined, but how do you define the social media return and how do you attach a dollar value to the return? We need to answer both questions before we can calculate the social media ROI.

Social Media Return Is the Return on Your Social Media Goals

The peculiar feature of the social media return is that you can define it to be essentially anything you want it to be!

Brian Solis from the Altimeter Group puts it even more succinctly in his article "ROI Doesn't Stand for Return on Ignorance: Everything Starts with an End in Mind."

In reality, social media return is the value that you derive from your social media campaign. For instance, if the goal of your social media campaign is to drive sales, then your social media return is the number of sales that you can attribute to your social media campaign.

Instead of sales, say your goal is to drive consumer insights. In this case, your social media return is the quantity and quality of the consumer insights you get from your fans and followers.

A third example of social media return is brand awareness. If your goal is to drive awareness of your brand, then your social media return is brand awareness.

Social media return is the value that you derive from social media based on the goals of your campaign. (Note that the number of followers, fans, Likes, and comments are not social media campaign goals.)

Quantifying Social Media Return

After we have defined our social media return, we need to quantify the social media return into dollars and cents. This is difficult, because you need to look at each type of social media return and develop a method for dollar quantification.

For instance, looking strictly at sales, we can quantify the social media return by looking at "last touch" sales, or we can use sales forecasting techniques or unique identifiers such as coupon codes.

Quantifying consumer insights is harder and requires different techniques to estimate value. One commonly used technique is to compare the quantity and quality of consumer insights from off-line focus groups to consumer insights from your social media campaign. The idea is that you know the value of consumer insights from off-line focus groups based on their cost. By comparing the quantity and quality of consumer insights from both channels, you arrive at a reasonable estimate of the value of consumer insights from your social media campaign.

Use Social Media ROI to Compare Apples to Apples

After estimating your return and your investment, you use the ROI formula to calculate your social media ROI.

Remember, ROI is a measurement of efficiency, so having calculated the ROI of your social media campaign, you use the ROI number to compare to other social media campaigns and also your TV, print, radio, and other campaigns.[29]

Tech and Trends

Where Is Twitter Going?

During its few years of existence, Twitter has seen exponential growth. Nevertheless, at least two problems have the potential to make the social media site's future less rosy than its brief past. First, Twitter has to deal with the same basic issue that has confounded many Web 2.0 media platforms—how to "monetize" the site (a fancy way to say make money from it). Second, the site's future popularity is not guaranteed—it could be overshadowed by the next social media darling idea, just as MySpace lost a lot of its lustre when many users defected to Facebook.

Twitter is hoping to address the monetization problem as it embarks on a program to sell advertising, or what it calls Promoted Tweets.[30] In much the same way that Google makes money when people use its site to search for information, ads will be activated when users search for keywords that advertisers have bought to link to their ads. If a Twitter user searches for

information on vacations in Bali, she may see a Promoted Tweet from an airline that offers—guess what?—special fares on flights to Bali. The messages will appear at the top of the posts no matter when they were added. Later, even when users don't search for those keywords, the ads that are relevant to a particular user based on her previous searches will be posted in a stream of Twitter posts. The program will also allow Twitter advertisers to respond to negative tweets. When a tweet about a brand is negative (Twitter already has the software to measure the sentiments of tweets), an ad can be inserted. For example, if a Twitter user says something negative about a movie, the studio can use its ads to link the user to a positive review.

Time will tell if Twitter's strategy is successful. One potential pitfall is, will users get turned off by the Promoted Tweets and defect to another site that (at least for now) offers an environment with no advertising? If so, cue up problem number two.

---

in real time. The blockbuster movie *Avatar* exposed many people to this basic idea as it told the story of a wounded soldier who takes on a new (10-feet tall and blue) identity in the world of Pandora.

In virtual worlds, residents can hang out at virtual clubs, shop for clothing and bling for their avatars, buy furniture to deck out virtual homes, and yes, even go to virtual colleges or universities (see Exhibit 10.7). Some people find it hard to believe, but it's common for people to spend real money to buy digital products that don't exist in the real world. Indeed, the **virtual goods** market is booming. In the United States alone, consumers will spend well over $2.11 billion in 2011 to buy items they use only in virtual worlds!

Second Life is one of the largest and best-known virtual worlds, although in reality there are several hundred of these environments up and running. This platform is one of many virtual worlds that has become a booming marketplace for budding fashion designers, musicians, and businesspeople who sell their products and services. A few have even become real-world millionaires by selling virtual goods to users who want to buy bling for their avatars. Following is a sampling of other virtual worlds:

- Coke Studios, a promotional virtual world for Coca-Cola that targets teens and young adults. Avatars called "V-egos" create their own customized music mixes in a virtual music studio and participate in games and contests for Coca-Cola and its partners.

- Disney's Toontown offers kids a brightly coloured cartoon environment where they can outfit their toon avatars and play games. Like off-line Disney World, Toontown is designed to be a place where kids feel they are in charge.

- Habbo Hotel is a virtual world where teens and young adults inhabit a room (a "habbo") and decorate it with furniture they purchase with Habbo credits.

- FooPets, especially popular with 12- to 14-year-old girls, allows users to "adopt" digitally animated pets, then care for them and feed them. If the pets are not properly cared for, they will be taken to a virtual shelter.[31]

virtual goods
Digital products bought and sold in virtual worlds that don't exist in the real world.

Exhibit 10.7

In anticipation of the 2011 launch of the *Cars 2* movie—a sequel to the original 2006 hit, *Cars*—Disney launched an online community it calls, "World of Cars." Subscribers to the community interact with characters from the movie, design their own car, and race it on an online track.

Most virtual goods, whether sold in virtual worlds or through other social media sites, have microprices—from less than $1 to $3. So what's in it for real-world marketers? Some firms enter the market for virtual goods to keep in touch with consumers, improve the brand's image, and develop loyal customers. MTV Networks gave away virtual replicas of celebrity accessories such as Beyoncé's diamond ring in its campaign to increase viewership for the Video Music Awards. H&M showed viewers its collection of denim and blue garments and encouraged consumers to visit H&M retail stores on the iPhone app Mytown. And Volvo Cars of North America offered virtual goods on MyTown in a program to improve its image.[32]

Product Review Sites

product review sites
Social media sites that enable people to post stories about their experiences with products and services.

Product review sites are social media sites that enable people to post stories about their experiences with products and services. Marketers hope that product review sites create a connection between the consumer and the brand. Product review sites give users both positive and negative information about companies:

- TripAdvisor provides unbiased hotel reviews complete with photos and advice. The site gives consumers an opportunity to rate and comment on a hotel that they recently stayed in or to use other consumers' comments to select a hotel for an upcoming trip.

- Yelp is a product review site that provides reviews of local businesses such as places to eat, shop, drink, or play. Consumers can access Yelp either through the Internet or a mobile phone. Businesses can create pages to enable them to track reviews.

- The *Zagat Survey* began in 1979 in off-line form. Today the online version provides consumer survey-based information on restaurants, hotels, nightspots, and leisure activities in over 100 countries based on surveys of more than 375 000 consumers. Zagat reviews are available to consumers online, through tablets, mobile phones, and in-car personal navigation devices.

Mobile Apps and Geospatial Platforms

It's obvious to almost anyone who's conscious today that the future of marketing communications lies in that magic little device you practically sleep with—whether it's a smartphone or a touchscreen device like the iPad. Combine Web browsing capability with built-in cameras and the race is on to bring to the world to your belt or purse. Apple lit up this market when it introduced the iPhone and now everyone is scrambling to "monetize" the mobile market through sales of on-demand video, online coupons, and "apps" that entertain or educate. A few to watch are included here:[33]

- Shop Savvy finds the lowest prices online and at nearby brick-and-mortar retailers, as well as coupons, and lets users make transactions.

- RetrevoQ uses texts and tweets to provide information about electronics products. Shoppers can text 41411 or tweet @retrevoq, including the make and model of the electronics product they're considering, and RetrevoQ will respond with advice on whether it's a good buy, a fair price, the price range available online for that product, and a link to reviews at Retrevo.com, a consumer-electronics shopping and review site.

- FastMall provides interactive maps of malls, highlights the quickest route to stores, and even helps shoppers remember where they parked their cars. Even better, shake your phone and it shows you the nearest restroom location.

geospatial platforms
Digital applications that integrate sophisticated GPS technology to enable users to alert friends of their exact whereabouts via their mobile phones.

Geospatial platforms integrate sophisticated GPS technology (like the navigation system you may have in your car) that enables users to alert friends of their exact whereabouts via their mobile phones. Foursquare is one of the most popular of these new sites with over 10 million users; one of its addicting features is that users compete to become "Mayor" of a location by checking in from there more than anyone else. Other hot location-based services include Loopt, Gowalla, Facebook Place, and Google Latitude. Victoria's Secret launched their Bombshell Collection with a foursquare promotion where users who follow Victoria's Secret on foursquare and check in at three of their Canadian or US stores earn a Victoria's Secret badge and two free panties with any $40 Bombshell Collection purchase. Details of the tour were on a Victoria's Secret Facebook page.[34] Businesses can ride this wave by offering discounts or free services to people who check in to their locations, or, in foursquare's case, to those who reach the rank of "Mayor," which obviously encourages consumers to visit the place frequently. Foursquare also provides a "dashboard" to businesses that tells them who checks into their locations and at what times so they can get a handle on how specific marketing communications such as a time-limited sales promotion are working (or not) to drive traffic.[35]

3 Promotional Planning in a Web 2.0 World

OBJECTIVE

Describe the steps in traditional and multichannel promotional planning.
(pp. 373–380)

Now that we've talked about communications and the traditional and new tools marketers can use to deliver messages to their customers, we need to see how to make it all happen. How do we go about the complex task of developing a promotional plan—one that delivers just the right message to a number of different target audiences when and where they want it, in the most effective and cost-efficient way?

Just as with any other strategic decision-making process, the development of this plan includes several steps, as Figure 10.4 shows. First, we'll go over the steps in promotional planning. Then we'll take a look at how marketers today are developing multichannel promotional strategies.

Step 1: Identify the Target Audience(s)

An important part of overall marketing planning is to identify the target audience(s). Remember, IMC marketers recognize that we must communicate with a variety of stakeholders who influence the target market. Of course, the intended customer is the most important target audience and the one that marketers focus on the most.

Step 2: Establish the Communication Objectives

The whole point of communicating with customers and prospective customers is to let them know in a timely and affordable way that the organization has a product to meet their needs. It's bad enough when a product comes along that people don't want or need. An even bigger marketing sin is to have a product that they *do* want—but you fail to let them know about it. Of course, seldom can we deliver a single message to a consumer that magically transforms her into a loyal

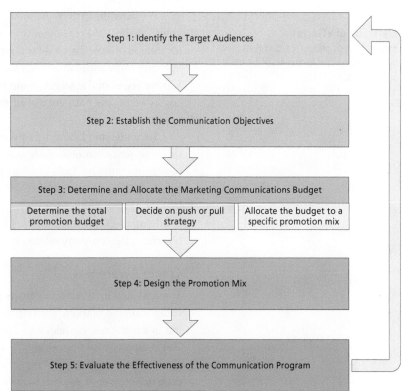

Figure 10.4 Steps in Developing the Promotional Plan

Development of successful promotional plans involves organizing the complex process into a series of several orderly steps.

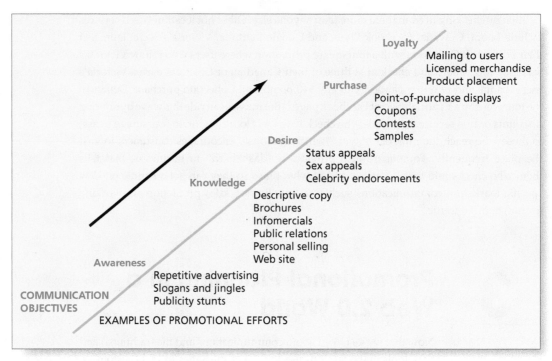

Figure 10.5 The Hierarchy of Effects

Communication objectives seek to move consumers through the hierarchy of effects.

hierarchy of effects

A series of steps prospective customers move through, from initial awareness of a product to brand loyalty.

customer. In most cases, it takes a series of messages that moves the consumer through several stages.

We view this process as an uphill climb, such as the one Figure 10.5 depicts. The marketer "pushes" the consumer through a series of steps, or a **hierarchy of effects**, from initial awareness of a product to brand loyalty. The task of moving the consumer up the hierarchy becomes more difficult at each step. Many potential buyers may drop out along the way, leaving fewer of the target group inclined to go the distance and become loyal customers. Each part of this path entails different communication objectives to "push" people to the next level.

To understand how this process works, imagine how a firm would have to adjust its communication objectives as it tries to establish a presence in the market for Hunk, a new men's cologne. Let's say that the primary target market for the cologne is single men, age 18 to 24, who care about their appearance and who are into health, working out, and looking ripped. The company would want to focus more on some promotion methods (such as advertising) and less on others (such as personal selling). Here are some communication objectives the company might develop for its Hunk promotion.

Create Awareness

The first step is to make members of the target market aware that there's a new brand of cologne on the market. The fragrance's marketers might place simple, repetitive advertising in magazines, on television, and on the radio to push the brand name (Exhibit 10.8). The company could develop a "teaser" ad campaign, in which messages heighten interest because they don't initially reveal the exact nature of the product (for example, a Facebook page or newspaper ads that simply proclaim, "Hunk is coming!"). The promotion objective might be to create an 80-percent awareness of Hunk cologne among 18- to 24-year-old men in the first two months. Note how this objective is worded; objectives are best when they are quantitative (80 percent), when they specify the target consumer or business group

(18- to 24-year-old men), and when they specify the time frame during which the plan is expected to reach the objective (in the first two months).

Inform the Market

The next step is to provide prospective users with knowledge about the benefits the new product has to offer—to *position* it relative to other colognes (see Chapter 6). Perhaps the cologne has a light, slightly mentholated scent with a hint of a liniment smell to remind wearers of how they feel after a good workout. Promotion would focus on communications that emphasize this position. The objective at this point might be to communicate the connection between Hunk and muscle building so that 70 percent of the target market develops some interest in the product in the first six months of the communication program.

Create Desire

The next task is to create favourable feelings toward the product and to convince at least some members of this group that they would rather splash on some Hunk than other colognes. Communications at this stage might consist of splashy advertising spreads in magazines, a YouTube video, or tweets, or perhaps with an endorsement by a well-known celebrity "hunk" such as The Rock (@TheRock). The specific objective might be to create positive attitudes toward Hunk cologne among 50 percent of the target market and brand preference among 30 percent of the target market in the first six months.

Encourage Purchase and Trial

As the expression goes, "How do ya know 'til ya try it?" The company now needs to get some of the men who have become interested in the cologne to try it. A promotion plan might encourage trial by mailing samples of Hunk to members of the target market, inserting "scratch-and-sniff" samples in bodybuilding magazines, placing elaborate displays in stores that dispense money-saving coupons, or even sponsoring an online contest on RedFlagDeals.com in which the winner gets to have The Rock as his personal trainer for a day. The specific objective now might be to encourage trial of Hunk among 25 percent of 18- to 24-year-old men in the first two months (Note: we have *not* cleared this plan with The Rock).

Build Loyalty

Of course, the real test is loyalty—convincing customers to stay with Hunk after they've gone through the first bottle. Promotion efforts must maintain ongoing communications with current users to reinforce the bond they feel with the product. As before, this step will include some mix of strategies, such as Twitter campaigns, direct-mail advertising to current users, product placements in popular television programs or movies, and maybe even the development of a workout clothing line that sports a Hunk logo. The objective might be to develop and maintain regular usage of Hunk cologne among 10 percent of men from 18 to 24 years old.

Step 3: Determine and Allocate the Marketing Communication Budget

While setting a budget for marketing communication might seem easy—you just calculate how much money you need to accomplish your objectives—in reality it's not that simple. To set a budget, three distinct determinations must be made:

1. Determine the total communications budget.

2. Decide whether to use a push strategy or a pull strategy.

3. Allocate spending to specific promotion activities.

Exhibit 10.8

Attention-getting messages ("fat is sexy") capture consumers' attention and inform them about new products.

Exhibit 10.9

Many brands have discovered that a great way to build loyalty is to give back to worthy causes.

top-down budgeting
Allocation of the promotion budget based on management's determination of the total amount to be devoted to marketing communication.

percentage-of-sales budgeting
A method for promotion budgeting that is based on a certain percentage of either last year's sales or on estimates of the present year's sales.

competitive-parity budgeting
A promotion budgeting method in which an organization matches whatever competitors are spending.

bottom-up budgeting
Allocation of the promotion budget based on identifying promotion goals and allocating enough money to accomplish them.

objective-task budgeting
A promotion budgeting method in which an organization first defines the specific communication goals it hopes to achieve and then tries to calculate what kind of promotional efforts it will take to meet these goals.

push strategy
The company tries to move its products through the channel by convincing channel members to offer them.

Determine the Total Promotion Budget

In the real world, firms often view communication costs as an expense rather than as an investment leading to greater profits (shame on them!). When sales are declining or the company is operating in a difficult economic environment, it is often tempting to cut costs by reducing spending on advertising, promotion, and other "soft" activities whose contributions to the bottom line are hard to quantify. When this is the case, marketers must work harder to justify these expenses.

Economic approaches to budgeting rely on *marginal analysis* (as was discussed earlier in the book), in which the organization spends money on promotion as long as the revenues it realizes through these efforts continue to exceed the costs of the promotions themselves. This perspective assumes that a company always intends promotions solely to increase sales, when in fact these activities may have other objectives such as enhancing a firm's image (Exhibit 10.9).

Also, the effects of marketing communication often lag over time. For example, a firm may have to spend a lot on advertising and other forms of marketing communication when it first launches a product, without seeing any immediate return. Because of these limitations, most firms rely on two budgeting techniques: top-down and bottom-up. **Top-down budgeting** techniques require top management to establish the overall amount that the organization allocates for promotion activities.

The most common top-down technique is **percentage-of-sales budgeting**, in which the promotion budget is based on last year's sales or on estimates for the present year's sales. The percentage may be an industry average provided by trade associations that collect objective information on behalf of member companies. The advantage of this method is that it ties spending on promotion to sales and profits. Unfortunately, this method can imply that sales cause promotional spending rather than viewing sales as the *outcome* of promotional efforts.

Competitive-parity budgeting is a fancy way of saying "keep up with the Joneses." In other words, match whatever competitors spend. Some marketers think this approach simply mirrors the best thinking of others in the business. However, this method often results in each player simply maintaining the same market share year after year. This method also assumes that the same dollars spent on promotion by two different firms will yield the same results, but spending a lot of money doesn't guarantee a successful promotion. Firms certainly need to monitor their competitors' promotion activities, but they must combine this information with their own objectives and capacities.

The problem with top-down techniques is that budget decisions are based more on established practices than on promotion objectives. Another approach is to begin at the beginning—identify promotion goals and allocate enough money to accomplish them. That is what **bottom-up budgeting** techniques attempt.

This bottom-up logic is at the heart of the **objective-task budgeting**, which is gaining popularity. Using this approach, the firm first defines the specific communication goals it hopes to achieve, such as increasing by 20 percent the number of consumers who are aware of the brand. It then tries to figure out what kind of promotional efforts—how much advertising, sales promotion, buzz marketing, and so on—it will take to meet that goal. Although this is the most rational approach, it is hard to implement because it obliges managers to specify their objectives and attach dollar amounts to them. This method requires careful analysis—and a bit of lucky "guesstimating."

Decide on a Push or a Pull Strategy

The second important decision in promotion budgeting is whether the company will primarily push or pull. A **push strategy** means that the company wants to move its products by convincing channel members to offer them and entice their customers to select these items—it pushes them through the channel. This approach assumes that if consumers see the product on store shelves, they will be motivated to make a trial purchase. In this case, promotion efforts will "push" the products from producer to consumers by focusing on personal selling, trade advertising, and trade sales promotion activities such as exhibits at trade shows.

In contrast, a company that relies on a **pull strategy** is counting on consumers to demand its products (Exhibit 10.10). This popularity will then convince retailers to respond by stocking these items. In this case, efforts focus on media advertising and consumer sales promotion to stimulate interest among end consumers who will "pull" the product onto store shelves and then into their shopping carts.

Whether a push or a pull strategy is used and how the promotion mix for a product is designed must vary over time, because some promotion strategies work better than others at different points in the product life cycle (which we outlined back in Chapter 8).

As an example, we might think about the state of electronics in today's market and the relative positions in the product life cycle. In the *introduction phase*, the objective is to build awareness of and encourage trial of the product among consumers, often by relying on a pull strategy. That's the situation today with 3G (third generation) mobile telephone technology that allows voice and data transmission at incredible speeds. This enables you to watch television, have video conversations with your friends, log into your bank account to pay your bills, view video clips of local tourist attractions, and manage your inventory of items that need restocking from your home's "smart" refrigerator—all from your 3G mobile phone. Advertising is the primary promotion tool to create awareness, and a publicity campaign to generate news reports about the new product may help as well. A company may use sales promotion to encourage trial. Business-to-business marketing that emphasizes personal selling—the marketing that a manufacturer does to retailers and other business customers—is important in this phase in order to get channel members to carry the product. For consumer goods that retailers sell, trade sales promotion may be necessary to encourage retailers to stock the product.

In the *growth phase*, promotions stress product benefits. For products such as MP3 players, advertising increases, while sales promotions that encourage trial usually decline because people are more willing to try the product without being offered an incentive.

The opposite pattern often occurs with products now in their *maturity phase* such as DVD players. In these situations many people have already tried the product. The strategy now shifts to encouraging people to switch from competitors' brands as sales stabilize. This can be tough if consumers don't see enough differences among the options to bother. Usually, sales promotion activities, particularly coupons and special price deals, have greater chances of success than advertising. In some cases, an industry revamps a widely used technology when it introduces one or more new versions or formats that force consumers to convert (sometimes kicking and screaming), thus transforming a mature category back to a new one. That's what's happening now in the "DVD format wars," a high-stakes showdown between the HD DVD and Blu-ray disk formats that Blu-ray won after it gained the backing of a large number of consumer electronics and entertainment companies.[36] (For another example, see Exhibit 10.11.)

All bets are off for VCR players, now in their *decline phase*. As sales plummet, the company dramatically reduces spending on all elements of the promotion mix. Sales will be driven by the continued loyalty of a small group of users who keep the product alive until it is sold to another company or discontinued.

pull strategy
The company tries to move its products through the channel by building desire for the products among consumers, thus convincing retailers to respond to this demand by stocking these items.

Exhibit 10.10
Small businesses need to budget carefully to be sure they get the bang for their scarce bucks. This food delivery company in Brazil decided to invest in an eye-catching print ad.

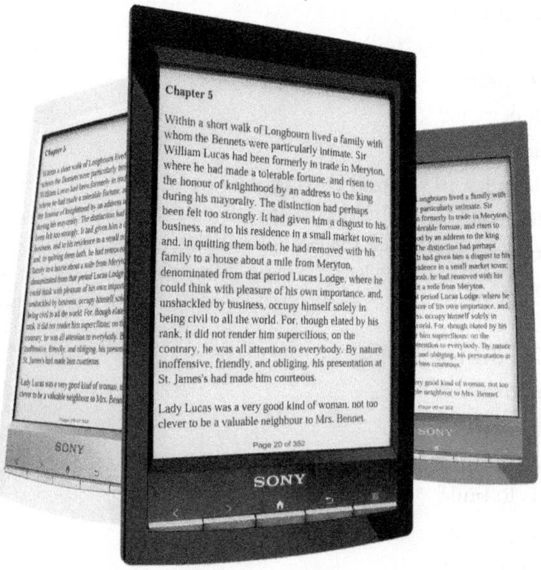

Exhibit 10.11

Consumers can't wait to read their novels and newspapers on a tablet instead of toting around all those hard copies but it's unclear which format will prevail. Will it be Amazon's Kindle, the Kobo eReader, the Apple iPad, the Barnes & Noble Nook, the Sony Reader—or maybe some upstart we haven't seen quite yet?

AIDA model
The communication goals of attention, interest, desire, and action.

Allocate the Budget to a Specific Promotion Mix

Once the organization decides how much to spend on promotion and whether to use a push or a pull strategy, it must divide its budget among the elements in the promotion mix. Although advertising used to get the lion's share of the promotion budget, today sales promotion and digital marketing such as buzz building and the use of social media we talked about earlier in this chapter are playing a bigger role in marketing strategies. Overall advertising spending in Canada, for example, increased 3.6 percent in 2010 compared to spending in 2009, while at the same time companies were investing more in Internet display ads (up 16 percent) ahead of newspapers and direct marketing.[37] In one study, up to 60 percent of marketers said they were shifting funds from traditional media to interactive marketing, including social media and mobile marketing. While only 12 percent of those surveyed said they were cutting TV-ad budgets, 40 percent were cutting direct mail, and more than 25 percent were cutting newspapers and magazines.[38]

In today's dynamic media environment, there are few clear guidelines for how to divide up the promotional pie. In some cases, managers may simply have a preference for advertising versus sales promotion or other elements of the promotion mix. Also, consumers vary widely in the likelihood that they will respond to various communication elements. Some thrifty consumers like to clip coupons or stock up with two-for-one offers, while others throw away those Sunday newspaper coupons without a glance. College and university students are especially likely to spend most of their time on the Internet (but you knew that). The size and makeup of a geographic market also influence promotion decisions. In larger markets, the cost of buying media, such as local TV, can be quite high. If only a small percentage of the total market includes potential customers, then mass media advertising can be a very inefficient use of a promotion budget.

Step 4: Design the Promotion Mix

Designing the promotion mix is the most complicated step in marketing communication planning. It includes determining the specific communication tools to use, what message to communicate, and the communication channel(s) on which to send the message. Planners must ask how they can use advertising, sales promotion, personal selling, and public relations most effectively to communicate with different target audiences. Each element of the promotion mix has benefits and shortcomings, so—as we've seen—often a combination of a few techniques works the best.

The message, ideally, should accomplish four objectives (though a single message can rarely do all of these): get attention, hold interest, create desire, and produce action. We call these communication goals the **AIDA model**. Here, we'll review some different forms the message can take as well as how we might structure the message.

There are many ways to say the same thing, and marketers must take care when they choose how they will encode their message. To illustrate, consider two strategies rival car companies used to promote similar automobiles. Toyota's advertising for its Lexus model used a rational appeal that focused on the technical advancements in the car's design. This approach is often effective for promoting products that are technically complex and require a substantial investment. Nissan, in contrast, focused on the spiritual fulfillment a driver might feel tooling down the road in a fine machine.

Step 5: Evaluate the Effectiveness of the Communication Program

The final step to manage marketing communications is to decide whether the plan is working (Exhibit 10.12). It would be nice if a marketing manager could simply report,

"The $3 million campaign for our revolutionary glow-in-the-dark surfboards brought in $15 million in new sales!" It's not so easy. There are many random factors in the marketing environment: a rival's manufacturing problem, a coincidental photograph of a movie star toting one of the boards, or perhaps a surge of renewed interest in surfing sparked by a cult movie hit like *Blue Crush*.

Still, there are ways to monitor and evaluate the company's communications efforts. The catch is that it's easier to determine the effectiveness of some forms of communication than others. As a rule, various types of sales promotion are the easiest to evaluate because they occur over a fixed, usually short period, making it easier to link to sales volume. Advertising researchers measure brand awareness, recall of product benefits communicated through advertising, and even the image of the brand before and after an advertising campaign. The firm can analyze and compare the performance of salespeople in different ter-

Exhibit 10.12

This Turkish ad for bird seed gets attention and holds interest!

ritories, although, again, it is difficult to rule out other factors that make one salesperson more effective than another. Public relations activities are more difficult to assess because their objectives relate more often to image building than to sales volume.

Multichannel Promotional Strategies

As we said early in this chapter, marketers today recognize that the traditional one-to-many communications model in which they spent millions of dollars broadcasting ads to a mass audience is less and less effective. At the same time, it isn't yet clear how effective the new many-to-many model is—or what marketing metrics we should use to measure how well new media campaigns are working. (See Exhibit 10.13.) Thus, many marketers opt for multichannel promotional strategies where they combine traditional advertising, sales promotion, and public relations activities with online buzz-building activities. For marketers who choose multichannel marketing there are important benefits. First, multichannel strategies boost the effectiveness of either online or offline strategies used alone. And multichannel strategies allow marketers to repeat their messages across various channels, letting them strengthen brand awareness and providing more opportunities to convert customers.

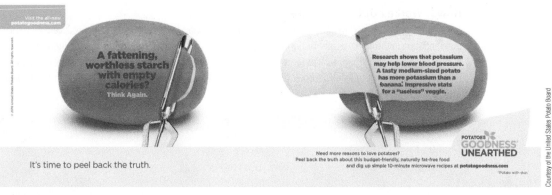

Exhibit 10.13

A communication objective may focus on educating consumers about a product like potatoes. The sponsor can measure the effectiveness of a campaign by assessing people's knowledge before and after the messages have run, to determine if they had any impact.

Perhaps the best way to really understand how marketers develop multichannel strategies is to look at how some actually do it:

- To promote ING Direct's new Thrive chequing account, the bank combined traditional TV, print, and outdoor media with online messages. The campaign featured four celebrities, a.k.a. the "THRIVEtastic Four," that were sent out on the road with $7000 in their account to pay for acts of kindness. This multichannel campaign also included streetcar and bus wraps in four major Canadian cities, and mobile ad placements on the Weather Network. The team tweeted about their experiences and ING Direct also used Facebook to spread the word about the celebs' philanthropy.[39]

- Mexican restaurant chain Del Taco created a Facebook-based entertainment webisode, "The Del Taco Super Special Show." Traditional TV and radio ads promoted the webisode and offered consumers a coupon for a free Classic Taco.[40]

- Ghiradelli Chocolate combined an online sweepstakes, a 10-city sampling tour, promotional packaging, in-store displays, an online banner campaign, and a month-long Times Square billboard in its "Million Moments of Timeless Pleasure" campaign. Consumers were asked to visit a Web site and create a 75-character message about the "sweet little moments" when they enjoyed Ghiradelli. The comments were then streamed live. Selected posts were also shown in lights on a billboard in New York City's Times Square. To sweeten the campaign even more, Ghiradelli distributed one million Ghiradelli squares in a sampling program. Hungry consumers were able to find out where the sampling was taking place by following the campaign on Twitter.[41]

Why do you think Mike chose option 3?

Here's my choice. . .

Real **People**, Real **Choices**

1 Option   2 Option   3 Option

How It Worked Out at Campfire
Mike and his partners declined the account. They felt that moving in that direction would reduce the agency's differentiation in the marketplace. Today the agency has grown to 25 employees and works on innovative forms of marketing and storytelling, such as recent work for Discovery Channel's Shark Week, a transmedia experience that used influencer outreach, Facebook Connect, and a chilling Web site to bring the visceral terror of a shark attack directly to its audience.

To learn the whole story, visit www.mypearsonmarketinglab.com.

Objective Summary → Key Terms → Apply

1. Objective Summary (pp. 356–363)

Understand the communication process and the traditional promotion mix.

Firms use promotion and other forms of marketing communication to inform consumers about new products, remind them of familiar products, persuade them to choose one alternative over another, and build strong customer relationships. Recognizing that consumers come in contact with a brand at many different touchpoints, firms today often practise integrated marketing communication to reach consumers through a multichannel promotional strategy. Because marketers understand the impact of word-of-mouth communication, they are likely to supplement the traditional one-to-many communication model with a newer many-to-many model and also talk one-to-one with consumers.

The traditional communication model includes a message source that creates an idea, encodes the idea into a message, and transmits the message through some medium. The message is delivered to the receiver, who decodes the message and may provide feedback to the source. Anything that interferes with the communication is called "noise."

The promotion mix refers to the marketing communication elements that the marketer controls. Advertising, sales promotion, and public relations use the mass media to reach many consumers at a single time while personal selling and direct marketing allow marketers to communicate with consumers one on one.

Key Terms

promotion, p. 356

integrated marketing communication (IMC), p. 357

multichannel promotional strategy, p. 357

word-of-mouth communication, p. 357

communications model, p. 358

encoding, p. 359

source, p. 359

message, p. 359

medium, p. 360

receiver, p. 360

decoding, p. 360

noise, p. 360

feedback, p. 360

promotion mix, p. 361

mass communication, p. 361

advertising, p. 362

2. Objective Summary (pp. 364–373)

Understand how marketers communicate using an updated communication model that incorporates buzz marketing activities and social media.

Because consumers spend more time online and less time watching TV or reaching magazines, traditional advertising has diminished as a way to talk to consumers. Consumers today are increasingly getting their information on products from one another rather than from firms as technology magnifies the spread of consumer buzz. Marketers use buzz-building activities to encourage consumers to share their opinions about products with friends and neighbours. While organic word-of-mouth (WOM) occurs naturally, buzz marketing campaigns create amplified WOM.

Viral marketing refers to activities that aim to increase brand awareness or sales by consumers passing a message along to other consumers. Marketers may recruit loyal customers, who care a great deal about a product and want it to succeed, to become brand ambassadors or brand evangelists to help create buzz.

Social media are Internet-based platforms that allow users to create their own content and share it with others. Social networking sites or social networks such as Facebook, Twitter, virtual worlds, product review sites, mobile apps, and geospatial platforms connect people with other similar people.

Key Terms

groundswell, p. 364

buzz, p. 365

viral marketing, p. 366

brand ambassadors or brand evangelists, p. 367

social media, p. 368

social networks, p. 368

twitter, p. 369

virtual worlds, p. 369

avatars, p. 369

virtual goods, p. 371

product review sites, p. 372

geospatial platforms, p. 372

3. Objective Summary (pp. 373–380)

Describe the steps in traditional and multichannel promotional planning.

Recognizing the importance of communicating with a variety of stakeholders who influence the target market, marketers begin the promotional planning process by identifying the target audience(s). Next they establish communication objectives. Objectives often are to create awareness, inform the market, create desire, encourage purchase and trial, and/or build loyalty.

Marketers develop promotion budgets from rules of thumb such as the percentage-of-sales method, the competitive-parity method, and the objective-task method. They then decide on a push or a pull strategy and allocate monies from the total budget to various elements of the promotion mix.

Next marketers design the promotion mix by deciding how they can use advertising, sales promotion, personal selling, and public relations most effectively to communicate with different target audiences. The final step is to evaluate the effectiveness of the communication program in order to determine whether the plan is working.

Marketers today often opt for multichannel promotional strategies where they combine traditional advertising, sales promotion, and public relations activities with online buzz-building activities. Multichannel strategies boost the effectiveness of either online or off-line strategies used alone and allow marketers to repeat their messages across various channels, thus strengthening brand awareness and providing more opportunities to convert customers.

Key Terms

hierarchy of effects, p. 374

top-down budgeting, p. 376

percentage-of-sales budgeting, p. 376

competitive-parity budgeting, p. 376

bottom-up budgeting, p. 376

objective-task budgeting, p. 376

push strategy, p. 376

pull strategy, p. 377

AIDA model, p. 378

Chapter **Questions** and **Activities**

Concepts: Test Your Knowledge

1. What is integrated marketing communication? What are multichannel promotional strategies? Why is word-of-mouth communication so important?
2. Describe the traditional communication model.
3. List the elements of the promotion mix and describe how they are used to deliver personal and mass appeals.
4. Explain the many-to-many communication model and why it is important for marketers today.
5. What is buzz? How do marketers practise buzz building?
6. What are some ethical problems in buzz marketing?
7. What is viral marketing? How do marketers use brand ambassadors or brand evangelists?
8. What is social media? What are social networks? Describe Facebook, Twitter, virtual worlds, product review sites, mobile apps, and geospatial platforms.
9. List and explain the steps in promotion planning.
10. Explain the hierarchy of effects and how it is used in communication objectives.
11. Describe the major ways in which firms develop marketing communication budgets.
12. Describe push versus pull strategies. How are push and pull strategies useful in different stages of the product life cycle?

Activities: Apply What You've Learned

1. Assume you are the director of marketing for a firm that markets one of the following products.
   i. Environmentally friendly household cleaning supplies
   ii. Hand-made wooden toys for 2- to 5-year-old children
   iii. A line of designer book bags for students

   You are developing a promotional plan. Develop suggestions for each of the following items.
   a. Marketing communication objectives
   b. A method for determining the communication budget
   c. The use of a push strategy or a pull strategy
   d. Elements of the traditional promotion mix you will use
   e. Use of buzz building and social media activities

   Then, in a role-playing situation, present your recommendations to your boss.

2. Many firms today are using a variety of buzz-building activities to encourage word-of-mouth communications about their products. Select a product that you and your classmates might purchase. You might, for example, think about (1) a specialty coffee shop, (2) a club where you and your friends might hang out on the weekends, or (3) a local theme or amusement park.

   For your selected product, develop ideas for at least three different buzz-building activities. Outline the details as to exactly how these activities would be implemented. Next, rank order the activities as to which you feel are the top three, and tell why you feel that way. Develop a report for your class on your ideas.

3. As a marketing consultant, you are frequently asked by clients to develop recommendations for marketing communication strategies. The traditional elements used include advertising, sales promotion, public relations, and personal selling. Which of these do you feel would be most effective for each of the following clients?
   a. A company that provides cellular phone service
   b. A hotel
   c. A university
   d. A new soft drink
   e. A sports equipment company

4. Assume that you are a marketing consultant for one of the clients in question 3 above. You believe that the client would benefit from non-traditional marketing. Develop several ideas for buzz building and social-media tactics that you feel would be successful for the client.

5. First, schedule an appointment with your college or university's marketing communications department to discuss their communications program. You will probably want to ask them about

   a. The target audiences for their communication program
   b. The objectives of their communications program
   c. The different types of traditional and nontraditional communication methods they use
   d. Their use of social media
   e. How they evaluate the effectiveness of their communication program(s)

   Based on your discussions, develop a report that (1) provides a critique of their communication program and (2) makes recommendations for improvement.

6. More and more firms are engaged in multichannel promotional programs. You can learn about many of these by searching library or Internet sources. Some Internet sources that may be useful are:

   strategyonline.ca (*Strategy* magazine)
   marketingmag.ca
   mediapost.com
   Adweek.com (*Adweek* magazine)
   Adage.com (*Advertising Age* magazine)

   Gather information on one or more multichannel promotional programs. Develop a report that describes the program(s) and makes suggestions for how it/they might be improved.

Choices: What Do You Think?

1. Some buzz marketing activities engage buzz "agents" to tell their friends about a product, ask store managers to stock the product, and in other ways purposefully create word-of-mouth. Do you think these activities are ethical?

2. There is increasing concern about consumer privacy on social networking sites such as Facebook. How do you feel about privacy on social networks? Is allowing personal information to be available to others without a user's specific permission unethical? Should the network owners do more to protect users' privacy? Should there be greater government regulation or should the sites be free to develop as they want to meet the needs of users? How much responsibility should users accept in protecting their own private information?

3. Marketing seems to be moving at breakneck speed toward greater use of the Internet. Where do you think this is headed? Will social media become even more important in the future? Will some types of social media grow in popularity and usefulness to marketers while others decline? What are the major factors in the growth or decline of an individual social media site?

4. Many companies are using brand ambassadors or brand evangelists to spread the word about their product. For what types of products do you think brand ambassadors are likely to be most useful? When would they be less useful? Would you be willing to be a brand ambassador for a product? If so, which product(s)? If not, why not?

5. Recently Twitter has joined other Internet sites in selling preferred positions on the site to generate revenue. Do you feel that such revenue-generating activities make sites such as Twitter less attractive? If you know that the top comments on a site have their positions because firms paid for them, are you likely to change your use of the sites? Are there other ways that an Internet site such as Twitter can generate revenue?

6. While marketers are spending less in mass media advertising today than in previous times, TV, radio, magazine, and newspaper advertising remains an important means of communicating with customers for many products. What products do you think most benefit from mass media advertising? Why is this so? Do you feel advertising will continue to decline in importance as a means for marketing communication or will it rebound in the future?

Miniproject: Learn by Doing

This miniproject is designed to help you understand how important word-of-mouth marketing is to consumers like yourself.

1. Ask several of your classmates to participate in a focus-group discussion about how they communicate with others about products. Some questions you might ask are the following:

   a. What products that you buy do you discuss with others at least from time to time?
   b. What experiences have you had discussing products face-to-face with others?
   c. What experiences have you had discussing products or reading comments of others about products on blogs, social networks, or other Internet sites?
   d. What are your experiences with product-related Web sites? Do you participate in games and entertainment opportunities on product-related Web sites?
   e. How do you think firms could improve their Web sites to provide more information for you?

2. Make a presentation of your findings and to your class.

Marketing in **Action** Case   Real Choices at American Express

What do Robert DeNiro, Ellen DeGeneres, Tiger Woods, Kate Winslet, and Laird Hamilton have in common? Let's see—Robert DeNiro is one of the greatest living actors, Ellen DeGeneres is a famous comedienne, Tiger Woods is arguably the best golfer ever, Kate Winslet is a multiple Academy Award nominee, and Laird Hamilton is perhaps the greatest surfer who ever lived. However, being famous and best in their fields are not the only things these folks have in common. They also all carry the American Express credit card and have appeared in television or print commercials to promote the card in the company's "My Life, My Card" campaign.

The fast pace of today's busy lifestyles and the rapid changes in information technology mean that, more than ever, companies like American Express have to rely on the familiar faces of celebrities to get its messages across. In late 2004, American Express started to feature famous and recognizable people as attractive spokespersons in the "My Life, My Card" advertising campaign in an attempt to capture the attention of current and potential consumers. Each of the AMEX ads included brief biographical information on the celebrity, such as where they live, profession, greatest triumphs or greatest disappointments, and basic philosophy on life. The final point of each ad showed how the American Express card helps enable individuals to pursue what is important to them. American Express sought to communicate to its current and potential customers that they are just like these celebrities—simply trying to live life at its best. So, the slogan of "My Life, My Card" was perfect for the ad campaign. Consumers loved the ads.

Unfortunately for American Express, its "My Life, My Card" advertising campaign had some serious competition. Visa had been running ads for some time with the slogan of "Life takes Visa," which is a clever variation on Amex's campaign theme. American Express's other main competitor, MasterCard, was using its "Priceless"-theme commercials that

are aimed at encouraging customers to use the card to create priceless moments.

In the end, however, the "My Life, My Card" campaign, while well-liked, really wasn't working. Measures of customer loyalty showed that American Express was first in its product category in 1997, but by 2007, the American Express card was fifth, trailing Discover, Capital One, Visa, and MasterCard.

So in 2007, American Express replaced its "My Life, My Card" ads with a campaign that that presented a product-oriented approach rather than the general image-oriented one. New ads asked consumers the question, "Are you a card-member?" Historically, American Express has not switched campaigns quickly. The "Do you know me?" campaign ran from 1974 to 1987 and is still a well-known advertising saying. "Membership has its privileges" was used from 1987 to 1996, and the "Do More" campaign ran from 1996 to 2004. With only three campaigns in thirty years, how could consumers respond to this quick change of focus? Was American Express risking confusing consumers about American Express's positioning? And what if the new "Are you a cardmember?" campaign didn't improve loyalty ratings. Should American Express move quickly to develop still another new campaign or stick with this one?

You Make the Call

1. What is the decision facing American Express?
2. What factors are important in understanding this decision situation?
3. What are the alternatives?
4. What decision(s) do you recommend?
5. What are some ways to implement your recommendation?

Sources: Brian Steinberg, "Now Showing: Clustered Ad Spots on Television," *The Wall Street Journal*, February 15, 2006, B3; Business Wire Inc., "American Express Launches the Restaurant Partnership Program with Savings, Access and Information," *Business Wire*, June 8, 2006; Centaur Communications Ltd., "Amex Expands Tourist Podcast After Turin Olympics Success," *New Media Age*, March 2, 2006, 2; Dan Sewell, "Companies Use Online Magazines to Woo Customers," *Associated Press Financial Wire*, January 2, 2006; Sentido Comun, "American Express Launches New Promotion Campaign in Mexico," *Latin American News Digest*, February 14, 2006; Stuart Elliott, "American Express Gets Specific and Asks, 'Are You a Cardmember?'" *New York Times*, April 6, 2007.

Advertising, Public Relations, Promotions, Direct Marketing, and Personal Selling

Real People **Profiles**

Hesham Shafie

▼ A Decision Maker at Brand Momentum Inc.

Hesham Shafie is the CEO and founding partner at Brand Momentum, a multi-million dollar company based in Mississauga, Ontario, with over 300 employees that provide sales and merchandising, experiential marketing, and work force automation services to leading global companies, including Lindt Chocolate, Volkswagen, Red Bull, Bell Mobility, L'Oréal, and Wrigley.

Hesham took a rather unusual route to get to a sales and marketing career. Prior to Brand Momentum, Hesham was the Vice President of Finance and Administration and a shareholder at Consumer Impact Marketing (CIM), another leading marketing organization. He helped build the organization from five employees in 1994 to over 2000 employees when he left in 2009. He also invented two leading technological solutions while at CIM, in the fields of sales-force automation and self-serve payroll services. Hesham also worked for diversified companies in various financial and management roles, including Scintrex, an international public company engaged in the research,

design, and manufacturing of military equipment and nuclear reactor components. Hesham had started his career in the retail industry with La Vie En Rose Lingerie, a national retailer where he assumed responsibilities as a sales auditor and an accountant.

Hesham studied Biochemistry at the University of Alexandria in Egypt before moving to Canada in 1987. Upon arrival, he realized that his university education was not recognized in Canada, and he had to redo his education. He decided to study accounting and finance at night while working during the day. Hesham obtained university credits from the University of Toronto and York University, qualifying him to pursue a CMA (Certified Management Accountant) designation, which he obtained in 1994.

Hesham exemplifies community service. He has demonstrated a long history of public involvement at both volunteer and executive levels. He has an extensive portfolio of leadership and public service commitments, including volunteer work at the Distress Center of Peel, with the CMA, and with Skills for Change, a non-profit organization.

Hesham finds his true calling in dynamic, fast-paced and innovative environments. He gets a great deal of satisfaction from delivering value to his clients while seeing his employees developing and growing. He is also passionate about delivering on his promises to clients, employees, and business partners. The tag line for his company is "Let's WOW them" and at Brand Momentum that is what they do every day!

Here's my ~~problem~~.

Brand Momentum Inc. (BMI) was launched in 2009 by a talented team of sales, marketing, and technology professionals who were united by a common vision: "To focus first on delivering on the promises we make to our employees and our clients." They also built their infrastructure, technology, and foundation to allow them to differentiate themselves by doing things smarter, better, and faster while at the same time providing the best value in the industry.

The core problem BMI faced as a company was how to best market themselves to potential B2B customers. Although they had individual reputations in the marketplace from their past experiences, they were unknown as a new company. BMI's core customers are other companies in need of third-party services including marketing, sales, merchandising, HR, and/or technologyaugmentation solutions.

Things to remember

There is no one "magic" marketing tool that can be successfully applied in all situations. Right now, new media is getting a lot of "media" but traditional marketing tools and personal selling still have a place in our tool chest.

Hesham needs to understand the differences between an organizational market and a consumer market in order to successfully promote BMI. He also needs to understand the differences between selling a service and selling a product.

Hesham considered his **Options** 1·2·3

1

Option

Use Traditional Marketing. Hesham considered buying ad space in magazines and newspapers such as *Strategy, Marketing Magazine,* and *The Globe & Mail* to share the BMI story, vision and how they differentiate themselves from the competition. He also considered hosting BMI-sponsored experiential events, inviting prospective clients to participate, and hiring a PR agency to spread the word to media outlets and influencers.

Hesham felt that this option would allow him get the message out to a very large audience quickly. Also, publishing their story in reputable publications would lend Brand Momentum a sense of legitimacy. However, this would be expensive to execute, and being a new company, they didn't really have a lot of case studies or stories to share.

2

Option

Employ new media. Hesham and his team considered contacting their extensive network of business associates and friends to see if they could help promote the new company via LinkedIn, Facebook, blogs, and other social media. Getting the story out by "word of mouth" would be a relatively easy and inexpensive way of contacting and connecting with possible influencers. The only thing missing was the "personal touch," which Hesham felt was important when selling a service. Influencers likely receive many messages daily, and not having that personal connection might affect BMI's chances of building solid relationships, a trademark of Hesham and his team.

3

Option

Get out there and do some personal selling. Each of the partners has significant track records with key decision makers at several companies with which they could seek sales opportunities. Personally calling on these contacts could lead to face-to-face meetings during which they could talk about their services, share their vision and values, and really put a face on the new company. This would be time consuming, as a lot of energy would have to be spent on one specific contact and the result might not necessarily be positive.

Now, put yourself in Hesham's shoes. Which option would you choose, and why?

You Choose

Which **Option** would you choose, and **why**?

1. ☐YES ☐NO   **2.** ☐YES ☐NO   **3.** ☐YES ☐NO

See what **option** Hesham chose on **page 432**

387

1

OBJECTIVE

Tell what advertising is, describe the major types of advertising, and discuss some of the criticisms of advertising.
(pp. 388–394)

Advertising: The Image of Marketing

Advertising is so much a part of marketing that many people think of the two as the same thing. Remember, product, price, and distribution strategies are just as important as marketing communications. And, as we saw in Chapter 10, there are many ways to get a message out to a target audience in addition to advertising. Make no mistake—traditional advertising is still very important. In 2009, Canadian marketers spent just over $9.3 billion on advertising, down 8.4 percent from the previous year.[1] In today's competitive environment, even the big guys like Procter & Gamble and General Motors are rethinking how much they want to invest in pricey ad campaigns as they search for alternative ways to get their messages out there. Indeed, while total ad spending declined, spending on mobile advertising skyrocketed 169 percent to almost $32 million.[2]

One thing is sure—as the media landscape continues to change, so will advertising. Sales of Internet-ready and 3D TVs are booming, as is the number of households with digital video recorders (DVRs) that let viewers skip through the commercials. ComScore reported that in the last quarter of 2010, persons aged 18–24 years were spending more than 20 hours watching an average of 267 videos per month.[3]

With all of this bleak news, is traditional advertising dead? Don't write any obituaries yet. Mass media communications are still the best way to reach a large audience. For that reason, producers of FMCGs (fast-moving consumer goods) such as P&G and Unilever will continue to rely on these traditional channels of communication to reach their customers. They will just be more creative as they mix and match different platforms to reach various target markets.

Indeed, wherever we turn advertising bombards us. Television commercials, radio spots, banner ads, and huge billboards scream, "Buy me!" Advertising, as we said in Chapter 10, is nonpersonal communication an identified sponsor pays for that uses mass media to persuade or inform an audience.[4] Advertising can be fun, glamorous, annoying, informative, and, hopefully, an effective way to let consumers know what a company is selling and why people should run out and buy it *today*. Advertising is also a potent force that creates desire for products; it transports us to imaginary worlds where the people are happy, beautiful, or rich. In this way, advertising allows the organization to communicate its message in a favourable way and to repeat the message as often as it deems necessary to have an impact on receivers.

A long-running Virginia Slims cigarettes advertising campaign proclaimed, "You've come a long way, baby!" We can say the same about advertising itself. Advertising has been with us a long time. In ancient Greece and Rome, ad messages appeared on walls, were etched on stone tablets, or were shouted by criers, interspersed among announcements of successful military battles or government proclamations. Would the ancients have believed that today we get messages about products almost wherever we are, whether we cruise down the road or around the Web? Some of us even get advertising messages on our mobile phones or in public restrooms. It's hard to find a place where ads don't try to reach us.

Types of Advertising

Although almost every business advertises, some industries are bigger spenders than others. Retail advertising tops the list with spending on measured advertising (magazines, newspapers, radio, television, and the Internet) of over $15 billion in 2009, down 11.5 percent from 2008. The automotive industry with its recent problems cut measured ad spending 23 percent to a little over $12 billion in 2009. In contrast, the telecommunications industry's 2009 spending was up 1.5 percent from the previous year to $10.2 billion, while medicine and remedies and financial services finished up the top five ad spenders with a little over $8 billion each, down 4.9 and 16.4 percent, respectively.[5] Because they spend so much on advertising, marketers must decide which type of ad will work best to get their money's worth given their organizational and marketing goals. As Figure 11.1 shows, the advertisements an organization runs can take many forms, so let's review the most common kinds.

Figure 11.1 Types of Advertising

Advertisements that an organization runs can take many different forms.

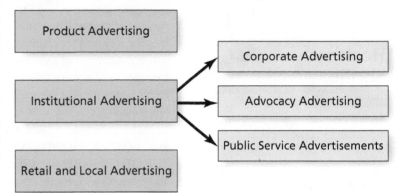

product advertising
Advertising messages that focus on a specific good or service.

institutional advertising
Advertising messages that promote the activities, personality, or point of view of an organization or company.

Product Advertising

When people give examples of advertising, they are likely to recall the provocative poses in Victoria's Secret ads or the colourful creatures in the Telus commercials. These are examples of **product advertising**, where the message focuses on a specific good or service. While not all advertising features a product or a brand, most of the advertising we see and hear is indeed product advertising.

Institutional Advertising

Rather than a focus on a specific brand, **institutional advertising** promotes the activities, personality, or point of view of an organization or company (see Exhibit 11.1). **Corporate advertising** promotes the company as a whole instead of the firm's individual products. Some firms, in fact, do not advertise specific products at all but have built their businesses with only corporate advertising. Cisco, for example, uses corporate advertising to brand itself as "the human network." Other firms like Dow Chemical use corporate advertising in addition to product advertising. Dow boosted its brand equity 25 percent through its "Human Element" corporate advertising campaign that said it is the human element that can solve some of the world's problems, such as climate change and lack of clean water.[6]

Some institutional messages state an organization's position on an issue to sway public opinion, a strategy we call **advocacy advertising.** For example, US governors joined together in a campaign to get Congress to pass climate change legislation. The

Exhibit 11.1

This corporate ad supports Irving's 'What If' brand positioning and its community involvement in "helping kids in our communities realize their dreams". Created by Target Marketing & Communications Inc.

Hesham Shafie

Hesham's team needs to decide if it wants to promote the personality of the company. ▶

corporate advertising
Advertising that promotes the company as a whole instead of a firm's individual products.

advocacy advertising
A type of public service advertising where an organization seeks to influence public opinion on an issue because it has some stake in the outcome.

public service advertisements (PSAs)
Advertising run by the media for not-for-profit organizations or to champion a particular cause without charge.

advertising campaign
A coordinated, comprehensive plan that carries out promotion objectives and results in a series of advertisements placed in media over a period of time.

limited-service agency
An agency that provides one or more specialized services, such as media buying or creative development.

full-service agency
An agency that provides most or all of the services needed to mount a campaign, including research, creation of ad copy and art, media selection, and production of the final messages.

account executive (account manager)
A member of the account management department who supervises the day-to-day activities of the account and is the primary liaison between the agency and the client.

account planner
A member of the account management department who combines research and account strategy to act as the voice of the consumer in creating effective advertising.

campaign included a 30-second TV commercial starring three governors, including former California governor and *Terminator* movie star Arnold Schwarzenegger.[7]

Other messages take the form of **public service advertisements (PSAs)** that the media run free of charge. These messages promote not-for-profit organizations that serve society in some way, or they champion an issue such as increasing literacy or discouraging drunk driving. Advertising agencies often take on one or more public service campaigns on a *pro bono* (for free, not the U2 singer) basis. Little League baseball aired a 15-second PSA on ESPN that featured a 10-year-old at the plate. In the stands the father yells, "Come on, son. Hit the ball." The boy rolls his eyes, turns around to face his dad, and yells back, "DAD, IS THAT THE BEST YOU CAN DO?! THAT'S PATHETIC. I DON'T EVEN KNOW WHY YOU BOTHER SHOWING UP! WHY CAN'T YOU BE MORE LIKE JIMMY'S DAD?! ALL THE OTHER PARENTS ARE GOING TO LAUGH AT YOU! YOU MAKE ME SICK!" The ad ends with a supertitle, "Now you know how it feels. Just let them play."[8]

Retail and Local Advertising

Both major retailers and small, local businesses advertise to encourage customers to shop at a specific store or use a local service. Local advertising informs us about store hours, location, and products that are available or on sale. These ads may take the form of popup ads online or perhaps newspaper circulars that fill out your local newspaper once or twice a week.

Who Creates Advertising?

An **advertising campaign** is a coordinated, comprehensive plan that carries out promotion objectives and results in a series of advertisements placed in various media over a period of time. Although a campaign may be based around a single ad idea, most use multiple messages with all ads in the campaign having the same look and feel. Some campaigns run for only a short period of time while others remain with us for many years. Take, for example, GEICO's advertising campaigns. In recent years, the insurance company has mounted a total of four different advertising campaigns; the messages often run simultaneously. These four are (1) the GEICO gecko campaign, (2) the caveman campaign that even spawned a short-lived TV sitcom ("so easy a caveman can do it"), (3) the "money you could be saving" campaign with the googly-eyed dollar bills, and (4) the "Rhetorical Questions" campaign that includes ads featuring Charlie Daniels, Elmer Fudd, and the Waltons. While all of these campaigns promote the same company and its products and all use the same tag line, "Fifteen minutes could save you 15 percent or more on car insurance," they are each creatively distinct. Each includes multiple ads (there have been at least 22 caveman TV commercials), but each ad is obviously part of a coordinated campaign.

Although some firms create their own advertising in-house, in many cases several specialized companies work together to develop an advertising campaign. Typically, the firm retains one or more outside *advertising agencies* to oversee this process. A **limited-service agency** provides one or more specialized services, such as media buying or creative development. In contrast, a **full-service agency** supplies most or all of the services a campaign requires, including research, creation of ad copy and art, media selection, and production of the final messages. The largest global agencies are Dentsu (based in Japan), BBDO Worldwide, McCann-Erickson Worldwide, and the J. Walter Thompson Co.[9]

A campaign has many elements; it requires the services of many different people to pull it all together. Big or small, an advertising agency hires a range of specialists to craft a message and make the communication concept a reality:

- *Account management:* The **account executive,** or account manager, is the "soul" of the operation. This person supervises the day-to-day activities on the account and is the primary liaison between the agency and the client. The account executive has to ensure that the client is happy while verifying that people within the agency execute the desired strategy. The **account planner** combines research and account strategy to act as

CHAPTER 11 | ADVERTISING, PUBLIC RELATIONS, PROMOTIONS, DIRECT MARKETING, AND PERSONAL SELLING**391**

the voice of the consumer in creating effective advertising. It is the job of the account planner to use market data, qualitative research, and product knowledge to become intimately familiar with the consumer and to translate what customers are looking for to the creative teams who create the ads.

- **Creative services:** *Creatives* are the "heart" of the communication effort. These are the people who actually dream up and produce the ads. They include the agency's creative director, copywriters, and art director. Creatives are the artists who breathe life into marketing objectives and craft messages that (hopefully) will interest consumers.

- **Research and marketing services:** *Researchers* are the "brains" of the campaign. They collect and analyze information that will help account executives develop a sensible strategy. They assist creatives in getting consumer reactions to different versions of ads or by providing copywriters with details on the target group.

- *Media planning:* The **media planner** is the "legs" of the campaign. She helps to determine which communication vehicles are the most effective and recommends the most efficient means to deliver the ad by deciding where, when, and how often it will appear.

As we saw in Chapter 10, more and more agencies practise *integrated marketing communication (IMC)*, in which advertising is only one element of a total communication plan. Because IMC includes more than just advertising, client teams composed of people from account services, creative services, media planning, research, public relations, sales promotion, and direct marketing may work together to develop a plan that best meets the communication needs of each client.

User-Generated Advertising Content: Do-It-Yourself Advertising and Crowdsourcing

The latest promotional craze is to let your customers actually create your advertising for you. **User-generated content (UGC)**, also known as consumer-generated content, includes the millions of online consumer comments, opinions, advice, consumer-to-consumer discussions, reviews, photos, images, videos, podcasts and webcasts, and product-related stories available to other consumers through digital technology. Marketers that embrace this strategy understand that it's okay to let people have fun with their products. For example, join the millions of others who checked out the infamous YouTube videos where "mad scientists" mix Mentos candies with Diet Coke for explosive results (such as http://www.youtube.com/watch?v=hKoB0MHVBvM>).

Marketers need to monitor (and sometimes encourage) UGC for two reasons. First, consumers are more likely to trust messages from fellow consumers than what companies tell them. In fact, they're more likely to say they "trust completely" product information they receive from other consumers than from any other source.[11] Second, we've already seen in the last chapter how proliferate social media is; a person who searches online for a company or product name is certain to access any number of blogs, forums, homegrown commercials, or online complaint sites that the product manufacturer had nothing to do with. Some companies resist this trend when they restrict access to their material or even sue consumers who talk about them, because they fear they will lose control over their brand messages. They really need to recognize that in our digital world their messages (like your Facebook page) are almost impossible to control. In Web 2.0, you're either on the train or under it!

To take advantage of this phenomenon, some marketers encourage consumers to contribute their own **do-it-yourself (DIY) ads.** When Frito-Lay sponsored a contest for 2010 Super Bowl ads, two of the winners, "House Rules" and "Underdog," turned out to be the most watched ads of the game.[11] In its "Priceless" campaign, MasterCard invited

creative services
The agency people (creative director, copywriters, and art director) who dream up and produce the ads.

research and marketing services
Advertising agency department that collects and analyzes information that will help account executives develop a sensible strategy and assist creatives in getting consumer reactions to different versions of ads.

media planner
Agency personnel who determine which communication vehicles are the most effective and efficient to deliver the ad.

user-generated content (UGC)
Online consumer comments, opinions, advice and discussions, reviews, photos, images, videos, podcasts, webcasts, and product-related stories available to other consumers.

do-it-yourself (DIY) ads
Product ads that are created by consumers.

consumers to write their own ad copy for two filmed commercials—all entries had to end with the word "Priceless." Converse allowed customers to send homemade commercials to its Web site, then ran several of them on television.[12] Other companies that have experimented with do-it-yourself (DIY) advertising are L'Oréal ("You Make the Commercial"), JetBlue ("Travel Stories"), and McDonald's ("Global Casting").[13]

For advertisers, DIY advertising offers several benefits. First, consumer-generated spots cost only one-quarter to one-third as much as professional TV and Internet ads—about $60 000 compared to the $350 000 or more to produce a traditional 30-second spot. This can be especially important for smaller businesses and emerging brands. Equally important, even to large companies with deep pockets, is the feedback on how consumers see the brand and the chance to gather more creative ideas to tell the brand's story.[14]

Crowdsourcing is a practice in which firms outsource marketing activities (such as product development) to a community of users; that is, to a crowd. TechSmith, the makers of Snagit, were developing a version for the Mac and wanted to get information on the features and feel that its users and targeted customer base wanted. They used Get Satisfaction's online community-building platform to get ideas and feedback on their beta software from over 450 000 participants (and saved around $500 000 in research costs).[15]

To get the ball rolling, an agency typically solicits ideas from online communities that people access because they are fans of a product or a specific brand. The idea behind crowdsourcing is that if you want to know what consumers think and what they like, the most logical thing to do is to ask them. First, the agency shares a challenge with a large number of people who have varying degrees of expertise. Whether motivated by money, competition, or obsession, individuals then submit their solution to the problem.

Ethical Issues in Advertising

Advertising, more than any other part of marketing, has been sharply criticized for decades. Such criticism certainly may be based less on reality than on the high visibility of advertising and the negative attitudes of consumers who find ads an intrusion in their lives. The objections to advertising are similar to those some people have to marketing in general as we discussed in Chapter 1. Here are the main ones:

- **Advertising is manipulative:** Advertising causes people to behave like robots and do things against their will—make purchases they would not otherwise make were it not for the ads. However, consumers are not robots. Since they are consciously aware of appeals made in advertising, they are free to choose whether to respond to an ad or to not. Of course, consumers can and often do make bad decisions that advertising may influence, but that is not the same as manipulation.

- **Advertising is deceptive and untruthful:** Deceptive advertising means that an ad falsely represents the product and that consumers believe the false information and act on it. Indeed, there is some false or deceptive advertising, but, as a whole, advertisers try to present their brands in the best possible light while being truthful. In Canada, both government regulation and the industry itself, through the not-for-profit Advertising Standards Canada self-regulatory body, strongly encourage honesty.

To protect consumers from being misled, the Competition Bureau has specific rules regarding unfair or deceptive advertising. Some deceptive ads make statements that can be proven false. For example, as a result of complaints by Wind Mobile and Mobilicity and their own investigation, the Competition Bureau charged Rogers Communications Inc. for allegedly "misleading advertising" in their promotion of the discount Chatr wireless service, which stated that Chatr customers would experience "fewer dropped calls than new wireless carriers." The matter is now in court.[16]

In addition to fining firms for deceptive advertising, the Competition Bureau also has the power to require firms to run **corrective advertising,** messages that clarify or qualify

corrective advertising
Advertising that clarifies or qualifies previous deceptive advertising claims.

previous claims. Curry's Art Store was found to have allegedly misled consumers by ticketing items with a manufacturer's suggested list price and a lower Curry's price even though Curry's never had sold the items at the suggested list price. A Competition Bureau ruling required Curry's Art Store to display a corrective notice in its retail stores and on its Web site, along with paying a $60 000 penalty."[17]

Other ads, although not illegal, may create a biased impression of products when they use **puffery**—claims of superiority that neither sponsors nor critics of the ads can prove are true or untrue. For example, Nivea bills itself as "the world's number 1 name in skin care," Neutrogena claims that its cream cleanser produces "the deepest feeling clean," and DuPont says that its Stainmaster Carpet is "a creation so remarkable, it's practically a miracle."

Does this mean that puffery is an unethical marketing practice? Not really. In fact, both advertisers and consumers generally accept puffery as a normal part of the advertising game. Although a little exaggeration may be reasonable, in most cases the goal is to create marketing communications that are both honest and that present the products in the most positive way possible. This approach works to the firm's advantage in the long run since it prevents consumers from becoming overly cynical about the claims it makes.

puffery
Claims made in advertising of product superiority that cannot be proven true or untrue.

Ethical and Sustainable Decisions in the Real World

Many consumers today are concerned about "greenwashing," a practice in which companies promote their products as environmentally friendly when in truth the brand provides little ecological benefit. This practice may refer to a company that boasts in its corporate image advertising of the cutting-edge research it does to save the planet, when in fact this work accounts for only a small fraction of its activities. Hotels claim they are "green" because they allow guests to choose not to have clean sheets and clean towels in their rooms every day. And grocery stores claim to be green because you can return your plastic bags there.

Critics of greenwashing single out Huggies Pure and Natural disposable diapers because the brand claims to be more environmentally friendly and safer for a baby. Its advertising claims that it offers parents the "pure bliss of a diaper that includes gentle, natural materials." However, the only real difference in the Pure and Natural Huggies from the original is a piece of

organically grown cotton fabric that is on the outside of the diaper, not where it touches the baby's skin.

But are such claims ethical? Are consumers being deceived into buying products that they think make a real difference to the environment when in reality the products are not substantially different? Those who are accused of greenwashing would argue that even small efforts toward "going green" are important and that such claims are justified. If you were a marketer, would you try to promote your product as more environmentally friendly even though differences between your product and those of the competition are very minor?

ETHICS CHECK: Find out what other students taking this course **would do** and **why** on **www.my pearsonmarketinglab.com**

If you worked for an advertising agency, would you approve an ad that implies a product is environmentally friendly when there is little to support such claims?

☐YES ☐NO

- **Advertising is offensive and in bad taste:** To respond to this criticism, we need to recognize that what is offensive or in bad taste to one person may not be to another. Yes, some TV commercials are offensive to some people, but then news and program content in the media can be and often is even more explicit or in poor taste. While advertisers seek to go the distance using humour, sex appeals, or fear appeals to get an audience's attention, most shy away from presenting messages that offend the very audience they want to buy their products.

- **Advertising creates and perpetuates stereotypes:** Some advertising critics assert that advertising portrays certain groups of consumers in negative ways. For example, advertising has portrayed women more often as homemakers than as industry leaders. While there is evidence that advertising (and media program content) is guilty of perpetuating stereotypes, it is important to recognize that these stereotypes already exist in the culture. Advertising doesn't create them so much as it reflects them.

- **Advertising causes people to buy things they don't really need:** The truth of this criticism depends on how you define a "need." If we believe that all consumers need is the basic functional benefits of products—the transportation a car provides, the nutrition we get from food, and the clean hair we get from shampoo—then advertising may be guilty as charged. If, on the other hand, you think you need a car that projects a cool image, food that tastes fantastic, and a shampoo that makes your hair shine and smell ever so nice, then advertising is just a vehicle that communicates those more intangible benefits.

2 Develop the Advertising Campaign

OBJECTIVE

Describe the process of developing an advertising campaign and how marketers evaluate advertising.
(pp. 394–410)

The advertising campaign is about much more than creating a cool ad and hoping people notice it. The campaign should be intimately related to the organization's overall communication goals. That means the firm (and its outside agency if it uses one) must have a good idea of who it wants to reach, what it will take to appeal to this market, and where and when it should place its messages. Let's examine the steps required to do this, as Figure 11.2 shows.

Step 1: Understand the Target Audience

The best way to communicate with an audience is to understand as much as possible about them and what turns them on and off. An ad that uses the latest "hip-hop" slang may relate to teenagers but not to their parents—and this strategy may backfire if the ad copy reads like an "ancient" 40-year-old trying to sound like a 20-year-old.

As we discussed in Chapter 6, marketers often identify the target audience for an advertising campaign from research. Researchers try to get inside the customer's head to understand just how to create a message that he will understand and to which he will respond. Sometimes they even get inside the customer's home! For example, a major coffee company had created an expensive TV campaign in the Philippines that featured smiling people drinking coffee in the shelter of their homes while the rain dropped on their roof. This campaign, celebrating the rainy season, had flopped . . . sales decreased and no one could understand why. The coffee company brought in a consultant who spent 10 days living in five different family homes, experiencing life in the Philippines, including the act of drinking coffee there. One night, during a rain storm, the consultant realized that the sound of rain on a tin roof in the Philippines was not the same as the stock rain sound often heard in Hollywood movies. No wonder the campaign did not work—the average Filipino did not connect with the sound and it, therefore, did not evoke the emotional stirrings that the brand had hoped for.[18]

Figure 11.2 Steps to Develop an Advertising Campaign
Developing an advertising campaign includes a series of steps that will ensure that the advertising meets communication objectives.

Step 1: Understand the Target Audience

↓

Step 2: Establish Message and Budget Objectives

↓

Step 3: Create the Ads

↓

Step 4: Pretest What the Ads Will Say

↓

Step 5: Choose the Media Type(s) and Media Schedule

↓

Step 6: Evaluate the Advertising

Step 2: Establish Message and Budget Objectives

Advertising objectives should be consistent with the overall communication plan. That means that both the underlying message and its costs need to relate to what the marketer is trying to say about the product and what the marketer is willing or able to spend. Thus, advertising objectives generally will include objectives for both the message and the budget. (See Exhibit 11.2.)

Set Message Objectives

As we noted earlier, because advertising is the most visible part of marketing, many people assume that marketing is advertising. In truth, advertising alone is quite limited in what it can achieve. What advertising *can* do is inform, persuade, and remind. Accordingly, some advertisements are informational—they aim to make the customer knowledgeable about features of the product or how to use it. At other times, advertising seeks to persuade consumers to like a brand or to prefer one brand over the competition. But many, many ads simply aim to keep the name of the brand in front of the consumer—reminding consumers that this brand is the one to choose when they look for a soft drink or a laundry detergent.

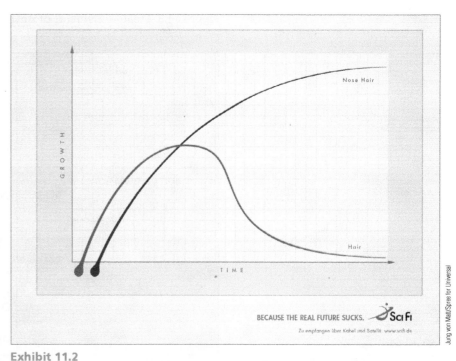

Exhibit 11.2

This German ad speaks to many of the viewers the SciFi channel hopes to reach.

Set Budget Objectives

Advertising is expensive. Procter & Gamble, which leads all US companies in advertising expenditures, spends almost $5 billion per year while second- and third-place ad spenders AT&T and General Motors spend well over $3 billion each.[19]

An objective of many firms is to allocate a percentage of the overall communication budget to advertising, depending on how much and what type of advertising the company can afford. The major approaches and techniques to setting overall promotional budgets, such as the percentage-of-sales and objective-task methods we discussed in Chapter 10, also set advertising budgets.

Major corporations like General Motors advertise heavily on expensive media such as television to promote multiple products throughout the year. Other companies may be more selective, and smaller firms may want to put their advertising dollars into cheaper media outlets such as direct mail, trade publications, or online via a service like Google AdWords. Or a firm may decide to blow its entire advertising budget in one grand gesture—as the webhosting company GoDaddy.com does when it buys airtime during the Super Bowl.

Step 3: Create the Ads

The creation of the advertising begins when an agency formulates a **creative strategy** which gives the advertising creatives (art directors, copywriters, photographers, and others) the direction and inspiration they need to begin the creative process. The strategy is summarized in a written document known as a **creative brief**, a rough blueprint that guides but does not restrict the creative process. It provides only the most relevant information and insights about the marketing situation, the advertising objective, the competition, the advertising target and, most importantly, the message that the advertising must deliver.

It's one thing to know *what* a company wants to say about itself or its products, and it's another to figure out *how* to say it. The role of the creative brief is to provide the spark that helps the ad agency come up with "the big idea," the visual and/or verbal concept that delivers the message in an attention-getting, memorable, and relevant manner. From this,

creative strategy
The process that turns a concept into an advertisement.

creative brief
A guideline or blueprint for the marketing communication program that guides the creative process.

Figure 11.3 Creative Elements of Advertising
Creating good ads includes making decisions about the four different ad elements.

Creative Element	Element Options
Appeals	Rational (Unique Selling Proposition) Emotional Reminder Advertising Teaser Ads
Execution Formats	Comparison Demonstration Testimonial Slice of Life Lifestyle
Tonality	Straightforward Humorous Dramatic Romantic Apprehension/Fear
Creative Tactics and Techniques	Animation and Art Celebrities Music, Jingles, and Slogans

advertising appeal
The central idea or theme of an advertising message.

unique selling proposition (USP)
An advertising appeal that focuses on one clear reason why a particular product is superior.

What will it take to make you care about the environment? Earth Day CANADA

Courtesy of Earth Day Canada and DDB Canada.

Exhibit 11.3
DDB Canada has created a memorable photo illustration and slogan that gets the consumer thinking about the environment.

the creatives develop the ads by combining already-known facts, words, pictures, and ideas in new and unexpected ways. Specifically, and as shown in Figure 11.3, to come up with finished ads, they must consider four elements: the appeal, the format, the tonality, and the creative tactics and techniques.[20]

Advertising Appeals

An **advertising appeal** is the central idea of the ad and the basis of the advertising messages. It is the approach used to influence the consumer. Generally, we think of appeals as informational or emotional (Exhibit 11.3).

Informational or rational appeals relate to consumers' practical need for the product. They emphasize the features of the product and/or the benefits we receive from using it. Often, informational appeals are based on a **unique selling proposition (USP)** that gives consumers a clear, single-minded reason why the advertiser's product is better than other products at solving a problem. For example, "M&Ms melt in your mouth, not in your hands" is a USP. In general, a USP strategy is effective if there is some clear product advantage that consumers can readily identify and that is important to them.

Because consumers often buy products based on social or psychological needs, advertisers frequently use emotional appeals instead where they try to pull our heartstrings rather than make us think differently about a brand. Emotional appeals focus on an emotional or social benefit the consumer may receive from the product, such as safety, love, excitement, pleasure, respect, or approval.

Of course, not all ads fit into these two appeal categories. Well-established brands often use **reminder advertising** just to keep their name in people's minds or to be sure that consumers repurchase the product as necessary. For example, Arm & Hammer baking soda reminds us to replace the open box, which many of us keep in our refrigerators to absorb odours, on a regular basis.

Sometimes advertisers use **teaser** or **mystery ads** to generate curiosity and interest in a to-be-introduced product. Teaser ads draw attention to an upcoming ad campaign without mentioning the product. Before the creative team can craft and polish the words and visuals to bring the big idea to life, they still must choose the most appropriate format and tonality of the advertising. We'll turn to those ideas next.

Execution Formats

Execution format describes the basic structure of the message. Some of the more common formats, sometimes used in combination, include the following:

- *Comparison:* A comparative advertisement explicitly names one or more competitors. Pizza Hut's recent US-based "America's Favorite Pizza" spots claimed that consumers preferred its hand-tossed pizzas 2 to 1 over both number two Domino's and number three Papa John's. Ads showed rival pizza delivery drivers eating Pizza Hut pizza at the Pizza Hut driver's home. Papa John's countered with claims that its crust was made fresh while Pizza Hut's was frozen.[21]

  Comparative ads can be very effective, but there is a risk of turning off consumers who don't like the negative tone. While in many countries comparative advertising is illegal, it's a widely used tactic in the United States. This format is best for brands that have a smaller share of the market and for firms that can focus on a specific feature that makes them superior to a major brand. When market leaders use comparative advertising, there is the risk consumers will feel they are "picking on the little guy." One exception is the "cola wars" advertising by Coca-Cola and Pepsi. In the Pepsi Max ad which features the song "Why Can't We Be Friends?" by War, delivery drivers for Coke and Pepsi meet in a diner; the Coke driver samples Pepsi Max and prefers it.

- *Demonstration:* The ad shows a product "in action" to prove that it performs as claimed: "It slices, it dices!" Demonstration advertising is most useful when consumers are unable to identify important benefits except when they see the product in use. You may remember ads like the ShamWow and Slap Chop featuring Vince Shlomi, which have gone viral.

- *Testimonial:* A celebrity, an expert, or a "man in the street" states the product's effectiveness. The use of *celebrity endorsers* is a common but expensive strategy. It may also be risky, if the celebrity endorser behaves in a way that is inconsistent with the brand positioning.

- *Slice of life:* A *slice-of-life* format presents a (dramatized) scene from everyday life. This advertising can be effective for everyday products such as peanut butter and headache remedies that consumers may feel good about if they see "real" people buy and use them.

- *Lifestyle:* A *lifestyle* format shows a person or persons attractive to the target market in an appealing setting. The advertised product is "part of the scene," implying that the person who buys it will attain the lifestyle. For example, a commercial might depict a group of "cool" California skateboarders who take a break for a gulp of milk and say, "It does a body good."

Tonality

Tonality refers to the mood or attitude the message conveys. Some common tonalities include:

- *Straightforward:* Straightforward ads simply present the information to the audience in a clear manner. Informative ads are frequently used in radio but less often in TV.

---

reminder advertising
Advertising aimed at keeping the name of a brand in people's minds to be sure consumers purchase the product as necessary.

teaser or mystery advertising
Ads that generate curiosity and interest in a to-be-introduced product by drawing attention to an upcoming ad campaign without mentioning the product.

execution format
The basic structure of the message such as comparison, demonstration, testimonial, slice of life, and lifestyle.

tonality
The mood or attitude the message conveys (straightforward, humorous, dramatic, romantic, sexy, and apprehensive/fearful).

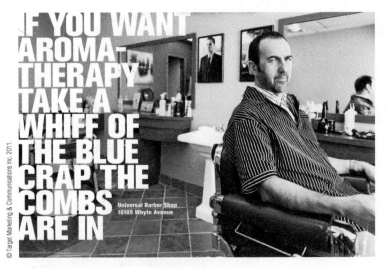

Exhibit 11.4

Humorous, witty, or outrageous ads can be an effective way to break through advertising clutter.

- *Humour:* Humorous, witty, or outrageous ads can be an effective way to break through advertising clutter (Exhibit 11.4). But humour can be tricky, because what is funny to one person may be offensive or stupid to another. Different cultures also have different senses of humour. A recent Reebok commercial showed women at a basketball game checking out the all-male cheerleading squad. The spot was witty, but people from countries that don't feature cheerleaders at sports events (you don't find too many pom-poms at soccer matches) might not "get it."

  Perhaps the major benefit of humorous advertising is that it attracts consumers' attention and leaves them with a pleasant feeling. Of course, humour in advertising can backfire. In the United Kingdom, a Renault Megane 225 ad that featured people in everyday situations shaking uncontrollably as the car passed was banned by the government's Office of Communications: Viewers complained that the ad mocked people with illnesses such as Parkinson's disease.[22]

- *Dramatic:* A dramatization, like a play, presents a problem and a solution in a manner that is often exciting and suspenseful—a fairly difficult challenge in 30 or 60 seconds.

- *Romantic:* Ads that present a romantic situation can be especially effective at getting consumers' attention and at selling products people associate with dating and mating. See Exhibit 11.5. That's why fragrance ads often use a romantic format.

- *Sexy:* Some ads appear to sell sex rather than products. In a Guess jeans ad, a shirtless man lies near an almost shirtless woman. Ads such as these rely on sexuality to get consumers' attention. *Sex appeal* ads are more likely to be effective when there is a connection between the product and sex (or at least romance). For example, sex appeals will work well with a perfume but are less likely to be effective when you're trying to sell a lawn mower.

- *Apprehension/Fear:* Some ads highlight the negative consequences of *not* using a product. *Fear appeal* ads focus on physical harm, while others try to create concern for social harm or disapproval. Mouthwash, deodorant, and dandruff shampoo makers and life insurance companies successfully use fear appeals, as do ads aimed at changing behaviours, such as messages discouraging drug use or encouraging safe sex. In general, fear appeals can be successful if the audience perceives there to be an appropriate level of intensity in the fear appeal. For example, horrible photos of teens lying on the highway following an auto accident can be quite effective in PSAs designed to persuade teens not to drink and drive, but they are likely to backfire if an insurance company tries to "scare" people into buying life insurance.

Creative Tactics and Techniques

In addition to ad formats and tonality, the creative process may also include a number of different creative tactics and techniques. Some of these are

- *Animation and art:* Not all ads are executed with film or photography. Sometimes, a creative decision is made to use art, illustration, or animation to achieve the desired

Exhibit 11.5

Gillette uses a romantic theme in China.

look of a print ad or TV commercial or to attract attention. For example, Coke used the popular Simpsons cartoon characters in its Super Bowl ads in 2010.[23]

- *Celebrities:* Sometimes they just appear in testimonials or endorsements, such as Sidney Crosby's work with Timbits Hockey. At other times, using a celebrity is simply a casting decision—a technique to make an ad more interesting or appealing, such as when the model Chi-Ling Lin and actors Kate Winslet and Aishwarya Rai show up in a commercial for Logines' Dolce Vita watch collection.

- *Music, jingles, and slogans:* **Jingles** are original words and music written specifically for advertising executions. Many of us remember classic ad jingles such as "I wish I were an Oscar Mayer Wiener" (Oscar Mayer) and ad slogans such as "Finger lickin' good" (KFC), "I am Canadian" (Molsons), and "Just do it" (Nike). Jingles aren't used as often as they were in the past, but many advertisers still like to set their slogan to original music at the end of a commercial. These are called "musical buttons" or "tags." A currently popular technique is to add a few appropriate measures of a popular song near the end of a commercial to emphasize the message.

jingles
Original words and music written specifically for advertising executions.

Slogans link the brand to a simple linguistic device that is memorable (jingles do the same but set the slogan to music). We usually have no trouble reciting successful slogans (sometimes years after the campaign has ended); think of such die-hards as "Please don't squeeze the Charmin," "Double your pleasure, double your fun," and "Roll up the rim." Firms such as Clorox, Allstate, and Procter & Gamble find that the songs they use in their commercials can become popular on their own—now they offer consumers the opportunity to purchase full-length versions of the music.[24]

slogans
Simple, memorable linguistic devices linked to a brand.

Step 4: Pretest What the Ads Will Say

Now that the creatives have performed their magic, how does the agency know if the campaign ideas will work? Advertisers try to minimize mistakes by getting reactions to ad messages before they actually place them. Much of this **pretesting**, the research that goes on in the early stages of a campaign, centres on gathering basic information that will help planners be sure they've accurately defined the product's market, consumers, and competitors. As we saw in Chapter 3, this information comes from quantitative sources, such as surveys, and qualitative sources, such as focus groups.

pretesting
A research method that seeks to minimize mistakes by getting consumer reactions to ad messages before they appear in the media.

In addition, some researchers use physiological measures to pretest ads. For example, the ad agency Bark Group employs eye movement tracking, skin responses, and brain responses to gauge consumers' emotional responses to ads in order to produce ad campaigns that result in a stronger emotional reaction.[25] The idea is to be able to identify the colours, sounds, images, and words that elicit the strongest responses—even in some cases when viewers aren't consciously aware of how they're feeling.

Step 5: Choose the Media Type(s) and Media Schedule

Media planning is a problem-solving process that gets a message to a target audience in the most effective way. Planning decisions include audience selection and where, when, and how frequent the exposure should be. Thus, the first task for a media planner is to find out when and where people in the target market are most likely to be exposed to the communication. Many university and college students read the campus newspaper in the morning (believe it or not, sometimes even during class!), so advertisers may choose to place ad messages aimed at students there.

media planning
The process of developing media objectives, strategies, and tactics for use in an advertising campaign.

There is no such thing as one perfect medium for advertising. The choice depends on the specific target audience, the objective of the message, and, of course, the budget. For the advertising campaign to be effective, the media planner must match the profile of the target market with specific media vehicles. For example, many Indo-Canadian consumers, even those who speak English, are avid users of Hindi-language media. Marketers that wish to reach this segment might allocate a relatively large share of their advertising budget to buying Hindi language newspapers, magazines, TV, and Hindi webcasts available to broadband Internet users.

The choice of the right media mix is no simple matter, especially as new options including videos and DVDs, video games, personal computers, the Internet, MP3 players, hundreds of new TV channels, and even satellite radio now vie for our attention. Consider that in 1965, advertisers could reach 80 percent of 18–49-year-olds in the United States with three 60-second TV spots! That kind of efficiency is just a pipe dream in today's highly fragmented media marketplace.

Where to Say It: Traditional Mass Media

What does a 46-inch 1080p LED HDTV with 4 HDMI ports have in common with the back of a cash register receipt? Each is a media vehicle that permits an advertiser to communicate with a potential customer. Depending on the intended message, each medium has its advantages and disadvantages. In this section, we'll take a look at the major categories of traditional mass media. Then, we'll look at Internet advertising and some less-traditional indirect forms of advertising. Table 11.1 summarizes some of the pros and cons of each type.

- **Television:** Because of television's ability to reach so many people at once, it's often the medium of choice for regional and national companies. However, advertising on a television network can be very expensive. The cost to air a 30-second ad on a popular prime-time network TV show one time normally ranges between $200 000 and $750 000 or more depending on the size of the show's audience. In 2008, ads for a near-finale episode of *American Idol*, the number-one TV show for four years, went for $1 million or more.[26] Advertisers may prefer to buy cable, satellite, or local television time rather than network time because it's cheaper or because they want to reach a more targeted market, such as "foodies," who are into cooking. Nevertheless, 78 percent of advertisers say TV advertising has become less effective as DVRs and video-on-demand grow in popularity.[27]

  While viewing of traditional broadcast TV is down dramatically in recent years, people spend a lot more time watching cable and satellite channels. This explains why the companies that own broadcast networks also are buying up major cable channels— Rogers, for example, owns TV stations across the county, and specialty channels like SportsNet and TVtropolis. Bell Canada owns BRAVO!, CablePulse24, CTV News Channel, E!, MTV (Canada), MuchMusic, Space, The Comedy Network, FTV, Discovery Science Canada, and Animal Planet Canada, to name a few.[28]

- **Radio:** Radio as an advertising medium dates back to 1922, when a New York City apartment manager went on the air to advertise properties for rent. One advantage of radio advertising is flexibility. Commercials can be changed quickly, often on the spot by an announcer and a recording engineer.[29]

- **Newspapers:** The newspaper is one of the oldest communication platforms. Retailers in particular have relied on newspaper ads since before the turn of the 20th century to inform readers about sales and deliveries of new merchandise. While most newspapers are local, *The Globe and Mail* and the *National Post* have national circulations and provide readerships in the millions. Newspapers are an excellent medium for local advertising and for events (such as store sales) that require a quick response. Today, most newspapers also offer online versions of their papers to expand their exposure. Some, such as *The Globe and Mail*, offer online subscribers downloads of the actual newspaper including all the ads at a much lower cost than the paper version. Rates for newspapers vary depending on the circulation of the paper. Most newspapers help advertisers in putting their ads together, a real advantage to the small business. However, the newspaper

Table 11.1	Pros and Cons of Media Vehicles	
Vehicle	Pros	Cons
Television	• TV is extremely creative and flexible. • Network TV is the most cost-effective way to reach a mass audience. • Cable and satellite TV allow the advertiser to reach a selected group at relatively low cost. • A prestigious way to advertise. • Can demonstrate the product in use. • Can provide entertainment and generate excitement. • Messages have high impact because of the use of sight and sound.	• The message is quickly forgotten unless it is repeated often. • The audience is increasingly fragmented. • Although the relative cost of reaching the audience is low, prices are still high on an absolute basis—often too high for smaller companies. A 30-second spot on a primetime TV sitcom costs well over $250 000. • Fewer people view network television. • People switch from station to station and zap commercials. • Rising costs have led to more and shorter ads, causing more clutter.
Radio	• Good for selectively targeting an audience. • Is heard outside the home. • Can reach customers on a personal and intimate level. • Can use local personalities. • Relatively low cost, both for producing a spot and for running it repeatedly. • Because of short lead time, radio ads can be modified quickly to reflect changes in the marketplace. • Use of sound effects and music allows listeners to use their imagination to create a vivid scene.	• Listeners often don't pay full attention to what they hear. • Difficulty in buying radio time, especially for national advertisers. • Not appropriate for products that must be seen or demonstrated to be appreciated. • The small audiences of individual stations means ads must be placed with many different stations and must be repeated frequently.
Newspapers	• Wide exposure provides extensive market coverage. • Flexible format permits the use of colour, different sizes, and targeted editions. • Provides the ability to use detailed copy. • Allows local retailers to tie in with national advertisers. • Readers are in the right mental frame to process advertisements about new products, sales, etc. • Timeliness; i.e., short lead time between placing ad and running it.	• Most people don't spend much time reading the newspaper. • Readership is especially low among teens and young adults. • Short life span—people rarely look at a newspaper more than once. • Offers a very cluttered ad environment. • The reproduction quality of images is relatively poor. • Not effective in reaching specific audiences.
Magazines	• Audiences can be narrowly targeted by specialized magazines. • High credibility and interest level provide a good environment for ads. • Advertising has a long life and is often passed along to other readers. • Visual quality is excellent. • Can provide detailed product information with a sense of authority.	• With the exception of direct mail, it is the most expensive form of advertising. The cost of a full-page, four-colour ad in a general-audience magazine typically exceeds $100 000. • Long deadlines reduce flexibility. • The advertiser must generally use several magazines to reach the majority of a target market. • A cluttered ad environment.

(continued)

| Table 11.1 | Pros and Cons of Media Vehicles *(continued)* | |

Vehicle	Pros	Cons
Directories	• Customers actively seek exposure to advertisements. • Advertisers determine the quality of the ad placement because larger ads get preferential placement.	• Limited creative options. • May be a lack of colour. • Ads are generally purchased for a full year and cannot be changed.
Out-of-home media	• Most of the population can be reached at low cost. • Good for supplementing other media. • High frequency when signs are located in heavy traffic areas. • Effective for reaching virtually all segments of the population. • Geographic flexibility.	• Hard to communicate complex messages because of short exposure time. • Difficult to measure advertisement's audience. • Controversial and disliked in many communities. • Cannot pinpoint specific market segments.
Internet Web sites	• Can target specific audiences and individualize messages. • Web user registration and cookies allow marketers to track user preferences and Web site activity. • Is interactive—consumers can participate in the ad campaign; can create do-it-yourself ads. • An entertainment medium allowing consumers to play games, download music, etc. • Consumers are active participants in the communication process, controlling what information and the amount and rate of information they receive. • Web sites can facilitate both marketing communication and transactions. • Consumers visit Web sites with the mindset to obtain information. • Banners can achieve top of mind awareness (TOMA), even without click-throughs.	• Limited to Internet users only. • Banners, pop-ups, unsolicited e-mail, etc., can be unwanted and annoying. • Declining click-through rates for banners—currently less than 0.03 percent. • If Web pages take too long to load, consumers will abandon the site. • Phishing: e-mail sent by criminals to get consumers to go to phony Web sites that will seek to gain personal information such as credit card numbers. • Because advertisers' costs are normally based on the number of click-throughs, competitors may engage in click fraud by clicking on a sponsored link. • Difficult to measure effectiveness.
Place-based media	• Effective for certain markets, such as pharmaceutical companies, to reach their target audience. • In retail locations it can reach customers immediately before purchase; this provides a last opportunity to influence the purchase decision. • In locations such as airports, it receives a high level of attention because of lack of viewer options.	• Limited audience. • Difficult to measure effectiveness.
Branded entertainment	• Brand presented in a positive context. • Brand message presented in a covert fashion. • Less intrusive and thus less likely to be avoided. • Connection with a popular movie plot or TV program and with entertaining characters can help a brand's image. • Can build emotional connection with the audience. • Can create a memorable association that serves to enhance brand recall.	• Little control of how the brand is positioned—is in the hands of the director. • Difficult to measure effectiveness. • Costs of placement can be very high.

Table 11.1	Pros and Cons of Media Vehicles (*continued*)	
Vehicle	**Pros**	**Cons**
Advergaming	• Companies can customize their own games or incorporate brands into existing popular games. • Some game producers now actively pursue tie-ins with brands. • Millions of gamers play an average of 40 hours per game before they tire of it. • Millions of consumers have mobile phones "in their hands."	• Audience limited to gamers.
Mobile phones	• A large variety of different formats using different mobile phone apps.	• Consumers may be unwilling to receive messages through their phones.

Source: Adapted from J. Thomas Russell and Ron Lane, *Kleppner's Advertising Procedure*, 15th ed. (Upper Saddle River, NJ: Prentice Hall, 2002); Terence A. Shimp, *Advertising, Promotion and Supplemental Aspects of Integrated Marketing Communications*, 8th ed. (Australia: Thomson Southwestern, 2010); and William Wells, John Burnett, and Sandra Moriarty, *Advertising: Principles and Practice*, 6th ed. (Upper Saddle River, NJ: Prentice Hall, 2003).

industry is in serious trouble as more people choose to get their news online, and many major papers are closing their doors or struggling.

• **Magazines:** Today, in addition to general audience magazines such as *Reader's Digest*, there are literally thousands of special-interest magazines. Approximately 92 percent of adults look through at least one magazine per month. New technology such as *selective binding* allows publishers to personalize their editions so that they can include advertisements for local businesses in issues they mail to specific locations. For advertisers, magazines also offer the opportunity for multipage spreads as well as the ability to include special inserts so they can deliver samples of products such as perfumes and other "scratch-and-sniff" treats. Kimberly Clark's Viva brand paper towels, for example, included samples of the product stitched into copies of *Reader's Digest* as part of a six-page spread.[30]

Where to Say It: Digital Media

The term **digital media** refers to any media that are digital rather than analogue. The more popular types of digital media advertisers use today include Web sites, mobile or cellular phones, tablets, and digital video such as YouTube.

Owned, Paid, and Earned Media

Internet media can be classified as owned, paid, and earned.[31] Companies can control their **owned media** that includes Web sites, blogs, Facebook, and Twitter accounts. The advantage of these owned media is that they are effective means for companies to build relationships with their customers. **Paid media**, the most similar model to traditional media, includes display ads, sponsorships, and paid key word searches. Consumers generally dislike the paid ads, making their effectiveness less of a sure thing. **Earned media** refers to word of mouth (WOM) or buzz using social media. The positive of earned media is that it is the most credible to consumers. The challenge is that marketers have no control over earned media; they can only listen and respond.

Web Site Advertising

Online advertising no longer is a novelty; companies now spend over $21 billion a year to communicate via digital media. Major firms like General Mills and Kraft Foods are boosting

Hesham Shafie

APPLYING ⌄ Owned Media

Hesham's team can build a relationship with customers through the Brand Momentum Web site and Facebook account. They can control what is communicated and how it is communicated! ➥

digital media
Media that are digital rather than analogue, including Web sites, mobile or cellular phones, and digital video such as YouTube.

owned media
Internet sites such as Web sites, blogs, Facebook, and Twitter accounts that are owned by an advertiser.

paid media
Internet media such as display ads, sponsorships, and paid key word searches that are paid for by an advertiser.

earned media
Word-of-mouth or buzz using social media where the advertiser has no control.

© Shutterstock

Exhibit 11.6

Alaska Airlines developed a system to create unique ads for individual Web surfers based on their geographic location, the number of times that person has seen an Alaska Airlines ad, the consumer's purchase history with the airline, and his experience with lost bags, delays, and flight cancellations. The program can offer different prices to different customers, even prices below the lowest published fares.[32]

their spending and the number of brands they promote online.[33] The reason? About 68 percent of the Canadian population is online. Canadians have the highest penetration of Internet access, highest consumption of YouTube videos, highest usage of Wikipedia, and are significant users of Facebook.[34]

Online advertising offers several advantages over other media platforms. First, the Internet provides new ways to finely target customers (see Exhibit 11.6). Web user registrations and *cookies* allow sites to track user preferences and deliver ads based on previous Internet behaviour. In addition, because the Web site can track how many times an ad is "clicked," advertisers can measure in real time how people respond to specific online messages.

Finally, online advertising can be interactive—it lets consumers participate in the advertising campaign, and in some cases they can even become part of the action. Viewers who logged on to a special Web site were able to "direct" TV commercials for the Ford Probe by picking the cast and plotlines that Ford's ad agency then used to create actual spots. Similarly, during its "whatever.com" campaign, Nike sent consumers to the Web to pick the endings of three cliffhanger TV spots.[35]

Specific forms of Internet advertising include banners, pop-up ads, buttons, search engines and directories, and e-mail:

banners
Internet advertising in the form of rectangular graphics at the top or bottom of Web pages.

- **Banners**, rectangular graphics at the top or bottom of Web pages, were the first form of Web advertising.

pop-up ad
An advertisement that appears on the screen while a Web page loads or after it has loaded.

- A **pop-up ad** is an advertisement that appears on the screen while a Web page loads or after it has loaded. Because these messages take up part of the screen's "real estate" while surfers wait for the desired page to load, they are difficult to ignore. Many surfers find pop-ups a nuisance, so most Internet access software provides an option that blocks all pop-ups. Web advertisers are typically charged only if people actually click through to the ad.

buttons
Small banner-type advertisements that can be placed anywhere on a Web page.

- **Buttons** are small banner-type advertisements that a company can place anywhere on a page.

search engines
Internet programs that search for documents with specified keywords.

- **Search engines** and directory listings are ways for people to find Web pages of interest to them. A Web search engine is a program that searches for documents with specified keywords. Because there are millions of Web pages that include a particular word or phrase, most search engines use some method to rank their search results and provide users with the most relevant results first. As we discussed in Chapter 4, firms are increasingly paying search engines for more visible or higher placement on results lists. Google, which has 65 percent of all US Web searches, has total global revenues of nearly $30 billion. In June 2010, BP spent nearly $3.6 million for Google advertising following the Gulf oil spill, while Google's top client, AT&T, spent $8.08 million on Google's AdWords to support its launch of the iPhone 4.[36] Unlike search engines, a **Web directory** does not display lists of Web pages based on keywords but instead lists sites by categories and subcategories. Google, for example, offers its users the Google Directory in addition to its search engine. Who have you Googled today?

Web directory
Internet program that lists sites by categories and subcategories.

e-mail advertising
Advertising messages sent via e-mail to large numbers of people simultaneously.

- **E-mail advertising** that transmits messages to very large numbers of inboxes simultaneously is one of the easiest ways to communicate with consumers—it's basically the same price whether you send ten messages or ten thousand. Recipients might be drawn from an organization's list or they may have "opted in" to receive notifications of a company's discounts and promotions. One downside to this platform is the explosion of **spam.** The industry defines this practice as sending unsolicited e-mail to five or more people not personally known to the sender. Many Web sites that offer e-mail give surfers the opportunity to refuse unsolicited e-mail via junk e-mail blockers. This **permission marketing** strategy gives the consumer the power to *opt* in or out. Marketers in the United States send about 200 billion e-mails to consumers every year, so they, as do Canadian marketers, hope that a good portion of these will be opened and read rather than being sent straight to the recycle bin.[37]

Mobile Advertising

The Mobile Marketing Association defines **mobile advertising** as "a form of advertising that is communicated to the consumer via a handset."[38] Mobile marketing offers advertisers a variety of ways to speak to customers, including mobile Web sites, mobile applications, mobile messaging, and mobile video and TV.

Mobile advertising has just begun to boom, much energized by Apple's iPhone and all the apps that go with it. Begun with Apple's iAd, today's mobile advertising has moved from tiny static banner ads to rich media that brings motion, interactivity, sound, video, or Flash to mobile advertising.[39] In the UK, Kellogg used mobile advertising for its "The Big Bake" campaign.[40] Messages on Kellogg's cereal boxes encouraged consumers to use their mobile phones to send in photos of them cooking recipes that include Kellogg's cereals. Winners of the contest were given the opportunity to star in a Kellogg's TV or print ad. And, while Oprah left network TV, she is still available to fans through a smartphone app that offers access to articles and photos from Oprah.com and *O* magazine and to her tweets.[41] Newer phones with global positioning system (GPS) features that pinpoint your location allow additional mobile advertising opportunities. Outdoor apparel retailer North Face, for example, used location-based mobile ads to lure consumers to its stores.[42] When customers who opt in are close to one of the chain's stores, they receive a text message about new arrivals or an in-store promotion such as a free water bottle with a purchase.

Video Sharing: Check It Out on YouTube

Video sharing describes the strategy of uploading video recordings or **vlogs** (pronounced vee-logs) to Internet sites such as YouTube so that thousands or even millions of other Internet users can check them out. These videos are a powerful way to break through the clutter. To understand how, let's take a look at how Blendtec, a small electric blender manufacturer, used this strategy to grab a lot of attention quickly and cheaply. The company uploaded a vlog that showed its president dropping a brand-new iPhone into one of its appliances—presto! Within 24 hours, over a million people had watched as presto! purée of phone resulted.[43]

For marketers, YouTube provides vast opportunities to build relationships with consumers. For example, Home Depot provides do-it-yourselfers with free educational videos that promote Home Depot products and position the company as a trusted expert. The University of Phoenix uses YouTube to post hundreds of video testimonials. The Boone Oakley advertising agency has established its Web site on YouTube. The interactive video allows potential clients to view its work in an easily accessible way and is especially appealing to companies that want a nontraditional marketing communications program.

Where to Say It: Branded Entertainment

As we noted earlier, more and more marketers rely on paid product placements in TV shows and movies to grab the attention of consumers who tune out traditional ad messages as fast as they see them. These placements are an important form of **branded entertainment,**

---

spam
The use of electronic media to send unsolicited messages in bulk.

permission marketing
E-mail advertising in which online consumers have the opportunity to accept or refuse the unsolicited e-mail.

mobile advertising
A form of advertising that is communicated to the consumer via a handset.

video sharing
Uploading video recordings on to Internet sites such as YouTube so that thousands or even millions of other Internet users can see them.

vlogs
Video recordings shared on the Internet.

branded entertainment
A form of advertising in which marketers integrate products into entertainment venues.

Tech and Trends

The World of Augmented Reality

Ever wonder how they make those yellow first-down lines in televised football games that spectators in the stadium can't see? Or how about the trail of the puck in broadcasts of hockey games? The answer is **augmented reality (AR)**, a form of technology where a view of a real-world environment joins a layer of virtual computer-generated imagery to create a mixed reality.

Adidas is one of several companies experimenting with AR in its marketing program.[44] Adidas.com used augmented reality to create three online games for Adidas sneaker customers. One is a skateboard game where the gamer's sneaker navigates through the city. Other Adidas games include a *Star Wars*–like game and a music game. To play all three games, the consumer holds the tongue of the sneaker up to a computer webcam and an implanted code activates a virtual 3D world that the person sneaks into.

augmented reality (AR)
A form of technology where a view of a real-world environment joins a layer of virtual computer-generated imagery to create a mixed reality.

a strategy where marketers integrate products into all sorts of venues including movies, television shows, video games, novels, and even retail settings. For one promotion, a group of 7-Eleven convenience stores literally became Kwik-E-Marts just like the store Homer loves to frequent in the TV show *The Simpsons*. Real-world customers could buy such exotic delicacies as Squishees, Buzz Cola, and Krusty-Os cereal. The KFC fast-food chain paid two cities in Indiana to put founder Colonel Sanders's face on their hydrants and fire extinguishers to promote its new "fiery" chicken wings.[45] And the Twentieth Century Fox movie studio even managed to place a plug for the romantic comedy *I Love You, Beth Cooper* in a high school valedictorian's speech (she got paid $1800 to mention one of the main characters).[46] Music videos often show brands, and artists even mention products like Air Force One (Nelly); Patron Tequila (Paradiso Girls); and Kodak (Pitbull featuring Ne-yo, Afrojack, and Nayer). Product placement has also moved to social media as many firms are paying YouTube celebrities to push their products. Because consumers trust what these YouTubers say, companies including giants AT&T, GE, Ford, Colgate, Lancôme Paris, McDonald's, and Coca-Cola are paying $75 000 or more to some YouTube stars.[47]

Is branded entertainment a solid strategy? The idea is that when consumers see a popular celebrity who uses a specific brand in their favourite movie or TV program, they might develop a more positive attitude toward that brand. Successful brand placements include the BMW Z3 James Bond drove, the Nike shoes Forrest Gump wore, and the custom-made Blinde sunglasses worn by the actors in *The Matrix*. Audi recently promoted its R8 sports car in the movie *Iron Man*: Superhero Tony Stark drives the car, while Gwyneth Paltrow as Virginia "Pepper" Potts drives the Audi S5 sports sedan.[48]

But placing a Pepsi can in a TV show is only one form of branded entertainment. Today advertisers also take a more active role in developing new television programs to showcase their products. For example, TNT and Dodge paired up to produce *Lucky Chance*, a branded miniseries about an undercover Drug Enforcement Agency agent who drives a 2009 Dodge Challenger to transport money to a mob boss.[49]

Beyond movies and television shows, what better way to promote to the video generation than through brand placements in video games? The industry calls this technique **advergaming**. If you are a video game hound, watch for placements of real-life brands such as Ford, Radio Shack, General Motors, Toyota, and Sony embedded in the action of your game. Quiksilver, a clothing manufacturer for extreme-sport participants, now puts its shirts and shorts into video games such as Tony Hawk's *Pro Skater 3*.

advergaming
Brand placements in video games

Where to Say It: Support Media

While marketers (and consumers) normally think of advertising as mass media messages, in reality many of the ads we see today show up in our homes, our workplaces, and in public venues like restroom walls, on signs that trail behind airplanes, or in movies and television programs. **Support media** reach people who may not have been reached by mass media advertising, and these platforms also support the messages traditional media delivers. Here we'll look at some of the more important support media advertisers use.

support media
Media such as directories or out-of-home media that may be used to reach people who are not reached by mass media advertising.

- **Directories**: Directory advertising is the most "down to earth," information-focused advertising medium. In 1883, a printer in Wyoming ran out of white paper while printing part of a telephone book, so he substituted yellow paper instead. Today, the Yellow Pages, including the online Yellow Pages, posts revenues of more than $16 billion in the United States and over $45 billion globally.[50] Often consumers look through directories just before they are ready to buy.

directories
Books that list organizations alphabetically or thematically with contact information.

- **Out-of-home media** includes outdoor advertising (billboards and signs), transit advertising (signs placed inside and/or outside buses, taxis, trains, train stations, and airports) and other types of messages that reach people in public places. In recent years, outdoor advertising has pushed the technology envelope with **digital signage** that enables the source to change the message at will. In a first for out-of-home media, CBS Outdoor installed a high-definition 3D projection display in New York's Grand Central Terminal, where 70 000 commuters a day were able to view 3D commercials (yes, with 3D glasses) for Visa.[51] Of course, many consumers dislike out-of-home media, especially outdoor advertising, because they feel it is unattractive.

out-of-home media
Communication media that reach people in public places.

digital signage
Out-of-home media that use digital technology to change the message at will.

- **Place-based media** like the "airport channel" transmit messages to "captive" audiences in public places, such as doctors' offices and airport waiting areas. Place-based video screens are now in thousands of shops, offices, and health clubs across the country including stores like Canadian Tire, Best Buy, Metro, Foot Locker, and Target. The Walmart TV Network has more than 125 000 screens in 2850 Walmart stores, and patients who wait in over 10 800 doctors' offices watch medical programming and ads. NBC Universal has its shows on screens installed in office building elevators and on United Airlines flights.[52]

place-based media
Advertising media that transmit messages in public places, such as doctors' offices and airports, where certain types of people congregate.

- And now, some retailers can even follow you around the store to deliver more up-close and personal messages: *RFID* technology (radio frequency identification) uses tiny sensors embedded in packages or store aisles to track customers as they pass. An unsuspecting shopper might hear a beep to remind him that he just passed his family's favourite peanut butter.[53] You're not paranoid; they really *are* watching you. This is *Minority Report* in real life!

When to Say It: Media Scheduling

After she chooses the advertising media, the planner then creates a **media schedule** that specifies the exact media the campaign will use as well as when and how often the message should appear. Figure 11.4 shows a hypothetical media schedule for the promotion of a new

media schedule
The plan that specifies the exact medium to use and when to use them.

Figure 11.4 Media Schedule of a Video Game

Media planning includes decisions on where, when, and how much advertising to do. A media schedule such as this one for a video game shows the plan visually.

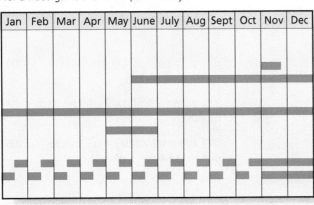

video game. Note that much of the advertising reaches its target audience in the months just before Christmas, and that much of the expensive television budget focuses on advertising during specials just prior to the holiday season.

The media schedule outlines the planner's best estimate of which media will be most effective to attain the advertising objective(s) and which specific media vehicles will do the most effective job. The media planner considers qualitative factors such as the match between the demographic and psychographic profile of a target audience and the people a media vehicle reaches, the advertising patterns of competitors, and the capability of a medium to adequately convey the desired information. The planner must also consider factors such as the compatibility of the product with editorial content. For example, viewers might not respond well to a lighthearted ad for a new snack food during a sombre documentary on world hunger.

There are also a number of quantitative factors, which the media planner uses to develop the media schedule. **Reach** is the percentage of the target market that will be exposed to the media vehicle at least once during a given period of time, usually four weeks. For example, if the target market includes 10 million adults age 18 and over and a specific TV program has an audience that includes 500 000 adults in this age group, the program has a reach of 5. Developing a media plan with high reach is particularly important for widely used products when the message needs to get to as many consumers as possible.

Frequency is the average number of times that an individual or a household will be exposed to the message. Note that this is the *average*. For example, while some members of a target market may be exposed to an ad 2 or 4 or 20 times and others see an ad only once, the average and thus the frequency might be 4. High levels of frequency are important for products that are complex or those that are targeted to relatively small markets for which multiple exposures to the message are necessary to make an impact.

Gross rating points (GRPs) are a measure of the quantity of media included in the media plan. Just as we talk about buying 50 litres of gas or 500 g of coffee, media planners talk about a media schedule that includes the purchase of 250 gross rating points of radio and 700 GRPs of TV. We calculate gross rating points by multiplying a media vehicle's rating by the number of planned ad insertions. As we see in Table 11.2, if 30 percent of a target audience watches *American Idol* and you place eight ads on the show, you buy 240 GRPs of that show.

reach
The percentage of the target market that will be exposed to the media vehicle.

frequency
The average number of times a person in the target group will be exposed to the message.

gross rating points (GRPs)
A measure used for comparing the effectiveness of different media vehicles: average reach × frequency.

Table 11.2	A (Hypothetical) Media Schedule

Media Vehicle	Rating (Percentage of Target Audience Reached)	Number of Ad Insertions During the Period	GRPs (Rating × Number of Insertions)
Hockey Night in Canada	30	8 (2 ads on each week's show for 4 weeks)	240 GRPs
The National CBC news	10	40 (2 ads each weeknight for 4 weeks)	400
Canada AM	20	40 (2 ads each weekday morning for 4 weeks)	800
Maclean's magazine	20	4 (1 ad in each of 4 editions during the 4-week period)	80
Canadian Business magazine	12	2 (1 ad in each of the 2 editions each month)	24
The National Post newspaper	7	8 (1 ad each Monday and Thursday during the 4-week period)	56
Total GRPs			1600

Although some media vehicles deliver more of your target audience, they may not be cost efficient. More people will see a commercial aired during the Super Bowl than during a 3:00 AM rerun of a *Gremlins* movie. But the advertiser could run late-night commercials every night for a year for the cost of one 30-second Super Bowl spot. To compare the relative cost effectiveness of different media and of spots run on different vehicles in the same medium, media planners use a measure they call **cost per thousand (CPM).** This figure reflects the cost to deliver a message to 1000 people.

Assume that the cost of each 30-second commercial on *Hockey Night in Canada* is $400 000 but the number of target audience members the show reaches is 20 million, or 20 000 × 1000. The CPM of *Hockey Night in Canada* is $400 000/20 000 = $20 CPM. Compare this to the cost of advertising in *Fortune* magazine: A full-page, 4-colour ad costs approximately $115 000 and the readership includes approximately 2 million members of our target audience. The cost per thousand for *Fortune* is $115 000/2000 = $57.50. Thus, *Hockey Night in Canada*, while having a much higher total cost, actually is a more efficient buy.

cost per thousand (CPM)
A measure used to compare the relative cost effectiveness of different media vehicles that have different exposure rates; the cost to deliver a message to 1000 people or homes.

Media Scheduling: How Often to Say It

After she decides where and when to advertise, the planner must decide how often she wants to send the message. What time of day? And what overall pattern will the advertising follow?

A *continuous schedule* maintains a steady stream of advertising throughout the year. This is most appropriate for products that we buy on a regular basis, such as shampoo or bread. The American Association of Advertising Agencies, an industry trade group, maintains that continuous advertising sustains market leadership even if total industry sales fall.[54] On the downside, some messages can suffer from advertising wear-out, because people tune out the same old ad messages.

A *pulsing schedule* varies the amount of advertising throughout the year, based on when the product is likely to be in demand. A suntan lotion might advertise year-round but more heavily during the summer months. *Flighting* is an extreme form of pulsing, in which advertising appears in short, intense bursts alternating with periods of little to no activity. It can produce as much brand awareness as a steady dose of advertising at a much lower cost, if consumers noticed the messages from the previous flight and these made an impact.

Step 6: Evaluate the Advertising

John Wanamaker, a famous Philadelphia retailer, once complained, "I am certain that half the money I spend on advertising is completely wasted. The trouble is, I don't know which half."[55] Now that we've seen how advertising is created and executed, let's step back and see how we decide if it's working.

There's no doubt that a lot of advertising is ineffective. Ironically, as marketers try harder and harder to reach their customers, these efforts can backfire. Many consumers have a love-hate relationship with advertising. Over half the respondents in a survey said they "avoid buying products that overwhelm them with advertising and marketing," and 60 percent said their opinion of advertising "is much more negative than just a few years ago."[56] With so many messages competing for the attention of frazzled customers, it's especially important for firms to evaluate their efforts to increase the impact of their messages. How can they do that?

Posttesting means conducting research on consumers' responses to advertising messages they have seen or heard (as opposed to *pretesting*, which as we've seen collects reactions to messages *before* they're actually placed in "the real world"). Ironically, many creative ads that are quirky or even bizarre make an advertising agency look good within the industry (and on the résumé of the art director) but are ultimately unsuccessful, because they don't communicate what the company needs to say about the product itself. We may remember that weird ad but have no idea what product it advertised.

posttesting
Research conducted on consumers' responses to actual advertising messages they have seen or heard.

unaided recall

A research technique conducted by telephone survey or personal interview that asks whether a person remembers seeing an ad during a specified period without giving the person the name of the brand.

aided recall

A research technique that uses clues to prompt answers from people about advertisements they might have seen.

attitudinal measures

A research technique that probes a consumer's beliefs or feelings about a product before and after being exposed to messages about it.

Three ways to measure the impact of an advertisement are *unaided recall, aided recall,* and *attitudinal measures*:

1. **Unaided recall** tests by telephone survey or personal interview whether a person remembers seeing an ad during a specified period without giving the person the name of the brand.

2. An **aided recall** test uses the name of the brand and sometimes other clues to prompt answers. For example, a researcher might show a group of consumers a list of brands and ask them to choose which items they have seen advertised within the past week.

3. **Attitudinal measures** probe a bit more deeply by testing consumers' beliefs or feelings about a product before and after they are exposed to messages about it. If, for example, Pepsi's messages about "freshness dating" make enough consumers believe that the freshness of soft drinks is important, marketers can consider the advertising campaign successful.

public relations (PR)

Communication function that seeks to build good relationships with an organization's publics, including consumers, stockholders, and legislators.

3

OBJECTIVE

Explain the role of public relations and the steps in developing a public relations campaign. (pp. 410–416)

Public Relations

Public relations (PR) is the communication function that seeks to build good relationships with an organization's *publics*; these include consumers, stockholders, legislators, and other stakeholders in the organization. Today marketers use PR activities to influence the attitudes and perceptions of various groups not only toward companies and brands but also toward politicians, celebrities, and not-for-profit organizations.

The basic rule of good PR is, *do something good, and then talk about it.* A company's efforts to get in the limelight—and stay there—can range from humanitarian acts to sponsoring band tours. The big advantage of this kind of communication is that when PR messages are placed successfully, they are more credible than if the same information appeared in a paid advertisement. As one marketing executive observed, "There's a big difference between hearing about a product from a pitchman or from your trusted local anchorman."[57]

Public relations strategies are crucial to an organization's ability to establish and maintain a favourable image. *Proactive PR* activities stem from the company's marketing objectives. For example, marketers create and manage **publicity**, unpaid communication about an organization that gets media exposure. It's interesting to note that this aspect of PR is blending into other promotional strategies as social media continue to mushroom. Essentially, buzz marketing is also one form of public relations because it tries to motivate consumers to talk up a brand or service to one another (ideally for free).

As many of the other functions of public relations blend into buzz marketing activities, perhaps the most important function it still "owns" is **crisis management**. This refers to the process of managing a company's reputation when some negative and often unplanned event threatens the organization's image. Think about the unfortunate BP executives, for example, who had to communicate to the public as the explosion of an oil rig in the Gulf of Mexico took the shape of an epic environmental disaster, or those who had to reassure a formerly loyal Toyota customer base that faulty accelerator pedals would not in fact cause their cars to speed out of control.

The goal in such situations is to manage the flow of information to address concerns so that consumers don't panic and distributors don't abandon the product. Although some organizations don't seem to learn this lesson, typically, the best strategy is to be honest about the problem and to quickly take responsibility for correcting it. For example, a few years ago PepsiCo was rocked by claims that consumers had found hypodermic needles in Diet Pepsi cans. The company assembled a crisis team to map out a response and supplied

publicity

Unpaid communication about an organization that appears in the mass media.

crisis management

The process of managing a company's reputation when some negative event threatens the organization's image.

video footage of its bottling process to show that it was impossible for foreign objects to find their way into cans before they were sealed at the factory. The claims proved false, and PepsiCo ran follow-up ads reinforcing the findings. Pepsi's calm, coordinated response averted a PR disaster.

Even a single negative event can cause permanent damage to a company, the success of its products, and its stockholder equity. While it didn't have the magnitude of a massive oil spill such as the one BP confronted, Wendy's was faced with a similar public image disaster when a customer said she found a finger in a bowl of its chili.[58] The woman and her husband were both sent to prison after investigators discovered that he had actually obtained the finger from a coworker who had lost it in a workplace accident. While the claim proved false, it still cost the company $2.5 million in lost sales.[59] In another incident, a man stuffed a dead mouse in a Taco Bell burrito in an attempt to extort money from the fast-food chain. Supersize that![60]

Public relations professionals know that when a firm handles a crisis well, it can minimize damage and help the company make things right. Thus, a vitally important role of PR is to prepare a *crisis-management plan*. This is a document that details what an organization will do *if* a crisis occurs: who will be the spokesperson for the organization, how the organization will deal with the press, and what sort of messages it will deliver to the press and the public.

Plan a Public Relations Campaign

A **public relations campaign** is a coordinated effort to communicate with one or more of the firm's publics. This is a three-step process that develops, executes, and evaluates PR objectives. Let's review each step and then we'll examine some of the more frequently used objectives and tactics shown in Figure 11.5.

Like an advertising campaign, the organization must first *develop* clear objectives for the PR program that define the message it wants people to hear. For example the International Apple Institute, a trade group devoted to increasing the consumption of apples, had to decide if a campaign should focus on getting consumers to cook more with apples, drink more apple juice, or simply to buy more fresh fruit. Because fresh apples brought a substantially higher price per pound to growers than apples used for applesauce or apple juice, the group decided to push the fresh fruit angle. It used the theme "An apple a day..." (sound familiar?) as it mounted a focused campaign to encourage people to eat more apples by placing articles in consumer media extolling the fruit's health benefits.

public relations campaign
A coordinated effort to communicate with one or more of the firm's publics.

Figure 11.5 Objectives and Tactics of Public Relations
Successful PR campaigns include clearly defined objectives and the use of the right PR activities.

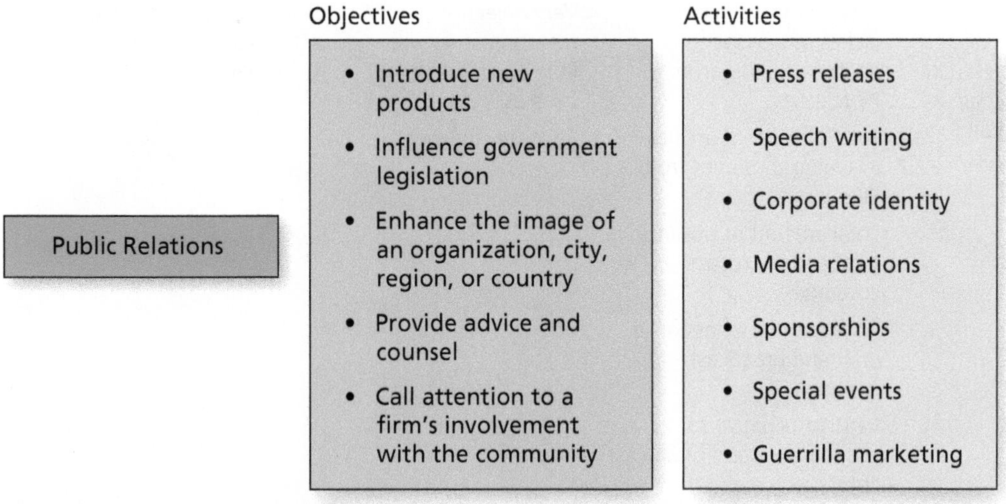

Public Relations	Objectives	Activities
	• Introduce new products	• Press releases
	• Influence government legislation	• Speech writing
	• Enhance the image of an organization, city, region, or country	• Corporate identity
	• Provide advice and counsel	• Media relations
	• Call attention to a firm's involvement with the community	• Sponsorships
		• Special events
		• Guerrilla marketing

Execution of the campaign means deciding precisely how to communicate the message to the targeted public(s). An organization can get out its positive messages in many ways: news conferences, sponsorship of charity events, and other attention-getting promotions.

One of the barriers to greater reliance on PR campaigns is *evaluation*; compared to many other forms of marketing communications, it's difficult to devise metrics to gauge their effectiveness. Who can say precisely what impact an appearance by Steve Carell on *The Tonight Show* to plug his new movie will exert on ticket sales, or whether Virgin's sponsorship of the London Marathon boosted purchases of airline tickets? It is possible to tell if a PR campaign gets media exposure, though compared to advertising it's much more difficult to assess bottom-line impact. Table 11.3 describes some of the most common PR measurement techniques.

Table 11.3	Measuring the Effectiveness of Public Relations (PR) Tactics			
Method	**Description**	**Example**	**Pros**	**Cons**
Personal (subjective) evaluation of PR activities.	Evaluation of PR activities by superiors may occur at all levels of the organization.	Items in employee annual reviews relate to the successful fulfillment of PR role.	Simple and inexpensive to complete; ensures an annual assessment will be completed.	Subjective nature of the evaluation may result in biased appraisal. Employees may focus on the annual review to the exclusion of some important PR goals.
Matching of PR activity accomplishments with activity objectives.	Simple counts of actual PR activities accomplished compared with activity goals set for the period.	Goal: to achieve publication of three feature articles in major newspapers in the first quarter of the year. Result: four articles published.	Focuses attention on the need for quantitative goals for PR activities and achievements. Easy and inexpensive to measure.	Focuses on activity goals rather than image or communication goals. Ignores image perception or attitudes of the firm's publics.
Evaluation of communication objectives through opinion surveys among the firm's publics.	Surveys are used to determine if image/communication goals are met within key groups.	Goal: to achieve an improved image of the organization among at least 30 percent of financial community stakeholders.	Causes PR professionals to focus on actual communication results of activities.	May be difficult to measure changes in perceptions among the firm's publics. Factors not under the control of PR practitioners may influence public perceptions. It is relatively expensive. Results may take many months, thus delaying corrective actions.
Measurement of coverage in print and broadcast media, especially those generated by PR activities in PR activities.	Systematic measurement of coverage achieved in print media (column inches/pages) and broadcast media (minutes of air time).	Total number of column inches of newspaper articles resulting from PR releases. Total number of articles including those not from PR releases. Total amount of positive print and broadcast coverage. Total amount of negative print and broadcast coverage. Ratio of negative to positive print and broadcast coverage.	Very objective measurements with little opportunity for bias. Relatively inexpensive.	Does not address perceptions, attitudes, or image issues of the organization.

| Impression measurement. | Measure the size of the audience for all print and broadcast coverage. Often assessment includes comparisons in terms of advertising costs for same number of impressions. | Network news coverage during the time period equalled over 15 million gross impressions. This number of impressions through advertising would have cost $4 500 000. | Objective, without any potential bias in measurement. Provides a monetary measure to justify the expenditures of the PR office or consultant. Relatively inexpensive. | Does not differentiate between negative and positive news coverage. Does not consider responses of publics to the coverage. Assumes advertising and PR communication activities are equal. |

Public Relations Objectives

Marketing communication experts know that PR strategies are best used in concert with advertising, sales promotion, and personal selling to send a consistent message to customers and other stakeholders. As part of the total marketing communication plan, they often rely on PR to accomplish the following objectives:

- *Introduce new products to retailers and consumers.* To make the most of the introduction of the iPad in January 2010, Apple staged a live press conference hosted by CEO Steve Jobs in his trademark blue jeans and black turtleneck.[61]

- *Influence government legislation.* Airplane maker Boeing spent over a decade in public relations activities to persuade regulators that jetliners with two engines are as safe as those with three or four engines even for nonstop international flights, some as long as 16 hours.[62]

- *Enhance the image of an organization.* The Ladies Professional Golf Association (LPGA) used a variety of public relations and other promotion activities, from product endorsements to player blogs to sexy calendars, in its "These Girls Rock" campaign. The program to change the image of ladies' golf to a hip sport seems to be working, as both tournament attendance and television audiences have increased.[63]

- *Provide advice and counsel.* Because of their expertise and understanding of the effects of communication on public opinion, PR professionals also provide advice and counsel for top management. When a firm needs to shut down a plant or to build a new one, to discontinue a product or add to the product line, to fire a vice president, or to give an award to an employee who spends hundreds of hours a year doing volunteer work in his community, it needs the advice of its PR staff. What is the best way to handle the situation? How should the announcement be made? Who should be told first? What is to be said and how?

- *Enhance the image of a city, region, or country.* To promote Vancouver, British Columbia, and Canada around the world, the not-for-profit business organization Tourism Vancouver used a large variety of PR activities to make the most of the Winter Olympics in Vancouver in 2010.[64]

- *Manage a crisis.* PR specialists handle the crucial but often difficult task of communicating with stakeholders when something goes wrong, such as when BP is involved in a massive oil spill or Toyota issues a massive recall of cars with faulty accelerator pedals. Organizations respond in many ways, ranging from (unfortunately) complete denial or silence to full disclosure. For example, when Toyota started to receive reports of unsafe cars in the UK, the director of the car maker's operations there posted a five-minute video apologizing to consumers.[65]

- *Call attention to a firm's involvement with the community.* US marketers spend about $15 billion a year to sponsor sporting events, rock concerts, museum exhibits, and the ballet. PR specialists work behind the scenes to ensure that sponsored events receive ample press coverage and exposure. We'll talk more about sponsorships later in this section.

Next, the PR specialists must develop a campaign strategy that includes the following:

- A situation analysis

- A statement of objectives

- Specification of target audiences (publics), messages to be communicated, and specific program elements to be used

- A timetable and budget

- Discussion of how to evaluate the program

Public Relations Tactics

In order to accomplish their objectives, PR professionals choose from a variety of tactics as shown in Figure 11.5. These activities include press releases, speech writing and corporate communications, sponsorships and special events, and guerilla marketing activities.

Marketing Metrics

Share of Voice

In the age of social media, share of voice (SOV) has gone beyond simply collecting and counting the number of clips or mentions that a brand or company gets due to PR. Now, according to Molly McWhinnie of Communiqué PR, it's about analyzing the sentiment value of not only clients, but competitors as well. She offers some best practices when analyzing share of voice:

- **Identify your top competitors**. We recommend selecting two or three top competitors in the industry that closely match your core business offerings. If you select more than this, or competitors who have a broader scope of services, your share of voice will be smaller as a result and much more difficult to monitor long term.

- **Identify the key messages**. Presuming your company has developed effective key messages, measuring how often these messages percolate through your media coverage should be easy to quantify. If they are not being picked up, it is an indicator that either they are not resonating with media or perhaps the spokesperson may need a refresher on media training.

- **Determine values for tone and types of coverage**. Creating consistent values for measurement of tone are key to understanding sentiment. For instance, did the article position your company positively or negatively? It is also important to assign values to consistently rank the types of coverage. As an example, consider that a feature story will have more weight, especially if a third-party influencer is included in the coverage, as compared to a re-posting of a press release. However, do not discount the value of re-posts of a press release as it can help to increase your search engine optimization.

- **Determine your share of discussion**. Finally, if the coverage features both you and a direct competitor, examine how much of the story focuses on your company and/or quotes from your company executive. If your competitor receives more air time, examine if it is because the piece is a sponsored post or perhaps a suggested topic your competitor presented to the reporter, a detail your PR partner may be able to identify when evaluating the media opportunity beforehand.[66]

Press Release

press release
Information that an organization distributes to the media intended to win publicity.

The most common way for PR specialists to communicate is by a **press release**. This is a report of some event or activity that an organization writes and sends to the media in the hope that it will be published for free. A newer version of this idea is a *video news release (VNR)* that tells the story in a film format instead. Some of the most common types of press releases include the following:

- *Timely topics* deal with topics in the news, such as Levi Strauss's efforts to promote "Casual Fridays" to boost sales of its Dockers and Slates casual dress pants by highlighting how different corporations around the country are adopting a relaxed dress code.

- *Research project stories* are published by universities to highlight breakthroughs by faculty researchers.

- *Consumer information releases* provide information to help consumers make product decisions, such as helpful tips from Butterball about how to prepare dishes for Thanksgiving dinner.

Speech Writing and Corporate Communications

An important job of a firm's PR department is **speech writing**; specialists provide speeches for company executives to deliver. While some executives do actually write their own speeches, it is more common for a speechwriter on the PR staff to develop an initial draft of a speech to which the executive might add his or her own input. PR specialists also provide input on **corporate identity** materials—such as logos, brochures, building design, and even stationery—that communicates a positive image for the firm.

One of the tasks of the PR professional is to develop close **media relations** to ensure the organization will receive the best media exposure possible for positive news, such as publicizing the achievements of an employee who has done some notable charity work or for a product the company developed that saved someone's life. And, as we've seen, good media relations can be even more important when things go wrong. News editors are less inclined to present a story of a crisis in its most negative way if they have a good relationship with PR people in the organization.

Sponsorships and Special Events

Sponsorships are PR activities through which companies provide financial support to help fund an event in return for publicized recognition of the company's contribution (see Exhibit 11.7). Many companies today find that their promotion dollars are well spent to sponsor a golf tournament, a NASCAR driver, a symphony concert, or global events such as the Olympics or World Cup soccer competition. These sponsorships are particularly effective because they allow marketers to reach customers during their leisure time; people often appreciate these efforts because the financial support makes the events possible in the first place.

A related task is to plan and implement **special events**. Companies find special events useful for a variety of purposes. For example, a firm might hold a press conference to increase interest and excitement in a new product or other company activity. A city or province may hold an annual event such as Montreal's Festival International de Jazz de Montreal, or "Jazzfest" as it has come to be known, or Vancouver's VISAFF Vancouver International South Asian Film Festival to promote tourism. A company outing like the huge road rallies Harley-Davidson's Harley Owner's Group (H.O.G.) sponsors reinforces loyalty toward an existing product. Other special events aim simply to create buzz and generate publicity. For New York City shoppers, Unilever created its "All Small & Mighty Clothes Bus," a 40-foot bus it covered in all the shirts, shorts, and socks that one bottle of super-concentrated All laundry detergent can wash. Consumers who spotted the bus during its 12-day campaign could "clean up" if they entered a sweepstakes to win a $5000 shopping spree or $200 gift cards.

Guerilla Marketing

Organizations with tiny advertising budgets need to develop innovative—and cheap—ways to capture consumers' attention. **Guerrilla marketing** activities are an

speech writing
Writing a speech on a topic for a company executive to deliver.

corporate identity
Materials such as logos, brochures, building design, and stationery that communicate an image of the organization.

media relations
A PR activity aimed at developing close relationships with the media.

sponsorships
PR activities through which companies provide financial support to help fund an event in return for publicized recognition of the company's contribution.

special events
Activities—from a visit by foreign investors to a company picnic—that are planned and implemented by a PR department.

guerrilla marketing
Marketing activity in which a firm "ambushes" consumers with promotional content in places they are not expecting to encounter this kind of activity.

Exhibit 11.7

McDonald's, a sponsor of the FIFA World Cup since 1994, built on its sponsorship of the FIFA World Cup South Africa to create promotions in its restaurants around the world. In Brazil, McDonald's restaurants offered customers sandwiches with flavours from countries competing in the World Cup. World Cup beverage cups were available for customers in some countries, including China and the United States, and some locations in Europe ran a "Feed The Passion" promotion featuring a series of special offers including "Fan Meals." The McDonald's Player Escort Program is a global program that sends 1,408 children ages 6 to 10 to the World Cup where they escort players onto the field for the start of all 64 FIFA matches.[67]

increasingly popular way to accomplish this objective. No, this term doesn't refer to marketers making monkeys out of themselves (that's "gorilla marketing"). A guerrilla marketing strategy involves "ambushing" consumers with promotional content in places where they don't expect to encounter these.

Today, big companies buy into guerrilla marketing strategies, big time. Burger King recently decided to increase sales in its Asia-Pacific stores by 25 percent.[68] The company sent CDs with quirky marketing suggestions to local restaurant managers. These included putting "I♥BK" on T-shirts and placing the shirts on Ronald McDonald, placing large footprints from McDonald's stores to Burger King outlets, placing signs on empty benches saying "gone to BK—Ronald," and placing large signs at BK locations that are near KFC locations that read, "It's why the chicken crossed the road."

Companies use guerrilla marketing to promote new drinks, cars, clothing styles, or even computer systems. Much to the annoyance of city officials in San Francisco and Chicago, IBM painted hundreds of "Peace Love Linux" logos on sidewalks to publicize the company's adoption of the Linux operating system. Even though the company got hit with a hefty bill to pay for cleaning up the "corporate graffiti," one marketing journalist noted that they "got the publicity they were looking for."[69] Given the success of many of these campaigns that operate on a shoestring budget, expect to see even more of these tactics as other companies climb on the guerrilla bandwagon.

4 Sales Promotion

OBJECTIVE

Explain what sales promotion is, and describe the different types of consumer sales promotion activities.

(pp. 416–419)

sales promotion
Programs designed to build interest in or encourage purchase of a product during a specified period.

When you walk through your student union on campus you might get assaulted by a parade of people eager for you to enter a contest, taste a new candy bar, or take home a free T-shirt with a local bank's name on it. These are examples of **sales promotion**, programs that marketers design to build interest in or encourage purchase of a good or service during a specified period.[70]

How does sales promotion differ from advertising? Both are paid messages from identifiable sponsors to change consumer behaviour or attitudes. In some cases, a traditional advertising medium actually publicizes the sales promotion, as when Denny's restaurant used Super Bowl advertising to tell consumers about its free breakfast offer. But while marketers carefully craft advertising campaigns to create long-term positive feelings about a brand, company, or store, sales promotions are more useful if the firm has an *immediate* objective, such as bolstering sales for a brand quickly or encouraging consumers to try a new product.

Marketers today place an increasing amount of their total marketing communication budget into sales promotion. Several reasons account for this increase. First, due to the growth of very large grocery store chains and mass merchandisers such as Walmart, there has been a shift in power in the channels. These large chains can pressure manufacturers to provide deals and discounts. A second reason for the growth in sales promotion is declining consumer brand loyalty. This means that consumers are more likely to purchase products based on cost, value, or convenience. Thus, a special sales promotion offer is more likely to cause price-conscious customers to switch brands.

Marketers target sales promotion activities either to ultimate consumers or to members of the channel, such as retailers that sell their products. Thus, we divide sales promotion into two major categories: consumer-oriented sales promotion and trade-oriented sales promotion. You'll see some examples of common consumer-oriented sales promotions in Table 11.4.

Sales Promotion Directed toward Consumers

As we said, one of the reasons for an increase in sales promotion is because it works. For consumer sales promotion, the major reason for this is that most promotions temporarily

Table 11.4	Consumer Sales Promotion Techniques: A Sampler	
Technique	Description	Example
Coupons: newspaper, magazine, in-the-mail, on product packages, in-store, and on the Internet	Certificates for money off on selected products, often with an expiration date, are used to encourage product trial.	Crest offers $5 off its WhiteStrips.
Price-off packs	Specially marked packages offer a product at a discounted price.	Tide laundry detergent is offered in a specially marked box for 50 cents off.
Rebates/refunds	Purchasers receive a cash reimbursement when they submit proofs of purchase.	Uniroyal offers a $60 mail-in rebate for purchasers of four new Tiger Paw tires.
Continuity/loyalty programs	Consumers are rewarded for repeat purchases through points that lead to reduced price or free merchandise.	Airlines offer frequent fliers free flights for accumulated points; a carwash offers consumers a half-price wash after purchasing 10 washes.
Special/bonus packs	Additional amount of the product is given away with purchase; it rewards users.	HP provides a bonus cartridge pack with the purchase of a particular model of printer.
Contests/sweepstakes	Offers consumers the chance to win cash or merchandise. Sweepstakes winners are determined strictly by chance. Contests require some competitive activity such as a game of skill.	Publisher's Clearing House announces its zillionth sweepstakes.
Premiums: free premiums include in-pack, on-pack, near-pack, or in-the-mail premiums; consumers pay for self-liquidating premiums	A consumer gets a free gift or low-cost item when a product is bought; reinforces product image and rewards users.	A free makeup kit comes with the purchase of $20 worth of Clinique products.
Samples: delivered by direct mail, in newspapers and magazines door-to-door, on or in product packages, and in-store	Delivering an actual or trial-sized product to consumers in order to generate trial usage of a new product.	A free small bottle of Clairol Herbal Essences shampoo arrives in the mail.

change the price–value relationships. A coupon for 50 cents off the price of a bottle of ketchup reduces the price while a special "25 percent more" jar of peanuts increases the value. And if you get a free hairbrush when you buy a bottle of shampoo, this also increases the value. Even the prize in the bottom of the box of cereal increases its value exponentially as every mother (unfortunately) knows. As shown in Figure 11.6, we generally classify consumer sales promotions as either price-based or attention-getting promotions.

Price-Based Consumer Sales Promotion

Many sales promotions target consumers where they live—their wallets. They emphasize *short-term price reductions or rebates* that encourage people to choose a brand—at least during the deal period. Price-based consumer promotions, however, have a downside similar to trade promotions that involve a price break. If a company uses them too frequently, this "trains" its customers to purchase the product at only the lower promotional price. Price-based consumer sales promotion includes the following:

- *Coupons:* Try to pick up any Thursday newspaper without spilling some coupons. These certificates, redeemable for money off a purchase, are the most common price promotion. Indeed, they are the most popular form of sales promotion overall. Companies distribute billions of them annually in newspapers, magazines, in the mail, in stores, by e-mail, and through the Internet. One company, ValPak, has created an entire

Figure 11.6 Types of Consumer Sales Promotions

Consumer sales promotions are generally classified as price-based or attention-getting promotions.

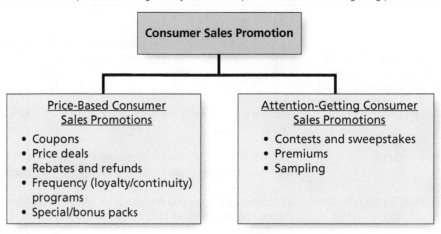

Consumer Sales Promotion

Price-Based Consumer Sales Promotions
- Coupons
- Price deals
- Rebates and refunds
- Frequency (loyalty/continuity) programs
- Special/bonus packs

Attention-Getting Consumer Sales Promotions
- Contests and sweepstakes
- Premiums
- Sampling

business around coupons. You've probably received a ValPak envelope in the mail—it's the one with dozens of coupons and other offers inside. Even industries such as pharmaceuticals that never tried this approach before now use it in a big way. This industry mails coupons that customers can redeem for free initial supplies of drugs. Coupons are also available through sites such as Viagra.com and Purplepill.com. Companies use the coupons to prompt patients to ask their physician for the specific brand instead of a competing brand or a more economical generic version.[71]

rebates

Sales promotions that allow the customer to recover part of the product's cost from the manufacturer.

frequency programs

Consumer sales promotion programs that offer a discount or free product for multiple purchases over time; also referred to as loyalty or continuity programs.

- *Price deals, refunds, and rebates*: In addition to coupons, manufacturers often offer a temporary price reduction to stimulate sales. This price deal may be printed on the package itself, or it may be a price-off flag or banner on the store shelf. Alternatively, companies may offer **rebates** that allow the consumer to recover part of the purchase price via mail-ins to the manufacturer. Today, many retailers such as Best Buy print the rebate form for you along with your sales receipt. After you mail it in, you can track whether the cheque has been sent to you by visiting the retailer's Web site.

- *Frequency (loyalty/continuity) programs*: **Frequency programs**, also called *loyalty or continuity programs,* offer a consumer a discount or a free product for multiple purchases over time. Mike Gunn, former vice president of marketing at American Airlines, is widely credited with developing this concept in the early 1980s when he coined the phrase "frequent flyer" miles. Of course, all the other airlines were quick to follow suit, as were a host of other firms, including retailers, auto rental companies, hotels, restaurants—you name it, and they have a customer loyalty program. Virgin Atlantic has gone one step farther with its frequent flyer program, allowing Virgin Atlantic Flying Club members the chance to redeem miles for a trip to outer space—only 2 million miles required![72] La Croissanterie, a French-style fast-food chain in Paris, offers an enhanced customer loyalty program that allows customers to identify themselves with a paper pass, a smartphone application, or their public transportation pass—no problem if you happen to leave the loyalty card at home.[73]

Exhibit 11.8

Marketers are constantly finding ways to attract some attention. Mobile billboards, hitting the streets of major cities like Montréal, Toronto, and Vancouver, represent a high-impact advertising strategy.

- *Special/bonus packs*: Another form of price promotion involves giving the shopper more product instead of lowering the price.[74] How nice to go to a Shoppers Drug Mart and find a 300 mL bottle of Nivea lotion packaged with another 50 mL for free! A special pack also can be in the form of a unique package such as a reusable decorator dispenser for hand soap.

Exhibit 11.9
Ben & Jerry's uses a game as part of its campaign to combat global warming.

Attention-Getting Consumer Sales Promotions

Attention-getting consumer promotions stimulate interest in a company's products (See Exhibit 11.8.). Some typical types of attention-getting promotions include the following:

- *Contests and sweepstakes*: According to their legal definitions, a contest is a test of skill, while a sweepstakes is based on chance.

- Ben & Jerry's, famous for ice cream flavours such as Chunky Monkey and Phish Food, launched a contest for consumers to create an original-flavour ice cream. Consumers enter the "Do Us a Flavour" contest by submitting their flavour name and description through Ben & Jerry's Web site.[75] See Exhibit 11.9.

- As part of the kickoff of Disney's global marketing campaign themed "Where Dreams Come True," Disney offered consumers an online "Keys to the Magic Kingdom" sweepstakes. The winning family received a trip to Walt Disney World Resort and a day at the Magic Kingdom.[76]

- Oreo included consumers as not only the contestants, but also the judges in its "Oreo & Milk Jingle" contest. The top five contestants' renditions of the Oreo song were posted on the Oreo.com Web site. Consumers entered part of an Oreo package UPC to vote for their favourite; the winner received $10 000 and a recording session for an Oreo radio spot and a trip to Los Angeles to visit with *American Idol* judge Randy Jackson.[77]

- *Premiums*: **Premiums** are items you get free when you buy a product. The prize in the bottom of the box of cereal—the reason many students open the box from the bottom—is a premium. Prepaid phone cards have become highly popular premiums. Companies that jump on the phone card bandwagon offer cards emblazoned with pictures of sports heroes, products, and rock bands. Phone cards make ideal premiums because they are compact, they can display brand logos or attractive graphics, and they provide opportunities for repeat exposure. And an important benefit for the marketer is the ability to build databases by tracking card usage.[78] Your "good neighbour" State Farm agent used to send you a calendar on your birthday—now you're likely to get a phone card with 30 long-distance minutes on it, adorned with a reminder of your agent's phone number to be sure you won't forget who sent it to you.

premiums
Items offered free to people who have purchased a product.

- *Sampling*: How many starving students haven't, at one time or another, managed to scrape together an entire meal by scooping up free food samples at their local grocery store or Costco? **Product sampling** encourages people to try a product by distributing trial-size and sometimes regular-size versions in stores, in public places such as student unions, or through the mail. Many marketers now distribute free samples through sites on the Internet.[79] Companies like Procter & Gamble, Unilever, S.C. Johnson, and GlaxoSmithKline are readily taking advantage of Web sites such as www.freesamples.com and www.startsampling.com that distribute the firms' samples and then follow up with consumer-satisfaction surveys.

product sampling
Distributing free trial-size versions of a product to consumers.

5 OBJECTIVE
Identify the sales promotion elements that are aimed at other channel members rather than at consumers.
(pp. 420–422)

Sales Promotions Directed toward the Trade

In the previous section, you learned about a variety of sales promotion techniques aimed directly at consumers. Now, we turn our attention to a different type of approach to sales promotion in which the consumer is decidedly *not* the primary target. Here, the target is the B2B customer—located somewhere within the supply chain. Such entities are traditionally referred to as "the trade." Hence, **trade promotions** focus on members of the supply chain, which include distribution channel members, such as retail salespeople or wholesale distributors with whom a firm must work to sell its products.

Trade promotions take one of two forms: (1) those designed as discounts and deals, and (2) those designed to increase industry visibility. Let's take a look at both types of trade promotions in more detail. To help you follow along, Figure 11.7 portrays several of the most important types of trade sales promotion approaches, and Table 11.5 provides more details about each approach. You will note that some of the techniques, although primarily targeted to the trade, also appeal to consumers.

Discount Promotions

Discount promotions (deals) reduce the cost of the product to the distributor or retailer or help defray its advertising expenses. Firms design these promotions to encourage stores to stock the item and make sure it gets a lot of attention.

Allowances, Discounts, and Deals

One form of trade promotion is a short-term *price break*. A manufacturer can reduce a channel partner's costs with a sales promotion that discounts its products. For example, a manufacturer can offer a **merchandising allowance** to reimburse the retailer for in-store support of a product, such as when a store features an off-shelf display for a brand. Another way in which a manufacturer can reduce a channel partner's cost is with a **case allowance** that provides a discount to the retailer or wholesaler during a set period based on the sales volume of a product the retailer or wholesaler orders from the manufacturer.

However, allowances and deals have a downside. As with all sales promotion activities, the manufacturer expects these to be of limited duration, after which the distribution channel partner will again pay full price for the items. Unfortunately, some channel members engage in a practice the industry calls *forward buying*—they purchase large quantities of the product during a discount period, warehouse them, and don't buy them again until the manufacturer offers another discount. Some large retailers and wholesalers take this to an extreme when they engage in *diverting*. This describes an ethically questionable practice where the retailer buys the product at the discounted promotional price and warehouses it. Then, after the promotion has expired, the retailer sells the hoarded inventory to other retailers at a price that is lower than the manufacturer's non-discounted price but high enough to turn a profit. Obviously, both forward buying and diverting go against the manufacturer's intent in offering the sales promotion.

trade promotions
Promotions that focus on members of "the trade," which include distribution channel members, such as retail salespeople or wholesale distributors, that a firm must work with in order to sell its products.

merchandising allowance
Reimburses the retailer for in-store support of the product.

case allowance
A discount to the retailer or wholesaler based on the volume of product ordered.

Figure 11.7 Trade Sales Promotions
Trade sales promotions come in a variety of forms. Some are designed as discounts and deals for channel members and some are designed to increase industry visibility.

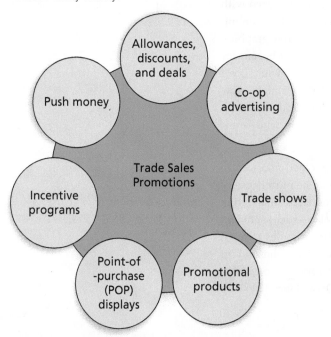

Table 11.5	Characteristics of Trade Sales Promotion Approaches		
Technique	Primary Target	Description	Example
Allowances, discounts, and deals	Trade	Retailers or other organizational customers receive discounts for quantity purchases or for providing special merchandising assistance.	Retailers get a discount for using a special Thanksgiving display unit for Uncle Ben's Stuff 'N Such Harvest Chicken with Vegetables stuffing mix.
Co-op advertising	Trade and consumers	Manufacturers pay part of the cost of advertising by retailers who feature the manufacturer's product in their ads.	Toro pays half of the cost of Alexander's Hardware Store newspaper advertising that features Toro lawn mowers.
Trade shows	Trade	Many manufacturers showcase their products to attendees.	The National Kitchen and Bath Association trade shows allow manufacturers to display their latest wares to owners of kitchen and bath remodelling stores.
Promotional products	Trade and consumers	A company builds awareness and reinforces its image by giving out "premiums" with its name on them.	Molson distributors provide bar owners with highly sought-after "Molson Canadian" neon signs. Caterpillar gives customers caps with the Caterpillar logo.
Point-of-purchase (POP) displays	Trade and consumers	In-store exhibits attract consumers' attention. Many POP displays also serve a merchandising function.	The Beauti-Tone paint display in Home Hardware stores allow consumers to select from over 2700 colours.
Incentive programs	Trade	A prize is offered to employees who meet a pre-specified sales goal or who are top performers during a given period.	Mary Kay cosmetics awards distinctive pink cars to its top-selling representatives.
Push money	Trade	A particular type of incentive program in which salespeople are given a bonus for selling a specific manufacturer's product (also known as a "spiff").	A retail salesperson at a cosmetics counter gets $5 every time she sells a bottle of Glow perfume by JLo.

Co-op Advertising

Another type of trade allowance is **co-op advertising.** These programs offer to pay the retailer a portion, usually 50 percent, of the cost of any advertising that features the manufacturer's product. Co-op advertising is a win–win situation for manufacturers, because most local media vehicles offer lower rates to local businesses than they do to national advertisers. Both the retailer and the manufacturer pay for only part (normally half) of the advertising, plus the manufacturer gets the lower rate. Normally, the amount available to a retailer for co-op advertising is limited to a percentage of the purchases the retailer makes during a year from the manufacturer.

co-op advertising
A sales promotion where the manufacturer and the retailer share the cost.

Sales Promotion Designed to Increase Industry Visibility

Other types of trade sales promotions increase the visibility of a manufacturer's products to channel partners within the industry. Whether it is an elaborate exhibit at a trade show or a coffee mug with the firm's logo that it gives away to channel partners, these aim to keep the company's name topmost when distributors and retailers decide which products to stock and push. These forms of sales promotion include the following:

trade shows
Events at which many companies set up elaborate exhibits to show their products, give away samples, distribute product literature, and troll for new business contacts.

- *Trade shows:* The thousands of industry **trade shows** in Canada and around the world each year are major vehicles for manufacturers to show off their product lines to wholesalers and retailers. Usually, large trade shows are held in big convention centres where many companies set up elaborate exhibits to show their products, give away samples, distribute product literature, and troll for new business contacts. Today we also see more and more online trade shows that allow potential customers to preview a manufacturer's products remotely. This idea is growing in popularity, though many industry people find it a challenge to "schmooze" in cyberspace. (It's also a little harder to collect all the great *swag*—promotional products—they give out at real-life shows!) An important benefit of traditional trade shows is the opportunity to develop customer leads that the company then forwards to its sales force for follow up.

promotional products
Goodies such as coffee mugs, T-shirts, and magnets given away to build awareness for a sponsor. Some freebies are distributed directly to consumers and business customers; others are intended for channel partners such as retailers and vendors.

- *Promotional products:* We have all seen them—coffee mugs, visors, T-shirts, ball caps, key chains, refrigerator magnets, and countless other doodads emblazoned with a company's logo. They are examples of **promotional products**. Unlike licensed merchandise we buy in stores, sponsors give away these goodies to build awareness for their organization or specific brands. In many industries, companies vie for the most impressive promotional products and offer their business customers and channel partners upscale items such as watches, polar fleece jackets, and expensive leather desk accessories.

point-of-purchase (POP) displays
In-store displays and signs.

- *Point-of-purchase (POP) displays:* **Point-of-purchase (POP) display** materials include signs, mobiles, banners, shelf ads, floor ads, lights, plastic reproductions of products, permanent and temporary merchandising displays, in-store television, and shopping cart advertisements. Manufacturers spend over $17 billion annually on POP displays, because it keeps the name of the brand in front of the consumer, reinforces mass-media advertising, calls attention to other sales promotion offers, and stimulates impulse purchasing. Generally, manufacturers must give retailers a promotion allowance for use of POP materials. For retailers, the POP displays are useful if they encourage sales and increase revenues for the brand.

    It's a challenge for marketers to come up with new and innovative POP displays that will grab attention, such as the now classic promotion Bausch & Lomb ran in Spain some years ago. The company wanted to encourage consumers with good vision to buy contact lenses that changed their eye colour. By letting shoppers upload their pictures to a computer in the store and digitally alter the photos, the promotion allowed people to see how they would look with five different eye colours without actually inserting the contacts.[80]

push money
A bonus paid by a manufacturer to a salesperson, customer, or distributor for selling its product.

- *Incentive programs:* In addition to motivating distributors and customers, some promotions light a fire under the firm's own sales force. These incentives, or **push money**, may come in the form of cash bonuses, trips, or other prizes. Mary Kay cosmetics, the in-home party plan cosmetics seller, is famous for giving its more productive distributors pink cars to reward their efforts. Another cosmetics marketer, Clinique, provides push money to department store cosmeticians to demonstrate and sell the full line of Clinique products. This type of incentive has the nickname *SPIF,* short for sales promotion incentive funds. Even Starbucks has gotten into the incentive program business by offering gift cards that companies can purchase and provide for their salespeople to give to clients as a small "thank you" for closing a sale.

OBJECTIVE

Understand the elements of direct marketing.

(pp. 423–428)

Direct Marketing

Are you one of those people who love to get lots of catalogues in the mail, pore over them for hours, and then order just exactly what you want without leaving home? Do you download music from iTunes or order books from Chapters Indigo? Have you ever responded to an infomercial on TV? All these are examples of direct marketing, the fastest-growing type of marketing communication.

Direct marketing refers to "any direct communication to a consumer or business recipient that is designed to generate a response in the form of an order, a request for further information, or a visit to a store or other place of business for purchase of a product."[81] The Direct Marketing Association (DMA) reports that direct-marketing-driven sales represent about 10 percent of the total US gross domestic product (GDP)—an astounding figure! Spending on direct marketing is increasing, while at the same time spending on traditional advertising has declined—largely the result of cutbacks during the recent economic downturn. And the projections for growth in outlays on direct marketing during the decade beginning in 2010 are very bullish.[82]

Clearly, direct marketing has the potential for high impact. Let's look at the four most popular types of direct marketing as portrayed in Figure 11.8: mail order (including catalogues and direct mail), telemarketing, direct-response advertising, and m-commerce. We'll start with the oldest—buying through the mail—which is still incredibly popular!

direct marketing
Any direct communication to a consumer or business recipient designed to generate a response in the form of an order, a request for further information, and/or a visit to a store or other place of business for purchase of a product.

Mail Order

In 1884 Timothy Eaton produced a 32-page catalogue for distribution at the Industrial Exhibition in Toronto, and the following year he created a mail-order department. While not the first catalogue to be distributed in North America, it was "one of the first to be distributed by a Canadian retail store."[83] The mail-order industry was born, and today consumers can buy just about anything through the mail. Mail order comes in two forms: catalogues and direct mail.

Figure 11.8 Key Forms of Direct Marketing

Key forms of direct marketing are mail order (including catalogues and direct mail), telemarketing, direct-response advertising, and m-commerce.

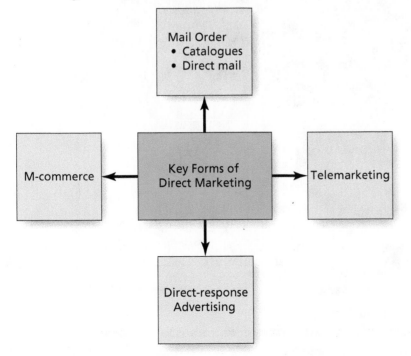

catalogue

A collection of products offered for sale in book form, usually consisting of product descriptions accompanied by photos of the items.

Catalogues

A **catalogue** is a collection of products offered for sale in book form, usually consisting of product descriptions accompanied by photos of the items. Catalogues came on the scene within a few decades of the invention of movable type over 500 years ago, but they've come a long way since then.[84]

The early catalogues Montgomery Ward and other innovators such as Eatons, Hudson's Bay, Simpson's, and JC Penney pioneered targeted people in remote areas who lacked access to stores. Today, the catalogue customer is likely to be an affluent career woman with access to more than enough stores but without the time or desire to go to them. According to the DMA, over two-thirds of US adults order from a catalogue at least once a year.[85] Catalogue mania extends well beyond clothing and cosmetics purchases. PC marketers HP and Dell both aggressively send out promotional catalogues that feature their own products along with accessories from a variety of manufacturers.

Many stores use catalogues to complement their in-store efforts—Neiman-Marcus is famous for featuring one-of-a-kind items like diamond-encrusted bras or miniature working versions of Hummers in its mailings as a way to maintain the store's image as a purveyor of unique and upscale merchandise. These upscale features change regularly, and avid Neiman's fans love to get the new catalogue to find out what the next one is.

A catalogue strategy allows the store to reach people in Canada who live in areas too small to support a store (Exhibit 11.10). But also, more and more firms use catalogues

Exhibit 11.10

The Simpson's catalogue allowed the company to reach consumers that lived in remote areas.

to reach overseas markets as well. Companies like Lands' End and Eddie Bauer do brisk sales in Europe and Asia, where consumers tend to buy more goods and services through the mail in the first place than do North Americans. Lands' End opened a central warehouse in Berlin and attacked the German market with catalogues. The company trained phone operators in customer service and friendliness and launched an aggressive marketing campaign to let consumers know of the Lands' End lifetime warranty (German catalogue companies require customers to return defective merchandise within two weeks to receive a refund). Although local competitors protested and even took the company to court, the case was settled in the American company's favour, and the Yankee invasion continues.

Catalogue Choice started in 2007 as a Web site that enabled consumers to opt out of receiving catalogues by big companies (much like a "do not call" list for telemarketers). By 2010 the Web site (www.cataloguechoice.org) claimed to be used by over 1.2 million people in communicating with nearly 3000 cataloguers! Part of the site's motivation is to reduce the waste that unwanted paper catalogues create. Back when the 2007 holiday season came around, many catalogue marketers initially didn't heed the requests of the consumers who signed up at Catalogue Choice and mailed to them anyway. Since then, additional pressure has been put on the cataloguers to comply, and the Direct Marketing Association (DMA) itself has begun an initiative to help firms better police their own practices.[86]

Direct Mail

Unlike a catalogue retailer that offers a variety of merchandise through the mail, **direct mail** is a brochure or pamphlet that offers a specific good or service at one point in time. A direct mail offer has an advantage over a catalogue because the sender can personalize it. Charities, political groups, and other not-for-profit organizations also use a lot of direct mail.

Just as with e-mail spamming, many Canadians are overwhelmed with direct-mail offers—"junk mail" that mostly ends up in the trash. Traditional direct mail marketers are finding it increasingly difficult to get their promotional pieces to rise above the din of competitors' offers. See Exhibit 11.11. A perfect example of overwhelming direct mail was the seemingly endless offers for new credit cards that bombarded consumers earlier in the 2000s, often resulting in the receipt of multiple promotional letters the same week (or even the same day!). However, this trend was cut short by the tightened credit markets and new regulations of the financial markets that followed the recession that began in 2008. The direct-mail industry constantly works on ways to monitor what companies send through the mail and provides some help when it allows consumers to opt out of at least some mailing lists.

direct mail
A brochure or pamphlet that offers a specific good or service at one point in time.

Telemarketing

Telemarketing is direct marketing an organization conducts over the telephone (but why do they always have to call during dinner?). It might surprise you to learn that telemarketing actually is more profitable for business markets than for consumer markets. When B2B marketers use the telephone to keep in contact with smaller customers, it costs far less than a face-to-face sales call yet still lets small customers know they are important to the company.

The Canadian Radio-television and Telecommunications Commission (CRTC) established the National Do Not Call List (DNCL) to allow consumers to reduce the number of telemarketing calls they receive. The idea is that telemarketing firms check the registry at least every 31 days and clean their phone lists accordingly. Some direct marketers initially challenged this action; they argued that it would put legitimate companies out of business while unethical companies would not abide by the regulation and continue to harass consumers. However, the National Do Not Call List now is an accepted part of doing business through direct marketing.

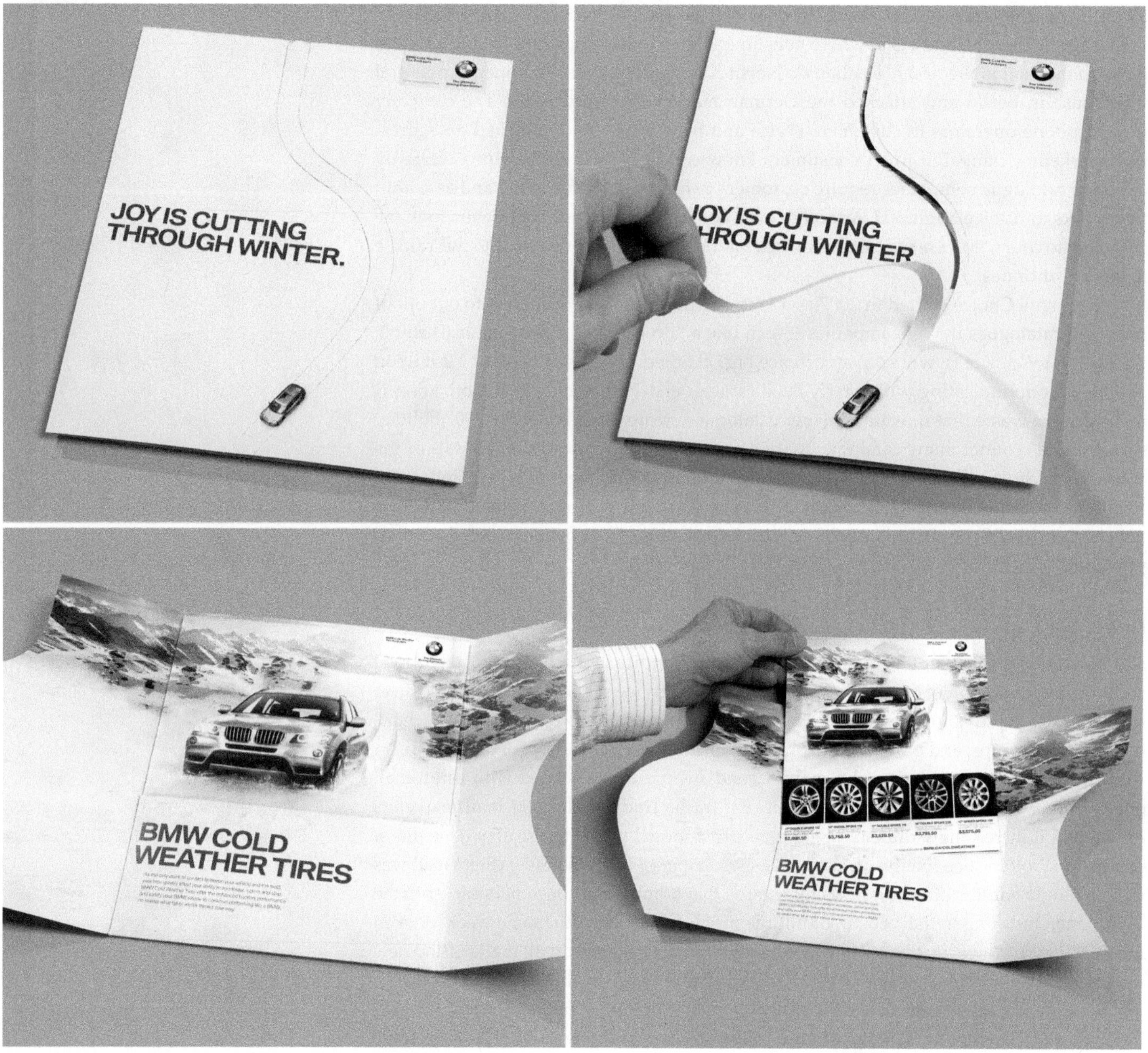

Courtesy of BMW Group Canada and Cundari

Exhibit 11.11

BMW's direct mail flyer promoting their cold weather tire packages had recipients pulling on the "tire tracks" tab to illustrate how cold weather tires can cut through snow. Once the flyer was opened the recipient would view detailed information about BMW Approved Cold Weather Tire Packages, BMW Accessories, and BMW Lifestyle products.

The major issue on the horizon for telemarketers is whether they will be able to access cell phone numbers, as many consumers fear. In fact, rumours crop up from time to time that it's now necessary to place your cell number on the do not call lists to avoid telemarketing calls (so far, that's not true). Especially for many young people, their cell phone often is their *only* phone, which makes the lack of penetration of this media a glaring hole in a telemarketing strategy.[87] Recently, the CRTC and Rogers Communication had reached a settlement over Rogers's use of automated calling devices to sell more airtime to their prepaid wireless customers. They are to make a payment of $175 000 to the École polytechnique de Montréal and $100 000 to the British Columbia Institute of Technology. They are not alone; Bell donated $266 000 to Concordia University and Telus gave $200 000 to Carleton University related to these so-called "robo calls."[88]

Direct-Response Advertising

Direct-response advertising allows the consumer to respond to a message by immediately contacting the provider to ask questions or order the product. This form of direct marketing can be very successful. Although for many companies the Internet has become the medium of choice for direct marketing, this technique is still alive and well in magazines, newspapers, and television.

As early as 1950, the Television Department Stores channel brought the retailing environment into the television viewer's living room when it offered a limited number of products the viewer could buy when he or she called the advertised company. Television sales picked up in the 1970s when two companies, Ronco Incorporated (you may have seen Ron Popeil on TV) and K-Tel International began to hawk products such as the Kitchen Magician, the Mince-O-Matic, and the Miracle Broom on television sets around the world.[89] And who can forget Billy Mays' enthusiastic hawking of Oxy Clean, Jupiter Jack, and nearly 20 other products on TV? Make a simple phone call and one of these wonders could be yours. **Direct-response TV (DRTV)** includes short commercials of less than two minutes, 30-minute or longer infomercials, and home shopping network shows such as The Shopping Channel and ShopTV. Top-selling DRTV product categories include exercise equipment, self-improvement products, diet and health products, kitchen appliances, and music.

The primitive sales pitches of the old days have largely given way to the slick **infomercials** we all know and love (?) today. These half-hour or hour-long commercials resemble a talk show, often with heavy product demonstration and spirited audience participation; but of course they really are sales pitches. Although some infomercials still carry a low-class, sleazy stereotype, in fact, over the years numerous heavyweights from Apple Computer to Volkswagen have used this format.

M-Commerce

One final type of direct marketing is m-commerce. The "m" stands for "mobile," but it could also stand for massive—that's how big the market will be for this platform. **M-commerce** refers to the promotional and other e-commerce activities transmitted over mobile phones and other mobile devices, such as smartphones and touchscreen tablets. With over 4.5 billion mobile phones in use world-wide, and more and more of them Internet-enabled, it makes sense that marketers would want to reach out and touch this large audience.[90] In fact, nearly 70 percent of the world's population has a mobile phone today! In Russia there are far more mobile phones in use than there are people! The top five countries in total mobile phones in use are (the second number is the percentage of population with a mobile phone):

1. China—786 million, 59.6 percent

2. India—636 million, 53.8 percent

3. United States—286 million, 91.0 percent

4. Russia—214 million, 147.3 percent

5. Brazil—185 million, 96.6 percent[91]

M-commerce through text messages (such as an ad for a concert or a new restaurant) is known as *short-messaging system* (SMS) marketing. In terms of unwanted "junk mail," m-commerce has the same potential dark side as other forms of direct marketing such as snail mail and e-mail. And the rise of the all-in-one smartphone, on which the user engages in 24/7 social networking, has created an up-and-coming industry of social networking activity tracking and analytics such as Google Analytics and similar programs. The feature on ethics and sustainability highlights the new-age science of *predicting* Web buying behaviour.

direct-response advertising
A direct marketing approach that allows the consumer to respond to a message by immediately contacting the provider to ask questions or order the product.

direct-response TV (DRTV)
Advertising on TV that seeks a direct response, including short commercials of less than two minutes, 30-minute or longer infomercials, and home shopping networks.

infomercials
Half-hour or hour-long commercials that resemble a talk show but actually are sales pitches.

m-commerce
Promotional and other e-commerce activities transmitted over mobile phones and other mobile devices, such as smartphones and touchscreen tablets.

Every once in a while in most Web surfers' lives, a suggestion pops up on the screen that leads them to wonder, how did they know that about me? The moment can seem magical, and a bit creepy. Most of us have experienced this phenomenon when shopping on sites such as Amazon.com: the site recommends items similar to the ones you have been browsing through. Sometimes, however, the connections between what you are looking at and the suggested items may not seem obvious. This type of surprising connection will happen more often as e-marketers adopt a new generation of predictive technology fuelled by growing rivers of behavioural data, from mouse clicks to search queries—all crunched by ever more powerful computers.

The surprising connections are the result of the information in the e-commerce database which tracks the types of purchases made by certain types of shoppers at certain times of day. Marketers are working towards having computers "read" customers in the same way salespeople do: just as in the customer's first five minutes in a store when the salesperson is observing the customer's body language and tone of voice, now machines are being taught to pick up those same insights from movements online.

This dissection of online shopping comes amid growing fears about invasions of privacy online and especially concerns about social media sites like Facebook's access to our personal data and online behaviours. But unlike the most controversial advertising technology, which tracks Web surfers' wanderings from site to site, many of these "preference prediction" methods limit their scrutiny to behaviour on a retailer's own Web page. Much of the analysis looks simply at the patterns of clicks, purchases, and other variables, without including personal information about the shopper. In most cases, personal details are incorporated only if a customer registers on the site and supplies them.

ETHICS CHECK:
Find out what other students taking this course **would do** and **why** on **www.mypearsonmarketinglab.com**

Should firms be able to use your online activities to attempt to predict your buying behaviour? Does "being watched" (virtually at least) make you feel uncomfortable?

☐ YES ☐ NO

Hesham Shafie

APPLYING ▽ Personal Selling

Hesham has to ensure he balances the benefits of speaking directly with the decision makers against the costs of having everyone travelling across the globe. Would the use of Skype or Google Chat take away from the "personal touch" that he feels is necessary to promote Brand Momentum? ➥

personal selling
Marketing communication by which a company representative interacts directly with a customer or prospective customer to communicate about a good or service.

7

OBJECTIVE
Understand the important role of personal selling and how it fits into the promotion mix.
(pp. 428–432)

Personal Selling: Adding the Personal Touch to the Promotion Mix

Companies increasingly supplement traditional advertising with other communication methods, such as public relations campaigns and various forms of social media, as they work harder and harder to cut through the clutter of competitors' marketing communications. In this chapter, so far we've looked at three other forms of promotion—consumer sales promotion, trade-directed sales promotion, and direct marketing. Now we turn our attention to one of the most visible, and most expensive, forms of marketing communication—personal selling.

Personal selling occurs when a company representative interacts directly with a customer or prospective customer to communicate about a good or service. This form of promotion is a far more intimate way to talk to customers. Another advantage of personal selling is that salespeople are the firm's eyes and ears in the marketplace. They learn which competitors talk to customers, what they offer, and what new rival goods and services are on the way—all valuable competitive intelligence.

Many organizations rely heavily on personal selling because at times the "personal touch" carries more weight than mass-media material. For a B2B market situation, the personal touch translates into developing crucial relationships with clients. Also, many industrial goods and services are too complex or expensive to market effectively in impersonal ways (such as through mass advertising). An axiom in marketing is *the more complex, technical, and intangible the product, the more heavily firms tend to rely on personal selling to promote it.*

Personal selling has special importance for students (that's *you*) because many graduates with a marketing background will enter professional sales jobs. Jobs in selling and sales management often provide high upward mobility if you are successful, because firms value employees who understand customers and who can communicate well with them. The old business adage "nothing happens until something is sold" translates into many firms placing quite a bit of emphasis on personal selling in their promotion mixes. And the sales role is even more crucial during tricky economic times, when companies look to their salespeople to drum up new business and to maintain the business they already have.

Sold on selling? All right, then let's take a close look at how personal selling works and how professional salespeople develop long-term relationships with customers.

The Role of Personal Selling in the Marketing Mix

When a woman calls the MGM Grand Hotel in Vegas' 800 number to book a room for a little vacation trip and comes away with not just a room but with show tickets, a massage booking at the hotel spa, and a reservation for dinner at Emeril's, she deals with a salesperson. When she sits in on a presentation at work by a Web site renewal consultant who proposes a new content management system for her firm's Web site, she deals with a salesperson. And when that same woman agrees over lunch at a swanky restaurant to invest some of her savings with a financial manager's recommended mutual fund, she also deals with a salesperson.

For many firms, some element of personal selling is essential to land a commitment to purchase or a contract, so this type of marketing communication is a key to the success of their overall marketing plan. To put the use of personal selling into perspective, Figure 11.9 illustrates some of the factors that make it a more or less important element in an organization's promotion mix.

Figure 11.9 Factors That Influence a Firm's Emphasis on Personal Selling

A variety of factors influence whether personal selling is a more or less important element in an organization's overall promotion mix.

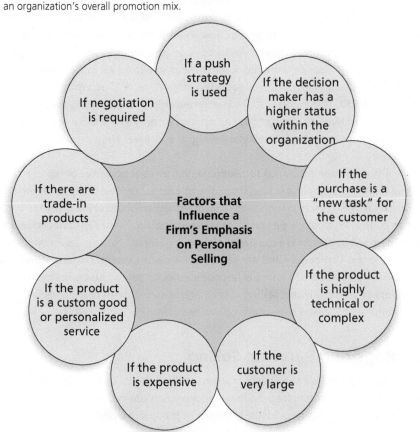

Exhibit 11.12

Salespeople, even the really energetic types, can make only so many calls a day. Thus, reliance on personal selling is effective only when the success ratio is high. Telemarketing, sometimes called teleselling, involves person-to-person communication that takes place on the phone. Because the cost of field salespeople is so high, telemarketing continues to grow in popularity (much to the dismay of many prospects when calls interrupt their dinner). Of course, as we've seen, do-not-call lists have given consumers a powerful weapon to ward off unwanted telephone selling.

In general, a personal selling emphasis is more important when a firm engages in a *push strategy*, in which the goal is to "push" the product through the channel of distribution so that it is available to consumers. As a vice president at Hallmark Cards once observed, "We're not selling *to* the retailer, we're selling *through* the retailer. We look at the retailer as a pipeline to the hands of consumers."[92]

Personal selling also is likely to be crucial in B2B contexts where the firm must interact directly with a client's management to clinch a big deal—and often when intense negotiations about price and other factors will occur before the customer signs on the dotted line. In consumer contexts, inexperienced customers may need the hands-on assistance that a professional salesperson provides. Firms that sell goods and services consumers buy infrequently—houses, cars, computers, lawn mowers, even postsecondary educations—often rely heavily on personal selling. (*Hint:* Your school doesn't have a Facebook page just to broadcast to the masses!) Likewise, firms whose goods or services are complex or very expensive often need a salesperson to explain, justify, and sell them—in both business and consumer markets.

If personal selling is so useful, why don't firms just scrap their advertising and sales promotion budgets and hire more salespeople? There are some drawbacks that limit the role personal selling plays in the marketing communication mix. First, when the dollar amount of individual purchases is low, it doesn't make sense to use personal selling—the cost per contact with each customer is very high compared to other forms of promotion (see Exhibit 11.12). Analysts estimate that in 2010 the average total cost for a sales call with a *consultative* (problem solving) approach to selling was about $350, and this cost will continue to increase at a rate of 5 percent per year. And, of course, this figure is an *average*—depending on the industry, some sales calls are much more expensive to make. The per-contact cost of a national television commercial is minuscule by comparison. A 30-second prime-time commercial may run $300 000 to $500 000 (or even around $3 million during the Super Bowl), but with millions of viewers, the cost per contact may be only $10 or $15 per 1000 viewers.[93] For low-priced consumer goods, personal selling to end users simply doesn't make good financial sense.

Ironically, consumer resistance to telemarketing gives a powerful boost to a form of selling that has been around for a long time: direct selling. *Direct selling is not the same thing as direct marketing.* Direct sellers bypass channel intermediaries and sell directly from manufacturer to consumer through personal, one-to-one contact. Typically, independent sales representatives sell in person in a customer's home or place of business. Tupperware, Avon, Mary Kay, and the Pampered Chef are some well-known examples. Many direct selling firms use a *party plan* approach where salespeople demonstrate products in front of groups of neighbours or friends. Direct selling is on a big upswing, with domestic sales volume doubling in the past 10 years to over $30 billion annually.

Technology and Personal Selling

Personal selling is supposed to be, well, "personal." By definition, a company uses personal selling for marketing communications in situations when one person (the salesperson) interacts directly with another person (the customer or prospective customer) to communicate about a good or service. All sorts of technologies can enhance the personal selling process and, clearly, today the smartphone is the communication hub of the relationship between salesperson and client. However, as anyone making sales calls knows, technology itself cannot and should not *replace* personal selling. Today, a key role of personal selling is to manage customer *relationships*—and remember, relationships occur between people, not between computers (as much as you love your Facebook friends or checking in on Foursquare).

However, there's no doubt that a bevy of technological advancements makes it easier for salespeople to do their jobs more effectively. One such technological advance is *customer relationship management (CRM) software*. For years now, *account management software* such as ACT and GoldMine has helped salespeople manage their client and prospect base. These programs are inexpensive, easy to navigate, and they allow salespeople to track all aspects of customer interaction. Currently, many firms turn to *cloud computing* CRM applications, which are more customizable and integrative than ACT or GoldMine, yet are less expensive than traditional client-server-based CRM installations. A market leader in such products is salesforce.com, whose Salesforce CRM is particularly user-friendly for salespeople (Exhibit 11.13). A key benefit of cloud computing versions of CRM systems is that firms "rent" them for a flat fee per month (at salesforce.com, monthly prices are as low as $2 per user) so they avoid major capital outlays.[94] Recently, some sales organizations have turned to a new-generation system called *partner relationship management (PRM)* that links information between selling and buying firms. PRM differs from CRM in that both supplier and buyer firms share at least some of their databases and systems to maximize the usefulness of the data for decision-making purposes. Firms that share information are more likely to work together toward win-win solutions.

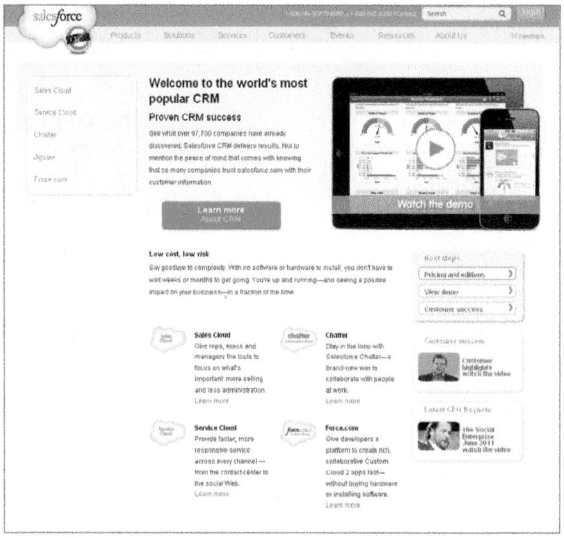

Beyond CRM and PRM, numerous other technology applications enhance personal selling, including teleconferencing, videoconferencing, and improved corporate Web sites that offer FAQ (frequently asked questions) pages to answer customers' queries. Many firms also use intranets and blogs to facilitate access to internal and external communication.

Voice-over Internet protocol (VoIP)—systems that rely upon a data network to carry voice calls—get a lot of use in day-to-day correspondence between salespeople and customers. With VoIP, the salesperson on the road can just plug into a fast Internet connection and then start to make and receive calls just as if she is in the office. Unlike mobile phones, there are no bad reception areas, and unlike hotel phones there are no hidden charges. One popular VoIP product is Skype, whose tagline is "The whole world can talk for free." According to its Web site, Skype "is a little piece of software that allows you to make free calls to other Skype users and really cheap calls to ordinary phones." Skype even offers bargain rates to fixed lines and cell phones outside Canada.[95]

Thanks to Skype, webcams, instant messaging, and the like, customers of all types are becoming more comfortable with the concept of doing business with a salesperson who is not actually in the same room. As such, a good portion of the future of face-to-face sales calls may occur on your own computer screen. Consider the following hypothetical transaction related to buying a set of solar panels for your roof—a complex and expensive purchase.

The sales consultant calls at an appointed time. You open her e-mail message, click a link to start the presentation, and a picture of your roof appears, courtesy of satellite imaging. Colourful charts show past electricity bills and the savings from a solar-panel system. A series of spreadsheets examine the financing options available—and these are dynamic documents, not static images, so the salesperson can tinker with the figures right before your eyes. Would more panels be justified? A few keystrokes later, new

Exhibit 11.13

Salesforce CRM is a popular CRM application.

charts displayed the costs and savings. Could they be shifted to another part of the roof? With a mouse, she moves some black panels from the east to the west side. How about more cash upfront? She scrolls to the spreadsheets, highlights three payment options, and computes the numbers over the next 15 years. In less than an hour, the exchange is over.

Perhaps for a few days or a week you mull over the choices and study the fine print in the contract, but the sale was essentially closed by the time you hung up the phone. You decided to make a major, complex purchase, worth thousands of dollars, without ever meeting anyone in the flesh and without holding any product in your hands. And unlike many purchases, you had no *buyer's remorse* despite the fact it was done online—or maybe *because* it was online.[96]

For years now, all of us have been shopping online, taking in the bargains and wide selection, usually for relatively straightforward products and services and without any human contact unless a problem arises with the ordering technology itself. The brave new world of virtual selling adds another dimension and is yet another example of how the Internet transforms business and remakes job descriptions. These more sophisticated virtual selling capabilities won't replace all face-to-face salesperson/client encounters any more than e-commerce replaced brick-and-mortar retailers. But smart sales organizations can find the right blend of technology and personal touch, tailored to their particular clientele and product offerings, that makes the most of building strong customer relationships.

Why do you think Hesham chose option 3?

Here's my choice...

Real **People**, Real **Choices**

1 Option   2 Option   3 Option

How It Worked Out at Brand Momentum

Hesham selected Option 3. Because of the strong personal relationships and credibility that the Brand Momentum management team has in the market it was time well spent. Many of these meetings resulted in significant opportunities for the company.

Brand Momentum grew from revenue of $8K in its first year of operation to a multimillion dollar company in just under two years of operation. Companies like to conduct business with people they trust and respect. Their reputation and dollars are on the line, and awarding significant contracts to people and organizations that you have no experience with or knowledge of is a risk that many would prefer not to take. Hesham said that BMI is fortunate because of their solid reputation in the marketplace.

To learn the whole story, visit www.mypearsonmarketinglab.com.

Objective Summary ➡ Key Terms ➡ Apply

1. Objective Summary (pp. 388–394)

Tell what advertising is, describe the major types of advertising, and discuss some of the criticisms of advertising.

Advertising is nonpersonal communication from an identified sponsor using mass media to persuade or influence an audience. Advertising informs and reminds consumers and creates consumer desire. Product advertising is used to persuade consumers to choose a specific product or brand. Institutional advertising is used to develop an image for an organization or company (corporate advertising), to express opinions (advocacy advertising), or to support a cause (public service advertising). Retail and local advertising informs customers about where to shop. Most firms rely on the services of advertising agencies to create successful advertising campaigns. Full-service agencies include account management, creative services, research and marketing services, and media planning, while limited-service agencies provide only one or a few services.

User-generated content (UGC), also known as consumer-generated media (CGM), includes online consumer comments, opinions, advice, consumer-to-consumer discussions, reviews, photos, images, videos, podcasts and webcasts, and product-related stories available to other consumers through digital technology. To take advantage of this phenomenon, some marketers encourage consumers to contribute their own do-it-yourself (DIY) ads. Crowdsourcing is a practice in which firms outsource marketing activities (such as selecting an ad) to a community of users, that is, a crowd.

Advertising has been criticized for being manipulative, for being deceitful and untruthful, for being offensive and in bad taste, for creating and perpetuating stereotypes, and for causing people to buy things they don't really need. While some advertising may justify some of these criticisms, most advertisers seek to provide honest ads that don't offend the markets they seek to attract.

Key Terms

product advertising, p. 389

institutional advertising, p. 389

corporate advertising, p. 389

advocacy advertising, p. 389

public service advertisements (PSAs), p. 390

advertising campaign, p. 390

limited-service agency, p. 390

full-service agency, p. 390

account executive (account manager), p. 390

account planner, p. 390

creative services, p. 391

research and marketing services, p. 391

media planner, p. 391

user-generated content (UGC), p. 391

do-it-yourself (DIY) ads p. 391

corrective advertising, p. 392

puffery, p. 393

2. Objective Summary (pp. 394–410)

Describe the process of developing an advertising campaign and how marketers evaluate advertising.

Development of an advertising campaign begins with understanding the target audiences and developing objectives for the message and the ad budget. To create the ads, the agency develops a creative strategy that is summarized in a creative brief. To come up with finished ads, they must decide on the appeal, the format, the tonality, and the creative tactics and techniques. Pretesting advertising before placing it in the media prevents costly mistakes.

Media planning gets a message to a target audience in the most effective way. The media planner must decide whether to place ads in traditional mass media or in digital media including Web site advertising, mobile advertising, and video sharing, variously referred to as owned media, paid or bought media, and earned media. Product placements, a type of branded entertainment, integrate products into movies, television shows, video games, novels, and even retail settings. Support media include directories, out-of-home media, and place-based media. A media schedule specifies the exact media the campaign will use and when and how often the message should appear.

The final step in any advertising campaign is to evaluate its effectiveness. Marketers evaluate advertising through posttesting. Posttesting research may include aided or unaided recall tests that examine whether the message had an influence on the target market.

Key Terms

creative strategy, p. 395

creative brief, p. 395

advertising appeal, p. 396

unique selling proposition (USP), p. 396

reminder advertising, p. 397

teaser or mystery advertising, p. 397

execution format, p. 397

tonality, p. 397

3. Objective Summary (pp. 410–416)

Explain the role of public relations and the steps in developing a public relations campaign.

The purpose of PR is to build good relationships between an organization and its various publics and to establish and maintain a favourable image. Crisis management is the process of managing a company's reputation when some negative and often unplanned event threatens the organization's image.

The steps in a PR campaign begin with setting objectives, creating and executing a campaign strategy, and planning how the PR program will be evaluated. Public relations is useful to introduce new products; influence legislation; enhance

the image of a city, region, or country; polish the image of an organization; provide advice and counsel; and call attention to a firm's community involvement.

PR specialists often use print or video news releases to communicate timely topics, research stories, and consumer information. Internal communications with employees include company newsletters and internal TV programs. Other PR activities include investor relations, lobbying, speech writing, developing corporate identity materials, media relations, arranging sponsorships and special events, and guerrilla marketing.

Key Terms

4. Objective Summary (pp. 416–419)

Explain what sales promotion is, and describe the different types of consumer sales promotion activities.

Sales promotions are programs that marketers design to build interest in or encourage purchase of a good or service during a specified period. Marketers target sales promotion activities either to ultimate consumers or to members of the channel such as retailers that sell their products. Price-based consumer sales promotion include coupons; price deals, refunds, and rebates; frequency (loyalty/continuity) programs; and special/bonus packs. Attention-getting consumer sales promotions include contests and sweepstakes, premiums, and sampling.

Key Terms

5. Objective Summary (pp. 420–422)

Identify the sales promotion elements that are aimed at other channel members rather than at consumers.

A sales promotion is a short-term program designed to build interest in or encourage purchase of a product. Trade sales promotions come in a variety of forms. Some are designed as discounts and deals, including co-op advertising, for channel members and some are designed to increase industry visibility. Approaches aimed at increasing industry visibility include trade shows, promotional products, point-of-purchase (POP) displays, incentive programs, and push money.

Key Terms

trade promotions, p. 420

merchandising allowance, p. 420

case allowance, p. 420

co-op advertising, p. 421

trade shows, p. 422

promotional products, p. 422

point-of-purchase (POP) displays, p. 422

push money, p. 422

6. Objective Summary (pp. 423–428)

Understand the elements of direct marketing.

Direct marketing refers to any direct communication designed to generate a response from a consumer or business customer. Some of the types of direct marketing activities are mail order (catalogues and direct mail), telemarketing, and direct-response advertising, including infomercials and home shopping networks.

Key Terms

direct marketing, p. 423

catalogue, p. 424

direct mail, p. 425

direct-response advertising, p. 427

direct-response TV (DRTV), p. 427

infomercials, p. 427

m-commerce, p. 427

7. Objective Summary (pp. 428–432)

Understand the important role of personal selling and how it fits into the promotion mix.

Personal selling occurs when a company representative interacts directly with a prospect or customer to communicate about a good or service. Many organizations rely heavily on this approach because at times the "personal touch" can carry more weight than mass-media material. Generally, a personal selling effort is more important when a firm engages in a push strategy, in which the goal is to "push" the product through the channel of distribution so that it is available to consumers. Today's salespeople are less likely to use transactional selling (hard-sell tactics) in favour of relationship selling, in which they pursue win-win relationships with customers.

Key Term

personal selling, p. 428

Chapter **Questions** and **Activities**

Concepts: Test Your Knowledge

1. What is advertising and what types of advertising do marketers use most often? What is an advertising campaign?
2. Firms may seek the help of full-service or limited-service advertising agencies for their advertising. Describe each. What are the different departments of a full-service agency?
3. What is consumer-generated advertising and why is it growing in importance? What is crowdsourcing and how is it used in advertising?
4. What are some of the major criticisms of advertising? What is corrective advertising? What is puffery?
5. Describe the steps in developing an advertising campaign. What is a creative brief? What is meant by the appeal, execution format, tonality, and creative tactics used in an ad campaign?
6. What is media planning? What are the strengths and weaknesses of traditional media, that is, television, radio, newspapers, and magazines?
7. What is digital media? How do marketers use Web site advertising, mobile advertising, and video sharing in their digital media activities? What are owned, paid, and earned media?

8. How do marketers use branded entertainment and support media such as directories, out-of-home media, and place-based media to communicate with consumers?
9. How do marketers pretest their ads? How do they posttest ads?
10. What is media planning? How do media planners use reach, frequency, gross rating points, and cost per thousand in developing effective media schedules? What are continuous, flighting, and pulsing media schedules?
11. What is the purpose of public relations? What is a crisis-management plan? What are the steps in planning a PR campaign? Describe some of the activities that are part of PR.
12. Explain some of the different types of consumer sales promotions marketers frequently use.
13. Explain some of the different types of trade sales promotions marketers frequently use.
14. What is direct marketing? Describe the more popular types of direct marketing.
15. What is m-commerce?
16. What role does personal selling play within the marketing function?

Activities: Apply What You've Learned

1. Assume that you are the head of PR for a regional fast-food chain that specializes in fried chicken and fish. A customer has claimed that he became sick when he ate a fried roach that was in his chicken dinner at one of your restaurants. As the director of PR, what recommendations do you have for how the firm might handle this crisis?

2. As we discussed in this chapter, many consumers are highly critical of advertising. In order to better understand this, conduct a short survey of (1) your college classmates and (2) a different group of consumers such as your parents and their friends. In the survey ask the respondents about the criticisms of advertising discussed in this chapter, that is, that advertising (1) is manipulative, (2) is deceptive and untruthful, (3) is offensive and in bad taste, (4) creates and perpetuates stereotypes, and (5) causes people to buy things they don't really need. Be sure to ask respondents to give you examples of ads that they feel fall in these categories. Develop a report that summarizes your results and compares the attitudes of the two consumer groups.

3. Watch three of your favourite TV programs. While you watch the programs, take notes on each product placement in the programs. Be sure to record how many seconds (approximately) the product is in view and where the product is located (e.g., was an actor holding the product, was it in the background, on a table, etc.). Develop a report that summarizes your findings.

4. Look through some magazines to find an ad that fits each of the following categories:

   a. USP strategy
   b. Demonstration
   c. Testimonial
   d. Slice-of-life
   e. Sex oriented
   f. Humour oriented

   Critique each ad. Tell who the target market appears to be. Describe how the message is executed. Discuss what is good and bad about the ad. Do you think the ad will be effective? Why or why not?

5. Assume that you are a member of the marketing department for a firm that produces several brands of household cleaning products. Your assignment is to develop recommendations for trade sales promotion activities for a new laundry detergent. Develop an outline of your recommendations for these sales promotions. In a role-playing situation, present and defend your recommendations to your boss.

6. Timing is an important part of a sales promotion plan. Trade sales promotions must be properly timed to ensure channel members fully maximize the opportunity to sell your product. Assume that the introduction of the new laundry detergent in question 1 is planned for April 1. Place the activities you recommended in question 1 onto a 12-month calendar of events. (Hint: The calendar needs to start *before* the product introduction.) In a role-playing situation, present your plan to your boss. Be sure to explain the reasons for your timing of each trade sales promotion element.

7. Consider carefully the potentially annoying downsides of various forms of direct marketing to consumers. As a marketer, what would you do to ensure that your firm's direct marketing efforts don't turn customers off your product?

Marketing Metrics: Exercise

Media planners use a variety of metrics to help in making decisions on what TV show or which magazines to include in their media plans. Two of these are gross rating points (GRPs) and cost per thousand (CPM).

Assume you are developing a media plan for a new brand of gourmet frozen meals. Your target market includes females ages 25–64. Following is a list of six possible media buys you are considering for the media plan. The plan is based on a four-week period.

1. Calculate the GRPs for each media buy based on the information given.
2. Calculate the CPM for each media buy.
3. Based on the cost of each buy, the reach or rating of each buy, and any qualitative factors that you feel are important, select four of the media buys that you would recommend.
4. Tell why you would select the four.

Media Vehicle	Rating	Cost per Ad or Insertion	Number of Insertions	CPM	GRPs for This Number of Insertions
American Idol	30	$500 000	4 (1 per weekly episode)		
NCIS	20	$400 000	4 (1 per weekly episode)		
CBC Evening News	12	$150 000	20 (1 per weeknight news program)		
Time magazine	5	$40 000	4 (1 per weekly publication)		
Canadian Living magazine	12	$30 000	1 (1 per monthly publication)		
The National Post	4	$10 000	12 (3 ads per week)		

Choices: What Do You Think?

1. Firms are increasing their use of search engine marketing in which they pay search engines such as Google and Bing for priority position listings. And social media sites such as Twitter are generating revenue by offering to sell "search words" to firms so that their posting appears on top. Are such practices ethical? Are consumers being deceived when a firm pays for priority positioning?

2. Because of concerns about the effectiveness of mass media advertising, more and more firms are using product placements, also referred to as branded entertainment, to put their product in front of consumers. But is this practice really ethical? Are consumers deceived when they see a can of Diet Coke on the *American Idol* judges' table? Or what about the can of Dr. Pepper on the table of Tony Stark's house in *Iron Man 2*? Does the average consumer believe the can is there because it is the favourite of a TV or movie celebrity or are most consumers savvy enough to recognize it as a paid product placement? Should the government regulate product placements, perhaps requiring TV programs and movies to inform consumers about the paid placements? Are consumers really harmed by such practices?

3. Some people are turned off by advertising because they say it is deceptive or offensive, that it creates stereotypes, and that it causes people to buy things they don't need. Others argue that advertising is beneficial and actually provides value for consumers. What are some arguments on each side? How do you feel?

4. Today, advertisers are spending less on mass media advertising and more on alternative media, that is, online, mobile, entertainment, and digital out-of-home media. How has this affected the advertising industry so far, and do you think this will affect it in the future? What are some ways that advertising has so far responded to this? What ideas do you have for how they can respond in the future?

5. User-generated content (UGC), also known as consumer-generated media (CGM), includes online consumer comments, opinions, advice, consumer-to-consumer discussions, reviews, photos, images, videos, podcasts and webcasts, and product-related stories available to other consumers through digital technology. What are the prob-

lems and benefits for marketers of UCG? How should marketers respond to UCG? Do you think marketers should encourage UCG or attempt to discourage it? Why do you feel that way?

6. Companies sometimes teach consumers a "bad lesson" with the overuse of sales promotions. As a result, consumers expect the product always to be "on deal" or have a rebate available. What are some examples of products for which this has occurred? How do you think companies can prevent this?

7. Some critics denounce PR specialists, calling them "flacks" or "spin doctors" whose job is to hide the truth about a company's problems. What is the proper role of PR within an organization? Should PR specialists try to put a good face on bad news?

8. M-commerce allows marketers to engage in location commerce when they can identify where consumers are and send them messages about a local store. Do you think consumers will respond positively to this? What do you think are the benefits for consumers of location commerce? Do you see any drawbacks (such as invasion of privacy)?

Miniproject: Learn by Doing

The purpose of this miniproject is to give you an opportunity to experience the advertising creative process.

1. First, you should create (imagine) a new brand of an existing product (such as a laundry detergent, toothpaste, perfume, or soft drink). If you are doing a marketing plan project in your course, you might use the same product for this miniproject.

2. Next, you should decide on your creative strategy. What appeal, execution format, tonality, and creative tactics do you think are best?

3. Create a series of at least three magazine ads for your product, using the appeal you selected. Your ads should have a headline, a visual, and copy to explain your product and to persuade customers to purchase your brand.

4. Present your ads to your class. Explain your ad execution and the reasons for the various decisions you made in developing the ads.

Marketing in **Action** Case   Real Choices at Frito-Lay

Chips, chips, and even more chips! This might be the mantra for Frito-Lay salespeople as they carry out their daily assignments. Although it may not seem like it on the surface, it is a challenge to be effective in the salty snack sales environment. As with most forms of selling, the secret to success lies in finding ways to be both efficient and effective. There is only so much shelf space for all those tempting crunchy bags in grocery and convenience stores and lots of manufacturers that want their products to be on them. The salty snack industry includes potato chips, tortilla chips, snack nuts and seeds (including corn nuts), popcorn, pretzels, extruded cheese snacks, corn snacks, and more. Retail sales in the United States alone totalled over $17 billion in 2009.

Frito-Lay is one of the world's leading producers of salty snacks. Frito-Lay North America is a division of PepsiCo Inc. Based in Plano, Texas, the company's most popular brands include Fritos, Lay's, Doritos, Cheetos, and Tostitos. In 1932, C. E. Doolin purchased the recipe for Fritos and began to sell corn chips in San Antonio from his Ford Model T. In the same year, Herman W. Lay began his potato chip business in Nashville by purchasing a snack food manufacturer.

The Frito Company and the H. W. Lay Company merged in 1961 to become Frito-Lay Inc. Eventually, in 1965 Frito-Lay Inc. and the Pepsi-Cola Company combined and created PepsiCo Inc. Today, PepsiCo is organized into four divisions: Frito-Lay

(continued)

Marketing in **Action** Case   Real Choices at Frito-Lay

North America, PepsiCo Beverages North America, PepsiCo International, and Quaker Foods North America.

In the retail atmosphere, Frito-Lay faces competition from many sources. These include large multinational companies such as ConAgra (DAVID Seeds, Crunch 'n Munch, Orville Redenbacher), Kraft Foods (Nabisco, Honey Maid), and Procter & Gamble (Pringles). In addition, there are numerous regional manufacturers such as Cape Cod Potato Chip (chips, popcorn), Snyder's of Hanover (chips, pretzels), and Jay's Foods (chips, popcorn). Relationships with retailers are critical as all these formidable competitors jockey for limited shelf space. The leadership of Frito-Lay's sales organization believes that knowledge management is the key to success, so that salespeople in the field can constantly update what they know about each store and tailor their offerings accordingly. The challenge is that important information must be captured in many different places and systems. This can inhibit the sharing of knowledge across members of the sales organization.

Frito-Lay's solution was to develop a knowledge management portal on the company's intranet. The portal provides a central point of access to the database that integrates customer and internal corporate information. The goals for the Frito-Lay portal are to provide knowledge that is more efficient, make use of customer-specific data, and promote team collaboration. Given the company's size, this is no easy task.

During the mid-2000s, the salty snack market grew slowly, and changes in consumers' eating habits might result in an even slower future. A trend toward healthier snacking and concerns about weight loss will increase the competitiveness among the different snack food sales organizations. Salespeople have to continue to develop customer loyalty as consumers experiment with new products to enhance the at-home experience. Frito-Lay needs to decide just what pieces of information its sales force needs to know while not burdening them with too much data to be effective.

You Make the Call

1. What is the decision facing Frito-Lay?
2. What factors are important in understanding this decision situation?
3. What are the alternatives?
4. What decision(s) do you recommend?
5. What are some ways to implement your recommendation?

Based on: Esther Shein, "Frito-Lay Sales Force Sells More Through Information Collaboration," CIO.com, May 01, 2001, http://www.cio.com/article/30167/Case_Study_Frito_Lay_Sales_Force_Sells_More_Through_Information_Collaboraton; Frito-Lay, Wikipedia, http://en.wikipedia.org/wiki/Frito-Lay; Kat Fay, "Salty Snacks," PreparedFoods.com, April 1, 2009, http://www.preparedfoods.com/Articles/Feature_Article/BNP_GUID_9-5-2006_A_10000000000000569180; Sonia Reyes, "Strategy: Frito-Lay Gets Wise to Rival's Revamp," Brandweek, June 21, 2004, http://www.allbusiness.com/marketing-advertising/branding-brand-development/4686710-1.html.

Deliver Value through Supply Chain Management, Channels of Distribution, and Logistics

Real People **Profiles**

Heather Mayo

Profile

▼A Decision Maker at Sam's Club

With over 16 years of operations and merchandising experience in the warehouse club industry, at Sam's Club Heather Mayo has responsibility for the grocery business with sales of over $5 billion. As Vice President of Merchandising, she focuses on creating solutions to meet the needs of the 47 million members Sam's serves in over 600 locations across North America. Additionally, she represented the company as a Supplier Diversity Lead on Walmart's Supplier Diversity Internal Steering Committee and was captain of Walmart's Packaging Sustainable Value Network. Most recently, she has added the role of Executive Sponsor of the Wood and Paper Sustainable Value Network. In February 2009, she was honoured as Divisional Merchandise Manager of the Year for Sam's Club.

Prior to joining Sam's in 2004, Heather was an executive consultant/ associate partner focusing on business strategy for IBM. In this capacity, she provided C-level executives of Fortune 500 companies with business advice and counsel regarding strategic direction and operational capability of their business, marketplace, and partners. Notable clients include REI, Godiva, Hallmark, the United States Mint, and Coca-Cola.

Heather also has 10 years of experience with a wholesale club competitor where she successfully managed 33 accounts representing the petroleum, financial, travel, communications, automotive, insurance, and foodservice industries. As assistant VP of Specialty Business, she identified, developed, and implemented entrepreneurial business concepts and lucrative strategic partnerships for increased revenue, visibility, and customer satisfaction. Heather successfully negotiated multi-million-dollar contracts with both local and national companies, resulting in significant mutually rewarding financial gain.

She holds a Bachelor of Science degree in business management from Bentley College in Waltham, Massachusetts.

Like other high-volume retailers that operate on razor-thin margins, Sam's Club always looks for ways to shave costs and improve efficiency in order to distribute large amounts of grocery and other items to its hundreds of stores quickly and inexpensively. Heather, at the time, oversaw the dairy category along with eight other merchandise categories for Sam's Club. Collectively, her team had the responsibility to source over 600 items, negotiate costs, and specify delivery methods and prices for the chain's more than 47 million club members across the US.

Ironically, milk is one of the most basic staple items the team stocks in its stores, but it is difficult to supply economically, because it takes up a lot of space and is highly perishable. Heather and her team tried to address the problem of the high cost of shipping milk using traditional distribution methods. Shippers and end consumers tend to stick with what they know, and what they know is that the milk people use every day will come out of familiar gallon jugs, just as it always has—the jug's design has not changed since 1953!

But Heather knew that something had to give. Competitors were cutting costs and using milk as a *loss leader* (deliberately selling the product below cost) in order to drive traffic into their stores. Sam's was at a competitive disadvantage, and it was losing market share on an important staple item. Sam's had to look closely at every step in the supply chain to find ways to trim costs. Heather realized that the tried-and-true method of shipping milk to stores was inefficient and that this could be a link in the chain that she might tighten.

Typically, a dairy truck will "weight out" before it "cubes out"; that is, will hit the maximum weight it can carry well before it's full of jugs. In early 2007, the company was approached by one of its supplier partners that had developed a simple design change to the gallon milk jug that would allow the jug to be *palletized*; that is, the item is shipped on a 40" × 48" platform (pallet) and a forklift or pallet jack moves the entire pallet from warehouse to truck and then from truck to cooler in the store.

Here's my problem.

The design modification also would eliminate the need to *back haul* empty racks and cases (milk crates) to the supplier for cleaning and reloading; typically, the empties are trucked back to where they came from, at great expense. This innovation promised to make milk cheaper to ship so that Sam's Club could reduce its "food miles" (an industry term that refers to how far the product has to travel from supplier to retailer). The company could deliver fresher milk to its stores, giving the product a longer shelf life in the dairy case. Additionally, this change would allow the company to pass a cost savings to the tune of 10 to 20 cents per gallon on to its members.

These new square, or *caseless,* milk jugs did not require crates or racks for shipping and storage. Instead, the newly designed milk gallon was self-stacking; the spout is flatter and each gallon can rest on another during transport, as well as while on display in the store. The company estimated that trucks used for shipping from the processor to a Club could accommodate 9% more product—a total of 4704 gallons per truck, or approximately 384 more containers—without the metal racks. In addition, the flat top and wider spout do not come in contact with equipment during the fill process. This reduces the risk of contamination or introduction of bacteria that shortens shelf life. To be sure, the new-and-improved technique had a lot of advantages over the tried-and-true method, but Heather knew she would have to swim against the tide if she advocated the change. You always have to think twice before you mess with such an important and traditional product!

Things to remember
Every link in the distribution chain adds cost to the final product.

Big companies like Sam's Club operate with very high volumes, so shaving a few cents off at different stages in a distribution process can result in significant savings.

Distribution processes are entrenched and it's costly to make changes. Also, consumers are reluctant to accept changes to products like milk cartons that they buy on a regular basis over a long period of time.

Heather considered her **Options** 1·2·3

1 Option

Continue doing business as usual and don't make any changes. Sam's Club's distribution network was very familiar with the current system, so with this option, workers would not have to be retrained to handle a different process. Similarly, the club managers wouldn't have to learn a new way to receive and merchandise a staple product. And Club members would continue to find what they expected to see on the dairy shelves. However, storage space is at a premium in the packed Sam's Club stores. Under the current system, the club has to store empty milk crates and racks until the milk supplier picks them up. Racks and crates tend to get stolen when they are placed outside for suppliers to pick up. The receiving process is slow because an employee needs to physically lift every crate and count it to verify the correct amount of product is there. In addition, floor space in the cooler is very tight as this is where product is stored and sold. Workers need to carefully maneuver milk rack "bossies" around in order to be able to stock other dairy items and get to needed stock for replenishment.

2 Option

Sam's Club's parent, Walmart, maintains large perishable distribution centres where full trucks of milk could be delivered and then reshipped to the appropriate locations. Walmart's fleet of trucks could help realize economies of scale as deliveries to stores would be made 24/7. Since the trucks deliver many other dairy products than just milk, the trucks could be loaded more efficiently if the warehouse workers loaded different kinds of refrigerated products together—the heavier milk jugs could be intermingled with lighter, smaller containers so that the trucks could be more tightly packed without exceeding weight restrictions. On the other hand, this process would involve shipping the milk products twice; first to the distribution centre and then to the Sam's Club stores. Each time the product is touched adds cost to the process. And multiple touches also multiply the opportunities for product damage.

3 Option

Change Sam's Club product and pallet configuration to embrace the new caseless design. This change would result in delivery of better-quality milk products with a longer shelf life and reduce the retail price members paid for gallons of milk. The net result would be 9 percent more product on a truck, leading to a 50 percent cut in the number of weekly deliveries each store would require—an elimination of 32 000 deliveries per year. On the "green" front, the supplier would save 100 000 gallons of water every day, because it wouldn't have to clean and sanitize returnable milk crates. The new container is recyclable; pallets are used for other products, while shrink wrap and cardboard are recycled at each Club location. And less labour is required at the Club to restock the milk jugs.

On the other hand, change can be difficult for managers and employees, and Club shoppers would have to accept a radically different container in place of their beloved milk jug. And if Sam's Club converted to this process it would be dependent on the supplier that invented it to stay in business and maintain its capacity to supply Sam's Club needs.

Now, put yourself in Heather's shoes. Which option would you choose, and why?

You Choose
Which **Option** would you choose, and **why**?

1. ☐YES ☐NO 2. ☐YES ☐NO 3. ☐YES ☐NO

See what **option** Heather chose on **page 490**

Objective Outline

1

Place: The Final Frontier

When talking about logistics, it's difficult not to mention Walmart Canada as an example. Walmart entered the Canadian market in 1994 with the purchase of Woolco and is still going strong. It has opened several supercentres and many stores around the country. Walmart Canada is a model of global supply chain effectiveness. Walmart Canada is increasing the proportion of goods that it buys directly from manufacturers rather than through third-party procurement companies or suppliers. As part of its effort to combine purchasing for the 15 countries in which it operates, Walmart Canada has established four global merchandising centres for general goods and clothing. These include a centre in Mexico City focused on emerging markets and a centre in the UK to serve its George brand. It is also shifting to direct purchasing of its fresh fruit and vegetables on a global basis in the United States, and it plans to do the same in Canada by 2015. The same is true for sheets and towels for its stores in Canada, the United States, and Mexico; its Faded Glory clothing line; its licensed Disney character clothing; and eventually other categories including seafood, frozen food, and dry packaged groceries.[1]

Walmart Canada clearly understands the potential for supply chain practices to enhance organizational performance and profits, and they have become the benchmark of other firms for best practices. The truth is, distribution may be the "final frontier" for marketing success. After years of hype, many consumers no longer believe that "new and improved" products really *are* new and improved. Nearly everyone, even upscale manufacturers and retailers, tries to gain market share through aggressive pricing strategies. Advertising and other forms of promotion are so commonplace they have lost some of their impact. Even hot, new social media strategies can't sell overpriced or unavailable products, at least not for long. Marketers have come to understand that *place* (the "distribution P") may be the only one of the *four Ps* to still offer an opportunity for real, long-term competitive advantage— especially since many consumers now expect "instant gratification" in getting just what they want when the urge strikes. Savvy marketers are, therefore, always on the lookout for novel ways to distribute their products.

This chapter is about the science and art of getting goods and services to customers. A large part of the marketer's ability to deliver a value proposition rests on the ability to understand and develop effective distribution strategies. In this chapter, we will begin with a broad view of the company through the lens of the value chain concept.

Recall from Chapter 1 that the concept of value chain is a useful way to identify all the players that typically work together to create value. This term refers to a series of activities involved in the design, production, marketing, delivery, and support of any product or service. In addition to marketing activities, the value chain includes business functions such as human resource management and R&D (research and development).

Each link in the chain has the potential to either add or remove value from the product the customer eventually buys.

Then we focus on the supply chain, which spans activities across multiple firms. The **supply chain** includes all the activities necessary to turn raw materials into a good or service and put it into the hands of the consumer or business customer. Often, of course, firms may decide to bring in outside companies to accomplish these activities—this is *outsourcing*. In the case of supply chain functions, outsource firms are most likely organizations with whom the company has developed some form of partnership or cooperative business arrangement.

Next, we talk about *distribution channels*, which are a subset of the supply chain. Distribution channels are important because a large part of the marketer's ability to deliver the value proposition rests on her ability to understand and develop effective distribution strategies. Finally, we look at *logistics management*, which is the process of actually moving goods through the supply chain. We will define each of these terms in greater detail in subsequent sections of this chapter, but for now let's look at the broader activities of the value chain.

supply chain
All the activities necessary to turn raw materials into a good or service and put it in the hands of the consumer or business customer.

The Value Chain and Supply Chain Management

As we saw in Chapter 1, the value chain concept is a way to look at how firms deliver benefits to consumers. Firms do this when they coordinate a range of activities that result in the customer's receipt of a satisfactory good or service. As we can see in Figure 12.1, the value chain consists of five primary activities (inbound logistics, operations, outbound logistics, marketing and sales, and service) and four support activities (procurement, technology development, human resource management, and firm infrastructure).

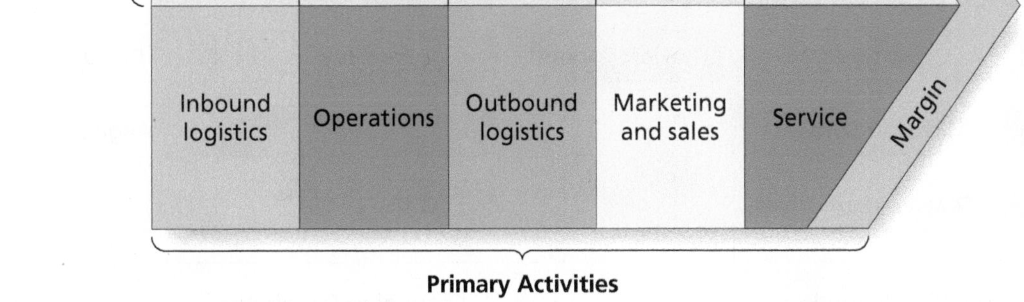

Figure 12.1 The Generic Value Chain

The value chain (a concept first proposed by Professor Michael Porter) encompasses all the activities a firm does to create goods and services that, in turn, create value for the consumer and make a profit for the company.

Source: Reprinted with the permission of the Free Press, a Division of Simon & Schuster Adult Publishing Group, from Michael E. Porter, *Competitive Advantage: Creating and Sustaining Superior Performance.* Copyright 1985–98 by Michael Porter.

Specifically, during the stage of *inbound logistics* activity, the company receives materials it needs to manufacture its products. This activity includes taking delivery of the input materials, warehousing, and inventory control. In *operations*, activities transform the materials into final product form, such as by machining, packaging, and assembly. *Outbound logistics* activities ship the product out to customers, while *marketing and sales* handle advertising, promotion, channel selection, and pricing. *Service* activities enhance or maintain the value of the product, such as by installation or repair. We call this process a *value chain* because each of these activities adds value to the product the customer eventually buys.

Links in the Supply Chain

supply chain management
The management of flows among firms in the supply chain to maximize total profitability.

The value chain is an overarching concept of how firms create value. Similarly, the supply chain also encompasses components external to the firm itself, including all activities necessary to convert raw materials into a good or service and put it in the hands of the consumer or business customer. Thus, **supply chain management** is the coordination of flows among the firms in a supply chain, to maximize total profitability. These "flows" include not only the physical movement of goods but also the sharing of information about the goods—that is, supply chain partners must synchronize their activities with one another. For example, they need to communicate information about which goods they want to purchase (the procurement function), about which marketing campaigns they plan to execute (so that the supply chain partners can ensure there will be enough product to supply the increased demand that results from the promotion), and about logistics (such as sending advance shipping notices to alert their partners that products are on their way). Through these information flows, a company can effectively manage all the links in its supply chain, from sourcing to retailing.

insourcing
A practice in which a company contracts with a specialist firm to handle all or part of its supply chain operations.

In his book *The World Is Flat: A Brief History of the Twenty-First Century*, which we mentioned in an earlier chapter, Thomas Friedman addresses a number of high-impact trends in global supply chain management.[2] One such development is that of companies we traditionally know for other things remaking themselves as specialists who take over the coordination of clients' supply chains for them. UPS is a great example of this trend. UPS, which used to be "just" a package delivery service, today is much, much more, because it specializes in **insourcing**. This is the process of a company contracting with a specialist who services their supply chains. Unlike the *outsourcing process* we reviewed earlier where a company delegates nonessential tasks to subcontractors, insourcing means that the client company brings in an external company to run its essential operations.

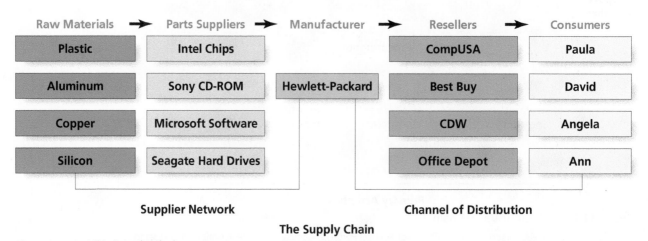

Figure 12.2 | HP's Supply Chain

The supply chain for computer maker HP's line of notebooks includes firms that supply component parts for the machines as well as retailers such as Best Buy. Each firm in the chain adds value through its inputs to provide the notebook the consumer wants at the lowest cost.

The major difference between a supply chain and a channel of distribution is the number of members and their functions. A supply chain is broader; it consists of those firms that supply the raw materials, component parts, and supplies necessary for a firm to produce a good or service, *plus* the firms that facilitate the movement of that product to the ultimate users of the product. This last part—the firms that get the product to the ultimate users—is the **channel of distribution**. (There will be more on channels of distribution in a bit.)

Now, let's take a closer look at one company's supply chain—that of Hewlett-Packard (HP) for its notebook computers as shown in Figure 12.2. HP uses hundreds of suppliers to manufacture its notebooks, and it sells those items at hundreds of online and off-line retailers world-wide. It's worth noting here that the perceived role of individual firms within the supply chain depends on one's perspective. If we look at Hewlett-Packard's supply chain, Intel is a supplier, and Best Buy is a member of its channel of distribution. From Intel's perspective, however, Hewlett-Packard is a customer. And from the perspective of Best Buy, HP is a supplier.

In our example, Intel takes raw materials such as silicon and adds value when it turns them into chips, which it brands with names such as "Core," "Centurion," "Celeron," and "Pentium." Intel then ships chips to HP, which combines them with the other components of a computer (and places the famous "Intel Inside" stickers on the outside), again adding value. Best Buy takes the finished product and adds value when it provides display, sales support, repair service, and financing for the customer.

Now that you understand the basics of the value chain and the supply chain, let's dig into the nitty-gritty and understand how products actually get from point A to point B.

channel of distribution
The series of firms or individuals that facilitates the movement of a product from the producer to the final customer.

2 Distribution Channels: Get It There

OBJECTIVE
Explain what a distribution channel is and what functions distribution channels perform.
(pp. 445–448)

So you've created your product—priced it, too. And you've done the research to understand your target market—you've even set up a Facebook page to attract legions of brand fans. Sorry, you're still not done—now you need to get what you make out into the marketplace. As we noted earlier, a channel of distribution is a series of firms or individuals that facilitates the movement of a product from the producer to the final customer. In many cases, these channels include an organized network of producers (or manufacturers), wholesalers, and retailers that develop relationships and work together to make products conveniently available to eager buyers.

Distribution channels come in different shapes and sizes. The bakery around the corner where you buy your cinnamon rolls is a member of a channel, as is the baked goods section at the local supermarket, the Starbucks that sells biscotti to go with your double mocha cappuccino, and the bakery outlet store that sells day-old rolls at a discount.

A channel of distribution consists of, at a minimum, a producer—the individual or firm that manufactures or produces a good or service—and a customer. This is a *direct channel*. For example, when you buy a loaf of bread at a mom-and-pop bakery, you're buying through a direct channel. Firms that sell their own products through Web sites, catalogues, toll-free numbers, or factory outlet stores use direct channels.

But life (and marketing) usually isn't that simple: Channels often are *indirect* because they include one or more **channel intermediaries**—firms or individuals such as wholesalers, agents, brokers, and retailers who in some way help move the product to the consumer or business user. For example, a baker may choose to sell his cinnamon buns to a wholesaler that will, in turn, sell boxes of buns to supermarkets and restaurants that, in turn, sell them to consumers. Another older term for intermediaries is *middlemen*.

channel intermediaries
Firms or individuals such as wholesalers, agents, brokers, or retailers who help move a product from the producer to the consumer or business user; an older term for intermediaries is middlemen.

© Juice Images/Jupiter Images

Exhibit 12.1

Sometimes firms "delegate" part of the distribution function to the customer. And many customers are happy to cooperate when they can save on shipping charges and get that 60" LCD TV set up immediately.

breaking bulk
Dividing larger quantities of goods into smaller lots in order to meet the needs of buyers.

creating assortments
Providing a variety of products in one location to meet the needs of buyers.

facilitating functions
Functions of channel intermediaries that make the purchase process easier for customers and manufacturers.

Heather Mayo

APPLYING ▽ Utility

Walmart's dairy distribution channel provides utility to shoppers who no longer need to obtain milk from farms. ➤

Functions of Distribution Channels

Channels that include one or more organizations or intermediaries often can accomplish certain distribution functions more effectively and efficiently than can a single organization. As we saw earlier, this is especially true in international distribution channels where differences among countries' customs, beliefs, and infrastructures can make global marketing a nightmare. Even small companies can succeed in complex global markets when they rely on distributors that know local customs and laws. (See Exhibit 12.1.)

Overall, channels provide the time, place, and ownership utility we described in Chapter 1. They make desired products available when, where, and in the sizes and quantities that customers desire. Suppose, for example, you want to buy that perfect bouquet of flowers for a special someone. You *could* grow them yourself or even "liberate" them from a cemetery if you were *really* desperate (very classy!). Fortunately, you can probably accomplish this task with just a simple phone call or a few mouse clicks, and, like magic, a local florist delivers a bouquet to your honey's door.

Distribution channels provide a number of logistics or physical distribution functions that increase the efficiency of the flow of goods from producer to customer. How would we buy groceries without our modern system of supermarkets? We'd have to get our milk from a dairy, bread from a bakery, tomatoes and corn from a local farmer, and flour from a flour mill. And forget about specialty items such as Twinkies or Coca-Cola; the companies that make these items would have to handle literally millions of transactions to sell to every individual who craves a junk-food fix.

Distribution channels create *efficiencies* because they reduce the number of transactions necessary for goods to flow from many different manufacturers to large numbers of customers. This occurs in two ways. The first is **breaking bulk**. Wholesalers and retailers purchase large quantities (usually cases) of goods from manufacturers but sell only one or a few at a time to many different customers. Second, channel intermediaries reduce the number of transactions when they **create assortments**—they provide a variety of products in one location—so that customers can conveniently buy many different items from one seller at one time.

Figure 12.3 provides a simple example of how distribution channels work. This simplified illustration includes five producers and five customers. If each producer sold its product to each individual customer, 25 different transactions would have to occur—not exactly an efficient way to distribute products. But with a single intermediary who buys from all five manufacturers and sells to all five customers, we quickly cut the number of transactions to 10. If there were 10 manufacturers and 10 customers, an intermediary would reduce the number of transactions from 100 to just 20. Do the math: channels are efficient.

The transportation and storage of goods is another type of physical distribution function. Retailers and other channel members move the goods from the production point to other locations where they can hold them until consumers want them. Channel intermediaries also perform a number of **facilitating functions** that make the purchase process easier for customers and manufacturers. For example, intermediaries often provide customer services such as offering credit to buyers. Many of us like to shop at department stores because if we are not happy with the product we can take it back and cheerful customer service personnel are happy to give us a refund (at least in theory). These same customer services are even more important in B2B markets where customers purchase larger quantities of higher-priced products. And channel members perform a risk-taking function; if a retailer

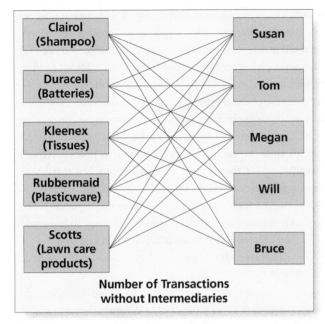
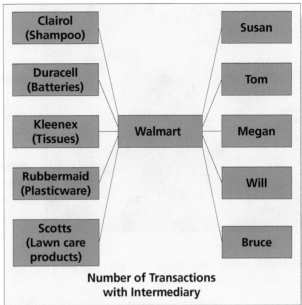

Figure 12.3 Reducing Transactions via Intermediaries

One of the functions of distribution channels is to provide an assortment of products. Because the customers can buy a number of different products at the same location, this reduces the total costs of obtaining a product.

buys a product from a manufacturer and it just sits on the shelf because no customers want it, he is stuck with the item and must take a loss. Perishable items present an even greater risk of spoilage.

Finally, intermediaries, like the Nerds On Site perform communication and transaction functions (Exhibit 12.2). Wholesalers buy products to make them available for retailers, and they sell products to other channel members. Retailers handle transactions with final consumers. Channel members can provide two-way communication for manufacturers. They may supply the sales force, advertising, and other types of marketing communication necessary to inform consumers and persuade them that a product will meet their needs. And the channel members can be invaluable sources of information on consumer complaints, changing tastes, and new competitors in the market.

The Internet in the Distribution Channel

Obviously, many consumers choose the Internet to shop for everything from tulip bulbs to exotic vacations. By using the Internet, even small firms with limited resources enjoy the same market opportunities as their largest competitors to make their products available to customers around the globe.

E-commerce creates radical changes in distribution strategies. Manufacturing firms like Dell, HP, and Apple in the personal computer space rely heavily on Internet-driven direct-to-end-user distribution strategies, although all three are very active outside this channel (consider Apple Stores and Dell Kiosks). In most cases, though, end users still don't obtain products directly from manufacturers. Rather, goods flow from manufacturers to intermediaries and then on to the final customers.

With the Internet, this need for intermediaries and much of what we assume about the need and benefits

Exhibit 12.2

Some wholesalers and retailers assist the manufacturer when they provide setup, repair, and maintenance service for products they handle. Nerds On Site partners with companies such as Dell, Microsoft, and Google.

Courtesy of Michael Hausman Artist Management

Exhibit 12.3

Recording artist Aimee Mann licenses her music rather than work with a major record label in order to retain creative control over her product.

disintermediation (of the channel of distribution)
The elimination of some layers of the channel of distribution in order to cut costs and improve the efficiency of the channel.

knowledge management
A comprehensive approach to collecting, organizing, storing, and retrieving a firm's information assets.

online distribution piracy
The theft and unauthorized repurposing of intellectual property via the Internet.

of channels changes. As you know, an increasing number of consumers buy (or pirate?) their music as an Internet download, making retail music stores less necessary. Then too, as more and more consumers have access to faster broadband Internet service, downloadable movies soon will become the norm.[3]

In the future, channel intermediaries that physically handle the product may become obsolete. Already companies are eliminating many traditional intermediaries because they find that they don't add enough value in the distribution channel—a process we call **disintermediation (of the channel of distribution)**. For marketers, disintermediation reduces costs in many ways: fewer employees, no need to buy or lease expensive retail property in high-traffic locations, and no need to furnish a store with fancy fixtures and decor. You can also see this process at work when you pump your own gas or withdraw cash from an ATM. Are there any full-service gas stations left?

Some companies use the Internet to make coordination among members of a supply chain more effective in ways that end consumers never see. These firms develop better ways to implement **knowledge management**, which refers to a comprehensive approach that collects, organizes, stores, and retrieves a firm's information assets. These assets include both databases and company documents and the practical knowledge of employees whose past experience may be relevant to solving a new problem. If a firm shares this knowledge with other supply chain members, this more strategic management of information results in a win-win situation for all the partners.

But as with most things cyber, the Internet as a distribution channel brings pain with pleasure. One of the more vexing problems with Internet distribution is the potential for **online distribution piracy**, which is the theft and unauthorized repurposing of intellectual property via the Internet. The university and college textbook industry has high potential for online piracy. It's not uncommon for US-produced textbooks to make their way to un-scrupulous individuals outside the country who translate the core content into the native language and post it online for distribution. And obviously, unauthorized downloading of music is a predominant issue for the "recording" industry—to the point where the whole nature of the industry has turned topsy-turvy. Many in the music business are rethinking exactly what—and where—is the value-added for what they do. If the value is just to sell CDs in plastic cases, the industry is likely doomed. More and more musical artists opt to defect from traditional record labels and introduce their tunes online where they can control some or the entire channel of distribution.[4] (See Exhibit 12.3.)

So far, we've learned what a distribution channel is and about some of the functions it performs. Now let's find out about different types of channel intermediaries and channel structures.

3

OBJECTIVE

Describe the types of wholesaling intermediaries found in distribution channels.
(pp. 448–452)

Wholesaling Intermediaries

How can you get your hands on a new Lady Gaga T-shirt? You could pick one up at your local music store, at a trendy clothing store like Hot Topic, or maybe at its online store. You might join hoards of other "little monsters" and buy an "official Lady Gaga concert T-shirt" from vendors during a show. Alternatively, you might get a "deal" on a bootlegged, unauthorized version of the same shirt that a shady guy standing *outside* the concert venue sells from a battered suitcase. Perhaps you shop online at www.ladygaga.com. Each of these distribution alternatives traces a different path from producer to consumer. Let's look at the different types of wholesaling intermediaries and at different channel structures. We'll hold off focusing on retailers, which are usually the last link in the chain, until the next chapter.

Wholesaling intermediaries are firms that handle the flow of products from the manufacturer to the retailer or business user. There are many different types of consumer and B2B wholesaling intermediaries. Some of these are independent, but manufacturers and retailers can own them, too. Figure 12.4 portrays key intermediary types and Table 12.1 summarizes the important characteristics of each.

Independent Intermediaries

Independent intermediaries do business with many different manufacturers and many different customers. Because no manufacturer owns or controls them, they make it possible for many manufacturers to serve customers throughout the world while they keep prices low.

Merchant wholesalers are independent intermediaries that buy goods from manufacturers and sell to retailers and other B2B customers. Because merchant wholesalers **take title** to the goods (that is, they legally own them), they assume certain risks and can suffer losses if products are damaged, become outdated or obsolete, are stolen, or just don't sell. On the other hand, because they own the products, they are free to develop their own marketing strategies, including setting the prices they charge their customers. Wait, it gets better: There are several different kinds of merchant wholesalers:

- *Full-service merchant wholesalers* provide a wide range of services for their customers, including delivery, credit, product-use assistance, repairs, advertising, and other promotional support—even market research. Full-service wholesalers often have their own sales force to call on businesses and organizational customers. Some general-merchandise wholesalers carry a large variety of different items, whereas specialty wholesalers carry an extensive assortment of a single product line; for example, a candy wholesaler carries only candy and gum products, but he stocks enough different varieties to give your dentist nightmares for a year.

- In contrast, *limited-service merchant wholesalers* provide fewer services for their customers. Like full-service wholesalers, limited-service wholesalers *take title* to merchandise but are less likely to provide services such as delivery, credit, or marketing assistance to retailers. Specific types of limited-service wholesalers include the following:

- *Cash-and-carry wholesalers* provide low-cost merchandise for retailers and industrial customers that are too small for other wholesalers' sales representatives to call on. Customers pay cash for products and provide their own delivery. Some popular cash-and-carry product categories include groceries, office supplies, and building materials.

- *Truck jobbers* carry their products to small business customer locations for their inspection and selection. Truck jobbers often supply perishable items such as fruit and vegetables to small grocery stores. For example, a bakery truck jobber calls on supermarkets, checks the stock of bread on the shelves, removes outdated items, and suggests how much bread the store needs to reorder.

- *Drop shippers* are limited-function wholesalers that take title to the merchandise but never actually take possession of it. Drop shippers take orders from and bill retailers and industrial buyers, but the merchandise is shipped directly from the manufacturer. Because they take title to the merchandise, they assume the same risks as other merchant wholesalers. Drop shippers are important to both the producers and the customers of bulky products such as coal, oil, or lumber.

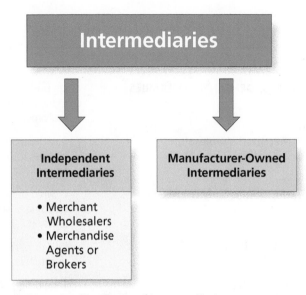

Figure 12.4 Key Types of Intermediaries
Intermediaries can be independent or manufacturer owned.

wholesaling intermediaries
Firms that handle the flow of products from the manufacturer to the retailer or business user.

independent intermediaries
Channel intermediaries that are not controlled by any manufacturer but instead do business with many different manufacturers and many different customers.

merchant wholesalers
Intermediaries that buy goods from manufacturers (take title to them) and sell to retailers and other B2B customers.

take title
To accept legal ownership of a product and assume the accompanying rights and responsibilities of ownership.

Table 12.1	Types of Intermediaries

Intermediary Type	Description	Advantages
INDEPENDENT INTERMEDIARIES	Do business with many different manufacturers and many different customers	Used by most small- to medium-sized firms
• **Merchant Wholesalers**	Buy (take title to) goods from producers and sell to organizational customers; either full or limited function	Allow small manufacturers to serve customers throughout the world; they keep costs low
• Cash-and-carry wholesalers	Provide products for small-business customers who purchase at wholesaler's location	Distribute low-cost merchandise for small retailers and other business customers
• Truck jobbers	Deliver perishable food and tobacco items to retailers	Ensure perishable items are delivered and sold efficiently
• Drop shippers	Take orders from and bill retailers for products drop-shipped from manufacturer	Facilitate transactions for bulky products
• Mail-order wholesalers	Sell through catalogues, telephone, or mail order	Provide reasonably priced sales options to small organizational customers
• Rack jobbers	Provide retailers with display units, check inventories, and replace merchandise for the retailers	Provide merchandising services to retailers
• **Merchandise Agents and Brokers**	Provide services in exchange for commissions	Maintain legal ownership of product by the seller
• Manufacturers' agents	Use independent salespeople; carry several lines of noncompeting products	Supply sales function for small and new firms
• Selling agents, including export/import agents	Handle entire output of one or more products	Handle all marketing functions for small manufacturers
• Commission merchants	Receive commission on sales price of product	Provide efficiency primarily in agricultural products market
• Merchandise brokers, including export/import brokers	Identify likely buyers and bring buyers and sellers together	Enhance efficiency in markets where there are many small buyers and sellers
MANUFACTURER-OWNED INTERMEDIARIES	Limit operations to one manufacturer	Create efficiencies for large firms
• Sales branches	Maintain some inventory in different geographic areas (similar to wholesalers)	Provide service to customers in different geographic areas
• Sales offices	Carry no inventory; availability in different geographic areas	Reduce selling costs and provide better customer service
• Manufacturers' showrooms	Display products attractively for customers to visit	Facilitate examination of merchandise by customers at a central location

- *Mail-order wholesalers* sell products to small retailers and other industrial customers, often located in remote areas, through catalogues rather than a sales force. They usually carry products in inventory and require payment in cash or by credit card before shipment. Mail-order wholesalers supply products such as cosmetics, hardware, and sporting goods.

- *Rack jobbers* supply retailers with specialty items such as health and beauty products and magazines. Rack jobbers get their name because they own and maintain the product display racks in grocery stores, drugstores, and variety stores. These wholesalers visit retail customers on a regular basis to maintain levels of stock and refill their racks with merchandise. Think about how quickly magazines turn over on the rack—without an expert who pulls old titles and inserts new ones, retailers would have great difficulty ensuring you can buy the current issue of *Maclean's* magazine on the first day it hits the streets.

Merchandise Agents or Brokers

Merchandise agents or brokers are a second major type of independent intermediary. Agents and brokers provide services in exchange for commissions. They may or may not take possession of the product, but they *never* take title; that is, they do not accept legal ownership of the product. Agents normally represent buyers or sellers on an ongoing basis, whereas clients employ brokers for a short period of time.

- *Manufacturers' agents, or manufacturers' reps*, are independent salespeople who carry several lines of noncompeting products. They have contractual arrangements with manufacturers that outline territories, selling prices, and other specific aspects of the relationship but provide little if any supervision. Manufacturers normally compensate agents with commissions based on a percentage of what they sell. Manufacturers' agents often develop strong customer relationships and provide an important sales function for small and new companies.

- *Selling agents,* including *export/import agents,* market a whole product line or one manufacturer's total output. They often work like an independent marketing department because they perform the same functions as full-service wholesalers but do not take title to products. Unlike manufacturers' agents, selling agents have unlimited territories and control the pricing, promotion, and distribution of their products. We find selling agents in industries such as furniture, clothing, and textiles.

- *Commission merchants* are sales agents who receive goods, primarily agricultural products such as grain or livestock, on *consignment*—that is, they take possession of products without taking title. Although sellers may state a minimum price they are willing to take for their products, commission merchants are free to sell the product for the highest price they can get. Commission merchants receive a commission on the sales price of the product.

- *Merchandise brokers,* including export/import brokers, are intermediaries that facilitate transactions in markets such as real estate, food, and used equipment, in which there are lots of small buyers and sellers. Brokers identify likely buyers and sellers and bring the two together in return for a fee they receive when the transaction is completed.

Manufacturer-Owned Intermediaries

Sometimes manufacturers set up their own channel intermediaries. In this way, they can operate separate business units that perform all the functions of independent intermediaries while at the same time they can still maintain complete control over the channel.

- *Sales branches* are manufacturer-owned facilities that, like independent wholesalers, carry inventory and provide sales and service to customers in a specific geographic area. We find sales branches in industries such as petroleum products, industrial machinery and equipment, and motor vehicles.

- *Sales offices* are manufacturer-owned facilities that, like agents, do not carry inventory but provide selling functions for the manufacturer in a specific geographic area. Because they allow members of the sales force to locate close to customers, they reduce selling costs and provide better customer service.

merchandise agents or brokers
Channel intermediaries that provide services in exchange for commissions but never take title to the product.

- *Manufacturers' showrooms* are manufacturer-owned or leased facilities in which products are permanently displayed for customers to visit. Merchandise marts are often multiple buildings in which one or more industries hold trade shows and many manufacturers have permanent showrooms. Retailers can visit either during a show or all year long to see the manufacturer's merchandise and make B2B purchases.

4   Types of Distribution Channels

OBJECTIVE

Describe the types of distribution channels and how *place* fits in with the other three Ps in the marketing mix.
(pp. 452–456)

Firms face many choices when they structure distribution channels. Should they sell directly to consumers and business users? Would they benefit if they included wholesalers, retailers, or both in the channel? Would it make sense to sell directly to some customers but use retailers to sell to others? Of course, there is no single best channel for all products. The marketing manager must select a channel structure that creates a competitive advantage for the firm and its products based on the size and needs of the target market. Let's consider some of the factors these managers need to think about.

channel levels
The number of distinct categories of intermediaries that populate a channel of distribution.

When they develop distribution (place) strategies, marketers first consider different **channel levels**. This refers to the number of distinct categories of intermediaries that make up a channel of distribution. Many factors have an impact on this decision. What channel members are available? How large is the market? How frequently do consumers purchase the product? What services do consumers require? Figure 12.5 summarizes the different structures a distribution channel can take. The producer and the customer are always members, so the shortest channel possible has two levels. Using a retailer adds a third level, a wholesaler adds a fourth level, and so on. Different channel structures exist for both consumer and B2B markets.

And what about services? As we saw earlier, services are intangible, so there is no need to worry about storage, transportation, and the other functions of physical distribution. In most cases, the service travels directly from the producer to the customer. However, an intermediary we call an *agent* can enhance the distribution of some services when he helps the parties complete the transaction. Examples of these agents include insurance agents, stockbrokers, and travel agents (no, not everyone books their travel online).

Consumer Channels

As we noted earlier, the simplest channel is a direct channel. Why do some producers sell directly to customers? One reason is that a direct channel may allow the producer to serve its customers better and at a lower price than is possible if it included a retailer. A baker who uses a direct channel makes sure his customers chew on fresher bread than if he sells the loaves through a local supermarket. Furthermore, if the baker sells the bread through a supermarket, the price will be higher because of the supermarket's costs of doing business and its need to make its own profit on the bread. In fact, sometimes this is the *only* way to sell the product, because using channel intermediaries may boost the price above what consumers are willing to pay.

Another reason to use a direct channel is *control*. When the producer handles distribution, it maintains control of pricing, service, and delivery—all elements of the transaction. Because distributors and dealers carry many products, it can be difficult to get their sales forces to focus on selling one product. In a direct channel, a producer works directly with customers so it gains insights into trends, customer needs and complaints, and the effectiveness of its marketing strategies.

Major Types of Channels of Distribution

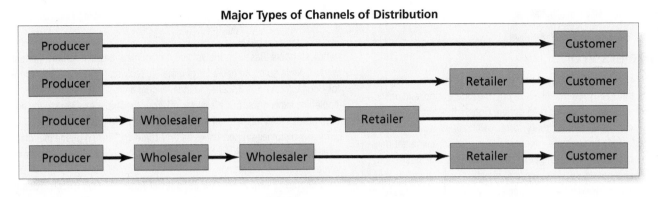

Typical Consumer Channels

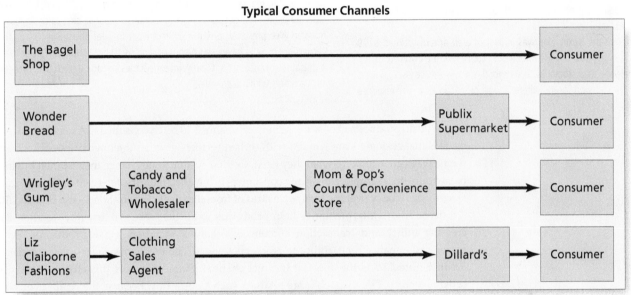

Business-to-Business Channels

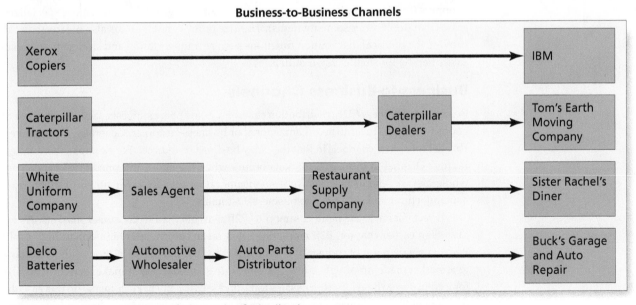

Figure 12.5 Different Types of Channels of Distribution

Channels differ in the number of channel members that participate.

Tech and Trends

The Wireless World

The wireless industry sells phones through several channels: company-owned stores, third-party retailers like Best Buy and Future Shop, and online, where customer telephone service is an option. Google thought it could sell phones in a new way—without retail stores or customer-service reps to hold shoppers' hands through the experience. Think again. Just eight days after Google opened its online store to sell the new Nexus One Smartphone (which runs their Android operating system) directly to customers, its support forums became overloaded with complaints. Customers vented about coverage and delivery problems, network compatibility, dropped calls, and operation woes.

Even though the Nexus One was initially offered at a discounted $179 with a two-year contract from T-Mobile, T-Mobile wasn't involved in the marketing, delivery, or customer service beyond wireless service issues. Issues were posted on a support forum, where Google promised an e-mail response within 48 hours. Based on the volume on Google's message forums the first week, Google no doubt had a lot of e-mail to reply to. "This is an epic failure for Google," says Rob Enderle, an independent analyst. "It tried to create an Apple-like experience, but it's so far off from the Apple experience, it's not even on the same planet." In a statement, Google said it works "quickly to solve any customer-support issues as they come up." It said phone manufacturer HTC would provide telephone support for "device troubleshooting and warranty, repairs and returns."

Charles Golvin, an analyst at Forrester Research, says Google "clearly neglected" to realize what was involved in being a retailer. "It needs to make sure the experience gets better going forward." Google, says Enderle, has a massive Web presence, and if it doesn't want to offer phone support as the carriers do, it could have used Web tools and social networking to better communicate with customers. Clearly, intermediaries can add a great deal of value to customers within a channel.[5]

Why do producers choose to use indirect channels to reach consumers? A reason in many cases is that customers are familiar with certain retailers or other intermediaries—it's where they always go to look for what they need. Getting customers to change their normal buying behaviour—for example, convincing consumers to buy their laundry detergent or frozen pizza from a catalogue or over the Internet instead of from the corner supermarket—can be difficult.

In addition, intermediaries help producers in all the ways we described earlier. By creating utility and transaction efficiencies, channel members make producers' lives easier and enhance their ability to reach customers. The *producer–retailer–consumer channel* in Figure 12.5 is the shortest indirect channel. Panasonic uses this channel when it sells flat-screen TVs through large retailers such as Best Buy. Because the retailers buy in large volume, they can obtain inventory at a low price and then pass these savings on to shoppers (this is what gives them a competitive advantage over smaller, more specialized stores that don't order so many items). The size of these retail giants also means they can provide the physical distribution functions such as transportation and storage that wholesalers handle for smaller retail outlets.

Business-to-Business Channels

Business-to-business (B2B) distribution channels, as the name suggests, facilitate the flow of goods from a producer to an organizational or business customer. Generally, B2B channels parallel consumer channels in that they may be direct or indirect. For example, the simplest indirect channel in industrial markets occurs when the single intermediary—a merchant wholesaler we refer to as an *industrial distributor* rather than a retailer—buys products from a manufacturer and sells them to business customers.

Direct channels are more common to B2B markets than to consumer markets. As we saw in an earlier chapter, B2B marketing often means a firm sells high-dollar, high-profit items (a single piece of industrial equipment may cost hundreds of thousands of dollars) to a market made up of only a few customers. In such markets, it makes sense financially for a company to develop its own sales force and sell directly to customers—in this case the investment in an in-house sales force pays off.

Dual and Hybrid Distribution Systems

Figure 12.5 illustrates how simple distribution channels work. But, once again we are reminded that life (or marketing) is rarely that simple. Producers, dealers, wholesalers, retailers, and customers alike may actually participate in more than one type of channel. We call these *dual* or *multiple distribution systems*.

The pharmaceutical industry provides a good example of multiple-channel usage. Pharmaceutical companies distribute their products in at least three types of channels. First, they sell to hospitals, clinics, and other organizational customers directly. These customers buy in quantity, and they purchase a wide variety of products. Because hospitals and clinics dispense pills one at a time rather than in bottles of 50, these outlets require different product packaging than when the manufacturer sells medications to other types of customers. Pharmaceuticals' second channel is an indirect consumer channel where the manufacturer sells to large drug store chains, like Shoppers Drug Mart, that distribute the medicines to their stores across the country. Alternatively, some of us would rather purchase our prescriptions in a more personal manner from the local independent drugstore. In this version of the indirect consumer channel, the manufacturer sells to drug wholesalers that, in turn, supply these independents.

Instead of serving a target market with a single channel, some companies combine channels—direct sales, distributors, retail sales, and direct mail—to create a **hybrid marketing system**.[6] For example, at one time you could buy a Xerox copier only directly through a Xerox salesperson. Today, unless you are a very large business customer, you likely will purchase a Xerox machine from a local Xerox authorized dealer, or possibly through the Xerox "online store." Xerox turned to an enhanced dealer network for distribution because such hybrid marketing systems offer companies certain competitive advantages, including increased coverage of the market, lower marketing costs, and a greater potential for customization of service for local markets.

hybrid marketing system
A marketing system that uses a number of different channels and communication methods to serve a target market.

Distribution Channels and the Marketing Mix

How do decisions regarding place relate to the other *three Ps*? For one, place decisions affect pricing. Marketers that distribute products through low-priced retailers such as Walmart Canada will have different pricing objectives and strategies than will those that sell to specialty stores or traditional department stores. And of course, the nature of the product itself influences the retailers and intermediaries that we use. Manufacturers select mass merchandisers to sell mid-price-range products while they distribute top-of-the-line products such as expensive jewellery through high-end department and specialty stores.

Distribution decisions can sometimes give a product a distinct position in its market. For example, Enterprise Rent-a-Car avoids being overly dependent on the cutthroat airport rental car market as it opens retail outlets in primary locations in residential areas and local business centres. This strategy takes advantage of the preferences of customers who are not flying and who want short-term use of a rental vehicle, such as when their primary vehicle is in the repair shop. Enterprise built such a successful following around this business model that loyal customers began to clamour for more Enterprise counters at airports, which the company is all too happy to provide. Now Enterprise is a rising competitive threat to traditional airport car rental agencies such as Hertz and Avis.

Ethics in the Distribution Channel

Companies' decisions about how to make their products available to consumers through distribution channels can create ethical dilemmas. For example, because their size gives them great bargaining power when they negotiate with manufacturers, many large retail chains force manufacturers to pay a slotting allowance—a fee in exchange for agreeing to place a manufacturer's products on a retailer's valuable shelf space. Although the retailers claim that such fees pay the cost of adding products to their inventory, many manufacturers feel that slotting fees are more akin to highway robbery. Certainly, the practice prevents smaller manufacturers that cannot afford the slotting allowances from getting their products into the hands of consumers.

Another ethical issue involves the sheer size of a particular channel intermediary—be it manufacturer, wholesaler, retailer, or other intermediary. Giant retailer Walmart Canada, increasingly criticized for forcing scores of independent competitors (i.e., "mom-and-pop stores") to go out of business, has begun a very visible program to help its smaller rivals. The program offers financial grants to hardware stores, dress shops, and bakeries near its new urban stores, training on how to survive with a Walmart Canada in town, and even free advertising in Walmart Canada stores. Of course, Walmart Canada hopes to benefit from the program in cities like Montreal and Quebec City, where its plan to build new stores in urban neighbourhoods has met high resistance from local communities.[7] Walmart Canada has also launched buy-local campaigns to support local suppliers across the country.

Overall, it is important for all channel intermediaries to behave and treat each other in a professional, ethical manner—and to do no harm to consumers (financially or otherwise) through their channel activities. Every intermediary in the channel wants to make money, but behaviour by one to maximize its financial success at the expense of others' success is a doomed approach, as, ultimately, cooperation in the channel will break down. Instead, it behooves intermediaries to work cooperatively in the channel to distribute products to consumers in an efficient manner—making the channel a success for everybody participating in it (including consumers)!

5 Plan a Channel Strategy

OBJECTIVE

Understand the steps to plan a distribution channel strategy.
(pp. 456–462)

Do customers want products in large or small quantities? Do they insist on buying them locally, or will they purchase from a distant supplier? How long are they willing to wait to get the product? Inquiring marketers want to know!

Distribution planning works best when marketers follow the steps in Figure 12.6. In this section, we will first look at how manufacturers decide on distribution objectives and then examine what influences distribution decisions. Finally, we'll talk about how firms select different distribution strategies and tactics.

Firms that operate within a channel of distribution—manufacturers, wholesalers, and retailers—do *distribution planning*. In this section, our perspective focuses on distribution planning by producers and manufacturers rather than intermediaries because they, more often than intermediaries, take a leadership role to create a successful distribution channel.

Step 1: Develop Distribution Objectives

The first step to decide on a distribution plan is to develop objectives that support the organization's overall marketing goals. How can distribution work with the other elements of the marketing mix to increase profits, market share, and sales volume? In general, the overall objective of any distribution plan is to make a firm's product available when, where, and in the quantities customers want at the minimum cost. More specific distribution objectives, however, depend on the characteristics of the product and the market.

For example, if the product is bulky, a primary distribution objective may be to minimize shipping costs. If the product is fragile, a goal may be to develop a channel that minimizes handling. In introducing a new product to a mass market, a channel objective may be to provide maximum product exposure or to make the product available close to where customers live and work. Sometimes, marketers make their product available where similar products are sold so that consumers can compare prices.

Step 2: Evaluate Internal and External Environmental Influences

After they set their distribution objectives, marketers must consider their internal and external environments to develop the best channel structure. Should the channel be long or short? Is intensive, selective, or exclusive distribution best? Short, often direct channels may be better suited for B2B marketers for whom customers are geographically concentrated and require high levels of technical know-how and service. Companies frequently sell expensive or complex products directly to final customers. Short channels with selective distribution also make more sense with perishable products, since getting the product to the final user quickly is a priority. However, longer channels with more intensive distribution are generally best for inexpensive, standardized consumer goods that need to be distributed broadly and that require little technical expertise.

The organization must also examine issues such as its own ability to handle distribution functions, what channel intermediaries are available, the ability of customers to access these intermediaries, and how the competition distributes its products. Should a firm use the same retailers as its competitors? It depends. Sometimes, to ensure customers' undivided attention, a firm sells its products in outlets that don't carry the competitors' products. In other cases, a firm uses the same intermediaries as its competitors because customers expect to find the product there. For example, you will find Harley-Davidson bikes only in selected Harley "boutiques" and Piaggio's Vespa scooters only at Vespa dealers (no sales through Walmart Canada for those two!), but you can expect to find Coca-Cola, Colgate toothpaste, and a Snickers bar in every possible outlet that sells these types of items.

Finally, when they study competitors' distribution strategies, marketers learn from their successes and failures. If the biggest complaint of competitors' customers is delivery speed, developing a system that allows same-day delivery can make the competition pale by comparison.

Step 3: Choose a Distribution Strategy

Planning a distribution strategy means making at least three decisions. First, of course, distribution planning includes decisions about the number of levels in the distribution channel. We discussed these options earlier in the section on consumer and B2B channels, and Figure 12.6 illustrates them again. Beyond the number of levels, distribution strategies also involve decisions about channel relationships—that is, whether a conventional system or a highly integrated system will work best—and the distribution intensity or the number of intermediaries at each level of the channel.

Conventional, Vertical, or Horizontal Marketing System?

Participants in any distribution channel form an interrelated system. In general, these marketing systems take one of three forms: conventional, vertical, or horizontal.

1. A **conventional marketing system** is a multilevel distribution channel in which members work independently of one another. Their relationships are limited to simply buying and selling from one another. Each firm seeks to benefit, with little concern for other channel members. Even though channel members work independently, most conventional channels are highly successful. For one thing, all members of the channel work toward the same goals—to build demand, reduce costs, and improve customer satisfaction. And each channel member knows that it's in everyone's best interest to treat other channel members fairly.

2. A **vertical marketing system (VMS)** is a channel in which there is formal cooperation among channel members at two or more different levels: manufacturing, wholesaling, and retailing. Firms develop vertical marketing systems as a way to meet customer needs better by reducing costs incurred in channel activities. Often, a vertical marketing system can provide a level of cooperation and efficiency not possible with a conventional channel, maximizing the effectiveness of the channel while also maximizing efficiency

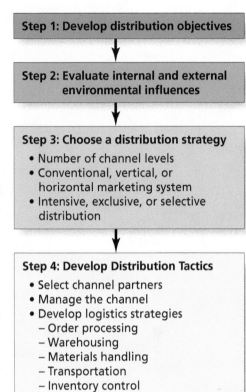

Figure 12.6 Steps in Distribution Planning

Distribution planning begins with setting channel objectives and includes developing channel strategies and tactics.

conventional marketing system
A multiple-level distribution channel in which channel members work independently of one another.

vertical marketing system (VMS)
A channel of distribution in which there is formal cooperation among members at the manufacturing, wholesaling, and retailing levels.

and keeping costs low. Members share information and provide services to other members; they recognize that such coordination makes everyone more successful when they want to reach a desired target market.

In turn, there are three types of vertical marketing systems: administered, corporate, and contractual:

3.a. In an *administered VMS*, channel members remain independent but voluntarily work together because of the power of a single channel member. Strong brands are able to manage an administered VMS, because resellers are eager to work with the manufacturer so they will be allowed to carry the product. Here are some examples of companies using an administered VMS:

Walmart Canada

Toys "R" Us

Kellogg Canada

PepsiCo

Coca-Cola

General Electric

Procter & Gamble

McKesson Canada

Campbell Company of Canada

3.b. In a *corporate VMS*, a single firm owns manufacturing, wholesaling, and retailing operations. Thus, the firm has complete control over all channel operations. Retail giant Loblaw Companies, for example, owns a nation-wide network of distribution centres and retail stores.

3.c. In a *contractual VMS*, cooperation is enforced by contracts (legal agreements) that spell out each member's rights and responsibilities and how they will cooperate. This arrangement means that the channel members can have more impact as a group than they could alone. In a wholesaler-sponsored VMS, wholesalers get retailers to work together under their leadership in a voluntary chain. Retail members of the chain use a common name, cooperate in advertising and other promotion, and even develop their own private-label products. Examples of wholesaler-sponsored chains are Sobeys food stores and Home Hardware stores.

In other cases, retailers themselves organize a cooperative marketing channel system. A *retailer cooperative* is a group of retailers that establish a wholesaling operation to help them compete more effectively with the large chains. Each retailer owns shares in the wholesaler operation and is obligated to purchase a certain percentage of its inventory from the cooperative operation. Associated Grocers and True Value Hardware stores are examples of retailer cooperatives.

Franchise organizations are a third type of contractual VMS. Franchise organizations include a *franchiser* (a manufacturer or a service provider) who allows an entrepreneur (the *franchisee*) to use the franchise name and marketing plan for a fee. In these organizations, contractual arrangements explicitly define and strictly enforce channel cooperation. In most franchise agreements, the franchiser provides a variety of services for the franchisee, such as helping to train employees, giving access to lower prices for needed materials, and selecting a good location. In return, the franchiser receives a percentage of revenue from the franchisee. Usually the franchisees are obligated to follow the franchiser's business format very closely in order to maintain the franchise.

From the manufacturer's perspective, franchising a business is a way to develop widespread product distribution with minimal financial risk while at the same time maintaining control over product quality. From the entrepreneur's perspective, franchises are a helpful way to get a start in business.

In a **horizontal marketing system**, two or more firms at the same channel level agree to work together to get their product to the customer. Sometimes unrelated businesses forge these agreements. Most airlines today are members of a horizontal alliance that allows them to cooperate when they provide passenger air service. For example, Air Canada is a member of the Star Alliance, which also includes Lufthansa, Scandinavian Airlines, Thai Airways International, and United Airlines. Star Alliance is the world's first and largest airline alliance, headquartered in Frankfurt am Main, Germany. These alliances increase passenger volume for all airlines, because travel agents who book passengers on one of the airline's flights will be more likely to book a connecting flight on the other airline. To increase customer benefits, they also share frequent-flyer programs and airport clubs.[8]

horizontal marketing system
An arrangement within a channel of distribution in which two or more firms at the same channel level work together for a common purpose.

Intensive, Exclusive, or Selective Distribution?

How many wholesalers and retailers should carry the product within a given market? This may seem like an easy decision—distribute the product through as many intermediaries as possible. But guess again. If the product goes to too many outlets, there may be inefficiency and duplication of efforts. For example, if there are too many Honda dealerships in town, there will be a lot of unsold Hondas sitting on dealer lots and no single dealer will be successful. But if there are not enough wholesalers or retailers to carry a product, this will fail to maximize total sales of the manufacturer's products (and its profits). If customers have to drive hundreds of miles to find a Honda dealer, they may instead opt for a Toyota, Mitsubishi, Mazda, or Nissan. Thus, a distribution objective may be to either increase or decrease the level of distribution in the market.

The three basic choices are intensive, exclusive, and selective distribution. Table 12.2 summarizes five decision factors—company, customers, channels, constraints, and competition—and how they help marketers determine the best fit between distribution system and marketing goals.

Intensive distribution aims to maximize market coverage by selling a product through all wholesalers or retailers that will stock and sell the product. Marketers use intensive distribution for products such as chewing gum, soft drinks, milk, and bread that consumers quickly consume and must replace frequently. Intensive distribution is necessary for these products because availability is more important than any other consideration in customers' purchase decisions.

intensive distribution
Selling a product through all suitable wholesalers or retailers that are willing to stock and sell the product.

Table 12.2	Characteristics That Favour Intensive Versus Exclusive Distribution	
Decision Factor	Intensive Distribution	Exclusive Distribution
Company	Oriented toward mass markets	Oriented toward specialized markets
Customers	High customer density	Low customer density
	Price and convenience are priorities	Service and cooperation are priorities
Channels	Overlapping market coverage	Nonoverlapping market coverage
Constraints	Cost of serving individual customers is low	Cost of serving individual customers is high
Competition	Based on a strong market presence, often through advertising and promotion	Based on individualized attention to customers, often through relationship marketing

exclusive distribution
Selling a product only through a single outlet in a particular region.

selective distribution
Distribution using fewer outlets than intensive distribution but more than exclusive distribution.

In contrast to intensive distribution, **exclusive distribution** means to limit distribution to a single outlet in a particular region. Marketers often sell pianos, cars, executive training programs, television programs, and many other products with high price tags through exclusive distribution arrangements. They typically use these strategies with products that are high-priced and have considerable service requirements, and when a limited number of buyers exist in any single geographic area. Exclusive distribution enables wholesalers and retailers to better recoup the costs associated with long-selling processes for each customer and, in some cases, extensive after-sale service.

Of course, not every situation neatly fits a category in Table 12.2. (You didn't *really* think it would be that simple, did you?) For example, consider professional sports. Customers might not shop for games in the same way they shop for pianos. They might go to a game on impulse, and they don't require much individualized service. Nevertheless, professional sports use exclusive distribution. A team's cost of serving customers is high because of those million-dollar player salaries and multimillion-dollar stadiums.

The alert reader (and/or sports fan) may note that there are some exceptions to the exclusive distribution of sports teams. We call market coverage that is less than intensive distribution but more than exclusive distribution **selective distribution**. This model fits when demand is so large that exclusive distribution is inadequate, but selling costs, service requirements, or other factors make intensive distribution a poor fit.

Selective distribution strategies are suitable for so-called *shopping products*, such as household appliances and electronic equipment for which consumers are willing to spend time visiting different retail outlets to compare alternatives. For producers, selective distribution means freedom to choose only those wholesalers and retailers that have a good credit rating, provide good market coverage, serve customers well, and cooperate effectively. Wholesalers and retailers like selective distribution, because it results in higher profits than are possible with intensive distribution, in which sellers often have to compete on price.

Step 4: Develop Distribution Tactics

As with planning for the other marketing Ps, the final step in distribution planning is to develop the distribution tactics necessary to implement the distribution strategy. These decisions are usually about the type of distribution system to use, such as a direct or indirect channel or a conventional or an integrated channel. Distribution tactics relate to the implementation of these strategies, such as how to select individual channel members and how to manage the channel.

These decisions are important, because they often have a direct impact on customer satisfaction—nobody wants to have to wait for something they've bought! When Toyota first introduced the now wildly successful Scion, the company wisely came up with a new approach to distribute this youth-oriented vehicle that differs from its traditional Toyota distribution system. The company's overall goal was to cut delivery time to its impatient young customers to no more than a week by offering fewer model variations and doing more customization *at the dealer* rather than at the factory. The continuing resounding success of the Scion brand shows the power of tailoring distribution tactics differently for different markets.[9]

Select Channel Partners

When firms agree to work together in a channel relationship, they become partners in what is normally a long-term commitment. Like a marriage, it is important to both manufacturers and intermediaries to select channel partners wisely, or they'll regret the match-up later (and a divorce can be really expensive!). In evaluating intermediaries, manufacturers try to answer questions such as the following: Will the channel member contribute substantially to our profitability? Does the channel member have the ability to provide the services customers want? What impact will a potential intermediary have on channel control?

Ethical and Sustainable Decisions in the Real World

Walmart Canada announced in 2010 that it would cut some 20 million metric tons of greenhouse gas emissions from its supply chain by the end of 2015 throughout North America—the equivalent of removing more than 3.8 million cars from the road for a year. The company plans to achieve that goal in part by pressing its suppliers to rethink how they source, manufacture, package, and transport their goods. Essentially, the chain is asking suppliers to examine the carbon lifecycle of their products, from the raw materials used in manufacturing all the way through to the recycling phase. Walmart Canada's sustainability executives will work with suppliers to help them figure out what measures to take. But any costs related to making products more energy efficient—for example, for redesigning packaging or using a different fertilizer—will be the responsibility of each supplier, not of Walmart Canada.

The initiative is good for the environment, but it's also good for Walmart Canada as it follows the sustainability mantra of "doing well by doing good." Driving costs out of the supply chain could result in savings for Walmart Canada that the stores can pass along to consumers—enabling the company to enhance its reputation as a destination for rock-bottom prices. Walmart Canada said supplier participation in its effort to reduce greenhouse gas emissions would not be mandatory. But the giant retailer, with sales of more than $400 billion, made it clear that it was interested in doing business only with suppliers that share its goals. Critics argue, though, that rather than change its business model, Walmart Canada pressures suppliers to change theirs, which can lead them to cut corners and produce shoddier products.

For its part, Walmart Canada has started many environmental initiatives in recent years that include improving the efficiency of its truck fleet, creating a global index to measure the environmental impact of products, and changing the labels on clothing it sells to indicate the products can be washed in cold water (therefore lowering customers' electricity bills). The company said the 20 million metric tons of greenhouse gas emissions it intends to cut from its supply chain by the end of 2015 is 150 percent of the estimated growth in carbon emissions from its own operations over the next five years.

ETHICS CHECK: ✎
Find out what other students taking this course **would do** and **why** on **www.mypearsonmarketinglab.com**

Should Walmart Canada aggressively force its suppliers to comply with its green goals?

☐ YES ☐ NO

For example, what small to midsize firm wouldn't jump at the chance to have retail giant Walmart Canada distribute its products? With Walmart Canada as a channel partner, a small firm could double, triple, or quadruple its business. Actually, some firms that recognize size means power in the channel actually decide against selling to Walmart Canada, because they are not willing to relinquish control of their marketing decision making. There is also a downside to choosing one retailer and selling only through that one retailer. If that retailer stops carrying the product, for example, the company will lose its one and only customer (perhaps after relinquishing other smaller customers), and it will be back to square one.

Another consideration in selecting channel members is competitors' channel partners. Because people spend time comparing different brands when purchasing a shopping product, firms need to make sure they display their products near similar competitors' products. If most competitors distribute their electric drills through mass merchandisers, a manufacturer has to make sure its brand is there also.

A firm's dedication to social responsibility may also be an important determining factor in the selection of channel partners. Many firms run extensive programs to recruit minority-owned channel members. Starbucks' famous organizational commitment to good corporate citizenship translates in one way into its "supplier diversity program" that works to help minority-owned business thrive.[10]

Manage the Channel

Once a manufacturer develops a channel strategy and aligns channel members, the day-to-day job of managing the channel begins. The **channel leader**, sometimes called a *channel captain*, is the dominant firm that controls the channel. A firm becomes the channel leader because it has power relative to other channel members. This power comes from different sources:

channel leader
A firm at one level of distribution that takes a leadership role, establishing operating norms and processes based on its power relative to other channel members.

- A firm has *economic power* when it has the ability to control resources.
- A firm such as a franchiser has legitimate power if it has legal authority to call the shots.
- A producer firm has *reward* or *coercive power* if it engages in exclusive distribution and has the ability to give profitable products and to take them away from the channel intermediaries.

In the past, producers traditionally held the role of channel captain. Procter & Gamble, for example, developed customer-oriented marketing programs, tracked market trends, and advised retailers on the mix of products most likely to build sales. As large retail chains evolved, giant retailers such as Best Buy, Home Depot, Target, and Walmart began to assume a leadership role because of the sheer size of their operations. Today it is much more common for the big retailers to dictate their needs to producers instead of producers controlling what products they offer to retailers.

Because producers, wholesalers, and retailers depend on one another for success, channel cooperation helps everyone. Channel cooperation is also stimulated when the channel leader takes actions that make its partners more successful. High intermediary profit margins, training programs, cooperative advertising, and expert marketing advice are invisible to end customers but are motivating factors in the eyes of wholesalers and retailers.

Of course, relations among members in a channel are not always full of sweetness and light. Because each firm has its own objectives, channel conflict may threaten a manufacturer's distribution strategy. Such conflict most often occurs between firms at different levels of the same distribution channel. Incompatible goals, poor communication, and disagreement over roles, responsibilities, and functions cause conflict. For example, a producer is likely to feel the firm would enjoy greater success and profitability if intermediaries carry only its brands, but many intermediaries believe they will do better if they carry a variety of brands.

In this section, we've been concerned with the distribution channels firms use to get their products to customers. In the next section, we'll look at the area of logistics—physically moving products through the supply chain.

Logistics: Implement the Supply Chain

OBJECTIVE

Explain logistics and how it fits into the supply chain concept.
(pp. 462–467)

Some marketing textbooks tend to depict the practice of marketing as 90 percent planning and 10 percent implementation. Not so! In the "real world" (our world) many managers argue that this ratio should be reversed. Marketing success is very much the art of getting the timing right and delivering on promises—*implementation*.

That's why marketers place so much emphasis on efficient **logistics**: the process of designing, managing, and improving the movement of products through the supply chain. Logistics includes purchasing, manufacturing, storage, and transport. From a company's viewpoint, logistics takes place both *inbound* to the firm (raw materials, parts, components, and supplies) and *outbound* from the firm (work-in-process and finished goods). Logistics is also a relevant consideration regarding product returns, recycling and material reuse, and waste disposal—*reverse logistics*.[11] As we saw in earlier chapters, that's becoming even more important as firms start to more seriously consider *sustainability* as a competitive advantage and put more effort into maximizing the efficiency of recycling to save money and the environment at the same time. So you can see logistics is an important issue across all elements of the supply chain. Let's examine this process more closely.

logistics
The process of designing, managing, and improving the movement of products through the supply chain; it includes purchasing, manufacturing, storage, and transport.

The Lowdown on Logistics

Have you ever heard the saying, "An army travels on its stomach"? *Logistics* was originally a term the military used to describe everything needed to deliver troops and equipment to the right place, at the right time, and in the right condition. In business, logistics is similar in that its objective is to deliver exactly what the customer wants—at the right time, in the right place, and at the right price. The application of logistics is essential to the efficient management of the supply chain.

The delivery of goods to customers involves **physical distribution**, which refers to the activities that move finished goods from manufacturers to final customers. Physical distribution activities include order processing, warehousing, materials handling, transportation, and inventory control. This process impacts how marketers physically get products where they need to be, when they need to be there, and at the lowest possible cost. Effective physical distribution is at the core of successful logistics.

When a firm does logistics planning, however, the focus also should be on the customer. When managers thought of logistics as physical distribution only, the objective was to deliver the product at the lowest cost. Today, forward-thinking firms consider the needs of the customer first. The customer's goals become the logistics provider's goals. And this means that when they make most logistics decisions, firms must decide on the best trade-off between low costs and high customer service. The appropriate goal is not just to deliver what the market needs at the lowest cost but rather to provide the product at the lowest cost possible *as long as the firm meets delivery requirements*. Although it would be nice to transport all goods quickly by air, that is certainly not practical. But sometimes air transport is necessary to meet the needs of the customer, no matter the cost.

Logistics Functions

When they develop logistics strategies, marketers must make decisions related to the five functions of logistics Figure 12.7 depicts: order processing, warehousing, materials handling, transportation, and inventory control. For each decision, managers need to consider how to minimize costs while maintaining the service customers want.

Order Processing

Order processing includes the series of activities that occurs between the time an order comes into the organization and the time a product goes out the door. After a firm receives an order, it typically sends it electronically to an office for record keeping and then on to the warehouse to fill it. When the order reaches the warehouse, personnel there check to see if the item is in

Heather Mayo

APPLYING ▼ Materials Handling

Heather needs to consider whether a new process that reduces the times a milk carton is handled is worth the hassles it may create if Sam's Club changes its distribution strategy for milk. ➡

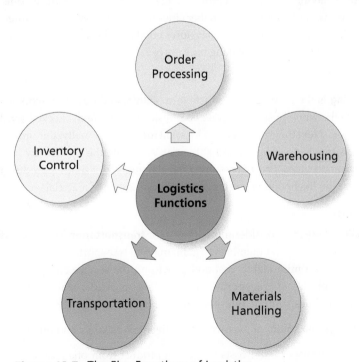

Figure 12.7 The Five Functions of Logistics

When they develop logistics strategies, marketers must make decisions related to order processing, warehousing, materials handling, transportation, and inventory control.

enterprise resource planning (ERP) system

A software system that integrates information from across the entire company, including finance, order fulfillment, manufacturing, and transportation and then facilitates sharing of the data throughout the firm.

warehousing

Storing goods in anticipation of sale or transfer to another member of the channel of distribution.

stock. If it is not, they put the order on back-order status. That information goes to the office and then to the customer. If the item is available, the company locates it in the warehouse, packages it for shipment, and schedules it for pickup by either in-house or external shippers.

Fortunately, many firms automate this process with **enterprise resource planning (ERP) systems**. An ERP system is a software solution that integrates information from across the entire company, including finance, order fulfillment, manufacturing, and transportation. Data need to be entered into the system only once, and then the organization automatically shares this information and links it to other related data. For example, an ERP system ties information on product inventories to sales information so that a sales representative can immediately tell a customer whether the product is in stock.

Warehousing

Whether we deal with fresh-cut flowers, canned goods, or computer chips, at some point goods (unlike services) must be stored. Storing goods allows marketers to match supply with demand. For example, toys and other gift items are big sellers at Christmas, but toy factories operate 12 months of the year. **Warehousing**—storing goods in anticipation of sale or transfer to another member of the channel of distribution—enables marketers to provide *time utility* to consumers by holding on to products until consumers need them.

Part of developing effective logistics means making decisions about how many warehouses we need and where and what type of warehouse each should be. A firm determines the location of its warehouse(s) by the location of customers and access to major highways, airports, or rail transportation. The number of warehouses often depends on the level of service customers require. If customers generally demand fast delivery (today or tomorrow at the latest), then it may be necessary to store products in a number of different locations from which the company can quickly ship the goods to the customer.

Firms use private and public warehouses to store goods. Those that use *private warehouses* have a high initial investment, but they also lose less of their inventory due to damage. *Public warehouses* are an alternative; they allow firms to pay for a portion of warehouse space rather than having to own an entire storage facility. Most countries offer public warehouses in all large cities and many smaller cities to support domestic and international trade. A *distribution centre* is a warehouse that stores goods for short periods of time and that provides other functions, such as breaking bulk.

Materials Handling

materials handling

The moving of products into, within, and out of warehouses.

Materials handling is the moving of products into, within, and out of warehouses. When goods come into the warehouse, they must be physically identified, checked for damage, sorted, and labelled. Next they are taken to a location for storage. Finally, they are recovered from the storage area for packaging and shipment. All in all, the goods may be handled over a dozen separate times. Procedures that limit the number of times a product must be handled decrease the likelihood of damage and reduce the cost of materials handling.

Transportation

transportation

The mode by which products move among channel members.

Logistics decisions take into consideration options for **transportation**, the mode by which products move among channel members. Again, making transportation decisions entails a compromise between minimizing cost and providing the service customers want. As Table 12.3 shows, modes of transportation, including railroads, water transportation, trucks, airways, pipelines, and the Internet, differ in the following ways:

- **Dependability:** The ability of the carrier to deliver goods safely and on time

- **Cost:** The total transportation costs to move a product from one location to another, including any charges for loading, unloading, and in-transit storage

- **Speed of delivery:** The total time to move a product from one location to another, including loading and unloading

Table 12.3 | A Comparison of Transportation Modes

Transportation Mode	Dependability	Cost	Speed of Delivery	Accessibility	Capability	Traceability	Most Suitable Products
Railroads	Average	Average	Moderate	High	High	Low	Heavy or bulky goods, such as automobiles, grain, and steel
Water	Low	Low	Slow	Low	Moderate	Low	Bulky, nonperishable goods, such as automobiles
Trucks	High	High for long distances; low for short distances	Fast	High	High	High	A wide variety of products, including those that need refrigeration
Air	High	High	Very fast	Low	Moderate	High	High-value items, such as electronic goods and fresh flowers
Pipeline	High	Low	Slow	Low	Low	Moderate	Petroleum products and other chemicals
Internet	High	Low	Very fast	Potentially very high	Low	High	Services such as banking, information, and entertainment

- **Accessibility:** The number of different locations the carrier serves

- **Capability:** The ability of the carrier to handle a variety of different products such as large, small, fragile, or bulky

- **Traceability:** The ability of the carrier to locate goods in shipment

Each mode of transportation has strengths and weaknesses that make it a good choice for different transportation needs. Table 12.3 summarizes the pros and cons of each mode.

- **Railroads:** Railroads are best to carry heavy or bulky items, such as coal and other mining products, over long distances. Railroads are about average in their cost and provide moderate speed of delivery. Although rail transportation provides dependable, low-cost service to many locations, trains cannot carry goods to every community.

- **Water:** Ships and barges carry large, bulky goods and are very important in international trade. Water transportation is relatively low in cost but can be slow.

- **Trucks:** Trucks or motor carriers are the most important transportation mode for consumer goods, especially for shorter hauls. Motor carrier transport allows flexibility because trucks can travel to locations missed by boats, trains, and planes. Trucks also carry a wide variety of products, including perishable items. Although costs are fairly high for longer-distance shipping, trucks are economical for shorter deliveries. Because trucks provide door-to-door service, product handling is minimal, and this reduces the chance of product damage.

- **Air:** Air transportation is the fastest and also the most expensive transportation mode. It is ideal to move high-value items such as important mail, fresh-cut flowers, and live lobsters. Passenger airlines, air-freight carriers, and express delivery firms such as

FedEx provide air transportation. Ships remain the major mover of international cargo, but air transportation networks are becoming more important as international markets continue to develop.

- **Pipeline:** Pipelines carry petroleum products such as oil and natural gas and a few other chemicals. Pipelines flow primarily from oil or gas fields to refineries. They are very low in cost, require little energy, and are not subject to disruption by weather.

- **The Internet:** As we discussed earlier in this chapter, marketers of services such as banking, news, and entertainment take advantage of distribution opportunities the Internet provides.

Inventory Control: JIT, RFID, and Fast Fashion

inventory control
Activities to ensure that goods are always available to meet customers' demands.

Another component of logistics is **inventory control**, which means developing and implementing a process to ensure that the firm always has sufficient quantities of goods available to meet customers' demands—no more and no less. That explains why firms work so hard to track merchandise so they know where their products are and where they are needed in case a low-inventory situation appears imminent.

radio frequency identification (RFID)
Product tags with tiny chips containing information about the item's content, origin, and destination.

Some companies are even phasing in a sophisticated technology known as **radio frequency identification (RFID)**. RFID lets firms tag clothes, pharmaceuticals, or virtually any kind of product with tiny chips that contain information about the item's content, origin, and destination. This technology is revolutionizing inventory control and helping marketers ensure that their products are on the shelves when people want to buy them. Great for manufacturers and retailers, right? But some consumer groups are creating a backlash against RFID, which they refer to as "spy chips." Through blogs, boycotts, and other anti-company initiatives, these groups proclaim RFID a personification of the privacy violations George Orwell predicted in his classic book *1984*.[12]

Firms store goods (that is, they create an *inventory*) for many reasons. For manufacturers, the pace of production may not match seasonal demand. It may be more economical to produce snow skis year-round than to produce them only during the winter season. For channel members that purchase goods from manufacturers or other channel intermediaries, it may be economical to order a product in quantities that don't exactly parallel demand. For example, delivery costs make it prohibitive for a retail gas station to place daily orders for just the amount of gas people will use that day. Instead, stations usually order truckloads of gasoline, holding their inventory in underground tanks. The consequences of stock-outs may be very negative. Hospitals must keep adequate supplies of blood, IV fluids, drugs, and other supplies on hand to meet emergencies, even if some items go to waste.

Inventory control has a major impact on the overall costs of a firm's logistics initiatives. If supplies of products are too low to meet fluctuations in customer demand, a firm may have to make expensive emergency deliveries or lose customers to competitors. If inventories are above demand, unnecessary storage expenses and the possibility of damage or deterioration occur. To balance these two opposing needs, manufacturers turn to **just in time (JIT)** inventory techniques with their suppliers. JIT sets up delivery of goods just as they are needed on the production floor. This minimizes the cost of holding inventory while it ensures the inventory will be there when customers need it.

just in time (JIT)
Inventory management and purchasing processes that manufacturers and resellers use to reduce inventory to very low levels and ensure that deliveries from suppliers arrive only when needed.

A supplier's ability to make on-time deliveries is the critical factor in the selection process for firms that adopt this kind of system. JIT systems reduce stock to very low levels, or even zero, and time deliveries very carefully to maintain just the right amount of inventory. The advantage of JIT systems is the reduced cost of warehousing. For both manufacturers and resellers that use JIT systems, the choice of supplier may come down to one whose location is nearest. To win a large customer, a supplier may even have to be willing to set up production facilities close to the customer to guarantee JIT delivery.[13]

Supply Chain Metrics

Companies track a wide range of metrics within the supply chain area. Some of the most common ones are the following:

- On-time delivery

- Forecast accuracy

- Value-added productivity per employee

- Returns processing cost as a percentage of product revenue

- Customer order actual cycle time

- Perfect order measurement

Let's take a look at the last measure in more detail. The perfect order measurement calculates the error-free rate of each stage of a purchase order.[14] This measure helps managers track the multiple steps involved in getting a product from a manufacturer to a customer so that they can pinpoint processes they need to improve. For example, a company can calculate its error rate at each stage and then combine these rates to create an overall metric of order quality. Suppose the company identifies the following error rates:

- Order entry accuracy: 99.95 percent correct (five errors per 1000 order lines)

- Warehouse pick accuracy: 99.2 percent

- Delivered on time: 96 percent

- Shipped without damage: 99 percent

- Invoiced correctly: 99.8 percent

The company can then combine these individual rates into an overall perfect order measurement by multiplying them together: $99.95 \times 99.2 \times 96 \times 99 \times 99.8 = 98.7$ percent.

7 Retailing: Special Delivery

OBJECTIVE

Define retailing;
understand how
retailing evolves and
some ethical issues in
retailing.
(pp. 467–474)

Shop 'til you drop! For many people, obtaining the product is only half the fun. Others, of course, would rather walk over hot coals than spend time in a store. **Retailing** is the final stop on the distribution path—the process by which organizations sell goods and services to consumers for their personal use.

Planning for distribution of product offerings includes decisions about where to make the product available. Thus, when marketers of consumer goods and services plan their distribution strategy, they talk about the retailers they will include in their channel of distribution. This, of course, means they need to understand retailing and the retailer landscape.

retailing
The final stop in the distribution channel in which organizations sell goods and services to consumers for their personal use.

Of course, retailers also develop their own marketing plans. While our sample marketing plan represents the plan of a producer, the same elements are also seen in marketing plans for retailers. They must decide which consumer groups they can best serve, what product assortment and services they will provide for their customers, what pricing policies they will adopt, how they will promote their retail operations, and where they will locate their retail outlets. This section of the chapter will explore the many different types of retailers as we keep one question in mind—how does a retailer, whether store or nonstore (selling via television, phone, or the Internet), lure the consumer? The answer to this question isn't getting any easier as the competition for customers continues to heat up, fuelled by the explosion of Web sites that sell branded merchandise (or that auction it like eBay), the "overstoring" of many areas as developers continue to build elaborate malls and strip shopping centres, and improvements in communications and distribution that make it possible for retailers from around the world to enter local markets. Let's start with an overview of where retailing has been and where it's going.

Retailing: A Mixed (Shopping) Bag

Retailing is big business. Although we tend to associate huge stores such as Walmart Canada and Sears Canada with retailing activity, in reality most retailers are small businesses. Certain retailers, such as Home Depot, also are wholesalers because they provide goods and services to businesses as well as to end consumers.

Retailers belong to a channel of distribution, and as such they provide time, place, and ownership utility to customers. Some retailers save people time or money when they provide an assortment of merchandise under one roof. Others search the world for the most exotic delicacies; they allow shoppers access to goods they would otherwise never see. Still others, such as Chapters bookstores, provide us with interesting environments in which to spend our leisure time and, they hope, our money.

Globally, retailing may have a very different face. In some European countries, don't even think about squeezing a tomato to see if it's too soft or picking up a cantaloupe to see if it smells ripe. Such mistakes will quickly gain you a reprimand from the store clerk who will choose which oranges and bananas you should have. In developing countries like Egypt, retailing often includes many small butcher shops where sides of beef and lamb proudly hang in store windows so everyone will be assured that the meat comes from healthy animals; vendors sell lettuce, tomatoes, and cucumbers on the sidewalk or neatly stack watermelons on a donkey cart; and women sell small breakfast items they cook out of the front of their homes for workers and schoolchildren who pass by in the mornings. Neat store shelves stacked with bottles of shampoo may be replaced by hanging displays that hold one-use size sachets of shampoo—the only size that a woman can afford to buy and then only for special occasions. Street vendors may sell cigarettes one at a time. The local pharmacist also gives customers injections and recommends antibiotics and other medicines for patients who come in with a complaint and who can't afford to see a doctor. Don't feel like cooking tonight? There's no drive-through window for pick up but, even better, delivery from Swiss Chalet, McDonald's, Hardees, KFC, Pizza Hut, Boston Pizza, Chili's, and a host of local restaurants via motor scooters that dangerously dash in and out of traffic is just a few minutes away.

The Evolution of Retailing

Retailing has taken many forms over time, including the peddler who hawked his wares from a horse-drawn cart, a majestic urban department store, an intimate boutique, and a huge "hyperstore" that sells everything from potato chips to snow tires. But now the cart you see at your local mall that sells new-age jewellery or monogrammed golf balls to passersby has replaced the horse-drawn cart. As the economic, social, and cultural pictures change, different types of retailers emerge—and they often squeeze out older, outmoded types. How can marketers know what the dominant types of retailing will be tomorrow or 10 years from now?

The Wheel of Retailing

wheel-of-retailing hypothesis
A theory that explains how retail firms change, becoming more upscale as they go through their life cycle.

One of the oldest and simplest explanations for these changes is the **wheel-of-retailing hypothesis**. Figure 12.8 shows that new types of retailers begin at the entry phase where they find it easiest to enter the market with low-end strategies as they offer goods at lower prices than their competitors.[15] After they gain a foothold, they gradually trade up. They improve their facilities and increase the quality and assortment of merchandise. Finally, retailers

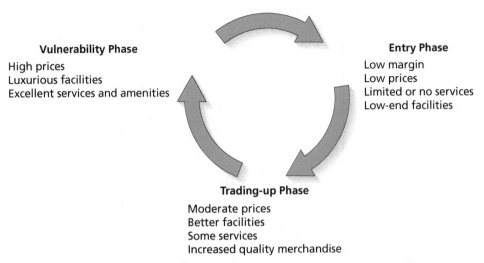

Vulnerability Phase

High prices
Luxurious facilities
Excellent services and amenities

Entry Phase

Low margin
Low prices
Limited or no services
Low-end facilities

Trading-up Phase

Moderate prices
Better facilities
Some services
Increased quality merchandise

Figure 12.8 The Wheel of Retailing

The wheel of retailing explains how retailers change over time.

move on to a high-end strategy with even higher prices, better facilities, and amenities such as parking and gift wrapping. Upscaling results in greater investment and operating costs, so the store must raise its prices to remain profitable, which then makes it vulnerable to still newer entrants that can afford to charge lower prices. And so the wheel turns.

That's the story behind Pier 1 Imports. Pier 1 started as a single store in San Mateo, California, that sold low-priced beanbags, love beads, and incense to post–World War II baby boomers. These days it sells quality home furnishings and decorative accessories to the same customers, who are now the most affluent segment of the American population.[16] Today, even low-cost retailer Walmart Canada is moving up, as it tries to broaden its appeal to upscale shoppers. The retail giant opened a new upscale supercentre in Plano, Texas, that boasts a Wi-Fi-enabled coffee shop, a sushi bar, quieter cash registers, and grocery selections that include more than 1200 choices of wine and gourmet cheeses.[17]

Retailers, however, must be careful not to move too quickly and too far from their roots. Earlier attempts by Walmart to upgrade its clothing lines from basic T-shirts, tank tops, and tube socks to brand-name apparel alienated many of its loyal core customers who found the new items out of reach. Today, Walmart Canada reinvents its clothing offerings by adding some higher fashion apparel while it maintains its general focus on everyday apparel.[18]

Marketing Metrics

Measuring Value

Retail stores like Canadian Tire typically measure store performance by looking at sales per square foot and by looking at comparable store sales on a year-to-year basis. While the comp-store sales have proven useful in measuring the progress of new stores and the value of locations, sales metrics are not enough. Unlike catalogue retailers that can measure catalogue fill rates to determine whether they are meeting customer demand, bricks-and-mortar retailers have a difficult time tracking the number of customers who enter a store with the intent to purchase but who walk out with nothing. Now, companies are developing customer intelligence programs that use video camera systems as a way to count traffic in retail stores. These programs count the number of shoppers that enter the store and compare these data with the number of transactions the POS system processes during the same time frame. This new measure allows retailers to understand the conversion rate of customers walking through the door. To further track why conversion rates are less than 100 percent, retailers can use the POS system to monitor each stock-keeping unit (SKU) and record the exact time stock runs out. By judging the demand for a SKU on a weekly basis, retailers can use a metric they call weighted in-stock percentage to help them assess just how "hot" a given item is compared to other merchandise the store is selling at the same time.

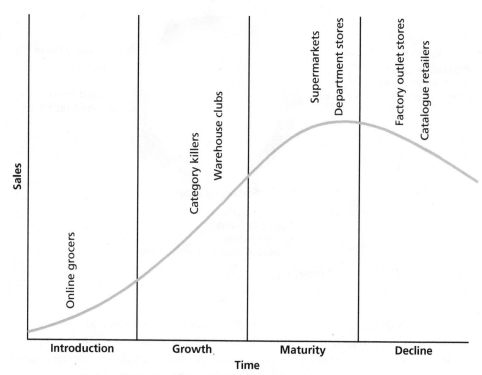

Figure 12.9 The Retail Life Cycle

The retail life cycle explains how retailers are born, grow, mature, and (most) die.

retail life cycle

A theory that focuses on the various stages that retailers pass through from introduction to decline.

BETHENNY FRANKEL FOR PeTA

FUR? I'D RATHER GO NAKED

Exhibit 12.4

Like other marketers, retailers need to stay on top of cultural trends that affect demand for the merchandise they sell, such as fur-free vegan, or sustainable products.

The wheel of retailing helps us explain the development of some but not all forms of retailing. For example, some retailers never trade up; they simply continue to occupy a niche as discounters. Others, such as upscale specialty stores, start out at the high end. Of course, some retailers move down after they experience success at the high end. Sometimes they open sister divisions that sell lower-priced products (as when Gap Stores opened Old Navy).

The Retail Life Cycle

Of course, retailers sell products. But in a way retailers also *are* products, because they provide benefits such as convenience or status to consumers, and they must offer a competitive advantage over other retailers to survive. And sometimes, *where* a product is bought either adds to or takes away from its allure (which explains why some people secretly replace shopping bags from bargain stores with those from upscale stores to create the "right" impression).

So another way to understand how retailers evolve is the **retail life cycle**. Like the *product life cycle* we discussed in an earlier chapter, this perspective, depicted in Figure 12.9, recognizes that (like people, soft-drink brands, and vacation destinations) retailers are born, they grow and mature, and eventually most die or become obsolete. The life cycle approach allows us to categorize retail stores by the conditions they face at different points in the cycle.[19]

In the *introduction* stage, the new retailer often is an aggressive entrepreneur who takes a unique approach to doing business (Exhibit 12.4). This may mean it competes on the basis of low price, as the wheel of retailing suggests. However, the new guy on the block may also enter the market by offering a distinctive assortment or a different way to distribute items, such as through the Internet. Internet grocery stores, for example, are in the introduction stage. In the introduction stage, profits usually are low because of high development costs (pop-up stores are an exception!). As the business enters the *growth* stage, the retailer (hopefully) catches on with shoppers, and sales and profits rise. But a new idea doesn't stay new for long. Others start to copy it and competition increases, so the store needs to expand what it offers. Often the retailer responds by opening more outlets and develops systems to distribute goods to these new stores—which may in turn cut profits, as the firm invests in new buildings and fixtures.

By the time the business reaches the *maturity* stage, many other individual retailers have copied the unique idea of the original entrepreneur to form an entire industry. The industry probably has over expanded and intense competition makes it difficult to maintain customer loyalty. Profits decline as competitors resort to price cutting to keep their customers. We observe this pattern in department stores like The Bay and fast-food chains like McDonald's.

During the maturity stage, firms seek to increase their share of the market or attract new customers. That has been the case with fast-food retailers for a number of years. In order to meet changing customer tastes, KFC offers grilled chicken for customers who want a finger-lickin' lower fat meal and McDonald's sells a Mac Snack Wrap for those who want less bread. Supermarkets respond to consumers' demand for healthy, locally grown food with organic alternatives.

Other retailers use mergers to survive when their retail category matures. (See Exhibit 12.5.) **Mergers** are when two or more separately owned retail firms combine. For example, Sears, a department store chain, merged with Kmart, a discount chain. Another strategy a firm in a mature industry may choose is **downsizing** where it closes unprofitable stores or sells off entire divisions. In the *decline* stage, retail businesses, like the general store or the peddler, become obsolete as newer ways of doing business emerge. Of course, the outmoded retailer does not have to fold its tent at this stage. Marketers who anticipate these shifts can avert decline if they change to meet the times. Some retailers, such as Starbucks, find growth opportunities in foreign markets. Starbucks now operates over 16 000 stores in 50 countries.[20]

Exhibit 12.5

One form of retailing can be at different points in its life cycle in different business environments. In China, the department store is still in its growth stage. Chains like PCD are benefiting from a boom in China's retail market and from shoppers' growing love affair with luxury items. They flock to department stores to buy them because e-commerce isn't well established in the mainland— and department stores have a reputation for avoiding the sale of counterfeit goods that pop up elsewhere around the country.

mergers
When two or more separately owned retail firms combine.

downsizing
When a firm in a mature industry closes or sells off unprofitable stores or entire divisions.

The Evolution Continues: What's "In Store" for the Future?

As our world continues to change rapidly, retailers scramble to keep up. Four factors motivate innovative merchants to reinvent the way they do business: the economic environment, changing demographics, technology, and globalization (Exhibit 12.6).

The Changing Economy

As we noted in Chapter 4, all marketers, including retailers, must understand and respond to changes in the marketing environment (Exhibit 12.4). Recently, changes in the economic environment have been especially important. The 2008–2009 downturn meant that consumers world-wide were less willing to spend discretionary income. Instead they chose to lower their level of debt and to save.

Exhibit 12.6

Atmosphere stores are a great example of specialty stores that can be found all across Canada.

Retail sales, including the all-important Christmas sales, fell in nearly all retail segments.[21] Sales for most upscale retailers were especially vulnerable while stores such as Stokes, The Body Shop, online retailer Amazon.com, Rossy, or Hart that offer consumers low prices or discounted merchandise thrived.

Other stores changed their merchandise assortment to meet consumers' preferences. Private-label brands reached an all-time high in sales in 2009, thanks to prices that can be 20 to 40 percent lower than national brands. Walmart, Sobeys, and Metro have all revamped or expanded their in-house offerings. Other mass merchandisers have responded to this trend by allocating more shelf space to their own private-label brands and less to national brands.

Demographics

As we noted in Chapter 6, keeping up with changes in population characteristics is at the heart of many marketing efforts. Retailers can no longer afford to stand by and assume that their customer base is the same as it has always been. They must come up with new ways to sell their products to diverse groups.

Here are some of the ways changing demographics are altering the face of retailing:

- *Convenience for working consumers:* Some retailers expand their operating hours and services to meet the needs of working consumers who have less time to shop. Other retailers, including dry cleaners and pharmacies, add drive-up windows. In some areas, mobile furniture stores replace design studios; designers pick out 8 or 10 sofas from their large inventories and bring them to your home so you can see how each will actually look in your living room. And walk-in medical clinics located at retailer, pharmacy, or grocery stores not only provide convenience but also save both patients and insurers money on routine care.[22]

- *Recognize ethnic diversity:* Although members of every ethnic group can usually find local retailers that cater to their specific needs, larger companies must tailor their strategies to the cultural makeup of specific areas. For example, in Quebec and New Brunswick where there are large numbers of customers who speak only French, retailers make sure that there are sales associates who *parlent français*.

Technology

In addition to demographics, technology is revolutionizing retailing. As we all know, the Internet has brought us the age of e-tailing. Whether it's a store that sells only on the Web or a traditional retailer such as Banana Republic or the Garage that also sells on the Web, retailing is steadily evolving from bricks to clicks. Our personal computers have turned our homes into virtual malls.

Some of the most profound changes are not even visible to shoppers, such as advanced electronic **point-of-sale (POS) systems**. These computerized devices collect sales data and connect directly into the store's inventory-control system. Stores may use POS systems to create **perpetual inventory unit control systems** that keep a running total on sales, returns, transfers to other stores, and so on. This technology allows stores to develop computerized **automatic reordering systems** that are automatically activated when inventories reach a certain reorder level.[23] The store of the future will use RFID tags (and other technology) to assist the shopper in ways we haven't even thought of. For example, an RFID tag on a bottle of wine can tip off a nearby plasma screen that will project an ad for Barilla pasta and provide a neat recipe for fettuccine with bell peppers and shrimp. Don't remember what number printer ink cartridge you need? No problem. In-store kiosks will allow consumers to ask questions of a product "expert" in another city via a video-enabled screen, alleviating customer complaints about lack of knowledgeable store personnel while creating a cost-efficient way to provide expertise to dozens of customers at one time.[24]

point-of-sale (POS) system
Retail computer systems that collect sales data and are hooked directly into the store's inventory-control system.

perpetual inventory unit control system
Retail computer system that keeps a running total on sales, returns, transfers to other stores, and so on.

automatic reordering system
Retail reordering system that is automatically activated when inventories reach a certain level.

Some restaurants already use technology to let diners order their food tableside directly from a screen complete with photos of the dishes it offers. The *e-menus* help customers because they can see what every item on the menu will look like and, hopefully, avoid a surprise when the order arrives.[25] This innovation also increases sales for the restaurant—who can avoid that mouth-watering picture of the four-layer chocolate cake with peppermint stick ice cream on top?

Of course, technology is important to service industries also. Banking, for example, has become much simpler for both consumers and business customers because of electronic banking. For many years electronic banking has offered ATMs and Web sites where consumers can check their bank balance, transfer funds, and set up automatic bill payments.

Globalization

As we saw in Chapter 2, the world is becoming a much smaller (and flatter) place. Retailers are busy expanding to other countries and they bring with them innovations and new management philosophies. McDonald's, Casey's, Montana's, and Starbucks join the Hard Rock Café as they become global success stories for retailers in Canada. Similarly, Spanish fashion retailers Zara and Mango are now global brands, while Swedish home goods company IKEA furnishes homes around the world.

Ethical Problems in Retailing

Retailers must deal with ethical problems that involve both their customers and their employees. Losses due to **shrinkage** are a growing problem. Shrinkage is the term retailers use to describe stock losses due to shoplifting, employee theft, and damage to merchandise. A 2009 world-wide survey of large retailers in 41 countries found that shrinkage cost retailers $114.8 billion or 1.43 percent of all retail sales.[26] That's $208.39 per family.

shrinkage
Losses experienced by retailers due to shoplifting, employee theft, and damage to merchandise.

Shoplifting

Shoplifting has grown in recent years to giant proportions. In 2009, shoplifting in the United States was estimated at $15.1 billion or more than 35 percent of all shrinkage.[27]

These thefts in turn drive consumer prices up and hurt the economy, and sometimes even cause smaller retailers to go out of business. For department stores, discount stores, and specialty stores, the items lifted include high-price-tag electronics, clothing, and jewellery. For food stores, razor blades, condoms, pregnancy tests, cigarettes, and pain relievers are shoplifters' common targets. The problem is so bad that many small stores now keep high-theft items such as analgesics under lock and key.

At its worst, shoplifting can be an organized criminal activity. Groups of thieves that use store floor plans and foil-lined bags to evade security sensors get away with thousands of dollars in goods in a single day. One survey found that 92 percent of retailers said they had been the victim of organized retail crime.[28] Ironically, the growth of online retailing boosts shoplifting from bricks and mortar stores because it facilitates a wide distribution of stolen goods—no longer do thieves have to fence their loot in the local market. Of course, some shoplifting is more amateurish and nakedly obvious—as when a nude man walked into a Montreal convenience store on a hot August day and did a hula dance to divert attention while his partner stole a case of beer from the store.[29]

Employee Theft

A second major source of shrinkage in retail stores is employee theft of both merchandise and cash. On a case-by-case basis, dishonest employees steal 6.6 times the amount shoplifters do.[30] A current trend in employee theft involves the use of store gift cards. Employees not only have access to products, but they also are familiar with the store's security measures. "Sweethearting" is an employee practice in which a cashier consciously undercharges, gives a cash refund, or allows a friend to walk away without paying for items.[31] Sometimes, a dishonest employee simply carries merchandise out the back door to a friend's waiting car.

Retail Borrowing

retail borrowing
Consumer practice of purchasing a product with the intent to return the nondefective merchandise for a refund after it has fulfilled the purpose for which it was purchased.

A third source of shrinkage is an unethical consumer practice the industry calls **retail borrowing**. Merchants over recent decades have developed liberal policies of accepting returns from customers because the product performs unsatisfactorily or even if the customer simply changes her mind. Retail borrowing refers to the return of nondefective merchandise for a refund after it has fulfilled the purpose for which it was purchased.[32] Popular objects for retail borrowing include a dress for a high school prom, a new suit for a job interview, and a boom box for a weekend picnic on the beach. One study suggests that 12 percent of merchandise returns involve an intent to deceive the retailer. For the consumer, the practice provides short-term use of a product for a specific occasion at no cost. For the retailer, the practice results in lower total sales and often in damaged merchandise, unsuitable for resale.

Ethical Treatment of Customers

On the other side of the retail ethics issue is the question of how retailers and their employees treat customers. While it may be illegal if a store doesn't provide equal access to consumers of different ethnic groups, behaviour that discourages customers who appear economically disadvantaged or socially unacceptable is not. As a classic scene in the movie *Pretty Woman* starring Julia Roberts depicted, stores that seek to maintain an image of elite sophistication may not offer assistance to customers who enter the premises not meeting the requirements for that image—or they may actually ask the customer to leave.

Similarly, many would suggest that retailers have an obligation not to sell products to customers if the products can be harmful. For example, for many years some teens and young adults abused potentially harmful over-the-counter medicines. While government regulations removed many of these drug products from store shelves in recent years, retailers still have to carefully police their distribution. The same is true for products such as alcohol and cigarettes, which by law are limited to sale to adult customers.

Ethical and Sustainable Decisions in the Real World

Retailers know that if they create a better shopping experience for their customers, they create higher sales for themselves. But retailers need to know what's wrong in order to "fix" it. What if customers find the aisles in stores too narrow, the merchandise on the top shelves too hard to reach, or no place to sit to tie a shoelace? Today, hundreds of retailers around the world use *observational research technology* to improve the way they serve customers. This means they install video cameras, motion sensors, and other monitoring devices in their stores not to catch thieves, but to observe how their customers shop and then to make improvements.[33] But some critics are concerned about customer privacy. People don't know they are being taped. We all behave differently when we think we are alone (which is the argument for using the technology in the first place). And what will happen when facial recognition technology allows a store to identify the individual customers they watch? Should retailers use cameras to monitor their shoppers without letting them know? Why or why not?

ETHICS CHECK:
Find out what other students taking this course **would do** and **why** on www.mypearsonmarketinglab.com

If you were a retailer looking to improve your store for your customers, would you install video cameras, motion sensors, and other monitoring devices to monitor customer behaviour?

☐YES ☐NO

8

OBJECTIVE
Understand how we
classify retailers.
(pp. 475–479)

From Mom-and-Pop to Super Walmart: How Marketers Classify Retail Stores

Retail marketers need to understand all the possible ways they might offer their products in the market, and they also need a way to benchmark their performance relative to other similar retailers.

Classify Retailers by What They Sell

One of the most important strategic decisions a retailer makes is *what* to sell—its **merchandise mix**. This choice is similar to settling on a market segment (as we discussed in Chapter 6). If a store's merchandise mix is too limited, it may not have enough potential customers; whereas if it is too broad, the retailer runs the risk of being a "jack of all trades, master of none." Because what the retailer sells is central to its identity, one way we describe retailers is in terms of their merchandise mix.

While we learned in Chapter 8 that a manufacturer's product line consists of product offerings that satisfy a single need, in retailing a *product line* is a set of related products a retailer offers, such as kitchen appliances or leather goods. A retailer that wants to identify direct competition simply looks for other firms with the same NAICS classification codes.

However, a word of caution—as retailers experiment with different merchandise mixes, it's getting harder to make these direct comparisons. For example, even though marketers like to distinguish between food and nonfood retailers, in reality these lines are blurring. **Combination stores** offer consumers food and general merchandise in the same store. **Supercentres** such as Walmart Supercentres are combination stores that combine an economy supermarket with other lower-priced merchandise. Other retailers like Target and Shoppers Drug Mart carry limited amounts of food. In Japan, the major department stores have one floor that, like freestanding supermarkets, sells meats, vegetables, and other fresh food items, while another entire floor offers customers a wide range of prepared foods ready for the modern Japanese working woman (or man) to carry home for dinner.

Classify Retailers by Level of Service

Retailers differ in the amount of service they provide for consumers. Firms recognize that there is a trade-off between service and low prices, so they tailor their strategies to the level of service they offer. Customers who demand higher levels of service must be willing to pay for that service, and those who want lower prices must be willing to give up services. Unfortunately, some consumers don't understand this trade-off and still expect top-level service while they pay bottom-dollar prices!

Retailers like Rona that promise cut-rate prices often are self-service operations. When customers shop at *self-service retailers*, they make their product selection without any assistance, they often must bring their own bags or containers to carry their purchases, and they may even handle the checkout process with self-service scanners. Contrast that experience to visiting a *full-service retailer*. Many of us prefer to shop at major department stores like The Bay and specialty stores like Victoria's Secret, because they provide supporting services such as gift wrapping and they offer trained sales associates who can help us select that perfect gift. Other specialized services are available based on the merchandise the store offers. For example, many full-service clothing retailers will provide alteration services. Retailers like Sears Canada that carry china, silver, housewares, and other items brides might want also offer bridal consultants and bridal gift registries.

merchandise mix
The total set of all products offered for sale by a retailer, including all product lines sold to all consumer groups.

combination stores
Retailers that offer consumers food and general merchandise in the same store.

supercentres
Large combination stores that combine economy supermarkets with other lower-priced merchandise.

Limited-service retailers fall in between self-service and full-service retailers. Stores like Walmart Canada, Target, Old Navy, and Le Chateau offer credit and merchandise return but little else. Customers select merchandise without much assistance, preferring to pay a bit less rather than be waited on a bit more.

Classify Retailers by Merchandise Selection

Another way to classify retailers is in terms of the selection they offer. A retailer's **merchandise assortment**, or selection of products it sells, has two dimensions: breadth and depth. These concepts strongly resemble the product lines we discussed in Chapter 8. **Merchandise breadth**, or variety, is the number of different product lines available. A *narrow assortment* such as we encounter in convenience stores means that shoppers will find only a limited selection of product lines such as candy, cigarettes, and soft drinks. A *broad assortment*, such as a warehouse store like Costco offers, means there is a wide range of items from eyeglasses to barbecue grills.

Merchandise depth is the variety of choices available within each specific product line. A *shallow assortment* means that the selection within a product category is limited, so a factory outlet store may sell only white and blue men's dress shirts (all made by the same manufacturer, of course) and only in standard sizes. In contrast, a men's specialty store may feature a *deep assortment* of dress shirts (but not much else) in varying shades and in hard-to-find sizes. Figure 12.10 illustrates these assortment differences for one product, science fiction books.

Major Types of Retailers

Now that we've seen how retailers differ in the breadth and depth of their assortments, let's review some of the major forms these retailers take. Table 12.4 provides a list of these types and their characteristics.

Convenience Stores

Convenience stores carry a limited number of frequently purchased items, including basic food products, newspapers, and sundries. They cater to consumers willing to pay a premium for the ease of buying staple items close to home. In other words, convenience stores meet the needs of those who are pressed for time, who buy items in smaller quantities, or who shop at irregular hours. But these stores are starting to change, especially in urban areas, where many time-pressed shoppers prefer to visit these outlets even for specialty

---

merchandise assortment
The range of products a store sells.

merchandise breadth
The number of different product lines available.

merchandise depth
The variety of choices available for each specific product line.

convenience stores
Neighbourhood retailers that carry a limited number of frequently purchased items and cater to consumers willing to pay a premium for the ease of buying close to home.

Breadth

	Narrow	Broad
Shallow	Airport Bookstore: A few *Lord of the Rings* books	Sam's Club: A few *Lord of the Rings* books and a limited assortment of *Lord of the Rings* T-shirts and toys
Deep	www.legendaryheroes.com: Internet retailer selling only merchandise for *Lord of the Rings*, *The Highlander*, *Xena: Warrior Princess*, *Legendary Swords*, *Conan*, and *Hercules*	www.Amazon.ca: Literally millions of current and out-of-print books plus a long list of other product lines including electronics, toys, apparel, musical instruments, jewellery, motorcycles, and ATVs

(Depth axis labelled on left: Shallow, Deep)

Figure 12.10 Classification of Book Retailers by Merchandise Selection

Marketers often classify retail stores on the breadth and depth of their merchandise assortment. In this figure, we use the two dimensions to classify types of bookstores that carry science fiction books.

Table 12.4	Major Types of Retailers				
Type	Merchandise	Level of service	Size	Prices	Examples
Convenience stores	Limited number of choices in narrow number or product lines; frequently purchased and emergency items	Self-service	Small	Low-priced items sold at higher than average prices	7-Eleven
Supermarkets	Large selection of food items and limited selection of general merchandise	Limited service	Medium	Moderate	Sobeys, Zehrs
Box stores	Limited selection of food items; many store brands	Self-service Bag your own purchases	Medium	Low	ALDI
Specialty stores	Large selection items in one or a few product lines	Full service	Small and medium	Moderate to high	Claire's (accessories) Yankee Candle Co., Things Remembered
Leased departments	Limited selection of items in a single product line	Usually full service	Small	Moderate to high	Picture Me portrait studios in Walmart stores
General merchandise discount stores	Large selection of items in a broad assortment of product lines	Limited service	Large	Moderate to low	Walmart, Kmart
Off-price retailers	Moderate selection of limited product lines; buy surplus merchandise	Limited service	Moderate	Moderate to low	Winners, HomeSense
Warehouse clubs	Moderate selection of limited product lines; many items in larger than normal quantities	Self-service	Large	Moderate to low	Costco, Sam's Club
Factory outlet stores	Limited selection from a single manufacturer	Limited service	Small	Moderate to low	Gap Factory Outlet, Liz Claiborne Outlet
Department stores	Large selection or many product lines	Full service	Large	Moderate to high	The Bay, Sears
Hypermarkets	Large selection of items in food and a broad assortment of general merchandise product lines	Self-service	Very large	Moderate to low	Real Canadian/ Loblaw Superstore

items. Store chains such as Couche-Tard and 7-Eleven now offer customers a coffee bar, fresh sandwiches, and pastries.

Supermarkets

Supermarkets are food stores that carry a wide selection of edible and nonedible products. Although the large supermarket is a fixture in North America, it has not caught on to the same extent in other parts of the world. In many European countries, for example, consumers walk or bike to small stores near their homes. They tend to have smaller food orders per trip and to shop more frequently, partly because many lack the freezer space to store a huge inventory of products at home. Although wide variety is less important than quality and local ambiance to Europeans, their shopping habits are starting to change as huge hypermarkets become popular around the globe.

supermarkets
Food stores that carry a wide selection of edibles and related products.

Box Stores

Box stores are food stores that have a limited selection of items, few brands per item, and few refrigerated items. Generally, they are open fewer hours than supermarkets and are smaller and carry fewer items than warehouse clubs. Items are displayed in open boxes (hence the name) and customers bag their own purchases. ALDI stores, for example, carry only about 1400 regularly stocked items, while a typical supermarket may carry up to 50 000 items.[34] (About 95 percent of ALDI items are store brands with a few national brands that are special-buy purchases and are available for limited periods.)

Specialty Stores

Specialty stores have narrow and deep inventories. They do not sell a lot of product lines, but they offer a good selection of brands within the lines they do sell. The *category killer* is one type of specialty store that has become especially important in retailing today. A category killer is a very large specialty store that carries a vast selection of products in its category. Some examples of category killers are Home Depot, Toys "R" Us, Best Buy, and Staples. For many women with less-than-perfect figures, shopping at a store that sells only swimsuits means there will be an adequate selection so they can find a suit that really fits. The same is true for larger, taller men who can't find suits that fit in regular department stores but have lots of choices in stores that cater to big-and-tall guys. Specialty stores can tailor their assortment to the specific needs of a targeted consumer, and they often offer a high level of knowledgeable service.

Leased Departments

Leased departments are departments within a larger retail store that an outside firm rents. This arrangement allows larger stores to offer a broader variety of products than they would otherwise carry. Some examples of leased departments are in-store banks, photographic studios, pet departments, jewellery departments, and watch and shoe repair departments.

Discount Stores

General merchandise discount stores such as Target, Kmart, and Walmart Canada offer a broad assortment of items at low prices and with minimal service and are the dominant outlet for many products. Discounters are tearing up the retail landscape because they appeal to price-conscious shoppers who want easy access to a lot of merchandise. These stores increasingly carry designer-name clothing at bargain prices as companies like Kohl's create new lines just for discount stores.[35]

We also have **off-price retailers**. These stores obtain surplus merchandise from manufacturers and offer brand-name, fashion-oriented goods at low prices.

Warehouse clubs such as Costco are a newer version of the discount store. These establishments do not offer any of the amenities of a full-service store. Customers buy many of the products in larger-than-normal packages and quantities—nothing like laying in a three-year supply of paper towels or two-kilogram boxes of pretzels, even if you have to build an extra room in your house to store all this stuff! These clubs often charge a membership fee to consumers and small businesses. A recent survey showed that the typical warehouse shopper shops about once a month, is intrigued by bulk buying, hates long lines, and is drawn to the club retailer because of specific product areas such as fresh groceries.[36] And, consistent with the wheel of retailing, even these stores "trade up" in terms of what they sell today; shoppers can purchase fine jewellery and other luxury items at many warehouse clubs. The **factory outlet store** is still another type of discount retailer. A manufacturer owns these stores. Some factory outlets enable the manufacturer to sell off defective merchandise or excess inventory, while others carry items not available at full-price retail outlets and are designed to provide an additional distribution channel for the

---

box stores
Food stores that have a limited selection of items, few brands per item, and few refrigerated items.

specialty stores
Retailers that carry only a few product lines but offer good selection within the lines that they sell.

leased departments
Departments within a larger retail store that an outside firm rents.

general merchandise discount stores
Retailers that offer a broad assortment of items at low prices with minimal service.

off-price retailers
Retailers that buy excess merchandise from well-known manufacturers and pass the savings on to customers.

warehouse clubs
Discount retailers that charge a modest membership fee to consumers who buy a broad assortment of food and nonfood items in bulk and in a warehouse environment.

factory outlet store
A discount retailer, owned by a manufacturer, that sells off defective merchandise and excess inventory.

manufacturer. Although the assortment is not wide because a store carries products only one manufacturer makes, we find most factory outlet stores in *outlet malls* where a large number of factory outlet stores cluster together in the same location.

Department Stores

Department stores sell a broad range of items and offer a deep selection organized into different sections of the store (Exhibit 12.7). Department stores dominated urban centres of North America in the early part of the twentieth century. In many countries, department stores continue to thrive and they remain consumers' primary place to shop. In Japan, department stores are always crowded with shoppers who buy everything from a takeaway sushi dinner to a string of fine pearls. In Spain, a single department store chain, El Corte Inglés, dominates retailing. Its branch stores include store-size departments for electronics, books, music, and gourmet foods, and each has a vast supermarket covering one or two floors of the store.

In Canada, however, department stores have struggled in recent years. On the one hand, specialty stores lure department-store shoppers away with deeper, more cutting-edge fashion selections and better service. On the other hand, department stores have also been squeezed by discount stores and catalogues that offer the same items at lower prices because they don't have the expense of rent, elaborate store displays and fixtures, or high salaries for salespeople.

Exhibit 12.7

The Bay store has been a trend setter in Canada, particularly around major events like the Olympics.

department stores
Retailers that sell a broad range of items and offer a good selection within each product line.

Hypermarkets

Hypermarkets combine the characteristics of warehouse stores and supermarkets. A European invention, these are huge establishments several times larger than other stores. A supermarket might be 40 000 to 50 000 square feet, whereas a hypermarket takes up 200 000 to 300 000 square feet, or four football fields. They offer one-stop shopping, often for over 50 000 items, and feature restaurants, beauty salons, and children's play areas. Hypermarkets such as those the French firm Carrefour runs are popular in Europe and Latin America where big stores are somewhat of a novelty. More recently, Carrefour is expanding to developing countries such as China where a burgeoning population and a lack of large retailers provide "hyper opportunities." Hypermarkets have been less successful in Canada where many other shopping options including discount stores, malls, and supermarkets are available. Consumers in Canada find the hypermarkets to be too large and shopping in them too time consuming.

hypermarkets
Retailers with the characteristics of both warehouse stores and supermarkets; several times larger than other stores, that offer virtually everything from grocery items to electronics.

Nonstore Retailing

9

OBJECTIVE

Describe the more common forms of nonstore retailing including B2C e-commerce.

(pp. 479–485)

As the founder of the Neiman-Marcus department store once noted, "If customers don't want to get off their butts and go to your stores, you've got to go to them."[37] Indeed, many products are readily available in places other than stores. Think of the familiar Avon lady who sells beauty products to millions of women around the world. Avon allows customers to place orders by phone, fax, or through a sales representative.

nonstore retailing
Any method used to complete an exchange with a product end user that does not require a customer visit to a store.

Avon's success at giving customers alternatives to traditional store outlets illustrates the increasing importance of **nonstore retailing**, which is any method a firm uses to complete an exchange that does not require a customer to visit a store. Indeed, many conventional retailers, from upscale specialty stores such as Birks to discounter Walmart Canada, offer nonstore alternatives such as catalogues and Web sites for customers who want to buy their merchandise. For other companies, such as Internet retailer Amazon.com, nonstore retailing is their entire business. Catalogue companies have, perhaps, had the easiest time making the transition to the Web. Many have been able to use their experience delivering goods directly to consumers and make a successful jump to online sales. Earlier, we talked about direct marketing done through the mail, telephone, and television. In this section, we'll look at two other types of nonstore retailing: direct selling and automatic vending.

Direct Selling

direct selling
An interactive sales process in which a salesperson presents a product to one individual or a small group, takes orders, and delivers the merchandise.

Direct selling occurs when a salesperson presents a product to one individual or a small group, takes orders, and delivers the merchandise. The Direct Selling Association reported that in 2009, 15 million people engaged in direct selling in the United States and these activities generated $29.6 billion in sales.[38] Similar numbers can be found in Canada. Of this, 66.3 percent of revenues came from face-to-face sales and 25.7 percent from party plan or group sales. Female salespeople accounted for 86.4 percent of all direct salespeople. The major product categories for direct sales include home/family care products (such as cleaning products), wellness products (such as weight loss products), and personal care products (such as cosmetics, jewellery, and skin care products).

Door-to-Door Sales

Green River Ordinances
Community regulations that prohibit door-to-door selling unless prior permission is given by the household.

Door-to-door selling is still popular in some countries, such as China. But it's declining in North America, where two-income households are the norm, because fewer people are home during the day, and those who *are* home are reluctant to open their doors to strangers. Door-to-door selling is illegal in communities that have **Green River Ordinances**; they prohibit door-to-door selling unless prior permission is given by the household.

Parties and Networks

At *home shopping parties* a company representative makes a sales presentation to a group of people who have gathered in the home of a friend.[39] One reason that these parties are so effective is that people who attend may get caught up in the "group spirit," and buy things they would not normally purchase if they were alone—even Botox injections to get rid of those nasty wrinkles. We call this sales technique a **party plan system**. Perhaps the most famous home shopping parties were the Tupperware parties popular in the 1950s.

party plan system
A sales technique that relies heavily on people getting caught up in the "group spirit," buying things they would not normally buy if they were alone.

Multilevel Marketing

multilevel or network marketing
A system in which a master distributor recruits other people to become distributors, sells the company's product to the recruits, and receives a commission on all the merchandise sold by the people recruited.

Another form of direct selling, which the Amway Company epitomizes, is **multilevel or network marketing**. In this system, a *master distributor* recruits other people to become distributors. The master distributor sells the company's products to the people she entices to join, and then she receives commissions on all the merchandise sold by the people she recruits. Today, Amway has over 3 million independent business owners who distribute personal care, home care, and nutrition and commercial products in more than 80 countries and territories.[40] Amway and other similar network marketers use revival-like techniques to motivate distributors to sell products and find new recruits.[41]

One of the advantages of *multilevel marketing* is that it allows firms to reach consumers who belong to tightly knit groups that are not so easy to reach. Salt Lake City–based Nu Skin Enterprises relies on Mormons to sell its products in Mormon communities. Shaklee (which sells food supplements, cleaning products, and personal care items) recruits salespeople in isolated religious communities, including Amish and Mennonite people (who receive "bonus buggies" instead of cars as prizes for superior salesmanship).[42]

Despite the growing popularity of this technique, some network systems are illegal. They are really **pyramid schemes**: illegal scams that promise consumers or investors large profits from recruiting others to join the program rather than from any real investment or sale of goods to the public. Often large numbers of people at the bottom of the pyramid pay money to advance to the top and to profit from others who might join. At recruiting meetings, pyramid promoters create a frenzied, enthusiastic atmosphere complete with promises of easy money. Some pyramid schemes are disguised as multilevel marketing—that is, people entering the pyramid do not pay fees to advance, but they are forced to buy large, costly quantities of merchandise. Of course, in these organizations, little or no effort ever goes into actually marketing the products.[43] That's one of the crucial differences between pyramid schemes and legitimate network marketers.

> **pyramid schemes**
> An illegal sales technique that promises consumers or investors large profits from recruiting others to join the program rather than from any real investment or sale of goods to the public.

Automatic Vending

Coin-operated vending machines are a tried-and-true way to sell convenience goods, especially cigarettes and drinks. These machines are appealing, because they require minimal space and personnel to maintain and operate. Some of the most interesting innovations are state-of-the-art vending machines that dispense everything from Ore-Ida French fries to software. French consumers purchase Levi's jeans from a machine called Libre Service that offers the pants in 10 different sizes. In the United States, vending machines that utilize touch screens and credit cards dispense pricey items like digital cameras and Elizabeth Arden cosmetics.[44]

In general, however, vending machines are best suited to the sales of inexpensive merchandise and food and beverages. Most consumers are reluctant to buy pricey items from a machine. New vending machines may spur more interest, however, as technological developments loom on the horizon, including video kiosk machines that let people see the product in use, have the ability to accept credit cards as payment, and have inventory systems that signal the operator when malfunctions or stock-outs occur.

B2C E-Commerce

Business-to-consumer (B2C) e-commerce is online exchange between companies and individual consumers. Forrester Research reports that in 2009 shoppers bought $155 billion worth of consumer goods online.[45] Furthermore, Forrester estimates $917 billion in off-line consumer sales were Web influenced. These two categories accounted for 42 percent of all retail sales. Forrester also estimates that off-line Web-influenced sales will increase to $1.4 trillion by 2014 while online sales will top $250 billion.[46]

> **business-to-consumer (B2C) e-commerce**
> Online exchanges between companies and individual consumers.

A number of factors prevent online sales from growing even more. Most consumers prefer stores where they can touch and feel items and avoid issues with returns and shipping costs. Also, many consumers don't like to buy online because they want the product immediately. To address some of these issues, retailers such as Best Buy have merged their online and in-store sales functions. Consumers can select an item and pay for it online, then pick it up at their local store within hours—no wandering over the store to find the item or waiting in line to pay and no concerns about stock-outs. We'll talk more about these limitations and the benefits of B2C e-commerce next.

Benefits of B2C E-Commerce

For both consumers and marketers, B2C e-commerce provides a host of benefits and some limitations. Table 12.5 lists some of these.

From the consumer's perspective, electronic marketing increases convenience as it breaks down many of the barriers time and location cause. You can shop 24/7 without leaving home. Consumers in even the smallest of communities can purchase funky clothing from Aritzia.com just like big-city dwellers. In less-developed countries, the Internet lets consumers purchase products that may not be available at all in local markets. The Web

Table 12.5	Benefits and Limitations of E-Commerce

Benefits	Limitations
For the consumer:	**For the consumer:**
Shop 24 hours a day	Lack of security
Less travelling	Fraud
Can receive relevant information in seconds from any location	Can't touch items
More product choices	Exact colours may not reproduce on computer monitors
More products available to less developed countries	Expensive to order and then return
Greater price information	Potential breakdown of human relationships
Lower prices, so less affluent can purchase	**For the marketer:**
Participate in virtual auctions	Lack of security
Fast delivery	Must maintain site to reap benefits
Electronic communities	Fierce price competition
For the marketer:	Conflicts with conventional retailers
The world is your marketplace	Legal issues not resolved
Decreases costs of doing business	
Very specialized businesses can be successful	
Real-time pricing	

La Cage aux Sports

Exhibit 12.8

The Canadian restaurant chain La Cage aux Sports is known for putting an airplane in all of its restaurants. The aircraft is part of the chain's image strategy and enhances the customer experience.

experiential shoppers
Consumers who engage in online shopping because of the experiential benefits they receive.

site Ideeli offers its customers the chance to buy heavily discounted luxury items in a kind of online "blue-light special" on your cell phone. Thus, the Internet can improve the quality of life without the necessity of developing costly infrastructure, such as opening retail stores in remote locations.

For some consumers, online shopping provides an additional benefit because it fulfills their experiential needs; that is, their desire to shop for fun. Consumers who are collectors or who enjoy hobbies are most likely to be **experiential shoppers**. While most online consumers engage in goal-directed behaviour—they wish to satisfy their shopping goal as quickly as possible—between 20 and 30 percent of online consumers shop online because they enjoy the "thrill of the hunt" as much as or more than the actual acquisition of the item. Experiential shoppers linger at sites longer and a desire to be entertained is what motivates them. Consequently, marketers who wish to attract these customers must design Web sites that offer surprise, uniqueness, and excitement. (See Exhibit 12.8 for an example of in-person experiential commerce.)

Marketers realize equally important benefits from e-commerce. Because an organization can reach such a large number of consumers via electronic commerce, it is possible to develop very specialized businesses that could not be profitable if limited by geographic constraints. The Internet provides an excellent opportunity to bring merchants with excess merchandise and bargain-hunting consumers together.[47] When retailers become

Tech and Trends

Be Your Own Virtual Stylist

Think shopping's a bore? Hate hours of trying on outfits to see what looks best? Coutourious.com tried changing that.[48] At Coutourious.com you became your own clothing stylist by virtually styling 3D models. Visitors to the site first chose a photo of a model with a body style like their own. Next they selected tops, bottoms, dresses, shoes, bags, accessories, and other items from 100 brands and placed them on a fairly realistic model—just the way they wanted it. To enhance the experience, Couturious even made styles from six designers that were shown at New York City's Fall 2010 Fashion Week but not yet in stores available to site visitors. The best part—for both Couturious and you—was that you could buy the clothes online and then share your outfit with friends on Facebook or Twitter.

concerned that, due to economic downturns or other factors, consumers may not buy enough, they may utilize online liquidators such as CHLI Distribution Inc. that offers consumers great bargains on apparel and accessories, items retailers refer to as "distressed inventory."

Even high-fashion designers whose retail outlets we associate with Rodeo Drive in Los Angeles, Fifth Avenue in New York, and the Magnificent Mile in Chicago are setting up shop on the Internet to sell $3000 skirts and $5000 suits.[49] Forrester Research predicts that soon luxury apparel online sales will approach $1 billion per year. Armani, for example, offers its entire Emporio collection at EmporioArmani.com. The high-end Neiman Marcus department store finds it can easily sell items like $7900 Valentino gowns and $5500 Carolina Herrera jackets online.

As we discussed in Chapter 9, one of the biggest advantages of e-commerce is that it's easy to get price information. Want to buy a new Hellboy action figure, a mountain bike, an MP3 player, or just about anything else you can think of? Instead of plodding from store to store to compare prices, many Web surfers use search engines or "shop-bots" like Ask.com that compile and compare prices from multiple vendors. With readily available pricing information, shoppers can browse brands, features, reviews, and information on where to buy that particular product. This means that consumers can find all of this information in one central location, which makes shopping more efficient.

E-commerce also allows businesses to reduce costs. Compared to traditional bricks-and-mortar retailers, e-tailers' costs are minimal—no expensive mall sites to maintain and no sales associates to pay. And, for some products, such as computer software and digitized music, e-commerce provides fast, almost instantaneous delivery. Music fans responded by buying over 30 million downloads from sites including iTunes, Dell, and Walmart Stores Inc. Newer entertainment downloads have gone a step further with sites such as iTunes that offers online shoppers the opportunity to purchase or rent movies. Just download with a flick to your iPod, plug it into your new flat-screen TV, and pop some corn. You're set for the evening.

Limitations of B2C E-Commerce

But all is not perfect in the virtual world. E-commerce does have its limitations. One drawback compared to shopping in a store is that customers must wait a few days to receive most products, which are often sent via private delivery services, so shoppers can't achieve instant gratification by walking out of a store clutching their latest "finds."

Of course, some e-commerce sites still suffer from poor design that people find irritating. Customers are less likely to return to sites that are difficult to navigate or that don't provide easy access to customer-service personnel such as the online chats that better sites provide. Customers are often frustrated with sites where their shopping baskets "disappear" as soon as they leave the site. Retailers need to take these navigational problems seriously. When consumers have problems shopping on a site, they are less likely to return to shop another day.

Security is a concern to both consumers and marketers. We hear horror stories of consumers whose credit cards and other identity information have been stolen. Although in North America an individual's financial liability in most theft cases is limited because credit card companies usually absorb most or all of the loss, the damage to one's credit rating can last for years.

Consumers also are concerned about Internet fraud. Although most of us feel competent to judge a local bricks-and-mortar business by its physical presence, by how long it's been around, and from the reports of friends and neighbours who shop there, we have little or no information on the millions of Internet sites offering their products for sale—even though sites like eBay and the Better Business Bureau try to address these concerns by posting extensive information about the reliability of individual vendors.

Another problem is that people need "touch and feel" information before they buy many products. Although it may be satisfactory to buy a computer or a book on the Internet, buying clothing and other items for which touching the item or trying it on is essential may be less attractive. As with catalogues, even though most online companies have liberal return policies, consumers can still get stuck with large delivery and return shipping charges for items that don't fit or simply aren't the right colour.

Developing countries with primarily cash economies pose yet another obstacle to the global success of B2C e-commerce. In these countries, few people use credit cards, so they can't easily pay for items they purchase over the Internet. Furthermore, banks are far less likely to offer consumers protection against fraudulent use of their cards, so a hacked card number can literally wipe you out. For consumers in these countries, there are a growing number of alternatives for safely paying for online purchases. PayPal is a global leader in online payments. Founded in 1998 and acquired by eBay in 2002, PayPal has 81 million active accounts and services customers in 190 markets and 24 currencies around the world.[50] Twitpay is a service that permits consumers to send payments using the social network site Twitter. Twitpay's RT2Give service offers consumers the opportunity to easily make payments to nonprofits. After the disastrous earthquake in Haiti in 2010, consumers were able to donate money to the Red Cross for Haiti using Twitter.

As major marketers beef up their presence on the Web, they worry that inventory they sell online will *cannibalize* their store sales (we discussed the strategic problem of cannibalization in Chapter 8). This is a big problem for companies like bookseller Barnes & Noble, which has to be careful as it steers customers toward its Web site and away from its chain of stores bursting with inventory. Barnes & Noble has to deal with competitors such as Amazon.com (with 40 million world-wide customers and annual sales of not only books but myriad products from apparel to cell phones of over $14.84 billion in 2007), which sells its books and music exclusively over its six global Web sites and so doesn't have to worry about this problem.[51] Of course, today books, including textbooks like this one, have gone digital and can be purchased and downloaded online. Tablet e-book readers such as Amazon.com's Kindle, Sony's Reader, and Apple's iPad have made e-books even more attractive.

B2C's Effect on the Future of Retailing

Does the growth of B2C e-commerce mean the death of bricks-and-mortar stores as we know them? Don't plan any funerals for your local stores prematurely. Although some argue that virtual distribution channels will completely replace traditional ones because of their cost advantages, this is unlikely. For example, although a bank saves 80 percent of its costs when customers do business online from their home computers, Wells Fargo found that it could not force its customers to use PC-based banking services. For now, clicks will have to coexist with bricks.

However, this doesn't mean that physical retailers can rest easy. Stores as we know them will continue to evolve to lure shoppers away from their computer screens. In the future, the trend will be *destination retail*; that is, consumers will visit retailers not so much to buy a product but for the entertainment they receive from the total experience. Many retailers are already developing ways to make the shopping in bricks-and-mortar stores an experience rather than just a place to pick up stuff. At the General Mills Cereal Adventure in the Mall of America, children of all ages cavort in the Cheerios Play Park and the Lucky Charms Magical Forest. Sony's Metreon in San Francisco is a high-tech mall that features futuristic computer games and cutting-edge electronics.[52]

10 Develop a Store Positioning Strategy: Retailing as Theatre

OBJECTIVE

Understand the importance of store image to a retail positioning strategy and explain how a retailer can create a desirable image in the marketplace.

(pp. 485–490)

A "destination retail" strategy reminds us that shopping often is part buying, part entertainment, and part social outlet. So far, we've seen that we distinguish stores in several ways, including the types of products they carry and the breadth and depth of their assortments. But recall that a store is itself a product that adds to or subtracts from the goods the shopper came to buy there.

When we decide which store to patronize, many of us are less likely to say, "I'll go there because their assortment is broad," and more likely to say, "That place is so cool. I really like hanging out there." Stores can entertain us, bore us, make us angry, or even make us sad (unless it's a funeral parlour), otherwise it probably won't be in business for long. In today's competitive marketplace, retailers have to do more than offer good inventory at reasonable prices. They need to position their stores so that they offer a competitive advantage over other stores that also vie for the shopper's attention—not to mention the catalogues, Web sites, and shopping channels that may offer the same or similar merchandise. Let's see next how bricks-and-mortar retailers compete against these alternatives.

Walk into Atmosphere, a Canadian-based retailer with over 20 stores in 10 provinces, and you'll find gear for camping, climbing, cycling, skiing, outdoor cross-training, paddling, snow sports, and travel. Atmosphere is more than that, though. One of its Toronto stores, for example, features a 65-foot-high, artificial climbing rock, while other Atmosphere stores include a vented area for testing camp stoves and an outdoor trail to check out mountain bikes. Buying a water pump? Test it in an indoor river. Want to try out those boots before you walk in them? Take a walk on hiking boot test trails.[53]

In Chapter 9 we saw that staging a service is much like putting on a play. Similarly, many retailers recognize that much of what they do is theatre. Shoppers are an audience to entertain. The "play" can cleverly use stage sets (store design) and actors (salespeople) that together create a "scene." For example, think about buying a pair of sneakers. Athletic shoe stores are a far cry from the old days, when a tired shoe salesman (much like Al Bundy in the TV show *Married with Children*) waded through box after box of shoes as kids ran amok across dingy floors.

Now salespeople (actors) dress in costumes such as black-striped referee outfits at stores like Foot Locker. Foot Locker stores are ablaze with neon, and they display their shoes in clear acrylic walls so they appear to be floating.[54] All these special effects make the buying occasion less about buying and more about having an experience. As one marketing strategist commented, "The line between retail and entertainment is blurring." In this section, we'll review some of the tools available to the retailing playwright.

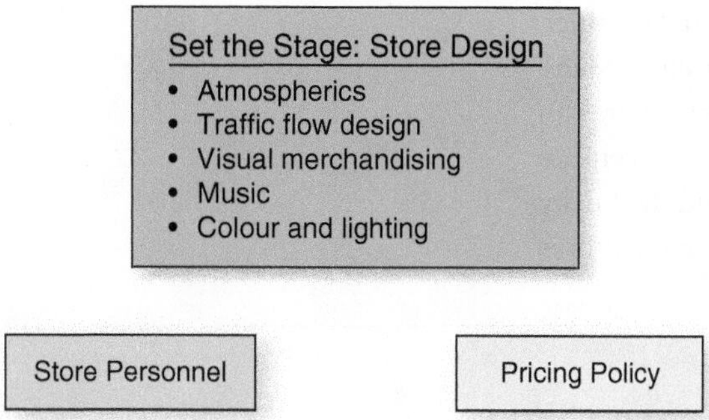

Figure 12.11 Elements of a Store Image

A store's image is how the target market perceives the store relative to the competition. Marketers have many tools to use in creating a desirable store image.

store image
The way the marketplace perceives a retailer relative to the competition.

atmospherics
The use of colour, lighting, scents, furnishings, and other design elements to create a desired store image.

traffic flow
The direction in which shoppers will move through the store and which areas they will pass or avoid.

Store Image

When people think of a store, they often have no trouble describing it in the same terms they might use to describe a person. They might come up with labels like *exciting, boring, old-fashioned, tacky,* or *elegant.* **Store image** is how the target market perceives the store—its market position relative to the competition. Restaurants provide a good example. While Outback's decor attempts to look like an Australian steakhouse, complete with "Kookaburra Wings" and "Jackaroo Chops" on the menu, Olive Garden restaurants use foliage, stucco walls, and Italian background music to remind the diner of an Italian farmhouse. Just as brand managers do for products, store managers work hard to create a distinctive and appealing personality.

To appreciate this idea, consider the dramatic makeover now in place at Selfridges, long a well-known but dowdy British department store chain. At the newly renovated flagship store in London, shoppers can wander over to a body-piercing salon where store associates are teenagers in dreadlocks. Periodic events that "scream" cutting edge accent the store's makeover, which included a "Body Craze" promotion when thousands of shoppers flocked to see 650 naked people ride the escalators.[55] Not every store can have (or wants to have) naked people running around, but even more modest strategies to enliven the atmosphere make a big difference. When a retailer decides to create a desirable store image, it has many tools including those shown in Figure 12.11 at its disposal. Ideally, all these elements work together to create a clear, coherent picture that meets consumers' expectations of what that particular shopping experience should be.

Store Design: Set the Stage

The elements of store design should correspond to management's desired image. A bank lobby needs to convey respectability and security, because people need to be reassured about the safety of their money. In contrast, a used bookstore might create a disorderly look so that shoppers think treasures lie buried beneath piles of tattered novels.

Atmospherics is the use of colour, lighting, scents, furnishings, sounds, and other design elements to create a desired setting. Marketers manipulate these elements to create a certain "feeling" for the retail environment.[56] Today many retailers seek to create a "playground" for adults in their stores, often through the sophisticated use of lighting, more intimate retail spaces, and even strategic smells they pump into the space.[57]

At Levi's stores, and other retailers, consumers experience a Jetsons-like virtual fitting room. A shopper steps into the cylindrical unit where holographic imaging technology performs a 360-degree body scan in less than 10 seconds. The customer then gets a printout with the store's styles and sizes that will best fit his particular body type.[58]

Here are some other design factors that retailers consider:

- *Store layout:* This is the arrangement of merchandise in the store. The placement of fixtures such as shelves, racks, and cash registers is important because store layout determines **traffic flow**—how shoppers will move through the store and which areas they will pass or avoid. A typical strategy is to place staple goods shoppers purchase more frequently in more remote areas. Retailers stock impulse goods in spots shoppers will pass on their way to look for something else, to encourage them to stop and check them out.

  A *grid layout* we usually find in supermarkets and discount stores consists of rows of neatly spaced shelves that are at right angles or parallel to one another. This configuration is useful when management wants to move shoppers systematically down each aisle, being sure that they pass through such high-margin sections as deli and meat. Figure 12.12 illustrates how a grid layout in a supermarket helps regulate traffic flow.

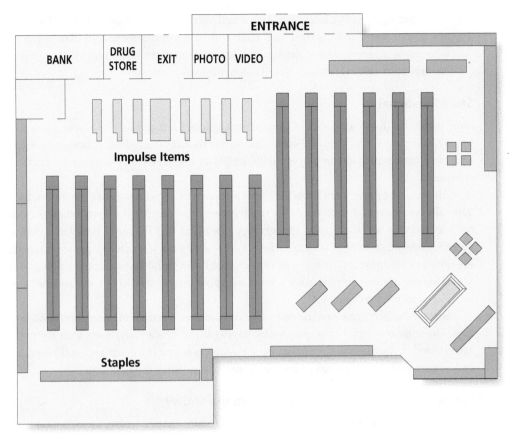

Figure 12.12 Grid Layout

A grid layout encourages customers to move up and down the aisles, passing many different products, and supermarkets and many discount stores often use it.

In contrast, department and specialty stores typically use a *free-flow layout* because it is more conducive to browsing. A retailer might arrange merchandise in circles or arches or perhaps in separate areas, each with its own distinct image and merchandise mix.

- *Visual merchandising:* Just as we form impressions of people from their home decor, our feelings about stores are affected by furnishings, fixtures (shelves and racks that display merchandise), and even how much "stuff" is packed into the sales area. **Visual merchandising** includes all the things customers see both inside and outside the store. Generally, clutter conveys a store with lower-priced merchandise. Upscale stores allocate space for sitting areas, dressing rooms, and elaborate displays of merchandise. Before customers even enter the store, the **storefront** or physical exterior and the sign that shows the store's name, called a **marquee**, contribute to the store's image. Retailers try to create a unique design that customers will associate with the personality of the store. The Toys"R"Us marquee, for example, uses a backward "R" reminiscent of a mistake a child learning to write the alphabet might make.

- The *sound of music:* An elegant restaurant softly playing Mozart in the background is worlds apart from a raucous place such as the Hard Rock Café, where loud rock-and-roll is essential to the atmosphere. The music a store plays has become so central to its personality that many retailers, including Ralph Lauren, Victoria's Secret, Starbucks, and Pottery Barn even sell the soundtracks specially designed for them.[59] Muzak, the premier provider of commercial music for over 70 years, uses its library of over three million songs to create "audio architecture" for businesses including retail stores. For a clothing store, the music may be fun and upbeat, while a bar may want romantic music to encourage late-night couples to stay and have another drink.[60]

visual merchandising
The design of all the things customers see both inside and outside the store.

storefront
The physical exterior of a store.

marquee
The sign that shows a store's name.

- *Colour and lighting:* Marketers use colour and lighting to set a mood. Red, yellow, and orange are warm colours (fast-food chains use a lot of orange to stimulate hunger), whereas blue, green, and violet signify elegance and cleanliness. Light colours make one feel more serene, whereas bright colours convey excitement.

Store Personnel

Store personnel (the actors) should complement a store's image. Each employee has a part to play, complete with props and costumes. Movie theatres often dress ushers in tuxedos, and many stores provide employees with scripts to use when they present products to customers.

Although the presence of knowledgeable sales personnel is important to shoppers, they generally rate the quality of service they receive from retail personnel as low. Retailers work hard to maintain service quality, though they often find that the rapid turnover of salespeople makes this a difficult goal to achieve. Perhaps they can learn from Japanese retailers. A visitor to a Japanese restaurant or store is greeted by an enthusiastic, cheerful, polite, and immaculately dressed employee who, no matter how busy she is, says "*Irasshaimase*" and bows to welcome the customer.

Some Canadian firms have turned superior customer service into a competitive advantage. The store motivates its employees by paying them substantially more than the average rate and deducting sales commissions if customers return the merchandise. This policy encourages the salesperson to be sure the customer is satisfied the first time.

Pricing Policy: How Much for a Ticket to the Show?

When consumers form an image of a store in their minds, the *price points,* or price ranges, of its merchandise often play a role. Discount stores and general merchandisers are likely to compete on a price basis by offering brand names for less.

In recent years, consumers' desires for bargains have hurt department stores. Many retailers responded by running frequent sales, a strategy that often backfired because they trained consumers to buy *only* when the store held a sale. Some stores have instead reduced the number of sales they run in favour of lowering prices across the board. As we saw in Chapter 9, some stores, including Home Depot and Walmart Canada, offer an *everyday-low-pricing (EDLP) strategy;* they set prices that are between the list price the manufacturer suggests and the deeply discounted price offered at stores that compete on price only.

Build the Theatre: Store Location

Any real estate agent will tell you the three most important factors when they sell a home are "location, location, and location." The same is true in retailing. Walmart's success is due not only to what it is but also to *where* it is. It was the first large discount retailer to locate in small and rural markets. When they choose a site, Walmart's planners consider factors such as proximity to highways and major traffic routes. By carefully selecting "undiscovered" areas, the company has been able to negotiate cheap leases in towns with expanding populations. This is an important strategic advantage for Walmart, because it means access to markets hungry for a store that offers such a wide assortment of household goods. In this section, we'll review some important aspects of retail locations.

Types of Store Locations

There are four basic types of retail locations. Stores locate in a business district, in a shopping centre, as a freestanding entity, or in a nontraditional location.

central business district (CBD)
The traditional downtown business area found in a town or city.

- **Business districts:** A **central business district (CBD)** is the traditional downtown business area you'll find in a town or city. Many people are drawn to the area to shop or work, and public transportation is usually available. CBDs have suffered in recent years because of concerns about security, lack of parking, and the lack of customer traffic on evenings and weekends. To combat these problems, cities typically provide incentives such as tax breaks to encourage the opening of stores and entertainment areas. These vibrant developments or *festival marketplaces* have done a lot to reverse the fortunes of aging downtown areas.

- **Shopping centres:** A **shopping centre** is a group of commercial establishments owned and managed as a single property. They range in size and scope from strip malls to massive *super-regional centres* such as the West Edmonton Mall, which offers over 3 million square feet of shopping plus many attractions. Strip malls offer quick and easy access to basic conveniences such as dry cleaners and video rentals, though shoppers seeking more exotic goods need to look elsewhere. Shopping malls offer variety and the ability to combine shopping with entertainment. Rents tend to be high in shopping malls, making it difficult for many stores to be profitable. In addition, small specialty stores may find it hard to compete with a mall's *anchor stores,* the major department stores that typically draw many shoppers.

A *lifestyle centre* combines the feel of a neighbourhood park with the convenience of a strip mall. These more intimate centres typically are located in affluent neighbourhoods and feature expensive landscaping; they are an appealing way for retailers to blend in to upscale residential areas.

- **Freestanding retailers:** Some stores, usually larger ones such as IKEA, occupy their own facility. These retailers benefit from lower rents and fewer parking problems. However, the store must be attractive enough on its own to be a destination point for shoppers, because it can't rely on spillover from consumers visiting other stores at the same place.

- **Nontraditional store locations:** Innovative retailers find new ways to reach consumers. For example, many entrepreneurs use *carts* or *kiosks* to sell their products. Carts are small, movable stores that can be set up in many locations, including inside malls, in airports, or in other public facilities. Kiosks are slightly larger than carts and offer store-like facilities, including telephone hookups and electricity. Carts and kiosks are relatively inexpensive and a good way for new businesses to get started. (See Exhibit 12.9.)

shopping centre
A group of commercial establishments owned and managed as a single property.

trade area
A geographic zone that accounts for the majority of a store's sales and customers.

popup store
A temporary retail space a company erects to build buzz for its products.

Site Selection: Choose Where to Build

A story from the past is that Sam Walton, the founder of Walmart, used to fly over an area in a small plane until he found a spot that appealed to him. Now factors such as long-term population patterns, the location of competitors, and the demographic makeup of an area enter into retailers' decisions. The choice of where to open a new store should reflect the company's overall growth strategy. It should be consistent with long-term goals and be in a place that allows the company to best support the outlet. For example, a chain with stores and an extensive warehouse system in Ontario may not be wise to open a new store in British Columbia because the store would be an "orphan," cut off from the company's supply lines.

Location planners look at many factors when they select a site. They want to find a place that is convenient to customers in the store's **trade area**, the geographic zone that accounts for the majority of its sales and customers.[61] A *site evaluation* considers specific factors such as traffic

Exhibit 12.9

A **popup store** is a temporary retail space a company erects to build buzz for its products. As the sour economy creates a glut of commercial real estate, this concept is an increasingly popular way to test new product ideas or perhaps even to test if a neighbourhood will be a good fit for a new store. A range of marketers, from eBay and Seven for All Mankind to upscale Hermés, have bought into the concept.

Frances M. Roberts/Newscom.

flow; number of parking spaces available; ease of delivery access; visibility from the street; local zoning laws that determine the types of buildings, parking, and signage allowed; and cost factors such as the length of the lease and the amount of local taxes.

Planners also consider population characteristics such as *age profile* (is the area witnessing an influx of new families?), *community life cycle* (is the community relatively new, stable, or in decline?), and *mobility* (how often do people move into and out of the area?). Planners also have to consider the degree of competition they will encounter if they locate in one place versus another. One strategy that fast-food outlets follow is to locate in a *saturated trade area*. This is a site where a sufficient number of stores already exist so that high customer traffic is present but where the retailer believes it can compete successfully if it goes head-to-head with the competition. As one fast-food industry executive put it, "Customers are lazybones. They absolutely will not walk one more step. You literally have to put a store where people are going to smack their face against it." However, that task is getting harder and harder because at this point many of the good sites are already taken. The United States has 277 208 fast-food outlets from coast to coast—one for every 1000 people in the country. Subway restaurants opens a new store in the United States every three hours on average. Starbucks unveils a new store every 11 hours, and Quiznos opens a new door every 16 hours.[62]

Another strategy is to find an *understored trade area*, where too few stores exist to satisfy the needs of the population (this was Walmart Canada's strategy), and the retailer can establish itself as a dominant presence in the community. Over time, these areas may become *overstored* so that too many stores exist to sell the same goods. Those that can't compete are forced to move or close, as has happened to many small mom-and-pop stores that can't beat the Walmarts of the world at their sophisticated retailing games.

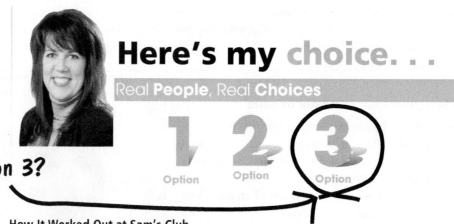

Why do you think Heather chose option 3?

How It Worked Out at Sam's Club

Heather chose Option 3. Sam's Club launched the caseless program in November of 2007 and expanded the program during 2008 when milk prices began to soar due to the higher cost of fuel, feed for cattle, and other factors.

The new jug was a radical change from the traditional container. It's actually easier to use as you "tilt and pour" the milk as opposed to lifting the traditional milk jug. Still, Sam's had to teach shoppers how to use the new jug—if they lifted and poured as they did with the old container, the milk would dribble down the side. People had to learn to just tilt the jug instead, so Sam's performed product demonstrations in all Clubs when the new product launched, to teach members how to use it. Since the initial launch, the jug has gone through numerous versions to improve "pourability" so the spillage problem has been eliminated.

The switch was so large-scale and innovative that over 1000 news stories about it ran around the world. Major TV news shows featured the new process, including NBC's *Today Show*, NBC *Nightly News*, CBS *Evening News*, *Good Morning America* and *Fox*.

How Sam's Club Measures Success

Sam's Club tracks the effectiveness of the caseless program by using metrics in different categories. These include:

- *Price and sales volume efficiencies:* It monitors the number of units sold over time and how fresh they are when they arrive at the store (i.e., an improved shelf life of 6 days due to better processor control). Heather observed that members buy more milk; Sam's is taking back market share from competitors and attracting more traffic into the club. Sam's Club has been able to maintain a lower cost structure due to the innovation and resulting lower labour costs. As a result the price spread between the company's milk prices and those of its key competitors has increased.

- *Logistical efficiencies:*
  - 9% more product on a truck
  - 51% improvement in cube utilization
  - Number of weekly deliveries cut in half
  - Pallets hold 3 times as much product as a milk rack
  - Back haul opportunities created as racks and cases are no longer returned to the production facility for cleaning and reloading. Under the traditional method of delivery, out-bound full loads and in-bound return loads require the same amount of cube. Now the supplier can use the truck's return trip to haul more merchandise instead of empty racks and cases.

- *The environmental impact of innovations.* In this case, sustainability metrics include
  - Fewer food miles driven
  - Elimination of need to clean racks and cases (milk crates), saving thousands of litres of water and detergents from going into the sewer system
  - Recycling of milk carton, shrink wrap, and cardboard slip sheets
  - Reuse of pallets for other products

To learn the whole story, visit www.mypearsonmarketinglab.com.

Objective Summary ➡ Key Terms ➡ Apply

1. Objective Summary (pp. 442–445)

Understand the concept of the value chain and the key elements in a supply chain.

The value chain consists of five primary activities (inbound logistics, operations, outbound logistics, marketing and sales, and service) and four support activities (procurement, technology development, human resource management, and firm infrastructure). The process is called a value chain because each of these activities adds value to the product the customer eventually buys. Whereas the value chain is an overarching concept of how firms create value, the supply chain also encompasses components external to the firm itself, including all activities that are necessary to convert raw materials into a good or service and put it in the hands of the consumer or business customer.

Key Terms

supply chain, p. 443

supply chain management., p. 444

insourcing, p. 444

channel of distribution, p. 445

2. Objective Summary (pp. 445–448)

Explain what a distribution channel is and what functions distribution channels perform.

A distribution channel is a series of firms or individuals that facilitates the movement of a product from the producer to the final customer. Channels provide time, place, and ownership utility for customers and reduce the number of transactions necessary for goods to flow from many manufacturers to large numbers of customers by breaking bulk and creating assortments. Channel members make the purchasing process easier by providing important customer services. Today the Internet is becoming an important player in distribution channels.

Key Terms

channel intermediaries, p. 445

breaking bulk, p. 446

creating assortments, p. 446

facilitating functions, p. 446

disintermediation (of the channel of distribution), p. 448

knowledge management, p. 448

online distribution piracy, p. 448

3. Objective Summary (pp. 448–452)

Describe the types of wholesaling intermediaries found in distribution channels.

Wholesaling intermediaries are firms that handle the flow of products from the manufacturer to the retailer or business user. Merchant wholesalers are independent intermediaries that take title to a product and include both full-function wholesalers and limited-function wholesalers. Merchandise agents and brokers are independent intermediaries that do not take title to products. Manufacturer-owned channel members include sales branches, sales offices, and manufacturers' showrooms.

Key Terms

wholesaling intermediaries, p. 449

independent intermediaries, p. 449

merchant wholesalers, p. 449

take title, p. 449

merchandise agents or brokers, p. 451

4. Objective Summary (pp. 452–456)

Describe the types of distribution channels and how _place_ fits in with the other three Ps in the marketing mix.

Distribution channels vary in length from the simplest two-level channel to longer channels with three or more channel levels. Distribution channels include direct distribution in which the producer sells directly to consumers, and indirect channels, which may include a retailer, wholesaler, or other intermediary. Decisions on what channels to utilize affect the price you can charge as well as overall positioning strategy for a product. The marketing mix is called a "mix" because each ingredient impacts the others as well as the whole marketing strategy.

Key Terms

channel levels, p. 452

hybrid marketing system, p. 455

5. Objective Summary (pp. 456–462)

Understand the steps to plan a distribution channel strategy.

Marketers begin channel planning by developing channel objectives and considering important environmental factors. The next step is to decide on a distribution strategy, which involves determining the type of distribution channel that is best. Distribution tactics include the selection of individual channel members and management of the channel.

Key Terms

conventional marketing system, p. 457

vertical marketing system (VMS), p. 457

horizontal marketing system, p. 459

intensive distribution, p. 459

exclusive distribution, p. 460

selective distribution, p. 460

channel leader, p. 461

6. Objective Summary (pp. 462–467)

Explain logistics and how it fits into the supply chain concept.

Logistics is the process of designing, managing, and improving supply chains, including all the activities that are required to move products through the supply chain. Logistics contributes to the overall supply chain through activities including order processing, warehousing, materials handling, transportation, and inventory control.

Key Terms

logistics, p. 462

physical distribution, p. 463

order processing, p. 463

enterprise resource planning (ERP) systems, p. 464

warehousing, p. 464

materials handling, p. 464

transportation, p. 464

inventory control, p. 466

radio frequency identification (RFID), p. 466

just in time (JIT), p. 466

7. Objective Summary (pp. 467–474)

Define retailing; understand how retailing evolves and some ethical issues in retailing.

Retailing is the process by which goods and services are sold to consumers for their personal use. The wheel-of-retailing hypothesis suggests that new retailers compete on price and over time become more upscale, leaving room for other new, low-price entrants. The retail life cycle theory suggests that retailing institutions are introduced, grow, reach maturity, and then decline. Three factors that motivate retailers to evolve are changing economic conditions, demographics, technology, and globalization. Some of the ethical issues retailers face include shrinkage due to shoplifting, employee theft, and retail borrowing. Retailers and their employees must also be cognizant of the ethical treatment of customers.

Key Terms

retailing, p. 467

wheel-of-retailing hypothesis, p. 468

retail life cycle, p. 470

mergers, p. 471

downsizing, p. 471

point-of-sale (POS) systems, p. 472

perpetual inventory
unit control system, p. 472

automatic reordering system, p. 472

shrinkage, p. 473

retail borrowing, p. 474

8. Objective Summary (pp. 475–479)

Understand how we classify retailers.

Retailers are classified by NAICS codes based on product lines sold; however, new retail models such as combination stores offer consumers more than one product line. Retailers may also be classified by the level of service offered (self-service, full-service, and limited-service retailers) and by the merchandise assortment offered. Merchandise assortment is described in terms of breadth and depth, which refer to the number of product lines sold and the amount of variety available for each. Thus, stores are classified as convenience stores, supermarkets, box stores, specialty stores, category killers, leased departments, variety stores, general merchandise discount stores, off-price retailers, warehouse clubs, department stores, and hypermarkets.

Key Terms

merchandise mix, p. 475

combination stores, p. 475

supercentres, p. 475

merchandise assortment, p. 476

merchandise breadth, p. 476

merchandise depth, p. 476

convenience stores, p. 476

supermarkets, p. 477

box stores, p. 478

specialty stores, p. 478

leased departments, p. 478

general merchandise discount stores, p. 478

off-price retailers, p. 478

warehouse clubs, p. 478

factory outlet store, p. 478

department stores, p. 479

hypermarkets, p. 479

9. Objective Summary (pp. 479–485)

Describe the more common forms of nonstore retailing including B2C e-commerce.

The two more common types of nonstore retailing are direct selling and automatic vending machines. In direct selling, a salesperson presents a product to one individual or a small group, takes orders, and delivers the merchandise. Direct selling includes door-to-door sales and party or network sales. State-of-the-art self-service vending machines can dispense products from French fries to iPods.

B2C e-commerce, online exchanges between companies and consumers, is growing rapidly. For consumers, B2C benefits include greater convenience, greater product variety, and increased price information. For marketers, B2C offers a world market, decreased costs of doing business, opportunities for specialized businesses, and real-time pricing. The downside of B2C e-commerce for consumers includes having to wait to receive products, security issues, and the inability to touch and feel products. For Internet-only marketers, success on the Internet may be difficult to achieve, whereas cannibalization may be a problem with traditional retailers' online operations.

Key Terms

nonstore retailing, p. 480

direct selling, p. 480

Green River Ordinances, p. 480

party plan system, p. 480

multilevel or marketing network, p. 480

pyramid schemes, p. 481

business-to-consumer (B2C) e-commerce, p. 481

experiential shoppers, p. 482

popup store, p. 483

10. Objective Summary (pp. 485–490)

Understand the importance of store image to a retail positioning strategy and explain how a retailer can create a desirable image in the marketplace.

Store image is how the target market perceives the store relative to the competition and results from many different elements working together to create the most desirable shopping experience and to ensure that shoppers view a store favourably relative to the competition. Colour, lighting, scents, furnishings, and other design elements, called atmospherics, are used to create a "feel" for a store environment. Use of atmospherics includes decisions on (1) store layout, which determines traffic flow and influences the desired customer behaviour in the store; (2) the use of store fixtures and open space; (3) the use of sound to attract (or repel) certain types of customers; and

(4) the use of colour and lighting that can influence customers' moods. The number and type of store personnel, pricing of products sold in the store, and store location contribute to a store's image. The major types of retail locations include central business districts, shopping centres, freestanding retailers, and nontraditional locations such as kiosks.

Key Terms

store image, p. 486

atmospherics, p. 486

traffic flow, p. 486

visual merchandising, p. 487

storefront, p. 487

marquee, p. 487

central business district (CBD), p. 488

shopping centre, p. 489

trade area, p. 489

Chapter **Questions** and **Activities**

Concepts: Test Your Knowledge

1. What is a value chain?
2. What is a supply chain, and how is it different from a channel of distribution?
3. What is a channel of distribution? What are channel intermediaries?
4. Explain the functions of distribution channels.
5. List and explain the types of independent and manufacturer-owned wholesaling intermediaries.
6. What factors are important in determining whether a manufacturer should choose a direct or indirect channel? Why do some firms use hybrid marketing systems?
7. What are conventional, vertical, and horizontal marketing systems?
8. Explain intensive, exclusive, and selective forms of distribution.
9. Explain the steps in distribution planning.
10. What is logistics? Explain the functions of logistics.
11. What are the advantages and disadvantages of shipping by rail? by air? by ship? by truck?
12. Define retailing. What is the role of retailing in today's world? How do the wheel of retailing and retail life cycle theories explain the evolution of retailing? How do the economic environment, demographics, technology, and globalization affect the future of retailing?
13. Explain retail store shrinkage and the ways shrinkage normally occurs. What are some of the ethical issues in retailers' treatment of consumers? What is "sweethearting"?
14. How do marketers classify retail stores? Explain merchandise breadth and depth.
15. Describe the differences in merchandise assortments for convenience stores, supermarkets, box stores, specialty stores, leased departments, general merchandise discount stores, off-price retailers, warehouse clubs, department stores, and hypermarkets.
16. Explain the different types of direct selling. What is the difference between a multilevel network and a pyramid scheme?
17. What is the role of automatic vending in retailing?
18. What is B2C e-commerce? What are some benefits of B2C e-commerce for consumers and for marketers? What are the limitations of B2C e-commerce?
19. What are some possible effects of B2C e-commerce on traditional retailing?
20. How is store-positioning strategy like theatre?
21. What is store image? Why is it important?
22. What is meant by store atmospherics? How can the elements of atmospherics be used to increase the store's success? How are store personnel part of a store's image?
23. What is visual merchandising? How do a retailer's store front and marquee participate in development of a store's image?
24. What are some of the different types of store locations? What are their advantages and disadvantages?

Activities: Apply What You've Learned

1. Assume that you have recently been hired by a firm that manufactures furniture. You feel that marketing should have an input into supplier selection for the firm's products, but the purchasing department says that should not be a concern for marketing. You need to explain to the department head the importance of the value chain perspective. In a role-playing exercise, explain to the purchasing agent the value chain concept, why it is of concern to marketing, and why the two of you should work together.
2. Assume that you are the director of marketing for a firm that manufactures cleaning chemicals used in industries. You have traditionally sold these products through manufacturer's reps. You are considering adding a direct Internet channel to your distribution strategy, but you aren't sure whether this will create channel conflict. Make a list of the pros and cons of this move. What do you think is the best decision?
3. As the one-person marketing department for a candy manufacturer (your firm makes high-quality, hand-dipped chocolates using only natural ingredients), you are considering making changes in your distribution strategy. Your products have previously been sold through a network of food brokers that call on specialty food and gift stores. But you think that perhaps it would be good for your firm to develop a corporate vertical marketing system (that is, vertical integration). In such a plan, a number of company-owned retail outlets would be opened across the country.

The president of your company has asked that you present your ideas to the company executives. In a role-playing situation with one of your classmates, present your ideas to your boss, including the advantages and disadvantages of the new plan compared to the current distribution method.

4. Assume that your firm recently gave you a new marketing assignment. You are to head up development of a distribution plan for a new product line—a series of do-it-yourself instruction videos for home gardeners. These videos would show consumers how to plant trees, shrubbery, and bulbs; how to care for their plants; how to prune; and so on. You know that as you develop a distribution plan it is essential that you understand and consider a number of internal and external environmental factors. Make a list of the information you will need before you can begin to write the distribution plan. How will you adapt your plan based on each of these factors?

5. Assume you are a business consultant for a chain of 37 traditional department stores located in 12 cities in central Canada. In recent years, the stores have seen declining revenues as specialty stores and hypermarkets have begun to squeeze the department stores out. The chain has asked you for suggestions on how to increase its business. Develop an outline of your recommendations and present your plan to your class.

6. Assume that you are the director of marketing for a national chain of convenience stores. Your firm has about 100 stores located in three provinces. The stores are fairly traditional both in design and in the merchandise they carry. Because you want to be proactive in your marketing planning, you are concerned that your firm may need to consider making significant changes because of the current demographic, technological, and global trends in the marketplace. You think it is important to discuss these things with the other executives at your firm. Develop a presentation that includes the following:
   a. A discussion of the demographic changes that will impact your stores
   b. A discussion of the technological changes that will impact your stores
   c. A discussion of how global changes may provide problems and opportunities for your organization
   d. Your recommendations for how your firm might meet the challenges faced in each of these areas

7. As a university graduate, you and a friend think the career you really would enjoy means being your own boss—you want to start your own business. You feel that e-commerce is the place for you to make your fortune. You and your friend are considering two options: (1) an online business that sells custom-made blue jeans based on customers' measurements, and (2) an online business that sells gourmet foods from around the world. In a role-playing exercise, debate with your friend the pros and cons of each of these two online retail businesses and make a decision about which is better.

8. All your life you've wanted to be an entrepreneur and to own your own business. Now you're ready to graduate from university, and you've decided to open a combination coffee shop and bookstore in a location near your university. You know that to attract both the student market and other customers from the local community, it will be necessary

to carefully design the store image. Develop a detailed plan that specifies how you will use atmospherics to create the image you desire.

9. In your job with a marketing consulting firm, you often are asked to make recommendations for store location. Your current client is a local caterer that is planning to open a new retail outlet for selling take-out gourmet dinners. You are examining the possible types of locations: the central business district, a shopping centre, a freestanding entity, or some nontraditional location. Outline the advantages and disadvantages of each type of location. In a role-playing exercise, present your recommendations to your client.

10. Retailers are faced with the problem of shrinkage and what to do about it. Shrinkage comes, of course, from shoplifting and employee theft. More subtle, however, is shrinkage such as "sweethearting" and "retail borrowing" that involves customers Many consumers feel such practices are okay. Conduct a survey of students in your school to study these two sources of shrinkage. You might want to include questions about the following:
    a. If and how frequently students engage in such practices
    b. The attitudes of students as to whether such practices are unethical and why or why not
    c. What harm comes from such practices
    d. What respondents think retailers should do to prevent such shrinkage

Develop a report on your findings and present it to your class.

11. One problem that traditional retailers face when they open online stores is cannibalization. Select a traditional retailer where you and your fellow students might normally shop that also sells products online. You might, for example, select Best Buy, Banana Republic, the Gap, or Walmart. Visit the retailer's online store and make notes on the site's product offering, pricing, customer service policies, and so on. (If the store you have chosen offers many different product lines, you might wish to limit your research to one or two different product lines.) Then visit the store and compare what is offered there with the online offerings. Develop a report that summarizes your findings and discusses the potential for cannibalization and its implications for the retailer.

Marketing Metrics: Exercise

Inventory management is an important aspect of retail strategy. For example, it is important to know when it is time to reorder and how much to order at a time.

This is the reorder point. As consumers buy a product day after day, the inventory level declines. The question for retailers is how low they should allow the inventory level to decline before they place an order; that is, when is it time to reorder? If you order too late, you take a chance of losing sales because you are out of stock. If you order too soon, consumer tastes may change and you will be stuck with excess and unsellable merchandise. The decision of when to order and how much to order is critical to a retailer's bottom line.

The simplest formula to determine the reorder point is

Reorder point = Usage rate × Lead time

But, of course, a retailer can't exactly estimate the usage rate, so it needs to keep some "safety stock" on hand. Then the formula becomes

Reorder point = (Usage rate × Lead time) + Safety stock

The Healthy Day Organic Food Store sells 20 containers of yogurt a day. It takes 6 days to place an order and receive a new shipment of yogurt. But to be prepared for the possibility of extra sales or a late shipment, they need to have a safety stock equal to three days' sales.

What is the reorder point for yogurt for Healthy Day Organic Food Store?

Choices: What Do You Think?

1. Pyramid-scheme promoters specialize in recruiting new members of the pyramid with exciting, even frenzied meetings where potential members are made fearful that they may pass up a great opportunity if they don't join. Why do people continue to be lured into these schemes? What do you think should be done to stop these unethical promoters?

2. Most retail store shrinkage can be attributed to shoplifting, employee theft, and retail borrowing. What are some ways that retail store managers can limit or stop shrinkage? What are some problems inherent in security practices? Should retailers create stricter merchandise return policies?

3. Experts predict the future of B2C e-commerce to be very rosy indeed, with exponential increases in Internet sales of some product categories within the next few years. What effect do you think the growth of e-retailing will have on traditional retailing? In what ways will this be good for consumers, and in what ways will it not be so good?

4. The wheel-of-retailing theory suggests that the normal path for a retailer is to enter the marketplace with lower-priced goods and then to increase quality, services, and prices. Why do you think this happens? Is it the right path for all retailers? Why or why not?

5. Walmart has become a dominant retailer in the American marketplace, accounting for over 30 percent of the total sales of some products. Is this a good thing for consumers? For the retail industry as a whole? Some communities try to prevent Walmart from building a store in their area. Why do you think people feel this way?

6. Some stores are using vending machines to sell electronics such as iPods. What are some other opportunities for vending-machine sales? What are the negative and positive elements of vending-machine sales?

Miniproject: Learn by Doing

This project is designed to help you understand how store atmospherics play an important role in consumers' perceptions of a retail store.

1. First, select two retail outlets where students in your university are likely to shop. It will be good if you can select two outlets that you feel are quite different in terms of store image but that sell the same types of products. You might consider two specialty women's clothing stores, two jewellery stores, two department stores, or two coffee shops.

2. Visit each of the stores, and write a detailed description of the store atmosphere—the storefront and marquee, colours, materials used, types of displays, lighting fixtures, product displays, store personnel, and so on.

3. Survey some of the students in your university. Develop a brief questionnaire asking about the perceptions of the two stores you are studying. You may want to ask about things such as the quality of merchandise, prices, competence and friendliness of the store personnel, the attitude of management toward customer service, and so on. What is the "personality" of each store?

4. Develop a report of your findings. Compare the description of the stores with the results of the survey. Attempt to explain how the different elements of the store atmosphere create each store's unique image.

Marketing in **Action** Case   Real Choices at Walmart

Walmart began as "Walton's Five and Dime" in Bentonville, Arkansas, operated by Sam Walton. Walton was able to be successful against the market by achieving higher sales volume through competitive pricing. In 1962, the first Wal-Mart Discount City store opened in Rogers, Arkansas. Through careful expansion and effective merchandising, Wal-Mart Stores Inc. (branded as Walmart since 2008), has become the world's largest public corporation by revenue according to *Forbes* magazine. While beginning as a discount general merchandise store, it has also become the largest grocery retailer in the United States. In addition, Walmart is the largest majority private employer in the United States.

In the past, Walmart has requested and was granted different concessions from members of its supply chain, such as environmentally friendly packaging, cooperative advertising, and radio frequency identification tags on products. Due to its enormous size and purchasing power, Walmart is able to make burdensome demands on its suppliers. This allows the company to achieve its main customer objective of providing the lowest possible price for its general merchandise and groceries. One of the challenges of this type of strategy is that it may be impossible to sustain because it has no endpoint. Therefore, Walmart is constantly pressuring suppliers to continually lower their price to the firm.

In its latest efforts to reduce its costs, Walmart wants to provide transportation services for its domestic suppliers. Walmart searches for those situations where it believes that it can provide delivery services for less money than the supplier charges. The company intends to use its scale to take advantage of shipping efficiencies that will ultimately lead to lower prices offered to customers. This process will lead to lower margins for the suppliers by eliminating an opportunity to provide services. Since Walmart generally represents a notable part of the suppliers' sales, they may offer little resistance. For instance, Walmart accounts for over 30 percent of Vlasic's pickle business. It is unlikely that Vlasic will not go along with the new policies.

When it comes to handling, moving, and tracking merchandise, Walmart has a reputation that includes continuous improvement in its methods. Walmart has a fleet of 6500 trucks and 55 000 trailers that would be supplemented with contractors to pick up products from the manufacturer and deliver the items to its regional centres and individual stores. Walmart would receive lower wholesale prices from the manufacturer as compensation for its transportation services. However, some retailers are complaining that the discount requested by Walmart is more than the cost of transporting goods by the manufacturer. This new arrangement represents another point of tension in its supplier relationships.

Walmart is not able to provide transportation services for all of its business partners' products. Therefore, Walmart still has to effectively manage these relationships. Having a relationship with Walmart affords each supplier an opportunity for increased sales and market share growth. Does this potential success come at too high a cost to the supplier? For many companies, they will have to pass on the additional costs from Walmart to partners in other supply chains in which they participate. Nevertheless, for many suppliers, they believe that they may have no choice in the matter. It has been stated before that "For many suppliers, though, the only thing worse than doing business with Wal-Mart may be not doing business with Wal-Mart."

You Make the Call

1. What is the decision facing Walmart?
2. What factors are important in understanding this decision situation?
3. What are the alternatives?
4. What decision(s) do you recommend?
5. What are some ways to implement your recommendation?

Source: Based on Chris Burritt, Carol Wolf, and Matthew Boyle, "Why Wal-Mart Wants to Take the Driver's Seat," *Bloomberg BusinessWeek,* May 27, 2010, pp. 17–18; Walmart, *Wikipedia,* http://en.wikipedia.org/wiki/Wal-Mart; Charles Fishman, "The Wal-Mart You Don't Know," *Fast Company,* December 1, 2003 (http://www.fastcompany.com/magazine/77/walmart.html).

CBC Video Case

BOOMERS

There is a shift in attitude—a change in how advertisers are addressing the aging population. The focus is not on aging but rather on lifestyles.

Canada's population is steadily aging and changing. While most magazine covers and TV commercials still feature the traditional, ideal, young and fresh image of beauty, the picture is beginning to change. Grey hair, wrinkles, and menopausal skin are becoming commonly used visuals and terms in cosmetic advertising.

Louis Vitton, one of the most successful luxury brands in the world, is focusing on a personal journey campaign where older people are portrayed in ads. It features older celebrities such Catherine DeNeuve, Keith Richards, and Sean Connery.

Zoomer magazine is a medium targeted specifically to the Boomer generation. This flashy magazine features famous Canadians of a certain age, such as Wayne Gretzky. *Zoomer* is successful not only in drawing advertisers from the medical and financial services, but also in attracting advertisers from luxury and high-end cosmetic companies.

Boomers define the society we live in and drive the trends in business because there are so many of them. One-third of Canada's population is considered baby boomers. Born between 1947 and 1966, they are now aged between 46 and 65, and are experiencing the ailments of advancing years. The concern is whether the boomers can make old age cool.

Boomers were abandoned in the last decade in a rush to target youth. The belief was that the younger population was more likely to switch brands and that because of their age, the youth could provide more years of long term loyalty. But recent data indicate the predisposition to change brands is just as high with a 25-year-old as it is with a 55-year-old. Furthermore, since the young are likely to switch brands, the long-term loyalty is not always there.

The 50+ crowd also have more money to spend due to their accumulated wealth. The 50+ market is attractive because most have paid mortgages, educated children, and are in the market for luxuries, even after the economy crash. They seek spa baths, high-end kitchens, and attractive landscaping. They are a huge market for goods and services related to home decorating, cooking, and gardening. They are receptive to new ideas and are a lucrative market.

Human life expectancy is also growing by two years every decade, so boomers are expected to live longer. The estimate is that the average 65-year-old has a decade into retirement.

The current boomer self-image is that 50 is the new 40. Boomers are active, engaged, and adventurous; they have many more spending years left than any other generation before them.

Questions

1. Why are boomers such an important market that it is creating a shift in attitude for many advertisers? Describe the shift in attitude that is being adopted by advertising agencies. Identify the reasons why this demographic change is affecting marketing decisions?

2. If you were a media planner, which Canadian media vehicles would you choose to reach the baby boomers? Would you use traditional and/or digital media vehicles? Which specific tools would you select? Justify your choices in terms of the target market.

3. If you were a sales agent for *Zoomer* magazine, which type of advertisers would you seek? What companies would you wish to include as advertisers in your magazine? Consider your target market as you formulate your response.

Source: This case was prepared by Kelly Crowe and is based on "Boomers," *National*, CBC video, Toronto, 17 August 2009 (time: 6:58 min).

MyMarketingLab

To view the CBC videos go to
pearsoned.ca/mymarketinglab.com

Marketing Plan: The S&S Smoothie Company

Executive Summary

Situation Analysis

S&S Smoothie Company is an entrepreneurial organization that produces fruit-and-yogurt–based beverages with superior flavour and nutritional content and unique packaging. Within Canada, S&S has targeted a consumer market of younger, health-conscious, upscale consumers who frequent gyms and health clubs, and two broad reseller markets: (1) gyms and health clubs, and (2) smaller upscale food markets. S&S distrib utes its product through manufacturers' agents in Canada, the United States, and the United Kingdom and through Internet sales. An analysis of the internal and external environments indicates the firm enjoys important strengths among its product, employees, and reputation, while weaknesses are apparent in its limited size, financial resources, and product capabilities. S&S faces a supportive external environment, highlighted by a growing interest in healthy living, and limited threats, primarily from potential competitive growth.

Marketing Objectives

The S&S marketing objectives are to increase awareness, gross sales (50 percent), and distribution, and to introduce two new product lines over the next three years:

- Gourmet flavoured smoothies
- Low-carb smoothies

Marketing Strategies

To accomplish its growth goals, S&S will direct its marketing activities toward the following strategies:

1. Target Market Strategy: S&S will continue to target its existing consumer markets while expanding its organizational markets to include hotels and resorts, golf and tennis clubs, and university campuses.

2. Positioning Strategy: S&S will continue to position its products as the first-choice smoothie beverage for the serious health-conscious consumer, including those who are seeking to lower their carbohydrate intake.

3. Product Strategy: S&S will introduce two new product lines, each identifiable through unique packaging/labelling:
   a. S&S Smoothie Gold: a product similar to the original S&S Smoothie beverages but in six unique flavours
   b. Low-Carb S&S Smoothie: a product with 50 percent fewer grams of carbohydrates

4. Pricing Strategy: S&S will maintain the current pricing strategy for existing and new products.

5. Promotion Strategy: S&S will augment current personal selling efforts with television and magazine advertising, sponsorships of marathons in major cities, and a sampling program.

6. Supply Chain Strategy: S&S will expand its distribution network to include the organizational markets targeted. In addition, to encourage a high level of inventory in larger health clubs, S&S Smoothie will offer free refrigerated display units.

Implementation and Control

The Action Plan details how the marketing strategies will be implemented, including the individual(s) responsible for each item, the timing, and the budget necessary. The measurement and control strategies provide a means of measurement of the success of the plan.

The following sections provide typical content for a marketing plan. Note that in the right margin, the relevant book part for each section is referenced. Please refer to each Part Opener for "Tricks of the Trade" for developing content for the related marketing plan section.

Situation Analysis

The S&S Smoothie Company[1] was founded in September 2004 in Toronto with the goal of creating and marketing healthy "smoothie" beverages for sale to health-conscious consumers. S&S Smoothie expects to take advantage of an increasing desire for healthy foods both in Canada and internationally—and to ride the wave of consumer interest in low-carb alternatives. While there are other companies, large and small, competing in this market, S&S Smoothie feels it has the expertise to create and market superior products that will appeal to its target market.

Internal Environment

PART ONE

Mission Statement

The strategic direction and actions of the S&S Smoothie Company are driven by its mission:

> S&S Smoothie seeks to meet the needs of discriminating, health-conscious consumers for high-quality, superior-tasting smoothie beverages and other similar products.

Organizational Structure

As an entrepreneurial company, S&S Smoothie does not have a very sophisticated organizational structure. Key personnel include the following:

- Peng Shen, co-founder and President. Shen is responsible for the strategic planning of S&S Smoothie and the creation and production management of all S&S Smoothie products.

[1]S&S Smoothie Company is a fictitious company created to illustrate a sample marketing plan.

- William "Bill" Sartens, co-founder and Vice President Marketing. Sartens is responsible for all marketing decisions, including international and domestic distribution, packaging, and marketing communications.

- Silvia Vlasenko, Chief Financial Officer. Humphries develops financial strategy and keeps the company's books.

- Baljit Arora, National Sales Manager. Arora is responsible for maintaining the sales force of independent sales reps. He also advises on product development.

- Alex Johnson, Pam Sartens, and Paul Sartens, shareholders. Next to Peng Shen and William Sartens, Alex, Pam, and Paul own the largest number of shares. They consult and sit on the company's board of directors. Alex is a lawyer and also provides legal services.

Corporate Culture

S&S Smoothie is an entrepreneurial organization. Thus, a key element of the internal environment is a culture that encourages innovation, risk taking, and individual creativity. The company's beginning was based on a desire to provide a unique, superior product, and company decisions have consistently emphasized this mission.

Current Products

The original S&S Smoothie product, introduced in mid-2004, is a fruit-and-yogurt–based beverage that contains only natural ingredients (no additives) and is high in essential nutrients. Because of the company's patented manufacturing process, S&S Smoothie beverages do not have to be refrigerated and have a shelf life of over a year. Therefore, the product can be shipped and delivered via nonrefrigerated carriers. S&S Smoothie currently sells its beverages exclusively through gyms, health clubs, and smaller upscale food markets. As a producer of dairy-based beverages, S&S Smoothie's NAICS (North American Industry Classification System) classification is 311511—Fluid Milk Manufacturers.

At present, the single product line is the S&S Smoothie fruit-and-yogurt beverage. This healthy beverage product has a flavour and nutritional content that makes it superior to competing products. The present product comes in five flavours: strawberry, blueberry, banana, peach, and cherry. S&S offers each in 355-ml and 590-ml sizes. S&S packages the product in a unique hourglass-shaped, frosted-glass bottle with a screw cap. The bottle design makes the product easy to hold, even with sweaty hands after workouts. The frosted glass allows the colour of the beverage to be seen, but at the same time it communicates an upscale image. The labelling and cap visually denote the flavour with an appropriate colour. Labelling includes complete nutritional information. In the future, S&S Smoothie plans to expand its line of products to grow its market share of the health drink market.

The suggested retail prices for S&S Smoothie beverages are $4.00 for the 355-ml size and $6.00 for the 590-ml container. S&S's prices to distributors are $1.20 and $1.80, respectively.

At present, S&S Smoothie outsources actual production of the product. Still, the company takes care to oversee the entire production process to ensure consistent quality of its unique product. With this method of production, variable costs for the 355-ml S&S Smoothie beverages are $0.63, and variable costs for the 590-ml size are $0.71.

Markets

The consumer market for S&S Smoothie products is made up of anyone who is interested in healthy food and a healthy lifestyle. Although, according to published research, nearly 70 percent of Canadian consumers say they are interested in living a healthy lifestyle, the number of those who actually work to achieve that goal is much smaller. It is estimated that approximately 9 million Canadians and 80 million Americans actually engage in exercise

Table A.1 | Company Sales Performance

Year	Gross Sales
2004	$ 287,850
2005	$ 638,770
2006	$1,211,445
2007	$1,586,228
2008	$1,918,376
2009	$1,895,120

and/or follow nutritional plans that would be described as healthy. As experts expect the trend toward healthier living to grow globally, the domestic and international markets for S&S Smoothie products are expected to expand for some time.

Customers/Sales

Sales of S&S Smoothie products showed steady growth through 2008 but suffered some decline due to a downturn in the economy in 2009. Actual sales figures for 2004 through 2009 are shown in Table A.1.

These sales figures plus S&S customer research show a strong and growing loyal customer base. This customer asset is important to the future of S&S. Nevertheless, research indicates that only about half of all consumers in the target market are aware of the S&S brand.

Within the Canadian consumer market, S&S Smoothie targets upscale consumers who frequent gyms and health clubs. Based on research conducted by S&S Smoothie, these consumers are primarily younger; however, there is also an older segment that seeks to be physically fit and patronizes health clubs.

Distribution

In order to reach its target market, S&S Smoothie places primary distribution emphasis on health clubs and other physical fitness facilities and small, upscale specialty food markets. The company began developing channel relationships with these outlets through individual contacts by company personnel. As sales developed, the company solicited the services of manufacturers' agents and specialty food distributors. Manufacturers' agents are individuals who sell products for a number of different noncompeting manufacturers. By contracting with these agents in various geographic regions, the company can expand its product distribution to a significant portion of Canada and the United States. Similar arrangements with agents in the United Kingdom have allowed it to begin distribution in that country.

The company handles large accounts such as Gold's Gym and World Gyms directly. While total sales to these chains are fairly substantial, when considering the large number of facilities within each chain, the sales are very small with much room for growth.

The Internet is a secondary channel for S&S Smoothie. Online retail outlets currently account for only 5 percent of S&S Smoothie sales. Although this channel is useful for individuals who wish to purchase S&S Smoothie products in larger quantities, S&S does not expect that online sales will become a significant part of the business in the near future.

External Environment

Competitive Environment

S&S Smoothie faces several different levels of competition. Direct competitors are companies that also market smoothie-type beverages, and include the following:

1. Franchise smoothie retail operations

2. Online-only smoothie outlets

3. Other smaller manufacturers

4. Larger companies such as Nestlé that produce similar products

Indirect competition comes from the following:

1. Homemade smoothie drinks made from powders sold in retail outlets and over the Internet

2. Homemade smoothie drinks made using a multitude of available recipes

3. Other healthy beverages, such as juices

4. A growing number of energy drinks that are especially popular with younger consumers

Economic Environment

S&S Smoothie first introduced its products during a period of economic downturn following the dot.com bust and 9/11. Despite this, the product quickly gained momentum and sales steadily increased. With the 2008–2009 recession, sales have correspondingly shown some decreases. Analysts estimate that the recovery will be slow and take a number of years, during which time GDP and consumer sales overall will increase at a similarly low pace.

Technological Environment

Because S&S Smoothie produces a simple food product, technological advances have minimal impact on the firm's operations. Nevertheless, the use of current technology enables and enhances many of the company's activities. For example, S&S Smoothie uses the Internet to enhance its operations in two ways. As noted previously, the Internet provides an additional venue for sales. In addition, manufacturers' agents and channel members can keep in contact with the company, allowing for fewer problems with deliveries, orders, and so on. Finally, in recent years, the company has established a presence on social media sites Facebook and Twitter, through which it can communicate with consumers in a more personal way while monitoring consumers' feedback communication.

Political and Legal Environment

Because they are advertised as nutritional products, all S&S Smoothie products must be approved by Health Canada (and before selling in the United States, by the FDA). Labelling must include ingredients and nutritional information. In addition, S&S Smoothie products are regulated by Agriculture Canada and the U.S. Department of Agriculture.

While there are no specific regulations about labelling or advertising products as low-carb, there is potential for such regulations to come into play in the future. In addition, in current and prospective global markets there are numerous country-specific regulations of which the company must constantly remain aware. Any future advertising campaigns developed by S&S Smoothie will have to conform to regulatory guidelines in Canada (following the guidelines of the industry-based Advertising Standards Canada) and internationally.

Sociocultural Environment

S&S Smoothies uses marketing research to monitor the consumer environment. This research shows that changing cultural values and norms continue to provide an important opportunity for S&S Smoothie. The trend toward healthy foods and a healthier lifestyle has grown dramatically for the past decade or longer. In response to this, the number of health clubs across the country and the number of independent resorts and spas that offer patrons a healthy holiday have also grown. In addition, many travellers demand that hotels offer health club facilities.

During the past decade, consumers around the globe have become aware of the advantages of a low-carbohydrate diet. Low-carb menu items abound in restaurants, including fast-food chains such as McDonald's. A vast number of low-carb foods, including low-carb candy, fill supermarket shelves.

There are approximately 13.7 million Canadian adults aged 15 to 44 (and 125 million American adults aged 15 to 44). Demographers project that this age group will remain stable for the foreseeable future, with an increase of less than 8 percent projected to 2025. Similarly, incomes should neither decrease nor increase significantly in the near future in this segment of the population.

SWOT Analysis

SWOT analysis provides a summary of the strengths, weaknesses, opportunities, and threats identified by S&S Smoothie through the analysis of its internal and external environments.

Strengths

The following are the strengths identified by S&S Smoothie:

- A creative and skilled employee team

    Enabling S&S Smoothie to compete on innovation and new product development

- A high-quality product recipe that provides exceptional flavour with high levels of nutrition

    Providing a basis of differentiation that is partially protected by trade secret

- Because of its entrepreneurial spirit, the ability to remain flexible and to adapt quickly to environmental changes

    Providing a source of competitive and comparative advantage

- A strong network of manufacturers' agents and distributors

    Providing a basis for expansion by leveraging current relationships and facilitating new product introduction

- The growth of a reputation for a high-quality product among health clubs, other retail outlets, and targeted consumer groups

    Facilitating new product introduction and expansion through the use of referrals

Weaknesses

The following are the weaknesses identified by S&S Smoothie:

- Limited financial resources for growth and for advertising and other marketing communications

    Requiring strategic investments, creativity, and leveraging of others' resources

- Little flexibility in terms of personnel due to size of the firm

    Making it difficult to develop new capabilities or expand quickly

- Reliance on external production to maintain quality standards and to meet any unanticipated surges in demand for the product

    Creating the strategic risk of not being able to adequately supply growth aspirations

Opportunities

The following are the opportunities identified by S&S Smoothie:

- A strong and growing interest in healthy living among both young, upscale consumers and older consumers

    Providing multiple high-growth segments for niche targeting

- Continuing consumer interest in low-carb alternatives

    Offering opportunities for additional product lines

Threats

The following are the threats identified by S&S Smoothie:

- The potential for competitors, especially those with large financial resources who can invest more in promotion, to develop products that consumers may find superior

    Innovation may not be a sustainable source of competitive advantage for S&S Smoothie; alternative sources of competitive advantage are needed

- The continuation of a slowed economy

    Reductions in consumer discretionary spending might affect sales, unless a niche can be found that is less impacted by the economic slowdown

- Fizzling of the low-carb craze if other forms of dieting gain in popularity

    New positioning may become necessary

- Increase in popularity of energy drinks like Rockstar, etc.

    Late entry into a crowded market may become necessary

PART TWO

Marketing Objectives

The following are the marketing objectives set by S&S Smoothie:

- To increase the awareness of S&S Smoothie products by at least 10 percent among the target market

- To increase gross sales by 50 percent over the next two years

- To introduce two new product lines: low-carb smoothies and gourmet flavoured smoothies

- To increase distribution of S&S Smoothie products to include 150 new retail outlets both in Canada and globally in the next two years.

Marketing Strategies

Young, Healthy-Living Segment

Who They Are

Demographics

- Male and female teens and young adults, but more likely female

- Ages 15–28

- High disposable income (their own or their parents)

- Heading to, in, or recently graduated from university or college
- Primarily located in midsize to large urban areas

Psychographics

- Health conscious and interested in living a healthy lifestyle
- Frequent gyms and participate in a wide range of physical activities
- Live very busy lives and need to use time wisely to enjoy all they want to do
- Enjoy spending time with friends
- Tend to be highly environmentally conscious
- According to the VALS2™ typology, many are in the Achievers and Experiencers categories

Behaviour

- Work out about three times a week either on campus or their local gym, often with a friend for mutual motivation support
- Have a circle of friends who are also active, and organize sports or recreation activities for each other
- Moderate to heavy Facebook users
- Care about what they eat, read labels, and choose organics when possible
- Wear trendy athletic clothing brands like lululemon, and when they find a sport they like, they buy top of the line equipment and clothing to pursue it

What They Want

- To be seen as making healthy choices, but still caring about taste
- Social status of consuming the "right" products.
- To "treat" themselves without feeling too guilty
- Shared experiences with their friends

When/Where They Buy and Consume

- Purchase in social settings and consume health beverages with friends after exercise
- Frequent Starbucks and other high-end coffee shops if a healthier alternative is not readily available

How They Buy and Consume

- Low involvement, impulse decisions
- Influenced by immediate group / friends
- Could become routine, part of the social contract
- Would feel guilty if they drank smoothies too often
- Heavy Internet users, particularly for news and social networking
- Don't watch a lot of TV but prefer edgier shows such as *Weeds* and *Californication*
- The women occasionally read magazines such as *Women's Health, Flare,* or their mother's *Chatelaine* and the men occasionally read *Men's Health, Maxim,* and *Sports Illustrated* if these magazines are lying around

Young Professional Healthy-Living Segment

A secondary target market for S&S Smoothie is the Young Professional Healthy-Living Segment. This segment is similar to the one above, only they are older (age 29 to 45), have professional careers (or professional spouses), may have young families of their own, and spend considerable time and money taking care of their bodies. They belong to high-end gyms (like Curves or Goodlife Fitness) or golf and tennis clubs, and drive to them in a luxury sedan or SUV. This segment is less environmentally conscious than the Young Healthy Living Segment, but they care about, and donate money to, health causes such as breast cancer and heart disease research. Exercise and physical fitness are scheduled into their busy days, and they are willing to pay a premium for convenience and personal coaching or training so they make the most of their time. This segment is also fitness-fashion conscious. They have a strong desire to stay young looking, but most will eschew surgery, Botox, and other interventions, believing that health and vitality are more important than "looks." This segment will occasionally drink a healthy smoothie as a treat (with friends), but they are more conscious of the calories that they consume and would be concerned about "undoing" the benefits of their workout or physical activity. They are, however, interested in brands that are consistent with a healthy-living lifestyle and are not very price sensitive. They shop, for example, at upscale specialty food markets and will pay a premium for locally grown food and organic products. This segment is more likely to use LinkedIn than Facebook, but they are infrequent users of social media. They skim two newspapers (a local daily and a national, such as *The Globe and Mail*), and read *Chatelaine*, *Maclean's* magazine, and *Canadian Business* magazine. They are most likely to get their news from drive-time radio but otherwise listen either to soft rock or CBC radio.

Organizational Markets

In the past, S&S Smoothie has targeted two categories of reseller markets: (1) health clubs and gyms, and (2) small, upscale specialty food markets. To increase distribution and sales of its products, S&S Smoothie will target the following in the future:

1. Hotels and resorts in Canada and the United States and in selected international markets

2. Golf and tennis clubs

3. College and university campuses

Positioning the Product

S&S Smoothie seeks to position its products as the first-choice smoothie beverage for the serious health-conscious consumer, including those who are seeking to lower their carbohydrate intake. The justification for this positioning is as follows. Many smoothie beverages are available. The S&S Smoothie formula provides superior flavour and nutrition in a shelfstable form. S&S Smoothie has developed its product, packaging, pricing, and promotion to communicate a superior, prestige image. This positioning is thus supported by all its marketing strategies.

PART THREE

Product Strategies

To increase its leverage in the market and to meet its sales objectives, S&S Smoothie needs additional products. Two new product lines are planned:

1. S&S Smoothie Gold: This product will be similar to the original S&S Smoothie beverage but will come in six unique flavours: Piña colada, Chocolate banana, Apricot nectarine madness, Pineapple berry crush, Tropical tofu cherry, and Peaches and dreams

Table A.2 | Nutritional Information: S&S Smoothie Beverage

	S&S Smoothie Gold		Low-Carb S&S Smoothie	
	Amount per Serving	% Daily Value	Amount per Serving	% Daily Value
Calories	140		130	
Calories from fat	6		7	
Total fat	< 0.5 g	1%	< 0.5 g	1%
Saturated fat	< 0.5 g	2%	< 0.5 g	2%
Cholesterol	6 mg	2%	6 mg	2%
Sodium	70 mg	3%	70 mg	3%
Potassium	100 mg	3%	100 mg	3%
Total carbs	20 g	8%	10 g	4%
Dietary fibre	5 g	20%	5 g	20%
Protein	25 g	50%	25 g	50%
Vitamin A		50%		50%
Vitamin C		50%		50%
Calcium		20%		20%
Iron		30%		30%
Vitamin D		40%		40%
Vitamin E		50%		50%
Thiamin		50%		50%
Riboflavin		50%		50%
Niacin		50%		50%
Vitamin B^6		50%		50%
Vitamin B^{12}		50%		50%
Biotin		50%		50%
Pantothenic acid		50%		50%
Phosphorus		10%		10%
Iodine		50%		50%
Chromium		50%		50%
Zinc		50%		50%
Folic acid		50%		50%

Serving Size: 355 ml
For 590 ml sizes, multiply the amounts by 1.67.

The nutritional content, critical to the success of the new products, will be similar to that of the original S&S Smoothie beverages. Nutritional information is shown in Table A.2. The packaging for the new S&S Smoothie product will also be similar to that used for the original product, utilizing the unique, easy-to-hold, hourglass-shaped, frosted glass bottle and providing the new beverage with the same upscale image. To set the product apart from the original-flavour Smoothie beverages in store refrigerator cases, labels will include the name of the beverage and the logo in gold lettering. The bottle cap will be black.

2. Low-Carb S&S Smoothie: As shown in Table A.2, the Low-Carb S&S Smoothie beverage will have approximately 50 percent fewer grams of carbohydrates than the original

Smoothie beverage or the S&S Smoothie Gold. Low-Carb S&S Smoothie will come in the following four flavours: strawberry, blueberry, banana, peach. Packaging for the Low Carb S&S Smoothie will be similar to other S&S Smoothie beverages but will include the term "Low-Carb" in large type. The label will state that the beverage has 50 percent fewer carbohydrates than regular smoothies.

Pricing Strategies

The current pricing strategy will be maintained for existing and new products. This pricing is appropriate for communicating a high-quality product image for all S&S Smoothie products. The company feels that creating different pricing for the new beverages would be confusing and create negative attitudes among consumers. Thus, there is no justification for increasing the price of the new products. Pricing through the channel, including margins, is shown in Table A.3.

S&S Smoothie will continue to outsource actual production of the new offerings, as it does with its existing product. As noted earlier, with this method of production, variable costs for the 355-ml S&S Smoothie beverages are $0.63 and variable costs for the 590-ml size are $0.71. Anticipated annual fixed costs for S&S Smoothie office space, management salaries, and expenses related to sales, advertising, and other marketing communications are as follows:

Sales of the two sizes of all S&S products are expected to be approximately equal; that is, half of sales will be for the 355-ml size and half will be for the 590-ml size. Thus, there will be an average contribution margin of $0.83 per bottle. Based on this, to achieve break-even, S&S Smoothie must sell

$$\frac{\$1,231,600}{.83} = 1,483,856 \text{ units}$$

Again, assuming equal sales of the two sizes of products, the break-even point in dollars is $2,225,784.

Table A.3	Pricing of S&S Smoothie Beverages		
		355 ml	590 ml
Suggested retail price		$4.00	$6.00
Retailer margin		50%/$2.00	50%/$3.00
Price to retail outlets (health clubs, etc.)		$2.00	$3.00
Distributor/sales agent margin		40%/$0.80	40%/$1.20
Price to distributor/discount to sales agent		$1.20	$1.80
Variable costs		$0.63	$0.71
S&S contribution margin		$0.57	$1.09
Salaries and employee benefits		$525,000	
Office rental, equipment, and supplies		$124,600	
Expenses related to sales (travel, etc.)		$132,000	
Advertising and other marketing communications		$450,000	
Total fixed costs		**$1,231,600**	

Promotion Strategies

In the past, S&S Smoothie has used mainly personal selling to promote its products to the trade channel. To support this effort, signage has been provided for the resellers to promote the product at the point of purchase. Posters and stand-alone table cards show appealing photographs of the product in the different flavours and communicate the brand name and the healthy benefits of the product. Similar signage will be developed for use by resellers who choose to stock the S&S Smoothie Gold and the Low-Carb Smoothies.

Selling has previously been handled by a team of over 75 manufacturers' agents who sell to resellers. In addition, in some geographic areas, an independent distributor does the selling. To support this personal selling approach, S&S Smoothie plans for additional promotional activities to introduce its new products and meet its other marketing objectives. These include the following:

1. Television advertising: S&S Smoothie will purchase a limited amount of relatively inexpensive and targeted cable channel advertising. A small number of commercials will be shown during prime-time programs with high viewer ratings by the target market. Television advertising can be an important means of not only creating awareness of the product but also of enhancing the image of the product. Indeed, consumers are prone to feel that if a product is advertised on prime-time TV, it must be a good product.

2. Magazine advertising: Because consumers in the target market are not avid magazine readers, magazine advertising will be limited and will supplement other promotion activities. During the next year, S&S Smoothie will experiment with limited magazine advertising in such titles as *Men's Health.* The company will also investigate the potential of advertising in university newspapers.

3. Sponsorships: S&S Smoothie will attempt to sponsor several marathons in major cities. The advantage of sponsorships is that they provide visibility for the product while at the same time showing that the company supports activities of interest to the target market.

4. Digital Marketing: S&S Smoothie will continue its use of social media to communicate with consumers and to monitor customers' postings about S&S products. In addition, S&S TV commercials will be available on the company Web site and on YouTube. In the latter part of the year, the company will sponsor a do-it-yourself ad competition through its Web site. The winning ads will be aired on cable TV.

5. Sampling: Sampling of S&S Smoothie beverages at select venues will provide an opportunity for prospective customers to become aware of the product and to taste the great flavours. Sampling will include only the two new products being introduced. Venues for sampling will include the following:
   a. Marathons
   b. Weight-lifting competitions
   c. Gymnastics meets
   d. Student unions located on select college and university campuses

Supply Chain Strategies

As noted earlier, S&S Smoothie distributes its beverages primarily through health clubs and gyms and small, upscale specialty food stores. S&S Smoothie plans to expand its target reseller market to include the following:

1. Hotels and resorts in Canada and the United States and in targeted international markets

2. Golf and tennis clubs

3. University and college campuses

To increase leverage in larger health clubs, S&S Smoothie will offer free refrigerated display units. This will encourage the facility to maintain a high level of inventory of S&S Smoothie beverages.

Table A.4	Action Items to Accomplish Marketing Objective Regarding Supply Chain

Objective: Increase Distribution Venues

Action Items	Beginning Date	Ending Date	Responsible Party	Cost	Remarks
1. Identify key hotels and resorts, golf clubs, and tennis clubs where S&S Smoothies might be sold	July 1	September 1	Bill Sartens (consulting firm will be engaged to assist in this effort)	$25,000	Key to this strategy is to selectively choose resellers so that maximum results are obtained from sales activities. Because health club use is greater during the months of January to May, efforts will be timed to have product in stock no later than January 15.
2. Identify 25 key universities where S&S Smoothies might be sold	July 1	August 1	Bill Sartens	0	IInformation about colleges and universities and their health club facilities should be available on the university Web pages.
3. Make initial contact with larger hotel and resort chains	September 1	November 1	Bill Sartens	Travel: $10,000	
4. Make initial contact with larger individual (nonchain) facilities	September 1	November 1	Bill Sartens	Travel: $5,000	
5. Make initial contact with universities	August 15	September 15	Manufacturers' agents	0	Agents will be assigned to the 25 universities and required to make an initial contact and report back to Bill Sartens on promising prospects.
6. Follow up initial contacts with all potential resellers and obtain contracts for coming six months	September 15	Ongoing	Bill Sartens, manufacturers' agents	$10,000	$10,000 is budgeted for this item, although actual expenditures will be on an as-needed basis, as follow-up travel cannot be preplanned.

Implementation

The action plan details the activities necessary to implement all marketing strategies. In addition, the action plan includes the timing for each item, the individual(s) responsible, and the budgetary requirements. Table A.4 shows an example of one objective (to increase distribution venues) and the action items S&S Smoothie will use to accomplish it.[2]

Measurement and Control Strategies

A variety of activities will ensure effective measurement of the success of the marketing plan and allow the firm to make adjustments as necessary. These include targeted market research and trend analysis.

Research

Firms need continuous market research to understand brand awareness and brand attitudes among their target markets. S&S Smoothie will, therefore, continue its program of focus group research and descriptive studies of its target consumer and reseller markets.

Trend Analysis

S&S Smoothie will do a monthly trend analysis to examine sales by reseller type, geographic area, chain, agent, and distributor. These analyses will allow S&S Smoothie to take corrective action when necessary.

---

[2]Note that the final marketing plan should include objectives, action items, timing information, and budget information necessary to accomplish all marketing strategies. We have only one objective in this sample marketing plan.

► Notes

CHAPTER 1

1. S&S Smoothie Company is a fictitious company created to illustrate a sample marketing plan.
2. *American Marketing Association*: www.marketingpower.com.
3. Rebecca Camber, *Daily Mail*, May 2, 2006: 29.
4. Peter F. Drucker, *Management* (New York: Harper & Row, 1973).
5. Peter F. Drucker, *Management: Tasks, Responsibilities, Practices* (New York: Harper & Row, 1972): 64–5.
6. "Church ad builds on idea," *TheStar.com*, January 30, 2009.
7. Matt Semansky, "New campaign asks Nova Scotians to sort things out," *Marketing Magazine*, October 01, 2010.
8. "Tim Hortons Charts Course for Global Expansion," *Marketing Magazine*, May 14, 2010.
9. Adapted from Carly Fiorina's talk given at the Schulich School of Business, York University, October 28, 2003.
10. http://www.finewaters.com/Newsletter/The_Water_Connoisseur_Archive/Claridges_to_offers_Comprehensive_Water_Menu.asp
11. "Menthol used to attract new smokers: study," *Marketing Magazine*, July 17, 2008.
12. Michael E. Porter, *Competitive Advantage: Creating and Sustaining Superior Performance* (New York: Free Press, 1985).
13. Melita Kuburas, "Students 'scream cheese' at Doritos Guru coronation," *Media Canada*, May 4, 2009. www.mediaincanada.com/articles/mic/20090504/doritosguru.html.
14. Jeff Beer, "Superfans produce super content, says Jimmy Wales," *Media News*, November 2, 2010. www.marketingmag.ca/news/media-news/digital-day-superfans-produce-super-content-says-jimmy-wales-5739
15. Max Chafkin, "The customer is the company," *Inc. Magazine*, June 1, 2008. www.inc.com/magazine/20080601/the-customer-is-the-company.html.
16. Laurie Burkitt, "Need to build a community? Learn from Threadless," *Forbes*, January 6, 2010. www.forbes.com/2010/01/06/threadless-t-shirt-community-crowdsourcing-cmo-network-threadless.html.
17. Jeff Surowiecki, *The Wisdom of Crowds* (New York: Anchor, 2005).
18. "Gap ditches new logo," *Marketing Magazine*, Oct 13, 2010. www.marketingmag.ca/news/marketer-news/chatter-gap-ditches-new-logo-5343.
19. Kunur Patel, "That Coke can you're holding could be your new media channel: StickyBits app lets users 'check in' to objects via barcodes," *Advertising Age*, April 28, 2010. www.adage.com/digital/article?article_id=143566.
20. Tom Espiner, "IE slips further as Firefox, Safari, Chrome gain," *CNET*, February 2, 2009. http://news.cnet.com/8301-1023_3-10154447-93.html.
21. Stephanie Rosenbloom, "Wal-Mart unveils plan to make supply chain greener," *New York Times*, February 25, 2010, www.nytimes.com/2010/02/26/business/energy-environment/26walmart.html.
22. Mountain Equipment Co-op Web site: www.mec.ca/Main/content_text.jsp?FOLDER%3C%3Efolder_id=2534374302885110.
23. "Our approach," *MEC 2007 Accountability Report*: 10. http://images.mec.ca/media/Images/pdf/accountability/MEC_Acct_Report_Ch1_v1_m56577569830738018.pdf.
24. "Microsoft to buy Skype for $8.5B," *Vancouver Sun*, May 10, 2011; Agence France-Presse. www.vancouversun.com/technology/Microsoft+Skype/4754460/story.html.
25. Bob Tedeschi, "Brand building on the internet," *The New York Times*, August 25, 2003. www.nyt.com.
26. "McCain drops genetically altered spuds," *Calgary Herald*, November 29, 1999: D5.
27. Beth Graddon-Hodgson, "Feel good ripple: A Canadian project built on kindness and giving back," *Investor Spot.Com*. http://inventorspot.com /articles/feel _good_ripple_canadian_project_built_kindness_and_giving_back_33850.
28. Cf. M.K. Khoo, S.G. Lee, and S.W. Lye, "A design methodology for the strategic assessment of a product's eco-efficiency," *International Journal of Production Research*, 39, 2001: 2453–74; C. Chen, "Design for the environment: A quality based model for green product development," *Management Science*, 47(2), 2001: 250–64; McDonough Braungart Design Chemistry LLC, "Cradle to cradle design paradigm," www.mbdc.com/c2c_home.htm; Elizabeth Corcoran, "Thinking green," *Scientific American*, 267(6), 1992: 44–46; Amitai Etzioni, "The good society: Goals beyond money," *The Futurist*, 2001: 68–69; M.H. Olson, "Charting a course for sustainability," *Environment*, 38(4), 1996: 10–23.
29. Sindya N. Bhanoo, "Those earth-friendly products? Turns out they're profit-friendly as well," *The New York Times*, June 12, 2010: B3.
30. Jeff Lowe, "The marketing dashboard: measuring marketing effectiveness," *Venture Communications*, February 2003, www.brandchannel.com/images/papers/dashboard.pdf; G.A.Wyner, "Scorecards and more: The value is in how you use them," *Marketing Research*, 15(3), Summer 2003: 6–7; C.F. Lundby and C. Rasinowich, "The missing link: Cause and effect linkages make marketing scorecards more valuable," *Marketing Research*, Winter 2003: 14–19.
31. Adapted from C.F. Lundby and C. Rasinowich, "The missing link," *Marketing Research*, Winter 2003: 18.
32. Archie B. Carroll and Ann K. Buchholtz, *Business and Society: Ethics and Stakeholder Management*, 7th edition (South-Western, Division of Thomson Learning: 2008).
33. *The Report of the Canadian Democracy and Corporate Accountability Commission*, 2002. Document #11650, Canadian Democracy Commission.doc.
34. Parts of this section are adapted from Michael R. Solomon, *Consumer Behavior: Buying, Having and Being*, 7th edition (Upper Saddle River, NJ: Prentice Hall, 2007).
35. "Columbine video game upsets victim's father," *CNN.com*, May 17, 2006.
36. William Leiss, Stephen Kline, and Sut Jhally, Social Communication in *Advertising: Persons, Products, and Images of Well-Being* (Toronto: Methuen, 1986).
37. Thomas C. O'Guinn and Ronald J. Faber, "Compulsive buying: A phenomenological explanation," *Journal of Consumer Research*, 16, September 1989: 154.
38. "Center tries to treat web addicts," *New York Times*, September 5, 2009, www.nytimes.com/2009/09/06/us/06internet.html; Samantha Manas, "Addicted to Chapstick: The world of Chapstick addicts revealed," *Associated Content*, July 5, 2006, www.associatedcontent.com/article/41148/addicted_to_chapstick.html.
39. Consumer Association of Canada: www.consumer.ca/index.php4.
40. "Take action to change the world," *Yahoo! Green*. http://green.yahoo.com/pledge/.
41. "What Is A Carbon Footprint?" *Carbon Footprint*. www.carbonfootprint.com/carbonfootprint.html.

Chapter 2

1. "Mission Statement," *MADD*. www.madd.org/About-Us/About-Us/Mission-Statement.aspx.

2. Danielle Sacks, "How Jack Abraham is reinventing EBay," *Fast Company*, June 22, 2011.

3. "Aspiring to be extraordinary," *Campbell Soup Company*. www.campbellsoupcompany.com/pdf/campbell_2007_annual_report.pdf.

4. A.G. Lafley and Ram Charan, *The Game Changer* (New York: Crown Business, 2008).

5. Anath Hartman, "Senior citizens wowed by Nintendo's Wii," *Gazette.Net*, December 20, 2007. www.gazette.net/stories/122007/laurnew142319_32358.shtml.

6. Christina Binkley, "Hotels? 'Go to the mattresses': Marriott is latest to make huge bet on better bedding," *Wall Street Journal*, January 25, 2005: D1.

7. Michael Arndt, "McDonald's 24/7," *BusinessWeek*, February 5, 2007: 64–72.

8. B. Mainprize, K. Hindle, B. Smith, and R. Mitchell, "Caprice versus standardization in venture capital decision making," *The Journal of Private Equity* 7(1), Winter 2003: 15–25.

9. Based on Lisa Schmidt, "How WestJet lost its shine," *Calgary Herald*, May 30, 2006.

10. Patrick Barwise and John U. Farley, "Which marketing metrics are used and where?" *Working Paper Series*, Report No. 03-111, (Cambridge, MA: Marketing Science Institute, 2003).

11. Flyertalk: www.flyertalk.com/forum/air-canada-aeroplan/940671-new-air-canada-tv-advertising-campaign.html.

12. "What else can social media do for your campaign?" *Marketing VOX*, January 7, 2010. www.marketingvox.com/what-else-can-social-media-do-for-your-campaign-045919/.

13. Gordon A. Wyner, "Beyond ROI: Make sure the analytics address strategic issues," *Marketing Management*, May/June 15, 2006: 8–9.

14. Tim Ambler, "Don't cave in to cave dwellers," *Marketing Management*, September/October 2006: 25–29.

15. Carol Matlack, "Auchan: Walmart's tough new global rival," *BusinessWeek*, October 23, 2009. www.businessweek.com/globalbiz/content/oct2009/gb20091023_414708.htm.

16. Chery International: http://www.cheryinternational.com/Chery-International.php.

17. "Chinese automaker coming to the U.S.," MSN.com, http://autos.msn.com/as/article.aspx?xml_Geely&shw_autoshow2006. Updated April 26, 2007, http://www.msnbc.msn.com/id/18307624/ns/business-autos/t/chinese-automakers-are-looking-west/.

18. Tom Gilbert, "An 'Idol' by any other name," *Television Week*, May 29, 2006: 2.

19. Saritha Rai, "Tastes of India in U.S. wrappers," *New York Times*, April 29, 2003. www.nytimes.com/2003/04/29/business/tastes-of-india-in-us-wrappers.html?pagewanted=all&src=pm.

20. Douglas McIntyre, "GM forecasts 2 million car sales in China this year," *DailyFinance*, January 24, 2010. www.dailyfinance.com/story/company-news/gm-forecasts-2-million-car-sales-in-china-this-year/19329149/.

21. Jim Thompson, "Twenty years later: What McDonald's in Russia says about the brand's future," Brandchannel, February 1, 2010. www.brandchannel.com/home/post/2010/02/01/Twenty-Years-Later-What-McDonalds-In-Russia-Says-About-The-Brands-Future.aspx.

22. Jeremy Kahn, "The world's most admired companies," *Fortune*, October 26, 1998: 206–16.

23. An influential argument for this perspective can be found in Theodore Levitt, "The globalization of markets," *Harvard Business Review*, May–June 1983: 92–102.

24. Juliana Koranteng, "Reebok finds its second wind as it pursues global presence," *Advertising Age International*, January 1998: 18.

25. Terry Clark, "International marketing and national character: A review and proposal for an integrative theory," *Journal of Marketing*, 54 (October 1990): 66–79.

26. Norihiko Shirouzu, "Snapple in Japan: How a splash dried up," *Wall Street Journal*, April 15, 1996: B1(2).

27. Sara Hope Franks, "Overseas, it's what inside that sells," *Washington Post National Weekly Edition*, 5(11), December 1994: 21.

28. Catherine McColl, "Saris and Levi's—the Indo-Western Youth Trend," Canvas8.com, August 4, 2009, http://docs.google.com/viewer?a_v&pid_sites&srcid_cGVhcnNvbi5jb218cmVhbC1wZW9wbGUtcmVhbC1jb2xsYWJvcmF0aW9uufGd4OjM0MWQxZDExNTUwOTAyZTk (accessed January 31, 2010).

29. International Energy Agency, "Access to electricity," *World Energy Outlook*, 2009. www.iea.org/weo/electricity.asp.

30. Aaron O. Patrick, "World Cup's advertisers hope one size fits all: Month-long tournament sets off scramble to reach huge global TV audience," *Wall Street Journal*, March 28, 2006: B7.

31. Natalie Zmuda, "Coke set to reveal 'open happiness' campaign," *Advertising Age*, January 14, 2009, http://adage.com/article/news/coke-set-reveal-open-happiness-campaign/133781/; Natalie Zmuda, "Sprite launches 'the spark,' its first global ad campaign," *Advertising Age*, February 11, 2010, http://adage.com/article/news/advertising-sprite-launches-global-ad-campaign/142073/.

32. Sinclair Stewart, "Tim Hortons brews new U.S. campaign," *Strategy Magazine*, September 27, 1999: 3.

33. "Kodak alleges Fuji photo is dumping color photographic paper in the U.S.," *Wall Street Journal*, February 22, 1993: B6.

34. *EcoLogo Program*: www.environmentalchoice.com.

35. Catherine Arnst, Stanley Reed, Gay McWilliams, and De'Ann Weimer, "When green begets green," *BusinessWeek*, November 10, 1997: 98–106.

36. "Canada's Competition Bureau scours online media for fraud: Deceptive ads on social media sites targeted", *CBC News*, September 24, 2010. www.cbc.ca/news/technology/story/2010/09/24/con-social-media-sweep.html.

Chapter 3

1. Alan J. Greco and Jack T. Hogue, "Developing marketing decision support systems in consumer goods firms," *Journal of Consumer Marketing* 7(1990): 55–64.

2. *Clark Marketing*, June 30 2010.

3. *The Q Scores Company*: www.qscores.com.

4. "CRTC slaps Bell with $1.3 million fine," *Canadian Business*, December 21, 2010.

5. Pan-Ning Tan, Michael Steinbach, and Vipin Kumar, *Introduction to Data Mining* (New York: Addison Wesley, 2005).

6. Catherine Holahan, "Battling data monsters at Yahoo!" *BusinessWeek*, December 14, 2007; Catherine Holahan, "Facebook: Marketers are your 'friends'," *BusinessWeek*, November 7, 2007.

7. Pan-Ning Tan, Michael Steinbach, and Vipin Kumar, *Introduction to Data Mining* (New York: Addison Wesley, 2005).

8. Arik Hesseldahl, "A rich vein for, `reality mining'," *BusinessWeek*, April 24, 2008.

9. Nate Nead, "Customer acquisition vs. retention," November 9, 2009. www.digitalsignage.com/blog/2009/11/09/signage-customer-acquisition-vs-retention.

10. Martin Brat, "The new nutritionist: Your grocer," *Wall Street Journal*, July 27, 2010: D1.

11. Hamilton Nolan, "Mercedes launches PR push," *PR Week*, February 6, 2006: 3.

12. *Experian.com*: www.smrb.com/web/guest/core-solutions/national-consumer-study.

13. Michael R. Solomon, *Conquering Consumer Space: Marketing Strategies for a Branded World* (New York: AMACOM Books, 2003).

14. Emily Steel, "The new focus groups: Online networks," *Wall Street Journal*, January 28, 2009: B6.

15. Matt Richtel, "The parable of the beer and diapers," *TheRegister.com*, August 15, 2006. www.theregister.co.uk/2006/08/15/beer_diapers.

16. World Business Academy, "'Spellcasters': The hunt for the 'buy-button' in your brain," *Truthout.org*, January 22, 2010. www.truthout.org/spellcasters-the-hunt-buy-button-your-brain56278.

17. "Where marketers can obtain state do-not-call lists," *Direct Marketing Association*. www.the-dma.org/government/donotcalllists.shtml.

18. The Praxi Group, Inc., "Research overview: Telephone versus online research—advantages and pitfalls," *praxigroup.net*. www.praxigroup.net/TPG%20Phone%20Versus%20Online%20WP.pdf.

19. Basil G. Englis and Michael R. Solomon, "Life/Style OnLine ©: A web-based methodology for visually-oriented consumer research," *Journal of Interactive Marketing* 14(1), 2000: 2–14; Basil G. Englis, Michael R. Solomon and Paula D. Harveston, "Web-based, visually oriented consumer research tools," *Online Consumer Psychology: Understanding and Influencing Consumer Behavior in the Virtual World*, ed. Curt Haugtvedt, Karen Machleit and Richard Yalch (Hillsdale, NJ: Lawrence Erlbaum Associates, 2005).

20. "The Nielson Homescan Panel," *Homescanecanada.ca*. www.homescancanada.ca/about_homescan.php.

21. Brian Steinberg, "Olympics give NBC universal first crack at cross-media metric: Network to provide data on audiences across all screens," *Advertising Age*, August 14, 2008. http://adage.com/mediaworks/article?article_id=130314.

22. Steven Baker, "The web knows what you want," *BusinessWeek*, July 16, 2009. www.businessweek.com/magazine/content/09_30/b4140048486880.htm.

23. *Canadian Marketing Association*: www.the-cma.org/.

24. Jack Neff, "Chasing the cheaters that undermine online research," *Advertising Age*, March 31, 2008: 12.

25. Bruce L. Stern and Ray Ashmun, "Methodological disclosure: The foundation for effective use of survey research," *Journal of Applied Business Research*, 7(1991): 77–82.

26. Michael E. Ross, "It seemed like a good idea at the time," *MSNBC.com*, April 22, 2005. www.msnbc.msn.com/id/7209828/.

27. Gary Levin, "New adventures in children's research," *Advertising Age*, August 9, 1993: 17.

28. "2009 Honomichl top 50 report," *Marketing News*, June 30, 2009. www.marketingpower.com/ResourceLibrary/Publications/MarketingNews/2009/43/6_30_09/Hono%20full.pdf.

Chapter 4

1. James R. Bettman, "The decision maker who came in from the cold," Presidential Address, in *Advances in Consumer Research*, vol. 20, ed. Leigh McAllister and Michael Rothschild (Provo, UT: Association for Consumer Research, 1990); John W. Payne, James R. Bettman and Eric J. Johnson, "Behavioural decision research: a constructive processing perspective," *Annual Review of Psychology*, 4(1992): 87–131; for an overview of recent developments in individual choice models, see Robert J. Meyer and Barbara E. Kahn, "Probabilistic models of consumer choice behaviour," in *Handbook of Consumer Behaviour*, ed. Thomas S. Robertson and Harold H. Kassarjian (Englewood Cliffs, NJ: Prentice Hall, 1991): 85–123.

2. Richard Pérez-Peña, "Newspaper guild files labor complaint against Reuters over compensation cuts," *New York Times*, February 17, 2010, http://mediadecoder.blogs.nytimes.com/; Stephanie Clifford, "Cable companies target commercials to audience," *New York Times*, March 3, 2009, www.nytimes.com/2009/03/04/business/04cable.html?_r=1.

3. Richard Gillis and Jonathan Clegg, "Ferrari scraps barcode logo," *Wall Street Journal*, May 9, 2010. http://online.wsj.com/article/NA_WSJ_PUB:SB10001424052748703674704575234083089692088.html.

4. Susannah Patton, "Web metrics that matter," *CIO Magazine*, November 2002.

5. Stuart Elliott, "TV commercials adjust to a shorter attention span," *The New York Times*, April 8, 2005.

6. Robert M. McMath, "Image counts," *American Demographics*, May 1998: 64.

7. Abraham H. Maslow, *Motivation and Personality*, 2nd edition, (New York: Harper & Row, 1970).

8. Robert A. Baron and Donn Byrne, *Social Psychology: Understanding Human Interaction*, 5th edition (Boston: Allyn & Bacon, 1987).

9. *Just For Me VIP Club - Mom Blog*: www.jfmvipclub.com/jfm_style-guide.pdf.

10. Andrea Chang, "Mattel taps into social media craze with puppy tweets," *Los Angeles Times*, February 11, 2010. http://articles.latimes.com/2010/feb/11/business/la-fi-puppy-tweets11-2010feb11.

11. Alfred S. Boote, "Psychographics: Mind over matter," *American Demographics*, April 1980: 26–29; William D. Wells, "Psychographics: A critical review," *Journal of Marketing Research*, 12 (May 1975): 196–213.

12. Alan R. Hirsch, "Effects of ambient odors on slot-machine usage in a Las Vegas casino," *Psychology & Marketing*, 12(7): 585–94.

13. James Vlahos, "Scent and sensibility," *New York Times*, September 9, 2007. http://query.nytimes.com/gst/fullpage.html?res=9D07EFDC1E3AF93AA3575AC0A9619C8B63&scp=1&sq=scent%20and%20sensibility&st=cse.

14. Marianne Meyer, "Attention shoppers!" *Marketing and Media Decisions* 23 (May 1988): 67.

15. GFK Group, "Many German consumers decide at the supermarket shelves," *Market Research World*, March 2009. www.marketresearchworld.net/index.php?option=com_content&task=view&id=2564&Itemid=77.

16. Eben Shapiro, "Need a little fantasy? A bevy of new companies can help," *The New York Times*, March 10, 1991: F4.

17. Quoted in John P. Cortez, "Ads head for bathroom," *Advertising Age*, May 18, 1992: 24.

18. Kerry Capel, "The Arab world wants its MTV," *Business Week*, October 11, 2007. www.businessweek.com/globalbiz/content/oct2007/gb20071011_342851.htm.

19. Adapted from Michael R. Solomon, *Consumer Behavior: Buying, Having, and Being*, 9th ed., (Upper Saddle River, NJ: Prentice Hall, 2010).

20. Richard W. Pollay, "Measuring the cultural values manifest in advertising," *Current Issues and Research in Advertising*, 1983: 71–92.

21. Emily Bryson York, "General Mills targets three groups to fuel growth," *Advertising Age*, February 16, 2010. http://adage.com/article?article_id=142138.

22. Ben Berkon, "Coca-Cola comes clean about going green at Olympic Games," *BrandChannel*, February 1, 2010. www.brandchannel.com/home/post/2010/02/01/Coca-Cola-Comes-Clean-About-Going-Green-At-Olympic-Games.aspx.

23. Stuart U. Rich and Subhash C. Jain, "Social class and life cycle as predictors of shopping behaviour," *Journal of Marketing Research* 5 (February 1968): 41–49.

24. Nathan Kogan and Michael A. Wallach, "Risky shift phenomenon in small decision-making groups: A test of the information exchange hypothesis," *Journal of Experimental Social Psychology*, 3 (January 1967): 75–84; Arch G. Woodside and M. Wayne DeLozier, "Effects of word-of-mouth advertising on consumer risk taking," *Journal of Advertising*, Fall 1976: 12–19.

25. Everett M. Rogers, *Diffusion of Innovations*, 3rd edition. (New York: Free Press, 1983).

26. Kathleen Debevec and Easwar Iyer, "Sex roles and consumer perceptions of promotions, products, and self: What do we know and where should we be headed," *Advances in Consumer Research*, ed. Richard J. Lutz (Provo, UT: Association for Consumer Research), 13(1986): 210–14; Lynn J. Jaffe and Paul D. Berger, "Impact on purchase intent of sex-role identity and product positioning," *Psychology & Marketing*, Fall 1988: 259–271.

27. Jennie Yabroff, "Girls going mild(er)," *Newsweek*, July 22, 2007. www.thedailybeast.com/newsweek/2007/07/22/girls-going-mild-er.html.

28. Vivian Manning-Schaffel, "Metrosexuals: A well-groomed market?" *Brandchannel*. www.brandchannel.com/features_effect.asp?pf_id=315.

29. Diego Rinallo, "Metro/fashion/tribes of men: Negotiating the boundaries of men's legitimate consumption," in B. Cova, R. Kozinets and A. Shankar, eds., *Consumer Tribes: Theory, Practice and Prospects*, (Burlington, MA: Elsevier/Butterworth-Heinemann, 2007); Susan Kaiser, Michael R. Solomon, Janet Hethorn, Basil Englis, Lewis Van Dyk and Wi-Suk Kwon, "Menswear, fashion, and subjectivity," paper presented in Special Session: Susan Kaiser, Michael Solomon, Janet Hethorn and Basil Englis (Chairs), "What Do Men Want? Media Representations, Subjectivity, and Consumption," at the *ACR Gender Conference*, Edinburgh, Scotland, June 2006.

30. Catharine Skipp, "Looks: A manly comeback," *Newsweek*, August 15, 2007. www.thedailybeast.com/newsweek/2007/08/15/looks-a-manly-comeback.html.

Chapter 5

1. Wikipedia: http://en.wikipedia.org/wiki/Bombardier_CRJ200#CRJ100.

2. F. Robert Dwyer and John F. Tanner, *Business Marketing: Connecting Strategy, Relationships, and Learning* (Boston: McGraw-Hill, 2008); Edward F. Fern and James R. Brown, "The industrial/consumer marketing dichotomy: A case of insufficient justification," *Journal of Marketing*, Spring 1984: 68–77.

3. "All Boxter models," *Porche*. www.porsche.com/usa/models/boxster/.

4. "North America industry classification system (NAICS)," U.S. Census Bureau. www.census.gov/eos/www/naics/.

5. Carol Krol, "Companies use fun and games to find serious business," *B2B: The Magazine for Marketing Strategists Online*, December 10, 2007. www.btobonline.com/apps/pbcs.dll/article?AID=/20071210/FREE/71210001/1109/FREE&template=printart; Andy Sernovits and Guy Kawasaki, *Word of Mouth Marketing: How Smart Companies Get People Talking*, (New York: Kaplan Publishing, 2006).

6. Ben Hanna, "Audience characteristics and social media use," *B2B: The Magazine for Marketing Strategists Online*, January 18, 2010.

7. April Joyner, "Nice meeting your avatar: Industry trade shows go virtual," *INC.com*, May 1, 2009.

8. Steve Fretzin, "Forget Facebook and Twitter … For B2B it's all about LinkedIn," *Enterprise Management Quarterly Online*, January 25, 2010; "B2B goes 007," *Marketing Profs Articles*, January 21, 2010; Gavin O'Malley, "LinkedIn debuts B2B network," *Media Post*, October 27, 2008.

9. Chris Lake, "10 kickass crowdsourcing sites for your business," *Econsultancy Digital Marketers United*, August 4, 2009. http://econsultancy.com/us/blog/4355-10-kickass-crowdsourcing-sites-for-your-business.

10. Patrick LaPointe, *Marketing by the Dashboard Light: How to Get More Insight, Foresight, and Accountability from Your Marketing Investments* (New York: ANA, 2005).

Chapter 6

1. Eve Lazarus, "Sizing up the sizzle," *Marketing Magazine*, June 5, 2000: 17.

2. "Converse's all-star image," *BusinessWeek*, April 25, 2008. www.businessweek.com/innovate/content/apr2008/id20080425_383266.htm?chan=search.

3. "Seizing the occasion," *Marketing Magazine*, August 13, 2001.

4. Craig Saunders, "Peachtree invests in brand-building," *Strategy Magazine*, March 27, 2000: 1.

5. "Lesson 3c: language & location targeting," *Google Learning Center*, http://adwords.google.com/support/aw/bin/static.py?page=guide.cs&guide=22793&topic=22804.

6. *Environics Research Group*: www.environics.ca/.

7. Caitlin Kelly, "A jones for a soda: Peter van Stolk is bottling success in Fufu Berry and Vanilla Coke flavours," *The Ottawa Citizen*, January 15, 2000: B2.

8. Jennifer Lawrence, "Gender-specific works for diapers almost too well," *Advertising Age*, February 8, 1993: S-10.

9. Keith Morgan, "Designed by women, Volvo concept car will please both sexes," *The Montreal Gazette*, March 30, 2004: E1.

10. Kathleen Martin, "Boys read," *Marketing Magazine*, January 20, 2003.

11. David K. Foot and Daniel Stoffman, *Boom, Bust and Echo 2000: Profiting from the Demographic Shift in the New Millennium* (Toronto: Macfarlane Walter & Ross, 1998): 124.

12. David K. Foot and Daniel Stoffman, *Boom, Bust and Echo 2000: Profiting from the Demographic Shift in the New Millennium* (Toronto: Macfarlane Walter & Ross, 1998).

13. "The kids are alright – 'lost' generation no more," *Investor's Group*. www.investorsgroup.com/english/aboutUs/news/2011/110104_kidsAlright.shtml.

14. Eleanor Beaton, "Your next big thing: Growth market - Generation Y", *Profit*, December 1, 2007.

15. Jaclyn Law, "First bank accounts: How to find the right savings account for your child," *Today's Parent*, November 2010. www.todaysparent.com/lifeasparent/article.jsp?content=20041105_144835_3936&page=1.

16. "Canadian demographics at a glance, 2006 census," *Statistics Canada*, Report # 91-003-X. www.statcan.gc.ca/pub/91-003-x/91-003-x2007001-eng.pdf.

17. Aaron Baar, "Ford builds buzz around upcoming Fiesta," *MediaPost News*, February 20, 2009. www.mediapost.com/publications/?fa=Articles.showArticle&art_aid=100693.

17. "Teen market to surpass $200 billion by 2011, despite population decline," *MC Marketing Charts*, 2007. www.marketingcharts.com/interactive/teen-market-to-surpass-200-billion-by-2011-despite-population-decline-817/

18. "Income in Canada," *Statistics Canada*, Report # 75-202-X: 75. www.statcan.gc.ca/pub/75-202-x/75-202-x2007000-eng.pdf.

19. "Canadian demographics at a glance, 2006 census," *Statistics Canada*, Report # 91-003-X. www.statcan.gc.ca/pub/91-003-x/91-003-x2007001-eng.pdf.

20. Danny Kucharsky, "Quebec's distinct specialty TV," *Marketing Magazine*, March 20, 2000: 22.

21. "Canadian demographics at a glance, 2006 census," *Statistics Canada*, Report # 91-003-X. www.statcan.gc.ca/pub/91-003-x/91-003-x2007001-eng.pdf.

22. Deannie Kolybabi, "Time for a closer look at the aboriginal market," *Marketing Magazine*, September 22, 2003.

23. Brian Morton, "Aboriginal businesses fostering strong income growth: report - Income of aboriginal households in Canada expected to rise sharply to $32 billion by 2016," *Vancouver Sun*, June 17, 2011.

24. "Canadian demographics at a glance, 2006 census," *Statistics Canada*, Report # 91-003-X. www.statcan.gc.ca/pub/91-003-x/91-003-x2007001-eng.pdf.

25. Eun-Mi (Liz) Adams, "The big piece of the mosaic," *Marketing Magazine*, June 21, 1999: 16-7.

26. "Canadian demographics at a glance, 2006 census," *Statistics Canada*, Report # 91-003-X. www.statcan.gc.ca/pub/91-003-x/91-003-x2007001-eng.pdf.

27. Astrid Van Den Broek, "Cozying up to kosher," *Marketing Magazine*, June 5, 2000: 18-9.

28. Jo Marney, "When the urge hits," *Marketing Magazine*, March 29, 1999.

29. *Canada Post*: www.canadapost.ca/cpo/mc/business/tools/geopostplus.jsf.

30. Sinclair Stewart, "Grand & Toy launches The Stockroom," *Strategy Magazine*, June 7, 1999: FE.01F.

31. Bruce Gillespie, "Get ready for the new wave," *National Post*, November 24, 2003: FE.01.F.

32. Anthony Ramirez, "New cigarettes raising issue of target market," *The New York Times*, February 18, 1990: 28.

33. Chrissie Thompson, "Buick counting on Greg and Laurie Robins," *Automotive News*, May 10, 2010.

34. Debbie Shork, "A matter of taste," *Marketing Magazine*, May 22, 2000: 14.

35. "Our business," Toyota. www.toyota.com/about/our_business/index.html.

36. *Blacksocks*: www.blacksocks.com; Jack Ewing, "A web outfit with socks appeal," *BusinessWeek*, July 24, 2002. www.businessweek.com/technology/content/jul2002/tc20020724_9718.htm?chan=search.

37. "Worldline," *Marketing Magazine*, May 21, 2001.

38. Michael Treacy and Fred Wiersama, "Customer intimacy and other value disciplines," *Harvard Business Review*, January-February 1993: 84-93.

39. Becky Ebenkamp, "No dollars for bowling," *Brandweek*, March 27, 2000: 56-8.

40. Eve Lazarus, "Lemon-aid," *Marketing Magazine*, October 11, 1999: 15.

41. Martin R. Lautman, "End-benefit segmentation and prototypical bonding," *Journal of Advertising Research*, June/July 1991: 9-18.

42. "Cassies awards: Listerine mouthwash and Pocketpaks," *Marketing Magazine*, November 18, 2002.

43. Chris Powell. "Selling together: A new study by Group M and CTV suggests TV ads achieve better recall when matched with product placement," *Marketing Magazine*, June 6, 2005.

44. Shawna Cohen, "Energizing elixirs," *Marketing Magazine*, April 3, 2000: 12-3.

45. "A crash course in customer relationship management," *Harvard Management Update* (Harvard Business School reprint U0003B), March 2000; Nahshon Wingard, "CRM definition-customer-centered philosophy," *CRM Definition*, October 26, 2009, www.crmdefinition.com/2009/10/crm-definition-customer-centered-philosophy/.

46. Don Peppers and Martha Rogers, *The One-to-One Future* (New York: Doubleday, 1996).

47. Don Peppers, Martha Rogers and Bob Dorf, "Is your company ready for one-to-one marketing?" *Harvard Business Review*, January-February 1999: 151-60.

48. Quoted in Cara B. DiPasquale, "Navigate the maze," Special Report on 1:1 Marketing, *Advertising Age*, October 29, 2011: S1(2).

49. Michael Bush and Rupal Parekh, "More marketers want to get to know you," *Advertising Age*, August 25, 2008, http://adage.com/article?article_id=130497.

50. Rebecca Harris. "Getting to know you," *Marketing Magazine*, July 3, 2006. www.marketingmag.ca/news/marketer-news/getting-to-know-you-19678.

51. Robert C. Blattberg, Gary Getz and Mark Pelofsky, "Want to build your business? Grow your customer equity," *Harvard Management Update* (Harvard Business School reprint U0108B), August 2001:

3: "What are your customers really worth?" *Forbes*, March 6, 2007. www.forbes.com/2007/03/06/gm-schwab-bmw-ent-manage-cx_kw_0306whartoncustomers.html.

Chapter 7

1. *Woodstream Corporation*: www.victorpest.com.

2. "Communities," *Microsoft Corporation*. www.microsoft.com/communities/default.mspx.

3. iRobot Corporation, *iRobot*. http://store.irobot.com/home/index.jsp.

4. "The story of cotton," *Cotton's Journey*. www.cottonsjourney.com/Storyofcotton/page7.asp.

5. "Business, consumer and property services," *Statistics Canada*, www.statcan.gc.ca/pub/11-402-x/2010000/chap/services/services-eng.htm; "GDP services-producing industries (NAICS 41-91)," *Industry Canada*, www.ic.gc.ca/eic/site/cis-sic.nsf/eng/h_00019.html.

6. Jennifer Pritchett, "Wyndham eliminates 300 call centre jobs," *CanadaEast Interactive*, February 9, 2011. http://telegraphjournal.canadaeast.com/rss/article/1378575.

7. John A. Czepiel, Michael R. Solomon and Carol F. Surprenant, eds., *The Service Encounter: Managing Employee/Customer Interaction in Service Businesses* (Lexington, MA: D.C. Heath, 1985).

8. Cengiz Haksever, Barry Render, Roberta S. Russell and Robert G. Murdick, *Service Management and Operations* (Englewood Cliffs, NJ: Prentice Hall, 2000): 25–26.

9. David H. Maister, *The Psychology of Waiting Lines*, in Czepiel et al., *The Service Encounter* (Lexington, MA: D.C. Heath, 1985): 113–24.

10. Lou W. Turley and Douglas L. Fugate, "The multidimensional nature of service facilities: Viewpoints and recommendations," *Journal of Services Marketing* 6 (Summer 1992): 37–45.

11. "WestJet named J.D. Power 2011 customer service champion," *WestJet Airlines Ltd.*, February 17, 2011. www.westjet.com.

12. Cynthia Webster, "Influences upon consumer expectations of services," *Journal of Services Marketing*, 5 (Winter 1991): 5–17.

13. Valarie A. Zeithaml, Mary Jo Bitner and Dwayne Gremler, *Services Marketing*, 4th edition, (Englewood Cliffs, NJ: Prentice Hall, 2005).

14. A. Parasuraman, Leonard L. Barry and Valarie A. Zeithaml, "SERVQUAL: A multiple-item scale for measuring consumer perceptions of service quality," *Journal of Retailing* 64(1), 1988: 12–40; A. Parasuraman, Leonard L. Barry and Valarie A. Zeithaml, "Refinement and reassessment of the SERVQUAL scale," *Journal of Retailing* 67(4), 1991: 420–50.

15. Valarie A. Zeithaml, Leonard L. Berry and A. Parasuraman, "Communication and control processes in the delivery of service quality," *Journal of Marketing* 52(April 1988): 35–48.

16. Debbie Delosa, "Social business: Customer perception becomes business reality," *Social Media Business Insights*, March 29, 2011. http://socialmediabusinessinsights.blogspot.com/2011_03_01_archive.html.

17. Jody D. Nyquist, Mary F. Bitner and Bernard H. Booms, *Identifying Communication Difficulties in the Service Encounter: A Critical Incident Approach*, in Czepiel et al., *The Service Encounter* (Lexington, MA: D.C. Heath, 1985): 195–212.

18. Nyquist et al., *Identifying Communication Difficulties in the Service Encounter: A Critical Incident Approach*, in Czepiel et al., *The Service Encounter* (Lexington, MA: D.C. Heath, 1985): 195–212.

19. Kristin Anderson and Ron Zemke, *Delivering Knock Your Socks Off Service* (New York: American Management Association, 1998).

20. Stephen L. Vargo and Robert F. Lusch, "Evolving to a new dominant logic for marketing," *Journal of Marketing* 68(January 2004): 1–17.

21. "Search Hyatt hotels & resorts," *Hyatt*. www.hyatt.com/hyatt/features/hotel-search-results.jsp?No=10&type=clear&N=409.

22. "Lexus self-parking car video and review," *GIZMODO*. http://gizmodo.com/gadgets/clips/lexus-self-parking-car-video-and-review-196551.php.

23. Roger Yu, "Airlines put mobile agents into service," *USA Today*, July 7, 2010. www.usatoday.com/money/industries/travel/2010-07-07-airlineagents07_ST_N.htm.

24. "Radar car collision systems put to test," *Gizmag*, February 25, 2008. www.gizmag.com/radar-car-collision-prevention-systems-put-to-the-test/8813/.

25. "iPod Classic Features," *Apple Inc.* www.apple.com/ipodclassic/features.html.

26. Tim Ambler, *Marketing and the Bottom Line*, 2nd edition. (Edinburgh Gate, UK: Pearson/Financial Times, 2004): 172.

27. Mary Bellis, "History of Sony Playstation," *About.com: Inventors*, http://inventors.about.com/library/inventors/bl_playstation.htm; "Sony Playstation," *CyberiaPC.com*, www.cyberiapc.com/vgg/sony_ps.htm; Steven L. Ken, *The Ultimate History of Video Games: From Pong to Pokémon—The Story Behind the Craze That Touched Our Lives and Changed the World* (Pittsburgh, PA: Three Rivers Press, 2001).

28. Natalie Zmuda, "Facebook turns focus group with Splenda product-sampling app," *Advertising Age*, July 13, 2009. http://adage.com/digital/article?article_id=137851.

29. Allison Enright, "There's nothing mellow about Sharp's new marketing mix," *Marketing News Exclusives*, April 1, 2010.

30. Simon Pitman, "Pfizer sues P&G over mouthwash ad claims," *CosmeticsDesign.com*, March 6, 2006. www.cosmeticsdesign.com/news/ng.asp?n=66236-pfizer-proctor-gamble-lawsuit-mouthwash.

31. Malcolm Gladwell, *The Tipping Point* (Newport Beach, CA: Back Bay Books, 2002).

32. *Amazon.ca*: www.amazon.ca/Brother-FAX-575-Personal-Phone-Copier/dp/B0007KI6PE/ref=sr_1_1?ie=UTF8&qid=1309270055&sr=8-1.

33. Allison Enright, "There's nothing mellow about Sharp's new marketing mix," *Marketing News Exclusives*, April 1, 2010.

34. "Jetta," *VW*, www.vw.com/jetta/en/us/; Neal E. Boudette and Lee Hawkins, "Volkswagen eyes young parents with newest version of Jetta," *Wall Street Journal*, January 11, 2005: D.9.

35. Bandai America Incorporated, "Products," *Tamagotchi Connections*. www.tamagotchi.com.

36. Amy Gilroy, "More players enter portable Nav market," *TWICE*, 28(2), April 5, 2004; Pioneer Electronics Co., "XM NavTraffic," *Pioneer: Car Electronics*, www.pioneerelectronics.com/pna/article/0,,2076_3149_269505659,00.html.

37. Bill Gerba, "Gamestop trials Dell kiosks," *Interactive Kiosk News*, September 30, 2005, http://kiosknews.blogspot.com/2005/09/gamestop-trials-dell-kiosks.html; "Dell completes acquisition of Alienware," *Allbusiness.com*, May 9, 2006, www.allbusiness.com/company-activities-management/company-structures-ownersip/5475507-1.html.

38. Everett Rogers, *Diffusion of Innovations* (New York: Free Press, 1983): 247–251.

39. Sources used in this section: "Wi-Fi's big brother," *Economist*, March 13, 2004: 65; William J. Gurley, "Why Wi-Fi is the next big thing," *Fortune*, March 5, 2001: 184; Joshua Quittner, "Cordless capers," *Time*, May 1, 2000: 85; Scott Van Camp, "Intel switches Centrino's gears," *Brandweek*, April 26, 2004: 16; Benny Evangelista, "SBC Park a hot spot for fans lugging laptops," *San Francisco Chronicle*, April 26, 2004: A1; Todd Wallack, "Santa Clara ready for wireless," *San Francisco Chronicle*, April 19, 2004: D1; Glenn Fleishman, "Three essays on Muni-Fi you should read," *WNN Wi-Fi Net News*, http://wifinetnews.com.

40. Christine Chen and Tim Carvell, "Hall of shame," *Fortune*, November 22, 1999: 140.

41. Carmen Nobel, "Clay Christensen's milkshake marketing," *HBS Working Knowledge*, February 14, 2011. http://hbswk.hbs.edu/item/6496.html?wknews=02142011.

42. Everett Rogers, *Diffusion of Innovations* (New York: Free Press, 1983): Chapter 6.

Chapter 8

1. David Kiley, "The MINI bulks up," *BusinessWeek*, January 17, 2006. www.businessweek.com/autos/content/jan2006/bw20060117_818487.htm?chan=search.

2. *Pepperidge Farm*: www.pfgoldfish.com/default.aspx.

3. *Dawn*: www.dawn-dish.com/en_US/home.do.

4. *Rolls-Royce Motor Cars*: www.rolls-roycemotorcars.com.

5. Matt Stone, "First drive: 2009 Hyundai Sonata," *MotorTrend*, www.motortrend.com/roadtests/sedans/112_0804_2009_hyundai_sonata/index.html; Joann Muller and Robyn Meredity, "Last laugh," *Forbes*, April 18, 2005: 98.

6. Daniel Thomas, "Relaunches: New life or last gasps?" *Marketing Week*, 20(2), 2004.

7. Lea Goldman, "Big gulp," *Forbes*, January 10, 2005: 68.

8. Geoffrey Colvin, "The ultimate manager," *Fortune*, November 22, 1999: 185–87.

9. "General information on ISO," *ISO*. www.iso.org/iso/support/faqs/faqs_general_information_on_iso.htm.

10. Al Ries and Laura Ries, *The Origin of Brands* (New York: Collins, 2005).

11. Laurie Burkitt and Ken Bruno, "New, improved ... and failed," *MSNBC.com*, March, 24, 2010. www.msnbc.msn.com/id/36005036/ns/business-forbescom/.

12. Brad Stone, "For Apple, iPad said more than intended," *New York Times*, January 29, 2010. www.nytimes.com/2010/01/29/technology/29name.html.

13. "'Apple' wins logo lawsuit against Beatles," *MacNN.com*, May 8, 2006. www.macnn.com/articles/06/05/08/apple.wins.logo.lawsuit.

14. "The most famous name in music," *Music Trades*, 118(12), September 2003.

15. Suzanne Vranica, "McDonald's vintage t-shirts sizzle," *Wall Street Journal*, April 27, 2006. www.post-gazette.com/pg/06117/685629-28.stm.

16. Susan Fournier, "Consumers and their brands: Developing relationship theory in consumer research," *Journal of Consumer Research*, 24 (March 1998): 343–373.

17. Stuart Elliott, "For one production company, it's all about the power of storytelling," *New York Times*, November 16, 2008. www.nytimes.com/2008/11/17/business/media/17adcol.html.

18. Kevin Lane Keller, "The brand report card," *Harvard Business Review* (Harvard Business School reprint R00104), January–February 2000.

19. Karl Greenberg, "Dodge cars to target lifestyles, Ram becomes sub-brand," *MediaPost*, November 4, 2009. www.mediapost.com/publications/?art_aid=116815&fa=Articles.showArticle.

20. Nicholas Casey, "Can new Quiksilver line reach beyond the beach," *Wall Street Journal*, March 6, 2008. http://online.wsj.com/article_email/SB120476311128015043-lMyQjAxMDI4MDA0NjcwNjYzWj.html.

21. John D. Stoll, "Eight-brand pileup dents GM's turnaround efforts," *Wall Street Journal*, March 4, 2008. http://online.wsj.com/article_email/SB120456874600508063-lMyQjAxMDI4MDA0NTUwNjU4Wj.html.

22. "Psst! wanna see Loblaws' new products?" *Private Label Buyer*, 10(1), January 2003; Len Lewis, "Turf war!" *Grocery Headquarters*, 13(6), November 2002.

23. "Why not try a nurse in a box," *Clark Howard*, January 11, 2007, http://clarkhoward.com/shownotes/category/11/65/315/;

"Pharmacy," *Walmart.com*, www.walmart.com/cp/Pharmacy/5431.

24. "TGI Friday's worldwide: Menus," *TGI Fridays*, www.tgifridays.com/menus/Menus.aspx; "Ultimate recipe showdown winners on Friday's menu," *SunSentinel.com*, http://weblogs.sun-sentinel.com/features/food/restaurants/blog/2009/02/ultimate_recipe_showdown_winne_1.html.

25. "Harry Potter," *Lego*. http://parents.lego.com/awards/awards.aspx?id=legoharrypotter.

26. D. C. Denison, "The Boston Globe business intelligence column," *Boston Globe*, May 26, 2002.

27. "Putting zoom into your life," *Time International*, March 8, 2004: 54.

28. Stephanie Thompson, "Brand buddies," *Brandweek*, February 23, 1998: 26–30; Jean Halliday, "L.L. Bean, Subaru pair for co-branding," *Advertising Age*, February 21, 2000: 21.

29. "EquiTrend," *Harris Interactive*. www.harrisinteractive.com/Products/EquiTrend.aspx.

30. "Best global brands for 2009," *Interbrand*. www.interbrand.com/best_global_brands.aspx.

31. Kusum L. Ailawadi, Donald R. Lehmann and Scott A. Neslin, "Revenue premium as an outcome measure of brand equity," *Journal of Marketing* 67(October 2003): 1–17.

32. *Pringles*: http://www.pringles.com/products.

33. "A package that lights up the shelf," *New York Times*, March 4, 2008. www.nytimes.com/2008/03/04/business/media/04adco.html?ex=1205298000&en=844d46791650b628&ei=5070&emc=etal.

34. Professor Jakki Mohr (personal communication), University of Montana, April 2004.

Chapter 9

1. Laura Pratt, "Trading places," *Financial Post Magazine*, March 1998: 97–100.

2. Glenda Luymes, "Blogger trades up from paper clip to house in rural Saskatchewan," *National Post*, July 10, 2006: A2.

3. Spencer Anderson, "Gas price wars hurting 'mom and pop' stations," *Comox Valley Echo*, June 10, 2011.

4. Kenneth Labich, "What will save the U.S. airlines," *Fortune*, June 14, 1993: 98–101; Chris Sorensen, "Are airlines taking off . . . or heading for a rough landing?" *National Post*, July 15, 2006: FP1.

5. "Canada's airlines: Risky business," *CBC News*, March 31, 2010. www.cbc.ca/news/business/story/2008/06/17/f-economy-airlines.html.

6. Leslie Vreeland, "How to be a smart shopper," *Black Enterprise*, August 1993: 88.

7. *Mega*: www.megagroup.ca/english/index.html.

8. John Dawes, "Sibling rivalry: When companies offer discounts, they too often ignore the impact on other products they sell," *Wall Street Journal*, August 17, 2009. http://online.wsj.com/article/SB10001424052970203353904574149120051802950.html?KEYWORDS=Sibling+Rivalry%3A+When+Companies+Offer+Discounts.

9. *Wikipedia*: http://en.wikipedia.org/wiki/Teen_Buzz.

10. Wendy Zellner, "Is JetBlue's flight plan flawed?" *BusinessWeek*, February 16, 2004: 56-58.

11. *Travelocity*: http://leisure.travelocity.ca/Promotions/0,,TCYCA%7C4818%7Cmkt_main,00.html.

12. Nick Bunkley and Bill Vlasic, "G.M. to close Saturn after deal fails," *New York Times*, September 30, 2009. www.nytimes.com/2009/10/01/business/01auto.html?scp-6&sq-saturn&st-cse.

13. Kristin Laird, "East Side Marios returns to budda-boom roots" *Marketing Magazine*, April 13, 2010.

14. Chris Woodyard, "High-tech gear disables car if borrower misses payment," *USA Today*, March 31, 2008. www.usatoday.com/money/autos/2008-03-30-repo-device-car-loans_n.htm.

15. Jack Neff, "Walmart reversal marks victory for brands," *Advertising Age*, March 22, 2010.

16. Ellen Byron, "P&G meets frugal shoppers halfway," *Wall Street Journal*, January 29, 2010, http://online.wsj.com/article/SB10001424052748704878904575030850236465716.html?KEYWORDS=PG+Meets+Frugal+Shoppers+Halfway; James Surowiecki, "Inconspicuous consumption," *The New Yorker*, October 12, 2009, www.newyorker.com/talk/financial/2009/10/12/091012ta_talk_surowiecki.

17. Claire Cain Miller, "Will the hard-core Starbucks customer pay more? The chain plans to find out," *New York Times*, August 20, 2009. www.nytimes.com/2009/08/21/business/21sbux.html?scp-1&sq-Will%20the%20Hard-core%20Starbucks%20Customer%20Pay%20More?%20The%20Chain%20Plans%20to%20Find%20Out&st=cse.

18. "Gas price regulation floated by Ontario NDP," *CBC News*, June 9, 2011. www.cbc.ca/news/canada/toronto/story/2011/06/09/ontario-ndp-gas-regulation.html.

19. "Government of Canada releases code of conduct for credit and debit card industry" (archived), *Department of Finance Canada*, April 16, 2010.

20. Quoted in Mercedes M. Cardonna, "Affluent shoppers like their luxe goods cheap," *Advertising Age*, December 1, 2003: 6.

21. Steve Mertl, "Forest industry battles switch to boardroom," *Times Colonist* (Victoria), October 12, 1999: E1.

22. Steward Washburn, "Pricing basics: Establishing strategy and determining costs in the pricing decision," *Business Marketing*, July 1985, reprinted in Valerie Kijewski, Bob Donath and David T. Wilson (eds.), *The Best Readings from Business Marketing Magazine*, (Boston: PWS-Kent Publishing Co., 1993): 257–69.

23. Ken Popovich and Mary Jo Foley, "Dell remains committed to pricing strategy," *eWeek*, April 9, 2001.

24. Tony Wong, "Some like it hot at Coca-Cola: Soft-drink maker exploring vending machines that raise the price of a can of pop when the weather warms up," *Toronto Star*, October 29, 1999: Section Head, NEWS.

25. Jennifer Merritt, "The belle of the golf balls," *BusinessWeek*, July 29, 1996: 6.

26. Sebastian Rupley, "The PowerPC revolution," *PC/Computing*, February 1994: 129–31; Marc Dodge, "New power chips," *PC/Computing*, February 1994: 116–7.

27. Jim Carlton, "Apple to launch Macintosh PowerPCs priced at level to gain market share," *Wall Street Journal*, March 14, 1994: B4.

28. Michael D. Mondello, "Naming your price," *Inc.*, July 1992: 159.

29. Annette Bourdreau, "Via targets future biz travel," *Strategy Magazine*, April 2007: 29

30. Susanne Craig, "Wal-Mart has radically changed the retail scene," *Financial Post*, December 21, 1996: 41.

31. "Challenging the high price at the pumps: Consumers force an inquiry on the gas industry," *Maclean's*, 109(23), June 1996: 17–19; Michael MacDonald, "Charge against Irving Oil just a distraction: Liberal MP," *Canadian Press Newswire*, October 1, 1999.

32. Betsy McKay, "Coca-Cola sets prices at premium," *The Globe and Mail*, November 16, 1999: B18.

33. Douglas Lavin, "Goodbye to haggling: Savvy consumers are buying their cars like refrigerators," *Wall Street Journal*, August 20, 1993: B1, B3.

34. Claire Cain Miller, "At checkout, more ways to avoid cash or plastic," *New York Times*, November 15, 2009. www.nytimes.com/2009/11/16/technology/start-ups/16wallet.html?_r=1&scp=1&sq=at%20chekout%20more%20ways%20to%20avoid&st=cse.

35. "iTunes music store downloads top a quarter billion songs," *Apple*, January 24, 2005. www.apple.com/pr/library/2005/jan/24itms.html.

36. Emma Ritch, "Mobile music is shooting up the charts," *San Jose Business Journal*, March 21, 2008.

37. This section is adapted from Chris Anderson, "Free! Why $0.00 is the future of business," *Wired*, March 2008.

38. *Shopbot.ca*: www.shopbot.ca/pp-viewsonic-vt2430-viewsonic-price-158735.html.

39. *Shopbot.ca*: www.shopbot.ca/pp-viewsonic-vt2430-viewsonic-price-158735.html.

40. "Bell Canada to pay $10 million fine for misleading ads," *Marketing Magazine*, June 29, 2011.

41. "Bogus bargains cost Suzy Shier $1 million," *The Times Colonist*, June 14, 2003: E2.

42. Naomi Lewis, "Bird dog video closes after Netflix surge," *Open File Calgary*, June 3, 2011. http://calgary.openfile.ca/calgary/file/2011/05/video-store-owners-project-differing-futures-rental-business.

43. "Price discrimination enforcement guidelines," *Industry Canada Competition Bureau*, August 17, 1992.

44. Chris Flanagan, "Gas price group takes on the giants," *The Telegram* (St. John's), May 20, 1999: 1; Ryan Cleary, "Price-fixing charge dismissed," *The Telegram* (St. John's), March 21, 2000: 1.

45. "Canadian court green lights worldwide diamond price-fixing case against De Beers," *Anti-Trust Today*, June 15, 2011. www.antitrusttoday.com/2011/06/15/canadian-court-green-lights-worldwide-diamond-price-fixing-case-against-de-beers/.

46. "Quebec gas price-fixing case nets more charges," *CBC News*, July 15, 2010.

47. "Jang Airlines fined $1.1-billion over price-fixing," *The Globe and Mail*, November 9, 2010.

48. "Refrigeration company guilty of bid rigging," *Times Colonist*, July 20, 2011: B4.

Chapter 10

1. Megan Mcilroy, "The hottest digital agencies around," *Advertising Age*, October 22, 2007. http://adage.com/digital/article?article_id=121406.

2. Schultz, Don E. and Heidi Schultz, *The Next Generation. Five Steps For Delivering Value And Measuring Returns Using Marketing Communication* (New York: McGraw Hill, 2003): 20-21.

3. Barbara Lippert, "Windows debut: Almost 7th Heaven," *Adweek*, October 26, 2009. www.adweek.com/aw/content_display/creative/critique/e3i7a4f853fe57e4c0b5bf8e3a501635ead.

4. Gert Assmus, "An empirical investigation into the perception of vehicle source effects," *Journal of Advertising*, 7 (Winter 1978): 4–10; for a more thorough discussion of the pros and cons of different media, see Stephen Baker, *Systematic Approach to Advertising Creativity* (New York: McGraw-Hill, 1979).

5. Charlene Li and Josh Bernoff, *Groundswell: Winning in a World Transformed by Social Technologies* (Boston, MA: Harvard Business School Publishing, 2008): 9.

6. Meghan Keane, "Pepsi Refresh: Will the social media halo extend to soda sales?" *EConsultancy*, February 5, 2010. http://econsultancy.com/blog/5391-pepsi-refresh-will-the-halo-extend-to-soda.

7. Natalie Zmuda, "Pepsi expands Refresh project," *Advertising Age*, September 7, 2010.

8. Lois Geller, "Wow—what a buzz," *Target Marketing*, June 2005: 21.

9. Dale Buss, "Volvo wants you to see its 'naughty' side," *Brandchannel*, March 4, 2010. www.brandchannel.com/home/post/2010/03/04/Volvo-Wants-You-to-See-its-e28098Naughtye28099-Side.aspx.

10. Matthew Creamer, "In era of consumer control, marketers crave the potency of word-of-mouth," *Advertising Age*, November 28, 2005: 32.

11. Todd Wasserman, "Word games," *Brandweek*, April 24, 2006: 24

12. Todd Wasserman, "Blogs cause word-of-mouth business to spread quickly," *Brandweek*, October 3, 2005: 9.

13. Richard Read, "2010 Honda Accord Crosstour sideswiped by Facebook, Twitter," *The Car Connection*, September 3, 2009. www.thecarconnection.com/marty-blog/1034885_2010-honda-accord-crosstour-sideswiped-by-facebook-twitter.

14. Wasserman, "Blogs cause word-of-mouth business to spread quickly," *Brandweek*, October 3, 2005: 9.

15. Abe Sauer, "Smith Vs. Southwest: Twitter again central to national debate," *Brandchannel*, February 16, 2010, www.brandchannel.com/home/post/2010/02/16/Smith-Vs-Southwest-Twitter-Again-Central-To-National-Debate.aspx.

16. "The WOMMA guide to disclosure in social media marketing," *word of mouth marketing association*, http://womma.org/ethics/disclosure/.

17. Todd Wasserman, "Word games," *Brandweek*, April 24, 2006: 24.

18. Tamar Weinbert, *The New Community Rules: Marketing on the Social Web* (Sebastopol, CA: O'Reilly Media, 2009).

19. Andrew McMains, "Consumers party on for major brands," *Adweek*, February 1, 2010. www.adweek.com/news/advertising-branding/consumers-party-major-brands-106989.

20. Aaron Baar, "Ford builds buzz around upcoming Fiesta," *Media Post News*, February 20, 2009. www.mediapost.com/publications/?fa=Articles.showArticle&art_aid=100693.

21. "Demandware survey reveals web-centric consumers have high brand volatility," *Demandware*, May 3, 2011. www.demandware.com/Demandware-Survey-Reveals-Web-Centric-Consumers-Have-Highly-Volatile-Brand-Loyalty/pr_2011_05_03,default,pg.html.

22. Hollie Shaw, "From pink to green." *Financial Post*, May 27, 2011.

23. Myra Frazier, "The networked boomer woman: Hear us roar," *Brandchannel*, December 18, 2009. www.brandchannel.com/features_effect.asp?pf_id=496.

24. "Facebook is college students' goto," *Center for Media Research*, December 18, 2009. www.mediapost.com/publications/?fa=Articles.showArticle&art_aid=119049.

25. "TELUS invites Canadian animal lovers to help select the next TELUS critter," *TELUS*, May 10, 2011. http://about.telus.com/cgi-bin/media_news_viewer.cgi?news_id=1398&mode=2&news_year=2011.

26. *Twitter Comms*, April 6, 2011. https://twitter.com/twitterglobalpr/status/55779434350907392.

27. "Tweeting is more than just self-expression," *Penn State Live*, September 10, 2009. http://live.psu.edu/story/41446.

28. Tamar Weinbert, *The New Community Rules: Marketing on the Social Web* (Sebastopol, CA: O'Reilly Media, 2009).

29. Dag Holmboe, "A simple way to calculate social media return on investment," *Social Media Examiner*, May 20, 2011. www.socialmediaexaminer.com/a-simple-way-to-calculate-social-media-return-on-investment/.

30. Claire Cain Miller, "Twitter unveils plans to draw money from ads," *The New York Times*, April 13, 2010: B1.

31. Sheila Shayon, "Kwedit promise: You can keep that virtual puppy, for a price," *Brandchannel*, February 8, 2010. www.brandchannel.com/home/post/2010/02/08/Kwedit-Promise-You-Can-Keep-That-Virtual-Puppy-For-A-Price.aspx.

32. Elizabeth Olson, "Marketing fanciful items in the lands of make believe," *The New York Times*, September 7, 2010: B3.

33. Natalie Zmuda, "An app for that, too: How mobile is changing shopping," *Advertising Age*, March 1, 2010, http://adage.com/print?article_id=142318; Jenna Wortham, "Telling friends where

you are (or not)," *New York Times*, March 14, 2010, www.nytimes. com/2010/03/15/technology/15locate.html.

34. "Victoria's Secret Bombshell tour", *Facebook*. www.facebook. com/victoriassecret?sk=app_208491619173847

35. "Five ways businesses can leverage foursquare in marketing efforts, from Affect Strategies," *BusinessWire*, April 16, 2010. www.businesswire.com/portal/site/home/permalink/ ?ndmViewId=news_view&newsId=20100416005542&newsLang =en.

36. John Borland, "All eyes on new DVDs' format war," *CNET News*, July 11, 2005. http://news.cnet.com/All-eyes-on-new-DVDs-format-war/2100-1026_3-5783387.html.

37. "Online is #2 media in Canadian ad spend," *Samuel Parent's Blog*, April 18, 2011. http://en.titaninteractif.com/index.php/2011/ 04/online-is-number-2-in-canadia/.

38. Center for Media Research, "Traditional marketing budgets lose to interactive," *Research Brief*, July 14, 2009. www.mediapost. com/publications/?fa=Articles.showArticle&art_aid=109611.

39. Melita Kuburas, "ING Direct pays strangers' bills," *Media in Canada*, March 9, 2011. www.mediaincanada.com/articles/ mic/20110309/ingdirect.html.

40. Sheila Shavon, "Del Taco goes online to bring customers in stores," *Brandchannel*, March 1, 2010. www.brandchannel.com/ home/post/2010/03/01/Del-Taco-Goes-Online-To-Bring-Customers-In-Stores.aspx.

41. Patricia Odell, "Ghirardelli gives out one million chocolates," *Promo Magazine*, March 11, 2010, http://promomagazine.com/ eventmarketing/news/0311-ghirardelli-gives-chocolates-/; Barry Silverstein, "Ghirardelli "Million Moments" combines live streaming with sweepstakes," *Brandchannel*, March 9, 2010, www.brandchannel.com/home/post/2010/03/09/Ghirardelli-Million-Moments-Combines-Live-Streaming-With-Sweepstakes. aspx.

Chapter 11

1. Hollie Shaw, "FP Marketing: Canadian ad spending to grow 5.4% in 2010," *Financial Post*, July 20, 2010. http://business.financial-post.com/2010/07/20/fp-marketing-canadian-ad-spending-to-grow-5-4-in-2010/.

2. Matt Hartley, "Canadian mobile ads to top $51M in 2010," *Financial Post*, April 11, 2011. http://business.financialpost. com/2011/04/11/canadian-mobile-ad-industry-to-top-51-million-for-2010/.

3. "The 2010 Canada digital year in review," *comScore*, March 23, 2011. www.comscore.com/Press_Events/Presentations_Whitepapers/ 2011/2010_Canada_Digital_Year_in_Review.

4. William Wells, John Burnett and Sandra Moriarty, *Advertising: Principles and Practice*, 5th edition. (Englewood Cliffs, NJ: Prentice Hall, 2000).

5. Bradley Johnson, "Top 100 outlays plunge 10% but defying spend trend can pay off" *Advertising Age*, June 21, 2010: 10–11.

6. Rance Crain, "Dow's corporate ads have great chemistry, but will respect follow?" *Advertising Age*, August 6, 2007. http://adage. com/columns/article?article_id=119676.

7. John M. Broder, "Governors join in creating regional pacts on climate change," *New York Times*, November 15, 2007. www.nytimes. com/2007/11/15/washington/15climate.html?scp=1&sq=gover nors+join+in+creating+regional&st=nyt.

8. Bob Garfield, "PSA won't change perennial parental bleacher creatures," *Advertising Age*, April 14, 2008. http://adage.com/ garfield/post?article_id=126354&search_phrase=PSA.

9. "Agency report 2007 index," *Advertising Age*, April 25, 2007. http://adage.com/article/datacenter-agency-2007/agency-report-2007-index/116344/.

10. "Global advertising: Consumers trust real friends and virtual strangers the most," *Neilsonwire*, July 7, 2009. http://blog.nielsen. com/nielsenwire/consumer/global-advertising-consumers-trust-real-friends-and-virtual-strangers-the-most/.

11. Stuart Elliott, "Do it yourself super ads," *The New York Times*, February 9, 2010: B3.

12. Michael R. Solomon, "The truth about what customers want: they think your product sucks—but that's not a bad thing," *Financial Times Press*, November 5, 2008.

13. "Customer-made," *trend-watching.com*, www.trendwatching. com/trends/CUSTOMER-MADE.htm; "Generation C," www. trendwatching.com/trends/GENERATION_C.htm.

14. Karen E. Klein, "Should your customers make your ads?" *BusinessWeek*, January 3, 2008: 9.

15. "Tech smith," *GetSatisfaction*. http://getsatisfaction.com/suc-cess-stories/techsmith.

16. "Competition Bureau, Rogers, go court in November," *The Wire Report*, March 31, 2009. www.thewirereport.ca/reports/ content/12554-competition_bureau_rogers_go_court_in_ november.

17. "Art supplies chain resolves Competition Bureau concerns over sale prices," *Competition Bureau Canada*, www.competitionbureau. gc.ca/eic/site/cb-bc.nsf/eng/03038.html.

18. Martin Lindstrom, "Want to sell product? Sleep with your customers," *Fast Company*, June 8, 2011. www.fastcompany. com/1758288/familiar-microscopic-consumer-insights-yet-to-be-discovered.

19. "Index to the 100 leading national advertisers," *Advertising Age*, June 20, 2007. http://adage.com/datacenter/article?article_ id=118652&search_phrase=top+ad+spenders+2007.

20. Peter Cornish, personal communication, March 2010.

21. Kate Macarthur, "Why big brands are getting into the ring," *Advertising Age*, May 22, 2007. http://adage.com/print?article_ id=116722.

22. Jeremy Lee, "Ofcom bans follow-up Renault Megane spot," *Campaign*, August 6, 2004: 10.

23. Russ Josephs, "I'd like to buy the world a (virtual) Coke, and keep it company," *Brandchannel*, January 28, 2010. www.brand channel.com/home/post/2010/01/29/Ie28099d-Like-To-Buy-The-World-A-%28Virtual%29-Coke-And-Keep-It-Company.aspx.

24. Stephanie Kant, "Magic of Clorox sells for a song," *Wall Street Journal*, March 28, 2008. http://online.wsj.com/article/ SB120666813235770629.html.

25. James Berrinder, "Tech box neuromarketing: Ad agency Bark gets emotional with neuromarketing technology," *Research*, April 28, 2010. www.research-live.com/news/new-business/ad-agency-bark-gets-emotional-with-neuromarketing-technology/4001806. article.

26. Christopher Rocchio, "Report: Writers strike spikes 'American Idol' ad rates to $1 million plus," *Radio-TV World*, January 14, 2008. www.realitytvworld.com/news/report-writers-strike-spikes-american-idol-ad-rates-1-million-plus-6390.php.

27. "TV advertising is less effective: Survey," *PROMO Magazine*, March 24, 2006. www.promomagazine.com/news/tvadvertis-ing_survey_032406/index/html.

28. "Simplified index of multiple ownership charts," *Canadian Radio-television and Telecommunications Commission*, www.crtc.gc.ca/ ownership/eng/title_org.htm.

29. Phil Hall, "Make listeners your customers," *Nation's Business*, June 1994: 53R.

30. Jack Neff, "Viva Viva! K-C boosts brand's marketing," *Advertising Age*, June 11, 2007: 4.

31. Sean Corcoran, "Defining earned, owned and paid media," *Forrester Blogs*, December 16, 2009. http://blogs.forrester.com/ interactive_marketing/2009/12/defining-earned-owned-and-paid-media.html.

32. Louise Story, "Online pitches made just for you," *The New York Times*, March 6, 2008: 7.

33. "Internet advertising revenues again reach new highs, estimated to pass $21 billion in 2007 and hit nearly $6 billion in Q4 2007," *Interactive Advertising Bureau*, February 25, 2008. www.iab.net/about_the_iab/recent_press_releases/press_release_archive/press_release/195115.

34. Michael Oliveira, "Web-savvy Canadians lead the world in time spent online," *TheStar.com*, December 28, 2010. www.thestar.com/news/sciencetech/technology/article/912790--web-savvy-canadians-lead-the-world-in-time-spent-online.

35. Michael McCarthy, "Companies are sold on interactive ad strategy," *USA Today*, March 3, 2000: 1B.

36. Michael Learmonth, "Inside the black box: What big brands are spending on Google," *Advertising Age*, September 6, 2010.

37. Ann M. Mack, "Got e-mail," *Brandweek*, March 20, 2000: 84–88.

38. "Mobile marketing industry glossary," *Mobile Marketing Association*. http://mmaglobal.com/uploads/glossary.pdf.

39. Kunur Patel, "How the iAd gave mobile marketing needed shot in arm," *Advertising Age*, September 13, 2010: M-2–M-3; Rich Karpinski, "Why mobile advertising networks are on the cusp of real change," *Advertising Age*, September 13, 2010: M-2–M-3.

40. Dan Butcher, "Kellogg runs MMS campaign for cereal recipes," *MobileMarketer.com*, April 9, 2009. www.mobilemarketer.com/cms/news/messaging/3002.html.

41. Giselle Tsirulnik, "Oprah grows mobile media empire," *MobileMarketer.com*, April 26, 2010. www.mobilemarketer.com/cms/news/media/6075.html.

42. Claire Cain Miller, "Take a step closer for an invitation to shop," *The New York Times*, February 24, 2010: B4.

43. Lon Safko and David K. Brake, *The Social Media Bible* (Hoboken, NJ: John Wiley & Sons).

44. Sheila Shavon, "Adidas steps into the world of augmented reality," *Brandchannel.com*, January 27, 2010. www.brandchannel.com/home/post/2010/01/27/Adidas-Steps-Into-The-World-Of-Augmented-Reality.aspx.

45. Bruce Schreiner and Emily Fredrix, "KFC pays Indiana cities for 'fiery' ad space," *Indystar.com*, January 6, 2010.

46. Ethan Smith and Sabrina Shankman, "Fellow graduates, before we greet the future, a word from my sponsor," *Wall Street Journal*, July 28, 2009.

47. Irina Slutsky, "Meet YouTube's most in-demand brand stars," *Advertising Age*, September 13, 2010: 8.

48. Karl Greenberg, "Audi ties R8 to promotion of 'Iron Man,' due out May 2," *Marketing Daily*, April 23, 2008.

49. Andrew Hampp, "In this year's upfront, it's all about branded entertainment," *Advertising Age*, May 26, 2008. http://adage.com/print?article_id=127312.

50. "Interactive advertising revenues to reach $147b globally, $62.4B in US," *The Kelsey Group*, February 25, 2008. www.marketingcharts.com/direct/interactive-advertising-revenues-to-reach-147b-globally-624b-in-us-3567.

51. Katy Bachman. "Visa tries 3-D display in Grand Central," *Adweek*, February 2, 2010. www.adweek.com/news/advertising-branding/visa-tries-3-d-display-grand-central-107007.

52. Louise Story, "Away from home, TV ads are inescapable," *The New York Times*, March 2, 2007: 6.

53. Jeremy Wagstaff, "Loose wire—bootleg backlash: Software industry groups are snooping for people using pirated software; But their assumptions about who's a pirate seem awfully mixed up," *Far Eastern Economic Review*, July 31, 2003: 31.

54. Bristol Voss, "Measuring the effectiveness of advertising and PR," *Sales & Marketing Management*, October 1992: 123–24.

55. This remark has also been credited to a British businessman named Lord Leverhulme; see Charles Goodrum and Helen Dalrymple, *Advertising in America: The First 200 Years* (New York: Harry N. Abrams, 1990).

56. Stuart Elliott, "New survey on ad effectiveness," *New York Times*, April 14, 2004. www.nytimes.com/2004/04/14/business/media-business-advertising-survey-consumer-attitudes-reveals-depth-challenge.html.

57. Kate Fitzgerald, "Homemade Bikini Contest Hits Bars, Beach for 10th Year," *Advertising Age*, April 13, 1998: 18.

58. Alan J. Liddle, "Guilty pleas end Wendy's finger-pointing, but will they inspire leniency in sentencing," *Nation's Restaurant News*, September 19, 2005: 202; Jonathan Birchall, "Jail for Wendy's finger claim couple," *Financial Times*, January 19, 2006: 25.

59. "Jail for Wendy's finger scam couple," *CBS News*, February 11, 2009. www.cbsnews.com/stories/2006/01/18/national/main1218315.shtml.

60. "Man who put dead mouse in burrito at Taco Bell given prison time," *FoxNews.com*, June 2, 2006. www.foxnews.com/story/0,2933,197993,00.html.

61. The Star-Ledger Continuos News Desk, "Apple iPad tablet is unveiled at live press conference," *nj.com*, January 27, 2010. www.nj.com/business/index.ssf/2010/01/apple_ipad_tablet_is_unveiled.html.

62. Andy Pasztor, "FAA ruling on long-haul routes would boost Boeing's designs," *Wall Street Journal*, June 5, 2006: A.3.

63. Amy Chozick, "Star power: The LPGA is counting on a new marketing push to take women's golf to the next level," *Wall Street Journal*, June 12, 2006: R.6.

64. Michael R. Solomon, Greg W. Marshall and Elnora W. Stuart, *Marketing: Real People, Real Choices*, 6th edition (Upper Saddle River, NJ: Prentice Hall, 2009).

65. Carol Driver, "Five-minute YouTube apology from Toyota boss as first lawsuit filed over faulty pedal recall," *Mail Online*, February 5, 2010. www.dailymail.co.uk/news/article-1248588/Five-minute-YouTube-apology-Toyota-boss-lawsuit-filed-faulty-pedal-recall.html.

66. Molly McWhinnie, "Determining your share of voice," *Communiqué PR*, June 8, 2011. www.communiquepr.com/blog/?p=2490.

67. "Global outreach, global impact," *McDonald's*. www.aboutmcdonalds.com/mcd/csr/about/community/sponsorships.html.

68. Jaimie Seaton, "Burger King guns for rivals in guerilla push," *Media*, September 9, 2005: 6.

69. Quoted in Michelle Kessler, "IBM graffiti ads gain notoriety," *USA Today*, April 26, 2001: 3B.

70. Howard Stumpf and John M. Kawula, "Point of Purchase Advertising," in *Handbook of Sales Promotion*, ed. S. Ulanoff (New York: McGraw-Hill, 1985); Karen A. Berger, *The Rising Importance of Point-of-Purchase Advertising in the Marketing Mix* (Englewood Cliffs, NJ: Point-of-Purchase Advertising Institute).

71. Gardiner Harris, "Drug makers offer consumers coupons for free prescriptions–but patients still have to get their physician's approval, and most don't pay for pills," *Wall Street Journal*, March 13, 2002: B1.

72. "Virgin Atlantic rolls out space miles," *PROMO Magazine*, January 11, 2006. http://promomagazine.com/incentives/virgin_atlantic_miles_011106/index.html.

73. Michael Fielding, "C'est délicieux," *Marketing News*, September 15, 2010: 10.

74. This section based on material presented in Don E. Schultz, William A. Robinson and Lisa A. Petrison, *Sales Promotion Essentials*, 2nd edition (Lincolnwood, IL: NTC Business Books, 1993).

75. "Ben & Jerry's launches ice cream flavor contest," *PROMO Magazine*, March 16, 2006. http://promomagazine.com/news/benjerry_contest_031606/index.html.

76. "Lengthy research leads Disney to global 'dreams' theme," *PROMO Magazine*, June 12, 2006. http://promomagazine.com/research/disney_research_061206/index.html.

77. "Consumers vote for Oreo idol," *PROMO Magazine*, June 12, 2006. http://promomagazine.com/contests/news/oreo_idol_contest_061206/index.html.

78. Kerry J. Smith, "It's for you," *PROMO Magazine*, 41(4), 1994; Sharon Moshavi, "Please deposit no cents," *Forbes*, August 16, 1993: 102.

79. Amanda Beeler, "Package-goods marketers tune in free-sampling sites," *Advertising Age*, June 12, 2000: 58.

80. "Bausch & Lomb makes eyes with consumers in Spain," *PROMO Magazine*, October 1994: 93.

81. *Direct Marketing Association*: www.the-dma.org/index.php.

82. David Liberman, "Ad spending forecast to shift to more direct marketing," *USA Today*, August 5, 2008. www.usatoday.com/money/media/2008-08-04-media-forecast_N.htm.

83. "Canadian mail order catalogues," *Library and Archives Canada*. www.collectionscanada.gc.ca/mailorder/029006-200-e.html.

84. Paul Hughes, "Profits due," *Entrepreneur*, 74(4), 1994.

85. *DMA Statistical Fact Book*, 31st edition (New York: Direct Marketing Association, 2010).

86. Burt Helm, "Cutting the stack of catalogs," *BusinessWeek*, December 20, 2007. www.businessweek.com/magazine/content/07_53/b4065035213195.htm?chan=search.

87. Robert Longley, "Truth about cell phones and the Do Not Call Registry," *Federal Trade Commission*, April 2005. www.ftc.gov/donotcall.

88. Iain Marlow, "Rogers pays $275,000 after telemarketing probe," *The Globe and Mail*, March 24, 2011. www.theglobeandmail.com/globe-investor/rogers-pays-275000-after-telemarketing-probe/article1955368/.

89. Alison J. Clarke, "'As seen on TV': Socialization of the tele-visual consumer," paper presented at the *Fifth Interdisciplinary Conference on Research in Consumption*, University of Lund, Sweden, August 1995.

90. "Measuring the information society 2010," *International Telecommunications Union*, 2010; "Mobile phone use reaches 50% worldwide," *Romow Shopping Blog*, February 28, 2008.

91. "List of countries by number of mobile phones in use," *Wikipedia*. http://en.wikipedia.org/wiki/List_of_countries_by_number_of_mobile_phones_in_use.

92. Quoted in Jaclyn Fierman, "The death and rebirth of the salesman," *Fortune*, 38(7), 1994: 88.

93. "Super Bowl commercials cost plenty, deliver little," *TransWorldNews*, February 4, 2008. www.transworldnews.com/NewsStory.aspx?id=35308&cat=2.

94. *Salesforce*: www.salesforce.com.

95. *Skype*: www.skype.com.

96. Adapted from Mitchell Schnurman, "The game-changing reality of virtual sales pitches," *Star-Telegram*, April 9, 2010.

Chapter 12

1. Jonathan Birchall, "Walmart aims to cut supply chain cost," *Financial Times*, January 3, 2010. www.ft.com/cms/s/0/891c7878-f895-11de-beb8-00144feab49a.html.

2. Thomas L. Friedman, *The World Is Flat 3.0: A Brief History of the Twenty-First Century* (New York: Picador, 2007).

3. "How it works," *Netflix*. http://ca.netflix.com/HowNetflixWorks.

4. David Byrne, "David Byrne's survival strategies for emerging artists—and megastars," *Wired*, 16(1), December 2007.

5. Jefferson Graham, "Google may be missing the middleman after all," *USA Today*, January 13, 2010: B3.

6. Rowland T. Moriarty and Ursula Moran, "Managing hybrid marketing systems," *Harvard Business Review*, November–December 1990: 2–11.

7. Michael Barbaro, "Walmart offers aid to rivals," *The New York Times*, April 5, 2006: C1.

8. *Oneworld*: www.oneworld.com/home.cfm.

9. John Neff, "Scion may break promise to itself, add fourth model," *AutoBlog*, May 25, 2007. www.autoblog.com/2007/05/25/scion-may-break-promise-to-itself-add-fourth-model/.

10. "About us," *Starbucks*. www.starbucks.com/about-us.

11. Toby B. Gooley, "The who, what, and where of reverse logistics," *Logistics Management* 42(February 2003): 38–44; James R. Stock, *Development and Implementation of Reverse Logistics Programs* (Oak Brook, IL: Council of Logistics Management, 1998: 20).

12. "Spychipped Levi's brand jeans hit the U.S.," *RFID Nineteen Eighty-Four*, April 27, 2006. www.spychips.com/press-releases/levis-secret-testing.html; Katherine Albrecht and Liz McIntyre, *Spychips: How Major Corporations and Government Plan to Track Your Every Purchase and Watch Your Every Move* (New York: Plume, 2006).

13. Faye W. Gilbert, Joyce A. Young and Charles R. O'Neal, "Buyer-seller relationships in just-in-time purchasing environments," *Journal of Organizational Research*, 29(February 1994): 111–120.

14. "Perfect order measure," *Supply Chain Metric.com*. www.supplychainmetric.com/perfect.htm.

15. Stanley C. Hollander, "The wheel of retailing," *Journal of Retailing*, July 1960: 41.

16. "About us," *Pier 1 Imports*. www.pier1.com/SideMenu/AboutUs/tabid/65/Default.aspx.

17. "Wal-Mart fishes upstream," *Businessweek*, March 24, 2006. www.businessweek.com/investor/content/mar2006/pi20060324_117687.htm; Stuart Elliott and Michael Barbaro, "Walmart on the hunt for an extreme makeover," *The New York Times*, May 4, 2006: C1.

18. Ann Zimmerman and Cheryl Lu-Lien Tan, "After misstep, Walmart revisits fashion," *Wall Street Journal*, April 24, 2008. http://online.wsj.com/article/SB120899828876040063.html.

19. William R. Davidson, Albert D. Bates and Stephen J. Bass, "The retail life cycle," *Harvard Business Review*, November–December 1976: 89.

20. "Financial release," *Starbucks*. http://investor.starbucks.com/phoenix.zhtml?c=99518&p=irol-newsArticle&ID=1515804&highlight=.

21. Stephanie Rosenbloom and Jack Healy, "Retailers post weak earnings and July sales," *The New York Times*, August 13, 2009. www.nytimes.com/2009/08/14/business/14shop.html?scp_2&sq_christmas%20sales%20percentage%20of%20annual&st_cse.

22. Thomas M. Anderson, "Checkups on the run," *Kiplinger Personal Finance*, May 2006: 96.

23. Barry Berman and Joel R. Evans, *Retail Management: A Strategic Approach*, 11th edition (Upper Saddle River, NJ: Pearson Education, 2010).

24. Mya Frazier, "The store of the future," *Advertising Age*, January 16, 2006: 23.

25. Rebecca Harrison, "Restaurants try e-menus," *Reuters*, February 25, 2008. http://uk.reuters.com/article/internetNews/idUKL204599320080226.

26. "Key findings from the Global Retail Theft Barometer 2009," *Center for Retail Research*.

27. Kathy Grannis, "Troubled economy increases shoplifting rates, according to National Retail security survey," *National Retail Federation*, June 16, 2009.

28. Jessica Silver-Greenberg, "Shoplifters get smarter," *BusinessWeek*, November 19, 2007. www.businessweek.com/magazine/content/07_47/b4059051.htm?chan_search.

29. "Weird but true, the naked truth," *Convenience Store News*, October 22, 2007: 13.

30. "Shoplifter and Dishonest Employee Theft on Rise," *Jack L. Hayes International, Inc.*, http://www.hayesinternational.com/thft_srvys.html

31. Kelly Gates and Dan Alaimo, "Solving Shrink," *Supermarket News*, October 22, 2007, 43.

32. Francis Piron and Murray Young, "Retail Borrowing: Insights and Implications on Returning Used Merchandise," *International Journal of Retail & Distribution Management*, 28(1), 2000: 27–36.

33. Stephanie Rosenbloom, "In bid to sway sales, cameras track shoppers," *The New York Times*, March 19, 2010. www.nytimes.com/2010/03/20/business/20surveillance.html?th&emc_th.

34. "About ALDI," *Aldi.* http://aldi.us/us/html/company/about_aldi_ENU_HTML.htm?WT.z_src=main.

35. Mark Albright, "Kohl's Debut with Fresh New Look," *The St. Petersburg Times*, September 28, 2006: 1D.

36. "Proof of club popularity in the 64-ounce pudding," *DSN Retailing Today*, December 19, 2005: 64.

37. Quoted in Stratford Sherman, "Will the information superhighway be the death of retailing?" *Fortune*, 99(5), 1994: 110.

38. "Direct selling by the numbers—calendar year 2008," *Direct Selling Association.* www.dsa.org/research/industry-statistics/#SALES.

39. "Direct selling by the numbers—calendar year 2006," *Direct Selling Association.* www.dsa.org/research/industry-statistics/#SALES.

40. "About Amway," *Amway.* www.amway.com/about-amway/our-company.

41. "Amway Corporation Company Profile," *Yahoo Finance.* http://biz.yahoo.com/ic/103/103441.html.

42. H. J. Shrager, "Close social networks of Hasidic women, other tight groups, boost Shaklee sales," *Wall Street Journal*, November 19, 2001.

43. "Pyramid schemes," *Direct Selling Association.*

44. Aili McConnon, "Vending machines go luxe," *BusinessWeek*, January 29, 2008: 17.

45. Erick Schonfeld, "Forrester Forecast: Online Retail Sales Will Grow to $250 Billion by 2014," *TechCrunch*, March 8, 2010.

46. Helen Leggatt, "Double-Digit Growth Ahead for U.S. and European Online Retail," *BizReport*, March 9, 2010, www.bizreport.com/2010/03/double-digit_growth_ahead_for_us_and_european_online_retail.html.

47. Bob Tedeschi, "A quicker resort this year to deep discounting," *New York Times*, December 17, 2007. www.nytimes.com/2007/12/17/technology/17ecom.html?scp_41&sq_forrester_research&st_nyt.

48. Leena Rao, "Like.com expands digital fashion empire with virtual styling tool Couturious," *TechCrunch*, February 23, 2010.

49. Bob Tedeschi, "$7,900 Valentino Gowns, a Click Away," *The New York Times*, November 5, 2007.

50. "Fact sheet," *PayPal.* www.paypal-media.com.

51. "Amazon.com announces fourth quarter sales up 42% to $5.7 billion; 2007 free cash flow more than doubles, surpassing $1 billion for the first time," *Amazon.com.* http://phx.corporate-ir.net/phoenix.zhtml?c=176060&p=irol-corporateTimeline_pf.

52. Westfield Metreon: http://www.westfield.com/metreon.

53. Atmosphere: http://en.atmosphere.ca/.

54. "A wide world of sports shoes: Fixtures enhance appeal of World Foot Locker," *Chain Store Age Executive*, January 1993: 176–81.

55. Tracie Rozhon, "High fashion, from front door to the top floor," *New York Times*, July 31, 2003. www.nytimes.com/2003/07/31/business/high-fashion-from-front-door-to-the-top-floor.html?scp_1&sq_High_Fashion%2C_from_Front_Door_to_the_Top_Floor&st_nyt.

56. L. W. Turley and Ronald E. Milliman, "Atmospheric effects on shopping behavior: A review of the experimental evidence," *Journal of Business Research*, 49(2000): 193–211.

57. Eric Newman, "Retail design for 2008: Thinking outside the big box," *Brandweek*, December 17, 2007: 26.

58. Samantha Murphy, "A contemporary future," *Chain Store Age*, April 2007: 62.

59. Julie Flaherty, "Music to a retailer's ears; Sorry, Springsteen won't be playing at Pottery Barn today," *The New York Times*, July 4, 2001.

60. *Muzak*: www.muzak.com; "Sound of Muzak," *CBS TV Sunday Morning*, March 21, 2010.

61. Michael Levy and Barton A. Weitz, *Retailing Management*, 3rd edition (Boston: Irwin/McGraw-Hill, 1998).

62. Quoted in Shirley Leung, "A glutted market is leaving food chains hungry for sites," *Wall Street Journal*, September 1, 2003.

Glossary

A

account executive (account manager) A member of the account management department who supervises the day-to-day activities of the account and is the primary liaison between the agency and the client.

account planner A member of the account management department who combines research and account strategy to act as the voice of the consumer in creating effective advertising.

actual product The physical good or the delivered service that supplies the desired benefit.

advergaming Brand placements in video games.

advertising Nonpersonal communication from an identified sponsor using the mass media.

advertising appeal The central idea or theme of an advertising message.

advertising campaign A coordinated, comprehensive plan that carries out promotion objectives and results in a series of advertisements placed in media over a period of time.

advocacy advertising A type of public service advertising where an organization seeks to influence public opinion on an issue because it has some stake in the outcome.

affect The feeling component of attitudes; refers to the overall emotional response a person has to a product.

AIDA model The communication goals of attention, interest, desire, and action.

aided recall A research technique that uses clues to prompt answers from people about advertisements they might have seen.

AIOs Measures of consumer activities, interests, and opinions used to place consumers into dimensions.

atmospherics The use of colour, lighting, scents, furnishings, and other design elements to create a desired store image.

attention The extent to which a person devotes mental processing to a particular stimulus.

attention economy A perspective that consumer spending, and hence the economy, is driven by psychological attachment to brands, the relevancy of information and solutions. Consumers choose where to spend their attention and their money.

attitude A learned predisposition to respond favourably or unfavourably to stimuli on the basis of relatively enduring evaluations of people, objects, and issues.

attitudinal measures A research technique that probes a consumer's beliefs or feelings about a product before and after being exposed to messages about it.

attributes Include features, functions, benefits, and uses of a product. Marketers view products as a bundle of attributes that includes the packaging, brand name, benefits, and supporting features in addition to a physical good.

augmented product The actual product plus other supporting features such as a warranty, credit, delivery, installation, and repair service after the sale.

augmented reality (AR) A form of technology where a view of a real-world environment joins a layer of virtual computer-generated imagery to create a mixed reality.

augmented services The core service plus additional services provided to enhance value.

automatic reordering system Retail reordering system that is automatically activated when inventories reach a certain level.

avatars Graphic representations of users of virtual worlds.

average fixed cost The fixed cost per unit produced.

B

baby boomers The segment of people born between 1946 and 1964.

back-translation The process of translating material to a foreign language and then back to the original language.

backward invention Product strategy in which a firm develops a less advanced product to serve the needs of people living in countries without electricity or other elements of a developed infrastructure.

bait and switch An illegal marketing practice in which an advertised price special is used as bait to get customers into the store with the intention of switching them to a higher-priced item.

banners Internet advertising in the form of rectangular graphics at the top or bottom of Web pages.

BCG growth–market share matrix A portfolio analysis model developed by the Boston Consulting Group that assesses the potential of successful products to generate cash that a firm can then use to invest in new products.

behaviour The doing component of attitudes; involves a consumer's intention to do something, such as the intention to purchase or use a certain product.

behavioural learning theories Theories of learning that focus on how consumer behaviour is changed by external events or stimuli.

behavioural segmentation A technique that divides consumers into segments on the basis of how they act toward, feel about, or use a good or service.

behavioural targeting The marketing practice by which marketers deliver advertisements for products a consumer is looking for by watching what the consumer does online.

benefit The outcome sought by a customer that motivates buying behaviour that satisfies a need or want.

benefit segmentation A segmentation approach that groups consumers or customers based on the benefits or value they seek in buying and using products.

bid rigging Collusion between suppliers responding to bid requests to lessen competition and secure higher margins.

blue ocean strategy A positioning strategy where you create a new market and get to define the playing field before competitors enter.

bottom-up budgeting Allocation of the promotion budget based on identifying promotion goals and allocating enough money to accomplish them.

box stores Food stores that have a limited selection of items, few brands per item, and few refrigerated items.

brand One particular company's version of a product (good or service). A name, a term, a symbol, or any other unique element of a product that identifies one firm's product(s) and sets it apart from the competition.

brand ambassadors or brand evangelists Loyal customers of a brand recruited to communicate and be salespeople with other consumers for a brand they care a great deal about.

brand concept How the marketer wants the brand to be positioned.

brand equity The value of a brand to an organization.

brand extensions A new product sold with the same brand name as a strong existing brand.

brand image How consumers perceive the positioning of the brand.

brand loyalty A pattern of repeat product purchases, accompanied by an underlying positive attitude toward the brand, based on the belief that the brand makes products superior to those of its competition.

brand manager An individual who is responsible for developing and implementing the marketing plan for a single brand.

brand meaning The beliefs and associations that a consumer has about the brand.

brand personality A distinctive image that captures a good's or service's character and benefits.

brand storytelling Marketers seek to engage consumers with compelling stories about brands.

branded entertainment A form of advertising in which marketers integrate products into entertainment venues.

break-even analysis A method for determining the number of units that a firm must produce and sell at a given price to cover all its costs.

break-even point The point at which the total revenue and total costs are equal and beyond which the company makes a profit; below that point, the firm will suffer a loss.

breaking bulk Dividing larger quantities of goods into smaller lots in order to meet the needs of buyers.

B2B marketers Marketers who work in business-to-business markets.

business analysis The step in the product development process in which marketers assess a product's commercial viability.

business cycle The overall patterns of change in the economy—including periods of prosperity, recession, depression, and recovery—that affect consumer and business purchasing power.

business ethics Rules of conduct for an organization.

business plan A plan that includes the decisions that guide the entire organization.

business planning An ongoing process of making decisions that guide the firm both in the short term and for the long term.

business portfolio The group of different products or brands owned by an organization and characterized by different income-generating and growth capabilities.

business-to-business (B2B) e-commerce Internet exchanges between two or more businesses or organizations.

business-to-business (B2B) marketing The marketing of those goods and services that business and organization customers need to produce other goods and services for resale or to support their operation.

business-to-business (B2B) markets The group of customers that includes manufacturers, wholesalers, retailers, and other organizations.

business-to-consumer (B2C) e-commerce Online exchanges between companies and individual consumers.

buttons Small banner-type advertisements that can be placed anywhere on a Web page.

buyclass One of three classifications of business buying situations that characterizes the degree of time and effort required to make a decision.

buying centre The group of people in an organization who participate in a purchasing decision.

buzz Word-of-mouth communication that customers view as authentic.

C

cannibalization The loss of sales of an existing brand when a new item in a product line or product family is introduced.

capacity management The process by which organizations adjust their offerings in an attempt to match demand.

captive pricing A pricing tactic for two items that must be used together; one item is priced very low, and the firm makes its profit on another, high-margin item essential to the operation of the first item.

case allowance A discount to the retailer or wholesaler based on the volume of product ordered.

case study A comprehensive examination of a particular firm or organization.

catalogue A collection of products offered for sale in book form, usually consisting of product descriptions accompanied by photos of the items.

causal research A technique that attempts to understand cause-and-effect relationships.

central business district (CBD) The traditional downtown business area found in a town or city.

channel intermediaries Firms or individuals such as wholesalers, agents, brokers, or retailers who help move a product from the producer to the consumer or business user; an older term for intermediaries is middlemen.

channel leader A firm at one level of distribution that takes a leadership role, establishing operating norms and processes based on its power relative to other channel members.

channel levels The number of distinct categories of intermediaries that populate a channel of distribution.

channel of distribution The series of firms or individuals that facilitates the movement of a product from the producer to the final customer.

classical conditioning The learning that occurs when a stimulus eliciting a response is paired with another stimulus that initially does not elicit a response on its own but will cause a similar response over time because of its association with the first stimulus.

clickstream analysis A means of measuring a Web site's success by tracking customers' movement around the company Web site.

cluster analysis Computer software that groups survey respondents based on the commonality of their answers to questions, putting respondents with similar answers in the same group, while maximizing the differences between the groups or segments.

co-op advertising A sales promotion where the manufacturer and the retailer share the cost.

cobranding An agreement between two brands to work together to market a new product.

code of ethics Written standards of behaviour to which everyone in the organization must subscribe.

cognition The knowing component of attitudes; refers to the beliefs or knowledge a person has about a product and its important characteristics.

cognitive dissonance The anxiety or regret a consumer may feel after choosing from among several similar attractive choices.

cognitive learning theory Theory of learning that stresses the importance of internal mental processes and that views people as problem solvers who actively use information from the world around them to master their environment.

combination stores Retailers that offer consumers food and general merchandise in the same store.

commercialization The final step in the product development process in which a new product is launched into the market.

communication The coordination of communication efforts by a marketer to influence consumers or organizations about goods, services, or ideas.

communications model The process whereby meaning is transferred from a source to a receiver.

comparison shopping agents or shopbots Web applications that help online shoppers find what they are looking for at the lowest price and provide customer reviews and ratings of products and sellers.

compatibility The extent to which a new product is consistent with existing cultural values, customs, and practices.

competitive advantage The ability of a firm to outperform the competition, providing customers with a benefit the competition cannot.

competitive-parity budgeting A promotion budgeting method in which an organization matches whatever competitors are spending.

complexity The degree to which consumers find a new product or its use difficult to understand.

component parts Manufactured goods or subassemblies of finished items that organizations need to complete their own products.

concentrated targeting strategy Focusing a firm's efforts on offering one or more products to a single segment.

consideration set The set of alternative brands the consumer is considering for the decision process.

consumer The ultimate user of a good or service.

consumer addiction A physiological or psychological dependency on goods or services.

consumer behaviour The process involved when individuals or groups select, purchase, use, and dispose of goods, services, ideas, or experiences to satisfy their needs and desires.

consumer goods The tangible products that individual consumers purchase for personal or family use.

consumer orientation A business approach that prioritizes the satisfaction of customers' needs and wants.

consumer satisfaction/dissatisfaction The overall feelings, or attitude, a person has about a product after she purchases it.

consumer-generated content Everyday people functioning in marketing roles, such as participating in creating advertisements, providing input to new product development, or serving as wholesalers or retailers.

consumerism A social movement that attempts to protect consumers from harmful business practices.

continuous innovation A modification of an existing product that sets one brand apart from its competitors.

contribution per unit The difference between the price the firm charges for a product and the variable costs.

convenience product A consumer good or service that is usually low priced, widely available, and purchased frequently with a minimum of comparison and effort.

convenience sample A nonprobability sample composed of individuals who just happen to be available when and where the data are being collected.

convenience stores Neighbourhood retailers that carry a limited number of frequently purchased items and cater to consumers willing to pay a premium for the ease of buying close to home.

conventional marketing system A multiple-level distribution channel in which channel members work independently of one another.

convergence The coming together of two or more technologies to create a new system with greater benefits than its separate parts.

cookies Text files inserted by a Web site sponsor into a Web surfer's hard drive that allows the site to track the surfer's moves.

core product All the benefits the product will provide for consumers or business customers.

core service The basic benefit of having a service performed.

corporate advertising Advertising that promotes the company as a whole instead of a firm's individual products.

corporate identity Materials such as logos, brochures, building design, and stationery that communicate an image of the organization.

corrective advertising Advertising that clarifies or qualifies previous deceptive advertising claims.

cost of ownership A pricing strategy that considers the lifetime cost of using the product.

cost per thousand (CPM) A measure used to compare the relative cost effectiveness of different media vehicles that have different exposure rates; the cost to deliver a message to 1000 people or homes.

cost-plus pricing A method of setting prices in which the seller totals all the costs for the product and then adds an amount to arrive at the selling price.

creating assortments Provide a variety of products in one location to meet the needs of buyers.

creative brief A guideline or blueprint for the marketing communication program that guides the creative process.

creative services The agency people (creative director, copywriters, and art director) who dream up and produce the ads.

creative strategy The process that turns a concept into an advertisement.

credence qualities Product characteristics that are difficult to evaluate even after they have been experienced.

crisis management The process of managing a company's reputation when some negative event threatens the organization's image.

critical incident technique A method for measuring service quality in which marketers use customer complaints to identify critical incidents—specific face-to-face contacts between consumer and service providers that cause problems and lead to dissatisfaction.

cross-elasticity of demand When changes in the price of one product affect the demand for another item.

cross-sectional design A type of descriptive technique that involves the systematic collection of quantitative information.

crowdsourcing A practice in which firms outsource marketing activities (such as selecting an ad) to a community of users.

culture The values, beliefs, customs, and tastes a group of people values.

cumulative quantity discounts Discounts based on the total quantity bought within a specified time period.

custom marketing strategy An approach that tailors specific products and the messages about them to individual customers.

custom research Research conducted for a single firm to provide specific information its managers need.

customer equity The financial value of a customer relationship throughout the lifetime of the relationship.

customer intimacy A strategy concerned with creating tailored solutions for narrowly defined market segments.

customer reference program A formalized process by which customers formally share success stories and actively recommend products to other potential clients, usually facilitated through an on-line community.

customer relationship management (CRM) A systematic tracking of consumers' preferences and behaviours over time in order to tailor the value proposition as closely as possible to each individual's unique wants and needs. CRM allows firms to talk to individual customers and to adjust elements of their marketing programs in light of how each customer reacts.

customer value The benefits a customer receives from buying and using a good or service in relation to the costs and sacrifices of buying and using it.

D

data mining Sophisticated analysis techniques to take advantage of the massive amount of transaction information now available.

decline stage The final stage in the product life cycle during which sales decrease as customer needs change.

decoding The process by which a receiver assigns meaning to the message.

demand Customers' desires for products coupled with the resources to obtain them.

demand-based pricing A price-setting method based on estimates of demand at different prices.

demand curve A plot of the quantity of a product that customers will buy in a market during a period of time at various prices if all other factors remain the same.

demographics Variables that describe objective characteristics of a population or group.

department stores Retailers that sell a broad range of items and offer a good selection within each product line.

derived demand Demand for business or organizational products caused by demand for consumer goods or services.

descriptive (quantitative) research A tool that probes more systematically into the problem and bases its conclusions on large numbers of observations.

differential benefit Providing an outcome or result valued by customers that competitors are not able to offer as well.

differentiated targeting strategy Developing one or more products for each of several distinct customer groups and making sure these offerings are kept separate in the marketplace.

diffusion The process by which the use of a product spreads throughout a population.

digital media Media that are digital rather than analogue, including Web sites, mobile or cellular phones, and digital video such as YouTube.

digital signage Out-of-home media that use digital technology to change the message at will.

direct mail A brochure or pamphlet that offers a specific good or service at one point in time.

direct marketing Any direct communication to a consumer or business recipient designed to generate a response in the form of an order, a request for further information, and/or a visit to a store or other place of business for purchase of a product.

direct selling An interactive sales process in which a salesperson presents a product to one individual or a small group, takes orders, and delivers the merchandise.

directories Books that list organizations alphabetically or thematically with contact information.

direct-response advertising A direct marketing approach that allows the consumer to respond to a message by immediately contacting the provider to ask questions or order the product.

direct-response TV (DRTV) Advertising on TV that seeks a direct response, including short commercials of less than two minutes, 30-minute or longer infomercials, and home shopping networks.

discontinuous innovation A totally new product that creates major changes in the way we live.

disintermediation A service that requires the customer to obtain an outcome without the intervention of a human provider.

disintermediation (of the channel of distribution) The elimination of some layers of the channel of distribution in order to cut costs and improve the efficiency of the channel.

distribution The availability of the product to the customer at the desired time and location. Also known as channels of distribution.

distinctive competency A capability of a firm that is superior to that of its competition.

diversification strategies Growth strategies that emphasize both new products and new markets.

do-it-yourself (DIY) ads Product ads that are created by consumers.

downsizing When a firm in a mature industry closes or sells off unprofitable stores or entire divisions.

dumping Pricing products lower in a foreign market than they are offered at home.

durable goods Consumer products that provide benefits over a long period of time, such as cars, furniture, and appliances.

dynamic pricing A pricing strategy in which the price can easily be adjusted to meet changes in the marketplace.

dynamically continuous innovation A change in an existing product that requires a moderate amount of learning or behaviour change.

E

e-commerce The buying or selling of goods and services electronically, usually over the Internet.

e-mail advertising Advertising messages sent via e-mail to large numbers of people simultaneously.

early adopters Those who adopt an innovation early in the diffusion process, but after the innovators.

early majority Those whose adoption of a new product signals a general acceptance of the innovation.

earned media Word-of-mouth or buzz using social media where the advertiser has no control.

80/20 rule A marketing rule of thumb that 20 percent of purchasers typically account for 80 percent of a product's sales.

elastic demand Demand in which changes in price have large effects on the amount demanded.

emergency products Products we purchase when we are in dire need.

encoding The process of translating an idea into a form of communication that will convey meaning.

enterprise resource planning (ERP) system A software system that integrates information from across the entire company, including finance, order fulfillment, manufacturing, and transportation and then facilitates sharing of the data throughout the firm.

environmental stewardship A position taken by an organization to protect or enhance the natural environment as it conducts its business activities.

environmentalism A broad philosophy and social movement that seeks conservation and improvement of the natural environment.

equipment Expensive goods, which last for a long time, that an organization uses in its daily operations.

ethnography An approach to research based on observations of people in their own homes or communities.

evaluative criteria The dimensions consumers use to compare competing product alternatives.

exchange The process by which some transfer of value occurs between a buyer and a seller.

exclusive distribution Selling a product only through a single outlet in a particular region.

execution format The basic structure of the message such as comparison, demonstration, testimonial, slice of life, and lifestyle.

experience qualities Product characteristics that customers can determine during or after consumption.

experimental pricing A strategy of experimenting with prices until the price that generates the highest profitability is found.

experiential shoppers Consumers who engage in online shopping because of the experiential benefits they receive.

experiments A technique that tests predicted relationships among variables in a controlled environment.

exploratory research A technique that marketers use to generate insights for future, more rigorous studies.

export merchants Intermediaries a firm uses to represent it in other countries.

exposure The extent to which a stimulus is capable of being registered by a person's sensory receptors.

external environment The uncontrollable elements outside an organization that may affect its performance either positively or negatively. These include macro environment factors like regulatory or technology factors, consumer behaviour trends, industry factors such as industry concentration, and competitive factors such as the number and sophistication of competitors.

extranet A private, corporate computer network that links company departments, employees, and databases to suppliers, customers, and others outside the organization.

F

F.O.B. delivered pricing A pricing tactic in which the cost of loading and transporting the product to the customer is included in the selling price and is paid by the manufacturer.

F.O.B. origin pricing A pricing tactic in which the cost of transporting the product from the factory to the customer's location is the responsibility of the customer.

facilitating functions Functions of channel intermediaries that make the purchase process easier for customers and manufacturers.

factory outlet store A discount retailer, owned by a manufacturer, that sells off defective merchandise and excess inventory.

family brand A brand that a group of individual products or individual brands share.

family life cycle A means of characterizing consumers within a family structure on the basis of different stages through which people pass as they grow older.

feedback Receivers' reactions to the message.

fixed costs Costs of production that do not change with the number of units produced.

focus group A product-oriented discussion among a small group of consumers led by a trained moderator.

four Ps Product, price, promotion, and place.

franchising A form of licensing involving the right to adapt an entire system of doing business.

freenomics The business model of offering a basic good or service for free in order to build a customer base to which added value offerings can be sold.

freight absorption pricing A pricing tactic in which the seller absorbs the total cost of transportation.

frequency programs Consumer sales promotion programs that offer a discount or free product for multiple purchases over time; also referred to as loyalty or continuity programs.

frequent discounting A strategy of frequently using sale prices to increase sales volume.

frequency The average number of times a person in the target group will be exposed to the message.

full-service agency An agency that provides most or all of the services needed to mount a campaign, including research, creation of ad copy and art, media selection, and production of the final messages.

functional planning A decision process that concentrates on developing detailed plans for strategies and tactics for the short term, supporting an organization's long-term strategic plan.

G

gap analysis A marketing research method that measures the difference between a customer's expectation of a service quality and what actually occurred.

gender roles Society's expectations regarding the appropriate attitudes, behaviours, and appearance for men and women.

general merchandise discount stores Retailers that offer a broad assortment of items at low prices with minimal service.

Generation X The group of consumers born between 1965 and 1978.

Gen Y The children of baby boomer parents is the second largest demographic segment in Canada.

generic branding A strategy in which products are not branded and are sold at the lowest price possible.

geodemography A segmentation technique that combines geography with demographics.

geospatial platforms Digital applications that integrate sophisticated GPS technology to enable users to alert friends of their exact whereabouts via their mobile phones.

good A tangible product that we can see, touch, smell, hear, or taste.

government markets The federal, provincial, regional, and municipal governments that buy goods and services to carry out public objectives and to support their operations.

grey market goods Items manufactured outside a country and then imported without the consent of the trademark holder.

green marketing The development of marketing strategies that support environmental stewardship by creating an environmentally grounded differential benefit in the minds of consumers.

Green River Ordinances Community regulations that prohibit door-to-door selling unless prior permission is given by the household.

greenwashing A practice in which companies promote their products as environmentally friendly when in truth the brand provides little ecological benefit.

gross margin The markup amount added to the cost of a product to cover the fixed costs of the retailer or wholesaler and leave an amount for a profit.

gross rating points (GRPs) A measure used for comparing the effectiveness of different media vehicles: average reach × frequency.

groundswell A social trend in which people use technology to get the things they need from each other, rather than from traditional institutions like corporations.

growth stage The second stage in the product life cycle, during which consumers accept the product and sales rapidly increase.

guerrilla marketing Marketing activity in which a firm "ambushes" consumers with promotional content in places they are not expecting to encounter this kind of activity.

H

heuristics A mental rule of thumb that leads to a speedy decision by simplifying the process.

hierarchy of effects A series of steps prospective customers move through, from initial awareness of a product to brand loyalty.

hierarchy of needs An approach that categorizes motives according to five levels of importance, the more basic needs being on the bottom of the hierarchy and the higher needs at the top.

horizontal marketing system An arrangement within a channel of distribution in which two or more firms at the same channel level work together for a common purpose.

hybrid marketing system A marketing system that uses a number of different channels and communication methods to serve a target market.

hypermarkets Retailers with the characteristics of both warehouse stores and supermarkets; several times larger than other stores and offer virtually everything from grocery items to electronics.

I

idea generation The first step of product development in which marketers brainstorm for products that provide customer benefits and are compatible with the company mission.

impulse products A product people often buy on the spur of the moment.

impulse purchase A purchase made without any planning or search effort.

inbound calling A customer-initiated call to place an order or get some information about a product or a service.

independent intermediaries Channel intermediaries that are not controlled by any manufacturer but instead do business with many different manufacturers and many different customers.

industrial goods Goods that individuals or organizations buy for further processing or for their own use when they do business.

industrial psychographics The application of psychographics to the business-to-business context.

inelastic demand Demand in which changes in price have little or no effect on the amount demanded.

infomercials Half-hour or hour-long commercials that resemble a talk show but actually are sales pitches.

information search The process whereby a consumer searches for appropriate information to make a reasonable decision.

ingredient branding A form of cobranding that uses branded materials as ingredients or component parts in other branded products.

innovation A product that consumers perceive to be new and different from existing products.

innovators The first segment (roughly 2.5 percent) of a population to adopt a new product.

inseparability The characteristic of a service that means that it is impossible to separate the production of a service from the consumption of that service.

insourcing A practice in which a company contracts with a specialist firm to handle all or part of its supply chain operations.

institutional advertising Advertising messages that promote the activities, personality, or point of view of an organization or company.

intangibility The characteristic of a service that means customers can't see, touch, or smell good service.

intangibles Experience-based products.

integrated marketing communication (IMC) A strategic business process that marketers use to plan, develop, execute, and evaluate coordinated, measurable, persuasive brand communication programs over time to targeted audiences.

intelligent agents Computer programs that find sites selling a particular product.

intensive distribution Selling a product through all suitable wholesalers or retailers that are willing to stock and sell the product.

internal environment The controllable elements inside an organization—including its people, its facilities, and how it does things—that influence the operations of the organization.

internal reference price A set price or a price range in consumers' minds that they refer to in evaluating a product's price.

interpretation The process of assigning meaning to a stimulus based on prior associations a person has with it and assumptions he or she makes about it.

intranet An internal corporate communication network that uses Internet technology to link company departments, employees, and databases.

introduction stage The first stage of the product life cycle in which slow growth follows the introduction of a new product in the marketplace.

inventory control Activities to ensure that goods are always available to meet customers' demands.

involvement The relative importance of perceived consequences of the purchase to a consumer.

ISO 14000 Standards of the International Organization for Standardization concerned with "environmental management" aimed at minimizing harmful effects on the environment.

ISO 9000 Criteria developed by the International Organization for Standardization to regulate product quality in Europe.

J

jingles Original words and music written specifically for advertising executions.

joint demand Demand for two or more goods that are used together to create a product.

joint venture A strategic alliance in which a new entity owned by two or more firms allows the partners to pool their resources for common good.

judgment A pricing strategy that draws on past experience of the marketer in setting appropriate prices.

just in time (JIT) Inventory management and purchasing processes that manufacturers and resellers use to reduce inventory to very low levels and ensure that deliveries from suppliers arrive only when needed.

K

knockoff A new product that copies, with slight modification, the design of an original product.

knowledge management A comprehensive approach to collecting, organizing, storing, and retrieving a firm's information assets.

L

laggards The last consumers to adopt an innovation.

late majority The adopters who are willing to try new products when there is little or no risk associated with the purchase, when the purchase becomes an economic necessity, or when there is social pressure to purchase.

learning A relatively permanent change in behaviour caused by acquired information or experience.

leased departments Departments within a larger retail store that an outside firm rents.

licensing An agreement in which one firm sells another firm the right to use a brand name for a specific purpose and for a specific period of time.

licensing agreement An agreement in which one firm gives another firm the right to produce and market its product in a specific country or region in return for royalties.

lifestyle The pattern of living that determines how people choose to spend their time, money, and energy and that reflects their values, tastes, and preferences.

lifetime value of a customer The potential profit a single customer's purchase of a firm's products generates over the customer's lifetime.

limited-service agency An agency that provides one or more specialized services, such as media buying or creative development.

list price or manufacturer's suggested retail price (MSRP) The price the end customer is expected to pay as determined by the manufacturer; also referred to as the suggested retail price.

logistics The process of designing, managing, and improving the movement of products through the supply chain; it includes purchasing, manufacturing, storage, and transport.

long tail A new approach to segmentation based on the idea that companies can make money by selling small amounts of items that only a few people want, provided they sell enough different items.

longitudinal design A technique that tracks the responses of the same sample of respondents over time.

loss-leader pricing The pricing policy of setting prices below cost to attract customers into a store.

M

m-commerce Promotional and other e-commerce activities transmitted over mobile phones and other mobile devices, such as smartphones and personal digital assistants (PDAs).

maintenance, repair, and operating (MRO) products Goods that a business customer consumes in a relatively short time.

mall intercept A study in which researchers recruit shoppers in malls or other public areas.

marginal analysis A method that uses cost and demand to identify the price that will maximize profits.

marginal cost The increase in total cost that results from producing one additional unit of a product.

marginal revenue The increase in total income or revenue that results from selling one additional unit of a product.

market All the customers and potential customers who share a common need that can be satisfied by a specific product, who have the resources to exchange for it, who are willing to make the exchange, and who have the authority to make the exchange.

market development strategies Growth strategies that introduce existing products to new markets.

market fragmentation The creation of many consumer groups due to a diversity of distinct needs and wants in modern society.

market manager An individual who is responsible for developing and implementing the marketing plans for products sold to a particular customer group.

market penetration strategies Growth strategies designed to increase sales of existing products to current customers, nonusers, and users of competitive brands in served markets.

market potential The maximum demand expected among consumers in a segment for a product or service.

market segment A distinct group of customers within a larger market who have similar needs, wants, preferences, and behaviours, who seek similar product solutions, and whose needs differ from other customers in the larger market.

market segmentation A process of dividing the overall market into groups of consumers who seek very different solutions for their needs and wants than other groups of consumers.

marketing Marketing is the activity, set of institutions, and processes for creating, communicating, delivering, and exchanging offerings that have value for customers, clients, partners, and society at large.

marketing concept A business orientation that focuses on achieving organizational objectives by understanding customer needs, and creating and delivering value in exchanges that satisfy the needs of all parties.

marketing decision support system (MDSS) The data, analysis software, and interactive software that allow managers to conduct analyses and find the information they need.

marketing information system (MIS) A process that first determines what information marketing managers need and then gathers, sorts, analyzes, stores, and distributes relevant and timely marketing information to system users.

marketing intelligence system A method by which marketers get information about everyday happenings in the marketing environment.

marketing mix A combination of the product itself, the price of the product, the place where it is made available, and the activities that introduce it to consumers, which creates a desired response among a set of predefined consumers.

marketing plan A document that describes the marketing environment, outlines the marketing objectives and strategy, and identifies who will be responsible for carrying out each part of the marketing strategy.

marketing research The process of collecting, analyzing, and interpreting data about customers, competitors, and the business environment in order to improve marketing effectiveness.

marketing research ethics Taking an ethical and above-board approach to conducting marketing research that does no harm to the participant in the process of conducting the research.

marketplace Any location or medium used to conduct an exchange.

markup An amount added to the cost of a product to create the price at which a channel member will sell the product.

marquee The sign that shows a store's name.

mass communications Relates to television, radio, magazines, and newspapers.

mass market All possible customers in a market, regardless of the differences in their specific needs and wants.

mass-class The hundreds of millions of global consumers who now enjoy a level of purchasing power that's sufficient to let them afford high-quality products—except for big-ticket items like college educations, housing, or luxury cars.

materials handling The moving of products into, within, and out of warehouses.

maturity stage The third and longest stage in the product life cycle, during which sales peak and profit margins narrow.

media blitz A massive advertising campaign that occurs over a relatively short time frame.

media planners Agency personnel who determine which communication vehicles are the most effective and efficient to deliver the ad.

media planning The process of developing media objectives, strategies, and tactics for use in an advertising campaign.

media relations A PR activity aimed at developing close relationships with the media.

media schedule The plan that specifies the exact media to use and when to use it.

medium A communication vehicle through which a message is transmitted to a target audience.

merchandise agents or brokers Channel intermediaries that provide services in exchange for commissions but never take title to the product.

merchandise assortment The range of products a store sells.

merchandise breadth The number of different product lines available.

merchandise depth The variety of choices available for each specific product line.

merchandise mix The total set of all products offered for sale by a retailer, including all product lines sold to all consumer groups.

merchandising allowance Reimburses the retailer for in-store support of the product.

merchant wholesalers Intermediaries that buy goods from manufacturers (take title to them) and sell to retailers and other business-to-business customers.

mergers When two or more separately owned retail firms combine.

message The communication in physical form that goes from a sender to a receiver.

metrics Measurements or "scorecards" marketers use to identify the effectiveness of different strategies or tactics.

metrosexual A straight, urban male who is keenly interested in fashion, home design, gourmet cooking, and personal care.

microcultures Groups of consumers who identify with a specific activity or art form.

mission statement A formal statement in an organization's strategic plan that describes the overall purpose of the organization and what it intends to achieve in terms of its customers, products, and resources.

mobile advertising A form of advertising that is communicated to the consumer via a handset.

modified rebuy A buying situation classification used by business buyers to categorize a previously made purchase that involves some change and that requires limited decision making.

motivation An internal state that drives us to satisfy needs by activating goal-oriented behaviour.

multichannel promotional strategy A marketing communication strategy where they combine traditional advertising, sales promotion, and public relations activities with online buzz-building activities.

multilevel or marketing network A system in which a master distributor recruits other people to become distributors, sells the company's product to the recruits, and receives a commission on all the merchandise sold by the people recruited.

multiple sourcing The business practice of buying a particular product from several different suppliers.

N

national or manufacturer brands Brands that the product manufacturer owns.

need The recognition of any difference between a consumer's actual state and some ideal or desired state.

new dominant logic for marketing A reconceptualization of traditional marketing to redefine service as the central (core) deliverable and the actual physical products purveyed as comparatively incidental to the value proposition.

new product development (NPD) The phases by which firms develop new products including idea generation, product concept development and screening, marketing strategy development, business analysis, technical development, test marketing, and commercialization.

new-task buy A new business-to-business purchase that is complex or risky and that requires extensive decision making.

niche marketing A type of concentrated targeting strategy where the market segment chosen is relatively small.

noise Anything that interferes with effective communication.

noncumulative quantity discounts Discounts based only on the quantity purchased in individual orders.

nondurable goods Consumer products that provide benefits for a short time because they are consumed (such as food) or are no longer useful (such as newspapers).

nonprobability sample A sample in which personal judgment is used to select respondents.

nonstore retailing Any method used to complete an exchange with a product end user that does not require a customer visit to a store.

North American Industry Classification System (NAICS) The numerical coding system that the United States, Canada, and Mexico use to classify firms into detailed categories according to their business activities.

not-for-profit organizations Organizations with charitable, educational, community, and other public service goals that buy goods and services to support their functions and to attract and serve their members.

O

objective-task budgeting A promotion budgeting method in which an organization first defines the specific communication goals it hopes to achieve and then tries to calculate what kind of promotion efforts it will take to meet these goals.

observability How visible a new product and its benefits are to others who might adopt it.

observational learning Learning that occurs when people watch the actions of others and note what happens to them as a result.

off-price retailers Retailers that buy excess merchandise from well-known manufacturers and pass the savings on to customers.

online auctions E-commerce that allows shoppers to purchase products through online bidding.

online distribution piracy The theft and unauthorized repurposing of intellectual property via the Internet.

online social networking Using Internet technology to keep in contact with friends, relatives, and business associates.

open source model A practice used in the software industry in which companies share their software codes with one another to assist in the development of a better product.

operant conditioning Learning that occurs as the result of rewards or punishments.

operational excellence A strategy focused on cost effectiveness, efficiency, and customer convenience.

operating cost Costs involved in using a product.

operational planning Planning that focuses on the day-to-day execution of the functional plans and includes detailed annual, semiannual, or quarterly plans.

operational plans Plans that focus on the day-to-day execution of the marketing plan.

opinion leader A person who is frequently able to influence others' attitudes or behaviours by virtue of his or her active interest and expertise in one or more product categories.

opportunity cost The value of something that is given up to obtain something else.

order processing The series of activities that occurs between the time an order comes into the organization and the time a product goes out the door.

organizational markets Another name for business-to-business markets.

outbound calling Encompasses telemarketing, lead generating, and other steps necessary in the sales process.

out-of-home media Communication media that reach people in public places.

outsourcing The business buying process of obtaining outside vendors to provide goods or services that otherwise might be supplied in-house.

owned media Internet sites such as Web sites, blogs, Facebook, and Twitter accounts that are owned by an advertiser.

P

package The covering or container for a product that provides product protection, facilitates product use and storage, and supplies important marketing communication.

paid media Internet media such as display ads, sponsorships, and paid key word searches that are paid for by an advertiser.

parity pricing strategy A pricing strategy where organizations keep their prices about equal to key competitors' prices.

party plan system A sales technique that relies heavily on people getting caught up in the "group spirit," buying things they would not normally buy if they were alone.

patent A legal mechanism to prevent competitors from producing or selling an invention, aimed at reducing or eliminating competition in a market for a period of time.

penetration pricing A pricing strategy in which a firm introduces a new product at a very low price to encourage more customers to purchase it.

perceived risk The belief that choice of a product has potentially negative consequences, whether financial, physical, and/or social.

percentage-of-sales budgeting A method for promotion budgeting that is based on a certain percentage of either last year's sales or on estimates of the present year's sales.

perception The process by which people select, organize, and interpret information from the outside world.

perceptual map A picture of where brands are "located" in consumers' minds.

perishability The characteristic of a service that makes it impossible to store for later sale or consumption.

permission marketing E-mail advertising in which online consumers have the opportunity to accept or refuse the unsolicited e-mail.

perpetual inventory unit control system Retail computer system that keeps a running total on sales, returns, transfers to other stores and so on.

personal selling Marketing communication by which a company representative interacts directly with a customer or prospective customer to communicate about a good or service.

personality The set of unique psychological characteristics that consistently influences the way a person responds to situations in the environment.

PESTO Political (including legal or regulatory), economic, social or cultural, technological, or other trends or issues that might impact a particular industry and business.

physical distribution The activities that move finished goods from manufacturers to final customers, including order processing, warehousing, materials handling, transportation, and inventory control.

place-based media Advertising media that transmit messages in public places, such as doctors' offices and airports, where certain types of people congregate.

point-of-purchase (POP) displays In-store displays and signs.

point-of-sale (POS) systems Retail computer systems that collect sales data and are hooked directly into the store's inventory-control system.

pop-up ad An advertisement that appears on the screen while a Web page loads or after it has loaded.

popular culture The music, movies, sports, books, celebrities, and other forms of entertainment consumed by the mass market.

popup store A temporary retail space a company erects to build buzz for its products.

portfolio analysis A tool management uses to assess the potential of a firm's business portfolio.

positioning How an organization wants its brand to be known to its customers as being different and better than competing brands.

positioning maps Illustration of the positioning of competing brands that draws on facts about each brand, such as characteristics or key attributes.

posttesting Research conducted on consumers' responses to actual advertising messages they have seen or heard.

predatory pricing Illegal pricing strategy in which a company sets a very low price for the purpose of driving competitors out of business.

predictive technology Analysis techniques that use shopping patterns of large numbers of people to determine which products are likely to be purchased if others are.

premium pricing When firms choose to price their products higher than competitive offerings.

premiums Items offered free to people who have purchased a product.

press release Information that an organization distributes to the media intended to win publicity.

prestige pricing A strategy where prices are set significantly higher than competing brands.

prestige products Products that have a high price and that appeal to status-conscious consumers.

pretesting A research method that seeks to minimize mistakes by getting consumer reactions to ad messages before they appear in the media.

price The seller's assignment of value to a product.

price bundling Selling two or more goods or services as a single package for one price.

price discrimination The illegal practice of offering the same product of like quality and quantity to different business customers at different prices, thus lessening competition.

price elasticity of demand The percentage change in unit sales that results from a percentage change in price.

price fixing The collaboration of two or more firms in setting prices, usually to keep prices high.

price-floor pricing A method for calculating price in which, to maintain full plant operating capacity, a portion of a firm's output may be sold at a price that covers only marginal costs of production.

price leadership (follower) A pricing strategy in which one firm first sets its price and other firms in the industry follow with the same or very similar prices.

price lining The practice of setting a limited number of different specific prices, called price points, for items in a product line.

price maintenance The collaboration of two or more firms in setting prices, usually to keep prices high.

price subsidies Government payments made to protect domestic businesses or to reimburse them when they must price at or below cost to make a sale. The subsidy can be a cash payment or tax relief.

primary data Data from research conducted to help make a specific decision.

private exchanges Systems that link an invited group of suppliers and partners over the Web.

private-label brands Brands that a certain retailer or distributor owns and sells.

probability sample A sample in which each member of the population has some known chance of being included.

problem recognition The process that occurs whenever the consumer sees a significant difference between his current state of affairs and some desired or ideal state; this recognition initiates the decision-making process.

processed materials Products created when firms transform raw materials from their original state.

producers The individuals or organizations that purchase products for use in the production of other goods and services.

product Any good, service, or idea that can be marketed. A tangible good, service, idea, or some combination of these that satisfies consumer or business customer needs through the exchange process; a bundle of attributes including features, functions, benefits, and uses.

product adoption The process by which a consumer or business customer begins to buy and use a new good, service, or idea.

product advertising Advertising messages that focus on a specific good or service.

product category managers Individuals who are responsible for developing and implementing the marketing plan for all the brands and products within a product category.

product concept development and screening The second step of product development in which marketers test product ideas for technical and commercial success.

product development strategies Growth strategies that focus on selling new products in served markets.

product leadership A strategy of competing by continually bringing innovative and useful new products or technologies to market.

product life cycle (PLC) A concept that explains how products go through four distinct stages from birth to death: introduction, growth, maturity, and decline.

product line A firm's total product offering designed to satisfy a single need or desire of target customers.

product line length Determined by the number of separate items within the same category.

product management The systematic and usually team-based approach to coordinating all aspects of a product's marketing initiative including all elements of the marketing mix.

product mix width The number of different product lines the firm produces.

product mix The total set of all products a firm offers for sale.

product orientation A management philosophy that emphasizes the most efficient ways to produce and distribute products.

product quality The overall ability of the product to satisfy customers' expectations.

product review sites Social media sites that enable people to post stories about their experiences with products and services.

product sampling Distributing free trial-size versions of a product to consumers.

product specifications A written description of the quality, size, weight, and other details required of a product purchase.

profit objectives Pricing products with a focus on a target level of profit growth or a desired net profit margin.

promotion mix The major elements of marketer-controlled communication, including advertising, sales promotion, public relations, personal selling, and direct marketing.

promotion The coordination of a marketer's communication efforts to influence attitudes or behaviour.

promotional products Goodies such as coffee mugs, T-shirts, and magnets given away to build awareness for a sponsor. Some freebies are distributed directly to consumers and business customers; others are intended for channel partners such as retailers and vendors.

prototypes Test versions of a proposed product.

psychographic segmentation A segmentation approach that groups people based on their attitudes, beliefs, values, lifestyles, or other psychological orientations.

psychographics The use of psychological, sociological, and anthropological factors to construct market segments.

psychological costs The stress, anxiety, or mental difficulty of buying and using a product.

public relations (PR) Communication function that seeks to build good relationships with an organization's publics, including consumers, stockholders, and legislators.

public relations campaign A coordinated effort to communicate with one or more of the firm's publics.

public service advertisements (PSAs) Advertising run by the media for not-for-profit organizations or to champion a particular cause without charge.

publicity Unpaid communication about an organization that appears in the mass media.

puffery Claims made in advertising of product superiority that cannot be proven true or untrue.

pull strategy The company tries to move its products through the channel by building desire for the products among consumers, thus convincing retailers to respond to this demand by stocking these items.

push money A bonus paid by a manufacturer to a salesperson, customer, or distributor for selling its product.

push strategy The company tries to move its products through the channel by convincing channel members to offer them.

pyramid schemes An illegal sales technique that promises consumers or investors large profits from recruiting others to join the program rather than from any real investment or sale of goods to the public.

Q

quantitative research A tool that probes more systematically into the problem and bases its conclusions on large numbers of observations.

quantity discounts A pricing tactic of charging reduced prices for purchases of larger quantities of a product.

QR code (quick response) A two-dimensional code consisting of modules arranged in a square pattern that can be read by a QR barcode reader (and camera phones); hold more data than a typical barcode and don't have to be scanned at one particular angle.

R

radio frequency identification (RFID) Product tags with tiny chips containing information about the item's content, origin, and destination.

raw materials Products of the fishing, lumber, agricultural, and mining industries that organizational customers purchase to use in their finished products.

reach The percentage of the target market that will be exposed to the media vehicle.

rebates Sales promotions that allow the customer to recover part of the product's cost from the manufacturer.

receiver The organization or individual that intercepts and interprets the message.

reciprocity A trading partnership in which two firms agree to buy from one another.

reference group An actual or imaginary individual or group that has a significant effect on an individual's evaluations, aspirations, or behaviour.

relative advantage The degree to which a consumer perceives that a new product provides superior benefits.

reliability The extent to which research measurement techniques are free of errors.

reminder advertising Advertising aimed at keeping the name of a brand in people's minds to be sure consumers purchase the product as necessary.

repositioning Modifying a brand image to keep up with changing times.

representativeness The extent to which consumers in a study are similar to a larger group in which the organization has an interest.

research and marketing services Advertising agency department that collects and analyzes information that will help account executives develop a sensible strategy and assist creatives in getting consumer reactions to different versions of ads.

research design A plan that specifies what information marketers will collect and what type of study they will do.

resellers The individuals or organizations that buy finished goods for the purpose of reselling, renting, or leasing to others to make a profit and to maintain their business operations.

retail borrowing Consumer practice of purchasing a product with the intent to return the nondefective merchandise for a refund after it has fulfilled the purpose for which it was purchased.

retail life cycle A theory that focuses on the various stages that retailers pass through from introduction to decline.

retailer margin The margin added to the cost of a product by a retailer.

retailing The final stop in the distribution channel in which organizations sell goods and services to consumers for their personal use.

return on investment (ROI) The revenue or profit margin generated by an investment, divided by the cost of the investment.

return on marketing investment (ROMI) The revenue or profit margin generated by investment in a specific marketing campaign or program, divided by the cost of that program at a given risk level.

reverse marketing A business practice in which a buyer firm attempts to identify suppliers who will produce products according to the buyer firm's specifications.

S

sales or market share objective Pricing products to maximize sales or to attain a desired level of sales or market share.

sales promotion Programs designed to build interest in or encourage purchase of a product during a specified period.

sampling The process of selecting respondents for a study.

SBU A semi-autonomous entity that operates as an independent business with its own mission and objectives—and its own marketing strategy.

search engine marketing (SEM) Search marketing strategy in which marketers pay for ads or better positioning.

search engine optimization (SEO) A systematic process of ensuring that your firm comes up at or near the top of lists of typical search phrases related to your business.

search engines Internet programs that search for documents with specified keywords.

search marketing Marketing strategies that involve the use of Internet search engines.

search qualities Product characteristics that the consumer can examine prior to purchase.

secondary data Data that have been collected for some purpose other than the problem at hand.

segment profile A description of the "typical" customer in a segment.

segmentation The process of dividing a larger market into smaller pieces based on one or more meaningfully shared characteristics.

segmentation variables Dimensions that divide the total market into fairly homogeneous groups, each with different needs and preferences.

selective distribution Distribution using fewer outlets than intensive distribution but more than exclusive distribution.

self-concept An individual's self-image that is composed of a mixture of beliefs, observations, and feelings about personal attributes.

selling orientation A managerial view of marketing as a sales function, or a way to move products out of warehouses to reduce inventory.

sensory marketing Marketing techniques that link distinct sensory experiences such as a unique fragrance with a product or service.

service encounter The actual interaction between the customer and the service provider.

services Intangible products that are exchanged directly between the producer and the customer.

servicescape The actual physical facility where the service is performed, delivered, and consumed.

SERVQUAL A multiple-item scale used to measure service quality across dimensions of tangibles, reliability, responsiveness, assurance, and empathy.

share of customer The percentage of an individual customer's purchase of a product that is a single brand.

shopping centre A group of commercial establishments owned and managed as a single property.

shopping products Goods or services for which consumers spend considerable time and effort gathering information and comparing alternatives before making a purchase.

shrinkage Losses experienced by retailers due to shoplifting, employee theft, and damage to merchandise.

single sourcing The business practice of buying a particular product from only one supplier.

Six Sigma A process whereby firms work to limit product defects to 3.4 per million or fewer.

skimming price A very high, premium price that a firm charges for its new, highly desirable product.

slogans Simple, memorable linguistic devices linked to a brand.

slotting allowance A fee paid by a manufacturer to a retailer in exchange for agreeing to place products on the retailer's shelves.

SMART objectives Objectives that are specific, measurable, attainable, relevant, and time-bounded.

social class The overall rank or social standing of groups of people within a society according to the value assigned to factors such as family background, education, occupation, and income.

social marketing concept A management philosophy that marketers must satisfy customers' needs in ways that also benefit society and also deliver profit to the firm.

social media Internet-based platforms that allow users to create their own content and share it with others who access these sites.

social networks Sites used to connect people with other similar people.

source An organization or individual that sends a message.

spam The use of electronic media to send unsolicited messages in bulk.

special events Activities—from a visit by foreign investors to a company picnic—that are planned and implemented by a PR department.

specialty products Goods or services that have unique characteristics and are important to the buyer and for which she will devote significant effort to acquire.

specialty stores Retailers that carry only a few product lines but offer good selection within the lines that they sell.

speech writing Writing a speech on a topic for a company executive to deliver.

sponsored search ads Paid ads that appear at the top or beside the Internet search engine results.

sponsorships PR activities through which companies provide financial support to help fund an event in return for publicized recognition of the company's contribution.

stakeholder People or organizations who influence or are influenced by marketing decisions.

staples Basic or necessary items that are available almost everywhere.

status symbols Visible markers that provide a way for people to flaunt their membership in higher social classes (or at least to make others believe they are members).

store image The way the marketplace perceives a retailer relative to the competition.

storefront The physical exterior of a store.

straight rebuy A buying situation in which business buyers make routine purchases that require minimal decision making.

strategic alliance Relationship developed between a firm seeking a deeper commitment to a foreign market and a domestic firm in the target country.

strategic business units (SBUs) Individual units within the firm that operate like separate businesses, with each having its own mission, business objectives, resources, managers, and competitors.

strategic orientation The overall approach to how you plan to compete and create value for your customers.

strategic planning A managerial decision process that matches an organization's resources and capabilities to its market opportunities for long-term growth and survival.

strategy What a firm is going to do to achieve an objective.

sub-branding Creating a secondary brand within a main brand that can help differentiate a product line to a desired target group.

subculture A group within a society whose members share a distinctive set of beliefs, characteristics, or common experiences.

subliminal advertising Supposedly hidden messages in marketers' communications.

supercentres Large combination stores that combine economy supermarkets with other lower-priced merchandise.

supermarkets Food stores that carry a wide selection of edibles and related products.

supply chain All the activities necessary to turn raw materials into a good or service and put it in the hands of the consumer or business customer.

supply chain management The management of flows among firms in the supply chain to maximize total profitability.

support media Media such as directories or out-of-home media that may be used to reach people who are not reached by mass media advertising.

sustainable development Meeting present needs without compromising the ability of future generations to meet their needs.

SWOT analysis An analysis of an organization's strengths and weaknesses and the opportunities and threats in its external environment.

switching costs Costs involved in moving from one brand to another.

symbolic-expressive value Differentiating your brand by the psychological meaning associated with it.

syndicated research Research by firms that collect data on a regular basis and sell the reports to multiple firms.

T

tactics How a strategy is going to be enacted.

take title To accept legal ownership of a product and assume the accompanying rights and responsibilities of ownership.

target costing A process in which firms identify the quality and functionality needed to satisfy customers and what price they are willing to pay before the product is designed; the product is manufactured only if the firm can control costs to meet the required price.

target market The group(s) of consumers or customers on which an organization focuses its marketing plan and toward which it directs its marketing efforts.

target marketing strategy Dividing the total market into different segments on the basis of customer characteristics, selecting one or more segments, and developing products to meet the needs of those specific segments.

teaser or mystery advertising Ads that generate curiosity and interest in a to-be-introduced product by drawing attention to an upcoming ad campaign without mentioning the product.

technical development The step in the product development process in which company engineers refine and perfect a new product.

telemarketing The use of the telephone to sell directly to consumers and business customers.

test marketing Testing the complete marketing plan in a small geographic area that is similar to the larger market the firm hopes to enter.

time poverty Consumers' belief that they are more pressed for time than ever before.

tipping point In the context of product diffusion, the point when a product's sales spike from a slow climb to an unprecedented new level, often accompanied by a steep price decline.

tonality The mood or attitude the message conveys (straightforward, humourous, dramatic, romantic, sexy, and apprehensive/fearful).

top-down budgeting Allocation of the promotion budget based on management's determination of the total amount to be devoted to marketing communication.

total costs The total of the fixed costs and the variable costs for a set number of units produced.

total quality management (TQM) A management philosophy that focuses on satisfying customers through empowering employees to be an active part of continuous quality improvement.

touchpoint Point of direct interface between customers and a company (online, by phone, or in person).

trade area A geographic zone that accounts for the majority of a store's sales and customers.

trade or functional discounts Discounts off list price of products to members of the channel of distribution who perform various marketing functions.

trade promotions Promotions that focus on members of the "trade," which include distribution channel members, such as retail salespeople or wholesale distributors, that a firm must work with in order to sell its products.

trade shows Events at which many companies set up elaborate exhibits to show their products, give away samples, distribute product literature, and troll for new business contacts.

trademark The legal term for a brand name, brand mark, or trade character; trademarks legally registered by a government obtain protection for exclusive use in that country.

traffic flow The direction in which shoppers will move through the store and which areas they will pass or avoid.

transportation The mode by which products move among channel members.

trial pricing Pricing a new product low for a limited period of time in order to lower the risk for a customer.

trialability The ease of sampling a new product and its benefits.

triple bottom line A business perspective that measures economic, social, and environmental value creation.

tweens Boys and girls aged 9-12 who are "in-between" stages in their development, when they are considered "too old for toys" but "too young for dating."

Twitter A free microblogging service that lets users post short text messages with a maximum of 140 characters.

U

umbrella pricing A strategy of ducking under a competitor's price by a fixed percentage.

unaided recall A research technique conducted by telephone survey or personal interview that asks whether a person remembers seeing an ad during a specified period without giving the person the name of the brand.

undifferentiated targeting strategy Appealing to a broad spectrum of people.

uniform delivered pricing A pricing tactic in which a firm adds a standard shipping charge to the price for all customers regardless of location.

unique selling proposition (USP) An advertising appeal that focuses on one clear reason why a particular product is superior.

Universal Product Code (UPC) The set of black bars or lines printed on the side or bottom of most items sold in grocery stores and other mass-merchandising outlets. The UPC, readable by scanners, creates a national system of product identification.

unobtrusive measures Measuring traces of physical evidence that remain after some action has been taken.

unsought products Goods or services for which a consumer has little awareness or interest until the product or a need for the product is brought to her attention.

usage occasions Indicator used in one type of market segmentation based on when consumers use a product most.

usage segmentation A segmentation approach that groups consumers or business customers based on the amount of a product purchased or consumed or how the product is used.

user-generated content (UGC) Online consumer comments, opinions, advice and discussions, reviews, photos, images, videos, podcasts, webcasts, and product-related stories available to other consumers; see also *consumer-generated content*.

V

validity The extent to which research actually measures what it was intended to measure.

VALS (Values and Lifestyles) A psychographic system that divides the entire U.S. population into eight segments.

value chain A series of activities involved in designing, producing, marketing, delivering, and supporting any product. Each link in the chain has the potential to either add or remove value from the product the customer eventually buys.

value-based pricing A pricing strategy in which a firm sets prices that provide ultimate value to customers.

variability The characteristic of a service that means that even the same service performed by the same individual for the same customer can vary.

variable costs The costs of production (raw and processed materials, parts, and labour) that are tied to and vary, depending on the number of units produced.

variable pricing A flexible pricing strategy that reflects what individual customers are willing to pay.

venture teams Groups of people within an organization who work together to focus exclusively on the development of a new product.

vertical marketing system (VMS) A channel of distribution in which there is formal cooperation among members at the manufacturing, wholesaling, and retailing levels.

video sharing Uploading video recordings on to Internet sites such as YouTube so that thousands or even millions of other Internet users can see them.

viral marketing Marketing activities that aim to increase brand awareness or sales by consumers passing a message along to other consumers.

virtual goods Digital products bought and sold in virtual worlds that don't exist in the real world but that consumers buy for use in online contexts.

virtual worlds Online, highly engaging digital environments where avatars live and interact with other avatars in real time.

visual merchandising The design of all the things customers see both inside and outside the store.

vlogs Video recordings shared on the Internet.

W

want The desire to satisfy needs in specific ways that are culturally and socially influenced.

warehouse clubs Discount retailers that charge a modest membership fee to consumers who buy a broad assortment of food and nonfood items in bulk and in a warehouse environment.

warehousing Storing goods in anticipation of sale or transfer to another member of the channel of distribution.

Web directory Internet program that lists sites by categories and subcategories.

wheel-of-retailing hypothesis A theory that explains how retail firms change, becoming more upscale as they go through their life cycle.

wholesaler margin The amount added to the cost of a product by a wholesaler.

wholesaling intermediaries Firms that handle the flow of products from the manufacturer to the retailer or business user.

word-of-mouth communication Consumers providing information about products to other consumers.

Y

yield-management pricing A practice of charging different prices to different customers in order to manage capacity while maximizing revenues.

Z

zone pricing A pricing tactic in which customers in different geographic zones pay different transportation rates.

Name Index

Notes: Page numbers followed by *f* indicate figures and those followed by *t* indicate tables.

Subject Index

Notes: Page numbers followed by *f* indicate figures and those followed by *t* indicate tables.